Turkey

written and researched by

Rosie Ayliffe, Marc Dubin, John Gawthrop and Terry Richardson

with additional research and contributions by

John Gorvett, Paul Sentobe, Martin Stokes
and Lizzie Williams

ROUGH
GUIDES

www.roughguides.com

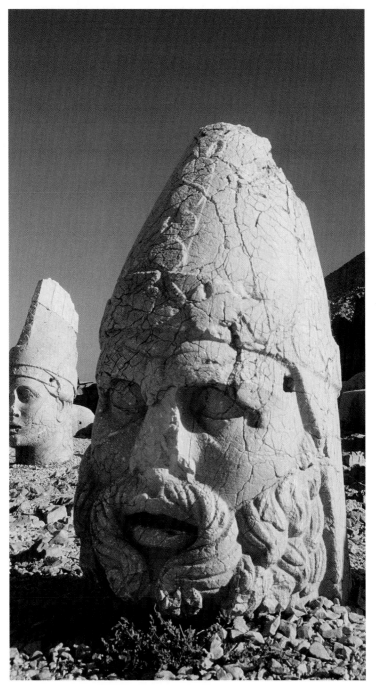

Introduction to

Turkey

Turkey is a country with a multiple identity, poised uneasily between East and West – though, despite the tourist brochure cliché, it is less a bridge between the two than a battleground, a buffer zone whose various parts have been invaded and settled from every direction since the beginning of recorded history. The country is now keen to be accepted on equal terms by the West: long the only NATO member in the Middle East region and a major recipient of US military aid, it is now also vigorously pursuing EU membership as a means of assuring future prosperity and democracy. But despite Turkish involvement with Europe dating back to the twelfth century, it is by no stretch of the imagination a thoroughly Western nation, and the contradictions – and fascinations – persist.

Turkey is a vast country – France would fit within its boundaries with plenty of room to spare – incorporating characteristics of Middle Eastern and Aegean, as well as Balkan and trans-Caucasian, countries. Mosques coexist with Orthodox churches; Roman theatres and temples crumble alongside ancient Hittite cities; and dervish ceremonies or gypsy festivals are as much a part of the social landscape as classical music concerts or delirious sports fans. The one constant in all this – and one of the things that makes Turkey such a rewarding place

iii

to travel – is the **Turkish people**, whose reputation for friendliness and hospitality is richly deserved; indeed you risk causing offence by refusing to partake of it, and any transaction can be the springboard for further acquaintance. Close to the bigger resorts or tourist attractions, much of this is undoubtedly mercenary, but in most of the country the warmth and generosity is genuine – all the more amazing when recent Turkish history has demonstrated that outsiders usually only bring trouble in their wake.

Politically, modern Turkey was a bold experiment, founded on the remaining Anatolian kernel of the **Ottoman Empire**, once among the world's largest, and longest-lasting, imperial states. The country arose from defeat after World War I, almost entirely the creation of a single man of demonic energy and vision – **Kemal Atatürk**. The Turkish War of Independence, fought against those victorious Allies intending to pursue imperialistic designs on Ottoman territory, has (with slightly stretched analogy – Turkey was never a colony) often been seen as the prototype for all Third World "wars of liberation". It led to an explicitly secular **Republic**,

iv

■

though one in which almost all of the inhabitants are at least nominally **Muslim** (predominantly Sunni). Turkey's heritage as home to the caliphate and numerous dervish orders, plus contemporary Islamist movements, still often deflects its moral compass south and east rather than northwest.

Turks, except for a small minority in the southeast, are not Arabs, and loathe being mistaken for them; despite a heavy lacing of Persian and Arabic words, the **Turkish language** alone, unrelated to any neighbouring one except Azeri, is sufficient to set its speakers apart. The **population** is, however, in spite of official efforts to enforce uniformity, remarkably heterogeneous ethnically. When the Ottoman Empire imploded early in the twentieth century, large numbers of Muslim Slavs, Kurds, Greeks, Albanians, Crimean Tatars, Azeris, Daghestanlis, Abkhazians and Circassians – to name only the most numerous non-Turkic groups – streamed into Anatolia, the safest refuge in an age of anti-Ottoman Nationalism. This process has continued in recent years from formerly Soviet or Eastern Bloc territories (including even a few Christian Turks or Gaugaz from Moldavia), so

Fact file

- Besides Russia, Turkey is the only nation incorporating both Asian and – albeit just 3 percent of its **total area** of 814,578 sq km – European territory. An 8333-kilometre **coastline** is lapped by four seas; the Black Sea, the Sea of Marmara, the Aegean and the Mediterranean. Numerous **peaks** exceed 3000m, the highest being 5165-metre Ararat (Ağrı Dağ) near the Armenian border. The largest Turkish **lake** is Lake Van (3713 square km) in the far southeast.

- The **population** of about 67 million is 98 percent Muslim (Sunni or Alevî sect), with dwindling **religious minorities** of the Armenian Apostolic, Greek Orthodox, Syrian Orthodox, Jewish and Catholic faiths. Besides standard Turkish, two dialects of Kurdish are widely spoken, while other **languages** heard include Arabic, Laz, Circassian, Albanian, Macedonian, Bulgarian, Romany and Greek. Well over half the inhabitants live in **urban areas**; the four largest cities, İstanbul, Ankara (the capital), İzmir and Adana, account alone for about 21 million people.

- Since 1922, when the last sultan was deposed, Turkey has been a **Republic**. The single-chamber *Büyük Meclis* or **Grand National Assembly** in Ankara has 550 seats, and the head of state (elected by this parliament) is the **president**. Both, however, are answerable to a **National Security Council** dominated by elements of the armed forces.

- Since 1950 the Turkish **economy** has often been in crisis, with inflation savaging the value of the currency and unemployment rates approaching one in four. Recovery from the 2001 crash is slowly proceeding, helped by tourism, with Turkey also poised to become a major exporter of automobiles and other consumer durables.

that the diversity of the people endures, constituting one of the surprises of travel in Turkey.

There are equally large disparities in levels of **development and income**. İstanbul boasts clubs as expensive and exclusive as any in New York or London, while town-centre shops are full of imported luxury goods, yet in the chronically backward eastern interior you'll encounter standards and modes of living scarcely changed from a century ago. Following a severe crash in early 2001, the Turkish economy languishes on the ropes and the country is heavily in debt, threatening the modernization process begun during the late nineteenth century. It's make-or-break time for a country aspiring to full EU membership: has Westernization struck deep roots in the culture, or does it extend no further than a mobile-phone- and credit-card-equipped urban élite?

Turkey has been continuously inhabited and fought over for close on ten millennia, as the layer-cake arrangement of many **archeological sites** and the numerous fortified heights testify. The juxtaposed ancient monuments mirror the bewildering **succession of states** – Hittite,

Urartian, Phrygian, Hellenistic, Roman, Byzantine, Armeno-Georgian – that held sway here before the twelfth century. There is also, of course, an overwhelming number of graceful **Islamic monuments** dating from the eleventh century onwards, as well as magnificent city **bazaars**, still holding their own despite the encroachments of chain stores and shopping malls. The country's modern architecture is less pleasing, the consequence both of government policy since 1950 and of returned overseas workers eager to invest their earnings in real estate – an ugliness manifest at the **coastal resorts**, where the beaches are rarely as good as the tourist-board hype. Indeed it's **inland** Turkey – Asiatic expanses of mountain, steppe, lake, even cloud forest – that may leave a more vivid memory, especially when accented by some crumbling *kervansaray*, mosque or castle.

Camels in Turkey

Despite stereotypes overseas, **camels** play a diminished role in modern Turkey. Most are now just tourist attractions, used for pleasure-riding or as photographic props in places like Pamukkale and Side. The last (just barely) working herd is resident on the Turquoise Coast, moving materials into and out of a roadless area near Kekova. It wasn't always so, however; camel caravans hauling freight still crisscrossed most of Anatolia until the 1960s, though in their last years the cargo tended to be salt, figs, cotton or light flints instead of the gemstones, spices and woven finery of yore. Before the Balkan Wars of 1912–1913, camel caravans extended northwest as far as Bosnia; beyond this point the beasts contracted fatal respiratory conditions brought on by the damp central European climate. In Muslim folklore the perceived haughty demeanour of camels is attributed to their knowledge of the hundredth, mystical epithet of Allah – humans only know the conventional ninety-nine.

Where to go

Western Turkey is not only the more economically developed but also by far the more visited half of the country. **İstanbul**, straddling the straits linking the Black and Marmara seas, is touted as Turkish mystique par excellence, and understandably so: it would take months to even scratch the surface of the old imperial capital, still the cultural and commercial centre of the country. Flanking it on opposite sides of the **Sea of Marmara** are the two prior seats of the Ottoman Empire, Bursa and Edirne, each with their complement of attractions and regal atmosphere. The sea itself is flecked with tranquil, frequently overlooked islands, ideal havens when the cities get too much – and just beyond the Dardanelles and its World War I battlefields lie two larger Aegean islands, only opened to outsiders during the late 1980s.

As you move south, the Classical character of the **Northeast Aegean** comes to the fore in the olive-swathed country around Bergama and Ayvalık, perhaps the two most compelling points in the region. Just outside İzmir, the old Ottoman princely training ground of Manisa and the originally Lydian city of Sardis, lost in vineyards, make a fine pair, while İzmir itself is the functional introduction to the **Central and Southern Aegean**, a magnet for travellers since the eighteenth century. The archeological complex at Ephesus overshadows in visitors' imaginations the equally deserving ancient Ionian sites of Priene and Didyma, or the ruins of Aphrodisias and

Labranda in old Caria. Also inland are the tranquil expanse of Bafa Gölü, and the architectural showcase town of Muğla. Be warned that the coast itself is heavily developed, though the star resorts – of which Çeşme is perhaps the quietest and Bodrum the most characterful – make comfortable bases from which to tour the interior. Don't overlook such evocative hill towns as Şirince, Birgi or Tire, which still exist in something of an Ottoman time warp.

Beyond the huge natural harbour at Marmaris, the Aegean becomes the Mediterranean; tourism levels drop slightly and the shore becomes more convoluted and piney. Yacht and schooner cruises are popular and easily arranged in brazen Marmaris or the more pleasant town of Fethiye, principal centre of the **Turquoise Coast**. Two of the finest and largest beaches in the country sprawl at Dalyan and Patara, close to the eerie tombs of the Lycians, the fiercely independent locals of old. Further east, Kaş and Kalkan are small but busy resorts, good places to rest up between explorations into the mountainous hinterland. Beyond the relatively untouched beaches around ancient Olympos, Antalya is Turkey's fastest growing city, a sprawling place located at the beginning of the **Mediterranean Coast** proper. This lengthy shore, reaching as far as the Syrian border, boasts extensive sands and archeological sites – most notably at Perge, Side and Aspendos – though its western parts get swamped in high season. Once past castle-topped Alanya, however, tourist numbers diminish, and the stretch between Silifke and Adana offers innumerable minor points of interest, particularly the Roman city of Uzuncaburç and the

Turkey's youth

About half of Turkey's estimated population of 67 million is under thirty years old, a far younger profile than any of its potential stablemates in the EU. This distribution may, however, age in coming decades, as the birthrate has declined from a high of 4.7 percent during the 1950s to just 1.5 percent in 1999. The country's youth are not, however, especially well educated: though literacy approaches 90 percent for both genders, only 10 percent of adolescents complete secondary education, and perhaps 5 percent receive some sort of higher education. Despite this, there are far too many qualified graduates at present for the shrunken job market, with underemployment as common as unemployment. So a very likely consequence of EU membership and full freedom of movement within Europe is substantial emigration from Turkey, either permanent or temporary.

Storks

Between May and September, storks in their nests balanced atop domes, utility poles or dead trees are a common sight across western Turkey, which is near the northern end of a migratory flyway connecting winter quarters in Africa with a summer habitat in the Balkans. The clattering of the birds' beaks is an equally common sound. Storks mate for life, and the breeding pair often returns to the same nest year after year to raise new chicks, preferably near a lake or swamp which provides an ample food supply of frogs and small fish. They are considered lucky in both Christian and Islamic belief, and rarely harmed (especially once local hunters are informed that their meat is unappetizing); some municipalities even go so far as to build special platforms to augment favourite stork-nesting perches.

romantic offshore fortress at Kızkalesi. Further east, Arab-flavoured Antakya is the heart of the **Hatay**, once part of Syria.

There are spectacular attractions inland in **South Central Anatolia**, where you're confronted with the famous rock churches, subterranean cities and tuff-pinnacle landscapes of Cappadocia. The dry, bracing climate, excellent local wine, the artistic and architectural interest of the area, plus the chance to go horse-riding or hot-air ballooning, could occupy you for as much as ten days, taking in the largest town in the area, Kayseri – with its bazaar and tombs – on the way north. You might also pause at Eğirdir or Beyşehir – historic towns fronting two of the numerous lakes that spangle the region – or in Konya, which, for both its Selçuk architecture and associations with the Mevlevî dervishes, makes for an appealing stopover on the way to or from the coast.

Ankara, hub of **North Central Anatolia**, is Turkey's capital, a planned city whose contrived Western feel gives some concrete (in all senses) indication of the priorities of the Turkish Republic; it also has the outstanding Museum of Anatolian Civilizations. Highlights of the region include the bizarre, isolated temple of Aezani, near Kutahya to the west; the Ottoman museum-town of Safranbolu; the exquisitely decorated early Turkish monuments at Divriği; and the remarkable Hittite sites of Hattuşaş and Alacahöyük. If you're travelling north to the Black Sea, you should also look in on the Yeşilırmak valley towns of Sivas, Tokat and Amasya, each with its quota of early Turkish monuments. The **Black Sea** shore itself is surprisingly devoid of architectural interest other than a chain of Byzantine-Genoese castles, but the beauty of the landscape goes some way to compensate. The oldest and most interesting towns between utilitarian Samsun and industrial Zongul-dak are Sinop, the northernmost point of Anatolia, and Amasra, also easily reached from Safranbolu. East of Samsun, a new four-lane highway brings you to fabled Trabzon, once a seat of empire and today a base for visits to the marvellous monasteries of Aya Sofya and Sumela.

The Ankara–Sivas route also poises you for the trip along the Euphrates River and into the hitherto invisible "back half" of Turkey – the East. Your first stop in **Northeastern Anatolia** is likely to be Erzurum, highest and bleakest major city of Turkey, from where you can head on to visit the temperate and church-studded valleys of southern medieval Georgia or go trekking in the Kaçkar mountains – Turkey's most popular hiking area – that wall off the area from the Black Sea. Dull Kars is worth enduring for the sake of nearby Ani, the ruined medieval Armenian capital, and various other Armenian monuments in the area – though many of these require some ingenuity and resourcefulness to seek out.

South of here, the **Euphrates and Tigris Basin** represents Turkey at its most Middle Eastern. Gaziantep, approached from points west, is the func-tional gateway to some centres of genuine interest. Urfa and nearby Harran are biblical in both appearance and history; Mardin, with its surrounding monasteries, is the homeland of Turkey's Syrian Orthodox minority. The colossal heads of Nemrut Dağı, however, reproduced endlessly on brochures and travel posters, are the real attraction here, and mightily impressive despite heavy commercialization. Diyarbakır, a swarming, vivid metropolis on the Tigris, is the last real urban centre before the largely Kurdish-popu-lated areas around **Lake Van**, an unearthly blue alkaline expanse just beyond the canyon-flank town of Bitlis. After some years as a no-go area, it is again possible – with a judicious ear to the ground – to travel the main routes through this rewarding region. Urartian, Selçuk and Armenian monuments abound within sight of the water, most notably at Çavuştepe, Ahlat and Akdamar, though you almost certainly will have to stay in **Van** town, an oasis sprawling on the eastern shore behind its ancient, rock-hewn citadel. East of Van looms the fairy-tale Kurdish castle of Hoşap, though excursions into the spectacular Cilo-Sat mountains beyond have long been limited by the prevailing political situation. A day's journey north of Van, just outside of Doğubeyazit, you'll find another isolated folly, the Işak Paşa Sarayı, staring across to **Mount Ararat** – the very end of Turkey.

When to go

Turkey has a wide variety of climates, and there's a good chance that no matter when you want to go, somewhere in the country will be at least tolerable, if not ideal – although you should also pay attention to the basic seasonal patterns of tourist traffic.

Of the coastal areas, **İstanbul** and the area around the **Sea of Marmara** have a relatively damp, Balkan climate, with muggy summers and cool, rainy (though seldom snowy) winters. Bear in mind that competition for facilities between June and August can be stiff. Things are similarly busy during summer on the popular **Aegean and Mediterranean coasts**; climatic conditions, too, can be difficult during July and August, especially between İzmir and Antakya, where the heat is tempered only slightly by offshore breezes. Perhaps the best time to visit these coastal regions is in spring or autumn, when the weather is gentler and the holiday crowds rather thinner. Late October and early November sees the **pastırma yazı**, or "Indian summer", an idyllic time with the scarcity of charter flights and open facilities as the only drawbacks. Indeed, even during winter, the **Turquoise** and Mediterranean coasts are – except for brief rainy periods in January and February – still fairly pleasant, and beyond Alanya up to the Hatay, winters can be positively balmy, though you may still not be able to brave the water. The **Black Sea** is something of an anomaly, with temperate summers and exceptionally mild winters for so far north, and rain likely during the nine coolest months of the year, lingering as mist and subtropical humidity during summer – but it does have the advantage of being less crowded than the Mediterranean or Aegean during the summer.

Anatolia forms a natural fortress, its entire coast backed by mountains or hills, cutting off the interior from any moderating maritime influences. **Cen-**

tral Anatolia is mostly semi-arid steppe, with a healthy, bracing climate – warm but not unpleasant in summer, cool and dry in the relatively short winters – though Ankara is exceptionally nasty during the central-heating season, when noxious soft coal is burnt (though

this is being gradually phased out in favour of natural gas). Cappadocia in particular makes a colourful, quiet treat throughout spring and autumn – indeed well into December, when its rock formations dusted with snow are especially beautiful. As you travel east, into **Northeast Anatolia** and around **Lake Van**, the altitude increases and conditions are deeply snowy between October and April, making late spring and summer by far the best (in some cases the only) time to visit, when you'll also find it more comfortable and less populated than on the teeming coast. As you move into the lower **Euphrates and Tigris Basin**, a more pronounced Middle Eastern influence exerts itself, with winters that are no worse than in central Anatolia but torrid summers – and without the compensation of a nearby beach.

Average midday temperatures in °C &°F

	Jan	Feb	Mar	Apr	May	Jun	Jul	Aug	Sep	Oct	Nov	Dec
İstanbul												
(°C)	6	6	7	12	17	21	24	24	20	16	12	8
(°F)	43	43	45	54	63	70	75	75	68	61	54	47
İzmir												
(°C)	9	10	12	16	21	25	28	28	24	19	15	11
(°F)	48	50	54	61	70	77	82	82	75	66	59	52
Antalya												
(°C)	11	12	13	17	21	23	29	29	25	21	16	12
(°F)	52	54	56	63	70	77	84	84	77	70	61	54
Ankara												
(°C)	1	1	5	12	17	20	24	24	19	13	8	3
(°F)	34	34	41	54	63	68	75	75	66	56	47	37
Trabzon												
(°C)	8	8	9	12	16	20	23	24	20	17	14	10
(°F)	47	47	48	54	61	68	73	75	68	63	57	50
Diyarbakır												
(°C)	2	4	9	14	20	26	31	31	25	18	10	5
(°F)	35	39	48	57	68	79	88	88	77	65	50	41

36

things not to miss

It's not possible to see everything Turkey has to offer in one trip – and we don't suggest you try. What follows is a selective and subjective taste of the country's highlights: outstanding buildings and historic sites, natural wonders and exciting activities. They're all arranged in five colour-coded categories to help you find the very best things to see, do and experience. All entries have a page reference to take you straight into the guide, where you can find out more.

xiv

01 Ancient Ephesus Page • **366** This major Aegean city was inextricably linked with the history of early Christianity; St Paul addressed one of his epistles to its citizens.

02 **White-water rafting on the Köprülü Çayı** Page • 554 This scenic river, tumbling down from the Toros mountains to the Mediterranean, is perfect for novice rafters.

04 **Hittite capital of Hattuşaş** Page • 730 The second-millennium-BC capital of the Hittites still impresses, with perimeter walls extending to six kilometres.

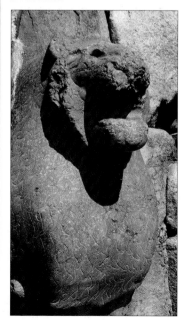

03 **Cruising the southwest coast** Page • 521 The deeply indented coastline between Bodrum and Olympos is the venue for multi-day cruises on a gület, or traditional wooden motor-schooner.

05 Roman theatre at Aspendos Page • **552** The best way to appreciate the largest and best-preserved theatre in Anatolia is by attending the summertime opera and ballet festival.

06 Oil wrestling Page • **226** Though a popular sport across Turkey, the best time to see olive-oil-coated contestants get to grips with each other is during Edirne's Kırkpınar Festival.

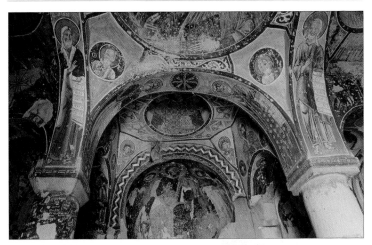

07 Byzantine frescoes, Cappadocia Page • **635** About 150 of Cappadocia's rock-hewn churches contain fine examples of early Christian frescoes; shown is an example from the most-visited Göreme complex.

08 Acropolis of ancient Pergamon Page

• **302** Pergamon was one of the chief Roman cities of Anatolia, and extensive ruins remain; shown here is the restored Trajan temple.

09

Museum of Anatolian Civilizations, Ankara Page •

698 Housing finds of all native cultures from the Stone Age to about 700 BC, this superb museum is the one must in the capital.

10 Camel-wrestling Pages •
273–321 These seasonal bouts between two male camels in rut draw vast crowds across the Aegean region.

11 Outdoor restaurants
Page • **51** The Ottomans introduced the concept of dining al fresco to Europe, and outdoor seafood restaurants especially do a roaring trade in warmer weather.

13 Gözleme Page • 52
The Turkish-village version of crêpes have enjoyed a comeback since the 1980s; watching their concoction is part of the fun.

12 Lycian Way long-distance path Page • 465
This marked path passes through some of the most scenic portions of the Turquoise Coast; shown is the medieval cobbled section between Ovacık and Kozağaçı.

14 Underground city, Kaymaklı
Page • 644 Burrowed out of soft volcanic tuff, this subterranean labyrinth provided refuge for Cappadocians from the Hittite through to the Byzantine eras.

15 Acropolis of ancient Assos Page • 290
At the summit, with views of Greek Lesvos, stands this restored Doric Athena temple; the architecturally preserved medieval village occupies the slopes below.

16 **"Beehive" houses, Harran** Page • **881** These timeless, mud-built dwellings at Harran, close to the Syrian border between the Euphrates and Tigris rivers, are inhabited by ethnic Arabs.

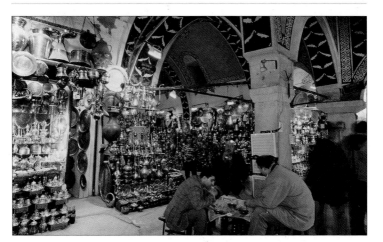

17 **Kapalı Çarşı, İstanbul** Page • **141** The hard sell reaches its apotheosis in what's claimed to be the largest covered bazaar in the world. Touristy but still compelling.

18 **Ihlara Valley, Cappadocia** Page • **669** Take a streamside walk along the lushly vegetated valley floor, pausing to visit painted cave-churches up the slopes.

19 Aya Sofya museum, İstanbul Page • **116** The seemingly unsupported dome of Aya Sofya, built during the sixth century as a Byzantine church, is one of the architectural marvels of the world.

20 Orthodox monastery of Sumela Page • **790** Built into the side of a palisade high up in the Pontic mountains, this Byzantine foundation harbours excellent if damaged frescoes.

21 Koza Hanı, Bursa Page • **255** The silk-cocoon auction which takes place in this fifteenth-century *han* during early summer is the basis for one of Turkey's distinctive natural crafts.

22 Whirling dervishes Page • **628** Members of a sect founded by the Konya-based Sufi mystic Mevlâna conduct "turning" ceremonies to effect union with God.

23 **Ölüdeniz beach** Page • **462** This lagoon-enclosing beach is just one among dozens of little-developed strands along Turkey's coast between Marmaris and Mersin.

24 **Football** Page • **82**
The loyalty of Turkey's football fans was finally rewarded when the national team finished third in the 2002 World Cup Finals.

25 **Fairy chimneys** Page • **637** Cones of volcanic tuff, often with basalt slabs teetering on top, make a bizarre spectacle in the geological fantasy landscape of Cappadocia.

26 Scuba-diving Pages • **453, 492 & 498** A burgeoning industry, scuba-diving off Turkey's coast offers up the chance to see marine life and go wreck exploring.

27 Topkapı Palace, İstanbul Page • **118** From 1453, the Ottoman Empire was governed from within this ornate and labyrinthine complex for four centuries.

xxii**28 Kaçkar Dağları** Page • **853** Lying just inland from the Black Sea, this glacially sculpted granite mountain range, spangled with dozens of lakes, is Turkey's premier trekking venue.

29 Orchids at Lake Van

Page • **919** Early summer sees the highland meadows around Van carpeted with wildflowers, including these rare orchids.

30 Churches of the Georgian valleys

Page • **843** Numerous medieval churches northeast of Erzurum are among the most striking monuments in northeastern Anatolia; shown is İşhan, one of the largest and oldest.

31 Visiting a hamam

Page • **50** Bathers relaxing on the central heated stone of a hamam are enjoying one of the traditional sensual comforts of Turkey.

32 İşak Paşa Sarayı

Page • **951** Strategically situated on the Silk Route, this architecturally eclectic seventeenth-century palace is one of eastern Turkey's most emblematic sites.

34 **Antakya Archeological Museum** Page • **594** A unique collection of mosaics unearthed from the villas of Roman and Byzantine Antioch are well displayed in one of Turkey's finest provincial museums.

33 **Drinking tea** Page • **797** Tea from the Black Sea has been the Turkish national drink since the 1930s, and it's available everywhere, at almost any hour.

35
Riverbank culture at Amasya
Page • **736** The tombs of the ancient Pontic kings are juxtaposed with graceful Ottoman mansions along the Yeşilırmak in Amasya.

36 **Hot-air ballooning over Cappadocia** Page • **635** A lighter-than-air float gives you an unrivalled perspective on the "fairy chimneys" and other aspects of the landscape.

Contents

Using this Rough Guide

We've tried to make this Rough Guide a good read and easy to use. The book is divided into six main sections, and you should be able to find whatever you want in one of them.

Colour section

The front colour section offers a quick tour of Turkey. The **introduction** aims to give you a feel for the place, with suggestions on where to go. We also tell you what the weather is like and include a basic country fact file. Next, our authors round up their favourite aspects of Turkey in the **things not to miss** section – whether it's great food, amazing sights or a special hotel. Right after this comes a full **contents** list.

Basics

The Basics section covers all the **pre-departure** nitty-gritty to help you plan your trip. This is where to find out which airlines fly to your destination, what paperwork you'll need, what to do about money and insurance, about Internet access, food, security, public transport, car rental – in fact just about every piece of **general practical information** you might need.

Guide

This is the heart of the Rough Guide, divided into user-friendly chapters, each of which covers a specific region. Every chapter starts with a list of **highlights** and an **introduction** that helps you to decide where to go, depending on your time and budget. Likewise, introductions to the various towns and smaller regions within each chapter should help you plan your itinerary. We start most town accounts with information on arrival and accommodation, followed by a tour of the sights, and finally reviews of places to eat and drink, and details of nightlife. Longer accounts also have a directory of practical listings. Each chapter concludes with **public transport** details for that region.

Contexts

Read Contexts to get a deeper understanding of what makes Turkey tick. We include a brief history, articles about **music** and **cinema**, and a detailed further reading section that reviews dozens of **books** relating to the country.

Language

The **language** section gives useful guidance for speaking Turkish and pulls together all the vocabulary you might need on your trip, including a comprehensive menu reader. Here you'll also find a glossary of words and terms peculiar to the country.

Index + small print

Apart from a **full index**, which includes maps as well as places, this section covers publishing information, credits and acknowledgements, and also has our contact details in case you want to send in updates and corrections to the book – or suggestions as to how we might improve it.

Map and chapter list

3

Contents

Colour section

Basics

Guide

Contexts   955–1085

Language   1087–1105

Index & small print   1107–1120

Map symbols

Maps are listed in the full index using coloured text

┅┅┅	International boundary	⋇	Marshland
┄┄┄	Chapter boundary	⚡	Skiing
▬▬▬	Motorway	♛	Castle
══	Major road	⚲	Church (regional maps)
══	Minor road	⚑	Monastery
▬▬▬	Pedestrianized road	✡	Synagogue
───	Unpaved road	⚑	Mosque
⊓⊓⊓⊓	Steps	⊙	Statue
┈┈┈	Path	⚠	Campsite
▬▬▬	Railway	◉	Accommodation
┈┈┈	Tramway	▣	Restaurant/café
───	Metro line	♦	Museum
─ ─ ─	Ferry route	ⓘ	Tourist office
───	Waterway	⊠	Post office
▪▪▪▪	Wall	@	Internet access
✈	Airport	⊞	Hospital
♦	Point of interest	⬗	Swimming pool
⌃⌃	Mountain range	★	Bus stop
▲	Mountain peak	Ⓜ	Metro stop
⌐Ⴑⴟⴤⴖⴗⴖ	Cliffs	▬█▬	Gate
∴	Ruins	▬	Building
⌂	Cave	⊞	Church
⩔⩔	Spa	⬭	Stadium
⚶	Waterfall	▦	Park
⊤	Lighthouse	▦	Beach
≍	Pass	⟨Y⟩	Muslim cemetery

Basics

Basics

Getting there

The easiest way to get to Turkey from the UK or Ireland is to fly, a journey of three-and-a-half to five hours depending on your starting/ending point. There are several gateway airports at each end, though London and İstanbul are still the busiest year-round. Just two carriers currently fly direct to Turkey from North America (down to one in winter), so most North Americans travel to a gateway European city, and pick up an onward connecting flight with an associated airline. It's fairly easy to track down flights from Australia to İstanbul or nearby Athens, much less so from New Zealand. But given most people's travel plans, you might be better off with a Round-the-World (RTW) ticket that includes İstanbul. The long trans-Europe train journey to Turkey is not straightforward and always much more expensive than flying; InterRail/Eurail passes are not a great help either. Driving overland through Europe can also be expensive and time-consuming, but once inside the country the effort can prove worthwhile. Using any overland means, you'll save bother and time by taking ferries between Italy and Turkey, or between outlying Greek islands and the Turkish coast, thus avoiding long detours through Eastern Europe and the ongoing turmoil in ex-Yugoslavia.

Airfares to Turkey from Europe and North America always depend on the **season**, with the highest during Easter week and from June to early September; fares drop during the "shoulder" seasons – April/May and late September/October – and you'll get the best prices during the low season, November to March (excluding Christmas and New Year weeks, when seats are at a premium). Note also that flying on weekends from North America can add $50 or so to the round-trip fare; prices quoted below assume midweek travel. Australian and New Zealand fares have their low season from mid-January to the end of February and October/November; high season is mid-May to August, plus December to mid-January; and shoulder season the rest of the year.

The cheapest of the airlines' **published fares** is an APEX (Advance Purchase Excursion) ticket, which has certain restrictions. You may be expected to book – and pay – at least 14–21 days before departure, keep to a maximum limit on your stay (typically 30 or 60 days), and be liable to penalties (including total loss of ticket value) if you change your schedule. Some airlines also issue "student" tickets to those under 26,

often extending the maximum stay to a year. There are also "Senior" or "Golden" fares available for those over 60.

You can often cut costs by going through a **specialist flight agent** – either a consolidator, who buys up blocks of tickets from the airlines and sells them at a discount, or a **discount agent**, who in addition to dealing with discounted flights may also offer special **student and youth fares** and a range of other travel-related services such as travel insurance, rail passes, car rental and tours. Some UK agents specialize in **charter flights**, which may be cheaper than anything available on a scheduled flight, but departure dates are fixed and withdrawal penalties high. For Turkey, you may find it more cost-effective (especially from the UK) to pick up a **package deal**, with accommodation and flights included.

Booking flights online

Many airlines and discount **travel websites** offer you the opportunity to book your tickets online, cutting out the costs of agents and middlemen. Good deals can often be found and most airlines offer discounts of £5–10 for booking return journeys on their website. But even if you don't end up actually buying your ticket online, the websites are worth visiting anyway to size up current fares (although the sites often don't have the really inexpensive deals). When exploring a quoted fare on a website, always click the "Rules" link – all conditions will be spelled out in small print. Some of the general travel sites offer moderately discounted "mystery fares" – the problem with these is you don't get to see the scheduling, or the airlines used, until after you've bought the ticket. Any reputable site will have a secure, encrypted facility for making credit-card payments – if it doesn't, you're better off not using the site to purchase.

Online booking agents and general travel sites

ⓦ **www.cheapflights.com** The most comprehensive source of flight deals: not a booking site itself, but maintains links to sites of travel agents offering the deals, or at least includes their phone number.

ⓦ **www.cheaptickets.com** or ⓦ **www.cheaptickets.co.uk** Discount flight specialists.

ⓦ **www.etn.nl/discount.htm** A hub of consolidator and discount agent web links, maintained by the non-profit European Travel Network.

ⓦ **www.expedia.com**, ⓦ **www.expedia.ca** or ⓦ **www.expedia.co.uk** Discount airfares, all–airline search engine and daily deals.

ⓦ **www.hotwire.com** Bookings from the US only. Last-minute savings of up to forty percent on regular published fares. Travellers must be at least 18 and there are no refunds, transfers or changes allowed.

ⓦ **www.lastminute.com** Offers good last-minute holiday package and flight-only deals.

ⓦ **www.priceline.com** or ⓦ **www.priceline.co.uk** Bookings from the US/UK only. Name-your-own-price website that has deals at around twenty percent off standard website fares. You don't know which airline you're bidding for, nor can you specify flight times (although you do specify dates) and the tickets are non-refundable, non-transferable and non-changeable.

ⓦ **www.princeton.edu/Main/air800.html** Has an extensive list of airline toll-free numbers and websites.

ⓦ **www.skyauction.com** Bookings from the US only. Auctions tickets and travel packages using a "second bid" scheme. Best strategy is to bid the maximum you're willing to pay, since if you win you'll pay just enough to beat the runner-up regardless of your maximum bid.

ⓦ **www.smilinjack.com/airlines.htm** An up-to-date compilation of airline website addresses.

ⓦ **www.travel.com.au** Australian website with a good range of discounted air fares; no-nonsense, easy to use and interpret.

ⓦ **http://travel.yahoo.com** Incorporates a lot of Rough Guide material in its coverage of destination countries and cities across the world, with information about places to eat and sleep etc.

ⓦ **www.travelselect.com** Useful and fairly easy-to-use, without most of the guff and banner adverts of the better-known sites. Linked to a walk-in travel agency in the UK (London) if you want to talk to a human.

ⓦ **www.travelshop.com.au** Australian website offering discounted flights, packages, insurance and online bookings.

ⓦ **www.travelocity.co.uk** Destination guides, hot web fares and deals for car rental, accommodation and lodging. Based on the North American SABRE central reservations system.

Flights and tours from the UK and Ireland

Most of the cheaper flights from Britain and Ireland to Turkey are charters, which are sold either with a package holiday or (less commonly) as a flight-only option. For longer stays or more flexibility, or if you're travelling out of season (when few charters are available), you'll need a scheduled flight. Useful advertisements for discounted flights of all types are found in the weekend-supplement travel sections of newspapers such as *The Independent*, *The Guardian*, *The Observer* and *The Sunday Times*.

You can **fly direct from the UK** to İstanbul, İzmir, Bodrum, Dalaman and Antalya. Reaching any other destination in Turkey involves a change of flights in İstanbul, though if you're flying with Turkish Airlines you can get a heavily discounted **domestic connecting flight** to most of the internal airports which they serve. It's also worth considering **indirect (ie, one-stop) flights** with other European airlines. These may well be cheaper than direct flights, and on the likes of Swiss, Air France or Lufthansa (which serves several Turkish airports direct from Germany), in-flight service may be superior. You can also use **Frequent**

Flyer miles to reach İstanbul from the UK: on most programmes just 20,000 miles are required, and if you need to change the return date this is usually possible – unlike with cheap APEX tickets – for a £50 fee.

Charter flights

Travel agents throughout Britain sell charter flights to Turkey, which usually operate from late April/early May to late October to İzmir, Dalaman, Bodrum and Antalya, with occasional winter charters to Antalya only. Late-night or dawn departures are common, though you may have a choice of more civilized hours.

The flights have fixed and unchangeable outward and return dates, and usually a maximum stay of two weeks, but occasionally you can pay a supplement and get a period of three, four or even more weeks. **Charter airlines** serving Turkey include Air 2000, Just, JMC and Monarch, but you can only book tickets on these through their designated agents (see list on p.14), and you may find that flight-only deals are not possible in peak season.

Departures are most commonly from London (Gatwick), Birmingham and Manchester. In summer, additional regional airports, such as Belfast, Edinburgh, Norwich, Bristol, Cardiff, East Midlands, Glasgow or Newcastle, are served.

Charter flight **fares** are often scarcely cheaper than scheduled services with Turkish Airlines, but you do get the convenience of non-stop service from a regional airport. As an example for the most common route, budget £230 for a Gatwick–Dalaman ticket in spring or autumn, £290 in peak season. Many charter airlines offer assorted upgrades – pre-bookable seats, extra legroom, "enhanced" in-flight meals, etc – for a typical supplement of £7–30 per person.

Remember that **reconfirmation** of return flights is vital and should be done at least 72 hours before departure. If you've travelled out with a package company, this service will usually be included as part of the rep's duties, but you should not assume that it has been done. Personal visits to the airline's representative office are best, as phone numbers given on ticket wallets are typically engaged.

Scheduled flights

Scheduled flights have longer ticket validities (30, 60, 90 or even 180 days), involve fewer or (occasionally) none of the typical restrictions applicable to charters, and often leave at more sociable hours. However, many of the cheaper, shorter-duration fares do have advance-purchase and/or minimum-stay requirements, and severe restrictions on date changes or refunds. Unlike charters, scheduled tickets usually don't require reconfirmation for the return.

The widest choice of scheduled flights from the UK is with the Turkish national carrier, **Turkish Airways** (THY), and with **Cyprus Turkish Airways** (KTHY).

THY links London Heathrow with İstanbul three times daily year-round, and Manchester with İstanbul four to five times weekly depending on the season. Thirty-day fares don't vary much across the year: London or Manchester to İstanbul costs £246, taxes included, though if you're willing to use the less popular dawn departures at both ends you can fly out of season for £166. Discounted Turkish domestic add-ons with THY are good value – eg, İstanbul–Dalaman return for £60, instead of the stand-alone price of over £100.

KTHY is a better, if rather less comfortable, bet for direct flights to the southwest coast; they operate useful services out of several UK airports. Typical winter patterns are twice-weekly London Stansted–Antalya, once weekly London Stansted–İzmir, and twice weekly London Heathrow–İzmir. During summer schedules become rather more elaborate: more or less daily Stansted–Antalya; two to three weekly Stansted–Dalaman and Stansted–İzmir; two weekly Heathrow–İzmir and Manchester–Dalaman; and one weekly Gatwick–Dalaman, Gatwick–Antalya, and Heathrow–Antalya. Depending on the season, thirty-day return fares run £250–290 for Stansted–Dalaman, £220–350 for Heathrow–İzmir. One-way tickets cost about seventy percent of these prices, while tickets valid for six weeks cost slightly more. Note that KTHY (airline code KY) doesn't show up on most travel-website searches;

you must usually book with the airline or its agents direct.

British Airways has twice-daily summer services (three daily in winter) from London Heathrow to İstanbul. One-month fares considerably undercut those of THY, averaging £164 with all taxes year-round, except for August/September when they rise to £224.

From Belfast, there are year-round daily scheduled services on combinations of BMI, British Airways and Lufthansa (potentially involving two stops) for a fairly hefty £234 winter/£318 summer. **From Dublin**, you'll do better on one-stop itineraries with Air France or KLM for €455–460; sometimes a more obscure carrier such as CSA will undercut this at €415. These fares prevail all year, without seasons, and may compare badly to direct summer charter prices.

KTHY has one weekly direct flight from Belfast to Antalya from April to October, and may begin a scheduled service out of Dublin in the near future. Otherwise, about the cheapest way to reach Turkey by air is to get a budget Ryanair flight to Stansted, which is a principal hub of KTHY (see p.13 for onward services).

Airlines

Aer Lingus Republic of Ireland ℡01/705 3333 or 844 4777, ⊛www.aerlingus.ie.
Air 2000 UK ℡0870/757 2757, ⊛www.air2000.com.
Air France UK ℡0845/0845 111, Republic of Ireland ℡01/605 0383, ⊛www.airfrance.co.uk.
BMI UK ℡0870/607 0555, Northern Ireland ℡0845/755 4554, Republic of Ireland ℡01/283 8833, ⊛www.flybmi.com.
British Airways UK ℡0845/773 3377, Republic of Ireland ℡0141/222 2345, ⊛www.britishairways.com.
Cyprus Turkish Airlines (KTHY) UK ℡020/7930 4851, ⊛www.kthy.net.
KLM UK ℡08705/074 074, ⊛www.klmuk.com.
Lufthansa UK ℡0845/773 7747, Republic of Ireland ℡01/844 5544, ⊛www.lufthansa.com.
Ryanair UK ℡0870/156 9569, Republic of Ireland ℡01/609 7800, ⊛www.ryanair.com.
Swiss UK ℡0845/601 0956, Republic of Ireland ℡01890/200515; ⊛www.swiss.com.
Turkish Airlines (THY) UK ℡020/7766 9300 or 0161/489 5289, ⊛www.turkishairlines.com.

Flight and travel agents

Alternative Travel UK ℡020/7923 3230, ⊛www.alternativeturkey.com. Specialist Turkish travel agency that's good for flight-only deals.
Aran Travel International Dublin ℡01/562 595, ⊛www.iol.ie/~aran/aranmain.htm. Good-value flights to all parts of the world.
Avro UK ℡0870/036 0111, ⊛www.avro.co.uk. Seat-only sales of all Monarch charter flights to Dalaman from Gatwick.
Co-op Travel Care Belfast ℡028/9047 1717. Flights and holidays around the world.
Gemstone Travel UK ℡01344/353807. Cheap flights to coastal Turkey, especially Bodrum and Dalaman.
JMC UK ℡0870/758 0194 or 555 0440, ⊛www.jmc.com. Good selection of flights only to Dalaman, Antalya and Bodrum from as many as 14 UK airports, plus three routes to İzmir.
Joe Walsh Tours Dublin ℡01/872 2555 or 676 3053, Cork ℡021/427 7959, ⊛www.joewalshtours.ie. General budget fares agent.
Just UK ℡0870/60 60 789, ⊛www.just.co.uk. Flight-only deals on the charter arm of Thomson Holidays, from 13 UK airports to Dalaman and Bodrum.
Lee Travel Cork ℡021/427 7111, ⊛www.leetravel.ie. Flights and holidays worldwide.
Liffey Travel Dublin ℡01/878 8322 or 878 8063. Package-tour specialists.
The London Flight Centre UK ℡020/7244 6411, ⊛www.topdecktravel.co.uk. Long-established agent dealing in discount flights.
North South Travel UK ℡01245/608291, ⊛www.nstravel.demon.co.uk. Flight agency offering discounted fares – profits are used to support projects in the developing world, especially the promotion of sustainable tourism.
Rosetta Travel Belfast ℡028/9064 4996, ⊛www.rosettatravel.com. Flight and holiday agent.
STA Travel UK ℡0870/160 6070, ⊛www.statravel.co.uk. Worldwide specialists in low-cost flights and tours for students and under-26s, though other customers welcome. A dozen branches across England, especially on or near university campuses.
Student & Group Travel Dublin ℡01/677 7834. Student and group specialists, mostly to Europe.
Trailfinders UK ℡020/7628 7628, Republic of Ireland ℡01/677 7888, ⊛www.trailfinders.com. One of the best-informed and most efficient agents for independent travellers, for scheduled flights only; branches in all the UK's largest cities, plus Dublin.

Tulip Holidays UK ☎ 020/7734 0484. Specialist Turkish flight consolidators; can also make full-scale arrangements (car rental, hotels, etc).

Package tours and special interest holidays

Over seventy companies in the UK offer some sort of Turkish beach, city or sailing holiday. The bulk of these target İstanbul and the coast between Çeşme and Alanya, but you needn't feel tied to a rigid programme since most outfits also feature fly-drive plans. As southern Turkey has such short, balmy winters, coastal yachting (*gület*) and accommodation packages are available from April to November (though you may have to use scheduled airlines rather than charters for the months cited). A few companies handle inland holidays, particularly to Cappadocia, while special-interest programmes include trekking, bird-spotting, scuba-diving, white-water rafting and battlefield tours.

A three- or four-night **city break** to İstanbul starts at around £400 for three-star bed-and-breakfast accommodation (including flights and transfers), rising to around £550 for the same break in one of the city's classic hotels. City-break prices tend not to vary much over the year.

Prices for a cheap-and-cheerful, two-week **beach package**, staying in a resort pension or two-star hotel (with breakfast), start at around £300 per person (double occupancy) in low season, including flights; a four-star hotel will set you back about £550–650. Quality self-catering villas tend to cost over £650 per person for the same low-season period (flight included), increasing to almost £800 at peak periods. **Fly-drive**-only deals weigh in at around £400 per person for four adults travelling for two weeks in high season, around £500 if there are only two of you.

A week's **yachting or cruising** holiday (plus two days on land) will cost £470–600 per person (double occupancy basis) depending on season, booked in the UK through an agent, but only £280–450 if arranged in Turkey directly with skippers. **Overland/hiking** trips range from £250–300 for a week along the Lycian Coast arranged locally, to £700–750 for a higher-quality

land/sea adventure booked in the UK. **Specialist holidays**, relying on the services of expert natural history/archeological guides, tend to be priciest of all, say £1500–1600 for two weeks. All these figures exclude the cost of the flight to Turkey.

General tour operators

Anatolian Sky ☎ 0121/325 5500, ⓦ www.anatolian-sky.co.uk. Middle-of-the-road-to-upmarket hotels and apartments on the southwest coast (particularly Kalkan, Dalyan, Akyaka, İçmeler, Orhaniye, Selimiye, Fethiye and Ölüdeniz), classic hotels in İstanbul, and tailor-made and fly-drive programmes.

Cachet Travel ☎ 020/8847 3846, ⓦ www.cachet-travel.co.uk. Small selection of classy (but very reasonably priced) premises, including exclusive representation of idyllic Turquoise Coast properties in remote locales such as Karaağaç, the Montenegro Ranch near Antalya, and Taşbükü; also somewhat more usual properties at Dalyan, Göcek, Ovacık Üzümlü and Cappadocia, plus guided special interest tours, fly-drives and select İstanbul hotels.

Mark Warner ☎ 0870/770 4222, ⓦ www.markwarner.co.uk. Two all-inclusive clubs on the Bodrum peninsula; sports and childcare laid on, thus excellent venues for families with kids.

Simply Turkey ☎ 020/8541 2204, ⓦ www.simply-travel.com. Quality self-catering villas or restored cottages in exclusive coastal locations such as Gümüşlük, Karakaya and Yalıkavak on the Bodrum peninsula, and Akyaka, Dalyan, Ölüdeniz and Kalkan, as well as gourmet hotels in İstanbul and Cappadocia (with hot-air ballooning an option there). Guided walking and botanical tours, plus painting and birdwatching courses; also a tailor-made and fly-drive department.

Sunquest ☎ 0870/366 1553, ⓦ www.sunquestholidays.co.uk. Long-established beach-hols outfit, with a budget-to-mid-range presence in most coastal resorts between Çeşme and Patara. Now owned by First Choice, so clients fly with Air 2000.

Tapestry Holidays ☎ 020/8235 7777, ⓦ www.tapestryholidays.com. Currently the best-quality Turkey operator, with a state-of-the-art website that permits virtual 3D tours of prospective accommodation. Selection of smallish but top-drawer *pansiyons* and hotels along the Turquoise Coast, with emphasis on the Bozburun peninsula, Kalkan, Kaş, Göcek, the Ölüdeniz area (including exclusive representation of Ocakköy), Akyaka and Turunç Bay. Also *gület* cruises, watersports, special-interest (hiking, drawing-and-painting) holidays plus a tailor-made department and fly-drives. Inland, well-selected accommodation in İstanbul and Cappadocia (where troglodytic hotels and ballooning are featured).

Turkish Collection (Ilios Travel)
℡01403/259788, 🌐 www.iliostravel.com. Very high-quality (and thus pricey) villas-with-pool on the Bodrum and Datça peninsulas, plus somewhat more conventional accommodation at Akyaka.

Trekking and adventure operators

Adrift ℡01488/684509, 🌐 www.adrift.co.uk.
Whitewater rafting on the Çoruh River from late May to late July; ten-day programme.

Exodus Travel ℡020/8675 5550,
🌐 www.exodus.co.uk. Strong on mountain-biking, hiking and *gület* cruises along the Lycian coast; well priced at under £700 for nine to twelve days, including flights, with accommodation in small hotels and village houses.

Explore Worldwide ℡01252/760 000,
🌐 www.explore.co.uk. Camping treks in Lycia, the Toros ranges and Cappadocia, plus a range of less strenuous overland minibus tours (one-, two- or three-week) across the country, which can be combined with one- or two-week *gület* cruises.

The Imaginative Traveller ℡020/8742 8612,
🌐 www.imaginative-traveller.com. Nine-to-seventeen-day explorations of the best of Turkey, travelling by bus, *gület* or even bicycle, camping out or staying at *pansiyon*s. Some unusual stops, opportunities for light walking and keen pricing, make this about the best overland group-tour operator for Turkey. Tie-in programmes around ANZAC Day, for London-based Antipodeans.

Travelbag Adventures ℡01420/541 007,
🌐 www.travelbag-adventures.com. Stands out for its "Family Adventures" programme pitched at veteran overland travellers, now with children, who want to introduce their offspring to the delights of expeditions. An eight-day Lycian Coast adventure includes Kekova and Tahtalı Dağ; 20 percent off for kids over 5.

Upcountry ℡01298/26760,
🌐 www.upcountryturkey.com. Tailor-made treks on long-distance walking routes created by Upcountry – see the website for their latest routes and projects.

Sailing and cruising operators

Day Dreams ℡020/7637 8921,
🌐 www.daydreams-travel.com. Twenty-strong fleet of *gület*s and schooners, which host "house parties" for singles and couples; ten days aboard in June or September cost a bit under £900, flights exclusive.

Nautilus Yachting ℡01732/867445,
🌐 www.nautilus-yachting.co.uk. Bare-boat charters out of Marmaris, Bodrum and Göcek, plus set one- or two-week flotilla itineraries between Selimiye, Göcek and Kalkan.

Setsail ℡01737/764443, 🌐 www.setsail.co.uk.
Flotilla holidays between Göcek, Fethiye and Orhaniye; also bare-boat charter.

Sunsail ℡023/9222 2222, 🌐 www.sunsail.com.
Flotilla holidays out of Göcek, Marmaris and Bodrum, taking in the Turquoise Coast and the peninsulas between Bodrum and Marmaris.

Tussock Cruising ℡020/8510 9292,
🌐 www.tussockcruising.com. Has a fleet of nine wooden *gület*s specially adapted so that you actually travel under sail power rather than (as with most such craft) with merely decorative rigging. Vessels accommodate parties of six to eighteen.

Special interest holidays

British Museum Traveller ℡020/7436 7575,
🌐 www.britishmuseumtraveller.co.uk. Most years offers a pair of ten- to fifteen-day archeological tours in spring and autumn, led by experts. Past outings have focused on lesser-known Ottoman or Selçuk sites, the standard Aegean classical ruins, or very early settlements of inner Anatolia by way of Byzantine or Armenian monuments.

Cox & Kings ℡020/7873 5018,
🌐 www.coxandkings.co.uk. Botanical tour operators which have at least one trip annually to Turkey, usually in early July to the Kaçkar mountains.

Gölköy Centre 🌐 www.yogaturkey.co.uk,
marketed through Neal's Yard Agency ℡0870/444 2702, 🌐 www.nealsyardagency.com. Yoga "farm" on Bodrum peninsula, which offers week-long courses, also encompassing painting, walking, shiatsu and assorted "personal growth" themes, from May to October; budget £365–400 per person per week, including full board and activities but not flights.

Greentours ℡01298/83563,
🌐 www.greentours.co.uk. Offers up to three annual, two-week natural-history holidays (emphasis on birds, orchids and butterflies), typically to Lakeland, the Kaçkar foothills and the Van basin. Enthusiastic English guides know their subject in incredible depth.

Gullivers Natural History Holidays
℡01525/270100. Birdwatching, botany and general springtime natural history tours; past (and annually changing) bases/areas have included Antalya with the lakes and river deltas nearby, and Kuşadası with its surrounding mountains, lakes and deltas.

Holt's Tours ℡01304/612248,
🌐 www.holts.co.uk. Battlefields specialist with a

one-week tour of western Turkey, focused on Gallipoli and the Dardanelles, in autumn (thus avoiding ANZAC Day mayhem).

Huzur Vadisi ⊛ www.huzurvadisi.com, marketed through Neal's Yard Agency ☎ 0870/444 2702, ⊛ www.nealsyardagency.com. One- and two-week programmes of light walks (May & Oct only) and yoga at a secluded, three-acre complex consisting of felt yurts or nomad dwellings around a renovated farmhouse and stone-clad pool, 10km inland of Göcek. Around £400 a week, including full board and activities but not flights; cheaper for non-participants.

Flights and tours from North America

No matter where you're flying from, it will almost certainly be cheapest to fly to İstanbul, as competition on routes results in heavy discounts off the published fares. If you can pick up a bargain transatlantic fare to Europe, you may discover that it's cheaper to arrange the final Turkey-bound leg of the journey yourself; onward flights from the UK are detailed on p.13.

Turkish Airways (THY) is the only carrier flying direct year-round from North America, with daily flights from New York (JFK) to İstanbul, and three weekly out of Chicago. There are half-a-dozen code-share feeder flights to these hubs on its partner, American Airlines, from several major cities, including San Francisco and Miami. Direct THY service from Miami was suspended in April 2002 but may re-appear if demand does. **Delta Airlines** is the only other airline offering a direct service (April–Oct), from New York to İstanbul, while **United Airlines** generally has the cheapest stopping fares via Frankfurt. All other flights route through **European hubs**, such as London, Paris, Frankfurt, Milan and Zürich, with the likes of British Airways, Air France, KLM, Alitalia and Swiss.

THY has the most comprehensive selection of **connecting flights** within Turkey, a major incentive to booking with them at least part of the way. THY normally charges about US$80 extra for these cities when the domestic leg is purchased as part of an international itinerary, but specialists, such as Turkish Tursan Tours (see "Flight and travel agents" overleaf), can often book you straight through for no extra charge, or book you through with a stop in İstanbul for an extra US$40 or so.

Tax-inclusive one-month fares out of **New York** vary from $537–604 in winter, up to $1020–1046 in peak season; it's usually worth paying the paltry difference for the non-stop service with Delta or THY, while United often has cheap summer deals at just under $800, via Frankfurt. For **Chicago**, the corresponding ranges are $621–646 winter, but $1097–1121 in summer (with THY's non-stop flight at the higher end of the band). Again, United has periodic deals for under $1000. From **San Francisco**, the seasonal bands are $709–757/$1203–1299, plus United's summer bargain at $1066. From **Miami**, expect to pay $616–666/$1121–1149, with United undercutting at $842, while from **Dallas/Fort Worth** the range is $691–717/$1209, again with United summer offers starting at $903.

There are no direct flights from Canada to Turkey, but several airlines do fly to İstanbul via major European hubs. From **Montréal** to İstanbul winter fares start at C$1003 on British Airways via London and C$1338 on United via Washington DC and Frankfurt, climbing to C$1350–1420 in summer with the same airlines. Out of **Vancouver**, winter fares start at C$1163 on British Airways via London, rising to C$1706 on a combination of Air Canada and either British Airways, Air France, Lufthansa or KLM. Depending on where you are, and current exchange rates, you might well be better off getting yourself cheaply to New York JFK, Chicago, or Seattle and arranging Turkey-bound travel originating there.

Specialist tour operators can take you off the beaten track in Turkey, or simply offer some companionship on your travels, but the best of the cultural or adventure tours do not come cheap. You can expect to pay a minimum of $2400 for a 14-day land-and-sea combo (inevitably with a couple of days in İstanbul at the start and end). Flights are never included in the tour price, but most tours include all meals (excluding drinks), guides and ground transport.

Round-the-world tickets rarely include Turkey because North American consolidators can't access discounted onward one-way tickets out of İstanbul. You'll find it much easier to get a ticket with a stopover in Athens, starting at about US$2200, and treat Turkey as a side-trip.

B

Airlines

Air Canada Airlines ☏1-888-247-2262, ⒲www.aircanada.ca.
Air France ☏1-800/237-2747, Canada ☏1-800/667-2747, ⒲www.airfrance.com.
Alitalia ☏1-800/223-5730; Canada ☏1-800/361-8336, ⒲www.alitalia.com.
American Airlines ☏1-800/433-7300, ⒲www.aa.com.
British Airways ☏1-800/247-9297, ⒲www.british-airways.com.
Delta Air Lines ☏1-800/241-4141, ⒲www.delta.com.
KLM/Northwest ☏1-800/447-4747, Canada ☏514/397-0775, ⒲www.klm.com.
Lufthansa ☏1-800/645-3880; Canada ☏1-800/563-5954, www.lufthansa.ca.com.
Swiss ☏1-877-FLY-SWISS, ⒲www.swiss.com.
Turkish Airlines (THY) ☏1-800/874-8875, ⒲www.turkishairlines.com.
United Airlines ☏1-800/538-2929, ⒲www.ual.com.

Flight and travel agents

Air Brokers International ☏1-800/883-3273 or 415/397-1383, ⒲www.airbrokers.com.
Consolidator and specialist in RTW and Circle-Pacific tickets.
Airhitch ☏1-800/326-2009 or 212/864-2000, ⒲www.airhitch.org. Standby seat broker. For a set price (currently $165–233, depending on where you live, plus taxes and a $29 fee), they guarantee to get you on a flight as close to your preferred western European destination as possible, within a week.
Airtech ☏212/219-7000, ⒲www.airtech.com. Standby seat broker; also deals in consolidator fares and courier flights.
Educational Travel Center ☏1-800/747-5551 or 608/256 5551, ⒲www.edtrav.com. Student/youth discount agent.
High Adventure Travel ☏1-800/350-0612 or 415/912-5600, ⒲www.airtreks.com. Round-the-world and Circle-Pacific tickets. The website features an interactive database that lets you build and price your own RTW itinerary
New Frontiers/Nouvelles Frontières ☏1-800/677 0720 or New York 212/986 6006, ⒲www.NewFrontiers.com. French discount-travel firm. Other branches in LA, San Francisco and Québec City.
Skylink US ☏1-800/AIR-ONLY or 212/573-8980, Canada ☏1-800/SKY-LINK. Consolidator.

STA Travel ☏1-800/777-0112 or 1-800/781-4040, ⒲www.sta-travel.com. Worldwide specialists in independent travel; also student IDs, travel insurance, car rental, rail passes, etc.
Student Flights ☏1-800/255-8000 or 480/951-1177, ⒲www.isecard.com. Student/youth fares, student IDs.
TFI Tours International ☏1-800/745-8000 or 212/736-1140. Consolidator.
Travac ☏1-800/872-8800, ⒲www.thetravelsite.com. Consolidator and charter broker, with offices in New York and Orlando.
Travel Avenue ☏1-800/333-3335, ⒲www.travelavenue.com. Full-service travel agent that offers discounts in the form of rebates.
Travel Cuts Canada ☏1-800/667 2887, US ☏416/979 2406, ⒲www.travelcuts.com. Canadian student-travel organization.
Turkish Tursan Travel New York ☏212/888-1180. Turkish specialist consolidator.
Worldtek Travel ☏1/800-243-1723, ⒲www.worldtek.com. Discount travel agency for worldwide travel.

Specialist tour operators

Adventures Abroad ☏1-800/665-3998 or 604/303-1099, ⒲www.adventures-abroad.com. Offers moderately active 7–10-day jaunts in western Turkey, 13–20-dayers in the east of the country.
Cultural Folk Tours ☏1-800935–TURK or 858/566-5951, ⒲www.boraozkok.com. Up to nine annual departures by this 1978-established San Diego-based company, lead (and musically accompanied) by Bora Özkök himself. A cut above the usual bus-tour dross, it offers some real insight into seldom-visited regions of the country (and central Asia as an add-on, if numbers permit).
Geographic Expeditions ☏1-800/777-8183 or 415/922-0448, ⒲www.geoex.com. Spring and autumn departures for their 17- and 21-day trek-plus-*gület*-cruises (10 days afloat off the Turquoise Coast), led by genial Turkish-American Enver Lucas and friends; 5-day Cappadocia add-on available.
Mythic Travel ☏1-800/228-0593 pin 12 or 831/438-3031, ⒲www.mythic-travel.com. Distinctly New Age "Magic Carpets" (as opposed to tours) with themed tags like "Mary and the Divine Feminine", "Jewish Life" and "Sufi Solstice".
Wilderness Travel ☏1-800/368-2794 or 510/558-2488, ⒲www.wildernesstravel.com. Offers two trips: 17 days encompassing İstanbul, Cappadocia and the far southeast, plus a 16-dayer incorporating a 10-day cruise using the same personnel and itinerary as Geographic Expeditions.

Flights and tours from Australia and New Zealand

There are no direct flights from Australia or New Zealand to Turkey. However, several weekly scheduled flights will get you there after either a plane change or short layover in the airline's hub – typically Bahrain, Bangkok, Singapore or Milan – before the final leg of the journey. A marginally less expensive, but far more time-consuming strategy would involve taking a flight to London and then proceeding from there with the benefit of the well-developed package industry (see p.15).

Flights booked directly through the airlines tend to be more expensive than those bought from discount agents, who will have the latest information on limited specials offered throughout the year. **Round-the-world tickets** including Turkey use combinations of airlines, and could be worth considering for a long trip taking in many destinations; generally some free stopovers are allowed, with fares starting at A$2000/NZ$2500.

Three-stop return fares to İstanbul tend to be rather cheaper than two-stoppers. Low-season, three-city fares, tax inclusive, run $A1700–1900 from **Melbourne** or **Sydney** to İstanbul, on assorted combinations of Aeroflot, British Airways, Qantas, Lufthansa, Singapore Airlines, Thai Airways, Emirates, Royal Jordanian and Turkish Airlines. In high season this climbs to $A2150 with British Airways, Qantas and Turkish Airlines, which is usually the cheapest two-stop itinerary (via Bangkok or Singapore, 5 weekly departures via either); others tend to exceed $A2350.

From New Zealand, Malaysia Airlines flies to İstanbul via Kuala Lumpur for NZ$2200–2800, depending on the season; linking flights to Australian or Asian centres are provided where needed by code-sharing.

Airlines

Aeroflot Australia ℡02/9262 2233, ⓦwww.aeroflot.com
Air New Zealand Australia ℡13 24 76, New Zealand ℡0800/737 000 or 09/357 3000, ⓦwww.airnz.com.
Alitalia Australia ℡02/9244 2400, New Zealand ℡09/302 1452, ⓦwww.alitalia.it.

British Airways Australia ℡02/8904 8800, New Zealand ℡09/356 8690, ⓦwww.britishairways.com.
Emirates Australia ℡02/9290 9700 or 1300/303 777, New Zealand ℡09/377 6004, ⓦwww.emirates.com.
Gulf Air Australia ℡02/9244 2199, New Zealand ℡09/308 3366, ⓦwww.gulfairco.com.
KLM Australia ℡1300/303 747, New Zealand ℡09/309 1782, ⓦwww.klm.com.
Lufthansa Australia ℡1300/655 727 or 02/9367 3887, New Zealand ℡09/303 1529 or 008/945 220, ⓦwww.lufthansa.com.
Malaysia Airlines Australia ℡13 26 27, New Zealand ℡0800/657 472, ⓦwww.mas.com.my.
Qantas Australia ℡13 13 13, New Zealand ℡0800/808 767 or 09/357 8900, ⓦwww.qantas.com.au.
Royal Jordanian Airlines Australia ℡02/9244 2701, New Zealand agent: Innovative Travel ℡03/365 3910, ⓦwww.rja.com.jo.
Singapore Airlines Australia ℡13 10 11 or 02/9350 0262, New Zealand ℡0800/808 909 or 09/303 2129, ⓦwww.singaporeair.com.
Thai Airways Australia ℡1300/651 960, New Zealand ℡09/377 3886; ⓦwww.thaiair.com.
Turkish Airlines Australia ℡02/9299 8400, ⓦwww.turkishairlines.com.

Flight and travel agents

Anywhere Travel Australia ℡02/9663 0411 or 018/401 014, ⓔanywhere@ozemail.com.au.
Budget Travel New Zealand ℡09/366 0061 or 0800/808 040, ⓦwww.budgettravel.co.nz.
Destinations Unlimited New Zealand ℡09/373 4033.
Flight Centres Australia ℡02/9235 3522 or 13 16 00, New Zealand ℡09/358 4310, ⓦwww.flightcentre.com.au.
Northern Gateway Australia ℡08/8941 1394, ⓦww.northerngateway.com.au.
STA Travel Australia ℡1300/360 960, ⓦwww.statravel.com.au, New Zealand ℡0508/782 872, ⓦwww.statravel.co.nz.
Student Uni Travel Australia ℡02/9232 8444, ⓔaustralia@backpackers.net.
Thomas Cook Australia ℡13 17 71 or 1800/801 002, ⓦwww.thomascook.com.au, New Zealand ℡09/379 3920, ⓦwww.thomascook.co.nz.
Trailfinders Australia ℡02/9247 7666.

Specialist tour operators

Adventures Abroad New Zealand ℡0800/800434, ⓦwww.adventures-abroad.com.

Offers 7–10-day jaunts in western Turkey, 13–20-dayers in the east of the country.

Adventure World Sydney ☎02/8913 0755, Perth ☎08/9226 4524, ⦿www.adventureworld.com.au, New Zealand ☎09/524 5118, ⦿www.adventureworld.co.nz. Not, in fact, very adventurous 8-day road trips of western Turkey, or 14 days including Cappadocia; 3-day add-on for the ANZAC sites available.

Sun Island Tours Australia ☎02/9283 3840, ⦿www.sunislandtours.com.au. Offers 3-to-5-day land tours in the west and, more compellingly, a week-long *gület* cruise from Bodrum to the Marmaris peninsula and back.

Tempo Holidays Australia ☎03/9646 0277, ⦿www.yallatours.com.au. Specialist agent for the entire eastern Mediterranean, with a good range of air tickets, car rental and accommodation in Turkey.

World Expeditions Australia ☎1300/720 000 for closest of five branches; New Zealand ☎0800/350354, ⦿www.worldexpeditions.com.au. Probably the most interesting Antipodean adventure operator for Turkey: does a 22-day "Turkey Panorama", including 5 days trekking and 3 days cruising, plus a 16-day botany tour in the Toros mountains.

By rail from Europe

Travelling to Turkey by rail makes very little sense unless you're equipped with a rail pass, and/or are determined on a longish holiday taking in several other countries en route.

By the most direct route **from the UK**, you're looking at a three-night, four-day journey, starting with the Eurostar service from London Waterloo to Brussels, then an overnight sleeper to Vienna, followed by a day-time Euro-City departure to Budapest, and finally two more nights aboard a sleeper to İstanbul. British and Irish citizens no longer require visas to transit Hungary, Romania or Bulgaria, but there are long waits at the Romanian–Bulgarian border, and you'll have to disembark at the Bulgarian/Turkish frontier to buy a Turkish tourist visa.

It's also not an especially cheap option. Unless you want a return fare good for six months (see p.21 for agents), you'll need a rail pass for starters (see opposite); throw in £79 for a return fare to Brussels, plus £33 per person for three nights of couchette supplements (£83 if you treat yourself to a proper sleeper compartment), and you're looking at a minimum total of £341–481 return.

An alternative strategy, potentially cheaper if slower, is to get to Italy by train and then proceed by ferry to Greece or even all the way to Turkey (see opposite).

Rail passes

The best train deal, though still more expensive than many airfares, is provided by an **InterRail pass**, which offers unlimited travel (except for express-train supplements and reservation fees) on a zonal basis within 28 European rail networks. These passes are only available to European residents, and you must provide proof of residency before being allowed to purchase one. To reach Turkey from the UK or Ireland, you'll need a pass valid for at least two zones: Turkey falls in Zone G, together with Italy, Greece and Slovenia, plus most of the Brindisi-Igoumenítsa ferries; to reach Italy from Britain, you'll need a Zone E pass to cross France; and to reach Thracian Turkey via Brussels, Vienna, Budapest and Bucharest, you'll need so many other zones (C, D and H) that you'll be obliged to buy an all-zone pass. For under-26s, you're looking at £229 for an all-zone pass valid for one month's second-class travel, £319 if you're over 26.

InterRail passes do not allow free travel between Britain and the continent, although InterRail Pass holders are eligible for discounts on rail travel in Britain and Northern Ireland, the cross-Channel ferries, and the London–Paris Eurostar service.

However, for North Americans, Australians and New Zealanders, a standard **Eurail Pass** (available from many discount and youth/student travel operators) is unlikely to pay for itself, whether going to, or travelling in, Turkey. This is among the many reasons for the popularity of the Fez Bus pass scheme (see "Getting around", p.36). For the record, the pass, which must be purchased before arrival in Europe, allows unlimited free first-class train travel in Turkey and 16 other countries, and is available in increments of 15 days, 21 days, 1 month, 2 months and 3 months. If you're under 26, you can save money with a Eurail Youthpass, which is valid for second-class travel in the same increments as the Eurail Pass. You stand a better chance of getting your money's worth out of a Eurail Flexipass, which is good for 10 or 15 days' travel within a two-month period. Like the standard pass, this comes in first-class and under-26/second-class versions.

Rail contacts

Deutsche Bahn ☏0870/243 5363. Sells passes and tickets, and can arrange the trans-Balkan rail itinerary.
Euro Railways ☏1-800-533-3341, ⊚www.eurorailways.com. Really good all-in-one outlet for all sorts of passes and tickets (though you can't get a simple fare to İstanbul).
Ffestiniog Travel ☏01766/512400. Assistance with the trans-Balkan rail itinerary.
InterRail ⊚www.inter-rail.co.uk. You may save some money by booking your pass via the InterRail website.
The Man in Seat 61 ⊚www.seat61.com. Named after British rail buff Mark Smith's favourite seat on the Eurostar, this non-commercial site is full of practical advice and planning on any train journey from the UK to just about anywhere in Eurasia (including Turkey). You can't buy tickets here, but all the necessary contacts are provided.

By car and ferry from Europe

In theory you can **drive from the UK** to Turkey in three to four days. However, this allows little time for stopping and sleeping, and it makes sense to slow down and take in a few places en route. For the full story on customs formalities and car insurance cover once in Turkey, see "Getting around", pp.42–43.

Given Serbia's war-damaged infrastructure, and the poor road links from Hungary to Bulgaria via Romania, the safest, if not exactly most direct, route is **through France, Italy and Greece**. You can cut the driving time by planning to take a ferry from Italy, direct to Turkey; and there are also short-hop ferry or hydrofoil services from five Greek islands to the southwestern Turkish coast.

The fastest way to start your journey is by using the **Eurotunnel** service (☏0870/535 3535, ⊚www.eurotunnel.com) via the Channel Tunnel, though some may prefer the traditional **cross-Channel ferry/hovercraft** links between England or Ireland and France. For full route and fare details, it's best to contact your local travel agent.

Ferries from Italy

Turkish Maritime Lines (TML, though known as TDİ in Turkish), the most consistent operator, runs a weekly, year-round ferry from **Venice to İzmir**. The 63-hour crossing costs £164/$252 per person for a third-class double cabin; small cars cost an additional £105/$161 (one-way, low-season fares, meals and taxes inclusive). On TML's 32-hour **Brindisi–Çeşme** crossing (to the second westernmost point of Anatolia), fares run about 25 percent cheaper than the Venice–İzmir run (mid-June to late Sept, 2 weekly). At present the only competition on the Brindisi–Çeşme route is offered by **Med Link Lines** (late June to mid-Sept, 2 weekly), with fares starting at £84/$129 per car in low season, £82/$127 per person in the cheapest double cabin. Agents for Med Link in the UK are Viamare Travel (see list below).

Useful contacts

Med Link Lines c/o Discovery Shipping Agency, Costa Morena, 72100 Brindisi, Italy ☏0831/548116, ⊚www.mll.gr.
TML UK, c/o Alternative Travel ☏020/7241 2687; Italy, c/o Bassani, Via XXII Marzo 2414, Venice ☏041/522 9544, or Brindisi ☏0831/568633; ⊚www.tdi.com.tr or www.tdi.gov.tr.
Viamare Travel Ltd UK ☏020/7431 4560, ⊚www.viamare.com.

Other useful websites

Agoudimos Lines ⊚www.agoudimos-lines.com.
ANEK ⊚www.anek.gr.
Blue Star ⊚www.bluestarferries.com.
Fragline ⊚www.fragline.gr.
Marlines ⊚www.marlines.com.
Minoan Lines ⊚www.minoan.gr.
Superfast ⊚www.superfast.com.
Ventouris ⊚www.ventouris.gr.

Ferries and hydrofoils from Greece

Many travellers take the short-hop ferries or hydrofoils over from the **Greek islands of Lésvos, Híos, Sámos, Kós and Rhodes**, to the respective Turkish ports of Ayvalık, Çeşme, Kuşadası, Bodrum, Marmaris and Fethiye. Services are daily in season (early May to early Oct) and, except for the Lésvos- and Fethiye-based services, they still run after a fashion in winter, but you may have to wait a week between departures. One-way prices of US$25–40 (plus, usually, US$10 more for Turkish port taxes) make

them vastly overpriced for the distances involved; full details of every service are given at the end of the North Aegean and the Central and Southern Aegean chapters.

Note that at the time of writing the only reliable **car-shuttle service** is from Híos to Çeşme. The Sámos–Kuşadası and Kós–Bodrum car services may resume in 2003, but don't count on this.

Red tape and visas

To enter Turkey you'll need a full passport, and a number of countries require visas, available only at the port of entry – do not pester Turkish embassies or consulates in your home country. Visas for citizens of the UK and Ireland cost £10/€15; US citizens are charged US$45; and Australians and New Zealanders pay US$5 for their visa. Citizens of Israel, Italy, Portugal and Spain currently also require visas to enter Turkey.

Note that while cashiers at much-frequented ports of entry, such as İstanbul's Atatürk airport, nonchalantly convert between different currencies (usually to your disadvantage) and give change for large notes, officials at less-used land or sea border crossings can be highly inflexible. For example, UK nationals may be required to pay in sterling only, and change for £20 notes will *not* be given.

Tourist visas are multiple entry and valid for three months from the date of issue – if you leave on a day-trip, for example to Greece, you should not have to pay for a new visa on re-entry. Most visitors are allowed to remain in Turkey for three months (South Africans, however, are given only one month); during this time it is forbidden to take up employment.

Once inside the country, you can **extend your visa** once only, for a further three months, by applying to the Foreigners' Department (*Yabancı Bürosu*) of the Security Division (*Emniyet Müdürlüğü*) in any provincial capital. Do this well before your time expires; it may take several weeks to process. If you know in advance that you want to stay longer, you should apply to the consulate in your own

country for a **long-stay visa**. On arrival in Turkey, the *Yabancı Bürosu* will convert it to a residence permit (*ikamet tezkeresi*), valid initially for one year (two with a work permit). Further renewals will be for three or five years. In either case, you will be required to show means of support (savings, a regular income from abroad or legal work in Turkey) and relinquish your passport until the permit is issued. Until recently, many people nipped across to a Greek island, Bulgaria or Northern Cyprus every three months and re-entered with a new three-month stamp, rather than go through the trouble of applying for a residence permit. Regulations have been tightened up since the millennium and you will now probably have to stay out of the country for at least 24 hours. Also, if the police have received a complaint that you are working, they may not re-admit you.

Turkish embassies and consulates abroad

Australia 60 Mugga Way, Red Hill, Canberra ACT 2603 ☎ 02/6295 0227.

Canada 197 Wurtemburg St, Ottawa, Ontario K1N 8L9 ☏613/789-4044.
Ireland 11 Clyde Road, Ballsbridge, Dublin 4 ☏01/668 5240.
New Zealand 15–17 Murphy St, Level 8, Wellington ☏04/472 1290.
South Africa 1067 Church St, Hatfield 0181, Pretoria ☏012/342 5063.
UK 43 Belgrave Square, London SW1X 8PA ☏020/7393 0202.
USA 2525 Massachusetts Ave NW, Washington DC 20008 ☏202/612 6700.

Customs and border inspections

Since Turkey's customs union with the European Union in the year 2000, travellers are now free to bring in valuable electronic gadgets, such as laptops and personal stereos, without having them written into their passport. But since Turkey is not yet actually an EU member, **duty-free limits** – and sales – for alcohol and tobacco are still prevalent. Limits are posted clearly at İstanbul's Atatürk airport, and apply for all frontiers: 2 litres of spirits or 2 litres of wine, plus 1000 cigarettes. If you haven't exploited your allowance at your departure airport, it's as well to know that you can usually buy duty-free goods at your Turkish port of arrival, at prices considerably cheaper than northern European airports.

Checks on the way out may be more thorough, and you should arrive at the airport or ferry dock in good time in case the customs officers decide to be slow and inquisitive. Only an idiot would try and take **drugs** through Turkish customs, although it's more likely that the guards will be on the lookout for **antiquities** and **fossils** – there is a ready market in Turkey and abroad for rare specimens. Penalties for trying to smuggle these out include long jail sentences, plus a large fine. For a discussion on what constitutes an antiquity, see "Bazaars and shopping", p.69.

Health

No special inoculations are required for visiting Turkey, although if you don't want to take any chances, jabs against typhoid and tetanus are suggested, particularly if you're travelling to eastern Anatolia. Some visitors also take the precaution of getting injections against hepatitis A. For a summer visit it's probably worth the discomfort – the risk is possibly greater in İstanbul than in remote rural areas. Malaria is generally a seasonal (April–July) problem in the regions between Adana and Mardin (mainly the area covered in Chapter 11), and incidence has skyrocketed recently around Şanlıurfa in areas newly irrigated by the Southeastern Anatolian Project (see box on p.869). However, for brief visits you shouldn't need prophylactic drugs. For up-to-date advice consult a travel clinic with experience in exotic diseases.

Health problems

You're unlikely to encounter many health problems in Turkey. **Tap water** is heavily chlorinated and probably safe to drink, though not exactly delectable (except in restaurants, which serve it chilled and minimally filtered). In İstanbul, where it comes out of the tap an off-putting orange colour, it is absolutely to be avoided in favour of bottled water. **Rural springs** are labelled *içilir*, *içilbelir* or *içme suyu* (all meaning "potable"), or *içilmez* (not drinkable).

Many people experience bouts of mild **diarrhoea**, and the chances of this happen-

23

ing increase the longer you stay in the country. As a precaution take anti-diarrhoea tablets with you (you'll be able to buy a locally produced variant if you forget). Lomotil or Imodium, trade names for the antiparastaltic diphenoxylate, are easily available in Turkey and will allow you to travel without constantly running to the bathroom, but do not kill the bug that ails you. Buscopan, also on sale locally, is particularly good for stomach cramps resulting from food poisoning and sunstroke. For electrolyte replacement resulting from dehydrating diarrhoea, Ge-Oral powder dissolved in pure water is a good local remedy.

Particularly during the hot summer months, more serious **food poisoning** is a possibility – even in the biggest cities and resorts. In restaurants, avoid dishes that look as if they have been standing around and make sure meat and fish are well grilled. Don't, whatever you do, eat stuffed mussels in summer. If you're struck down, the best thing is to let the bug run its course and drink lots of fluids; eating plain white rice and yoghurt also helps. Stubborn cases will need a course of antibiotics – pharmacists (see opposite) are trained to recognize symptoms and can put you in touch with the nearest state clinic for free treatment.

Health information and travel clinics

UK

British Airways Travel Clinics 28 regional clinics, call ☎01276/685 040 for the nearest, ✆www.britishairways.com. All clinics offer vaccinations, tailored advice from an online database and a complete range of travel healthcare products.
Communicable Diseases Unit Brownlee Centre, Glasgow ☎0141/211 1074. Travel vaccinations.
Hospital for Tropical Diseases Mortimer Market Centre, off Capper St, London WC1 ☎020/7388 9600, Health Line ☎09061/337 733. A consultation costs £15, which is waived if you have your injections here. The recorded Health Line gives hints on hygiene and illness prevention as well as listing appropriate immunizations.
Liverpool School of Tropical Medicine Pembroke Place, Liverpool ☎0151/708 9393, Malaria Helpline 24-hr recorded message ☎0891/600 350. Walk-in clinic Mon–Fri 1–4pm.
MASTA (Medical Advisory Service for Travellers Abroad), London School of Hygiene and Tropical

Medicine ☎0906/822 4100. Pre-recorded 24-hr Travellers' Health Line, giving written information tailored to your journey by return of post.
Trailfinders 194 Kensington High St, London W8 ☎020/7938 3999. Immunization clinics (no appointments necessary).

Ireland

Dun Laoghaire Medical Centre 5 Northumberland Ave, Dun Laoghaire, Co Dublin ☎01/280 4996. Advice on medical matters abroad.
Travel Health Centre Department of International Health and Tropical Medicine, Royal College of Surgeons, Mercers Medical Centre, Stephen's St Lower, Dublin ☎01/402 2337. Expert pre-trip advice and inoculations.
Travel Medicine Services ☎028/9031 5220. Offers medical advice before a trip and help afterwards in the event of a tropical disease.

USA and Canada

Canadian Society for International Health ☎613/241-5785, ✆www.csih.org. Distributes a free pamphlet, "Health Information for Canadian Travellers", containing an extensive list of travel health centres in Canada.
Centers for Disease Control ☎1-800/311-3435 or 404/639-3534, International Travelers Hotline ☎1-877/FYI-TRIP, ✆www.cdc.gov. Publishes suggested inoculations, precautions and other background information for travellers.
International Association for Medical Assistance to Travellers US ☎716/754-4883, ✆www.sentex.net/~iamat, Canada ✆519/836-0102. A non-profit organization that can provide a list of English-speaking doctors in Turkey, climate charts and leaflets on various diseases, and inoculations.
International SOS Assistance ☎1-800/523-8930, ✆www.intsos.com. Members receive pre-trip medical referral info, as well as overseas emergency services designed to complement travel insurance coverage.
Travel Medicine ☎1-800/872-8633, ✆www.travmed.com. Sells first-aid kits, mosquito netting, water filters, reference books and other health-related travel products.
Travelers Medical Center ☎212/982-1600. Consultation service on immunizations and treatment of diseases for people travelling to developing countries.

Australia

Travellers' Medical and Vaccination Centres Adelaide ☎08/8212 7522; **Brisbane** ☎07/3221

9066; Canberra ☎02/6257 7156; Darwin ☎08/8981 2907; Hobart ☎03/6223 7577; Melbourne ☎03/9602 5788; Perth ☎08/9321 1977; Sydney ☎02/9221 7133.

New Zealand

Travellers' Medical and Vaccination Centres Auckland ☎09/373 3531; Christchurch ☎03/379 4000; Wellington ☎04/473 0991.

Animal hazards

Snakes and **scorpions** can lurk among the rocks and stones at archeological sites, and in the nooks and crannies of ground-floor accommodation. There are two kinds of vipers (*engerek* in Turkish): the very deadly, metre-long Ottoman viper, fortunately quite rare, and the smaller, more common and less dangerous asp viper. Neither is particularly aggressive unless disturbed, and both are most commonly seen during long, but not too hot, spring days.

Mosquitoes are a problem in some places, and since no good topical repellents are available locally, you should bring your own. At night mozzies are most easily dispatched with locally sold incense coils (*spiral tütsü*) or an *Esem Mat*, a small, electrified tray that slowly vapourizes an odourless disc during the course of a night. The word for mosquito netting is *çibindirik*; provision of which by hotels and *pansiyons* in areas of heavy infestation is becoming almost standard.

Rabies is perhaps the greatest potential danger, and the giant Sivas-Kangal sheepdogs are the most obvious possible source, though they are rarely aggressive unless their flock is closely approached. Be wary of any animal that bites, scratches or licks you, particularly if it's behaving erratically. First aid involves flushing a wound with soap and water after encouraging limited bleeding. Apply antiseptic and bandage if necessary, but do not suture, and seek medical attention immediately. A six-injection course of human diploid cell vaccine (HDCV) – given in the arm – needs to be started within 72 hours, followed by a single jab of human rabies immunoglobulin (HRIG).

Medical treatment

For minor complaints, head for the nearest **pharmacy** (*eczane*). Even the smallest town will have at least one, where you'll be able to obtain remedies for ailments such as diarrhoea, sunburn and flu. In larger towns, *eczane* staff may know some English or German. Pharmacists in Turkey are able to dispense medicines, invariably locally produced, that would ordinarily require a prescription abroad. Medication prices are low, but you may find it difficult to find exact equivalents to your home prescription, so bring it, and a good supply of the actual medication you may need, along. **Night-duty pharmacies**, often found near main hospitals, are known as *nöbet(çi)*; a list of the current rota is posted in Turkish in every chemist's front window, as "Nöbetçi Eczaneleri".

For more serious ailments you'll find well-trained **doctors** in larger towns and cities. Most of these are specialists, advertising themselves by means of signs outside their premises. A *diş tabibi* or *hekimi* is a dentist; a *tıbbî doktor* will treat ailments of all kinds; while an *operatör* is a qualified surgeon.

If you're not sure what's wrong with you, it's best to go instead to one of the free **state clinics** (*sağlık ocağı*), which can give diagnoses and prescriptions, or a **hospital** (*hastane*), indicated by a blue street sign with a large white "H" on it. Hospitals are either public (*Devlet Hastane* or *SSK Hastanesi*) or private (*Özel Hastane*); the latter are vastly preferable in terms of cleanliness and standard of care, and since all foreigners must pay for any attention anyway, you may as well get the best available. Fees are lower than in northern Europe and North America but still substantial enough to make insurance cover essential. The medical faculties of major universities – eg, in İstanbul, İzmir, Edirne and Bursa – also have affiliated teaching hospitals that are infinitely better than the state hospitals, but less expensive than the private ones. Admission desks of private hospitals can also recommend their affiliated doctors if you don't want or need to be an in-patient, and your consulate or the tourist office may also be able to provide you with the address of an **English-speaking doctor**.

If you're too ill to move, but must summon a doctor, hotel-room visits will cost about US$50, with perhaps another US$25 for medication delivered from a local pharmacy.

If you're on an all-inclusive **package tour**, the better companies will have arrangements with competent, English-speaking doctors in or near the resort.

In a medical **emergency** summon an ambulance by dialing ☏ 112.

Contraception and feminine hygiene

About a dozen international brands of **birth control** pills (*doğum kontrol hapı*) are sold over the counter at pharmacies. **Condoms** are also sold in most pharmacies super-market chains such as Gima and the larger branches of Migros, which stock a good range of imported brands; don't buy off street carts, where stock may be tampered with or expired. The "proper" word is *preservatif*, the slang term *kılıf* ("hood"). AIDS and other sexually transmitted diseases are now prevalent in Turkey.

Tampons are available from pharmacies and supermarkets for the same price as in the UK; Orkid is the much-improved domestic brand of "sanitary towel".

Insurance

There are not yet any reciprocal health-care privileges between Turkey and the European Union, so it's essential to take out an insurance policy before travelling to cover against theft, loss, illness or injury. Before paying for a new policy, however, it's worth checking whether you are already covered: some all-risks home-owners' or renters' insurance policies may cover your possessions when overseas, and many private medical schemes offer coverage extensions for abroad.

A specialist travel insurance company can sell you a suitable policy, or consider the travel insurance deal we offer (see box opposite). A typical travel insurance policy usually provides cover for the loss of baggage, tickets and – up to a certain limit – cash, cards or travellers' cheques, as well as cancellation or curtailment of your journey.

Most policies exclude so-called **dangerous sports** unless an extra premium is paid: in Turkey this can mean scuba-diving, whitewater rafting, paragliding, windsurfing and trekking, though probably not kayaking or jeep safaris. Many policies can be chopped and changed to eliminate coverage you don't need – for example, sickness and accident benefits can often be excluded or included at will. If you do take **medical coverage**, ascertain whether benefits will be paid as treatment proceeds or only after return home, and whether there is a 24-hour medical emergency number. When securing **baggage cover**, make sure that the per-article limit – typically under £500/US$750 – will cover your most valuable possession. Travel agents and tour operators are likely to require travel insurance when you book a package holiday – you're not obliged to take theirs, though you may be required to sign a declaration saying that you already have a policy with a particular company.

If you need to make a medical **claim**, you should keep receipts for medicines and treatment, and in the event you have anything **stolen or lost**, you must obtain an official statement from the police (or the airline that lost your bags). In the wake of growing numbers of fraudulent claims, most insurers won't even entertain a claim unless you have a police report. There is usually also a time limit for submitting claims after the end of your journey.

Rough Guide travel insurance

Rough Guides offers its own **travel insurance**, customized for our readers by a leading UK broker and backed by a Lloyds underwriter. It's available for anyone, of any nationality, travelling anywhere in the world.

There are two main Rough Guide insurance plans: **Essential**, for basic, no-frills cover; and **Premier** – with more generous and extensive benefits. Alternatively, you can take out **annual multi-trip insurance**, which covers you for any number of trips throughout the year (with a maximum of 60 days for any one trip). Unlike many policies, the Rough Guides schemes are calculated by the day, so if you're travelling for 27 days rather than a month, that's all you pay for. If you intend to be away for the whole year, the Adventurer policy will cover you for 365 days. Each plan can be supplemented with a "Hazardous Activities Premium" if you plan to indulge in sports considered dangerous, such as skiing, scuba-diving or trekking. Rough Guides also does good deals for older travellers, and will insure you up to any age, at prices comparable to SAGA's.

For a policy quote, call the **Rough Guide Insurance Line** toll-free on ☎0800/015 09 06 (in the UK); on ☎1-866/220 5588 (in the USA); or, if you're calling from elsewhere ☎+44 1243/621 046. Alternatively, get an online quote at ⓦwww.roughguides.com/insurance

Information, maps and websites

Before you set off on your trip it's worth a visit to a Turkish tourist office (official-ly known as the Information Office of the Embassy), where you'll be able to pick up a few very basic maps and glossy brochures. Don't overload your luggage with these, however, as much the same choice is available within Turkey itself. What you should take with you are decent regional maps, since those on sale locally are generally inadequate. Turkey-related sites on the internet are not wild-ly exciting; many are in Turkish only and/or have a very short life span.

Tourist offices

Most Turkish towns of any size will have a *Turizm Danışma Bürosu* or **tourist office** of some sort, often lodged inside the public library or *Belediye* (city hall) in the smaller places. However, outside the larger cities and obvious tourist destinations there's often very little actual information to be had, and the staff may well try to dismiss you with a selection of useless brochures. Lists of accommodation for all budgets are some-times a useful feature of the more heavily patronized offices; the staff, however, will generally not make bookings. In the more

frequented spots – with some sterling exceptions – staff made world-weary by the steady stream of visitors can be perfunctory at best in the discharge of their duties. On the other hand, staff in out-of-the-way places can be embarrassingly helpful.

The best plan is to have a specific ques-tion – about bus schedules, festival ticket availability or museum opening hours – although in remote regions there is no guar-antee that there will be anyone who can speak English.

Tourist office **opening hours** generally adhere to a standard schedule of 8.30am to 12.30pm and 1.30pm to 5.30pm, Monday to Friday. Between May and September in big-name resorts and large cities, these hours extend well into the evening and through much of the weekend. In winter, by contrast, many tourist offices in out-of-the-way spots will be shut most of the time.

Turkish information offices abroad

Australia Room 17, Level 3, 428 George St, Sydney, NSW 2000 ☎02/9223 3055, @turkish@ozemail.co.au.
Canada Constitution Square, 360 Albert St, Suite 801, Ottawa, ON K1R 7X7 ☎613/230-8654, @www.magi.com/~toturcan.
Ireland Refer to the embassy (see p.23).
New Zealand Refer to the embassy (see p.23).
UK 1st Floor, 170–173 Piccadilly, London W1V 9DD ☎020/7766 9300, @www.gototurkey.co.uk.
USA 821 United Nations Plaza, NY 10017 ☎212/687-2194; 2525 Massachusetts Ave NW, Washington DC 20008 ☎202/612-6800, @www.turkey.org/turkey.

Turkey on the internet

We've indicated relevant websites throughout the Guide – mostly for hotels and adventure-tour companies – but the websites listed below provide general background for Turkey. The bulk of the following sites are travel-arrangement-related, though there are also a few good general ones, as well as some sites featuring current events and news. With the single noted exception of Kalkan most local resort-based sites are poor, with scanty or obsolete information.

Useful websites

General

@www.hitit.co.uk
An excellent "alternative" on-line guide, readable and generally sound, though weak on anything east of Cappadocia since the authors are based on the Turquoise Coast.
@www.turkey.com
Sophisticated portal with links grouped into channels (business, travel, news, culture, etc), plus forums that you have to register for – and which attract some lively debate.
@www.turkeycentral.com
Essentially a portal to a claimed figure of nearly 5000 other sites; most of the links are useful –

"diving" gets you a list of dive operators and venues, "skiing" gets an assortment of winter resorts – but some (eg, "maps") are clunkers.
@www.twarp.com
İstanbul-based site that offers regional thumbnail sketches and a very limited accommodation-booking facility.

Antiquities and architecture

@www.exploreturkey.com
Excellent background on the country's historical monuments, written by an archeologist, though coverage is strongly biased towards İstanbul, Cappadocia and the southwest coast.
@www.patriarchate.org/ ecumenical_patriarchate/chapter_4
Literate coverage of İstanbul's numerous Byzantine monuments, though loads at glacial pace because of the lavish illustrations.

Specific destinations

@www.galata.net
Covers the Galata and Beyoğlu districts of İstanbul – lots of interesting maps, photos and video clips, with English text.
@www.kackarmountains.com
Despite the name, also offers well-written, lavishly photographed coverage of the Aladağlar, Mt Ararat and volcanos of the central plateau, as well as the Pontic Kaçkar range. Maintained by recommended domestic trekking agency Middle Earth, but offers plenty of sensible advice for those who want to set off on their own.
@www.kalkan.org.tr
Probably the best resort-specific site, with features on the village and surrounds and a good selection of profiled lodging.

News and views

@www.ntv.com.tr/news/ENGLISH_Front.asp
The only domestic website offering good news coverage in passable English; updated almost daily.
@www.turkey.org
The official party line, maintained by the Turkish Embassy in the US; also good for customs and visa rules, etc.
@www.turkishdailynews.com
Updated daily in theory, this gives abridged versions of all this English-language paper's print-version stories, both current and archived.
@www.turkishnews.com
A site nominally run by Turkish alumni of American universities, but hitting the "Turkish News" links takes you to the utterances of the government's press and information office.

Miscellaneous

⊛ www.tapu.co.uk
Been to Turkey on holiday a dozen times, can't tear yourself away? This site flogs real estate, though most properties are in the Fethiye area.

⊛ www.turkeygaytravel.com
As it says; fill in the on-line form with your criteria and it will help you find gay-friendly accommodation, particularly in İstanbul. Also a few useful reviews of clubs and discos in that city.

Touring and city maps

Stock up on maps *before* you leave, as Turkish-produced ones are neither detailed nor accurate. That said, very few of those available outside – or inside – the country are remotely reliable, since ordnance-survey-based cartography and/or large-scale coverage is completely absent.

The least bad **touring maps**, more or less accurately showing many smaller villages, are the series of seven folding maps put out by Kartographischer Verlag Reinhard Ryborsch (Frankfurt, Germany), which cover the entire country at a scale of 1:500,000. They are currently unavailable in the UK, but both original and pirated versions can still be found at better bookshops in İstanbul, Ankara and the larger resorts like Bodrum or Kusadası; the Turkish distributor is Koreks (☎0212/236 4893 or 0312/256 5523).

An alternative, also difficult to obtain, is a series originally produced by the German Reise und Verkehrsverlag, but distributed in the UK and North America by GeoCenter. This covers the entire country in a variety of formats, including "Western Turkey" and "Eastern Turkey", each at 1:800,000, and the entire country on the same scale, double-sided. **Drivers** are best off with the ring-bound EuroAtlas version, which divides the country into manageable pages. There are also regional GeoCenter folding offerings: "South Coast", "West Coast", "Southeast Turkey" and "Black Sea and West", all at a scale of 1:600,000. Some of these may be on sale at Turkish resorts, but don't count on it. Otherwise, marginally the best of a rather bad lot is the Shell Eurokarte/Marco Polo double-sided 1:750,000 sheet.

Tourist offices in İstanbul, Ankara, Antalya, Bursa and İzmir (as well as overseas offices) stock reasonable, free **city street plans**,

although the İstanbul one is restricted to the centre and lacks detail. The quality of local sketch plans available at provincial tourist offices varies widely though, as a rule of thumb, the more tourists a place gets the better the maps tend to be.

There are very few maps of Turkish cities on sale, and when available they are rarely good value. Notable exceptions are GeoCenter's easy-to-read 1:7500 EuroCity plan of central İstanbul, plus their exhaustive, ring-bound A–Z atlas (harder to find), including pages at scales of 1:15,000 and 1:7500. The latter is available only in good İstanbul bookshops, alongside the slightly less accurate, locally published Asya A–Z atlas. One or the other is a worthwhile investment if you plan to spend a lot of time in the city. Otherwise, the Canadian-produced ITMB map (1:11,000) has the best street-grid depiction and shows both banks of the Bosphorus, although it's one of the flimsiest products; Hallwag's 1:10,500 offering is the better-jacketed runner-up. Failing these, you're stuck with the Cartographia offering, or the laminated Insight Fleximap (both 1:12,500). Note that only the Asya atlas shows the Asian side of the city in any detail.

Map outlets

UK

Blackwell's Map and Travel Shop 50 Broad St, Oxford OX1 3BQ ☎01865/793 550, ⊛http://maps.blackwell.co.uk/index.html.
Heffers Map and Travel 20 Trinity St, Cambridge CB2 1TJ ☎01223/568 568, ⊛www.heffers.co.uk.
John Smith & Son 100 Cathedral St, Glasgow G4 0RD ☎0141/552 3377, ⊛www.johnsmith.co.uk.
The Map Shop 30a Belvoir St, Leicester LE1 6QH ☎0116/247 1400, ⊛www.mapshopleicester.co.uk.
National Map Centre 22–24 Caxton St, London SW1H 0QU ☎020/7222 2466, ⊛www.mapsnmc.co.uk.
Newcastle Map Centre 55 Grey St, Newcastle-upon-Tyne, NE1 6EF ☎0191/261 5622.
Stanfords 12–14 Long Acre, WC2E 9LP ☎020/7836 1321, ⊛www.stanfords.co.uk.

Ireland

Easons Bookshop 40 O'Connell St, Dublin 1 ☎01/873 3811, ⊛www.eason.ie.

Hodges Figgis Bookshop 56–58 Dawson St, Dublin 2 ☎01/677 4754, ⓦwww.hodgesfiggis.com.

USA

Adventurous Traveler Bookstore 102 Lake Street, Burlington, VT 05401 ☎1-800/282-3963, ⓦwww.adventuroustraveler.com.
Book Passage 51 Tamal Vista Blvd, Corte Madera, CA 94925 ☎1-800/999-7909, ⓦwww.bookpassage.com.
Distant Lands 56 S Raymond Ave, Pasadena, CA 91105 ☎1-800/310-3220, ⓦwww.distantlands.com.
Elliot Bay Book Company 101 S Main St, Seattle, WA 98104 ☎1-800/962-5311, ⓦwww.elliotbaybook.com.
Forsyth Travel Library 226 Westchester Ave, White Plains, NY 10604 ☎1-800/367-7984, ⓦwww.forsyth.com.
Globe Corner Bookstore 28 Church St, Cambridge, MA 02138 ☎1-800/358-6013, ⓦwww.globercorner.com.
GORP Books & Maps ☎1-877/440-4677, ⓦwww.gorp.com/gorp/books/main.htm.
Map Link 30 S La Patera Lane, Unit 5, Santa Barbara, CA 93117 ☎805/692-6777, ⓦwww.maplink.com.
Omni Resources 1004 South Mebane St, Burlington NC 27216 ☎336/227 8300, ⓦwww.omnimap.com
Phileas Fogg's Travel Center #87 Stanford Shopping Center, Palo Alto, CA 94304 ☎1-800/533-3644, ⓦwww.foggs.com.
Rand McNally Around thirty stores across the US ☎1-800/333-0136 ext 2111, or ⓦwww.randmcnally.com for the nearest store.
Traveler's Choice Bookstore 22 W 52nd St, New York, NY 10019 ☎212/664-0995, ⓔtvlchoice@aol.com.

Canada

Open Air Books and Maps 25 Toronto St, Toronto ON M5C 2R1 ☎416/363-0719.
Ulysses Travel Bookshop 4176 St-Denis, Montréal, PQ H2W 2M5 ☎514/843-9447, ⓦwww.ulysses.ca.
World of Maps 118 Holland Ave, Ottawa, Ontario K1Y 0X6 ☎613/724-6776, ⓦwww.itmb.com.
World Wide Books and Maps 1247 Granville St, Vancouver V6Z 1G3 ☎604/687-3320, ⓦwww.worldofmaps.com.

Australia

The Map Shop 6 Peel St, Adelaide ☎08/8231 2033, ⓦwww.mapshop.net.au.
Mapland 372 Little Bourke St, Melbourne ☎03/9670 4383, ⓦwww.mapland.com.au.
Perth Map Centre 1/884 Hay St, Perth ☎08/9322 5733, ⓦwww.perthmap.com.au.
Travel Bookshop Shop 3, 175 Liverpool St, Sydney ☎02/9261 8200.
Worldwide Maps & Guides 187 George St, Brisbane ☎07/3221 4330.

New Zealand

Mapworld 173 Gloucester St, Christchurch ☎03/374 5399, ⓦwww.mapworld.co.nz.
Specialty Maps 46 Albert St, Auckland ☎09/307 2217, ⓦwww.ubd-online.co.nz/maps.

Trekking maps

It is virtually impossible to obtain large-scale topographical maps of specific areas for **trekking** (except for the Lycian Way, see p.464), though restrictions in Turkey were lifted in 1993 enabling visitors in theory to obtain 1:50,000 topographic sheets from the Harita Genel Müdürlügü (General Mapping Ministry) in the Dikimevi district of Ankara. However, you will need to speak reasonable Turkish to get in the door – it's best to have a local get them on your behalf.

Overseas, it is possible to obtain photocopies of a 1:200,000 series prepared with German assistance in 1944, but again with some difficulty: the Turks have security or copyright protocols with other NATO countries, and permission must be obtained from relevant military authorities before copying commences. In Britain you should consult the Map Room at the Royal Geographical Society (1 Kensington Gore, London SW7 2AR ☎020/7591 3050), which will then refer you to the Directorate of Geographic Information in Surrey for a permit. This may not be granted automatically – you will need to present yourself as a serious researcher or someone organizing an expedition. If you're part of a decently funded expedition, contact Omni Resources in the US (see "Map outlets" opposite); they have copies of large-scale Soviet topographic/geological maps for most areas of the country, but the cost – several thousand dollars for a full set – is prohibitive for most punters.

Usable enough maps for the most popular trekking areas can be found in Trekking in

Turkey (Lonely Planet, o/p). Barring that, the Turkish Tourist Office's A4-sized brochure entitled "Mountaineering" includes six sketch maps at varying scales of popular alpine areas, but these were issued in the early 1980s by the Turkish Mountaineering Federation and are now woefully out of date. The Mountains of Turkey (Cicerone/Hunter) reproduces these sketches without correction or elaboration.

Costs, money and banks

While no longer as rock-bottom cheap as it was, much of Turkey is still less expensive than other Mediterranean travel destinations and travellers with foreign currency find themselves at a considerable advantage, especially after the 2001 devaluation of the Turkish currency and subsequent economic crash. There's a wide disparity in costs between relatively unvisited spots in the interior and the coastal resorts, where over the long term, prices have steadily crept up to scarcely less than those in Greece, Spain and Portugal. Domestic inflation runs at sixty–ninety percent annually, depending on which set of statistics you believe; outsiders are spared the full effect of this by a constant devaluation of the Turkish currency against hard currencies, amounting to about seventy percent a year. We've therefore quoted all prices in the Guide in US$ (or £ sterling in some British-dominated resort areas) and, with minor adjustments from year to year, these should give a fairly reliable idea of what you'll be paying on the spot.

Average costs

In terms of a **daily budget**, a frugal existence relying exclusively on bus travel, food from simple eateries and the cheapest grades of accommodation won't set you back more than £13/US$20 a day per person. Incidentally, you won't save much by assembling picnic materials at a grocer's – even the poorest Turks eat out frequently, and you may as well too. If you're entitled to one, a student identity card – FIYTO being more influential than ISIC – will shave a healthy chunk off the cost of selected museum or entertainment tickets, and state-owned transport (planes, trains and long-haul ferries – but *not* buses). For any degree of comfort, including rooms with en-suite bath and the occasional splurge on a boat outing or at the bazaar, allow an average daily expenditure of £24/$37. And for £49/$75 a day you could be staying in four- and five-star hotels – especially east of Ankara – renting a car and splurging in fashionable restaurants.

As for specifics, **accommodation** costs range from about £2.50/$4 per person in the most basic dosshouses to £65/$100 a head for five-star resort hotels with every mod con; mid-range hotels with decent amenities weigh in somewhere around £9.50/$15 per person in large provincial towns and coastal centres. **Food** also varies widely in price: it's difficult to spend more than £4/$6 apiece for a two-course meal with a beer once off the tourist circuit, but easy to get through three times that amount in a resort town. **Transport** is more consistent – bus fares vary between £2.50/$4 and £3/$4.50 per 100km travelled, with shorter distances proportionately more expensive. The better long-distance trains charge about the same as a good bus company, with small supplements for sleeping facilities, but still represent excellent value for the extra comfort gained. Domestic air ticket prices are on a par with those in northern Europe, but a reclining seat or low-class cabin on the limited long-haul ferry network is still excellent value.

A service charge of ten to fifteen percent is levied at the fancier restaurants, but as this goes directly to the management, the waiters and busboys should be left five percent again if they deserve it. In some places a mandatory tip (*garsoniye*) accompanies the service charge. Round odd taxi fares upwards (you may not have a choice, as the driver may genuinely not have small change); hotel and train-sleeper porters should be tipped appropriately, the latter often presenting you with a chit stating the required amount.

Currency, cash and travellers' cheques

The Turkish currency is the **lira**, abbreviated as TL. **Coins** still exist in denominations of 50,000 and 100,000TL, but have strictly nuisance value except in paying for public toilets or newspapers. **Notes** come in denominations of 250,000 (soon to vanish), 500,000, 1,000,000, 5,000,000, 10,000,000 and 20,000,000; the 5,000,000 and now-withdrawn 100,000 notes in particular are confusingly similar in colour and size, giving an opportunity for unscrupulous money-changers to substitute one for the other. As in other countries that have suffered from **hyperinflation**, it seems only a matter of time before Turkey knocks off some zeros from these denominations and issues new notes – already this has occurred informally, with most shops and restaurants posting prices with the last three zeroes omitted.

Rates for foreign currency are always better inside Turkey, so don't bother buying TL at home before you leave. Conversely, don't leave Turkey with unspent TL – it's not illegal to export up to the equivalent of $5000, but you won't get a decent exchange rate for them anywhere outside of the country.

It's wise to take a fair wad of **hard currency** with you to Turkey (either US dollars, euros or, travelling to the UK-dominated resorts, sterling), as you can often use it to pay directly for souvenirs or accommodation (prices for both are frequently quoted in hard currency). Although theft and pickpocketing are on the increase in tourist areas, leaving a money belt in hotel lockers is safe enough under normal circumstances.

Travellers' cheques are, frankly, not worth the bother: most exchange offices (see below) refuse them, and any bank you try must have a specimen for the brand you carry, or they'll refuse to serve you. This is less of a problem with Thomas Cook and American Express cheques, which are the most widely recognized brands. US$, pounds sterling or euros are the preferred currencies.

Banks and other exchange services

Because of the TL's constant devaluation you should only **change money** every few days, unless of course you're going to disappear into bank-less regions for weeks at a time. You should also keep all foreign exchange slips with you until departure, if only to prove the value of purchases made in case of queries by customs.

Most **banks** are open Monday to Friday, 8.30am to noon and 1.30 to 5pm, though the Garanti Bankası operates throughout the day and on Saturday mornings; foreign exchange transactions won't, however, be undertaken after 4.45pm. Exchange rates and commissions (*komisyon*) vary widely, though most banks (and hotels) charge a hefty three percent.

The best rates and (usually) commission-free transactions are to be had at the **döviz**, or exchange houses, found all over western Turkey and along the Black Sea. They're open very long hours, especially in resorts, and buy or sell foreign currency of most sorts instantly, though very few take travellers' cheques, and those that do will charge two-percent commission.

Outside normal banking hours, you can also use the special exchange booths run by banks in coastal resorts, airports and ferry docks. The local **post and telephone office** (PTT), particularly in a sizable town, is often able to change foreign currency without commission. In small towns where no bank is authorized to take foreign currency, the PTT will also give a reasonable rate of exchange for travellers' cheques, but levies the usual commission.

Value added tax

The Turkish variety (*Katma Değer Vergisi* or *KDV*), ranging from eight to twenty-three percent depending on the commodity, is included in the price of virtually all goods and services (except car rental, where the fifteen-percent figure is usually quoted separately). Look for the notice *Fiatlarımız KDV Dahildir* (VAT included in our prices) if you think someone's trying to do you for it twice. There is a VAT refund scheme for large souvenir purchases made by those living outside Turkey, but it's such a rigmarole to get that it's probably not worth pursuing; if you insist, ask the shop to provide a *KDV İade Özel Fatura* (Special VAT Refund Invoice), assuming that it participates – very few do, and they tend to be the most expensive shops.

ATMs and credit/debit cards

The simplest way to get hold of money in Turkey is to use the widespread **ATM** (cashpoint) network, now found even in the smaller towns of the east. Bank ATMs – most reliably those of Garanti Bankası, Yapı Kredi Bankası, İşbank, Akbank, Pamukbank, Halk Bank, Ziraat Bankası, Koçbank, Vakıf Bank, Oyak Bank and HSBC – will accept any debit cards that are part of the Cirrus, Maestro or Plus systems. Screen prompts are given in English on request. The daily ATM withdrawal limit for most cards is about £250/$400 equivalent (or £80–200 /$125–310 per transaction), depending on the bank or even individual ATM.

An increasing number of shopkeepers are also able to process debit or credit cards on swipe readers (though use of credit cards in particular will attract commissions of three to five percent).

A major **credit card** is invaluable for domestic ferry and plane tickets, and also for waiver of a huge cash deposit when renting a car. You can also normally get cash advances (in TL only) at any bank displaying the appropriate sign. You can also use Visa or Mastercard to get cash from ATMs, though American Express holders are currently restricted to those of Akbank. All use of a credit card to obtain cash attracts a 2.75 percent fee back home.

However, don't rely entirely on plastic, as Turkish ATM networks are prone to crashing (though the "down" periods are seldom long). Avoid "stand-alone" booths found on resort quays, as these may only be serviced once weekly, so if it eats your card (not unknown), too bad. It's safest to use ATMs during normal working hours so help can be summoned if needed. Also, spurious "transaction declined" messages are common; try another bank or try again during off-peak phone hours.

Getting around

Public transport is fairly comprehensive in Turkey, and only on major routes and during public holidays do you need to book tickets in advance. Although the train network is rather skeletal, there's an all-embracing network of buses that spans the country, offering reasonably priced, comfortable and efficient long-distance travel. Shorter distances within towns and cities or between rural villages are covered by the Turkish institution of the dolmuş (shared transport). The domestic ferry and sea bus network is confined to the Sea of Marmara and the north Aegean or Black Sea coasts, while state airline THY links Ankara and İstanbul with most major Turkish towns. Car rental is also an option, though rates are among the highest in the Mediterranean, and road conditions can be challenging. However, driving yourself is often the only way to reach remote spots, and will enable you to see more of the country during a brief visit.

"Travel details" at the end of each chapter rounds up all the relevant routes and schedules.

By train

Turkey's train network is run by **Turkish State Railways** (TCDD; ⊕www.tcdd.gov .tr/tcddwebenglish/index.html). This English-language website provides full timetable and ticket information.

Turkish trains are best used to span the distances between the three main cities (İstanbul, Ankara and İzmir) and the provincial centres. Turkey's first rail lines were built by the British in the mid-nineteenth century, in part to get the fig harvest to İzmir; later, German companies built the line to Europe used by the Orient Express, as well as the Turkish section of the Berlin-to-Baghdad railway. Limited construction budgets meant that lines were forced to follow tortuous routes around Turkey's many mountain ranges (rather than tunnel through them) and this, coupled with chronic subsequent under-investment, means that Turkish trains may take up to twice as long as buses on the same route. However, they do have the considerable advantage of additional comfort at comparable or lower prices. Short-hop journeys in the Aegean region may be downright frustrating, though longer, intercity express journeys can be delightful and wonderfully scenic.

Takeaway **timetables** are only sporadically issued – apparently, to make life more diffi-cult for terrorists intent on derailing or attacking locomotives. Sometimes a small printed timetable is available, detailing İstanbul commuter trains and local services, as well as intercity and some international departures, but it does not cover other major routes. Neither is the internationally published Thomas Cook handbook reliable, so in fact the only way to get accurate **information** is to go to the station in person, scan the placards and then confirm departures with staff.

The better **services** west of Ankara, denoted *mavı tren* or *ekspresi*, are reasonably quick, though still much slower than buses. In the east, however, punctuality and service standards begin to slip. Avoid any departure labelled *yolcu* (local) – they're excruciatingly slow.

On long-haul journeys you may still have a choice between a first- and second-class seat, though this distinction is being slowly phased out in favour of a single standard of service. **First class** features pullman-style seats and air conditioning/heating according to season; **second-class** wagons have pullman seating or (in the east) continental-style, six-person compartments with narrow corridors on one side. In second-class carriages, single **women travelling alone** will be looked after by the conductor, which generally means delivery into a family or mixed-gender compartment. **Non-smoking cars** are always available; ask for an *içmeyen vagon* when booking.

There's almost always a **dining car** on trains west of Ankara – the limited menus aren't so bad or expensive as to require bringing your own food. All long-distance services are supposed to have a licensed *büfe* wagon. In the east you'd be well advised to check on the availability of food and drink, and bring your own if necessary.

On major train routes it's essential to make a **reservation** in advance. This can be done anytime between one month and three hours before departure, but the most popular services sell out long in advance, as does just about everything at public holidays. Though the TCDD booking system is theoretically computerized, in practice it may be difficult to book an Ankara–İstanbul journey from İzmir, for example, and almost impossible to arrange sleeper facilities from a station that's not your start-point. **Credit cards** are not yet accepted as payment for train fares.

Fares and passes

Regular **fares** on the better trains cost about the same per kilometre as the buses. Typical prices are $14 first-class on the Ankara–İstanbul route, $6 second class from the Bandırma ferry dock to İzmir. Buying a return ticket brings the fare down by twenty percent, while foreign **students** with appropriate identification are entitled to a thirty-percent discount on train tickets. InterRail, Eurail and Eurodomino **passes** are valid all over Turkey, though you're unlikely to get full value from any of these trans-European passes; the one-month **TrenTur** card, purchased from major stations in Turkey, is potentially better value at around $35 a month for unlimited second-class travel.

There are three different kinds of **sleeping facilities** on Turkish trains. *Küşetli* is a couchette in a six-seat, second-class compartment, where bunks pull down from the wall at night and you share with strangers; you'll pay a supplement of about fifteen percent on the basic ticket price for pillow only, thirty percent for full bedding. *Örtülü küşetli* is a better category with usually only four bunks per compartment, with bedding provided. *Yataklı* first-class suites have one or two (sometimes three) beds with full linen supplied; reckon on paying around $25, İzmir–Ankara, for a single bed in such a compartment, $21 each for two sharing. Given that this will barely amount to three times the supplement for *küşetli*, you may as well coddle yourself.

By long-distance bus

An immensely popular form of transport, the Turkish **long-distance bus** is a crucial part of the country's modern culture. There is no single, national bus company in Turkey and most routes are covered by several firms, which usually have ticket booths both at the **otogars** (bus terminals) and in the city centre. If you buy your ticket at a sales office (*yazıhane*) in the centre you should ask about free service buses to the *otogar*, especially if it's located a few miles out. Most companies provide small minibuses even for a single passenger; the question to ask is *servis araba var mı?* These buses will often also take passengers from *otogars* into town centres, but this is a more erratic system – the transfer cannot be guaranteed within the long-distance ticket price and may be charged extra.

There's no such thing as a comprehensive national bus **timetable**, although individual companies often provide their own. **Prices** vary considerably between top- and bottom-drawer companies, though convenience of departure and onboard service are equally important criteria. If in doubt, inspect the vehicle out in the loading bay (*peron* in Turkish) and ask at the ticket office how long the trip will take. It's worth bearing in mind that long-haul journeys (over 10hr) generally take place at night, and that because of rest stops buses never cover more than 60km an hour on average, no matter what you're told. As a broad example of fares, İzmir–Antalya costs around $17, Konya–Göreme $6, Fethiye–İstanbul $28.

Otogars, especially in touristed areas, are full of **touts** waiting to escort you to their company's window once you state your destination – though it may not have the most convenient departure, nor the best service and seats. Common, fallacious ploys to get you to sign on with a particular company include a promise of "free breakfasts" on early morning departures (which means tepid tea in a PVC cup and a soggy, cellowrapped bread roll) or transfer to the lodging of your choice at your destination (which may end up being accommodation owned by the driver's relatives, where you're taken for an extra fee).

When buying tickets, ask to see the **seating plan**: if you crave fresh air, request front-row seats behind the driver, whose window may be the only open ventilation on the coach. **Non-smoking** is now the rule on long-haul coaches, though this can't be implicitly assumed on the dilapidated coaches linking county towns; most Turks hate open windows or vents, with the latter often welded shut on the more down-at-heel Turkish buses. Seats over the wheels (usually numbers 5–8 and 33–36 on the standard Mercedes O302 model) have cramped legroom and take the worst of the road bumps. Unacquainted women and men are not allowed to sit next to each other, and you may be asked to switch your assigned seat to accommodate this convention.

To avoid the disadvantages of Turkish bus travel, make use of the country's three **premium coach companies**: Ulusoy, Bosfor and Varan. Their seats are more comfortable than most, with non-smoking strictly enforced, and they don't segregate single passengers by sex. Kamil Koç and Pamukkale, while not quite as enlightened, are two of the best standard outfits, in that order of preference. There have been some horrific accidents on buses – directly related to the practise of paying drivers a low base salary, plus a top-up fee for every trip done. Thus the temptation is to drive beyond the fatigue barrier, and it's of course the better companies who are likely to pay more for relief drivers.

Be warned that most buses play music – either electronic Turkish pop or a Western equivalent – until the lights go out. Some buses also show films (strictly in Turkish), an additional nuisance/diversion depending on your mood. Partial compensation for this is the attention of the **muavin**, or driver's assistant, who can supply drinking water on demand, and will appear several times in a journey with aromatic cologne for freshening up. Every ninety minutes there will be a fif-teen-minute **rest stop** (*mola*) for tea and toilet visits, and there are less frequent half-hour pauses for meals at purpose-built roadside cafeterias. Many of the better companies supply free coffee/tea/soft drinks as well as cling-wrapped cakes.

By backpacker bus

An alternative to the standard long-distance bus is the backpacker-oriented **Fez Bus**, which operates a seasonal pass scheme connecting the most popular spots in the western half of the country: the Turquoise Coast, Antalya, Side, Cappadocia, Pamukkale, Ephesus, Bergama and Gallipoli. The passes are valid for an entire tourist season (departures every two days; late April to early November) and are used on a hop-on, hop-off basis, though you must re-book onward seats 48 hours in advance to guarantee a seat. Further advantages are door-to-door service to designated budget accommodation, non-smoking vehicles, and the services of an English-speaking steward/tour guide. The obvious disadvantage is that this is a guaranteed way of getting stuck in assorted overlanders' ghettos, and being pretty insulated from the host country.

The pass extends over two zones, north and south, with the divide being a line connecting Cappadocia, Pamukkale and Kuşadası; A two-zone pass costs £115/$177, the northern zone alone £75/$115, the southern zone £65/$100, with small discounts for students plus assorted possible add-ons (eg, a *gület* cruise or Gallipoli battlefield tour). It's a moderately stiff price tag for what's usually a three-to-four-week itinerary, but the issuers claim the passes are transferable in the presence of a Fez rep, so you could sell unused months on.

Fez Bus agents

Fez Travel Akbıyık Cad 15, Sultanahmet, İstanbul ☏212 516 9024, ⓦ www.fezbus.com.
Interest and Activities Holidays Hartfield House, 173 Hartfield Rd, Wimbledon, London SW19 3TH ☏020/8251 0208. Sole UK agent for Fez Bus.

By dolmuş

The Turkish institution of the **dolmuş**, or shared transport, could profitably be imitated in the West: it's practical, economical and ecologically sound. The idea is that a vehicle – a car or small van (*minibüs* in Turkish) – runs along set routes, picking passengers up and dropping them off along the way. You will be expected to switch seats so that women do not sit next to strange males. To stop a dolmuş, give a hand signal as for a normal taxi and if there's any room at all (the word *dolmuş* means "stuffed"), they'll stop and let you on. To get out, say *inecek var* (literally, "there's a getting out") or *müsait bir yerde* ("at a convenient place"). Eight-seater diesel transit vans with windows serve as dolmuşes in most cities, particularly İzmir, but in Trabzon the dolmuşes are ordinary taxi-lookalikes. In İstanbul, the classic American 1950s cars, which long had the monopoly on most routes, have now been banned except for use as "special tourist taxis" and wedding limos.

On busy **urban routes** it's better to take the dolmuş from the start of its run, at a stand marked by a blue sign with a black-on-white-field "D", sometimes with the destination indicated – though usually you'll have to ask to find out the eventual destination, or look at the dolmuş' windscreen placard. On less popular routes the driver will often depart before the vehicle is full, making it easier to hail in mid-route.

Inter-town and -village services are always provided by twelve- to fifteen-seater minibuses, and in these instances the term "dolmuş" is seldom used. For the remotest villages there will only be two services a day: to the nearest large town in the morning and back to the village in mid-afternoon. Generally, though, minibuses run constantly between 7 or 8am and 7pm in summer, stopping at sunset in winter or extending until 10 or 11pm (or even later) near popular resorts.

Fares are low, hardly more than urban bus prices and about the same as coaches between towns, but it's always difficult to know how much to pay if you're only going part of the way. However, everybody else on board will know; just state your destination and hand over a roughly appropriate stack of coins or notes (not too large in denomination), and you'll invariably get the right change. If you sit near the front, you'll have

to relay other people's fares and repeat their destinations to the driver – no mean feat if you don't speak the language.

By city bus and taxi

In larger towns the main means of transport are the red-and-white **city buses**, which take pre-purchased tickets available from kiosks near the main terminals, newsagents or from kerbside touts (at slightly inflated prices). The only exceptions are **private buses** in İstanbul, which look the same as those run by the *Belediye* (city hall) and whose drivers issue tickets in exchange for cash.

Yellow city **taxis** are everywhere, with ranks at appropriate places, though in rush hour finding a free cab can be difficult. Hailing one in the street is the best way to get a cab, but in suburban areas there are useful street-corner telephones from which you can call (if you can make yourself understood). Urban vehicles all have working, digital-display meters and **fares** are among the lowest in the Mediterranean – the flag falls at about \$0.70, with double tariff applicable between midnight and 6am. In cities, it's illegal to ask for a flat fare, though attempted rip-offs of foreigners aren't unheard of. Out in the country, you'll have to bargain. Taxi drivers may remind you to fasten your seat belt (*kemer* is the word) if there's an ongoing campaign of police spot-checks, though strangely the drivers themselves aren't required to use them – perhaps, as some cynics say, there are too many taxis and the lawmakers consider their drivers expendable.

Hitchhiking

As in most other countries these days, **we do not recommend hitching in Turkey** as a safe method of getting around. However, you may be forced to exercise this option where public transport is scarce or nonexistent, and lifts tend to be frequent and friendly – you may be expected to share tea with the driver on reaching your destination. Rural Turks hitch too – if you see a group at the roadside waving you down in your own car, it's a good bet that no bus or dolmuş is forthcoming any time soon, and you'd be performing a useful service by giving them a lift.

On routes that are well served by buses or minibuses, the general consensus among Turks is that there's little point in hitching since public transport is so cheap, and they will be less inclined to view hitchhikers favourably.

You do sometimes see Turkish women – older, conservatively dressed villagers – hitching near the Aegean coast. However, you also see prostitutes soliciting truck drivers along the main highways, and on balance it's not a good idea for foreign women to hitch alone, especially in the east of the country. With male company, it need be fraught with no more peril, and possibly less, than elsewhere around the Mediterranean.

By car

Given the excellent bus services, you don't need to drive in Turkey to get between the major centres, but having a car does add some flexibility to your travels. However, you really need to be an experienced, level-headed driver in order to tackle the challenging highway conditions. You could bring your own car, though this creates administrative hurdles; many people choose to rent instead, though you'll find rates on a par with most of Europe.

Road regulations

You **drive on the right**, and yield to those approaching from the right, even on the numerous roundabouts. **Speed limits**, seldom observed, are 50km/hr within towns and 40km/hr if towing a trailer or caravan; while on the open road, limits are 90km/hr for saloon cars, 80km/hr for vans, 70km/hr if you're towing something; and on motorways (*otoyol* in Turkish), 120km/hr for saloon cars, 100km/hr for vans and small trucks. Turkey has the second highest European **accident rate** (after Portugal), and it's easy to see why: Turkish drivers are in the main an impatient bunch who lean on the horn and tailgate brazenly if they feel the traffic isn't moving fast enough. **Drink-driving laws** are in line with those of the European Union – 50mg of alcohol per 100ml of blood

(roughly equal to one hard drink or two glasses of wine) is the upper limit for private drivers.

Traffic control points at the approaches to major cities are frequent, and although the police manning them are mostly interested in overweight trucks, they may halt foreigners. They can be rude and unnerving, and if things get sticky you should pretend total ignorance of Turkish, whatever your linguistic abilities. However, you might well be waved through simply upon showing your foreign ID. If it's your own vehicle, it may be inspected for real or imagined equipment defects (especially lights), though you'll probably be sent to the nearest repair shop rather than cited. If you've rented a car, make sure the rental company provides the insurance certificate, the pollution compliance certificate (*eksoz muayene tasdiknamesi*) and the vehicle registration, or certified copies thereof.

Despite the deficiencies of many Turkish drivers, don't expect to get away with blatant **driving offences** without being noticed. Radar stake-outs are predictably located, usually at the edge of busy resorts or towns. Major violations, such as jumping red lights, speeding or turning illegally, carry spot fines of up to $40; less serious stuff, like passing on hills or failing to wear your seat belt, nets a token $20 fine. You should always receive a receipt for any fine paid, otherwise it goes straight into the cop's pocket.

Do heed the signposted **no-parking zones**, especially in resorts. Local police are very industrious with tow trucks, though you usually get advance warning in the form of slowly cruising patrol cars yelling out the plate numbers of offenders over their loudspeakers. Fines of about $20 ($30 if you've been towed) are not outrageous by European standards, but you will waste considerable time hunting down the pound where your vehicle has been taken, not to mention overcoming the language barrier with staff. Generally, it's wisest to patronize the covered (*katlı*) or open *otoparks*. If you **park on the street** you may be approached by roving attendants demanding parking fees (about $0.70 for all day); don't pay up unless an official ticket is produced – this is a popular beggars' scam.

Road conditions

Ordinary **main roads** are usually adequately paved, but often dangerously narrow. This is not so much of a problem in the relatively uncrowded east, but it makes driving quite hair-raising in the west. The most popular archeological sites and other points of interest are admirably marked by large **black-print-on-yellow-field signs**; however, side roads to minor sites or villages are often poorly signposted and inaccurately shown on maps. Moreover, roads optimistically shown on maps may be unfinished or submerged under one of the many new reservoirs.

Toll highways, marked with white-on-green signs, are springing up and, especially for novice foreign drivers, are well worth the modest tolls ($1.50–4) to use. Main ones finished at the moment include İstanbul–Ankara, bypassing the hilly, curvy nightmare between Gerede and Adapazarı and missing only one section of tunnel; İstanbul–Edirne; Adana–Gaziantep; İzmir–Çeşme; and İzmir–Denizli, cutting through the mountains to skirt the horrific E-24 between Selçuk and Denizli.

Typical **hazards** include the local flair for overtaking right, left and centre, preferably on a curve; failure to signal turns; and huge trucks (the ubiquitous TIRs) either ambling along at walking pace or whizzing past at kamikaze speeds. Additionally, small-town driving features all the following: trotting horsecarts, pedal bicyclists in the fast lane (with no lights), blithely reversing tractors, pedestrians or livestock strolling heedlessly out in front of you, and buses and minibuses halting without warning to take on passengers invisible to you.

The commonest **minor mishaps** involve smashed windscreens, for which passing lorries churning up barrages of gravel are the main culprit, and shredded tyres. If you rip a tyre (not difficult to do on the many rocky tracks), go to a *lastıkçı* (tyre workshop). In many cases the damage can be skilfully repaired; otherwise a new tyre for a compact A- or B-group car runs to about $50, a slightly used but acceptably treaded specimen around half that amount. Always check that the spare tyre and tool kit are sound and complete before leaving the rental agency.

Turks wrestle ordinary saloon cars up and down some appalling **dirt roads**, and so do most foreigners, especially with rental cars (one reason the price of car rental is fairly steep). Dirt-surface roads throughout the country are so rough that driving them is barely quicker than walking, and you will at

Road signs

Dur	Stop
Tek yön	One way
Çıkmaz sokak	Dead end/cul-de-sac
Yol kapalı	Road closed
Yol boyunca	Road narrows
Tırmanma şeridi	Overtaking lane
Araç çıkabilir	Vehicles exiting
Yaya geçidi	Pedestrian crossing
Yol yapımı	Roadworks
Bozuk satıh	Rough surface
Düşük banket	Abrupt verge/shoulder
Şehir merkezi	City centre
Park yapılmaz/edilmez	No parking
Araç giremez	No entry
Aracınız çekilir	Your car will be towed
Giremez	No entry
Askeri bölge	Military zone
Heyelan bölgesi, heyelanlı bölge	Landslide zone

the very least abrade the mud flaps and various other plastic shields off the front of the car. Do not assume that because a minibus gets through that your 2WD model automatically can as well – Turkish minibuses typically have twice the ground clearance and twice the engine displacement that you do.

Night driving is best not attempted by beginners – be prepared for ill-lit vehicles (especially tractors), flocks of sheep or goats (distinguished by massed green-eye shine) and an extra quota of lumbering trucks. If you're forced to drive after dark in isolated areas, it's not a bad idea to open windows enough to smell goat flocks and tractor exhaust in front of you! Oncoming cars will typically flash their lights at you whether or not your high beams are on – contrary to British or North American convention, this actually means "Don't even think of overtaking, *I'm* coming through". **Safety equipment**, such as flares or warning triangles, is nonexistent, and usually the first hint you'll have of a breakdown or wreck ahead, night or day, are either piles or lines of stones on the asphalt.

Fuel and repairs

Filling stations are ubiquitous throughout most of the country and open long hours, so it's pretty difficult to run out of fuel. Diesel is *mazot* or *diezel*, while petrol is *benzin*, available in normal or (more usually) *süper* grades, costing $0.75, $1.05 and $1.05 per litre respectively; car rental firms like you to fill up with *süper*. Lead-free (*kursunsuz*), suitable for catalytic convertors (same price as *süper*), is pretty common in the west of Turkey, but can be difficult to come by in the remote east. The fuel trade is set to be deregulated in the near future, with uncertain effect – possibly price hikes, followed by dips when cheap imported fuel arrives.

In western Turkey, roadside **rest-stop culture** conforming to Italian or French notions has arrived in a big way. You can eat, pray, patch a tyre, phone home, shop at mini-marts and, sometimes, even sleep at what amount to small hamlets (essentially the descendants of the medieval *kervansarays*) in the middle of nowhere. In the impoverished east, however, you'll find much less

basic amenities – nothing more than a few bottles of oil, cans of soft drinks and rather grim diners.

Credit cards (mainly Visa and Mastercard but also American Express) are widely honoured for fuel purchases in much of Turkey, but you'll find this facility less often southeast of a line connecting Gaziantep, Elazığ and Rize, especially in cases where the phone link to the bank (to get transaction approval) fails – in which case you're out of luck. Signs prominently advertise *Kredi Kart Komisyonu Sıfır* or *0%* (no commission on credit cards), since the amount is charged virtually immediately to your account via the same sort of online apparatus prevalent in Europe and North America. If the filling station doesn't have such a notice, it's best to take your business elsewhere if you have a choice.

Car **repair workshops** and spare-part dealers are located in industrial zones called *sanayis* at town outskirts. Fiat, Renault, Ford, Skoda, Mercedes and Fargo are the most common brands catered for, usually instantly, though Turkish mechanics will attempt to fix anything and are getting progressively more used to repairing exotic foreign models, especially Peugeot, Hyundai and Toyota, all manufactured in Turkey. It's easy and cheap to get parts for most big-name brands, though you may have problems outside the largest towns for less common models, such as Citroen or Rover. If possible, seek out a factory-authorized workshop in a large town; if not in stock, parts can be ordered on a day's notice, while labour charges are very cheap by foreign standards – a third to a half of the cost in northern Europe or North America.

Car rental

To rent a car you need to be at least 21 (27 for Groups E and above), with a **driver's licence** held for at least one year. An **International Driving Permit**, from the RAC or AA in Britain/Australasia or the AAA/CAA in North America, is not essential – your own home licence will do at a pinch – but is very helpful, especially at traffic-control points (show the cops your IDP, not your main home licence, in case they decide to keep it for any reason).

Rental rates are usually exorbitant, usually at least as much as in the UK. The minimum over-the-counter rates of the largest international chains are close to $70 a day in summer, all inclusive; Turkish chains may charge fifteen to twenty percent less, and often you'll find a one-off outlet that's willing to let a Group A car go for under $40 per day outside of peak season. Weekly rates are hardly any better, ranging from $300 with small local outfits to almost $500 with a multinational in summer. There is some **regional variation**: south-coast locations (Antalya, Fethiye) are noticeably cheaper than west-coast resorts (Kuşadası, İzmir), and either is far less expensive than relatively untouristed towns such as Erzurum or Van, where monopoly situations prevail, or İstanbul, where overheads are high.

Especially if you rent from Hertz, Avis, Budget, Sixt, Europcar or Thrifty (branded as Decar in Turkey), you'll have to exploit every discount scheme available to bring the price down: Frequent Flyer membership programme partner-codes, THY boarding passes presented at airport agency desks and discount vouchers obtained at home before departure are all effective bargaining chips. You'll also need to flash a **credit card** or leave a **cash deposit** to cover the estimated rental total.

Rental companies will usually allow you to rent in one town and drop off in another, provided they have an office in your destination, though you may have to pay a hefty **drop-off charge** – which will also be levied if you are renting from an airport or town where the company concerned does not maintain a permanent office. **Unlimited kilometrage** is invariably a better deal than any time-plus-distance rate. Basic **insurance** is usually included, but CDW (Collision Damage Waiver) is not, and given typical driving conditions taking this out is virtually mandatory. Along with KDV (Value Added Tax), all these extras can push up the final total considerably.

If you can commit to a rental period of one to four weeks, you should **pre-book**, either as part of a fly-drive scheme with a tour operator, or with a major **car-rental agency** (see below). Promotional deals come and go, so call as many agencies as possible

and ask for a complete itemization of charges. Reserving from North America, count on a minimum of US$280 per week, all-inclusive; the most advantageous UK rates (£175–200 weekly, all-inclusive, according to season) are available through Autos Abroad, Holiday Autos or Transhire. Otherwise, you're best off dealing in person with small Turkish companies, especially off-season. Beware of the booking request functions on the websites of the major chains such as Avis or Hertz, which do exactly that – make requests only. All too often in peak season, the booking, although initially accepted, will come back after several days marked "denied, car category unavailable". Particularly if you have an esoteric rental need, get cracking on it weeks, if not months, in advance. Have companies fax or email you a formal confirmation form, with a reference code, to make it more difficult for staff to deny all knowledge of your booking upon arrival.

The bottom-of-the-range Group A **models**, now offered only by small local outlets, are either the barely adequate Serçe, the Turkish equivalent of a Fiat 124, or the sturdier but now discontinued Toros Renault 12. If you've pre-booked from overseas with a chain, you'll be furnished with the slightly more powerful Şahin (equivalent to a Fiat 131) or Doğan (same as a Fiat 131 SLX). But these licensed Turkish clones of Fiat and Renault are on the way out and for scarcely any more money you'll probably end up with an imported Fiat Palio or Fiat Siena – the latter with a nifty fifty-litre fuel tank – or perhaps a Ford Fiesta (D-group) or Ford Focus (G-group), any of them with better design, space and overtaking power than their predecessors. The domestically produced Toyota Corolla four-door or the Hyundai Accent four-door are also well worth the extra outlay as Group B/C cars, when available. If you want a **4WD** to bash along the rough roads of eastern Anatolia, the only model usually offered is the Suzuki Vitara jeep (typically Group E), and these go quickly in season.

When checking a car out, agency staff should make a thorough diagrammatic notation of any **blemishes** on the vehicle – it's in your interest to make sure they do this. If you have an accident of any kind, go immediately to the nearest police station and get them to type out and validate an **accident report** (*kaza raporu*) – otherwise you'll invalidate the insurance. If it's something serious enough to immobilize you and/or cause major damage to other people's property, the traffic police will appear and administer alcohol tests to all drivers, results of which must also be submitted along with the *kaza raporu*. Incidentally, it's an offence to move a vehicle involved in a car-crash before the police give the all-clear – leave it where it is, even if you're blocking traffic, otherwise all drivers involved risk a $40 spot fine for "leaving the scene of an accident". For **minor scratches or dents** – especially if you're at fault – it's far less of a palaver to go to the nearest *sanayi* and have them repaired for a few dollars. Rental insurance never covers smashed windscreens or ripped tyres; it's up to you to fix these as cheaply as possible.

Car rental agencies

Autos Abroad UK ☎0870/066 7788, ⓦwww.autosabroad.co.uk.
Avis Australia ☎13 63 33, Canada ☎1-800/272-5871, Republic of Ireland ☎01/605 7500, New Zealand ☎09/526 2847 or 0800 655 111, UK ☎0870/606 0100, US ☎1-800/331-1084; ⓦwww.avis.com.
Budget Australia ☎1300/362 848, Republic of Ireland ☎01/9032 7711, New Zealand ☎0800/652 227 or 09/976 2222, UK ☎0800/181 181, US ☎1-800/527-0700; ⓦwww.drivebudget.com.
Cosmo Thrifty Northern Ireland ☎028/9445 2565, ⓦwww.thrifty.co.uk.
Dollar Australia ☎02/9223 1444 or 1800/358 008, US ☎1-800/800-6000; ⓦwww.dollar.com.
Europcar Republic of Ireland ☎01/614 2800, UK ☎0845/722 2525; ⓦwww.europcar.com
National UK ☎08705/365 365, ⓦwww.nationalcar.com.
Hertz Australia ☎13 30 39, Canada ☎1-800/263-0600, Republic of Ireland ☎01/813 3416, New Zealand ☎0800/654 321, UK ☎08708/44 88 44, US ☎1-800/654-3001; ⓦwww.hertz.com.
Holiday Autos Republic of Ireland ☎01/872 9366, UK ☎08704/00 00 99; ⓦwww.holidayautos.co.uk.
National Australia ☎13 10 45, New Zealand ☎0800/800 115 or 03/366 5574, US ☎1-800/227-7368; ⓦwww.nationalcar.com.
Sixt Republic of Ireland ☎1850/206 088, UK no

general phone number, consult website; ⓦwww.e-sixt.com.
Thrifty Australia ☎1300/367 227, New Zealand ☎09/309 0111, UK ☎01494/751 600, US ☎1-800/367-2277, ⓦwww.thrifty.com.
Transhire UK ☎0870/789 8000, ⓦwww.transhire.com

Bringing your own car

Arriving at the frontier in your own car, you'll be asked for the following **documentation**: an International Driving Permit or home licence, registration papers or log book (originals or certified copy), and a Green Card or other proof of internationally valid third-party insurance. You'll be issued with a Turkish temporary registration (*araba tezkeresi*), separate from the passport stamp, valid for six months and to be mandatorily surrendered at your point of exit.

Your car will be **registered in your passport** for a maximum stay of 180 days, and must leave the country when you do (if you have to return home by plane for an emergency, the vehicle can be safely stored in a customs lock-up for a daily charge). Since tourist visas are typically only for three months, border officials may only grant ninety days unless you can offer a convincing reason why you're staying longer, and explain that you intend to get your visa renewed with the Security Division (*Emniyet Müdürlüğü*). If you leave Turkey briefly and then return in the vehicle, you'll get a shorter allowance the second time around – only six months of tourist use in any twelve-month period is permitted.

A vehicle can only be used on foreign plates for six months; after this time they must be changed to Turkish plates. This procedure is only available to those legally employed in Turkey and involves a police inspection, an expensive bank guarantee and a fat sheaf of forms. In general, if you plan to spend more than six months in the country, leave your car at home and lease or buy one in Turkey. Similarly, you should also apply for a Turkish driving licence after six months; the police don't seem to care, but if you have a crash you'll find that your insurance is invalid.

If your car is written off while in Turkey, the remains must be transported to a customs compound, and the full-page stamp in your passport cancelled. Similarly, if it's stolen, you'll have to get a report from the *Vilayet* (Provincial Authority) to get rid of the passport endorsement. Bring a fluent Turkish-speaker along, as none of the officialdom concerned are likely to speak English.

The British Green Card **insurance** system is still required in Turkey until or unless it becomes a full member of the EU. With either the AA or RAC, a thirty-day Green Card is provided free to members, but for longer stays there is an additional charge. You must keep the receipt of such payments for display to Turkish officials; it may be requested at the frontier, and your Green Card will not be considered valid beyond the initial month without it.

British motoring associations provide comprehensive cover, including breakdown and recovery service, legal aid and car replacement. In Turkey they occasionally work in conjunction with the **Turkish Touring and Automobile Association** (TTOK; Büyükdere Cad, Oto Sanayi Sitesi Yanı, Seyrantepe, Dördüncü Levent, İstanbul %0212/282 8140), which can advise on Turkish insurance and related matters. You will always have to pay to be towed, and you'll also pay for their breakdown service unless you've equipped yourself with an insurance policy prior to arrival. North Americans will have to pay on the spot in any case since the AAA has no reciprocal agreement with the TTOK.

The 24-hour TTOK nationwide **emergency breakdown number** is ☎0212/280 4449; there are unfortunately no toll-free services or numbers for each province. If an English speaker is unavailable, you'll have to find someone to translate for you, or contact the main İstanbul headquarters during office hours.

Motoring organisations

AA Ireland ☎01/617 9988, ⊛www.aaireland.ie; UK ☎0800/44 45 00, ⊛www.theaa.co.uk.
American Automobile Association (AAA) ☎1-800/222-4357, ⊛www.aaa.com.
Australian Automobile Association ☎02/6247 7311.
Canadian Automobile Association (CAA) ☎613/247-0117, ⊛www.caa.com.
New Zealand Automobile Association ☎09/377 4660.
RAC UK ☎0800/55 00 55, ⊛www.rac.co.uk.

By bicycle and motorbike

Touring Turkey by **bicycle** isn't as daft as it sounds, so long as you avoid the hottest months and the busiest roads. Flying in with a bike in your luggage is no more complicated than it is to any other destination, and sometimes it's not even charged as excess baggage.

You do, however, have to be prepared for the lack of maintenance facilities, and your own novelty value. The only pushbikes rural Turks are used to seeing are old clunkers used strictly for sedate pedalling around town. A homegrown mountain-bike industry has emerged in most of the major cities, but you should bring **spares** of everything small or light and not count on the admittedly ingenious local mechanics to improvize parts. Because you'll probably opt for back roads, where few foreigners pass by, you'll draw crowds at any rest stop. Accept the inevitable and reckon that bike and bags are usually more, rather than less, secure guarded in this manner while you go to have a tea.

The main **dangers** to you and your bike will be potholed pavements and the elements. Most back-road drivers are surprisingly courteous, perhaps because they're so stunned at the sight of you, though be prepared for some gratuitous horn-honking. You can skirt many potential trouble-spots or skip boring stretches by judicious use of the ferry and train network, on which you can usually transport your machine for free. With a bit of forethought and common sense, it's even possible and enjoyable to pedal through İstanbul (though you're not allowed to cycle across the Bosphorus bridges). Choose routes so as to avoid traffic; after 10am on a normal workday you should be fine, though avoid going up the Bosphorus coast roads in rush hour or at weekends. **Rental facilities** are as yet few and far between in Turkey; the few outlets we know about are mentioned in the text.

Much the same advice applies to riding around Turkey on a **motorbike**, though these are not transported free on the ferries, but charged at their own special rates. In larger resorts and big cities there will be least one motorbike **rental agency**, or a car rental company which also rents out motor-scooters and mopeds (*mobilet*). You'll need an appropriate driving licence, and most companies insist that it has been held for at least a year. Before renting any kind of bike, make sure it's physically capable of coping with the terrain you want to use it for.

By ferry

Turkey's domestic ferries are run by Türkiye Denizcilik İşletmesi (TDİ; ®www.tdi.com.tr) – literally "Turkey Maritime Enterprises" – known in English as **Turkish Maritime Lines** (TML). Ferries to Italy and Greece are covered on p.21.

İstanbul **city shuttle services** (see Chapter 1), mainly serving foot passengers, are frequent, cheap and efficient. Timetables (*saat tarifeleri*) are available cheaply from the ticket window (*gişe*) at the various docks. The municipality of İstanbul also operates *deniz otobüsleri*, or **sea buses** (schedules on ®www.ido.com.tr), both along the Bosphorus and across the Sea of Marmara to Yalova, Bandırma and the Marmara islands (Chapter 2). In general, they're twice as fast – and twice as costly – as conventional boats. Other **short-hop ferry services** run from İstanbul to the Princes' Islands (Chapter 1), across the Gulf of İzmit, or across the Marmara to the Marmara Islands. Any of the trans-Marmara car-ferry links, specifically to Armutlu or the islands, saves time compared to the dreary, circuitous road journey, but are relatively expensive with a vehicle.

Long-haul ferries are restricted to the coastal stretches where the road network remains substandard, specifically along the Black Sea coast between İstanbul and Rize, via Zonguldak, Sinop, Samsun and Trabzon (once weekly), and with equal frequency direct from İstanbul to İzmir (see "Travel details", Chapter 1, for both services). Reservations must be made well in advance through one of the authorized agencies in the appropriate ports, though the İstanbul TDİ headquarters at Karaköy, right behind the jetty on Rıhtım Caddesi, is the best equipped.

Timetables are subject to change and the most current resource is always the TDİ website (as above) where you can – in theory, at least – book tickets. There are four classes of **cabin** on long-haul ferries, containing two to four berths. All are comfortable enough, if ruthlessly air-conditioned, with en-suite showers and toilets. It's also possible to reserve a **reclining chair** (*pulman koltuk*), but if you leave booking to the last minute you won't even get one of these. No one will mind if you sleep on deck – bring a sleeping bag and mat, or just crash out on the loungers provided – but you do need a confirmed seat reservation to be allowed on the boat in the first place.

Fares are extremely reasonable – about $20 in a fourth-class, three-bunk cabin on the İstanbul–İzmir run, $27 for the same facilities İstanbul–Trabzon, for example – and students with proper ID enjoy discounts ranging from ten to thirty percent, depending on the route; there are also concessions for groups and children up to the age of 12. **Cars** cost at least as much again as a passenger berth (eg $23 İstanbul–İzmir, $32 İstanbul–Trabzon), but most drivers consider the expense to be well worth it in terms of wear and tear (as well as fuel) saved.

Once aboard, the atmosphere is extremely convivial: the long-haul services are essentially budget cruises. However, the mediocre food and drink, whether at the bar, the self-service cafeteria or in the formal dining room, is exorbitantly marked up – the locals take picnic food along, even though this is technically forbidden.

Both TDİ and private competitors offer services from Taşucu, Mersin and (some years) Alanya to Girne and Famagusta in **Northern Cyprus**, details of which are given in the relevant town accounts. TDİ's year-round Mersin–Famagusta services are the most reliable and comfortable, as well as the priciest.

By plane

Türk Hava Yolları (THY), the state-run airline that's soon to be privatized, has undergone something of a transformation since the 1990s. Heavy investment has resulted in a noticeable rise in service standards and punctuality – a far cry from the days when local wags swore that THY stood for "They Hate You".

THY **destinations** tend to change yearly as the market fluctuates, and current schedules reflect the general post-September-11 travel-industry depression. There are regular services between İstanbul, Ankara and İzmir, and from İstanbul to most other major Turkish centres (and quite a few minor ones). Many airports, however (eg, Ağrı and Edremit), have been opened for blatantly political reasons, see a maximum of three flights weekly, and may not survive – Bursa and Isparta have already closed down. Most journeys to the east (except to Adana, and certain Diyarbakır, Gaziantep, Van and Malatya flights) involve a connection in Ankara, with frequently long layovers there – try to avoid stopping flights when booking.

With little effective competition from private airlines (which have a very short life span), **fares** remain high compared to Europe. For example, the full return fare from İstanbul to Antalya is over $160 (tax inclusive), though THY does offer variable student, youth and family discounts.

Regardless of what you may be told, appearing at the airport an hour before your scheduled flight departure is adequate leeway for completing the strict security procedures. Rarely posted in English is the requirement for you to identify your luggage from amongst a pile of bags on the runway before getting on; this is a measure to prevent terrorists from checking in a bomb and then not boarding, so if you don't point out your bag it won't be loaded on, and may be destroyed. All flights, domestic and international, as well as most of Atatürk airport in İstanbul, are (amazingly for Turkey) **non-smoking**.

Accommodation

Finding a bed for the night is generally no problem in Turkey, except in high season at the busier coastal resorts and larger towns. Lists of category-rated hotels, motels and the better *pansiyons* (pensions) are published by local tourist offices, and we've listed the best options throughout the Guide. Prices, while cheap by most Western European standards, are no longer rock-bottom, and can be downright exorbitant in İstanbul. To some extent facilities have improved correspondingly, though not surprisingly you often get less for your money in the big tourist resorts, and little choice between fleapits or four-star luxury in relatively untouristed towns of the interior. However, with the Turkish economy as it is, backpackers can often afford to go mid-range, and those on mid-range budgets can sometimes secure rooms at the best hotels available east of Cappadocia, so there's absolutely no reason to slum it in the mistaken belief that you're seeing the "authentic" Turkey.

If you take your chances with a **tout** rather than our recommendations, note that certain outfits, particularly in İstanbul, Kuşadası, Selçuk, Antalya, Kaş and Cappadocia, have generated serious complaints from ex-clients, ranging from dangerous plumbing to extortion and false imprisonment. If, on the other hand, you like where you have stayed, you may very well find that your accommo-dation proprietor keeps business cards on hand for similar establishments in other towns; often they have visited each other, or have some idea of what's on offer. This informal network can work very well indeed, with proprietors making a simple phone call to arrange both a stay and a transfer from the *otogar* for you.

Rooms are, almost without exception, on

Accommodation price codes

In this book, hotels, motels and *pansiyons* have been categorized according to the price codes outlined below. The short description appended to each code should give a rough idea of what you'll get for your money.

Category price ranges are given in **US dollars**, since the high domestic Turkish inflation rate makes TL prices meaningless. They represent the minimum you can expect to pay for a **double room in high season**. For backpackers' hostels, trekkers' lodges and coastal "treehouses", where guests are charged per person, US\$ rates, rather than a numerical code, are given in the Guide.

By law prices for rooms at any establishment must be displayed at the reception desk. Most places in band ❷ and above will have **en-suite bathroom facilities** of some kind. For band ❸ and up **breakfast** (see p.52) will be automatically included, while below that taking it is negotiable. At slack times, **bargaining** is virtually expected and usually productive; for example, lone travellers may be able to upgrade to a double room for the single price.

It is strongly recommended that if possible you book establishments in bands ❺–❽ as part of a package, since by doing so you will guarantee yourself better service (particularly choice of rooms) and may actually see the effective price code drop a category.

❶ **up to \$12** Budget hotels in untouristed areas without en-suite facilities; also, so-called "treehouse" accommodation along the southwestern coast, and trekkers' lodges in the Kaçkar mountains.

❷ **\$13–21** The few surviving 1970s-vintage *pansiyons* – some with sink or shower cubicles added at a later date – plus more recent purpose-built *pansiyons*. The latter often have balconies, bedside furniture and sometimes other individual touches, as well as en-suite baths, toilets,

linen and towels. Slightly more salubrious hotels in the interior, though these may not have full attached bathrooms.

❸ **\$22–30** Establishments in touristed areas that straddle the border between a *pansiyon* and a one-star hotel, often with roof terraces for breakfast, and perhaps a bar and small swimming pool; occasionally handled by package tour operators. Relatively hygienic hotels in the interior, with fully equipped bathrooms, room phones

the small side by European standards, with rarely enough power points or places to sit down other than the bed itself, even in the newer, three- to five-star establishments. **Single rooms** generally go for just over half the price of a double, since proprietors are well used to lone (male) business travellers. Rooms with **en-suite bath** are generally about twenty-five percent more than unplumbed ones; triples are also usually available, costing about thirty percent more than a double.

To avoid **noise**, pick a room away from main thoroughfares or mosque minarets (not easy), or one with double-glazing. You'll never cause offence by asking to see another room, and you should never agree on a price for a room without seeing it first.

Though break-ins aren't the norm in Turkey, **security** should be at least a token consideration; paradoxically, some rooms in fancier hotels cannot be locked with a latch or button from the inside, only by key from outside – a particular hazard for women travelling alone.

Prostitution is another likely source of noise or at least comings and goings (so to speak) at all hours. It's a potential issue during the off-season, when hotels have to find ways of paying the bills, and can affect any grade of accommodation. That said, the phenomenon seems to have abated considerably since the boom years immediately after the opening of the ex-Communist-bloc borders.

Water should be tested to verify claims of *devamlı/24 saat sıcak su* (constant/24 hour and TV. Hot water more reliable than in lower categories, but still not guaranteed.

4 **$31–45** Good-value two-star hotels and *pansiyons* in resorts, sometimes in restored old buildings; invariably has some package-tour presence. Often with extra touches such as attached restaurant and rural-antique decor. Air-conditioning /heating makes its appearance.

5 **$46–60** Comfortable, if sometimes small-roomed, three-star hotels and *pansiyons*; this category includes many (often overpriced) places in İstanbul's Sultanahmet district, top-end establishments in the Anatolian interior and restored *kervansarays*, which may appear to be underpriced but often suffer from creeping damp or on-site nightclub noise. Attached bar/restaurant is more or less mandatory, as are room phones and winter heating. Ottoman antiques in common areas, kilims in rooms etc, more or less de rigueur.

6 **$61–80** Four-star hotels and the smaller holiday villages, plus *özel* (special) architectural revival projects. Full-sized bathtubs usually present, as well as extra facilities

such as a pool, private beachfront, watersports gear and tennis courts.

7 **$81–110** More exclusive four-star hotels and bungalow complexes. All of the preceding amenities will be provided, probably duplicated (ie two pools, two restaurants, two snack cafés, two drinks bars) and more grandly laid out – rooms may resemble small suites. Additional touches such as telecom services, hairdresser, organized excursions etc. Standard of breakfast starts to be higher than usual; there should be no excuse for lack of hot water.

8 **over $110** Restored classics, such as the *Pera Palas* or *Çırağan Palace* in İstanbul, plus five-star de luxe behemoths often affiliated to an international chain. At coastal resorts, luxury digs are often rather remote, necessitating use of the hotel's shuttle or a local taxi to get into the nearest town (the idea being to encourage you to spend more money on-site). Breakfasts, ideally, will be generous and varied. All other creature comforts and distractions to hand. Prices in this range can run as high as $300 a night or more per room; the Guide notes the actual price of anything higher than $150.

---

hot water) – always to be treated sceptically. If provided by a solar heater, it will be exhausted with astonishing reliability after 5pm or so even in multi-starred hotels; in the absence of an electric back-up system, there is little you can do short of moving. Before giving up completely, however, try the right-hand tap; the nominal "hot" and "cold" convention is sometimes reversed in Turkey. Bathtubs and sinks almost never have plugs, so a universal plug is worth bringing from home. Especially on the south and south-west coast, **air-conditioning** is almost always found in most establishments of category **4** and above. It's invariably of the "split-level" variety, doubling as heating during the cooler months.

Double beds for couples are relatively

rare, but slowly catching on; the magic words are *Fransız yatak* ("French" bed), not *çift yatak* ("double" bed), which actually refers to the number of beds in the room. Incidentally, in many conservative (read Islamist-dominated) rural areas, hotel management may refuse to let a heterosexual couple share a room, let alone a bed, unless there is documentary evidence that they are married (just a ring may not work, especially if passport names remain different). The police may make trouble for them if proprietors are lenient on this point, as a law exists to this effect, so there's little you can do in this situation short of finding other lodgings that will accept you as you are.

Button and light coding in **lifts/elevators** is a potential source of mystification. "Ç" stands for *çagır* or "call"; a lit-up "K" means *katta*, that is, the car is already on your floor; illuminated "M" is *meşgül* or "in use"; "Z" stands for *zemin kat*, the ground floor, while "A" means *asma kat* or mezzanine.

Hotels and motels

Turkish hotels are graded on a scale of one to five stars by the Ministry of Tourism; there is also a lower tier of un-starred establishments rated by municipalities. At the **four-and five-star** level you're talking international-standard mod cons and prices. **Two- or three-star** outfits are less expensive and may have slightly more character; of late there has been a veritable craze to restore historic buildings as unique lodgings, with decidedly mixed results. While on the face of it turning a disused *kervansaray* into a hotel may seem commendable, in practice the presence of a noisy nightclub in the central courtyard completely negates their function as accommodation. **Restored-mansion accommodation** in Anatolian towns such as Amasya, Sinasos and Safranbolu, or **village-house inns**, increasingly found along the Turquoise Coast and southwest Aegean, are generally more successful, although preservation considerations may mean that not every room is en-suite. Least costly are the wide variety of acceptable no- or **one-star** establishments, whose exact price depends on location, the presence or absence of bath and, to some extent, the season – out of season you can bargain prices down considerably. Breakfast, on the occasions when it's available, is often included in the rates, but it's almost invariably unexciting.

Motels, also graded from one to five stars, tend to be more expensive than hotels of the same class, and conform more to American notions of the term. They're essentially aimed at the drive-in trade, and often have imposing beachfront or panoramic settings to compensate for a nondescript layout. However, unless you're touring by car, their locations – generally way outside city centres – are inconvenient. Be warned that the term "motel" is sometimes used to add a touch of class to an otherwise mediocre establishment, or can be a tip-off that it's a haven of roadside prostitution for truckers.

The **un-rated hotels** licensed by municipalities can be virtually as good as the lower end of the one-star class, sometimes with wall-to-wall carpeting, en-suite baths and phones. On average, though, expect spartan rooms with possibly a washbasin and certainly a shower (never a tub), with a squat toilet down the hall. Count on $5–7 per person for such comforts, with showers sometimes carrying an additional $1–2 charge. Some places, especially in the east or interior, are jail-like dosshouses where the bedding, winter or summer, tends to be yellowed sheets topped by a thick quilt wrapped in a seldom-laundered slipcover anchored with safety pins. These establishments are listed only when a town has nothing better.

At the roughest end of the spectrum – not recommended in this guide – you may pay by the bed ($3–4 apiece) rather than the room, so potentially you'd be sharing quarters with strangers unless you buy up all the beds. There will often be no shower in the building, certainly not a hot one. Such places tend to be patronized by villagers in town on business and thus attract an exclusively male clientele.

Pansiyons and apartments

Often the most pleasant places to stay are **pansiyons** (pensions), small guesthouses that proliferate anywhere large numbers of holidaymakers do. If there are vacancies in season, touts in the coastal resorts and other tourist targets descend on every incoming bus, dolmuş or boat. Or look for little signs with the legend *Boş oda var* ("empty rooms free").

Pansiyons almost universally have en-suite facilities, and many feature common gardens or terraces where breakfast (about $2–4 a head when not included in the room price) is served. Rooms tend to be spartan but clean, furnished in one-star hotel mode and always with two sheets (*çarşafs*) on the bed. Hot water is generally solar-heated at seaside locations, or supplied out of wood- or coal-fired boilers elsewhere. Hot showers are rarely charged for separately; if they are, count on paying an extra dollar or so. Laundry facilities – even if just a drying line and a plastic bucket – are almost always present, and washing will often be done for you cheaply, a big advantage over most low-grade hotels. In addition, the proprietors are apt to be younger and friendlier than hotel staff – though this may be manifested in an unduly attentive attitude to lone female guests. Prices are often rigidly controlled by the local tourist authorities, set according to the establishment's rating.

Self-catering apartments are becoming widespread in coastal resorts, and are mostly pitched at vacationing Turks or foreigners arriving on pre-arranged packages. Some are available to walk-in trade – local tourist offices maintain lists – and apart from the weekly price the major (negotiable) outlay will be for the large gas bottle feeding the stove. Ensure, too, that kitchens are equipped well enough to make them truly self-catering.

Hostels, lodges and treehouses

With the abundance of budget *pansiyons* and downmarket working-men's hotels, there are relatively few **hostels** outside İstanbul. Sometimes a *pansiyon* in a major resort will have roof space or a "group room" set aside. Most other supposed "hostels" – called *yurts* – are rather poky dormitories aimed at local students on summer holiday and are unlikely to cater for you; this, and the fact that there is only one *bona fide* IYHF-affiliated hostel in the country, makes the purchase of an IYHF card before you leave a total waste of money.

The lack of official, foreigner-pitched youth hostels has been amply filled by **backpackers' hostels**, found most notably in İstanbul, Çanakkale, Selçuk, Köyceğiz and Fethiye. Basically 1970s *pansiyons* which have been adapted to feature multi-bedded rooms, laundry and internet facilities, self-catering kitchen, tours and lively bars, they can be fair value – costs rarely exceed $6 a head in a dorm – but also do a pretty good job of insulating clients from the host country.

In recent years a large number of **trekkers' lodges** have sprung up in the foothills of the Kaçkar mountains, especially on the south slope, and along the Lycian Way. These generally offer a choice between communal sleeping on mattresses arrayed on a wood-en terrace, or more enclosed double-to-quadruple, non-en-suite rooms – strangely, cooking facilities may often be absent. Costs are comparable to the backpacker's hostels.

Found principally on the southwestern coast between Antalya and Fethiye are the so-called **"treehouses"**, often ramshackle collections of elevated shacks or even just open platforms made of rough timber. These may have bedding inside, but equally often just provide sleeping-bag space for up to twenty people, at hostel/trekking lodge prices. Some of the more luxurious models provide proper, pricier rooms for two, with doors, windows and electric current provided.

Campsites and chalets

Wherever *pansiyons* are found, there will probably also be **campsites** – often run by the same people, who in the absence of a proper site may simply allow you to crash out in the *pansiyon's* garden. Charges per head run from a couple of dollars for such an arrangement to $5 in a well-appointed site at a major resort, plus fees of around $1–4 per tent. You may also be charged for your vehicle – anything from $2 to $7, depending on the site and season.

Campsites often **rent out tents** for a dollar or two to those showing up without canvas. They also sometimes provide A-frame **chalet accommodation**, which can be anything from a stuffy garden shed with a bed inside to a fairly luxurious affair with bathroom. Prices vary (from $10 to $20 per night), as does construction quality; most sleep a maximum of two.

The most appealing campsites are well-amenitied ones managed by the **Ministry of Forestry**; look for brown wooden signs with yellow lettering. There are 25 of them in shady groves at strategic locations (mostly coastal) across the west of the country, and they make an ideal choice if you have your own transport, especially a combi-van or car and caravan. Most are open April to October inclusive, with maximum charges of $4 per tent, $5 per van and $1 per person; inland sites are much cheaper, and fifty-percent discounts apply to holders of IYHF or FIYTO cards.

Various makeshift roadside **"kampings"**, essentially nothing more than some clumps of trees with parking and picnic space for Turkish weekenders, are unlikely to appeal to most foreigners. **Camping rough** is not illegal, but hardly anybody does it except when trekking in the mountains, and, since you can expect a visit from curious police or even nosier villagers, it's not really a choice for those who like privacy.

Hamams

One of the highlights of a stay in Turkey, especially during the cooler months, is a visit to a hamam or Turkish bath. A nearby hamam will also make a showerless, but otherwise bearable, budget hotel more palatable. Many tourists never partake because they (usually wrongly) anticipate sexual hassles or intense culture shock. In fact, after a day at the ruins or in the bazaar, a corner of a bathhouse is likely to be an oasis of tranquillity in comparison.

Virtually all Turkish towns have at least one hamam per neighbourhood. The only exceptions to this are some of the coastal resorts, which were formerly populated by Orthodox Christians, who didn't build such structures. Baths are usually signposted, but if in doubt look for the distinctive external profile of the roof domes, visible from the street. Baths are either permanently designated for men or women, or sexually **segregated** on a schedule – look for the words *erkekler* (men) and *kadınlar* (women), followed by a time or day range written on a placard by the door. Women, alas, tend to be allotted far more restricted hours, usually mid-week during the day.

On entering, you leave your **valuables** in a small locking drawer, the key of which (often on a wrist/ankle-thong) you keep with you for the duration of your wash. Bring soap, shampoo and a shaving mirror, which are either not supplied or are expensive to buy on the spot. The basic **admission charge** varies depending on the level of luxury, but except in posh or tourist-oriented baths it should never be more than $4–5 a head, and is normally clearly indicated by the front desk. Men will be supplied with a *peştamal*, a thin, wraparound sarong; women usually have to specifically request one but, in fancier spas, more often wear bathing costumes.

Both sexes get *takunya*, awkward wooden clogs, and later a *havlu* or proper drying towel. Changing cubicles (*camekân* in Turkish), equipped with a reclining couch, are sometimes shared and rarely lock except in the better hamams – thus the safe-drawer.

The *hararet* or **main bath chamber** varies from plain to ornate, though any hamam worth its salt will be dressed in marble at least up to chest height. Two or more *halvets*, semi-private corner rooms with two or three *kurnas* (basins) each, lead off from the main chamber. The internal temperature varies from tryingly hot to barely lukewarm, depending on how well run the baths are. Unless you're with a friend, it's one customer to a set of taps-and-basin; refrain from making a big soapy mess in the basin, which is meant for mixing pure water to ideal temperature. Use the scoop-dishes provided to sluice yourself, being careful not to splash your neighbours; on Fridays especially they may have just completed their *abdest* (ritual ablution), and would have to start all over again if touched by an "infidel's" water. It's also considered good etiquette to clean your marble slab with a few scoopfuls of water before leaving.

It's not done for men to drop their *peştamal*: **modesty** is the order of the day, and washing your lower half through or under the cloth is an important acquired technique. Women are less scrupulous about covering up, though they too keep their knickers on. Communal bathing in Turkey is essentially a chaste business, though unsolicited male-to-male advances are a potential – if rare – hazard, especially in unsophisticated rural areas.

More than one foreign female visitor has been brought up short by the sight of a matronly figure advancing on them, beckoning with a straight razor: religious Turkish women **shave** all over, though usually not at the baths. Alternatively, the locals stalk about swathed to waist height in green depilatory paste, like New Guinea mud-women. Men, incidentally, are expected to shave their faces in the *tıraşlık*, a section of the *soğukluk* cooling-down room located between the foyer and the main chamber.

At the heart of the hamam is the *göbek taşı* or "navel stone", a raised platform positioned directly over the wood- or coal-fired furnaces that heat the premises. In a good bath the *göbek taşı* will be piping hot, and covered with prostrate figures using their scoop-dishes or special pillows as headrests. It's also the venue for vigorous (to say

the least) **massages** from the *tellâk* or masseur/masseuse, whose technique is inspired more by medieval rack-and-wheel practices than by New Age touchie-feelie methods – be warned. A *kese* (abrasive mitt) session from the same person, in which untold layers of dead skin and grime are whisked away, will probably be more to most people's tastes. Agree terms in advance with the *tellâk*, which should be about equal to the basic bath charge. If you prefer, you can buy a *kese* at any chemist's and rub yourself down. Traditionally, only male *tellâks* massaged men, and female masseusses women, but since the 1990s there has been increased incidence of men massaging women in the more touristy baths. If this is not to your liking, decline offers or even request a same-sex masseur from the management.

Upon return to your cubicle you'll be offered tea, soft drinks or mineral water, any of which is a good idea since the baths dehydrate you. These, like a massage, are charged as extra; if in doubt, consult the price placard over the reception desk. Except in the heavily touristed establishments, **tips** above and beyond the listed fees are not required or expected.

Food and drink

At its finest, Turkish food is among the best in the world. Indeed, gourmets often rank it as one of the three classic cuisines (along with French and Chinese), with many venerable dishes descended from Byzantine or Ottoman palace cuisine. There are enough climate zones in the country to grow or raise most ingredients locally; and the quality of the raw materials has not yet been compromised by mass-marketing standards and regulations.

Prices, except for the fancier cuts of meat and for seafood, aren't going to break your budget either, with full meals starting at around £4/$6, often even cheaper if you eat where the locals do. However, you'll pay more (often a lot more) at the major resorts, where

standards have sadly declined as tourism has taken hold. Unadventurous travellers are prone to get stuck in a kebab rut and come away moaning about the monotony of the cuisine; in fact, all but the strictest vegetarians should find enough variety to satisfy them.

A run-down of eating places and specialities follows, but for a full **menu reader**, turn to p.1095.

Breakfast

The so-called "Turkish" **breakfast** (*kahvaltı*) served at modest hotels and *pansiyons* is almost invariably a pile of spongy white bread slices with a pat of margarine, a slice of processed cheese, a dab of pre-packed jam and a couple of olives. Only tea is likely to be available in quantity; seconds are likely to be charged for, as are extras such as *sahanda yumurtalar* (fried eggs). In the better hotels and top-end *pansiyons* you can anticipate iced butter, preserves that actually contain fruit chunks, a variety of breads and pastries, fresh fruit slices, a choice of olive and cheese types, and an array of cold and hot meats, plus eggs in various styles.

You can breakfast better on a budget by simply using street stands or snack joints, many of which serve some of Turkey's best food. Many workers start the morning with a **börek**, a rich, flaky, layered pastry containing bits of mince or cheese; these can be found either at a tiny *büfe* (stall-café) or from a street cart. Others content themselves with a simple **simit** (bread rings speckled with sesame seeds) or a bowl of **çorba** (soup) with lemon.

Street snacks

With breakfast over, vendors hawk **lahmacun**, small, round Arab-style pizzas with a thin meat-based topping. Visitors from Britain may find to their surprise that **kebabs** (*kebap* in Turkish) per se are not generally considered takeaway food unless wrapped in a section of *dürüm*, an increasingly popular type of paratha-like bread; more often you'll find *döner* or *köfte* in takeaway stalls, served on a baguette or hamburger bun. Alternatively, try a **sandwich** (*sandviç*), a baguette chunk with various fillings (often *kokoreç* – offal – or fish), though it is extremely unwise to eat street fish in İstanbul; most of it comes from the pollutant-laced waters of the Sea of Marmara. In coastal cities deep-fried **mussels** (*midye tava*) are often available, as are *midye dolması* (mussels stuffed with rice, pine nuts and allspice) – though

these are best avoided in summer months, especially when offered un-refrigerated by street vendors.

Not to be confused with *lahmacun* is **pide**, Turkish pizza – flat bread with various toppings, served to a sit-down clientele in a *pideci* or *pide salonu*. The big advantage of this dish is that it's always made to order: typical styles are *kaşarlı* or *peynirli* (with cheese), *yumurtalı* (with egg), *kıymalı* (with mince), and *sucuklu* (with sausage). Most *pidecis* don't light their ovens until 11am or so, thus making it an obvious lunchtime treat.

Other specialities worth seeking out are **mantı** – the traditional Central Asian, meat-filled ravioli, served drenched in yoghurt and spice-reddened oil – or **gözleme**, a crêpe-like delicacy for which there is now a veritable craze in tourist resorts and Turkish towns alike. In any sizable town you'll also find at least one **kuru yemiş** stall, also known as a *leblebeci*, where nuts and dried fruit are sold by weight – typically 100g a shot. Aside from the usual offerings, keep an eye out for *cezeriye*, a bar made of carrot juice, honey and nuts; the east-Anatolian winter/spring snack of **peştil** (dried fruit), most commonly apricot and peach, pressed into sheets; and **tatlı sucuk**, a fruit, nut and molasses roll (not to be confused with meat *sucuk* or sausage).

Restaurants

Various types of eatery fill the need for more substantial sit-down food. A **lokanta** is a restaurant emphasizing *hazır yemek*, pre-cooked dishes kept warm in a steamtray. Here also can be found *sulu yemek*, "watery food" – which is just that, hearty chunks swimming in broth or sauce. Despite their often clinical appearance, food at the best *lokantas* (especially in İstanbul) may well prove your most delicious and memorable taste of Turkish cooking.

A **"restoran"**, a self-bestowed title for anything from a motorway bus pit-stop to a white-tablecloth affair, will provide *ızgara yemek* or meat dishes grilled to order. A **çorbacı** is a soup kitchen; **kebapcıs** and **köftecis** specialize in the preparation of kebab and *köfte* respectively, with a limited number of side dishes – usually just an array of salad, yoghurt and desserts. **İskembe** salonus are a Turkish institution, aimed at revellers as they emerge from clubs or taverns in the early hours, and open until 5 or 6am. Their main dish is tripe soup laced liberally with garlic oil, vinegar and red pepper flakes, an effective hangover antidote/preventative. They also sell *piliç* (small chickens), which can usually be seen spit-roasting in the window.

At an **ocakbaşı**, the grill and its hood is placed centre-stage, so that the diners can watch their meat being prepared. Even more interactive is the **kendin pişir kendin ye** (cook-it-and-eat-it-yourself) establishment, where a *mangal* (barbecue with coals), a specified quantity of raw meat, and condiments such as *kekik* (oregano) and *kimyon* (cumin) are brought to your outdoor table. Such places are excellent value, and you get to inspect the state of the meat; they also occasionally offer *tandır kebab*, a side of lamb or goat roasted in an oven.

Most budget-priced restaurants are **alcohol-free** (*içkisiz*); any **licensed** place (marked *içkili*) is likely to be more expensive. A useful exception is a **meyhane** (tavern), in its truest incarnation a smoky dive where eating is considered secondary to tippling. In the fancier ones, though, the food – mostly unusual delicacies – can be very good and not always drastically marked up in price. No self-respecting Turkish woman, however, would be caught dead in most of them, and unfortunately very few *meyhanes* are the sort of spot where an unaccompanied foreign woman can go without comment, and some will seem dodgy to Western men too. That said, any foreign men or couples bold enough to visit the more decorous *meyhanes* will be treated with the utmost courtesy. In restaurants, unaccompanied women may be ushered into the *aile salonu* (family parlour), usually upstairs or discreetly behind a curtain.

Prices vary widely according to the type of establishment: from $2–3 a head at a simple boozeless soup kitchen up to $20–25 at the flashier resort restaurants and İstanbul establishments. The fancier places will inevitably levy a ten-percent extra *servis* (service) charge and, to compound the pain, add on a separate *garsoniye* (waiter's tip).

Portions, especially in *meyhanes*, tend to be tiny, so if you're a big eater you may need to order two main courses. Many places don't have **menus**: you'll need to ascertain the prices beforehand and review bills carefully when finished. Tallying up items you never ate, or presenting diners with dishes they didn't order, are fairly common gambits; so is having your plate whisked away before you're done with it. This last habit is not so much a ploy to hurry you along, but derives from the Turkish custom of never leaving a guest with an "empty" or "dirty" plate before them. *Kalsın* ("may it remain") is the term to stop this practice in mid-air.

Dishes and specialities

In a *çorbacı*, soup (*çorba*) and salad (*salata*) predominate. The most frequently encountered **soups** are *mercimek* (lentil), *ezo gelin* (rice and vegetable broth – thick enough to be an appetizing breakfast), *paça* (trotters) or *işkembe* (tripe). Çoban (shepherd's) *salatası* is the generic term for the widespread cucumber, tomato, onion, pepper and parsley **salad** (approach the peppers with caution); *yeşil* (green) salad, usually just some *marul* (lettuce), is only seasonally available. A range of soups and salads can also be found in *lokantas* and high-class restaurants; here the so-called *mevsim salatası* or seasonal salad – perhaps tomato slices, watercress, red cabbage and lettuce hearts, sprinkled with cheese and drenched in dressing – resembles a Western salad and makes a welcome change from "shepherd's" salad.

In any *içkili restoran* or *meyhane*, you'll find more of the **mezes** (appetizers) for which Turkey is justly famous – usually a bewildering array of rich purees, vinaigrettes and fried-then-chilled dishes kept (sometimes for too long) in refrigerated display cases. These are the best dishes for vegetarians to concentrate on, since many are free of meat, while the variety of vegetables and pulses used, combined with vitamin-retentive cooking methods, will sustain your dietary needs.

Along with dessert (see overleaf), *mezes* are really the core of Turkish cuisine. The best and most common include *patlıcan salatası* (aubergine mash), *piyaz* (white haricot vinaigrette), *semizotu* (purslane weed, usually in

53

yoghurt), *mücver* (courgette croquettes), *sigara böreği* (tightly rolled cheese pastries), *beyin salatası* (whole lamb's/sheep's brain), *turşu* (pickled vegetables), *imam bayıldı* (cold baked aubergine with onion and tomato) and *dolma* (any stuffed vegetable, but typically peppers or tomatoes).

Bread is good if an hour or two old, but otherwise is spongy and stale, best for scooping up *mezes* and the like. Flat unadorned *pide* is served with soup, during Ramadan and at *kebapcıs*; while loaves of *kepekli* (wholemeal) or *çavdar* (rye bread; only from a *fırın* or bakery) afford relief in the largest cities. In villages, cooked *yufka* – the basis of *börek* pastry – makes a welcome respite, as does *bazlama* (similar to an Indian paratha).

Main courses are nutritious if often plainly presented. In *hazır yemek* restaurants, *kuru fasulye* (bean soup – rather like baked beans in tomato sauce), *taze fasulye* (French beans), *sebze turlu* (vegetable stew) and *nohut* (chickpeas) are the principal **vegetable** dishes. Vegetarians should, however, be aware that even though no meat may be visible in these dishes, they're almost always made with lamb- or chicken-based broth; even bulgur and rice may be cooked in meat stock. You might ask *İçinde et suyu var mı?* (Does it contain meat stock?), but it's best to confine yourself to *mezes* and salads, when available.

Dishes containing meat include *mussaka* (not as good as the Greek rendition), *karnı-yarık* (a much better Turkish variation), *güveç* (clay-pot fricassee), *tas kebap* (a meat and vegetable combo), *hunkar beğendi* (beef stew on a bed of pureed eggplant and cheese), *saray kebap* (beef stew topped with bechamel sauce and oven-browned), *macar* (Hungarian) *kebap* (stewed meat and vegetables topped with mashed potato and cheese, then baked) and *saç kavurma*, an inland Anatolian speciality made from meat, vegetables, spices and oil, fried up in a *saç* (the Turkish wok).

Grilled meat dishes from the *ızgara* (grill) include several variations on the stereotypical kebab. *Adana kebap* is spicy, with a sprinkling of purple sumac herb betraying Arab influence; *İskender kebap*, best sampled in Bursa, is heavy on the flatbread and

yoghurt. *Köfte* (meatballs), *şiş* (stewed meat chunks, usually mutton or beef) and *çöp* (bits of lamb or offal) are other options. When ordering, if you've any appetite, specify *bir buçuk* (a portion and a half – adequate) or *çift* (double portion – generous). Grilled dishes normally come with a slice or two of *pide* and raw vegetable garnish – never inside pitta bread as in Britain. Potentially more exciting are titbits such as *pirzola* (lamb chop), *böbrek* (kidney), *yürek* (heart), *ciğer* (liver) and *koç yumurtası* (ram's egg) or *billur* (crystal) – the last two euphemisms for testicle, less commonly found of late. A *karışık ızgara* (mixed grill) is always good value. Chicken (*piliç* or *tavuk*) is widely available, though not as cheap as you'd think.

Fish and seafood is good, if usually pricey, and sold by weight more often than by item ($16–20 per kilo is the rule). Buy with an eye to what's in season (as opposed to farmed or frozen and imported), and don't turn your nose up at humbler items, which in all likelihood will be fresher because they turn over faster. Budget mainstays include *sardalya* (sardines – grilled fresh), *palamut* (autumn tuna), *akya* (amberjack), *kefal* (grey mullet, a south Aegean speciality) and *sarıgöz* (black bream). *Çipura* (gilt-head bream) and *levrek* (sea bass), when suspiciously cheap, are almost invariably farmed.

Desserts and sweets

After the occasionally functional presentation of main dishes, Turkish chefs pander shamelessly and elegantly to the sweet tooth. Sticky-cake addicts and pudding freaks will find every imaginable concoction at the closest **pastane** (sweet-shop).

The syrup-soaked **baklava**-type items are pretty self-explanatory on a glance into the glass display cabinet – all permutations of a sugar, flour, nut and butter mix. More mysterious, less sweet and healthier are the **milk-based** dishes, which are popular all over the country. *Süpangile* ("süp" for short, a corruption of *soupe d'Anglais*) is an incredibly dense, rich chocolate pudding with sponge or a biscuit embedded inside. More modest dishes are *keşkül* (a vanilla and nut-crumble custard), and *sütlaç* (rice pudding) – one dessert that's consistently available in ordinary restaurants. The most convoluted dish

Asure

Aşure is the Turkish variant of a food with deep religious symbolism, found in Muslim, Christian and Jewish communities throughout Anatolia and the Balkans. The word is derived from the Arabic word for "ten", referring to *aşure günü*, or the tenth of the month of Muharrem, when Hasan and Hussein, sons of the fourth caliph Ali and grandsons of Mohammed, were slain, becoming martyrs for the Shiites and their allied sects in Turkey, the Alevîs and the Bektaşis. The latter have incorporated *aşure* fully into their ritual: after fasting for the first ten days of Muharrem, Bektaşi elders invite initiates to a private ceremony where the fast is broken over a communal meal of *aşure*. It is supposed to be made from forty different ingredients, courtesy of a legend which claims that after the Ark's forty-day sail on the Flood, and the first sighting of dry land, Noah commanded that a stew be made of the remaining supplies on board – which turned out to number forty sorts of food. An alternative name for the dish is thus "Noah's pudding", but today you'll be fortunate to find half that number of ingredients, even in a devotional recipe. You can also buy bags of prepackaged *aşure* mix in Turkish markets, and many kebab joints or *pastanes* serve it much of the year.

is *tavukgöğsü*, a cinnamon-topped morsel made from hyper-boiled and strained chicken breast, semolina starch and milk. *Kazandibi* (literally "bottom of the pot") is *tavukgöğsü* residue with a dark crust on the bottom – not to be confused with *fırın sütlaç*, which looks the same but is actually *sütlaç* pudding with a scorched top baked in a clay dish.

Grain-based sweets are some of the best that the country has to offer. Especially if you coincide with the appropriate holiday, you'll get to sample *aşure* (see box above), a sort of rosewater jelly laced with pulses, wheat berries, raisins and nuts. The best-known Turkish sweet, *lokum* or **"Turkish Delight"**, is pretty much ubiquitous, available from *pastanes* and the more touristy shops. It's basically solidified sugar and pectin, flavoured (most commonly) with rosewater, sometimes pistachios, and sprinkled with powdered sugar.

There are also nearly a dozen recognized sorts of **helva**, including the *tahini*-paste chew synonymous with the concoction in the West, although in Turkey the term usually means any variation on the basic theme of baked flour or starch, butter, sugar and flavoured water.

Ice cream is an excellent summer treat, provided it's genuine *Maraşlı döşme dondurma* (whipped in the Kahraman Maraş tradition – a bit like Italian *gelato*), not factory-produced rubbish. Consistent warm weather prompts the stationing at public parks, sea promenades and so on of outlandishly costumed young men with swords selling the stuff. Being served is half the fun: you may be threatened or cajoled at (blunted) sword point into buying, after which the cone is presented to you on the point of the sword after a twirl or three, and a bell rung loudly to celebrate the transaction.

Final choices include *kabak tatlısı* (candied squash usually served in autumn with walnut chunks and *kaymak*, or clotted cream); *ayva tatlısı* (stewed quince served with nuts or dried fruit, topped with *kaymak* and dusted with grated pistachio); or **summer fruit** (*meyve*), which generally means *kavun* (Persian melon, honeydew) or *karpuz* (watermelon).

Tea, coffee and soft drinks

Tea, grown along the Black Sea since the 1930s, is the national drink and an essential social lubricant – you'll inevitably be offered some within twenty minutes of your arrival in Turkey. Tea is properly prepared in the *çaydanlık*, a double-boiler apparatus, with a larger water chamber underneath the smaller receptacle containing dry leaves, to which a small quantity of hot water is added. After a suitable wait the tea is decanted into tiny tulip-shaped glasses, then diluted with more water to taste: *açık* is weak, *demli* or *koyu* steeped. Sugar comes as cubes on the side; milk is never added. If you're frustrated by the usual tiny glass at breakfast, ask for a *düble çay* (a "double tea", served in a juice glass).

Herbal teas are also popular in Turkey, particularly *ıhlamur* (linden flower), *kuşburnu* (rose hip), *papatya* (camomile) and *ada çay* ("island" tea), an infusion of a type of sage common in all coastal areas. Most of the much-touted **apple tea** (*elma çay*) in fact contains chemicals and not a trace of apple essence, though it is becoming possible to find natural (*doğal*) formulas as opposed to artificial (*sintetik*).

Coffee is not as commonly drunk in Turkey, despite the fact that the Ottomans first introduced the drink to Europe from Yemen. Instant is increasingly popular, now available in several brands besides the inevitable Nescafé. It's much stronger, however, than Anglo-Saxon formulas, brewed more in line to German tastes. The traditional, fine-ground Turkish coffee is preferable, brewed up *sade* (without sugar), *orta şekerli* (medium sweet) or *çok şekerli* (cloying). For an extended session of drinking either tea or coffee, you retire to a **çay bahçesi** (tea garden), which often will also serve ice cream and soft drinks.

Only in the very largest cities and most cosmopolitan resorts will you find western notions of coffee, such as filtered or cappuccino, though the EU customs union has made the raw materials easier to find in the appropriate aisles of major supermarkets.

Certain traditional beverages tend to accompany particular kinds of food or appear at set seasons. *Sıcak süt* (hot milk) is the perennial complement to *börek*, though in winter it's fortified with *salep*, the ground-up tuber of *Orchis mascula*, a phenomenally expensive wild orchid gathered in coastal areas between Antalya and İzmir. **Salep** is a good safeguard against colds (and also reputedly an aphrodisiac), though because of its cost most pre-packaged varieties are heavily adulterated with powdered milk, starch and sugar – only in the İzmir bazaar will you find the real thing at full strength. **Ayran** (watered-down yoghurt), is always on offer at *pidecis* and *kebapcis*, and is good cold but not so appetizing if – as it sometimes is – lukewarm and lumpy. In autumn

and winter, you'll find stalls selling **boza**, a delicious, mildly fermented millet drink flavoured with grape juice. Similarly tangy is **şıra**, a lightly alcoholic grape juice acceptable to religious Muslims and available in late summer and autumn.

Fruit juice (*meyva suyu*) can be excellent if it comes as pulp in a bottle, available in such flavours as *kayısı* (apricot), *şeftali* (peach) and *vişne* (sour cherry). The recent wave of thin, preservative-spiked cardboard-packaged juice drinks is distinctly less thrilling, though there are a few, more pricey, locally produced pure fruit juices in packets. The good stuff is so thick you might want to cut it with **spring water** (*memba suyu*), or fizzy **mineral water** (*maden suyu*). A PVC bottle of water costs about $0.50 in a restaurant; in many establishments chilled, potable tap water in a glass bottle or a jug is routinely provided at each table, for which there should be no extra charge. You can request lemon wedges to squeeze into this for improved taste. *Meşrubat* is the generic term for all types of carbonated **soft drinks** – available pretty much everywhere now.

Alcoholic drinks

Despite inroads made by Islamic fundamentalists, **alcoholic drinks** (*içkiler*) are available virtually without restriction in resorts – even being sold within 100m of a mosque, normally a no-no – though you will indeed have some thirsty moments in conservative interior towns such as Afyon, Konya, Erzerum or Diyarbakır. Even with the new Islam-friendly government, this situation promises to remain unchanged as they're keen to encourage tourism, and will probably settle for a few more local bans where the municipality is under their control. One likely development, however, is the sale and break-up of the *Tekel*, or state alcohol-producing monopoly.

Beer (*bira*) is sold principally in returnable bottles but also in cans (expensive) and on draught (*fıcı bira* in Turkish), which is cheaper. There are two principal domestic brands, both at about five-percent alcohol content. **Efes Pilsen**, the most popular beer in Turkey, can be over-yeasty; it's normally sold as a half-litre bottle, though in resort areas comes as 33cl bottles or cans of "Lite" (low alcohol), "Dark", and "Extra" (seven percent). Efes has an alternate label (Marmara 34, available in 70cl bottles or 50cl cans) and is also the local licensee-brewer of Becks (33cl bottles, 50cl cans) and Miller (same sizes). **Tuborg** also generates varying opinions, though since foreign backer Carlsberg began brewing Carlsberg per se locally (33/50cl bottles, 50cl cans, also draught) its market share has improved – their sub-label Troy is a decent pilsener beer. **Imported** bottled beers (such as Corona, Bud or Heineken) are now available in the largest cities, though at a price. There are, as yet, very few relatively civilized **pubs** (*birerrie*) as opposed to the ubiquitous **beer hall** (*birahane*), imitation-German-style establishments, which often have a distinctly aggressive atmosphere – best avoided.

Wine (*şarap*), from vineyards scattered across western Anatolia between Cappadocia, the Euphrates Valley, Thrace and the Aegean, is often better than average. There has lately been a huge upswing of interest in fine wine, with expensive imported labels available in most large international-chain hotels, and some upmarket town-centre restaurants. Local wines are also now better distributed, resulting in a huge variety in the bigger cities, though quality remains variable. Red wine is *kırmızı*, white *beyaz*, rose *roze*. In shops, count on paying $3.50–10 for a bottle of mid-range wine, or as much as $20 for a bottle from some obscure, self-styled boutique winery that may be scarcely better than the major players.

The market is currently dominated by two large vintners: Doluca (try their Moskado Sek, from 1999 onwards) and Kavaklıdere (whose Çankaya white and Lâl rose are especially commendable). Kavaklıdere also produces a sparkling white, İnci Damalası, the closest local thing to champagne. Other smaller, regional brands to watch for include Turasan (red is excellent, though their white's a bit too sweet), Narbağ, Peribacası

(Cappadocia) and Kavalleros (Sea of Marmara), though Merih Rosé is disgusting and eminently avoidable. Feyzi Kutman red in particular is superb, though alas rarely found outside the largest centres. Similarly confined to their areas of production are cheap-and-cheerful whites from Bozcaada and Şirince, plus Majestik red, available only around İzmir. A new producer worth seeking out is Sevilen, which makes organic reds – Merlot and Cabernet – at premium prices.

The Turkish national aperitif is **rakı**, not unlike Greek ouzo but rougher and stronger. The *Tekel* state monopoly remains the sole distiller until its plants are sold off in 2004. Rakı comes in four grades, which in roughly ascending order of price and quality are Yeni, Külübe, Altıbaş and Tekirdağ (the last not to be confused with the superior grade of Yeni distilled at Tekirdağ, using recycled sherry casks). It's usually drunk over ice and topped up with bottled water. The *meyhane* routine of an evening is for a group of men to order a big bottle of *rakı,* a bucket of ice and a few bottles of water, and then slowly drink themselves under the table between bites of seafood *meze* or nibbles of *çerez* – the generic term for pumpkin seeds, chickpeas, almonds etc, served on tiny plates.

Stronger **spirits** – domestically produced *cin* (gin), *votka* (vodka) and *kanyak* (cognac) – were long the province of the *Tekel* government monopoly, but since the mid-1990s import duties on foreign-bottled items have plummeted. However, there is still a sharp price (as well as quality) difference between imported spirits and those of the *Tekel* (designated as *yerli* or "local" on bar placards). Expect domestic distillery quality to remain low even after the *Tekel* is replaced by private enterprises. Domestically produced **liqueurs** are often given on the house at the end of a meal. For the most part they are quite cloying, but bearable exceptions include Mocca and Acıbadem (almond liqueur).

Communications

The Turkish postal and telephone service was historically run by the state-owned PTT (*Posta Telefon ve Telegraf*), with its black-on-yellow livery. However, since 1996 most of its telecommunications functions have been hived off as TT (*Türk Telekom*), distinguished by its blue-on-turquoise call boxes. In the largest towns and tourist resorts, the phone division of the main PTT building is open until midnight (7pm on Sundays), with mail accepted daily from 8am until 5pm; separate TT buildings, where present, tend to keep roughly the same hours. Elsewhere, the PTT adheres to standard civil-service hours, with complete closure on Saturday afternoon and Sundays.

Postal services

Stamps are only available from the PTT, whose website (🅦www.ptt.gov.tr) has full English-language listings of current services and prices. **Overseas letter** rates are rapidly approaching uniformity with those in EU countries; air mail (*Uçakla*) rates to Europe are about $0.50 for up to 20g, up to $14 for 2kg, the maximum weight for letters. Delivery to Europe or North American can take seven to ten days, but *acele* (express) service is available for a surcharge assessed in 50-gramme increments (in a range of $0.70–$32), cutting delivery time for the EU to about three days. Registered (*taahuklu*) service costs about $0.50 extra and by itself is enough to guarantee somewhat faster as well as secure delivery.

The best advice on sending **packages** is to find a private cargo company; they exist in all sizeable cities, and most of them handle overseas parcels. The best known are Yurtiçi Kargo and Aras Kargo, plus the more expensive international companies DHL and UPS. You will have to complete a declaration of the contents; it will cost about $22 for three-working-day delivery of a 500-gramme package to the UK. If you opt instead for the PTT, which is cheaper, do it in a medium-sized town with an airport and enlist the help of a sympathetic supervisor who understands the rules. For non-EU destinations, boxes should be presented unsealed for potential inspection; at main branches folded cardboard packing kits are usually sold. Though most of these may be supplied, it's best to come prepared with tape, twine, indelible marker, scissors, supporting invoices and certificates – and plenty of patience. There is no *acele* parcel service and rates vary for each country, but as an example, an air parcel to the UK costs $22 for the first kilo, plus $4 for each additional kilo, while surface (not really worth the scant savings) is $19 for the first kilo, $3 for each additional one.

Posting slots are clearly labelled – *yurtdışı* for overseas, *yurtiçi* for inland, *şehiriçi* for local. Street-corner post boxes are just about non-existent these days. To receive mail **poste restante** (general delivery), articles should be addressed to you, c/o "Postrestant, Merkez Postanesi, [city name], Turkey".

Telephones

PTT or TT premises are the best place to make phone calls. The **Türk Telekom** website (🅦www.turktelekom.com.tr) has an English-language page listing all services and tariffs. Inside the PTT/TT, or just adjacent, there is usually a row of card (*telekart*) phones and/or a *kontürlü* (metered, clerk-attended) phone, the latter sometimes in a closed booth. **Public phones** elsewhere are fairly common, typically found on resort quays, in public parks and at filling stations or street corners. The standard Turkish phone replies are the Frenchified *Allo* or the more local *Buyurun* (literally, "Avail yourself/at your service"). Connection standards in rural areas are far worse than in the big cities, and you will typically have to dial two or three times to reach your party, even within the same area code.

Jetons, or tokens, to work old-style phones theoretically still exist, but you're unlikely to encounter them. Instead, for interurban or overseas calls, two breeds of **phonecards** (*telekarts*) are available: ordinary *telekarts* in denominations of 30, 60, 100 and 120 units ($1, $2, $2.60 and $3.20 respectively) and so-called "smart" *telekarts* in denominations of 50, 100 and 350 units ($2, $2.60 and $9.40). A 100-unit card, for example, yields 35 minutes of peak-time chat from İstanbul to Ankara, 41 minutes off-peak; for overseas calls to North America and most of Europe, you'll get just 6 minutes at peak rates, 9 minutes 20 seconds off-peak. *Telekarts* are used in exactly the same manner as British or North American ones, though you have little warning before being cut off; wait for the number of units remaining to appear on the screen before dialling. A steadily increasing number of phones have also been adapted to accept foreign **credit cards**.

Metered booths inside PTTs or TTs, or at street kiosks (look for signs reading *kontürlü telefon bulunur*) work out more expensive than cards, but are certainly far cheaper than hotels, but also tend to be quieter (plus you won't be cut off). Their disadvantage is that you can't see the meter ticking over, and instances of overcharging are not unknown.

Turkey uses a system of eleven-digit **phone numbers** nationwide, consisting of four-digit area or mobile-provider codes (all starting with "0") plus a seven-digit subscriber number. To call a number in Turkey **from overseas**, dial your country's international access code, then 90 for Turkey, next the area or mobile code minus the initial zero, and finally the subscriber number. To call home **from Turkey**, dial ☎00 followed by the relevant international dialling code (see list below), then the area code (without the initial zero if there is one), then the number.

Overseas call rates are still not anywhere near EU rates: $0.70/min peak to Europe or North America, $0.40/min off-peak (daily 10pm–8am and all day Sunday). Try not to make anything other than local calls from a hotel room – there's usually a minimum 100-percent surcharge on phonecard rates.

Charge-card call services from Turkey back to your home country are provided by a variety of operators (UK, BT and Npower; North America, Canada Direct, AT&T, MCI and Sprint; Australia, Optus and Telstra; New Zealand, Telecom NZ). Local-dial numbers with some charge-card operators (see list below) enable you to connect to the international network for the price of a one-unit call and then charge the call to your home number.

Most hotels in our categories ❸ and above have **faxes** and it is usually simpler to send and receive one there than to use the PTT's fax service. At about a minute per transmitted page, this is a far cheaper way of staying in touch transcontinentally than chatting – as well as being a reliable way of making reservations.

Useful telephone numbers

Directory assistance ☎118
International operator (reverse charges) ☎115
Postal code assistance ☎119
Inter-city operator ☎131

International dialling codes

Australia ☎61
Ireland ☎353
Netherlands ☎31
New Zealand ☎64
UK ☎44
US and Canada ☎1

Charge-card access numbers from Turkey

AT&T USA Direct ☎00 800 12277
British Telecom ☎00 800 890900
Canada Direct ☎00 800 16677
Ireland ☎00 800 3531177
MCI ☎00 800 11177
Sprint ☎00 800 14477
Telestra Australia ☎00 800 611177

Mobile phones

Given the shortcomings of the fixed-phone system, **mobile phones** have become an essential accessory in Turkey. Numbers are prefixed ☎0542, ☎0543, ☎0532, ☎0535 and ☎0555, and as ever it's pricey to dial into them – use a *kontürlü* phone, or another mobile, so you won't get cut off. Coverage is fairly good, except in alpine or thinly populated areas.

There are four **networks** at present – Turkcell, Telsim, Aria and Aycell – the last-named a TT subsidiary, confined thus far to big cities but offering cheaper rates to fixed phones. All networks offer a bewildering array of pay-as-you-go packages, available at any mobile phone outlet advertising *kontürlü* phonecards; registering, allocation of a number and your first 100-unit chat card costs as little as $10, a 200-unit top-up $11. Rates depend on whom you're calling and which package you choose, but compare favourably to *telekart* use and roaming with a foreign mobile number (see below): typically $0.80/min to Europe, $1.20/min to North America, $2/min to Australia.

Any GSM mobile home-based in northern Europe, Australia or New Zealand should work fine in Turkey; North American users will only be able to use tri-band rigs. You also may need to inform your provider before going abroad to get international access ("roaming") switched on. Some price-plans charge extra for this, and you will definitely be charged extra for incoming calls when abroad, though discount plans are available to reduce the cost by as much as seventy percent. If you want to retrieve voicemail while away, you'll need to ask your provider for a new access number, as your home one (or one-stroke "mail" key) is unlikely to work abroad.

In terms of the four existing Turkish networks (which show themselves on your screen abbreviated as TR-01, TR-02, TR-03 or TR-04), there's little to distinguish between the first two as roaming partners – TR-03 and TR-04 have markedly less coverage – or the eventual (often horrendous) bill to be paid back home after using any of them. Not being subject to EU rules means that Turkish mobile providers seem to charge guest users what they like, to the tune of £1.10 per minute for calls to Britain (including voicemail retrieval), 33p per minute for incoming calls, even with a discount plan (over double that without one). Ringing either a Turkish landline or mobile with an overseas SIM card will cost about 45–50p per minute.

The best way to avoid high roaming bills is to use your foreign-purchased mobile with a SIM card from a Turkish network. It's easily

done – pop out the original SIM and replace with the Turkish SIM. Some mobile operators, however, "block" their phones to prevent their being used on other networks; "unblocking" the phone is not illegal and will not void your existing home-based contract. Legions of mobile repair shops, especially around Sirkeci in İstanbul, will oblige you – about $10 for a simple two-minute procedure that permits subscribing to a Turkish number without keying in any special unblocking code. If you're going to be in the country anything longer than a week or so, this is well worth pursuing.

Email and internet

Email and internet use has caught on in a big way in Turkey, especially in the bigger towns where Türk Telekom has invested in infrastructure; elsewhere low-capacity phone lines mean chronic frustration in maintaining ISP connections. Email addresses or websites are given in this guide for the growing number of travel companies and hotels that have them. For your own email needs, you can use the various **internet cafés** that have sprung up in the larger coastal resorts and interior towns – addresses are given where appropriate. Rates tend to be $1.50 per hour maximum, with shorter periods often available.

Ideally you should sign up in advance for a free web-based email address that can be accessed from anywhere, for example Yahoo (@www.yahoo.com) or Hotmail (@www.hotmail.com). Once you've set up an account, you can use these sites to pick up and send mail from any internet café or hotel with internet access. One big disadvantage of Hotmail is that your mailbox storage quota is very small, so it must be collected regularly or you will lose messages.

Alternatively, you can lug your own laptop around, not such a burden as they get progressively lighter. You will need about 2m of North American-standard cable (UK ones will *not* work), lightweight and easily purchasable in Turkey, with RJ-11 male terminals at each end. Many newer hotel rooms have RJ-11 sockets, but some older ones still have their phones hard-wired into the wall. You can sometimes get around this problem with a female–female adaptor, either RJ-11- or 6P6C-configured, available at better electrical retailers. They weigh and cost next to nothing, so carry both (one is sure to work) for making a splice between your cable and the RJ-11 end of the cable between the wall and phone (which you simply unplug). You will usually have to dial an initial "9" or "0" to get around the hotel's central switchboard for a proper external dial tone. No international ISPs maintain points of presence in Turkey, so if you don't have Yahoo or Hotmail service you're looking at an international call to retrieve your mail.

The media

Newspapers and magazines weren't even allowed in the country until the middle of the nineteenth century; since then, however, lost time has been made up for with a vengeance. A score of mastheads, representing the full gamut of public tastes from elevated to gutter, compete for readers' attention. The airwaves were controlled exclusively by the government until the late 1980s, but with satellite dishes widely available and overseas transmitters a reality, a vast quantity of private, cable and digital stations – mostly of poor quality – flourishes across Turkey.

Turkish-language publications

An independent press didn't exist in Turkey until the middle of the nineteenth century, when an Englishman, William Churchill, started the first non-official publication, the *Cerde-I-Havadis* (Journal of News). Today, it's estimated that out of a population of over 63 million, fewer than ten percent actually read newspapers, with circulation figures – at best a few hundred thousand daily – boosted by those collecting special promotional coupons for consumer goods.

Around seventy percent of the **newspapers** sold are produced by two giant media conglomerates, the Doğan group and the Sabah group. Three titles – **Sabah**, **Hürriyet** and **Milliyet** – dominate the middle market, mixing gossip, sleaze and plenty of football with serious political and economic news. All three include weekly TV guides with their Saturday editions. Slightly to the left of these stands **Radikal**, the best paper to pick up in the big cities for listings of cinema, exhibitions and concerts (often with discount coupons for the latter).

The only surviving high-end newspaper is venerable **Cumhuriyet**, founded as the mouthpiece of the Turkish republic in 1924. Nowadays, it mixes conservative nationalism with old-style socialism and struggles to survive. Distinctly downmarket are heavily illustrated **Posta**, **Star**, **Akşam** and **Vatan**, which offer rather dubious news coverage – and principally something for corner shops to wrap vegetables in, thus the idiom "asparagus news" for these rags.

Of more interest are Turkey's Islamist papers, which give surprisingly intelligent coverage. Of the biggest sellers, **Yeni Şafak** and **Zaman**, the former is currently a strong supporter of the Justice and Development (AK) Party elected to power in 2002, while the latter takes a more independent line. Distinctly nasty is the bigoted **Vakit**, which delights in "outing" prominent non-Muslims among Turkey's business and political communities.

On the far right, **Türkiye** usually sticks to a predictable ultra-nationalist line. On the far left, two titles – **Evrensel** and the "pro-Kurdish" **Özgür Politika** – stand out. Both

Censorship and the press

The forcible closure of publications, confiscation of assets and prosecutions of journalists or editors, at the behest of the **State Security Tribunal** (*Devlet Güvenlik Mahkemesi*), were depressingly common in Turkey during the 1980s and 1990s. Most "infractions" were related to alleged insults or impertinence to government officials, accounts of official misdeeds and financial scandals, highlighting the history or current status of Kurds or Armenians, and anything resembling advocacy of communism (banned in Turkey). Judicious self-censorship in the Turkish press was further encouraged by even more direct threats to journalists' well-being. Throughout the 1990s the staff of pro-Kurdish publications were physically attacked, often fatally, by shadowy groups alleged to have links with security forces; most egregious was the assassination of *Cumhuriyet* columnist and national pundit Uğur Mumcu in 1993. In late 1999 a watershed of sorts was finally crossed when, after more than forty "unsolved" killings of journalists since 1990, six police officers were sentenced to short jail terms for the beating to death in 1995 of *Evrensel* photographer Metin Göktepe.

The far more open political climate that has prevailed since the late 1990s has made it safer for journalists to criticize the establishment without consequences. Early in 2002, American professor Noam Chomsky appeared as a witness and co-defendant in the trial of a pro-Kurdish publisher charged with "disseminating separatist propaganda", and all charges were gratifyingly dropped. Turkey's campaign to enter the EU has also prompted changes to various laws restricting press and political freedom, including a redraft (though not a repeal) of the infamous Article 8 of the so-called Anti-Terror Law, often dubbed Turkey's "thought crime" statute. This has narrowed the conditions under which writers, editors and publishers can be prosecuted, though it's still unclear how the redrafted law will be interpreted by the courts.

have had their problems with the authorities; *Özgür Politika* in particular is the direct descendant of four successive publications that were closed down between 1994 and 1999.

The principal weekly **magazines** are the picture-driven **Tempo** and **Aktuel**, which serve up a diet of showbiz gossip, news and features, including politics. Usually good for a laugh are two pages of pics from celebrity bashes featuring the famous, the nearly famous and the wannabes, shrink-wrapped into atrocious "designer" garb. A vast range of other weekly and monthly glossies includes Turkish versions of most major women's magazines, and even the lads' mag *FHM*.

Turkey also has an insatiable market for weekly **satirical comics** whose content invariably revolves around sex and other foibles of the human condition, often delivering a subtle, or not-so-subtle, political message. Turkey's caricature artists are among the cruellest and most graphic in the world, but seem miraculously immune from legal proceedings. However, title turnover is fairly rapid, with artist-management disputes resulting in frequent walkouts and the establishment of spin-offs. During the late 1980s, pioneer **Gırgır** was the third biggest-selling adult comic in the world after America's *Mad* and the Soviet Union's *Krokodil*, until the cartoonists responsible decamped to other titles. More recent big-sellers included *Limon*, victim of another walkout, which produced *Leman*, which itself gave birth to current favourite **Le Manyak**, whose star character is a politically incorrect tom-cat, Şerafettin. The latest entrant is the far more political – and arguably less funny – **Penguen**, which lampoons the ruling elite.

English-language publications

The only surviving local English-language newspaper, sold wherever foreigners congregate, is the long-running **Turkish Daily News**, now majority-owned by the Doğan group, and with useful cinema listings for

İstanbul, İzmir and Ankara. If you're interested in Turkish politics, the *TDN* serves as a good resource, though its failure to contextualize can be frustrating for those unfamiliar with the country. The Sunday edition (confusingly called *Turkish Probe*) has little news and consists mainly of tedious "analysis" articles penned by "experts" in fractured English.

Glossy magazines include the bimonthly **Istanbul: The Guide**, sold at newsstands or available free in many of the city's larger hotels – features are weak but listings are OK. The same is true for **Time Out Istanbul**, the local imprint of the London listings mag, which comes with a forty-page English-language supplement of what's-on listings and useful coverage of new bars clubs and restaurants. The monthly travel and culture mag **Atlas** boasts good Turkish-language travel features on Turkey and overseas, plus excellent photography; its excellent twice-yearly supplement, *Arkeo*, has English summaries of all pieces. The surprisingly good Turkish Airlines bilingual in-flight magazine **Skylife** (free on the plane, otherwise on sale at larger newsagents) has a wide variety of features on little-known Turkish destinations, crafts and historical episodes. Any of these is cheaper and more down-to-earth than bi-monthly **Cornucopia**, which dwells in its own bubble-world of property restoration, decadent food and auction-house interiors, plus sound-bite features by writers commissioned more for their name or connections than anything else.

British and American newspapers are easily available in Anglophone resorts and the three largest cities, generally arriving late in the evening of publication day. Easiest to find are usually *The Guardian* (European edition), the *International Herald Tribune* and *USA Today*.

Television

Turkish TV has come a long way since the early 1980s, when it was restricted to a single, closely controlled, state-run channel. The advent of satellite dishes essentially broke the public-broadcasting monopoly, as it became possible to beam Turkish-language (and, sporadically, Kurdish-language) programmes in from European transmitters. Private terrestrial channels were not slow to proliferate and

have now largely overtaken public stations in terms of viewer numbers. According to the national broadcasting authority, RTUK, there are about 260 licensed channels, public and private, throughout the country, though the overwhelming majority are local services restricted to one town and not noted for adventurous programming.

Quality in the private sector is fairly low, and the political/religious affiliation of the proprietors – often newspaper moguls or banks – is seldom in doubt. Politically biased reporting, as well as a multitude of other RTUK-defined misdemeanours, are treated severely, with the normal punishment being to take the channel off the air for a couple of days, replacing programmes with a screen explaining which law has been infringed. The latest legal reforms specifically allow for broadcasting in "non-Turkish" languages, specifically Kurdish, though as yet nobody has dared act on this possibility.

Up to four television channels of the **state-owned TRT** (Turkish Radio and Television) are available, depending on where you are and what time it is. Public programming veers between foreign historical drama series dubbed in Turkish, American films (also dubbed) and talking-heads panel discussions, punctuated by classical Turkish musical interludes, variety shows, soaps and chirpy, US-style advertisements. TRT-1 has a fairly balanced output not dissimilar to British channels, while TRT-2 is the arts and cultural channel; TRT-3 offers live coverage of parliament, and TRT-4 is nominally educational. Another state channel, GAP (*Güney Anadolu Programı* or "South Anatolian Programme"), is reserved for reruns and easy-watching pap aimed at those whose first language is Kurdish or Arabic.

Among **private channels** offering light entertainment, film reruns and current affairs, Show, Star, ATV, Kanal D and Kanal Altı are generally the easiest to pick up. Number 1 and Kral devote their time mainly to Turkish pop videos and short "youth"-related features. Best (Turkish-only) **news coverage** is generally reckoned to be that of NTV and CNN Türk. CNN Türk's output is a mix of news, reviews and interviews similar to its international namesake, although its output is almost exclusively in Turkish. NTV's sister channel CSNBC, a joint venture with America's NBC, devotes evenings and weekends to a bizarre mix of B-movies and US TV shows such as *Seinfeld*, *South Park* and ancient re-runs of *Saturday Night Live*, all in English with Turkish subtitles.

Ideological bias is most apparent on the **religious and far-right-wing channels**. Generally reckoned to be the most Islamic is *Saman Yolu* ("Milky Way"), also known as STV, while Kanal 7 and Flash also maintain a religious stance. TGRT and HBB offer a mixed diet of programmes but are well to the right – although the former's current-affairs coverage is very professionally put together.

Satellite TV is common in homes, bars and restaurants, particularly in the Aegean and Mediterranean resorts where live English Premier League soccer is a big attraction. Otherwise you'll find BBC World, CSNBC, BBC Prime, Cinebeş (all-films), CNN and other usual suspects on hotel-room TVs.

Live Turkish Premier League football is now exclusive to Turkey's only **digital TV** platform, Digiturk, which you'll find in many bars and cheaper restaurants, predictably packed on match nights. Occasionally terrestrial channels buy the rights to show a big-league game live, but they mostly – especially CNN Türk – make do with a highlights package. National team games and second division matches still appear live on TRT, while European club matches go out live on certain private channels such as Star or Show.

Radio

Frequency-crowding on the effectively unregulated airwaves means that even popular channels are almost impossible to pick up without interference. The cacophony seems set to continue as a long-promised frequency auction has been postponed by successive governments.

Up to four **public radio stations** broadcast between 7am and 1am, though certain channels start earlier or end later. Radyo Üç (The Third Programme or TRT-3), most commonly found at 88.2, 94 and 99MHz, broadcasts the highest proportion of Western music. It also airs **news bulletins in English** at 9am, noon, 2pm, 5pm, 7pm and 10pm, though these tend to be heavily edited propaganda snippets focusing on the move-

ments and utterances of government ministers.

As with television, mediocre **private radio** stations have multiplied almost unbearably, but by playing dial roulette on your personal stereo or car radio, you can often snare some decent jazz, rock, blues or classical programmes. In İstanbul, Açık Radyo (FM 94.9) provides a mixed diet of Western rock, jazz and soul, while Radio Blue (FM 94.5) offers Latin and jazz. Other big names offering Western music and production values include Capitol FM (99.5), Kiss FM (90.3) and Metro FM (97.2), which can be received across much of the country. Many resorts have their own local station on which you may find some programming in English. **English-language foreign services** – including Voice of America and the BBC World Service – can be picked up on short wave, although you'll need to be fairly adept at tuning. The BBC World Service can also theoretically be received on medium wave along the south coast closest to the BBC transmitter on Cyprus.

Cinema

The arrival of TV in Turkey cut the number of cinema screens in the country from around three thousand at the start of the 1970s to just a few dozen by the early 1990s. Thanks to new modern multi-screen complexes being created in big shopping centres, the number has since inched back up to over a hundred, mostly in İstanbul (with almost half the total), Ankara, İzmir, Adana and Antalya, but also in such previously unlikely spots as Antakya, Kayseri, Gaziantep, İskenderun, Diyarbakır and even Van.

Western first-run releases and quality Turkish films supplement the old diet of shoot-em-ups and kung-fu flicks. **Foreign films** are invariably shown in the original language with Turkish subtitles; screenings (a *seans* in Turkish), up to five daily, generally start at 11.30am or noon, following at around 3pm, 6pm, 9pm and usually midnight. **Tickets** usually cost around $3 equivalent, with reductions for students and teachers. Most films have a fifteen-minute break mid-action, to allow cigarette-smokers to satisfy their habit in the stairways and cafés. For a detailed overview of the homegrown Turkish film industry, see Contexts, p.1049.

Admission to museums, sites and mosques

Museums are generally open from 8.30 or 9am until 5.30 or 6pm, and closed on Monday, though in the case of some smaller museums you may have to find the *bekçi* (caretaker or warden) and ask him to open up. All sites and museums are closed on the mornings of public holidays (see p.66), while İstanbul's palaces are generally closed on Mondays and Thursdays. Some of İstanbul's most fascinating smaller Byzantine monuments are only accessible by permission from the Directorate of Aya Sofya, located in the grounds of Aya Sofya. Certain isolated monuments beside the Armenian border also require permission to visit, which can be granted only by the military authorities in Ankara.

Admission prices

Admission prices for foreigners – formerly a pawn in arcane battles between whichever political party controlled the Ministry of Culture and its opponents – seem to have settled down to something like what's charged in neighbouring Greece and Cyprus. Current charges are the equivalent of $0.70 for minor sites, $2 at sites of middling interest and $7.50–10 for major attractions such as Ephesus, Cappadocian cave-churches and İstanbul's Aya Sofya. FIYTO student cards should ensure **free admission** to museums and sites; ISIC cards will usually – though not always – net you a fifty to sixty percent **reduction**. In theory, those over 65 are also supposed to gain free entrance to museums and sites; bring your passport as proof of age. A few minor sites not administered by the Ministry of Culture, such as private museums or ones managed by Islamist municipalities, may charge foreigners much more than locals and not recognize any discount schemes.

Archeological sites

Major archeological sites are generally open daily from just after sunrise until just before sunset; owing to budgetary constraints, current schedules feature later opening and earlier closing than in previous years. Some smaller archeological sites are only guarded during the day and left unfenced, permitting (in theory) a free wander around in the evening. Others are staffed until dark by a solitary warden, who may have enough English to give you a guided tour, for which he will probably expect a tip. However, in recent years surveillance at sites both fenced and unenclosed has been improved in the wake of antiquities theft and furtive visits after posted closing hours can result in your being picked up by the *jandarma*.

Never pay **entrance fees** unless the wardens can produce a ticket, whatever other documentation they may have. If you don't take a ticket, crooked sellers can resell the same ticket over and over again, pocketing the proceeds. Keep tickets with you for the duration of your visit and even afterwards, as sites often straddle the route to a good beach – in theory the ticket is valid for the entire day (sometimes even several days or a week), sparing you repayment if you re-cross the area.

Mosques

There's no admission fee for entry to mosques, but you may be asked by the caretaker or *imam* to make a small donation. If so, put it into the collection box rather than someone's hand. Larger mosques frequented by tourists are open all the time – others only for *namaz*, or Muslim prayer, five times a day. **Prayer times**, which last around twenty minutes, vary according to the time of year, but generally occur at dawn, late morning, midday, late afternoon and sundown; often a chalkboard will be posted outside the door with exact hours for that day. Outside prayer times it's sometimes possible to find the *imam* and ask him to open up; just ask passers-by where his house is.

Whether or not you're required to, it's a courtesy for women to cover their heads before entering a mosque, and for both men and women to cover their legs (shorts are considered particularly offensive) and upper arms – in some mosques pieces of material are distributed at the door. In some of the larger mosques women will be encouraged to view the premises from the women's galleries upstairs. Shoes should always be removed: unless there's an attendant outside, pick your shoes up, carry them inside and place them on the racks near the door. It's better to wait until prayer is finished and then go in, rather than enter while it's in progress, although at any time you will find a few individuals at prayer. As long as you keep a distance and speak quietly you won't disturb anyone unduly.

Opening hours and public holidays

White-collar workers keep conventional Monday to Friday 9am to 6pm schedules, with a full lunch hour; civil servants (including tourist offices and museum staff) in theory work 8.30am to 5.30pm, but in practice hours can be much more erratic, including two-hour lunches – don't expect to get important official business attended to the same day after 2.30pm. Ordinary shops, including those in malls and large department stores, are open continuously from 8.30 or 9am until 7 or 8pm, depending on the owner. Craftsmen and bazaar stallholders keep marathon hours, often working from 9am to 8 or 9pm, Monday to Saturday, with only the hastiest of breaks for meals, tea or prayers. Even on Sunday the tradesmen's area may not be completely shut down – though don't count on this.

National secular public holidays are generally marked by processions of schoolchildren or the military, or else by some demonstration of national strength and dignity, such as

Turkish public holidays

January 1 *Yılbaşı* – New Year's Day.
April 23 *Ulusal Egemenlik ve Çocuk Bayramı* – Independence Day, celebrating the first meeting of the new Republican parliament in Ankara, and Children's Day.
May 19 *Gençlik ve Spor Günü* – Youth and Sports Day, also Atatürk's birthday.
May 29 Festival to commemorate İstanbul's capture by Mehmet the Conqueror in 1453 (İstanbul only).
July 1 *Denizcilik Günü* – Navy Day (banks and offices open).
August 26 *Silahlı Kuvvetler Günü* – Armed Forces Day (banks and offices open).
August 30 *Zafer Bayramı* – Celebration of the Turkish victory

over the Greek forces at Dumlupınar in 1922.
September 9 *Kurtuluş Günü* Liberation Day, with parades and speeches marking the end of the Independence War (İzmir only).
October 29 *Cumhuriyet Bayramı* – commemorates the proclamation of the Republic by Atatürk in 1923.
November 10 The anniversary of Atatürk's death in 1938. Observed at 9.05am (the time of his death), when the whole country stops whatever it's doing and maintains a respectful silence for a minute. It's worth being on a Bosphorus ferry this morning, when all the engines are turned off, and the boats drift and blow their foghorns mournfully.

a sports display. Banks and government offices will normally be closed on these days; where they are not, we say so in the list on p.66. Many shops, and all banks and offices, also close during the main religious festivals (see "Festivals", below).

Festivals

There are two kinds of celebration in Turkey: religious festivals, observed all over the Islamic world on dates determined by the Muslim Hijra calendar; and annual cultural or harvest extravaganzas held in various cities and resorts across the country.

Religious festivals

As the Islamic calendar is lunar, the dates of the four important religious festivals drift backwards eleven days each year relative to the Gregorian calendar.

Perhaps the most important is **Ramadan** (*Ramazan* in Turkish), the Muslim month of daylight abstention from food, water, tobacco and sexual relations, occurring during late autumn during the first decade of the new millennium. Ramadan is not a public holiday: life carries on as normal despite the fact that half the population is fasting from sunrise to sunset (with a huge incidence of traffic accidents during the last hour or so of fasting – drivers beware). Some restaurants close for the duration, others discreetly hide their salons behind curtains, but at most establishments you will be served with surprisingly good grace. Koranic injunction allows pregnant and nursing mothers, the infirm and travellers to be excused from obligatory fasting; immediately after dark there's an orgy of eating by the famished in places public and private, and you may well find restaurants sold out of everything within an hour of sunset.

Kadir Gecesi (The Eve of Power) takes place between the 27th and 28th days of the month of Ramadan, the time when Mohammed is supposed to have received the Koran from Allah. The mosques are full all night, as it's believed that prayers at this time have special efficacy; those who can't make it out tend to stay home reading the Koran and praying.

The three-day **Şeker Bayramı** (Sugar Holiday) is held at the end of Ramadan, celebrated by family get-togethers and the giving of presents and sweets to children, and restrained general partying in the streets and restaurants; on the first night, known as *Arife*, you will have to book well in advance for tables at better restaurants. The four-day **Kurban Bayramı** (Festival of the Sacrifice), in which the sacrificial offering of a sheep represents Abraham's son Ishmael (a Koranic version of the Old Testament story) is marked by the slaughter of over 2.5 million sheep. Only the wealthiest families can afford to buy a whole animal, so part of the meat is distributed to the poor of the neighbourhood. Sheep are brought from all over Anatolia to the big cities (as depicted in the Yılmaz Güney film *The Herd*), and sold on street corners in the weeks leading up to the festival. They are killed by the traditional Islamic method of a slit gullet, in any open space available – now legally restricted, with use of apartment-building gardens now forbidden.

During *Şeker* and *Kurban Bayram*s, which are also public holidays (see list on p.68 for dates), travel becomes almost impossible: from the afternoon leading up to the first evening of the holiday (a Muslim festival is reckoned from sunset) – and on the first and last days themselves – public transport is completely booked up, and unless you plan in advance you won't get a seat on any long-distance coach, train, plane or ferry.

Many shops and all banks, museums and government offices close during the holiday periods (although corner grocery stores and most shops in resorts stay open). When these festivals occur close to a national holiday, the whole country effectively grinds to a halt for up to a week, with resorts packed for the duration.

Şeker Bayramı dates

Nov 25–27, 2003
Nov 14–16, 2004
Nov 2–4, 2005

Kurban Bayramı dates

Feb 11–14, 2003
Jan 31–Feb 3, 2004
Jan 20–23, 2005

Cultural festivals

Cultural festivals are most interesting in the cities and resorts with the resources to attract international name acts. Just about every sizeable town will have some sort of yearly bash, though many are of limited interest to outsiders. We've highlighted the best below, most of which are described in fuller detail in the Guide. Be aware that some of the relatively minor events do not take place in slack years.

İstanbul's most important festivals are organized by the **İstanbul Foundation for Culture and Arts** (see p.189), which promotes a heavyweight annual programme. There's a full festival calendar for İstanbul on p.188, but – as a taster – the season kicks off in mid-April with the **İstanbul International Film Festival**, followed by the **International İstanbul Theatre Festival** (May) and the **International İstanbul Music Festival** (June). The city also sees two major jazz festivals, separate pop, rock and blues events, and the **İstanbul Biennial**, an autumn art exhibition held every two years, usually revolving around a set theme.

The **International İzmir Festival** (June & July) also manages to attract name acts, with many performances at Ephesus theatre and Çeşme castle. The **Aspendos Opera and Ballet Festival** (usually 10 performances from mid-June to early July) is

the Mediterranean Coast's big high-brow event.

Less spectacular, but still meriting a look if you happen to be in the area, are: the **Ephesus Festival** (second or third week of May); the **Pamukkale Song Festival** (late June); the **Bursa Festival** (last three weeks of July); the **Bodrum Festival** (early September); and the **Antalya Altın Portakal** ("Golden Orange") **Film Festival** (late September to early October).

A number of more unusual events are also worth coinciding a visit with, not least the **camel wrestling** at Selçuk in mid-January, though bouts (between two male camels in rut) occur throughout Aydın province during December and January, as well as at Kumluca on the Turquoise Coast towards the end of January. You might also try and see the **oil-wrestling** (yağlı güreş) in Kırkpınar near Edirne in early summer (usually mid-June; and see p.226), and the **bull-fighting** – again between randy beasts – which forms the climax of the Kafkasör festival at Artvin in late June.

One of the few public performances of a religious nature – with emphasis on the word "performance" – is the **Mevlâna (Dervish) Festival** at Konya on December 10–17 (p.628), almost the only occasion when the so-called "Whirling Dervishes" appear in public. Preferable, however, are the more genuine Mevlevî turning ceremonies that take place at the same time in İstanbul – a marked contrast to the basketball-court setting at Konya. The only other public devotional observance is the **Hacı Bektaş Veli** commemoration at Hacıbektaş village in Cappadocia, during the latter half of August, when Bektaşis and their affiliates, the Alevîs, meet for a weekend of ritual singing and dancing. This is preceded by a similar festival in early June, honouring the second most important Alevî saint, **Pir Abdal Musa**, in Tekke village near Elmalı in Antalya province.

Folk-dance festivals are always worth a detour, providing an opportunity to see some of the country's best dance groups performing a sample of the varied repertoire of Turkish dances in traditional costumes. There are folk festivals in Silifke in May, in Foça in June and in Samsun in July. More spontaneous, and therefore more difficult to track down, are the music-and-dance gatherings of the Gypsies in Thrace during spring and early summer, though Edirne's Spring Festival and Kırklareli's Takava Festival are both permanent fixtures.

Agricultural festivals play an important part in Turkish rural life. The Diyarbakır Watermelon Festival in mid- or late September is basically a competition for the most outsized of the region's fruit. Ürgüp's Grape Harvest Festival in mid-September culminates a season of celebrations in the Cappadocia region, including a Handicrafts and Pottery Festival at Avanos during August. The trodden grape is honoured by drinking some of Turkey's finest white wines from the local thimble-sized, earthenware vessels. Other agricultural products are ingested at Bolu's Mengen Chefs' Contest in August – the region is purportedly home to the country's best cooks.

Bazaars and shopping

Consuming interests are high on the agenda of most visitors to Turkey. Even those who come determined not to buy will be shortly persuaded otherwise by the myriad street merchants, store owners and affiliated touts who cannot resist the hard sell – as intrinsic to Turkish culture as tea and hospitality – and by the occasionally high quality of goods available.

Bazaars, shops, department stores and malls

There are several types of traditional bazaar in Turkey, which continue to coexist with the modern American/European-style shopping malls that have lately spread across the wealthier districts of every large town.

First are the **covered bazaars**, found in large towns such as İstanbul, Bursa and Kayseri. These are essentially medieval Ottoman shopping malls, comprising several *bedesten*s, or domed buildings, at which particular types of goods were sold, linked by various covered arcades, which in turn were also originally assigned to a particular trade – though strict segregation has now broken down.

Surrounding these covered bazaars are large areas of **small shops**, basically open-air extensions of the covered areas and governed by the same rules: each shop is a separate unit with an owner and apprentices, and successful businesses are not allowed to expand or merge. Prices on the street are often a bit lower than in the *bedesten*s owing to lower rents.

In addition there are weekly or twice-weekly **street markets** in most towns or in different areas of cities, arranged on the same lines as those in northern Europe and selling roughly similar everyday household products. More exotic are the semi-permanent **flea markets** (*bit pazarı*, literally "louse markets"), ranging in quality from street stalls where old clothes are sold and resold among the homeless, to lanes of shops where you can buy secondhand clothes, furniture or occasionally an antique of real aesthetic or monetary value.

In the cities, particularly in İstanbul, shopping for everyday household goods, clothes, furniture and accessories is increasingly done in Western-style department stores and shopping malls. They're often situated some way from the centre, but we've picked out the most useful in the Guide. The main **department store** chain is Yeni Karamürsel, with outlets in İstanbul, İzmir and Ankara, plus several other large towns. For a run-down of İstanbul's major **shopping malls**, see p.194.

Best buys

The best selection of good-quality wares is to be found in the major tourist centres: İstanbul, Cappadocia, Bursa and the coastal resorts. Don't think that you'll find bargains in the production centres for a particular craft in the interior: wholesalers and collectors have been there long before you.

Apart from the variety and visual impact of goods on sale in Turkish bazaars, and the tantalizing prospect of picking up something worthwhile, the main reason to visit is for the challenge of **bargaining**. As a guideline, begin at a figure rather lower than whatever you are prepared to pay, perhaps around half of your shopkeeper's starting price. Once a price has been agreed on, you are ethically committed to buy, so don't commence haggling unless you are reasonably sure you want the item. There are other psychological tactics to engage in, such as enquiring about several articles in a shop before you even look at the thing you really want, or proposing to go elsewhere for some comparison shopping, but you'll only perfect your act with practice. "Assistance" from touts will automatically bump up the price thirty to fifty percent, as they will be getting a commission. Also, be prepared to hand over between three and seven percent extra if paying by credit card; your bargaining position is strongest with crisp, bunched foreign notes.

Carpets and kilims

Turkish **carpets and kilims** are world famous, though they are no longer necessarily cheaper in Turkey than overseas. The selection is best in İstanbul, whose shopkeepers scour the countryside; thus there are relatively few rugs on sale near their source. A *kilim*, or pile-less rug, is flat-woven and double-sided (that is, the pattern should look much the same top or bottom); a *cicim* is a kilim with additional designs stitched onto it; while *sumak* technique, confined in Turkey to saddlebags, involves wrapping extra threads around the warp.

Vigilance is the rule when shopping for any kind of floor covering; it's easy to pay over

the odds for inferior quality. One useful test, ensuring that the colours aren't going to run the first time you try to clean off a coffee stain, is to wet a white rag and rub the carpet, then check to see if any colour has come off. If it has, it doesn't bode well for the future, and the dyes certainly aren't natural. Since older, handmade, natural-dyed rugs are getting rarer all the time, genuine collector's items are often salvaged from deteriorated larger works, and more or less skilfully repaired; saddle or cradle bags may be opened to become small rugs. A hand-woven rug will usually show its pattern clearly on the reverse, unlike a machine-made one. Hand-spun yarn can be identified by the fringe, which is unevenly twisted, tight and ravelled to the ends.

You can buy a new, artificially dyed *çeyrek* ("quarter", 1m by 1.5m) kilim for around $60–100, and **prices** go up according to quality, age and design. A small woollen rug made with natural dyes would be $80–200 bought new, a larger one around $250–350. Silk carpets start in the hundreds of dollars for a tiny one, and go up to hundreds of thousands.

Natural dyes, especially in earth tones, are now being used in manufacturing again, and they tend not to fade as quickly as chemical ones. This renaissance was pioneered by DOBAG, a co-operative with headquarters in Ayvacık (see box on p.290), dedicated both to ethical treatment of the weavers and traditional methods, pigments and designs. All of their carpets bear a distinctive leather certification tag.

Chemical dyes first appeared during the 1870s, and their use up until the 1980s is easy to spot because the colours are either garish (especially the oranges) or fade muddily except at the roots. Overly bright rugs are often left out for sun-fading or are bleached in lye or chlorine. The latter two processes are particularly undesirable as they weaken the fabric; bleach-faded rugs will smell of chlorine when you rub a wet finger on the pile.

It's now difficult to find a carpet vendor who will admit that his stock is anything other than natural-dyed. However, such claims are usually spurious, since most carpets are still made using artificial dyes, albeit the so-called "natural-identical" ones with more subtle, light-fast, gradually fading pigments.

The test for pure **wool** is setting light to a fine strand. If the charred remains are crumbly, it's wool; if they're sticky, it's synthetic fibre. A strand of **silk** will not flame, but makes an ash and smells organic when it burns; synthetic silk glows and smells of chemicals. The price of a silk carpet depends on the number of knots per square centimetre – this is usually 64 or 81, but very fine ones are made with 144 or 196 per square centimetre. There should be no flaws visible on the back of a silk rug.

It's worth finding out as much as you can about the origins of the carpet, the symbolic meanings of its motifs and the production methods. This will increase the nostalgic value of the product, and during such discussions you should be able to decide if your dealer is trustworthy, and whether his final price will be fair or not. If you're very serious about carpet-buying, preliminary visits to carpet shops in your home country, to an ethnological museum or two and a perusal of some of the recommended titles on the subject (listed under "Books" in Contexts) will be worthwhile.

Jewellery

Jewellery should also be bought with care, since imitations abound. Fake amber melts on exposure to an open flame, but a test isn't advisable without the permission of the proprietor. Gold, silver and semi-precious stones, of which amber and turquoise are the most common, are sold by weight, with almost total disregard for the disparate level of craftsmanship involved. One particularly intricate method is *telkâri* or wire filigree, most of which comes from eastern Turkey, particularly Diyarbakır and Trabzon. Bear in mind that the price per gramme of silver or gold can be bargained down, making a substantial difference to the eventual total. Also remember that sterling silver items should bear a hallmark – anything else could well be a nickel or pewter alloy.

Copperware

Copperwork is not as common as in the days when it was an essential part of a newly-

wed couple's household furnishings, and very little of it is still hammered out from scratch, or of really heavy gauge. Still, the articles are very handsome and if you want to buy at source, keep an eye out in the bazaars of eastern Anatolia. Since copper is mildly toxic, vessels intended for use in the kitchen must be tinned inside – one layer for use as a tea kettle, three for use with food. If the layer is absent or deteriorated, have it (re)done at the nearest *kalaycı* or tinsmith for a nominal fee. If you live in a hard-water area, or the vessel is from such a place in Turkey, a layer of mineral deposits will quickly build up, serving the same protective function.

Antique copperware is a cult in itself, though not quite as exalted as that of the carpet. Pieces from the Republican (post-World War I) era are sold roughly by weight at about $6 per kilo; for Ottoman trays and vessels, you'll be asked whatever the dealer thinks he can get away with, based loosely on age, weight and provenance. Cheap, newer thin-gauge ware with machine-pressed designs comes from Kayseri, Gaziantep or Kahramanmaraş and won't be older than 1960 or cost more than $30. At the opposite end of the price/quality scale is embossed work from Bosnia, such as a late nineteenth-century *sefer tası* (lunchbox set, tiffin) for about $50–70; older Greek- or Armenian-produced trays or vessels, identifiable by their distinctive lettering, for $120–240; and incredibly heavy, early nineteenth-century Persian or Anatolian trays or vessels with a sultan's monogram, for which asking prices of $1000 and up are not unheard of. Best deals have historically been in Ankara's Bakırcılar Çarşısı, though staff from embassies and multinational corporations living locally have had a predictable effect on prices. Antique shops in Kalkan, Kaş, Cappadocia and Bergama are well presented but usually vastly overpriced, while İstanbul's old copper market, near the Nuruosmariye Camii, is now completely gentrified.

Clothing

Turkey's **clothing** industry has raised its profile somewhat since Rifat Özbek and half-Turkish Nicole Farhi appeared on the scene with their lines of orientally influenced designer togs, and Turkish designs are beginning to match the quality of local fabrics – including Bursa silk and Angora wool. Nowadays you will pay near-Western prices for decent locally designed items at reputable shops, which rarely sale fakes – local brands are aggressively protected, if necessary by police raids at the behest of corporate lawyers.

Only street vendors peddle **imitation** Lacoste, Polo, Ralph Lauren, Quiksilver, Tommy Hillfiger, Adidas, Nike, Levi Strauss and Benetton items of decidedly varying quality, some made in Turkey under licence but much of it merchandise bootlegged in the best pirating tradition of Asia. Occasionally this is done with panache and humour (eg, a sign in Bodrum reading "Genuine Fake Rolexes"), but most of the time the marketing and results are furtive and shabby: real Italian- or English-language labels slapped onto local products that shrink two sizes or fade at the first washing. Prices too good to be true are the dead giveaway; neither should you be taken in by "near" brand-names like Benelton or Adidos with copy-cat logos. Some fake soccer shirts (mostly Turkish, English, German and Dutch clubs) do make good buys, as their material is fairly robust.

In general the best bargains are to be had from **street markets** and oddments stores where you can fetch seconds, samples or overstock of Western brands (including British high-street chains) produced for export but not generally marketed locally.

Bear in mind that T-shirts or other articles of clothing prominently featuring the **Turkish flag** are, bizarrely, illegal at present. A long-forgotten law banning the use of the national flag in clothing was "rediscovered" in 2001 and used to prosecute sellers of red tees bearing the Turkish star and crescent. Their disappearance from shops prior to the 2002 World Cup, coupled with the appearance of vast numbers of cheap vintage football shirts for export, led many Turks to support their national team decked out in red "CCCP" and "England 1966" shirts. The law is due for repeal, though it's unclear when.

Leather goods

There are always a number of well-stocked **leather** outlets in any important tourist centre, though the industry was originally based in western Anatolia where alum deposits and acorn-derived tannin aided the tanning process. Today, İzmir and İstanbul still have the largest workshops, though the retail business also booms on the Mediterranean coast, particularly in Antalya and Alanya. Jackets are the most obvious purchase, the prices of which vary from a paltry $60 to over $300, with a minimum of about $120 for anything half-decent. If you're not interested in big outlays, men's or women's wallets are excellent and durable; Maraş brand may be the best in quality, but the Marchila, Guard or Pikaldi lines are very nearly as good for half the price. The variety of designs is staggering, so allow for plenty of browsing time. Women's **shoes** come in a wide range of colours, but curiously only up to about European size 40.

Nargiles

The **nargile**, or hookah, is doubtless one of those Ottoman hangovers, like fezzes and dervishes, that Atatürk might have wished to consign to the dustheap of history. However, it's still around, indulged in for hours along the central and north Aegean coasts by cafés-full of contentedly puffing gentlemen.

A functional *nargile* is not a plastic toy nor *objet d'art* as sold in so many trinket shops, but should have a lamb's-leather, wire-reinforced tube, all-brass or lathed hardwood plumbing and a clear glass or crystal chamber. If you find an older, crystal item, it will be an antique and worth upwards of $100. Expect to pay $35 for an 18-inch model with a blown glass bowl; cast ones with visible mould marks aren't so valuable. A wood superstructure looks better, but brass ones last longer.

If you intend to use the *nargile* when you get home, remember to buy *tömbeki*, or compressed tobacco, as you won't find it easily outside Turkey. You'll also have to convince customs authorities that your *nargile* isn't narcotics paraphernalia and you'll need a source of live coals to drop into the *sönbeki* or brazier end – matches don't work well. Also, the *sönbeki* tends to be fitted with meltable plastic mesh inside, so for practical use you'll need to install a small copper mesh, easily available for a few pennies in north European and American head shops or hippy boutiques.

Music and musical instruments

Traditional Turkish **musical instruments** are sold cheaply all over Turkey. The most easily portable are the *ney*, the Mevlevî flute made from a length of calamus reed, the *davul* or drum, and the *saz*, the long-necked Turkish lute. In İstanbul the main sales points are along Atatürk Bulvarı below the Valens Aqueduct, especially the IMC centre in Unkapanı, and along the upper reaches of Yüksek Kaldırım and its continuation Galipdede Caddesi, across from the Mevlevi *semahane*, near the top station of the Tünel in Beyoğlu. You are less likely to get a "toy" version if you buy instruments at specialist shops like these, or from the craftsmen themselves. A *kaval* (end-blown flute) is compact and inexpensive at about $10, and a *saz* is good value for around $40 and up.

Since Turkey joined the EU customs union in 2000, the available selection of imported **cassettes** and, especially, **CDs** has grown dramatically, with specialist shops in cities catering for jazz, world and dance music springing up in bigger towns. Decreased sales in the wake of the 2001 economic crisis prompted a marked drop in prices, while the rapid spread of CD copiers has spurred a boom in the sale of secondhand genuine CDs, as collectors buy, duplicate and then sell on their original. Currently, imported new CDs cost the equivalent of $12–15, secondhand foreign CDs $6–8 and cassettes around $4. The burgeoning interest in world music has led to a simultaneous rediscovery of Turkey's native music traditions. A steady stream of new CD issues and re-issues of long-forgotten ethnic music has followed, with locally produced cassettes and CDs of Turkish music costing $4 and $6–8 respectively; see p.1040 for a discography of recommended items.

If your conscience doesn't nag you, Turkey has a flourishing **pirating industry** for every sort of CD – computer games, DVD and Playstation as well as music – for about $2 each. Not only street traders, but supposedly reputable shops keep lists of titles available for pirating under the counter – all of which keeps the police busy.

Games, mementoes and accessories

A **tavla** or backgammon set makes another good souvenir of Turkish popular culture, since it's played in coffeehouses and gaming halls all over the country. The cheapest wooden sets cost around $4; a medium-size apparatus of inlaid, painted cedar wood (*şedir*) runs to about $20, and you can easily pay anything up to $100 for inlaid mother-of-pearl and ivory. Most boards come from Damascus, as any reputable dealer will admit; if you're not confident that the inlay material is genuine and not just stencilled on, it's better to settle for the painted wood kind, which is more difficult to fake. Dice and pieces should be included, and many boards have a chess/checkers grid on the exterior; an olive-wood set of chessmen will set you back another $6.

Mavi boncuk (blue bead) key rings, lintel ornaments and animal collars are sold all over the place to ward off *nazar* (the evil eye). Bath **loofahs** are common in the coastal resorts; even at tourist prices, they cost one-third to one-half of what they would at home, and weigh next to nothing in your luggage.

Other possible memorabilia, easily found in the shops of any covered bazaar, are probably best obtained from the towns in which they originate. These include **meerschaum pipes** carved from *lületaşı* stone quarried near Eskişehir; **Karagöz puppets**, representing the popular folk characters Karagöz and Hacıvat, preferably made from camel skin in Bursa; **towelling and silk goods**, again in Bursa – although the all-cotton bedding and towels at dedicated retail outlets nationwide are excellent value; **onyx**, available all over Cappadocia, but especially Hacıbektaş; and **Kütahya ceramics**, which may not be the finest ever produced in Turkey, but since the kilns of İznik closed down are the best available. Middle-grade enamelled tiles suitable for fireplace surrounds won't cost more than $2 apiece at either of the two Kütahya factories making them – in tourist resorts, boutiques will demand up to $7 for the same, so it's worth loading up a car with some if you're passing through Kütahya. Tiles, as opposed to kitsch objects, may not be found easily in the town itself – you have to ask to be taken to the factories outside of town. In another league entirely are the products of the **İznik Foundation**, whose patterns are subtly altered to prevent counterfeiting by others; they can cost upwards of $150 each and are startlingly different from anything else on offer.

Spices and foodstuffs

Acknowledging the slight risk of having certain goods confiscated on return to the European Union or North America, locally produced **spices, condiments and foodstuffs** can be recommended as a compact, lightweight souvenir purchase. Low-grade saffron (*zafran*), the stamen of a particular kind of crocus, is still gathered in northern Anatolia. Sumac (*sumak*) is a ground-up purple leaf for sprinkling on barbecued meats, much encountered in districts with an Arab heritage. Vanilla (*vanilya*) pods are bigger and cheaper in Turkey than elsewhere, and pure *salep* powder (ground-up orchid root; see p.56), while not cheap by any standard, can be found nowhere else (easiest in İzmir). *Pekmez* (grape molasses) is phenomenally nutritious and, though a potential mess in your baggage, makes a splendid ice-cream topping or baking ingredient; rural people typically mix it with *tahini* (sesame paste) to make an appetizing, high-calorie snack. Olive oil, most famously from Gemlik, is a worthwhile purchase, as is olive-oil soap (excellent for getting grease stains off clothes). Both hot and sweet peppers are made into concentrated pastes, while dried aubergine/eggplant shells are convenient for stuffing. Pomegranate seeds are the basis of *nar ekşisi*, sour grenadine syrup, which can either flavour drinks, garnish aubergine slices

or liven up stews (Migros supermarkets stock it). Many visitors acquire a taste for Black Sea tea; the best blends change from year to year, with little quality control within a single brand, but go for the best available and it still won't break the bank.

Antiques and smuggling: a warning

Some of the more popular archeological sites, particularly Ephesus and Pamukkale, are periodically the haunt of characters peddling **"antiks"** of doubtful authenticity. These freelance salesmen are remarkably tenacious, but in the majority of cases you would simply be throwing money away; in the unlikely event you were sold something genuine, you would be liable for prosecution. Under Turkish law it is an offence to buy, sell, attempt to export or even possess museum-calibre antiquities (which includes fossils). Exact age limits are not specified in lawbooks, suggesting that decisions by customs officials are arbitrary and subjective, though a principal measure of antiquity is rarity.

In the case of **carpets** handled by established dealers, you run a very slight risk of investing a lot of money in a supposed "collector's item" that turns out to be collectable only by the Turkish Republic. If you're apprehensive about a proposed purchase, ask the dealer to prepare both a *fatura* (invoice) recording the exact purchase price – also necessary to satisfy customs – and a declaration stating that the item is not an antiquity. If you're still not reassured, you may want to consult staff at the nearest museum.

Should you be caught **smuggling** out anything restricted, the Turkish authorities will be unimpressed by any excuses or connections and will very likely make an example of you – as they did an American woman in 1986, who unsuccessfully claimed ignorance of a purchase's vintage and served six months of a much longer prison sentence before escaping with the assistance of her legal counsel.

Crime, personal safety and etiquette

Despite popular, *Midnight-Express*-type stereotypes, you're unlikely to encounter any trouble in Turkey. Violent street crime is uncommon, theft is rare (though pickpocketing and purse-snatching are on the rise) and the authorities generally treat tourists with courtesy. Keep your wits about you and an eye on your belongings just as you would anywhere else, and make sure your passport is secure at all times, and you shouldn't have any problems. Indeed, most people are still scrupulously honest: it is far more likely that someone draws your attention to money fallen from your wallet onto the pavement, rather than pocket it themselves, or for a merchant to point out that you've handed over a ten-million lira note rather than one million lira.

The police, army and gendarmerie

Civilian police come in a variety of sub-divisions, treated with a healthy respect – mixed with fear and contempt – by the locals. Many of the attitude problems stem from the fact that most police are recruited from the slums, poorly trained and risibly paid; in addition, since many attended the *imam hatip* religious schools fostered by past Islamist governments, they are unabashedly anti-European in outlook. **If you are arrested** for any reason, the best general rule is to stay polite and patient – getting irate tends to be counterproductive. While waiting for the commanding officer to arrive, engage your captor in small talk; you'll find that matters get much more relaxed. You have **the right to make a phone call** to a friend, hotelier or consul; if you are refused this, asking for or getting the officer's name often brings about a swift attitude adjustment.

The blue-uniformed **Polis** are the everyday security force in cities and towns with populations over 2000; the most you'll probably have to do with them is a request for help in finding a street. The **Trafik Polis**, recognized by their white caps and two-toned vehicles (usually Renault Clios or Fords), are a branch of this service and their main responsibility seems to be controlling intersections and doing spot checks on vehicles at approaches to towns. İstanbul and several other large towns have a rapid-response squad of red-and-black-uniformed motorbike police known as the *yunus* (dolphin) *polis*; they are

generally courteous and helpful to tourists and have effectively replaced the former designated corps of *Turizm Polis*. The *Trafik Polis* in İstanbul also have a black-and-yellow-liveried motorbike branch, not particularly known for their courtesy towards anyone. In the towns you're also likely to see the **Belediye Zabıtası**, the navy-clad market police, who patrol the markets and bazaars to ensure that tradesmen aren't ripping off customers – approach them directly if you have reason for complaint.

Although the country nominally returned to civilian rule in 1983, Turkey's huge armed forces still play a fairly high-profile role in maintaining law and order. In most rural areas where villages do not exceed 2000 in population, law enforcement is in the hands of the **jandarma** or gendarmerie, a division of the regular army charged with law enforcement duties. Gendarmes, despite their military affiliation, are often kitted out not in fatigues but well-tailored gear, modelled on the French uniform, to make them appear less threatening; most of them are conscripts who will be courteous and helpful if approached. However, their officer corps can be less than cooperative in complicated or touchy cases such as rape complaints and they are often in the hip pockets of powerful local interests – so complaining to them about illegal buildings, desecration of archeological sites or rip-off roadside restaurants is often a futile exercise.

Another branch of the army much in evidence is the **military police** or *Askeri İnzibat*.

You'll recognize them by their white helmets bearing the letters *As İz*, white holsters and lanyards. Officially they are supposed to keep order among the large numbers of conscripts you'll see on the streets of many Turkish towns.

Restricted areas

In the two **southeastern provinces** (Diyarbakır and Sırnak) still under martial law (due to end during 2003) the army or gendarmerie patrol the streets in the towns and cities and man numerous checkpoints on rural roads. In the mountains around the towns of Hâkkari and Siirt, all around Mardin, Doğubeyazit, Bitlis, Diyarbakır, Muş and Bingöl, and between Kemah and Tunceli, there was – until the 1999 arrest of PKK leader Abdullah Öcalan – a full-scale insurrection underway, and while the Guide includes coverage of areas previously omitted, it will be some time before matters return completely to normal in the affected regions. You can find more details about the situation on p.921.

In **remote areas of the east** you're likely to attract the attention of the *jandarma*, who'll want to know what you're doing and where you're going. This may involve, at most, a rather tedious day or evening of polite interrogation. The only areas where you absolutely need a **permit** are within a few hundred metres of the eastern border, especially the ever-tense frontier with Armenia; we've detailed specific instances in the Guide. The **Kurdish-populated areas** along the border with Iraq and Syria fall into a sort of grey zone: while it's not forbidden for outsiders to visit them – tourism authorities are often loath to admit that there's any lingering problem – local authorities may try to prevent you from going and will take no responsibility for your safety. That said, the Turkish army has established a line of control well inside northern Iraq and no rogue factions of the PKK have yet emerged within Turkey.

Avoiding trouble

In addition to the expected caveats on drugs and exporting antiquities, there are a number of other situations to avoid. **Don't insult** Atatürk or Turkey in any way, even in jest, nor should you deface, degrade, or tear up currency or the flag; drunkenness will likely be considered an aggravating, not a mitigating factor. Try not to be drawn into **serious disputes**, since while things rarely turn violent in Turkey, when they do they can turn *very* violent – if anybody seems to be insulting or provoking you, walk away. **Don't take photographs** near the numerous, well-marked military zones. Don't "raid" **archeological sites** after posted closing hours (see "Admission to museums, sites and mosques" on p.65). And last but not least, don't engage in any **missionary or proselytization activities** among the locals, or attempt to import evangelical literature. Touring the Christian sites with the Bible or a scholarly work is certainly OK, but any tract intended for distribution isn't. A number of foreigners were arrested and/or deported for offending Muslim sensibilities on this point during previous Islamist governments; at the very least you will seriously offend the object of your proselytizing.

A late-1990s wave of refugees from Africa landing in Turkey and attempting to find a back door into Schengen Europe, coupled with racist reports in the local media blaming them for bringing heroin into the country, made many people (especially policemen) poorly disposed towards anyone who appeared African. Most of the Africans concerned have now moved on to Europe and **black EU citizens** should expect – at the very most – a careful inspection by immigration authorities, who retain a reputation for harassing nationals of African countries.

Despite the courtesy and honesty of most Turks, certain crimes aimed specifically at tourists should be guarded against: there have been an increasing number of **gas-and-rob** operations in train compartments, and of **knockout drugs** being introduced into food and drink. Be suspicious, especially if travelling alone, of young men working in pairs or trios who befriend you too assiduously – by proposing to share a hotel with you, for example – and then ply you with comestibles procured out of sight. You're quite likely to wake up hours later with a splitting headache, minus your bags and valuables.

More seriously, there is a thriving black market in **stolen EU passports** in Turkey, furnished to refugees from further east in Asia; a direct consequence of this is that significant numbers of solo male Britons with Latin or Asian surnames and appearance were murdered during the late 1990s, in İstanbul particularly, to obtain their passports. If you fit this description, we would advise you to use hotels or *pansiyons* several notches up from the bottom – proprietors of İstanbul budget lodgings have been implicated in some incidents – and to be especially vigilant against drug-and-rob scams.

Touts

The Turkish argot for **touts** – *avcılar*, "hunters" – gives a good idea of how these individuals, who haunt bus stations, restaurants, ferry quays and bazaars in particular, view foreigners. Whether and how you decide to use their services is a personal matter; just occasionally, they may lead you to acceptable or better accommodation, but 95 percent of the time they will be collecting hefty commissions on accordingly marked-up lodging, food and goods, all of which may be dodgy, so it's best to stick to our listings whenever possible. Especially in Cappadocia, Pamukkale or at certain resorts on the southwest coast, they can be stubbornly persistent or even abusive if spurned; at such times, it's best to rely on some of the survival techniques mentioned above on p.76, without, however, being too provocative.

With every edition, our post-bag contains letters replete with horror stories from folk who fell victim to touts: most frequently, physical intimidation to guarantee payment of inflated bills, or dismissal of anyone with the temerity to ask for restitution of money paid for substandard accommodation. From time to time measures have been mooted by the more successful hoteliers and restaurateurs to control a practice that gives certain tourist areas a bad name, but intense competition within the tourist industry – and Turkey's stubbornly high unemployment rate – together guarantee that the art and its practitioners will be around indefinitely.

Sexual harassment

Mutual attraction mixed with apprehension are the hallmarks of relationships between Western women and Turkish men. Each approaches the other with stereotypes in mind fuelled partly by myth, partly by reality. Turkish men, especially the hairy-chested, Brut-scented, gold-chained *magandas* or street spivs of urban folklore are seen as lecherous wide-boys always on the lookout for a *manita* ("dolly-bird"), while foreign women are considered an easy lay and rich to boot. Successful marriages between the two are rare and generally confined to mature individuals who have had some experience of each other's countries.

Turkish society is deliberately gender-segregated in many public areas (though this is decreasing each year), as well as in private life, so even if a **woman travelling alone** wants to avoid the company of men, it's not too difficult. Simply seek the company of Turkish women at every opportunity and you will generally be protected by them. Places where you will *not* find unaccompanied Turkish women include the streets, bars and restaurants at night, so this policy does actually limit your options of independent enjoyment.

Turkish women have over the years adopted successful tactics to protect themselves from **harassment**. To imitate them, avoid eye contact with men and try and look as confident and purposeful as possible. When all else fails, the best way of neutralizing harassment is to make a public scene. You won't elicit any sympathy by swearing in Turkish, but the words *Ayıp* ("Shame!") or *Beni rahatsız ediyorsun* ("You're disturbing me"), spoken very loudly, generally have the desired effect – passersby or fellow passengers will deal with the situation for you. *Defol* ("Piss off!") and *Bırak beni* ("Leave me alone") are stronger retorts. In general, Turkish men will back down when confronted and cases of violence against strangers are very rare; the back streets of most Turkish towns are a lot safer at night than those of (say) London. This is partly due to excessive police presence; do not hesitate to ask them for help.

Etiquette and body language

Hospitality, *misafirperverlik* in Turkish, remains one of the pillars of rural Turkish culture away from touristed areas and dealing gracefully with invitations is crucial to avoid causing offence. Such offers usually have no ulterior motives, with nothing expected in return except your company and possible entertainment value. If you really can't spare the time, you can mime "thanks" by placing one hand on your chest and pointing with the other to your watch and then in the direction you're headed. Even a **tea-break** will take a while, because you should stop for at least two, or none at all; drinking only one glass may be interpreted as casting aspersions on their tea. The first offer of **food** or a full meal should be declined on your part – if it's sincere it will be repeated at least twice and convention demands that you accept the third offer. Attempting to reciprocate in kind is extremely bad form; far more appreciated than grubby food from your pack will be a postcard from your hometown after your return, or a print of a snapshot you take of your new friends.

If you're **invited into a home**, remove your shoes at the door and if a meal is served at a low table with seating on the floor, hide your stockinged feet under the table or a dropcloth provided for the purpose. You should in fact **never point your feet**, shod or otherwise, at anyone, as they're considered unclean in every sense. When scooping food with bread sections from a communal bowl, **use your right hand** – the left is reserved for intimate toilet operations. Do not openly pick your teeth or blow your nose at table or on the street; if you use tooth-picks provided at restaurants, cover your mouth while doing so, like a harmonica-player.

Couples should refrain from making excessive **gestures of affection** in public; canoodling on a park bench, for instance, could result in an open, half-full soft drink can (or worse) being lobbed in your direction by the irate. **Nudism** at the beach is not on, though at resorts such as Assos frequented by Turkish "entels" (trendies) or any Mediterranean beach resort with a large for-

eign presence you can get away with some discreet topless sunning. **Beachwear** (as in bikini tops and bottoms, briefs etc) should be confined to the beach and, except in the most tolerant resorts, wearing halter tops or ultra-tight shorts on the street is just asking for abuse.

If you venture much off the tourist track, you will have to accept that being **stared at** is part of the experience and not considered rude, as is possibly being mobbed by small children who may or may not wish to guide you to the local ruins, beg for pens and candy or even pelt your car with stones.

People of colour may find themselves ogled in remoter areas in an unnerving fashion, as well as receiving unsolicited comments – ranging from *Arap!* (a Black!) to the notionally more appreciative *çok güzel* (very pretty!). Turkey is in fact one of the least racist countries around the Mediterranean; read the box about "The Sudanese of Turkey" on p.335 to get an idea of what place blacks occupy in the Turkish psyche. The situation has improved greatly since the arrival of numerous African and South American footballers, with most teams boasting a couple of black players in their squad. For some years in İstanbul, all dark-skinned players were affectionately referred to as *amokatchilar*, after a popular Nigerian player for Beşiktaş.

Turks employ a variety of **body language** not immediately obvious to most outsiders. Clicking the tongue against the roof of the mouth and simultaneously raising the eyebrows and chin means "no" or "there isn't any"; those economical of movement will rely on their eyebrows alone. By contrast, wagging the head rapidly from side to side means "Explain, I don't understand", while a single, obliquely inclined nod means "yes". Rubbing bunched fingers and thumb together means "loadsamoney", usually when referring to nefarious dealings or local corruption. Clicking fingers sharply indicates "good, top quality (merchandise, football player, etc)". The length of things is measured on the outstretched arm, from the fingers up to the point where a flat hand is laid; chopping sharply at the elbow indicates hugeness.

Women in Turkey

Turkish women, particularly Western-style feminists, have been organizing to improve their status since the 1980s, picking up a thread that has always run through Turkish society. Among the pre-Islamic Turkic tribes, men were only allowed one wife (as they are in today's Republican Turkey) and the king and queen ruled as equals, so that a decree was only valid if issued in both their names. Historically, Turkish women have had support from some impressive quarters: the two best-known Sufi mystics, Hacı Bektaş Veli and Celaleddin Rumi (aka Mevlâna), both strongly endorsed the need to educate women and treat them as equals, and Atatürk, the founder of the Turkish Republic, made numerous speeches on the subject of women's rights, lending support to efforts that culminated in full women's suffrage in 1934. Between 1993 and 1996 Turkey had a woman prime minister, Tansu Çiller – something that would be anathema in other Middle Eastern countries.

Social roles and behaviour

There is a wide divergence of views on acceptable behaviour and roles for women, both according to social class and region of the country. Pornography is conspicuously exhibited daily on news-stands across Turkey, perhaps two racks down from the handful of women's magazines pitched at an urbanized, educated audience. Countrywide, most freedom exists in İstanbul and the west and south coasts, which are almost on a par with European (or at least generic Mediterranean) mores; in more devout, traditional areas women and girls enjoy far less freedom. Voluminous head coverings are becoming more prevalent in the religious enclaves of western towns as well as most points further east and women in these areas are rarely seen outdoors after dark or unaccompanied. In the rural areas, practicality takes priority, with many women working outside the home harvesting cotton, carnations or tea and bringing their own produce alone to local markets or wholesalers.

The pace of change is fast enough for most middle-class women, who enjoy basic rights of parity of education and equal pay for equal work. "The National Action Plan of Turkey", prepared in the light of the Fourth World Conference on Women in Beijing (1995), declared women's education, training, health and opposition to domestic violence as the top critical areas of concern. Middle-class women have long worked as public-sector employees (including the police and civil services) and in private white/blue-collar jobs including hotels and airlines, but are almost totally absent from the bazaars, restaurants and bars, even in tourist resorts, due partly to the fact that they need special permits to work anywhere alcohol is served. The spread of fast-food chains and supermarkets is, however, opening up more job opportunities in resorts and cities. A woman's right to work without her husband's consent was only guaranteed by a 1992 court decision, in which a bar waitress married to a spendthrift gambler successfully sued for the right to support herself.

Regtrograde as it may seem at first glance, the most galvanizing rallying-point in recent years has been the sustained campaign for the right of female state university students, civil servants and office-holders to wear **headscarves** in class or on the job. This seemingly trivial issue is actually highly charged, as the headscarf is a religious symbol on a par with a Sikh's turban, as well as a feminist issue. The highest-profile personality in this campaign to date has been Merve Kavakçı, elected in 1999 as an MP for the now-defunct Virtue Party. She arrived at the Turkish parliament wearing her headscarf, was immediately suspended, stripped of her parliamentary immunity and prosecuted. Once it became known that she was a dual US/Turkish national, but had neglected to mention this on her candidature forms, the authorities were only too happy to dodge the contentious headscarf issue by stripping Kavakçı of her Turkish nationality before her return to the US.

Both male and female university students have demonstrated vociferously for women's right to wear the headscarf in class; many girls have sacrificed their careers for their beliefs, or lately have resorted to exchanging their scarves for outlandish rasta wigs when they enter campuses. The AK Party campaigned strongly for a sensible resolution to the headscarf problem; now that they're in power they're not rushing into any decision likely to upset the military, but in the medium term will almost certainly allow university students to attend classes in scarves, and may try to overturn the ban on civil servants wearing them.

Family issues

In country areas parents still reserve the right to choose a wife for their son after he has completed his military service. Turkish women, knowing that they are **marrying** for status rather than companionship, are often content to respect their mother's advice. Amongst educated women in cities, a Western attitude prevails and couples are even beginning to live together outside marriage.

Abortion is available on demand, with or without the father's consent, contraceptives are readily available over the counter, and a baby can now be registered to unmarried parents. The **birthrate** is declining rapidly – though there's still a huge disparity between the east and west of the country – and is currently estimated at 2.8 children per married couple. The law awards men considerable say over the welfare of their children, including preventing them from going abroad with the mother without the father's permission. In mixed-nationality marriages this can lead to all sorts of problems, including (as in more formally Islamic countries) rather spectacular cases of offspring-kidnapping and disappearances. Once a separation has

taken place, **divorce** law is fairly even-handed, providing divorce in a minimum time as long as a settlement can be made for the children, equitable division of property acquired during the marriage and maintenance payments for the wife while the case is ongoing.

Despite laws to the contrary, girls' **education** is often neglected by poor families, most of whom are rural and who depend on their daughters for agricultural labour or child-care.

Prostitution

Nowhere is Turkish women's subordinate status more apparent, however, than in Turkey's numerous municipal **brothels**. Strange as it may seem in a nominally Muslim culture, prostitution is legal and highly organized by every large municipality – the idea being that some women protect the virtue of others by acting as foils for male lust. Organized prostitution tends to be a feature of certain obvious hotels in a town's bazaar area, or more commonly is concentrated in purpose-built compounds, complete with gate and police guard, known as the *genelev* (general or public house). İstanbul's notorious İkibuçuk *genelev*, just below the Galata Tower, is the largest such (and so named for the long-ago days when you could indulge for two-and-a-half – *ikibuçuk* – liras), managed until her death in 2001 by the Armenian Mathilde Hanım, for many years the nation's biggest taxpayer.

The **prostitutes** themselves are licensed, and supposedly examined regularly for STDs, but are effectively the chattel of the mobsters who run most of the business across Turkey. If they attempt to flee the brothels to which they are tied by a system of debt bondage, the police are likely to work them over before returning them to their workplace. Many of the women (estimated at 100,000 nationwide) have literally been sold by their families or ex-spouse for real or imagined transgressions of the rural moral code; others, if suspected of "immoral acts", are committed – like lunatics to an asylum – to the *genelevs* by shadowy tribunals, which operate in each province "for the maintenance of public morality". A high proportion use amphetamines or other drugs much of the time, some attempt suicide and few are able to save much money by the time they're forcibly retired between age 35 and 40. UK-based Anti-Slavery International has published two investigations of the industry (*Forced Prostitution in Turkey: Women in the Genelevs* and one other comparative study of prostitution in eight countries worldwide; ☎020/7501 8920 ⓔantislavery@gn.apc.org, £5 donation for both booklets). Perhaps the greatest obstacle to full civil rights for prostitutes is official policy; the Constitutional (Supreme) Court, for example, ruled in 1989 that the rape of a prostitute should carry a prison term only one-third as long as that for other rapes, though this was subsequently changed owing to outcry over the definition of a prostitute.

All of the foregoing, however, has been dwarfed by events since the collapse of the Soviet Union and Eastern Bloc in 1990. One of many consequences was the inundation of Turkey (and other countries) by legions of "professional" Russian, Ukranian, Romanian and Moldavian women or "**natashas**", as they are familiarly known. Undeniably exotic to Turkish male sensibilities, they soon dominated the local market, flaunting themselves openly in town centres, commanding prices many times that of *genelev* personnel and posing a serious commercial threat to the few Turkish call girls working outside of the *genelev* system. Particularly along the Black Sea and in northeast Anatolia, it became difficult to find a decent hotel where they didn't occupy an entire storey (or even the whole building) semi-permanently. Of late, however, the phenomenon is less visible – the post-2001 economic crash means that there's far less disposable income for local men to indulge.

If you wander through **red-light districts** such as Laleli/Aksaray in İstanbul, or stumble across known pickup points on major highways, you can expect to be followed by kerb-crawlers; it's usually enough to explain that you're not a *natasha*. They generally enter illegally on a tourist visa, or are smuggled in as "cabaret entertainers" and are thus barred from the *genelev* system and the minimal security and health protection that affords.

Organizations

You can find a list of Turkish women's organizations at ⓦwww. euronet.nl and there is even a Women's Studies Master's Program at Middle East Technical University in Ankara (ⓦwww.metu.edu.tr/home/www810/). Alternatively contact one of the organisations listed below.

Useful contacts

The Foundation for Women's Solidarity Hisarparkı Cad, Firuzağa Sok 9/3-4, 06240 Ulus, Ankara ☎0312/309 0484, ⓕ310 0670, ⓔkdndanis@prizma. net.tr. Provides refuges for women who are the victims of violence in the home.
National Council of Turkish Women Katıp Celebi Sok 5, 406680 Ankara ☎0312/426 2621, ⓕ223 0780.
Women for Women's Human Rights (WWHR) Plajyolu Sok, Camlıdağ Apt 12/9, Suadiye 81070, İstanbul ☎0216/357 2142, ⓕ385 1262, ⓔkihp@info-ist. comlink.de or wrpst@fenestra.comlink.de. Works in the legal and political field to improve women's rights.
Women's Library and Information Centre Foundation Fener Mahallesi, Fener Vapur Iskelesi Karşısı, Fener-Haliç, 34220 İstanbul ☎0212/534 9550, ⓕ523 7408. Women's library and information centre (Mon–Sat 9am–5.30pm), mainly used by women's organizations and activists and the media, and which includes foreign-language books and periodicals.

Gay life

It would be an understatement to say that Turkish society is deeply ambivalent about male homosexuality; it has been so since Ottoman times, when the imperial culture was rampantly bisexual and transvestite dancers and entertainers were the norm. Atatürk tried to stamp out such decadent holdovers, but in recent years transvestite – or transsexual – entertainers such as Bülent Ersoy and the late Zeki Müren have become national heroes. That has not, however, stopped macho males from verbally or physically abusing such personalities in public – and getting away with it.

Homosexual acts between adults over 18 are legal and any law against "spreading homosexual information" in print – ie advocating the lifestyle – is no longer enforced, otherwise *Time Out İstanbul* would have been banned from its first issue. However, the few gay bars in İstanbul have been raided in the past by the police, who forced customers to submit to STD testing; they still routinely beat drag queens on the streets. Aside from the adulated entertainers cited above, public attitudes are generally intolerant – or closeted – except in resorts such as Side or Alanya and, surprisingly enough, in the otherwise religious stronghold of Bursa,

considered the gay capital of Turkey. *İbne* (catamite, passive male partner) is a deadly Turkish insult, while there is no specific word for the active role.

Despite all the foregoing, there are currently three activist groups locally: a chapter of the gay rights group **Lambda** (ⓦwww .lambdaistanbul.org/), an "alternative" gay/lesbian group, **Kaos** (ⓦwww.geocities .com/kaosgl), which also publishes an eponymous "research" magazine; and a lesbian group called **Sappho'nin Kızlar** (Sappho's Girls, ⓦwww.geocities.com /WestHollywood/Chelsea/9070/).

Sports and outdoor activities

The Turks have been sports fanatics since the inception of the Republic, but success in the international arena was long confined to Naim Süleymanoğlu's spectacular Olympic weightlifting coup in 1988, when everyone in the country was treated to infinite television replays of his winning clean-and-jerk. He repeated this feat in the 1992 and 1996 Olympiads for a hat trick. Then in 2002, the Turkish national football team made it all the way to the World Cup semi-finals . . . .

Football

To the casual observer, it may appear that **football** (soccer) is more popular than Islam in Turkey, and the game certainly excites passions that discussing politics can't. Although the history of organized clubs in

İstanbul extends back to the first decade of the twentieth century, it wasn't until the 1960s that things really got going.

As in other countries, the British were mostly responsible for introducing the sport and many of the early teams were either largely expat or filled by the Greek or Armenian minorities. Galatasaray, however, was formed by Muslim students of the French-run Galatasary Lycee.

The stadiums hold up to 30,000 fans (all seated) and **matches** are usually on Saturday or Sunday afternoons between September and May, though during the season there seem to be televised matches from somewhere nearly every night of the week. Although there are well-supported **teams** in every town and village, most people profess allegiance to one of the "Big Four" first-division teams: the three İstanbul sides Galatasaray, Beşiktaş or Fenerbahçe (see p.169) – all established early in the 1900s – or the relative newcomer Trabzonspor, formed only in the 1960s.

Money is actually the biggest problem in Turkish football – not a lack of it, but the fact that top clubs have far too much and can buy up any emerging talent (especially African and South American). Of late, however, this traffic has become reciprocal, with many Turkish players playing for teams across Europe. Local teams have been more conspicuously successful in European competition, most notably when Galatasaray won the UEFA Cup in 2000 (the first Turkish side ever to do so), beating Arsenal 4–1 on penalties.

Sadly, Turkish football usually hits the headlines thanks to the less savoury aspects of the game. Charges of bribery and corruption are common and violence sporadically occurs. Unusually, this isn't a Western import; in a famous incident of 1967, a match between Kayserispor and Sivas resulted in forty dead and three hundred injured during running street-battles after the match. More recently in 2000, two English supporters of Leeds United were stabbed to death in Taksim Square, allegedly for insulting the Turkish flag, during running street-fighting with Galatasaray fans.

If you're (un)lucky enough to be caught in the aftermath of one of the bigger games, you're not likely to forget it. While a losing team occasionally gets attacked by its own supporters, more likely you'll witness delirious celebrations, with flag-waving fans leaning on the horns of cruising cars embroiled in massive traffic jams. An estimated 200,000 fans crammed İstanbul's Taksim Square to celebrate the Turkish national team reaching the finals of the 1995 European Championships, but this was nothing compared to the delirium that broke out in mid-2002 when Turkey reached the semi-finals of the World Cup for the first time since 1954; against all the odds the national team finished third, beating South Korea in the consolation match after being eliminated by eventual cup-winners Brazil. When the team returned to Turkey, an estimated three million people turned out to greet the players.

Skiing

Turkey is normally thought of as a summertime holiday destination, but there are a number of serviceable **ski resorts**, though as yet only a couple are up to European standards. The oldest, most famous and perhaps most overrated resort is **Uludağ**, above Bursa, with easy and intermediate runs, but maximum altitude is 2232m, slopes are prone to mist and snow turns slushy after February. The **Saklıkent** complex in the Beydarlağı near Antalya would seem potentially ideal for an early spring sea-cum-ski holiday, but snow cover tends to be thin and it's considered something of a joke amongst serious skiers – and omitted from most current tourist literature. Nearby, and opened in 2001, is the Davras centre near İsparta; it's meant primarily as a teachers' club, but is open to all. Roughly midway between İstanbul and Ankara, near Bolu, **Kartalkaya** is better than any of the foregoing, despite a modest top altitude of 2223m; facilities, with three chairlifts and seven T-bars, now nearly match those of Uludağ, plus there are several red and black runs (though again slush is a problem from February on).

The longest season and best snow conditions by far are at **Palandöken**, near Erzurum, where the top lifts goes over 3000m and the Turkish Olympic team trains; there are three chairlifts, one T-bar and a three-kilometre-long gondola car to service a mix of blue and red runs (there are only two advanced, half-hour runs for the team to sink its teeth into). At **Tekir Yaylası** on Erciyes Dağı near Kayseri, the season is nearly as long, the snow almost as powdery, and the top lift is 2770m (one to 3100m is planned), though thus far runs are only green and red grade, served by two chairlifts and two T-bars. **Sarıkamış**, near Kars, is having two new hotels built to augment the one existing, but only has two chairlifts and one T-bar to service a handful of runs (mostly red and blue grade); top lift is 2634m.

At present there are no ski packages offered from the UK, though Inghams is considering laying on winter charters to Erzurum for Palandöken. Your nearest overseas Turkish tourism office (see p.28) can provide you with lists of fancy resort hotels for each ski area, but if you're willing to forego doorstep skiing, it's surprisingly easy and cheap to do it based, say, in nearby Erzurum or Bursa rather than on the slopes.

Mountaineering and hiking

Although only Turks who have come through the university-linked walking and outing clubs trek and hike for pleasure, there is plenty of scope for these activities. You'll find details on specific hiking routes through the Kaçkar Dağları and a selection of walks on Bursa's Uludağ and along the Turquoise Coast, in the Guide, but if you're daunted at the prospect of going alone, contact one of the adventure travel companies listed in the "Getting there" section above.

At present, the **Kaçkar Dağları**, running parallel to the Black Sea, is the most rewarding area for treks and a number of companies organize expeditions there. The **Cilo and Sat massifs** along the Iraqi border are even more spectacular, but owing to Kurdish troubles were regrettably off-limits to outsiders for much of the past three decades. Most of it is now "open", barring any prolonged Iraq war – the first Turkish non-military expedition climbed Resko peak in 2002 – but expect trekking infrastructure to remain vestigial for a while yet. Next up in interest are the **Toros (Taurus) ranges**, which form a long chain extending from central Turkey to above the main Turquoise Coast resort areas; again various tour companies can take you to the best places. During the cooler months, the mountains of Lycia in particular offer some interesting

peak-bagging ascents, as well as – down in their foothills – Turkey's first official long-distance trail, the **Lycian Way** (see p.464).

Aside from this, high-altitude **mountaineering** in Turkey consists mostly of climbing the volcanoes of the central plateau – not nearly as satisfying; Ağrı Dağ (Ararat) – out of bounds for most of the 1990s, but now "open" again – is likely at the best of times to be a crashing non-event for most. By contrast, Erciyes and Hasan Dağı near Cappadocia are excellent for winter ascents, without any of the expense or bureacracy prevalent at Ararat.

If you go alone, you'll need to be fully kitted out, since alpine huts are nonexistent; if you've gaps in your equipment, note that only İstanbul and Ankara have European-standard mountaineering shops (as opposed to hunting-and-fishing gear outlets). **Water** can be a problem in the limestone strata of the Toros and on the volcanoes, detailed **maps** are very difficult to obtain (see p.30) and **trails** (when present) are faint, even where waymarking exists. But the unspoilt quality of the countryside and the friendliness of other mountaineers go a long way in compensation.

Birdwatching

Turkey attracts a tiny fraction of the birdwatchers that (for example) Israel does, but most of the same migrating birds pass over both countries. Because of the variety of Turkish terrain and temperature, and Turkey's role as a halfway house between the birds of the northern palearctic (the temperate zone across Eurasia) and those of the Middle East or Africa, in an active birdwatching holiday you could expect to tick off nearly three hundred different species.

Below is a suggested route for a birdwatching tour; sites marked * are also described in the main text. All of the sites lie within a few hours' drive of each other and form a neat circle based on Adana airport; Birecik is the furthest at five hours' drive from the airport. Spring arrives early here; the **best months** are February to May and, for the southbound migrations, late September to early October.

In the early morning, the steep scree slopes of the jagged **Aladağlar Mountains** are good for Caspian snowcock, Radde's and alpine accentor and crimson-winged finch.

The **Sultansazlığı marshes*** occupy a depression between Erciyes and the west flank of the Aladağlar. Because the salty marsh water doesn't freeze, it attracts many overwintering ducks. Migrating waders stop off here, and there are breeding Dalmatian and white pelicans. The **Ereğli marshes**, 80km southwest of Niğde, are similar, with a chance of spotting greater sand plover.

The **Göksu delta*** near Silifke is a huge area of canals, sand dunes and marsh. Rarities demonstrating the tremendous range of habitat include the black francolin, Smyrna kingfisher and Audouin's gull. The **Sertavul pass** 50km to the north is good for passing raptors, including flocks of vultures.

Durnalık, en route to Birecik, has dry valleys with eastern rock nuthatch, red-tailed wheatear, cinereous bunting and Upcher's warbler.

Birecik*, on the Euphrates River, offers a variety of dry habitats plus sandbanks; rarities include Bruce's scops owl, yellow-throated and pale rock sparrow, Menetrie's warbler, see-see partridge, black-bellied and pin-tailed sandgrouse, cream-coloured courser and a pair of eagle owls. Except for a few specimens in an aviary, the famous bald ibises that used to breed during the summer here have vanished since the 1950s, victims of pesticide poisoning and other human interference.

The **delta of the Tarsus Çayı** near Tarsus is good for any waders you didn't get at Göksu, plus the Smyrna kingfisher. Finally, **Belen**, the pass over the Nur mountains south of İskenderun, offers excellent raptor-watching opportunities, but you have to time it just right. The Turkish Forestry Ministry organizes a bird photography safari hereabouts during the first week of October.

Useful birdwatching contacts

Doğal Hayatı Koruma Derneği (DHKD) Büyük Postane Cad 43–45, Kat 5–6, Bahçekapı, Sirkeci, İstanbul ☎ 0212/528 2030, ⓕ 528 2040. The "Society for the Protection of Nature" (the local branch of the World Wildlife Fund), sells a book describing endangered Turkish environments,

including many of those cited above, plus bird charts and other publications, all in English.

Greentours See "Special Interest Holidays", p.16. Ian Green of Greentours has a book listing all Turkey's species, describing the sites above and with helpful sketch maps to get you to the right place.

Watersports, diving and rafting

Opportunities for engaging in various **watersports** abound at the Turkish coastal resorts. You can count on renting windsurfing, kayaking and snorkelling gear just about anywhere, and at the more developed sites waterskiing, sailing and yachting will be on offer – the yachts chartered either bare-boat or (more likely) as part of a guided, skippered three- to fifteen-day coastal cruise. For the possibilities of pre-booking such a cruise, see the "Getting there" sections starting on p.11; for advice on arranging something on the spur of the moment, see the box on p.415.

Because of the presumed number of antiquities still submerged off Turkey, **scuba-diving** is strictly regulated and is principally available out of Bodrum, Marmaris, Fethiye, Adrasan, Kalkan and Kaş, with appreciable fish numbers only at the last two spots. Of late, **wreck-diving** around the Gallipoli peninsula has also become popular and the nearby Gulf of Saros also supports a couple dive operators taking advantage of abundant local marine life.

Only three rivers – the Akköprü (or Dalaman Çayı) behind the Turquoise Coast, the Çoruh in the Kaçkar and the Göksu in the Toros mountains – are suitable for **whitewater rafting**, and all are chronically under threat from hydroelectric projects. The first two rivers receive regular attention from adventure travel operators; again, see "Getting there", p.11, for specifics.

Other activities

Kaş is the focus of **canyoning**, with a number of suitable gorges within a few hours' drive. The Kıbrıs Çayı, between Sütleğen and Kemer on the way to Gömbe, makes an excellent one-day beginners' outing after snowmelt is finished; the Kaputaş and Saklıkent gorges are more technical expeditions involving thirty-metre drops. Saklıkent can be traversed in two full days (summer only), Kaputaş in one-and-a-half (best April–June) – though it's also possible to do the lowest five drops only by using a side entrance. Elsewhere, the Köprülü canyon and another unnamed one near Manavgat on the Mediterranean coast are the main venues.

Paragliding is practiced at Ölüdeniz and Kaş on the Turquoise Coast; it's marginally cheaper to indulge at Kaş, though either is pricey compared to, say, the Pyrenees, as "tolls" and assorted other backhanders must be paid to the forest service and municipalities involved for crossing their land en route to the launching sites. That said, these are two of the most spectacular venues in the world, with clear, stable conditions most of the year. **Hot-air ballooning** is rather more elitist at $200 per person and restricted at present to Göreme in Cappadocia.

Work

Turkey has a chronically high unemployment rate even amongst graduates, variable but generally low wages and no special privileges for EU citizens – all factors intensified by the economic crash of 2001. It's hardly a bright picture for potential job-seekers, but many foreigners do work in Turkey for varying periods, even on a tourist visa, though this is strictly illegal.

Teaching is the most obvious employment, though the best-paid jobs involve working for a foreign employer, for example a contractor on a World Bank water project or a management job at a NATO base. You have to be pretty lucky, in the right place at the right time, to get one of these. If you have a skill that is in demand, large Turkish companies may be able to offer you employment, although there are various kinds of jobs, including medical work, which a foreigner is not allowed to do.

For qualified **nannies**, work is relatively easy to find, especially in İstanbul; agencies advertise in the *Turkish Daily News*.

The paperwork

If you intend to work from the start, it's far preferable to obtain a job offer and get a work permit before you arrive. Contact the Turkish embassy or consulate in your home country (see "Red tape and visas", p.22) or, failing that in a country bordering Turkey, to obtain a **work permit** (*çalışma tezkeresi*). As well as your written offer of employment from inside Turkey, you'll need proof of your educational qualifications, passport photos and the requisite embassy forms filled out and fees paid. Possession of a **work visa** for a permanent job automatically entitles you to a residence permit for an initial two-year period. It also entitles you to bring your car into Turkey for more than six months (see p.22).

Teaching

Most of the foreigners working in Turkey are **teaching English** as a foreign language in one of the major cities. Conditions and rates of pay vary according to the required qualifications, local cost of living and the attractiveness of the area; a job in İstanbul will pay more than twice that in a south-coast resort. The best rates are paid at the private universities teaching *hazırlık* (preparatory) classes – ie coaching rich, indolent teenagers through a year of intensive English.

Teaching in a state university or *Anadolu Lisesi* (the equivalent of old-style British grammar schools) is less stressful, but your first pay packet can be delayed until the vetting procedure (checking your credentials and political background) is completed by the appropriate ministry and in practice it's rare for foreigners to be employed. Both the above types of schools require an English degree and preferably a TEFL (teaching English as a foreign language) certificate.

*Dershane*s (private cramming academies) and private high schools may employ people with other degrees or no degree at all; a TEFL qualification is sometimes enough. Some may also provide accommodation, at least for an initial period. Examine contracts carefully (they're usually for one calendar year), checking the hours when you will have to actually be in the school for extra duties, as well as teaching hours. Turkish school terms are quite different from England; two long terms are separated by a fortnight's break and the summer break is for three months; you won't have Christmas or Easter off!

Teaching posts for the bigger outfits are advertised in *The Guardian*'s educational section and the *Times Educational Supplement* in Britain, in the *International Herald Tribune* and the *Turkish Daily News* in Turkey, but, especially if you are looking for temporary work, private schools are probably best approached on the spot. Check whether the job will enable you to apply for a work permit.

Tourism-related work

There is always work available at tourist resorts during the summer months, for example at the backpackers' treehouses on the Turquoise Coast. Very little of it is legal and after three months you will have either to leave the country to get a second entry visa or apply for a three months' extension inside the country (see p.22). In the view of the locals, you are taking a job away from a

Turk, so if you cause offence, they are likely to complain to the *jandarma*. If this happens, you will be initially warned not to work; if you persist, you'll definitely be deported. If you have any dispute with an employer (most commonly being under-paid or not paid at all), you obviously have no legal recourse.

Foreigners are not allowed to work as certified archeological **tour guides** – one rule that is enforced, as in most Mediterranean countries – though tour companies may employ you to do PR work in their office, or as a courier to meet groups from the airport and take them to their hotel. **Carpet and leather shops** will often employ English-speakers on a commission basis, in which case you will work long hours trying to pull in your quota of likely tourists. **Yacht and gület** captains may take on foreign staff to cook and clean, or host guests.

Voluntary work

Voluntary work at **rural aid projects** all over Turkey is organized by Gençtur, whose website contains a list of projects requiring volunteers. Their camps generally involve manual labour in Turkish villages. Basic accommodation is provided, either in guesthouses or dormitories, and food is prepared for you by the villagers.

Conservation volunteers are organized through the World Wildlife Fund and its Turkish branch the DHKD (see "Birdwatching", p.85); past projects have included bird habitat surveys and turtle protection.

Voluntary work contacts

Gençtur Yerebatan Cad 15/3 34410 Sultanahmet, İstanbul ☎0212/520 5274, ⓕ519 0864, ⓦ www.genctur.com.tr.
International Voluntary Service 162 Upper New Walk, Leicester LE1 7QA ☎01533/549430. Gençtur-affiliate organization.

Directory

Addresses In Turkish addresses, street names precede the number; if the address is on a minor alley, this will usually be included after the main thoroughfare it leads off. If you see a right-hand slash between two numbers, the first is the building number, the second the flat or office number. A letter following a right-hand slash is more ambiguous: it can mean either the shop or unit number, or be part of the general building number. Standard abbreviations, also used in this book, include "Cad" for *Cadde(si)* (avenue or main street), "Bul" for *Bulvarı* (boulevard), "Meyd" for *Meydan(ı)* (square), "Sok" for *Sokak/Sokağı* (alley) and "PK" for *Posta Kutu* (Post Box). Other useful terms are *kat* (floor), *zemin* (ground floor), *asma* (mezzanine), *han(ı)* (office block), *mahalle* (district or neighbourhood) and *çıkmaz(ı)* (blind alley). *Karşısı* means "opposite to", as in *PTT karşısı*. A five-digit postcode system exists, but is sporadically used; it is much more important to include the district when addressing mail. For example: Halil Güner, Kıbrıs Şehitler Cad, Poyraz Sok, Ulus Apartmanı 36/2, Kat 1, Delikliçınar, 34800 Direkköy, means that Halil Güner lives on Poyraz Sokak no. 36, just off Kıbrıs Şehitler Caddesi, on the first floor, Flat 2, of the Ulus apartments, in the Delikliçınar area of a larger postal district known as Direkköy.

Bargaining You can haggle for souvenir purchases, minor repair services, rural taxis where no rate is posted, car rental, hotels out of season and meals – especially seafood ones – at eateries where a menu is absent. You shouldn't have to bargain for dolmuş or bus tickets, though some of the stewards selling fares on long-distance coaches are less than honest; if in doubt, check to see what others are paying for the same distance.

Beaches All Turkish beaches are free in theory, though the luxury compounds that straddle routes to the sand will control access in various ways. Never pay a fee for a beach-lounger or umbrella, unless the seller can produce a ticket. Periodically there can be quite a lot of tar on south-coast beaches facing the Mediterranean shipping lanes. For tar globs on your feet, olive oil is a far more effective, ubiquitous – and safer – solvent than white spirit or nitro thinner.

Camping gas It's possible to find small 190ml cartridges for camping stoves relatively easily. Likely sales points include hunting and outdoor-sports shops in İstanbul, Migros supermarkets and many outlets of the Aygas and Milangas chain of gas-bottle storefronts. In the Guide, we give some confirmed addresses for towns near the Kaçkar mountains.

Children They're adored in Turkey; childless couples will be asked when they plan to have some and bringing children along guarantees red-carpet treatment almost everywhere. Three- or four-bedded hotel rooms are easy to find, and airlines, ships and trains offer substantial discounts. Baby formulas are cheap and readily available, as are disposable nappies.

Departure tax None is currently charged at airports – it's included in air-ticket prices – though İstanbul, Çeşme (long-haul dock), Kuşadası, Marmaris, Antalya, Taşucu and Mersin seaports, all controlled by Turkish Maritime Lines, do levy varying amounts on departing international passengers.

Disabled travellers Turkey makes poor provision for disabled travellers. Sidewalk corners and archeological sites do not have ramps, hotels below three stars in rating lack lifts and there is no adapted public transport. For advice, current information and specialist tours, contact: UK, Holiday Care ☎01293/774 535, Minicom ☎01293/776 943, ⊛www.holidaycare.org.uk; Ireland, Irish Wheelchair Association ☎01/833 8241,

@iwa@iol.ie; US, Mobility International ☎541/343-1284, ⊛www.miusa.org; Australia, Australian Council for Rehabilitation of the Disabled ☎02/6282 4333; New Zealand, Disabled Persons Assembly ☎04/801 9100.

Electric power 220 volts, 50 cycles, out of double round-pin sockets. British appliances need a 3-to-2 plug adaptor, with a minimum 5-amp fuse (7.5amp is better) to permit operation of a hair dryer or travel iron; North American ones both a square-to-round-pin adaptor and a transformer (except for dual voltage shavers, which need only the former).

Emergencies Police ☎155; rural gendarmerie ☎156; traffic police ☎154; fire brigade ☎110; rural forest fires ☎177; ambulance ☎112. These calls cost one small *jeton* or one card unit.

Essentials On most trips it's worth packing the following: universal bath plug (they're rarely supplied, to prevent you from doing laundry in the washbasin), camera film (see below); contact lens accessories (only a basic range of solutions is available locally); ear plugs (a godsend in noisy low-rent hotels); mosquito repellent; sunblock (at least factor 15); brand toiletries; a torch (flashlight); travel alarm clock; Walkman /Discman (invaluable on long bus journeys); and a water container. A multipurpose penknife and a small sewing kit can also be very useful, though pack these in your checked baggage not your carry-ons.

Film This is expensive in tourist resorts and provincial towns; a broad range of Fuji products are reasonable if bought in the bazaars of İstanbul, İzmir and Ankara, though it's best to bring enough with you. Note that you may not find anything faster than ASA 100 outside the three largest cities.

Laundry These are slowly appearing in tourist resorts, but there are dry-cleaning (*kuru temizleme*) establishments in most large towns, and *pansiyon*s and large hotels will do your washing for a small consideration.

Left luggage An *emanet* (left-luggage) service is available at virtually all bus and train stations and the largest international airports; there are no lockers, you pay the attendant upon return of article(s) in exchange for your claim ticket. Prices, usually for a maximum of 24 hours, vary according to the amount of insurance applicable – for nice foreign backpacks, suitcases or holdalls, you'll be charged the most expensive rate, about $2–3 per item.

Smoking Tobacco smoke can be a major nuisance, despite an ongoing nationwide anti-smoking campaign. Tangible results thus far include designated no-smoking cars on most trains, and prohibition of smoking on all domestic flights, İstanbul ferries and on the better-quality long-haul buses.

Time Turkey is two hours ahead of GMT in winter; as in Europe, daylight saving (ie, GMT + 3hr) is observed between the last weekend in March and the last one in October – clocks change at 2am of the Sunday concerned.

Toilets Except in the plusher resort hotels and restaurants, most public toilets are of the squat-hole variety, found either in public parks or (more infallibly) next to any mosque. They usually cost about $0.25, so keep a few coins or small notes handy. Also keep a supply of toilet paper with you (available in Turkey) – Turks wash themselves off either with the bidet or toilet-rim spout, or the special vessel filled from the handy floor-level tap. You may well become a convert to this method, reserving the paper – which shouldn't be thrown down the hole – for drying yourself off.

Guide

Guide

drivers willing to take you the short distance (2km) to the metro station at Yeni Bosna, the bus is the better option. Alternatively, a **taxi** from the airport to Sultanahmet or Taksim should cost $9 (though double this between midnight and 6am) – consult the tourism sign posted outside the arrivals hall for prices. However, fares *from* Sultanahmet back to the airport can creep over the $14 mark, with no logical explanation forthcoming.

By train

İstanbul has two mainline **train stations**, one in Europe at Sirkeci, the other, at Haydarpaşa, across the Bosphorus in Asia. The two are linked by ferry.

Two daily trains from Western Europe arrive at **Sirkeci train station**, located 250m above Eminönü ferry terminal: from Athens (23hr) via Thessaloniki (16hr) and Üzünköprü (6hr), and from Budapest (33hr) via Sofia (14hr) and Bucharest (18hr). The latter service connects with the rest of the European train network at Budapest. At Sirkeci it's easy to find a taxi, or catch the tram from outside the station directly uphill to Sultanahmet, Laleli and on to Aksaray (where you can change onto the metro to reach the main inter-city bus station at Esenler).

Trains from Asian Turkey arrive at **Haydarpaşa train station**, across the Bosphorus and a kilometre north of Kadıköy. To cross the Bosphorus to Sultanahmet, board a ferry immediately in front of the station to Eminönü, whose ferry terminal is directly below Sirkeci station. Alternatively, it's a kilometre walk to the hotels further along the waterfront in Kadıköy, or take a #12 bus to accommodation in Üsküdar. There's a taxi rank outside the main entrance, on the road between the station and the quay.

By bus

There are two major **otogars** (bus stations) in İstanbul, one in Esenler, 10km northwest of the centre on the E800 (İstanbul–Edirne toll road) and one at Harem on the Asian side of the city, on the coast road between Üsküdar and Kadıköy. All national bus services stop at both, regardless of their destination, and both bus stations are open 24 hours.

The **Esenler** bus station is well organized and some 150 companies have numbered ticket stands here. Most bus companies run free service buses to and from Taksim and those that don't should be able to arrange for you to travel on one run by another company. To get to Sultanahmet from Esenler, take the metro (every 15min, 6am–11.15pm) from the station in the centre of the *otogar* to Aksaray; from there you can switch to the tram to Sultanahmet, get a taxi, or walk to hotels in Laleli. If you arrive any later than 11.15pm, your only option is to take a taxi into town, which should cost around $4. Travelling from the city centre to Esenler by metro, note that you should get off at *Otogar* station and not at *Esenler* station. If you have booked your ticket with a travel agent or with one of the bus company's city offices, they will arrange a shuttle service from Taksim or Sultanahmet to Esenler, usually an hour before the departure of your bus. Some of the larger companies even operate late-night departures direct from their city office near Taksim Square.

If you're arriving in İstanbul by bus from Asia, it's worth disembarking at **Harem**, saving yourself the tedious journey on to Esenler via one of the Bosphorus bridges and through the worst of the traffic snarl-ups. From Harem, regular ferries cross the Bosphorus to Eminönü (every hour, daily 7am–10pm) and there are private boats running to Beşiktaş and Kabataş. There are also dolmuşes every few minutes to Kadıköy and to Üsküdar, leaving from the south side of the complex, beyond the ticket offices surrounding the main courtyard. From either of these suburbs, it's an easy matter to take a ferry across to Eminönü, or from Üsküdar to Beşiktaş for Taksim. Taxis are available everywhere, but to cross the bridge by taxi is expensive, as you pay the bridge toll on top of the fare.

By ferry

Car ferries, operated by Turkish Maritime Lines, cross the Bosphorus from Harem to Eminönü. **Sea bus** car and passenger services from Yalova, Bandırma (on the İzmir–İstanbul route) and the islands of Avşı and Marmara arrive at the **Yenikapı ferry terminal**, off Kennedy Caddesi in Kumkapı, just south of Aksaray. From here, simply catch the train from Yenikapı station across the road from the ferry terminal; it's two stops to Sultanahmet or three to the main station at Sirkeci. Any number of buses go from Yenikapı to Taksim via Aksaray.

Cruise ship arrivals will go through customs and immigration procedures at **Karaköy International Maritime Passenger Terminal**, across the Galata bridge from Eminönü. This is also the arrival point for the **Karadeniz Feribot**, the car-ferry that runs up the Black Sea Coast during summer (see "Travel details", p.214). For Sultanahmet, cross the bridge by bus or foot to the tram stop at Eminönü; for Taksim, either take the Tünel up to Beyoğlu and then the tram to Taksim Square or (easier) take a taxi.

Information

By far the most helpful **tourist office** in the city is on Divan Yolu Caddesi, in Sultanahmet, near the Hippodrome (daily 9am–5pm; ☎0212/518 8754). Others can be found in the international arrivals area of **Atatürk airport** (daily 24hr; ☎0212/573 4136), in **Sirkeci train station** (daily 9am–5pm; ☎0212/511 5811), at **Karaköy International Maritime Passenger Terminal** (Mon–Sat 9am–5pm; ☎0212/249 5776) and in the **Hilton Hotel arcade** on Cumhuriyet Caddesi (Mon–Sat 9am–5pm; ☎0212/233 0592). Each hands out an abundance of city maps and leaflets and the staff have excellent working knowledge of most European languages.

The **Directorate of Tourism**, at Süleyman Cad 7, Beşiktas (Mon–Fri 9am–5pm; ☎0212/258 7032), won't answer run-of-the-mill queries from drop-in customers, but if you contact them in advance can help in the preparation of long trips and can recommend guiding companies.

City transport

For any one journey within İstanbul there's invariably a wide choice of means of transport, from horse and carriage to high-speed tram. All **public transport** tends to be overcrowded and pick-pocketing is not unknown; if you have any trouble with this, or with sexual harassment, make other passengers aware of the fact (try calling *imdat*, meaning "help") and invariably you will be assisted. Negotiating the bus system in particular can be daunting, but once you've mastered this you will find that you can travel just about anywhere cheaply. Trams and trains are efficient, while taxis and dolmuşes (shared taxis) are very reasonably priced with knowledgeable – if not necessarily good – drivers. However, by far the nicest way of exploring a city that, historically, has puts its best face towards the

akbils – automatic travel passes

An **akbil** (automatic travel pass) is worth considering if you're staying for a few days or more. After paying an initial, refundable, deposit of $4, these can be "charged" to whatever value you require at kiosks or at the automatic terminals in main *otogar*s. The passes are accepted on private buses, sea buses, ferries, trains on the European and Asian side (for local journeys only), the metro and the tram. All either have *akbil* machines or turnstiles; press the *akbil* against the receptor and the appropriate journey cost (including a small discount) is deducted. You can now even buy soft drinks at vending machines on some tram or metro platforms with an *akbil*.

water is by ferry, with the year-round **Bosphorus Tour** a favoured way of seeing the sights.

Traffic jams are very much a part of everyday life in İstanbul. You can avoid congestion problems only by staying around the historic Sultanahmet district, which can easily be explored on foot and is relatively traffic free. Otherwise, expect to spend time in tailbacks as you travel to and from other equally interesting areas – an hour in a bus or taxi from Sultanahmet to Ortaköy for example, isn't unusual. There are plans for another Bosphorus bridge (located between the existing two) and for underground links under the Golden Horn and between the suburban rail lines at Sirkeci and Haydarpaşa, but in the meantime, patience is required for most journeys you'll make, particularly by road.

Buses

The cheapest but slowest form of transport is provided by İstanbul's **buses** (*otobus* in Turkish), which are often full to the point of overflowing. They come in a range of colours, but the bulk are red-and-blue municipality buses, while a substantial number of green-and-white or orange-and-white ones are privately run (and usually older and shabbier looking). Main bus stops boast large route maps and lists of services. Most buses run daily from 6.30am to 11.30pm, though last buses depart from the outlying suburbs much earlier. For all municipality buses, either use an *akbil* or buy a ticket in advance, which you deposit in the metal box next to the driver on boarding.

Tickets are sold at *otogar* ticket kiosks next to main bus, tram or metro stops (regular ticket $0.50; longer routes may require two or three). Touts at most main stops also sell them for a small mark-up. It's as well to lay in a good supply of tickets whenever you get the chance, since you can walk for miles trying to find a ticket kiosk in more remote areas of the city. On a privately run bus you can either use an *akbil* or pay the conductor in cash; routes overlap with those of the municipal services and prices are the same.

On the European side **main bus terminals** are at Eminönü, Taksim Square, Beşikataş and Aksaray, and on the Asian side at Üsküdar and Kadıköy. Note that very few buses pass through the main tourist area of Sultanahmet, so the easiest thing to do is walk, or catch the tram three stops, down the hill to the bus station at Eminönü (sited in front of the ferry terminal). **From Eminönü** there are buses to Taksim, west-bound services to Aksaray and Topkapı, and services to the Bosphorus shore through Beşiktaş, Ortaköy and Arnavutköy to Bebek where you'll have to change to continue on through the suburbs as far as the village of Rumeli Kavağı. Buses **from Taksim Square** head through Mecidiyeköy to the northern suburbs, down along the Bosphorus through

Beşiktaş, Ortaköy and Aranvutköy, and across the horn to Topkapı and Aksaray.

Useful routes include: #12 and #14 (Kadıköy to Üsküdar); #15A (Üsküdar to Beylerbeyi, Kanlıca and Anadolu Kavağı); #22 and #22C (Eminönü to Karaköy, Beşikataş, Arnavutköy and Bebek); #25A (Eminönü to Beşikataş, Levent, Maslak, Sariyer and Rumeli Kavağı); #30 (Sultanahmet to Eminönü, Karaköy and Beşikataş); #84 (Eminönü to Sultanahmet, Aksaray and Topkapı); and #23B (Taksim to Beşikataş and Ortaköy).

Trains

The **municipal train network** – operated by *Türkiye Cumhuriyeti Devlet Demiryolları* (TCDD) – consists of one line on either side of the Bosphorus. It's hardly comprehensive, but elaborate plans exist to link the two via a tunnel crossing under the Sea of Marmara.

Trains are frequent and cheap, though crowded at morning and evening rush hours; daily hours of operation are 7am to 9.30pm. One line runs **from Haydarpaşa** (enquiries on ☎0212/336 0475) out to Göztepe and Bostancı, and along the Gulf of İzmit to Gebze; the other, **from Sirkeci** (☎0212/527 0051), runs to Halkala, along the shores of the Sea of Marmara, stopping at Kumkapı (known for its fish restaurants), Yenkapı (for the sea bus ferry terminal), Yedikule fortress and Yeşilköy, not far from the airport. Journeys cost the same flat **fare** ($0.50) and *akbils* are accepted on local lines. At Sirkeci, you buy a *jeton* (metal token) from the kiosk (insert it at the turnstile), but Haydarpaşa still uses tickets, again available from kiosks.

There is also a one-stop underground funicular train line, between Karaköy and İstiklâl Caddesi in Beyoğlu, known as the **Tünel** (every 15min, daily 8am–9pm); use an *akbil* or *jetons* ($0.50), available at the kiosks on entry.

Trams

The **main tram** service runs from Zeytinburnu and Merter via Topkapı Gate to Aksaray (where it connects with the metro), Laleli, the University, Beyazit, Cemberlitaş, Sultanahmet and downhill to Eminönü. Trams are frequent and operate from 7.30am to 9pm. Approaching trams signal their arrival with a bell and passengers must wait on the concrete platforms, placed at regular intervals along the tracks. *Jetons* ($0.50) are bought at booths next to the platforms and are deposited in turnstiles on entry, or you can use an *akbil*.

The other tramline provides a useful service between the Tünel station, at the Beyoğlu end of İstiklâl Caddesi, and Taksim Square. **Antique trams** (with ticket collectors in appropriately antiquated uniforms) run along the 1.5-kilometre route (every 15min, daily 9am–9pm; $0.50) and tickets can be purchased from kiosks at either end or at the one fixed stop halfway at Galatasaray School; *akbils* are also accepted.

The metro

Once the building of a tunnel underneath the Golden Horn has been completed, the **metro**, or *hızlı tramvay* (high-speed tram), will connect the whole of the European side of İstanbul. At present, though, the service is limited to a line on each side of the horn. The line on the **southern side** runs west from Aksaray via the inter-city *otogar* near Esenler, where the line splits. One branch continues to Esenler itself, the other to the end of the line at Yeni Bosna, which is a rather infuriating 2km from the airport. On the **northern side** of the Golden Horn, the newly opened Taksim to Levent section runs roof terrace where you can have a drink looking directly at the dome of the Blue Mosque. **4**

Hotel Ayasofya Demirci Reşit Sok 28, off Mehmet Paşa Sok ☏0212/516 9446, ⓔinfo@ayasofya.com. An indoor winter garden, kilims and old-world charm feature at this rebuilt nineteenth-century wooden Ottoman mansion. **6**

Optimist Guesthouse At Meydanı 68 ☏0212/638 9580, ⓕ638 8480. The small rooms here are good value and it's in a prime location right on the Hippodrome. It also has a street-side café/pub. **2**

Hotel Sokullupaşa Mehmet Paşa Sok 5/7 ☏0212/518 1790, ⓦwww.sokullupasa.com. Wooden-clad concrete copy of an original nineteenth-century mansion, featuring stained glass, Ottoman antiques, a Turkish bath, bar and garden. Not cheap, but special promotions are sometimes offered on the website (complimentary dinner, fifth night free, etc.). **7**

Hotel Spectra Şehit Mehmet Paşa Yokuşu ☏0212/516 3546, ⓦwww.hotelspectra.com. Concrete facsimile of an Ottoman house, with large, comfortable and nicely furnished rooms, good views from the terrace and free internet access in the lobby for guests. **6**

Turkoman Hotel Asmalı Çeşme Sok, Adliye Yana 2 ☏0212/516 2956, ⓦwww.turkomanhotel.com. Converted house in nineteenth-century Turkish style, right on the Hippodrome and opposite the Egyptian obelisk, with fine views of the Blue Mosque from the roof terrace. Each attractive room is named after one of the old Turkoman tribes and has a brass bed and wooden floors. Free airport transfers. **7**

Around Topkapı Palace

Ayasofya Pansiyonlar Soğukçeşme Sok ☏0212/513 3660, ⓔayapans@escourtnet.com. A row of pastel-coloured houses reconstructed in nineteenth-century style, in a peaceful cobbled street tucked away behind the back wall of the Aya Sofya. The setting is fantastic and lit up atmospherically at night, but the rooms (up to $120) are rather simply furnished, perhaps in an attempt to match the period feel. **6**

Inter Youth Hostel Caferiye Sok 6 ☏0212/513 6150, ⓦwww.yucelthostel.com. One of İstanbul's prime locations with a staggering 320 beds available in a mixture of dorms ($5), doubles and quads. All are basic but clean, with shared bathrooms (hot water mornings and evenings only). Facilities include a safe, laundry, roof terrace, garden bar, café and internet access. There's a $1 discount for IYHF members and regular promotions (free drink on arrival, sixth night free, etc). Advance booking essential. **2**

Merih Hostel Alemdar Cad 20 ☏0212/526 9708, ⓔmerihotel@superonline.com. Friendly hostel just down from Aya Sofya, with four-person dorms ($7) as well as a couple of spartan but clean doubles with their own bathrooms. Rooms at the front can be noisy early in the morning when the tram starts running. **3**

Around Divan Yolu Caddesi

And Hotel Yerebatan Cad, Camii Çıkmazı Sok 40 ☏0212/512 0207, ⓦwww.andhotel. Unremarkable rooms with Turkish TV in a modern building; there's room for negotiation out of season. The biggest attraction is the wonderful view of the Golden Horn and Bosphorus from the rooftop breakfast restaurant. **6**

Kybele Hotel Yerebatan Cad 35 ☏0212/511 7766, ⓦwww.kybelehotel.com. Colourfully painted house with beautifully furnished rooms with marble bathrooms. It's decorated with period antiques from the attached shop, including several hundred elaborate light fittings. Breakfast is served in a courtyard full of candelabras, cushions, empty bottles and other knick-knacks. **6**

Nomade Hotel Ticarethane Sok 15 ☏0212/511 1296, ⓦwww.hotelnomade.com. A reproduction townhouse run by twin sisters, this used to be one of the best budget options in the area but it has definitely seen better days, with scuffs, chips and dings on the walls and much of the period décor vanished. However, the breakfast is decent and the roof terrace pleasant. The low-season price drops a category. **5**

Cankurtaran

Alp Guesthouse Akbıyık Cad, Adliye Sok 4 ☏0212/517 9570, ⓔalpghouse@turk.net. Clean place with a range of rooms available. The pretty breakfast terrace commands views of palaces, mosques and the sea, and the service is excellent (as attested to by the wall of thank-you letters in reception). **5**

Berk Guesthouse Kutlugün Sok 27 ☏0212/517 6561, ⓔreservations@berkguesthouse.com. Family-run place with eight standard rooms, plus a couple of spacious luxury rooms with minibar, air-conditioning and TV. The nineteenth-century mansion has been lovingly restored, and has great views of the former prison – now converted into the *Four Seasons Hotel* – from the rooftop lounge and terrace. Standard rooms **5**, luxury rooms **7**

Empress Zoe Akbıyık Cad, Adliye Sok 10 ☏0212/518 2504, ⓕ518 5699. Owned by American Ann Nevans, who has decorated throughout with her personal touch – the nineteen rooms are in dark wood with richly coloured textiles, accessed by a narrow spiral staircase. Part of the basement walls belong to the remains of the Byzantine Palace and the sun terrace has panoramic views of the Blue Mosque and Aya Sofya. Ten-percent discount for cash. **❻**

Four Seasons Hotel Tevfikhane Sok 1 ☎0212/638 8200, ⓦwww.fourseasons.com. Until the early 1980s, this formidable building still served as the Sultanahmet Prison before being completely renovated as one of the city's leading hotels. The watch-towers and exercise court are still evident underneath the flowers and vines, but the 54 beautiful high-ceilinged rooms are unrecognizable as former cells. Excellent, attentive service at this five-star luxury establishment, with rooms starting at $320 and rising to $2000 in a suite. **❽**

Istanbul Hostel Kutlugün Sok 35 ☎0212/516 9380, ⓦwww.istanbul-hostel.com. Large hostel in a central location, with 64 dorm beds ($6), but only two double rooms, and spotless shared marble bathrooms. The cosy basement bar has satellite TV, video, fireplace and internet access, and there are more bars on the roof terrace, as well as regular entertainment from belly dancers. **❷**

Mavi Guesthouse Isakpaşa Cad, Kutlugün Sok 3 ☎0212/516 5878, ⓦwww.maviguesthouse.com. One of the cheapest options in town, this established backpacker-friendly hostel offers a mixture of basic but functional doubles and triples, alongside 26 dorm beds ($7) and 18 beds under canvas ($5) on the roof. The shared bathrooms have 24hr hot water; and there's internet access. **❷**

Orient Youth Hostel Akbıyık Cad 13 ☎0212/517 9493, ⓔorienthostel@superline.com. Friendly, popular hostel with a lively rooftop bar and a good restaurant (with telescopes provided to spy on all the other rooftop bars in the area). It's worth visiting for the Friday night party even if you are staying elsewhere. Dorms ($7) are basic but clean, and some of the doubles have en-suite bathrooms and satellite TV. **❷**

Seven Hills Tevkifhane Sok 8 ☎0212/516 9497, 516 9498 or 516 9499 ⓦwww.hotelsevenhills .com. Deluxe hotel in a newly restored mansion with all the trimmings and the usual stunning views from the sumptuous terrace. All rooms are furnished to the highest standard, with some sporting jacuzzis and balconies (for which you'll typically pay an extra $50 or so). **❽**

Side Hotel & Pension Utangaç Sok 20 ☎0212/517 2282, ⓦwww.sidehotel.com. Pricier en-suite rooms on the hotel side, cheaper ones with shared bathroom in the pension, both sharing the extensive breakfast terraces, which have great views of the Princes' Islands. The whole complex, owned by three charismatic brothers, is bright, spacious and friendly. Pension **❸**, hotel **❺**

Wooden House Inn Akbiyik Depirmen Sok 7, ☎0212/516 7132, ⓦwww.nazwoodenhouseinn.com. A commendable restoration of an original Ottoman house. During excavations, part of a city wall and marble from a Byzantine palace were discovered, which have all been incorporated into the design. Rooms are small but exquisite – cool whitewashed walls strewn with colourful kilims – and the only drawback is the railway line that runs at the back, though the double-glazed windows help keep some of the noise out. **❼**

Yeşil Ev Kabasakal Cad 5 ☎0212 517 6785, ⓦwww.turing.org.tr. On a leafy cobbled street between Aya Sofya and the Blue Mosque. Built in the style of the house that originally occupied the site, *Yeşil Ev* ("Green House") is furnished in period (mid-nineteenth century) style, with wood-panelled ceilings and antique rugs. Rooms (from $160) are good-value for this quality; *Pasha's Room* ($250) has its own Turkish bath and ostentatious Ottoman bedroom suite. There's a fine garden restaurant with a central marble fountain open to non-residents. **❽**

Aksaray and Laleli

Old İstanbul's other main concentration of hotels is situated in the area called **Aksaray**, where you arrive if coming from Esenler *otogar* by metro. Aksaray encompasses the smaller district of **Laleli**, immediately to the east of Aksaray Meydanı (where busy Turgut Özal Caddesi, Adnan Menderes Caddesi and Atatürk Bulvarı meet). It's a commercial textile district with little of interest for the visitor, but there are numerous reasonably priced hotels and Sultanahmet is only three stops away by tram. The main concentration of accommodation is in the north of Laleli, between Atatürk Bulvarı and Büyük Rezit Paşa Caddesi, up as far as Şehzade Camii. There are more hotels south of Ordu Caddesi, around Namik Kemal Caddesi, leading down towards Yenikapı train station, but these tend to be favoured by Russian businessmen and are best avoided as single women walking alone here may be mistaken for prostitutes.

The places reviewed below are marked on the "Old İstanbul" map on pp.100–101.

Hotel Burak Fethi Bey Cad, Ağa Yokuşu 1 ☎0212/511 8679, ℱ511 3066. Quite ordinary but cheap (so favoured by Russian shoppers), with not a bad street-side restaurant serving good-value and filling meals. ❸

History Hotel Gençtürk Cad, Şirvanizade Sok 14 ☎0212/520 6607, ⓦwww.historyhotel.com. Great value in a quiet backstreet, a handy location for buses (to Taksim from Atatürk Bul) and the tram. The comfortable rooms have TV, fridge and air-conditioning, and the staff are enthusiastic and friendly. ❹

Merit Antique Ordu Cad 226 ☎0212/513 9300, ⓦwww.meritantiquehotel.com.tr. Restored late nineteenth-century apartment building converted into a luxury hotel. The modern rooms (from $200) are fabulous, but have no real nostalgic charm, though the buildings are connected by an airy, bird-filled atrium. It has a poor setting on a busy main road, but with distractions such as health club, pool, shopping arcade, beauty salon and a variety of restaurants, that won't matter. ❽

Hotel Seren Yeşil Tulumba Sok 26 ☎0212/513 7982, ℱ519 2319. Good-value, two-star comfort whose rooms include a minibar and air conditioning. It's popular with Russian business people. ❸

Taksim and around

Taksim is the city's major business and shopping district, with a wide range of hotels aimed largely at tour groups and business travellers. Rates here are considerably higher than in other areas, but there are still one or two bargains to be found. It's not so convenient for sightseeing in Sultanahmet, but Taksim affords easy access to the Bosphorus and Beyoğlu, and comes into its own at night as the city's cultural, culinary and entertainment centre. At the northwestern end of İstiklâl Caddesi there are several hotels in **Tepebaşı**, centred on Meşrutiyet Caddesi, which you can reach by taking a tram along İstiklâl Caddesi to the halfway stop at Galatasaray School. There are also a couple of options close to the **Galata** tower; to get there, stay on the tram to the end of the line at Tünel. **Cihangir**, on the northern side of Sıraselviler Caddesi, is a bohemian backwater with splendid views of the Bosphorus, handy for the antiques district of Çukurcuma and boasting a fast-changing roster of small cafés and restaurants.

For the locations of hotels in this area, see the "Taksim and Beyoğlu" map on pp.162–163.

Off Taksim Square

Otel Avrupa Topçu Cad 32, Taksim ☎0212/250 9420, ℮otelavrupa@superonline.com. Small rooms with small beds and shared bathrooms – though some are en-suite with TV – but it's very friendly and there's a pleasant breakfast room. On a quiet street, this is a bargain in an area where most other hotels are in the luxury class. French and German spoken. ❸

Marmara Hotel Taksim Square ☎0212/251 4696 ⓦwww.themarmara.com.tr. Premier five-star hotel right on Taksim Square, one of İstanbul's landmark buildings – look up to the second floor and see guests working out in the gym. The 410 luxurious rooms (from $380) all have great views over Beyoğlu, and facilities include swimming pool, Turkish bath, spa and a number of restaurants – the best being the ground-floor *Brassiere* for some serious people-watching over coffee, pastries Turkish sweets. ❽

Hotel Perador Abdülhak Hamit Cad 54, Taksim ☎0212/238 8500, ℱ237 8337. Central location with rather dark and gloomy rooms, though they are furnished with fat armchairs in an additional lounge area. Favoured by European coach parties, rates are good value for the area. ❹

Otel Sato İstiklâl Cad, Bekar Sok 5, Beyoğlu ☎0212/245 2579. Very basic and unremarkable twin rooms, with bathrooms located in little more than a cupboard in the corner and no breakfast available. But it's clean and couldn't be better situated for İstanbul's nightlife. ISIC card carriers get an exceptional fifty-percent discount. ❸

Vardar Palace Hotel Sıraselviler Cad 54, Taksim ☎0212/252 2888, ⓦwww.vardarhotel.com. Renovated late nineteenth-century apartment building. There are no views at the back and rooms at the front are noisy, but it's a reasonable option for the Taksim area, with period furniture, spacious rooms and a friendly atmosphere. ❼

Tepebaşı and Galata

Büyük Londra Oteli Meşrutiyet Cad 117, Tepebaşı ☎0212/249 1025, ☏249 0438. Palatial, mid-nineteenth-century townhouse. The dusty rooms are a little worse for wear, cluttered with ancient junk, but some have fridges and the very top rooms have a view across the Golden Horn. Ernest Hemmingway stayed here in 1922 when he was a journalist covering the Turkish War of Independence. ❺

Galata Residence Bankalar Cad, Hacı Ali Sok 27, Galata ☎0212/292 4841, ☷www.galataresidence .com. Beautifully restored late-nineteenth-century building, offering one- and two-bedroom apartments with fully equipped kitchens. There's a roof-terrace restaurant and a café in the vaulted cellar, and cheaper apartments across the road more suited to business travellers. Monthly rates are $1500 for one to four persons in the main apartments and $750 for two in the cheaper apartments; overnight rates are expensive, but are discounted the longer you stay. ❽

Monopol Hotel Meşrutiyet Cad 223, Tepebaşı ☎0212/251 7326, ☏251 7333. Opposite the US Embassy, the comfortable rooms here have one to four beds, air-conditioning, satellite TV and a fridge. All in all, it's excellent value for such a prominent area, but the front rooms can get noisy at night when the Beyoğlu bars turn out. ❹

Pera Palas Meşrutiyet Cad 98–100, Tepebaşı ☎0212/251 4560, ☷www.perapalas.com. A contender for the most atmospheric hotel in İstanbul, the *Pera* deserves a visit if only for a coffee in the chandeliered American Bar or the exquisite tea-rooms and a visit to the "powder room". Built in the nineteenth century to accommodate Orient Express passengers, its rooms are marked with the names of famous occupants such as Agatha Christie and Graham Greene. Rooms start from $220, but package deals booked through tour operators abroad are better value. ❽

Cihangir

Cihangir Hotel Sıraselviler Cad, Arslan Yatağı Sok 33 ☎0212/251 5317, ☷www.cihangirhotel.com. Situated in a quiet backstreet in one of the town's more atmospheric quarters: excellent service, large rooms (some with tremendous Bosphorus views) with TVs, air-conditioning and minibars, and a huge buffet breakfast served on a commanding terrace. ❻

Family House Kutlu Sok 53 ☎0212/249 7351, ☏249 9670. Good value for small self-catering groups, since these apartments accommodate up to four people and have fully equipped kitchens. The interiors are rather gloomy and cheaply furnished, but the building is in a pleasant backstreet. Advance bookings essential in high season. ❼

Villa Zurich Akarsu Yokuşu Cad 44–46 ☎0212/293 0604, ☏249 0232. Delightful, good-value hotel offering large, well-equipped doubles with satellite TV, air-conditioning and a baby-sitting service. Breakfast is served on the rooftop terrace, which during the day serves an odd combination of Turkish and Japanese snacks. ❼

On the Bosphorus

The suburbs along the shores of the Bosphorus make an interesting alternative to staying in the city centre and are fairly easy to reach by bus or ferry. There are several cheap hotels on the Asian side, in **Kadıköy** and **Üsküdar** in particular, though despite being friendly, the staff here have little experience of tourists and English is unlikely to be spoken. There are no budget options on the European side of the Bosphorus – you pay a massive premium for the waterfront location at **Beşiktaş**, in one of the best hotels in İstanbul (and the same again at Bebek, further up the Bosphorus; see p.199).

Beşiktaş

Çırağan Palace & Kempinski Hotel Çırağan Cad 84 ☎0212/258 3377, ☷www.ciragan-palace .com. Twelve suites in an elaborately restored Ottoman palace right on the Bosphorus, on the European side, with every luxury imaginable for upwards of $1500 per night. For mere mortals, there are spacious rooms in the adjacent modern five-star *Kempinski*, though even here rooms cost from $750. Guests at both have use of the several restaurants serving gourmet cuisine, large outdoor pool and health club. ❽

Kadıköy

Hotel Eysan Rıhtım Cad 26 ☎0216/346 2440, ☏418 9582. In a prominent position opposite the ferry, this four-star hotel offers old-fashioned comfort, an attached restaurant and great views from of disorder, in fact the arrangement is meticulously logical. The first courtyard was the service area of the palace and open to all, while most of the second court and its attendant buildings were devoted to the Divan, or Council of State, and to those who had business with it. The pavilions of judges were located at the Orta Kapı (the entrance to the palace proper, between the first and second courtyards), in accordance with the tradition that justice should be dispensed at the gate of the palace.

The third courtyard was mainly given over to the palace school, an important imperial institution devoted to the training of civil servants, and it is only in the fourth courtyard that the serious business of state gives way to the more pleasurable aspects of life. Around the attractive gardens here are a number of pavilions erected by successive emperors in celebration of their victories. Here, the glorious views and sunsets could be enjoyed in privileged retreat from their three- to four-thousand-member retinue.

The various adjustments made to the structure and function of the buildings were indicative of the power shifts in the Ottoman Empire over the centuries. During the "Rule of the Harem" in the sixteenth century, for example, a passageway was opened between the Harem and the Divan, while in the eighteenth century, when the power of the sultan had declined, the offices of state were transferred away from the "Eye of the Sultan" (the window in the Divan through which a sultan could monitor proceedings) to the gateway that led to the palaces of the Grand Vezir known as the Sublime Port.

The **entrance** to Topkapı Palace is to the right and behind Aya Sofya, up Babıhümayun Caddesi. There is no entry fee to enter the first courtyard, while the first **ticket booth** is located to the right of the middle gate that leads through to the second courtyard, where you pay the $5 entry fee. Another ticket booth is located at the entrance of the Harem, where you pay a further $3 for the additional guided tour.

The first courtyard and Aya Irene

Entering the first courtyard from the street through Mehmet the Conqueror's **Bab-ı Hümayün**, the great defensive imperial gate opposite the fountain of Ahmet III, it's hard to believe that this is the outer courtyard of a former imperial palace: all is taxi ranks and coaches and their disembarking tour parties. Such a melee, however, is entirely in keeping with the origins of the first courtyard, which, as the palace's service area, was always open to the general public. The **palace bakeries** are behind a wall to the right of the courtyard and the buildings of the **imperial mint and outer treasury** (all currently closed) are behind the wall north of the church of Aya Irene. In front of Aya Irene were located the quarters of the straw-weavers and carriers of silver pitchers, around a central courtyard in which the palace firewood was stored. The church itself was variously employed as an armoury and storage space for archeological treasures.

Today, **Aya Irene**, "the Church of the Divine Peace", is generally closed to visitors, but can be opened for large groups by special request at the Directorate of Aya Sofya, located at the entrance of Aya Sofya. Otherwise, the only way to get in is during one of the occasional exhibitions or concerts held here, such as those during the summer İstanbul music festival. The original church was one of the oldest in the city, but it was rebuilt along with Aya Sofya after being burnt down in the Nika riots of 532. Around the semicircular apse is the only **synthronon** (seating space for clergy in the apse of a church) in İstanbul to have survived the Byzantine era. It has six tiers of seats with an ambulatory running behind the fourth tier.

TOPKAPI PALACE

1. Ortakapi or Middle Gate
2. Kitchens and cooks' quarters (Porcelain & glass collection)
3. Reconstructed kitchen
4. Stables and Harness rooms
5. Barrack of the Halberdiers
6. Hall of the Divan
7. Offices of the Divan
8. Inner Treasury (Arms & armour collection)
9. Gate of Felicity (Bab-üs Saadet)
10. Quarters of the White Eunuchs (Costume collection)
11. Throne room
12. Ahmet III library
13. Mosque of the school, now the library
14. Harem mosque
15. Court of the Room of the Robe
16. Room of the Robe of the Prophet
17. Rooms of the Relics of the Prophet
18. Hall of the Treasury (Sultans' portraits & miniature collection)
19. Hall of the Pantry (Museum Directorate)
20. Pavilion of Mehmet II, now the Treasury
21. Disrobing chamber of Selim II hamam
22. Site of Selim II hamam
23. Site of Selim II hamam boilers
24. Hall of the Expeditionary Force
25. Circumcision Köşkü
26. Terrace and bower

HAREM		
67	Pool	
68	Baghdad Köşkü	
69	Pool	
70	Revan Köşkü	
71	Tulip garden	
72	Mustafa Paşa Köşkü	
73	Physician's tower	
74	Mecidiye Köşkü-restaurant	
75	Third Gate	
76	Entry to the Harem (Carriage Gate)	
37	Mosque of the Black Eunuchs	
38	Court of the Black Eunuchs	
39	Barrack of the Black Eunuchs	
40	Princes' school	

41	Quarters of the Chief Black Eunuchs
42	Quarters of the Treasurer
43	Quarters of the Chamberlain
44	Aviary Gate (Kuşhane Kapisi)
45	Courtyard of the Women of the Harem
46	Kitchen of the Women
47	Hamam of the Women
48	Stairs to bedrooms
49	Laundry
50	Women's dormitory
51	Apartments of senior women
52	Court of women's hospital
53	Hospital hamam
54	Hospital kitchen quarters

55	Sultan Ahmet Kiosk
56	Harem Garden
57	Valide court
58	Valide's dining-room
59	Valide's bedroom
60	The Valide's hamam
61	Kadin's quarters
62	Golden Road
63	Ahmet III dining-room
64	The Throne Room Within
65	The Sultan's hamam
66	Osman III Terrace
67	Terrace of Selâmlik Garden
68	Apartment of the Selamlik (Sultan's Rooms)

Ortakapı, the second courtyard and the Divan

To reach the second courtyard you pass through the Bab-üs Selam, "the Gate of Salutations", otherwise known as the **Ortakapı**, or middle gate (where the entry fee is collected). Entering through Ortakapı, with the gateway to the third courtyard straight ahead of you, the Privy Stables of Mehmet II (closed to the public) are on your immediate left, while beyond them are the buildings of the Divan and the Inner Treasury and the entrance to the Harem. Opposite the Divan, on the right side of the courtyard, is the kitchen area.

The gardens between the paths radiating from the Ortakapı are planted with ancient cypresses and plane trees, rose bushes and lawns. Originally they would also have been resplendent with peacocks, gazelles and, most importantly, fountains. Running water, considered to have almost mystical properties by Muslims, was supplied in great quantity to the palace from the Byzantine cistern of Yerebatan Saray (see p.130). This **second courtyard** would have been the scene of pageantry during state ceremonies, when the sultan would occupy his throne beneath the Bab-üs Saadet, "the Gate of Felicity". At all times, even on one of the three days of the week when the courtyard was filled with petitioners to the Divan, silence reigned here, as people obeyed the rules of conduct imposed in the presence – actual or potential – of the sultan.

As you enter the buildings of the **Divan**, to the left of the courtyard, you'll see the metal grille in the Council Chamber (the first room on the left), called "the Eye of the Sultan". Through this he could observe the proceedings of the Divan, where the eminent imperial councillers sat in session and which took its name from the couch running around the three walls of the room. The building dates essentially from the reign of Mehmet the Conqueror, and the Council Chamber was restored to its sixteenth-century appearance in 1945, with some of the original İznik tiles and arabesque painting. The other two rooms of the Divan have retained the Rococo decorations of Ahmet III.

The **Divan tower** is visible from many vantage points all over the city. Rebuilt in 1825, the classical lines of the octagonal structure, with its tall windows between engaged Corinthian columns and its lead-covered conical spire, look rather out of place here, but it's certainly an impressive landmark and a nice foil for the domes of the Divan. The tower is opened for strictly chaperoned guided tours twice a day: admission to the balconies is not allowed, but the panoramic Bosphorus views through the windows are exceptional. Ask at the main ticket booth at the entrance of the second courtyard for times of tours.

Next to the Divan is another building from Mehmet the Conqueror's original palace, the **Inner Treasury**, a six-domed hall preceded by a double-domed vestibule and supported internally by three piers. The **arms and armour collection** here juxtaposes much exquisite craftsmanship with barbaric-looking exhibits, such as a seventeenth-century executioner's sword and some seven-foot-long double-handed swords of which wearied Europeans were relieved during one Turkish campaign or another. It is also interesting to compare the swords of various Ottoman sultans: that of the Conqueror appears altogether more effective than the finely wrought example attributed to that patron of the arts, Süleyman the Magnificent.

Across the courtyard are the **palace kitchens and cooks' quarters**, with their magnificent rows of chimneys, best seen in profile from a distance (for example from Kennedy Caddesi, which runs around the Marmara shore). Much of this complex was destroyed by fire in 1574, though the chimneys were reconstructed by Mimar Sinan, as were eight of the ten domes behind them (the two southernmost domes date to the reign of Mehmet the Conqueror). The ten kitchens, which had a staff of 1500, all served different purposes. The two at the far end, where sweets and *helva* were made, have been restored complete with a fascinating array of utensils. The other rooms house a collection of some of the finest porcelain in the world, an ever-changing display continually replenished from the vast Topkapı collection.

The third courtyard

As you pass through the **Bab-üs Saadet**, "the Gate of Felicity", the **Throne Room** is immediately in front of you. This building, mainly dating from the reign of Selim I, was where the sultan awaited the outcome of sessions of the Divan in order to give his assent or otherwise to their proposals. The grey marble building at the centre of the third courtyard, the **Ahmet III Library**, is not generally open to the public. It is restrained and sombre compared to his highly decorative fountain outside the gates of the palace.

The room to the right of the gate and throne room and library, southwest of the courtyard, is the **Hall of the Expeditionary Force**, sometimes referred to as the Hall of the Campaign Pages (Seferli Koğuşu), which houses a collection of embroidery and a very small selection from the imperial costume collection. The latter includes a charming little outfit of Selim I's – red with yellow circles – prompting the question of where he could have acquired his epithet "the Grim". Behind the hall is the hamam of Selim II, who fell there in a drunken stupor and died later of his injuries.

The Cage

The Cage was adopted by Ahmet I as an alternative to fratricide, which had become institutionalized in the Ottoman Empire since the days of Beyazit II. To avoid wars of succession, Beyazit ruled that a sultan should execute his brothers upon his accession to the throne. The Cage was introduced as a way around this practice, but in the event proved a less than satisfactory solution. After the death of their father, the younger princes would be incarcerated along with deaf mutes and a harem of concubines, while their eldest brother acceded to the throne. They remained in the suite of rooms of the Harem known in Turkish as *Kafes* (the Cage) until such time as they were called upon to take power themselves. The concubines never left the Cage unless they became pregnant, and great care was taken to prevent this, either by the removal of their ovaries or by the use of pessaries, since if it did occur they were immediately drowned.

The decline of the Ottoman Empire has in part been attributed to the institution of the Cage. The sultans who spent any length of time there emerged crazed, avaricious and debauched. Osman II, for example, enjoyed archery, but only when using live targets, including prisoners of war and his own pages. He was assassinated by the janissaries, to be replaced by Mustafa I, who had all but died of starvation in the Cage and was even more mad than his predecessor. He too was assassinated. The worst affected of all, however, was İbrahim, better known as Deli İbrahim (İbrahim the Mad). He spent 22 years in the Cage, and when they came to take him out he was so sure he was about to be assassinated that he had to be removed forcibly. His reign was characterized by sexual excess and political misrule (his mother Köşem once complained that there was not enough wood for the Harem fires and he responded by having his grand vizier executed). Eventually, in response to a rumour of harem intrigue, İbrahim had all of his 280 concubines (excluding his favourite, Şeker Para) drowned in the Bosphorus.

The Treasury

The **Imperial Treasury** is housed in the rooms that once functioned as the Pavilion of Mehmet II, which takes up most of the southeast side of the third courtyard, to the right of the entrance. The building is on two floors and a colonnaded terrace leads from the courtyard into the lower rooms, whose interior plasterwork, including shell-shaped niches, stalactite capitals and ogee (slightly pointed) arches over the windows, is typical of the fifteenth century. The first two rooms – the right-hand one of which was used as the *camekan* or disrobing chamber of the hamam of Selim II – are beautifully proportioned and domed. The last two rooms are at right angles, with an attractive loggia at the angle where they meet.

The first room contains a number of highly wrought and extremely beautiful objects, including a delicate silver model of a palace complete with tiny birds in the trees, a present to Abdül Hamid II from Japan. The next two rooms – memorials to the excess and bad taste of the megalomaniacal – are always thronged and there are certainly plenty of thrills to be had if you like your gemstones big and your precious metals abundant.

The big crowd-puller in room two is the **Topkapı Dagger**, which starred alongside Peter Ustinov in the Sunday matinee classic *Topkapı*. A present from Mahmut I to Nadir Shah that was waylaid and brought back when news of the shah's death reached Topkapı, the dagger is decorated with three enormous emeralds, one of which conceals a watch. In the third room the **Spoonmaker's Diamond**, the fifth largest diamond in the world, is invariably surrounded by a gawping crowd, which perhaps gives some impression of the effect it must have had during its first public appearance, adorning Mehmet IV's turban at his coronation in 1648. The rest of this room is a succession of increasingly grotesque and jewel-studded exhibits and you might well be tempted to make good your escape.

The fourth room boasts a jewel-encrusted throne and the hand and occipital bone of John the Baptist, but otherwise it's a relative haven of restraint and good taste. Ivory and sandalwood objects predominate, refreshingly simple materials whose comparative worth is determined by craftsmanship rather than quantity.

Across the courtyard from the Treasury, the Pavilion of the Holy Mantle houses the **Rooms of the Relics of the Prophet**, holy relics brought home by Selim the Grim after his conquest of Egypt in 1517. The relics were originally viewed only by the sultan, his family and his immediate entourage on days of special religious significance, but were opened to the public in 1962. They include a footprint, hair and a tooth of the Prophet Mohammed, as well as his mantle and standard, swords of the first four caliphs and a letter from the Prophet to the leader of the Coptic tribe. The most precious of the relics are kept behind glass, attractively arranged and lit.

Next to this, the former **Hall of the Treasury** houses a selection from Topkapı's **collection of paintings and miniatures**, but this is currently closed for restoration, with no clear indication as to when it will reopen. The miniatures date from the reign of Süleyman the Magnificent to that of Ahmet III, the Tulip Age, but above all they come from the reign of Murat III. He commissioned three works, the *Hünername* (the "Book of Accomplishments"), the *Shahanshahname* (the "Book of the King of Kings") and the *Surname* (the "Book of Festivals"), the first two of which glorified the exploits of the sultans, while the last was a depiction of the glorious parade that followed the circumcision ceremony of the sultan's son (nowadays Turks make home videos on the same theme).

The fourth courtyard

The **fourth courtyard** is entered through a passageway running between the Hall of the Treasury and the display of clocks and watches in the Silahdar Treasury. It consists of several gardens, each graced with pavilions, the most attractive of which – from where you get a totally new perspective of the city from Galata to Fatih – are located around a wide marble terrace beyond the tulip gardens of Ahmet III.

The **Baghdad Köşkü**, the cruciform building to the north of the terrace, is the only pavilion presently open to the public. It was built by Murat IV to celebrate the conquest of Baghdad in 1638. The exterior and cool, dark interior are tiled in blue, turquoise and white, and the shutters and cupboard doors are inlaid with tortoiseshell and mother-of-pearl. If you think this is redolent of unseemly excess, take a look at the attractive pool and marble fountain on the terrace, scene of debauched revels among İbrahim I and the women of his harem. Deli İbrahim, or **İbrahim the Mad**, emerged dangerously insane from 22 years in the Cage, his reign culminating in a fit of sexual jealousy when he ordered death by drowning in the Bosphorus for the 280 concubines of his harem – only one of them lived to tell the tale, when she escaped from the sack in which she was bound and was picked up by a passing French ship and taken to Paris.

The **Circumcision Köşkü**, in the Portico of Columns above the terrace, also dates from the reign of İbrahim the Mad. You'll have to peer through the windows to get any idea of the interior, but outside it's covered in İznik tiles of the sixteenth and early seventeenth centuries. There doesn't seem to be much of a design about these – any number of different patterns are represented – but they include some of the most beautiful panels from the very best İznik period. At the other end of the Portico of Columns is the **Revan Köşkü**, built to commemorate the capture of Erivan in the Caucasus by Mehmet IV.

The **Mecidiye Köşkü** – the last building to be erected at Topkapı – commands the best view of any of the Topkapı pavilions. It's been opened as the *Konyalı Café* (see p.176) and on a clear day from its garden terrace you can identify most of the buildings on the Asian shore of the Bosphorus.

The Harem

The **tour of the Harem** (daily 10am–4pm, every 30min from the Harem entrance in the second courtyard; $3) is extremely popular, so arrive early as tickets sell out and queues are massive later in the day. The tour (which lasts 1hr 40min) is conducted at breakneck speed, but can be interesting with a little background knowledge and a few pertinent questions.

The word "harem" means "forbidden" in Arabic; in Turkish it refers to a suite of apartments in a palace or private residence where the head of the household lived with his wives, odalisques (female slaves) and children. The Harem in Topkapı lies between the sultan's private apartments and the quarters of the Chief Black Eunuch. It consisted of over four hundred rooms, centred on the suites of the sultan and his mother, the Valide Sultan. Around these, in descending order of rank, were the apartments of the wives, favourites, sultan's daughters, princes, housekeepers, maids and odalisques. The Harem was connected to the outside world by means of the **Carriage Gate**, so-called because the odalisques would have entered their carriages here when they went on outings. To the left of the Carriage Gate as you enter the Harem is the Barracks of the Halberdiers of the Long Tresses, who carried logs and other loads into the Harem. The Halberdiers, who also served as imperial guardsmen, were only

The women of the harem

The women of the harem were so shrouded in mystery that they became a source of great fascination to the world in general. The most renowned among them was probably Haseki Hürrem, or Roxelana as she was known in the West, wife of Süleyman the Magnificent. Prior to their marriage, it was unusual for a sultan to marry at all, let alone to choose a wife from among his concubines. The marriage, and the subsequent installation of the harem women in the palace, established the women of the harem, and especially the **Valide Sultan** (the mother of the reigning sultan), in a position of unprecedented power. This was the beginning of a new age of harem intrigue, in which women began to take more control over affairs of state, often referred to as the "Rule of the Harem".

Roxelana began this new order in characteristic vein: she persuaded Süleyman to murder both his grand vizier, İbrahim Paşa, and his son, the heir apparent, Mustafa – the latter in order to make way for her own son, Selim the Sot. The favourite of Selim the Sot, **Nur Banu**, made a significant change to the layout of the harem when she became Valide Sultan in her turn. She moved her suite of apartments from one end of the Golden Road to the other, so that it was located next to that of her son, Murat III. She was now lodged near to the entrance of the Divan and could easily listen in on affairs of state. Nur Banu encouraged her son in debauchery (he fathered a total of 103 children, 54 of whom survived him) and persuaded him to murder his most able minister, the grand vizier Sokollu Mehmet Paşa.

The number of **odalisques** (female slaves) employed in the harem increased steadily with the decline of the Ottoman Empire and by the reign of Abdülaziz (1861–1876) there were 809 in Topkapı. Many were imported from Georgia and Caucasia for their looks, or were prisoners of war, captured in Hungary, Poland or Venice. Upon entering the harem, they would become the charges of the *haznedar usta*, who would teach them how to behave towards the sultan and the other palace inhabitants. The conditions in which the majority of these women lived were dangerously unhygienic and many of them died from vermin-carried and waterborne diseases, or from the cold of an İstanbul winter. The women who were chosen to enter the bedchamber of the sultan, however, were promoted to the rank of imperial odalisque, given slaves to serve them and pleasant accommodation. If they bore a child, they would be promoted to the rank of favourite or wife, with their own apartments. If the sultan subsequently lost affection for one of these women, he could give her in marriage to one of his courtiers. The following account of life in the Topkapı harem, given by Hafsa Sultan, a wife of Mustafa II (1695–1703), dispels a couple of popular myths about life there:

The claims that the sultan throws a handkerchief at the girl he prefers are quite untrue. The sultan asks the Chief Black Eunuch to call whichever of the girls he desires and his other women take her to the baths, perfume her body and dress her gracefully in clothes appropriate to the circumstances. The sultan sends the girl a gift and afterwards goes to the room where she is. There is no truth either in the claim that the girl crawls to the sultan's bed.

employed at certain hours and even then they were blinkered. The Carriage Gate and the Aviary Gate were both guarded by black eunuchs, who were responsible for running the harem, but only allowed to enter in daylight hours. At night the female housekeepers took charge and reported any unusual occurrences to the Chief Black Eunuch.

The **Court of the Black Eunuchs**, the first area to be visited on a tour, dates mainly from a rebuilding programme begun after the great fire of July 24, 1665. The fire, started by a malicious servant, damaged most of the Harem as well as the Divan. The tiles in the eunuchs' quarters date from the seventeenth century, suggesting that the originals were destroyed in the fire.

The *Altın Yol* or **Golden Road** ran the entire length of the Harem, from the quarters of the Black Eunuchs to the fourth courtyard. It was down this road in 1808 that the last of the great Valide Sultans, Aimée Dubbucq de Rivery, fled with her son Mahmut to escape the deaf mutes, hired assassins of the janissaries. The life of the prince was saved by a Georgian odalisque called Cevri Khalfa, who flung a brazier of red-hot coals into the faces of the pursuers. The prince escaped to become Mahmut II, later given the title of "Reformer". Strategically located at the beginning of the Golden Road were the **apartments of the Valide Sultan**, also rebuilt after 1665. They include a particularly lovely domed dining room. A passageway leads from her apartments to those of the women she controlled, the senior women of the court. These were well-designed, compact apartments, with an upper gallery in which bedding was stored, windows and a hearth.

Beyond the Valide Sultan's apartments, to the north, are some of the most attractive rooms of the palace. These were the apartments and reception rooms of the *selamlik*, the sultan's own rooms. The largest and grandest of them is the **Hünkar Sofrası**, the Imperial Hall, where the sultan entertained visitors. Another important room in this section is a masterwork of the architect Sinan: the **bedchamber of Murat III**, covered in sixteenth-century İznik tiles and kitted out with a marble fountain and, opposite, a bronze fireplace surrounded by a panel of tiling representing plum blossom.

The northernmost rooms of the Harem are supported by immense piers and vaults, providing capacious basements that were used as dormitories and storerooms. Below the bedchamber is a large indoor **swimming pool**, with taps for hot and cold water, where Murat is supposed to have thrown gold to women who pleased him. Next to the bedchamber is the light and airy **library of Ahmet I**, with windows overlooking both the Bosphorus and the Golden Horn; beyond this is the **dining room of Ahmet III**, whose walls are covered in wood panelling painted with bowls of fruit and flowers, typical of the extravagant tulip-loving sultan. To the southwest of the bedchamber are two rooms originally thought to be the notorious **Cage** (see box on p.123), though this is no longer believed to be the case. The Cage was actually situated in various rooms on the floor above. Other areas often visited on a tour include the **dormitories** of the favourite women, located up stone stairs on a beautiful terrace overlooking the fourth courtyard, and the **boating pool** of Murat III.

It's usual to depart from the Harem by way of the **Aviary Gate**, or Kuşhane Kapısı. One of the most infamous of all the Valide Sultans, Mahpeyker Sultan, also known as *Köşem*, "the leader", was assassinated here. She was the effective ruler of the Ottoman empire during the reigns of her two sons, Murat IV and İbrahim the Mad, and since she was not banished to the old palace after the death of İbrahim (as was customary), she also ruled during the reign of her grandson Mehmet IV. She was eventually murdered on the orders of a jealous rival, the new Valide Turhan Hatice, by the Chief Black Eunuch. At the age of 80 the toothless old woman was stripped naked and strangled, after allegedly putting up a ferocious struggle.

Gulhane Parkı and around

Gulhane Parkı surrounds Topkapı Palace on all sides and was once the extended gardens of the sultans. It is now a public park (open sunrise–sunset; $0.50) with a relaxed atmosphere, particularly at weekends when the crowds of families indulge in cheap traditional Turkish fast foods and listen to free concerts by *arabesk* musicians or pop performers. The park is also home to a rather sordid little zoo, with caged dogs and threadbare camels, though other nearby attractions are worthier of attention: the Darphane, or Royal Mint; the city's Archeology Museum; and the ceramics on display in the Çinili Köşk, or Tiled Pavilion.

The Darphane

Located next to Gulhane Parkı, though also entered from the first courtyard of Topkapı Palace, the **Darphane** (Royal Mint; Wed–Sun 9.30am–5.30pm; free; Ⓦwww.tarihvakfi.org.tr) was moved to this site in 1715, although there is some evidence that coins were struck in the vicinity as early as the sixteenth century. Most of the current buildings date from the 1830s and the reign of Mahmut II. The monetary reforms introduced by Abdülmecit between 1839 and 1861 saw the introduction of modern steam-powered machinery to improve the quality of coins produced. However, the whole place was largely abandoned in 1967, with the buildings and remaining equipment left undisturbed until the mid-1990s. It's now run by the Turkish Economic and Social History Foundation, which has lovingly restored the complex, opening part as a fascinating museum where smelting equipment, imported European coin presses and assorted artefacts are displayed. There's also exhibition space and a theatre where high-brow Turkish plays are performed during the summer.

The Archeology Museum

The Archeology Museum complex, which includes the Museum of the Ancient Orient and Çinili Köşk (see p.129 & p.130 respectively), can be entered either through Gulhane Parkı or from the first courtyard of the Topkapı Palace.

The **Archeology Museum** itself (Arkeoloji Müzesi; daily except Mon 9.30am–5.30pm; $3) is centred on the excavations at Sidon in 1887 of Hamdi Bey, the Director of Ancient Antiquities. These brought to light a group of sarcophagi, together with other monuments of Phoenician origin but of quite disparate styles – evidence of the variety of influences absorbed into Phoenician culture from neighbouring civilizations.

The sarcophogi are housed in the two rooms to the left of the entrance on the ground floor. The **Lycian Sarcophagus**, in the room immediately on your left, depicts centaurs, sphinxes and griffons, as well as scenes from Greek mythology. It is in the Lycian style, but the carvings show a Peloponnesian influence in the stocky bodies and broad faces of the human figures. In the same room are the anthropoid sarcophagi from Sidon, which illustrate the fifth-century BC fashion for Egyptian models in Greek sculpture. The **Tabnit Sarcophagus**, the oldest Sidon discovery, is in fact Egyptian in origin. A hieroglyphic inscription on the chest of this alabaster mummy case states that it belonged to an Egyptian commander named Penephtah and a later inscription suggests that Tabnit, himself the father of a pharaoh, was its second occupant.

The **Sidamara Sarcophagus**, again in the first room on the left, dates from the third century AD and is the most important remaining example of its type. This room is full of similar sarcophagi, discovered elsewhere in Anatolia; on many of them a hand-held drill has been used for much of the carving, especially of the foliage, which is roughly executed in comparison with the Sidon sarcophagi.

The **Alexander Sarcophagus** is in the second room to the left of the entrance lobby. It's covered with scenes of what is presumed to be Alexander the Great hunting and in battle, but since Alexander himself is known to have been buried in Alexandria this is no longer believed to be his sarcophagus. Despite its Hellenistic influences, it is ascribed variously by different sources to a ruler of the Seleucid dynasty or to the Phoenician Prince Abdolonyme, but there seems to be agreement in dating the sarcophagus to the end of the fourth century BC. The metal weapons originally held by warriors and huntsmen on the sarcophagi were stolen prior to the excavations of Hamdi Bey, presumably when the burial chambers were looted.

The Ionic architecture of another of the Sidon sarcophagi, the **Sarcophagus of the Mourning Women**, is repeated in the exterior of the museum itself. This one shows eighteen members of the harem of King Straton (who died in 360 BC) in various poses of distress and mourning. To drive the point home, a funeral cortege is shown proceeding around the lid of the sarcophagus. As with the Alexander Sarcophagus, traces of the original paintwork can still be seen on the surface of the marble.

The museum's **upper rooms** are a joy: beautiful, well-lit displays, thorough explanatory aids, audio-visual back-up and a comfortable environment that encourages visitors to linger, a far cry from Turkey's provincial museums where nervous curators follow you about switching lights on and off. Exhibits worth mentioning range from jewellery discovered at Troy – some beautiful gold work including a head ornament with leaves as fine as paper – and Phrygian finds from near Arslantaş, the lion rock-cut tomb near Afyon Karahisar.

The Museum of the Ancient Orient

The **Museum of the Ancient Orient** (Eskı Şark Eserleri Müzesi; daily except Mon 9.30am–4.30pm; $3) – just to the north of the main entrance to the museum complex – contains a small but dazzling collection of Anatolian, Egyptian and Mesopotamian artefacts. The late Hittite basalt lions flanking the entrance look newly hewn, but they actually date from the ninth century BC, giving a taste of the incredible state of preservation of some of the exhibits inside.

These include the oldest peace treaty known to mankind, the **Treaty of Kadesh** (1280–1269 BC), which was signed when a battle fought on the River Orontes (today's Ası Nehri in Anatolia), between Pharaoh Ramses II and the Hittite king Muvatellish, ended in a stalemate. The treaty includes a cease-fire agreement and pledges of a mutual exchange of political refugees, and was originally engraved onto silver tablets. None of these survive, though the treaty was also inscribed in hieroglyphics on the mortuary temple of Ramses II in Thebes and the copy on display in the museum was uncovered during excavations at the site of the Hittite capital of Hattuşaş (see p.730). A copy of the treaty decorates the entrance to the UN building in New York.

The blue-and-yellow **animal relief** in the corridor beyond the first room dates from the reign of Nebuchadnezzar (604–562 BC), the last hero-king of Babylonia, when it would have lined the processional way in Babylon, leading from the Ishtar Gate to a sanctuary where New Year festivities were held. Other exhibits in the museum were taken from the palace-museum of Nebuchadnezzar, located at the Ishtar Gate. Another massive relief, in Room 8, depicts the **Hittite king Urpalla** presenting gifts of grapes and grain to a vegetation god, who is three times his own size and wearing a rather attractive pair of curly-toed boots. This is a plaster copy of a relief found at İvriz Kaya near Konya, dating from the eighth century BC.

Other exhibits include a **Sumerian** love poem and a tablet of Sumerian proverbs dating from the eighteenth century BC, and a figure of a duck, with an inscription that identifies it as a standard weight belonging to a priest called Musallim Marduk. It weighs about 30kg and has been dated to around 2000 BC, making it the oldest known standard measure.

Çinili Köşk

The graceful **Çinili Köşk** (Tiled Pavilion) – a few metres north of the Museum of the Ancient Orient – is the oldest secular building in İstanbul, its design and decoration influenced by Selçuk art. Built in 1472 as a kind of grandstand, from which the sultan could watch sporting activities such as wrestling or polo, it now houses the **Museum of Turkish Ceramics** (daily except Mon 9.30am–4.30pm; free). Tiles of equal quality to those in Topkapı Palace and İstanbul's older mosques can be seen here and, while there is no substitute for seeing tile panels *in situ*, here they can be inspected at close quarters and in good lighting conditions, along with well-written explanations of the different periods in the history of Turkish ceramics. Look particularly for polychrome tiles of the mid-sixteenth to mid-seventeenth centuries, dating from the longest and most successful period of tile production. Interesting exhibits include a mosque lamp from the Sokollu Mehmet Paşa Camii (see p.135), a ceramic coffee cooler in which beans were placed after roasting and before grinding and Murat III's attractive little fountain in the wall of the last room of all, after the İznik collection.

Yerebatan Sarayı

From Topkapı Palace or the Aya Sofya, it's a quick stroll across the tram tracks on Caferıye Sok and down the hill for a few metres to the entrance of the **Yerebatan Sarayı** (daily 9am–6pm; $6), the "Sunken Palace" – also known as the Basilica Cistern. It's one of several underground cisterns, this one buried under the very core of Sultanahmet (underneath the tramline, the Tourist Police headquarters and, possibly, part of the grounds of Aya Sofya) and is the first to have been extensively excavated. Although generally crowded, it still warrants a prolonged exploration: the entrance is on Caferıya Sok, with the exit on Yerebatan Caddesi, above the largest hall of the cistern.

Probably built by the emperor Constantine in the fourth century, and enlarged by Justinian in the sixth, the cistern was supplied by aqueducts with water from the Belgrade Forest and it in turn supplied the Great Palace and later Topkapı Palace. The cistern fell into disuse in the century after the Ottoman conquest and its existence was only brought to public attention in 1545 by the Frenchman **Petrus Gyllius**. He had been led to it by local residents, whose houses were built over the cistern and who had sunk wells into it. They even kept boats on the water from which they could fish its depths – it is said that Gyllius' interest was first aroused when he found fresh fish being sold in the streets nearby.

Restorations were undertaken in 1987: 50,000 tons of mud and water were removed, the walls were covered to make them impermeable and eight of the columns were sheathed in concrete to fortify the structure. The construction of raised pathways to replace the rowboats used by early tourists may seem a desecration, but they do facilitate a leisurely examination of interesting bits of masonry, as does the careful spotlighting.

The largest covered cistern in the city, at 140m by 70m, Yerebatan held 80,000 cubic metres of water. The small brick **domes** are supported by 336 columns, many of which have Corinthian capitals. The columns' varied styles – one is even carved with a tree-trunk pattern, resembling the remains of columns found beyond the University on Ordu Caddesi – probably indicate that they were made from the recycled remnants of earlier structures. The two **Medusa heads** at the southwest corner, brought to light when the cistern was drained, are simply thought to have been used as construction material – this would explain the fact that they would have been totally submerged and invisible.

The Hippodrome

The arena of the **Hippodrome**, formerly the cultural focus of the Byzantine Empire, is now the site of a long and narrow municipal park known as **At Meydanı**, or Square of Horses. This rather unprepossessing strip of land, with a road running around its perimeter, is overshadowed by the Palace of İbrahim Paşa on one side and Sultanahmet Camii on the other, but its historical significance predates that of most other major monuments in İstanbul.

A stadium was first constructed by the Roman emperor Septimius Severus in 200 AD and later enlarged by Constantine the Great for the performance of court ceremonies and games. Estimated to have held up to 100,000 people, the original orientation and dimensions of the 480-metre-long arena have been more or less preserved by the present-day park, although its amphitheatre was destroyed in the construction of the Sultan Ahmet mosque. Nonetheless, the Hippodrome continued to be a focus of state ceremony for the Ottoman sultans.

The large open space would now be little more than a pleasant respite from the surrounding hubbub if interest were not aroused by the monuments strewn, in seemingly haphazard fashion, along its length. Down at the south end of the park are three survivors of the array of obelisks, columns and statues that originally adorned the *spina*, the raised central axis of the arena, around which chariots raced.

The northernmost of these, the **Egyptian Obelisk**, was originally 60m tall, but only the upper third survived shipment from Egypt in the fourth century. The obelisk was commissioned to commemorate the campaigns of Thutmos III in Egypt during the sixteenth century BC, but the scenes on its base commemorate its erection in Constantinople under the direction of Theodosius I. Among the figures depicted are dancing maidens with musicians,

Crowd trouble in Constantinople

The **Hippodrome factions** originated in ancient Roman trade guilds, which in Byzantine times developed further associations: "the Blues" were generally upper-class, politically conservative and orthodox regarding religion; while "the Greens" were from the lower classes and more radical in their political and religious views.

The factions were a focus for serious rivalry in Constantinople, centred on the circus events in the Hippodrome. In 532 the rivalry was forgotten when members of the Blue faction combined forces with the Greens against the emperor Justinian in protest at heavy taxation and in the resulting **riots** – which derived their name from the battle cry *Nika* (Victory) – much of the city, including the church of Aya Sofya, was destroyed. It was the former courtesan, Empress Theodora, who eventually shamed Justinian to action and, as a result, 30,000 Greens and a few hundred Blues were trapped and massacred by the forces of General Belisarius in the Hippodrome. Chariot racing was banned for some time after this and it was a number of years before the Green faction recovered to the extent that they could compete in either the sporting or the political arena.

Theodosius and his family watching a chariot race (south side) and a group of captives kneeling to pay homage to Theodosius (west side).

The **Serpentine Column** comes from the Temple of Apollo at Delphi, where it was dedicated to the god by the 31 Greek cities that defeated the Persians at Plataea in 479 BC. The column was brought to Constantinople by Constantine the Great. The three intertwining bronze serpents originally had heads, which splayed out in three directions from the column itself. The jaw of one of the serpents was lopped off by Mehmet the Conqueror on his arrival in Constantinople as an act of defiance against such symbols of idolatry and the remaining heads were probably removed in an act of vandalism at the beginning of the eighteenth century. However, one of the heads is on display in the "İstanbul through the ages" exhibit at the Archeology Museum.

The third ancient monument on the *spina* is a huge lump of masonry, a 32-metre-high column of little or no decorative or practical worth. The emperor Constantine Porphyrogenitus was presumably of this opinion in the tenth century, since he restored the pillar and sheathed it in gold-plated bronze. This ornamentation was taken and melted down by the Crusaders during the sacking of Constantinople in 1204. The origins of the column, known as the **Column of Constantine**, are uncertain, but an inscription records that it was already decayed when Constantine restored it.

Sultanahmet Camii: the Blue Mosque

It is impossible to remain for long in the Hippodrome without becoming aware of the **Sultanahmet Camii**, the Blue Mosque, on its southeastern side. In the unlikely event that the mosque's imposing size fails to impress, your attention will doubtless be drawn to it by some persistent youth who wishes to guide you around it. Despite its fame, however, Sultanahmet is not really the place to start developing a taste for oriental interiors: here, it is size and visibility that count, rather than any architectural or aesthetic merit.

Before construction was begun, in 1609, objections were raised to the plan of a six-minareted mosque – partly because it was said to be unholy to rival the six minarets of the mosque at Mecca, but also because it would be a great drain on state revenues. The true cause of the objections, however, probably had more to do with the need to destroy several palaces belonging to imperial ministers to make way for construction.

From the **outside**, the building is undeniably impressive, particularly on the all-important approach from Topkapı Palace on the opposite side of the Hippodrome. The imposing mass of grey stone is visible for miles around on its hilltop vantage point and is instantly recognizable thanks to the six minarets. Above the level of the courtyard the mosque is a mass of shallow domes and domed turrets, hardly broken by a single straight line. The **courtyard**, best approached from the attractive and graceful west portal, is surrounded by a portico of thirty small domes and has the same dimensions as the mosque itself.

You can enter through the courtyard, despite signs in English and German asking visitors to use the side entrance facing Aya Sofya. Lone tourists, as opposed to groups, will not create ill-will by entering here as long as they are suitably covered (limbs for men and women, heads for women) and do not intrude on worshippers. At the side entrance, you will invariably encounter large crowds.

Inside, four **"elephant foot" pillars** (so called because of their size) of five metres in diameter impose their disproportionate dimensions on the interior, appearing squashed against the outer walls and obscuring parts of the building from every angle. But it's the predominantly blue colour of the internal decoration that is the biggest draw, from which the name "Blue Mosque" is derived. The **tiles** – over twenty thousand of them – constituted such a tall order that the İznik kilns were practically exhausted. Still in evidence are the clear bright colours of the best period of İznik ware, including flower and tree panels as well as more abstract designs. However, they are often difficult to see in the gloomy interior and the best panels, in the galleries, are all but obscured by the columns of the arcades.

At the northeast corner of the Sultanahmet complex is the richly decorated and elegant **royal pavilion**, approached by ramp and giving access to the sultan's loge inside the mosque – the ramp meant that the sultan could ride his horse right up to the door of his chambers. The royal pavilion now houses a **Museum of Carpets** (Halı Müzesi; Tues–Sat 9am–4pm; $1.50), which traces the history of Turkish carpets through the ages and includes some ancient, priceless pieces.

Between May 1 and September 30 there is a free **sound and light show** conducted from the small seating area in the park between the Blue Mosque and Aya Sofya. Images are projected onto the surrounding buildings to a musical and spoken accompaniment – performed in English, French, Turkish and German on alternate evenings from 7.30pm onwards. Unfortunately, the event attracts a large number of hustlers.

The tomb of Sultan Ahmet

Outside the precinct wall to the northwest of the mosque is the *türbe* or **tomb of Sultan Ahmet** (Tues–Sat 9am–4pm; free), decorated, like the mosque, with seventeenth-century İznik tiles. Buried here along with the sultan are his wife and three of his sons, two of whom (Osman II and Murat IV) ruled in their turn. This successive rule of brothers was only possible because Sultan Ahmet had introduced the institution of the Cage (see box on p.123), thus relieving himself and his sons of the burden of fratricide upon accession to the throne. Unfortunately, both Ahmet's own brother Mustafa and his son Osman were completely mad and unfit to rule by the time they left the Cage to take up the reins of office and Murat IV only escaped this fate by succeeding to the throne at the age of 10, before the conditions in the Cage had affected him.

İbrahim Paşa Sarayı: the Museum of Turkish and Islamic Art

The **İbrahim Paşa Sarayı** (Palace of İbrahim Paşa), on the eastern side of the Hippodrome, is now the **Museum of Turkish and Islamic Art** (Türk ve İslam Eserleri Müzesi; daily except Mon 9am–5pm; $1.50), an attractive, well-planned museum, containing one of the best-exhibited collections of Islamic artefacts in the world. The sixteenth-century setting of cool, darkened rooms around a central garden courtyard obviates the necessity for expensive technology to keep the sun off the remarkable exhibits, which highlight the wealth and complexity of Islamic art and culture. The museum also boasts an excellent courtyard **café**.

The palace itself is one of the few private Ottoman residences to have survived – at least in part – the fires that periodically destroy large areas of the city. Much of the building has, however, disappeared and what remains was rebuilt in stone – to the original plan – in 1843. Originally completed in 1524 for İbrahim Paşa, Süleyman the Magnificent's newly appointed grand vizier, the palace is a fitting memorial to one of the most able statesmen of his time, whose abilities were matched only by his accumulation of wealth and power. His status can be judged from the proportions of the palace's rooms and by its prominent position next to the Hippodrome: later sultans were to use its balconies to watch the festivities below. İbrahim controlled the affairs of war and state of the Ottoman Empire for thirteen years and fell from grace partly as a result of the schemings of Süleyman's wife, Roxelana. Even so, it doesn't seem unreasonable that Süleyman should distrust a servant who could say to a foreign ambassador: "If I command that something should be done, and he [the sultan] has commanded to the contrary, my wishes and not his are obeyed." The strangled body of İbrahim Paşa was found in a room of Topkapı Palace. Süleyman the Magnificent ordered it to be buried in an unmarked grave and İbrahim Paşa's possessions, not least the palace, reverted to the crown.

The museum exhibits

The main concentration of exhibits in the museum deals with Selçuk, Mamluk and Ottoman Turkish art, but there are also several important Timurid and Persian works on display.

The **Selçuk Empire**, centred in Konya, preceded that of the Ottomans in Anatolia and it is interesting to trace influences from one to the other. Ceramic techniques, for example, were obviously well developed by the Selçuks, judging from the wall tiles on display in the museum, and the wood-carvings from Konya also suggest a high level of craftsmanship and artistry, which may have influenced later Ottoman work.

Other impressive exhibits include sixteenth-century Persian miniatures, which like many Ottoman works defy the Islamic stricture against depicting human or animal forms. Pictures in lacquer and leather-bound Persian manuscripts feature a tiger ripping into an antelope and another of a dancing girl dated 1570. The tiny Sancak Korans were meant for hanging on the standard of the Ottoman imperial army in a jihad (holy war), so that the word of God would precede the troops into battle.

The **Great Hall** of the palace is occasionally devoted to special exhibitions about aspects of Islamic art, but more usually it houses a collection of **Turkish carpets** that is among the finest in the world. These range from tattered remains dating from the thirteenth century to carpets that once adorned İstanbul's palaces, some so massive that they weigh in at thousands of kilograms. On the basement floor, there is an exhibition of the **folk art** of the *Yörük* tribes of Anatolia, which includes examples of a *kara çadır* (literally "black tent", a domicile woven from goat hair that can still be seen in central and eastern Anatolia) and a *topakev* (a tent constructed around a folding frame, used by nomads in Anatolia and Mongolia for over a thousand years). There is also a fascinating display of what life was like in a late-Ottoman wooden house in Bursa.

The Hamam of Roxelana

The double-domed building between the Sultanahmet Camii and Aya Sofya is the **Hamam of Roxelana** (Haseki Hürrem Sultan Hamami; daily except Tues 9.30am–5pm; free), built by Mimar Sinan in 1556 to replace the Byzantine baths of Zeuxippus on the same site and named in honour of Süleyman's wife, Roxelana. The 75-metre-long hamam served the worshippers at the mosque of Aya Sofya. The hamam has been restored with stained-glass windows and varnished wooden doors and original marble fountains in the changing rooms.

Administered by the Ministry of Culture, the building now serves as a show-room for traditional handwoven carpets and kilims. Despite its atmospheric setting, it's nothing more than a glorified carpet shop. The pieces on sale are produced to traditional designs from different regions, each one being the work of a single, named weaver. Prices aren't cheap, with regular knotted carpets selling at $300 per metre and finer examples for as much as $650. There is also a small photo display of the dyeing and weaving processes.

Sokollu Mehmet Paşa Camii

A pleasant couple of minutes' walk from the southwest corner of the Hippodrome leads down the steep Mehmet Paşa Yokuşu to **Sokollu Mehmet Paşa Camii** (open at prayer times only, but the *imam* may be around to unlock it during the day). This, one of Mimar Sinan's later buildings (1571), appears to have been omitted almost entirely from tourist itineraries. Sokollu Mehmet Paşa, who commissioned the mosque, was the last grand vizier of Süleyman the Magnificent and it was his military expertise that later saved the Ottoman Empire from the worst effects of the dissolute rule of Selim the Sot. He was eventually assassinated as a result of the intrigues of Nur Banu, the mother of Murat III, who was jealous of his power.

The large mosque **courtyard** is surrounded on three sides by the rooms of the *medrese*, now occupied by a boys' Koran school (the boys inhabit the dervish lodge at the back of the mosque and can be seen seated in the porch studying the Koran during term time). At the centre of the courtyard is a handsome fountain with a pretty upcurved parapet to its dome.

The **interior** of the mosque is distinguished by the height of its dome and by the impressive display of İznik tiles on its east wall. These are from the best period of Turkish ceramics: the white is pure, the green vivid and the red intense. Calligraphic inscriptions are set against a jungle of enormous carnations and tulips, and the designs and colours are echoed all around the mosque and in the conical cap of the *mimber*, the tiling of which is unique in İstanbul. While the stained-glass windows are copies, some of the original, extremely delicate **paintwork** can be seen in the northwest corner below the gallery and over the entrance. Embedded in the wall over the entrance and above the *mihrab* are pieces of the Kaaba from Mecca.

Around three sides of the mosque, a **gallery** is supported on lozenge-capitalled marble columns. With permission from the *imam*, who will hover during your visit, you can have a look up here and see the mosque interior from a different angle.

Küçük Ayasofya Camii

Located a couple of hundred metres below the Blue Mosque, downhill along Mehmet Paşa Yokuşu, is **Küçük Ayasofya Camii**, the "small mosque of Aya Sofya" (open prayer times only). Like its larger namesake on the opposite side of the Hippodrome, it was built as a church in the sixth century. It was originally named after two Roman soldiers, **Sergius** and **Bacchus**, who were martyred for their faith and later became the patron saints of Christians in the Roman army, but it was renamed because of its resemblance to Aya Sofya. It is believed to have pre-dated the larger church, but this is not certain; all that is known is that it was built between 527 and 536 to service the palace of Hormisdas. The church was converted into a mosque comparatively early in the sixteenth century during the reign of Beyazit II.

Despite imperfections in its execution, this is an attractive building and it makes an interesting comparison with Aya Sofya since it is virtually a scale model of the larger building. Like most Byzantine churches of this era, its **exterior** is unprepossessing brick and only inside can the satisfying proportions be properly appreciated. It is basically an octagon with semicircular niches at its diagonals, inscribed in a rectangle, but both these shapes are extremely irregular. This has been variously ascribed to a pragmatic solution to an awkward space at planning stage, or to shoddy workmanship, and while the latter seems to be the more likely explanation, the irregularities certainly don't detract from the general effect. The original marble facing and gold leaf have vanished, but a frieze honouring Justinian, Theodora and St Sergius runs around the architrave under the gallery. It's worthwhile, for the sake of the view, to ask permission to visit the **gallery**, but put on a pair of wooden clogs before you go up as it's filthy upstairs.

The sea walls and the Great Palace

At Küçük Ayasofya Camii you're almost down at the Sea of Marmara and close to the best-preserved section of the **sea walls**, built in 439 by Cyrus, prefect of the East. They originally stretched from Saray Burnu to the city walls of Constantine the Great and were later extended by Theodosius to meet his land walls, with thirteen gates piercing the eight-kilometre course. Theophilus, the last Iconoclast emperor, rebuilt the walls in the ninth century to hold off a possible Arab invasion.

Nowadays the best way to see the walls is by train, since the tracks run along their length and on out of the city; indeed parts were destroyed when the rail lines were built. The best-preserved remains are a stretch of a couple of kilometres between Ahır Kapı, near the Cankurtaran train station, and Kumkapı, with a walkway along Kennedy Caddesi.

The Palace of Bucoleon and the Great Palace

About halfway between Küçük Ayasofya Camii and the Cankurtaran train station the facade of the Palace of Bucoleon, a seaside annex to the **Great Palace of the Byzantine emperors**, is one of the most melancholy and moving survivors of Constantinople. The Great Palace was an immense structure, covering around five square kilometres from Sultanahmet to the sea walls. At its height it consisted of several separate palaces, including the Palace of Bucoleon and the Magnaura Palace – substantial sections of which also survive. In 1204 the palace was taken over by the Crusaders and a description by one illuminates the splendours they discovered:

Within the palace there were fully 500 halls all connected with one another and all made with gold mosaic. And in it were fully 30 chapels, great and small, and there was one of them that was called the Holy Chapel, which was so rich and noble that there was not a hinge or a band nor any other small part that was not all of silver, and there was no column that was not of jasper or porphyry or some other precious stone.

By the time the Latins left in 1261, the palace was virtually destroyed, and funds were never found to repair it.

It's easy to miss what's left of the **Palace of Bucoleon**, especially if you pass at speed along Kennedy Caddesi. It is draped in beautiful red vine and set back from the road with a little park in front. Three enormous marble-framed windows set high in the wall offer glimpses of the remains of a vaulted room behind. Below the windows, marble corbels give evidence of a balcony that would have projected over a marble quay (the waters of the Marmara once reached almost as far as the palace walls). For the rest of the Great Palace you'll need a lively imagination: you could wander 200m along Kutlugün Sokak to visit the **Başdoğan carpet centre**, where shop owners allow free access to the impressive complex of vaulted basements, or travel further down towards the coast where fragments of wall and ancient palace, on streets or tucked away in back-lots, are all that survive. Further sections of the palace exist under land currently belonging to the *Four Seasons Hotel*. Excavated in 1998, these are said to contain a vaulted chapel with some frescoes still intact.

The Mosaic Museum

The other substantial reminders of the Great Palace are the mosaics displayed in the **Mosaic Museum** (Büyüksaray Mozaik Müzesi; daily except Mon 9am–4.30pm; $1), 500m inland from the Palace of Bucoleon, on Torun Sokak. It can be reached by running the gauntlet of salespeople in the **Arasta Çarşısı** – a renovated street-bazaar selling tourist gifts, whose seventeeth-century shops were originally built to pay for the upkeep of the nearby Sultanahmet Camii.

Many of the mosaics in the museum are presented *in situ*, so that some idea of their original scale and purpose can be imagined. The building has been constructed so that some of the mosaics are viewed from a catwalk above, but can also be examined more closely by descending to their level. These remains were part of a mosaic peristyle, an open courtyard surrounded by a portico. To the south of the portico and down to the Palace of Bucoleon were the private apartments of the emperor, while the public sections of the palace were located to the north. Among the mosaics, which probably date from Justinian's rebuilding programme of the sixth century, are various portrayals of animals in their natural habitats, as well as domestic scenes. These include a vivid portrayal of an elephant locking a lion in a deadly embrace with its trunk and two children being led on the back of a camel. More hefty chunks of Byzantine marble, again from the palace, are contained in the museum garden, while a further section of palace wall can be seen in the car park opposite.

Eminönü and around

Once the maritime gateway to the city, **Eminönü** remains one of the largest and most convenient transport hubs, where buses, ferries, trams and trains converge. **Sirkeci train station** here is effectively the first and last station of the European rail network (there's a helpful tourist office inside the station); while the Eminönü **waterfront** – with its line of ferry terminals and small fishing boats serving up fried-fish sandwiches to passing commuters – is likely to be most people's first introduction to the **Golden Horn** (see box on p.139), the inlet of water that divides the European shore. Eminönü is the place to catch a ferry up the Bosphorus or a bus across Galata bridge, but there are also several notable attractions in the area, especially the famous spice bazaar and a couple of worthy mosques, including the prominent landmark, the Yeni Camii.

Eminönü is within easy reach of Sultanahmet. Simply catch the tram for three stops to the end of the line, or walk the couple of kilometres down the hill, through the area's commercial backstreets, invariably thronged with *hamals* (stevedores) bent double under burdens twice their size.

Cağaloğlu

From Sultanahmet, it's a simple matter to follow the tramline past the northern walls of Topkapı Palace down to Eminönü. But the alternative route is to continue along Yerebatan Caddesi as it climbs the hill into the district of **Cağaloğlu** and then turn down Ankara Caddesi into Eminönü. Cağaloğlu was traditionally the centre of Turkey's newspaper industry, but with the exception of the old and well-respected *Cumhuriyet*, the press has long since moved into hi-tech media centres on the outskirts of town.

The major attraction here, is the **Cağaloğlu Hamamı** on Kazım Ismail Gürkan Caddesi (daily: men 7am–10pm; women 8am–9pm; $10 for self-service bath, $15–30 for assisted baths and massages; ⓦ www.cagalogluhamami.com.tr); the women's entrance to the haman is around the corner on Cağaloğlu Hamam Sok. These are the most popular baths this side of town, famous for their beautiful *hararet*s or steam rooms – open cruciform chambers with windowed domes supported on a circle of columns. The baths were built in 1741 by Mahmut I to pay for the upkeep of his library in Aya Sofya, and the arches, basins and taps of the hot room, as well as the entries to the private cubicles, are all magnificently Baroque. Florence Nightingale is said to have bathed here, while in more recent years the haman has appeared in several movies, including scenes in an *Indiana Jones* adventure.

Yeni Camii

The **Yeni Camii**, or "new mosque", is one of the more familiar landmarks of the city, sited across the horrendously busy road from Eminönü's ferry terminal. A large, grey and rather ugly building, whose pigeon-covered steps are a popular stamping ground for hawkers and pickpockets, it was the last of Istanbul's imperial mosques to be built and its history gives an interesting perspective on harem power struggles. It was erected for the Valide Sultan Safiye ("the light one", a beautiful Venetian woman who some said was a Venetian spy), mother of Mehmet III and one of the most powerful of the Valide Sultans, who effectively ruled the whole empire through the weakness of her son. This was the only imperial mosque to be built during the reign of Mehmet III and the site chosen by Safiye was regarded as wholly inappropriate. It occupied a slum neighbourhood inhabited by a sect of Jews called the Karaites, who were relocated across the Horn to Hasköy, and a synagogue and church had to be demolished to make room for it. The site was also dangerously close to the water's edge and the building programme was constantly plagued by seepage from the Horn. The foundations that eventually withstood this seepage are a series of stone "bridges" reinforced with iron.

An even greater plague to the building programme was court politics. The original architect was executed for heresy and the work was interrupted again by the death of Mehmet III and the banishment of his mother to the Old Palace. Construction had reached as far as the lower casements when it was halted, and the Karaites returned to camp out in the rubble. It was another sixty years before the Valide Sultan Turhan Hatice, mother of Sultan Mehmet IV, completed the building. Today the mosque is characterized above all by its gloominess, partly due to the heavy eaves that cover the washing area, but also a result of the thick layer of soot that covers its walls and windows.

The lower chambers of the Kasir (royal entrance), at the northeast corner of the mosque, now house the **Ayvalik and Aydin Agricultural Foundation** shops (Mon–Fri & Sun 8am–noon & 1–5pm, Sat 8am–1pm), selling good-quality olives, olive oil and other produce more cheaply than regular shops.

Mimar Sinan, master builder

Many of the finest works of Ottoman civil and religious architecture throughout Turkey can be traced to one man, a genius who had the good luck to come of age in a rich, expanding empire willing to put its considerable resources at his disposal. **Mimar Sinan** (1489–1588) served as court architect to three sultans – Süleyman the Magnificent, Selim II and Murat III – but principally to the first, who owed much of his reputation for "magnificence" to this gifted technician.

Little is known of Sinan's early life except that he was born in a small village near Kayseri, the son of Greek or Armenian Christian parents. Even his birthdate is open to question, since it is established that he was conscripted into the janissaries in 1513, which would have made him a good ten years older than the typical recruit. In any case, prolonged military service in all of the major Ottoman campaigns of the early sixteenth century compelled Sinan to travel the length and breadth of south-eastern Europe and the Middle East, giving him the opportunity to become familiar with the best Islamic – and Christian – monumental architecture there. Sinan was immediately able to apply what he had learned in the role of military engineer, building bridges, siegeworks, harbours and even ships, which earned him the admiration of his superiors. These included Sultan Süleyman, who in recognition of his abilities appointed him court architect in April 1536.

During Sinan's first twelve years in the job, he did little out of the ordinary, undertaking only relatively minor public works throughout Anatolia and the Balkans. In 1548 he completed his first major religious commission, İstanbul's Şehzade Camii, and shortly thereafter embarked on a rapid succession of ambitious projects in and around the capital, including the waterworks leading from the Belgrade Forest and the Süleymaniye Camii. After exhausting the potential of the great city Sinan turned his matured attention to the provinces, gracing Edirne with the Selimiye Camii in 1569–1575, and a decade later fulfilling a longstanding wish as a devout Muslim by overseeing the restoration of the Harem-i-Zerif mosque in Mecca.

Unusually for his time, Sinan could make an objective assessment of his talents: he regarded most of his pre-1550 works as apprentice pieces and posterity has generally agreed with the self-evaluations in his memoirs, the *Tezkeret-ül-Bünyan*. Despite temptations to luxury he lived and died equally modestly, being buried in a simple tomb he made for himself in his garden in the grounds of the Süleymaniye Camii – the last of more than five hundred constructions by Sinan, large and small, throughout the empire.

Behind the shop fronts in this street is the **Süleymaniye Library** (Mon–Sat 8.30am–5pm), housed in the Evvel and Sani *medreses*. These buildings, mirror images of each other, are situated around shady garden courtyards. Süleyman established the library in an effort to bring together collections of books scattered throughout the city: works were gathered from eleven palaces and date from the reigns of six different sultans. The library is open to the public, though – to protect the originals – all of the works are preserved on microfilm. There is also a book restoration department, where the original bindings are closely imitated.

Other buildings of interest in the vicinity include the **Tomb of Mimar Sinan**, on Mimar Sinan Caddesi. The tomb is in a triangular garden, which was the location of the architect's house during construction work. At the corner of the triangle is an octagonal eaved fountain. Perhaps there is no nicer way of being remembered than by providing the gift of water to passing strangers, but in Sinan's case it nearly caused his downfall: the fountain, as well as Sinan's house and garden, were liberally supplied with water, but when the mosques further down the pipeline began to run short, Sinan was charged with diverting the water supply for his household needs. The garden beyond the fountain now houses the tomb of Sinan, with its magnificent carved turban, a measure of the architect's high rank. The eulogy written on the south wall of the garden picks out the bridge at Büyükçekmece as Sinan's greatest achievement.

Otherwise, the buildings of the Süleymaniye complex served the usual functions. On Şifahane Sokak is the *imaret* (soup kitchen), which despite its ornate design was constructed as a public kitchen supplying food for the local poor (fittingly, it now houses the very reasonable *Darüzziyafe* restaurant, p.178) and a *kervansaray* (hotel). A *mektep* (primary school) stands on the corner of Saddak Sami Onal Caddesi and Süleymaniye Caddesi, and there are Koran schools and a language school, which taught the proper pronunciation of Arabic for reading the Koran. There's also a triangular wrestling ground (now used as a car park), located to the south of the cemetery.

The **Süleymaniye hamam**, built by Sinan in 1557, is on the corner of Mimar Sinan Caddesi and Dökmeciler Hamamı Sokak (daily 6.30am–midnight; $10, $15 with massage; Ⓦwww.suleymaniyehamami.com). Legend has it that the great architect took all his baths here from 1557 to 1588. It is a beautiful building, but in a terrible state of repair.

The mosque itself, **Süleymaniye Camii**, is preceded by a rectangular courtyard, whose portico stands on columns of porphyry, Marmara marble and pink Egyptian granite (which are said to have come from the royal box of the Hippodrome), and by four tapering minarets. Semi-domes supporting the huge central dome to east and west alternate with arches, in front of which is a set of three domes. The east and west flanks of the mosque are distinguished by two-storey loggias, accessible from within the mosque, which support an eave protecting those performing their ablutions at the taps below.

The doorway into the mosque is high and narrow, its wooden doors inlaid with ebony, mother-of-pearl and ivory. Move inside, and the sense of light and space is paramount – a dome 53m high (twice its diameter), surmounting a perfect square of 26.5m. There are no side aisles and the double panes of 200 windows ensure a softly filtered light. The dome collapsed during the earthquake of 1766, while in the nineteenth century further damage was done by the Fossati brothers, whose attempt at Ottoman Baroque redecoration jars with the inherent simplicity of the building. The original crystal lamps have also been replaced by glassware supported on a rather cumbersome iron frame, though the stained glass of İbrahim the Mad remains, above a graceful marble *mimber*.

In the adjacent **cemetery** (daily 5.30am–8pm) are located the tombs of Süleyman the Magnificent and of Haseki Hürrem, or Roxelana, his powerful wife. Süleyman's tomb is particularly impressive: as you enter, passing through doors inlaid with ebony and ivory, silver and jade, you are confronted by the huge turban of Süleyman the Magnificent. Above, the spectacular inner dome has been faithfully restored in red, black and gold inlaid with glittering ceramic stars. Both here, and in the neighbouring tomb of Roxelana, original tiles and some fine stained glass have survived the centuries.

Laleli and Aksaray

Heading west from Beyazit up Ordu Caddesi, you arrive at an appalling tangle of road intersections where Adnan Menderes Caddesi crosses Ordu Caddesi.

This is the main focus of the districts of **Aksaray** and **Laleli**, whose atmosphere is distinctly different from anywhere else in İstanbul. In part, it's the dispiriting effect of the constant roar of traffic, but it's also because - in Laleli especially – there's no real sense of community. Many of the inhabitants are Iranian refugees and Arab students, and, more recently, Russians and Eastern Europeans buying everything and anything the Turks might have a mind to sell.

Both districts have sights worth seeing and it's certainly worth wandering away from the main road to explore some of them. Laleli, in particular, is a big import/export area for textiles, cheap clothes and shoes, car parts and leather, attracting coach loads of shoppers from the former eastern bloc. You are more likely to hear Russian spoken here than Turkish and the unique sound of brown parcel tape being ripped off the roll reverberates throughout the district – even from hotel rooms late at night – as shoppers pack up their goods to transport them back home. To eavesdrop on all the shopping action, sit and have a beer at the *Hotel Burak* on the corner of Fethi Bey Caddesi and Ağa Yokuşu Sokak.

Laleli Camii

The **Laleli Camii** complex, on Ordu Caddesi opposite the Laleli tram stop, is in the Ottoman Baroque tradition of Nuruosmaniye and the Ayazma Camii in Üsküdar, but the mosque itself owes more to traditional Ottoman architecture. It was founded by Mustafa III, whose octagonal tomb is located at the southeast gate. Selim III, who was assassinated by his janissaries, is also buried there.

The main Baroque elements in the mosque complex are the use of ramps (including one which the reigning sultan would have used to ride up to his loge), the grand staircases and the detail, for example in the window grilles of the tomb and in the carved eaves of the *sebil* (drinking fountain). Inside, a mass of pillars dominates, especially to the west, where the columns beneath the main dome seem to crowd those supporting the galleries into the walls. Back outside, the foundations of the mosque are used as a covered **market**, selling the cheapest of clothes and acting as an inducement for the local populace to worship at the mosque.

At the back of the Laleli complex, between Fethi Bey and Gençturk *caddesi*s, is another smaller covered bazaar, the **Taşhan**, originally built as an inn in 1793 by Sultan Mustafa III to entertain his guests. The building has been restored as a two-tiered bazaar surrounding two open courtyards, with a couple of restaurants (including the atmospheric *Taşhan Restaurant*, p.178), located in the vaults underneath. Because the bazaar specializes in cheap clothing, there are hundreds of mannequins standing to attention around the walkways and courtyards, wearing anything from fur coats to shell-suits, granting rather a surreal atmosphere to what is otherwise a fine specimen of sixteenth-century architecture.

The Aqueduct of Valens and Kalenderhane Camii

An alternative route from Beyazit into Laleli takes you up Şehzadebaşi Caddesi towards the Şehzade Camii (another creation of the ubiquitous Mimar Sinan), following the line of the magnificent **Aqueduct of Valens**. Recently renovated, the aqueduct was originally built during the late fourth-century waterworks programme carried out by the emperor Valens, part of a distribution network that included reservoirs in the Belgrade Forest and various cisterns located around the city centre. It was in use right up to the end of the nineteenth century, having been kept in good repair by successive rulers, who maintained a constant supply of water to the city in the face of both drought and siege (which is more than can be said for the present administration). More than six hundred of its original thousand metres are still standing and the best view is from where the aqueduct crosses Atatürk Bulvarı, where it reaches a height of eighteen-and-a-half metres.

The ninth-century Byzantine Church of Kyriotissa, near where the aqueduct now ends, was renamed **Kalenderhane Camii** after the Kalender dervishes who converted it into a *tekke* (Dervish monastery) after the conquest. It has the cruciform ground plan typical of Byzantine churches of its time, with much of the marble revetment and sculpture still in place. The apse has been closed off, but the mosque toilet keeper will usually unlock the crypt, which still boasts extensive frescoes.

Zeyrek

Crossing Atatürk Bulvarı brings you into **Zeyrek**, an attractive area notable for its steep, cobbled streets and ramshackle wooden houses interspersed with small mosques. There are also wonderful views of the Süleymaniye mosque complex. Crossing the road is something of an ordeal (local drivers seem to regard it as a Grand Prix test track) and the convoluted streets of Zeyrek can be confusing, but it's worth persevering in order to track down a handful of interesting sights, including two former Byzantine churches in contrasting states of repair.

Museum of Caricatures

The **Museum of Caricatures** (Karikatür ve Mizah Müzesi; Mon–Fri 9am–6pm; $1) stands on Atatürk Bulvarı between Cemal Yener Tosyalı Caddesi and the aqueduct, housed in the rooms of Gazanfer Medrese around a pretty garden courtyard with a marble fountain. Cartoons are an important popular art form in Turkey: most papers employ a number of cartoonists and the weekly *Gırgır* was the third best-selling comic in the world before many of its employees left to set up the rival *Avni*. The collection includes pieces dating back to 1870, with many exhibits concentrating on political satire, such as the image of a musustachioed and larger-than-life Prime Minister Bülent Ecevit on magazine covers from the 1960s. Temporary exhibitions change every week and feature work by both international and Turkish cartoonists, while the museum also organizes silk-screen and other workshops, including some for children.

Çinili Hamami

The **Çinili Hamamı** (daily 8.30am–8pm; $8, $10 with massage) or "tiled baths", on İtfaiye Caddesi, provide a welcome respite from sightseeing. This double hamam, which was built for the great sixteenth-century pirate-admiral Barbarossa, has been beautifully restored to working order and has a particularly friendly atmosphere. Notice the huge dome and the marble floors and fountain of the *camekan* (changing room), the enormous octagonal marble massage table in the main room of the *hararet* (steam room) and the toilets, which are continually flushed by water draining from the *hararet*. There are still a few of the original tiles on the walls in the men's section, but none are evident through the continual clouds of steam in the women's baths. The blissful bath experience can be nicely rounded off in the *Gül Lokantası*, behind the basket-ball court on the other side of Atfaiye Caddesi. This little basement kebab joint has a discreet but friendly atmosphere peculiar to establishments in areas slightly off the tourist agenda and as such is a rarity in İstanbul.

Zeyrek Camii

In the heart of Zeyrek nestles **Zeyrek Camii**, the former Church of the Pantocrator, built in the twelfth-century and converted into a mosque at the time of the conquest. To get here, take İtfaiye Caddesi northwards, then turn left on to İbadethane Arkası Sokak.

The building is officially open only at prayer times, though you may be able to persuade the *imam* to open the door for you (his house is up the stone steps behind the wooden door, next to the mosque). It originally consisted of two churches and a connecting chapel, built between 1118 and 1136 by John II Comnenus and Empress Irene. The chapel was built as a mausoleum for the Comnenus dynasty and continued to be used as such by the Paleologus dynasty. Although the tombs have been removed, there is still evidence of the graves beneath the pavement. Empress Irene also founded a monastery nearby, which was to become one of the most renowned religious institutions in the empire and later the official residence of the Byzantine court, after the Great Palace had been reduced to a ruin. No trace remains of the monastery, nor of its hospice, asylum or hospital.

The **mosque**, which occupies the south church, is also in an advanced state of dilapidation and it's difficult to believe that it was once an imperial mausoleum. Among the surviving features are the revetments of the south apse and the original marble doorframes. The floor, naturally, is covered in carpets but the *imam* may pull one of these back to give a glimpse of the coloured marble underneath: an interlacing geometric pattern with figures of animals in its borders.

Eski İmaret Camii

Another attractive Byzantine church can be found within walking distance, albeit by a rather convoluted route. To get there, return to İbadethane Sokak and follow it to Çırçır Caddesi. Take a right off here onto Nevşehirli İbrahim Paşı Caddesi, then a left into Hanedan Sokak, and you'll see the church, now known as the **Eski İmaret Camii**, ahead of you. To get in you'll need to arrive at prayer time or hope to find the *imam* at home (his house is connected to the mosque down a flight of stone steps). Founded at the end of the twelfth century by Empress Anna Delessena, the mother of Alexius I Comnenus, this four-column structure is similar to the south church of the Pantocrator, evidence of a return to traditional Byzantine forms, perhaps in reaction to the encroaching political threat from east and west.

Eski İmaret has one of the most interesting exteriors of all the Byzantine churches in İstanbul. As ever, it's hemmed in by surrounding buildings, but in this case the wooden houses provide an attractive frame as you approach down Küçük Mektep Sokak. The roof and twelve-sided dome retain their original curved tiles, while the eaves are decorated with a zigzag of bricks. Other designs in the brickwork include swastikas and Greek keys. Inside, some of the original fittings remain, notably the red marble doorframes and a floral decoration around the cornice supporting the dome. The two side apses also retain their original windows and marble cornice.

Fatih

The reputation of **Fatih** ("the Conqueror") as a very conservative Islamic area, associated with intolerance towards visitors of different religious and cultural persuasions, is not especially deserved. If you make the effort to come and see its two important mosques, you're much more likely to be greeted with polite curiosity than outright hostility. Fatih was one of the first districts to elect an Islamist mayor and you may notice more covered women about the streets, many of them wearing headscarves or full *chador*, and men sporting long white beards, but the majority of people will be dressed as in the rest of İstanbul. However, locals may be more likely to take exception to naked limbs and (perhaps understandably) to having their picture taken without due warning.

To get to Fatih, simply follow the line of the Valens aqueduct from the north side of Atatürk Bulvarı and keep going in the same direction when you run out of aqueduct. Or from Eminönü or Sultanahmet, take any bus going to Edirnekapı and get off at the Fatih mosque complex.

Fatih Camii

Fatih Camii, the "Mosque of the Conqueror", on İslambol Caddesi, was begun ten years after the conquest of İstanbul, in 1463, and completed in 1470. In 1766, however, it was almost completely destroyed in an earthquake: only the courtyard, the entrance portal of the mosque, the south wall of the graveyard and the bases of the minarets survived; the rest was rebuilt.

The **outer precinct** of the mosque is large enough to accommodate the tents of a caravan. It is enclosed by a wall and, to north and south, by the *medrese* (theological academy) buildings, which accommodated the first Ottoman university. The **inner courtyard** of the mosque is one of the most beautiful in the city. Verd antique and porphyry columns support a domed portico with polychrome edges, while an eighteenth-century fountain is surrounded by four enormous poplar trees. Over the windows outside the courtyard in the west wall the first verse of the Koran is inscribed in white marble on verd antique, while at either end of the mosque portico there are inscriptions in the early İznik *cuerda seca* technique, whereby coloured glazes were prevented from running into each other by a dividing line of potassium permanganate, which outlined the design. The inscription over the mosque portal records the date and dedication of the mosque, and the name of the architect, **Atık Sinan**, who was supposedly executed the year after its completion on the orders of Mehmet, because the dome wasn't as large as that of Aya Sofya.

The **interior**, painted in drab colours without a tile in sight, is rarely empty, even outside prayer times. It appears to be a social meeting place as well as a centre of serious Koranic study for both women and men. As in all mosques, the men occupy the main body of the building while the women's section is confined to the anterior regions, where you'll find an unusual old bronze water pump with silver cups.

The **tombs** of Mehmet II and of one of his wives, Gülbahar (Wed–Sun 9am–4.30pm), are situated to the east of the mosque. The originals were destroyed in the earthquake and while that of Gülbahar is probably a facsimile of the original, the *türbe* of the Conqueror is sumptuous Baroque. **Çorba Kapısı**, the "Soup Gate", to the southeast of the mosque, is original, inlaid in porphyry and verd antique.

Yavuz Selim Camii

Built on a terrace on the crest of one of İstanbul's seven hills (the fifth, count-ing from Topkapı's), **Yavuz Selim Camii** – also called the Selimiye – holds a commanding position over the surrounding suburbs. It lies on Yavuz Selim Caddesi and is a twenty-minute walk from Fatih Camii, though a nicer approach is to take a ferry up the Golden Horn from Eminönü to Aykapı ferry terminal and walk up to the mosque, again about twenty minutes.

Viewed on the approach down Yavuz Selim Caddesi, the mosque presents one of the most impressive facades to be seen in the city. This is in part because of its position next to the **Cistern of Aspar**, one of three open cisterns built during the fifth and sixth centuries in Constantinople. For centuries this space housed market gardens and a village, but these were cleared years ago and sec-tions are now in use as an attractive park, as well as basketball and tennis courts.

The mosque of Yavuz Selim, or Selim the Grim, was probably begun in the reign of Selim and completed by Süleyman, but its dates are not certain. Close up, the exterior is rather bleak, a fitting memorial to a man with such a repu-tation for cruelty. There's no pretty cascade of domes and turrets, just a large dome atop a square room with a walled courtyard in front of it. Once inside the courtyard walls, however, this simple, restrained building emerges as one of the most attractive of all the imperial mosques. A central fountain is surround-ed by tall cypress trees, the floor of the portico is paved with a floral design, while its columns are a variety of marbles and granites.

The **domed rooms** to the north and south of the mosque – which served as hostels for travelling dervishes – are characteristic of early Ottoman archi-tecture. In the mosque itself, under the sultan's loge (supported on columns in a variety of rare marbles) is paintwork in designs reminiscent of the delicacy of Turkish carpets or ceramics; in places there are bunches of flowers tied with painted bows, which cannot predate the eighteenth century, but the rest of the paintwork may be original.

The **tomb of Selim the Grim** (daily except Tues 9.30am–4.30pm), beside the mosque, has lost its original interior decoration, but retains two beautiful tiled panels on either side of the door. Other tombs in the complex include that of four of Süleyman the Magnificent's children, probably the work of Sinan.

Along the city walls

Theodosius II's **city walls** are among the most fascinating Byzantine remains to be found in Turkey. Well-preserved remnants can still be found along the whole of their six-and-a-half-kilometre length, despite the 1999 earthquake, which caused several unrestored portions to collapse. Sadly, the on-going ren-ovation process gives barely a nod to historical accuracy: some sections have been completely rebuilt in newly dressed stone and cement bricks; while cer-tain additional details, such as medieval-style flourishes, quite possibly never existed.

The land walls were named after Theodosius II, even though he was only 12 years old when their construction was started in 413. The walls – stretching from the Marmara to Tekfur Saray, 2km further out than the previous walls of Constantine – were planned by Anthemius, Prefect of the East, to accommo-date the city's expanding population. They were almost completely destroyed

THE CITY WALLS

0   400 m

by an earthquake in 447 and had to be rebuilt in haste, since Attila's forces were on the point of attack. An ancient edict was brought into effect whereby all citizens, regardless of rank, were required to help in the rebuilding, and the Hippodrome factions of Blues and Greens (see box on p.131) provided 16,000 labourers and finished the project in just two months. The completed construction consisted of the original wall, 5m thick and 12m high, plus an outer wall of 2m by 8.5m, and a 20-metre-wide moat. This was sufficient to repel Attila's Huns who numbered several thousand but did not have the skill or patience for siege warfare.

A **walk along the walls** and around the adjacent sites easily takes all day, but it is well worth the effort. Most of the outer wall and its 96 towers are still standing; access is restricted on some of the restored sections, though elsewhere there's the chance to scramble along the crumbling edifice. The stone used is limestone and the bricks, about 30cm square and 5cm thick, were sometimes stamped with the name of the manufacturer or donor and bear the name of the emperor in whose reign they were made. Mortar mixed with brick dust was used liberally to bind the masonry; the towers had two levels, separated by brick barrel vaults.

There are still plenty of run-down **slum dwellings** along the Theodosian city walls, the worst of which are in Topkapı, which is dangerous after dark. However, it's highly unlikely you'll encounter any problems in daytime.

If time is limited, the three best **sites** to visit are the Yedikule fortifications and surrounding district, Kariye Museum, a former Byzantine church containing some of the best-preserved mosaics and frescoes in the world, and Mihrimah Camii, a Mimar Sinan mosque. **Buses** from Eminönü or Sultanahmet include the #80 to Yedikule, #84 to Topkapı and #39 or #86 to Edirnekapı, but the best way of reaching the walls is to take a local **train** from Sirkeci to Yedikule on the Marmara shore.

Yedikule and around

Yedikule – at the southern end of the walls, around 5km from Sultanahmet – is an attractive quarter, full of churches since it is a centre of Rum Orthodoxy: the dwindling congregations of such churches, scattered throughout İstanbul, are the last remaining descendants of the Byzantine Greeks. When you leave the train station, on Yedikule İstasyon Caddesi, head away from the sea along Halit Efendi Sokak and you reach İmrahor İlyas Bey Caddesi, Yedikule's main street. Here you'll find a concentration of quaint, Greek-influenced houses and some pretty churches.

The name Yedikule ("seven-tower") refers to the fortifications in this area, namely the triumphal arch of the Golden Gate – constructed here by Theodosius I in 390, even before the walls themselves – and the towers and walls later added by Mehmet the Conqueror.

İmrahor Camii

The only ancient building of any note in the vicinity of Yedikule is the **İmrahor Camii**, the former Church of St John of Studius, at İmam Aşır Sokak, off İmrahor İlyas Bey Caddesi. Even this is almost completely ruined. To get there, walk straight up Halit Efendi Sokak from the train station and you'll see the remains on your right. Whatever anyone may suggest to the contrary, there is no entrance fee.

The church, built in 463, was connected to a monastery of the *akoimetai* or "unsleeping", whose inhabitants prayed in relay around the clock. The monks lived according to the strict rules of St Basil: even melancholy was considered a sin and the monks were required to keep before them the spectre of death by repeating the words "We shall die!" over and over. They still found time, however, to transcribe books for mass circulation and monks even came to the monastery from Russia to learn the trade. The monastery gained particular renown under the auspices of **Abbot Theodore**, an outspoken defender of images and critic of the Byzantine court, who established it as the centre of a renaissance in Byzantine scholarship. Although he died in exile on the Princes' Islands, the reputation of the institution survived him and the monastery was home to the University of Constantinople during the first half of the fifteenth century. Its greatest claim to historical fame, though, came in 1042, when the tyrant **Michael V** took refuge here from a popular revolution. He made his way to the church by ship, but was discovered, dragged from the altar and blinded.

As you approach the **church entrance** you'll see four large columns with acanthus capitals, supporting a horizontal carved entablature. This is the entrance to the narthex and the east wall of the atrium, which was square and probably colonnaded. The interior of the church was a simple, almost square basilica: the aisles were partitioned off by rows of columns, six of which have survived; these too are capped with acanthus capitals and support a horizontal entablature. The interlace floor is twelfth-century, but what remains of the original fittings suggests that the church was sumptuously decorated, in contrast to its simple structure.

The Yedikule Museum

The most impressive sections of wall have been designated the **Yedikule Museum** (Yedikule Müzesi; daily except Mon 9am–4pm; $0.50), situated to the southwest of İmrahor Camii on Yedikule Meydanı Sokak, Yedikule Caddesi. Follow Kuyulu Bakkal Sokak (or, from the station, Yedikule İstasyon Cad) straight to the entrance.

The so-called **Golden Gate**, flanked by two marble towers, stood alone – a triumphal arch in the path of important visitors of state and of conquering emperors (generals were never permitted to pass through the gate, even after successful campaigns). Nowadays, the shape of the three arches is still visible on both sides of the wall, but it takes a degree of imagination to invest the structure with the glamour and dignity it must once have possessed. Michael Palaeologus was the last emperor to ride through the gate in triumph, when the city was recaptured from occupying Crusaders. After the empire went into decline, the gold-plated doors were removed and the entryway bricked up.

The other five towers of the Yedikule fortifications were added by Mehmet the Conqueror, and with their twelve-metre-high curtain walls they form the enclave that can be seen today. Despite its design this was never actually used as a castle, but two of the towers served as prisons and others were used as treasuries and offices for the collection of revenue of the *Vakıf* or pious foundation.

The two **prison towers** are those immediately to the left of the entrance: the "tower with inscriptions" and the tower on the north side of the Golden Gate. The inscriptions around the outside of the first of these were carved into the walls by prisoners, many of whom were foreign ambassadors on some hapless errand. The prison in the second tower doubled as an execution chamber: the wooden gallows and "well of blood", into which heads would roll, are still to be seen, and the odd instrument of torture can be found lying about outside in the courtyard. The most famous victim of the execution chamber was Osman II, deposed and murdered in 1622 by his janissaries, thus providing Ottoman history with its first case of regicide.

It's worth spending some time climbing around the battlements with the lizards. You can look across to the Marble Tower, where the sea and land walls meet beyond the railway line on the Marmara coast, and also see a good stretch of the walls to the north.

Yedikule, Belgrat, Silivri and Mevlana gates

North along the walls, the first of the public gateways is the **Yedikule Kapı**. This is still in use: traffic wardens compete to direct traffic through the narrow entry, while a Byzantine eagle cut in the blackened marble overhead remains serenely oblivious to the commotion below.

The land in and around the first section between Yedikule and **Belgrat Kapı** is in use as market gardens, and access is difficult because of fences, deep ditches and so forth. Belgrat Kapı was a military gate, different from a public gateway in that there was no bridge crossing the moat beyond the outer walls. It was named for the captives who were settled in this area by Süleyman the Magnificent after his capture of Belgrade in 1521. The walls here have been substantially renovated and are floodlit at night. North from Belgrat Kapı to **Silivri Kapı** the walls are largely untouched, though the sections around Silivri Kapı itself have been extensively renovated.

There is more restoration work at the **Mevlanakapı**, and also some interesting inscriptions on the outer wall. The Theodosian walls reached completion at this gate, since it was here that the Greens, building from the Marmara, met the Blues, who were working southwards from the direction of the Golden Horn. A Latin inscription to the left of the gate celebrates this fact: "By the command of Theodosius, Constantine erected these strong fortifications in less than two months. Scarcely could Pallas [Athena] herself have built so strong a citadel in so short a time."

Topkapı

A road system dominates the outer side of the one-kilometre Mevlanakapı to Topkapı section of wall and a pleasant pavement has been constructed along the moat, but again it's difficult to walk along the walls themselves. Just south of Topkapı the walls have been destroyed to make way for the enormous thoroughfare of Turgut Özal Caddesi and you will somehow have to cross this to reach Topkapı itself. Continue inside the walls, until you reach the area called Kaleiçi and the **Topkapı** (the "Gate of the Cannonball"), named after the most powerful cannon of Mehmet the Conqueror (see below), some of whose enormous stone cannonballs have been placed around the inside of the gate. To get here by public transport, take a tram from Sirkeci, Sultanahmet or Aksaray.

At Kaleiçi you can get a decent midday meal at any of the *lokanta*s and *pide* or kebab salons on Topkapı Caddesi. At the southern end of this street, on the left, is the **Ahmet Paşa Camii**, a Sinan mosque dating from 1554. In the porch there are original tiles made in the *cuerda seca* technique and despite some heavy-handed renovation it's worth having a look inside at the original arabesque painting under the galleries.

Another delightful mosque lies on Topkapı-Davutpaşa Caddesi (south off Davutpaşa Caddesi). The wooden **Takkeci İbrahim Çavuş Camii** (open for *prayers* only) retains much that is original, including its wooden dome and some fine tile panels from the best İznik period. The mosque was founded in 1592 by the eponymous *takkeci*, a maker of the distinctive felt hats (*takke*) worn by dervishes. The income of an artisan could not have been equal to the cost of building a mosque, however modest, and around this fact no doubt has grown the myth of its origins.

It is said that the hatmaker was told in a dream to go to Baghdad, where he would find a great treasure buried under a vine tree in the garden of an inn. He duly set off on his donkey and, arriving at the place of his dream, he began to dig under said vine. The innkeeper came out and enquired his business, admonished him and advised him to return to the place from which he had started his journey. On arriving back in Topkapı, the *takkeci* found two bags of gold on the present site of the mosque. Burying one in the ground, he used the other to finance the building of his mosque, the idea being that if this mosque were destroyed then another could be built in its place with the buried gold. The *imam* who tells this story to visitors points out a panel of faience tiles depicting plump red grapes hanging on vines, jokingly suggesting that these are corroborative evidence of his story. And in such a poor parish who can blame him for clinging to the fond hope that sufficient funds are buried beneath the wooden mosque to finance its rebuilding should the need arise?

Edirnekapı

Between Topkapı and Edirnekapı there is a pronounced valley, formerly the route of the Lycus river, now taken by Vatan Caddesi. At this point the walls are at their least defensible, since the higher ground outside gives the advantage to attackers. The famed **Orban cannon** of Mehmet the Conqueror was trained on this part of the walls during the siege of 1453 – hence their ruinous state – and it was here that Constantine XI rode into the midst of the Turkish army after he realized that all hope of holding out was gone.

Edirnekapı itself is a small-time suburb with a large *otogar* for local buses and no decent restaurants. The gate of Edirnekapı takes its name from the route to modern Edirne, which passed through even in Byzantine times. Also left over from the Byzantine era is the smallest of the ancient city's open cisterns, located about 50m from the *otogar* on the left of Fevzi Paşa Caddesi (Edirnekapı's main street), below the level of the road. It's now the site of the Vefa football stadium, but the original dimensions of the cistern can still be seen. Buses straight to Edirnekapı from town include the #34 or #39 from Eminönü and #86 from Eminönü and Sultanahmet.

The **Mihrimah Camii** is a little to the left of the *otogar* as you face the walls. Mihrimah, the favourite daughter of Süleyman the Magnificent, had a passion for architecture as great as that of her husband Rüstem Paşa and the couple commissioned many of Sinan's early works. Mihrimah Camii, situated on the highest of İstanbul's seven hills, dates from somewhere around the middle of the sixteenth century. Raised on a platform, the area beneath is occupied by shops and can be seen from all over the city and especially as you approach from Edirne.

The mosque and its dependencies have suffered in two earthquakes, the second of which brought the minaret tumbling down onto the mosque itself. During renovation the interior was filled with twentieth-century arabesque stencilling, though other aspects compensate, especially the light flooding in through the windows and the graceful white marble *mimber*. Note the skilful fake marbling of the arches under the eastern gallery. The mosque's nearby **hamam** has also been poorly restored but at least is still functioning.

The Kariye Museum

The **Kariye Museum** (Kariye Müzesi; daily except Wed 9am–6pm; $3.50), formerly the church of St Saviour in Chora, is decorated with a superbly preserved series of **frescoes and mosaics** portraying the life and miracles of Christ. It's among the most evocative of all the city's Byzantine treasures, thought to have been built in the early twelfth century on the site of a much older church far from the centre: hence "in Chora", meaning "in the country". Between 1316 and 1321 the statesman and scholar Theodore Metochites rebuilt the central dome and added the narthexes and mortuary chapel.

To reach the museum from Edirnekapı, take Vaiz Sokak off Fevzi Paşa Caddesi and a second right onto Kariye Bostanı Sokak, a street with a number of picturesquely renovated wooden houses, painted in pastel colours. There's no direct transport from the city centre.

The narthexes

The mosaics and frescoes date from the same period as the renovations carried out by Metochites and depict the life of Christ in picture-book sequence. The first series to be followed is a set of dedicatory and devotional panels located in the two narthexes. Inside the church, the most prominent of the mosaics is that of **Christ Pantocrator**, bearing the inscription "Jesus Christ, the Land of the Living". Opposite this, above the entrance, is a depiction of the Virgin and angels, with the inscription "Mother of God, the Dwelling Place of the Uncontainable". The third in the series is located in the inner narthex and depicts Metochites offering a model of the building to a seated Christ. The hat he is wearing is called a *skiadon*, or "sunshade". SS Peter and Paul are portrayed on either side of the door leading to the nave, and to the right of the door are Christ with his Mother and two benefactors, Isaac (who built the original church) and a female figure, described in the inscription as "Lady of the Mongols, Melane the Nun".

In the two domes of the inner narthex are medallions of Christ Pantocrator and the Virgin and Child, and in the fluting of the domes, a series of notable figures – starting with Adam – from the **Genealogy of Christ**. The **Cycle of the Blessed Virgin** is located in the first three bays of the inner narthex. These mosaics are based on the apocryphal gospel of St James, which gives an account of the birth and life of the Virgin and was very popular in the Middle Ages. Episodes depicted here include the first seven steps of the Virgin (taken when she was six months old), the Virgin caressed by her parents, with two beautiful peacocks in the background, the Virgin presented as an attendant at the temple (where she remained from the age of 3 to 12), the Virgin receiving a skein of purple wool, as proof of her royal blood, Joseph taking the Virgin to his house, in which is also depicted one of Joseph's sons by his first wife, and Joseph returning from a six-month business trip to find his wife pregnant.

The next cycle, to be found in the lunettes of the outer narthex, is that of the **Infancy of Christ**. The mosaics can be followed clockwise, starting with Joseph dreaming, the Virgin and two companions and the journey to Bethlehem. Apart from well-known scenes such as the Journey of the Magi and the Nativity, there are depictions in the seventh bay (furthest right from the main entrance) of the Flight into Egypt, which includes the apocryphal Fall of Idols (white and ghostly-looking figures) from the walls of an Egyptian town as the holy family passes by. In the sixth bay is the Slaughter of the Innocents, complete with babies impaled on spikes.

The **Cycle of Christ's Ministry** fills the vaults of the outer narthex and parts of the south bay of the inner narthex. It includes wonderful scenes of the Temptation of Christ, with dramatic dialogue (Matthew 4: 3–10) that could almost be in speech bubbles, beginning:

Devil: If thou be the Son of God, command that these stones be made bread.
Christ: It is written, Man shall not live by bread alone, but by every word that proceedeth out of the mouth of God.

The nave and funerary chapel

In the nave, the main frescoes echo the mosaics, featuring the death of the Virgin, over the door and, to the right of this, another depiction of Christ. The best known of all the works in the church, however, are the frescoes in the **funerary chapel** (known as the parecclesion) to the south of the nave. These comprise depictions of the Resurrection, the Last Judgement, Heaven and Hell and the Mother of God. Below the cornice are portraits of the saints and martyrs.

The most spectacular of the frescoes is the **Resurrection**, also known as the Harrowing of Hell. This is a dramatic representation of Christ in action, trampling the gates of Hell underfoot and forcibly dragging Adam and Eve from their tombs. A black Satan lies among the broken fetters at his feet, bound at the ankles, wrists and neck, but still writhing around in a vital manner. To the left of the painting, animated onlookers include John the Baptist, David and Solomon, while to the right Abel is standing in his mother's tomb, behind him is another group of the righteous.

Other frescoes in the chapel, in the vault of the east bay, depict the **Second Coming**. In the east half of the domical vault Christ sits in judgement, saying to the souls of the saved, on his right, "Come ye blessed of my Father, inherit the kingdom prepared for you from the foundation of the world". To the condemned souls on the left he says, "Depart from me, ye cursed, into everlasting fire, prepared for the devil and his angels". Below, a river of fire broadens into a lake in which are the souls of the damned. Their torments are illustrated in the lunette of the south wall and comprise the Gnashing of Teeth, the Outer Darkness, the Worm that Sleepeth Not and the Unquenchable Fire.

The tomb in the north wall of the parecclesion has lost its inscription, but is almost certainly the **tomb of Metochites**, the donor of the church.

Eyüp

Eyüp is one of the holiest places in Islam, its mosque being the site of the tomb of Eyüp Ensari, the Prophet Mohammed's standard-bearer. The district itself is controlled by the Islamic Virtue Party, which has carried out an extensive restoration programme in the suburb, spending large amounts of money to create a showcase for the party.

Muslims come here from all over the Islamic world on pilgrimage – if you're going to come, try not to visit on Fridays, out of respect for conservative worshippers. The mosque is most easily reached by boat up the Golden Horn from Eminönü – it's the last **ferry** stop before the Horn peters out into two small streams, and the mosque and tomb are about a ten-minute walk from the ferry terminal on Camii Kebir Caddesi. Or catch the #39A **bus** from Eminönü, which drops you off at the ferry terminal.

Eyüp Camii

One of the small group of companions of the Prophet, **Eyüp Ensari** was killed during the first Arab siege of Constantinople (674–678); a condition of the peace treaty signed following the siege was that his tomb be preserved. Later, the mosque here, **Eyüp Camii**, hosted the investiture ceremonies of the Ottoman sultans: indeed, mosque and tomb face each other across the court-yard that was used for the ceremony, the exact site marked by a raised platform surrounded by railings, from which two plane trees grow.

The original mosque, built by Mehmet the Conqueror in honour of Eyüp Ensari, was destroyed in the eighteenth century, probably by the same earth-quake that put paid to Fatih Camii. The present Baroque replacement, filled with light, gold, pale stone and white marble, was completed in 1800. The **tomb of Eyüp Ensari** (Tues–Sun 9.30am–4.30pm) is far more compelling, however (footwear should be removed and women should cover their heads before entering). Its facade and vestibule are covered in tile panels from many different periods and, although the overall effect is a bit overwhelming, the panels constitute a beautiful and varied display of the art form; you could spend weeks visiting individual buildings to see as many different designs and styles.

Other tombs and Eyüp cemetery

There are a number of other important tombs in the Eyüp district, as it was a popular place of burial for Ottoman dignitaries. Two of these, the **tombs of Sokollu Mehmet Paşa and Siyavus Paşa** (Tues–Sun 9.30am–4.30pm), stand opposite each other on either side of Cami Kebir Caddesi, five minutes' walk from Eyüp Camii towards the Golden Horn. Five years before his assassination, Sokollu Mehmet Paşa commissioned Mimar Sinan to build his tomb. It is an elegantly proportioned octagonal building of around 1574, notable for its stained glass, some of which is orig-inal; connected to the tomb by an elegant three-arched colonnade is a for-mer Koran school. Siyavus Paşa's tomb, on the other hand, was probably actually built by Sinan for the children of Siyavus Paşa, who had died young. It's decorated with İznik tiles.

Eyüp is still a popular burial place and the hills above the mosque are cov-ered in plain modern stones interspersed with beautiful Ottoman tombs. To the north of the mosque, off Silahtarağa Caddesi, Karyağdı Sokak leads up into the **Eyüp cemetery**. Following the signs up this lane through the graveyard – most beautiful at sunset with an arresting view of the Golden Horn – it takes about twenty minutes from Eyüp Camii to reach the romantic **Pierre Loti Café** (daily 8am–midnight) overlooking the Horn, where waiters in Ottoman costume serve up Turkish coffee. The café was made famous by the autobio-graphical novel of Pierre Loti (the pen name of Julien Marie Viaud), a young French naval officer and writer of romantic novels and travel books, who fell in love with the green eyes of a Circassian harem girl called Aziyade in nineteenth-century İstanbul.

Karaköy, Galata and Beyoğlu

Directly across the Golden Horn from Eminönü is the district of **Karaköy**, reached via the Galata bridge. It's been a port area since Byzantine times, when the north shore of the Horn was a separate settlement from Constantinople and where, in the late nineteenth century, the dockside was home to İstanbul's most insalubrious rooming-houses and seediest taverns.

Above Karaköy's docks the settlement at **Galata**, initially known as Sykai, is as old as Constantinople itself. The **Genoese occupation** of Galata began when they gave active support to Byzantine emperor Michael Paleologus in his attempt to drive out the Crusaders. In return, he signed a treaty in March 1261, signing Galata over to them as a semi-independent colony. The Byzantines no doubt lived to regret the privileges granted to the colony when the Genoese repaid them with neutrality during the final siege of Constantinople by Mehmet the Conqueror. The new sultan showed his gratitude by allowing the Genoese to retain their commercial and religious establishments, although arms were to be handed over and the walls torn down. The Genoese subsequently built one of the city's most famous landmarks here, the **Galata Tower**.

During the early centuries of Ottoman rule, many Spanish Jews, Moorish traders, Greeks and Armenians settled in Galata, which became established as the city's **European quarter**. In time, foreign powers set up their embassies in the area, and it was also a popular haunt of visiting merchants, traders, seamen and adventurers.

While Galata was used exclusively to define the area within the city walls, the word **Pera** (Greek for "beyond" or "across") was originally used interchangeably with Galata to refer to the area across the Horn from Constantinople. Later it came to denote the district above Galata, present-day **Beyoğlu**, to which the European quarter gradually spread as Galata became too crowded. By the mid-nineteenth century Pera was the area of choice for the main European powers to build ambassadorial palaces. The declining empire increasingly relied on the skills of the Galata bankers to secure funds from abroad. The fiscal boom led to the construction of new buildings, designed to reflect the power and status of their owners, and it is this imported **architecture** that still dominates Beyoğlu. The completion of the Orient Express Railway in 1889 encouraged an influx of tourists, accommodated by a growing number of large hotels, such as the splendid *Pera Palas Hotel*. Around the same time Pera became a favoured haunt – and subject matter – of a school of **artists** heavily influenced by European "salon" painting of the nineteenth century.

The **nightlife** of the quarter was notoriously riotous even in the seventeenth century, when one Evliya Çelebi could write that "Whoever says Galata says taverns". By the nineteenth and early twentieth centuries, the area had become fashionable for its operettas, music halls, inns, cinemas and restaurants, and it was only after the exodus of the Greek population from İstanbul in the 1920s that Galata and Pera began to lose much of its cosmopolitan flavour. Other minorities left too, partly as a result of the wealth tax imposed on ethnic communities between 1942 and 1944 and until recently it looked as if the area would be entirely destroyed by office building and lack of planning.

In recent years, however, there have been moves to restore the appearance of Beyoğlu. The most visible change was the pedestrianization in 1990 of Beyoğlu's main boulevard, **İstiklâl Caddesi**, and the reinstallation of its tramway (see "City transport", p.106). The sleazier side of Beyoğlu culture has not completely disappeared, but the "adult" cinemas, hostess bars and unofficial brothels that remain have been exiled to a few streets between İstiklâl Caddesi and the parallel Tarlabaşı Bulvarı.

Crossing the Golden Horn

Any number of **buses** cross the Golden Horn via two bridges: **Galata Köprüsü** (from Eminönü) and **Atatürk Köprüsü** (from Aksaray). Most useful is the #T1 from Eminönü, which crosses Galata Köprüsü to Karaköy and follows the coast road around to the ferry terminal at Kabataş before climbing the hill to Taksim Square. From there the route continues in a loop to cross the other Golden Horn bridge, Atatürk Köprüsü, travelling on under the Aqueduct of Valens on Atatürk Bulvarı to Aksaray, where it takes a left turn along Ordu Caddesi through to Beyazit before skirting around Sultanahmet back to Eminönü. The #T4 follows exactly the same route but in the opposite direction.

From Eminönü there are regular commuter **ferries** on the short hop across to Karaköy, though there is little need to catch one when the easiest and most interesting way to cross the Horn is to **walk over the bridge** from Eminönü past the fishermen and hawkers.

Across Galata bridge to Karaköy

Despite being the vital link between the two sides of European İstanbul, the **Galata Köprüsü** (Galata bridge) is a bit of an eyesore. An ugly concrete and steel ramp, it features an abandoned shopping centre beneath the surface road that has remained un-let since it was built in the 1980s. But, despite the traffic fumes, the stroll across is very pleasant – past the throngs of anglers and with great views of both shores. Once on the northern side, look out for the small market on the left where bucket-loads of live fish and crabs are sold.

Once over the bridge, you will have reached the port area of **Karaköy**, from where you can either walk up to Beyoğlu on the steep Yüksek Kaldırım Caddesi, past the Galata Tower, or take the **Tünel** underground train (daily 9am–9pm; $0.50); the Tünel entrance is on Tersane Caddesi, just to the left of the first road junction beyond the bridge. There is also a useful **tourist office** in Karaköy's main ferry terminal to the right of the bridge.

Karaköy's port and Ottoman shipyard was once enclosed within the walls of the Castle of Galata and in 1446 the Byzantines stretched a great chain across the mouth of the Horn to prevent enemy ships from entering. Originally constructed around 580, the subterranean keep of the castle is thought to be preserved as the **Yeraltı Camii**, or "Underground Mosque", on Kemankeş Caddesi. Inside is a forest of thick columns, supporting a low, vaulted ceiling. Two tombs in one corner purport to be those of Muslim martyrs killed in the first Arab siege of Byzantium (674–678 AD).

At the far end of the port area is another mosque, the **Kılıç Ali Paşa Camii**, constructed in 1580 by Sinan and essentially a reduced-size copy of Aya Sofya. Kılıç Ali Paşa was one of the great Ottoman admirals, an Italian by birth who was captured by Algerian pirates and converted to Islam.

Galata and the Galata Tower

The most obvious landmark in the area is the Galata Tower, but there are a few other interesting places to stop and break the steep ascent on the way up from Galata bridge to İstiklâl Caddesi.

The newest addition to the area is a small museum that has recently opened in the Zülfaris Synagogue on Meydanı Perçemli Sokak. The **Jewish Museum** (Mon & Thurs 10am–4pm, Fri & Sun, 10am–2pm; $0.70) contains a small but interesting display of exhibits – mostly documents and photographs donated by

TAKSIM AND BEYOĞLU

ACCOMMODATION

Avrupa	3
Büyük Londra	2
Cihangir	11
Family House	10
Galata Residence	9
Marmara	7
Monopol	4
Perador	5
Pera Palas	1
Sato	6
Vardar Palace	8
Villa Zurich	12

local Jewish families – chronicling Turkish Jews since they first came to Turkey over seven hundred years ago.

About 400m below the Galata Tower, on Yanık Kapı (or "Burned Gate") Sokak, is the only remaining Genoese **city gate**. Somewhat the worse for wear, it still boasts a marble slab bearing the Cross of St George. Of the many churches that once crowded the narrow streets of Galata, few original structures now remain. One notable exception is the unusual building on Fütühat Sokak, now a mosque known as **Arap Camii**. With its tall square tower and pyramidal roof, it was, under the Genoese, the largest church in Galata. It was converted into a mosque to serve the needs of the Moorish community that settled here in the early sixteenth century following their expulsion from Spain. It stands on one side of an attractive closed courtyard, decorated with assorted pieces of ancient marble and in one corner are the remains of a raised water system, now a fish pool.

About 100m below the tower, at Galata Külesi Sokak 61, is an even more unusual relic, the **British prison**. Under the capitulations granted by the Ottomans, Western powers had the right to try their citizens under their own law, rather than the draconian Ottoman code, so consulates possessed their own courthouses and prisons. The court as an institution of the consulate originated in the 1600s, but the current building dates from 1904 and today is the **Galata House** restaurant-café (see p.176). The owners will happily show you

Military Museum, Şişli & Hilton Hotel ▲

Dolmabahçe & Beşikaş ▼

graffiti left by former inmates, including a sketch of the Rock of Gibraltar and the poignant words, "An unfavourable wind has brought the ship of my life to this shore."

The Galata Tower

Built in 1349 by the Genoese, on the site of a former tower built by Justinian in 528, the **Galata Tower** (Galata Kulesi; daily 9am–8pm; $1.50) was originally known as the Tower of Christ and stood at the apex of the several sets of fortifications that surrounded the Genoese city-state. It has had a number of functions over the centuries, including a jail, a fire tower and even a spring-board for early adventurers attempting to fly. Nowadays, there's a restaurant on the top floor.

At 61m high, the tower's **viewing gallery** – reached by elevator – offers magnificent panoramas of the city and views across the Sea of Marmara and Golden Horn. The best view of Eminönü in particular is from here: the boats that nudge in and out of the ferry terminal form a foreground to the skyline of Beyazit and Sultanahmet, with Yeni Cami directly below Nuruosmaniye, the Spice Bazaar below Beyazit Camii and Rüstem Paşa Camii below the Beyazit fire tower. For photographs, it is best to go early or late in the day, as the haze and pollution over the city is at its most intense during the middle of the day.

Along İstiklâl Caddesi

The exit from the **upper Tünel station** in Beyoğlu is fronted by a small square from which **İstiklâl Caddesi** heads 1.5km north towards Taksim Square. Make a brief detour a few metres down to the right, along Galipdede Caddesi, and an unassuming doorway on the left leads to the courtyard of the **Galata Mevlevihane**, also referred to as the Divan Literature Museum (daily except Tues 9.30am–4.30pm; $0.70). A former monastery and ceremonial hall of the whirling dervishes (see p.628), the building now serves as a museum to the Mevlevi sect, which was banned by Atatürk along with other Sufi organizations because of its political affiliations. Exhibitions include musical instruments and dervish costumes and the building itself has been beautifully restored to late eighteenth-century splendour, complete with the fake marbling that was so popular at the time. The Whirling Dervishes perform *sema* dances to Sufi music at 5pm on the last Sunday of every month, with the main ceremony on December 17, the annual Mevlana holiday (further information is available at the museum).

Further along İstiklâl Caddesi, on your right, is the **Botter House**, a fine Art Nouveau apartment building with a carved stone façade and wrought-iron balcony. Commissioned in 1901 as a showroom, workshop and family house by Dutchman Jan Botter, tailor and couturier to Sultan Abdülhamid II, it is one of a number of structures around İstanbul designed by the Italian architect Raimondo D'Aronco. Further up on the right is the newly restored **Palais de Hollande** at İstiklâl Caddesi 393. Built in 1858 on the site of the home of Cornelis Haga, the first Dutch diplomat in Constantinople during the fifteenth century, the impressive building now houses the Consulate to the Netherlands.

Many other buildings lining İstiklâl Caddesi are also typically European, like the **Mudo** shop at no. 401, whose beautifully preserved Art Nouveau interior sells very expensive toys and retro or kitsch ornaments. The oldest church in the area is **St Mary Draperis** at no. 429, which dates from 1789, although the Franciscans built their first church on the site in the early fifteenth century. Better known is the Franciscan **church of St Antoine** at no. 325, a fine example of red-brick neo-Gothic architecture. Originally founded in 1725 it was demolished to make way for a tramway at the beginning of the century and rebuilt in 1913.

Further along İstiklâl Caddesi you can detour down Nura Ziya Sok to see the imposing **French Palace**, with its large central courtyard and formally laid-out gardens, the residence of ambassadors and consuls from 1831 until the present day. Below the Palace, on Tom Tom Kaptan Sok, stands the **Italian Consulate**, originally the Palazzo di Venezia, built in the seventeenth century. Casanova stayed here in 1744, but according to his memoirs he didn't make a single conquest, although one Ismail Efendi claims to have been seduced by him. Turning left off İstiklâl Caddesi, along Hamalbaşı Sok, leads in 100m to the **British Consulate**, an impressive Renaissance style structure, designed by Charles Barry, who also designed the British Houses of Parliament.

The northernmost stretch of İstiklâl Caddesi and its offshoots boasts most of the area's bars and restaurants, all within easy walking distance of one another (see p.182 for reviews). The famous **Çiçek Pasaj** (Flower Passage) had its heyday in the 1930s when the music and entertainment was supplied courtesy of anti-Bolshevik Russian emigrés. These days it's home to a collection of attractive but rather overpriced and touristy restaurants – it's far better to head through to the **Balik Pazarı** (fish market), notably on **Nevizade Sokak**, a street dedicated to fish restaurants, all with outside tables.

In the barber's chair

A trip to the *kuaförü* or *berber* plays an important role in Turkish male grooming and is a part of daily social life, especially as Turkish barbers tend to double up as layman psychiatrists. The ritual starts with a read of the newspaper and a glass of apple tea – or a chat about football if you speak some Turkish – whilst you wait your turn.

Once you are in the chair, much hairwashing and rubbing down with fluffy towels follows until it is time to try to communicate with the barber what you'd like to look like when you leave. Important phrases to remember include the following: *Ucundan azıcık* (don't take too much off); *Sıfıra vur* (take it all off); *Sakalı alalım* (give me a shave, literally "take my beard"); *Sinek kaydı* ("a fly would slide") or *Kaymak gibi* ("like cream") both meaning clean shaven; *Pis sakal* (designer stubble); and *Sıhhatler olsun!* ("good health to you", an expression only used after a haircut or shave). A good tactic is to ask for something short in the first place and be ready to modify your expectations – remember that clippers are an especially valued item in the Turkish barbering world.

After the haircut there may well be a pause for more tea and/or a cigarette, by both the client and the barber, before he lathers you up for a shave with a cut-throat razor. This is followed by a dousing down with jaw-stinging cologne before the grooming stage begins in earnest. Ear hairs are zapped with a lit cotton bud soaked in methylated spirits, wayward cheek hairs are attacked with twisted cotton, and nose hairs are plucked with such dexterity the numbness lasts only a fraction of a second. The whole process is rounded off by a massage of the neck and shoulders, and possibly another hairwash and dabbing of the eardrums to remove any unwanted wax.

The whole experience will last about an hour and cost little more than $5. There are *kuaförü* or *berbers* all over İstanbul; try Cihangir Erkek Kuaförü, Akarsu Cad 49, Cihangir, just below Beygolü ☏0212/251 1660 (Mon–Sat 9am–7pm), which is used to foreigners and where some English is spoken.

Taksim Square and around

At the northern end of İstiklâl Caddesi is **Taksim Square**, the heart of modern İstanbul. The size of Taksim Square is undeniably impressive, which is just as well since there's little else to be said in its favour. As an imitation of a grand Western plaza, it's not a great success, lacking the essential monumental architecture to balance its broad expanse and robbed of any real atmosphere by its confusing traffic system. It is however, a central pivot of İstanbul's, and indeed Turkey's, main business area and is often regarded as a symbol of the Turkish republic – so much so that when, in 1997, the fleeting Islamist Virtue Party's government unveiled plans to build a mosque in the square, they were soon forced to abandon the idea in the face of public disapproval.

Taksim Square

Taksim in Turkish means "distribution" and the low **stone reservoir** on the south side is the building from which Taksim Square takes its name. Constructed in 1732 to distribute water brought from the Belgrade Forest by aqueduct, the *taksim*'s octagonal annex, located on the İstiklâl Caddesi side, has stone bird houses above its door that are carved to look like miniature Ottoman houses.

Steps on the north side of the square above the main bus terminal lead up to the pleasant **Taksim Parkı**, with its bench-lined paths and open-air tea gardens. The rare occurrence of a park here – wholly untypical of traditional towards Kadıköy (Bağdat Caddesi is one-way, so you can't tour it from Kadıköy). Dolmuşes can be hailed anywhere along the street, which is just as well since the shops are quite far apart. The best shopping areas are Şaşkan Bakkal and Suadiye, while there are good restaurants the whole way along.

In Kadıköy itself, the best place for clothes is **Gen Azim Gündüz Caddesi** (formerly Bahariye Caddesi), which is a right turn off Söğütlüçeşme Caddesi, the wide, steep street leading uphill from the ferry jetty. There's more fun to be had sorting through the great mounds of junk, old carpets and kilims that can be found for sale in the **bit pazar** (flea market) on Özellik Sokak.

Directly south of Kadıköy is the more upmarket suburb of **Moda**, reached by taking Moda Caddesi off Söğütlüçeşme Caddesi and turning left up any of its side-streets. It's a pleasant area for aimless wandering, particularly popular with courting couples who cruise Moda Caddesi, calling in at establishments such as the *Benadam* art gallery, the *Café Bonjour* and, at no. 266, *Ali Usta*, a very well-known ice-cream parlour that attracts vast queues on summer evenings.

North of Kadıköy, across the bay, is the mainline **Haydarpaşa train station**, a noticeable building jutting out into the Bosphorus. Trains to the rest of Turkey, with the exception of the European side, all depart from here and you can reach it directly by ferry from Eminönü, or it's a ten-minute walk from Kadıköy ferry terminal.

Directly north of the station, between the sea and Tıbbiye Caddesi, is the Marmara University and the **British War Cemetery** (daily 7am–7pm), a beautifully kept spot sheltering the dead of the Crimean War and the two world wars. To find it, turn off Tıbbiye Caddesi into Burhan Felek Caddesi, between the university building and the military hospital. A few minutes' walk northeast of the university, along Kavak Iskele Caddesi, is the imposing **Selimiye Barracks** (closed to the public), whose northwest wing was used as a hospital by the British during the Crimean War (1854–1856). **Florence Nightingale** lived and worked in the northern tower, where she reduced the death toll among patients from twenty percent to two percent, and established universally accepted principles of modern nursing.

Opposite the barracks, across Çeşme-i Kebir Sokak on Selimiye Camii Sokak, the **Selimiye Camii** was constructed, along with the nearby hamam, for the use of the barracks' soldiers. The largest Muslim graveyard in İstanbul, the **Karaca Ahmet Mezarlığı**, is a ten-minute walk away on Tıbbiye Caddesi, in the direction of Üsküdar. It's a sprawling place shadowed by ancient cypress trees, thought to have been founded in the mid-fourteenth century and now with an estimated one million graves. Any number of buses, including the useful #12 and #14, head north from Kadıköy, past the train station and slightly inland, to Üsküdar, passing the **Capitol** shopping mall (see p.195) in Altunizade.

Üsküdar

There's plenty of evidence of religious conservatism in **Üsküdar** (a corruption of "Scutari" – the name used for what was a separate town in the late Byzantine era), particularly in the dress of its inhabitants. The area has been characterized by wholesale migration from the more Islamic regions of Anatolia and has long been a centre of Islamic mystical sects. Nevertheless, it is still a more comfortable and friendly place than other similarly conservative suburbs, such as Fatih.

To get to Üsküdar simply take a ferry from Eminönü or Beşiktaş, or a #12 or #14 bus or a dolmuş from Kadıköy. Üsküdar's main square and quayside is an enormous bus park. Buses up the Bosphorus, as far as Anadolu Kavağı, leave from in front of İskele Camii on Paşa Liman Caddesi and it's also possible to get buses from here to the Black Sea resorts of Ağva and Şile (see "Around İstanbul, p.198).

Although there are some fine imperial mosques in and around the suburb, modern Üsküdar is primarily renowned as a shopping centre – famed for its street stalls offering fresh produce, particularly fish and vegetables, and innumerable family-run supermarkets that stock obscure varieties of Anatolian cheeses. Secondhand furniture and ornaments are sold at the **Üsküdar bit pazar** (flea market) in Büyük Hamam Sokak and there are also some reasonable jewellery and clothes shops. Along the quayside at **Salacak** are some good pavement cafés and bars, offering fantastic views of Topkapı Palace and İstanbul.

Most obvious mosque is **İskele** or **Mihrimah Camii**, opposite the ferry landing on İskele Meydanı. This sits on a high platform, fronted by an immense covered porch that is the perennial haunt of old men in knitted hats complaining about the changing times while they peruse the square below. Designed by Mimar Sinan and built in 1547–1548, this is the only Ottoman mosque with three semi-domes (rather than two or four), a result of the requirements of a difficult site against the hillside behind.

Directly across the main square from the İskele Camii is the **Yeni Valide Camii**, and it's worth being in the vicinity of these two mosques for the call to prayer: the two muezzins call and answer each other in a poignant refrain across the bus park below. The Yeni Valide Camii, built between 1708 and 1710 by Ahmet III in honour of his mother, is most easily identified by the Valide Sultan's green, birdcage-like tomb, the meshed roof of which was in fact designed to keep birds out while allowing rain in to water the garden tomb below (now rather untidily overgrown). There is an attractive *şadırvan* (ablutions fountain) in the courtyard; the grilles of its cistern are highly wrought, their pattern echoed in the stone carvings above.

One of the most attractive mosques in Üsküdar is the **Çinili Cami**, or Tiled Mosque, which dates from 1640. To get there on foot, take Hakimiyet-i Milliye Caddesi out of the centre and do a left into Çavuşdere Caddesi; after passing Çavuşdere fruit and veg market, continue to climb the same street and you'll see the mosque on your right. The tiles are mainly blues and turquoise, but there's a rare shade of green to be found in the *mihrab*. Below the mosque, in the same street, is the beautifully restored **Çinili Hamamı** (men 8am–10pm, women 8am–8pm; $8), which retains its original central marble stones for massage and acres of marble revetments. It's an extremely clean hamam and the pride of its workers.

The **Atık Valide Külliyesi** is just a short walk from Çinili Camii: go back down Çavuşdere Caddesi and turn left into Çinili Hamam Sokak and you'll find the mosque on the right. Dating from 1583, the complex is a work of the master architect Mimar Sinan, built for Nur Banu, wife of Selim II and mother of Murat III. The mosque courtyard, meant to be the most beautiful in İstanbul, has been closed for restoration for a number of years and the mosque is entered through a side-door. Worth inspecting are the underside of the wooden galleries on three sides of the interior, which are beautifully painted, and the İznik tiles covering the *mihrab*.

From Üsküdar's main square, İskele Meydanı, minibuses to Ümraniye run past the foot of **Büyük Çamlıca**, the highest hill on the Asian side. If you get off at

Kısıklı Camii you can walk up Kısıklı–Büyük Çamlıca Caddesi, turning right just before the *Büyük Çamlıca Et Lokantası* to reach the park – a walk of fifteen minutes or so. The effort is rewarded by refreshingly cooler temperatures and by spectacular views of the Bosphorus and the European shore. The **café** on the hill (daily 9am–midnight) has been tastefully refurbished.

Eating

Eating out is an everyday activity for most Turks, and the best restaurants in Turkey are located in İstanbul, including several that lavish time and skill on old Ottoman cuisine. The city has its fair share of top-class international restaurants and, thanks to the lengthy coastline, fish is a firm menu favourite. Snacks, too, are ubiquitous, with kebab stands, pastry shops, fast-food outlets and cafés across the city catering to locals, workers and tourists alike. You'll rarely be stuck for somewhere to eat, though it's worth remembering that whilst venues in the main tourist areas, such as Sultanahmet, may be close to the sights, they're likely to charge three or four times more for a cup of coffee or a simple kebab than in places further off the tourist trail.

Workers' **cafés** and *lokantas* tend to open early at 6am and serve until 4pm; other cafés generally open daily between 9am and 9pm. **Restaurants** open for lunch and dinner, with last orders at 10 or 11pm, with more popular live-music venues staying open until the early hours. In the more commercial districts eateries follow suit of the shops and close on a Sunday. **Credit cards** are widely accepted in all but the smallest of restaurants. We've included telephone numbers for places where it's wise to **reserve a table**.

Cafés and restaurants are located on the relevant **maps**: Sultanahmet (p.110); Eminönü, Beyazit, Kumkapı and Laleli on the Old İstanbul map (p.100); and Galata, Beyoğlu and Taksim on the map on p.162.

Cafés and budget eating

Until recent times, café society in İstanbul was limited to a glass of tea, a puff on a nargile or a shot of raki in a male-dominated teahouse. But today's cafés are as wide-ranging as in any other European city, from traditional workers' taverns and student beer halls, where cafeteria-type fare is dished out, to sophisticated continental cafés serving trendy coffees and imported alcoholic drinks.

Budget options include *lokanta*-style buffets (where what you see is what you get), and *pide* or *kebap salonu* for cheap and filling meat- and bread-based staples. Barrow-boys all over the city offer simple pretzels, fishermen in Kadıköy, Karaköy and Eminönü serve dubious fish sandwiches off their boats, while sizzling tangles of sheep innards (*kokoreç*) are sold from booths and push-carts in the more salubrious areas. **Prices** vary depending on the establishment and location, but range from a few cents for a *börek* (cheese-, spinach- or meat-filled pastry) to a dollar or two for a takeaway kebab, or five dollars or more for coffee and cake in an upmarket café.

Sultanahmet

Ahırkapi Börekçisi Ahırkapi Sok 64, Cankurtaran. Tiny *börek* bakery in the backstreets towards Kennedy Cad. Dispenses traditional Turkish meat, cheese or spinach pastries, which make great snacks or cheap lunches.

Buhara Sıfa Hamamı Sok 12. Wide range of traditional fare – kebab, salad and beer for around $9 – and consistently full of locals at lunchtime.

Café Ağa Medresesi Caferiye Sok, Soğukkuyu Çıkmazı. A peaceful café next to *Inter Youth Hostel*, set in the courtyard of a former *medrese* that now sells Turkish handicrafts in its beautifully renovated rooms. A good place for a budget breakfast or to quench the thirst after a trip round Aya Sofya.

Çiğdem Patisserie Divan Yolu Cad 62. For over forty years has offered a good selection of both Turkish and non-Turkish pastries and sweets. It's opposite the tourist office.

Doy Doy Sıfa Hamamı Sok 13. A backpacker's favourite (off Küçükayasofya Cad at the Hippodrome end), with a well-deserved reputation for cheap and well-prepared kebabs and *pide*. Dining is on four floors, including a roof terrace with great views of the harbour and night-time light show over the Blue Mosque. No alcohol served, but unusually vast portions, particularly the lunchtime *mezes*.

Karadeniz Pide Salonu Divan Yolu Cad, Bıçkı Yurdu Sok 1. Cheap and unremarkable with plastic tables and plates, but the food – particularly a good *kiremit kebap* (lamb cooked on a clay dish) – is very popular with locals.

Konyali Café Mecidiye Pavilion, Topkapı Palace. Open during palace hours for coffee and pastries and set-priced buffet lunches geared towards coach parties. Some compensation for the ridiculous prices – there is little other choice of refreshments inside the palace – is the terrace set amongst the palace gardens, with a great view over the Bosphorus. Closed Tues.

Sultan Pub Divan Yolu Cad 2. Pleasant café-bar in a prominent position, with tables outside in summer, offering international dishes for $6–8 a head and plenty of cold beer on tap.

Eminönü

Konyali Ankara Cad 233, Sirkeci. Excellent pastry and cake shop opposite the train station, open by 7am and frequented by the quarter's businesspeople, who eat their breakfast standing at the marble-topped counters. An affordable $3 for coffee and pastry. Closed Sun.

Beyazit

Subaşı Restaurant Nuruosmaniye Cad 48, Çarşı Kapı. Behind Nuruosmaniye Camii, just inside the main entrance of the covered bazaar, this spit-and-sawdust place (with real sawdust) serves excellent lunchtime food to the market traders, far better than anything else in the same price range in the area. Go early (noon–1pm) as it gets packed and food may run out.

Galata

Galata House Café Galata Külesi Sok 61 ℡0212/245 1861. A café housed in the former British prison, serving good coffee, homemade *börek*s, cakes and jams. Full meals are available – Turkish or Georgian cuisine – if booked at least two days in advance. Closed Mon.

Güney Opposite Galata Tower. A workers' favourite with *saray kebap* (beef stew topped with bechamel sauce and oven-browned) that has to be tasted to be believed. It's one of the best *lokanta*s in town; you'll be lucky to find a seat at lunchtime.

Beyoğlu

Afacan İstiklâl Cad 331. Best of the area's many self-service *lokanta*s, with a wide selection of meat and some vegetarian dishes, prepared to a high standard at very reasonable prices (from $2 per plate). Opens early for a traditional Anatolian breakfast of lentil soup and home-cooked *börek*.

Dilek İstiklâl Cad 341. Homemade chocolates, yummy desserts and to-die-for cakes, served on three air-conditioned levels. It's the haunt of Istanbul's ladies who meet for coffee.

Ekmek Arası İstiklâl Cad 28. Eat-in or takeaway joint serving Turkish-style fast-food – chips, soft drink and *döner* special deals for under $2.

Gina Margarino İstiklâl Cad 316. Modern, Western-style café/pub, with good lunchtime pizza deals.

Nizam Pide İstiklâl Cad, Büyükparmakkapı Sok. Offers the best beans and rice in town, and excellent *pide*. A second branch is on Kalyoncu Kulluğu Cad, behind Nevizade Sok in the fish market.

Patisserie de Pera *Pera Palas Hotel*, Meşrutiyet Cad 98–100, Tepebaşı ℡0212/251 4560. It would be worth splashing out for the Art Nouveau elegance alone, though the delicious cakes and coffee and the excellent service also appeal. Booking advised for the traditional afternoon tea.

Pia İstiklâl Cad, Bekar Sok 7. Pleasant split-level café attracting a trendy clientele. It's a popular pre- and post-cinema hangout (there's good pasta), but a *café latte* doesn't come cheap – though there's a nice selection of English-language magazines to browse through.

Saklıkent İpek Sok 18, 2nd Floor. The "Hidden Town" is the place for an inventive, mainly veggie, spin on Turkish cuisine, excellent value at around $4–5 a head. Located above the *Babil* bar and next to the *Madrid* bar, both of which serve cheap beer – a tailor-made budget night out.

Saray İstiklâl Cad 102–104. The emphasis is on classic, cheap milk-based desserts such as *fırın sütlaç* (baked rice pudding) and *irmik helvası* (semolina with nuts). Other branches are at

Teşvikiye Cad 105, just east of the police station, a 10–15min walk from Taksim's Military Museum, and in the Galleria shopping centre in Ataköy.

Yağmur Şeyh Bender Sok 18, İsmalımescit. Stylish internet café with a quiet, library-type atmosphere, away from the bustle of İstiklâl Cad. Not a bad place to go just for coffee and a read of the paper, and with a useful notice board advertising long-term accommodation for teachers and the like.

Taksim

Café de Flose French Cultural Centre, İstiklâl Cad 2. Authentic fresh baguettes, *café au lait* and *pain au chocolat*, served in the calming whitewashed courtyard of the French Cultural Centre, just off

Taksim Square. You need to show your passport to get in.

Ocakbaşı Sıraselviler Cad 52. Specializes in kebabs cooked on a grill in the middle of the restaurant. Friendly service and good value at under $10 a head with beer.

Kadiköy

Divan Pastanesi Bağdat Cad 361, Erenköy. Very classy joint selling the best pastries and cakes, and with a good line too in attractively boxed sweets and *lokum* (Turkish delight). Sit outside and watch the Bağdat people as you indulge yourself. Other branches all over the city, including inside the *Divan Hotel* in Taksim.

Restaurants

Restaurants in **Taksim** and **Beyoğlu** cater for theatre- and cinema-goers and young people filling up before a night out, as well as for those who want to spend all evening over a meal and a bottle of *rakı*. The most atmospheric spot is undoubtedly the **Balık Pazarı**, or fish market, on Nevizade Sokak, where restaurants serve *meze*s, kebabs and fish, accompanied by the sound of serenading street musicians. The restaurant situation in the old city has improved significantly in recent years, though establishments in **Sultanahmet** and elsewhere still don't compare with Beyoğlu for variety or quality. Instead, it's worth seeking out **Kumkapı**, south of Laleli, off the coast road, Kennedy Caddesi, a charming area of narrow streets where wandering *fasıl* bands – musicians playing traditional Turkish instruments – will serenade you over a *rakı*. There are some fifty fish restaurants here, surrounding the small square, Kumkapı Meydanı, serving up anything that scuttles or swims, from swordfish, seabass and red mullet to lobster, giant prawns and calamari. It's a popular spot on a balmy summer evening, with candlelit tables spilling out on to the traffic-free streets. Otherwise you can try your luck in the cobbled streets around the ferry terminal in **Ortaköy**, where there are numerous trendy options rubbing shoulders with older, more traditional establishments.

Restaurant **prices** vary considerably depending on what and where you eat. Expect to pay more for extras, such as live music or to dine on a terrace overlooking the Bosphorus, while fish is always pricier than meat. Main courses start from $4 at a cheap restaurant frequented by locals, though run up to $20 or more at a swish restaurant with all the trimmings. Set meals at $15–25 represent the best value, with a wide choice of *meze*s followed by a substantial main course, Turkish desserts and, usually, half a bottle of wine or *rakı*.

Sultanahmet

Alzer At Meydani Sok. Good central hotel restaurant, on the Hippodrome, with excellent *et sote* (sautéed meat). It's not too outrageously priced, considering the location, and main courses start from as little as $4.

Ayazma Akbıyık Cad 40. Relaxed pizza and oven-cooked kebab restaurant and bar. Good food and service with antique-style decor.

House of Medusa Yerebatan Cad, Muhterem

Efendi Sok 19. Indoor and outdoor tables offering a wide selection of Turkish dishes and Western breakfasts. Good-value fixed dinner menus $8–12.

Kathisma Restaurant Yeni Akbıyık Cad 26. Fish and meat dishes, excellent sweets to follow, and a wine menu, with meals served in a cavernous bare-brick dining room. On Wednesday lunchtimes you'll coincide with the street market outside the front door.

Mosaik Restaurant Divan Yolu Cad, İncili Çavuş Sok 1. Nicely restored late nineteenth-century house, with tables on the street and a separate downstairs bar. Serves a range of less common Turkish dishes, such as *elbasan tava* – beef cooked with *kaşar* cheese and vegetables – with a separate, pricier menu for fish.

Rami Restaurant Utangaç Sok 6 ☏0212/517 6593. Restored Ottoman townhouse full of antiques, with great views from the roof terrace. Offers a mixture of stews, *mezes* and oven-baked dishes – including some fish. Excellent food but at $10–15 for a main course alone, it's expensive. It's opposite the Arasta bazaar, near the Mosaic Museum.

Rumeli Café Divan Yolu Cad, Ticarethane Sok 8. Friendly, cosmopolitan atmosphere in nicely restored bare-brick and wood surroundings – there are also a few candlelit tables on the street. Simple filling food: breakfasts, omelettes, salads, and steak and mash, in addition to a Turkish menu, with main courses starting from $7.

Türkistan Aşevi Tavukhane Sok 36. A rather garish rebuild of a nineteenth-century family house, with some quaint customs, usually reserved for the home, such as removing your shoes as you enter and eating at low tables. Mum prepares traditional Turkish and Turkestan dishes; the *düğün çorbası* (wedding soup) is especially good. The staff touts aggressively to passing tourists and prices reflect its popularity with tour groups.

Beyazit

Cennet Divan Yolu Cad 90. Specializes in *gözleme* (filled filo-pastry pancakes) and *mantı* (dough parcels filled with meat), served at low tables surrounded by cushions. Turkish women sit in the centre rolling out pastry for the *gözleme*, while a band of extremely noisy live musicians does the rounds. It's reasonably priced at around $15 a head, but you might want to look elsewhere for better cooking without the gimmicks. It's near the Çemberlitaş Hamamı.

Darüzziyafe Şifahane Cad, Süleymaniye Camii. Ottoman cuisine cooked in the original kitchen of the Süleymaniye Camii and served in arched halls of the mosque or under the ancient plane tree in the courtyard. It's unexceptional *lokanta* fare – around $12 for lunch or dinner – but the location more than makes up for it. There's live sixteenth-century-style music, and non-alcoholic Ottoman drinks available, such as *salep* (a cinnamon-laced concoction made from powdered orchid root).

Padaliza Kapalı Çarşı, off Yağlıkcılar Cad. Easily the best eating establishment in the covered bazaar (near the main entrance, at the entrance to

Cebeci Han), with reasonably priced, authentic Turkish dishes and excellent service in a beautifully restored barrel-vaulted *han*.

Eminönü

Pandeli Mısır Çarşısı 51, Hamıdıye Cad ☏0212/527 3909. Go through the main entrance of the spice bazaar on the shore side and turn back towards the doorway; on your right is a staircase leading up to the restaurant. Over seventy years old, decorated throughout with blue and white tiling and run by Greek and Turkish owners, the food here is some of the best in İstanbul. Known for its fish, particularly seabass, though the succulent lamb dishes are also worth trying – main courses from $12. Lunch only, noon–3.30pm, closed Sun.

Laleli

Dynasty Asian Restaurant *Hotel Merit Antique,* Ordu Cad 226 ☏0212/513 9300. Well-cooked Chinese food: *dim sum* lunch, popular with businessmen, is served from noon to 3pm for around $15, though an evening meal will set you back $20–30.

Taşhan Fethi Bey Cad 55 ☏0212/526 8734. Located in the vaults of a restored historic *han* built in 1763, the main dining area is a converted Ottoman stable. The menu is typically Turkish, with a two-course *meze* and kebab meal for around $9. The courtyard tables are overlooked by hundreds of mannequins from the surrounding clothes shops.

Kumkapı

Evren Çapariz Sok 4. Choose from a huge fish menu, with main courses from $5 and cooked to your specifications, or spoil yourself with lobster priced by the kilo. Late-night restaurant, open until 2am, frequented by large Turkish families celebrating at tables spilling out onto the street.

Fener Telli Odalar Sok 5 ☏0212/516 4002. Unusual fish on the menu include bluefish, barbel, gurnard and turbot. Not only that, there's a great atmosphere, live music and – theoretically – a free pick-up and drive-back service, which seems too good to be true but is worth asking about.

Kör Agop Ördekli Bakkal 7–9 ☏0212/517 2334. Third-generation Armenian-owned fish restaurant, one of the oldest in town (since 1938) and hugely popular. Offers a standard selection of seasonal fish, *mezes* and salads, accompanied by a *fasıl* band in the evening. Not cheap, at about $20 a head, but a reliable night out.

Olimpiyat 2 Kumkapı Meyd. A favourite among locals for its excellent service, guaranteed high quality and large range of fish, from bluefish to sea bass.

Şehzade Restaurant Kennedy Cad, Balakçalar Çarşısı 28. Right by the sea, with a waterside terrace, so you can watch the boats go out to the sound of the *fasıl* band. The menu specializes in lobster, crab and prawn, with main courses starting at $12.

Edirnekapı

Asithane *Kariye Hotel*, Kariye Camii Sok 18 ☏0212/534 8414. Garden-restaurant next door to the Kariye Museum. It's expensive, but you may feel like splashing out for good service and food in such a peaceful (if distant) location. The menu is described as nouvelle Ottoman cuisine – plenty of meat- and fruit-based stews from $8, or try the *hükar beğendi* (tender lamb with aubergine puree). Meals served on a lovely terrace swamped by roses, accompanied by classical Turkish music.

Galata

Galata Kulesi Restaurant Galata Tower, top floor ☏0212/293 8180. Despite the belly dancing and the spectacular views, at $50 per person (fixed menu, including the show, served at 8.30pm) this is an expensive place with little real atmosphere. It's better to go up in the daytime for the views and eat elsewhere.

Beyoğlu

Çatı İstiklâl Cad, Orhan A. Apaydan Sok 17, Tünel ☏0212/251 0000. Crowded at weekends (when you might want to book), but deserving of its glowing reputation, this restaurant-bar spreads over two floors. Live music and reasonably priced food, including unusual dishes such as desserts made from tomatoes and aubergines. Main courses start at $12 but the set meals represent much better value, with all-you-can-eat *mezes*. Closed Sun.

Cumhuriyet Meyhanesi Sahne Sok 47, Balık Pazarı. Excellent selection of *mezes* and fish dishes from $15 a head, in a restaurant located at the heart of the fish market. Sit upstairs for a bird's eye view of the fish stalls in the market below and try to avert your eyes from the offal shop across the alleyway whilst you're eating.

Degustasyon Sahne Sok 41, Balık Pazarı ☏0212/292 0667. Fish-market tavern run by Nazim, Turkish TV's star chef. Dishes mix Turkish and international flavours, such as the chicken soya stir-fry, and set menus are $18 (meat) or $25 (fish). Lesser-known Turkish wines available, plus a selection of imports from Bulgaria and Georgia. There are cheaper options in the surrounding fish market, but a lot of thought has been put into this menu.

Four Seasons İstiklâl Cad 509, Tünel ☏0212/293 3941. Popular with expats for its classy, English-style, old-world charm and sweet trolley. Not cheap, but you get what you pay for. Lunchtime set menus are better value at around $10. Closed Sun.

Hacı Abdullah İstiklâl Cad, Sakızağacı Cad 17 ☏0212/293 8561. One of the best traditional restaurants in town sports a high-ceiling atrium salon at the back. Main courses from $7 – try the *hunkar beğendili kebab* (beef stew on a bed of aubergine and cheese purée) and the *ayva tatlı* (stewed quince with clotted cream), not forgetting the preserved fruit dished out by the staff from the huge jars on display. Strictly no alcohol served. The entrance is opposite the Ağa Camii, just off İstiklâl Cad.

Nature and Peace İstiklâl Cad, Büyükparmakkapı Sok 21. Earthy vegetarian restaurant on a lively street, where specialities include green lentil balls, falafels and nettle soup, from around $6 a dish. Some chicken dishes served, too; the only alcohol available is wine. Service is slow at times but it's worth the wait.

Parsifal Kurabiye Sok 13. Sophisticated, inexpensive menu blending Turkish and international styles, with an imaginative menu of non-meat dishes, such as leek and soya burgers.

Refik's Sofyalı Sok 10–12, Tünel. Modest *rakı*-infused Turkish joint, specializing in Black Sea cuisine. *Kara lahana dolmasi* is an unusual stuffed cabbage, popular with the locals. Refik Baba, the good-natured owner, likes to chat in numerous languages, though he doesn't speak much of any. Full dinner with booze, $20. Closed Mon.

Rejans İstiklâl Cad, Emir Nevruz Sok 17 ☏0212/243 3882. Opposite the church of St Antoine and frequented by diplomats from the nearby consulates, this famous establishment was founded by White Russians in the 1930s and thrives on its nostalgic reputation. It's somewhat shabby and staid, but, considering the quality of the food, not too expensive. Main courses (barbecued salmon, grilled quail) start from $10, accompanied by the excellent lemon vodka. *Zindan* in the basement is an upmarket tavern with a more informal atmosphere, for post-dinner drinks and coffees. Both closed Sun.

Zencefil Kurabiye Sok 3. The ever-changing menu includes vegetarian versions of various Turkish dishes from as little as $4, plus some chicken and fish specials, great salads, homemade breads, herbal teas and local wines. Closed Sun.

Taksim

Ayaspaşa İnönü Cad 77 ☏0212/143 4892. Famous basement Russian restaurant that's been cooking for over fifty years, with a friendly atmosphere and good service. It offers a selection of Russian favourites, such as *borscht* and *palaçinka*.

C.Fisher İnönü Cad 51. Atmospheric restaurant-bar of questionable nationality, where wizened old men discuss the woes of the world over *rakı*. Grills, schnitzels and *borscht* available from $5 a dish, though you may want to pass on the fried brains starter.

The China Lamartin Cad 17. There are a number of Chinese restaurants on this street, but this was the first Chinese restaurant in Turkey. Excellent food – their speciality is chicken with vegetables and almonds – and a friendly atmosphere. Closed Sun.

Hong Bin Lou İnönü Cad 53 ☎0212/243 6379. Chinese restaurant with good-value lunch and evening set menus and good service. Popular with the local Chinese community, so booking advised at weekends.

Udonya Tarlabaşı Bul 26 ☎0212/256 9318. Sushi, sashimi and tempura prepared by two Japanese

GALATA, TAKSIM & BEYOĞLU: EATING & DRINKING

CAFÉS & RESTAURANTS

Afacan	23	Dilek	25	Hong Bin Lou	38
Ayaspaşa	39	Ekmek Arasi	11	Kallavi Taverna (Turkish music)	8
C.Fisher	37	Four Seasons	26	Nature and Peace	32
Café Cute (gay)	17	Galata (Turkish music)	15	Nizam Pide 1	28
Café de Flose	31	Galata House Cafe	35	Nizam Pide 2	1
Çatı	16	Galata Kulesi	34	Ocakbaşı	36
The China	12	Gina Margarino	13	Parsifal	21
Cumhuriyet	5	Güney	33	Patisserie de Pera	2
Degustasyon	4	Hacı Abdullah	20	Pia	24
Demğah (Turkish music)	6	Han Café (gay)	27	Refik's	14

chefs. It's pricey – $25–30 a head with drinks – but cheaper than other Japanese options in town. Closed Sun.

Beşiktaş

Tuğra *Çıragan Palace & Kempinski Hotel*, Çaragan Cad 84 ☎0212/258 3377. Ottoman restaurant with one of the most spectacular settings in the city, providing a stunning view over the Bosphorus. Expect to pay Western prices, up to $23 for a main course alone – though these include unexpected

menu items such as *Çerkez tavuğu* (chicken in walnut sauce) and a laden dessert trolley. Dress to impress. Dinner only; closed Mon.

Hanedan Balik Babaros Meyd. Large, fairly formal establishment (meat served downstairs – the roast lamb is especially good – and fish and seafood upstairs), popular with locals and tourists alike for its reliable food, served with abundant fresh *pide*. It's on the front next to the ferry jetty, so the window tables afford good views of the Bosphorus. Expect to pay $25–30 a head with drinks.

Dolmabahçe & Beşikatş ▼

		BARS & CLUBS		Jazz Stop	**K**
Rejans	**7**	5.Kat (gay)	**W**	Kaktüs	**I**
Saklıkent	**30**	Andon	**U**	Line	**N**
Sal Bar (Turkish music)	**29**	Babil	**P**	Madrid	**Q**
Saray	**18**	Babylon Performance Centre	**H**	Mojo	**R**
Süheyla (Turkish music)	**3**	Buenos Aires	**C**	My Moon	**J**
Udonya	**19**	Club 14 (gay)	**E**	Neo (gay)	**D**
Yakup (Turkish music)	**10**	Gizli Bahçe	**A**	Pano Şaraphanesi	**B**
Yağmur	**9**	Gramafon	**M**	Prive (gay)	**F**
Zencefil	**22**	Hayal Kahvesi	**O**	Roxy	**V**
		James Joyce Irish Pub	**L**	Şarabi	**G**
		Jazz Café	**S**	Yaga	**T**

Ortaköy

Carne Muallim Naci Cad 41 ☎0212/260 8425.
Supposedly the only *kosher* restaurant in Turkey.
Sophisticated decor, and a strong emphasis on
Mediterranean dishes, such as *falafel* and tradi-
tional Jewish *köfte*. Bookings essential. Closed Fri
evening & Sat lunch.

İlhamenin Yeri Osmanzade Sok 6. One of the last
of the original Ortaköy *meyhane*s and still one of
the best places in the area, serving a reasonably
priced selection of *mezes*, kebabs and fish – the
set menu is $15. It's on the corner of a busy main
road, so ask for a table inside.

Üsküdar

Huzur (Arabin Yeri) Salacak Iskelesi 20. Run by a
group of Arabic-speaking Turks from the Hatay,
serving grilled fish or seafood with salad for a reasonable $8. The restaurant has a rather faded
charm and an undeniably wonderful view of the
European side of the Bosphorus at sunset.

Kanaat Selmanipak Cad 25. One of the city's more
famous *lokanta*s established in 1933, featuring
copies of İznik tile panels from the Selimiye Camii
in Edirne and a copper chimney-piece. Meals are
reasonably cheap at about $7 a head; no alcohol
served.

Nightlife

Traditionally, İstanbul nightlife meant **meyhanes** (taverns) and **gazinos**
(drinking clubs serving *mezes*, with entertainment from singers and oriental
dancers). The latter have largely faded away and have been replaced by overpriced and tacky all-singing, all-dancing **cabarets** geared towards coach-loads
of tourists. Some traditional and atmospheric *meyhanes* still exist, where a *fasıl*
band might accompany your bottle of *rakı*, but these too are slowly being
eclipsed by café-bars and modern nightclubs. The main locations for **bars and
clubs** are around Taksim, in Ortaköy and the richer European Bosphorus suburbs (where bright young things turn up for a night out in BMWs or even
yachts), and over the water in Kadıköy.

İstanbul listings

The monthly magazine *Time Out İstanbul* is available from newsstands all over the
city for $2. A thirty-odd page English edition is enclosed within the Turkish one
and is the best source of listings and features on what to see in city. Other
English-language publications include the bi-monthly *İstanbul: The Guide*, available in hotel lobbies or bookshops for $5, and the quarterly *City Plus* (✆www
.cityplus-turkey.com) from newsstands for $2. Both have a useful listings section
plus reviews of expensive restaurants and designer clothes shops. **Cornucopia**, a
glossy bi-monthly covering the Ottoman arts scene, auctions, galleries and exhibitions, costs $10 and is available from bookshops that stock foreign newspapers
and publications.

Bars

For a Muslim city, İstanbul is far from dry, and away from conservative Islamic
areas (forget Fatih and Eyüp, for example) you'll find bars ranging from the
dangerously seedy to the chic and overpriced. While **Sultanahmet** favours
rather staid, touristy bars that close early, **Beyoğlu** is the better late-night
choice. There's a variety of bars along the lively *soks* leading off **İstiklâl
Caddesi**, at the Taksim Square end – from jazz joints to sophisticated cafés,
and from basement bars where Turkish youth practice their guitars to a fair
number of dubious establishments that should be avoided altogether. (All
Beyoğlu bars are marked on the map on pp.180–181.) On the Bosphorus,
Ortaköy on the European shore and **Kadıköy**, on the Asian side, have both

seen a recent blossoming of drinking haunts. For the Ortaköy joints, take a taxi or bus the short distance from Taksim Square; to reach Kadıköy's Kadife Sokak, walk or take a taxi from the Kadıköy ferry terminal south down Moda Caddesi, until it turns into Doktor Esat Işık Caddesi – Kadife Sokak is on the left.

The line between İstanbul's bars and cafés tends to blur, with most open during the day to serve food and coffee, becoming more alcoholic as the evening progresses, and often introducing a cover charge between 10pm and 2am if there is live music.

Sultanahmet

Bodrum Bar Divan Yolu Cad, Seftali Sok 3. Small, unremarkable basement bar, but one of the few options in the area for a late-night drink.

Cozy Pub Divan Yolu Cad 66. Modern, Western-style pub that appeals to tourists – hence the high prices. Outside tables are not a bad place to watch the world go by on the Divan Yolu Cad.

Orient Youth Hostel Bar Yeni Akbıyık Cad 13. Rooftop bar at the hostel, with a cheap menu and good views of the Bosphorus and Sea of Marmara. It's frequented by travellers from surrounding hostels in the evening; there are belly-dancing shows on Friday nights.

Beyoğlu

Babil İpek Sok 18. Small bar on a couple of floors of a narrow house, attracting quite the bohemian set.

Buenos Aires Meşrutiye Cad 251. Turkey's only Argentinean café-bar has a fun atmosphere and plenty of tequila, with tango and Latin nights from Wed to Sat. Tango lessons available for a fee in the afternoons.

Gramafon Tünel Meyd 3. At the very end of İstiklâl Cad, right next to Tünel station. Stylish, late-night bar with occasional jazz performances and good people-watching opportunities from the outside tables. Small cover charge if there's a band on.

Hayal Kahvesi İstiklâl Cad, Büyükparmakkapı Sok 19. Attractive brick-and-wood joint with good live jazz and blues every night from 11pm.

James Joyce Irish Pub İstiklâl Cad, Zambak Sok 6. An authentic stab at an Irish pub thanks to owner Eamonn, who hails from Ireland's west coast. Live Irish music from 10pm Thurs–Sun, plus English-language book exchange, travellers' message board and big-screen sports TV. The traditional all-day brunches include pork sausages and black pudding imported from Ireland. The loud, crowded downstairs bar rocks until 4am at the weekends when a band is on (cover charge $8).

Kaktüs İstiklâl Cad, Imam Adnan Sok 4. Favoured drinking, meeting and eating haunt of the TV and advertising crowd, and prominent (but not exclusively) gay venue. Good coffee and salads available, plus a selection of imported beers.

Madrid İpek Sok 20. The only one of Beyoğlu's Spanish-themed bars to have a Spanish owner. The converted four-storey house, with a tight iron spiral staircase, boasts the cheapest beer in the area, good music and a raucous weekend atmosphere. It's next door to *Saklıkent* vegetarian restaurant.

My Moon İstiklâl Cad, Bekar Sok 16. Long, low wooden room with a line of bar stools along a well-stocked bar for *Cheers*-style drinking.

Pano Şaraphanesi İstiklâl Cad, Hamalbaşı Cad 26, Galatasaray. Beautifully restored century-old Greek wine bar, on the opposite corner to the British Consulate. Beer, local wine and excellent, light Turkish food available. The owners also run *Cumhuriyet Meyhane*, another historical drinking den, just round the corner in the Fish Market.

Şarabi İstiklâl Cad 174. One of the swishest places around – a basement wine-bar with an international menu and Guinness on tap, attracting a professional clientele.

Ortaköy

Rock House Café *Princess Hotel*, Dereboyu Cad. İstanbul's answer to the *Hard Rock Café*. Bar and restaurant (serving ribs, chilli, steaks and burgers), with live bands after 10pm. It's a barn of a place, but gets very busy at weekends.

Wall Bar Kaymakça Sok 14. Drinking downstairs, dancing upstairs, in a brightly painted house with fat sofas outside on the pavement. It's friendly enough, but check your bill carefully.

Kadıköy

Hera Kadife Sok 10, Caferağa Mah. The rock and jazz grooves don't quite gel with the pseudo-Ottoman decoration, but it's a popular spot. Hot food is served, too, including tasty *börek*.

Isis Kadife Sok 26, Caferağa Mah. Three-storey townhouse that's café by day and bar-disco at night. Cutting-edge music and good food, plus a

garden open during the summer months.
Lal Kadife Sok 19, Caferağa Mah. Relaxed
café/bar, open all day from breakfast until 2am,

with intimate seating and lighting, Latin grooves,
and good *börek* and salads.

Clubs and live music

İstanbul's dance **clubs** may surprise Western visitors. The best ones are imaginative in decor with sounds that are bang up to date, while **live music** – jazz, rock, blues, R&B, reggae and salsa – is plentiful around the backstreets of Beyoğlu. Expect to spend no less than you would in London, New York or Sydney on a night out. Most places have entry charges (anything from $2 to $20) and tend to be open from around 9pm until 2am or 4am.

Local and visiting foreign bands also play at a welter of annual **festivals** – including two jazz festivals, an international music festival, plus separate dance and techno and blues events: see the festival calendar on p.188 for more details.

Beyoğlu

Babylon Performance Centre Şeybender Sok 3, Asmalımescit, Tünel ☎0212/292 7368, ⓦwww.babylon-ist.com. İstanbul's premier live music club (one of the "Best 100 Jazz Clubs of the World", according to US magazine *Downbeat*) with a regular programme of local and foreign groups playing jazz, reggae and cutting-edge dance. Drinks are expensive and concert tickets last $10–30 (booking office across the street, open daily from noon); performances start at around 10pm.

Gizli Bahçe İstiklâl Cad, Nevizade Sok 27. In the fish market – enter through an unmarked rusty wrought-iron door and head up to the second and third floors of an Ottoman town house for extremely loud dance music and a deliciously illicit atmosphere. Daily 9pm–4am.

Jazz Café Hansun Galip Sok 20, off Büyükparmakkapı Sok ☎0212/252 0694, ⓦwww.jazzcafeistanbul.com. More blues than mainstream jazz, despite the name, in an intimate club with high tables overlooking the tiny stage. A real mix of talent from new bands to studio artists. Shows start at 10.30pm. Daily 4pm–2am.

Jazz Stop Tel Sok 2, off Büyükparmakkapı Sok ☎0212/252 9314. Stylish, atmospheric, barebrick basement club with steep cover charge – one of Istanbul's leading venues for jazz and flamenco. Owned by the band members of the local jazz group *Moğollar* who perform regularly. Performances start at about 11pm. Mon–Sat 4.30pm–4am.

Line İstiklâl Cad, Büyükparmakkapı Sok 14. Sophisticated dance club, with live music from 11pm, currently attracting Istanbul's top bands. Daily 10pm–2am.

Mojo İstiklâl Cad, Büyükparmakkapı Sok 26. Ultra-modern basement club, recently revamped, with live music most nights – best when the blues bands turn up. Daily 9pm–4am.

Taksim

Andon Sıraselviler Cad 89 ☎0212/251 0222. Massively popular with İstanbul's fashionable set, this features five overwhelming floors, each with their own personality: dancing in *Pera* to İstanbul's best DJs; wine and cheese in the second-floor *Wine House*; live Turkish music and belly-dancing in *Müdavim Bar*, a fourth-floor *meyhane* with seafood snacks, *fasıl* band and *rakı*; and fifth-floor roof-terrace restaurant. Booking advised if you want to eat; the Wine House and terrace open at 5pm, the others at 7pm, and the whole circus closes at 3am.

Gossip *Hyatt Regency Hotel*, Taşkışla Cad. Expensive hotel club sporting avant-garde decor. Mainstream bands play from May to Sept, but there's a nicer atmosphere in the relaxing garden area, decorated with trailing ivy and oil lamps. Mon–Sat 8pm–4am.

Roxy Arslan Yatağı Sok 113, Sıraselviler Cad ☎0212/245 6539, ⓦwww.roxy.com.tr. DJs and live bands play rock, R&B, jazz and dance music in this posy, pricey bar-disco, which attracts a mixed crowd – rich students to 1980s throwbacks. It's unmarked and not easy to find, close to the German Hospital, and sometimes closes for a few weeks over summer if business is slow – so call first. Daily 6pm–3.30am.

Yaga Sıraselviler Cad 67. An unassuming entrance opens up inside to all sorts of treats – several levels of bars, a dance floor, giant TV screen and garden with comfy cushions. Bands play Wed–Sun at 10pm. Café and restaurant open during the day, cover charge levied after 9pm, when things liven up. Daily noon–4am.

Ortaköy

Q Club & Bar *Çırağan Palace Hotel Kempinski,
Çarağan Cad 32* ☎ *0212/258 3377,* ⓦ *www
.infoqjazzclub.com.* With its beautiful Bosphorus
views from the terrace, this is a class joint in a
sumptuous hotel and you won't get in unless they
like the look of you. Past performers have included
Whitney Houston and Ray Charles so expect to pay
insanely high cover charges and drinks prices.
Different sections feature jazz, Latin and salsa

sounds, while famous Turkish club DJs appear
most nights. Daily 10pm-4am.
Reina *Muallim Nacı Cad 120.* Summer drinking
outside until dawn for the bright young things who
manage to get through the door. There are dance
floors, video screens and bars all directly overlooking the Bosphorus, and overpriced sushi – early
birds get 30 percent off drinks between 6 and
8pm. June–Sept only, daily 6pm–4am.

Gay and lesbian İstanbul

Despite the widespread enthusiasm for transvestite and transsexual singers and
entertainers in Turkey, homosexuality is still taboo and it is possible to be arrested for cruising (see Basics, p.82). The main centre of the **Turkish gay scene** is
in and around Taksim, where most of the places reviewed below can be found.

A rundown of the İstanbul scene can be found at ⓦwww.qrd.org/qrd
/world/europe/turkey/guide, the homepage of **Lambda** (Turkey's foremost gay
liberation group). Lambda also issues a bi-monthly magazine called *cins* but
it's almost impossible to get hold of – try asking for it at the *Pandora* bookshop
(p.190). Otherwise, the *Time Out İstanbul* magazine offers the best advice with
a rundown of gay and lesbian venues.

Cafés

Café Cute *2nd floor, İstiklal Cad, Yeni Çarşı Cad
26, Galatasaray, Beyoğlu.* Though not exclusively
gay, this comfortable café is one of the few alternatives to the late-night scene. Daily 11am to midnight.
Han Cafe *Cumhuriyet Cad 9, Taksim.* In a prominent position in Taksim Square (next to
McDonalds), this huge cafe-bar is busy all day
from breakfast. Gays and lesbians frequent the
back bar. Daily 10am–midnight.

Bars and clubs

Club 14 *Abdulhakhamit Cad, Belediye Dükkanları
14, Taksim.* Tiny late-night spot with a young
crowd, lively atmosphere, good music and friendly
staff. Daily except Mon 11pm–4am.
5.Kat *5th Floor, Siraselviler Cad, Soğancı Sok 7,
Taksim.* Established venue, close to the German
Hospital, for the older crowd – a sophisticated and
stylish place with good food. Also houses *Bar*

Bahçe, a first-floor bar with the occasional weekend drag show by an Audrey Hepburn look-a-like.
Both open daily except Mon 9pm–2am.
Love Bar *Cumhuriyet Cad 349, Harbiye.* Spacious
new club (free admission) where DJs spin a wide
range of sounds from garage to traditional Turkish.
It's opposite the Military Museum and near the
Osmanbey metro station. Daily except Mon
11pm–4am.
Neo *Lamartin Cad 40, Taksim.* Popular bar with
upmarket professionals, quite yuppyish but one of
İstanbul's consistently crowded gay venues. Daily
except Mon 10pm–2am.
Prive *Tarlabasi Bul 28, Taksim.* Gay-only dance
club, with a devoted following due to its reputation as a pick-up place. It's a bit more middle-
aged and less trendy than Club 14, its sister club,
and the ancient Western pop tunes will appeal to
people who like words with their music.
Admission charge only at weekends. Daily
midnight-4am.

Cabaret and Turkish music

Cabaret is probably the most expensive way to develop a feel for the Orient.
Even in the more reputable places an exorbitant entrance fee is levied, you are
overcharged for anything you eat or drink and belly-dancers expect to be given
generous amounts of money (stuffed in their bras) by foreign tourists. It's wise
to avoid the touts, particularly around the *Hilton* and other five-star hotels on
Cumhuriyet Caddesi, who may lead you to less salubrious places – it's better

to stick to the more established venues, the best of which are reviewed below. Unless otherwise stated, the cabaret venues have daily **performances**, with dinner served at 7.45pm, the show running from 8.30pm to around midnight.

A less expensive and more authentic alternative to cabaret is a night of **traditional Turkish music** (see Contexts, p.1026) in a friendly bar-restaurant. Most venues offer either *bağlama*, played on the *saz* (a long-necked stringed lute), or *fasıl*, heavy on the violin with *ud* (lute), *darabuka* (drum) and maybe a *zurna* (clarinet). In bars featuring livelier music, you'll be expected to dance. As well as the places around Beyoğlu listed below, most of the fish restaurants in Kumkapı on the Sultanahmet side of the Horn have live *fasıl* music in the evenings. Expect to pay $15–20 per head for *meze*s and a couple of drinks in a restaurant that provides traditional live music.

Cabaret venues

Gar Music Hall Mustafa Kemal Paşa Cad 3, Yenikapı ☎0212/588 4045. Folk dancing, belly dancing and a three-course meal for around $50, or $30 without food, and free pick-ups from major hotels. It's one of the cheaper options but the show resembles a badly organized school play. The venue is near Yenikapı train station.

Kervansaray Cumhuriyet Cad 30, Harbiye ☎0212/247 1630, ⓦwww.kervansaraytr.com. Not far from the *Hilton*, it's a huge pillared, chandeliered hall where you won't feel comfortable unless you dress up a bit. Expensive at $75 a head, $50 without food, but the club has a good reputation for its floor-show, which includes oriental and folk dancers.

Orient House *President Hotel*, Tiyatro Cad 27, Beyazıt ☎0212/517 6163, ⓦwww .orienthouseistanbul.com. Traditional Turkish and folk music, plus belly-dancing. A four-course meal with wine and show is $75 a head; show and wine but no meal costs $50.

Sultana's Cumhuriyet Cad 16, Harbiye ☎0212/219 3904-5, ⓦwww.sultanas-nights.com. Oriental and folklore show, costing $75 with dinner, $45 without, plus free transport from any hotel (cheaper rates can be negotiated if you just turn up at the door). Members of the audience are expected to participate in the *Harem* dance.

Turkish Cultural Dance Theatre Firat Culture Centre, Divan Yolu, Sultanahmet ☎0212/517 8692, ⓦwww.dancesofcolours.com. Presents *Dances of Colours* from ten different regions of Turkey, including belly-dancing and Whirling Dervishes, in an air-conditioned auditorium next to the Çemberlitaş tram stop. This is purely theatre, with no dinner or the other trappings of a club. Twice-weekly shows ($25) on Tues at 5.15pm and Fri at 7pm.

Fasıl and bağlama venues

Demğah Nevizade Sok 18, Beyoğlu. Overpriced *meyhane* in this hugely popular street of restaurants in the fish market, but there's live music nightly and you can sit outside.

Galata İstiklâl Cad, Orhan Apaydın Sok 11, Tünel, Beyoğlu ☎0212/293 1139. Old-style *meyhane* with a set menu of a succession of quality *meze*s, including *raki* or wine, for around $16. Tables surround the *fasıl* band; bookings essential. Closed Sun.

Kallavi Taverna İstiklâl Cad, Kallavi Sok 20, Beyoğlu. Small, traditional restaurant near Galatasaray School with tables and *fasıl* band on the street. It's very popular with the locals; there's another branch at Şefik Bey Sok, Kadıköy. Closed Sun.

Sal Bar İstiklâl Cad, Büyükparmakapı Sok 18, Beyoğlu. A relaxed atmosphere in a low-ceilinged room with coffee tables and couches. The *bağlama* band starts early, from 5pm, often inspiring *halay*s, Turkish line-dancing. There are a number of other similar venues on Hasnun Galip Sok, around the corner.

Süheyla Kalyoncu Kulluk Cad 45, Beyoğlu. Friendly late-night *lokanta* behind the fish market, serving *meze*s accompanied by live band. Closed Sun.

Yakup Asmalı Mescit Sok 35, Tünel, Beyoğlu ☎0212/249 2925. Casual and noisy, one of the last of the old brigade of *meyhane*s. It has a faded charm and smoke-stained decor and is still frequented by artists, journalists and intellectuals. *Meze*s and kebabs served, with *raki* by the bottle. It's a small venue – booking required on a Friday evening.

Arts, entertainment and festivals

İstanbul hosts a decent variety of annual cultural **festivals** and matches other European cities for the breadth of its **arts scene**. State-subsidized theatre, opera and ballet make performances affordable for all and there's something going on almost every night at various venues around the city. Music features heavily over the summer months when international festivals draw musicians from all over the world.

Art exhibitions

In addition to the galleries listed below, **Atatürk Cultural Centre** (see "Theatres and concert halls", p.189) hosts temporary exhibitions, as do a number of hi-tech galleries sponsored by banks and large corporations. Many of these are found along İstiklâl Caddesi in Beyoğlu, where you are quite likely to stumble on an art exhibition when you use an ATM at one of the banks. The most important event for artists is the **International İstanbul Biennial** held in odd-numbered years in October, when works of art are displayed in some of the oldest and most historic buildings in Sultanahmet, notably in Topkapı Palace.

Aksanat Cultural Centre İstiklâl Cad 16–18, Beyoğlu ☏0212/252 3500, ⓦwww.akbank.com.tr/sanat. Changing exhibitions of art and sculpture from well-known local artists, and interesting films of jazz and classical concerts shown on a giant screen.

Borusan Arts & Cultural Centre İstiklâl Cad 421, Tünel, Beyoğlu ☏0212/292 0655, ⓦwww .borusansanat.com. Also home to the Borusan Philharmonic Orchestra (p.189), with state-of-the-art exhibition space showing established Turkish artists as well as international names.

Garanti Bankasi Güncel Culture Centre İstiklâl Cad 276, Beyoğlu ☏0212/233 2238. Changing art

and photography exhibitions sponsored by the bank of the same name.

İstanbul Arts Fair Tuyap Exhibition Centre, Sergi Sarayı, Meşrutiyet Cad, Tepebaşi ☏0212/241 6535, ⓦwww.tuapfair.com. This annual week-long sales fair takes place in October, when both domestic and international art companies rent exhibition stands.

Yapı Kredi Cultural Centre İstiklâl Cad 285, Beyoğlu ☏0212/293 3710, ⓦwww.yapikredi .com.tr. International photography exhibitions in a large space on one floor, next to the Galatasaray School.

Film

There are hundreds of **cinemas** (*sinemasi*) all over İstanbul showing Hollywood and Bollywood releases with Turkish sub-titles. Many of the modern complexes are situated in the large shopping malls but there are a few old classic movie theatres left where, for a tip, white-coated attendants show you to your seat and a ten-minute interval pacifies the smokers. Tickets cost around $3; there are discounts before 6pm and for students. The annual **International Film Festival** (mid-April to May) takes place mainly at cinemas in Beyoğlu.

AFM Akmerkez Akmerkez Shopping Mall, Etiler ☏0212/282 0505. The city's largest multiplex, surrounded by a vast food court and Akmerkez's palatial shops. Sound and screen quality is the best in town.

AFM Fitaş İstiklâl Cad 24–26, Beyoğlu ☏0212/292 1111. A popular ten-screen cinema not far from Taksim Square, showing the newest films, with a trendy pub upstairs and a vast range of CDs in the shop out front.

Atlas İstiklâl Cad 209, Beyoğlu ☏0212/252 8576. Newly restored comfy cinema with an arty

atmosphere in the adjoining bar. Offbeat Hollywood movies and homespun Turkish farces.

Emek Yeşilçam Sok 5, İstiklâl Cad, Beyoğlu ☏0212/293 8439. This huge atmospheric auditorium (875 seats) built in the 1920s is a popular venue during the International Film Festival.

Şafak Yeniçeriler Cad, at the Çemberlitaş tram stop ☏0212/516 2660. The closest cinema to Sultanahmet, buried in the bowels of a shopping centre, with seven screens showing the latest Western releases.

The annual festival calendar is pretty full – at least between April and October, when most of the best events take place. The highlights are detailed below; for more information, consult the city tourist offices or the İstanbul Foundation for Culture and Arts (see "Theatres and concert halls", opposite).

April
International Film Festival Turkish, European and Hollywood movies premiere at İstanbul's cinemas, plus the best of the non-English-speaking world's releases from the previous year and new prints of classic films – visiting celebrities add glitz and glamour.

May
Conquest Celebrations Week-long celebration of the Ottoman conquest of old Constantinople (May 29, 1453) – concerts by the Ottoman Mehter military band, fancy dress processions and fireworks.

International Puppet Festival A celebration of Turkish Shadow Theatre, or *karagöz* – silent puppets tell their tale behind a two-dimensional screen.

International Theatre Festival The year's best Turkish plays (both local avant-garde and established theatre groups) and performances by visiting foreign theatres – some plays enacted out at open-air venues.

June
H2000 Music Festival İstanbul's answer to Woodstock, an open-air festival and campsite attracting 25,000 revellers to see top bands and DJs.

International Bosphorus Festival A bizarre range of musical and dance events from rock, pop and ballet, to big band sounds and disco divas.

June/July
The International Music Festival Concerts, recitals, dance and opera – this hugely successful festival was launched in 1973 to celebrate Turkey's fifty years of independence and brings top-notch orchestras and soloists from all over the world to perform in such atmospheric venues as the church of Aya Irene.

July/August
International Jazz festival Two-weeks of gigs and jamming sessions from world-class performers (with the definition of jazz stretched in recent years to include rock artists such as Lou Reed and Marianne Faithful).

Rumeli Hisarı Fortress Concerts Nightly summer concerts within the walls of this Ottoman fortification overlooking the Bosphorus – a varied programme from classical to rock.

September
Akbank International Jazz Festival Concentrates on traditional jazz rather than the mainstream music and big names of July's festival – events include film screenings, informal jamming sessions and drum workshops.

İstanbul Arts Fair A weeklong fair selling the work of some fifty or so İstanbul galleries and visiting foreign artists – paintings, sculptures, pottery and fabrics.

J&B Dance and Techno Festival The name says it all, a 24-hour non-stop rave for 20,000 party goers – guest DJs spin a variety of sounds from trip hop to garage in three giant dance arenas.

October
Efes Pilsen Blues Festival Two-day late-night blues festival – a showcase of new local talent and famous foreign bands.

International İstanbul Biennial Every two years (odd-numbered), artists from over thirty countries exhibit at some evocative locations – Sultanahmet's Yerebatan Saray, and the Aya Irene and Royal Mint buildings in Topkapı Palace.

Theatres and concert halls

There are regular **classical music**, **ballet** and **opera** performances in İstanbul, held at Taksim's Atatürk Cultural Centre and at other venues across the city. The main annual event is the **International Music Festival** during June and July, which includes jazz, classical and world music concerts, as well as performances by the İstanbul State Symphony Orchestra. **Theatre** is popular, but it's mostly Turkish plays that are performed on the thirty or so stages in the city. The **State Theatre Company** puts on occasional plays in English at the Atatürk Cultural Centre and foreign theatre groups such as the Royal Shakespeare Company perform in İstanbul during May's **International Theatre Festival**. Information on all music and theatre events, and on the various cultural festivals, is available from the **İstanbul Foundation for Culture and Arts**, İstiklâl Cad 146, Beyoğlu ☎0212/334 0700, ⓦ www.istfest.org.

Atatürk Cultural Centre (AKM) Taksim Square, Theatre ☎0212/251 5600; Opera & Ballet ☎0212/243 2011; Symphony Orchestra ☎0212/243 1068. Multi-purpose venue shared by the Symphony Orchestra, State Theatre Company, and State Opera and Ballet. Leading venue during the various international festivals and has regular performances of classical music on Friday evenings and Saturday mornings, plus opera and ballet on Thursday and Friday nights throughout the year. Ticket prices are subsidized by the government, so remain low ($5–8) – box office open daily 10am–6pm, student discounts available, no credit cards.

Borusan Arts and Cultural Centre İstiklâl Cad 421, Tünel, Beyoğlu ☎0212/292 0655, ⓦ www.borusansanat.com. Home to the Borusan Philharmonic Orchestra, one of Turkey's most successful private orchestras, which performs two monthly concerts (tickets $10–15). Also boasts one of the country's most extensive CD libraries.

Cemal Reşit Rey (CRR) Darülbedai Cad 1, Harbiye ☎0212/231 5497, ⓦ www.crrks.org. Chamber music, classical, jazz and Turkish music, plus regular performances by visiting international orchestras. Venue for the International Music festival in June and the CRR Piano Festival in December. Daily performances (season Oct–May; $5–10) at 8pm; no credit cards.

Kenter Theatre Halaskargazi Cad 35, Harbiye ☎0212/246 3589. Theatre founded by the famous Turkish actress Yıldız Kenter who appears in most of the plays. Some English-speaking performances such as Shakespeare and Chekhov, and venue for the Turkish Shadow Play performed on most weekend mornings. Box office daily 11am–6pm, tickets $5–10.

Shopping

Shopping in İstanbul is part of the cultural experience, and drinking tea with a merchant whilst feverishly bargaining over a carpet may be one of the fondest memories you will take back home. At times the city seems like one enormous bazaar, so knowing where to look is the trick. No one should miss the Kapalı Çarşı, the **covered bazaar**, a hive of over four thousand little shops selling the contents of a lifetime of shopping lists. But scattered around the city are a number of other shopping districts, which are just as interesting – **Ortaköy**, for arts and crafts; **Nişantası** for international fashion; and the Mısır Çarşısı, or **spice bazaar**, for spices and sweets.

İstiklâl Caddesi in Beyoğlu is İstanbul's equivalent to London's Oxford Street and is traffic-free save for an antique tram. Many major Turkish and international chain stores can be found along here, as well as a few interesting covered markets, bootleg CD stalls, and clothing and secondhand-book markets. For upmarket shopping try **Nuruosmaniye Caddesi**, the modern pedestrianized street that leads to the main entrance of the covered bazaar. Here, every alternate shop seems to sell either top-of-the-range carpets or gold jewellery – this has got to be one of the most valuable streets in the city.

There are **carpet shops** all over İstanbul, particularly in and around the covered bazaar (Takkeciler Caddesi has a good concentration), but also in the flea markets of Kadıköy and Üsküdar, and secondhand shops around Altıpatlar Sokak, off İstiklâl Caddesi. Buying a carpet involves the psychological game of bargaining; play it with the right people, otherwise you will be ripped off (see "Basics", p.70). Out of the centre, **shopping malls** have taken off in a big way, good for homeware and furniture as well as clothes, though in malls prices are clearly marked and there's no room for bargaining.

Opening hours for most shops are Monday to Saturday 10am to 7pm, though the modern shopping malls stay open daily until 10pm. Supermarkets and hypermarkets open 9am to 10pm every day but smaller food shops close much earlier. The covered bazaar opens Monday to Saturday 9am to 7pm and is credit-card friendly, as are all shops save for the smallest of grocers (*bakals*) or kiosks.

Books, maps and prints

There are some good stockists of English-language **books** around the city, and it's also rewarding to browse through the secondhand-book markets and shops. The best-known **Sahaflar Çarşısı** (old book market) is the one at Beyazit (see p.143), at the Beyazit side of the covered bazaar, next to Beyazit Camii – though these days it's probably better for finding old prints of İstanbul. Numerous secondhand bookstores cluster in **Beyoğlu**, especially in the backstreets off the east side of İstiklâl Caddesi and down towards the Çukurcuma antique district. The annual **İstanbul Book Fair** in late October is held in the İstanbul Sergi Sarayı on Meşrutiyet Cad, near the *Pera Palas Hotel*.

Aypa Kitabevi Mimar Mehmet Ağauu Cad 19, Sultanahmet. Broad range of books, cards and maps. For some inexplicable reason, it opens at 6.30am.

Beyoğlu Sahaflar Çarşısı İstiklâl Cad, Beyoğlu. Good book market in the streets surrounding the Balık Pazarı (fish market), where some of the shops specialize in English-language texts.

Denizler Kitabevi İstiklâl Cad 395, Beyoğlu. Specialists in nautical books and charts, plus an extensive range of collectors' books on Turkey and the Ottomans.

Dünya Kitabevi İstiklâl Cad 469, Beyoğlu. Upmarket outlet specializing in coffee-table hardbacks and a broad range of English-language newspapers and magazines. Café on site for leisurely reading.

Eren Sofyala Sok 34, Tünel, Beyoğlu. Art and history books, old maps and miniatures.

Galeri Kayseri Divan Yolu Cad 58, Sultanahmet. The biggest distributor of English-language books in Turkey, with a vast range of books on Ottoman history and all other imaginable Turkish topics.

Homer Yeni Çarşşı Cad 28, Beyoğlu. Wide range of books on academic subjects, especially archeology and ancient history – has been known to stock the odd Rough Guide.

Librairie de Pera Galapdede Cad 22, Tünel, Beyoğlu. Excellent selection of antiquarian books, including English-language ones, plus maps of the Ottoman Empire, prints and photographs.

Natural Akbiyik Cad 31, Sultanahmet. Secondhand foreign-book exchange a few doors along from the *Orient Youth Hostel* – buy, sell, or swap two for one.

Pandora İstiklâl Cad, Büyükparmakkapı Sok 3, Beyoğlu. Excellent selection of foreign-language books on three storeys; carries some gay literature and will order books on request.

Remzi Kitabevi Basement Floor, Akmerkez Shopping Mall, Etiler. A good selection of foreign newspapers, and books and magazines in English, for adults and children.

Robinson Crusoe İstiklâl Cad 389, Tünel, Beyoğlu. Reasonably priced, extensive collection of English-, French-, and German-language books, and a number of guides and maps.

Fashion: clothes, fabrics and leather

Turkish fashion designs are beginning to compete on the catwalks, thanks to Rıfat Özbek, the darling of the European fashion world. Other names to watch out for in Turkish *haute couture* are Bahar Korçan, Gönül Paksoy, Ferruh Karakaşli and Murat Taşin, all of whom are working with the best Turkish fabrics: leather so fine that it is now processed for the Italian market and sold at inflated prices under Italian labels, Bursa silk and the universally famous Angora wool. Paksoy also uses hand-processed vegetable dyes. While Turkish designers often imitate European styles, they do occasionally flirt with eastern motifs and designs, creating more of a distinctive effect.

Bargain clothing

Many Western high-street stores have their clothes produced in Turkey and a number of stalls and markets across the city specialize in seconds, production overruns and samples – often at ludicrously cheap prices ($1–2 for T-shirts and tops, $5–7 for trousers and $7–10 for casual jackets). Fakes abound (be wary of *Elvis* jeans – an anagram of *Levis*), but garments that belong to Western high-street brands not marketed in Turkey are probably genuine. Cheap, locally made clothes can be found in any number of shops, particularly in the whole-sale backstreets of Laleli.

Beşiktaş Pazar Beşiktaş. Saturday bazaar held in a warren of streets on either side of Şair Nedim Cad at the back of Beşiktaş (follow Şair Nedim Cad for about ten minutes from the ferry terminal). It's pot-luck what you'll find, as just about any kind of clothing can turn up here.

Salıpazar Kuşdili Cad, Kadıköy. Held on Tuesdays, Fridays and Sundays, reached by going uphill from the ferry terminal along Söğütlüçeşme Cad until it becomes Kuşdili Cad. Similar to Beşiktaş Pazar, but with a European style Sunday fleamarket selling jewellery and antiques.

Sirkeci Pazar Yeni Cami Meydanı, opposite Mısır Çarşısı (spice bazaar). Held on Sundays on the open square opposite the bazaar and in the adjacent backstreets. Cheap Turkish clothes and sportswear, though anything with a Western label is likely to be a fake.

Terkoz Çıkmaz Beyoğlu. A side-street off İstiklâl Cad; next to the Paşabahçe glass store, down towards Tünel. Open daily and crammed with stalls selling overruns bearing British, French and German high-street names.

Ulus Pazar Nispetiye Cad, Etiler. Held on Thursdays on the opposite side of Nispetiye Cad from Akmerkez shopping mall. High-street labels, more expensive than in the other street markets.

High-street and designer clothes

You'll find all the usual **high-street fashion stores** in İstanbul, including Benetton, Diesel, DKNY, Escada, Lacoste, Levi's and Polo Ralph Lauren, as well as the more upmarket Armani, Versace and Gucci. **Turkish stores** (with multiple branches) to watch out for include: Beymen, Damat Tween, Homestore, Karaca, La Luna, Mudo City, Mudo, OXXO, Silk and Cashmere, and Yargıcı. Vakko is one of the oldest and best-known fashion chains in İstanbul; Vakkorama is its youth-market offshoot. For **shoes**, look for Desa, Hotiç and Vetrina.

Designer clothing outlets in İstanbul are mainly located in the shopping malls (see overleaf) or in the streets around the districts of **Nişantaşı**, **Osmanbey** and **Şişli** (take any bus north from Taksim square, from outside *McDonalds*). There are more stores on **İstiklâl Caddesi**, and on **Bağdat Caddesi** on the Asian side of the Bosphorus near Kadıköy. Bursa **towelling**, among the best in the world, is available all over town, with many shops grouped in Nişantaşı and Şişli.

Beyman Akmerkez Shopping Mall, Etiler. Quality chain store for tailored men and women's suits, dress shirts, silk ties and scarves and other accessories for the well turned out executive.

Mavi İstiklâl Cad 117, Beyoğlu; and in all shopping malls. Gap-inspired jeans label, good quality denimwear, T-shirts, sweat tops and funky bags.

Silk & Cashmere Akmerkez Shopping Mall, Etiler; and other branches, including a duty-free shop at Atatürk airport. Scarves, hats, gloves, sweaters and shirts, using imported fabrics from China.

Vakko İstiklâl Cad 123–125, Beyoğlu; Akmerkez Shopping Mall, Etiler, and other branches; ⓦ www.vakko.com.tr. Classy fifty-year old Turkish fashion label renowned for its sense of style and use of fine fabrics. The clothes don't come cheap though, and you have to dress up a bit simply to get in the flagship store on İstiklâl Cad where you may come under some scrutiny from the rather snooty assistants. Vakkorama is the younger version aimed at wealthy teenagers. At the Vakko Sales Store, at Seylülislam Hayri Cad in Eminönü, items here can be picked up for a quarter of the regular price.

Yargıcı Akmerkez Shopping Mall, Etiler, and other branches. Turkey's answer to Marks & Spencers – well-made and reasonably priced clothing from work suits to sportswear and underwear.

Leather

Leather is big business in Turkey, with raw pelts imported for processing from as far away as Australia and New Zealand. Turks wear a lot of leather and, increasingly, designs are matching the quality of the raw material. Prices can be attractive to foreign buyers and if you go home without buying a leather item then count yourself in the minority. The classiest outlets are listed below, but if you are prepared to do the leg-work, cheaper shops can be found in Aksaray and Laleli, and in the covered bazaar, particularly in Vezirhan Sokak.

BB Kuyulu Sok 9–12, covered bazaar; and Yağlıkçalar Cad 143, covered bazaar. European designers, competitive prices.

Derishow Akmerkez Shopping Mall, Etiler; Bağdat Cad 381, Suadiye; and Akkavak Sok 18, Nişantaşı. Fine quality leather goods.

Desa İstiklâl Cad 140, Beyoğlu; and Akmerkez, Capitol and Galleria shopping malls. Top-quality Turkish designs; representatives of Samsonite.

De-Sa Ortakazlar Cad 8–10, covered bazaar. Good selection of leather and kilim bags.

Taki Nuruosmaniye Cad 96, Sultanahmet. Sophisicated shop with prices to match, near the covered bazaar.

Markets, arts, crafts and antiques

Bit pazarları or flea markets (literally "louse markets") make for excellent shopping, whether you're settling in the city and need furniture or simply looking for souvenirs. İstanbul is also a wonderful place for antique collectors. The choices run from traditional Turkish pieces to more obscure items from Europe. Remember, though, that while Turkish antiquities may be bought and sold, it's illegal to export them (punishable with five to ten years' imprisonment). An item under a hundred years old will pose few problems, but exporting a seventeenth-century Ottoman sword is another matter altogether. Storeowners are always ready with explanations on the history of specific items.

Below is listed an assortment of markets and odd shops selling arts, crafts and antiques.

Sultanahmet

Caferağa Medresesi Caferiye Sok. Next to the Inter Youth Hostel, the central courtyard is a pleasant tree-shaded café, while the surrounding shops sell leather, jewellery, calligraphy, carpets and miniatures.

İstanbul Handicrafts Centre Kabasakal Cad 5, next to the Yeşil Ev Hotel. Restored medrese where artists and craftsmen are keeping alive traditional skills such as ebru marbling, calligraphy, lace-making and embroidery.

Food shopping

The best places for food shopping are the weekly street markets in just about every residential area, or the municipality-run **Halk Paşarlar** (people's markets). The latter are permanent markets with small cubicle-like shops (including grocers, butchers and delicatessens), usually open from Monday to Saturday and specializing in fresh, cheap produce.

You can find **imported Western foods** in the major supermarket chains, such as *Migros* or *Macrocenter*, which have branches throughout the city, or in many of the delis that crowd the narrow streets behind Kadıköy harbour on the Asian shore.

The **Balak Pazarı**, or fish market off İstiklâl Caddesi in Beyoğlu, is a fascinating daily market with much more for sale than just fish. There's everything from fresh ducks, quails, regional cheeses, coffee beans and spices to farm-fresh eggs, *crème fraiche* and Beluga caviar scooped from a bucket. Pork, bacon and other hard-to-find ingredients are sold at a shop called Şutte (no. 21); while at Bunsa (no. 26) sun-dried tomatoes, fresh ginger, and a wide selection of health foods are available.

Dried fruit and exotic herbs can be found in the **Mısır Çarşısı** (spice bazaar) in Eminönü; while the **Eminönü Pazarı** (to the right of the spice bazaar) is a crowded market selling olives, olive oil, fresh vegetables, cheeses and pastrami. Also here is *Kurukahveci Mehmet* (Tahmiş Cad 66), the most famous outlet for **Turkish coffee**.

For a taste of **boza**, the Anatolian drink made from fermented *dari* (a type of wheat) flavoured with grape juice and cinnamon, try the oldest producer in Turkey, Vefa Bozacısı (Vefa Katip Çelebi Cad 102), just down from the Süleymaniye mosque. For traditional **Turkish cheese and meat products** visit one of the many family-owned supermarkets in Üsküdar, where you'll find specialities from all over Turkey.

Beyazit and the covered bazaar

Beyazit Pazar Beyazit Meyd. Held on Sundays in the square and the surrounding streets, with everything from stolen mobile phones to Russian army surplus gear. Also the odd stall selling kilims, embroidery and other handicrafts from Central Asia.

Emin Çömez Yağlıkçılar Cad 101–103, covered bazaar. Excellent hat stall, well-stocked in winter with Russian and Turkish wool, leather and fur. This street is also good for traditional Anatolian textiles.

İç Bedesten Covered bazaar. The "Old Bazaar" is where the most precious objects have traditionally been kept. It's the place to go for antiques, reproductions and souvenirs of every kind, from Ottoman hamam slippers to pistols and silver jewellery.

Kato Export Halıcılar Cad 55, covered bazaar. Ottoman copper and Byzantine icons from the eighteenth and nineteenth centuries.

May Kolancilar Kapısı Sok 7, covered bazaar. Kilim bags, belts, purses and so forth, as well as ceramics.

Sarnıçlı Han Çadırcılar Cad 5, covered bazaar. A wholesale and handicraft bazaar: lots of copperware.

Sivaslı İstanbul Yazmacısı Yağlıkçılar Cad 57, covered bazaar. Hand-woven and hand-embroidered textiles, both old and new.

Sofa Nuruosmaniye Cad 42, Cağaloğlu. Old prints, maps, calligraphy, contemporary art and quality ceramics.

Yurt Antika Cebeci Han 51, covered bazaar. Central Asian carpets, kilims and textiles, some antique. It supplies to many other shops, so prices tend to be lower, and smaller items, such as cushions, go from $2.

Fatih

Deli Kızın Yeri Halıcılar Cad 42. Opposite the main entrance of Fatih Camii, "Crazy Lady's Place" sells a vast amount of junk and collectibles, including limited-edition clothes, wall-hangings, scarves, Christmas decorations and unusual objects from Turkish artists. Linda is the crazy lady and she plans to open another branch in the covered bazaar. Closed Sun.

Horhor antique market Kırık Tulumba Sok. The famous weekend market behind Fethiye Camii with its rare Ottoman furniture is beyond most pockets, but it's a fascinating place to browse.

Beyoglu

Atlas Pasaj İstiklâl Cad 209. An arcade behind the Atlas cinema filled with shops selling bric-a-brac, antiques and all sorts of kitsch – model cars, fur-trimmed lamps, ship's lanterns. One useful shop sells international brands of backpacks.

Aznavur Pasaj İstiklâl Cad. Opposite Galatasaray Yapı Kredi bank, two floors of small shops and stalls selling crafts, clothing, music and bric-a-brac.

Nobonb Çukuurlu Çeşme Sok 12. A real treasure trove, with anything from antiques to secondhand costumes, and with a café on site.

Çukurcuma

Antikarnas Kuloğlu Mah, Faik Paşa Yokuşu 15. Turkish, Ottoman and European antiques – it specializes in religious icons.

Çukurcuma bit pazar In the streets below the Galatasaray Hamam. There are a number of antique shops here selling everything from valuable paintings, prints and carved wooden doors to bric-a-brac and books. To get there walk down Yeniçarsi Cad from İstiklâl Cad and turn left into Çukurcuma Sok.

Ortaköy

Artisan İskele Sok 9. Extensive range of antique silverware.

Entel Ortaköy Boardwalk, waterfront square, next to the ferry terminal. The daily market sells just about everything, from arts and crafts to junk and antiques and is an enjoyable experience if you don't mind the crowds. The best day to go is Sunday for the Ortaköy "intellectual market" when the best stalls sell obscure music cassettes and dissident literature.

Pegasus İskele Sok 4. Designer jewellery, some inspired by Ottoman motifs, some contemporary.

Kenser Canfener Sok 14. Specializes in Kütahya potter; it's an easy shop to find because of the beautiful tiles on the outside walls.

Hazal Halı Mecidiye Köprüsü Sok 9. Some colourful, quality carpets and kilims, beautifully displayed.

Kadiköy

Kadıköy bit pazar Özellik Sok, off Soğutluçeş me Cad. Daily street market where there's fun to be had sorting through the great mounds of furniture, household junk and old carpets and kilims, with some clothes on Tuesdays and fresh food on Fridays.

Üsküdar

Üsküdar bit pazar Büyük Hamam Sok, off Hakimiyet-i Milliye Cad. A 10-min walk uphill from the ferry terminal – a bargain damaged or second-hand carpet can sometimes be picked up in this warren of antique shops full of junk and collectibles.

Music and musical instruments

Turkish music aside, you'll find a good general selection of world music, classical, pop and jazz in the music shops listed below and in the many outlets on İstiklâl Caddesi and in the shopping malls. Bulgarian-made bootlegs are sold along the backstreets of Taksim Square and Eminönü. Traditional musical instruments are sold in the covered bazaar, but prices are much better at any one of the myriad of instrument shops on and around Galipdede Caddesi, near the upper Tünel station in Beyoğlu.

Akusta CD and Hi-fi Showroom Abdi İpekçi Cad 40, Nişantaşı. Classical, jazz, rock and world music, and state-of-the-art hi-fi equipment to play it on.

IMÇ Atatürk Bul, Unkapını. This dingy concrete shopping precinct just over the Atatürk bridge on the Golden Horn is the nerve centre of the Turkish music business. CD and tape prices tend to be 25 percent lower here than elsewhere.

Metropol İstiklâl Cad 140, Beyoğlu. A fine selection of Turkish sounds, many released on its own label.

Shopping malls

Akmerkez Nisbetiye Cad, Etiler, 5km north of Taksim. The largest of the new Western-style shopping centres, with restaurants and a cinema, and shops carrying most top Turkish brands, plus quality European and American outlets. Take bus #58N or #59N from Eminönü, #59N or #559C from

Taksim, or a free twice-daily shuttle bus if you are staying in one of the five-star hotels. **Capitol** Altunizade, on the Asian side of the Bosphorus. Take the ferry from Eminönü to Üsküdar or Kadıköy, then any dolmuş or bus that runs between these two ferry terminals via Altunizade. More user-friendly than Akmerkez, with a more affordable mix of Turkish chain stores and international brands (including British Home Stores and

Mothercare), two cinemas, giant food-court in the basement, and large Migros hypermarket. **Galleria** Ataköy. Five minutes' walk south along the coast road, Rauf Orbay Cad, from the Bakarköy train station and sea bus terminal. It incorporates an ice-skating rink surrounded by fast-food cafés, a bowling alley and the best of Turkish and European shops.

Listings

Airlines Most airlines have their offices around Taksim Square, or Elmadağ and Nişantaşı, the suburbs further north along Cumhuriyet Cad. THY (Turkish Airlines) ☎0212/663 6363, ⓦwww .turkishairlines.com, is the only airline offering domestic flights. For other services, contact: Air France ☎0212/256 4356; Alitalia ☎0212/231 3391; Air Portugal ☎0212/240 4575; Austrian Airlines ☎0212/240 5032; Balkan Bulgarian Airlines ☎0212/245 2456; British Airways ☎0212/234 1300; Egypt Air ☎0212/231 1126; El-Al ☎0212/246 5303; Emirates Airlines ☎0212/293 5050; Gulf Air ☎0212/231 3450; KLM ☎0212/230 0311; Kuwait Airlines ☎0212/240 4081; Lufthansa ☎0212/288 1050; Northern Cyprus–Turkish Airlines ☎0212/267 0973; Olympic Airways ☎0212/247 3701; Qantas ☎0212/231 2850; Singapore Airlines ☎0212/232 3706; Swissair ☎0212/219 6419.
Airport Atatürk airport, Yeşilköy, flight enquiries ☎0212/663 0793. Havaş (☎0212/465 4700) runs buses to the airport from Cumhuriyet Cad, Taksim, next to the DHL office, a few doors up from the THY (Turkish Airlines) office; departures every half-hour, on the hour (daily 5am–11pm; $3), journey time 20–40min, depending on traffic. Konuş Turizm (☎0212/660 1706, ⓦwww.konusturizm.com), and a number of travel agents on Divan Yolu Cad, as well as most hotels in Sultanahmet and Taksim, can arrange an airport transfer for around $4.
Banks and exchange Exchange offices (*döviz*) around Eminönü, Sultanahmet and Taksim, and on most main city thoroughfares, change cash without commission and usually at good rates, are open daily from 9am to 8pm (sometimes later in peak season) and are generally more efficient than banks. Some will change travellers' cheques, but charge a commission for this. There are also exchange offices at the airport (24hr), Esenler *otogar* (daily 8.30am–11pm) and Sirkeci station (daily 9am–5pm, also takes travellers' cheques). Opening hours for banks are Mon–Fri

9am–12.30pm & 1.30–5pm, though the larger branches of Garanti Bankası stay open through lunch and open between 9am–11.30am on Saturday mornings; most major banks have ATMs, some of which also dispense US$ and euros. The PTT (post office) operates an exchange booth outside Sultanahmet Camii in the summer (April–Sept daily 9am–5pm) and there's a 24-hour ATM next to it.
Bus companies All the following are based at Esenler *otogar*. Barış (☎0212/658 4002), for the Black Sea coast; Birçik (bay 154 ☎0212/658 1714), for the Black Sea coast; Kamil Koç (bays 144–146 ☎0212/252 7223, ⓦwww.kamilkoc.com.tr), to Ankara and southern resorts; Mersin (☎0212/658 3527), for the east; Metro (bays 51–52 ☎0212/658 3235), for the Black Sea coast; Nevtur/Göreme (bay 24 ☎0212/658 0771), for Cappadocia; Pamukkale (bays 41–42 ☎0212/249 2791), to the west and southern coasts; Ulusoy (bay 127 ☎0212/471 7100, ⓦwww.ulusoy.com.tr), to major cities and the Black Sea Coast; Varan (bays 1–2 ☎0212/251 7474, ⓦwww.varan.com.tr), for western and southern destinations including non-stop luxury services to Ankara, Izmir and south coast resorts. Also, see "Travel details" at the end of the chapter.
Car rental Avis, Atatürk airport ☎0212/663 0646, and the *Hilton Hotel*, Cumhuriyet Cad, Harbiye ☎0212/241 7896, ⓦwww.avis.com.tr; Beyaz Rent-a-car, Yeşim Sok 20, Akatlar ☎0212/351 2660, ⓦwww.beyazrentacar.com; Budget, Atatürk airport ☎0212/663 0858, and Cumhuriyet Cad 19, Harbiye ☎0212/253 9200; Decar (Thrifty), Yıldız Posta Cad 52, Esentepe ☎212/288 4243, ⓦwww.decar.com.tr/eng/; Europcar, Atatürk airport ☎0212/254 7788, and Topçu Cad 1, Taksim ☎0212/254 7788; Green Rent-a-car, Cumhuriyet Cad 23, Taksim ☎0212/232 6767; Hertz, Atatürk airport ☎0212/663 0807, and Cumhuriyet Cad 295, Harbiye ☎0212/233 1020; Plan Tur, Cumhuriyet Cad 131, Elmadağ ☎0212/230 8118;

Sixt Rent a Car, Atatürk airport ☎0212/663 8788, and Kışıklı Cad, Nurbaba Sok 1, Üsküdar ☎0216/318 9040, ⊛www.sunrent.com.

Consulates Australia, Tepecik Yokuşu 58, Etiler ☎0212/257 7050; Canada, Büyükdere Cad 107/3, Gayretepe ☎0212/272 5174; New Zealand, Yesilçimen Sok 75, Ihlamur ☎0212/327 2211; United Kingdom, Meşrutiyet Cad 34, Tepebaşı, Beyoğlu ☎0212/293 7540; United States, Meşrutiyet Cad 104–108, Beyoğlu ☎0212/251 3602.

Cycling Cyclists should make a point of visiting Yeşil Bisiklet (Lalezar Cad 8, Selamiçeşme, Kadıköy ☎0216/363 5836), a cycling club and shop, which offers a maintenance service, rents out bikes and organizes trips.

Dentists Reliable options where English, German or French are spoken include: German Hospital Dental Clinic, Sıraselviler Cad 119, Taksim ☎0212/293 2150; Hakan Kaya, Çamlık Girişi 6, Etiler ☎0212/263 1649; Prodent Can Ergene, Valikonağı Cad 109, Nişantaşi ☎0212/230 4635; Reha Sezgin, Halazkargazi Cad 48, Şeker Apt, 5th floor no. 9, Harbiye ☎0212/240 3332.

Emergencies Ambulance ☎112; Fire ☎110; Police ☎155.

Hamams Most central, and the most frequented by tourists, are the Çemberlitaş Hamam (see p.141) near the covered bazaar and Cağaloğlu Hamam; other good ones include the Çinili Hamami, off İtfaiye Cad in Zeyrek (p.148), the Çinili Hamami, opposite the Çinili Cami in Üsküdar (p.174) and the Galatasaray Hamam on Turnacıbaşı Sok, Beyoğlu (daily: men 8am–8pm, women 8am–8pm; bath $15, massage $8 extra).

Hospitals The Taksim First Aid Hospital at Sıraselviler Cad 112, Taksim ☎0212/252 4300, is state-run and deals with emergencies only; patients are often referred on to one of the hospitals listed below. For emergencies, as well as regular doctor's appointments, private foreign hospitals are better, though more expensive than the state hospitals, which are under staffed and overcrowded. One of the city's best-equipped is the American Hospital, Güzelbahçe Sok 20, Nişantaşı (☎0212/231 4050); while the European Hospital, off Mehmetçik Cad, Mecidiyeky (☎0212/212 8811), is modern and more female-friendly than others. The German Hospital, at Sıraselviler Cad 119, Taksim (☎0212/293 2150), also has a dental and eye clinic.

Internet access Internet cafés have sprung up everywhere, catering predominantly to students, and generally open daily 9am–9pm, sometimes as late as 11pm. Well-located places include: Internet Club, İstiklâl Cad, Bekar Sok 20, Beyoğlu; Kirtasiye

Internet, Suterazisi Sok 5, Sultanahmet; Net@Net Internet Cafe, Divan Yolu Cad, İncili Çavuş Sok 33, Sultanahmet; Otanik Internet Café, Alayköşkü Cad 2, Cağaloğlu, Sultanahmet; and Yağmur, Şeyh Bender Sok 18, İsmalımescit, Beyoğlu.

Language classes Bosphorus University (☎0212/257 5039, ⊛www.boun.edu.tr), offers an intensive eight-week summer course for around $300, and a regular two-term Turkish course. For a range of courses throughout the year (and class size usually limited to twelve), try: Turkish Time, in the same offices as English Time, İstiklâl Cad 251, Beyoğlu (☎0212/293 9723, ⊛www.turkishtime.com), or the Tömer school, Halaskargazi Cad 330, Şişli (☎0212/232 5832, ⊛www.tomer.com.tr).

Laundry You might find a laundry service in your hotel or *pansiyon*, otherwise try: Active Laundry, Divan Yolu Cad, Dr Eminpaşa Sok 14, behind the *Cozy Pub* (daily 8am–8pm); or Star Laundry, Yeni Akbıyık Cad 18, Çankurtaran, opposite the *Orient Hostel* (daily 8am–7pm). Dry cleaners (*kuru temizlemecisi*) include: Morve-Site, Üçler Sok 4/A, at the far end of the Hippodrome (Mon–Sat 9am–6pm); and Safi, İstiklâl Cad, Bekar Sok 24, Beyoğlu (Mon–Fri 10am–7pm). There is an expensive drive-in laundry and dry cleaners at the *Hyatt Regency Hotel*, north of Taksim Square, which has a 3hr express service.

Left luggage Left-luggage offices (*Emanet* in Turkish) can be found at Atatürk airport (open 2hr, $3.50 per item) and in both Sirkeci and Haydarpaşa train stations.

Libraries American Library & Computer Centre, American Embassy, Meşrutiyet Cad 108, Tepebaşi, Beyoğlu (Mon–Fri 10am–3.30pm; ☎0212/251 2675); British Council Library, Barbaros Bul, Beşiktaş (Tues–Fri 10am–5.30pm, Sat 9.30am–2.30pm; members only, $10 to join, which includes free internet access; ☎0212/327 2700). The Süleymaniye Library, Ayşekadın Hamam Sok 35, Beyazit (Mon–Sat 8.30am–5pm; ☎0212/520 6460) has a rich reference collection on Ottoman history and culture. The Turkish Touring and Automobile Association, Soqukçeşme Sok, Sultanahmet (Mon, Wed & Fri 10am–noon & 1.30–4.30pm; ☎0212/513 3660) has a library of books concerning the history of İstanbul.

Newspapers and magazines The kiosk just off Taksim Square at the top of Siraselviler Cad has a broad range of European publications at reasonable prices. For women's, men's, music and lifestyle magazines try: Dünya bookshop, İstiklâl Cad 469, Beyoğlu; the Metropol music shop, İstiklâl Cad 140, Beyoğlu; or Pandora bookshop, and delightful **fish restaurants** clustered around the ferry terminal on İskele Caddesi. Particular favourites include *Ayder Balik*, a classy place where you order fish specials off a big tray, the cheaper *Süper Yedigün*, which has an open terrace on the roof; and *Yedi Gün*, whose shrimp casserole is excellent. There's also a small private swimming **beach** here, one of the very few along the Bosphorus, though it is often restricted to women and children only.

The easiest way to get here is on the Bosphorus Tour, when restaurant owners expectantly await the arrival of the ferry. If you're intending to make an evening of it, however, it is worth remembering that the last bus from Rumeli Kavağı to Eminönü, the #25A, leaves at 10pm from the bus stop near the jetty, while the last dolmuş to Sariyer leaves at 11pm, from where there are later buses back to Taksim and Eminönü. There is also a local ferry connecting Rumeli Kavağı with Anadolu Kavağı on the opposite Asian shore, and with Sariyer.

Belgrade Forest

Lying several kilometres to the west of Sariyer, off the main road to Kılyos in the Istranca mountains, **Belgrade Forest** (Belgrad Ormanları) was originally a hunting preserve of the Ottomans. The only sizeable piece of woodland in the vicinity of İstanbul, the forest has always been a popular retreat from the rigours of the city and it's a pleasant place for a few hours' romp through the oaks, pines and beech trees. Unfortunately it's really only accessible by car, though determined non-drivers can take a dolmuş from Sırmacılar Sok in the suburb of Büyükdere, on the Bosphorus, to the village of **BAHÇEKÖY**, which lies on the east side of the forest. From here it is a 1.5km walk to **Büyük Bend reservoir** and the largest picnic ground in the forest, where there's a tea garden, first-aid stand and gymnastic equipment in the trees for joggers and athletes.

A sophisticated system of dams, reservoirs, water towers and aqueducts is still in evidence around the forest, which supplied İstanbul with most of its fresh water during Byzantine and Ottoman times. The most impressive of the aqueducts is the *Uzun* or **Long Aqueduct**, a 1km walk south of Büyük Bend beyond Kemer Burgaz. Its tiers of tall, pointed arches were built by Sinan for Süleyman the Magnificent in 1563. Close to the reservoir are the remains of Belgrade village; the name came about after the capture of Belgrade in 1521, when a community of Serbian well-diggers, prisoners-of-war of Süleyman, were settled here to take over the upkeep of the water-supply system. In the seventeenth century the forests' attractions were discovered by the foreign community of İstanbul, who came to seek refuge from a particularly nasty pestilence that was wiping out half the city, and for the next century or so many wealthy Christians had second homes here. In the 1890s the village was evacuated by Abdül Hamid II who, in his paranoia, believed that the inhabitants were polluting the city's water supply.

The Asian shore

On the Asian side of the Bosphorus are vast suburbs and small villages that all have one thing in common: they are virtually unknown to tourists. The Bosphorus Tour (see p.108) calls in at some of the villages on the way to Anadolu Kavağı, which is the last stop and last village on the Asian side. Alternatively, you can travel by bus from the suburb of Üsküdar (see p.173); services leave regularly to all the other villages up and down the Bosphorus from Üsküdar's main bus station in front of the İskele Camii and ferry termi-

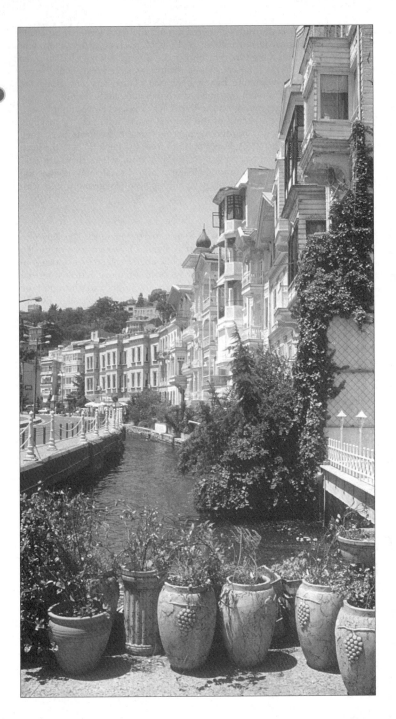

restaurants and shops are just a short walk away. With motor vehicles banned, there are **bike rental** shops ($10 per day) everywhere. **Phaeton** (horse-and-carriage) tours (for up to four people; short tour $7, long tour $10) leave from the *phaeton* park off the main square on Isa Çelebi Sok, 50m above the ferry terminal. **Donkey rides** (about $2 per ride) up the hills start from a little park found just up Kadayoran Caddesi from the centre of town.

Accommodation is uniformly expensive, though the chance to stay in a grand restored mansion may be appealing. There are lots of good fish **restaurants** along the shore to the left of the ferry terminal, but the closer they are to the terminal, the more expensive they are. One street back from the shore road, Iskele Caddesi, is a selection of cheaper **cafés**, selling all the usual Turkish dishes.

Accommodation

Büyükada Princess İskele Meyd ☏216/382 1628, ℱ382 1949. Offers neatly furnished air-conditioned rooms with TV and minibar in a nineteenth-century building with pool. Prices may be negotiable, and drop anyway at the beginning and end of the season by up to twenty percent. **❼**

Saydam Planet II İskele Meyd ☏0216/382 2670, ℱ382 3848. Beautiful (if overpriced) renovated mansion with comfortably furnished rooms and great bathrooms. **❼**

Hotel Splendid Nisan Cad 23 ☏216/382 6950, ℱ382 6775. Serious *fin de siècle* grandeur, with cupolas, balconies, a good restaurant, excellent service and a garden with a swimming pool. Unless you want to fork out an extra $20 for a corner suite, bathroom arrangements are in an odd plastic cabinet in the corner of the room. **❻**

Turing Evi Çankaya Cad 55 ☏0216/382 8304, ℱ517 6780. Italianate palace that was once the summer home of the Ottoman governor of Lebanon, and where Leon Trotsky lived in exile from 1929 to 1933. It's a listed building, so most rooms don't have an en-suite bathroom. **❼**

Villa Rifat Pansıyon Yilmazturk Cad 80 ☏0216/382 6068. Quite a walk from the town centre and beaches, on the shore road running round the east side of the island, but pleasant and comfortable. **❹**

Eating and drinking

Hamdi Baba Gülistan Cad 18. Immediately to the left of the ferry on landing – the best thing to have here is *kiremette balık*, fish baked in a clay dish.

Kaptan Restaurant Liman Çıkmaşı Sok 11. A white-tablecloth affair, right beside the ferry landing. It's a good place for fish, though there are cheaper options around.

Heybelıada

Heybeliada, or the "Island of the Saddlebag", has managed to retain much of its village identity, and there is a strong community spirit among its permanent residents. It's a beautiful place, known for the beaches to which İstanbul residents flock in their hundreds at weekends. It's also the location of the only five-star hotel on the islands, as well as a highly fashionable watersports club, situated near Değirmen Burnu to the northwest of the island.

On an island tour (see "Practicalities" p.210) you'll see (though not have access to) the nineteenth-century **Greek Orthodox School of Theology**, the Aya Triada Manastiri, majestically situated on the peak of the island's northernmost hill and the site of an important collection of Byzantine manuscripts. Other buildings you'll be shown include the Heybeliada Sanatorium, a private home for TB sufferers located off Çam Limanı Yolu on the south side of the island. The **Naval High School** (Deniz Harp Okulu), on the east side of the island, along the coast road from the main jetty, was originally the Naval War Academy, situated on the island since 1852.

The best way to find an isolated **beach** is to head up Refah Şehitler Caddesi, out of the village, until you arrive at Alp Görüngen Yolu, which is the road that encircles most of the island. The northern shore, especially, before you reach Alman Köy, is a good bet for a quiet swim if you climb down off the road to one of the tiny pebble beaches below. You can also reach Yeni İskele from Refah Şehitler Caddesi, and from here it costs around $3 to take a small boat across to **Kaşıkadı** ("Spoon Island", so called because of its shape), although the new holiday complex on this island has scarred its former wildness.

Practicalities

Ferries and **sea buses** arrive at Heybeliada ferry terminal on the main quayside of Rıhtım Caddesi. Walking and cycling are good ways to enjoy Heybeliada, its pine forests and hills making for scenic rides and rambles; there's **bike rental** near the quayside at Imralı Sok 3. Prices for **phaetons** from Ayyıldız Caddesi (which runs parallel to the front) to various destinations around the island are posted on a board in the street; **tours of the island** are also available (short tours for $3, longer ones $5).

There are some cheaper **accommodation** options here than on Büyükada, though you'll have to book in advance to secure a room. The **restaurants** cater to locals all year round and consequently there are plenty to choose from – generally good, simple and cheap, offering standard *lokanta*, kebab and *pide* fare; most are situated on Ayyıldız Caddesi.

Merit Halki Palas Refah Şehitler Cad 88 ☎0216/351 0025, ⊛www.merithotels.com. Nineteenth-century villa, restored in dubious taste by the Merit Hotel group as the only five-star hotel on the islands, incorporating gymnasium, jacuzzi and outdoor pool. In the restaurant you can get a three-course meal, usually featuring fish, for around $25 a head, served in a lovely poolside setting. ❽

Panorama Hotel Ayyıldız Cad ☎0216/351 8543. In dire need of refurbishment, but comfortable, with friendly staff and situated on the seafront with an outdoor café. Rooms have their own bathrooms. It's one of the cheapest options on the islands, so booking is essential. ❸

Prenset Pansiyon Ayyıldız Cad 74 ☎216/351 9388. This converted apartment building with wood-trimmed exterior is the best value on the islands, despite most rooms not having views. Friendly management, comfortable rooms with immaculate modern bathrooms and central heating in winter. They've also got a tiny splash pool on the roof terrace. Usually closed Dec–Feb if business is slow. ❹

Burgazada and Kınalıada

The other two islands served by public ferry are Burgazada and Kınalıada, both small and relatively unspoilt, although development is proceeding apace. They are still popular with escapees from the strict Islamic codes more evident in mainland İstanbul and, on both, holiday homes already outnumber those of permanent residents. In winter the villages around their jetties are practically ghost towns, with little to see or do.

Burgazada

Burgazada has a fascinating small **museum** (Tues–Fri 10am–noon & 2–5pm, Sat 10am–noon; free) at Burgaz Çayırı Sok 15, on the other side of the square from the Church of St John the Baptist (the dome of which is the town's most prominent landmark). The museum is dedicated to the novelist **Sait Faik** (often described as the Turkish Mark Twain), who lived here, and the house has been so carefully preserved – as if the writer were still there – that you get an unsettling sense that you're trespassing. This becomes stronger when you go up to the bedroom and find a pair of pyjamas neatly folded on the bed and a towel on the rack beside it. You get an immediate impression of the man, whose exceptional character is evidenced by the simple bohemian style of furnishings in his island home (the floor, for example, is covered in reed matting, generally associated with impoverishment).

Around the Sea of Marmara

CHAPTER 2

Highlights

✳ **Selimiye Camii** The masterpiece of architect Mimar Sinan, considered to be the finest mosque in Turkey. See p.225

✳ **Kırkpınar festival** Wrestlers slicked down head to toe in olive oil battle it out every July in a 600-year-old tournament at Edirne. See p.226

✳ **Battlefield sites and cemeteries** The Gelibolu peninsula pays testament to the Allied defeat during World War I, remembered each year on Anzac Day. See p.235

✳ **Termal** Get steamy in winter at Termal's near-scalding hot springs – ancient baths where people have come to take the cure since Byzantine times. See p.243

✳ **İznık** Sleepy town nestled in an olive-mantled valley, famous for its sixteenth-century tiles. See p.244

✳ **Bursa's Silk-Cocoon Hall** Centrepiece of Bursa's covered bazaar, occupied by silk-breeders at the auction held every June. See p.255

✳ **Cumalikizik** A finely preserved Ottoman village, its cobbled streets full of charmingly dilapidated houses. See p.260

THEIR NAME LIVETH FOR EVERMORE

Around the Sea of Marmara

Despite their proximity to İstanbul, the shores and hinterland of the **Sea of Marmara** are neglected by most foreign travellers. This is not altogether surprising – here the country is at its most Balkan and, at first glance, least exotic – but there are good reasons to come: above all the exquisite early Ottoman centres of **Edirne** and **Bursa**. If your appetite is whetted for more of the same, the historic towns of **Lüleburgaz** and **İznik** make good postscripts to the former imperial capitals.

For many citizens of the Commonwealth nations and Ireland, a pilgrimage to the extensive and moving World War I battlefields and cemeteries on the **Gelibolu (Gallipoli) peninsula** may involve personal as well as national history. The northern Marmara port of **Gelibolu** is one starting-point for guided excursions of the memorial sites, although it's **Eceabat** (along with Çanakkale, described in the next chapter) that is the better base for either an organized or do-it-yourself tour.

With more time at your disposal you might consider venturing up to northern **Thrace**, which offers a rolling landscape of forests and slow-moving rivers, dotted with prehistoric and Iron Age tombs and the remains of Byzantine frontier towns – most notably the coastal fortress of **Kıyıköy**. The region boasts a large settled Romany population whose annual spring celebration at **Kırklareli** is one of the most memorable festivals held anywhere in Turkey.

The four inhabited **Marmara islands** on the south side of the Sea of Marmara attract local tourism due to their proximity to İstanbul, Edirne and Bursa. Their short summer season and unglamorous image mean that the islands – and indeed much of the Marmara coastline – are relatively unspoilt, and you may enjoy the status of being the only foreigner in town. Meanwhile, for evocative inland scenery, visit **Uluabat Gölü** and **Manyas Gölü** – shallow lakes that support a dwindling fishing community and a bird sanctuary respectively – or **Uludağ**, a mountain resort popular with skiers in winter and hikers in summer.

Before 1923, much of the Marmara region's population was Greek Orthodox. Following the establishment of the Turkish Republic and the exchange of populations massive immigration – both internal and from abroad – changed the mix. The result is an ethnic stew that includes people of Çerkez (Circassian), Artvinli and Greek Muslim descent, but consists predominantly of

Pomak, **Bosnian** and **Macedonian Muslims**, and especially **Bulgarian Turks**. All of them had in fact been trickling in for decades, as Austro-Hungarian or Christian nationalist victories in the Balkans made their previous homes inhospitable to Turks or Slavic Muslims. This trend was reinforced following the disturbances in Bulgaria during 1989, when hundreds of thousands of ethnic Turks fled to Turkey, though many of the new arrivals subsequently returned to post-Communist Bulgaria.

Thrace

Thrace (Trakya in Turkish), the historic term for the territory bounded by the rivers Danube and Nestos and the Aegean, Marmara and Black seas, is today divided roughly equally among Turkey, Greece and Bulgaria. In ancient times it was home to warlike stock-breeding tribes, whose bizarre religions and unruly habits presented a continual headache for rulers bent on subduing them. Contemporary life is decidedly less colourful, though until the late 1960s nearly all of Thrace was a military security zone and strictly off-limits to foreigners. Most of the area is open to travel now, but all the towns remain heavily garrisoned.

To the south, the flatter land has long since been denuded of trees, while much of the coast has fallen prey to estates of concrete holiday homes – seasonal barbecue pads for İstanbul's lower middle classes. Inland is staunchly agricultural and in summer a sea of yellow sunflowers, grown for oil, spreads for mile after mile. Further west, in the wetter lands around Üzünköprü, rice is predominant. The north, though, is a different story: rolling hills and dense forests of scrub oak hide itinerant charcoal burners and myriad fish farms growing rainbow trout. Hidden away across the whole region are open-cast workings extracting the sand and gravel that accumulated on the seabed that once covered Thrace.

The E80 highway from İstanbul to the main Thracian town of **Edirne** follows almost exactly the route of the Roman and Byzantine **Via Egnatia**, which later became the medieval route to the Ottoman holdings in Europe. Many towns along the road not surprisingly began life as Roman staging-posts, a role continued under the Ottomans who endowed all of them with a civic monument or two. Few places have much to detain you, though you should keep an eye out for various fine **old bridges**, which like the road itself may be Ottoman re-workings of Roman or Byzantine originals. The best of these is the quadruple Büyükçekmece span, crossing the neck of an estuary a few kilometres west of İstanbul and built by the great architect Mimar Sinan in 1563.

Edirne

More than just the quintessential border town, **EDİRNE** – 230km northwest of İstanbul – is one of the best-preserved Ottoman cities and makes an impressive and easily digestible introduction to Turkey. It's a lively and attractive spot of around 120,000 people, occupying a rise overlooking the meeting of the Tunca, Arda and Meriç rivers, a short distance from the Greek and Bulgarian frontiers. The life of the place is derived from day-tripping foreign shoppers, from a growing number of discerning tourists and from the presence of students (the University of Thrace is here). **Downtown**, teeming bazaars and elegant domestic architecture almost distract you from the clutch of striking Ottoman monuments that lifts Edirne out of the ranks of the ordinary. The best of these Ottoman offerings, crowning the town hillock and sufficient reason in itself for a detour here, is the **Selimiye Camii**, the crowing achievement of the imperial architect Mimar Sinan.

Some history

There has always been a settlement of some kind at this strategic point and its military importance has fated it to be captured – and sometimes sacked for good measure – repeatedly over the centuries. Thracian Uscudama was refurbished as Hellenistic Oresteia, but the city really entered history as **Hadrianopolis**, designated the main centre of Roman Thrace by the emperor Hadrian. Under the Byzantines it retained its significance, not least as a forward base en route to the Balkans – or, more ominously from the Byzantine point of view, first stop on the way to attempts on the imperial capital itself. Unsuccessful besiegers of Constantinople habitually vented their frustration on Hadrianopolis as they retreated and a handful of emperors met their end here in pitched battles with Thracian "barbarians" of one sort or another.

The **Ottomans** had by the mid-fourteenth century enmeshed the Byzantines in a web of mutual defence treaties and links by marriage and gained their first permanent foothold on the coast of Thrace. In 1361 Hadrianopolis surrendered to the besieging Murat I and the provisional Ottoman capital was effectively transferred here from Bursa. A century later, Mehmet the Conqueror trained his troops and tested his artillery here in preparation for the march on Constantinople; indeed the Ottoman court was not completely moved to the Bosphorus until 1458. Because of its excellent opportunities for hunting and falconry, Edirne, as the Turks renamed it, remained a favourite haunt of numerous sultans for three more centuries, earning the title *Der-I Saadet* or "Happiness Gate" – when, it's said, there were enough victory celebrations, circumcision ceremonies and marriages to make even Constantinople jealous.

Decline set in during the eighteenth century, prompted largely by an **earthquake** in 1751. During each of the **Russo–Turkish wars** of 1829 and 1878–1879 the city was occupied and pillaged by Tsarist troops; far worse were the Bulgarians, who in 1913 presided over a four-month spree of atrocities. The Greeks, as one of the victorious World War I Allies, **annexed Edirne** along with the rest of Turkish Thrace from 1920 to 1922 and Turkish sovereignty over the city was only confirmed by the 1923 Treaty of Lausanne.

Arrival and information

Buses from elsewhere in Turkey arrive at Edirne's **otogar**, just over 2km southeast of the centre; a free service minibus will whisk you to points opposite the *Belediye* (town hall). The **train station**, a more likely entry point from abroad, is another kilometre out in the same direction; from here, the only transport into the centre is a red city bus, but these are infrequent and

EDİRNE

N

0 ____ 500 m

ACCOMMODATION

Aksaray	6
Efe	5
Park	3
Rüstem Pasa Kervansarayı	4
Şaban Açıkgöz	2
Sultan	1

CAFÉS & RESTAURANTS

Balkan Piliç	A
Edirne Lahmacun	B
Lalezarğ	E
London Cafe	C
Yuva	D

Muradiye Camii

Archeological & Ethnographic Museum

Museum of Turkish & Islamic Arts

Selimiye Camii

Bulgarian Consulate

MİTHAT PAŞA CAD

ESKİ İSTANBUL CAD

Edirne Train Station ▶

Ruins of Hamam of Janısserien

Dilaver Bey Parkı

Bus to Kapıkule

Belediye ★

Eski Camii

MİMAR SİNAN CAD

SABUNİ CAD

KIYIK CAD

Üç Şerefeli Camii

Police

Hürriyet Meyd

Bedesten

★ Minibuses to border
Nokta Internet

2

4

@

@ Eska

B
C

A

Internet @

SARAÇLAR CAD

Great Synagogue

Yeni Bridge

Meriç Bridge

D

E

Meriç River

Tunca River

▶ Pazarkule & Greece & Karaagac

Sokullu Paşa Hamamı

HÜKUMET CAD

Semiz Ali Paşa Çarşıksı

3

5
6

Etur El Sanatlar Mağazası

BALIKPAZAN CAD

MAARİF CAD

CUMHURİYET CAD

KALE İÇİ

ORTAKAPI CAD

Kule Kapısi

HOROZLU BAYIR CAD

1

i

TALAT PAŞA CAD

i

Beyazit Bridge

İkinci Beyazit Küllıyesi

Tunca River

Gazi Mihal Bridge

▲ Ay ay ay

▲ Bulgaria & Kapıkule (18 km)

◀ Kapıkule ▶

Gazi Mihal Camii

221

a taxi ($3) is the easiest option. If you're coming directly **from the Greek or Bulgarian highway border posts**, see the box on "Border crossings", below.

There are two fairly unhelpful **tourist offices** in Edirne, the first at Hürriyet Meydanı 17 (Mon–Fri 8.30am–5pm; ℡0284/213 9208), the second – the office of the Tourism Directorate – at Talat Paşa Caddesi 76 (Mon–Fri 8.30am–5pm, until 7pm in summer; ℡0284/225 5260), about 500m west of the first office, towards the Gazi Mihal bridge. There's also a booth at the Bulgarian (Kapıkule) frontier gate (daily 8.30am–5pm; ℡0284/238 2019). All three outlets supply tourism ministry brochures and an excellent **map** of Edirne – the latter also sometimes stocked by hotels in town.

Border crossings

At the time of writing, the Turkish–Greek and Turkish-Bulgarian frontier posts are **open 24 hours**. The current trend is for lifting all restrictions on travelling **between Greece and Turkey**, but if in any doubt you can check the current situation at the tourist offices in Edirne before setting out. In **Bulgaria**, the government has lifted the visa restriction for stays of thirty days or less by holders of EU, US, Canadian, Australian and New Zealand passports. The only general proviso is that the expiry date of your passport should not fall within three months of entering the country.

Turkey–Greece

The Turkish frontier post of **Pazarkule**, separated from the Greek one at Kastaniés by a kilometre-wide no-man's-land, is 7km west of Edirne and 2km beyond the last Turkish village of **Karaağaç**.

Red city **buses to Karaağaç** ($0.25) run from behind the *Belediye* building in Edirne every twenty minutes; minibuses ($0.50) depart with similar frequency from behind the Rüstem Paşa Kervansarayı. At present, you can walk the final 2km from Karaağaç to Pazarkule, though buses through to Kastaniés in Greece leave regularly from Karaağaç; look for signs for *Yunanistan* ("Greece" in Turkish), in travel agent windows in both Karaağaç and Edirne.

Alternatively, take a taxi ($3) directly from Edirne **to Pazarkule**. Once through the Turkish post, you'll have to take a Greek taxi to the **Kastaniés** post, as you're not allowed to walk; this applies coming from Greece too – budget on $5 per car for the one-kilometre gap. From Kastaniés, on the Greek side, three trains daily, and about as many buses, make the three-hour run down to Alexandhroúpoli, the first major Greek city, between 8am and 1pm, with a couple more later in the day. If all this seems too much bother, compare the more southerly rail and road crossings into Greece described from Kapıkule.

Turkey–Bulgaria

Crossing the **Bulgarian–Turkish border** is slightly less problematic. The vast complex at **Kapıkule**, 18km northwest of Edirne (and 320km south of the Bulgarian capital Sofya) straddles the busy E800 expressway.

Minibuses to Kapıkule ($0.75) ply the route half-hourly from 6.30am to 9pm, leaving from behind the Rüstem Paşa Kervansarayı in Edirne. City buses also make the journey for under $1, departing from next to the *Belediye* building. Hakiki Koç runs six **coaches** daily to Kapıkule ($1.50), departing from opposite the Bulgarian consulate, while a **taxi** will set you back well over $8. (In the unlikely event that you get stuck at the border, note that there are a few basic motel rooms catering for TIR truck drivers at *Londra Camping* on the Turkish side.)

Balkan Express **trains** depart daily at 2pm from Kapıkule for Bucharest, Sofya and Budapest – you can check current timetables at the tourist offices in Edirne.

The main annual event in Edirne is the **Kırkpınar festival** in July (see box on p.226), hosting the famous oil-wrestling. The festival lasts two or three days and is preceded by a couple of days of folkloric exhibitions laid on by the Edirne municipality. For more information, and for tickets to the wrestling events, it's best to contact either tourist office well in advance.

Accommodation

With most hotels booked solid either by truck drivers, Turkish workers on their way back to Germany or car-loads of eastern Europeans, **accommodation** is always tight in Edirne. During the main Turkish holidays and the Kırkpınar festival you'll probably need to book at least a month in advance. Most places are expensive, too, as Edirne's strategic location brings it sufficient, and comparatively undemanding, custom. However, high US$ prices on display in hotel lobbies should be taken with a pinch of salt – bargaining commonly achieves discounts of up to fifty percent. For cheaper options, Maarif Caddesi is lined with reasonable choices, though there are also a few serious dives along here that are best avoided.

Hotels and pansiyons

Aksaray Pansiyon Alipaşa Ortakapı Cad 9 ℡0284/212 6035, ℻225 3901. Good-value place with both en-suite and cheaper, waterless, rooms available. ❷

Efe Hotel Maarif Cad 13 ℡0284/213 6166, ⓦwww.efehotel.com. Delightful family-run hotel – it's clean and modern, with stylish air-conditioned rooms, satellite TV and an English-style pub on the ground floor. ❸

Park Maarif Cad 7 ℡0284/213 5276, ℻225 4635. Not quite as spruce as the *Efe*, a few doors down, but nevertheless a clean and calm hotel with a reasonable kebab joint attached. ❸

Rüstem Paşa Kervansarayı İki Kapalıhan Cad 57 ℡0284/215 2489, ℮k.saray@netone.com. A beautifully restored *kervansaray* whose cool, cell-like rooms are set around a pleasant garden-courtyard; noise is minimal as the substantial walls of the *kervansaray* are quite soundproof,

though water supplies aren't all they could be. Also houses a dodgy nightclub and seedy internet café. Staff freely admit to charging higher rates for foreigners, so bargain hard. ❼

Otel Şaban Acikgöz Çilingirler Cad 9 ℡0284/213 1404, ℻213 4516. Recommended for comfort (rooms have TVs, air-conditioning and minibars) and good service. ❺

Sultan Hotel Talat Paşa Cad 42 ℡0284/225 1372, ℻225 5763. Two-star hotel with an imposing exterior, though with dreary rooms on gloomy corridors. It's really only worth considering if you can't get a room in one of the others. ❺

Motel and campsite

Fifi Lokanta Mocamp 8km along the E80 towards İstanbul ℡0284/226 0101, ℻212 9888. The best campsite in the region. It also has en-suite motel rooms and a pool. ❸

The City

You can tour the main sights of Edirne on foot, but as the Ottoman monuments are widely scattered you'll need a full day to do it. Many lie to the north and west of town, deliberately rusticated by the early sultans to provide a nucleus for future suburbs. Because of the depopulations suffered by the city during the last three centuries, urban growth has never caught up with some of them and many have a rather forlorn atmosphere. Still, if the weather's fine, the walk is a pleasure, especially since you'll follow the willow-shaded banks of the **Tunca River** for some distance. Public transport doesn't connect up the more far-flung sites, so hiring a taxi is your only other option.

Eski Camii and the Bedesten

The logical starting point is **Eski Camii**, the oldest mosque in town, right across from the *Belediye*. This boxy structure, topped by nine vaults arranged three-square, is reckoned a more elaborate version of Bursa's Lulu Camii. Emir Süleyman, son of the luckless Beyazit I, began it in 1403, but it was his younger brother Mehmet I – the only one of three brothers left alive after a bloody succession struggle – who dedicated it eleven years later. The mosque is famous for its giant works of calligraphy, the most prolific being the large Arabic inscriptions on either side of the front door, one in the name of Allah, the other of Mohammed.

Just across the way Mehmet I constructed the **Bedesten** (closed Sun), Edirne's first covered market, a portion of whose revenue went to the upkeep of the nearby mosque. The barn-like structure with its fourteen vaulted chambers – again indebted to a Bursa prototype – has recently been restored, but modern shops and poor paintwork make the interior drab and unimpressive.

Semiz Ali Paşa Çarşısı and Kale İçi

The other main covered bazaar in Edirne is the nearby **Semiz Ali Paşa Çarşısı** (closed Sun), whose north entrance lies about 250m west, on the corner of Talat Paşa and Saraçlar caddesis. The bazaar was established by Mimar Sinan in 1568 at the behest of Semiz Ali, one of the most able and congenial of the Ottoman grand viziers. A massive fire in 1992 burned out many of its 130 shops, but renovations have been administered with care – particularly impressive is the beautiful multi-domed ceiling.

Just opposite the north entrance looms the **Kule Kapısı** (Tower Gate), sole remnant of the town's Roman/Byzantine city walls; the Ottomans, in a burst of confidence after expanding the limits of empire far beyond Edirne, demolished the rest. The gate was partially restored some years ago and, with a team of archeologists scrabbling around in the excavations, the site promises to become more of a fixture on Edirne's sightseeing list.

West of the Semiz Ali market sprawls the **Kale İçi** district, a rectangular grid of streets dating from Byzantine times and lined with much-interrupted terraces of medieval houses. A stroll through here will uncover some surviving stumps of Byzantine wall.

Üç Şerefeli Camii and the Sokullu Paşa Hamamı

Slightly north of Semiz Ali and Hürriyet Meydanı stands **Üç Şerefeli Camii**, which replaced the Eski Camii as Edirne's Friday mosque in 1447. Ten years in the making, its conceptual daring represented the pinnacle of Ottoman religious architecture until overshadowed by the Selimiye Camii (see opposite) a short time later. Ongoing restorations mean that the courtyard and outer complex are still closed, though the prayer hall has reopened.

The mosque's name – "three-balconied" – derives from the presence of three galleries for the muezzin on the tallest of the four whimsically idiosyncratic **minarets**; the second highest has two balconies, the others one, and their bases are all different. Each of the multiple balconies is reached by a separate stairway within the minaret. The **courtyard**, too, was an innovation, centred on a şadırvan (ritual ablutions fountain) and ringed by porphyry and marble columns pilfered from Roman buildings. The experimental nature of the mosque is further confirmed by its **interior**, much wider than it is deep and covered by a dome 24m in diameter. It was the largest that the Turks had built at the time and, to impart a sense of space, the architect relied on just two freestanding columns, with the other four recessed into front and back walls to form a hexagon.

Right across from the mosque is the sixteenth-century **Sokullu Paşa Hamamı** (daily 6am–10pm; separate wings for men and women; $3, massage

$3 extra), built by Mimar Sinan, though it's not as friendly, hot or well maintained as it might be.

Selimiye Camii and nearby museums

The masterly **Selimiye Camii**, widely considered to be the finest mosque in Turkey, was designed by the 80-year-old Mimar Sinan (see box on p.144) in 1569 at the command of Selim II. The work of a confident craftsman at the height of his powers, it's visible from some distance away on the Thracian plain and is virtually the municipal symbol, reproduced on the sides of Edirne's buses, among other places.

You can approach the Selimiye across the central park, Dilaver Bey, then through the **Kavaflar Arasta** (Cobbler's Arcade; closed Sun), which was built by Sinan's pupil Davut and is still used as a covered market, full of household goods and cheap clothing – every day, under the market's prayer dome, the shopkeepers promise that they will do their business honestly. The mosque **courtyard**, approached from the Kavaflar Arasta up a flight of stone steps, is surrounded by a colonnaded portico with arches in alternating red and white stone, ancient columns and domes of varying size above the arcades. Its delicately fashioned *şadırvan* is the finest in the city. The four identical slender **minarets** each has three balconies – Sinan's nod to his predecessors – and at 71m are the second tallest in the world after those in Mecca. The detailed carved portal once graced the Ulu Camii in Birgi and was transported here in pieces, then reassembled.

But it is the celestial **interior**, specifically the dome, which impresses most. Planned expressly to surpass that of Aya Sofya in İstanbul, it manages this – at 31.5m in diameter – by a bare few centimetres, and Sinan thus achieved a lifetime's ambition. Supported by eight mammoth but surprisingly unobtrusive twelve-sided pillars, the cupola floats 44m above the floor, covered in calligraphy proclaiming the glory of Allah. Immediately below the dome the muezzin's platform, supported on twelve columns, is an ideal place from which to contemplate the proportions of the mosque. The delicate painting on the platform's underside is a faithful restoration of the original, and gives some idea of how the mosque dome must once have looked. The water of the small marble drinking fountain beneath symbolizes life, under the dome of eternity. The most ornate stone carving is reserved for the *mihrab* and *mimber*, backed by fine İznik faience illuminated by sunlight streaming in through the many windows allowed by the pillar support scheme.

An associated *medrese*, at the northeastern corner of the mosque, is now the **Museum of Turkish and Islamic Arts** (Türk ve İslam Eserleri Müzesi; May–Oct Tues–Sun 8.30am–5.30pm; Nov–April Tues–Sun 8am–noon & 1.30–5.30pm; $0.70), consisting of fifteen rooms around a pleasant garden courtyard and housing assorted wooden, ceramic and martial knick-knacks from the province. One of the rooms is dedicated to oil-wrestling (see box on p.226), including a portrait gallery of its stars, a pair of oil-wrestler's leather trousers and blow-ups of miniatures depicting this 600-year-old sport through the ages.

The main **Archeological/Ethnographic Museum** (Arkeoloji/ Etnografya Müzesi; May–Oct Tues–Sun 8.30am–5.30pm; Nov–April Tues–Sun 8am–noon & 1.30–5.30pm; $0.70) – the modern building just northeast of the mosque precincts – contains a predictable assortment of Greco-Roman fragments. The ethnographic section focuses on carpet-weaving and other local crafts, including colourful village bridal wear, which preceded the bland white confectionery that's been adopted from the West.

Oil-wrestling and the Kırkpınar festival

Oil-wrestling (*yağlı güreş*) is popular throughout Turkey, but reaches the pinnacle of its acclaim at the doyen of tournaments, the annual **Kırkpınar festival**, staged early each summer on the Saray İçi islet outside Edirne. The preferred date is the first week of July, but the five-day event is moved back into June if it coincides with Ramadan or either of the two major *bayram*s (religious holidays) following it.

The wrestling matches have been held annually, except in times of war or Edirne's occupation, for more than six centuries and their origins are shrouded in legend. The most commonly repeated story asserts that Süleyman, son of Orhan Gazi, was returning from a battle in 1360 with forty of his men and decided to camp at a village near Edirne. To pass the time the soldiers paired off to wrestle; the last two were unable to best each other after several days of tussling, and in a final elimination match expired simultaneously after midnight. Their companions buried them on the spot and, returning to visit the graves the next season, were astonished to find instead a lush meadow with forty springs (*kırk pınar* in Turkish) bubbling away. Forty is one of the sacred numbers of Islam and the Ottomans needed little encouragement to inaugurate a commemoration.

Despite the less than atmospheric environment of the stadium that now hosts the wrestling, tradition still permeates the event. The contestants – up to a thousand per year – dress only in leather knickers called *kispet* and are slicked down head to toe in diluted olive oil. Wrestlers are classed by height, not by weight, from toddlers up to the *pehlivan* (full-size) category. Warm-up exercises, the *peşrev*, are highly stereotyped and accompanied by the *davul* (deep-toned drum) and *zurna* (single-reed Islamic oboe). The competitors and the actual matches are solemnly introduced by the *cazgır* or master of ceremonies, usually himself a former champion.

The bouts, several of which take place simultaneously, can last anything from a few minutes to a couple of hours, until one competitor collapses or has his back pinned to the grass. Referees keep a lookout for the limited number of illegal moves or holds and victors advance more or less immediately to the next round until, after the second or third day, only the *başpehlivan* (champion) remains. Despite the small prize purse, donated by the *Kırkpınar Ağaları* – the local worthies who put on the whole show – a champion is usually well set-up in terms of appearance and endorsement fees and should derive ample benefit from the furious on- and off-site betting. In the main, gladiators tend to be villagers from all over Turkey who have won regional titles, starry-eyed with the prospect of fame and escape from a rural rut.

In addition to providing the music of the *peşrev*, the local Romany population descends in force during the Kırkpınar, setting up a combination funfair, circus and carnival on the outskirts of town. They also have their own **Romany spring festival** (similar to the bigger Takava festival in Kirklareli, p.230), which takes place in the fields around the stadium during the first week of May. The Romany King lights a bonfire on the evening of May 6, and a flaming torch is paraded around to light a number of other bonfires in the area; a dish of meat and rice is given to the gathered picnickers. The next morning, young Romany girls are paraded through the streets on horseback around the Muradiye Camii (where a number of settled Romanies live) to the accompaniment of *davul* and *zurna*, wearing their own or their mothers' wedding dresses.

Muradiye Camii

Northeast of the centre, but simple enough to reach, the **Muradiye Camii** (admission only at prayer times) is an easy ten-minute, down-then-up walk along Mimar Sinan Caddesi from the Selimiye mosque. According to legend Celaleddin Rumi, founder of the Mevlevi dervish order, appeared in a dream to the pious Murat II in 1435, urging him to build a sanctuary for the Mevlevis in Edirne. The result is this pleasing, T-shaped *zaviye* (dervish convent) crouched on a hill looking north over vegetable patches and the Tunca River; the grassy entry court lends a final bucolic touch. The interior is distinguished by the best İznik tiles outside Bursa: the *mihrab* and walls up to eye level are solid with them. Higher surfaces once bore calligraphic frescoes, but these have probably been missing since the catastrophic earthquake of 1751. The dervishes initially congregated in the *eyvan*s (transepts), which form the ends of the T's cross-stroke; Murat later housed them in a separate *tekke* (gathering place) in the garden.

Along the Tunca River

At Edirne, the **Tunca River** is crossed by the greatest concentration of historic bridges in Thrace, better suited to pedestrians and horse carts than the motor vehicles that jostle to use them. The best way to see them is to take a stroll along the riverbank parallel to the dykes and water meadows of the Tunca's right bank. A good place to start is at the pair furthest upstream, the fifteenth-century **Saray (Süleyman)** and **Fatih** bridges, which join the respective left and right banks of the Tunca with the river island of **Saray İçi**. The island once supported the **Edirne Sarayı**, a royal palace begun by Murat II, which was blown to bits by the Turks in 1877 to prevent the munitions stored inside from falling into Russian hands. Today nothing is left of this pleasure pavilion except the rubble of some baths and a tower, next to which is a modern concrete stadium, venue for the Kırkpınar wrestling matches (see box, opposite).

Following the riverbank west and downstream for half an hour brings you to the double-staged **Beyazit bridge** that crosses another small island in the Tunca River. The seventeenth-century bridge is more commonly known as the Tek Göz Köprüsü ("one-eyed bridge"), referring to its single hump. Across the bridge on the left bank is the **İkinci Beyazit Külliyesi**, built between 1484 and 1488 by Hayrettin, court architect to Beyazit II. This is the largest Ottoman spiritual and physical welfare complex ever constructed. Within a single irregular boundary wall, and beneath a hundred-dome silhouette, are assembled a mosque, food storehouse, bakery, *imaret*, dervish hostel, medical school and insane asylum. Unfortunately, most of the buildings are closed to the public these days, though the *imam* or his son may appear in order to give you a short tour (which will mean peering frustratedly though windows and gates). Except for its handsome courtyard and the sultan's loge inside, the **mosque** itself is disappointing, and more interesting is the **medical school** in the furthest northwest corner of the complex. This was conveniently linked to the *timarhane*, or madhouse, built around an open garden, which in turn leads to the magnificent **darüşşifa** (therapy centre). This hexagonal, domed structure consists of a circular central space with six *eyvan*s (side-chambers) opening onto it; the inmates were brought here regularly, where musicians would play to soothe the more intractable cases. Strange five-sided rooms with fireplaces open off three of the *eyvan*s. The complex is open as the well-intentioned but fairly dull **Trakya University Museum of Health** (Tues–Sun 9am–5pm; $0.70), boasting a collection of old medical equipment and photographs.

Another twenty minutes' walk south along the river will bring you to the **Gazi Mihal bridge**, an Ottoman refurbishment of a thirteenth-century Byzantine span and hence the oldest around Edirne. Gazi Mihal was a Christian nobleman who became an enthusiastic convert to Islam – hence the epithet *Gazi*, "Warrior for the Faith". His namesake mosque is at the western end of the bridge. From here it's an easy 500-metre stroll back into town.

Eating and drinking

Restaurants cater mainly to pass-through trade and do little to encourage return custom; most are adequate but not especially cheap. Exceptions include the booths and **street stalls** around Saraçlar Caddesi, serving up the city's speciality, deep-fried liver, as well as every imaginable kind of pudding, pastry and ice cream. You can also get cheap snacks from the acres of **tea gardens** in front of the Selimiye Camii.

Balkan Piliç Saraçlar Cad 14. Plenty of wholesome *lokanta* fare, not just chicken but enticing vegetable dishes and good roast lamb. A plateful of various dishes will cost around $10.

Edirne Lahmacun Salonu Çilingirler Cad 2. Offers a good variety of *pide* and grilled kebabs in a canteen environment (no alcohol) to the local bazaar traders.

Lalezarğ 1.5km south of town (Karaağaç road), on the Meriç River. Unlicensed restaurant with beautiful views of the Meriç and its elegant, honey-coloured bridge. Food – kebabs and *mezes* – is substantial and reasonably priced, served in waterfront gardens. One table is located in the branches of a tree. The licensed *Villa Restaurant* next door is similar. Take the Karaağaç minibus from in front of the PTT, or any red city bus heading south along Saraçlar Cad.

London Café Saraçlar Cad 74. An unexpected find, this two-storey affair (opposite the PTT) is incongruously decorated with Wild West photographs, cowboy boots and stetsons. There's a wide range of imported alcoholic drinks and a non-Turkish menu including things like chicken schnitzel and spaghetti.

Yuva 1.3km south of town (Karaağaç road), between the Yeni and Meriç bridges. Friendly place, with inexpensive *mezes* and kebabs, accompanied by *raki* and (very occasionally) live music. It's one of a line of lively *meyhanes* (taverns) between the bridges, an area dubbed *Bülbül Adası* – "nightingale island" – by the locals. For transport, see *Lalezarğ* opposite.

Listings

Banks and exchange There are several banks with ATMs along Talat Paşa Cad. None will change Turkish lira for drachma, so you'll need to do this at one of the *döviz* offices on and around Hürriyet Meydanı and the Semiz Ali Paşa Çarşısı – though their rates aren't particularly good.

Buses From the *otogar* ⊕0284/225 1979. Services with Kamil Koç, Pamukkale, Varan and Uludar Hakiki Koç (and several other companies) to Çanakkale, İstanbul, Kapıkule, Keşan, Kirklareli and Lüleburgaz (see "Travel details" at end of chapter for schedules).

Consulates Bulgarian consulate, Mithat Paşa Cad, about halfway to the *otogar* (Mon–Fri 9am–noon; ⊕0284/214 0617); Greek consulate, further out towards the *otogar* at 2 Caddesi (Mon–Fri 9am–noon; ⊕0284/235 5808) – turn off the main E80 highway opposite the *Çağlar Gazoz* factory.

Hospital Behind the Bulgarian consulate.

Internet access Facilities generally open daily 9am–9pm, at the café in the *Rüstem Paşa Kervansarayı*, as well as the *Eska Internet Café*, just round the corner from the hotel on Cilingirler Çarşısı, and the *Nokta Internet Café*, further down the same street opposite the dolmuş stand.

Police Karanfiloğlu Cad, behind the Üç Şerefeli Camii.

Post office The PTT is on Saraçlar Cad (Mon–Sat 8am–midnight for telephone and telegrams, 8am–8pm for letters, and 9am–5.30pm for full postal services).

Shopping Etur el Sanatları Mağazasi, Saraçlar Cad 85, is a classy handicrafts shop, selling a vast range of high-quality products, including inlaid backgammon boards, patchwork quilts, homemade dolls and jewellery.

South of Edirne: Greek border crossings

There's little reason to stop at any point south along the E87 highway as it heads down from **Havsa**, the junction 27km southeast of Edirne. This road does, however, connect **Uzunköprü**, **İpsala** and **Keşan**, one of which you're likely to pass through if in transit to or from Greece.

Uzunköprü

UZUNKÖPRÜ (Long Bridge), a little over 60km south of Edirne, formerly the Thracian and later Greek town of Plotinopolis, gets its current name from the 1.4km-long, 174-arched Ottoman aqueduct at the north end of town; however, you wouldn't make a special trip to see it.

Today the town is an official rail entry and exit post for Turkey – the daily Athens "express" from İstanbul passes through Uzunköprü's station in the early hours of the morning, before crossing the Greek border to **Píthio** where passengers disembark and wait an hour for the connecting Greek service. The Turkish train re-crosses the border and returns to Uzunköprü roughly two hours later, continuing from there back to İstanbul. The line runs through the all but deserted wetlands around the **Meriçnehri River** before crossing the "long bridge", but you're unlikely to see any of it from the train at night.

Uzunköprü station is 4km north of town. If you miss the train, you'll have to take a taxi into the centre where the one-star *Ergene Oteli* (☎0584/513 5440; ❷), on the main square, is the only **accommodation** worth considering. It has a reasonable restaurant attached.

İpsala

The main Turkish–Greek road crossing, far busier and somewhat less paranoiac than the Edirne–Kastaniés one, is between **İPSALA**, astride the E25/110 highway, and Kípi in Greece. The two posts here are open 24 hours, but the banking facilities on both sides and the tourist information booth in İpsala (☎0284/616 1577) only operate sporadically, so it's not a bad idea to show up with a certain amount of currency for the country you'll be entering (though if you have dollars, the Turkish immigration officials will be happy to exchange it for Turkish lira). As at the Edirne frontier, there's a 500-metre-wide military zone that you're not allowed to cross on foot; during daylight hours at least, it's fairly easy to arrange a ride over.

From the village of **Kípi** there are six buses daily further into Greece; at the Turkish immigration post there are only taxis available to take you to İpsala.

Keşan

Crossing the border by public transport, it's easier to take a bus to **KEŞAN** (30km southeast of İpsala), whose *otogar* lies 3km north of town. It's a cipher of a place but has frequent bus connections from İstanbul, Edirne and Çanakkale, and into Greece via İpsala. As long-haul bus connections out of Edirne to anywhere but İstanbul are very poor, if you're making for Çanakkale, İzmir or Bursa, you'll almost always have a change of vehicle (with an hour or two's stopover) in Keşan.

Kirklareli

Although it's the capital of Thrace, **KIRKLARELİ** is often overlooked because of its relative proximity to the much larger Edirne. While historically not in the same league, it is nonetheless a pleasant little town clustered around a central main square with enough of interest to warrant at least a couple of hours' visit. It lies 62km east of Edirne: there are hourly **buses** from Edirne's *otogar* to the Kirklareli *otogar*, 1.5km out of town on the İstanbul road, and frequent dolmuşes depart from outside Edirne's *Rüstem Paşa Kervansarayı* to Kirklareli's main square.

The town **museum** (Kirklareli Müzesi; Tues–Sun 9am–12.30pm & 1.30–5pm; $0.50), on the north eastern corner of the square, neatly presents the history of the area. Pride of place goes to the second-century skeleton of a woman from one of the many local Thracian burial mounds. The museum also offers information about travel to the Neolithic and Iron Age **tombs** found hereabouts; there's a map of the area displayed on the first floor. The easiest tomb to reach, and the only one accessible by public transport, is in the village of Kapaklıköy (itself named after the stone-capped tomb), 8km north along the road to Dereköy; take a Dereköy-bound dolmuş ($0.50) from the dolmuş stand in the central square, and you'll find the immense Iron Age tomb in the copse on the far side of the village.

Ottoman Kirklareli is represented by five mosques, of which the fourteenth-century **Hışırbey Camii** on the central square is the most impressive, encompassing both a hamam, with separate entrances for men and women (still operating), and a shopping arcade.

With a large settled Romany population, Kirklareli is also the site of the immensely popular, three-day **Takava festival**, usually held over the first weekend after May 6. Families celebrate the arrival of spring by jumping over small bonfires for luck, while the local authorities organize painting competitions, concerts, bicycle races and a large public bonfire in the town centre on the Saturday night. On the Sunday, buses and coaches transport all and sundry to the banks of the Şeytandere River, southeast of town, for a day-long picnic and more concerts.

The most comfortable **accommodation** option in Kirklareli is the two-star *Best Otel Bilgiç* at Şukru Nail Sok 2 (☎0288/214 4671; ❷) just to the east of the square, towards the fruit and vegetable market, which has comfortable en-suite rooms with TV. It also has a licensed **restaurant**, but the food on offer rather depends on how many people are staying in the hotel. The unique *Kırklar Beyoğlu Sineması*, just north of the main square, screens Hollywood **movies** nightly in a converted Ottoman farmhouse.

Lüleburgaz

If you've become a Sinan-ophile, you can visit yet another of his substantial creations, which dominates the town of **LÜLEBURGAZ**, 76km east of Edirne on the main route to İstanbul.

The **Sokollu Mehmet Paşa Külliyesi**, originally commissioned by the governor of Rumeli in 1549, was built in fits and starts and wasn't completed until 1569, during Sokollu's term as grand vizier. What you see today is an imposing mosque and *medrese* abutted by a covered bazaar and guarded by two isolated towers. The mosque proper is peculiar, possessing only one minaret; where the others might be, three stubby turret-like towers jut instead, all joined by a mansard crenellation. The *medrese*, still used as a children's Koran school, is arrayed around the mosque courtyard, entered by two tiny arcades on the east and west sides; in the middle of the vast space stands the late Ottoman caprice of a *şadırvan* (ablutions fountain). The mosque's portico, built to square with the *medrese*, is far more impressive than the interior, and most visitors will soon drift out of the north gate to the **market promenade**, whose shops are still intact and in use. Just outside the gate, a huge dome with a stork's nest on top shades the centre of the bazaar.

Beyond, there was once a massive *kervansaray*, equal in size to the mosque complex. All of it has vanished save for a lone tower, balanced by another, the **Dar-ül-Kura**, at the south edge of the entire precinct, beyond the mosque's *mihrab*. The former **hamam**, across the street from the complex, is now chock-a-block with tiny **restaurants** in its outer bays, though the main dome has collapsed.

There are a few simple but acceptable **hotels** 200m south of Sokollu Mehmet, plus the *Yaman Oteli*, İstanbul Cad 12 (℡0288/417 1613, ℻417 1523; ❸), offering soulless, but very clean en-suite rooms with TV. There's little point stopping over, though, as the town is otherwise undistinguished and, given the frequent buses (every 30min or so to İstanbul or Edirne), moving on is an easy matter.

Vize

Buses to **VİZE** (originally Bizye) from İstanbul or Kirklareli drop you at the *otogar*, 300m from the town centre. Today an attractive backwater, with no hint of the tourist trade in evidence, Vize was formerly the capital of the Roman vassal kingdom of Eastern Thrace and later fortified as a Byzantine frontier town. The place is still overlooked by the **citadel's** remaining towers, ranged around modern radio antennae. Further downhill, back into the centre, stands a well-preserved **Byzantine church**, built on the foundations of an earlier Christian church. Designated as a museum, it houses surviving fragments of late Byzantine frescoes, but at the time of writing remains closed to the public. The remnants of a Byzantine bathhouse are situated close by, while carved into the hillside to the northwest of the town is a ninth-century Byzantine **cave monastery**.

Vize is a fair way to come from anywhere by bus just to say you've been, but drivers might well pass through en route to the Black Sea coast (see below). Should you find yourself stranded here, you'll need one of the town's only two **hotels**: the *Yeni Zafer Otel* (℡0288/318 2588; ❶), next to the *otogar*, which has very cheap, very basic waterless rooms; and the *Trak Otel*, a few doors down, that promises to be a tidy three-star establishment once the building work is finished.

Kıyıköy and the Black Sea coast

KIYIKÖY occupies an idyllic location, perched high on a rocky bluff, overlooking the Black Sea and flanked on both sides by slow-moving rivers and swathes of verdant green forest. It was fortified by the Byzantines around the sixth century, though most of what is still standing dates from the thirteenth and fourteenth centuries. Kıyıköy's Greek population left during the population exchange of the 1920s to be replaced by Bulgarian and Romany Muslims, but many inhabitants still use the former Greek name, "Midye" – after the mussels for which the town is famed. Today, gently crumbling half-timbered houses line the backstreets and part-mended fishing nets hang everywhere.

The main approach to the walled citadel of Kıyıköy is via the narrow south gate, sadly restored with pink cement bricks. The west gate opens onto what used to be the town's **agora**, now housing a pair of tea gardens (of which the *Kartal* also serves beer) and offering superb views to the west. Outside the west gate a road leads down the hill and 300m up the Kazandere River to the impressive **monastery of St Nicholas** – an elaborate structure carved into the rock of the hillside, complete with colonnaded aisles, barrel-vaulting and a semi-circular apse of tiered seats where the clergy once sat. On the northeast side of the village it's possible to see the part-brick **tunnel**, constructed to allow safe passage down to the harbour in time of siege – the only deep-water anchorage on this part of the coast. A mere fifteen-minute walk west of the village takes you to 2km of unspoilt **sandy beach**, backed by low cliffs oozing fossils.

Practicalities

The village is too tiny to have it's own *otogar* and direct **buses from İstanbul**, of which there are two a day (2hr 30min), drop you directly outside the narrow south gate. There are more frequent buses from İstanbul to **Saray**, a sleepy town 29km southwest of Kıyıköy, from where minibuses depart for Kıyıköy every hour.

You shouldn't have much trouble finding somewhere to stay in summer. The town boasts a good number of **pansiyons**, usually on the unoccupied floors of private houses: all are basic, offering shared bathroom and sometimes kitchen facilities, for as little as $4–6 per person a night. Typical of what's available is the *Hulya Pansiyon* (℡0288/388 6016; ❶), signposted to the west of the south gate, offering three-, four- and five-bed rooms and reductions for longer stays. The cliff-top *Deniz Motel* (℡0288/388 6452; ❶) has one-, two- and three-bed waterless rooms and generally fills up quickly at weekends; while the *Plaza Restaurant & Pansiyon* (℡0288/388 6177; ❷), outside town on the road to Saray, offers a nice view of cow-filled fields and the beach. West over the Kazandere River are a couple of simple, rubbish-strewn, summer-only **campsites**, but the untidy semi-permanent tents of Turkish families, camped here for the whole summer, have the air of a refugee camp.

Eating out is a more luxurious experience as Kıyıköy is famed for its fish: not only mussels, but locally caught salmon and trout as well. There are several rather good **restaurants** attracting day-trippers from İstanbul. Northeast of the village is the *Tevfiğin Yeri*, offering nice views to the east from its narrow terrace and a meal of *mezes*, salad and fish for about $10–15. The *Liman*, over the way, is a cheaper option.

The Thracian coast

If you're heading west from İstanbul, you don't really outrun the straggling suburbs until the junction where the Edirne-bound E80 splits off from the E25/110, headed for the İpsala frontier station. Fifty-five kilometres beyond the junction, the port of **Tekirdağ** marks the start of the little-visited **Thracian coast**. Here the main E25/110 steers the majority of the traffic inland to Keşan before joining the E87 south to the Gelibolu peninsula. But from Tekirdağ there is an alternative, little-used minor road that also heads eventually to the Gelibolu peninsula, following the coast through a run of fishing villages and small resorts.

Tekirdağ

TEKİRDAĞ, in a hilly setting at the head of a gently curving bay, is a fairly pleasant seaside port, with a few remaining wooden houses and a ferry service to the islands in the Sea of Marmara.

Time to kill between connections could be spent in the sixteenth-century **Rüstem Paşa Camii**, designed by Mimar Sinan and situated opposite the *Belediye* building on Hükümet Caddesi, or in the **Rakoczi Museum** (Rakoczi Müzesi; Tues–Sun 8.30am–4.30pm; $0.70). Prince Ferenc Rakoczi (1676–1735) was leader of an unsuccessful revolt against the Austrian Hapsburgs and the house, where he lived in exile as a Carmelite friar, was converted to a museum in his memory in 1932 by the Hungarian government. Among the exhibits are Hungarian weapons, paintings relating to Rakoczi's life and his flag.

Down on the shore boulevard there's a **tourist office** (Mon–Fri 8.30am–noon & 1–5.30pm; ☏0282/261 1698), next to the dockside. From here, ferries ply to and from the islands of the Sea of Marmara and on to Erdek on the Kapıdaği peninsula (for ticket details, see p.264). There are at least three car-ferry services to Marmara and Avşa every evening, though out of season the service drops to twice a week (weather permitting). The **otogar** is 200m from the ferry landing off Atatürk Bulvarı, on the road to İstanbul.

A few **hotels** stand opposite the ferry jetty. *Yat Hotel*, Ertuğrul Mah Cad 8 (☏0282/261 1054; ❷), off İskele Caddesi, is a reasonable option, where all rooms have toilets and some have full bathrooms.

Tekirdağ is known for its grilled meatballs, served in most of the local **restaurants**, although they are barely distinguishable from those sold elsewhere across Turkey. The **local wine** is a more exciting prospect, on sale in shops facing the seafront. The best are mature reds, perhaps in unlabelled bottles, some of which never make it out of the region. The bottling plants 3km to the west of town usually let you sample before buying.

Kumbağ, Hasköy and Şarköy

Regular minibuses depart from Tekirdağ's *otogar* towards **KUMBAĞ**, 8km southwest along the coast. There's a narrow beach here, but uncontrolled holiday-home development has made it another İstanbul-by-the-sea.

After Kumbağ, the coast road deteriorates distinctly and is flanked by precipitous and unprotected drops to the sea below. The journey is punctuated after 25km by the pretty fishing village of **HASKÖY**. Here, a pebbly beach is set against rolling, vine-covered hills and a few *pansiyon*s, mostly attached to fish restaurants, overlook the harbour.

Another 20km further southwest along the coast takes you to **ŞARKÖY**, a boring, over-developed resort attracting Turks from İstanbul and Thrace since the 1960s. The *otogar* is about a fifteen-minute walk from the beach, at the extreme northwest of town on the road to the E87/550 highway. In season (May–Sept) a semi-legal ferry service crosses three times a week to Avşa and the Marmara islands (see p.269) from the ferry terminal in the centre of town. **Accommodation** tends to be block-booked by Turkish families in season, and closed out of season, though one exception is the *Otel İmen* (☏0282/518 1188; ❷), which stays open throughout the year. The usual array of *pide*, kebab and fish **restaurants** covers the waterfront.

The Gelibolu peninsula

Burdened with a grim military history but endowed with some fine scenery and beaches, the slender **Gelibolu (Gallipoli) peninsula** – roughly 60km in length and between 4km and 18km wide – forms the northwest side of the **Dardanelles** (Çanakkale Boğazı in Turkish, the ancient Hellespont), the narrow strait connecting the Aegean with the Sea of Marmara. Whether you approach the peninsula from Şarköy or (more likely) Keşan, the road there is pretty, swooping down in long arcs past the Saros gulf.

Site of the 1915 **Gallipoli landings** by the Allied troops, the peninsula contains a mind-numbing series of battlefields and cemeteries that tell of the trag-

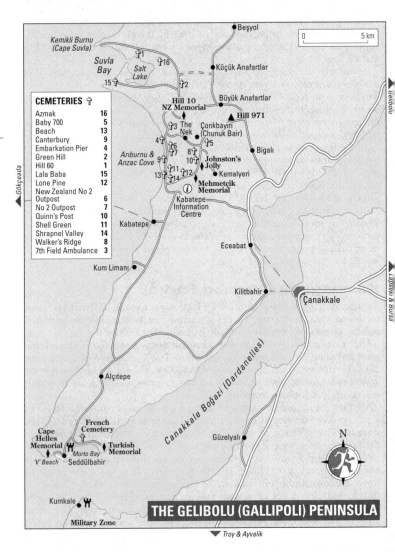

CEMETERIES †

Azmak	16
Baby 700	5
Beach	13
Canterbury	9
Embarkation Pier	4
Green Hill	2
Hill 60	1
Lala Baba	15
Lone Pine	12
New Zealand No 2 Outpost	6
No 2 Outpost	7
Quinn's Post	10
Shell Green	11
Shrapnel Valley	14
Walker's Ridge	8
7th Field Ambulance	3

THE GELIBOLU (GALLIPOLI) PENINSULA

ic defeat by the Turkish forces. For Turks the region also holds a great deal of significance, as the Gallipoli campaign made famous a previously unknown lieutenant-colonel, Mustafa Kemal, later to become Atatürk.

Some people visit the peninsula's main town, **Gelibolu**, intending to use it as a base to visit the battlefields. However, **Eceabat**, at the southern end of the peninsula, or Çanakkale (see p.277), across the strait, are much closer to the battlefield sites. If you're intending to join a tour or go under your own steam you'll almost certainly find Eceabat a better bet than Gelibolu.

Touring the battlefields and cemeteries

The **World War I battlefields and Allied cemeteries** scattered along the Gelibolu peninsula are a moving sight, the past violence made all the more poignant by the present beauty of the landscape. The whole area is now either fertile rolling country, or cloaked in thick scrub and pine forest alive with birds, making it difficult to imagine the carnage of 1915. Much of the flatter land is still farmed and ploughing often turns up pieces of rusting equipment, fragments of shrapnel, human bones and even unexploded munitions.

The open-air sites have no admission fees or restricted hours and there's now a reasonable choice of options for touring the peninsula. **Tours of the northern sites** (including the Kabatepe Information Centre) depart from Gelibolu, Eceabat and Çanakkale, and costs fluctuate between $15 and $25 per person, depending on the number of tourists around and general market conditions. Tours from İstanbul cost around $50 and should include transport to either Çanakkale or Eceabat and one night's accommodation. Length of tour, departure time and other conditions all vary, so the best policy is to shop around and try to talk to people who have been on specific tours. Check whether any extra costs apply, or if lunch is provided. You'll also want enough time to wander a little, take in the breathtaking beauty of the location and, most likely, swim. Distant sites are often omitted (the focus is very much on ANZAC), so also check that what you want to see is on the itinerary. All companies are supposed to be working with Ministry of Tourism licensed guides, who should have excellent English and a thorough knowledge of the sites.

You can also make **independent visits** to the sites in the northern and southern parts of the peninsula by a combination of short minibus rides and walking. **Minibuses** run from Gelibolu to Kilitbahir via Eceabat, from Eceabat to Kabatepe village and, less frequently, from Eceabat to Alçitepe via the Kabatepe Information Centre; there's also a sporadic service from Kilitbahir to Seddülbahir. From the Kabatepe Information Centre, you can walk around the main sites to the north inside a couple of hours. At Kilitbahir, minibuses meet the Çanakkale car ferries in summer and take passengers to Alçitepe and Seddülbahir, from where you can tour the surrounding cemeteries and memorials on foot. They also ferry passengers to the Turkish memorial (Çanakkale Abidesi in Turkish).

It's also usually possible to **rent bicycles** in Eceabat, which gives you all the freedom you could possibly require, but be warned – some roads are steep, and can be rough and muddy in winter.

Some history

Soon after the start of World War I it became obvious to the Allies that Russia could not be supplied by sea, nor a Balkan front opened against the Central

Powers, unless Ottoman Turkey was eliminated. **Winston Churchill**, in his earliest important post as First Lord of the Admiralty, reasoned that the quickest way to accomplish this would be to force the Dardanelles with a fleet and bombard İstanbul into submission. A combined Anglo–French armada made several attempts on the straits during November 1914, which were repulsed, but they returned in earnest on March 18, 1915. This time they managed to penetrate less than 10km up the waterway before striking numerous Turkish mines, losing half a dozen vessels and hundreds of men. The Allies retreated and command squabbles erupted over allocation of troops to the campaign. The generals saw the western front as paramount, whereas politicians – foremost among them, Churchill – wanted to knock Turkey out of the war first in order to weaken Germany, while at the same time exciting anti-Turkish feelings in Bulgaria and bringing it too into the war.

Regrouped at Mudros harbour on the Greek island of Limnos, the joint expeditionary forces took several months to prepare an amphibious assault on the Turkish positions along the peninsula. During this time the British had no way of knowing that Turkish forces defending the straits were cripplingly under supplied. Had they attempted it, another naval sprint down the Dardanelles might have succeeded, but instead the delay gave the Turks the chance to strengthen their own defences.

The plan eventually formulated by the British and French commanders called for an Anglo–French landing at Cape Helles, Seddülbahir and Morto Bay at the mouth of the straits, and a simultaneous **ANZAC** (Australia–New Zealand Army Corps) assault at Kabatepe beach 13km north. The two forces were to drive towards each other, link up and neutralize the Turkish shore batteries controlling the Dardanelles.

The Australians landed first at dawn on April 25, 1915, with the British and French making shore around an hour afterwards, followed by the New Zealanders later in the day. The rather hare-brained scheme ran into trouble from the start. Anglo–French brigades at the southernmost cape were pinned down by accurate Turkish fire and the French contingent was virtually annihilated; after two days they had only managed to penetrate 6.5km inland and never managed to move any further. The fate of the ANZAC landing was even more horrific: owing to a drifting signal buoy, the Aussies and Kiwis disembarked not on the wide, flat sands of Kabatepe, but at a cramped and Turkish-dominated cove next to Arıburnu, 2km north. Despite heavy casualties (around 2000 on the first day alone) the ANZACs advanced inland in staggered parties, as the Turks initially retreated. The next day, goaded by their commanders, they managed to threaten the Turkish strongpoint of Çonkbayırı overhead. It was here that one Mustafa Kemal, a previously unknown lieutenant-colonel, rushed in reinforcements, telling his poorly equipped troops, "I do not order you to fight, I order you to die." Amazingly it worked: the ANZAC force never made it further than 800m inland, despite a supplementary British landing at Cape Suvla to the north. With the exception of ferocious battles for the summit in early August, both sides settled into long-term trench warfare. Finally, around Christmas 1915, the Allies gave up, with the last troops leaving Seddülbahir on January 8, 1916. Churchill's career went into temporary eclipse, while that of Mustafa Kemal was only just beginning.

The reasons for the **Allied defeat** are many. In addition to the chanciness of the basic strategy, the callousness and incompetence of the Allied commanders – who often countermanded each other's orders or failed to press advantages with reinforcements – cannot be underestimated. With hindsight you cannot help but wonder why the Allies didn't concentrate more on Cape Suvla and the flat, wide valley behind, skirting the fortified Ottoman heights to reach the Dardanelles' northwest shore. On the **Turkish side**, much of the credit for the successful resistance must go to Mustafa Kemal, then relatively obscure, but later better known as **Atatürk**. His role in the Turkish victory at Çonkbayırı is legendary. Mustafa Kemal seemed to enjoy a charmed life, narrowly escaping death on several occasions and, aside from his tactical skills, is credited with various other extraordinary accomplishments, but primarily that of rekindling morale, by threats, persuasion or example, among often outgunned and outnumbered Ottoman infantrymen.

At various times, half a million men were deployed by defenders and attackers alike; of these well over fifty percent were killed, wounded or missing. Allied deaths were around 52,000 while incomplete records have led to estimates of Turkish dead to be anywhere between 50,000 and 200,000. The carnage among the ANZACs in particular was especially severe compared to the island nations' populations, but would in fact be dwarfed by the number of ANZACs killed on the western front later in the war. Only around 10,600 lost their lives in the Gallipoli campaign compared with around 60,000 for the entire war. Claims voiced in some quarters that the Allied top brass regarded the "colonials" as expendable cannon fodder have never fully been borne out. Indeed more British and Irish troops died at Gallipoli than ANZACs, with two Irish battalions suffering over fifty-percent casualties on the first day and the 42nd Manchester Division being almost completely wiped out. However, this baptism by blood had several long-term effects: a sense of Australia and New Zealand having come of age as sovereign countries; the designation of April 25 as Anzac Day, a solemn holiday in Australia and New Zealand; and a healthy antipodean scepticism, pending an evaluation of actual national interest in the face of blandishments to join international adventures.

Anzac Day

Anzac Day, April 25, is the busiest day of the year for the Gelibolu peninsula, as thousands of Australians and New Zealanders arrive to commemorate the Allied defeat, providing a huge annual boost to the local economy. In the days leading up to the 25th Eceabat and Çanakkale start to fill with visitors: Anzac Day tours are organized locally or from just about any travel agent in İstanbul, while all the European overland companies write Anzac Day into their itineraries.

The day itself begins with the **Dawn Service** at 5.30am at Anzac Cove, though most people arrive much earlier to camp out, as the police close all the roads around the grave sites to traffic from 3am. The service used to be a somewhat informal ceremony, but in recent years thousands have attended and the service now features official speeches, prayers and a representative from the Australian or New Zealand forces playing a poignant "Last Post" as the sun rises over Anzac Cove. An hour's breakfast break follows the Dawn Service before the rest of the morning's ceremonies resume – **wreath-laying** at the British, French and Turkish memorials, and more services at the Australian memorial at Lone Pine and the New Zealand memorial at Chunuk Bair.

For most people the experience of being at Gallipoli on Anzac Day is a solemn affair – many are here in remembrance of ancestors that lost their lives during World War I. However, some backpackers choose to celebrate the occasion through the bottom of a beer glass, and recent years have seen violent confrontations between alcohol-charged visitors and right-wing Turks – many bussing in from İstanbul especially. Local police seldom sympathize with those unable to explain their problems coherently from a vertical position.

Gelibolu

GELİBOLU – principal town of the peninsula and 35km north of the main battlefield sites – is a moderately inviting, if slightly windy, place perched just where the Dardanelles begin to narrow in earnest. It served as the Anglo–French headquarters during the Crimean War, though the town's history goes back at least as far as the fifth century BC when it was allied with Athens against the invading Persians. It's still a military outpost today, where young Turks on their two-year National Service practice for their passing-out parades at the various military installations around town.

At the heart of town is a colourful, square **fishing harbour**, ringed by cafés and restaurants, its two pools separated by a broad stone **tower**, which is all that remains of the fortifications of Byzantine Callipolis. The fortress was held by an army of rebelling Catalan mercenaries for seven years in the early fourteenth century and later fell to the Ottomans (1354), who rebuilt and expanded it. These days the tower houses the **Piri Reis museum** (Piri Reis Müzesi; Tues–Sun 9.30am–5.30pm; $0.50), dedicated to the legendary cartographer but also containing a small number of local archeological finds and some old photos of the straits. The only other significant monuments are a historic **mosque** in the marketplace and, well inland to the northeast, a few sturdy but otherwise unremarkable Ottoman tombs.

Practicalities

The **ferry jetty** is right at the inner harbour entrance; ferries cross on the hour, every hour (24hr service; $2, or $10 per car) to Lapseki, across the Dardanelles, providing one approach to Cannakkale. The **otogar** is 500m out of town on the Eceabat road. Currently, Gelibolu has no tourist office or exchange office, though both occasionally do re-open for business. However, all the main **banks** have ATMs and most will change currency and travellers' cheques, as will the **PTT** kiosk next to the ferry terminal.

For **accommodation**, *Yelkenci Pansiyon* (℡0286/566 1022; ❶), at Liman Meydanı on the harbour, offers pleasant rooms, without showers but with balconies overlooking the harbour. A short walk up the main street, Liman Caddesi, and then uphill along Taşçılar Caddesi, brings you to the *Otel Dilmaç* (℡0286/566 3212, ✉ilkerd@kabiline.com; ❷), whose well-appointed rooms have TV and minibar. There's an interesting display of brass ship fittings in the lobby of the *Hotel Oya* on Miralay Şeflik Aker Caddesi, the next street left off Liman Caddesi (℡ & ℻0286/566 0392; ❸). The rooms here are very clean, with TV and fridge, though you should ask for a room at the front with a balcony, as these are twice the size of those at the back. Between the lighthouse and an army camp extends a serviceable **beach**, with a free **campsite** operated by the local municipality.

Only contemplate staying at the unprepossessing, old-fashioned *Hotel Yılmaz* (℡0286/566 1256, ℻566 3598; ❷), on Liman Caddesi, if there is no room at one of the better options above. However, it is the only place in town to offer group **tours** (about $15, including taped commentary) of the World War I sites each morning or afternoon and a video showing of Peter Weir's *Gallipoli* every evening.

When eating out, don't miss the local catch of *sardalya* (sardines), grilled fresh before they find their way to Gelibolu's canneries. The *Yelkenci Pansiyon* has a good, inexpensive fish **restaurant**, where meals are served on a large rooftop balcony looking out to sea. Prices here, rather oddly, depend on how big a selection of fish there is to choose from; the more fish on offer, the cheaper it

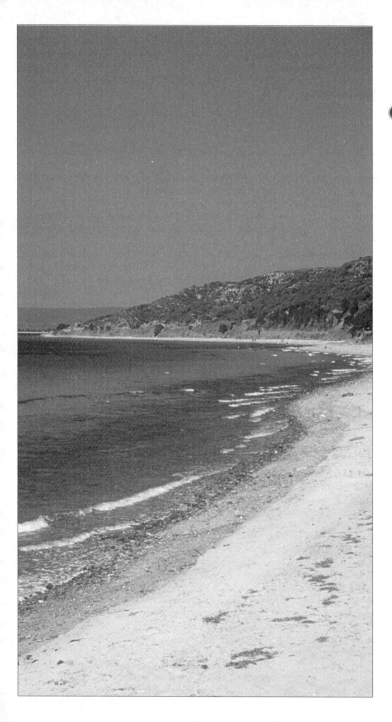

is (and there's a ten-percent discount if you're staying at the *pansiyon*). The excellent *Imren*, to the left of the harbour, is both cheap and licensed, as are the similar *Liman* and *Boğaz* restaurants next door. Expect to pay $5–10 for starters, fish and drinks at each of these.

Eceabat

ECEABAT – 40km south of Gelibolu – is less attractive than Gelibolu and smaller than Çanakkale, but is the best base for touring the battlefield sites, whether by yourself or on a tour.

The town doesn't have a proper *otogar* and most **buses** drop you near the ferry jetty, from where **car-ferries** run across the Dardanelles to Çanakkale (on the hour, 24hr service; $0.50, $5 per car; 40min). The bus company ticket offices are right in front of the jetty at Cumhuriyet Meydanı. There's a **PTT booth** by the jetty, changing money and offering a metered phone until 9pm. **Emails** can be picked up at the *Gina Internet Café*, across the road from *TJ's Hostel* on Cumhuriyet Caddesi, and **bike rental** can be arranged at both of these places.

Accommodation is plentiful but you'll need to book well ahead if you want to stay over for Anzac Day. Best budget option in town by far is the backpacker-friendly *TJ's Hostel*, Cumhuriyet Caddesi 5 (℡0286/814 3121, ⓦwww.anzacgallipolitours.com; ❷), run by the formidable TJ and his Australian wife. There are 55 beds available in clean, tidy rooms (most of them en suite), including dorm beds ($4). Extras include a laundry, book exchange, screenings of Mel Gibson in *Gallipoli*, and the lively rooftop *Boomerang* bar, offering a nightly barbecue-and-beer for $4. Otherwise, there's the *Hotel Eceabat*, also known as the *Down Under Hostel* (℡0286/814 2458, Ⓕ814 2461; ❷), on İskele Meydanı, overlooking the harbour, which has a pleasant breakfast room with picture windows looking out to sea. Also on İskele Meydanı is the *Ece* (℡0286/814 1210; ❷) offering simple rooms. The *Boss 1 Hotel*, near the jetty on Cumhuriyet Meydanı (℡0286/814 1464, Ⓔboss@heyboss.com; ❷), and the *Boss II* (℡0286/814 2311, Ⓔboss@heyboss.com; ❷), with adjoining **campsite**, 500m further west up the waterfront and slightly inland, both offer rooms with TV and on-site restaurants.

Eating and, more specifically, **drinking** aren't a problem in Eceabat. There is a line of simple *pide* and *kebap* salons in front of the jetty, plus a smattering of antipodean-named bars around *TJ's Hostel*, easily spotted by the Australian and New Zealand flags hanging outside. The best of the bunch is the *Vegemite Bar*, a veritable institution on the Aussie/Kiwi backpacker trail through Turkey.

Battlefield tours

TJ's Hostel runs informative half-day **tours** to the battlefield sites for $20 per person, which kick off with a screening of a documentary on Gallipoli, *The Fatal Shore,* to get you into the right frame of mind, and include a picnic lunch and a stop for a swim. For another $20, the battlefield tour can be combined with an additional half-day tour across the Dardanelles to Troy. TJ also offers diving tours to the 1915 **shipwrecks** around the peninsula (from $40 per dive, minimum two persons). In addition, the shop in the hostel reception sells a useful battlefield map and guide for $5, plus other Gallipoli-related gear. The Çanakkale-based *Anzac House* and the *Yellow Rose Pansiyon* also run organized tours of the battlefields with pick-ups in Eceabat (see p.278 for more details).

For exploring under your own steam, **local minibuses** depart from in front of the *Atlanta* restaurant for Gelibolu, Kabatepe village (this service can also drop you at the Kabatepe Information Centre) and Alçitepe. There are also services south to Kilitbahir (see below), where you can find regular dolmuşes to the southern battlefield sites.

Kilitbahir and around

The tiny village of **KİLİTBAHİR**, 5km south of Eceabat, is dwarfed by its massive and perfectly preserved **castle**. Unpublicized, privately run **car ferries** chug across to Çanakkale at regular intervals – generally departing when full – at this narrowest point (1300m) of the Dardanelles. In summer, regular **dolmuşes** meet the Çanakkale car ferries at Kilitbahir and take passengers to Alçitepe, Seddülbahir and the Turkish memorial at the southern end of the peninsula.

The central and northern sites

The first stop on most tours is at the **Kabatepe Information Centre and Museum** (daily 8.30am–5pm; $0.70), 9km northwest of Eceabat, which contains a well-labelled selection of war memorabilia, including touching letters home, photographs of the trenches, weapons and uniforms. The only sour note is the rather ghastly inclusion of some human, presumably Allied, remains.

The first points encountered along the coast road north of the centre are the **Beach**, **Shrapnel Valley** and **Shell Green** cemeteries – the latter 300m inland up a steep track, unsuitable for all but four-wheel drive vehicles, and consequently missed out by most tours. These are followed by **Anzac Cove** and **Arıburnu**, site of the first, bungled ANZAC landing and location of the dawn service on Anzac Day. At Anzac Cove a memorial bears Atatürk's famous quotation concerning the Allied dead, which, translated into English, begins: "Those heroes that shed their blood and lost their lives . . . you are now lying in the soil of a friendly country." Looking inland, you'll see the murderous badlands that gave the defenders such an advantage. Beyond Arıburnu, the terrain flattens out and the four other cemeteries (Canterbury, No. 2 Outpost, New Zealand No. 2 Outpost and Embarkation Pier) are more dispersed.

A couple of kilometres north of Arıburnu are the beaches and salt lake at **Cape Suvla**, today renamed Kemikli Burnu ("the bone-strewn headland"), location of another six cemeteries: 7th Field Ambulance, Hill 60 (with its memorial to the New Zealand forces), Green Hill, Azmak, Hill 10 and Lala Bala; all contain mainly English, Scottish, Welsh and Irish dead, with ANZAC graves also in the first two. The roads up here are little more than dirt tracks and most tours don't make it this far.

From Anzac Cove tours go uphill along the road north that roughly follows what was the front line, to the strong points (now cemeteries) scattered around **Çonkbayırı** hill. To the left of this road is **Shrapnel Valley** – the single, perilous supply line that ran up-valley from the present location of Beach Cemetery to the trenches. First up is **Lone Pine** (Kanlı Sırt), lowest strategic position on the ridge and the largest graveyard-cum-memorial to those buried unmarked or at sea. Action here was considered a sideshow to the main August offensive further up Çonkbayırı; a total of 28,000 men died in four days at both points. Just up from Lone Pine is the **Mehmetcik memorial** to the Turkish soldiers who perished and at **Johnston's Jolly** (named after an officer who liked to "jolly the Turks up" with his gun) is a heavily eroded section of **trench**, peaceful now beneath the pine trees.

From here the road forks. To the left is **The Nek** – the scene of Peter Weir's film *Gallipoli* – and the **Walker's Ridge** cemetery. To the right the road continues uphill to Baby 700 cemetery – the high-water mark of the Allied advance on April 25 – and to the massive New Zealand memorial obelisk and the five-monolith Turkish memorial on the crest of Çonkbayırı hill (Chunuk Bair). On the Turkish memorial are Atatürk's words and deeds – chief among the latter being his organization of successful resistance to the Allied attacks of August 6–10. The spot where the Turkish leader's pocket watch stopped a fragment of shrapnel is highlighted, as is the grave of a Turkish soldier discovered in 1990 when the trenches were reconstructed. On this part of the front, the trenches of the opposing forces lay within a few metres of each other and the modern road corresponds to the no-man's-land.

To the southern cape

The harbour of **KABATEPE** village, boarding point for the ferry to the Turkish Aegean island of Gökçeada (Imvros; twice weekly in winter; daily in the evening over summer), lies 2km south of the Kabatepe Information Centre. There's a good beach to the north of town – intended site of the ANZAC landing – but if you're after a swim wait until you reach **KUM LİMANI**, another 3km further south, where an even better strand fringes a warm, clean, calm sea, unusual this far north. There's been little development of this beautiful setting, but you probably won't be alone: a number of tour companies bring their clients here for a dip after battlefield sightseeing. There's recommended **accommodation** at the friendly *Kum Motel* (☎0286/814 1455-66, ⓔotelkum@superonline.com; ❹), which has an attractive bar on the beach. It also offers half-board for $45 per person, or you can camp in the grounds for $4. Call ahead and someone from the motel will pick you up from the Eceabat–Kabatepe dolmuş; otherwise it's a three-kilometre walk from Kabatepe harbour.

The British **Cape Helles Memorial** obelisk adorns the Turkish equivalent of Land's End, 16km beyond Kum Limanı and just past the village of Seddülbahir. From Cape Helles itself, the views south to Bozcaada (Tenedos), west to Gökçeada (Imvros) and east to Asia are magnificent, and abundant **Ottoman fortifications** hint at the age-old importance of the place. Tucked between the medieval bulwarks is an excellent beach, the **V Beach** of the Allied expedition, behind which is a **campsite** – and the biggest of five British cemeteries in the area. A turning just before Seddülbahir leads to the **French Cemetery** above Morto Bay, one of the most striking of all the memorials, with its serried rows of named black crosses, and to the nearby **Turkish Memorial**, resembling a stark, tetrahedral footstool. Locally organized tours rarely venture this far, so if you're intent on seeing these two you'll have to make your own arrangements.

The Southern Marmara shore

The **southern shoreline** of the Sea of Marmara is not as rewarding as the northern one. To the east it consists mainly of a heavily urbanized, polluted dormitory community for İstanbul. Much of the area was devastated by the **earthquake** of August 17, 1999, in which an estimated 30,000 people were killed – many the victims of rogue builders who ignored building regulations, skimped on materials and miraculously managed to pass official inspections. Since then, hurriedly constructed apartment blocks have been erected for the tens of thousands who were housed in makeshift tented camps after the quake. Fortunately, **İznik**, historically the most interesting town in the region, suffered little damage. Important as a centre of Christianity and, briefly, capital of the Nicaean Empire, it has many fascinating monuments and merits a stay. To the south, **Bursa**, once one of Turkey's most attractive cities, has succumbed to rapid industrial growth over the past ten years, bringing great wealth but destroying much of its colourful provincial atmosphere.

Sea bus services from İstanbul provide quick access to the region. For example, the bus from İstanbul to Bursa takes a congested five-hour route along the gulf shore through İzmit (badly hit by the quake), whereas it's less than three by sea bus and bus via Yalova. Departures are from İstanbul's Yenikapı ferry terminal to **Yalova** ($6), **Mudanya** ($8) and **Bandırma** ($12), as well as to the islands of **Avşa** and **Marmara**. For schedules, see İstanbul's "Travel details", p.213. Using these services, you could see all the sights on the southern Marmara shore over a three- or four-day period, though during July and August, it's advisable to pre-book sea bus tickets.

Southern Marmara ports and resorts

There's little of compelling interest in the **coastal ports** of the southern Marmara shore, from Yalova to Kumyaka. They like to call themselves resorts – which they are for numbers of locals – and for the most part this is rocky coast, with inland contours softened somewhat by ubiquitous olive groves. **Yalova** itself is the main transport hub, but there's no need to hang around longer than it takes to catch one of the buses outside the ferry terminal that depart for Bursa every half-hour or so ($2; 1hr). Across the road, dolmuşes to Iznik depart every hour on the hour ($1.50; 1hr).

Termal

There are regular dolmuşes from Yalova to the famous hot springs at **TERMAL**, 12km to the southwest (just inland from Çinarcik). Although visited by Byzantine and Roman emperors, Termal's springs only became fashionable again at the turn of the twentieth century and most of the Ottoman Belle Epoque buildings date from that era.

Atatürk had a house built here, now open as a **museum** (Atatürk Müzesi; Tues–Sun 8.30am–noon & 1–5pm; $0.70), which preserves a certain rustic charm, its original hand-crafted furniture still in place. Several **hamams** – popular for their beneficial effect on rheumatism and skin diseases – offer communal pools (daily 8am–11pm; $6) with separate compartments for tour groups. Water temperatures reach 65°C, so the best time to visit is during winter when the hot water provides a haven from the seasonal chill. In summer, you'll find yourself swimming, then jumping out to sunbathe in order to cool off.

The spa resort is completely dominated by two luxury **hotels**, both owned by the Turban hotel group: the *Turban* and the *Çamlık* (reservations for both ☎0226/675 7400, ℱ675 7413; ❼–❽) whose rooms vary in price according to size, facilities and location. The *Turban* is licensed and has a good, reasonably priced restaurant that serves trout.

A cheaper alternative can be found in an idyllic location in the village of **ÜVEZPİNAR**, on one of the surrounding hills: the *Dinana* (☎0226/675 7293; ❹) is family-run and clean, with pleasant rooms all with balconies overlooking the forested mountains; the hotel also has a restaurant serving simple meals. Üvezpınar is a two-kilometre hike up the road leading from the *jandarma* station to the left of the entrance to Termal, or up steps leading from within the resort itself.

Mudanya

MUDANYA is the closest harbour to Bursa, though the least useful transit point from İstanbul (Yalova is the better option). Bursa and Çanakkale buses and minibuses connect with the arriving ferries from İstanbul. Now rather dull and unappealing, the town's major moment in history was as the place where the provisional armistice between Turkey and the Allies was signed on October 11, 1922, in a nineteenth-century waterside wooden mansion that now houses a small (missable) museum to mark the occasion. More recently Mudanya served as the port of departure for those attending the trial of Kurdish separatist leader Abdullah Öcalan (held on the nearby island of İmralı).

There's one excellent **hotel** here: the *Montania*, Eski İstasyon Caddesi (☎0224/544 6000, ☒www.montaniahotel.com; ❼), a renovated 150-year-old station building on the seaside esplanade. It has indoor and outdoor pools, a sauna and well-equipped modern rooms, some with sea views. Rates are negotiable out of season.

Kumyaka and Zeytinbaği

KUMYAKA, 7km west of Mudanya, and **ZEYTINBAĞI**, 3km further on, both have **Byzantine churches** that are worth a look. The latter village was the Greek Trilya and the Fatih Camii here is thought to have started life as a thirteenth-century church – it is presently undergoing restoration. A more ruinous church just out of town dates from the eighth century. Once you've seen these, you can get a good fish meal by the little anchorage. Both villages are served by bus from Mudanya and Bursa.

İznik

It's hard to believe that **İZNİK**, today a somnolent farming community at the east end of the lake of the same name, was once the seat of empires and scene of desperate battles. But looking around the fertile olive-mantled valley, you can understand the attraction for imperial powers needing a fortified base near the sea-lanes of the Marmara. Today, İznik is firmly a backwater, slumbering away among its orchards and waking only recently to the demands of tourism. Tractors, rather than tour buses, are still the most common sight on İznik's streets. The town's famous sixteenth-century ceramics, the best ever produced in Turkey, are now all but absent from İznik's museums and mosques – even the tiles sheathing the minaret of Yeşil Camii, the town's most famous landmark, are poor substitutes made in Kütahya. Most people visit İznik as a long day out of İstanbul or Bursa, staying a night at most – just about enough time to sample the town's monuments.

Some history

Founded by Alexander's general Antigonus in 316 BC, the city was seized and enlarged fifteen years later by his rival Lysimachus, who named it **Nicaea** after his late wife. He also gave Nicaea its first set of walls and the grid plan typical of Hellenistic towns; both are still evident. When the Bithynian kingdom succeeded Lysimachus, Nicaea alternated with nearby Nicomedia as its capital until bequeathed to Rome in 74 BC. Under the Roman emperors the city prospered as capital of the province and it continued to flourish during the Byzantine era.

Nicaea played a pivotal role in early Christianity, by virtue of hosting two important **ecumenical councils**. The first, convened by Constantine the Great in 325AD, resulted in the condemnation of the Arian heresy – which maintained that Christ's nature was inferior to God the Father's – and the promulgation of the Nicene Creed, affirming Christ's divine nature, which is still central to Christian belief. The seventh council (the second to be held here) was presided over by Empress Irene in 787AD; this time the Iconoclast controversy was settled by the pronouncement, widely misunderstood in the West, that icons had their proper place in the church so long as they were revered and not worshipped.

Nicaea's much-repaired walls seldom repelled invaders and in 1081 the Selçuks took the city, only to be evicted by a combined force of Byzantines and Crusaders sixteen years later. The fall of Constantinople to the Fourth Crusade in 1204 propelled Nicaea into the spotlight once more, for the Byzantine heir Theodore Lascaris retreated here and made this the base of the improbably successful **Nicaean Empire**. The Lascarid dynasty added a second circuit of walls before returning to Constantinople in 1261, but these again failed to deter the besieging Ottomans, who, led by Orhan Gazi, the victor of Bursa, broke through in March 1331.

Renamed İznik, the city embarked on a golden age of sorts, interrupted briefly by the pillaging of Tamerlane in 1402. Virtually all of the surviving monuments predate the Mongol sacking, but the most enduring contribution to art and architecture – the celebrated **İznik tiles and pottery** – first appeared during the reign of Çelebi Mehmet I, who brought skilled potters from Persia to begin the local industry. This received another boost in 1514 when Selim the Grim took Tabriz and sent more craftsmen west as war booty; by the end of the sixteenth century ceramic production was at its height, with more than three hundred functioning kilns. It was to be a brief flowering, since within another hundred years war and politics had scattered most of the artisans. By the mid-eighteenth century the local industry had packed up completely, with products from nearby Kütahya serving as inferior substitutes. İznik began a long, steady decline, hastened by near-total devastation during the 1920–1922 war.

▲ Yeraltı Mezar, Yalova & İstanbul

İZNİK

ACCOMMODATION
Aydin	2
Babacan	3
Çamlık	5
Cem	1
Kaynarca	4

CAFÉS AND RESTAURANTS
Balıkçi	A
Çamlık	E
İskender Kebab	C
Karadeniz Pide Salon	D
Kar-pi	B

İznik Gölü

▼ Bursa

The Town

With its regular street plan, İznik is easy to navigate. The main north–south boulevard **Atatürk Caddesi** and its east–west counterpart **Kılıçaslan Caddesi** link four of the seven ancient gates, dividing the town into unequal quadrants. Only enthusiasts will want to walk the entire perimeter of the double **walls**, now missing most of their hundred original watchtowers, but three of the seven portals are worth some time. Heavy traffic has been rerouted through modern breaches in the fortifications to prevent vibration damage to the original openings, now restricted to tractors and pedestrians.

The **lake** provides decent swimming in summer, but the town beaches are scrappy and uninviting; you really need a car to reach the more attractive spots. Both roads out of town along the lakeshore stay close to the water and both offer swimming possibilities at various tiny beaches along the way.

The southeast quadrant

If your time is limited, head directly to İznik's central roundabout, southeast of which is the **Aya Sofya Museum** (Aya Sofya Müzesi; Tues–Sun 8.30am–noon

& 1–5pm; $0.70), housed in all that remains of the Byzantine Church of Holy Wisdom, founded by Justinian. The current structure was built after an earthquake in 1065 and, as the cathedral of the provisional Byzantine capital, hosted the coronations of the four Nicaean emperors. The Ottomans converted it to a mosque directly on taking the city and Mimar Sinan restored it, but the premises were already half-ruined when reduced to their present, sorry condition in 1922. Inside there's not much to see except some damaged floor mosaics and a faint but exquisite **fresco** of Christ, John and Mary, at ground level behind a glass panel to the left as you enter.

Returning to Kılıçaslan Caddesi, take a right before the tourist office and, opposite the İkinci Murat Hamamı, you'll see the excavations of the İznik **kilns**, still in progress. The site can be entered at any time with the kilns clearly visible; finds from the excavations are on display in the archeological museum (see p.248).

Three blocks east of the kilns, stands the **Süleyman Paşa Medresesi**, built in 1332 – the oldest such Ottoman structure in Turkey and the first example of a school with an open courtyard surrounded by eleven chambers and nineteen domes. For centuries it was used as a school of theology, but it was fully restored in 2001 and is now home to a **Ceramic Crafts Centre** (daily 10am–7pm; ☎0224/757 7588, ⓦwww.iznikdefteri.com), dedicated to the revival of İznik's traditional ceramic production. Seven artists (mostly women) have galleries in the chambers and there's a small café in the courtyard, so it's a pleasant place to drink tea and watch the women at work. Prices are not cheap, but are less than at the İznik Vafkı (see below), though the patterns employed here are copied and not original.

The fourteenth-century **Yakub Çelebi Zaviyesi**, three blocks south of the *medresesi* and one block southeast of the *otogar*, was founded by the luckless prince slain by his brother Beyazit I at Kosovo in 1389 (see p.260); it has been compromised by too many bad restorations. A block to the east, nothing but foundations remain of the **Kimisis Kilisesi** (Church of the Assumption), the presumed burial place of Theodore Lascaris, which was destroyed in 1922. Nearby is a dank, sunken **Ayazma** or sacred spring.

İznik Vafkı

The **İznik Vafkı**, or İznik Foundation, clearly signposted in the southwest quadrant on Halı Saha Arkası (July & Aug 6–11am; rest of year daily 8am–6pm; ☎0224/757 6025, ⓦwww.iznik.com) was established in 1995 with the dual intentions of researching the early techniques used to produce İznik tiles and restarting production using traditional methods. Today, tiles of extremely high quality are manufactured and sold on site (prices start from $150 each, credit cards accepted); exact replicas of original designs are not reproduced for fear of them being passed off as genuine. During a visit you'll see different production stages and receive a brief history of the İznik *oeuvre*. Occasional workshops are run on request for interested groups, with accommodation in the small hotel on site.

İznik tiles adorn various Turkish company headquarters, while in İstanbul you are likely to see them decorating the stations on the new metro line from Taksim to Levant, as well as in the Turkish bath of the *Ritz-Carlton Hotel* and at the new terminal buildings of Atatürk airport. They are also on display in the Montreal Peace Park in Canada.

The northeast quadrant

Just north of Kılıçaslan Caddesi squats the **Hacı Özbek Camii**, the earliest known Ottoman mosque, built in 1333 but much adulterated; the portico was senselessly pulled down in 1939, but is presently being restored by the Ministry of Culture.

Ambling along Kılıçaslan Caddesi you'll soon reach a vast landscaped park to the north, dotted with İznik's most famous monuments. The **Yeşil Camii**, or Green Mosque, erected toward the end of the fourteenth century, is a small gem of a building, its highlight the fantastic marble relief on the portico. Tufted with a stubby minaret that looks back to Selçuk models, the mosque takes its name from the green İznik tiles that once adorned this minaret; they've long since been replaced by mediocre, tri-coloured Kütahya work.

Across the park sprawls the **Nilüfer Hatun İmareti**, commissioned by Murat I in 1388 in honour of his mother, by all accounts a remarkable woman. Daughter of a Byzantine noble (some say of Emperor John VI Cantacuzenos himself), Nilüfer Hatun was married off to Orhan Gazi to consolidate a Byzantine–Ottoman alliance. Her ability was soon recognized by Orhan, who appointed her regent during his frequent absences. The T-form building, whose ample domes perennially play host to storks, is more accurately called a *zaviye* than a mere soup kitchen and is one of the few that never doubled as a mosque. It was originally the meeting place not of dervishes but of the Ahi brotherhood, a guild drawn from the ranks of skilled craftsmen that also acted as a community welfare and benevolent society.

Today the *imaret* contains the **Archeological Museum** (Arkeoloji Müzesi; Tues–Sun 8.30am–noon & 1.30–5pm; $2), which is sadly lacking in the expected İznik ware. The pieces of fourteenth-century İznik tiles excavated from the town's kilns have been painstakingly restored, but they are all incomplete and there are few of the beautiful sixteenth-century mosque ornaments and massive plates that are commonplace in the museums of İstanbul and abroad. More interesting is an exhibition of **Selçuk tile fragments** found in the area around the Roman theatre and in local kilns – this area was not known to be a centre of Selçuk occupation and it's uncertain whether these tiles were locally produced or imported, although evidence suggests that İznik ware is in part descended from that of the Selçuks. The museum also has such Roman bits as a bronze dancing Pan, some Byzantine gold jewellery and, standing out among the nondescript marble clutter, a sarcophagus in near-mint condition. For a more perilous adventure, and a fine view of Nilüfer Hatun's cupolas, climb the minaret of the adjacent **Şeyh Kubettin Camii**.

The walls and beyond

Closest gate to the Yeşil Camii is the eastern **Lefke Kapısı**, a three-ply affair including a triumphal arch dedicated to Hadrian between the two courses of walls. Just outside is a stretch of the ancient **aqueduct** that until recently supplied the town. It's possible to get up on the ramparts here for a stroll, as it is at the northerly **İstanbul Kapısı**, best preserved of the gates, the outer part of which was constructed as a triumphal triple arch to celebrate the visit of the Roman emperor Hadrian in 124. The inner gate is decorated by two stone-carved **masks**, probably taken from the nearby Roman theatre. Other traces of Roman Nicaea are evident in the southwestern quarter: a course of **ancient wall** delimits the so-called "Senatus court", extending from the surviving tower next to the **Saray Kapısı**, and an all-but-collapsed **theatre** lies just inside the gate.

If time permits, you might walk or drive to the obvious **Abdülvahap hill** 2.5km east of the Lefke Kapısı for a comprehensive view over İznik, its walls, the surrounding olive groves and lake. From March 21 to September 21, when the sun sets between the two distant hills on either side of the lake, the top of this hill is the best place to share a dramatic sunset with picnicking İznik families. The green-painted tomb on top belongs to a certain Abdülvahap, a semi-legendary character in the Arab raids of the eighth century.

Seven kilometres north of İznik in the village of **Elbeyli** is the **Yeraltı Mezar**, a subterranean tomb for which the archeological museum staff in İznik retain the keys. Thought to be the fourth-century burial chamber of a Roman couple (there are two graves here), the single chamber is covered in excellent frescoes, including a pair of peacocks. For a small consideration the museum custodian takes individuals and groups after the museum closes at 5pm. You'll need your own transport, or the willpower to haggle with a taxi driver, for a return trip.

Practicalities

You'll probably arrive at the tiny **otogar** in the southeast quarter, three blocks south of the German-speaking **tourist office**, opposite the *Belediye* on the ground floor at Kılıçaslan Cad 130 (May–Sept Mon–Fri & sometimes Sat 8am–noon & 1–5.30pm; Oct–April Mon–Fri 8.30am–noon & 1–5pm; ℡0224/757 1933). The town's only **internet café** is next door to the *Kaynarca Pansiyon* on Gündem Sok. Both men (evenings) and women (daytime) can get steam-cleaned at the **İkinci Murat Hamamı** (women 8am–2pm, men 4–10pm; bath $6, massage $3) just southeast of İznik's central roundabout and the Aya Sofya Museum.

Accommodation

Rooms, singles in particular, are at a premium and reservations are recommended between mid-June and mid-September – especially at the weekends, when inhabitants of neighbouring towns come to bathe in İznik lake. It's possible to **camp** in the shady site next door to the lakeside *Çamlık Motel* and there's another campsite on the lake just north of the city walls.

Hotel Aydın Kılıçaslan Cad ℡0224/757 7650, ⓦwww.iznikhotelaydin.com. Opposite the police station, with pleasant rooms, many with balconies overlooking the central square. ❸
Hotel Babacan Kılıçaslan Cad 86 ℡0224/757 1211, ℱ757 4281. Cheap en-suite rooms, but the hotel lacks any kind of charm. ❷
Çamlık Motel Sahili Cad 11 ℡ & ℱ0224/757 1631. Rooms are small but comfortable, with balconies overlooking the lake; there's also an excellent attached restaurant. ❸

Cem Pansiyon Sahili Cad 20 ℡0224/757 1687, ⓔcempansiyon@hotmail.com. Basic lakeside rooms; you pay $3 extra for a bathroom. ❷
Kaynarca Pansiyon Gündem Sok 1 ℡0224/757 1723, ⓦwww.kaynarca.s5.com. The most appealing midtown budget option, run by English-speaking Ali (one-man ambassador of tourism for İznik) and his charming family. Dorm beds ($5), as well as en-suite singles, doubles and triples – all rooms have satellite TV, breakfast ($2) is served on the rooftop terrace and there's a kitchen for guests' use. ❷

Eating and drinking

Maple-canopied Kılıçaslan Caddesi has a few good **restaurants**, including two or three good-value *pide* places next to each other near the *Belediye* building. Most outsiders, however, will want to eat **by the lakeshore**, where some of the restaurants are licensed; try grilled or fried *yayın*, the excellent local catfish. For snacks or dessert there are plenty of tea gardens, cafés and ice-cream parlours overlooking the lake.

Balıkçı Sahili Cad 22. Good-value licensed restaurant, with lakeside views and outside tables. Simple grilled or fried fish accompanied by bread and salad costs around $6.

Çamlık Motel Sahili Cad 11. The nicest of the waterside restaurants in a lovely shady setting, dishing up *mezes* and kebabs, including their speciality fish kebab, for around $10 a head with beer.

Iskender Kebab Kılıçaslan Cad. Fresh *pide*, tremendous local meatballs and steam-tray food, popular at lunchtime with office workers from the nearby town hall. A plate of varied *lokanta*-style dishes will set you back about $4.

Karadeniz Pide Salon Kılıçaslan Cad. Fresh and cheap *pides* washed down with *ayran* – you can watch the food being pulled into shape in the

kitchen at the back of this tiny cafeteria.

Kar-pi Kılıçaslan Cad. Fast-food joint that's not a bad place for an air-conditioned break in the middle of the day and makes a change from the male dominated teahouses; a *lahmacun* (round bread with tomato topping) and salad will cost no more than a couple of dollars.

Bursa

Draped ribbon-like along the leafy lower slopes of Uludağ, which towers more than 2000m above it, and overlooking the fertile plain of the Nilüfer Çayı, **BURSA** does more justice to its setting than any other Turkish city apart from İstanbul. Gathered here are some of the finest early Ottoman monuments in the Balkans, set within neighbourhoods that, despite being marooned in masses of concrete, remain among the most appealing in Turkey.

Industrialization over the last four decades, and the quadrupling in population to over a million, mean that the city as a whole is no longer exactly elegant. Silk and textile manufacture, plus patronage of the area's thermal baths by the elite, were for centuries the most important enterprises; they're now outstripped by automobile manufacture (both Renault and Tofaş have plants here), canneries and bottlers processing the rich harvest of the plain, and the presence of Uludağ University. Vast numbers of settlers from Artvin province have been attracted by job opportunities at the various factories, while the students provide a necessary leavening in what might otherwise be a uniformly conservative community. Some of this atmosphere derives from Bursa's role as first capital of the Ottoman Empire and burial place of the first six sultans, their piety as well as authority emanating from the mosques, social welfare foundations and tombs built at their command.

Bursa is sometimes touted as a long day out from İstanbul, but this is really doing both the city and yourself a disservice: it deserves at least one and preferably two nights' stay. The spirit of the place really can't be gauged amid the whisked-in coach parties gawping at the overexposed Yeşil Camii and Yeşil Türbe. And despite dire warnings in other guidebooks, Bursa is a good city for walking, whether through the hive of the bazaars, the linear parks of the Hisar district or the anachronistic peace of the Muradiye quarter.

Some history

Although the area had been settled at least a millennium previously, the first city was founded early in the second century BC by Prusias I, a king of ancient Bithynia, who in typical Hellenistic fashion named the town, **Proussa**, after himself. Legend claims that Hannibal helped him pick the location of the acropolis, today's Hisar.

Overshadowed by nearby Nicomedia (modern İzmit) and Nicaea (İznik), the city stagnated until the **Romans**, attracted by its natural hot springs, began spending lavish amounts on public baths and made it capital of their province of Mysia. Justinian introduced silkworm culture and Byzantine Proussa flourished until Arab raids of the seventh and eighth centuries, and the subsequent tug-of-war for sovereignty between the Selçuks and the Greeks, precipitated decline. During and after the Latin interlude in Constantinople (1204–1261), the Byzantines reconsolidated their hold on Proussa, but not for long.

The start of the fourteenth century saw a small band of nomadic Turks, led by one **Osman Gazi**, camped outside the walls of Proussa. After more than a decade of siege, the city capitulated in 1326 to Osman's son, Orhan, and the **Ottomans** ceased to be a wandering tribe of marauders. Orhan marked the acquisition of a capital and the organization of an infant state by styling himself sultan, giving the city its present name and striking coinage. Bursa began to enjoy a second golden age: the silk industry was expanded and the city, now outgrowing the confines of the citadel, graced with monuments.

In the years following Orhan's death in 1362 the imperial capital was gradually moved to Edirne, but Bursa's place in history, and in the hearts of the Ottomans, was ensured; succeeding sultans continued to add buildings, and to be laid to rest here, for another hundred years. Disastrous fires and earthquakes in the mid-nineteenth century, and the 1920–1922 war of independence, only slightly diminished the city's splendour.

Arrival, orientation and information

Bursa's position at the foot of the mountain has dictated an elongated layout, with most of the major boulevards running from east to west, changing their names several times as they go. The **otogar** lies 10km north of town on the Yalova road; from here special grey-and-blue service buses ferry visitors straight to **Heykel**, the local name for Cumhuriyet Alanı, nominal focal point of the city. Bursa's main **tourist office** (May–Sept Mon–Sat 8am–noon & 1–5.30pm; Oct–April Mon–Fri 8.30am–noon & 1–5pm; ☎0224/220 1848) is a 200m walk from Heykel, opposite Orhan Gazi Camii, in a row of shops under the north side of Atatürk Caddesi, where you can pick up a reasonable city map.

Bursa's main lengthwise thoroughfare begins life just east of Heykel as **Namazgah Caddesi**, below the district of **Yeşil** and its namesake mosque and tomb. West of İnönü Caddesi it becomes **Atatürk Caddesi** as it passes through the city's central bazaar and hotel district and changes its name again to **Cemal Nadir Caddesi** right below **Hisar**, the nucleus of the Byzantine settlement. After being fed more traffic by Cumhuriyet Caddesi, which divides the bazaar, and by the roundabout at the top of Fevzi Çakmak Caddesi, the boulevard metamorphoses into **Altıparmak Caddesi**, and then into **Çekirge Caddesi** as it heads west past the Kültür Parkı and to the thermal resort of **Çekirge**, 4km west of the centre. However, there are numerous other delightful secondary streets, noted in the city account, all better suited for walking between Bursa's historical sites.

City transport

Though Bursa is narrow, with many points of interest bunched together, it's sufficiently long enough for you to want to consider **public transport** to reach the outlying attractions. A new metro line is currently under construction, creating intense traffic problems that are likely to last for a number of years until the line is complete.

Of the **city buses**, only the #2/A (connecting Emir Sultan in the east of town with Çekirge to the west) and the #3/A (linking Heykel with the Uludağ *teleferik*) are of much use, and you need to buy tickets for them at designated booths. It's often simpler, and well worth the extra $0.50 or so, to avail yourself of Bursa's **dolmuşes** instead. Appearing in various colours, the cars all bear destination signs on their roofs, start from fixed points around the city and pick up and let down passengers at places clearly marked with a large "D". If your luggage won't fit in the boot, you'll have to buy a seat for it – still a lot cheaper than a private taxi.

▲ Çanakkale & Mudanya

MUDANYA CAD

HWY E-23/200 — ANKARA CAD

KIBRI

Yeni Kaplıca

& Çekirge ▲

B

Archeological Museum

Kültür Parkı

STADYUM CAD

A 1 2 3 4 5 6 & Çekirge ▲

7

▲ Uludağ

AROUND THE SEA OF MARMARA | Bursa

ÇEKİRGE CAD

Atatürk Stadium

HAMZABEY CAD

BEŞİKÇİLER CAD

İkinci Murat Hamamı

İKİNCİ MURAT CAD

Oxford Bookshop

Brr-Soft
@

ALTIPARMAK CAD

Muradiye Külliyesi

Hüsnü Züber House

MURADİYE

UZUNYOL SOK.

KAPLICA CAD

SAKARYA CAD

C D E

HASTALARYURDU CAD

Devlet (State) Hastanesi

N

ORHANELİ CAD

ORTAPAZAR CAD

F 8

HİSAR

Alaeddin Camii

Zindan Kapısı

Pınarbaşı Kapısı

ALACAHIRKA CAD

Cılımboz Deresi

ACCOMMODATION		CAFÉS & RESTAURANTS	
Ada Palas	1	Adanur Hacıbey	L
Atlas Termal	2	Arap Şükrü	E
Çeşmeli	11	Café M	C
Çelik Palas	7	Çiçek İzgara	J
Demirci	3	Grand Geye	N
Dikmen	14	Hacıbey İskender	M
Dilmen Murat	4	Kebapçı İskender	K
Efehan	9	Konyalı Lokantası	H
Guneş	13	Mercan	A
İpekçi	10	Piccolo	D
Kent	12	R.C. Cumurcul	B
Kervansaray Termal	5	Safran	F
Safran	8	Sezende	I
Yat	6	Üç Köfte	G

0 _____ 500 m

Useful routes, many starting at Heykel, are indicated where appropriate in the account of the city, starting on p.254, below; fares are set and average $1 a ride.

Accommodation

Reasonably priced hotel beds are generally plentiful in Bursa, not least because it's a little off the backpacking trail and because it's often treated as

▲ Otogar & Yalova

BURSA

2

AROUND THE SEA OF MARMARA | Bursa

▶ Ankara & Cumalıkızık

▶ Yıldırım Beyazıt Camii

Emir Sultan Camii

Teleferik for Uludağ ▼

a day-trip destination from İstanbul. Rich foreigners, particularly Arabs, gravitate toward the luxury spa hotels 4km out of the centre at **Çekirge**, but there is also a cluster of modest establishments out here, around the Birinci Murat Camii. If you're interested in seeing monumental Bursa, then staying in midtown accommodation, around **Atatürk Caddesi**, makes more sense.

Near Atatürk Caddesi

Hotel Çeşmeli Gümüşçeken Cad 6 ⊤ &
Ⓕ 0224/224 1511. Immaculate hotel run entirely
by women. Rooms have mini-bars, TVs and fans;
buffet breakfast included. ❸

Hotel Dikmen Maksem Cad 78 ⊤ 0224/224 1840,
ⓦ www.hoteldikmen.com. Slightly impersonal two-
star, with a garden courtyard where breakfast is
served. Most rooms have TVs, minibars, air-
conditioning and balconies, and all have pleasant
bathrooms; bargaining possible for the less luxurious
rooms. Secure underground parking available. ❹

Efehan Hotel Gümüşçeken Cad 34 ⊤ 0224/225
2260, ⓦ www.efehan.com.tr. Pleasant newly
restored three-star comfort in a central location.
Extras include minibars and satellite TV. Ask for
one of the top rooms for mountain views. ❺

Guneş Hotel İnebey Cad 75 ⊤ 0224/224 1404.
Cheap, clean and friendly, with centrally heated
(though waterless) rooms. ❶

Hotel İpekçi Çancılar Cad 38 ⊤ 0224/221 1935.
In the bazaar area west of İnönü Cad, with bright,
airy and surprisingly quiet rooms. En-suite rooms
fall into the next price category up. ❷

Kent Hotel Atatürk Cad 69 ⊤ 0224/223 5420,
Ⓕ 224 4015. The most prominent hotel in the
town centre, three-star comfortable rooms with
satellite TV, fridges and minibars. The front rooms
suffer badly from traffic noise, though. ❺

Tophane

Safran Hotel Ortapazar Cad, Arka Sok 4
⊤ 0224/224 7216, Ⓕ 224 7219. Beautifully
restored wooden house, in an atmospheric part of
the old town up on the Hisar. Rooms are modern
and there's a good restaurant (see p.262, below).
❺

Çekirge

Ada Palas Murat Cad 21 ⊤ 0224/233 3990,
Ⓕ 236 4656. Clean, smart two-star hotel. Extra
treats include Turkish bath and jacuzzi. ❹

Atlas Termal Hamamlar Cad 35 ⊤ 0224/234
4100, Ⓕ 236 4605. Comfortable rooms, excellent
bathrooms and good service. The decor is mock
Art Nouveau, including stained glass windows and
a glass lift, and downstairs there are two shiny
marble hamams, a reasonable restaurant, garden
courtyard and terrace. ❺

Hotel Çelik Palas Çekirge Cad 79 ⊤ 0224/233
3800, Ⓕ 236 1910. A refined, elegant hotel, which
still retains some of its original chandeliers and
other trimmings, though the rooms are ultra-
modern with air-con, cable TV and hot spring
water in the bathtubs. The Turkish bath is the
hotel's major selling point, with top-to-toe marble
and a magnificent domed ceiling. ❼

Demirci Otel Hamamlar Cad 33 ⊤ 0224/236
5104, Ⓕ 235 2436. Friendly, unpretentious and
good value, with en-suite rooms and a searingly
hot hamam in the basement. ❷

Hotel Dilmen Murat Cad 20 ⊤ 0224/233 9500,
ⓦ www.hoteldilmen.com. Four-star hotel, with
sauna, Turkish bath, rooftop terrace and all the
comforts you might expect at this price. Prices are
highest at weekends. ❽

Kervansaray Termal Hotel Çekirge Meyd
⊤ 0224/233 9300,
ⓦ www.kervansarayhotels.com. Sumptuous five-
star luxury, next to the Old Baths, with an assortment of swimming pools, Turkish baths and
saunas. There are five pricey restaurants and a
baby-sitting service. Prices rise to $140 over the
weekends, though you should be able to knock
$40 or $50 off the rate during the week. ❽

Yat Hotel Hamam Cad 31 ⊤ 0224/233 9335,
Ⓕ 233 9339. Modern hotel with rooms with TV,
plus small garden and Turkish bath. Buffet breakfast included. ❹

The City and around

There's little point in touring Bursa's monuments in strictly chronological
order, though not surprisingly many of the oldest ones are clustered just outside Hisar, in today's city centre. The places covered below under each heading
can be visited in a leisurely morning or afternoon. If you can't spare this much
time, you could just manage to see the most spectacular monuments around
the Koza Parkı and at Yeşil in a few rushed hours.

Central sites

Just across from the main tourist office stands the **Orhan Gazi Camii**, whose
1336 foundation makes it the second-oldest mosque in Bursa. Originally built
as a *zaviye* for itinerant dervishes, this is the earliest example of the T-form
mosque with *eyvan*s flanking the main prayer hall. **Karagöz puppets**, the

painted camel-leather props used in the Turkish national shadow play, are supposed to represent workers who were involved in building the Orhan Gazi Camii. According to legend, the antics of Karagöz and his sidekick Hacıvat so entertained their fellow workmen that Orhan had them beheaded to end the distraction. Later, missing the comedians and repenting of his deed, he arranged to immortalize the pair in the art form that now bears the name of Karagöz.

Just west of Orhan Gazi, the compact **Koza Parkı**, with its fountains, benches, strolling crowds and street-level cafés, is the real heart of Bursa – never mind what they say about Heykel. Though animated through the day and early evening, the plaza empties soon after, with the illuminated fountains dark and still and the walkways deserted by 11pm.

On the far side of the Koza Parkı looms the tawny limestone **Ulu Camii**, built between 1396 and 1399 by Yıldırım Beyazit I, from the proceeds of booty won from the Crusaders at Macedonian Nicopolis. Before the battle Yıldırım (Thunderbolt) had vowed to construct twenty mosques if victorious. The present building of twenty domes supported by twelve freestanding pillars was his rather loose interpretation of this promise, but it was still the largest and most ambitious Ottoman mosque of its time. The interior is dominated by a huge *şadırvan* pool in the centre, whose skylight was once open to the elements, and an intricate walnut *minber* pieced together, it's claimed, without nails or glue. Even less convincing is the tradition stating that the main north portal was remodelled by Tamerlane when he occupied Bursa in 1402–1403.

From the north porch you can descend stairs to the two-storeyed **Emir (Bey) Hanı**, originally a dependency of the Orhan Gazi Camii and now home to various offices and shops. A fountain plays under the trees in the courtyard, but with no teahouse or public seating it's not a place to linger. Beyond the Emir Hanı begins Bursa's **covered bazaar** (daily 9am–8pm; closed Sun) whose assorted galleries and lesser *han*s are a delight for shoppers hunting for ready-to-wear clothing, silk goods (scarves to jump suits), towels, bolts of cloth and furniture, all Bursa province specialities. The nearby **Bedesten** is given over to the sale and warehousing of jewellery and precious metals.

The centrepiece of the bazaar has to be the **Koza Hanı**, or "Silk-Cocoon Hall", flanking the park close to the Orhan Gazi Camii. Built in 1451 on two levels, it's still entirely occupied by silk and brocade merchants. In the middle of the cobbled courtyard, under the plane trees, a minuscule **mescit** (small mosque) perches directly over its *şadırvan*, while a U-shaped subsidiary court bulges asymmetrically to the east; there are teahouses and public benches to pause at.

Bursa silk and the cocoon auction

Highlight of the year is the **cocoon auction** of late June and early July, when silk-breeders from around the province gather to hawk their valuable produce. Then, Bursa's Koza Hanı becomes a lake of white torpedoes the size of a songbird's egg; the moth, when it hatches, is a beautiful, otherworldly creature with giant onyx eyes and feathery antennae. You can watch the melee from the upper arcades or, as long as you're careful, the merchants don't mind you walking the floor.

After being sent into a tailspin by French and Italian competition two hundred years ago, the Bursa silk trade has recently experienced a tentative revival. However, the quality of contemporary fabric cannot compare to museum pieces from the early Ottoman heyday and most of the better designs are made up in imported material, which is still better quality than the Turkish material. If you're buying silk here, make sure the label says *ipek* (silk) and not *ithal ipek* (artificial silk).

Bursa's most central **food market** is in the bazaar's Nilüfer Koylu Pasaja, just below Orhan Gazi Camii on Belediye Caddesi. This is the place to stock up for picnics, with an excellent selection of the fruits (strawberries and cherries in spring, peaches and pears in summer), nuts and dairy products for which the region is noted. In the same area, near the *Sezende Restaurant*, handmade lace and other handicrafts are on sale in **Hanamelsanatlar Sokak** ("the street of women's handicrafts").

Another area of the bazaar that has kept its traditions intact despite quake and blaze is the **Demirciler Çarşısı**, the ironmongers' market. This is just the other side of İnönü Caddesi, best crossed by the pedestrian underpass at Okcular Caddesi. Stall upon stall of blacksmiths and braziers attract photographers, but be advised that some expect a consideration for posing. From here you can easily continue past a small mosque and some cabinet-makers' workshops to **Fırın Sokak**, which is lined with some of the finest old dwellings in town. At the end of this short street a bridge spans the **Gök Dere**, one of two streams that tumble through Bursa, forming an approximate eastern boundary for the centre.

Yeşil

Across the stream, it's only a few minutes' walk up to **Yeşil**, as the eastern neighbourhood around the namesake mosque and tombs is known.

Designed by the architect Hacı Ivaz atop a slight rise, the **Yeşil Camii** was begun in 1413 by Çelebi Mehmet I, victor of the civil war caused by the death of Beyazit I. Despite being unfinished – work ceased in 1424, three years after Mehmet himself died – and despite catastrophic damage from two nineteenth-century earth tremors, it's easily the most spectacular of Bursa's imperial mosques. The incomplete entrance, faced in a light marble, is all the more easy to examine for the lack of a portico; above the stalactite vaulting and relief calligraphy you can see the supports for arches never built.

Next you'll pass through a foyer supported by pilfered Byzantine columns to reach the **interior**, a variation on the T-plan usually reserved for dervish *zaviye*s. A fine *şadırvan* occupies the centre of the "T", but your eye is monopolized by the hundreds of polychrome **tiles** that line not just the *mihrab* but every available vertical surface up to 5m in height, particularly two recesses flanking the entryway. Green and blue pigments matching the carpets predominate and praying amid this dimly lit majesty must be something like worshipping inside a leaf. Tucked above the foyer, and usually closed to visitors, is the **imperial loge**, the most extravagantly decorated chamber of all. Several artisans from Tabriz participated in the tiling of Yeşil Camii but the loge is attributed to a certain Al-Majnun, which translates most accurately as "intoxicated on hashish". On the same knoll as the mosque, and immediately across the pedestrian precinct separating them, the **Yeşil Türbe** (daily 8am–noon & 1–5pm; free) contains the sarcophagus of Çelebi Mehmet I and his assorted offspring. Inside, the walls and Mehmet's tomb glisten with the glorious original Tabriz material.

Regrettably, the immediate environs of the two monuments swarm with tour groups: the café nearby overcharges mercilessly for the view and a clutch of converted, vehemently repainted old houses are glutted with souvenir dross. There's not a genuine antique-seller to be found, with the possible exception of one eccentric old man next to the *medrese* (theology academy), which lies 100m from the summit. The academy now houses Bursa's **Museum of Turkish and Islamic Art** (Türk ve İslam Eserleri Müzesi; daily except Mon 8am–noon & 1–5pm; $0.70), set around a pleasant courtyard with fountain, trees and picnic tables. If the museum is short-staffed certain rooms may be closed, but in theory you can view İznik ware, Çanakkale ceramics, kitchen utensils, inlaid wooden articles, weapons and a mock-up of an Ottoman *sünnet odası*, or circumcision chamber. The exhibition of hamam paraphernalia has a local relevance because of the history of bathing in the area, which is probably why Bursa towelling has developed world prominence. In the nineteenth century, however, in place of towels, beautifully embroidered linen cloths were used as wraps. Other signs of wealth were silver bathbowls, bone or tortoiseshell combs and clogs inlaid with mother-of-pearl, all of which are on display here.

East of Yeşil: to Yıldırım Beyazit Camii

A 300-metre walk east of Yeşil leads to the **Emir Sultan Camii**, lost in extensive graveyards where every religious Bursan hopes to be buried. The mosque was originally endowed by a Bokharan dervish and trusted adviser to three sultans, beginning with Beyazit I, but it has just been restored again after enduring an Ottoman Baroque overhaul early last century, so you can only guess what's left of the original essence. The pious, however, seem to harbour no doubts, coming in strength to worship at the tombs of the saint and his family.

If you're short of time Emir Sultan Camii is the obvious site to omit: climb down steps through the graveyard instead and cross the urban lowlands to the **Yıldırım Beyazit Camii**, perched on a small hillock at the northeastern edge of the city. If you're coming directly from downtown, this is a substantial hike, so you might want to take a dolmuş (marked "Heykel–Beyazit Yıldırım" or the more common "Heykel–Fakülte"), which passes 200m below the mosque. Completed by Beyazit I between 1390 and 1395, the Beyazit Camii features a handsome, five-arched portico defined by square columns. The interior is unremarkable except for a gravity-defying arch bisecting the prayer hall, its lower supports apparently tapering away to end in stalactite moulding. The only other note of whimsy in this spare building is the use of elaborate niches out on the porch.

The associated **medrese**, exceptionally long and narrow because of its sloping site, huddles just downhill; today it's used as a medical clinic. The **türbe** (tomb) of the luckless Beyazit, kept in an iron cage by the rampaging Tamerlane until his death in 1403, is usually locked. Perhaps the mosque custodians fear a revival of the Ottoman inclination to abuse the tomb of the most ignominiously defeated sultan.

The Hisar

The **Hisar**, Bursa's original nucleus, nowadays retains just a few clusters of dilapidated Ottoman housing within its warren of narrow lanes and some courses of medieval wall along its perimeter.

From where Atatürk Caddesi becomes Cemal Nadir Caddesi in a whirl of traffic, you can climb up to the Hisar plateau via pedestrian ramps negotiating the ancient walls. En route, you'll pass **Zater Plaza**, a cavernous modern shopping mall, most of it underground but topped by an attractive square and glass pyramid. There are a number of places in here to grab a blast of air-conditioning, some cheesecake and a coffee. Alternatively, take a walk along Orhangazi Caddesi, home to a rather contrived artists' colony. Where Orhangazi stops climbing, the **Osman and Orhan Gazi Türbesı** stand side by side at the edge of the fortified acropolis that they conquered. The tombs – post-earthquake restorations in gaudy late Ottoman style – are on the site of a Byzantine church that has long since disappeared except for some mosaic traces near Orhan's sarcophagus.

Far better is the view from the cliff-top **park** sprawling around the tombs and clocktower, with reasonable cafés at the head of the walkways down to Cemal Nadir and Altıparmak *caddesi*s. Most of the city's posher shops and cinemas line Altıparmak Caddesi, but for now it's preferable to back away from the brink and explore Hisar itself, where the wreckers took a heavy toll of the vernacular houses before preservation orders went into effect.

You must choose whether to follow signs west to Muradiye, along the most direct route, or to veer inland on a random walk around the neighbourhood. At the southernmost extreme of the citadel you exit at the **Pınarbaşı Kapısı**, lowest point in the circuit of walls and the spot where Orhan's forces finally entered the city in 1326. From there you can stroll parallel to the walls, re-entering at the **Zindan Kapısı**, inside of which is the simple **Alâeddin Camii**, erected within a decade of the conquest and so the earliest mosque in Bursa.

A more straightforward route follows Hasta Yurdu Caddesi until another generous swathe of park studded with teahouses opens out opposite the public hospital. The furthest teahouses have fine views of the Muradiye district, and from the final café and course of wall, obvious stairs descend to the **Cılımboz Deresi**, the second major stream to furrow the city.

Muradiye

Across the stream lies medieval **Muradiye**, where Bursa's best-preserved dwellings line streets at their liveliest during the Tuesday **street market**. If you're coming directly from Heykel, take one of the frequent dolmuşes marked "Muradiye".

The **Muradiye Külliyesi** is easy enough to find and, if you were disappointed by the circus at Yeşil, this is the place to capture the early Ottoman spirit more accurately – while trinket sellers and an antique shop do show the flag, there's no pressure to buy and no coachloads to shatter the calm. The mosque complex, begun in 1424 by Murat II, was the last imperial foundation in Bursa, though the tombs for which Muradiye is famous were added piecemeal over the next century or so.

The ten **royal tombs** (Muradiye Külliyesi Türbesı; daily: May–Sept 8am–noon & 1–5pm; Oct–April 8am–5pm; free) are set in lovingly tended gardens and open on a rota basis; to get into the locked ones you must find the gardener-*bekçi* with the keys – no tip is expected for the service. The first tomb encountered is that of **Şehzade Ahmet** and his brother Şehinşah, both murdered in 1513 by their cousin Selim I to preclude any succession disputes. The luxury of the İznik tiles within contrasts sharply with the adjacent austerity of **Murat II's tomb**, where Roman columns inside and a wooden awning out front are the only superfluities. Murat, as much contemplative mystic as warrior-sultan, was the only Ottoman ruler ever to abdicate voluntarily, though pressures of state forced him to leave the company of his dervishes and return to the throne after just two years. He was the last sultan to be interred at Bursa and one of the few lying here who died in his bed; in accordance with his wishes, both the coffin and the dome were originally open to the sky "so that the rain of heaven might wash my face like any pauper's".

Next along is the tomb of **Şehzade Mustafa**, Süleyman the Magnificent's unjustly murdered heir; perhaps a sign of his father's remorse, the tomb is done up in extravagantly floral İznik tiles, with a top border of calligraphy. Nearby stands the tomb of **Cem Sultan**, his brother Mustafa and two of Beyazit II's sons, decorated with a riot of abstract, botanical and calligraphic paint strokes up to the dome. Cem, the cultured and favourite son of Mehmet the

Conqueror, was one of the Ottoman empire's most interesting might-have-beens. Following the death of his father in 1481, he lost a brief dynastic struggle with the successful claimant, brother Beyazit II, and fled abroad. For fourteen years he wandered, seeking sponsorship of his cause from Christian benefactors who in all cases became his jailers: first the Knights of St John at Rhodes and Bodrum, later the papacy. At one point it seemed that he would command a Crusader army organized to retake İstanbul, but all such plans came to grief for the simple reason that Beyazit anticipated his opponents' moves and each time bribed them handsomely to desist, making Cem a lucrative prisoner indeed. His usefulness as a pawn exhausted, Cem was probably poisoned in Italy by the pope in 1495, leaving nothing but reams of poems aching with nostalgia and homesickness.

A minute's walk from the Muradiye Külliyesi is the **Hüsnü Züber House**, at Uzunyol Sok 3, Kaplıca Caddesi (Tues–Sun 10am–5pm; $0.70). This former Ottoman guesthouse, built in 1836, sports a typical overhanging upper storey, wooden roof and beams and a garden courtyard. It now houses a collection of carved wooden musical instruments, spoons and farming utensils, many of which were made by Hüsnü Züber himself, the present owner, who inhabits the house still. The main exhibit, however, is the house itself, one of the few of its era to have been well restored and opened to the public.

The Kültür Parkı

From Muradiye it's just a short walk down to Çekirge Caddesi and the south-east gate of the **Kültür Parkı** (token admission charge when entry booths are staffed). Inside there's a popular tea garden, a small boating lake, a disgraceful mini-zoo, and a number of restaurants and *gazino*-style nightclubs. As you stroll, however, it soon becomes obvious that there's no potential for solitude – though courting couples try their best – and no wild spots among the regimented plantations and too-broad driveways.

At the west end of the park, just below Çekirge Caddesi, is the **Archeological Museum** (Arkeoloji Müzesi; daily except Mon 8am–noon & 1–5pm; $0.70). Inside the museum, exhibits in the right-hand Stone Room vary from the macabre (a Byzantine ossuary with a skull peeking out) to the homely (a Roman cavalryman figurine), but the adjacent hall featuring metal jewellery from all over Anatolia – watch chains, breastplates, belts, buckles, bracelets, anklets, chokers – steals the show. The left wing houses a modest coin gallery and miscellaneous small ancient objects, the best of which are the Roman glass items and Byzantine and Roman bronzes. Oil lamps, pottery, a token amount of gold and far too many ceramic figurines complete these poorly labelled exhibits; while a garden of sarcophagi, stelae and other statuary fragments surrounds the building.

Çekirge

The thermal centre of **Çekirge** ("Grasshopper" – presumably a reference to the natural soundtrack of a summer evening), is another twenty minutes' walk or so along Çekirge Caddesi from the west side of Kültür Parkı. Buses (including the #2/A), as well as dolmuşes (marked "Çekirge"), shuttle, to and from the dolmuş stand near the tourist office on Atatürk Caddesi.

Most visitors come here to experience the Çekirge hot springs, which flow out of Uludağ's mountainside and are tapped into by the various hotels and bathhouses. The **Yeni Kaplıca** (New Baths; daily 6am–10pm; $4 admission, $3–4 extra for a wash and massage) lie just beyond the Kültür Parkı, accessible by a steep driveway beginning opposite the *Çelik Palas Oteli*. There's actually a clutch of three facilities here: the **Kaynarca baths**, for women only, which is really rather grim and unappealing; the **Karamustafa spa**, for men only; and the Yeni Kaplıca itself, dating in its present form from the mid-sixteenth century, which has a women's section, but is still nothing like as splendid as the men's. According to legend, Süleyman the Magnificent was cured of gout after a dip in the Byzantine baths here and had his vizier Rüstem Paşa overhaul the building. Fragments of mosaic paving stud the floor and the walls are lined with once-exquisite but now blurred İznik tiles.

The **Eski Kaplıca** (Old Baths; daily 7am–10.30pm; $4.50 admission, $4 extra for a massage), huddled at the far end of Çekirge Caddesi, next to the *Kervansaray Termal Hotel*, are Bursa's most ancient baths (and much the nicest public bath for women). Byzantine rulers Justinian and Theodora first improved a Roman spa on the site and Murat I in turn had a go at the structure in the late fourteenth century. Huge but shallow keyhole-shaped pools dominate the *hararetler*, or hot rooms, of the men's and women's sections, whose domes are supported by eight Byzantine columns. Scalding (45°C) water pours into the notch of the keyhole, the temperature still so taxing in the main basin that you'll soon be gasping out in the cool room, seeking relief at the fountain in the middle. Afterwards, the bar in the men's *camekan*, where you recuperate swaddled in towels on a chaise longue, serves alcoholic beverages should you wish to pass out completely. Alternatively, head for the swimming pool of the *Kervansaray Termal Hotel* next door (daily 8am–11pm; $8), where you swim indoors and then under a partition to their heated outdoor section.

On a hillock just west of the thermal centre stands the **Hüdavendigar (Birinci) Murat Camii**, which with its five-arched portico and alternating bands of brick and stone seems more like a church teleported from Ravenna or Macedonia. Indeed tradition asserts that the architect and builders were Christians, who dallied twenty years at the task because Murat I, whose pompous epithet literally means "Creator of the Universe", was continually off at war and unable to supervise the work. The interior plan, consisting of a first-floor *medrese* above a highly modified, T-type *zaviye* at ground level, is unique in Islam. Unfortunately, the upper storey, wrapped around the courtyard that's the heart of the place, is rarely open for visits.

Murat himself lies in the much-modified **türbe** across the street, complete apart from his entrails, which were removed by the embalmers before the body began its long journey back from Serbia in 1389. In June of that year Murat was in the process of winning his greatest triumph over the Serbian king Lazarus and his allies at the **Battle of Kosovo**, in the former Yugoslavia, when he was stabbed to death in his tent by Miloş Obiliç, a Serbian noble who had feigned desertion. Murat's son Beyazit, later better known as Yıldırım, immediately had his brother Yakub strangled and, once in sole command, decimated the Christian armies. Beyazit's acts had two far-reaching consequences: the Balkans remained under Ottoman control until early in the twentieth century, and a gruesome precedent of blood-letting was established for most subsequent Ottoman coronations.

Cumalıkizik

With extra time to spare in Bursa, it's worth taking a trip out to the rural Ottoman village of **Cumalıkizik**, 10km east on the Ankara road – easily reached by any dolmuş heading towards İnegöl from the dolmuş stop on İnönü Caddesi. The journey takes around twenty minutes. Documents date the village to 1685, but it is thought to be considerably older, possibly established by the Turkish horseback tribes that flowed into the region during the formative years of the Ottoman principality.

Set on the lower slopes of Uludağ, the cobbled streets are full of dilapidated buildings, leaning brokenly into each other. The Cumalikizik residents once made a living from growing chestnuts, but a virulent disease annihilated the plantation that surrounded the village. Now, raspberries and blackberries are grown instead, but as the young have gradually drifted into Bursa in pursuit of work, Cumalikizik's population has shrunk. The village has pinned its hopes on tourism to survive, promoting itself as a living museum, and after the busy streets of Bursa Cumalikizik certainly makes a peaceful place to spend a couple of hours, drinking tea and watching the inhabitants gossip on the steps of their decaying houses.

The most prominent sights on arrival are the two enormous plane trees in the square at the entrance to the village where the dolmuş drops you. Following the alleys into the village, you'll find that the roads are only wide enough for pedestrians and pack animals – some are so narrow that two people cannot pass each other – and there is a myriad of fascinating alley ways, dead-ends and cobbled squares to explore. The ground and first floors of the houses harbour the storerooms, stables and inner courtyards; upstairs, the living quarters present bay or lattice windows and wide tiled eaves overhanging the street. Many of the existing original double-front doors are studded with large-headed nails and wrought-iron strips. Neither the **hamam** nor the **mosque** can be dated with any accuracy, though it's thought that they are around three hundred years old. There is a tiny **museum**, with no particular set opening times – if it's locked, ask anyone to fetch the curator. Inside, there's a ramshackle, but well-meaning, collection of village implements, from old radios, door-knockers and swords, to a pile of rusting farming equipment in the garden. Around the main square at the entrance of the village are a couple of **teahouses** with outside tables and a small bakery selling tasty *börek*.

Eating, drinking and entertainment

Bursa's **cuisine** is solidly meat-oriented and served in a largely alcohol-free environment – reflecting the city's conservative nature. The most famous local recipes are *İskender kebap* (essentially *döner kebap* soaked in a rich butter, tomato and yoghurt sauce) – named after its supposed inventor, İskender (Alexander) Usta, a Bursan chef – and *İnegöl köftesi*, rich little pellets of mince often laced with cheese (when they're known as *kaşaril köfte*) and introduced by Balkan immigrants in the 1930s. If you're hungry, ask for *bir buçuk porsiyon* ("one big portion") as normal size portions of either dish are not enough for a meal. The city is also famous for its chestnut-based sweets, and instead of eating Turkish white bread, look out for Bursan *kepekli* (whole bran) loaves at any bakery.

For alcohol with your evening meal, head for **Sakarya Caddesi** between Altıparmak Caddesi and the walls of the Hisar above, near the clocktower – the former fish market and main street of the Jewish quarter has been reborn as an atmospheric place for an outdoor fish dinner or a drink on a summer's evening. Otherwise, try the **Kültür Parkı**, where you can dine in a peaceful environment and then later take in some Turkish pop at one of the bar-cum-discos, or head up to the over-priced nightclubs in Çekirge's five-star hotels.

Bursa has relatively few nocturnal or weekend events and the student contingent is responsible for any concerts that do occur. The **Kültür Merkezi** or

Cultural Centre, on Atatürk Caddesi (☎0224/223 4461), hosts ever-changing art exhibitions and occasional concerts. The **open-air theatre** in the Kültür Parkı is the main venue for the touristy musical performances and folkloric presentations that form a big part of the annual **Bursa Festival** in the last three weeks of July.

Restaurants

Adanur Hacibey Unlu Cad, Yılmaz İşhanı Girişi, Heykel. Large, impersonal, plastic dining room but great service and excellent *İskender kebap*, much cheaper than at *Hacibey İskender* (see below) at around $4 a portion.

Arap Sükrü Kuruçeşme Mah, Sakarya Cad 6 & 29, Tophane. Fish in all shapes and sizes, with beer, wine or *rakı* to wash it down, served at tables on both sides of the cobbled street. Reasonable prices with set meal deals available from $15 – typical of places on this quaint pedestrianized street.

Çiçek İzgara Belediye Cad 5. The best midtown value for lunch and dinner is this popular place on the upper floor, behind the *Belediye* building (town hall). Flawless service, tablecloth elegance and extremely reasonable prices. The emphasis is on various variations of *İnegöl köftesi*. Closed Sun.

Hacibey İskender Taşkapı Sok 4, off Atatürk Cad. The original, famous *İskender* salon. It's a tiny, two-storey establishment opposite the *Belediye* building where the decor is old wood and fake Ottoman tiles and the *İskender* is excellent, but you pay for the ambience.

Kebapçı İskender Unlu Cad 7, Heykel. Another claimant to be the inventor of the namesake dish – and that's all they serve, not even salads. It's always crowded to feed-trough density, even though it's moderately expensive. There's another three-storey branch on Atatürk Cad, near the Kültür Merkezi. Lunch only.

Konyalı Lokantası Koza Hanı, covered bazaar. With its tree-canopied setting in the central courtyard, this is the most atmospheric of a dozen *pide* ovens, tea booths, *büfes* and tiny restaurants scattered throughout the bazaar. Excellent *saç kavurma* (lamb in onion and tomato sauce made and served in a Turkish wok), which locals mop up with bread. Lunch only, closed Sun.

Mercan Restaurant *Kervansaray Termal Hotel*, Çekirge Meyd, Çekirge. A rooftop restaurant with great views and an outdoor terrace. Dishes include smoked salmon, Chateaubriand and pineapple

flambé, but you can expect a bill in the region of $30–35 for two, with wine. It's one of five excellent restaurants in this five-star hotel.

R.C.Cumurcul Restaurant Kültür Parkı. One of many relaxed, licensed establishments in the park, where two can eat *mezes* and kebabs, with a bottle of wine, for around $15. Housed in a restored Ottoman building with a large terrace.

Safran Restaurant *Safran Hotel*, Ortapazar Cad, Arka Sok 4, Hisar. Chic little a-la-carte restaurant in a renovated Ottoman mansion. The menu includes cold and hot *mezes*, meat and mushroom stews, good salads and heavenly sweets such as the *kaymaklı ayva tatlısı* (quince with clotted cream). Expect to pay in the region of $15–20 a head for a three-course meal with drinks.

Sezende Restaurant Hamamlar Cad 37, off Belediye Cad. Restored Ottoman house in the bazaar area serving a wide selection of cheap worker's dishes, from soup and *pide* to *izgara*.

Üç Köfte İvaz Paşa Çarşısı 3, in the north of the covered bazaar. The name means "three meatballs", which is what you get, served up three times over for a portion so the food on your plate is always piping hot. Lunch only, closed Sun.

Cafés and bars

Café M Kuruçeşme Mah, Sakarya Cad 24, Tophane. *Nargile* (hubble-bubble pipe) and coffee bar, with comfortable sofas to smoke from and watch the world go by. This is a good place to try a *nargile* in an easy-going environment.

Grand Geye Setbaşı bridge, Namazgah Cad, Heykel. Reasonably priced café, which attracts a student crowd. There's no alcohol. The outdoor terrace looks downstream to the next bridge, or there's indoor seating on four other levels.

Piccolo Kuruçeşme Mah, Sakarya Cad 16, Tophane. Bursa's fashionable youth collect in this trendy bar, hiding behind the sort of windows you can see out of but not into. It serves snacks, but it's better to eat first at one of the surrounding fish restaurants. Stays open late, depending on the mood.

Listings

Banks and exchange There are plenty of banks with ATMs, including Garanti Bankası, on Atatürk Cad, and exchange offices (Mon–Sat 8am–8pm) in

the covered bazaar and on Altıparmak Cad.
Books Good stocks of English-language books and foreign magazines at the Oxford Bookshop,

Altıparmak Cad 48–50.

Buses Departures are from the *otogar* (☎0224/261 5400), 10km north of Bursa; regular city buses from Heykel run up there. Kamil Koç, Pamukkale and Varan (and several other companies) run to Ankara, Bandırma, Çanakkale, Erdek, İstanbul (with ferry transfer), İzmir, Kütahya, Mudanya and Yalova. See "Travel details" at the end of the chapter for schedules.

Car rental Avis, Çekirge Cad 139 ☎0224/236 5133; Budget, Çekirge Cad 39/1 ☎0224/223 4204; and Europcar, Çekirge Cad 41 ☎0224/223 2321.

Consulate UK (honorary consulate), Resam Şefik Bursalı Sok, Başak Cad ☎0224/221 2534.

Hamams See p.259, or try the central, historic Çakır Ağa, located just below Hisar on Cemal Nadir Cad (men and women; 6am–midnight; $5); or İkinci Murat, next to the Muradiye tomb complex (Fri & Sun men only, all other days women only; 10am–6pm; $6).

Hospitals Devlet (State) Hastanesi, Hasta Yurdu Cad, Hisar ☎0224/220 0020; and Üniversite Hastanesi, P. Tezok Cad, Hastane Sok, Çekirge ☎0224/442 8400.

Internet access Bursa is well endowed with cybercafés, including *Brr-Soft Internet*, Sakarya Cad, just past the fish restaurant district; *Café Cappuccino*, Maksem Cad 84, up from the PTT; *Rock Café*, Orhan Sok 10, near Orhan Gazi Camii; and *American Internet* and *Star Internet*, both off Ülü Cad in Heykel.

Left luggage At the *otogar*, open 24hr.

Police Police station at Cemal Nadir Cad.

Post office Main PTT branch at the corner of Atatürk and Maksem *caddesis* (daily 24hr for telephone and telegrams, 8am–8pm for letters, and 9am–5.30pm for full postal services).

Uludag

Presiding over Bursa, the 2543-metre-high **Uludağ** (or "Great Mountain") is a dramatic, often cloud-cloaked massif, its northern reaches dropping dizzyingly into the city. In ancient times it was known as the Olympos of Mysia, one of nearly twenty peaks around the Aegean so named (Olympos was possibly a generic Phoenician or Doric word for "mountain"), and it has a place in mythology as the seat from which the gods watched the battle of Troy. Early in the Christian era the range became a refuge for monks and hermits, who were replaced after the Ottoman conquest by Muslim dervishes.

These days the scent of grilling meat has displaced the odour of sanctity, since Bursa natives cram the alpine campsites and picnic grounds to the gills on any holiday or weekend. Getting there is definitely half the fun if you opt for the **cable car** (*teleferik*), which links the Teleferüç borough of Bursa with the **Sarıalan** picnic grounds at 1635m, where a cluster of *et mangals* (barbecue grillhouses) and *kendin pişin kendin ye* (rent-a-barbecue establishments) await your custom.

Much of the dense middle-altitude forest has been designated a **national park**, though there are only a few kilometres of marked hiking trails. In fact, the best part of the mountain lies outside the park to the east, where a few hours' walking will bring you to some glacial **lakes** in a wild, rocky setting just below the highest summit. The best months for a visit are May and June, when the wildflowers are blooming, or September and October, when the mist is less dense. However, due to its proximity to the Sea of Marmara, the high ridges trap moist marine air and whiteouts or violent storms can blow up during most months of the year. **Skiing** is possible from December to March (though it's better earlier in the season than later). There's a dense cluster of hotels, most with their own ski lift, at the 1800m level (a day pass for each lift costs around $10), and you can rent skis and ski clothes at booths in **Oteller**, as the accommodation and skiing area is known.

Practicalities

To reach the lower cable-car terminus, take a dolmuş labelled "Teleferik" from the corner of Ressam Şefik Bursalı and Atatürk *caddesis*. The wobbly **teleferik** gondolas make the trip up from Teleferüç to Sarıalan every half-hour or so (daily 8am–9pm; $4 each way), but are cancelled in high winds; the journey takes just under thirty minutes, with a pause part way up at Kadıyayla. Try to avoid travelling mid-afternoon, when students make the ascent after school, or at weekends when hour-long queues at either end are the norm. At Sarıalan, at the top, there is an army of dolmuşes waiting to take you to Oteller.

The alternative is to take a **dolmuş** all the way to Oteller, which winds the 32km of paved road up from Bursa's Orhangazi Caddesi. The one-way fee is $6 per person, though it can occasionally be difficult to muster the necessary number of passengers (six).

You'd follow the same route in your own vehicle, the road veering off above Çekirge and climbing rapidly through successive vegetation zones. Staff at the **Karabelen national park gate**, 20km into the park, charge $2 per car when they're in the mood and sometimes have **information** to hand out. The final stretch of road, from just below the gate to the hotels at Oteller, is very rough cobble, designed to prevent drivers from skidding – or speeding – so allow nearly an hour for the trip. In bad weather conditions you will be advised to put chains on your wheels and may not be allowed to make the journey without them.

Accommodation

There's little difference between the four- and five-star resort **hotels** at the road's end in Oteller, but since the national park campsites are squalid and full in summer and it's too cold to camp in winter, you might want to consider a room. There are some 7500 hotel beds in the area, and while out-of-ski-season rates can dip as low as $40 for a double, in the skiing season (ie, winter) you will find rates of up to $250 per night with full board – and no shortage of people prepared to pay.

Hotels include: the *Ergün* (☎0224/285 2100, ℱ285 2101; ❻); *Kar Otel* (☎0224/285 1121, ℱ224 1123; ❺); *Beceren* (☎0224/285 2111, ⓦwww .beceren.com; ❽); *Yazıcı Regency* (☎0224/285 2040, ℱ285 2045; ❽); and the *Grand Yazıcı* (☎0224/285 2050, ℱ285 2048; ❽). In summer, the *Ergün*, *Beceren* and *Grand Yazıcı* are generally open, but some of the others may be pressed into use as summer English camps for Turkish high-school kids.

Walking routes

From the top of the hotel zone, a jeep-track leads in an hour and a half to a **tungsten mine**. An obvious path, beginning behind the mine's guard-house, slips up onto the broad but barren watershed ridge, just below the secondary summit of **Zirve** (2496m); follow this trail for an hour and a half to a fork. Right leads to the **main peak** (2543m); the cairned left-hand choice is more rewarding, descending slightly to overlook the first of Uludağ's lakes, **Aynalıgöl**, reachable by its own side-trail a half-hour beyond the junction.

There are some campsites here but none at **Karagöl**, the second and most famous lake, fifteen minutes southeast of the first one, sunk in a deep chasm and speckled with ice floes. **Kilimligöl**, the third substantial lake, is tucked away on a plateau southeast of Karagöl and offers good high-altitude camping. There are two smaller, nameless tarns, difficult to find in the crags above Aynalıgöl.

Returning to Oteller, as long as the weather is good you can stay with the ridge rather than revisiting the tungsten works, passing below the ruined hut on Zirve to meet a faint trail. This soon vanishes and thereafter it's cross-country downhill along the watershed as far as **Cennetkaya**, a knoll above the hotels, served by a marked trail. High above the trees, crowds and jeep tracks here, you just might strike lucky and glimpse patches of the distant Sea of Marmara to the north.

West of Bursa: Uluabat Gölü and Manyas Gölü

The 120-kilometre route west from Bursa to Bandırma is enlivened by two large but shallow lakes, only really accessible by car – though diehard dolmuş enthusiasts may be able to reach them by taking a series of connecting dolmuşes from village to village along the main road. The rarely visited **Uluabat Gölü**, site of the ancient settlement of Apollonia and the diminishing ancient fishing community of **Gölyazı** is 38km west of Bursa, while **Manyas Gölü**, 18km southeast of Bandırma, supports a bird sanctuary where the robust twitcher will appreciate the annual migration as it stops over in April/May and again in November. Neither lake warrants a special visit, but they do provide a break during the tedious drive along the southern Marmara shore.

Uluabat Gölü and Gölyazı

GÖLYAZI proves to be an atmospheric community of half-timbered houses, with the odd daub of purple or green paint, built on an island now lashed by a causeway to the shore of **Uluabat Gölü**. Bits of Roman and Byzantine **Apollonia** – the lake's alias – have unconcernedly been pressed into domestic service, and extensive courses of wall ring the island's shoreline. On the mainland you can see a huge, ruined Greek cathedral, large enough for a few hundred parishioners. The lake itself, speckled with islets, is only two metres deep, murky and not suitable for swimming, though it does attract a number of water birds.

Appearances would lead you to pronounce Gölyazı the quintessential fishing village: there's a lively open-air **fish market** each morning at the island end of the causeway, nets and rowboats are much in evidence, and the women – who don't appreciate gratuitous snaps being taken of them – patiently mend their traps. All this conceals the fact that pesticide and fertilizer runoff from the surrounding fields is constantly diminishing the lake catch, and a handful of families now emigrate every year.

To get here, you need to keep an eye out for an inconspicuous sign, "Gölyazı", 38km west of Bursa, which marks the six-kilometre side road to the village. The only **accommodation** is at the *Apollonia Motel* (no phone; ❶) on the landward side of the causeway – it's very rough and ready, and open only if there is an inkling of a demand during July and August. Pick up a room key at the co-managed **restaurant** of the same name at the extreme north edge of the village, where you can sample inexpensive *turna* (lake pike) fresh from a tank. For a couple of dollars (and with proficient Turkish) you can arrange for one of the fisher families to take you out in a small boat to some remote ruins on the nearby islets.

Manyas Gölü

Manyas Gölü attracts visitors mainly because of the national park bird sanctuary established here in 1938 astride a stream delta and swamps at the northeast corner of the lake. The **Kuş Cenneti National Park** (Kuş Cenneti Milli

Parkı; daily 7am–5.30pm; $0.70) – or "bird paradise" – contains a small visitor centre full of dioramas, labelled in Turkish but with a handy poster giving translations into English, and stocked with stuffed geese, orioles, spoonbills, herons, pelicans, ducks, egrets and owls. Next you're directed to a wooden **observation tower**, with a pair of binoculars, unfortunately not powerful enough for the job in hand. The most spectacular sightings are of pelicans (white and Dalmatian, nesting in May), spoonbills, spotted eagles and night herons, with cormorants and gray herons commonplace. The best months to visit are November – after the first rains and coincident with various migratory species' southward movements – and April to May, when the swamps are at their fullest and the birds are flying north. During these migrations, up to three million birds and some 239 species stop by, including up to five hundred pairs of smew (an Asian duck). You'll have to be satisfied with the observation tower, as there are no walkways or boats provided to get you through or around the delta.

The park and sanctuary is 18km southeast of Bandırma (see below): 13km along the Balıkesir road and then 5km on the signposted side-road. There are no facilities in the park grounds, the closest being a simple **restaurant** with a couple of *pansiyon* rooms by the roadside at Eski Sığırcı, 1.5km before the gate.

Bandırma

BANDIRMA – knocked flat during battles in 1922 and now neighbour to a NATO airbase – is a definite finalist in the ugliest-town-in-Turkey sweepstakes. Given its status as a major transit point you may well have to spend some time here, but all you really need to know is how to get from one transport terminal to another.

The main **otogar** is on the southern outskirts of town, 800m above the **ferry terminal** (for sea bus services from İstanbul) and adjoining **train station** (for trains to and from İzmir). If you don't want to walk up the hill or take a taxi to the *otogar*, use the red-and-white city buses labelled "Garaj/600 Evler", which depart from a marquee 200m east of the ferry terminal. Frequent dolmuşes to Erdek leave from outside the ferry terminal.

In the unlikely event that you get stranded here for the night, a number of cheap **hotels** one block up from the ferry terminal, and a couple of mid-range ones on the front, can provide accommodation. Best is the three-star *Hotel Villa Marina* (☎0266/715 1260, @hotelmarina@ixir.com; ❺) with a rooftop bar and restaurant overlooking the harbour; breakfast costs $5 extra. A couple of minute's walk east of the terminal, centred on the mosque, are a few reasonable **restaurants** dishing up the usual Turkish dishes.

Erdek and the Kapıdağı peninsula

A leafy, cobbled pedestrianized shore esplanade sets the tone for **ERDEK**, tucked at the base of the Kapıdağı peninsula and the closest jump-off point for the Marmara islands (see p.268). It's a pleasant enough town, with its landscaping and patches of park – another of the "İstanbul-by-the-sea" resorts that crowds with the urban middle class in summer.

Approaching from Bandırma, across the two-kilometre-wide isthmus that joins the peninsula to the rest of Anatolia, you'll have already seen some of the rest of the **Kapıdağı peninsula**, though it's not a promising sight. The shore is almost wholly given over to military facilities, or to campsites firmly oriented toward automobile or caravan custom. The ruins of **ancient Kyzikos**, 3km off the main road, are so negligible that you'd have to be incredibly keen to make the effort to reach them. **Ocaklar**, 5km northwest of Erdek is still the best beach to the north, though development encroaches with every season. **Narli**, a further 4km to the northwest, has a ruined Greek church, and a few small *pansiyon*s, but not much of a beach.

Practicalities

Erdek's **otogar** is by the road in from Bandırma, at the northeast edge of town, and is just a few minutes' stroll away from the waterfront. Almost everything of interest stands either along the shore promenade or just behind it. There's a summer-only **tourist information** kiosk hidden in trees next to the **ferry terminal** (for ferries to the Marmara islands), though it's not always open, and a tiny private office in the *otogar* that offers an accommodation booking service, but unless you speak good Turkish you will struggle to communicate here.

There are **minibuses** out of Erdek to all the main villages, but as traffic is generally light it's probably best to **rent a bike** (around $10 a day from outlets all over town).

The **PTT** is on Neyyire Satka, opposite the ferry landing, while one street back from the front are several **internet cafés**. A number of **shops** on the seafront sell cheap clothes, mostly seconds and over-runs.

Accommodation

There's very little reasonable **accommodation** in town proper – most establishments have been converted to holiday apartments. If you're desperate you could try either the basic *Saner Hotel* (℡0266/835 7152; ❶), on Neyyire Satka opposite the ferry terminal, or the unfriendly and overpriced *Ümit Hotel*, on Balık Hanı Sokak, behind Cumhuriyet Meydani (℡0266/835 1092; ❷). Better value is to be had at the out-of-town *Erdek Otel* (℡0266/835 2963; ❷) next to the *otogar*; it has some en-suite rooms and stays open during the winter.

Along the beach, 500m north of town, there must be at least forty establishments – all large affairs aimed at the domestic package market – most of which close in winter. The best value for money is the two-star *Hotel Özgün* (℡0266/835 4722, ℻347 6867; ❸), a friendly establishment, with small well-furnished rooms. Towards the end of the promenade, the *Otel Gül Plaj* (℡0266/835 1947, ⓦwww.hotelgulplaj.com; ❺) is a swish option directly on the seafront, but the deal is half-board only. Top hotel is the luxury, four-star *Agregento* (℡0266/835 4973, ℻835 1399; ❼), with mock-classical trimmings, large indoor and outdoor pools and comfortable air-conditioned rooms. Right at the end of the beach, there's a **campsite**, *Ay Camping*, which heaves during the summer school holidays.

Eating and drinking

There's plenty of choice when it comes to eating, but nothing that particularly stands out. The seafront strip boasts dozens of small **stalls and cafés** (several on boats moored in the harbour) offering varieties of Turkish fast food, some serving alcohol. One block inland is a predictable array of *pide salonu* and *lokanta*s, though numerous outlets also offer locally produced olive oil, olives and honey.

KAPIDAĞI PENINSULA
AND THE
MARMARA ISLANDS

Hayırsız Ada

Saraylar

Çınarlı

Marmara
Adası
▲ 699 m
Asmalı

Marmara
Gündoğdu
Topağaç

Ekinlik Adası

N

Ekinlik

Mavıköy
Avşa Adası

SEA OF MARMARA

Manastır
Burnu
Turkeli

Yiğitler
Altınkum
Koyun Adası

Paşalimanı Adası

Doğanler

Paşalimanı
Poyrazlı

Ormanlı

Harmanlı
İlhan
Turan

Ballıpınar

Balıklı
Tuzla
Narlı

782 m
▲
Çayağzı
Kestanelik

Ocaklar
Kapıdağı Peninsula
Çakil

Gulf of Erdek
Karşıyaka

Erdek
Tatlısu

Kyzikos
Aşağıyapıcı   Gulf of Bandırma

0   10 km

Gönen & Biga ▼   ▼ Bandırma

The Marmara islands

The **Marmara islands** – in the western half of the Sea of Marmara – are well known to Turks, but rarely visited by foreigners. They exist in a 1970s time warp; the holiday centres have lost whatever pretence to trendiness they once claimed, bypassed in the stampede to the south. The major settlements are nondescript, with little conscious preservation ethic, but the swimming and cycling are fine, while the scenery – the horizon studded with islets – is as close to that of the Greek archipelagos as you'll see in Turkey. In all honesty, they're never going to attract many overseas visitors, not when the south Turkish resorts offer more of intrinsic interest and a longer season. But if you're happy with a night or two in a simple pension, and a day on the beach with an army of Turkish working-class families, the islands make for a convenient overnight stop between İstanbul or Bursa and the north Aegean.

Four of the seven islands are inhabited and can be visited with varying degrees of ease. The largest, **Marmara**, was a colony of Miletus in ancient times, as were Erdek (Artaki) and Kyzikos on the peninsula. A Greek identity persisted until this century and the old names are still used by the older generation: Elafonisos for Marmara, Ophioussa for **Avşa**, Haloni for **Paşalimanı**. As elsewhere in western Anatolia, the Greeks began leaving the archipelago at the turn of the twentieth century, with emigration acquiring a more compulsory character after some were caught co-operating with British submarine captains during World War I. Recent years have seen a surge in visits by elderly Greeks born on the island (or their descendants) searching for their former homes, but the islanders claim they rarely find them – too much has changed.

For such a tightly bunched group, the islands are markedly different. Avşa is the most commercialized – some say ruined, the tiny Ekinlik and Paşalimanı are the least spoiled, while Marmara falls somewhere in between. Incidentally, while cars are not expressly forbidden on the islands, neither are they encouraged, making the archipelago relatively quiet by Turkish standards. Finally, if you show up much before June 1 or after September 30, the sea will be cool – and hardly anything open.

Getting to the islands

The islands are accessible by ferry, either directly from İstanbul, from Tekirdağ or from Erdek, main town of the Kapıdağı peninsula.

Ferry timetables to the islands are notoriously changeable. Services are predominantly seasonal, with most running over the summer – June to September – and tailing off in April, May and October, before almost grinding to a halt between November and March. Throughout the year, services from Erdek are not as frequent as from Tekirdağ, due to the latter's proximity to the highway to İstanbul. See "Travel details" at the end of the chapter for routes and journey times.

High season sees Turkish Maritime Lines' car ferries running three times a day **from Erdek to Marmara and Avşa** (one early morning, one late morning and one early evening), dropping to one a day or less out of season. Other private, unlicensed car and passenger ferries also run to Marmara and Avşa, as well as **to Ekinlik**, and **Balıklı** and **Paşalimanı** (both on Paşalimanı island), several times a week, but tend to depart only when full. The cost on any of these craft to any of the islands is around $2 one-way per person, $16 per car.

From Tekirdağ there are up to three passenger boats a day in high season to Marmara and Çınarlı on Marmara island, or to Avşa, tailing off to one daily in shoulder season and three times a week out of season, weather permitting ($3 per person, $8 per car). There are also connections on to Erdek.

From İstanbul's **Yenkapı** ferry terminal, there's a summer sea bus service (daily except Sun at 10.30am; $16) to Marmara and Avşa; in winter, the service drops to twice weekly. In summer there's also an unlicensed private passenger ferry three times a week **from Şarköy** in Thrace to Avşa and Çınarlı on Marmara ($6 per person).

Marmara

Largest of the islands at roughly 17km by 8km, **Marmara** acquired its name during the Middle Ages thanks to the giant marble quarries (*ta marmara* in Greek) that are still worked on the north shore. Marmara is the ancient Proconnesus, from where the famous blue-grey streaked Proconnesian marble originates, used for many of the columns of Aya Sofya in İstanbul. Sailing in from the south, you'll see the rocky ridge of 700-metre Alyas Dağı, with a ruined Byzantine tower, plunging down to the west tip of the island. Except for its valley-bottom oases, Marmara is bleak – downright windswept and cliff-girt in the north – so most of its villages huddle on the southern, lee shore.

The ferry will stop first at the pretty but facility-less port of Gündoğdu; don't get off here, but wait to reach the main town. This, simply called **MARMARA**, is backed up against a hill with steep, stepped streets penetrating inland, an enchanting setting from a distance, though seen up close its modern domestic architecture is nothing special.

The **beach** is five minutes' walk to the northwest of Marmara town and is sandy, but you'll have to accustom yourself to the extremely low salinity of the Sea of Marmara and the occasional swarms of white jellyfish that plague all the islands from time to time. In cooler weather you might entertain thoughts of hiking up through the mostly barren **interior**, but there are only goat-trails along the ridges and most of the time you'll be restricted to the skeletal network of dirt roads that rings the island.

The only other village equipped to handle visitors is **ÇINARLI**, 6km northwest, or a fifteen-minute dolmuş ride along a dirt road from the main harbour of Marmara. Çınarlı is a pretty place, with cottage gardens bursting with flowers and a village green shaded by plane trees (*Çınar*) after which the village takes it's name, but its 700-metre swathe of sand and pebbles is backed by a scruffy esplanade so it's not particularly private. There's no permanent accommodation in Çınarlı, but Turkish families have been known to rent out a few *pansiyon* rooms in busier years, and there are a couple of summer-only fish and kebab restaurants on the front.

East from Marmara, dirt tracks lead several kilometres to the side of the island that has been quarried for centuries. The marble is still today cut into mammoth blocks and transported to the harbour at **Saraylar** – a village in the north of the island populated by migrant quarry workers from the Black Sea Coast. The sole attempt to attract tourists here is a haphazard collection of marble fragments collected together in what is referred to as an open air museum, though it's little more than a dumping ground for old rocks.

Practicalities

In Marmara town, **ferries** dock at the terminal in the centre from where it's a short walk to the **PTT**, **bank** and a number of small hotels and *pansiyon*s. The best **accommodation** is at the far west end of the shore esplanade, facing the sunset. The *Marmara Hotel* (☎0266/885 6140; ❷) has sparse rooms – you share expansive clean marble bathrooms – while the *Şato Motel* (☎0266/885 5003; ❸) has sea-view terraces and a good breakfast, but suffers from noise from the nearby *gazino*s. Next to the jetty and handy for early ferries, the friendly *Murat* (☎0266/885 5222; ❷) has small rooms with shared hot-water bathrooms up the corridor.

Restaurants are fairly unpretentious. The *Şato Motel* serves up a set menu (around $8) that changes each night and the *Birol*, the first establishment over the footbridge from the jetty, has excellent fish, meat and *mezes*. It's slightly more expensive than elsewhere on the island but worth it for the waterside location and good service. Also on the front near the jetty is the *Birsen*, which provides tasty soups and stews – hardly fitting meals for a hot summer's evening, but cheap and filling at $3 for a main course.

Avşa

Low-lying and partly covered in vineyards, **Avşa** – around 8km in length and 3–4km wide – is surrounded by beaches and crystal-clear water that are both its raison d'être and its curse. The island is heavily developed and virtually a suburb of İstanbul in season, with prime beachfront locations snapped up thirty years ago as holiday homes. The sole cultural point of interest is the abandoned **Aya Triada church**, awash somewhere in the concrete sprawl that is the main town of **TÜRKELI** – an unruly spread of apartment buildings along the west coast. A promenade dominates the front with its row of cavernous cafés, where families drink tea and play games in the evening.

Taxis and dolmuşes from Türkeli (from next to Hal Çarşısı on Okullar Caddesi) run the 2.5km to **YIĞITLER** on the east coast of Avşa, populated almost entirely by settlers from the former Yugoslavia. One kilometre southeast of the village, there's a large sandy beach called **Altınkum**, overlooked by a couple of summer-only restaurants. For more secluded swimming the only option is to head off by foot to the quieter coves to the south of here.

Practicalities

Ferries dock at the ferry terminal, roughly halfway along the Avşa urban strip, from where small private boats also cross to Paşalimanı – prices and frequency depending entirely on demand. The **PTT** is located to the north of town on Posthane Caddesi, on the road running uphill parallel to the beach.

Although there's loads of **accommodation**, most fills quickly during high season and tends to be in the form of unremarkable, basic *pansiyon* rooms, often with shared bathrooms, on the spare floors of people's holiday homes. A couple of exceptions include the *Geçim Pansiyon* (☎0266/896 1493; ④), 500m north of the Türkeli ferry jetty, with a wide choice of compact rooms from singles to family-sized fully equipped apartments – breakfast and dinner extra and on request – and the friendly, family-run *Yalı Pansiyon* (☎0266/896 2085; ②), immediately south of the jetty on the beachfront, with only twelve waterless rooms, but plenty of hot water in the communal bathroom and nice views out to sea.

Restaurants also abound though only the Yarar particularly stands out, also south of the jetty on the beachfront – a popular and established diner that opens most of the year, serving seafood and meat dishes from $6. Strangely, despite the island's vineyards, most of the wine on sale seems to come from Bozcaada.

Ekinlik and Paşalimanı

There is little to see or do – never mind anywhere to stay and eat – on Ekinlik and Paşalimanı, but if you are determined to go you can take at least one daily private ferry from Erdek in summer for each of these other two inhabited Marmara islands.

Ekinlik, also known as Kaşık Adası, or "spoon island", because of its shape, is little more than a kilometre in length and 500m across. Although there are no beaches, and consequently no tourism development here, the island has a pretty harbourside village. There are several old Greek houses and a ruined church to the left of the jetty. The harbour is full of fishing boats (no pleasure craft, for a change) and is overlooked by a shaded tea garden.

Again lacking enough beaches to make it the target of development, **Paşalimanı** – irregularly shaped but almost 10km in length – is a sleepy, friendly place, greener than Marmara and Avşa and distinguished mainly by its giant plane trees. There's very little to attract anyone to **BALİKLİ** village, the "capital", though a few people rent out their spare rooms over summer and occasional day-trippers visit on private boats to drink tea on the jetty before returning to Avşa.

Travel details

Trains

Bandırma to: İzmir (2 daily; 5hr 30min).
Edirne to: Budapest (1 daily; 25hr) via Sofia (10hr)
and Bucharest (14hr); İstanbul (2 daily; 5hr
30min);
Üzünköprü to: Athens (1 daily, 17hr). Note: this is
not a direct service; connections are made in
Thessaloniki.

Buses and dolmuşes

Bandırma to: Balıkesir (hourly; 1hr 45min); Bursa
(hourly; 2hr); Çanakkale (hourly; 3hr 30min); Erdek
(every 30min; 25min); İzmir (7 daily; 6hr); Manyas
(7 daily; 30min); Yalova (several daily; 3hr).
Bursa to: Ankara (every 30min; 7hr); Bandırma
(hourly; 2hr); Çanakkale (hourly; 5hr 30min); Erdek
(8 daily; 2hr); İstanbul, with ferry transfer (hourly;
5hr); İzmir via Balıkesir and often Ayvalık (every
hourly; 7hr); Kütahya (3 daily; 3hr); Mudanya
(every 30min; 40min); Yalova (every 30min; 1hr).
Edirne to: Çanakkale (5 daily; 4hr 30min); İstanbul
(every 30min; 3hr); Keşan (every 20min; 2hr);
Kapıkule (every 30min; 30min); Kırklareli (every
hour; 1hr); Lüleburgaz (every 30min; 1hr 15min).
Erdek to: Bandırma (every 30min; 25min); Bursa
(8 daily; 2hr).
Gelibolu to: Eceabat (hourly; 50min); Kilitbahir
(hourly; 1hr).
İznik to: Adapazarı (hourly; 1hr 30min); Bursa
(every 30min; 1hr 30min); İstanbul (1 daily; 3hr
30min); Yalova (several daily; 1hr).
Şarköy to: Edirne (1 daily; 3hr 30min); İstanbul
(every 30min; 4hr); Tekirdağ (20 daily; 1hr 30min).
Yalova to: Bursa (every 30min; 1hr); İznik (hourly;
1hr).

Short-hop ferries

Eceabat to: Çanakkale, car ferry (hourly, 24hr;
40min).
Gelibolu to: Lapseki, car ferry (hourly 24hr; 50min).
Kilitbahir to: Çanakkale, car ferry (according to
traffic, 6am–9pm; 10min).

Island & long-haul ferries and sea buses

Services are most frequent in summer (June–Sept),
tail off in the shoulder seasons (April–May & Oct)
and are greatly reduced during winter (Nov–March).
Avşa to: Erdek (summer 3 daily; winter 1 daily;
3hr); İstanbul (summer 1 daily except Sun; 2hr
45min).
Bandırma to: İstanbul (summer 4–6 daily; winter
2 daily; 2hr).
Erdek to: Avşa (summer 3 daily; winter 1 daily;
3hr); Ekinlik (summer 1 daily; winter 1 weekly; 2hr
30min); Marmara (summer 3 daily; winter 1 daily;
2hr 15min).
Kabatepe to: Gökçeada/Imvros (June–Oct 1 daily;
Nov–May 2 weekly; 1hr 30min).
Marmara to: Avşa (summer 3 daily; winter 1 daily;
1hr); İstanbul's Yenkapı terminal (summer 1 daily
except Sun; 2hr 45min).
Mudanya to: İstanbul (2 daily; 1hr 45min).
Şarköy to: Avşa (summer 3 weekly; 3hr); Çınarlı
on Marmara (summer 3 weekly; 1hr 30min).
Tekirdağ to: Avşa (summer 3–4 daily; winter 3
weekly; 3hr 30min); Erdek (summer 2 daily; 5hr
30min); Marmara (summer 3–4 daily; winter 3
weekly; 3hr).
Yalova to: İstanbul's Yenkapı ferry terminal (summer 6–7 daily; winter 2–3 daily; 1hr); Kartal (every
30min; 35min).

3

The North Aegean

CHAPTER 3 # Highlights

✳ **Troy** The most celebrated archeological site in Turkey boasts a bleak, windswept setting and an enduring mythology. **See p.285**

✳ **Bozcaada** Small island, famed for its elegant architecture, relaxing atmosphere and especially its wine. **See p.283**

✳ **Assos** The old town and ancient city occupy a rocky peak, with stunning views of the Aegean and Greece beyond. **See p.290**

✳ **Ayvalik** Relax in this former Greek fishing town, with its charming mix of derelict and restored Ottoman houses. **See p.295**

✳ **Ancient Pergamon** The renowned acropolis has a dramatic setting and wide-ranging ruins that easily rival more famous sights further south. **See p.302**

✳ **Foça** The former fishing village is now a popular resort that hasn't forgotten its maritime heritage. **See p.310**

✳ **Manisa** This working town has some particularly impressive mosques and makes a good base from which to explore the surroundings. **See p.313**

✳ **Sardis** Seat of King Croesus, and the first city to see the use of coins, these remote ruins warrant a lengthy visit. **See p.316**

The North Aegean

T urkey's **North Aegean** coast sees far fewer visitors than the shoreline further south. There are decent sandy beaches, though the lower sea temperature and lack of a major airport protect the region from widespread development. Most summer visitors are Turks and, while tourism is inevitably important to the local economy, even in August the number of visitors doesn't match those at the country's more renowned destinations. Away from the resort towns, life goes on much as it always has, with farming and fishing providing a livelihood for the bulk of the population.

This area, which roughly constitutes ancient Aeolia, has been settled since Paleolithic times; civilization bloomed early here under the Phrygians, who arrived in Anatolia during the thirteenth century BC. Later waves of Greek colonists established settlements on the coast, leaving the region rich in Classical and Hellenistic remains. Although the sparse ruins of **Troy** in the north don't quite live up to their literary and legendary reputation, the ancient cities of **Assos** and **Pergamon** (modern **Bergama**) display some tangible reminders of the power and wealth of the greater Greek empire. Less visited than any of these is the more isolated Lydian city of **Sardis**, the ancient capital of King Croesus (and Midas before him), one of Aegean Turkey's most impressive archeological sites.

Coming from İstanbul or anywhere else in northwestern Turkey, your most obvious entry point is **Çanakkale** is the obvious entry point – useful as a base for both the ruins at Troy and the World War I battlefields on the Gelibolu peninsula (see p.235). The road running south from Çanakkale is justifiably characterized as scenic on most maps, with much of the route wooded and gently hilly, giving way to a coastal strip with the mountains of the **Kaz Dağı** range rising behind. Further south, the best stretches of beach lie near **Ayvalık** – the area's longest-established resort – though there are also pleasant resorts and sands along the coastal strip running from **Assos** to **Ören**, on the northern shore of the **Gulf of Edremit**, as well as at the small port towns of **Dikili**, **Çandarlı** and **Foça**. Offshore, the Turkish Aegean islands of **Gökçeada** and **Bozcaada**, provide an easy escape from Çanakkale, though many people prefer the charms of smaller islands such as **Alibey**, a good day-trip destination from the resort of Ayvalik.

In general there's less to write home about further **inland**, where a mountainous landscape harbours a few predominantly industrial cities. However, the **İzmir–Bandırma railway line** provides an alternative approach to the region, passing through the otherwise unremarkable provincial capital of Balikesir (from where there are frequent buses to the Gulf of Edremit and Çanakkale), Soma (a short bus ride away from Bergama) and **Manisa** – the last

a town of some antiquity, often used by visitors as a base for seeing Sardis. Of these inland destinations only Manisa and, further east, the town of **Alaşehir** are really worth any kind of prolonged attention.

Çanakkale

Although celebrated for its superb setting on the Dardanelles straits, the functional modern town of **ÇANAKKALE** has little to detain you except for a good archeological museum and a pleasing seafront. However, it is the most popular base for visiting the World War I landing sites (Gallipoli) on the European side of the Dardanelles and for seeing the ruins of Troy. Also, if you're intent on going to the Turkish Aegean islands of Gökçeada or Bozcaada, then Çanakkale makes a convenient jumping-off point.

It's the **Dardanelles** (Çanakkale Boğazi in Turkish) that have defined Çanakkale's history and its place in myth. The area's Classical name, **Hellespont**, is owed to one Helle, who, while escaping from her wicked stepmother on the back of a winged ram, fell into the swift-moving channel and drowned. From Abydos on the Asian side, the youth Leander used to swim to Sestos on the European shore for trysts with his lover Hero, until one night he too perished in the currents; in despair Hero drowned herself as well. Byron narrowly escaped being added to the list of casualties on his swim in the opposite direction in 1810.

In 480 BC Xerxes' Persian hordes crossed the waters on their way to Greece; and in 411 and 405 BC the last two naval battles of the Peloponnesian War took place in the straits, the latter engagement ending in decisive defeat for the Athenian fleet. Twenty centuries later Mehmet the Conqueror constructed the elaborate fortress of Kilitbahir directly opposite the Çimenlik Kale in Çanakkale (which he also built), to tighten the stranglehold being applied to doomed Constantinople. In March 1915, an Allied fleet attempting to force the Dardanelles and attack İstanbul was repulsed, with severe losses, by Turkish shore batteries, prompting the even bloodier land campaign usually known as Gallipoli. These days the straits are still heavily militarized and modern Çanakkale is very much a navy town.

Arrival, information and tours

Arriving by **ferry** from Eceabat or Kilitbahir on the Gelibolu peninsula, or from the island of Gökçeada, you'll dock close to the start of Demircioğlu Caddesi, which barrels inland, roughly splitting the town in two. Most of what there is to see or do in Çanakkale, except for the archeological museum, is within walking distance of the ferry terminal.

The **otogar** is out on Atatürk Caddesi, the local name for the coastal İzmir–Bursa highway, a fifteen-minute walk from the centre. This is mainly of use for buses to North Aegean destinations, which start and terminate in Çanakkale. However, many buses pass straight through the town centre to cross the straits via ferry and travellers will often find it more convenient to board as they come off the ferry. The bus companies also arrange free transfers to the *otogar* from their respective offices, which lie opposite the tourist office. **Dolmuşes** to Troy run from the minibus garage, opposite the fairground on Atatürk Caddesi.

The **tourist office** on Cumhuriyet Meydanı (May–Sept Mon–Fri 8.30am–7.30pm, Sat & Sun 10.30am–6pm; Oct–April Mon–Fri 8.30am–5.30pm; ☏0286/217 1187), next to the main dock is, in summer at least, staffed by friendly, English-speaking students.

CENTRAL ÇANAKKALE

▲ Eceabat

ACCOMMODATION
Anafartlar	1
Anzac	4
Anzac House	3
Bakir	2
Efes	6
Kervansaray	5
Yellow Rose	7

RESTAURANTS & BARS
Boaz	C
Boğaz 2000	D
Efes Internet Café	B
Entellektual	A
Gaziantep	F
Kepenek	G
TNT	E

Dardanelles

Gökçeada

Kilitbahir

Police

Emniyet Müdürlüğü

Ferry Ticket Office

CUMHURIYET MEYDANI

Troy Anzac Tours

Clock Tower (Saat Kulesi)   See inset

Atatürk Statue

Main Police

Otogar

Lapseki & Bursa

Passport Police

Cinema

Naval Museum

Nusrat

Hamam

Çimenlik Kale

N

Friday Market

Dolmuşes for Troy ★

Fairground

0   200 m

Archeological Museum, Troy & Ayvalik ▼

Battlefield and Troy tours

Many people opt to **tour the World War I battlefields** on the Gelibolu peninsula from here. Tour prices fluctuate between $15 and $25 per person; for details of what to look out for when booking a tour, see p.235. Premier **tour company** is *TJ's Hostel* in Eceabat (see p.240), which you should call for details and arrangements. Çanakkale-based tours include *Hassle Free Tours*, operated by the *Anzac House Pansiyon*, at Cumhuriyet Meyd 61 (☎0286/217 1392, ⓔhasslefree@anzachouse.com), *Troy Anzac Tours*, just west of the Saat Kulesi (clocktower) at Yali Cad 2 (☎0286/217 5849, ⓕ217 0196) and the *Yellow Rose Pansiyon* at Yeni Sok 5 (☎0286/217 3343, ⓔyellowrosepension@hotmail

.com). Both *Anzac House* and *Yellow Rose* also offer daily **Troy tours** for $14 and $20 respectively, including transport and guide.

Accommodation

Except around Anzac Day, April 25, you'll have little trouble finding a room in town. The most obvious budget options are only a few minutes' walk from the ferry landing. Just south of the tourist office, the Saat Kulesi (clocktower) signals the entrance to a warren of alleys – Fetvahane Sokağı, Aralık Sokağı, Yeni Sokak – that are home to various inexpensive hotels and *pansiyon*s. Moving across Demircioğlu Caddesi, or closer to the water, you'll find the more upscale hotels.

Hotel Anafartlar Kayserili Ahmet Paşa Cad ☎0286/217 4454, ℱ217 4457. On the water next to the ferry landing, this offers up-market, "big hotel" service together with pleasant en-suite rooms with TV, air-con and minibar. Also a rooftop restaurant with sea view. ❹

Anzac Hotel Saat Kulesi Meyd 8 ☎0286/217 7777, ℱ217 2018. Practically opposite the clock tower, this two-star place has neat, plainly decorated en-suite rooms with satellite TV. ❸

Anzac House Cumhuriyet Bul 61 ☎0286/217 1392, ℮hasslefree@anzachouse.com. Well-equipped backpackers' hostel with basic dorms ($5) and doubles, some without windows. Also a bar and restaurant, internet access, video room and battlefield tours (and one night free to those on the Hassle Free tour). ❷

Otel Bakir Cumhuriyet Meyd ☎0286/217 4088, ℱ217 4090. Professionally run hotel with good-

value rooms and great harbour views. ❸

Efes Hotel Fetvahane Sok 15 ☎ & ℱ0286/217 3256. Clean, bright and reasonably modern rooms, communal TV room and a homely, friendly feel. Breakfast not included. ❶

Kervansaray Fetvahane Sok 13 ☎0286/217 8192. Quiet, polite and friendly family-run affair, housed in a rather neglected 200-year-old mansion. Rooms are a bit shabby, though the courtyard and kitchen are available for guests. No alcohol permitted on the premises. ❷

Yellow Rose Pansiyon Yeni Sok 5 ☎0286/217 3343, ℮yellowrosepension@hotmail.com. Fifty metres back from the clocktower. Rooms of varying size, though all are stark and basic, as well as dorms ($6) and a disappointing non-inclusive breakfast. Also laundry service, video room, internet access and battlefield tours. ❶

The Town

The name *Çanakkale* means "Pottery Castle", after the garish Çanakkale ware that finds its way into the ethnographic section of every Turkish museum. Fortunately none of this is conspicuous, the only nod to the local style being in a few appealing, early twentieth-century buildings in the tiny **bazaar**, just south of the nucleus of cheap hotels. There's more interesting shopping at the large **Friday market**, five minutes' walk south of the *otogar* on Atatürk Caddesi.

Continue past the bazaar area to **Çimenlik park** (daily 9am–10pm) and fortress (closed to public). The **Naval Museum** (Deniz Müzesi; daily except Mon & Thurs 9am–noon & 1.30–5pm; $0.70), at the northern end of the park, features archival photos – Seddülbahir in ruins after Allied shelling, Atatürk's funeral – and military paraphernalia, including (on the upper floor) Atatürk's shattered pocket watch, which stopped a shell fragment at Gelibolu and saved his life. Meanwhile, beached on the park esplanade – from where you get the best views of Kilitbahir fort across the way – is a replica of the minelayer **Nusrat** (same hours and ticket as museum), which stymied the Allied fleet by re-mining at night zones that the French and British had swept clean by day.

An hour should be enough to take in the **Archeological Museum** (Arkeoloji Müzesi; daily except Mon & Thurs 8.30am–noon & 1–5.30pm; $0.70), nearly 2km from the centre of town; flag down any dolmuş along

Çanakkale

❸

Atatürk Caddesi labelled "Kepez" or "Güzelyalı". The collection is strong on brass implements, delicate glass and glazed pottery, unfired lamps and figurines, and wooden objects, most of them from the nearby Bozcaada and Dardanos tumuli. There's also a coin case spanning all cultures from Lydian to Ottoman, but the most exquisite items are the gold and jewellery grave finds, and the bone and ivory work by the exit.

Eating, drinking and nightlife

Places to eat and drink tend to lie within a block or two of the straits. Most of the conspicuous quayside **restaurants**, south of the main ferry jetty, offer a wide variety of dishes, including freshly caught fish, though you may find views blocked by traffic queuing for the ferry. Further south along the waterfront, near the bazaar, a clutch of friendly, unpretentious outdoor restaurants are a cheaper option for food and drink. **Nightlife**, such as it is, centres on the clocktower, with a few places offering live music in an attempt to sweeten the bitter pill of the high bar prices. As with accommodation, this all changes around Anzac Day when the sheer weight of numbers alters the area's character beyond recognition.

Restaurants

Boaz Lokantası Saat Kule Meyd. Located next to the *Anzac Hotel*, this offers very good hot stews and an impressive range of lunchtime dishes for around $5.

Boğaz 2000 Saat Kule Meyd. One of the cheapest options, deservedly popular for both lunch and dinner. A dish with rice can cost as little as $4 (if you can get a seat).

Entellektüel South of the ferry terminal. The widest range of *meze* and fish in town – try the banded bream (*karagöz*), good value at around $12. They give you a handy chart of Turkish fish with their English names, and pictures, in case you're still in doubt.

Gaziantep Lokantası Fetvahane Sok 8. Special spicy dishes from the southeast of Turkey, including the best *İskender kebap* in town. It's near the *Kervansaray* hotel, with outdoor tables sandwiched between two buildings, friendly service and colourful wall murals.

Bars

Kepenek Keramik Fetvahane Sok. Hidden away in a courtyard, this *al fresco* joint is popular with young artists and musicians, and has the best pop music collection in town.

TNT Fetvahane Sok. A dark cavernous bar, popular with backpackers, with a courtyard restaurant and live music upstairs most evenings.

Listings

Banks and exchange A number of banks and ATMs line Fetvahane Sok and Cumhuriyet Meyd. Opening hours for most banks are Mon–Fri 9am–12.30pm & 1.30–5pm.

Car rental Delta Rent A Car, Cumhuriyet Meyd 21/1 ☏0286/814 1218.

Cinema One of the closest cinemas is housed below the new Tanşas shopping centre, next door to the *otogar*, showing mainstream releases in English with Turkish subtitles. There's also a much smaller cinema housed within the Belediye İş Merkezi, behind the Atatürk statue.

Internet access At the cheap *Efes Café*, along the seafront and opposite the Kilitbahir ferry terminal. The Belediye İş Merkezi also has many smaller

internet shops and cafés, and internet access is available from a few of the hostels (see "Accommodation" on p.279), though these tend to be overpriced.

Hospital Hasan Mevsuf Sok ☏0286/217 1098.

Newspapers English-language newspapers from Orka Kitabevi, Yali Cad 5, behind the *Entellektüel* restaurant.

Police Kayserili Ahmet Paşa Cad, opposite the ferry terminal.

Post office PTT on İnönü Cad (Mon–Sat 8am–11pm).

Telephones Booths can be found in Cumhuriyet Meyd and there's a small PTT shop within the Belediye İş Merkezi.

The Turkish Aegean islands

Strategically straddling the Dardanelles, **Gökçeada** and **Bozcaada** were the only Aegean islands to remain in Turkish hands after the 1923 Treaty of Lausanne, which concluded the Greek–Turkish war. Under the terms of the agreement the islands' predominantly Greek inhabitants were exempt from the population exchange of the same year, but after 1937 both Gökçeada and Bozcaada were re-militarized along with the Greek islands of Samothráki and Límnos, and in subsequent decades the Turkish authorities began to assert their sovereignty more forcefully. Access to foreigners was banned until 1987 and even now few overseas visitors make their way over from the mainland. What you find, if you make the effort, are inexpensive, basic facilities, good beaches and a rather uneasily shifted sense of identity. Both islands, incidentally, are short on banks and exchange shops, so make sure you have enough cash on you before departing the mainland.

Gökçeada

Gökçeada, the larger of the two Turkish Aegean islands, hovers just northwest of the Dardanelles, tantalizingly visible from any of the Gelibolu battlefields. Its previous name, Imvros, most likely derives from "Imbrasos", the pre-Hellenic god responsible for breathing life into infertile land. Today, the barren, hilly island – still heavily militarized – is a hotchpotch of the old and the new, Christian and Muslim. It's also large enough to make your own vehicle necessary. There are local dolmuş services, but they are few and unreliable, barely used by the wealthy Turkish and Greek visitors who make up the bulk of the island's small tourist trade.

During the Gallipoli campaign Gökçeada was occupied by the Allies. General Hamilton's command was based on the island and many troops were ferried from here to the battlefields. Assigned to Turkey for its strategic value after the 1923 peace conference, the island's majority population of seven thousand Orthodox Greeks was more or less left to itself for forty years, save for a token force of a hundred or so Turkish gendarmes and officials. When the Cyprus conflict came to a head in 1964, the Turkish government decided to "claim" the island more pointedly, instituting policies of forced land expropriation without compensation, heavy garrisoning, the closure of schools for Greek children, settlement of Turkish civilians from the mainland and the establishment of an open prison. These measures were taken specifically to make continued residence for the ethnic Greeks impossible, and they've had the desired effect: today there are only about two hundred Greeks left, the bulk of the population having left for Athens and further afield.

Getting there

In summer there is one **ferry** a day to Gökçeada **from Çanakkale** (June–Sept; $1.50 each way, $11 per car; 3hr), and one **from Kabatepe** on the Gelibolu peninsula (July & Aug; $0.80, $6 per car; 1hr 30min). In winter these times drop drastically to once a week from Çanakkale and twice a week from Kabatepe. However, ferry schedules are notoriously unreliable, so check carefully at Çanakkale tourist office. Weekend ferries tend to fill quickly in summer, and if you are taking a car over it is advisable to arrive at least two hours before departure. The busiest time to travel is around August 15 when the island's Greek festival is held.

Around the island

Ferries dock at **KUZU LİMANI**, which boasts a new yacht harbour. A dolmuş meets the boat and takes you the 6km inland to the island's small capital, generally known as **GÖKÇEADA MERKEZ**, but also as Çınarlı (and, formerly, by the Greek name, Panayia). The grim official architecture on the main drag is complemented by the old Greek vernacular in the back streets. There are a couple of hotels and restaurants here – including the *Belediye Otel* at Belediye Meydanı (T 0286/887 3375; ❷), with its own good *lokanta*, and the *Kanaat Otel* (T 0286/887 3027; ❷) – as well as two or three huge, shuttered Greek churches. The main square also holds at least two banks with ATMs.

Most visitors continue a further 5km by dolmuş to the island's former capital of **KALEKÖY** (previously Kastro) on the north shore, where a ruined castle built during Süleyman the Magnificent's reign overlooks a good beach and the Greek island of Samothraki. In the centre the *Gökçe Motel* (T 0286/887 3473, F 887 2059; ❷) has basic rooms with balcony. There's also the *Yakamoz Pansiyon & Restaurant* on the hill (T 0286/887 2057; ❷) which has simple double rooms with rustic charm and a quality restaurant serving things such as *kalamar* (calamari) and *tavuk şiş* (chicken shish). Another longstanding favourite is the *Kallmerhaba Otel* (T 0286/887 3648, F 887 2224; ❷), which also offers decent meals. Further up the hill is the slightly more upmarket *Kale Motel* (T 0286/887 3438, W www.kalemotel.com.tr; ❸), also with its own good restaurant. Along the quay a number of excellent, cheap fish tavernas feature roof-terrace seating.

The hamlet of **KALEKÖY ÜSTÜ**, ten minutes' up the hill, boasts the restored remains of the oldest church on the island and the *Güzelyali* restaurant offering unusually interesting cooking with home-grown vegetables, olives and cheese.

From Kaleköy you can easily walk the 1.5km south to Bademlı (Glyki), passing on the way the new settlement of **YENI BADEMLI**, which boasts a couple of good basic *pansiyon*s – the *Morgül* (T 0286/887 3490; ❶) and the *Gökçen* (T 0286/887 2250; ❶). The old town of **ESKI BADEMLI** is virtually deserted apart from the sumptuous *Poseidon Otel* (T 0286/887 4619, W www.poseidonotel.com; ❺), whose rooms have marvellous views.

There's more life at **ZEYTİNLİ** (Ayii Theodhori), 3km northwest of Gökçeada Merkez, where most of the island's remaining Greek Orthodox population lives, but you'll quickly notice that no one is younger than 60 (although younger family members return for regular visits especially during summer). They're understandably bitter about the turn of events and, in the past, have been reluctant to talk to – or be photographed by – outsiders for fear of subsequent Turkish interrogation. These days, though, things are more relaxed, with Turks as well as Greeks turning out in force for the island's **annual festival** of Greek culture held around August 15. The most typically Greek village is **TEPEKÖY**, 7km to the west, which also has the best and most popular *pansiyon*/taverna on the island, *Baba Yorgo* (T & F 0286/887 3592; ❷). The beautifully restored village house is run by a Greek man who returned after years working in İstanbul.

Kefalo Burnu (Kaleköy), the southeastern tip of the island, offers better beaches than those around Kale on Bozcaada (see opposite), but you'll need your own transport if you plan to visit. It also boasts the rusting remains of Allied shipping sunk during the Gallipoli campaign. Nearby, **AYDINCIK** has a good beach, a campsite and lake waters with supposed healing properties.

Bozcaada

The island of **Bozcaada** – formerly known as Tenedos (from Tenes, one of the heroes of the Trojan War) – is a more popular and cheerful place than Gökçeada, if only because it's far less militarized and more architecturally of a piece. It's too close to the mainland to have avoided the attention of Turkish rulers down the ages and the population, as evidenced by a handful of medieval mosques, has historically been about one-quarter Muslim. Covered mostly in vineyards that produce the justly famous Bozcaada **wine**, the island is small enough to walk around, and it has some excellent beaches, though the water is freezing cold until September.

Getting there

Ferries (June–Sept 3 daily, rest of the year 2 daily; $1 return, $5 per car; 1hr 30min) to Bozcaada leave from **Yükyeri İskelesi**, a tiny port with several kilometres of excellent beach, 60km southwest of Çanakkale. Direct dolmuşes from Çanakkale's *otogar* depart three times a day, timed to catch the 10am, 2pm or 6pm ferry.

If you miss the ferry and need to stop over, it's best to hole up in the village of **GEYIKLI**, 5km east of Yükyeri İskelesi, back towards Ezine. Regular dolmuşes ply the short route, though these dwindle considerably after the last ferry crossing. The *Gözde Hotel* here (☎0286/638 5086; ❶) has en-suite **rooms**, while Geyikli also boasts a bank with an ATM and a Thursday street market, where you can pick up the delicious local honey and olives. There is also a **campsite** a few kilometres further down the coast towards Alexandria Troas.

Around the island

The only town, **BOZCAADA** (also known as **KALE** – "castle"), is built on a grid plan along a slight slope. It's surprisingly elegant, with cobbled streets and a good number of preserved old houses with overhanging upper floors. The old Greek quarter extended east from the church to the sea, though nowadays fewer than a hundred elderly Orthodox inhabitants remain. Kale lies in the shadow of its **castle**, which was successively enlarged by Byzantine, Genoese, Venetian and Turkish occupiers, and most recently restored by the archeological service in the 1960s. The result is one of the largest citadels in the Aegean (easily the equal of that at Bodrum) and thankfully it's not a military area, so you can explore every inch – the locals use the keep to graze sheep and the lower courtyard as a football pitch. It also boasts a small **museum** of locally unearthed artefacts (May–Oct daily 10am–1pm & 2–7pm; $1.50).

The interior of the island consists of gently undulating countryside, flatter than Gökçeada and treeless except for the clumps marking the site of farms. The three best **beaches** are the consecutive strands of Ayazma, Sullubahçe and Habbele, 7km from Kale on the south coast; take the right at the first fork out of town and then two lefts, or catch one of the half-hourly dolmuşes to Ayazma. Just above Ayazma is an abandoned monastery, home to the *ayazma* (sacred spring) that gave it its name, while closer to the sand are a couple of restaurants. A dirt track leads thirty minutes east to the beach at **Ayiana**, a marvellous site if you're after complete solitude.

Taking the left turn instead at the first fork out of Kale leads to more beaches – narrower and more exposed – on the east shore, along the 4km of asphalt ending at **Tuzburnu**.

Arrival, orientation and transport

Ferries dock at the northeast tip of the island in Kale, where most accommodation is situated. As you leave the quay, the castle is situated nearby, to the right of the town, while to the left, in a tight arc, lies the small fishing **harbour**. Following the main road out of town takes you past the main square on the left, together with a small park often used as an outdoor café. **Dolmuşes** embark on their short journey around the island from behind here. The **PTT** is on the main square. At present the only bank on the island does not accept foreign cards, so change plenty of lira before you arrive.

The *Ada Café* (T 0286/697 8795), one street behind the harbour in town, **rents bikes** for around $12, as well as arranging **tours of the island** and renting out camping equipment. Boat excursions and scuba diving are currently outlawed, but accompanying a fisherman on a trip is permitted if the groups are kept small. As this is usually an impromptu affair its best to ask at one of the small fishing boats moored in the harbour.

Accommodation

A haven this convenient not surprisingly fills up in summer, but finding **accommodation** is not a big problem, except at weekends and on public holidays. All the same, advance booking is advisable if you want to stay in anything better than average. There are also numerous **rooms** available in people's houses, advertised as "*ev pansiyon*". Prices vary according to demand, but you can expect to pay from around $12.

The wonderfully quirky *Rengigül Pansiyon* on Atatürk Cad (T 0286/677 8171; ❸), near the Greek church and clearly signposted from the bank, comes highly recommended – good rooms in a restored Greek house, well looked after by its artist owner. The *Güler Hotel* on the front, to the left of the ferry landing (T 0286/697 8844; ❷) – and its similarly priced annex, the *Güler Ada* on Alsancak Sok, inland behind the PTT – is clean, modern and pleasant, with breakfast served by the waterside at the hotel. The *Gümüş Hotel* (T 0286/697 8252, F 697 0052; ❸), close to the ferry behind the harbour restaurants, is situated in an old Greek house with a more modern concrete annex. Some rooms boast original wooden floors and ceilings, while those in the new section have bathroom and TV. *Otel Tena* (T 0286/697 8880, F 697 0270; ❸), on Iğdeli Sok, has rooms with TV and shower in a fine old house, but breakfast is not included. The *Ergin Pansiyon* (T 0286/697 8429; ❷), on Şüran Sok, is visible from the coast road as you walk uphill from the castle and has good clean rooms with bathrooms. At the far end of the esplanade behind the harbour, the *Ege* (T 0286/697 8189, F 697 8389; ❸), on Mektep Sok, is located in a partially restored nineteenth-century Greek school. The rooms are too basic for the price, though some on the top floor have balconies with nice views.

More upmarket than all of these is the *Thenes* (T 0286/697 8888; ❺), 5km round the coast, south of town at **Alaybey**, with its own concreted "beach" and rather basic rooms for the price. Beyond here, the *Güler Pansiyon* (T 0286/697 8454; ❸), on Tekirbahçe Mevkii, is beautifully situated on its own strip of beach, with only vines between it and the sea. Rooms are very simple, but guests have use of a kitchen and there are boats to rent. Finally, **Ayazma** beach has a smattering of small **campsites** with attached restaurants, *Paşa Camping* (T 0286/697 8101) being the pick of the crop, well known for its freshly caught fish dishes.

Eating and drinking

There are numerous **restaurants** grouped around the harbour, mostly offering seafood. Of these, *Paşa* is particularly good, offering a quality selection of fresh fish, *güveç* (fish stew) and *mezes* including a fine sautéed calamari. Further east along the harbour street *Lisa's Café* serves an impressive range of wines together with favourites such as *mantı* and mouth-watering chocolate cake – there are occasional exhibitions of paintings here by resident island artists. The most stylish place for evening **drinking** is the *Salhane Bar*, along the coast behind the castle. *Polenta Café*, meanwhile, between the park and the quay, attempts to cater for the European market with Italian coffee and outdoor seating.

Local seafood is usually accompanied by the ubiquitous island **wine**. Traditional grapes include the white Vasilaki and Chavush (sweet table grapes) and the red Karasakez and Karalahna. Good brands include Ataol (try the '95 and '96 reds, '99 and 2000 whites, and 2001 rosé), Yunatular and Talay. The Talay **bottling plant** is at the back of Kale, up the hill behind the school. It is open to visitors and sells its own brand at half shop prices.

Troy

But Aunt Dot could only think how Priam and Hecuba would have been vexed to see the state it had all got into and no one seeming to care anymore. She thought the nations ought to go on working at it and dig it all up again, and perhaps do some reconstruction, for she belonged to the reconstruction school, and would have liked to see Troy's walls and towers rising once more against the sky like a Hollywood Troy, and the wooden horse standing beside them, opening mechanically every little while to show that it was full of armed Greeks.

Rose Macaulay, *The Towers of Trebizond* (1990)

Although by no means the most spectacular archeological site in Turkey, **TROY**, thanks to Homer, is probably the most celebrated. Known as Truva in Turkish, the remains of the ancient city lie around 20km south of Çanakkale, just west of the main road. It's a scanty affair on the whole, but if you lower your expectations and use your imagination, you may well be impressed. The ruins are now a lot less obscure than previously: using modern scientific methods to try to fill in the gaps left by earlier excavations, recent work led by Dr Manfred Korfman has served to clarify the site greatly, to the extent that laypeople can now at least grasp the basic layout and gain a knowledge of the different settlement periods discovered.

Some history

Until 1871 Troy was generally thought to have existed in legend only. The Troad plain, where the ruins lie, was known to be associated with the Troy that Homer wrote about in the *Iliad*, but all traces of the city had vanished completely. In 1868 **Heinrich Schliemann** (1822–1890), a German businessman who had made his fortune in America, obtained permission from the Ottoman government to start digging on a hill known to the Turks as Hisarlık, where earlier excavators had already found the remains of a Classical temple and signs of further, older ruins.

Schliemann was born into a poor Mecklenburg family and became obsessed at an early age with the myths of ancient Greece. Unable to pursue the interest professionally (although he did teach himself ancient Greek, in addition to several modern languages), he amassed his considerable fortune during the Californian Gold Rush of 1849, forsaking commerce at the age of 46 to become the world's most celebrated and successful amateur archeologist.

Schliemann's sloppy trenching work resulted in a certain amount of damage to the site, only rectified by the first professional archeologist to work at Troy, the respected Carl William Blegen, whose excavations began in 1932. Schliemann was also accountable for removing the so-called **Treasure of Priam**, a large cache of beautiful jewellery that was taken back to Berlin and subsequently displayed there until 1941, when it was squirrelled away for safety under Zoo Station. The hoard disappeared during the Red Army's sacking of the city in May 1945; long suspected of having been spirited back to the USSR, it resurfaced spectacularly in Moscow in August 1993. A legal tussle between Germany and the Russian Federation to determine ownership is now in progress – as well as careful forensic examination of the precious items to answer allegations that Schliemann fraudulently assembled the treasure from scattered sites in Asia Minor.

Whatever Schliemann's shortcomings, his initial, unsystematic excavations did uncover nine layers of remains, representing distinct and consecutive city developments that span four millennia. The oldest, **Troy I**, dates back to about 3600 BC and was followed by four similar settlements. Either Troy VI or VII is thought to have been **the city described by Homer**: the former is known to have been destroyed by an earthquake in about 1275 BC, while the latter shows signs of having been wiped out by fire about a quarter of a century later, around the time historians generally estimate the Trojan War to have taken place. **Troy VIII**, which thrived from 700 to 300 BC, was a Greek foundation, while much of the final layer of development, **Troy IX** (300 BC to 300 AD), was built during the heyday of the Roman empire.

Although there's no way of being absolutely sure that the **Trojan War** did take place, there's a fair amount of circumstantial evidence suggesting that the city was the scene of some kind of armed conflict, even if it wasn't the ten-year struggle described in the *Iliad*. It's possible that Homer's epic is based on a number of wars fought between the Mycenaean Greeks and the inhabitants of Troy, who, it seems, were alternately trading partners and commercial rivals. Homer's version of events, however, dispensed with these pedestrian possibilities, turning the war into a full-scale heroic drama, complete with bit parts for the ancient Greek gods.

The site

The **site** (daily: May–Sept 8am–7pm; Oct–April 8am–5pm; $7) is signalled by the ticket office – marked "Gişe" – just opposite the dolmuş drop-off point. It's well worth buying a copy of Dr Manfred Korfman's *A Tour of Troia* ($9) from a small shop by the entrance to the site, consisting of two books and a map, which will guide you around with pages of information corresponding to numbers on the signs at the site.

From the ticket office a long, straight road leads to a giant **wooden horse** (which would have delighted Macaulay's fictional Aunt Dot) and the **excavation house**, with a scale model of the site and an excellent video explaining the history of Troy and the excavations. Just beyond is the ruined city itself, a craggy outcrop overlooking the Troad plain, which extends about 8km to the sea. The circular trail takes you around the site, the twelve panels enlisting the help of schematic diagrams, going some way to bringing the ruins to life. It's a bleak spot, however, leaving you in no doubt as to the thinness of Troy's remains, but as you stand on what's left of the ramparts and look across the plain that stretches out at your feet, it's not too difficult to imagine a besieging army, legendary or otherwise, camped below.

Most impressive of the extant remains are the **east wall and gate** from Troy VI (1700–1275 BC), of which 330m remain, curving around the eastern and southern flanks of the city. The inward-leaning walls, 6m high and over 4m thick, would have been surmounted by an additional brick section. A ramp paved with flat stones from Troy II (2500–2300 BC), which would have led to the citadel entrance, also stands out. It was near here that Schliemann found what he believed to be Priam's treasure, using the evidence that Troy II had been burned down in a fire to come to the erroneous conclusion that this was Homer's city. Just inside the citadel entrance is the most impressive of the dwellings unearthed at Troy, the **Pillar House**, dating from Troy VI.

The most important monument of Roman Troy IX, or Ilium, is the **temple of Athena**, which was rebuilt on a promise of Alexander the Great by his general, Lysimachus, after Alexander himself had visited the temple and left his armour as a gift. Remains found by Schliemann proved the temple to be of the Doric order, and fragments of its coffered ceiling can still be seen on site. The most famous relief from the temple, however, depicting Apollo astride four pawing stallions, is now in Berlin. Troy was an important religious centre during Greek and Roman times, and the remains of two other **sanctuaries**, which were also renovated after the visit of Alexander the Great, can be seen at the westernmost point of the site. It's thought that the female deities Cybele and Demeter were worshipped here, because the layout, with altar and grandstand, is similar to the sanctuary in Pergamon.

Practicalities

Çanakkale is the most sensible base for seeing Troy. A couple of companies there offer **guided tours** for around $15–20 (see p.278) and may tell you that there is no dolmuş service to the site. In fact, **dolmuşes** run every twenty minutes from Çanakkale (from the minibus garage, opposite the fairground on Atatürk Caddesi) to the village of **Tefvikiye**, which sits at the gates of the site; it's a thirty-minute ride. If you're moving on further south, the best option is to take the Troy–Çanakkale minibus and jump off at the junction with the main road. From here, you can hop on to any passing southbound bus.

There is **accommodation** in Tevfikiye, in the form of the overpriced *Hisarlık Hotel* (☏0286/283 0026, ℻283 0087; ❷), with attached restaurant and bar, just before the ticket office on the road to the site.

Alexandria Troas

About 20km to the south of Troy, a minor road leaves the highway at Ezine and runs a further 15km down towards the coast to the extensive ruins of the ancient city of **Alexandria Troas**. There are **dolmuşes** every hour from Çanakkale's minibus garage to the small wayside town of Ezine, from where you take either the dolmuş to the holiday village of Dalyan, just before the ruins, or the less frequent service to Gülpınar (see p.288), which passes right by.

The city was founded in about 300 BC by Antigonus I, a general of Alexander the Great and ruler of one of the successor kingdoms established when Alexander's empire finally broke up. Antigonus forced the inhabitants of the surrounding area to move into his city, which he named Antigonia after himself. His stab at immortality was unsuccessful: Lysimachus, king of Macedonia, conquered Antigonia, after killing Antigonus and his son

Demetrius in battle, and renamed the city Alexandria Troas in honour of Alexander the Great. And it's by that name that it appears in the Bible, one of the ports of call of St Paul, who during his travels around Anatolia and Greece, chose to walk the 50km from Troas to Assos, rather than sail round the cape with his companions.

Apparently much of the thousand-acre city remained intact until as late as 1764, when the British traveller and antiquarian Richard Chandler visited and reported having seen substantial city walls and fortifications, enclosing what he assumed to be a ruined temple. A German and Turkish university collaboration plans to renew excavations at some point in the future, but as they stand today, the **ruins** (always open; $0.70 admission if the ticket booth is staffed), although spread over a vast area, are none too spectacular. As Eric Newby wrote in *On the Shores of the Mediterranean*, "it was perfectly possible . . . to walk into it through one of the now enormous gaps in the walls and walk out through a similar gap on the far side, without, apart from tripping over some low-lying remains or else bumping into something shrouded in vegetation which loomed unidentifiable overhead, seeing much of Alexandria Troas at all."

Gülpınar and Babakale

Heading south of Alexandria Troas you pass through some of the most fertile agricultural land in western Turkey, interspersed with tiny, unspoilt villages and dotted with ancient remains. The beautiful coastal road as far as Gülpınar is flat, well tarmacked and usually deserted – ideal for cycling, though four dolmuşes a day make the fifty-kilometre trip from Ezine to Gülpınar, where you change for the remaining 9km to Babakale. There's also an infrequent service to Gülpınar from the east, from Ayvacık, which passes out of Assos parallel to the ancient paved road and on through more barren, hillier country marked by attractive villages built of the local andesite rock.

Gülpınar

GÜLPINAR is notable mainly as the site of the **Temple of Apollo Smintheos**, signposted at the western edge of the village. The shrine is dedicated to one of the more bizarre manifestations of the god, as Lord of Mice. When the original Cretan colonists found themselves harassed by mice, they remembered a previous oracle advising them to settle wherever overrun by the "sons of earth". This they took to mean the rodents, founding the now mostly vanished ancient town of Chryse around the temple. Of the remaining Hellenistic temple, oddly aligned northeast, scarcely more remains, just the platform and some column stumps. It's an atmospheric, lonely site, with detailed on-site explanation panels and is well worth the detour.

Gülpınar itself is a bustling, friendly place, seemingly at odds with its remote position. There are a few reasonable eateries, a couple of beer houses and a single *pansiyon*. However, you might as well push on the 9km southwest to Babakale.

Babakale

BABAKALE – working fishing port and westernmost point of Asia – is one of the best-kept secrets on Turkey's Aegean coast and the perfect place to chill out. Referred to in the *Iliad* as Cape Lekton, and dominated by a fine, eighteenth-century Ottoman castle, it is still almost unknown to the chattering classes of İstanbul who flock to nearby Assos.

The village takes its name in part from the **castle** (always open; free), or *kale*, and part from a dervish saint (*baba* – literally "father") whose tomb is in the small graveyard next to the main square. There are some other Ottoman remains, such as a mosque, whose outer walls are curiously decorated with Ottoman gravestones, and a couple of carved marble *çeşme* (drinking fountains). The only local **beach** is about 3km before the port, overlooked by holiday villas, although the rocks on either side of Babakale harbour are ideal for swimming and are well populated with marine life.

Babakale boasts a handful of very reasonable **hotels** ranged on the hillside above the harbour, which tend to fill at weekends, when you may find rooms more expensive. All have their own restaurants offering fresh, locally caught fish. Most reasonably priced is the *Karayel* (☎0286/747 0497, ℻747 0358; ❶), which offers basic rooms with bathroom. The next-door *Uran Motel* (☎0286/747 0218; ❷) offers similar facilities, with the added attraction of a rooftop terrace. The *Lekton Motel* (☎0286/747 0281; ❷), further along, has pleasantly furnished three-person rooms with bathrooms.

Ayvacık

Thirty kilometres south of Ezine lies the market town of **AYVACIK**, gateway to the Classical settlement of Assos. No question but the best time to be in town is Friday – **market day** – when the local people, mostly settled *Yörük* nomads, converge from the surrounding villages to trade their produce at stalls adjacent to the *otogar* and ticket offices. It's a particularly noisy and colourful affair, worth spending some time at between minibus connections: women in traditional patterned *şalvar* (baggy pantaloons) and headscarves sell all kinds of fruit and vegetables, honey, cheese and pre-prepared *börek*. Late April in Ayvacık sees the more extensive annual **Paniyir**, a traditional gathering of the region's nomadic peoples, which revolves around drinking, dancing and horse-trading. Although the nomads are nominally Muslim the festival itself is probably descended from pagan celebrations for the arrival of spring, which pre-date even ancient Greece.

It's not likely that you'll find much else to detain you in town, although Ayvacık is the headquarters of the co-operative **DOBAG carpet project**, based in premises opposite the Elif petrol station on the Çanakkale road, on the outskirts of town. The project has had a profound effect on the Turkish carpet industry (see box on p.290), though it's worth noting that the cooperative only markets its products abroad – carpets sold in the Friday market in Ayvacık (and elsewhere in the bazaars of Turkey) may be produced in the area, but are not those of DOBAG. Another cooperative, **Yörük Hale**, sells reliable quality carpets – cheaper than DOBAG – from a small shop opposite the *otogar*.

There are hourly **buses** to the town from Çanakkale, and there's no reason to stay in Ayvacık with Assos (see p.290) so close; four or five dolmuşes a day run on there from the *otogar*. There are no **banks** in Assos, so Ayvacık is the place to exchange money if you need to.

DOBAG carpets

The **DOBAG carpet project** was initiated by a German schoolteacher and doctor of chemistry, **Harold Böhmer** who, together with his wife Renate, became interested in Turkish carpets while working in İstanbul in the 1960s. Returning in the 1970s, he started analysing traditional carpet dyes to try and find out why some older rugs were more attractive than newer ones, whose colours either faded to mud grey or remained garish. Böhmer discovered that older rugs used **traditional vegetable dyes**, while many of those made after the 1880 were coloured with **artificial analine dyes**, which had come to Turkey from Europe, primarily Germany.

Next came the more difficult task of trying to find out which plants had produced the more attractive natural colours. For the most part these turned out to grow wild in Anatolia, including: madder (*Rubia tinctorum*), a reed-like plant whose roots produce shades ranging from light red to violet; weld (*Reseda luteola*), one of around twenty plants that can produce yellow dye; as well as extract of oak apples and acorn cups mixed with iron, which produces black. The only exception was the blue produced by natural indigo (from the plant *Indigofera*), which was imported into the region from India as early as Roman times.

In 1981, Böhmer initiated the **Doğal Boya Araştırma ve Geliştirme Projesi** (natural dye research and development project). After devising commercial techniques for the preparation of dyes in a village setting, his newfound methods were taught to the nomads of Ayvacık. The vast majority of plants used in the dyeing process are now farmed in the region (the one exception being indigo).

The project is run as a **workers' cooperative** and under Turkish law only producers are allowed to be members. Thus, it's entirely run by the village women who do all the weaving, as well as choosing their own colours and patterns, adapted from traditional designs. Standards are high, and only carpets that retain their lustre (ie, those made from the best-quality, handspun long stapler winter wool and dyes) are accepted by DOBAG. A square metre of a DOBAG carpet has a hundred thousand knots, and consequently costs around $380. A second, similar project has been set up in Yuntdağ, near Manisa.

Although small in themselves, the two projects have had a far-reaching effect on the **Turkish carpet sector**, and it's now almost impossible to find any carpet-seller admitting that artificial dyes have been used in his products. But that doesn't mean they're all natural – many manufacturers simply switched to more sophisticated chemical dyes that give subtler shades and produce the sought-after "faded" effect.

Assos and around

Situated on and around the ancient Greek city of the same name, **ASSOS**, 25km south of Ayvacık, is a charmingly preserved old village where no new buildings are permitted and old buildings may only be restored using the attractive local stone. **Ancient Assos** sits on top of a steep rocky hill and spreads down the seaward side towards the Aegean. Modern Assos consists of two parts – the village of **Behramkale**, which wraps itself around the top rear of the hill, and the tiny settlement of former warehouses and fishing cottages grouped around the **harbour** below – but most people, including locals, just refer to it collectively as Assos. Further along the coast, 4km east of Assos, lies the fine shingle beach of **Kadırga**, though getting here can be difficult without your own vehicle.

Undiscovered until the mid-1980s, when it became an inexpensive bolt-hole for the İstanbul literati, Assos these days is anything but cheap.

Accommodation prices and availability fluctuate violently – on summer weekends booking in advance is essential, although on weekdays, and in May or late season, you can still find the place close to deserted, with its inimitable charm intact and rooms at realistic prices (though you should still make a point of bargaining). The ruins themselves attract a fair number of coach tours, but thankfully few stop overnight, leaving the village relatively peaceful by evening.

There are between four and five **dolmuşes** a day to Assos from Ayvacık. Be warned, though, that during the low season and at slack times they may take a couple of hours to fill, so if there are a few of you waiting it may be worth offering to pay for an early departure (it's roughly $1 per person and the minibus won't leave with fewer than eight).

The journey is through beautiful hills covered with olive trees and the Mediterranean oak, whose acorn cups are used to produce a substance for tanning leather, the export of which was the main business of Assos until early last century. The final stretch passes a fourteenth-century, hump-backed **Ottoman bridge**, built with masonry from the ancient settlement, and then leads up into the village square where local women sell traditional embroidery and women from surrounding *Yörük* villages sell small carpets.

Ancient Assos and Behramkale

According to some sources, Assos was the site of a thirteenth-century BC Hittite colony, although the earliest traces only really date from the eighth century, when Greek colonists from neighbouring Lesbos (Lésvos) established a settlement, later building a huge temple to Athena in 540 BC. Hermias, a eunuch and disciple of Plato, ruled here, attempting to put Plato's theories of the ideal city-state into practice. From 347 to 344 BC Aristotle made his home in Assos as the guest of Hermias, developing his philosophy further before the arrival of the Persians forced him to flee. Assos was also purportedly the source of much of the wealth of Croesus. During medieval times, the Ottomans plundered the town for dressed stone, as did local villagers. The site was only rediscovered in 1880 when it was stumbled on by a 25-year-old American, Francis Bacon. He returned in 1881 to conduct extensive excavations sponsored by the Antiquarian Society of Boston.

Take the road into the upper village until you reach the **Murat Hüdavendigar Camii**, an austere fourteenth-century mosque that probably began as a church, built with stone quarried from the earlier settlement. Beyond is the enclosed site of the sixth-century **Temple of Athena** (open daylight hours; $1.50), with Doric columns re-erected by an American university archeological team, and a partially rebuilt antique theatre. Unfortunately, both make use of unsightly concrete in places where the original stone proved insufficient. Anyway, it's still beautiful, although overshadowed somewhat by views to Lésvos and over the Gulf of Edremit.

The rest of ancient Assos is a jumble of ruins falling away from the temple, enclosed by the old and partly intact **city wall**, which is accented with towers and quite impressive. The most recognizable part is the old **necropolis**, littered with sarcophagi, which can be viewed on the way down from the village to the harbour.

Dolmuşes from Ayvacık call first at the upper village, dropping passengers in the small square.

The two cheapest *pansiyons* – *Tekin* (☎0286/721 7099; ❶) and *Sidar* (☎0286/721 7041; ❶) – lie on the road back out of the village, but this is one place where it pays to spend a little more, as **accommodation** in the upper village is much better value than down around the harbour. By the bridge is the *Old Bridge House Pension* (☎0286/721 7426, ✉oldbridgehouse @yahoo.com; ❸), which offers tastefully decorated rooms in a house personally designed by the Turkish/Dutch owners Cem and Diana. There are also beds in a windowless, airless dorm ($8), as well as a hammock garden, internet access and a moped for rent. In the village itself, just downhill from the ruins, *Timur Restaurant & Pansiyon* (☎0286/721 7449; ✉timurpansiyon@yahoo.com; ❸) has four small double rooms – two with bathrooms – in a beautifully restored 200-year-old house, with a walled garden and restaurant affording superb views over the coastline to Greece. Just around the corner, the *Eris Pansiyon* (☎0286/721 7080; ❸), owned by a retired American couple, offers local charm and five rooms with views north over the valley. Take the left lane at the square to find the *Assos Konukevi* (☎0286/721 7081; ❸), whose high-quality apartments have a large lounge, double bedroom and one single bedroom, superb views and a large walled garden. The *Dolunay* (☎0286/721 7172; ❷), next to the dolmuş stop in the centre of the village, is also attractive and comfortable, with an attached restaurant.

For good-value **food** there are a number of cheap *lokanta*s selling typical village dishes such as *mantı* and *gözleme*, washed down with a glass of *ayran*. The *Timur Restaurant* provides an unforgettable setting for tasty meals or just a drink.

Assos harbour

Having called at the upper village, the dolmuşes from Ayvacık then run down to **Assos harbour**, where they wait for return custom. It's well worth the twenty-minute walk down in any case, which will afford breathtaking views out over the Aegean to Lesbos. Despite the harbour, there's little yacht trade here and crossing to Greece is illegal, which probably explains the *jandarma* post down on the quayside.

The harbour is very compact and you'll have no trouble locating **accommodation**. A budget option is the *Dr No Pansiyon* (☎0286/721 7101; ❷), with simple, small doubles. *Plaj Pansiyon* (☎0286/721 7193; ❹), a group of small waterfront wooden chalets with basic shared bathrooms, seems expensive but the price includes breakfast and dinner. Next to it, *Hotel Mehtap* (☎0286/721 7221; ❸) also has basic rooms fronting the beach, but this time with en-suite hot-water bathrooms. Going up a notch, the *Küçük Ev* (☎0286/721 7011; ❹) is a nicely restored old village house, set back from the harbour. The immaculate, well-run *Behram* (☎0286/721 7016, ✉hotelbehram@yahoo.com; ❺), just as you enter the harbour area, is usually amenable to negotiation and has friendly service that belies its size; it's well worth the extra for a room overlooking the harbour.

If you're prepared to pay a bit more, consider the larger hotels, which offer reasonable half-board options. The grandest choices are the *Hotel Assos* (☎0286/721 7017, ✆721 7249; ❹), whose rooms are plainer than the exterior suggest, and the rather aloof *Assos Kervansaray* (☎0286/721 7093, ✆721 7200; ❼), with old-fashioned doubles. There are also four small **campsites** – just follow the lane through the harbour – which let space for a few dollars a night; *Erdoğan* camping will also rent you a tent for around $5.

Most of the hotels have good **restaurants**, serving excellent fish meals. The restaurant at the *Hotel Assos* has tables overlooking the water, though diners are in danger of forking a wing mirror rather than their food due to the proximity of the lane. Both the *Plaj Pansiyon* and the *Hotel Mehtap* have beachfront restaurants, while *Dr No Pansiyon* is the only cheaper option, serving reasonable *pide* and kebab meals. The *Feverlihan Restaurant*, next door to the *jandarma*, is one of the quietest spots, with dinner priced at around $13 plus drinks.

Kadırga

Less than an hour away on foot from Assos harbour is the beach resort of **KADİRGA**. Simply head east along the coastal footpath and cut across the headland by the ugly holiday village. Kadırga is also accessible by a paved four-kilometre road signposted from the upper village.

The beach itself is reasonable, over a kilometre of fine shingle and by Turkish standards still relatively undeveloped – but that means no showers. Currently, there are about half a dozen **accommodation** options lining the beach, mostly at the Assos end of the beach. Least pretentious is the spick-and-span *Huzur Otel* (☎0286/721 7189; ❸). More upmarket are the friendly *Assos Park Hotel* (☎0286/721 7163, ⓦwww.assospark.com; ❹), with extensive landscaped gardens, and the *Yildiz Saray* (☎0286/721 7204, ⓕ721 7025; ❹), the last offering double rooms with TV, and half-board is included. There is also a smattering of well-placed **campsites** including the large *Sahil Camping & Restaurant* (☎0286/721 7050), which rents out tents for $5, and *Kadirga 93 Camping* (☎0286/721 7321).

Well worth knowing about, and not properly shown on most maps, is the twenty-kilometre **shore road** east from Kadırga to Küçükkuyu (see below). Though narrow, it is entirely paved, travelled by the occasional dolmuş (or mountain bike) and it allows you to bypass the tortuous mountain curves of the main inland route.

Along the Gulf of Edremit

From Ayvacık, the main Çanakkale–İzmir road winds through pine-forested hills, offering occasional glimpses out across the **Gulf of Edremit**. The road straightens out at **Küçükkuyu**, the first major settlement and the only real town, before continuing past a succession of small resorts to the transport hub of **Edremit** itself.

Küçükkuyu

The small fishing port of **KÜÇÜKKUYU** – 20km southeast of Ayvacık – still has a fleet in evidence, and there are plenty of reasonable seafood restaurants. It's mostly Turkish tourists who swim from the nearby beaches, while on Fridays farmers from the surrounding villages come here to sell their produce at the street market.

The few **hotels** are affordable and never more than a few minutes' walk from the sea. Near the port, the *Marina Hotel* (☎0286/752 5686; ❷) is worth trying, though most of the actual beachfront premises are west of town, along the start of the minor coast road to Kadırga (see above). There are also a few **campsites** in the area, including *Filiz Camping*, *Truva*, *Kuçuk Kuyu Kamping* and *Zeus Motel Camping*.

East of Küçükkuyu a series of small resorts – one with the baldly descriptive name of Moteller ("motels") – is unlikely to appeal to foreigners. You're best off staying in your vehicle until Akçay, the next place of any size.

Akçay

From the main road, where long-distance buses will drop you (Edremit-bound dolmuşes continue to the centre), it's about a ten-minute walk into **AKÇAY**, a resort frequented by middle-class Turks. The hotels, restaurants and discos are packed during the school summer holidays, but deadly quiet out of season. The seafront is pleasant but otherwise there's nothing of interest unless you develop a hankering to see with what discreet charm bourgeois Turkey spends its summer.

The **tourist office** is on Edremit Caddesi (Mon–Fri 8.30am–noon & 1.30–5pm), clearly signposted on the left as you walk into town along the main road. With high demand in peak season, Akçay **hotels** are not particularly cheap. *Otel Linda* at Barbaros Meydanı (☎0266/384 3500, ⓔdemratour @hotmail.com; ❷) – opposite the PTT – has basic rooms (though with a balcony and sea view) and congenial hosts. *Otel Ozsoy* along the waterfront (☎0266/384 1190, Ⓕ384 2190; ❷) offers much the same, but it's just that bit closer to the beach.

The seafront esplanade abounds with cheap fast-food **cafés** and fish **restaurants** – the large *Tuana* is a popular example. Taner Nuran Sokak in the centre has numerous *lokantas*, *kebab* and *pide salonus*, such as the recommended *Faruk* where you can eat fish or meat. *Atlas* just off the seafront is one of the few dedicated **bars** in the area catering to a young mixed crowd.

Edremit

Easily reached by dolmuş from Akçay, **EDREMİT** is the Adramyttium of the *Iliad*, which was sacked by Achilles. After destroying the town, Achilles kidnapped Chryseis, the daughter of the priest at the Temple of Apollo Smintheos (see "Gülpınar", p.288), only to have her claimed by Agamemnon, leader of the Greek force. This provoked the "wrath of Achilles" (more like a long-drawnout sulk), one of the major subplots of the *Iliad*.

These days the legends far outshine the reality of the place and you're most likely to stop in Edremit only for services such as post and banks, as these are not widely available in the coastal resorts. Edremit is a major public transport node, with buses to destinations all over Turkey, including services 70km east to the provincial capital of Balıkesir (where you can pick up the İzmir–Bandırma train). The **otogar** is 800m out of town on Yılmaz Akpınar Bulvarı.

Should you get caught between connections you might require **rooms**, and those at the *Otel Balgçılar*, Menderes Bul 63 (☎0266/374 2255; ❷), opposite the Yunus Emre park, are pretty good value. Menderes Bulvarı – the main thoroughfare – is also location of the main **PTT** (summer 9am–11pm; winter 9am–7pm) and a couple of ATMs.

Ören

From Burhaniye, 14km south of Edremit, there are dolmuşes to **ÖREN**, another 4km northwest, a small resort popular with Turkish holidaymakers. During the summer you can also reach Ören by boat from Akçay (check with the tourist office in Akçay for current details).

Ören has a beautiful **beach** overlooked by Kaz Dağı, the ancient Mount Ida. It's a much smaller and sleepier town than Akçay, with development restricted to the outlying areas. In the centre there is little new building allowed, leaving space for flower-filled gardens and pine-covered walks between old-fashioned holiday villas. As with Akçay, though, the place is all but deserted once the schools go back. The town has a long history of wine- and olive-oil production, dating back to the Greek occupation, and there's an annual **olive festival** held between August 16 and 18.

There's a **tourist kiosk** (Mon–Fri 8.30am–noon & 1.30–5pm) next to the police station and the small *otogar*, while **accommodation** possibilities are mainly located on Çarşı Caddesi, the street running from the *otogar* to the beach. The *Kösem* (℡0266/416 3230; ❶) is friendly, if a little jaded. Nestling under the pine walkway to the beach is the *Pekcan Motel* (℡0266/416 3180; ❷), with small, but fairly modern rooms. There's also a **campsite**, 300m south of the centre on the main road, best thought of as a last resort.

For good-value food, head for the **market** that runs parallel to Çarşı Caddesi, where stands dish up *pide* and *lahmacun*, baked potatoes and kebabs. At the top of the lane, furthest from the beach, is the *Mesudun* **restaurant** with pleasant outdoor tables. Back towards the beach, the *Ida Yörük Çadiri* is a small café/bar under a large nomadic awning, with low tables, cushioned seating and *nargile*.

Ayvalık and around

AYVALİK, 56km south of Edremit, is growing in popularity with Turkish and European visitors for the charm of its cobbled streets lined with picturesque old Greek houses. In stark contrast to the resorts to the south that have been completely taken over by the holiday trade, the town has retained a fishing fleet, as well as its traditional crafts and markets, and tourism feels like just another string to its bow. The closest good beaches are in the recently developed resort of Sarımsaklı, with some remoter, less sandy ones on the island of Alibey, both easily reached from town. Ayvalık is also convenient for ruin-spotting at nearby Bergama – to which there's a fine back-country drive – and stands opposite the Greek island of Lésvos, connected to town in summer by a regular ferry service.

Ayvalık started life as the **Ottoman Greek settlement** of Kydonaie around three or four centuries ago. Both Turkish and Greek names refer to orchards of quince, the rock-hard pear-shaped fruit that grows all round the region but hardly features in its cuisine. In the late eighteenth century the town was granted special concessions by the then grand vizier, Cezayirli Hasan Paşa, who, as a captain in the Ottoman navy twenty years earlier, had been rescued by the Greeks of Ayvalık following a disastrous defeat at the hands of the Russian navy. The town grew to become the most prosperous and imposing on the Aegean coast after İzmir, boasting an academy, a publishing house and around twenty Orthodox churches, many of which still remain. The exchange of populations that followed the Greek–Turkish war of 1920–1922 saw the expulsion of the town's Greek Orthodox inhabitants and the conversion of the largest churches into mosques. Ironically, most of the people resettled here after 1923 were Greek-speaking Muslims from Crete and Mytilini (Lésvos), and many of Ayvalık's older inhabitants still speak Greek.

Arrival, information and tours

There are regular direct **buses** to Ayvalik along the main highway, either south from Çanakkale via Edremit, or north from İzmir. Unless explicitly stated these

AYVALIK

① ②

Ⓑ ③
Ⓒ ③ ⑤
④

Lesvos
(Greece)

N

0   200 m

Alibey
(Cunda)

Customs

See inset

*AEGEAN
SEA*

ACCOMMODATION

Ayvalık	1
Aziz Arslan	4
Bonjour	6
Chez Beliz	8
Kaptan	5
Kıyı	3
Taksiyarhis	7
Yalı	2

RESTAURANTS & BARS

Anadolu	A
Cennet Koya Sahil	G
Gaziantep	F
Kytaro Club	C
Osmanlı	E
Paşale	D
Sokak	B

Ⓐ
Ⓓ
Ⓔ

Ⓕ

Taksiyarhis
Kilisesi ⑥
⑦

Saatlı
Cami

Çınarlı
Cami

BAZAAR

★ Buses to
Sarımsaklı
& Şeytan
Sofrasi

İSKELE
MEYD.

ⓘ

ATATÜRK CAD

İzmir & Bergama ▼

Ⓖ *Çamlık, Sarımsaklı, Şeytan Sofrası & Sözer*

intercity buses will drop you 5km out of town at the Ayvalık highway junction. The main **otogar** is 1.5km north of the town centre, though any red-and-white city bus labelled "Çamlık" will take you into town for about $0.25. Ayvalık is a fairly small place and most of what you'll need is concentrated around **İskele Meydanı**, the small plaza with the Atatürk bust. Northbound buses coming from İzmir usually pass through the square and will drop you here if you ask.

The **tourist office** is in a booth on İskele Meydanı (May–Sept daily 9am–1pm & 2–7pm; ☎0266/312 3158), while just north of the square you'll find the banks, PTT and most midtown bus company offices.

From the fishing-harbour quay, regular summer ferries run across to **Alibey** (Cunda) island (see p.299), a vastly preferable route to the circuitous city bus trip there (across the bridge from the mainland). There are also seasonal **boat** tours ($5, includes lunch) around the other local islands, which last around six hours, taking in stops for swimming and sightseeing at Alibey harbour. Plenty of boats tout for custom between around 9.30am and 11am every morning, near the tourist office.

Ferries to Lésvos

There's a **ferry service to Lésvos** in Greece in summer, but schedules are the least reliable of any of the Greek island–Turkish mainland crossings. Moreover, you have to do the outward and return journeys with the same boat, whether Turkish or Greek. Given the short distance involved, prices are astronomical ($40 one-way, $50 return; cars $70; plus a $10 port tax on arrival in Greece), a reflection of the official policy on both sides to discourage travel between the two countries. Three agencies deal with the crossing (see "Listings", p.298) and the service runs from May to September, with six boats a week leaving Ayvalık at 9am and returning at 4pm. Departures are from the **ferry terminal** near the Customs building, 250m north of the fishing-harbour quay.

Accommodation

Down by the water, **Gümrük Meydanı**, a once-dilapidated district of old Greek mansions and stone-built warehouses, is being swiftly restored. If hotels around here or in town's **back streets** are full, you'll have to extend your search to the south, to the suburb of Çamlık, where a number of modest *pansiyon*s are clearly marked from the coast road (and where the summer villas of late nineteenth-century İzmir Greeks still peek out from between the pines). There are reports of taxi drivers taking unsuspecting tourists to a different hotel than the one requested; a firm yet polite insistence should clear up any "misunderstanding".

The back streets

Bonjour Pansiyon Maraşal Çakmak Cad, Beşinci Çeşme Sok 6 ℡0266/312 8085. Occupies one of the grandest houses in town; beautifully renovated with a charming courtyard where breakfast is served. ❸

Chez Beliz Pansiyon Maraşal Çakmak Cad 28, Fethiye Mah ℡0266/312 4897, ℻312 4609. Based in the family home of charming ex-actress Beliz, who provides inclusive breakfasts and lavish dinners at $12 a head. The interior is comfortable (though the rooms are basic, with no en-suites), and there's a nice garden courtyard where dinner is served. It's a stiff 10–15min uphill walk from town. ❸

Taksiyarhis Pansiyon Marasal Çakmak Cad 71 ℡0266/312 1494. One of the best pensions on the Aegean Coast, each room harmoniously decorated by Jasmin, the owner, and featuring two terraces and a kitchen for guests. The serene former Greek house, immediately behind the church of the same name, also serves as an information centre, bike-rental outlet and book exchange. Booking essential in summer. ❶

Gümrük Meydanı

Ayvalık Palas Gümrük Meyd ℡0266/312 1064, ℻312 7333. En-suite rooms with balconies overlooking the sea, buffet breakfast included. It also doubles as the office of the Ayvalık Diving Centre. ❸

Aziz Arslan Otel Gümrük Meyd ℡0266/312 5331, ℻312 6888. One of the cheaper waterfront options – a large hotel with ample rooms though fairly nondescript decor. ❷

Hotel Kaptan Balıkhane Sok 7 ℡0266/312 8834, ℻312 1271. These comfortable yet faded rooms are all en suite, some with air-con, some with sea views, and there's a seaside terrace where breakfast is served. ❸

Kıyı Motel Gümrük Meyd ℡0266/312 6677. Standard-issue 1970s-vintage Turkish hotel, though the owners try hard to please. Among the cheapest downtown lodgings, it's good value as all rooms are en suite with TVs and minibars. ❶

Yalı Behind the PTT ℡0266/312 2423. Large high-ceilinged rooms, antiques and a lush garden have recreated the ambience of a *fin-de-siècle* merchant's house. ❷

The Town

Ayvalık presents the spectacle – almost unique in the Aegean – of an almost perfectly preserved Ottoman Greek market town, its essential nature little changed despite the inroads of commercialization. Riotously painted horse-carts clatter through the cobbled **bazaar**, past the occasional bakery boy roaming the alleys in the early morning selling fresh bread and cakes. In the bazaar itself, crafts are still alive and well, as cobblers, copper- and tinsmiths and watch-repairers ply their trades from ramshackle wooden premises. Ayvalık is also famous for its fine yoghurt, cheese and *kepekli* (wholegrain) bread. Thursday is the special **market day**, when the back streets overflow with produce shipped in from surrounding villages. There's also a daily **fish market** next door to the Alibey ferry terminal, where the local fishermen exhibit the morning's catch. The main **İnönü Caddesi** is the location of numerous factory shops for the region's many olive producers, offering various qualities of olive oil, pickled and salted olives, and rough green olive-oil soap.

There are few other specific sights save for the converted nineteenth-century churches, which punctuate the warren of inland streets. There's little point in asking directions: just use the minarets as landmarks and give yourself over to the pleasure of wandering under numerous wrought-iron window grilles and past ornately carved doorways. The most conspicuous church, Ayios Ioannis, is now the **Saatlı Cami**, renamed after its clocktower. Just north of here and up the hill lies the **Taksiyarhis Kilisesi**, which never converted into a mosque – it's been closed for years, allegedly awaiting restoration as a museum. Southeast of the Saatlı Cami stands ex-Ayios Yioryios, now the **Çınarlı Cami**, mis-named given that not one of the half-dozen trees gracing its courtyard is a plane (*çınar* in Turkish).

Eating and drinking

The choice of **restaurants** in Ayvalık doesn't quite match the variety of hotels and *pansiyon*s. On the seafront, and around the southern end of Gümrük Meydanı, you'll find the usual mix of Turkish fast food, *pide* salons and *lokanta*s, as well as a couple of more expensive fish **restaurants**. Just east of the market on Sefa Caddesi a few **bakeries** produce excellent *helva*-soaked morning pastries. Squeezed amongst the hotels in Gümrük Meydanı the *Bar-Café Sokak* provides evening **drinks** and taped music, as does the *Kytaro Club* next door, with cosy seating overlooking the sea, ideal for watching the last of the sun's rays disappear.

Anadolu Pide ve Kebab Salonu İnönü Cad. Opposite the PTT, this serves nine different sorts of kebab, including *beyti* and *İskender* and delicious *pide*, unbeatable at $2.

Cennet Koya Sahil 3km south of Ayvalık, on the Sarımsaklı road. A worthwhile stop if you're returning late from the beach, this fish restaurant makes an ideal location for an enchanting meal with tables built out over the waterline.

Gaziantep Pide Talat Paşa Cad. *Pide* and spicy kebab specialities.

Osmanlı Mutfağı Talat Paşa Cad. Offers superior *lokanta*-style dishes, including filling meat stews and *köfte*.

Paşale Down a side street off Mareşal Çakmak Cad. This cosy café/bistro specializes in original homemade *çorba* (soup) recipes alongside the more usual *mercimek* (lentil) and *tavuk* (chicken) choices.

Listings

Banks and exchange All the main Turkish banks have branches in town with ATMs. Currency can be changed at *Gunaydın Döviz* on İnönü Cad, trav-

ellers' cheques at the PTT (see opposite).

Car rental Avis, Talatpaşa Cad 67/B ℗ 0266/312 2456; Duke, İskele Meyd, opposite the tourist office ☎0266/312 3794; and Light Rent-a-Car, next to the Lésvos ferry terminal ☎0542/533 0897.

Ferry agencies Tickets to Lésvos from: Ayvalık Tour, also known as Jale, Gümrük Cad 41/A ☎0266/312 2740; Yeni İstanbul Tur, next to the *Aziz Arslan Otel* off Cumhuriyet Meyd ☎0266/312 6123; and Miniotis Tours which has an office in the passage next to the ferry terminal.

Internet Ayvalık has a few small internet cafés,

catering for the games-hungry locals. Easiest to find is *C@fein Café Net*, located on Cumhuriyet Meyd, opposite the tourist office.

Laundry Ak Pak, Edremit Cad 38, is a self-service launderette.

Post office PTT at İnönü Cad, just north of the town centre (Mon–Sat 8am–11pm).

Newspapers There's an astonishing range of English-language newspapers and periodicals on sale at the newspaper booth on Cumhuriyet Meyd.

Sarimsakli

Some of the biggest beaches in the area are 7km south of Ayvalık at **SARIM-SAKLI** ("Garlic Beach"), a local resort accessible by frequent dolmuşes from the stand just south of İskele Meydanı. The sandy shore here is attractive, getting less crowded and developed as you head away from town in either direction along its three-to-four-kilometre length.

You could stay here too – there are plenty of big tourist **hotels** – but, in season at least, most of these cost an arm and a leg. A well-sited budget choice on the waterfront, heading north from the shops, is *Zafer Pansiyon* (☎0266/324 1760; ❷), with simple, clean rooms. There's a variety of reasonably priced *köfte*, *börek*, soup and *manti lokantas* on the seafront road, with more pricey **restaurants** on the beach itself. A couple of flash fast-food joints catering to a young Turkish crowd have also sprung up, including the pizza specialist *Brand New Prestij*.

Şeytan Sofrası

Just before Sarımsaklı a right turn leads 3km to the peninsula southwest of Ayvalık. The headland itself levels off at **Şeytan Sofrası** (the "Devil's Dinner Table"). This distinctive rocky outcrop sits virtually at the centre of a vast array of volcanic islands, of which Alibey and more distant Lésvos are just two. In clear weather it's certainly worth the trip here for views, which extend for a hundred kilometres around, and perhaps also to spot otherwise hidden beaches below, to be reached later with your own vehicle. At the northern edge of the headland there's a small cavity in a rock, supposedly Satan's footprint, into which people throw money for luck. More prominent, however, are the numerous votive rags tied onto bushes by the country folk to placate the presiding spirit, Satan or otherwise.

In summer a **bus** leaves Şeytan Sofrası at 7pm from the minibus stand near Ayvalık's PTT (returning after sunset), but if you come to watch the sun go down, you'll probably be accompanied by massive crowds intent on the same experience.

Alibey

Across the bay from Ayvalık, the island of **Alibey** – known also as **Cunda Adası** – constitutes either a good day-trip destination or an overnight halt. It's a quieter, less grand version of Ayvalık, with a couple of patches of beach and numerous quayside fish restaurants.

The best way to get here in summer is by **ferry from Ayvalık**: in addition to the daily tour boats, a regular ferry service runs every half-hour (June–Sept; $0.70 each way; 20min) from the quay directly behind the tourist information booth. At other times you'll have to rely on the half-hourly **bus** service from İskele Meydanı, or a **taxi** (at least $15), to cross the bridge linking island to mainland.

Around the island

Behind the island's **harbour** sprawls a grid of sleepy back streets lined by dilapidated, but still imposing, stone houses – remnants of life before 1922, when Cunda was known as Moskhonissi to its largely Greek-speaking inhabitants. After the Greeks were deported, the island was resettled with Cretan Muslims from around Hania, and you'll find that most people over 50 speak Greek as a matter of course. Recently the place has become the target of middle-class visitors from İstanbul bent on owning an Aegean retreat, with the inevitable consequences.

Halfway up the slope from the waterfront stands the Orthodox **Cathedral of the Taksiarhis**, now all but deserted and home only to a Greek-speaking caretaker, its interior retaining a few defaced and faded frescoes. The church was heavily damaged in the earthquake of 1944 and rumoured restoration has yet to materialize. Above the town on a hill, there's a small, roofless chapel, now used as a stable, from where you can gaze out across the bay to Ayvalık.

The northern half of Alibey, known as **Patrica**, has some relatively deserted sand and gravel beaches, though as ever they are blighted by the construction of villa complexes. Pleasure launches departing from the harbour offer trips to these coves, as well as to an enormous derelict Greek monastery accessible only by sea.

Practicalities

Ferries dock at the harbour from where everything is only a short walk away. **Accommodation** prices and comfort levels increase toward the waterside, where the best value is on offer at the *Artur Motel* (☎0266/327 1014; ❸), right on the quay, whose rooms sport TVs and fridges. *Altun Pansiyon* (☎0266/327 1554; ❷), further back from the shore, also has en-suite rooms available, though breakfast is extra.

Nicest choice by far, though, is the *Ortunç* (☎0266/327 1120, ℉327 2082; ❻), tucked away in a pine forest 4km from the harbour, on the **western shore** of the island, overlooking one of the thirty Blue Flag beaches in the Turkish Aegean. It's run by a retired opera singer, Orhan Tunç, and the recently renovated bungalows and attached restaurant sit nicely in a well-maintained garden. There's also a number of **campsites**, among them *ADA Camping* (☎0266/327 1211, ℉327 2065), 3km southwest of town on a rough road, which provides good facilities, beach access and slightly overpriced bungalows (❹).

For **restaurants**, the one attached to the *Artur Motel* is excellent and reasonably priced, with a great selection of *mezes* and servings of fresh *kalamari*. Keep an eye out for the inexpensive local seafood speciality, *papalina*, a sort of small, tasty smelt.

The old road to Bergama

The **old road from Ayvalık to Bergama** (75km) takes you through the pine forests and small villages of the Madra Dağı mountain range, and makes a worthwhile alternative to the monotonous main coastal route. With your own vehicle, and a few hours to spare, a pleasant time can be had exploring many of the small villages along the way. The area is famed for its pine nuts and wine, and conceals numerous unexplored ancient remains. The region is fairly

remote and the road, particularly in its later downhill stages, is narrow, twisting and demanding. Natural springs appear along the route at regular intervals and are perfectly safe to drink – in fact, a request for bottled water from any of the petrol stations en route will be met with a nonplussed stare.

Around 20km from Bergama, you could stop at the small village of **ÇİNAR** where the *Canli Alabalık* – a small fish restaurant with live trout and a fountain – is to the right of the main village square. If you stop for lunch, you'll have time to take a quick look at the ancient tomb, just outside in the car park.

Bergama

Although frequently touted as a day-trip destination from Ayvalık, **BERGA-MA**, site of the **ancient city of Pergamon**, rates a full day or two in its own right. The stunning acropolis of the tyrant, Eumenes II, is the main attraction, but there is a host of lesser sights and an old quarter of chaotic charm to detain you a little longer. Bergama is unpromising at first: the long approach to the centre reveals a dusty modern-looking place, and the monuments to which it owes its reputation are nowhere to be seen. In fact, most of ancient Pergamon is some distance from the modern town and takes a little effort to reach.

Some history

The first recorded mention of Pergamon dates from 399 BC, but the town only gained prominence when it became the base of Lysimachus, one of Alexander the Great's generals. He left some of his accumulated wealth in the hands of his officer Philetarus, who inherited the lot when Lysimachus was killed in battle fighting Syria for control of Asia Minor. By skilled political manoeuvring Philetarus was able to hang onto his new-found riches, passing them on to his adopted son Eumenes, who again defeated the Syrians at Sardis and extended further the domain of Philetarus.

Eumenes, generally recognized as the founder of the Pergamene dynasty, was succeeded in 241 BC by his nephew, Attalus I, whose immediate task was to defeat the Gauls; this he did with the help of the sacrifice of an animal whose liver turned out to bear the word "Victory". Attalus was a cunning ruler – it later emerged that he had secretly imprinted the word onto the liver with a specially made ring – and his authority was soon assured, the fame of his kingdom spreading across the Hellenistic world. Thus installed, he went on to build the **Temple of Athena** and the **Library** in Pergamon.

Attalus's son and successor, **Eumenes II**, consolidated his father's gains, allied himself with the Romans and set about building Pergamon into a great city. He later helped the Romans to defeat the Syrians at the battle of Magnesium, extending his sphere of influence. Under Eumenes II, the gymnasium and theatre were built and the acropolis was secured with a wall. The last king of Pergamon, Attalus III, was less interested in ruling than in chemistry (he spent a lot of time conducting experiments with poisons on criminals), and died after a short reign, perversely leaving his realm to the **Romans**. Under them Pergamon thrived, growing into a city of 150,000 people that was a renowned artistic and commercial centre. With the arrival of the Goths in 262 AD, the city began a gradual decline and passed through the hands of a succession of invaders before falling into ruin.

The German railway engineer **Karl Humann** rediscovered ancient Pergamon in 1871, when he found a strange mosaic in the possession of some local road workers that turned out to be part of the relief from the Altar of Zeus. Humann bought the mosaic from the farmers, gave notice to his Ottoman employers on the rail line and five years later began excavating the acropolis. Work was completed in 1886, and unfortunately most of the finds were carted off to Germany, not least the reliefs from the Altar of Zeus, which you can only view in the Pergamon Museum in Berlin.

Modern-day Bergama has been making the news thanks to the **discovery of gold** in the area. However, far from delighting the local inhabitants, they've been protesting long and hard at its extraction by means of "cyanide leeching" to separate the gold from the native rock.

Arrival, orientation, information and tours

The **acropolis**, the ancient city of the kings of Pergamon, sits atop a rocky bluff towering over modern Bergama, while just out of town, to the west, is the **Asclepion**, the ancient medical centre. The **old town** (site of most of the cheap accommodation) lies at the foot of the acropolis, about ten minutes' walk from the main **otogar**. If you're visiting on a **day-trip from Ayvalık**, note that the last direct dolmuş back departs from the main *otogar* at 5pm; if you miss it, there are a few more dolmuşes to Ayvalık until about 8pm (via a change and a wait at Dikili) with Dikili Ko-op.

There's a second *otogar* just south of the Kızıl Avlu (Red Basilica) on Istiklâl Meydanı, with bus services to and from points east and north. Most useful are the links with Bursa, and with Soma, 45km away on the main **train** line between İzmir and Bandırma (it's a short taxi ride between Soma's train and bus stations). A Metro service bus links the two *otogars*, saving you a long walk or a taxi ride.

When **leaving Bergama**, you can easily connect with either the morning or evening trains to Bandırma and the fast ferry to İstanbul – by far the easiest and cheapest way of reaching it from Bergama. The so-called "direct" night buses to İstanbul from the main *otogar*, incidentally, tend to be uncomfortable, slow and expensive.

Information and tours

Bergama's **tourist office** is on Atatürk Meydanı, next to the archeological museum (summer Mon–Fri 8.30am–7pm; winter daily 8.30am–5.30pm; ⊕0232/631 2851), though all it offers are the usual tourism ministry brochures and a rather feeble map of the town.

As soon as you get off the bus you'll probably be approached by a **taxi driver** offering to ferry you around the ruins for the extortionate sum of $25–30. If there are a few of you, or you're in a hurry, this can make sense, but otherwise it's a bit of a racket, limiting you to one hour at the acropolis (you'll almost certainly want to spend more time there), ten minutes at the Red Basilica and half an hour at the Asclepion.

Accommodation

The town's biggest and most expensive **hotels** announce themselves loudly enough on the approach to town along the İzmir Asfaltı, as do the two local **campsites** (these signposted just south of the town limits). Bergama's best budget accommodation is located in the old town, though taxi drivers might tell you some places are "closed" or "full" – a quick phone call ahead of your arrival should quash any such claims.

BERGAMA

Library
Royal Palaces
Ticket Booth
Temple of Trajan
Car Park
Theatre
City Gate
Heroön
Temple of Dionysus
Path
ACROPOLIS
Altar of Zeus
Temple of Athena
Upper Agora

KALE YOLU

Bergama Çayi

Wall Course

Gymnasium

Temple of Demeter

Lower Agora

Ulu Cami

Roman Amphitheatre

IMAM ÇIKMAZI ①

Path

İSTİKLÂL MEYDANI

Kızıl Avlu (Red Basilica)

B Ⓐ Ⓒ

Bergama Çayi

Otogar

② BANKALAR CAD

Hamam

Roman Theatre

Sacred Fountain

Propylon

Kurşunlu Cami

Ⓓ

Theatre

Sacred Way

i ATATÜRK MEYDANI

Archeological Museum

③

Car Park

Underground Passage

Main Otogar

Temple of Telesphorus

BÖBLINGEN CAD

Temple of Asclepios

ASKLEPION CAD

Army Camp

İZMİR ASFALTI

TANINAR SOK

Football Stadium ④

Army Camp

KAYMAKAM KEMAL BEY CAD

⑤

▲ Soma & Rail line

ACCOMMODATION
Anıl	3
Athena	1
Berksoy	5
Efsane	6
Manolya	4
Pergamon	2

RESTAURANTS
Arzu Pide	Ⓐ
Meydan	Ⓒ
Pala	Ⓑ
Sağlam 3	Ⓓ

N

0   500 m

▼ ⑥ , İzmir & Ayvalık

Hotel Anıl Hatuniye Cad 4, off İzmir Asfaltı ☏0232/631 1830, ⊛www.anilhotel.com. Very pink and very plush. All rooms have tasteful co-ordinated furnishings, TVs and air-conditioning. ❺

Athena Pension Imam Çıkmazı 5, Barbaros Mah ☏0232/633 3420. Enduringly popular place, with rooms in a 150-year-old Greek house as well as in a new annex with en-suite bathrooms. Facilities are fairly basic, but it's cosy, convivial and serves capacious breakfasts, ably overseen by Aydin. Good maps and restaurant information provided. Advance bookings essential. ❶

Berksoy İzmir Asfaltı, 2km west of town ☏0232/633 2595, ℻633 5345. The most comfortable of the more expensive hotels, with extensive grounds, outdoor pool, tennis court and internet facilities. ❺

Efsane İzmir Asfaltı 86 ☏0232/632 6351, ⊛www.efsanehotel.com. Large hotel, twinned with the more central *Anıl*, with hardwood fittings and TV in the rooms, plus rooftop pool and bar. The air-conditioned restaurant serves an impressive *meze* selection. ❹

Manolya Pension Tanpinar Sok 11 ☏0232/633 4488. Small, centrally located hotel, behind the main *otogar*, bedecked with Turkish carpets – there's a small pool out back. Some rooms have balcony TV and air-conditioning. ❷

Pergamon Pansiyon Bankalar Cad 5 ☏0232/633 4343. Atmospheric old house, with some en-suite rooms (though those at the front suffer from traffic noise). The courtyard restaurant is a good option whether or not you're staying. ❷

The Town

The foremost attraction in Bergama itself is the **Kızıl Avlu** or "Red Basilica" (daily 8.30am–5.30pm; $2), a huge redbrick edifice on the river below the acropolis. Originally built as a second-century AD temple to the trinity of Egyptian gods Serapis, Harpokrates and Isis, it was converted into a basilica by the Byzantines. Early in Christianity it was one of the Seven Churches of Asia Minor addressed by St John in the Book of Revelation – he referred to it as home of the throne of the devil, perhaps a nod to the still-extant Egyptian cult. It's now a crumbling ruin containing a mosque in one of its towers, with the ancient **Selinus River** (today called the Bergama Çayı) passing underneath the basilica via two intact tunnels. Just downstream you'll see a handsome, equally well-preserved Ottoman bridge, built in 1384; and there are two equally well-preserved Roman bridges upstream.

The area around and uphill from the basilica, north of the river, is given over to the **old quarter** of the town, a jumble of Ottoman buildings, antique and carpet shops, mosques and maze-like streets full of vitality and colour. The antique stalls are full of very beautiful and very overpriced copperware, costing even more than in İstanbul – too many coach tours have had their effect. Similarly, the formerly good reputation of Bergama carpets has been besmirched by too much synthetic dye and machine-weaving – beware. However, Tahsin on Istıklal Meydanı, near the Kızıl Avlu, has a reliable reputation.

Back on the main drag into town you'll find the **Archeological Museum** (Arkeoloji Müzesi; Tues–Sun 8.30am–5.30pm; $2), which has a large collection of locally unearthed relics, including a statue of Hadrian from the Asclepion. Many of the statues exhibited mark a shift in style to a more naturalistic technique – incorporating accentuated body shape, form and muscle tone – which allowed for a wider range of expressions and therefore meaning to be shown. First developed in Pergamon, this style influenced the later European Baroque style. Also of interest, to the right of the statues, is an impressively complete Roman mosaic of Medusa. There's also a small model of the Altar of Zeus at the acropolis (see overleaf), and a large figurine of Aphrodite holding an oyster shell, found at the nearby site of Allianoi, 18km northeast of Bergama. The extensive remains of this once important hydrotherapy centre dedicated to Ascelepius is currently threatened by the building of the impending Yortanli dam.

The acropolis

The **acropolis** (daily: 8.30am–5.30pm; May–Sept until 7pm; $4) is readily accessible on foot from the old town – though this is one attraction you may want to reach by taxi, at least on the way up, since the path can be difficult to find in that direction. The trail begins on the far side of the second bridge upstream from the Kızıl Avlu, angling obliquely up to the road, crossing which takes you up a fairly steep incline into the lower agora. Set off early, before it gets too hot and, in any case, try not to walk there following the main road, which is steep and not particularly direct, doubling back on itself for about 5km.

Taxis ($6) drop you off in the site car park, by the ticket booth, from where a ramp leads up to the former **city gate**, though this has almost completely disappeared.

Altar of Zeus

The path leads southwest to the huge square **Altar of Zeus**, standing in the shade of two great pine trees. The altar was built during the reign of Eumenes II to commemorate his father's victory over the Gauls, and was decorated with reliefs depicting the battle between the Titans and the gods, symbolizing the triumph of order over chaos (and, presumably, that of Attalus over the Gauls). Even today its former splendour is apparent, though it has been much diminished by the removal of the reliefs to Berlin. The main approach stairway was on the west, though this is the most deteriorated side today.

The Temple of Athena and the Library

Directly northeast of and exactly parallel to the Altar of Zeus, on the next terrace up, lie the remains of the **Temple of Athena**, dating back to the third century BC. Only some of the stepped foundations on which it was built have survived, although the entrance gate, with the inscription recording its dedication by "King Eumenes to Athena the Bearer of Victories", has been reconstructed in Berlin.

The scanty north stoa of the temple once housed Pergamon's famous **Library**, which at its peak rivalled that of Alexandria. Founded by Attalus II, it came to have a catalogue of 200,000 books. Eumenes II was particularly active in building it up, augmenting the collection by borrowing books from other libraries and not returning them. He is also said to have paid for books by Aristotle and Theophrastus with their weight in gold. Eventually the Egyptian kings, alarmed at the growth of the Pergamon library, which they saw as a threat to their own library in Alexandria, banned the export of papyrus, on which all books were written – and of which they were sole producers – thereby attempting to stem the library's expansion.

In response Eumenes offered a reward to anyone who could come up with a replacement, and the old custom of writing on specially treated animal skins – parchment – was revived, leading to the invention of the codex or paged book, since it wasn't possible to roll up parchment like papyrus. The words "parchment" and the more archaic "pergamene" are both actually derived from "Pergamon". The library was ransacked by Mark Antony, who gave the choicest items to Cleopatra as a gift, but enough remained for it to be consulted up until the fourth century AD.

The Temple of Trajan and around

Still further north and higher up looms the Corinthian **Temple of Trajan**, where Trajan and Hadrian were both revered during Roman times – their busts were taken from the temple and are also now in Berlin. The Germans recently completed the re-erection of the temple columns, plus those from the stoa that surrounded the shrine on three sides. The north architrave is lined with Medusa heads, two of them modern re-castings.

Behind the temple are mounds of rubble and collapsed walls – the remains of barracks and the highest reaches of the city's **perimeter wall**. Nearby yawns a cistern with a pillar in the centre, either a level indicator or core of a vanished stairway – this was fed by an **aqueduct**, traces of which are still visible running parallel to a modern one on the hillside to the northwest. Finally, as you begin your descent back down toward the main entrance, you'll pass – east of the library and Athena temple – the extensive but jumbled ruins of the **Royal Palaces**.

The theatre

From the Temple of Athena a narrow staircase leads down to the **theatre**, the most spectacular part of the acropolis. Dating from Hellenistic times, it was cut into the hillside and was capable of seating 10,000 spectators. According to the architectural conventions of the day, the auditoria of Greek theatres were always greater than a semicircle, but at Pergamon the steepness of the site made this impossible, so the architects compensated by building upwards, creating a narrow, sharply raked auditorium with eighty rows of seats. The stage was built from wood and removed after performances – the holes into which supporting posts were driven can still be seen on the terrace at the foot of the auditorium. One of the reasons for the use of a portable stage was to allow free access to the **Temple of Dionysos**, built just off-stage to the audience's right.

The upper and lower agoras

Just south of the Altar of Zeus lies a terrace, formerly the **upper agora** of Pergamon. There isn't much to see today, other than Karl Humann's grave, although this was once the commercial and social focal point of the city. A path leads down from here to the **lower agora**, where the common people lived and went about their business.

In among the remains of various houses, at the foot of the path to the Lower Agora, is the **Temple of Demeter**, where the local variant of the Eleusinian Mysteries, a cultic ceremony supposed to guarantee a better life after death, was enacted. On the northern side of the temple are the remains of a building containing nine rows of seats with space for about a thousand people, which it's thought were for spectators at the ritual. Below the temple there's a fountain for ritual ablutions and a pit designed to receive the blood of animals sacrificed in the temple. Nearby is a **gymnasium**, spread out over three terraces, where the children of the city were educated. The upper level, with its sports ground, was for young men, the middle was used by the adolescents, while the lower served as a kind of playground for younger children.

Once you've reached the lower agora, it should be a simple matter to find the path from here back down to town – the circular blue waymarks are much easier to see on the way down.

The Asclepion

Bergama's other significant archeological site is the **Asclepion** (daily: 8.30am–5.30pm; May–Sept until 7pm; $4), the town's Greco-Roman medical centre. It can be reached along the road starting opposite the PTT, by the Kurşunlu Cami – a drive or walk of 1.5km. Note that the ruins lie within a large and clearly marked military zone, which is closed to traffic at dusk – avoid entering any surrounding army camps and don't take photographs away from the site itself.

The Asclepion was devoted to Asclepios, son of Apollo and the god of healing, who supposedly served as a doctor in the army of Agamemnon during the siege of Troy. According to myth, Asclepios learned how to bring the dead back to life using the blood of the Gorgon that Athena had given to him. Zeus, worried that Asclepios's activities were endangering the natural order of things, struck him down with a thunderbolt but elevated him to the stars in compensation.

In part, the healing methods practised at the Asclepion were ritualistic in nature, with patients required to sleep in the temple in order that Asclepios might appear to them in a dream to relay his diagnosis and suggest treatment. However, dieting, bathing and exercise also played an important role in the therapeutic regime. **Galen** (131–201 AD), the greatest physician of the ancient world, who laid down the basis of much of modern medical science and served as personal physician to the emperor Marcus Aurelius, was trained here.

Much of what can be seen today was built in the reign of the emperor Hadrian (117–38 AD), the early stages of the first- and second-century heyday of the Pergamene Asclepion, when its function was similar to that of a nineteenth-century spa. Some patients came here to be cured of ailments, but for others a visit to the Asclepion was simply a social event, part of the habitual existence of the wealthy and leisured.

The site

From the site entrance, a long, colonnaded sacred way known as the **Via Tecta** leads to the **propylon**, or monumental entrance gate. The propylon was built during the third century AD, after an earthquake that had seriously damaged the complex in the previous century. Northeast of the propylon is a square building that housed a **library** and the statue of Hadrian now on display in the local museum.

To the south of the propylon lies the circular **Temple of Asclepios**, dating from 150 AD and modelled on the Pantheon in Rome. The domed roof of this graceful structure was 24m in diameter and had a circular opening in the centre to allow light and air to penetrate. The floor and walls would have been decorated with mosaics and recesses housed statues of the gods. To the west of the propylon and temple, the broad, open area was originally enclosed by colonnaded walkways, the bases of which can still be seen. At the western end of the northern colonnade is a **theatre** with a seating capacity of 3500, which served to keep patients entertained. At the centre of the open area, the **sacred fountain** still gushes with weakly radioactive drinking water. Nearby, an 80m-long underground passage leads to the **Temple of Telesphoros** (a lesser deity associated with Asclepios) – a two-storey circular building, which, like the Temple of Asclepios, served as a place for patients to sleep while awaiting dream diagnoses. The lower storey survives in good repair.

Eating and drinking

You can eat well in Bergama provided you ignore the large, overpriced tourist **restaurants** along the approach to the Kızıl Avlu. Tour buses will often take you to a particular restaurant, but you're not obliged to eat there. There are a number of good cheap *pide* and kebab options around Istiklâl Meydanı, and some semi-outdoor **beer houses** opposite the archeological museum, near the small terraced public park.

Arzu Pide Istiklâl Meyd. Serves delicious *pide*, topping the usual tomato and cheese *pide* with *çöp şiş* (small scraps of lamb) and good salad.

Meydan Bankalar Cad. Popular local haunt offering a large selection of dishes, including fish, as well as beer and wine.

Pala Mescit Karacac. One of the oldest joints in town, with good-value *köfte* for $3. Upstairs at the cramped tables you ring a bell to summon a waiter.

Sağlam 3 Hükümeit Cad 89. Specializes in eastern food from the Urfa region, including oven-cooked *kiremit kebap* and *güveç* (meat and veg claypot casserole) as well as *beyti sarma* (a roll of spicy *Adana kebap* covered in unleavened bread, then sliced and served with salad). Garden courtyard out back and rooms upstairs where you dine seated on cushions around low tables.

Dıkılı

DİKİLİ is a sizable resort with a population of about 10,000, which offers a decent crescent-shaped sandy beach and a promenade lined with cafés and restaurants. Otherwise, though, there's little of interest unless you arrive in early autumn when local farmers descend on the town with their harvests of raw cotton to sell to wholesalers. Cruise liners occasionally dock in the harbour, allowing their passengers to make day excursions to Bergama and Ayvalık, or head for the beaches to the north.

The town is 30km west of Bergama (and 4km off the main Canakkale–İzmir highway) and well served by dolmuşes and intercity buses, with at least six daily **buses** from Bergama. Many of the **accommodation** possibilities lie just beyond the *otogar*, along Menderes Caddesi; among them is the marble-clad *Hotel Akçay*, Menderes Cad 6 (☏0232/671 8857, ℱ671 8858; ❶), a small hotel whose modern airy rooms have balconies, and there's a bright roof-top breakfast salon. At the main roundabout lies the *Dikili Hotel* (☏0232/671 9030, ℱ671 4222; ❸), good value if you're looking for air-con rooms with TV and the use of a pool. Heading away from the shore is the clean, reasonably decorated *Halat Pansiyon* (☏0232/671 4825, ℱ671 2940; ❷).

Of the seafront **restaurants**, *Gonca Café*, run by a retired music teacher, serves good *çir köfte* (raw spicy meatballs). Try to get a table at the back for an ocean view on three sides.

The coast road **north of Dikili** takes you near a number of undeveloped resort towns, heading up towards Ayvalık. The best stretch of sandy **beach** runs for about 15km from north of Dikili to Altınova. It is, however, only really accessible if you have your own transport, and in any case there are very few facilities en route.

Çandarlı

About half an hour to the south of Dikili is the small fishing port and resort of **ÇANDARLI**. It occupies a headland that was formerly the site of ancient Pitane, the northernmost Aeolian city, though nothing remains of this. Despite its pedigree, the oldest building in Çandarlı is a perfectly restored fourteenth-century **Genoese fortress** (not open to the public), incorporating recognizable chunks of the ancient city. This is one of several such forts dotting the northwestern Turkish coast and the Greek islands immediately opposite, a reminder of the days when the military and commercial might of Genoa dominated the North Aegean.

The **beach** here is coarse sand and – except in high summer – Çandarlı is not a bad place to get away from the crowds for a day or two. It's remarkably clean and well kept, with a welcoming atmosphere absent in some larger resort towns. The ordinary life of the town centres on the east side of the peninsula, near the bus stop. Here, the lively **market square** (market day is Friday) is surrounded by simple soup-and-*pide* kitchens, beer halls and old Greek houses. There's a **PTT** and a **bank** with an ATM. Hourly **buses** run here from Dikili and in summer there's an hourly service between Çandarlı and İzmir (less frequent out of season).

Best budget **accommodation** option – offering basic rooms with shared bathroom – is *Gül Pansiyon* (☎0232/673 3347; ❶), close to the beach, a ten-minute walk through the village and past the castle. The *Senger* (☎0232/673 3117; ❸), on the seafront past the castle, above the eponymous restaurant, has many repeat customers, particularly Germans, who enjoy its cosily furnished rooms (some with air-conditioning and sea views) and buffet breakfast. Or there's the quiet *Samyeli* on the seafront (☎0232/673 3428, ⓕ673 3461; ❸), also with en-suite rooms, some with air-conditioning.

The cheapest places to eat are in town, while most of Çandarlı's fancier **restaurants**, **cafés** and **bars** line the shore road: for reasonably priced seafood, look no further than the *Kalender Restaurant*. *Pitaneon* is a noisy bar right on the beach, catering manly for young Turkish weekenders.

Foça and around

FOÇA – 65km south of Çandarlı – is the modern successor (and linguistically a corruption) of ancient **Phocaea**, founded around 1000 BC by Ionian colonists; it was thus later reckoned a member of the Ionian confederation, despite lying squarely in Aeolian territory. The Phocaeans became renowned seafarers whose enormous, state-of-the-art boats plied the principal trade routes of the Mediterranean throughout the fifth century BC, establishing among other places the city of Massilia, now Marseilles. Powered by fifty oarsmen, the galleys were capable of carrying five hundred passengers or the equivalent in precious metals. On the basis of excavations carried out in 1913, it is claimed that the prodigious Phocaeans also introduced writing into southern France and were responsible for olive cultivation in the Mediterranean basin. In later times, the Byzantines gave Phocaea as a placatory present to the Genoese, who restored its castle and managed to retain the city during the fourteenth century by paying tribute to the Saruhan emirs and later the Ottomans.

The original name *Phocaea* is derived from the ancient Greek word for "seal" and the beast features in modern local statues, promotional signs and so forth. The small local colony of endangered **monk seals** – whose barking may have given rise to the myth of the sirens luring sailors onto the rocks that features in Homer's *Odyssey* – has now been afforded special protection by Turkey's council of ministers and was the target of a World Wildlife Fund conservation project. Frankly you'd have to *be* a seal to really enjoy the sea here, which owing to strong currents and a sharp drop-off is notoriously chilly most of the year. The other fortuitous restraint on development has been the pervasive military presence: Foça is an important naval base, and the land to the north is out of bounds.

None of this has prevented Foça from becoming a favourite summer retreat for İzmir and Manisa people, who own or rent holiday apartments here. They have been joined by a few European tour operators, but the town has accommodated the tourist swell fairly graciously and is still a pleasantly relaxed little place. A boat trip out to the local islets makes a good day-trip, or you can rent transport and head out into the scenic countryside north and east of town.

The Town

Today, sadly, little remains intact of **ancient Phocaea**. Nine kilometres before the modern town, just north of the main road, is the **Taş Kule**, an unusual-looking tomb believed to date from the fourth century BC, squatting beside an Ottoman bridge and a modern cemetery, while a small **ancient theatre** dating from 340 BC marks the east entry to Foça. Some mosaic pavements from a Roman villa, including an almost perfectly preserved portrayal of four Bacchus heads and birds, have been unearthed in what was to be a car park off 193 Sokak near a housing development called the Barişkent Evler. Local legend also maintains that a large black stone is hidden somewhere beneath the streets and those who walk unwittingly over it are destined someday to return to Foça to live.

The oldest structure in Foça itself is the **Genoese fortress** (not open to the public), which has recently been rather crudely restored, with stage-set towers added as a touristic backdrop. More authentic are some wonderful old Greek fishermen's cottages and a few more opulent Ottoman mansions lining the cobbled back streets. There are also two interesting mosques: the small, unheralded but beautiful, fifteenth-century **Fatih Camii**, and another at the very summit of the castle enclosure, sporting a distinctly lighthouse-like minaret. In the same street as the Fatih Camii are two **hamams**, one of which is 150 years old and has been converted into a bicycle repair shop, while the other continues to operate daily from 8am to midnight.

The castle headland lends Foça an interesting layout, splitting the bay into two smaller harbours: the northerly, more picturesque **Küçükdeniz**, where most of the action is; and the southern, rather bleak **Büyükdeniz**, which looks as if it could be anywhere in Turkey, and whose pair of hotel-restaurants is not really recommended, so go only for a view of the huge fishing fleet and the *kale* (castle) on its promontory. Neither bay has a decent beach, with the shore apt to be weedy.

Boat trips (May–Sept; around $15) run out from the Küçükdeniz to some of the small islets that dot the coastline to the north of Foça, within an area designated for Special Environmental Protection. Most of the ten boats follow similar itineraries, leaving by 10.30am returning by 6pm, with three stops for swimming (and lunch) throughout the day.

Practicalities

The town lies 26km west of the main Çanakkale–İzmir road. To reach it, take any İzmir-bound **bus** and ask to be let off at the turning for Foça. From here, a regular **dolmuş** should take you into town. There are also half-hourly direct buses from İzmir itself.

The very helpful **tourist office** (May–Sept Mon–Fri 8.30am–6.30pm, Sat & Sun 10am–1pm & 5–8pm; Oct–April Mon–Fri 8.30am–5.30pm; ℡0232/812 1222) is at the rear of the central square, opposite the **otogar**, at the south end of town. *Göçmen Motor Rent*, a cluttered workshop opposite the *otogar*, rents somewhat dilapidated **bikes** for $6 a day and **motorbikes** for $18 a day, with discounts for longer use. For **car rental** contact *Bir Tour*, Fevzi Pasa Mah 193/1 (☎0232/812 5050).

Accommodation

If you want to stay affordably by the sea, head straight through the town, down the right side of the harbour and along the esplanade towards 139 Sokağı, where many of the best **pansiyons and hotels** are located. The very cheap *Iyon Pansiyon* (☎0232/812 1415; ❶), run by a friendly retired schoolteacher, has basic rooms in a restored Greek house; there's a kitchen for guests. *Huzur* (☎0232/812 1203, ℉812 6647; ❷) has nicely furnished rooms and a waterside terrace, but breakfast is not included. The adjacent *Fokai* (☎0232/812 1765; ❷) is quiet and friendly, overlooks the water and comes highly recommended; the nearby *Sempatik Güneş* (☎0232/812 2195, ℉812 1915; ❷), one block back from the water, is also well-kept and comfortable. For ocean views from large bright rooms with huge windows, give the *Iyigun Pansiyon* (☎0232/812 1182; ❷) a try; or the *Ensar Pansiyon*, 200m back from the sea at 161 Sok 15 (☎0232/812 1401, ℉812 6159; ❶), which has sea views from the terrace and a kitchen for guests.

Of the mid-range premises, the *Akizmir Pansiyon* (☎0232/812 7102, ℉812 7103; ❸), right next to the castle, has large, basically furnished rooms and a good fish restaurant attached. You pay for the central location here rather than the room quality.

The local **campsites** all lie out of town, on the road to Yenifoça (see below).

Eating and drinking

Küçükdeniz harbour is lined with fish **restaurants** mostly along the small esplanade. Prices for kebabs and *mezes* are marked on boards outside, with main dishes ranging between $5 and $10, but those for fish vary daily and can be expensive, so check before ordering.

The *Bedesten* and *Celep* both offer a good range of fish dishes as does the *Kordon*, which is popular with the locals for its *çipura* (gilt-headed bream, a regional speciality) and lobster. At the extreme south end of the quay, inland among trees, the *Sedef* offers the best value in town; try the *kiremit kebap* (lamb cooked on a tile). Next to the *Kordon*, *Café Neco* is a popular evening hangout for younger residents and also does a good breakfast. To the right, down the ivy-covered alley, the simply titled *Café* caters for an older crowd, with snacks, good coffee and magazines.

Around the coast to Yenifoça

The scenic countryside around Foça is ideal for touring by rented car or bike, though any illusions of completely escaping development as the shore heads north are difficult to maintain. Nonetheless, there are some excellent **beaches**, often difficult to access, and a number of basic **campsites** between five and fifteen kilometres from town – namely, *Ferhat*, *Remzinin*, *Di-Ba* and *Acar Kamping*, in that order as you leave Foça. All have good beaches, the best is that at *Acar Kamping*. Further on *Mambo Beach* (no phone; ❷), 2km before Yenifoça, has a bar, campsite, restaurant and *pansiyon*, as well as a decent beach – a far better place to stay than Yenifoça itself.

YENİFOÇA, 23km by road from Foça, maintains a core of old Greek houses, but here the beach is grubby, rocky and suffers from full northern exposure. All in all, the town is merely the turnaround point for heading back to Foça via the **inland road**, past crumbling hamlets abandoned since 1923.

KOZBEYLI, around 10km before Foca, a small cluster of old Greek village houses centred on a mosque, makes for an evocative stopover. Many of the dilapidated houses and cobbled lanes are now being restored and a few antique shops have sprung up, in anticipation of visitors yet to arrive.

Manisa

The site of the ancient town of Magnesia ad Sipylus, **MANİSA** lies about 40km east of Menemen (on the main Canakkale–İzmir highway) and is easily reached from there, or from İzmir itself, by way of pleasant mountain roads. Over ninety percent of the historic centre was destroyed by the Greek army during its 1922 retreat, but despite this Manisa remains an interesting place with a few fine Selçuk and Ottoman monuments, reminiscent of Bursa as it spills out from the foot of the Manisa Dağı mountain range. This may not seem enough to pull you so far off the main route to the attractions of the central Aegean, but the nearby ruins of Sardis tip the balance in favour of a detour. An overnight stop suggests itself – arriving in Manisa at noon, visiting Sardis in the afternoon and spending the following morning looking around Manisa before moving on. In practice, however, there are limited sleeping and eating options in Manisa and Sardis-bound visitors may prefer to carry on to Salihli, beyond the ancient site.

According to Homer, Manisa was founded after the Trojan War by warriors from the area. Alexander the Great passed through during his campaign, while in 190 BC there was a huge battle here between the Romans and the Syrians, under King Antioch III. The day was decided in favour of the Romans by the cavalry of the king of Pergamon, who was given control over the city as a reward. The town finally came under direct Roman rule – and entered a period of great prosperity – after the death of Attalus III of Pergamon. For a short time during the thirteenth century Manisa was capital of the Byzantine empire, after the sacking of Constantinople by the Fourth Crusade. In 1313 the city fell into the hands of the Selçuk chieftain Saruhan Bey; from this century date the earliest of Manisa's surviving monuments. Later, the Ottomans sent heirs to the throne here to serve an apprenticeship as local governors, in order to ready them for the rigours of İstanbul palace life.

The Town

Manisa still has a lot to recommend it and the relatively modern town centre, with its extensive parklands, strikes visitors as clean, orderly and prosperous. The principal central attractions in Manisa are three mosques, which you could easily tour in half a day, while a local museum (temporarily closed), the remains of the castle and a few other minor sights help to pass any remaining time.

Sultan Camii and around

At the south end of Ören Caddesi, the extension of Ibrahim Gökçen Bulvarı, the **Sultan Camii** was built in 1522 for Ayşe Hafize, the mother of Süleyman the Magnificent, who lived here with her son while he was serving as governor. This rectangular mosque is much wider than it is deep, its single central dome flanked by two pairs of satellite domes. Late Ottoman Baroque paint decoration and a tiny wood-railed pulpit on the west enliven the porch – actually a *son cemaat yeri* (latecomers' praying place). The mosque was once the focus of a large *külliye* (mosque complex) that included a *medrese*, mental hospital and even an official clock-setting shop.

MANISA

▲ Balıkesir

Menemen ◀

İzmir ◀

Train Station

İZMİR ASFALTI

Otogar

AVNİGEMİCİOĞLU CAD

CUMHURİYET CAD

ATATÜRK BUL

Sardis ▶

Tarih Borsa Kahvesi Restaurant ▶

DOĞU CAD

❶

ⓘ

MUSTAFA KEMAL CAD

SEYFETTİN BEY CAD

❷

❸

Hatuniye Camii

İBRAHİM GÖÇEN BULVARI

DUMLUPINAR

✉

❹

Kurşunlu Han

ÇARŞI CADDESİ BUL

MURAT CAD

Sultan Camii

İZMİR CAD

Saruhan Bey Türbesi

Muradiye Cami

Museum

Yeni Alaca Hamam

Mevlevi Hane

Ulu Cami

ACCOMMODATION	
Arma	1
Atlas	4
Marmaris	2
Niobe	3

N

Niobe Ağalayan Kaya

Sandikkale

0   200 m

Every year on the third or fourth Sunday of April, the *Mesir Şenlikleri* **Power-Gum Festival** – now well into its fifth century – takes place around the Sultan Camii, to commemorate the occasion when a local doctor called Merkez Efendi concocted a special resin to cure Ayşe Hafize of an unspecified ailment. The gum, or *mesir macunu*, concocted from 41 herbs, is scattered from the minaret by the muezzin to the waiting crowd, who believe that consuming the paste will protect them from pain (especially snake and insect bites) until the next festival. It is also reputed to have an aphrodisiac effect.

Across from the Sultan Camii stands the **Saruhan Bey Türbesi**, the tomb of Saruhan Bey, who took Manisa in 1313, ending Byzantine sovereignty. His army is said to have attacked Sandıkkale, the city's castle, driving a flock of goats with candles on their horns before them to give the impression that a huge army was attacking. The defenders panicked and the castle fell – an event commemorated here by a festival each November 13.

The Muradiye complex

Barely 100m further east along the same side of Murat Caddesi you'll find the **Muradiye Camii**, built for Murat III in 1583–1585 while he was governor here. The interior, with its stained-glass windows and relatively restrained decoration – despite the use of 12kg of gold – is impressive: the carved wooden *mimber*, or pulpit, and the sultan's loge are particularly fine, as are the İznik tiles around the *mihrab* and the windows. Unusually, a large women's gallery runs the full length of the cross-stroke of the reverse-T groundplan, a design more typical of dervish *zaviye*s (hostels), and indeed the mosque, like the Sultan Camii, was originally part of a *külliye*.

Next door to the Muradiye Camii, housed in the former *imaret* (soup kitchen), is Manisa's **museum**. This is currently closed following the much-publicized theft of its antique coins, though when it does re-open you'll be able to view archeological and ethnological exhibits, including items retrieved from Sardis.

Further along the street, the still-used **Yeni Alaca Hamam** is one of the oldest bath-houses in town. On Thursdays the street itself, Murat Caddesi, is the site of the town's large **market**, where you'll find just about any kind of vegetable or fruit, as well as cheap household items and clothing.

The Ulu Cami and peripheral sites

Manisa's oldest surviving mosque, the **Ulu Cami**, sits on a natural terrace amid a panoramic park 250m above the museum. Built on the site of a Byzantine church in 1366 by Işak Çelebi, the grandson of Saruhan Bey, it is basically a square walled compound divided into two rectangles, with a *medrese* – still functioning as a children's Koran school – tacked onto the west side. Entering the open-roofed courtyard via the ornate portal, you confront the glory of the place, a forest of varied **antique columns**, some "double" and others carrying Byzantine capitals, many presumably recycled from the church that formerly stood on the site. There are more columns in the interior, supporting a very large central dome by means of pointed arches. Back outside, the **minaret** is striped with patterns of green- and grape-coloured İznik bricks. The view out north over the plain is truly spectacular and that alone is well worth the steep climb. For an even more spectacular panoramic view continue further uphill to the fairly unimpressive remains of Manisa's Byzantine citadel, **Sandıkkale**, parts of which date to the eighth and thirteenth centuries.

Follow the maze of streets leading west from here to the foot of Mount Sipylus (Sipil Dağ) and you'll eventually come to **Niobe Ağlayan Kaya**, the so-called "Weeping Rock of Niobe", in the form of a woman's head from which tears can supposedly be seen issuing every Friday. According to legend, Niobe was the daughter of Tantalus and had seven daughters and six sons. She taunted the nymph Leto – who had only borne the divine twins Apollo and Artemis – for her relative infertility until the latter became jealous and ordered her own offspring to kill Niobe's. Niobe wept for a long time over the bodies of her children until Zeus put an end to her suffering by turning her to rock.

Heading back downhill into town, you could take a detour to the **Mevlevihane** – a former *tekke* or gathering place of the Konya-based whirling dervish order, the only one in the region – housed in a solid stone building on the southeastern edge of town.

Practicalities

Upon arrival, walk south away from the **otogar** toward the mountains for about ten minutes until you come to **Doğu Caddesi** – the town's main commercial street, where most of the banks and larger shops are located. The **train station**, with regular daily services from İzmir, lies fifteen minutes north of here, along Atatürk Bulvarı.

Manisa's **tourist office** is on the sixth floor at Mustafa Kemal Cad 606 (Mon–Fri 8am–noon & 1–5pm; ☎0236/231 2541). They should be able to give you a town plan, and may even have someone on hand who can speak English.

On the **accommodation** front, Manisa leaves much to be desired and most of what exists fills with students between mid-September and June. However, the well-signposted *Marmaris Otel*, Anafartalar Mah 3, Sok 10 (☎0236/239 5835, ⓕ239 4686; ❷), is surprisingly good, with presentable modern rooms with TV, but no breakfast. The *Arma* on Doğu Caddesi (☎0236/231 1980, ⓕ232 4501; ❸) in the heart of town is reasonable value, but the rooms are in need of a revamp. The *Otel Niobe* (☎0236/231 3745, ⓕ238 9785; ❷), opposite the Belediye building on Sınema Park Caddesi, is cheaper, but rooms catch the full sun in summer. Finally, the *Atlas* at Dumulpınar Cad 22 (☎0236/231 1197; ❶) caters for students and impecunious backpackers alike, with bare, minimally furnished en-suite rooms.

Manisa isn't going to win any prizes in the gourmet stakes either, with little other than the usual range of **kebab and pide salons** and *lokanta*s. However, *Tarihi Borsa Kahvesi*, Borsa Cad 29, comes highly recommended for quality steamtray food and *meze*s. The area around the tourist office features a number of Western-style burger and pizza joints, where pizza and salad should set you back no more than $3. If you're lucky you might find a restaurant offering the traditional autumn recipe of stewed quince in *pekmez* (grape molasses), the latter courtesy of the province's vineyards.

Sardis

The ancient site of **Sardis** (Sart in Turkish) lies about 65km east of Manisa and is easily reached from there or from İzmir. It's another one of those places in Turkey that is so old that it's difficult to separate history from myth. The area was probably inhabited as far back as 1200 BC and was later settled by the Lydians, descended from native Anatolians and Greek invaders. Sardis grew to be incredibly wealthy thanks to the gold that was washed down from the nearby mountains and caught in sheepskins by the locals. According to legend, the source of these riches was the Phrygian king **Midas**, whose touch turned everything to gold. Unable to eat, his curse was lifted when the gods had him wash his hands in the River Pactolus, which flowed down to Sardis from the south. Wherever the gold came from, the Lydians were happy enough and celebrated their wealth by inventing coinage.

The first coins were issued under the city's most celebrated king, **Croesus**, during whose rule (563–546 BC) the kingdom's prosperity grew, attracting the attention of the Persians under Cyrus the Great. Worried about this threat, Croesus consulted the Delphic oracle as to whether or not he should attack first. The oracle replied that if he did he would destroy a great empire. Croesus went to war and was defeated, and after a two-week siege Sardis fell and Croesus was supposedly burned alive by the victors.

As a Persian city, Sardis was sacked during the Ionian revolt of 499 BC. It made a comeback under Alexander the Great and the Macedonians, but was destroyed by an earthquake in 17 AD. The Romans rebuilt it, having taken it at the same time as Manisa, and the town was the site of one of the Seven Churches of Asia addressed by St John in the Book of Revelation. This didn't save Byzantine Sardis from conquest by Saruhan and destruction at the hands of Tamerlane in 1401, after which the city never really recovered. It only came to light again early this century, when American archeologists began excavating mostly Roman and Byzantine remains.

The road to Sardis

If you're travelling by dolmuş, and fancy a stop on the way, you can visit a 3300-year-old relief, known as the **Taş Suret**, carved into the rock of **Mount Sipylus**, above the road about 7km east of Manisa. It's generally reckoned to be a Hittite version of Cybele, the mother goddess. Ask to be let out at the Akpınar pool and climb a few hundred metres up into the cliffs above the road. The image, none too distinct, is tucked into a five-metre-high niche and was probably placed here in the hope of making the valley of the Gediz River below more fertile.

Mount Sipylus, incidentally, is associated with the ancient king **Tantalus**, whose daughter Niobe was turned into the rock in Manisa. According to legend, Tantalus also had two sons, Pelops and Broteas, the latter of whom supposedly carved this image of Cybele on the mountainside. Pelops ended up being served up in a dish Tantalus prepared for the gods, and narrowly escaped with only his shoulder being eaten. He was later restored to life with a new ivory shoulder and Tantalus was punished by being sent to Hades, where water and food were kept eternally just out of his reach – hence the verb "to tantalize".

The onward journey takes you through an uneventful agricultural landscape. The fertile **Gediz plain**, stretching from Manisa until well past Alaşehir, is totally given over to the cultivation of grapes, particularly sultanas, for which the region is the number-one world producer. Things pick up once the **Boz Dağları** mountain range rears up to the south. When you see the ruins of ancient Sardis, get off at **Sartmustafa**, a small, traditional village centred on a cluster of teahouses, where local farmers like to put their feet up while their wives and daughters work the vineyards.

The sites

There are two main clusters of ruins, both easily reached on foot from the main road. The **first site** primarily made up of the gymnasium and synagogue (daily 8.30am–8pm; $0.70), lies just north of the road on the eastern edge of the village and includes the **Marble Way**, a Byzantine shopping street complete with latrines, whose holes and drainage channels are still visible. The various shops are labelled and include a restaurant, an office and a hardware shop. Foundations and low walls with discernible doorways are all that remain, although in some places Greek inscriptions and engraved basins with carved crosses can still be seen.

A left turn leads into the restored **synagogue**, whose walls are covered with impressive mosaics – though these are copies, the originals being housed in the Manisa Museum; the extensive floor mosaics are, however, original. The intact walls and pillars are covered with ornate patterned tiles and explanatory text includes a plaque honouring the donors, mostly North American Jews, for the renovation work.

Almost right next door to the synagogue is the third-century AD **gymnasium and bath complex**, the most prominent building in the city, covering five and a half acres. Its **Marble Court**, the entry from the palaestra to the baths, has been spectacularly restored to its original state when first built in 211 AD. The walls behind the columns would have had marble revetments and the podia would have supported statues, forming a multi-storeyed facade so visually splendid as to suggest that the baths must have been associated with observance of the imperial cult. Behind the court are the remains of a swimming pool and rest area.

From the Sartmustafa village teahouses, a paved track – very poorly marked on the far side of the highway, west of the synagogue – leads 1200m south from the main road to the other main site, the **Temple of Artemis** (daily 8.30am–8pm; $0.70). The temple, once among the four largest in Asia Minor, was built by Croesus, destroyed by Greek raiders during the Ionian revolt and later rebuilt by Alexander the Great. Today a baker's dozen of massive Ionic columns, dating from both Hellenistic and Roman times, remain standing, though only two are completely intact. Enough of the foundations are visible to make clear just how large the building, constructed to rival the temples of Ephesus, Samos and Didyma, used to be. In the southeastern corner of the site are the remains of a small brick Byzantine church. Small-scale excavations are continuing beneath a huddle of shelters on a small eastern ridge. More than anything, however, it's the beauty of the setting, enclosed by wooded and vined hills and accented by weird Cappadocia-like pinnacles, that leaves a lasting impression.

Practicalities

Sardis is easily reached by taking the Salihli dolmuş **from Manisa** – or the Salihli bus **from İzmir**. The site can also be reached by **train**: two morning services run from İzmir to Manisa, from where, in turn, there are three services (morning, lunchtime and evening) to Sahihli (see below). Taking the train is a more relaxed, though slower, way of doing the trip – trains also return to Manisa a bit later (7.15pm) than the dolmuşes. The dolmuş will drop you on the main highway, at the turn-off for Sartmustafa. The train station is 1km to the north, near the tiny hamlet of Sartmahmut.

As accommodation in Manisa is limited, you may prefer to stay instead in **SALIHLI**, a market town 8km beyond Sardis on the İzmir–Afyon road. There's nothing of historical interest here, but it's closer to the ruins. To get out to the site, take any of the regular Manisa-bound dolmuşes, which will drop you at the highway turn-off.

The *Otel Hakan* at Mithatpaşa Cad 192 (℡0236/713 0348; **❷**), is quiet and has some en-suite rooms overlooking a pleasant courtyard. At *Hotel Yener*, Dede Çelak Sok 7 (℡0236/712 5003, ℻714 1562; **❶**), just south of the *otogar*, the rooms at the front have showers but may suffer a little from traffic noise, especially on market day (Wednesday). The more upmarket *Berrak* is behind the *Yener* at Belediye Cad 59 (℡0236/713 1452, ℻713 1457; **❸**), while the *Akgül*, clearly visible from the marketplace next to the *otogar* (℡0236/713 3737,

ⓦwww.otelakgül.alem.com; ❷), has English-speaking management, rooms with TV and an open buffet breakfast included. Both places are extremely comfortable.

Alaşehir

Perched between high mountains and a vine-covered valley leading down to the Gediz flood plain, **ALAŞEHIR** is a pleasant, although nondescript, town easily reached from Sardis or Salihli. Founded originally by Attalus II of Pergamon, and later the Philadelphia of the early Church (one of St John's Seven Churches of Asia in Revelation), its residents always astonished historians by their loyalty to the site despite repeated destruction by earthquakes. This strategic location also wasn't spared the tug of war between Turks and Byzantines, though amazingly it held out as an enclave against the Ottomans until 1390.

Generally the only outsiders passing through today are North American Christians on whirlwind tours of St John's Seven Churches, though the sole evidence of the one here consists of four squat brick stumps that once supported the seventh-century dome of the **Basilica of St John**, in the Beş Eylül district. Finding it is easy enough: stand facing the mid-range *Hotel Benan* on Cumhuriyet Meydanı (☎0236/652 3026; ❷) – incidentally the only comfortable place to stay – and take the street leading diagonally uphill to the left, then look right just after the Atatürk obelisk. On Tuesdays the church neighbourhood is host to a lively street **market**.

If you're pressed for other things to do, visit the small Roman odeion up on **Toptepe**, the hill that overlooks town. The **Byzantine walls**, which only a few decades ago girded much of Alaşehir, have been allowed to crumble; what little remains can be seen at the northeast edge of town, by the bus stand.

Travel details

Trains

Balıkesir to: Bandırma (2 daily; 2hr); Kütahya (4 daily; 5hr).
Manisa to: Afyon (1 daily; 10hr); Alaşehir (1 daily 4hr); Ankara (2 daily; 12hr); Balıkesir (3 daily; 3hr); İzmir (5 daily; 1hr 30min); Salihli (3 daily; 1hr 30min); Sart/Sardis (2 daily; 1hr 30min).

Buses and dolmuşes

Alaşehir to: Denizli (4 daily; 1hr 45min); İzmir (hourly; 2hr); Salihli (hourly; 2hr).
Ayvalık to: Balıkesir (hourly; 2hr); Bergama via Dikili (11 daily; 1hr); Bursa (12 daily; 5hr); Çanakkale (hourly; 3hr 30min); İstanbul (10 daily; 8hr); İzmir (every 30min; 2hr 30min).
Bergama to: Afyon (1 daily; 7hr); Ankara (1 daily; 11hr); Ayvalik (6 daily; 1hr); İstanbul (2 daily;

10hr); İzmir (every 30min; 1hr 45min); Soma (hourly; 1hr).
Çanakkale to: Ayvacık (hourly; 1hr 30min); Ayvalik (every 1 hr; 3hr 30min); Bursa (hourly; 4hr); Ezine (hourly; 1hr); İstanbul (hourly via Thrace; 5hr); İzmir (hourly; 5hr); Lapseki (every 30min; 45min); Troy (every 20min; 30min); Yükyeri İskelesi (3 daily, timed to meet the Bozcaada ferry; 1hr).
Foca to: Çanakkale (hourly; 5hr); İzmir (hourly; 1hr 30min).
Manisa to: Alaşehir (2 daily; 2hr); İzmir (every 10min; 1hr); Salihli via Sart/Sardis (every 30min; 1hr 30min).

Ferries

Ayvalık to: Alibey (June–Sept, every 30min; 30min); Lésvos, Greece (May–Sept daily except Sun; 2hr).
Çanakkale to: Eceabat (hourly, on the hour,

7am–3am; 20min); Gökçeada (June–Sept 1 daily, rest of the year 1 weekly; 3hr); Kilitbahir (every 30min; 10min).

Kabatepe to: Gökçeada (daily in July & Aug, otherwise 2 weekly; 1hr 30min).

Ören to: Akçay (numerous small boats daily in season; 30min).

Yükyeri İskelesi to: Bozcaada (June–Sept 3 daily, rest of the year 2 daily; 1hr 30min).

The central and southern Aegean

✳ **Altınkum, Çeşme**
Altınkum's remote sun-baked coves conceal arguably some of the best beaches on the Aegean Coast. See p.340

✳ **Birgi** Amble through the evocative streets of a sleepy mountain village. See p.348

✳ **Selçuk** This small town is an increasingly popular base from which to explore the famous surrounding historical sights. See p.359

✳ **Priene** Scramble over the ruins of one of the country's best-preserved Hellenistic towns and gaze out over the Meander basin. See p.371

✳ **Heracleia ad Latmos** Former monastic village on Lake Bafa, which has had a compelling hold on the imagination of modern travellers and the Romantic poets alike. See p.381

✳ **Bodrum** Spend a few days sampling the nightlife at Turkey's most fashionable and sophisticated beach resort. See p.392

✳ **Aphrodisias** Ongoing excavations at this beautifully sited Roman city are revealing a site to rival Ephesus in grandeur and importance. See p.428

✳ **Pamukkale** Visit the geological oddity that has found its way onto every Turkish tourism poster. See p.432

Eating

Fast-food joints are thick on the ground and a local favourite is pizza served with fried chicken pieces and chips and topped with mayonnaise and ketchup. The obvious budget eateries within sight of Basmane station have tables on the street and offer the usual range of kebabs, *pide* and stews. They're also usually full of transient male travellers with nowhere else to go, making for a pretty depressing – and undistinguished – meal. There's a far better selection of inexpensive outfits in the **bazaar**, but unfortunately most of them close by 7.30pm. Meals eaten close to the Birinci Kordon **waterfront** represent a definite notch up in price, though not always as much as you'd think, since at most of these places the emphasis is on drinking. Best hunting ground by far, though, is among the restored inland mansions of **Alsancak**; restaurants, café-bars, bars and fast-food outlets abound along Kıbrıs Şehitler Caddesi and its side-streets.

İzmir is particularly noted for its **mussels**, and half a dozen stuffed with rice and pine-nuts make a wonderful cheap snack for well under a dollar – don't be conned into paying more. The street vendors are found everywhere, but it's a good idea not to patronize them between late May and early September, when you stand a good chance of food poisoning.

Bazaar

Doğu Karadeniz Lokantası Yeyisel Çıkmazi 39/E. A late-opening (11pm) *meyhane*, just off the beginning of Anafartalar Cad. All male as a rule, but decorous – outdoor seating and impromptu music with your grilled dishes and cold *mezes*.

Halikarnass Balık Lokantası Junction of 870, 871 and 873 *sok*s, overlooking the fountain. A simple fish restaurant near the Bazdurak Camii fish market, where a meal won't cost more than $7.

Pide Fabrika 857 Sok 5/B. Excellent *pide* starting at an incredibly cheap $0.50 a portion.

Between Konak and Alsancak

Café Browne 1379 Sok, next to *Karaca Hotel*. Popular bar-café in a quiet lane with outdoor seating, serving an excellent range of lunchtime veggie options.

Chinese Restaurant 1385 Sok. Not brilliant, but the least expensive and most central of the city's three oriental food outlets, with good-value lunch specials.

Ora Restaurant Akdeniz Cad. With a mainly young, student crowd, this small restaurant-bar is popular at lunchtimes and for early evening drinks.

Vejetaryen Restaurant 1375 Sok 11. Run by the city's Vegetarian Foundation, just across from the American Hospital. Tiny – about six tables indoors, seven out – but cheerful; count on $5 for a meal. The food sells out early.

Birinci Kordon and Alsancak

Altınkapı 1444 Sok 14/A. Good for *döner* and *piliç* (chicken) grills. It's long-established, and popular with the trendy set who, weather permitting, sit outside on the pedestrianized street.

Bonjour Cafe Bar Corner of Dr Ali Çetinkaya Bul and Pilevene Cad. Light meals and patisserie snacks for the *tikki* (young, rich and trendy) crowd. Ideally positioned amongst the quiet, wide leafy backstreets of chic İzmir, and open late.

Deniz Restaurant *İzmir Palas Hotel*, Vasif Çınar Bul ☎0232/422 0601. Local favourite offering a sophisticated range of seafood dishes, including its speciality fish soup. Reservations necessary at weekends.

Kemal'in Yeri 1453 Sok 20/A ☎0232/422 3190. One of several on this lane, and famous for its excellent (but expensive) seafood; reckon on $15 a head. Reservations recomended.

Liman Çay Salonu Birinci Kordon 128. An extremely varied crowd of locals frequents this place, for unbelievably cheap tea, soft drinks and juices. It's a good place to puff on a *nargile* (Turkish waterpipe).

1888 İkinci Kordon (Cumhuriyet Bul) 248. Turkish and Mediterranean seafood served in a restored eighteenth-century mansion. Set meals for $15, including alcohol.

Drinking and nightlife

Clustered around the Konak Meydanı are a number of bars offering live Turkish music and dancing. But it's upper **Alsancak** that has blossomed as the district for trendy nightlife, with assorted bars and clubs tucked inland along pedestrianized side-streets invisible from Birinci Kordon. It should be stressed that ownership and themes of each establishment tend to roll over on roughly a two-year cycle, so specific recommendations are subject to change.

Longest-lived, if hardly state-of-the-art, places include *Mask*, at 1435 Sok 18 – a bistro-bar with dance floor – and, for the better dressed, *Punta Bar*, in an old merchant's villa at 1469 Sok 26 (open Wed–Sat), with live music some nights. More recent additions include *Nektar*, on İkinci Kordon (Cumhuriyet Bul), offering live Turkish music and *Eko*, on the corner of Pilevne Bulvarı and Cumhuriyet Caddesi, popular with expats and the young and trendy gearing up for a long night out on the town. Also worth a search further north is a local watering-hole, the *Alem Bar*, on the corner of Cumhuriyet Caddesi and 1469 Sok.

The cafés, bars and upmarket teahouses, lining the shore on Birinci Kordon (Atatürk Caddesi) – such as *Despina* – are ideal for a quiet drink and a snack, while watching the sunset. House and trance together with some Turkish tracks can be heard at the best **club** in town, *Outside*, situated east of Alsancak on Şehitler Caddesi; cross the railway junction, take a right and follow round past the football stadium and it's on the left.

Arts and entertainment

The **Atatürk Cultural Centre** at Mithatpaşa Cad 92 (Atatürk Kültür Merkezi; ℡0232/483 8520) is home to the local symphony orchestra, which plays regularly on Friday evening and Saturday at noon and hosts occasional concerts by "serious" soloists. Tickets are not always sold on the spot – read the hoardings outside the building for directions or ask at the information desk. More varied is the programme offered by the **State Opera and Ballet** (Devlet Opera ve Balesi; ℡0232/484 3692), housed in a wonderful Ottoman Art Deco specimen on Milli Kütüphane Caddesi, which encompasses everything from chamber music to pop and jazz. Tickets are sold on the premises. Other **classical music concerts** are held at Dokuz Eylül University's Sabanci Cultural Centre, Mithatpaşa Caddesi (℡0232/441 9009 or 441 8477), while with the onset of the hot weather, events move to the open-air theatre in the **Kültür Parkı**.

Most of İzmir's small **cinemas** are located in and around Konak Meydanı, including Çınar in the SSK shopping arcade and Soma, Konak & San on Anafartalar Caddesi, to the right of the tourist information booth. Mid-April sporadically sees the holding of the **İzmir International Film Festival**, featuring foreign releases, all shown in their original languages with subtitles.

International İzmir Festival

Linchpin of the summer season is the **International İzmir Festival**, running from mid-June to early July. It's something of a misnomer since many events take place at various restored venues at Ephesus or Çeşme castle. Tickets tend to run to $10–18 a head, but fifty-percent student discounts are available and the acts featured are often world-class – past names have included Sarah Vaughan, the Moscow Ballet, Paco Peña, Ravi Shankar and Chris de Burgh. Get this year's programme from the **İzmir Culture Foundation** at Zair Ezref Bul, Park Apt 58/4, 35220 Alsancak (℡0232/463 0300), or from the city tourist offices. **Tickets** are usually available from the State Opera and Ballet box office, the museum in Selçuk, the İzmir *Hilton* or the tourist office in Kuşadası.

Eating

Fast-food joints are thick on the ground and a local favourite is pizza served with fried chicken pieces and chips and topped with mayonnaise and ketchup. The obvious budget eateries within sight of Basmane station have tables on the street and offer the usual range of kebabs, *pide* and stews. They're also usually full of transient male travellers with nowhere else to go, making for a pretty depressing – and undistinguished – meal. There's a far better selection of inexpensive outfits in the **bazaar**, but unfortunately most of them close by 7.30pm. Meals eaten close to the Birinci Kordon **waterfront** represent a definite notch up in price, though not always as much as you'd think, since at most of these places the emphasis is on drinking. Best hunting ground by far, though, is among the restored inland mansions of **Alsancak**; restaurants, café-bars, bars and fast-food outlets abound along Kıbrıs Şehitler Caddesi and its side-streets.

İzmir is particularly noted for its **mussels**, and half a dozen stuffed with rice and pine-nuts make a wonderful cheap snack for well under a dollar – don't be conned into paying more. The street vendors are found everywhere, but it's a good idea not to patronize them between late May and early September, when you stand a good chance of food poisoning.

Bazaar

Doğu Karadeniz Lokantası Yeyisel Çıkmazi 39/E. A late-opening (11pm) *meyhane*, just off the beginning of Anafartalar Cad. All male as a rule, but decorous – outdoor seating and impromptu music with your grilled dishes and cold *mezes*.

Halikarnass Balık Lokantası Junction of 870, 871 and 873 *soks*, overlooking the fountain. A simple fish restaurant near the Bazdurak Camii fish market, where a meal won't cost more than $7.

Pide Fabrika 857 Sok 5/B. Excellent *pide* starting at an incredibly cheap $0.50 a portion.

Between Konak and Alsancak

Café Browne 1379 Sok, next to *Karaca Hotel*. Popular bar-café in a quiet lane with outdoor seating, serving an excellent range of lunchtime veggie options.

Chinese Restaurant 1385 Sok. Not brilliant, but the least expensive and most central of the city's three oriental food outlets, with good-value lunch specials.

Ora Restaurant Akdeniz Cad. With a mainly young, student crowd, this small restaurant-bar is popular at lunchtimes and for early evening drinks.

Vejetaryen Restaurant 1375 Sok 11. Run by the city's Vegetarian Foundation, just across from the American Hospital. Tiny – about six tables indoors, seven out – but cheerful; count on $5 for a meal. The food sells out early.

Birinci Kordon and Alsancak

Altınkapı 1444 Sok 14/A. Good for *döner* and *piliç* (chicken) grills. It's long-established, and popular with the trendy set who, weather permitting, sit outside on the pedestrianized street.

Bonjour Cafe Bar Corner of Dr Ali Çetinkaya Bul and Pilevene Cad. Light meals and patisserie snacks for the *tikki* (young, rich and trendy) crowd. Ideally positioned amongst the quiet, wide leafy backstreets of chic İzmir, and open late.

Deniz Restaurant *İzmir Palas Hotel*, Vasif Çınar Bul ☏0232/422 0601. Local favourite offering a sophisticated range of seafood dishes, including its speciality fish soup. Reservations necessary at weekends.

Kemal'in Yeri 1453 Sok 20/A ☏0232/422 3190. One of several on this lane, and famous for its excellent (but expensive) seafood; reckon on $15 a head. Reservations recomended.

Liman Çay Salonu Birinci Kordon 128. An extremely varied crowd of locals frequents this place, for unbelievably cheap tea, soft drinks and juices. It's a good place to puff on a *nargile* (Turkish waterpipe).

1888 İkinci Kordon (Cumhuriyet Bul) 248. Turkish and Mediterranean seafood served in a restored eighteenth-century mansion. Set meals for $15, including alcohol.

Drinking and nightlife

Clustered around the Konak Meydanı are a number of bars offering live Turkish music and dancing. But it's upper **Alsancak** that has blossomed as the district for trendy nightlife, with assorted bars and clubs tucked inland along pedestrianized side-streets invisible from Birinci Kordon. It should be stressed that ownership and themes of each establishment tend to roll over on roughly a two-year cycle, so specific recommendations are subject to change. Longest-lived, if hardly state-of-the-art, places include *Mask*, at 1435 Sok 18 – a bistro-bar with dance floor – and, for the better dressed, *Punta Bar*, in an old merchant's villa at 1469 Sok 26 (open Wed–Sat), with live music some nights. More recent additions include *Nektar*, on İkinci Kordon (Cumhuriyet Bul), offering live Turkish music and *Eko*, on the corner of Pilevne Bulvarı and Cumhuriyet Caddesi, popular with expats and the young and trendy gearing up for a long night out on the town. Also worth a search further north is a local watering-hole, the *Alem Bar*, on the corner of Cumhuriyet Caddesi and 1469 Sok.

The cafés, bars and upmarket teahouses, lining the shore on Birinci Kordon (Atatürk Caddesi) – such as *Despina* – are ideal for a quiet drink and a snack, while watching the sunset. House and trance together with some Turkish tracks can be heard at the best **club** in town, *Outside*, situated east of Alsancak on Şehitler Caddesi; cross the railway junction, take a right and follow round past the football stadium and it's on the left.

Arts and entertainment

The **Atatürk Cultural Centre** at Mithatpaşa Cad 92 (Atatürk Kültür Merkezi; ☎0232/483 8520) is home to the local symphony orchestra, which plays regularly on Friday evening and Saturday at noon and hosts occasional concerts by "serious" soloists. Tickets are not always sold on the spot – read the hoardings outside the building for directions or ask at the information desk. More varied is the programme offered by the **State Opera and Ballet** (Devlet Opera ve Balesi; ☎0232/484 3692), housed in a wonderful Ottoman Art Deco specimen on Milli Kütüphane Caddesi, which encompasses everything from chamber music to pop and jazz. Tickets are sold on the premises. Other **classical music concerts** are held at Dokuz Eylül University's Sabanci Cultural Centre, Mithatpaşa Caddesi (☎0232/441 9009 or 441 8477), while with the onset of the hot weather, events move to the open-air theatre in the **Kültür Parkı**.

Most of Izmir's small **cinemas** are located in and around Konak Meydanı, including Çınar in the SSK shopping arcade and Soma, Konak & San on Anafartalar Caddesi, to the right of the tourist information booth. Mid-April sporadically sees the holding of the **İzmir International Film Festival**, featuring foreign releases, all shown in their original languages with subtitles.

International İzmir Festival

inchpin of the summer season is the **International İzmir Festival**, running from l. d-June to early July. It's something of a misnomer since many events take place at arious restored venues at Ephesus or Çeşme castle. Tickets tend to run to $10- 8 a head, but fifty-percent student discounts are available and the acts featured re often world-class – past names have included Sarah Vaughan, the Moscow Ballet, Paco Peña, Ravi Shankar and Chris de Burgh. Get this year's programme m the **İzmir Culture Foundation** at Zair Ezref Bul, Park Apt 58/4, 35220 Alsancak (0232/463 0300), or from the city tourist offices. **Tickets** are usually available fro the State Opera and Ballet box office, the museum in Selçuk, the İzmir *Hilton* or he tourist office in Kuşadası.

Altınkum is easily reached by dolmuş, and between June and September the service continues a kilometre or so from the bus stand at the first cove to the **central cove**, stopping opposite the tiny *jandarma* outpost. This is probably the best beach between Bozcaada and the Turquoise Coast, where multi-hued water laps hundreds of metres of sand and dunes. At one time, it was a stopover on the hippy trail and the cove is still host to a rash of seasonal wooden bars that spring up from the dunes. *Cennet Camping* (☎0532/394 0131; summer only), ten minutes' walk along the beach, is by far the best **campsite** and also rents out tents ($10). Run by the garrulous Okan, and popular with young İzmir weekenders, the site lies within an organic farm, set in gorgeous surroundings just off the beach. The attached **restaurant** is popular at weekends, serving assorted fish dishes ($8) and spicy *menemen*. In high season you can **rent kayaks and windsurfers** from the Fun Club on the beach; though it's often windy here, the water is very clear and warm. It's also permissible to camp on the beach.

In high summer you have to walk pretty far to the east to lose the crowds – possibly over the headland to the **easternmost cove**, equal in all respects to the central one. This is accessible along a direct, un-signposted road from Çiftlik (bear left at the north edge of town).

North: Daylan

The approach to **DALYAN**, 4km north of Çeşme, is announced by a strange, four-storey tower looming over the village's remaining Greek-built houses. This straggly fishing settlement, built on the west shore of an almost completely landlocked harbour, is becoming a popular location for retirement and holiday homes. There are, however, few short-term places to stay, and even less in the way of sandy beach, so for most people a clutch of fish restaurants, appealingly set by the narrow channel to the open sea, will be the extent of Dalyan's interest.

Dolmuşes from Çeşme (every 45min or when full) drop you at the small statue that acts as the main square for the village. Follow the channel round to find a group of nicely presented **restaurants** – the *Liman*, *Körfez*, *Köşem* and *Borsa Dalyanköy* – offering (not particularly cheap) *meze* and seafood with outside seating and fine views over the harbour. Less pricey options include the *Levant* and *Sülo Nun Yeri* near the statue. The *Köşem* is also a **hotel**, aimed at the yacht and weekend trade (☎0232/724 7358, ☏724 8800; ❸); or you might try the small family-run *Güven Pansiyon* (☎0232/724 7031; ❶), where breakfast isn't included in the price.

Northeast: Ildır and ancient Erythrae

ILDIR – 27km northeast of Çeşme – is a poky little village with minimal tourist facilities, its Greek houses either abandoned or unimproved. This is due to an archeological preservation order, since Ildır is built just to one side of the acropolis of **ancient Erythrae**, an important site during Hellenistic and Roman times. The ancient city was renowned for two local cults: that of a sibyl (or prophetess), second in importance only to the one at Cumae in Italy; and that of Hercules, venerated in a temple containing a miraculous statue of the god. All traces of both have long since vanished, along with quite a bit of the rest of Erythrae, since villagers of all subsequent eras simply helped themselves to the masonry. What was fortuitously rescued can be found in the archeological museum in İzmir.

A well-defined path leads from the edge of Ildır, up the conical hill behind, to the caretaker's white sentry box. If he's around he'll take you on a fifteeen-minute tour of the highlights, though the trodden paths lead obviously enough to most attractions. Only a few courses of wall and a recent, battered Greek church remain on the summit; the **theatre**, disfigured by concrete stairs, spills down the north slope. North of a wheatfield-cum-pear orchard, you'll be shown an old **tomb** and several houses standing to waist height, including a large **Roman villa** with a fieldstone floor and storage cistern. Panoramas west over the islet-flecked gulf, and north to the mountains looming over the Gerence Körfezi, are the main recompense for the trip up.

Dolmuşes leave Çeşme's *otogar* for Ildır when full. Because of the village's listed status, amenities are fairly limited, with **accommodation** provided either by the *Ildır Pansiyon* (☎0232/725 1109; ❷), to the north of the village; or the *Erythrae Hotel* (☎0232/725 1500, ⓦwww.otelerythrae.com.tr; ❻), one bay before the village. There are also a few fish **restaurants**, including the *Balıkçı Ramazanın Yeri* and the waterside *Ildır* (tasty but pricey at $25 for two).

The Karaburun peninsula

The little visited **Karaburun peninsula**, which spears northeast of Çeşme, provides a good day trip for anyone wanting to get off the beaten track. You'll need your own transport, though – while there is an unreliable **bus** service along the old İzmir–Çeşme highway to Karaburun town, 75km from İzmir, there's no public transport to the more isolated villages and beaches, or to the ancient site of Clazomenae, and there are few other facilities for the casual visitor.

The turn-off for the peninsula from the old highway is 12km west of Urla; from the new expressway, it's about 9km west of the Urla exit. The first place you'd be tempted to stop is **BALIKLIOVA**, a sheltered bay with some patches of beach and a restaurant or two. **MORDOĞAN**, about halfway up the east coast, is a proper town, but its sand beach is completely overshadowed by the renovated harbour and new development. The final stretch to Karaburun is dramatic, with villages and orchards clinging to the crags of 1218-metre Akdağ mountain, although **KARABURUN** itself is a letdown, with an exposed, rocky shore and a port redeemed only by a few fish restaurants.

Beyond here, the road – paved until Küçükbahçe village, dirt thereafter – makes a loop completely around the peninsula to Ildır (see p.345), winding through several crumbling, half-inhabited villages that were Greek before 1922. Several pebble **beaches** face Híos and Inoússes, but they're difficult to get at without a motorcycle. The most accessible and protected lie in the embrace of the **Gerence Körfezi** gulf, and by this point you're within 6km of Ildır, or only 10km from Balıklıova via another dirt road spanning the narrow neck of the peninsula.

Jutting into the İzmir Körfez, just east of the Karaburun peninsula, is the site of the Ionian city of **Clazomenae** (Klazomenai in Turkish; always open; free). Most interesting of the remaining ruins is the olive-oil factory dating from the sixth century BC. The mill with its cylindrical roller and three separation pits are clearly visible, and plans are afoot to open the structure as a working museum.

Sığacık and around

Southwest of İzmir, **SIĞACIK** huddles inside a low-slung Genoese castle, with many of its houses built right into the perimeter walls. Otherwise the village is of middling architectural interest and, although you might want to wander the maze of alleys inside, foreigners come to Sığacık primarily for the sake of its good yacht anchorage. Certainly, there are no decent beaches in sight and for a swim you'll need to continue 1.5km over the hill to the west to **Akkum**, a 150-metre-wide sandy cove that's gradually becoming oversubscribed.

The journey to Sığacık by bus is complicated by loop routes and the frequent need to change vehicles. From İzmir or Kuşadası (hourly services from either), you'll find you probably have to change in **Seferihisar**, a large town 40km southwest of İzmir and 6km east of Sığacık – here you can catch a red-and-white *Belediye* bus to cover the remaining distance to Sigacik and Akkum.

The best of Sığacık's **accommodation** is the Dutch-run *Teos Pension* near the castle (℡0232/745 7463; ❷), with well-kept doubles and a decent attached restaurant and bar. Otherwise there's the *Burg Pansiyon* (℡0232/745 7464, ℱ745 7306; ❶), a recent but traditional-style building right on the quay. Some of the rooms here have sea views. At Akkum there's a **campsite**, *Bungalow Kamping*, on the cape, just past the large *Neptun* windsurfing resort whose patrons crowd out the beach. There are a few fish **restaurants** overlooking the harbour, including the upmarket *Liman*, with quality fish meals for around $10.

Teos

The same road serving Akkum continues for just under 5km to **ancient Teos** (site unenclosed; $1.50 when kiosk manned), though approaching on foot you can miss out the final zigzags.

Teos was once one of the most important Ionian cities, renowned for its colossal temple to Dionysos, deity not only of wine but of the arts and the generative forces of nature. Accordingly, in early Roman times Teos was chosen to host the Guild of Dionysos, the union of all artists, actors and musicians who performed throughout Asia Minor. They soon proved so insufferable that the Teans exiled them to backwaters down the coast. An earlier, more genial embodiment of the Dionysian ethic was the city's famous son, the sixth-century poet **Anacreon**, who choked to death on a grape seed after a long life of wine, women and song.

Appropriately, the second-century BC **Temple of Dionysos** is the most interesting remnant, excavated – with three columns partly re-erected – in a bucolic setting of olive trees and grazing cattle. You can also pick your way 400m northeast to a hillside supporting the **Hellenistic theatre**, though only the stage foundations are left of this, and it's debatable whether it's worth snaking around the wheat fields and buzzing cow-pat flies for the view south over assorted islets to Sámos. About 100m southeast of the theatre you might find the eleven remaining rows of the Roman-era **odeion**. When you've finished sightseeing, call at the small drinks stand that operates in high season, at the road's end in front of the temple.

Inland: the Küçük Menderes valley

With a spare day, the inland towns and villages of the **Küçük Menderes valley**, southeast of İzmir, are easily seen by public transport, as connections from both İzmir and Selçuk are good. To reach Birgi village, the lake at Gölcük or the conservative town of Tire, you first have to travel via the undistinguished market town of **Ödemiş** – 80km southeast of İzmir – to which there are buses every two hours from İzmir's *büyük otogar*, a three-and-a-half-hour ride. From Ödemiş *otogar* there are hourly services to Birgi and Tire, while six or seven daily dolmuşes to Gölcük leave from the corner of Hatay and Namik Kemal *caddesi,* some 200m from the *otogar.* Failing these, anything plying the mountain road to Salihli passes within 3km of Gölcük and 1km of Birgi, or you'll have to arrange a taxi from Ödemiş ($3 per car to Birgi, $6 to Gölcük).

Birgi

A sleepy community of half-timbered houses lining both slopes of a narrow valley at the foot of Boz Dağ, **BİRGİ**, 9km east of Ödemiş, is an excellent example of what small-town Turkey looked like before the wars and cement mania of the twentieth century.

The main thing to see is the **Aydınoğlu Mehmet Bey Camii**, also called the Ulu Cami, an engaging fourteenth-century mosque on the site of an earlier church. It's across the ravine from the Çakırağa Konaği (see below), a little way upstream. Quite a lot of ancient Pyrgion, including a sculpted lion, is incorporated into the exterior walls; inside, it's an understated masterpiece, with the tiled *mihrab* and a single arch betraying a Selçuk influence. Most impressive, though, are the carved hardwood *mimber* and shutters, some of them replacements for those carted off to the Selimiye Camii in Edirne. The sloping wooden roof is supported by a forest of Roman columns, the whole effect more like Spanish Andalucia than Turkey. The minaret features zigzag belts of glazed green tiles, like the Yeşil Cami in İznik, while the dome of the adjacent *türbe* (tomb) of the Aydınoğlu clan is fashioned in concentric rings of alternating brick and the same faïence. A couple of other mid- to late-period Ottoman mosques perch next to or above the stream, along with some ruined baths and a *medrese*, but while these add to the atmosphere of the place none can compare to the Ulu Cami.

Birgi's houses – ensembles of wood and either brick, stone, lath-and-plaster or half-timbered mud – run the gamut from the simple to the sumptuous. Many are dilapidated, but the restored eighteenth-century **Çakırağa Konağı** (Tues–Sun 9am–noon & 1–6pm; $0.70) operates as a museum and has some explanatory panels in English. Built by one Zerif Aliağa in 1761, the mansion is one of the best surviving specimens of those built in the wake of the decentralizing reforms of the eighteenth century, which allowed local potentates (the *derebeys*) to rule and live in grand style. Many have burned down or simply rotted away owing to the widespread use of wood in coffered and painted ceilings, lattices and built-in cupboards (*mısandras*). Most *konaks* were two-storeyed, but the slope here dictates a three-storey plan: the ground floor in stone, the upper floors in lath-and-plaster. The extensive and vivid murals depict stylized skylines of favourite coastal cities; the presence or absence of particular structures allows dating of the paintings to the nineteenth century.

Despite the increased tourist traffic, attracted by the mansion, Birgi actually boasts fewer facilities for outsiders than in previous years, making Gölcük a more likely base. The only candidate for **accommodation** is the grim *Belediye Inn* (no phone; $6 per person), and you'll need plenty of time during weekday working hours to track down the warden with the key. Next to the *Çakırağa Konağı* the beautifully restored *Konak* **café** serves delicious coffee and cakes. It's run by a retired artist and schoolteacher, whose architect son is very active in restoring the local properties.

Gölcük

GÖLCÜK, 20km north of Birgi, is just about the last thing you'd expect to see in the Aegean region: a six-acre alpine **lake** in a wooded cavity tucked nearly halfway up 2129-metre Boz Dağ. The coolness and the greenery make it a favourite local summer and winter retreat. The lakeshore itself is surprisingly undisturbed, probably because swimming in the reedy, murky waters is forbidden.

Many come just for the day to eat **catfish** (*yayın* in Turkish) at the *Rıhtım Restaurant*, which has a gazebo built on stilts over the water. **Accommodation** is limited and liable to fill in high season, but you may want to try the *Kavaklı Pansiyon* (☎0232/558 1358; ➊; closed in winter), with clean, waterless doubles and the use of a kitchen. The very large *Otel Prenses* (☎0232/558 1115, ℱ558 1148; ➌), located in extensive lakeside grounds, seems expensive on the face of it but its large rooms, some with balcony views of the lake, and half-board facilities (with excellent chicken and lamb *şiş* and *köfte* meals) make it very good value; it's open all year.

Tire

Thirty kilometres across the valley floor from Ödemiş, **TİRE**, clustered at the base of Güme Dağı, is an altogether different proposition. Much fought over by Byzantines and Selçuks, it eventually became one of the Aydınoğlu clan's first important strongholds, and the conservatism and religious fervour of the inhabitants is still apparent (and disparaged by secular Turks). If you've had an overdose of the touristed coast, Tire makes the perfect antidote – though being stared at may be part of the experience.

There are hourly **dolmuşes** here from Ödemiş. The **old quarter** with its rickety houses is uphill from the main traffic roundabout in the northwest of town; you might have a look at the map posted outside the **museum** (daily except Mon 8.30am–noon & 1–5pm; $0.70), but the best strategy is just to wander around. First, find the **Yeşil Imaret Zaviyesi**, also known as the Yahşi Bey Camii, built in 1442 by a general of Murat II as the core of a dervish community. An unusual scallop-shell half-dome looms over the *mihrab*, as does stalactite vaulting over the front door. No other monument cries out for attention – your main impression will be of a staggering number (reputedly 37) of indifferently restored Ottoman mosques, and older *türbe*s or tombs, including two by the *otogar*.

Tire's atmosphere is, however, considerably enlivened by a large gypsy presence from the surrounding villages, most in evidence at the weekly **Tuesday market**, reputedly the best in the Aegean region. The gypsies are probably the source of the lace articles sold in the bazaar, and of the local horse-cart painting technique, imitated by some wealthy city-dwellers on their kitchen cabinets.

The heart of ancient Ionia

Although ancient **Ionia** – including half of the historic league of thirteen cities known as the Panionium – extended north of the Çeşme peninsula, what the term usually evokes is the often startlingly beautiful territory around the deltas of the Küçük and Büyük Menderes rivers. Few other parts of Turkey can match this region for the sheer concentration of ancient cities, which in their time were at the forefront in the emergence of the sciences, philosophy and the arts.

The Ionian coast was first colonized by Greek-speakers in the twelfth century BC and the culture reached its zenith during the seventh and sixth centuries BC. Enormous advantages accrued to those who chose to settle here: an amenable climate, fertile, well-watered terrain, and a strategic location between the Aegean – with its many fine harbours – and inland Anatolia. Local development was only temporarily hampered by the Persian invasions, Alexander the Great's contrary campaigns, and the chaos following his death, and under the Romans and the Byzantines the region perked up again. Indeed, urban life here might have continued indefinitely were it not for the inexorably receding coastline – thanks to the two silt-bearing rivers. By mid-Byzantine times virtually all of the Ionian cities had been abandoned, and with the declaration of Christianity as the state religion, religious centres and oracles met a similar fate.

Today's inhabitants have found the silver lining to the cloud of the advancing deltas, cashing in on the rich soil brought down from the hills. Vast tracts of cotton, tobacco, sesame and grain benefit from irrigation works, while groves of pine, olive and cypress, which need no such encouragement, adorn the hills and wilder reaches. And the sea, though more distant than in former times, still beckons when tramping the ruins palls. Indeed, tourism is now threatening to outstrip agriculture as a means of making a living.

This is nowhere more obvious than in **Kuşadası**, an unabashedly utilitarian base for excursions to the major antiquities. There are some beaches and minor sites to delay your progress inland, particularly to the north at **Pamucak** and **Claros**, but the main show of the area is undoubtedly the ensemble of ruins further south, spanning numerous eras: most notably at **Ephesus**; at **Priene** – perhaps the most dramatic site of all the Ionian cities; at **Miletus**, further south – probably the least impressive; and at **Didyma**, with its gargantuan temple. The beaches near these ruins unfortunately tend to be functional at best and always exposed; the immensely popular exception is **Altınkum**, now a densely developed and tatty package-holiday venue.

Kuşadası

KUŞADASI is Turkey's most bloated resort, a brash, mercenary and unpleasant Las Vegas-on-Sea that extends along several kilometres of coast and well inland. In just three decades its population has swelled from about 6000 to almost 40,000, though how many of these are year-round inhabitants is debatable.

The town – whose name means "Bird Island" – is many people's introduction to the country: efficient ferry services link it with the Greek island of Sámos, while the resort is an obligatory port of call for Aegean cruise ships,

which disgorge vast crowds in summer, who delight the local souvenir merchants after a visit to the ruins of Ephesus just inland. Not to be outdone by Bodrum and Marmaris, and in a studied attempt to siphon off some business from the Greek islands opposite, the local authorities have also constructed a huge yacht marina at the north end of town. It's the largest and best-equipped marina northwest of Marmaris, but it can't help but seem a strange venture, since the coast nearby is largely exposed leeward shore and unsuitable for cruising.

Not surprisingly, all this rapid development has affected local attitudes. New arrivals are besieged by touts offering accommodation, carpets and so forth, and unaccompanied women should be prepared for the shock of being singled out as targets. In recent years Kuşadası has promoted downmarket package tourism in a bid to bolster flagging visitor numbers, though the collapse in the tourism sector has badly affected even this trade. Reasons to stay here include the excellent connections to nearby attractions, the adjacent beaches and the lively and comparatively sophisticated nightlife, rather than the town's minimal charm. However, if beer-guzzling holiday-makers leave you cold, you might prefer Selçuk as a base.

Kuşadası's origins are obscure; no proven trace has been found of any ancient settlement. The Venetians and Genoese renamed the Byzantine anchorage of Ania as Scala Nuova when they established the harbour here to replace Ephesus's silted-up one, but only in the Ottoman era did the port acquire its current name, derived from the small fortified islet – Güvercin Adasi, or "Pigeon Island" – tethered to the mainland by a causeway. The little castle on the island is actually the southernmost of several Aegean fortresses built by the Genoese during the fourteenth and fifteenth centuries. Sepia-toned postcards for sale, reissued by the local Lions' Club, show the town as it was from the 1920s until the 1950s: handsome, tiered ensembles of tile-roofed nineteenth-century houses grouped in distinct neighbourhoods (of the Jews, the Greeks, the Muslim immigrants from Crete or the Peloponnese) – especially poignant souvenirs in light of what has transpired here since the 1970s.

Arrival and information

Arriving by **ferry** from Sámos, you'll exit customs directly onto Liman Caddesi, and walk right past the **tourist office** at no. 13 (June–Sept daily 8am–5pm; Oct–May Mon–Fri 8am–5pm; ☏0256/614 1103), which hands out town plans and keeps exhaustive lists of accommodation. For a better map of the town, buy a copy of the "City Plan, Kuşadası", from Kuydaş bookshop (see "Listings", p.356).

The **long-distance otogar**, where you're dropped if coming from the south, is over a kilometre out, past the end of Kahramanlar Caddesi on the ring road (*çevre yolu*) to Söke. **Dolmuşes** to and from Selçuk, Söke and the Dilek national park often accept passengers at a stop slightly closer to the centre, on the corner of Adnan Menderes Bulvarı and Candan Tarhan Bulvarı; all long-distance services make a stop near here too. **Local dolmuşes** linking the northern Tusan beach with the town centre and its southern annex of Kadınlar Denizi stop at the corner of Atatürk and İnönü *bulvarıs*.

If you're bound for İzmir on *Elbirlik*'s frequent shuttle service, you really have to trudge out to the *otogar* to be sure of getting a seat, since they often sell out. Little publicized is the fact that these buses pass the **airport** gate, 700m from the terminal proper; ask to be let off at *havalimanı kavşağı* ("airport junction"), and allow an hour and a half for the trip. Taxis usually wait to transfer you the final distance from the junction to the airport, and you pay $2.50 maximum per car. A taxi between Kuşadası and the airport will cost you a staggering $60.

Drivers should leave their cars fairly far north along Atatürk Bulvarı, or well out on Güvercin Adası Caddesi, or (for a fee) in the *kapanlı* (covered) **car park** on Inonu Bulvarı. Illegally parked vehicles will be towed to a remote pound and drivers fined a minimum of $20.

Accommodation

The tourist office lists over 400 **hotels and pansiyons** of all categories in Kuşadası, though some of these are used as brothels. One area for reasonably priced, hygienic accommodation is just south of the Kale – the core of the town – uphill from Barbaros Hayrettin Bulvarı, particularly the upper reaches of Yildirim, Aslanlar and Kıbrıs *caddesi*s. For a relatively central location with a sea view, try Bezirgan Sokak, above Kıbrıs Caddesi, reached quickest via the stairs behind the new shopping centre with its clocktower. For more comfort, there are a number of sea-view establishments scattered along the entire length of the shore road. Kadınlar Denizi (Ladies' Beach) may suggest itself as a cheap and cheerful base, but accommodation here can be squalid, and the poor beach can't compensate for its relative remoteness.

It's advisable to choose from the hotels and *pansiyon*s we recommend below, as we have received serious complaints about a number of establishments and proprietors, particularly those who tout at the *otogar* or the pier.

Bezirgan Sokak

Hasgül Bezirgan Sok 53 ☏0256/614 3641. At the quiet end of Bezirgan Sok, past the co-managed *Hotel Stella*. Some of the plainly decorated rooms overlook the bay; there's a terrific roof terrace, friendly staff plus pool privileges at the *Stella*. ❷

Hotel Neptun Alley off Bezirgan Sok ☏0256/614 1540. Very quiet position, with ocean glimpses from some of the rooms at this older hotel; breakfast not included. ❷

Hotel Stella Bezirgan Sok 44 ☏0256/614 1632, ⓦwww.stellatravelersinn.com. Kilim decor for the common areas, good-sized tile-floor rooms with balconies, rooftop bar, swimming pool and friendly management make this the choice establishment on this street. Breakfast not included. ❸

Kıbrıs Caddesi and Kale

Bahar Pansiyon Cephane Sok 12, Kale ☏0256/614 1191. Down in the flatlands in an area better known for nightlife than quiet sleep, but the double glazing in the well-appointed, air-conditioned rooms keeps the noise at bay. Closed in winter. ❸

Liman Otel Kıbrıs Cad, Buyral Sok 4 ☏0256/612 3149, ⓕ614 6913. Fair-sized rooms, some with air-conditioning and tiled bathrooms, in a small, modern building. It's central but relatively calm; ask for a sea-facing or side room. ❸

Özhan Pansiyon Kıbrıs Cad 5 ☏0256/614 2932. Small but reasonably kept *pansiyon*, whose quiet doubles with neutral decor represent good value. A nice terrace bar and heating in winter. ❷

Sammy's Palace Kıbrıs Cad 14 ☏0256/612 2588, ⓦwww.hotelsammyspalace.com. Part of the European Backpacker Network, this large hostel, favoured by antipodeans, has cramped dorms ($5) and basic doubles, and a rooftop restaurant/bar commanding enviable views of the shoreline. It's well organized, with internet and laundry facilities, and a street-level travel agent. ❷

Surtel Hotel Atatürk Bul 20, Hacivat Sok ☏0256/612 0606, ⓔsurtel@net.tr. Three-star comfort on a pedestrian alley bordering the *kale* wall. Attractively designed complex with a shaded café, large pool and restaurant. Rooms are spacious and comfortable, if rather heavy on the chintz. ❹

Yıldırım and Aslanlar caddesis

Cennet Pansiyon Yayla Sok 1, corner of Yildirim Cad ☏0256/614 4893. Spotless *pansiyon* with a small garden. *Table d'hôte* meals available by advance arrangement. ❷

Dileck Hotel Kahramanlar Cad 73 ☏0256/614 9262, ⓦwww.dilekhotel.com. A centrally located hotel with a small pool, spacious dining area and

well-stocked bar. Doubles are fairly minimally furnished, with dark-wood fittings, tiled floors and
air-conditioning. ❸
Golden Bed Aslanlar Cad, Uğurlu Birinci Çıkmazı 4
☎0256/614 8708,
ⓦwww.kusadasihotels.com/goldenbed.
Signposted from Yıldırım Cad, this laidback, friendly and quiet *pansiyon* is nicely decorated with kilims and home furnishings. Good views from both
the balconied rooms and the rooftop breakfast terrace. Book ahead in high season. ❸
Sempati Pansiyon Güvercin Sok 16 ☎0256/614
4388. Female-run establishment, offering plain en-
suite rooms and cheap home-cooked meals on the
terrace on request. ❷
Sezgin Hotel Aslanlar Cad 68 ☎0256/614 4225,
ⓔsezgin@ispro.net.tr. Run by the energetic Sezgin
("Mr Flash") and his multi-lingual staff, this
extremely well-organized hotel, popular with backpackers, has a breakfast garden with pool, satellite
TV, internet facilities, and a wide range of other
services including airport pickup and a ten-percent
discount on Samos tickets. ❶

On the seafront

Altınsaray Otel Yılancı Burnu Sok ☎0256/614
4939, ⓦwww.hotelaltinsaray.com. Attractively set
in landscaped gardens; with a *faux* İznik-tiled atrium and dining room. Only some of the smallish
rooms have balconies overlooking the medium-
sized pool, but the beach isn't far away. ❸

Ilyada Hotel Atatürk Bul 40 ☎0256/614 3807,
ⓔilyadakusadasi1@superonline.com.tr. Well-
maintained seafront hotel, of 1970s vintage but
recently refurbished; the surprisingly quiet rooms
have sea views, TV and air-conditioning. ❹
Kismet Hotel Yacht Marina ☎0256/618 1290,
ⓦwww.kismet.com.tr. Part owned by Hümeyra
Özbaş, a princess descended from the last
Ottoman sultan – a fact that rather sets the tone
for this elegant spot in well-kept gardens.
Ordinary rooms resemble small suites, while "de
luxe" rooms are palatial. Private lido and tennis
court; limited package presence (Simply Turkey
and Anatolian Sky). Prices run as high as $250,
though there are advantageous half-board rates.
❽
Köken Otel İstiklal Cad 5 ☎0256/614 1460,
ⓔinfo@hotelköken.com. Set back just inland from
noisy Atatürk Bul, this small, friendly two-star
hotel has balconied rooms with sea views. ❷

Campsites

Önder Atatürk Bul 74, behind the Yacht Marina
☎0256/618 1590, ⒻF618 1517. Popular, reasonably priced place with good facilities, including
tennis courts, a swimming pool and restaurant.
Open all year.
Tur-Yat Kamping Tusan beach ☎0256/618 0809.
A well-appointed spot for tenting down, though its
two/three-person bungalows (❹) are downright
unreasonably priced. Open May–Oct.

The Town

Liman Caddesi runs 200m from the ferry port up to the sixteenth-century
Öküz Mehmet Paşa Kervansaray, restored as a tawdry "luxury" hotel,
before turning hard left to become Atatürk Bulvarı, the main harbour
esplanade. Barbaros Hayrettin Bulvarı is a pedestrian precinct beginning next
to the *kervansaray* and homing in on a little **stone tower**, a remnant of the
town's medieval walls. To the left as you ascend lies the **Kale district**, huddled
inside the rest of the walls, with a namesake mosque and some fine traditional
houses that help lend the town what little appeal it has – most of these have
been done up as restaurants and bars. Bearing left down Sağlık Caddesi takes
you along the rear of Kale, where bits of old wall (including the landscaped
stretch parallel to Hacivat Sokak) are visible; bearing right leads up towards
some of Kuşadası's more desirable *pansiyons*, scattered among the largest
neighbourhood of handsome old dwellings. Continuing straight on, the walkway (emblazoned with a sign "Old Bazaar") changes its name to Kahramanlar
Caddesi, dividing (the left fork becomes Adnan Menderes Bulvarı) just past the
Hanım Camii. **Market day** is Friday, with the market area north of Adnan
Menderes Bulvarı inevitably skewed by tourist interests.

Out across the causeway, **Güvercin Adası** presents a series of landscaped terraces within its fortifications, dotted with tea gardens and snack bars – good
spots to wait for an afternoon ferry to Greece. Swimming off the islet is rocky;
for the closest decent sand, head 500m further south to the small beach north

of **Yılanci Burnu**, or patronize one of the **day-trips** offered by excursion boats moored along the causeway. Most offer a similar itinerary, leaving at 9am, visiting three isolated beaches and returning by 4pm. The price usually hovers around $16; chat with the skippers first before you make your choice.

The beaches

Kuşadası's most famous beach, **Kadınlar Denizi** (Ladies' Beach), just under 3km southwest of town, is a perplexingly popular strand, but is far too crowded in season and not really worth the effort. Dolmuşes for this beach trundle south along the seafront past Güvercin Adası, alert for custom. They continue to **Paradise Beach**, just one cove further along, which is smaller and quieter with only a few bars.

Tusan beach, a long stretch of hard-packed sand, 5km to the north of town, is probably more worthwhile, despite noise from the coast road; the *Tusan Hotel* at the northern end will rent you all manner of watersports equipment. All Kuşadası–Selçuk minibuses pass by, as well as the more frequent ones from the town centre labelled "Kadınlar Denizi" and "Şehir İçi", whose routes end near the *Tusan Hotel*.

Much the best beach in the area is **Pamucak**, at the mouth of the Küçük Menderes River, 15km north of town, a little way off the route to Selçuk. The dolmuş from Kuşadası's Atatürk Bulvarı to Selçuk (every half-hour) stops at the northern end of the beach. The main disadvantage of this exposed, four-kilometre-long stretch of sand is that it can't be used if the wind is up. Popular principally with local families, it's scarcely developed except for the two enormous complexes situated near the far south end.

Eating

Value for money is not the order of the day as far as **eating out** goes in Kuşadası, with most outfits being targeted at the hordes of tourists coming off the liners, but a bit of searching and a little legwork will be rewarded. For quality fish dishes, locals recommend one or two restaurants overlooking the harbour and ferry terminal, though prices can be daunting. Better value is offered by the establishments located inside the castle on Güvercin Adası.

Kale area

Avlu Cephane Sok 15/A. You'll do no better for traditional Turkish food than this unlicensed place with rear-courtyard seating. It serves low-priced grilled lamb and steamtray specialities, best at lunchtime.

Kapı Cephane Sok 20. *Meze* and kebab dishes available at this traditional establishment; often accompanied by live *fasıl* music.

Öz Urfa Kebapçısı Cephane Sok 9. Well spoken of locally for its reasonably priced and authentic Turkish dishes; particularly geared towards grilled meat. Expect to pay $5 per dish. Licensed.

Paşa Cephane Sok 21. Entertaining family affair set within the confines of a picturesque courtyard. Recommended for its seafood and very cheap *mezes*.

South of the tower

Albatros Restaurant Emek Sok 4, Belediye

Dükkanları Zabıta Karşısı. Squeaky clean unlicensed restaurant (the sign is obscured by a huge climbing vine), which serves outstanding stews and the like for just over $3, each accompanied by a complimentary dish of pickled chilli.

Holiday Inn Restaurant Kahramanlar Cad. Popular with discerning locals and tourists alike, this eastern Turkish outfit has made a name for its reasonably priced spicy dishes ($8) and professional service.

Orient Express Adnan Menderes Bul 17/1. A small, friendly, Dutch-run establishment with a nice garden. One of the better, more popular restaurants catering for the tourist trade, with fodder including pasta or steak and chips.

Saraydamları

Degirmen Saraydamlari, 3km from Davutlar, 12km south of Izmir t0256/681 2150. Meticulous recreation of an old mill, built from traditional and salvaged materials, with a menu featuring seldom-seen household breads, noodles and stews, as well as selections from the grill ($15) – chicken and quail are raised on the premises. Summer tables on the lawn overlook an artificial lake. Booking advised. Open all year.

Drinking and nightlife

After-dark activity in Kuşadası is distributed over perhaps three dozen **bars**, clumped into distinct groups: a dwindling number of arty, genteel bars of the Kale district; their more energetic neighbours, featuring live music sung in either Turkish or English; and Irish/British pubs with karaoke gear and record-ed house and techno tracks, culminating in the downmarket, foreigner-dominated "Barlar Sokak" area. As ever, making specific recommendations is futile, even invidious; if you pace the streets named below, guided by the cranked-up sound systems, you'll certainly find something to suit.

The most durable of the **Kale** watering holes, and congenial environments for meeting educated Turks on holiday, include *Jazz Bar*, Bahar Sok 18, and the perennially popular *She*, at the corner of Bahar and Sakarya *sokaks*. Dancers will want to gravitate towards the large *Heaven*; though *Extasy* nearby, with a mix of Turkish and Euro House is increasingly more popular, while *Ankara* on Cephane Sokak is a good representative of a live Turkish-music venue. *Big Bang Rock Café* at Kışla Sok 27 is true to its name.

Just off the foot of Yıldırım Caddesi, Eskipazaryeri Sokak has been officially renamed **Barlar Sokak** (Pub Lane), as the entry arch proclaims. The decibels emanating from the dozen or so "Irish" and "London" pubs are deafening, with the Union Jack T-shirt brigade and rugby-song choirs out in force. If this seems at all desirable then *Jimmy's Bar* is probably a good place to start and one of the few bars here actually owned by a Kuşadasın.

Listings

Banks and exchange Many of the bank booths and ATMs at the junction of Liman Cad and Atatürk Bul stay open until dark in the summer, while further up Barbaros Hayrettin are a few *döviz* offices.

Books Kuydaş, İnönü Bul 8/B, for secondhand English-language books, newspapers, magazines, CDs and tapes, and nautical charts.

Car rental Offices cluster along İnönü Bulvarı, just back from the sea; standard walk-in rates of $80 a day can be bargained down to $45–55 at slack times. Outlets include: Avis, Atatürk Bul 26/B ☎0256/614 4600; Budget, Sağlik Cad 58 ☎0256/614 4956; DeCar, Kaya Şavkay Meyd Paşa Han 106/A ☎0256/612 6844; and Start, İnönü Bul 6/1 ☎0256/614 3126.

Ferries The agency for *Sultan*, the Turkish morning boat to Samos, is Azim Tour, Liman Cad, Yayla Pasajı (☎0256/614 1553); all other boats, including the *Diana*, *Kuşadası Prenses*, and the Greek afternoon craft, are handled by Diana, Atatürk Bul 90 (☎0256/612 8888, ⓦwww.dianashipping .com). From April to October, ferries leave for Samos daily at 8.30am. For schedules and prices, see "travel details" at the end of the chapter.

Hamams Kale Hamamı, behind the Kale Camii, is very touristy, Belediye Hamam on Yıldırım Cad slightly less so. Both open daily 9am–9pm and both are expensive at $15–20.

Hospital The state hospital is at Atatürk Bul 32 ☎0256/613 1616, near the park.

Internet Kismet Internet Café, Liman Sok 1, 3rd floor (daily 9am–8pm).

Laundry Can Laundry, Özgür Sok 8, off the south side of Adnan Menderes Bul.

Post office The PTT is on Barbaros Hayrettin Bul (24hr from May–Sept; 8am–midnight otherwise).

Tours and travel agencies *Sammy's Palace* and *Sezgin Hotel* (see "Accommodation" above) organize day tours to some of the more popular tourist destinations, such as Ephesus ($38), Pamukkale ($32) and boat trips to Didim ($25). Sisan Tours, Yıldırım Cad 17 (☎0256/614 1188, ⓦwww .sisantours.com), is a long established tour company in the centre of town. Osman Turizm, Sağlık Cad, Öge Sok 63 ☎0256/614 4205, is a full-service agency for planes and buses, with computerized booking capability.

North of Kuşadası: Notion and Claros

North of Kuşadası are some relatively unspoiled beaches and the two archeological sites of ancient **Notion** and **Claros**, though you're really going to need your own transport to reach them. While neither site in itself justifies a detour, together with the chance for a swim they make a satisfying day-trip. At present both sites have unrestricted access, but restoration works are continuing and the admission situation will certainly change when excavations are completed.

Driving towards Seferihisar, after 25km there's a poorly marked junction, with a sign pointing inland to Ahmetbeyli and Menderes. This is a recognized stop for buses; in your own vehicle bear seaward for the moment and park behind the excellent 600-metre beach.

Notion

The artificially terraced promontory bounding the beach to the east, on the opposite side of a sluggish creek, is in fact the site of ancient **Notion**. This obscure settlement was founded as the port annex to the city of Colophon, 15km inland, at least as early as the eighth century BC. In time the littoral community attained greater importance than the inland one and came to be called Neocolophon. This process was accelerated when Lysimachus punished old Colophon for its support of Antigonus in the post-Alexandrian civil wars by semi-depopulating it in 302 BC. Both settlements dwindled as nearby Ephesus became prominent, and today Notion is ruinous in the extreme – the only recognizable monument, aside from the fragments of wall visible above the streambed, are the foundations and column fragments of a Corinthian **Temple of Athena Polias** erected during the second century AD. It's debatable whether the tricky scramble through the breaches in the walls is worth interrupting a tanning session, but the view over the sea from up top is superb.

Claros

The ancient oracle and temple of Apollo at **Claros**, 1.5km inland from Notion in a lushly vegetated valley, is more rewarding. Though overshadowed in popular imagination by the nearby oracle of Apollo at Didyma and the more remote one at Delphi, Claros, particularly during the Roman period, equalled the other two in importance.

Though there was mention of a temple here as early as the seventh century BC, its role as a prophetic centre did not begin until three hundred years later, notably with its approval of the relocation of Smyrna. The sacred precinct was a dependency of ancient Colophon, and was similarly punished by Lysimachus, but under Hadrian its fortunes revived spectacularly. The premises were handsomely reconstructed, with clients from throughout the Roman Empire arriving to consult the oracle. Despite this, most of what is visible today – most poignantly seen at dusk – dates from early or even pre-Hellenistic times.

To reach the site, turn right at the yellow-and-black signpost 1km along the asphalt road up to **Ahmetbeyli** village, then right again once over the bridge, following more crude signs. Beyond this point the track would be impassably muddy to two-wheel-drive cars after rain, but it's only 400m further to the makeshift car park. Repeated attempts have been undertaken since the turn of the century to keep the ruins clear of the silt deposited by the adjacent river, and to pump them free of water – an ongoing problem, which has resulted in a permanent resident population of frogs and terrapins.

The precinct was entered from the south via a **monumental gate**, of which half a dozen sunken columns remain, flanked by a semicircular bench and a small stoa. Originally, a **sacred way** – now half-buried under dirt and shrubbery, but still flanked by statue niches and adorned with inscriptions from grateful supplicants – led some 200m to the **Temple of Apollo**.

This, strewn with enormous toppled column drums, dates from the fourth or third century BC and – rare in Ionia – is of the Doric order. Pilgrims were admitted at night to the temple porch and their names were relayed by a priest to the prophet residing in a sunken sanctuary underneath the great hall. After the seer had drunk from a sacred spring within, his mutterings were then phrased in more artful verse by an assistant. You can still see the vaulting of the subterranean chamber's roof, which supported the shrine's colossal 7.6-metre statue of Apollo, of which only fragments remain. The current excavators are slowly piecing together some of these.

Immediately east of the temple are the remains of the sacrificial altar, while next door, on the northern side, rest the foundations of a smaller Ionic **Temple of Artemis**, also with the ruins of an altar.

Dilek Yarımadası Milli Parkı

The imposing outline of **Samsun Dağı**, otherwise known as Dilek Dağı (the ancient Mount Mycale), dominates the skyline south of Kuşadası and may inspire notions of a visit. Regular dolmuşes (8am–dusk; 1hr) make light work of the 28-kilometre trip to the national park established around the mountain.

The **Dilek Yarımadası Milli Parkı** (spring & autumn daily 8am–5pm; summer daily 8am–6.30pm; winter closed; $1, cars $3) was set aside in 1966 for, among other reasons, the protection of its thick forest and diverse fauna, which is said to include rare lynx, jackal and wild cats. However, you are unlikely to see any of the species in question, since much of the 28,000-acre park is an off-limits military zone; try to walk out towards the tempting bits at the very tip of the peninsula and armed conscripts will bar the way.

Arguably, the park performs its function as a wildlife preserve better than it does that of an all-purpose recreation area. The undeniable beauty of the terrain, certainly the most unspoiled along the Turkish Aegean, is owed entirely to the military presence. The most visited portion of the unrestricted zone consists of a ten-kilometre stretch of mostly paved road beyond the entrance and four good, but often windswept, beaches along it – **İçmeler** (hard sand shaded by plane trees), just beyond the gate; **Aydınlık Koyu** (pebbles); **Kavaklı Burun** (pebbles); and the last and prettiest one, **Karasu** (700m of pea gravel). Each beach has its own small snack bar or drinks kiosk operating in high season.

Immediately past Karasu the onward dirt track is signposted as "Yasak Bölge", and armed patrols will turn you back should you venture further. A lone jeep track, gated against wheeled traffic and signposted as "Kanyon", complete with walking-man symbol, does saunter inland between Aydınlık and Kavaklı beaches, curling up to the **summit ridge** east of 1237-metre Samsun Dağı (Dilek Tepesi).

Better access to the ridge is possible by trail from **ESKİDOĞANBEY**, a village to the south. This is an all-day outing, best done in spring or autumn to avoid the heat. Chances of wildlife-spotting, particularly badgers, jackals and birds of prey, are probably better here than within the confines of the national park on the other side of the mountain. Since the closure of most short-term accommodation in Eskidoğanbey, walkers tend to take an early dolmuş to one or other of the trailheads, hike over the mountain, and take an evening dolmuş back to Söke or Kuşadası from the walk's endpoint.

There are no facilities for staying overnight in the park, though it does provide WCs, barbecue areas and a small café. The closest *pansiyon*s and hotels, pitched at Turkish visitors, are in and around **GÜZELÇAMLI**, a village 1km outside the reserve boundaries. The pebble beaches 300m below Güzelçamlı are not as good as those in the park, and are hemmed in by massive over-development.

Selçuk and around

A laidback farming town only two decades ago, **SELÇUK** has been catapulted into the limelight of premier-league tourism by its proximity to the ruins of Ephesus. The flavour of tourism here, though, is markedly different from that at nearby Kuşadası, its less prestigious inland location, good-value accommodation and ecclesiastical connections (not least, burial place of St John the Evangelist) making it a haven for a disparate mix of backpackers and Bible Belters. Some may find this characterization a bit harsh, but it's not meant as out-and-out disparagement – it means, among other things, that the numerous carpet-shop hustlers and accommodation touts here have a more realistic idea of their audience's financial limits.

Although evidence of settlement as early as 2000 BC has been found atop Ayasoluk hill (a feature used as Selçuk's logo), the town only really flourished as a Byzantine enterprise during the fifth century AD, after the harbour of adjacent Ephesus had completely silted up. Like Birgi and Tire, the place was later a haunt of the Aydınoğlu clan, who yielded to the Ottomans in the early fifteenth century. Despite a role in the events of the early Church, including key events in the life of Paul, John and (supposedly) the Virgin, local Christianity thereafter was mostly restricted to the village of Kirkince, now Şirince (see p.365). In this century, the town's demographic profile has become an uneasy mix: of Rumeliot (south Balkan) and Bosnian emigrants, who arrived in successive waves between 1890 and 1960; settled Yörük nomads wont to idle in the teahouses; and Kurds and gypsies. Each group has its own designated quarter, socializing little with the others.

Arrival and information

At the base of the castle hill and across the busy E24/550 highway (known as Atatürk Caddesi in town), a mock arch marks the start of a pedestrian precinct, with Gengiz Topel Caddesi its main throughfare. This leads east to the **train station**, from where there are seven daily connections to İzmir, two to Denizli and one each to Afyon, İsparta and Söke. Along the way you'll pass the **PTT** and most of the town's restaurants. Following Atatürk Caddesi a bit further south brings you to the **otogar**; it's worth knowing that the Elbirlik shuttle between Kuşadası and İzmir airport always makes a stop on the main highway.

On the western side of Atatürk Caddesi, beyond the fountains of the central park, the cheerful **tourist office** (May–Sept daily 8.30am–noon & 1–5.30pm; Oct–April Mon–Fri 9am–noon & 1–5.30pm; ☏0232/892 6328) has extensive lists of accommodation. You will find the tourist office to be a more disinterested source of intelligence than the rug boys and *pansiyon* promoters (often one and the same person) who mob every bus arrival, sometimes boarding them at the town limits to deliver their sales pitch. Subsequent hustles are more refined, and some include the time-honoured offer of a lift to Ephesus and loan of a site guidebook – bracketed by "coincidental" stopovers at a relative's carpet shop for tea and a "chat".

Accommodation

Most recommended places to stay cluster around the central pedestrianized zone or just west of Ataturk Caddesi, near the museum, with additional desirable establishments scattered on and beyond Ayasoluk hill. Another concentration of *pansiyons* is found in the east of the town – five minutes' walk beyond the rail line – where life is lived at a more traditional pace. The increase in competition between Selçuk's hotels is good news for hotel hunters, though those with a "stork-view" option often charge a premium for the privilege.

Near the museum

Ak Hotel Uğur Mumcu Sevgi Yolu 14 ☏ 0232/892 2161, ⓕ 892 3142. Family-run operation with attached restaurant, spread over two (somewhat shabby) buildings; ask for a rear-facing room overlooking the garden to avoid street noise. Bargaining possible. ❷

Australian and New Zealand Pansiyon Miltner Sok 17 ☏ 0232/892 6050, ⓦ www .anzturkishguesthouse.com. Run by a family of returned Turkish-Australians, this *pansiyon* is proud of its courtyard-with-view and snug wooded bar. Dorms ($12) and doubles are fairly standard, but the tiled floors are covered with Turkish throws. Breakfast starts at $2. Also offers three-day trekking trips at $60 a head. ❷

Barım Pansiyon Turgut Reis Sok 34 ☏ 0232/892 6923. Restored, rambling old house complete with its own stork's nest and a lush courtyard/garden. Most of the kitschy doubles come as en-suite, breakfast is $2 extra. ❷

Pension Baykal Sevgi Yolu 2 ☏ 0232/892 6908, ⓕ 892 3157. Run by an English and archeology teacher, Şerif Baykal, who owns a carpet shop, lectures on carpet and kilim history, and organizes trips. Rooms are en-suite. ❷

Homeros Pansiyon Asmalı Sok 17 ☏ 0232/892 3995. Split over two adjoining buildings this family-run pension has a choice of rooms, all nicely decorated and furnished by their carpenter son Derviş. A nightly glass of complimentary wine enhances the fine sunsets from the roof terrace; breakfast and homecooked meals extra. ❷

Outback Pension Turgutreis Sok 5 ☏ 0232/892 2452. Friendly, moderately sized establishment, ably run by a returnee Turk from Down Under, offering kilim-bedecked en-suite doubles and singles. ❷

West of Ayasoluk

Hotel Akay Serin Sok 3 ☏ 0232/892 3172, ⓕ 892 3009. Affordable two-star choice, with rather unimaginative doubles but with decent bathrooms. Fine views of the mosque, castle and basilica from its cushioned rooftop restaurant and bar. ❷

East of Ayasoluk

Hotel Bella St Jean Cad 7 ☏ 0232/892 3944, ⓕ 892 7045. Suffers from some tour-bus and carpet-shop bustle and hustle en route, owing to its position near the basilica gate, but the hotel itself is well run, featuring smallish rooms with balconies and American power-showers. Good value and bargainable. ❷

Kalehan Hotel İzmir Cad, 5min north of central junction ☏ 0232/892 6154, ⓕ 892 2169. Bit of a tour mill, but luxurious for the price. The tastefully furnished double-glazed rooms, most with air-con, are attractively set around a small pool and mature gardens. ❹

Nazhan St Jean Cad 2 ☏ 0232/892 8731, ⓔ nazhan@superonline.com. A delightful small house packed with antiques and bric-a-brac, chosen by Nazhan and Kemal when they escaped the rat-race of İstanbul. Each of the five doubles is individually decorated to a high standard. ❷

Nazar Hotel Eski İzmir Cad 14 ☏ 0232/892 2222, ⓦ www.nazarhotel.com. Clean, friendly and well-run, with a good roof restaurant. The quiet spacious doubles, decorated with a domestic touch, come with either air-con or ceiling fan. It receives rave reviews and is good value for money. ❷

Gengiz Topel Cad and around

Artemis Guest House ("Jimmy's Place"), 1012 Sok 2 ☏ 0232/892 1982, ⓦ www

SELÇUK

RESTAURANTS & BARS

Aloe Vera	A
BarBa	D
Dilek	E
Eski Ev	B
Naturel	F
Pink Bistro	C
Selçuk	G

ACCOMMODATION

Ak	11
Akay	3
Artemis	9
Australian	14
Barim	15
Baykal	13
Bella	5
Diana	7
Homeros	10
Kalehan	1
Kiwi	16
Nazar	2
Nazhan	4
Nur	8
Outback	12
Ürkmez	6

Baptistry

Basilica of St John

Ayasoluk Hill

Isa Bey Camii

Gate of Persecution

ST JEAN CAD

SERIN SOK

Archaic Tomb

Hamam

Train Station

Byzantine Aqueduct

NAMIK KEMAL CAD

CENGIZ TOPEL CAD

DERE SOK

3004 SOK

1012 SOK

KÜÇÜK SOK

BIRINCI OKUL SOK

İKİNCI OKUL SOK

ATATÜRK CADDESİ (E24/550)

TURGUT REIS SOK

ASMALI SOK

UĞUR MUMCU SEVGI YOLU

Mosque

SAFFA SOK

MILTNER SOK

Archeological Museum

Market Place

Otogar

Artemision

N

0   200 m

▲ Şirince
◀ İzmir
◀ Ephesus, Pamucak, Kuşadası & Dereli Kamping
▼ Meryemana & Çamlık

.artemisguesthouse.com. Run by an irrepressible, well-travelled Turk, and offering standard and luxury (plushly furnished) en-suite rooms, plus laundry, kitchen, garden-café, internet access, and cheap breakfast options ($2). Women-only hamam trips can be arranged on request. Will arrange collection for Kuşadası ferry arrivals. Book ahead. Standard rooms ❶, luxury rooms ❸

Otel Ürkmez Namık Kemal Cad ☎0232/892 6312. The best by some way of several "storkview" hotels, overlooking a nest-laden Byzantine aqueduct. Some rooms have balconies, all have baths, but what makes the hotel is the non-pushy management style of the Özkan brothers, who speak excellent English. Roof terrace, laundry and kitchen facilities, and good breakfasts. ❸

South of the otogar

Kiwi Pension 1038 Sok 26 ☎0232/892 4892 ⓦwww.kiwipension.com. Deservedly popular backpackers', 5min south of the bus station. Basic but clean rooms (ask to look around as some are better than others) with balcony, and dorm beds ($4.50). Also has a swimming pool, located separately in the orchards on the road to Ephesus. Large breakfast included. ❷

East of the train station

Diana Pension 3004 Sok 30, Zafer Mah ☎0232/892 1265, ⓔjesseakin@hotmail.com. A small, quality pension with good views of Selçuk, popular with mature tourists. Run by the accommodating Jesse; some of the comfortable, homely rooms have air-conditioning. ❷

Nur Pansiyon Dere Sok 16, Zafer Mah ☎0232/892 6595. Run by a widow, and particularly appropriate for single women travellers. An optional breakfast is served in the garden, and excellent cheap evening meals available too. Will collect arrivals from the *otogar*. ❶

Campsites

Dereli Motel and Kamping Pamucak beach, 7km west of Selçuk ☎0232/893 1205. Large campsite set amongst palm trees, right on the beach; with attached restaurant and simple bungalows (❷) you could almost be in Thailand. Can arrange pick-up from *otogar* though the Pamucak dolmuş drops at entrance. Open all year.

Garden Selçuk, 300m beyond İsa Bey Camii ☎0232/892 6165, ⓕ892 2997. Shady, grassy campsite (used by caravans and tourers, too). Open all year.

The Town

Selçuk offers a variety of antiquities from diverse eras (not least in its excellent archeological museum), which can easily be toured in a single day. The town's sights are numerous and interesting enough to warrant another night's stay after visiting Ephesus, especially if you also plan on heading out to the shrine at Meryemana or the hill-village of Şirince.

Ayasoluk Hill

Lodestone of settlement in every era, **Ayasoluk** hill (daily 8am–6.30pm; $2) is the first point you should head for. You enter the site through the **Gate of Persecution**, so called by the Byzantines because of a relief of Achilles in combat that once adorned it, mistakenly thought to depict a martyrdom of Christians in the amphitheatre of nearby Ephesus.

St John the Evangelist – or "Theologian" as the Greeks knew him – came to Ephesus in the middle of the first century. He died here around 100 AD and was buried on Ayasoluk Hill, whose name is thought to be a corruption of "Ayios Theologos". The sixth-century Byzantine emperor Justinian decided to replace two earlier churches sheltering John's tomb with a basilica worthy of the saint's reputation, and until destruction by Tamerlane's Mongols in 1402 it was one of the largest and most ornate Byzantine churches in existence.

Today, various colonnades and walls of the **Basilica of St John** have been re-erected, courtesy of a religious foundation based in Lima, Ohio, giving just a hint of the building's magnificence in its prime. The purported tomb of the evangelist is marked by a slab on the former site of the altar. Beside the nave is the **Baptistry**, where fundamentalist tourists may pose in the act of dunking for friends' cameras.

The Archeological Museum

The **Archeological Museum** (Arkeoloji Müzesi; daily 8.30am–noon & 1–5.30pm, winter closes at 5pm; $2) is permanently packed out with visitors, but is well worth setting aside the time to visit. Its galleries of finds (mostly from Ephesus) are arranged thematically rather than chronologically. The first, small-finds hall contains some of the most famous bronze and ceramic objects in the collection, including Eros riding a dolphin, effigies of the phallic gods Bes and Priapus – perennial postcard favourites – a humane bust of the comedian Menander, and various excellent miniatures from the Roman terrace houses at Ephesus, one of the rooms from which is recreated at the far end.

Beyond here, past some relief and free-standing statuary from the fountains of Ephesus, there are a couple of courtyards, containing sarcophagi, column capitals and stelae, from which steps lead down to another courtyard with attractive fountains and a small souvenir stall.

Continuing through the main galleries, you'll enter a hall devoted to tomb finds and mortuary practices. Just beyond this is the famous **Artemis room**, with two renditions of the goddess studded with multiple testicles (not breasts, as is commonly believed) and tiny figurines of real and mythical beasts, honouring her role as mistress of animals. At Ephesus, Artemis adopted most of the attributes of the indigenous Anatolian mother-goddess Cybele, including a eunuch priesthood – the stone testicles possibly symbolize the ultimate votive offering.

The last gallery houses friezes and busts from imperial cult temples – the strangest fragments a giant forearm and head, the latter misshapen and infantile, part of a five-metre statue of Domitian (emperor 81–96 AD), and a small space set aside for touring exhibitions.

The Artemision

Beyond the museum, 200m along the road toward Ephesus and to the right, are the scanty remains of the **Artemision**, or the sanctuary of Artemis (daily 8.30am–5.30pm; free). The archaic temple here replaced three predecessors dedicated to Cybele, and was itself burned down in 356 BC by Herostratus, a lunatic who (correctly) reckoned his name would be immortalized by the act. The massive Hellenistic replacement was considered to be one of the Seven Wonders of the Ancient World, though this is hard to believe today: the Goths sacked it in 263 AD and the Byzantines subsequently carted off most of the remaining masonry to Ayasoluk and Constantinople, leaving just a lone column (re-erected in modern times) amid battered foundation blocks. It took the English archeologist J.T. Wood six years of trial soundings in the mud to locate the temple's foundations in 1869. Constant pumping is necessary to keep the area from flooding, and in winter the ducks come here for a swim anyway.

İsa Bey Camii

The **İsa Bey Camii** is the most distinguished of the various Selçuk monuments, the style that gives the town its name. It's a late fourteenth-century Aydınoğlu mosque and it represents a transition between Selçuk and Ottoman styles, with its innovative courtyard – where most of the congregation would worship – and stalactite vaulting over the entrance; the contemporary Ulu Cami in Manisa, though much smaller, is conceptually quite similar in its use of a courtyard. Although recently restored, the İsa Bey's two minarets were snapped off long ago and the ablutions fountain in the court is missing. If you can get inside the main hall, you'll see a high, gabled roof supported by Roman columns and some fine tile-work in the south dome.

Eating, drinking and entertainment

Restaurants in Selçuk, virtually all found in the town centre, tend to be rather similar: not nearly so exploitative as some in Kuşadası, though not nearly as refined either. Good value among establishments along pedestrianized Cengiz Topel Caddesi are the relatively elegant *Eski Ev*, offering good Turkish home cooking, and, further along, *Aloe Vera*, a cosy bar-bistro popular with locals and tourists alike for lunchtime food and evening drinks. A sweet tooth can be satisfied at the *Dilek Pastanesi*, also on Cengiz Topel Caddesi, or at the *Naturel Pastanesi*, Atatürk Mah, 1005 Sok 13. Further afield, near the *otogar* on Şahabettin Dede Caddesi, the cheap and abundant portions served at *Selçuk Köftecisi* are consistently good value.

After-hours tippling takes place at several noisy **pubs** near Cengiz Topel Caddesi. The *Pink Bistro* and *BarBa* have tables spilling out onto the street; though the *Aloe Vera* (above) is probably your best bet for late-night carousing.

For formal entertainment, the second or third week of July sees the **Ephesus Festival**, with various international music and dance performances occurring nightly at the Ephesus amphitheatre. Enquire at the tourist office for details and tickets (around $18). Mid-January brings **camel wrestling bouts**, between huge male camels, at the edge of town.

Around Selçuk

The main draw in the region is the ancient city of Ephesus (p.366), not to be missed if you are staying in Selçuk. However, a few other local diversions are worth considering, including the evocative village of **Şirince**, nestled in the hills 8km to the east. It's increasingly becoming a weekend bolthole for wealthy Turks and makes for an easily attainable day trip. **Meryemana**, on the other hand, only of any real interest to those on a biblical tour, requires your own transport or a taxi.

Meryemana

Eight kilometres southwest of Selçuk, beyond Ephesus and just below the summit of Bülbül Dağ, stands **Meryemana** (dawn–dusk; $5, plus car-park fees), a monument to piety and faith. Though most orthodox theologians maintain that the Virgin Mary died and was buried in Jerusalem, another school of thought holds that the mother of Jesus accompanied St John the Evangelist when he left Palestine in the middle of the first century on his way to Ephesus.

After the medieval turmoil around Ephesus nobody from abroad was inclined to delve further into the matter until **Catherine Emmerich** (1774–1824), a German nun and seer who never left her country, recorded her visions of a small stone house, where, she claimed, the Virgin had lived her last years. In 1891 Lazarist priests from İzmir decided to follow her descriptions and discovered a building that matched them – and which, in its role as the **chapel of Panayia Kapılı**, was already a focus of adoration by the Orthodox Greeks of nearby Kirkince (now Şirince) especially on August 15, the Feast of the Assumption. Things mushroomed predictably from there, spurred by a papal visit and imprimatur in 1967, and today the place is on the checklist of pilgrims from around the world.

The site is enclosed within a municipal park and subject to a generous dose of commercialism – though the dense forest and fountain are pleasant enough. The **house** itself, now a chapel aligned unusually southwest-to-northeast, probably dates from early Byzantine times, though its foundations may indeed be first-century. It overlooks a beautiful wooded valley and two terraces where a spring gushes forth; nearby, tree branches are festooned with the votive rag scraps left by Muslim pilgrims, for whom *Meryemana* (Mother Mary) is also a saint. Whatever you may believe about the historical likelihood of this being Mary's last home, the shrine is a tribute to the tenacity of mother-goddess veneration in Anatolia.

The site is accessible only by private car or taxi. If you want to come, it makes sense to combine a visit with a day at Ephesus, whose upper entrance is 5km to the north; see p.367 for details.

Şirince

ŞİRİNCE, a well-preserved, originally Greek-built hill village, situated 8km east of and above Selçuk, has a history going back 600 years. The village's lush orchards and vineyards are now worked by Muslim settlers from near Thessaloníki, who make assorted wines that pack quite a punch – you can buy them or even taste them at the village's few shops, wineries and restaurants. Dido Sotiriou, chronicler of the Greek Asia Minor experience and its post-1922 aftermath, visited here in 1990; much of her classic novel *Farewell to Anatolia*, perennially popular in Turkey, was set in the village. Not too surprisingly, the place has become a target of tour groups, but compared with Kuşadası it's low-key – though beware of invitations to private homes, which invariably serve as pretexts to foist lacework on you.

At the edge of Şirince stands a late nineteenth-century **church**, with a pebble-mosaic floor, plaster relief-work on the ceiling and wooden vaulting – though much is crumbling away. Nearer the middle of the village there's a larger stone **basilica** dating from 1839 and restored as an art gallery. But the main point of a visit is the idyllic scenery and the handsome domestic architecture, which, since the late 1980s, has attracted wealthy urban Turks in search of characterful vacation homes.

Six or seven daily **dolmuşes** serve Şirince, departing from the Selçuk *otogar* between 8.30am and 5pm, and dropping you in the centre of the village, where everything is no more than a few minutes' walk away. You could stay overnight here, though **accommodation** prices are higher than they should be. *Kirkinca Pansiyon* (☎0232/898 3117; ❸) has a small number of plainly decorated double rooms, while *Erdem Evleri* (☎0232/898 3069; ❸), with lovely rooms in a restored old house furnished with antiques, boasts the only espresso machine for miles. *Nişanyan Evleri* (☎0232/898 3117, ℻898 3209; ❻), in a restored mansion with serene views, five minutes' up on the eastern slopes, has superb singles and doubles, all furnished with inherited antiques. Travelwriter owners Sevan and Müjde also have a number of restored four-person apartments in the village (❼), some with *kerevets* (built-in wooden beds) and designer bathrooms.

At the east end of the single-lane bazaar, now mostly lined by shabby trinket shops, half a dozen **restaurants** – such as the well-established *Koy* – cluster around the main square.

Çamlık Open-Air Rail Museum

Some 12km south of Selçuk on the main highway to Aydın, the village of **ÇAMLIK** is the site of the **Çamlık Open-Air Rail Museum** (Buharlı Lokomotif Müzesi; open daily; $1.50), 50m southwest of the road after the village-limits sign. The museum occupies the sidings of a former train works and exhibits include more than two dozen steam locomotives, many pre-World War I; the majority German-made but also British, American, Czech, French and Swedish models. The locomotives are rust-proofed, mounted on sections of track, and have panels offering brief information. You are free to clamber up into the cabs and to operate the hand-wound turntable around which half-dozen of the most impressive are grouped. Other rail vehicles – such as hand-carts and cranes – are also on display. A particularly scenic, if slow, way of reaching the museum is by taking one of the three daily Selçuk–Aydın trains, getting off at the Çamlık station itself.

Ephesus

With the exception of Pompeii, **EPHESUS** (Efes in Turkish) is the largest and best-preserved ancient city around the Mediterranean; and, after the Sultanahmet district of İstanbul, it's the most visited tourist attraction in Turkey. The ruins are mobbed for much of the year, although with a little planning and initiative it's possible to tour the site in relative peace. Certainly, it's a place you should not miss, though you may come away disappointed at the commercialization and the extent of areas that are off-limits. You'll need two to three partly shady hours to see Ephesus, as well as a water bottle – the acres of stone act as a grill in the heat of the day, and there are only two drinking taps within the site, close by the main entrance.

Some history

Situated by a fine harbour at the terminus of overland trade routes, and beneficiary of the lucrative cult of the Anatolian mother-goddess Cybele/Artemis, Ephesus led a charmed life from earliest times. Legends relate that **Androclus**, son of King Kodrus of Athens, had been advised by an oracle to settle at a place indicated by a fish and a wild boar. Androclus and his entourage arrived here to find natives roasting fish by the sea; embers from the fire set a bush ablaze, out of which charged a pig, and the city was on its way. The imported worship of Artemis melded easily with that of the indigenous **Cybele**, and the Ephesus of 1000 BC was built on the north slope of Mount Pion (Panayır Dağı), very close to the temple of the goddess.

The Ephesians needed their commercial wealth, since they rarely displayed much common sense, military strength or political acumen. When the Lydian **King Croesus** appeared in the sixth century, the locals could muster no other defence than to rope off the Artemis temple and retreat behind the barrier. Croesus, perhaps amused by this naivety, treated the city leniently and even contributed to the temple. Still unfortified and un-garrisoned, Ephesus passed back and forth between Greek and Persian interests until the Hellenistic era.

Alexander the Great, on his visit in 334 BC, offered to fund the completion of the latest version of the Artemis shrine, but the city fathers tactfully demurred, saying that one deity should not support another, and dug deeper into their own pockets. Following Alexander's death his lieutenant **Lysimachus** moved the city to its present location – necessary because the sea had receded considerably – and provided it with its first **walls**, traces of which are still visible on Panayır Dağı and Mount Koressos (Bülbül Dağı) to the south.

In subsequent centuries, Ephesus displayed flashes of its old fickleness, changing allegiance frequently and backing various revolts against Roman rule. Yet it never suffered for this lack of principle: during the Roman imperial period it was designated the **capital of Asia** and ornamented with magnificent public buildings – the ones on view today – by a succession of emperors. Ephesus's quarter-million population was swelled substantially at times by the right of sanctuary linked to the sacred precinct of Artemis, allowing shelter to large numbers of criminals. Of a somewhat less lurid cast was the more stable, mixed population of Jews, Romans and Egyptian and Anatolian cultists.

Despite, or perhaps because of, this, **Christianity** took root early and quickly at Ephesus. St John the Evangelist arrived in the mid-first century, and **St Paul** spent the years 51–53 AD in the city, proselytizing foremost among the Jewish community. As usual, Paul managed to foment controversy even in this cosmopolitan environment, apparently being imprisoned for some time – in a tower bearing his name near the west end of the walls – and later provoking the famous silversmiths' riot, described in Acts 19:23–20:1. Paul preached that the silver votive images of Artemis were not divine. The head of the silversmiths' guild, seeing his livelihood threatened, assembled his fellows in the amphitheatre where they howled "Great is Artemis of the Ephesians!" – as well as calling for the apostle's blood. The authorities managed to calm the crowd, but Paul was obliged to depart for Macedonia.

Under the Byzantines, Ephesus was the venue for two of the **councils of the Church**, including one in 431 AD at which the Nestorian heresy (see p.946) was anathematized. However, the general tenor of the Byzantine era was one of decline, owing to the abandoning of Artemis-worship following the establishment of state Christianity, Arab raids and (worst of all) the final silting up of the harbour. The population began to siphon off to the nearby hill crowned by the tomb and church of St John, future nucleus of the town of Selçuk, and by the time the Selçuks themselves appeared the process was virtually complete.

Visiting the site

Approaching the **site** (daily 8.30am–6.30pm; winter closes 5.30pm; last ticket 30min before closing; $10, $2 parking fee) **from Kuşadası**, get the dolmuş to drop you at the *Tusan Motel* junction, from where it's another easy kilometre to the lower entrance and ticket office. **From Selçuk**, don't bother with wheeled transport unless you have your own or succumb to the blandishments of the horse-drawn cab drivers who ply the route to the site ($10 per cart) – it's a pleasant three-kilometre walk, the first two along a mulberry-shaded lane paralleling the busy highway. There is also a second, **upper entrance** on the southeastern side of Ephesus, on the way to Meryemana – perhaps a more sensible route in summer since it enables you to walk downhill through the site (tour buses tend to drop their clients here, retrieving them at the lower gate). Visiting Meryemana first by **taxi from Selçuk** will allow you to use the upper gate: $30 (per car) should include a half-hour wait at "Mary's house", then a final drop-off at the top of the Ephesus site.

The Cave of the Seven Sleepers

Before reaching the lower entrance, you can detour left off the approach road after 300m and then proceed about 1km to visit the **Cave of the Seven Sleepers**, the focus of a touching legend. Seven young Ephesian Christians, refusing to sacrifice to the second-century emperor Decius, took refuge in this cave, were walled in by the imperial guard and fell into a deep sleep. An earthquake shattered the wall and woke them; upon ambling down to town for food, they discovered that two hundred years had passed and that Christianity was now the state religion. When the seven men died soon after – presumably

EPHESUS

Selçuk & Magnesia Gate

Selçuk

Tusan Motel

MOUNT PION
(PANAYIR DAĞI)

Cave of the
Seven Sleepers

Magnesia
Gate

East
Gymnasium

Varius
Baths

Upper Entrance
& Ticket Office

Odeon

Vedius
Gymnasium

Stadium

Trajan's Fountain

Upper Agora

7

6

Theatre

Steps

Lower Entrance
& Ticket Office

CURETES STREET

Steps

Car & Coach
Park

MARBLE STREET

3 41 2

5

Domitian Temple

Museum of
Inscriptions

Wide Walk

Path

Lower Agora

Serapis Temple

Terrace
Houses

Library of Celsus

Hellenistic Wall

St Mary's
Church

Arcadian Way

Harbour
Baths &
Gymnasium

Old Port

Tower of
St Paul

MOUNT KORESSOS
(BÜLBÜLDAĞI)

Mervemana (5 km)

Kuşadası

1 Scholastica Baths
2 Temple of Hadrian
3 Brothel
4 Latrines
5 Byzantine Fountain
6 Gate of Hercules
7 Prytaneum

N

0   100 m

buildings – the ones on view today – by a succession of emperors. Ephesus's quarter-million population was swelled substantially at times by the right of sanctuary linked to the sacred precinct of Artemis, allowing shelter to large numbers of criminals. Of a somewhat less lurid cast was the more stable, mixed population of Jews, Romans and Egyptian and Anatolian cultists.

Despite, or perhaps because of, this, **Christianity** took root early and quickly at Ephesus. St John the Evangelist arrived in the mid-first century, and **St Paul** spent the years 51–53 AD in the city, proselytizing foremost among the Jewish community. As usual, Paul managed to foment controversy even in this cosmopolitan environment, apparently being imprisoned for some time – in a tower bearing his name near the west end of the walls – and later provoking the famous silversmiths' riot, described in Acts 19:23–20:1. Paul preached that the silver votive images of Artemis were not divine. The head of the silversmiths' guild, seeing his livelihood threatened, assembled his fellows in the amphitheatre where they howled "Great is Artemis of the Ephesians!" – as well as calling for the apostle's blood. The authorities managed to calm the crowd, but Paul was obliged to depart for Macedonia.

Under the Byzantines, Ephesus was the venue for two of the **councils of the Church**, including one in 431 AD at which the Nestorian heresy (see p.946) was anathematized. However, the general tenor of the Byzantine era was one of decline, owing to the abandoning of Artemis-worship following the establishment of state Christianity, Arab raids and (worst of all) the final silting up of the harbour. The population began to siphon off to the nearby hill crowned by the tomb and church of St John, future nucleus of the town of Selçuk, and by the time the Selçuks themselves appeared the process was virtually complete.

Visiting the site

Approaching the **site** (daily 8.30am–6.30pm; winter closes 5.30pm; last ticket 30min before closing; $10, $2 parking fee) **from Kuşadası**, get the dolmuş to drop you at the *Tusan Motel* junction, from where it's another easy kilometre to the lower entrance and ticket office. **From Selçuk**, don't bother with wheeled transport unless you have your own or succumb to the blandishments of the horse-drawn cab drivers who ply the route to the site ($10 per cart) – it's a pleasant three-kilometre walk, the first two along a mulberry-shaded lane paralleling the busy highway. There is also a second, **upper entrance** on the southeastern side of Ephesus, on the way to Meryemana – perhaps a more sensible route in summer since it enables you to walk downhill through the site (tour buses tend to drop their clients here, retrieving them at the lower gate). Visiting Meryemana first by **taxi from Selçuk** will allow you to use the upper gate: $30 (per car) should include a half-hour wait at "Mary's house", then a final drop-off at the top of the Ephesus site.

The Cave of the Seven Sleepers

Before reaching the lower entrance, you can detour left off the approach road after 300m and then proceed about 1km to visit the **Cave of the Seven Sleepers**, the focus of a touching legend. Seven young Ephesian Christians, refusing to sacrifice to the second-century emperor Decius, took refuge in this cave, were walled in by the imperial guard and fell into a deep sleep. An earthquake shattered the wall and woke them; upon ambling down to town for food, they discovered that two hundred years had passed and that Christianity was now the state religion. When the seven men died soon after – presumably

EPHESUS

Selçuk & Magnesia Gate

Cave of the Seven Sleepers

Magnesia Gate

East Gymnasium

Upper Entrance & Ticket Office

Varius Baths

Odeon

MOUNT PION (PANAYIR DAĞI)

Tusan Motel

Selçuk

Vedius Gymnasium

Stadium

Trajan's Fountain

Theatre

Upper Agora

Path

6 7

Steps

CURETES STREET

Lower Entrance & Ticket Office

Paved Access Road

Car & Coach Park

Wide Walk

MARBLE STREET

3 4 1 2

5

Steps

Domitian Temple Museum of Inscriptions

Meryemana (5 km)

Path

St Mary's Church

Lower Agora

Serapis Temple

Library of Celsus

Terrace Houses

Hellenistic Wall

Harbour Baths & Gymnasium

Arcadian Way

Old Port

MOUNT KORESSOS (BÜLBÜLDAĞI)

Tower of St Paul

Kuşadası

N

0   100 m

1 Scholastica Baths
2 Temple of Hadrian
3 Brothel
4 Latrines
5 Byzantine Fountain
6 Gate of Hercules
7 Prytaneum

from shock – they were re-interred in the grotto, and a commemorative church was built over their graves.

The place is in fact an extensive network of catacombs backed into the hillside on several levels, which was used until late Byzantine times. Since 1993, however, the complex has been tightly fenced and you can only view it from the perimeter path that snakes above it. On the approach road you run a gauntlet of *gözleme* and *çay* stalls, rather more relaxed and pleasant than those crowding the entries to Ephesus proper.

St Mary's church

The first hint of the city, well before you reach the tacky parking lot with its souvenir stalls and tour buses, is the rather eroded (and pilfered) remains of the **Vedius gymnasium** and the **stadium**, funded by Nero. Once past the entry gate, take a sharp right along a path signed "Meryem Kilisesi", which leads to **St Mary's Church**, an absurdly elongated hotch-potch constructed between the second and fourth centuries AD. The building, originally a Roman warehouse, was the venue of the ecumenical council in 431 AD; its baptistry is in good condition.

The Arcadian Way and the theatre

Beyond the church, the **harbour baths** and **gymnasium** are prominent, but overgrown and difficult to explore. They are usually approached along the splendid **Arcadian Way** (currently off-limits while adjacent digs are under way), so named after the fifth-century Byzantine emperor Arcadius who renovated it. Today tree- and bush-fringed, it's a forlorn echo of the era when it was lined with hundreds of shops and illuminated at night – although its neglect is refreshing when compared to the ancient **theatre**, brutally restored to provide additional seating for the various summer festivals, with material that would be more appropriate buttressing a California freeway flyover. If you bother to climb past the 20,000 seats of half-modern masonry to the top, it's for the views over the surrounding countryside.

Along Marble Street

The so-called **Marble Street** begins near the base of the theatre and heads almost due south; wheel-ruts in the road and the slightly elevated colonnade remnant to the right indicate that pedestrians and vehicles were kept neatly separated. Also to your right as you proceed is the **lower agora** (currently closed for excavations), with an adjoining **Serapis Temple**, where the city's many Egyptian merchants would have worshipped. About halfway along Marble Street, metal stanchions protect alleged "signposting" – a footprint and a female head etched into the rock – for a **brothel**. It's located in the very centre of the Roman city, at the junction with the other main street, Curetes Street (see p.370), named after a caste of priests at the Artemis shrine. Little remains above chest height at the house of pleasure, but there are some fine floor mosaics denoting the four seasons, and (appropriately enough) one of the priapic figurines in the Selçuk museum was found here.

The Library of Celsus

Directly across the intersection of the two major streets looms the **Library of Celsus**, originally erected by the consul Gaius Julius Aquila between 110 and 135 AD as a memorial to his father Celsus Polemaeanus, who is still entombed under the west wall of the structure. The elegant, two-storey facade was fitted with niches for statues of the four personified intellectual virtues, today filled with plaster copies (the originals are in Vienna). Inside, twelve thousand scrolls were stored in galleries designed to prevent damp damage – a precaution that didn't prevent the Goths burning them all when they sacked the area in 262 AD. Abutting the library, and designed to provide entry to the lower agora, is the restored triple **gate of Mazaeus and Mithridates**.

Along Curetes Street

Just uphill from the Roman city's main intersection, a **Byzantine fountain** looks across **Curetes Street** to the public **latrines**, a favourite with visitors owing to the graphic nature of their function. Continuing along the same side of the street, you'll come to the so-called **Temple of Hadrian**, actually donated in 118 AD by a wealthy citizen in honour of Hadrian, Artemis and the city in general. Currently a drinks stand occupies its left side. As in the case of the library facade, most of the relief works here are plaster copies of the originals, which reside in the Selçuk museum. The two small heads on the arches spanning the four columns out front are of Tyche and possibly Medusa, respectively installed for luck and to ward off evil influences.

Behind and above the temple sprawl the first-century **Scholastica baths**, named after the fifth-century Byzantine lady whose headless statue adorns the entrance and who restored the complex. There was direct access from here to the latrines and thence the brothel, though it seems from graffiti that the baths, too, were at one stage used as a bawdy house. Clay drainage pipes are still visibly lodged in the floor, as they are at many points in Ephesus.

The terrace houses

On the far side of Curetes Street from the Temple of Hadrian lies a huge patterned **mosaic**, which once fronted a series of shops. Nearby, a stepped street leads up to the **terrace houses** (same times as main site; $17), housed in a plexiglass-and-steel shelter designed to protect the fragile finds from the elements. Access is limited to a series of wooden walkways that guide you through the remains of six houses and 62 rooms, revealing something of daily life in imperial and early Byzantine times (though hardly worth the exorbitant extra charge).

The first house is built around an atrium with a fountain, paved in black-and-white mosaics; a room leading off this to the east has walls covered in murals, including one of Hercules battling the river-god Achelous. In the second dwelling, the central court features a fine mosaic of a triton cavorting with a nereid; just south of this, in an overhead vault, Dionysos and Ariadne are depicted in an excellent glass mosaic, which, while damaged, is still recognizable. Excavations of the large central dome, part of the Dionysus House built in 588 BC, revealed the tiny golden figurine of an Egyptian priest, now on display in the Selçuk museum.

To the upper entrance

Returning to Curetes Street, you pass **Trajan's Fountain**, whose ornamentation has been removed to the museum, and then the street splits just above the **Hydreion** (another fountain) and the **Gate of Hercules**, where a remaining column relief depicts the hero wrapped in the skin of the Nemean lion. Bearing right at the junction takes you to the **Domitian Temple**, of which only the lower floor of the complex is left intact, housing a **Museum of Inscriptions** (currently closed).

The main thoroughfare skirts the large, overgrown **upper agora**, which lies opposite the civic heart of the Roman community – the **prytaneum**. This housed the inextinguishable sacred flame of Ephesus and two of the Artemis statues in the Selçuk museum, in spite of Hestia (Vesta) being the presiding goddess; it also served as the reception area for official guests.

The adjacent **odeon**, once the local parliament, has been as insensitively restored as the main theatre, though presumably the 27 rows of seats are the original number. The **Varius baths** mark the end of the paved Roman street system, and also the location of the upper site entrance. Beyond the gate huddles the massive **east gymnasium**, next to which the **Magnesia Gate** signals the true edge of the old city. The asphalt road here leads 5km south to Meryemana (see p.364), but you'd have to hitch or hope for a passing taxi – it's too steep and car-infested a walk to be enjoyable.

Priene

Perched on a series of pine terraces graded into the south flank of Samsun Dağı, 35km south of Kuşadası, the compact but exquisite site of **Priene** enjoys a situation that bears comparison with that of Delphi in Greece. The original settlement, legendarily founded by refugee Athenians and dating from perhaps the eleventh century BC, was elsewhere in the Meander basin; the townspeople, following the receding shoreline – now just visible to the west – refounded the city on its present site during the fourth century BC, just in time for Alexander to stop in and defray the cost of the principal temple of Athena. The Panionion sanctuary, cult centre of the league of Ionian cities, had always lain in Priene's territory, just the other side of Samsun Dağı; as a result its priest was usually chosen from Priene, whose secular officials also presided over the regular meetings of the confederacy. Under Roman – and later Byzantine – rule, however, the city enjoyed little patronage from the emperors, with the result that Priene represents the best-preserved Hellenistic townscape in Ionia, without any of the usual later additions. The town was laid out by Hippodamus, an architect from nearby Miletus, who favoured a grid pattern made up of various *insulae* (rectangular units), each measuring roughly 42m by 35m. Within each rectangle stood four private dwellings; a public building had its own *insula*, sometimes two.

The site

The **site** (daily 8am–6.30pm, winter closes 5.30pm; $0.70) lies a few hundred metres west of the village of Güllübahçe (see "Practicalities", p.373). There's a site map posted at the entrance, but the labelling is incorrect and, in many cases, confusing. From the entrance, a gap in Priene's ancient walls at the eastern end of the central street leads into the city.

South of the central street

The first easily distinguished civic monument, on the south side of the central street, is the square **bouleuterion** or council house, the most intact in Turkey, consisting of seats on three sides enclosing the speakers' area, together with a sacrificial altar.

Just east of the bouleuterion are the scantier remains of the **prytaneion**, or town administration offices, with traces of a dining area for the highest municipal officials. On the next terrace down lie the **Temple of Zeus**, the **agora** and the **sacred stoa**, once graced by outer and inner series of Doric and Ionic columns, though nothing is left above knee level of any of these. The commanding views, however, suggest that this was the heart of public life in the city.

Clearly visible below, reached by way of a stairway from the agora, are the **gymnasium** and **stadium** – relatively neglected parts of the site due to the shadeless climb back up entailed by a visit. Some of the gymnasium walls are decorated with still-visible graffiti; nearby are **bathing basins**, complete with gutters and lion-head spouts, for use after athletics. On the west side of the stadium there are a few sets of **starting blocks** for foot races; spectators watched from the north side of the 190m-by-20m area, where some seats are still discernible.

Returning to the central street and continuing west down a gentle slope you are soon in the midst of the densest surviving residential district in Priene, where thick walls stand up to 1.5 metres in some places. Though many of the **houses** are choked by pine and shrubbery, others permit entry. The usual ground plan was that of a narrow passage leading to a large central court, surrounded by various rooms. The discovery of occasional stairways demonstrated that some dwellings had two storeys. Priene's **west gate** marks the end of both the main street and the blocks of houses.

North of the central street

The city's most conspicuous monument, the **Temple of Athena Polias**, stands two terraces above the main residential street. The temple took more than two centuries to complete and, in its time, was considered the epitome of Ionic perfection; a manual written by its designer Pytheos was still considered standard reading in Roman times. Five of the original thirty Ionic columns were re-erected in the 1960s and at certain seasons of the year they catch the sunset and glow in the dusk long after the rest of the archeological zone has been plunged into darkness.

Directly north of the Athena temple, reached by a faint trail through the pines, is the **Sanctuary of Demeter and Kore**, on the highest terrace of the urban grid. Other than the foundations – a good century or two older than those of any other shrine in Priene – little is visible today besides the few Doric column stumps and a pit for catching the blood of sacrificial animals.

The **theatre**, a little way southeast, is by contrast in an excellent state of preservation, its layout and seating (for 5000, Priene's entire population) unchanged from the Hellenistic original. Most prominent are five larger than average marble thrones for the municipal dignitaries. The stage buildings were extensively modified during the second century AD – virtually the only Roman tampering with Priene's public buildings. Just behind them are the waist-high remains of a **Byzantine basilica**.

If you're keen on scrambling and the weather is not too hot, take the path beginning above the theatre, which leads in stages to the **acropolis**, on the bluff known as Teloneia in ancient times. A head for heights is useful as the path dwindles, after passing an aqueduct and some cisterns, to a series of paint-splodge-marked steps and goat traces zigzagging steeply up the cliff. Allow an extra hour and a half for the round trip.

The mandatory exit from the site is the former **main (northeast) gate**, still mostly intact.

Practicalities

All-in tours can be arranged from Selçuk, usually from your hotel or hostel, and are a good idea if time is limited. The tour usually includes a reasonable guide and a 9.30am pick-up from your hotel, a lunch-stop and a 5pm return. The itinerary is open to alteration but often starts at Priene moving on to Didyma (p.376) and saving the shadeless Miletus (see below) until last. Prices average around $18 but it's worth shopping around as they do vary enormously.

Dolmuş services to Priene require a change of vehicle at Söke, 24km southeast of Kuşadasi and 44km south of Selçuk. Making connections is pretty hassle-free: you'll be deposited right next to vehicles leaving for Priene, Miletus and Didyma. The hourly **dolmuşes from Söke** take twenty minutes to reach the very spread-out village of **Güllübahçe**, scattered 200 to 700m east of the ruins.

It is tempting to save a visit to Priene for late afternoon, when it is at its most beautiful, but staying overnight can be a problem. There is only one small **pension** in the village, the *Priene* (☎0256/547 1725; ❶), which offers very reasonable en-suite rooms but requires advance booking in high season. Of the handful of **restaurants**, best is *Pınar*, at the far west end of the village, right below the site car park, though *Şelale*, in the village centre, has a wider menu.

Miletus

The position of **MILETUS** (Milet in Turkish), on an eminently defendable promontory jutting out into the ancient Gulf of Latmos, once outshone that of Priene. However, its modern setting, marooned in the seasonal marshes of the Büyük Menderes, is dreary, and there's little left to bear witness to the town's long and colourful past. Only the theatre, visible from some distance away, hints at former glories (and even this is often submerged under water in winter). Up close, the site is a confusing juxtaposition of widely scattered relics from different eras, often disguised by weeds, mud or water, depending on the season. Ironically, even the grid street plan championed by native son Hippodamus has largely failed to survive, swept away by the Romans and geological processes. If you're pressed for time, this might be the Ionian site to miss.

Some history

Miletus is at least as old as Ephesus and far older than Priene; German archeologists working locally since the 1890s have uncovered remnants of a Creto-Mycenaean settlement from the sixteenth century BC. Ionian invaders made their first appearance during the eleventh century, and by the seventh century BC Miletus was in the first flush of a heyday that was to last more than two hundred years, when the city was able to repulse the advances of the Lydians and found colonies all over Anatolia. It was also a highly evolved cultural centre, with a roll call of scholars and thinkers that included the mathematician Thales and the courtesan-orator Aspasia, friend of Socrates and Pericles.

While not strong enough to completely avoid Persian domination, Miletus did manage to secure favourable terms as an equal, and even took the opportunity to appropriate the nearby oracle of Didyma. But with Athenian instigation, the city was unwisely persuaded to take command of the abortive Ionian revolt against the Persians between 500 and 494 BC. After the rebels were finally defeated in the naval battle at nearby Lade Island, Darius punished the ringleader severely with wholesale massacre and pillage.

Within fifty years Miletus was rebuilt some distance to the northeast of its original site, but it was never again to be as great – or as independent. Alexander saw fit to "liberate" the city from a new, short-lived occupation by the Persians and their allies, including a huge fleet anchored hard by which sat motionless, perhaps in awe of the Macedonian's mystique. Later it was bequeathed to the Romans, under whose rule it enjoyed a brief renaissance – most of what you see today is a legacy of various emperors' largesse. The Byzantine town stubbornly clung to life, producing Isidorus, architect of İstanbul's Aya Sofya. In the ninth century Miletus was already dwindling and by the time the Menteşe emirs, and then the Ottomans, took control, there was little left to prize.

Visiting the site

The site lies 45km south of Selçuk and access by public transport is fairly easy from Söke (see "Priene: Practicalities" on p.373): all dolmuşes bound for Balat (2km from the ruins), Akköy or Altınkum run past Güllübahçe (for Priene) and Milet; the journey from Söke takes 40 minutes. At Akköy, 6km to the south, there are simple **eateries** (but no accommodation); otherwise some expensive snack-bars cater for a tour-bus clientele near the **site entrance** (daily: summer 8.30am–7pm; winter 8.30am–5.30pm; $0.70). Note that the **museum**, 1km south of the main ticket booth, is currently closed following the theft of various artefacts and is likely be relocated to Didyma in the future.

Theatre and castle

The most obvious attraction at Miletus is behind the ticket stall: a **theatre**, whose Hellenistic base was modified and enlarged during the second century

Museum & South Entrance ▼ *Akköy & Didyma*

AD to a capacity of 15,000. One of the first things you'll see on the orchestra floor is a stone block with two griffins carved in relief, one playing a lyre. The centre of the front row sports two pillars that once supported the emperor's canopy. Further up, the vaulted exit passageways are enormous and virtually intact; unfortunately the area above the *diazoma* (dividing terrace) is now off-limits.

An eighth-century **Byzantine castle** and some contemporaneous ramparts surmount the theatre, giving a marvellous 360-degree view over the flood plain, and the chance to get your bearings on the rest of the site. Visible on the plain a kilometre or so to the west is a scrubby hill, formerly the **Island of Lade**.

The harbour area

Descending from the walls, you pass a **Hellenistic tomb** featuring a circular burial chamber in the middle. Further east, a round base is all that remains of the **naval monument**, commemorating an unknown victory of the first century BC, that once overlooked the most impressive of Miletus's four harbours, the "Lion Bay", so called for the two **stone lions** that guarded the entrance – now embedded up to their haunches in marsh silt.

The end of the tongue-shaped bay was lined by a colonnade that extended east to the sixth-century **Delphinion**, dedicated to Apollo Delphinius, patron of sailors, ships and ports. Not surprisingly in such a maritime community, it was the most important religious establishment in town. Today you can still see the foundations of altars or semicircular benches and the enclosing colonnade. Immediately south squat some incongruous **Selçuk baths**.

Along and around the Sacred Way

Both the Delphinion and baths stand at the north end of a handsomely paved **Sacred Way**, which in its time linked Miletus with Didyma; after a rainy winter, though, it's likely to remain submerged for some months. On the same side of the pavement as you walk south stands a first-century AD **Ionic stoa**, conspicuous owing to its rather clinical partial restoration, which partly shields the enormous **Capito baths** and a **gymnasium** of the same era. The most satisfying monument east of the Sacred Way is the **nymphaeum**, the largest public fountain of Miletus, once extremely ornate but now standing at barely half its original height. Just south of here are the ruins of a sixth-century **Byzantine church**.

On the west side of the pavement, beginning at the harbour, are the jumbled and overgrown remains of the so-called **north agora**. Marginally more interesting is the second-century BC **bouleuterion**, which faces the nymphaeum. The Sacred Way skirts the **south agora**, unexcavated except for a monumental gateway, which was carted off to Berlin in 1908. West of the *agora* are the recessed premises of a third-century AD **Temple of Serapis**, where you can make out a bas-relief representation of the deity Serapis Helios on a fallen pediment.

The Roman **Baths of Faustina** (Marcus Aurelius' wife), west of here at the foot of the theatre hill, are distinctive for their position at an angle to what remains of the urban grid – and for their good state of repair. The most engaging sight inside is the two spouts that once fed the cold pool – one in the form of a now decapitated statue of local river deity Meander, the other an intact lion head.

İlyas Bey Camii

About 200m to the south and marked by dense vegetation, the early fifteenth-century **İlyas Bey Camii**, built by that Menteşe emir to give thanks for his safe return from captivity by Tamerlane, is arguably more interesting than anything at the ancient site except the theatre. The mosque, dressed entirely in marble pillaged from the ancient city, lost its minaret in the 1958 earthquake that levelled nearby Balat, but otherwise fared well, retaining its fine carved-marble *mihrab*, stalactite vaulting and Arabic inscriptions. The entrance is particularly enchanting, with a carved marble screen flanking the door and triple bi-coloured arches just outside. There was once a *medrese* and *imaret* adjacent, but only a peaceful, neglected courtyard with some adjoining cells and head stones has survived. It's a serene and contemplative corner, more frequented by storks than humans.

Didyma and around

By the time you reach **DIDYMA** (Didim in Turkish) site fatigue might be beginning to set in. However, the oracular sanctuary of Apollo, though half-ruined and besieged throughout the middle of the day by swarms of tour groups, rarely fails to impress. The best time to visit – and the hour when, having worked their way through either Priene or Miletus or both, many people tend to show up – is late afternoon or early evening, when the masonry glows in the sunset. The other great advantage of a visit is being able to combine seeing the ruins with hitting the nearby beach at **Altınkum**, just 5km to the south.

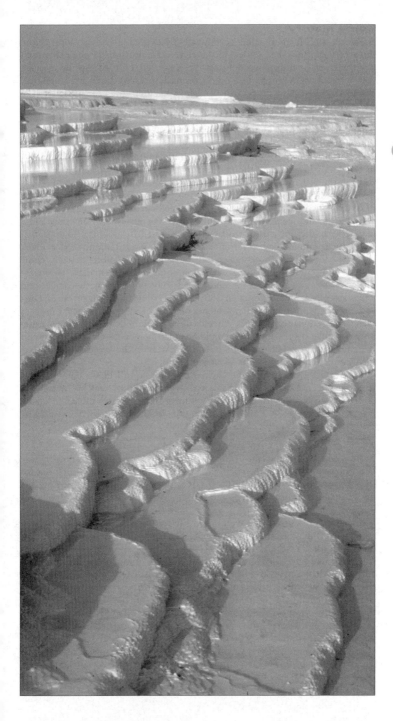

Some history

An oracle and shrine of some sort apparently existed at Didyma long before the arrival of the Ionian settlers in the eleventh century BC – the name itself is an ancient Anatolian word – but the imported **cult of Apollo** quickly appropriated whatever previous oracle, centred on a sacred well and laurel tree, had worked here. Didyma remained a sacred precinct, under the jurisdiction of a clan of priests originally from Delphi, and was never a town as such, though it eventually became a dependency of nearby Miletus. Every four years the sanctuary was also the venue for the Didymeia, a festival of music and drama as well as athletics.

The Archaic shrine, begun during the eighth century BC, was finished within two hundred years, and though similar in design to the current structure, it was half the size. After their defeat of the Ionian revolt in 494 BC, the Persians destroyed this first temple and plundered its treasures, including the cult statue of Apollo. The oracle puttered along in reduced circumstances until Alexander appeared on the scene, when the cult statue was retrieved from Persia and a new temple (the one existing today) commissioned.

Despite continuing subsidy from the Romans, work continued at a snail's pace for more than five centuries and the building was never actually completed – not entirely surprising when you consider the formidable engineering problems presented. In the end Christianity put paid to the oracle, and when the edict of Theodosius in 385 AD proscribed all pagan practices, construction ceased for good, after which a medieval earthquake toppled most of the columns. Inhabitants of the Greek village of Yeronda (the Ottoman name for the hamlet overlooking the temple precinct) helped themselves liberally to the ancient masonry in their midst, and blocks from the site can still be seen incorporated into some of the older village houses.

At its zenith Didyma was approached not only from Miletus but also from Panormos, a cove 6km west, via a sacred way whose final stretches were lined with statuary. Neither pavement nor statues are visible today, the latter having been spirited away to the British Museum in 1858.

The site

Entry to the **site** (daily 8am–7pm; closes 5.30pm winter; $1.50) is now by way of a gate to the north of the enclosure. At the bottom of the steps look out for the **Medusa head**, which fell from a Roman-era architrave and is now the unofficial logo of the place, repeated ad infinitum on posters and cards all over Turkey.

Pilgrims would first visit a **well** below the resting place of the Medusa head and purify themselves, then approach a still-prominent **circular altar** to offer a sacrifice before proceeding to the **shrine** itself. Even in ruins this is still intimidatingly large – the surviving column stumps alone are considerably taller than a man, and in its nearly complete state it must have inspired reverence. The effect was accentuated by the shrine's position on a steep, stepped base and enclosure in a virtual forest of 108 Ionic **columns** – though only three of these stand to their original height. The remaining twelve stumps supported the roof of the entry porch, reached by a steep flight of steps, where supplicants would deliver their queries to the priest of Apollo, who would reappear after a suitable interval on a terrace some six feet higher to deliver the prophetess's oracular pronouncement. Questions ranged from the personal to matters of state; prophecies were recorded and stored for posterity on the premises. The cult statue of Apollo, his sacred laurel and the sacred well were formerly enclosed in a miniature shrine of which only traces remain – though the **well** itself is still obvious, roped off to prevent accidents. As at Delphi in Greece, prophecies were formulated by a priestess, who either (accounts disagree) drank from, bathed in or inhaled potent vapours from the waters. Her subsequent ravings were rephrased more delicately to those waiting out front.

Petitioners did not normally enter the inner sanctum, except to watch the goings-on of the Didymeia from a monumental stairway providing access to the terrace from the interior. The steps still bear spectators' graffiti, though the terrace is currently off-limits – you enter the sanctuary proper by means of twin tunnels to either side. The innermost court was never roofed, though the height of the walls once exceeded 20m; today they're half that height.

Practicalities

Hourly **dolmuşes** and full-size buses cover the route between Söke and Altınkum beach (see below) via **Didim village**, the modern name for Didyma. It's a fifty-minute ride to the village; ask to be dropped off at the junction 200m from the ruins, otherwise buses will continue on to the *otogar*, 2km out of Didim village to the west. The village itself is something of a tourist trap, crammed with souvenir shops, and all three of the **restaurants** across from the archeological zone are expensive and poor in quality. For a good feed at reasonable prices you'll have to walk a kilometre northeast to **Yenihisar**, a much larger, more untouched village, where the *lokantas* are less touristy and a bit more authentic.

The **accommodation** choice is between the rooms at the *Pension Oracle* (☎0256/811 0270; ❷), offering breakfast on a terrace directly overlooking the ruins, and those at the more comfortable, if viewless, *Medusa Haus* (☎0256/811 0063; ❹), nearby. The latter is run by a German/Turkish couple and features rustic rooms in an old building restored with plenty of character.

South of Didyma: Altınkum

Five kilometres south of Didyma, the information placard at the road's end in **ALTINKUM** says it all, listing well over a hundred hotels and *pansiyons* arrayed behind a single kilometre of beach split by a headland. In midsummer it's standing room only on the sand, but at least it lives up to its name ("golden sand" in Turkish): a gently sloping beach with no surf, ideal for children and in total contrast to the exposed coast on the other side of Didyma. Of late the place has become the Turkish equivalent of Costa del Sol, with a large British package presence that has engendered a rash of "English" eateries with food (and prices) the way Turks imagine Brits like it ("Roast Beef and Yorkshire Pudding", as well as the widely advertised, and totally inedible, "T-bone steaks").

Altınkum is essentially the shore annex of Yenihisar (see above), which is where you'll find most of the amenities (such as proper shops). However, to the right of the T-junction marked by the accommodation placard there's a **bank** and **PTT** as well as a sporadically staffed **tourist information** booth further along. A seasonal (May–Oct) **ferry service** to Bodrum operates most days in the morning, which allows travellers to shortcut the tortuous journey there by land.

The least expensive **pansiyons**, such as the *Ankara* (☎0256/813 6895, ℱ813 7626; ❶) – where the price doesn't include breakfast – and the *Agais* (☎0256/813 1379; ❷), can be found on the upper, parallel street behind the far western jetty, but these are usually block-booked by Turkish families in season. Lodgings to the east of the accommodation placard are considerably more upmarket, though competition and lean tourist years have led to some three-star hotels dropping their prices considerably. Examples include the *Göçtur* (☎0256/813 2740 & 2744; ❷) – the rates are for half-board accommodation – and the *Majestic* (☎0256/813 4615, 🖷813 5018; ❷).

Ancient Caria: the coastal regions

In antiquity, **Caria** was an isolated, mysterious region purportedly inhabited by barbarous people indigenous to the area (a rarity in Anatolia), speaking a language distantly related to Greek. Following the advent of Alexander, and the Hecatomnid dynasty at Halicarnassus, Hellenization proceeded apace and the differences between the Carians and their neighbours diminished. After the Byzantine period, and the fifteenth-century absorption of the local Menteşe emirate by the Ottomans, the region again assumed backwater status. Until the early republican years, internal exile to the coast here was an habitual and feared sentence for political offenders. In a strange echo of the ancient tendency, the dialect of **Muğla province** – whose territory corresponds almost exactly to that of coastal Caria – is still one of the most eccentric and difficult to understand in the entire country.

Bafa Gölü (or Lake Bafa) and ancient **Heracleia ad Latmos** on its northeast shore make a suitably dramatic introduction to coastal Caria. **Euromos** and **Labranda** are two of the more satisfying minor ancient sites in Turkey, and both can be seen from **Milas**, the nearest substantial town. Nearby, at **Stratonikya**, a once-untouched ancient metropolis is almost engulfed by a lignite quarry. Southeast of Milas, **Peçin Kale** constitutes a Turkish oddity – a ruined medieval city, in this case the Menteşe capital. **Ören**, still further southeast on the same road, is another rare beast: an attractive coastal resort that has not yet been steamrollered by modern tourism. Southwest of Milas, however, neither **ancient Iassos**, nor the small resort of **Güllük**, live up to their hyped reputations. Most visitors bypass Güllük in favour of **Bodrum** and its peninsula, very much the big tourist event on this coast, with tentacles of development creeping over every available parcel of surrounding land – though what attracted outsiders to the area in the first place still shines through on occasion.

Moving on, **Muğla** makes for a pleasant stopover if you're passing through: one of the best-preserved Ottoman townscapes in Turkey, coexisting with an unobtrusive, well-planned new city.

Further south, **Marmaris** is another big – and rather overblown – resort, from which the **Loryma (Hisarönü) peninsula** beyond, bereft of a sandy shoreline but blessed with magnificent scenery, offers the closest escape. As a compromise,

Datça and its surroundings might fit the bill, with some remote beaches near-by more rewarding than the much-touted ruins of ancient **Knidos**.

Bafa Gölü

Bafa Gölü (Lake Bafa), one of the most entrancing spectacles in southwestern Turkey, was created when silt deposited by the Büyük Menderes River sealed off the Latmos gulf from the sea. The barren, weirdly sculpted pinnacles of ancient **Mount Latmos** (Beşparmak Dağı) still loom over the northeast shore, visible from a great distance west. Numerous islets dot the 100-square-kilometre lake, most of them sporting some sort of fortified Byzantine religious establishment, dating from the lake's days as an important monastic centre between the seventh and fourteenth centuries.

Bafa's separation from the sea is not perfect: canals link the lake's west end with an oxbow of the Büyük Menderes close by. As a result, the water is faintly brackish and fish species tolerant of both salt and fresh water shuttle back and forth, spawning in the lake. The most important are *levrek* (bass), *kefal* (grey mullet), *yayın* (catfish) and *yılan balığı* (eel) – all caught by a fishing co-operative based on the north shore and by numerous migratory waterfowl, for whom Bafa is an important stopover.

During dry years the water level falls by up to a metre and the weeds that always hover in the shallows can burgeon, making access difficult – which is a shame since the water temperature is ideal for swimming.

Practicalities

Bus services past the lake are frequent, but Söke–Milas dolmuşes (every 30min) are more flexible than the big coaches in terms of stopping. The southern shore of Bafa, which the main highway follows, is the location of a few combination **campsite-pansiyon-restaurants**, best thought of as a serene setting for lunch (at least for those in their own vehicle). Heading east, the most acceptable of these is *Ceri'nin Yeri* (☎0252/512 4498; ❶), run by proprietor Ceri, a rather basic, five-room *pansiyon* with a restaurant menu that varies with the catch. There are no shops anywhere along the lake (though Ceri sells perishables such as eggs and yoghurt), so bring what you need.

Swimming is best from the far side of the monastery-capped islet, which in dry years is joined to Ceri's restaurant by a muddy spit. On the islet, some flattish rocks offer a weed-free corridor out onto the lake when the water level is normal. Failing that, dive off the end of the wooden jetty constructed to outrun the weeds.

Heracleia ad Latmos

Across Lake Bafa, most easily seen from the *Ceri'nin Yeri pansiyon*-restaurant, is a patch of irregular shoreline with a modern village, Kapıkırı, whose lights twinkle at the base of Mount Latmos by night. This is the site of **Heracleia ad Latmos** (Heraklia in Turkish) one of Turkey's most evocatively situated ancient cities.

A settlement of Carian origin had existed here long before the arrival of the Ionians, and Carian habits died hard, though Latmos – as it was then known –

had far better geographical communication with Ionia than with the rest of Caria. Late in the Hellenistic period the city's location was moved a kilometre or so west, and the name changed to Heracleia, but despite adornment with numerous monuments and an enormous wall it was never a place of great importance. Miletus, at the head of the gulf, monopolized most trade and already the inlet was beginning to close up.

Heracleia owes its fame, and an enduring hold on the romantic imagination, to a legend associated not with the town itself but with Mount Latmos behind. **Endymion** was a handsome shepherd who, while asleep in a cave on the mountain, was noticed by Selene, the moon goddess. She made love with him as he slept and in time, so the story goes, bore Endymion fifty daughters without their sire ever waking once. Endymion was reluctant for all this to stop and begged Zeus, who was also fond of him, to be allowed to dream forever; his wish was granted and, as a character in Mary Lee Settle's *Blood Ties* flippantly observed, thus became the only known demigod of the wet dream. Later, Christian hermits who settled in the vicinity during mid-Byzantine times cleaned up Endymion's act, so to speak – in their version he was a mystic who after a lifetime of "communing" with the moon had learned the secret name of God. Once a year the anchorites, leaving their homes on the island cloisters, or in various caves on Latmos, converged upon an ancient tomb believed to be Endymion's. The sarcophagus lid would be opened and the bones inside would emit a strange humming noise, said to be the deceased saint's attempt to communicate the holy name.

The monastic communities, after producing a few minor saints, were dispersed for good early in the fourteenth century and little is now left of any of the Byzantine monuments. But when a full moon rises over the serrated peaks across the water, it is easy to suspend disbelief in all the legends pertaining to the place. Indeed Endymion's fate has exercised a fascination on many subsequent eras: Shakespeare declared "Peace, ho! The moon sleeps with Endymion/And would not be waked!", and four centuries later Keats added: "What is there in thee, Moon! that shouldst move my heart so potently? . . . Now I begin to feel thy orby power/Is coming fresh upon me."

The site

Arriving by car, park your vehicle either next to the *Agora Pansiyon* (see Practicalities opposite) or in another area about 200m up the hill. The site is not enclosed, though you may have to pay a dollar or so **admission** if the warden is in the ticket booth.

The crudely signposted **bouleuterion** lies 100m to the east of the first parking area, though only the retaining wall and some rows of benches are left of the second-century BC structure. The **Roman baths** visible in the valley below, and a crumbled but appealing **Roman theatre** off in the olives beyond, can be reached via an unmarked trail starting between the first and second parking areas. The path up to the **hermits' caves** on Mount Latmos begins at the rear of the second parking area. Stout boots are advisable, as is a cool day in early spring or late autumn – for a place still so close to the sea, Heracleia can be surprisingly hot and airless. Similar cautions apply for those who want to trace the course of the **Hellenistic walls**, the city's most imposing and conspicuous relics, supposedly built by Lysimachus in the late third century BC.

The *Agora*'s restaurant looks south over the **Hellenistic agora**, now mostly taken up by the village schoolyard; its south edge is buttressed by a row of **shops**, whose downhill side stands intact to two storeys, complete with windows. From the agora grounds you've a fine view west over the lake and assorted castle-crowned promontories. A box-like Hellenistic **Temple of Athena** perches on a hill west of the agora; less conspicuous is an inscription to Athena, left of the entrance.

From the agora a wide, walled-in path descends toward the shore and the final quota of recognizable monuments at Heracleia. Most obvious is the peninsula – or, in wet years, island – studded with **Byzantine walls** and a **church**. A stone causeway half-buried in the beach here allowed entrance in what must have been drier medieval times. Follow the shore southwest to the *Zeybek* restaurant, strategically astride another promontory, and then continue along its access drive to the junction with a slightly wider track. Across the way you should see the tentatively identified Hellenistic **Sanctuary of Endymion**, oriented unusually northeast to southwest. Five column stumps front the structure, which has a rounded rear wall – a ready-made apse for later Christians – with sections of rock incorporated into the masonry.

Striking out across the pasture opposite the Endymion shrine, and skimming the base of yet another Byzantine castle, you arrive at the ancient **necropolis**, which consists of a few dozen rectangular tombs hewn into boulders on the shore. Many are partly or completely awash, depending on the water level.

Practicalities

The most common access to Heracleia is by **boat** from *Ceri'nin Yeri* (see "Bafa Gölü: Practicalities" on p.381). Tours generally depart between 9.30 and 10.30am, take twenty minutes to cross the lake, and allow just under two-and-a-half hours at the ruins – enough for a look around and a quick meal. Reckon on paying about $5 a head round-trip, assuming a group of at least ten people, plus site admission.

Alternatively, if you have your own vehicle, drive east to Çamiçi village (6km beyond *Ceri'nin Yeri*) and then turn left at the signpost ("Herakleia"). The ten-kilometre paved road leads through fields and finally a wilderness of Latmian boulders to the modern village of **KAPIKIRI**, built higgledy-piggledy among the ruins. Scattered in and around Kapıkırı are a few simple **pansiyons** and **restaurants**, and a campsite. The opening periods of most establishments are erratic to say the least, though most will be open for the main May to September period. *Selene's*, near the waterfront (☎0252/543 5221, ⓦwww.bafalake3.netfirms.com; ❷), is a good choice for basic rooms and can also organize boat trips on the lake. The *Zeybek Restaurant-Camping* (☎0252/543 5158), on the lakeside, has good views and serves moderately priced fish. The most upmarket is the *Agora Pansiyon* (☎0252/543 5445, ⓦwww.heraklia.com; ❸), whose basically furnished doubles and attached restaurant are arranged around a verdant garden.

Milas

A small, initially nondescript town of some 35,000 people, and major regional transport hub, **MİLAS** is too often given short shrift by tourists intent on reaching the fleshpots of Bodrum as quickly as possible. This is a shame, for although it's unlikely that most foreigners would want to stay the night here, there are enough sights of interest to fill a few hours between buses.

First impressions – sprawling apartment buildings on the outskirts, traffic congestion in the bazaar – are not reassuring, but a stroll around reveals beautiful old houses tucked away behind the main thoroughfares. The town's market is at its best on Tuesdays, when organized tours visit from Bodrum. The local specialities – honey, olives and earth-toned carpets – are sold here; in winter and spring the stalls sell freshly picked wild herbs and sweet-tasting purple carrots.

Milas – or **Mylasa**, as it was formerly known – was an important Carian centre (its original location was at the nearby hill of **Peçin Kale**), but it was the Halicarnassus-based Hecatomnid dynasty that really put it on the map. The nearby quarries provided ample marble for numerous public monuments, while increased control over the sanctuary at Labranda brought the city additional benefits. Mylasa's assignment by the Roman republic to the jurisdiction of Rhodes in 190 BC was too much for the locals to stomach and they rebelled within twenty years, declaring a brief independence which lasted for two more decades before eventual incorporation into the Roman Empire. Details of the Byzantine period are obscure, but the city experienced a resurgence during the fourteenth century when the Menteşe emirs, a Turcoman clan, made it the capital of their realms in southwestern Anatolia.

The Town

An elaborate early Roman tomb known as the **Gümüşkesen** (literally "cuts-silver") is the most obviously impressive relic of ancient Mylasa. The way there is poorly marked from the town centre, but the monument is easy enough to find by heading 500m west along Kadıağa Caddesi, which soon becomes the slightly sloping Gümüşkesen Caddesi. There are no formal visiting hours nor an admission fee to the landscaped site, which lies in a slight depression south of Hıdırlık hill.

The monument consists of a square burial chamber surmounted by a Corinthian colonnade with a pyramidal roof – a design presumed to be a miniature of the now-vanished mausoleum at Halicarnassus. The ceiling sports elaborate carvings and some flecks of paint; a hole in the floor allowed mourners to pour libations into the sepulchre below.

Milas's lively tradesmen's **bazaar** covers the western slopes of Hisarbaşı hill, which has been the focus of settlement in every era. Once past the warren of alleys perpendicular to the main Cumhuriyet Caddesi, veer up to the summit and the late Ottoman **Belen Camii**. Immediately to its right stands the eighteenth-century **Çöllühanı**, one of the last semi-functioning, unrestored *kervansaray*s in western Turkey. Leaving here, go through the archways of the more modern *han* opposite and continue downhill to the grounds of the fine, grey-marble, late fourteenth-century **Firuz Bey Camii**, erected by the Menteşe emirs using bits of the ancient town.

Back past the Çöllühanı, heading southeast behind the PTT, there's a district of sumptuous **old houses**, the finest in Milas, built from the wealth engendered by tobacco and cotton during the nineteenth century, when the town boasted large Greek Orthodox, Armenian and Jewish populations. One of the finest houses on the hill is at Tabakhane Cad 9/A, which still boasts particularly impressive stone carving around the door. Watch for yellow arrow-signs with the legend "Uzunyuva" (Tall Nest) and the single Corinthian column, adorned with a stork's nest (hence the name), announcing the first-century BC **Temple of Zeus**, adjacent to which a sign cryptically reads "*Kutsal Alan*" (Holy Clearing). Much of the foundation has been incorporated into later houses, with pieces of carved masonry often reused as keystones above doors.

Downhill from here you'll pass a huge stretch of ancient **city wall** and at the

▲ Otogar & Labranda

MİLAS

Firuz Bey
Camii

Gümüşkesen (500 m)

GÜMÜŞLUK CAD

CUMHURIYET CAD

MERDIVENLI SOK

MIRKIN SOK

İNÖNÜ CAD

Baltalı Kapı

4

Produce
Market

A

Belediye

Belen
Camii

Orhan (Ağa)
Camii

SARDATLI CAD

GÜMÜŞKESEN CAD

GÜVERCINLIK CAD

MENTESE CAD

Bazaar

Çöllühanı

HİSARBAŞI
HILL

Temple
of Zeus

1

KADIAĞA CAD

TABAKHANE CAD

Dolmuş
Terminal

DAMLACIK CAD

PARK CAD

ONIKI EYLÜL CAD

CUMHURIYET CAD

Ulu Cami

SAIR ULVI AKGÜN CAD

Archeological
Museum

ACCOMMODATION

| Cınar | 1 |
| Sürücü | 2 |

B

MUŞTAK BEY CAD

İNÖNÜ CAD

RESTAURANTS

Kösem	C
Özcan Kebap	B
Pammukale	A
Ziyafet Pide	D

ZAFER CAD

BAG CAD

C ★ Otogar Drop off/
Pick up point

STAD CAD

0   100 m

THE CENTRAL AND SOUTHERN AEGEAN | Milas

▼ **2**, **D** & Airport Bus Stop

bottom of the slope an **Ottoman bridge** with an inscribed plaque. Across the bridge, a few minutes' walk past the **Orhan (Ağa) Camii**, oldest of the town's mosques (1330), stands the **Baltalı Kapı** (Gate-with-Axe) – the largest remaining section of the city walls. The axe in question, a double-headed attribute of Zeus, is faintly carved on the north-facing keystone.

The late fourteenth-century **Ulu Cami**, further south along Şair Ulvi Akgün Caddesi, is perhaps more engaging, an exotically asymmetrical building incorporating a vast quantity of plundered antiquities. Kufic inscriptions adorn the lintels, and a peculiar staircase leads up over the front door to a short and stubby minaret. In addition, the building has gables, buttressing and a dome over the *mihrab* end, and the whole effect is more that of a Byzantine church than a mosque.

Across the street, the **Archeological Museum** (Arkeoloji Müzesi; daily 8.30am–noon & 1–5.30pm; $2), labelled almost exclusively in Turkish, has a sparse collection considering the size of the hall – merely pottery and figurines from the immediate environs of Milas, plus two cases of mediocre gold diadems and slightly better jewellery. More interesting is the garden, which contains a large collection of ancient Jewish gravestones.

Peçin Kale

The original site of ancient Mylasa on the hill of **Peçin Kale** (*Beçin Kale* in local dialect and signposting), 5km east of Milas, lies just off the road leading southeast to the Gulf of Gökova. Mylasa's shift to its current position during the fourth century BC means that the hill is actually more interesting for its **castle** (daily 8am–8pm; $0.70), an unmistakable fortified bluff, originally Byzantine but adapted by the Menteşe emirs during their fourteenth-century tenure. However, the citadel does not fulfil the promise of its imposing exterior and the principal saving grace is the view of the plain, 200m below.

The Menteşe complex itself lies about 400m south from the castle. The main buildings are clearly marked: among the most interesting are the unusual two-storeyed **Kızıl Han**, and the fourteenth-century **Orhan Bey Camii**, featuring a far more ancient doorjamb and old hamam. Bearing right takes you to the **medrese and türbe of Ahmet Gazi**, from the same era – tombs of a Menteşe governor and his wife that are venerated as those of minor Islamic saints, with coloured rags and candles. Take any Ören-bound dolmuş from town (every 45min) and ask to be dropped at the *Beçin Kale* turn-off.

Practicalities

Milas's **otogar** is way out on the northern edge of town, near the junction for Labranda. You'll be left here unless you've come from Güllük or Ören, whose dolmuşes have a separate **terminal** close to the town centre. Getting into the centre from the *otogar*, take either a dolmuş marked "Şehir İçi" or the complimentary shuttle run by the big companies. The drop-off/pick-up point is the pavement south of the *Köşem* restaurant and city park; there's no fixed rank – just wait around. The Havaş bus to **Milas airport** stops at the roundabout at the end of Atatürk Bulvarıand is geared to the times of THY internal flights.

The only central, savoury budget **accommodation** you'll find is on Kadıağa Caddesi, just west of a T-junction at the base of Hisarbaşı hill: the *Çınar* (☎0252/512 5525, ℻512 2102; ❷) has comfortable, balconied rooms but is still no bargain. The surprisingly large *Sürücü Hotel* on Atatürk Bulvarı (☎0252/512 4001, ℻512 2548; ❷) is a few hundred metres out of the centre but far better value; its attached restaurant and café are frequented by students from the nearby university.

Simple **lunches** can be had at the *Pamukkale Pide Salonu*, near the market, or at several nearby hole-in-the-wall joints. Another good midday option is the *Özcan Kebap Salonu*, halfway up the main thoroughfare, Cumhuriyet Caddesi. The *Köşem* near the park and the *Sürücü Hotel*'s **restaurant** are licensed and not too expensive, while the *Ziyafet Pide*, opposite the school, serves enamel-corroding spiced *pide*.

Euromos, Labranda and Stratonikya

A short distance northwest of Milas lie two impressive Carian ruins that, together, make a good day out from the town. **Euromos** is easily reached by public transport, although you really need your own vehicle to visit isolated **Labranda**, as dolmuşes only take you halfway. To the east of Milas lies the ancient Roman city of **Stratonıkya**, again one for those with their own transport and a passion for ruins.

Euromos

Two-thirds of the way between Bafa Gölü and Milas, 4km southeast of the town of Selimiye, a Corinthian Temple of Zeus, north of the road in an olive grove, is virtually all that remains intact of the ancient city of **Euromos** (daily: May–Sept 9am–7pm; Oct–April 9am–5.30pm; $0.70 if warden present). However, it's sufficiently unusual – only two other temples in Turkey are in a comparable state of repair – to justify a detour.

You can get to the site **from Milas** by taking a dolmuş towards Selimiye – every twenty minutes between 7am and 7pm. If you are returning by public transport be warned that Selimiye–Milas dolmuşes, often full by this point, may refuse you. Be prepared to walk the 4km back to Selimiye to find one at the start of its run.

There was a sanctuary to a native Carian deity on this spot as early as the sixth century BC, together with a city originally known as Kyromus. By the fourth century, under the Hellenizing influence of nearby Halicarnassus, the name had changed to Euromos and the cult of Zeus had merged with that of the earlier god. The city attained its greatest importance during the Hellenistic and Roman periods, when it nearly rivalled nearby Mylasa, but by Byzantine times it had sunk back into obscurity.

The **Temple of Zeus** is a legacy of the generous Roman emperor Hadrian, though the fact that several of the remaining columns are unfluted suggests that the shrine was never finished. Of the original 32 columns, arranged six by eleven, only sixteen remain, though all of these are linked to one or more neighbours by portions of the architrave. The city itself was built several hundred metres to the northwest of the temple, but the only easily found trace of it is a stretch of wall with a **tower**, up on the ridge overlooking the sacred precinct. The city's badly eroded **amphitheatre** lies about ten minutes' walk north, on the far side of the ridge, down and right from the tower.

Labranda

The sanctuary of Zeus at **Labranda** (Labraynda in Turkish), perched in splendid isolation on a south-facing hillside overlooking the plain of Milas, is arguably the most beautifully set archeological zone of ancient Caria. It's also one of the least visited – it takes a very sturdy tour bus to brave the horrendous road in. The site lies over 15km north of Milas, but dolmuşes only go as far as the hamlet of **Kargıcak**, roughly halfway, beyond which you must walk or beg lifts from passing trucks. The road, though fully asphalted, is still a difficult drive with the gradient at times punishing and mud a problem. A **taxi from Milas** will set you back the better part of $20 return.

Excavations since 1948 have turned up no finds older than the seventh century BC, but it seems certain that some god was venerated here long before that. Oddly enough, the agreeable climate 600m up, coupled with a perennial spring, never prompted the founding of a city, but instead nurtured a grove of sacred plane trees that eventually became the precinct of Zeus Stratios (the Warlike), alias Zeus Labrayndus (the Axe-bearing), after his depiction on fourth-century coins struck at nearby Mylasa. The fourth-century BC Hecatomnid rulers of Halicarnassus and Mylasa did much to promote the cult, endowing various structures at the sanctuary that can still be seen. However, the priests of Zeus retained a large degree of autonomy, exerting their independence to advantage during the chaotic years after the death of Alexander. Roman and later Byzantine rule brought few material benefits to Labranda, and the place was finally abandoned during the late eleventh century.

The site

Just when you're beginning to wonder if you've made a wrong turn, a clump of poplars – replacing the long-vanished plane trees – heralds the location of the springs that still supply some of the water for modern Milas. A drinks stall and some beehives stand opposite the artificial terraces of the **sanctuary** (daily 8am–8pm; $0.70) and the rickety wooden gate giving onto them. The warden's family lives on the premises, and the children will usually escort you through the principal monuments in the following order, though they can only speak Turkish. In any case, the site is well marked and there's a helpful map-placard.

After skirting some unidentified ancient buildings, you climb up to the so-called **Andron A** – one of three such constructions at Labranda, used for sacred banquets held at the shrine. While roofless, it is otherwise complete, and includes a windowed niche in the back. Immediately adjacent are the **oikoi** (priests' residences), fronted by four Doric column stubs. Like the Andron A, this was another foundation of the Hecatomnids, though authorities disagree on whether it was the actual quarters of the cult priests or merely the repository of temple records.

The **Temple of Zeus**, originally laid out in the fifth century and rededicated by Idrieus, sprawls east of here. None of it stands more than knee high, yet it is appealing, especially when viewed from the near edge of the temple terrace, lined with the rudiments of a stoa. From its far corner a path leads up to the ruined **acropolis** and – more importantly – to a massive fourth-century **tomb** thought to be that of Idrieus and his family. This is divided in two, with three sarcophagi in the rear chamber and a damaged pair up front.

Just below the south rim of the temple terrace is the recessed **well house**, the original exit point of the spring; just across the flat area from here are **Andron B**, donated by Mausolus and relatively intact, and **Andron C**, a Roman contribution that has not weathered the ages as well.

From the level area in front of Andron C, it's a short distance to the prominent **monumental stairway** descending to the lowest terrace at the site. A right turn at the bottom of the steps leads to the **south propylaea**, one end of the sacred way to Mylasa, patches of which can still be followed; straight ahead takes you to the more prominent **east propylaea**, terminus of a processional way, long disappeared, from Alinda. Wedged in between the two propylaea are the remains of a so-called **Doric house**, some adjoining **Roman baths** and a **Byzantine church**, beyond which are the probable foundations of Labranda's famous **fish oracle**. The resident fish, bedecked with jewellery according to several ancient sources, were thrown bits of food by their custodians. Depending on whether they accepted the morsels or not, the enquirer's fortunes were in the ascendant or decline.

Stratonıkya

The ancient city of **Stratonıkya** (Stratoniceia in Turkish), 25km east of Milas, would be more acclaimed if it weren't for a giant, adjacent lignite quarry, whose noise and dust considerably reduce the peace and tranquillity. That the site continues to exist at all is a tribute to the Ministry of Culture's obstinance in the face of the coal company's demands to swallow it up.

The archeological zone occupies the site of tumbledown **Eskihisar village**, nearly all of whose population have moved 3km west to a new settlement. Still, if you have your own vehicle (there's no public transport) and time to spare, the ruins are worth a visit. Signs direct you through the crumbling houses, themselves worthy museum pieces of 1930s' architecture, past the abandoned teahouse and vandalized mosque to a parking area beside the makeshift museum (see below); $2 **admission** is payable when the portakabin is staffed.

Stratonikya was a third-century BC Seleucid foundation, but its heyday occurred during the Roman imperial period, so everything you can see now dates from that time. A few paces north of the empty teahouse is the Roman **gymnasium**, an elaborate structure with a colonnaded semicircular chamber sandwiched between three quadrangles of massive masonry. At the edge of the village, overlooking the opencast mine, is the **north city gate**, flanked by a lone, unfluted Corinthian column, just outside of which is a fragment of a **sacred way** that once led to a shrine of Hecate at nearby Lagina. By the pavement stands a **subterranean tomb** in good condition, the sole survivor of a necropolis, which, like the sacred way, has been sacrificed to mining interests. Bits of the substantial **city wall** are incorporated into houses on the west side of Eskihisar, with more chunks visible marching up the hillside to the south.

On the opposite side of the village is the most imposing remnant, a vast rectangular precinct identified either as a **bouleuterion** or a **shrine of Serapis**. The first thing you'll see is an isolated, rectangular **monumental gateway** erected a few metres west, but currently entry is via twin staircases bored through the south and north side walls; the north wall's interior is covered with inscriptions. Its possible role as a council house is supported by the five rows of seats, overlooking the countryside to the east. Southeast of here, the garden of an ochre-stained building serves as an impromptu **museum–cum–warehouse**, where finds from the excavation have been temporarily stored.

Ören

ÖREN is an endangered Turkish species – a coastal resort that's not completely overdeveloped. It's virtually the only sizeable village on the north coast of the Gulf of Gökova, and owes its pre-tourism history to the narrow, fertile, alluvial plain adjacent, and the lignite deposits in the mountains behind.

The route there is inauspicious, the landscape defaced by two giant power plants built with Polish aid. These installations are also one of the reasons tour operators have not seen fit to develop the area, although the industrial scenery of stacks and opencast mining stops well short of Ören itself, and pollution has not yet affected the crystalline waters offshore. Overall Ören makes a great hideout from the commercialism that has engulfed the rest of the coast, and is an excellent spot to recuperate from the rigours of overland travel. People, mostly from Ankara, come to stay for weeks on end: a single day is really pointless, and since there are fewer than 250 beds to go around, the place fills up in high season, when reservations are strongly advised.

The upper village and ancient Keramos

The **upper village**, on the east bank of a canyon mouth exiting the hills, is an appealingly homogenous settlement, scattered among the ruins of **ancient Keramos**. You can easily make out sections of wall, arches and a boat slip, dating from the time when the sea (now 1km distant) lapped the edge of town. Excavations are in progress, with some archeological fragments housed in a small fenced-off area, but a do-it-yourself tour through the village's old, mostly Ottoman Greek, houses should turn up some interesting oddments. The new resort area down on the coast (see below) has little in the way of relics, save for sections of column carted off from the main site by *pansiyon* owners for use as decoration.

The upper village has **shops** and a **post office** but no bank. Most **dolmuşes** from Milas continue the final short distance to the beach. For those driving themselves, a 45-kilometre **road** of sorts continues east from Ören past unspoiled, spectacular canyonland to the resort of Akyaka (see p.409), but only the first 8km or so at each end have thus far been widened or improved in any way, leaving a horrendous middle section capable of shearing off exhausts: explore at your own risk.

The beach

The **beach** is a more than acceptable kilometre of coarse sand, gravel and pebbles, backed by handsome pine-tufted cliffs; in clear weather you can spy the Datça peninsula opposite. Once there was a working harbour at the east end of the town, but since lignite is now burned locally rather than being shipped out, the lignite-loading conveyor has been demolished and what's left of the jetty now serves a few fishing boats and the occasional wandering yacht.

Practicalities

Dolmuşes from Milas take an hour to reach Ören. Having passed through the upper village you'll be dropped at the beach. Should you plan on **staying**, note that mid-range comfort is best represented by the *Dolunay Motel* (℡0252/532 2194, ℻532 3005; ❸), at the west end of the beach, with its own pier, pleasant garden and airy cottage units. Somewhat posher is *Kardelen* (℡0252/532 2678; ❷), though its slightly inland location is a drawback. Other alternatives include

Ortakent, Yahşi and around

The south peninsular trunk road continues to **ORTAKENT** (still known by its old name Müsgebi), an inland village crowned by the early seventeenth-century Mustafa Paşa tower and blessed with abundant water and orchards. From both Ortakent and **YAHŞI**, the next settlement, paved drives wind down several kilometres through oases to the longest, though not necessarily best, beach on the peninsula at **Yahşi Yalı**. Its two-kilometre length has been closed to wheeled traffic, and the clutter of shops, mediocre restaurants, motels and small hotels can make access problematic if you're not actually staying here. The resort is pitched almost totally to Turkish families, with lately a scattering of Czech and Russian tour groups. If you do choose to stay, you may as well plump for the top end of things here: the three-star *Club Petunya* (☎0252/348 3272, ⓦwww.clubpetunya.com; ❹), right on the beach, with lodging in six separate garden buildings. It's available through a couple of British package specialists, most consistently Sunquest. Dolmuşes to the beach bear the legend "Ortakent Yahşi Sahil" or "Yahşi Yali".

Kargı, Bağla and Karaincir

Beyond Yahşi, a turning flanked with hotel signs at Gürece leads high above **Kargi** – a beach more commonly reached by boat from Bodrum and usually referred to in day-trip-speak as "Camel Beach", since this is where they drop you for a spot of camel-riding. The beach and bay are sandy and gently sloping, overlooked by the ubiquitous villas and a handful of fish restaurants. The main **accommodation** option is the three-star *Javelin Hotel* (☎0252/348 3189; ❺).

Bağla, the next cove on, initially seems off-putting, with a water tank resembling an airport control tower planted amidst the villas that cover the cape. But if you've arrived with your own transport, persevere by going straight past the old Greek chapel to the beachfront parking space, rather than following signs to the fee-parking at a pair of mediocre restaurants. The sand here is the softest in the vicinity of Bodrum; accordingly, excursion boats arrive in force by noon.

Karaincir, the next bay with public access, is nearly as good – 600m of sand guarded by a pair of headlands. Canoes and windsurfers can be rented, and while mid-beach is completely crowded out by sunbeds and umbrellas, the south end of the strand inexplicably remains in its wild, natural state. The adjacent *Dorya* and *Bal Mahmut'in Yeri* **restaurants** divide most of the custom between them, with a handful of cafés and bars further south hemming in the beach a bit claustrophobically. Of a similar number of simple **motels** up by the main road, the *Bizimtepe* (☎0252/393 6322) is recommended, with either air-conditioned doubles (❷) or four-person apartments (❺) available.

Akyarlar and beyond

Surrounded by euclyptus trees, **AKYARLAR** (the former Greek port of Kefalouka), 30km from Bodrum, is more of an actual village – albeit one surrounded by estates of concrete villas – with a stone jetty, yacht harbour and mosque. The often breezy conditions here make it cooler and more comfortable in summer than sweaty Bodrum. Akyarlar's beach is small and hardpacked, mostly given over to windsurfing, but with both Karaincir and, in the opposite direction, the sandy cove at **Simin** – below the *Simin Hotel* – within walking distance, this is no great loss.

More to the point, Akyarlar is your passport to good local eating, with cuisine and a clientele far more Turkish, and prices far lower, than anywhere east of here. Current favourite **restaurants** include *Kücük Ev*, good for both meat and fish dishes, those attached to the *Akyarlar* and *Kılavuz* motels, and the *Mehtap*, particularly popular for fish. For **accommodation**, the *Kılavuz* (☎0252/393 6006; ❸), the *Babadan* (☎0252/393 6002; ❸), with simple rooms, some with sea views, and the *Candan* (☎0252/393 6035; ❷) offer the best value. There's **camping** at *Camping 86* (☎0252/393 6233).

Beyond Akyarlar the coast is lined with villas (and a very few *pansiyons*), all of which stare across at nearby Kós (just two nautical miles distant here) and assorted Turkish islets. The good **beach** on the peninsula's southwesternmost cape is partly occupied by the Armonia time-share village, but the far end, under the **Hüseyin Burnu** lighthouse, offers free access and is popular with Turkish free-campers and caravanners, as well as a few German windsurfers, who repair to the *Fener* **restaurant** for sustenance. The food is not that great, but it's still the only place for a bite between here and Turgutreis.

Turgutreis

Once the road rounds the point to skirt the peninsula's west shore, the wind becomes stronger and the sand disappears, with nothing aside from villas until **TURGUTREİS**. Frequent dolmuşes ply the route between the town and Bodrum, 18km to the east. As a strictly package resort, this runs a close second on the peninsula to Gümbet, with nearly a hundred hotels and a marina in development to attract the passing yachts. But the town is a sterile grid of streets, and the small exposed beach is closely pressed by the luckiest half-dozen **accommodation** outfits. Of these the *Ceylan* (☎0252/382 2376; ❷) is the cheapest, offering en-suite rooms but no breakfast. Alternatively, the nearby, jointly run *Monalisa* and *Kordon pansiyon*s (☎0252/382 2932, ℱ382 3969; ❹) can provide half-board.

Kadıkalesi

A recently asphalted side-road starting by the Turgutreis *otogar* leads north to better things, through a fertile landscape of the tangerine groves for which the region is famous. After 4km you reach **KADIKALESİ**, with its long, partly protected sand beach and unbeatable views over to assorted islets. The old Greek church on the hill is the most intact around Bodrum, but of the village's namesake "judge's castle" there seems to be no trace. As with Turgutreis, there is little **accommodation** available if you haven't arranged it in advance. Your best bet is the friendly *Club Blue Bodrum* (☎0252/382 2017; ❹), boasting a swimming pool and watersports equipment in addition to comfortable rooms. The beach is overlooked by a couple of fish restaurants.

Gümüşlük

If you've had a bellyful of villa phalanxes, then sleepy **GÜMÜŞLÜK**, 2km past Kadıkalesi or 6km along a direct road from a turning at Gürece, is perhaps the best bet. Easily the nicest spot on the peninsula (40min by dolmuş from Bodrum), it partly occupies the site of **ancient Myndos**, so most new development has been prohibited by the archeological service. The majority of the sparse ruins litter the flat isthmus that links a giant, towering cape to the rest of the peninsula; you can scrabble around the unrestricted site, assisted by a placard map. Yachties are drawn here by the excellent deep anchorage between the headland and Tavşan Adası (Rabbit Island), with more traces of ancient Myndos; the rabbits are shy, and only emerge at night. The kilometre-long sand and gravel **beach** extending south of the island is less protected but still attractive, with watersports gear for rent.

Among a bare handful of low-key **pansiyons**, those that cater well to independent travellers include the *Sisyphos* (☎0252/394 3016; ❸), at the south end of the beach, with a decent terrace restaurant and lush grounds. Mid-beach are the humble but recommended *Hera Pansiyon*, (☎0252/394 3065; ❸), and the *Gümüşlük Motel* (☎0252/394 3045; ❸), with standard doubles, some with sea views. The UK holiday operator Tapestry controls the best of the very characterful **self-catering villas** at the north end of the beach, overlooking the most sheltered part of the bay. Their presence has resulted in a surprising concentration of well-stocked shops in the shoreline hamlet. The actual village of Gümüşlük lies 2km inland, from where you can climb to an abandoned ridgetop monastery.

A dozen waterfront **restaurants** cater primarily to yacht passengers and seasonally resident Turks. Most are outrageously priced, with expensive *meze* and obligatory service charges, but of a good standard, specializing in freshly caught fish. *Ali Reza* is the oldest; nearby *Batı* does meat as well as fish, and has its own *pide* oven.

Yalıkavak

In general, the north flank of the peninsula, served by a loop road out of Ortakent (or the narrower coastal route from Gümüşlük) has poor swimming and a relative lack of facilities. The trip over to **YALIKAVAK** – 20km from Bodrum – with glimpses of sea from a windmill-studded ridge, is possibly more worthwhile than the destination itself. Formerly the area's main sponge-fishing port, it has now been ruthlessly gentrified with its shorefront windmill marooned in a pedestrian zone that extends through most of the commercial district; vehicles can get little further than the small *otogar*.

Few tourists choose to brave the windswept, scrappy coast here, with just a handful of **hotels** exiled to either side of the town. These include the very cheap but noisy *Yalıkavak Pansiyon* (☎0252/385 4035, ❶) and the reasonably priced *Yalıkavak Apart Otel* (☎0252/385 4660, ❷). Two kilometres north of town is the luxurious *Club Mirage* holiday village (☎0252/385 4437; ❼). The *Liman* **restaurant** next to the harbour, offers everything from steak to pizza, but its speciality is *meze* followed by steamed fish; expect to pay $10–15 for a full meal excluding drinks. A cheaper establishment *Margül*, further inland, serves good *pide*.

Gündoğan

GÜNDOĞAN (also known as Farilya), three bays east, represents something of an improvement on Yalıkavak. The long, mostly narrow but serviceable beach, divided by a small harbour, is little impinged upon by the surrounding villas. The tour company Sunworld Sailing maintains a big presence here, with its windsurfers and small craft; the constant breeze does not, however, prevent swimming. Restaurants and bars (mostly indifferent) extend right of the anchorage, while **accommodation** options clusters to the left. Of these, the most reasonably priced is the *Gürkaya* (☎0252/387 7007; ❷), overlooking the beach, while the *Yılınkaya Motel* (☎0252/387 8037; ❸) has air-conditioned rooms.

For a taste of the local Ottoman heritage, you can walk a kilometre inland to **Gündoğan village** proper, where there's a ruined monastery to climb to.

Gölköy and Türkbuku

The turning for **GÖLKÖY**, 1km further east, is easy to miss. Development here is low-rise, with the improbably slender beach doubling as the shore path.

Swimming platforms have been erected for diving into the cold, clear water by the half-dozen **motels**, which include the *Sahil Motel* (☎0252/357 7183; ❺), the *Antik* (☎0252/357 7115, ❹), and *Kaktüs Çiçeği*, on the beach (☎0252/377 5253, ℱ377 5248; ❼). The last has only sixteen rooms and booking in advance is essential, as many guests return every year.

TÜRKBÜKÜ, aka the St Tropez of the peninsula, lies just around the corner and on the same dolmuş route, but has lost what little beach it had following enlargement of the quay – everyone swims from platforms. The clientele is overwhelmingly from the İstanbul moneyed and media set, who often come ashore from their yachts at anchor – the indented local coast and island provide shelter for even more craft than at Gümüşlük. But accommodation is minimal, architecture relentlessly concrete and the restaurants indifferent. The only points of interest in Türkbüku are a ruined church and some partially collapsed rock tombs.

Muğla and around

Muğla, capital of the province containing several of the biggest resorts on the Aegean, is something of a showcase town and an exception to the Turkish rule of dire urban architecture. It's also the closest town to **Akyaka**, the first coastal settlement you encounter at the bottom of the winding grade descending south from Muğla's plateau.

Mugla

MUĞLA's well-planned modern quarter incorporates spacious tree-lined boulevards and accommodates some hillside **Ottoman neighbourhoods** that are among the finest in Turkey. A leisurely stroll through the lanes of well-maintained eighteenth-century white houses, with their tiled roofs, beaked chimneys and ornate doors, is well worth half a day.

The **bazaar**, encompassing a grid of neat alleys nestling at the base of the old residential slope to the north, is divided roughly by trade (blacksmiths predominating). South of the bazaar is the **Ulu Camii**, built in the fourteenth century by the Menteşeoğlu emir, İbrahim Bey. The serene **Yağcılar Hanı**, a restored *kervansaray* located on Kursunlu Caddesi, contains carpet shops and *çay* stalls, and a second restored *kervansaray*, **Konakaltı Hanı**, on Saatlı Kulealtı Caddesi, is in use as an art gallery. Meanwhile, the town's **museum**, on Yatağan Eskiser Caddesi (daily except Mon 8.30am–5.30pm; $0.70), houses a collection of locally found dinosaur fossils, including prehistoric rhinos, giraffe, horse and elephant.

Practicalities

The large **otogar** lies 400m southwest of the centre on Züybde Hanim Caddesi. There are regular services from Bodrum, Fethiye and Marmaris. Muğla's **tourist office**, Cumhuriyet Bul 24 (summer Mon–Fri 8am–7pm; winter Mon–Fri 8am–noon & 1–5.30pm; ☎0252/214 1261), is a fifteen-minute walk from the *otogar*, and willingly provides pamphlets and maps.

Accommodation covers the two extreme ends of the price range, with little choice in the middle, but since Muğla is not exactly deluged with tourists, this shouldn't be a problem. The quietest and least expensive mid-range option is the *Otel Saray* (☎0252/214 1950, ℱ214 3722; ❷), facing the produce market but dead calm at night, with comfortable rooms with baths and balconies.

A good-value cheapie to the north is the *Tuncer Hotel* at Kütüphane Sok 1 (☎0252/214 8251; ❶). If you're going to splash out try the *Hotel Grand Brothers* (☎0252/212 2700, ℱ212 2610; ❻), 1km on the road west out of town, complete with swimming pool, sauna and its own hamam.

Eating out in Muğla is unlikely to be memorable. There are plenty of *lokanta*, kebab and *pide* options, but few stand out. In the Mustafa Muğlali Işhanı (a large office complex) there's the licensed *Bulvar Ocakbaşi*, popular at lunchtimes and with a good line in spit-roasted chickens, but very limited for *meze* or steamtray food. Opposite, and serving excellent *döner* and kebab, is the more upmarket *Nazar*. A cheaper, more versatile option is the nearby *Sabah Lokantasi*, opposite the *Otel Saray*, licensed and serving *meyhane* fare and *hazır yemek* at pleasant outdoor seating opposite a fountain. Otherwise, the *Bulvar Muğla Kebab* restaurant on Cumhuriyet Bulvarı offers a good range of kebabs.

Akyaka

Situtated at the very head of the Gulf of Gökova, with steep Sakara Tepe looming overhead, scenic **AKYAKA** (Gökova) has always been popular with Turkish holiday-makers but is now attracting a small number of foreign tourists; in the UK, Turkish Collection, Anatolian Sky, Tapestry and Simply Turkey all represent properties here. The town is arrayed along an unobjectionable grid of streets on a slight slope amidst dense pine forest; private villas are interspersed between *pansiyon*s and small hotels, most built attractively in a sort of mock–Ottoman–*köşk* architectural style mandated by a local preservation code. Although Akyaka's town **beach** consists of hardpacked sand, merely suitable for getting into the clear waters of the gulf, there's a much better gravel beach 2.5km west of town, beyond the old jetty, and another more utilitarian strand to the east, beyond the river mouth.

Dolmuşes ply regularly to and from Muğla (30km to the north) and Marmaris (37km south), a thirty-minute journey from either. At the top end of the **accommodation** range, the three-star *Yücelen* (☎0252/248 5108, ☏243 5435; ❺), just inland at the village centre, has vast common areas and a large pool. The cosier and squeaky-clean *Engin* (☎0252/243 5727, ☏243 5609; ❷), with a small pool, is on the east of town towards the river, while the *Server Apartments* (☎0252/243 5497, ☏243 5570; ❸), on Gökova Caddesi, offers large 4–5 person apartments with self-catering kitchens. A cheaper option is the *Fatih* (☎0252/214 5786; ❷), offering suites for as little as $18 if business is slack. There's also a forestry **campsite** with good amenities in a gorgeous setting, though it's apt to fill with day-tripping school parties during term time – to get there, follow the main town road north, turning left just past the last houses.

In the village centre and overlooking the beach there are few **restaurants** independent of the hotels. The *Captain's* specializes in fish, while the *Köşem* offers spaghetti, omelettes and a few other non-meat options.

Marmaris

MARMARİS runs Kuşadası a close second as the largest and most developed Aegean resort. Boosters call it *Yeşil Marmaris* – "Green Marmaris" – which it certainly is, but they omit mention of the humidity, the ferocious mosquitoes and the amorphous concrete sprawl that extends for nearly 10km around the bay. Development has dwarfed the old village core of shops and *lokanta*s lining narrow, bazaar-like streets, an intricate warren contrasting strongly with the European-style marina and waterfront. According to legend, the place was named when Süleyman the Magnificent, not finding the castle here to his liking, was heard to mutter "*Mimarı as*" ("hang the architect"), later corrupted to "Marmaris" – a command that ought perhaps still to apply to the designers of the seemingly endless apartments and hotels.

Marmaris's **Netsel Yacht Marina**, Turkey's largest, has more than anything else shaped the town's character – this is the main base for most yacht charter organizations operating on the Turquoise Coast. Proximity to Dalaman airport also means that both foreign and domestic tourists pour in non-stop during the warmer months, and – the Netsel marina aside – the town remains very much a downmarket package resort.

Marmaris's **history** has been determined above all by the stunning local topography: a deep, fjord-like inlet surrounded by pine-cloaked hills. This did not seem to spur ancient Physcus, the original Dorian colony, to any growth or importance, but Süleyman comfortably assembled a force of 200,000 here in 1522, when launching the successful siege of the Knights of St John's base in Rhodes. Shortly after this campaign Süleyman endowed the old town nucleus with the tiny castle and a *han*. In 1798 Nelson's entire fleet sheltered here before setting out to defeat Napoleon's armada at the Battle of Aboukir Bay in Egypt.

Arrival and information

Marmaris's **otogar** is 2km outside the town centre on the Muğla road. A regular dolmuş service runs from the *otogar*, down the main Ulusal Egemenlik Caddesi, stopping outside the huge Tansaş shopping centre – from where all the town's **dolmuş** services start. The Havaş **airport bus** from Dalaman airport leaves you in front of the THY office on Atatürk Caddesi, the long shore road usually known as Kordon Caddesi. Marina Taxi has a booth in the Netsel Yacht Marina and will run you to Dalaman for around $45. If you show up

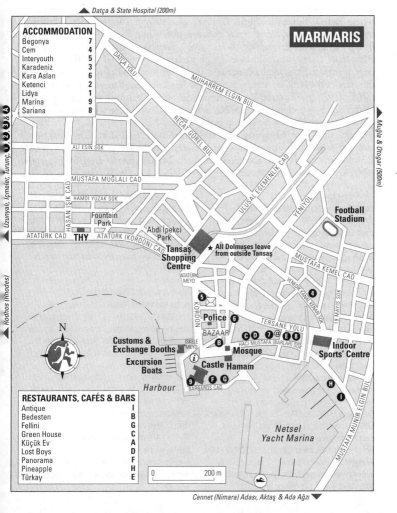

Datça & State Hospital (200m)

MARMARIS

ACCOMMODATION

Begonya	7
Cem	4
Interyouth	5
Karadeniz	3
Kara Aslan	6
Ketenci	2
Lidya	1
Marina	9
Sariana	8

Uzunyalı, İçmeler, Turunç, ➊ ➋ ➌ & ➍

Rodhos (Rhodes)

Muğla & Otogar (500m)

DATÇA YOLU

MUHARREM ELGİN BUL

RECAİ GÜREL BUL

ALİ ESİN SOK

MUSTAFA MUĞLALI CAD

HASAN IŞIK CAD

HAMDİ YUZAK SOK

Fountain Park

ATATÜRK CAD **THY** ATATÜRK (KORDON) CAD

Abdi İpekçi Park

ULUSAL EGEMENLİK CAD

YENİYOL

Football Stadium

★ All Dolmuşes leave from outside Tansaş

Tansaş Shopping Centre

ATATÜRK MEYD.

MUSTAFA KEMEL CAD

VENGİK KANAL KENAR SOK

19 MAYIS SOK

KORDON

Police ➏

BAZAAR

TERSANE YOLU

Customs & Exchange Booths

İSKELE MEYD.

➐ @ ➑

HACI MUSTAFA (BARLARI) SOK

Mosque

Indoor Sports' Centre

Excursion Boats

ⓘ **Castle Hamam**

Harbour

BARBAROS CAD

MUSTAFA MÜNİR ELGİN BUL

Netsel Yacht Marina

N

RESTAURANTS, CAFÉS & BARS

Antique	I
Bedesten	B
Fellini	G
Green House	C
Küçük Ev	A
Lost Boys	D
Panorama	F
Pineapple	H
Türkay	E

0   200 m

Cennet (Nimara) Adası, Aktaş & Ada Ağzı ▼

with your own car, be aware that no **parking** is allowed anywhere along the Kordon.

Arriving by **ferry** from the Greek island of Rhodes or **hydrofoil** from Bodrum, you dock by İskele Meydanı, on one side of which stands the extraordinarily knowledgeable **tourist office** (summer daily 8am–8pm; winter Mon–Fri 8am–noon & 1–5pm; ☎0252/412 1035), dispensing town plans, bus schedules and accommodation lists. This is also the best stop-off for details of the correct current **boat charter** prices (see box on p.415). **Boat-taxis** to İçmeler and Turunç leave from in front of the tourist office ($3.50–5 one-way).

Accommodation

Although there is no concentration of *pansiyon*s or small hotels in Marmaris, some apart-hotels have sprung up in the area inland from the marina, while a handful of very basic establishments (and a youth hostel) survive in the **town centre**. Better value for money can be had out at the west end of the Kordon, close to where **Kemal Seyfettin Elgin Bulvarı** splits away to run parallel to **Uzunyalı** beach. Further west, some three hundred hotels line the five-kilometre palm-fringed strip, with the luxury, all-inclusive complexes – the *Grand Azur*, *MGM*, *Altınyunus*, *Grand Yazıcı* and *Iberotel* – clustering at the far end. For the best value here, try the seafront establishments in the neighbourhood of the *Turban Hotel*, at the edge of the built-up area, or head a few blocks inland. **Kenan Evren Bulvarı**, incidentally, is the continuation of Kemal Seyfettin Elgin Bulvarı running parallel to the beach but slightly inland. Note that accommodation will be tight during the yachting regatta in the second week of May.

Your best bet for **camping** near the centre is to stroll along Uzunyalı beach and see who's operating this year between the building sites. Alternatively, 1.5km east of Marmaris, past the Günnücek forestry reserve, are *Dimet Camping* (☎0252/412 5601) and *Pekuz Camping* (☎0252/412 1963), both open all year.

Town centre

Hotel Begonya Hacı Mustafa Sok 101 ☎0252/412 4095, ℱ412 1518. Delightful renovated barn with designer architecture, air-conditioning and enclosed garden; it's double-glazed against loud music from nearby bars. ❹

Cem Apart Otel Venedik Kanal Kenari Sok 25/12 ☎0252/413 1725, ℱ413 1726. Self-catering units (sleep four) with averagely furnished rooms but well-fitted kitchens, arranged around the rather small pool and sauna. ❹

Interyouth Hostel 1 42 Sok 45 ☎0252/412 3687, ℮interyouth@turk.net. IYHF-accredited hostel within the covered bazaar. Clean, comfy but bare double rooms as well as dorms ($6) – it's hopelessly overcrowded in season. There's also an internet café and various short-term meal deals, such as free pasta for lengthy stays. ❷

Kara Aslan Otel Tepe Mah, 39 Sok 1 ☎0252/412 1867. Close to the action, with basic en-suite rooms with balcony. ❷

Hotel Marina Barbaros Cad 37 ☎0252/412 6598, ⓦwww.turkguide.net/marina. Neat rooms with intricate wooden ceiling designs (and surprisingly little street noise). The rooftop breakfast bar/restaurant commands breathtaking views of the bay. ❸

Sariana Apart Otel 24 Sok 4 ☎0252/412 1786, ℱ412 2656. Suites containing a starkly furnished double bedroom, modern bathroom, lounge and kitchen, as well as access to the hotel bar and pool. ❺

West of the centre

Hotel Karadeniz Atatürk Cad (Kordon) 68 ☎0252/412 3642, ℱ412 1064. Comfortable and well-run 59-room hotel (200m off our map) offering all the usual amenities. Rooms are large and bright, but the best aspect is its convenient location, just across from the beach. ❹

Ketenci Hotel Kemal Seyettin Elgin Bul ☎0252/412 6395, ℱ412 8996. Slightly inland (600m off our map) with modern rooms with balcony. Boasts a fair-sized pool and a restaurant. ❹

Hotel Lidya Kenan Evren Bul ☎0252/417 3350, ℱ412 1478. The oldest luxury hotel in Marmaris (800m off our map) still has the most character and smoothest service. Well-equipped rooms, and good beach facilities, complete with a nightclub on site. ❺

The Town

Ulusal Egemenlik Bulvarı cuts Marmaris roughly in half, and the maze of narrow streets to the east of it is home to most of the monuments and facilities – including the castle, bazaar, banks and PTT – of interest to the average tourist. Numerous travel agencies and bus-company ticket offices cluster a hundred or so metres to either side of **Atatürk Meydanı**, the seashore plaza at the southern end of Ulusal Egemenlik Bulvarı. Further west the weekly **Friday market** is held behind the THY office, where women from surrounding villages sell a range of homemade goodies, including delicious jams.

Little is left of the sleepy fishing village that Marmaris was a mere two decades ago. The **bazaar**, including its diminutive *kervansaray*, now rivals those at İstanbul and Kuşadası in its array of glitzy kitsch on offer, and only the **Kaleiçi** district, the warren of streets at the base of the tiny castle, offers a pleasant wander. The **castle** itself (daily 8am–noon & 1–5.30pm; $0.70) is open as a fully stocked museum with clearly annotated displays of local finds; it also serves as a venue for events during the May festival.

In any case, you don't come to Marmaris for cultural edification, and you swim off the badly polluted **Kordon beach** at your peril – though this doesn't seem to deter the hundreds of bathers who use it daily. It's far better to take a dolmuş (regular services from Ulusal Egemenlik Bulvarı) or boat-taxi (see opposite) out to **İçmeler**, 9km west of Marmaris, whose old village core survives precariously at the far edge of the recently developed resort. Here the sand is coarse but cleaner than at Kordon, as is the sea.

Boat excursions

Day-trips usually visit highlights of the inner bay, not venturing much beyond the straits separating Cennet and Keçi islands. Most skippers will take you to a beach on the north side of Cennet Adası, and to caves on the south shore, then complete the day with a visit to Kumlubükü or Turunç coves (see "Around Marmaris", p.414, for full descriptions). Since all of these spots are fairly difficult to reach by land, it's worth the effort – and the price of $12–20 per person may include a full lunch. Most of the boats are moored along Barbaros Caddesi and the castle peninsula and leave at 9am during the May to September summer season.

One offer that you definitely can refuse is an **excursion to Kaunos** (see p.472) from Marmaris: because of the distance involved, you'll spend six-plus hours sailing and, at best, two hours sightseeing. Kaunos is more usually reached from Dalyan or as part of a lengthy cruise.

Eating

Getting a decent meal at a reasonable price is something of a challenge in Marmaris. In town, the **restaurants** around the bazaar tend to offer fast food and English dishes. Simple pizzerias and other spots serving light meals abound along the Kordon and further west, where homesick Brits seek relief at various English-named outfits serving indifferently cooked "English" food. East of the castle, the waterfront spots along Barbaros Caddesi change names, management and cuisine frequently – here, a meal with wine will run to around $20 a head, more if you eat the seafood.

Antique Overlooking Netsel Yacht Marina ℡0252/413 2955. Smart Italian restaurant offering cosy atmosphere and impeccable service for about $30 per person. Book ahead as this place is busy in season.

Bedesten Café Below the mosque in the bazaar.

Lovely courtyard oasis for coffee and a *nargile* (waterpipe). With a choice of chairs or traditional cushions, and a trickling fountain, it's an "ethnic" kind of place aimed at tourists, but is at its best at night when the daytime awning is drawn back to reveal a star-studded view.

Fellini Pizza On the waterfront. Popular no-nonsense pizzeria, particularly recommended for its vegetarian options.

Küçük Ev İçmeler, 9km west of Marmaris. One of the area's longest-running restaurants, serving a wide selection of *hazır yemek* (set meals) for $10–20 per head, including beer.

Pineapple Netsel Yacht Marina ☎0252/412 0976. Ever-popular dressy Turkish/English eaterie, famous for its steak and kidney pie. With an attached English pub upstairs, things can get a bit noisy.

Türkay Restaurant Hacı Mustafa Sok 107. Combines Turkish themes with a French touch to excellent effect – at about $40 a head.

Drinking, nightlife and entertainment

Most of Marmaris's tippling takes place along **Hacı Mustafa Sokağı** (or Barlar Sok), which in recent years has become a fully fledged "Bar Street" along the lines of those in Kuşadası and Bodrum. More than two-dozen **bars and clubs** here feature increasingly sophisticated designer profiles and various sorts of (usually live) music, often in spacious inner courtyards. Names and favourites change yearly, if not more often, though a couple of long-termers include *Green House* and *Lost Boys*. Up above, behind the castle, the *Panorama* bar offers the best views. The yachties expand their liver capacities during the happy hour at a group of pubs and upmarket restaurants within the Netsel Yacht Marina.

An **open-air cinema**, behind the *Keyif Bar* at the western end of the marina, shows original-language international releases with Turkish subtitles. An annual **yachting and arts festival** takes place in the second week of May, aimed primarily at those of the sailing fraternity, and there's a large **yacht race** during the first week of November. For further details contact the Marmaris Yacht Club (☎0252/412 3835).

Listings

Airport THY has a Havaş service bus to Dalaman airport, 90km east, departing from its office at Atatürk Cad 50/B (☎0252/412 3751) 2hr 45min before flight departures. In addition, the Marmaris *Belediyesi* runs two daily buses to the airport.

Banks and exchange Assorted *döviz* booths along the Kordon and near the ferry jetty stay open late (sometimes until 9.30pm), including Sundays and holidays. Marmaris is also well endowed with credit/debit-card-accepting ATMs.

Bike and jeep rental Yoshimoto (☎0252/417 6237, ⓦwww.yoshimoto.de), delivers rental bikes (from $375 per week) to your hotel (and organizes guided motorbike safaris throughout Turkey, starting at $1000). Çağdaş Tour, behind 10 Kordon (☎0252/412 4125), rents bikes and cars; Best Motor, Kemal Elgin Cad opposite the *Balim Otel* (☎0252/412 4361), for bikes, mopeds, motorbikes and jeeps.

Books Arkadaş Kitap, in front of the Sabaci High School on Kordon, has a selection of secondhand books in English, French and German; Hittite, Hacı Mustafa Sok, is a book and music store; NET, in the bazaar, stocks nautical charts of the area; Şehrazat, across from Hacı Mustafa Sok 49, behind the castle, has some used English books to trade; and Marmaris International Bookstore, Talat Paşa Sok, has a selection of current English bestsellers.

Buses The main bus companies – Varan, Ulusoy, Pamukkale, Kamil Koç, Hakiki Koç – all have offices in or around Tansaş shopping centre at the Kordon Caddesi end of Ulusal Egemenlik Bul, and all run courtesy buses to the *otogar* to connect with their company's major routes.

Car rental Airtour, Kenan Evren Bul, Alter Sok 18/A ☎0252/412 3963; Avis, Kordon Cad 30 ☎0252/412 2771; DeCar, Ulusal Egemenlik Cad, Rodoslu Kemal İş Hanı 13 ☎0252/413 4669; Europcar/InterRent, Kordon Cad 12 ☎0252/412 2001; Hertz, İskele Meyd ☎0252/412 2552; Intercity, İskele Meyd 41 ☎0252/413 0106; LeMar, Kemal Seyfettin Elgin Bul 4 ☎0252/412 3222.

Consulate Honorary British Consulate, c/o Yeşil Marmaris Tourism & Yachting, Barbaros Cad 11, near the marina ☎0252/412 6486 or 24hr ☎0532/262 7661.

Coastal boat charters

Chartering either a **motor schooner** (*gület*) or a smaller **yacht** out of Marmaris will allow you to explore the convoluted coast between Bodrum and Kaş. Especially out of high season, the daily cost isn't necessarily prohibitive – no more than renting a medium-sized car, for example – and in the case of a *gület*, a knowledgeable crew will be included. Virtually all of the shore described in this chapter and the next is fair game, plus many other hidden anchorages accessible only by sea.

You can pre-book a yacht charter through **specialist holiday operators** (see Basics for details), or you can make arrangements on the spot; though prices are always quoted in US dollars or sterling, it's possible to pay in Turkish lira. Substantial deposits are required – usually fifty percent of the total price.

The best option for individual travellers or small groups is a **cabin charter**. Several companies set aside one schooner whose berths are let out individually. The craft departs on a particular day of the week with a fixed itinerary of seven days. Prices depend on demand but in April, May and October are around $350 per person, including all food and watersports equipment – excellent value. From June to September the cost jumps to around $415.

If you can assemble a large group, and have more time at your disposal, consider a **standard charter** of a twenty-metre motor schooner. A group of twelve, for example, will pay $34 each daily during May or October, not including food or sporting equipment, while a group of eight will be more comfortable and less crowded but will pay $38 a day. From June to September, count on $50–60 each per day for the same-sized groups.

Companies often offer to supply **food** for about $15 minimum per day for each passenger, though there's a sizable mark-up hidden in this and you'd spend about the same eating two meals a day on shore. Probably the best strategy is to dine in restaurants at your evening mooring and to keep the galley stocked for breakfast and snacks. If you tip the crew appropriately they're usually happy to shop for you.

For the greatest degree of independence, so-called **bareboat yacht charter** is the answer. Prices range from $1,120 for the smallest boat in the off-season, to $5,060 for the largest in high season. This assumes that at least one of your party is a certified skipper; otherwise count on at least $130 a day extra to engage one. Prices are usually quoted by the week, and in April or October work out at around $250 per person; during June or September allow $320 each per week. One of the oldest and more reliable **charter agencies** in Marmaris is Yeşil Marmaris, Barbaros Cad 11 (⌖0252/412 6486). For bareboat yachts, one of the larger local operators is Offshore Sailing at the Albatros Marina, 3km east of Netsel Marina (⌖0252/412 3430, Ⓦwww.offshore-sailing.net).

Ferries and hydrofoils From April to October there's a twice-weekly domestic hydrofoil to Bodrum via Gökova Bay and daily hops to Rhodes in Greece; there's also a twice-weekly car ferry; see "Travel details" at the end of this chapter for schedules and prices. Authorized agents include Yeşil Marmaris, Barbaros Cad 11 ⌖0252/412 2290, and Engin Turizm, G. Mustafa Muğlalı Cad 16, 3rd Floor ⌖0252/412 6944.

Hamam There's an old one in the rear of the bazaar at Eski Cami Arkası 3 (daily 8am–midnight for both sexes; $7), and the newer touristic Ottoman Hamam, off the Datça road, 1km north of the town centre (daily 8am–11pm; $20).

Hospitals The state hospital is at the junction of Yunus Nadı Cad and the Datça road ⌖0252/413 1445; Ahu Hetman private hospital is in Armutalan suburb, 167 Sok ⌖0252/ 413 1415.

Internet Internet Café, Kahve Evi, one block inland from the Netsel Marina; and Uyum, Tepe Mah 10/C (both daily 10am–10pm).

Laundry Marmaris laundry is located in the street behind the *Gün Café*, down in front of the castle.

Pharmacies The most central ones are: Dee Pharmacy, Datça Yolu E Devlet Hastane ⌖0252/412 3230; Ebru Pharmacy, Hasan Isik Cad, 103 Sok 49 ⌖0252/413 6666; and Fulya Pharmacy, K. Elgin Bul 53/3 ⌖0252/412 9314.

Police On Kordon Cad, next to the government house ☎ 0252/412 1872.

Post office PTT is within the bazaar on 49 Sok (mail services until 6pm, phones 24hr).

Rafting Alternatif Turizm, Çamlık Sok 10/1 (☎ 0252/417 2720, ⊛ www.alternatifraft.com),

offers regular springtime whitewater rafting trips on the Dalaman River, plus river and sea kayaking, and tailor-made Turkey-wide outdoor sports packages. Prices range from 5-day Coruh Rafting expedition (northeast Turkey) from $600, to 3-day sea kayking (Köycegiz-Enkincik) for $450.

Around Marmaris: the Rhodian Peraea

In ancient times the peninsula extending from the head of the Gulf of Gökova to a promontory between the Greek islands of Symi and Rhodes was known as the **Rhodian Peraea** – the mainland territory of the three united city-states of Rhodes, which controlled the area for eight centuries. Despite this, and the fact that the natives were granted full Rhodian citizenship, there is little evidence of the long tenure. The peninsula was (and still is) a backwater, today known as the **Hisarönü peninsula** – or the Loryma or Daraçya peninsula, depending on which map you look at or yacht skipper you ask. In fact, yachts have up to now been the principal means of getting around this irregular landmass and, although a proper road was completed in 1989, the difficulty of access has so far kept development to a minimum.

North: the Gökova gulf shore

The pristine shores of the **Gulf of Gökova** were badly affected by a massive forest fire in 1996, which roared along the southerly shore between the Muğla–Marmaris road and the Marmaris–Datça highway, reducing thousands of forested acres to ashes. Fortunately, natural re-growth and a reforestation policy have redressed much of the damage, though obvious remaining signs are the older trees, which bear visible scorching.

In Marmaris you'll probably notice signs pitching an excursion to "Cleopatra's Isle". This is actually **Sedir Adasi** (Cedar Island), an islet near the head of the Gulf of Gökova, which still sports extensive fortifications and a theatre from its time as Cedreae, a city of the Peraea. More evocative, however, is its alleged role as a trysting place of Cleopatra and Mark Antony, and the legend concerning the island's beach – the main goal of the day-trips; the sand was supposedly brought from Africa at Mark Antony's behest, and indeed analysis has shown that the grains are not from local strata.

The usual way of getting to the island (where you may well be charged an additional $4 admission by the resident warden) is by tour boat, departing between 10 and 11am from **Çamli İskelesi**, 6km down a side-road beginning 12km north of Marmaris. There's no public transport to the departure point, so you must use the tour operator's shuttle bus. The boats return at 4 or 5pm.

Alternative access is by much briefer boat excursion from the hamlet of **TAŞBÜKÜ**, 4km further along the same road and just opposite the islet. Again, there's no dolmuş service, but there are two **motel–campsites** with attached **restaurants**: the *Çamlı Motel* (☎ 0252/495 8085, ⓕ 495 8080; ❶) and the *Sedir Motel* (☎ 0252/495 8109; ❷) – both are friendly, year-round operations and the management might arrange to shuttle you in, if you phone ahead. It's quite idyllic little area, and the sand and gravel beach is not nearly as stony as the name Taşbükü (Stone Cove) implies. Just inland from the two beach motels stand the self-catering *Mandalin Villas*, represented by Cachet Travel and Simply Turkey in the UK.

Besides the obvious jaunt over to Sedir Adası, there are also boat outings available to **İNGİLİZLİMANI**, a beautiful inlet reachable only by sea. It got its name ("English Harbour") from a World War II incident when a British ship sought shelter from pursuing Germans in these nominally neutral waters.

Boats based at Çamlı İskelesi also call at **KARACASÖĞÜT**, accessible by land via a side-road 11km north of Marmaris. It's 13km (the occasional village-bound dolmuş will take you the first 11km) to this almost landlocked bay, girded by willows, with the wall of mountains north of the open gulf as a backdrop. It's a big yacht and *gület* haven, and you can watch the action from several restaurants overlooking the bay. The main beach, alas, is muddy and has two creeks draining onto it, so you can really only swim off the purpose-built platform jutting out into the water, well away from the boats and the shore.

South to Bozburun

Overland access to the bulk of the **Hisarönü peninsula** is by way of a paved road, which branches south from the main Datça-bound highway, 21km west of Marmaris, and describes a loop back to Marmaris via Selimiye, Bayar, Turunç and İçmeler. **Dolmuşes** from Marmaris leave several times daily for Orhaniye, and there are three daily services to Bozburun.

Orhaniye and Selimiye

ORHANİYE, 9km off the main highway, is visited mostly for its yacht anchorage. The beach here is confined to muddy, sumpy shallows, though further out in the bay lurks a celebrated curiosity: a long, narrow, submerged sand-spit known as **Kızkumu** (Maiden's Sand), extending halfway across the bay. Legend asserts that a local beauty, menaced by raiding pirates, filled her skirts with sand and attempted to escape across the water by creating her own causeway, but upon exhausting her supply at mid-bay, drowned herself rather than surrender her virtue to the marauders. Another version has her attempting to escape an unwanted arranged marriage to a rich landowners's son. There are two small **hotels** and a mere half-dozen *pansiyons* of note here, including the clean *Palmiye Motel* (☎0252/487 1134; ❸).

SELİMİYE, 9km further south, is the next coastal village where visitors tend to stop, again mostly by yacht. The remains of an Ottoman fort overlook the port here, at the head of an all-but-landlocked arm of the giant Delikyol bay. Numerous quayside restaurants are aimed mostly at the passing boat trade, as are the pleasant *pansiyons* that have sprouted since the road was paved. **Accommodation** may fill in season, so pre-booking is a good idea – try the *Beyaz Güvercin* (☎0252/446 4274; ❸) or the *Begovina Pansiyon* (☎0252/446 4069; ❹). Several daily dolmuşes leave Bozburun (below) for Selimiye from May to September, though outside the summer season the service is somewhat erratic.

Bozburun and beyond

BOZBURUN, 7km over the hill from Selimiye, is not much more than a yacht harbour: yacht repairs and supplies are conspicuously on offer, and *gület* boatyards occupy a large area. The settlement itself is undistinguished, slumbering in dusty heat six months of the year, but its setting, on a convoluted gulf with a fat islet astride its mouth and the Greek island of Sími beyond, is startling.

The place is unlikely to go the way of Datça (see p.420), since there is precious little level land for villas, even less fresh water and absolutely no sand beaches. Nonetheless Bozburun has long been an "in" resort for various eccentrics – ex-journalists turned bartenders, recording executives turned restaurant proprietors, diehard Turkish hippies – who collect in this most isolated corner of coastal Turkey.

In high season **pansiyon** proprietors will collar you as you alight from the thrice-daily dolmuş from Marmaris. *Suna Pansiyon* (☎0252/456 2119; ❷), which offers doubles with bathroom and kitchen access, is good value. If you fancy something more upmarket call for a boat to *Sabrina's House* (☎0252/456 2045, ⓦwww.sabrinashouse.com; ❹), a German-run, television- and traffic-free idyll set on the far edge of the harbour, represented in the UK by Dolunay Holidays; this tasteful haven amidst burgeoning gardens has huge bright and airy suite-like units and (of necessity) an excellent restaurant (meals around $12). Without the free boat shuttle, it's a thirty-minute walk to *Sabrina's*, partly along the road signposted to "Hotel Mete". Overlooking the shore, the *Pembe Yunus* (☎0252/456 2154; ❷) is a popular, cheaper alternative, with modest single and double en-suites (dinner can be arranged), as is the *Yilmaz Pension* (☎0252/456 2167; ❶).

The fifteen or so quayside **restaurants** offer a variable range and quality of food and service; best of the lot is probably the *Pink Dolphin* fish restaurant. The trendy set, whether Turkish landlubbers or yachties, gathers at the *Möwe Bar*, run by yet another refugee from the İstanbul rat-race.

The boat day-trips advertised in Bozburun rarely leave the confines of the bay. Instead, in cooler weather, you could walk east one valley to **SÖĞÜT**, essentially a farming oasis with a minimal shore settlement boasting two restaurants and a couple of *pansiyon*s. The dolmuş serving Söğüt terminates at **TAŞLICA**, a hilltop village girded by almonds and olives sprouting from what's otherwise a stone desert. From the square where the dolmuş minibus leaves you, a three- to four-hour trail leads south to ancient **Loryma**, where a Rhodian-built fort overlooks the magnificent harbour of **Bozukkale** – which in turn holds several restaurants. If you don't want to walk back the same way, you just might be able to hitch a boat ride out from here.

The east coast of the Hisarönü peninsula

From Selimiye, the main loop road climbs inland to **BAYIR**, a mountain village spread across an amphitheatre of rocky terraces, whose distinctive feature is a 2000 year-old tree on its main square. A local tradition states that circling it seven times will prolong the walker's life, a myth not gone unnoticed by the troop of jeep safaris that regularly invade. A side-road leads the 3km down from here to **Çiftlik** bay, a once-isolated beach now dominated by a huge holiday village. Occasional dolmuşes do brave the route from Turunç, but their infrequent times make having your own transport the only practical option.

Turunç

The main route curls north back towards Marmaris, with another spur road leading down to **TURUNÇ**, which, since the late-1980s, has been transformed from a few farms and two ramshackle restaurants into an exclusive package venue. It's stunningly beautiful, boasting a 500-metre beach of coarse sand, backed by impressive, pine-tufted cliffs. These are now dotted with hotels and villas, some of whose residents commute to sea level using cogwheel chair-lifts. UK-based Tapestry Holidays is well represented here, offering something for all tastes, from the exclusive *Physkos* and *Serena Suites* self-catering apartments down to the bare-bones *pansiyon*s *Sema* and *Alpin*. Three walk-in **hotel** options

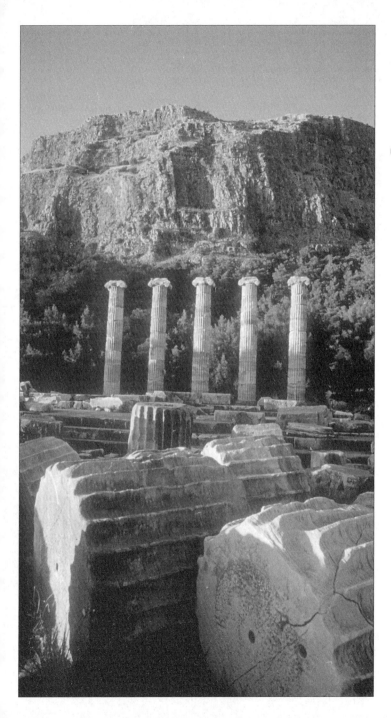

are the air-conditioned *Özcan Hotel* (☎0252/476 7140, ℗476 7036; ❹), the *Zeybek Hotel* (☎0252/476 7014, ℗476 7710; ❸), and the *Merhaba Motel* (☎0252/476 7285; ❸); owners of the latter also run the *Minem* restaurant-bar on the beach. **Pensions** include the *Gül Pansiyon* (☎0252/476 7003; ❸) and the overpriced *Çınar Motel* (☎0252/476 7088; ❸), both with en-suite doubles and kitchen access.

A spur road (and sometimes a dolmuş) heads south, past ancient **Amos** (only Hellenistic walls and theatre remain) to **KUMLUBÜKÜ**, another large bay with decent amenities. Along with the Çiftlik bay, 4km southwest of here by rough tracks or paths, it's the only really big patch of sand on the whole peninsula.

The Datça peninsula

Once past the turning for Bozburun, the main highway west of Marmaris ventures out onto the elongated, narrow **Datça (Reşadiye) peninsula**. There are glimpses through pine gullies of the sea on both sides, though the road is narrow and twisting and it's inadvisable to use it at night. Ongoing roadworks are continuing to straighten out some of the more treacherous bends, and delays of one to two hours can sometimes be experienced. There's nothing until **Datça** town except a pair of tiny villages, two huge, German-monopolized hotels and two private **campsites** that escaped fire damage: the *Öz-il* Karaincir (☎0252/723 3457), on Karaincir beach, and the *Aktur* (☎0252/724 6168), 18km before Datça behind a larger, sandy beach.

Beyond Datça the peninsula broadens considerably, and the scenery – almond or olive groves around somnolent, back-of-beyond villages at the base of pine-speckled mountains – is quite unlike that which came before. Towards **ancient Knidos**, the ancient site on the western cape, of the 32km of road beyond **Reşadiye** village the 24km to Yazıköy are paved (with more being currently surfaced), but the last 4km are appalling, although an ordinary car with good clearance should make it in dry weather.

Datça

Too built-up and commercialized to be the backpackers' haven it once was, **DATÇA** is still many times calmer than either Bodrum or Marmaris. It's essentially the shore annex of inland Reşadiye village but under the ministrations of visiting yachtspeople and tour operators it has outgrown its parent. Still, partly due to low local accommodation standards and the difficulty of access, prices are noticeably softer than in Bodrum or Marmaris, and most villa development lies out of town to the east. Carpet shops are big news, though – a round dozen appeal to the yacht and package trade.

Life in and around Datça mostly boils down to a matter of picking your swimming or sunbathing spot. The **east beach** of hardpacked sand, known locally as Kumluk, is oversubscribed but has some shade. The less crowded **west beach**, mixed pebble and sand and called Taşlık, is acceptable and gets better the further you get from the anchored yachts.

In contrast to the scenery on the drive in, the immediate surroundings of Datça are quite barren, softened only by a mineral spring-fed small **lake** halfway along the west bay. Warm-water seeps from the lake-bed, 2m down, making swimming here nicer than in the sea, and a line of appealing café-bars overlooks the stone dam that augments the water level.

Arrival and orientation

Apart from its setting, Datça's most striking feature is its layout: a single, kilometre-long high street meandering between two sheltered bays separated by a hillock and then a narrow isthmus, finally terminating at a cape. Along the way in you pass – more or less in this order – the **PTT**, most of the main **banks**, the tiny tourist office, a traffic circle dominated by a large tree, with **taxi rank** and **bazaar** grounds (Fri & Sat) adjacent, and **travel agencies**.

The **tourist office** (Mon–Fri 8am–6pm; ☏0252/712 3163) is hidden away in a large cream-coloured government building on the high street – identifiable by the police vans parked outside. It can supply maps and lists of accommodation for the whole peninsula.

The nine or so daily **buses** to and from Marmaris stop at the Pamukkale bus company office, just back from the harbour. Datça also has a small *otogar* on the outskirts of town, near the *jandarma* post; if you end up here **taxis** and service buses will compete to take you into town, but it's only a fifteen-minute walk. Except in high season, few of the big bus companies reach Datça, and you might be best off taking a short-hop dolmuş to either Marmaris or Muğla, from where there will be more frequent onward departures.

Ferries and **hydrofoils** from Bodrum arrive at Körmen Limani, 9km to the north; your ticket includes a shuttle bus service into Datça. It's worth taking the boat at least in one direction to avoid duplicating the wild bus journey in from the east. From Körmen Limani there are once-a-week direct return ferries to the Greek islands of Kós (Mon) and Rhodes (Fri). There are no ferry services to Simi, but you'll find small charter boats offering private return trips for around $50 person; likewise private trips at Datca are available to Knidos (about $10) and Koytur (about $20).

Accommodation

Accommodation, although limited, is generally sufficient to meet demand. The most obvious desirable location is the hillock separating the two bays, where there are several *pansiyon*s to choose from, including the *Huzur* (☏0252/712 3052; ❷), with the most modern rooms and an attractive terrace, and the *Karaoğlu* (☏0252/712 3079; ❷), with the best sea view and a pleasant attached restaurant. *Yılmaz Pansiyon* (☏0252/712 3188; ❷), close to the beach strip, is cheaper, though it doesn't serve breakfast.

The small, friendly **campsite**, *Ilıca Kamping* (☏0252/712 3400; open all year), perfectly located at the far end of the beach, is an ideal spot to relax, with a good restaurant, bar and serene views, five simple two-person bungalows (❶) and room for 27 tents.

Out **on the cape**, formerly an island called Esenada, the aging *Dorya Motel* (☏0252/712 3593, ℻712 3303; ❹) is home to such package trade as Datça gets. Rooms are hardly state of the art, but the place does offer well-kept gardens and common areas, a pool and a private lido. But probably the smartest choice in town is the *Villa Tokur* (☏0252/712 8728, ℻712 8729; ❺), up **on the hill** with unparalleled views of the beach, run by a Turkish-German family, with pool and nicely tended garden.

Eating and drinking

Various cafés overlooking the east beach offer full **breakfast** for as little as $2. Othwerwise, Datça's **restaurants** are fairly indistinguishable in terms of price and quality. The *Iskele*, *Karaca* and *Kapani Yeri*, on the bluff overlooking the harbour, and the *Hüsnünün Yeri*, down on the fishing boat dock, offer the usual list of kebabs and fish. Cheaper places include the nicely decorated *Defne Pide*

Salonu on the main drag and inland sidewalk eateries such as *Zekeriya Sofrası*, *Korsan*, *Valentino* and *Kemal*, on the west side of the main thoroughfare. Further inland from the main drag, the *06 Aspava Restaurant*, offering *pide* and kebab specialities from Adana at $2–3 a head, is a local favourite.

The most frantic activity you'll find in Datça is after dark at the handful of small **music pubs** and **bars** along the west harbour and beyond on the west beach. Among others there's *Bambu Bar* and *Maradonna's*, with *Eclipse* perhaps being the most popular of the lot.

Boat trips

The local **boat trips** advertised on the west harbour make a good day out. Groups generally depart between 9 and 9.30am, returning between 5 and 6pm. Standard stops include Palamut Bükü, Domuz Çukuru, Mesudiye Bükü and ancient Knidos – most of which are detailed below. The going price per person, excluding lunch (usually in a restaurant at Palamut Bükü) and allowing three swim stops, is around $10, which compares well, for example, with the price of taking a taxi to Knidos.

Eskidatça

Two kilometres from Datça, back on the road towards Marmaris, a left turn takes you along a minor paved road to the original hamlet, **ESKIDATÇA**. The cobbled road leading into the hamlet passes the teahouse before splitting into two, up and down hill. The sleepy maze of alleys – used mainly by cows – and ancient stone-built farmhouses have lately become a haven for artists and writers, who have renovated many of the delapidated country homes. One such example is now the *Antik Bar and Restaurant*, with a walled garden.

West to Knidos

Some 9km west of Datça signs point down the five-kilometre side road to the shore hamlet of **MESUDİYE BÜKÜ**. There is an occasional dolmuş to Mesudiye from Datça, leaving from the traffic circle. Accommodation prices here are slightly cheaper than in Datça, but not much happens after dark. Choose from the *Yıldırım Hotel and Camping* (☏0252/728 0221, ℻728 0224; ❷), the German speaking *Hoppala* (☏0252/728 0148; ❷) and the *Özdemir Pansiyon* (☏0252/728 0128; ❸), the last with air-conditioned rooms and decent attached restaurant.

HAYİT BÜKÜ, one cove east with the necessary road-fork left well marked, hasn't such a good beach, but the bay itself is well protected by a scenic, clawlike headland to the west. Accordingly, the place sees lots of boat traffic and there's a large dock, a few restaurants and some **motels** – such as the *Alp Otel* (☏0252/728 0219; ❶); and the *Gül Pansiyon* (☏0252/728 0027; ❶), where breakfast is $2.50 extra.

Nine kilometres of coast road, rough but just passable in an ordinary car in low gear, links Mesudiye with **PALAMUT BÜKÜ**. Most vehicles (but no dolmuşes) take the main road to the point in Yaka Köyü, about 20km out of Datça, where a side-road drops 4.5km south to Palamut. Without your own transport you'll need to take the dolmuş which leaves from behind the Ziraat Bankası in Datça. The stark setting is balanced by a kilometre-long beach of tiny pebbles lapped by brisk, clear water, with an islet offshore. Of a handful of **pansiyons**, mostly occupied for weeks on end by Turkish families, one of the most appealing is the *Bük* (☏0252/725 5136; ❶), at the far eastern end of the bay. The only drawback is that most **restaurants** are well to the west, by the harbour.

Knidos

Hard as it is to believe from its current state, **Knidos** (Cnidus), out on wind-lashed Tekir Burnu (the Cape Krio of antiquity), was one of the most fabled and prosperous cities of antiquity. With its strategic location astride the main shipping lanes of the Mediterranean it was a cosmopolitan city, and illustrious personalities hailing from here were legion. In its heyday it was also home to an eminent medical school, rival to the Hippocratic clinic across the straits on Kós. However, the city was most notorious for a splendid statue of Aphrodite and the cult (and sacred brothels) that surrounded it.

The catch is that very little remains of this former greatness, and it's probably not worth punishing any vehicle for the full distance from Datça to see it. At least until ongoing excavations are completed, a short halt on a **boat trip** (see opposite) is all that the site will merit for most visitors. You could take a **taxi from Datça**, but this will cost at least $50, and give you only an hour at the ruins.

Arriving by boat you dock in the south bay, backed by a single restaurant and a police post. Leave vehicles at the small **car park**; a nearby sign requests that, although the site is unenclosed, you should observe the official **visiting hours** of 8am to 7pm and pay admission – $2.50 – if the keeper is manning his booth.

The site

With the ruins still under excavation, the site-plan placard near the entrance is of little use, though labelling and signposting have improved in recent years.

The Aphrodisiac cult at Knidos

Like several cities in Asia Minor, Knidos was a Peloponnesian Dorian foundation, circa 1000 BC, its original site located near present-day Datça. The famous shrine of Apollo, religious focus of the Dorian Hexapolis, is thought to have been above today's Palamut Bükü. During the middle of the fourth century BC Knidos was moved to its present location – a shrewd step, taking advantage of the enforced stays of ships sheltering here from high local winds. The new town was built on both the tip of the mainland and what was then an island to the south. In ancient times the two were joined by a causeway, sluiced by a bridged channel, but the channel has long since silted up.

Undoubtedly Knidos's most famous "citizen" was an inanimate object, the **cult statue of Aphrodite** by Praxiteles, the first large-scale, freestanding nude of a woman (modelled by the famous Athenian courtesan, Phryne). This adorned the new city from its earliest days and became, even more than the menacing winds, Knidos's chief source of revenue. Set up in a sanctuary so that it could be admired from every angle, the marble Aphrodite attracted thousands of ancient tourists, not all of them mere art-lovers. According to legend the statue bore a dark stain in its crotch, not a flaw in the marble but the result of a youth conceiving such a passion for it that he hid in the temple until after closing time and made love to the effigy.

After paying their respects to the image, more conventional pilgrims were wont to observe the rites of love with one of the sacred prostitutes who worked in the temple precincts. Subsequently, customers bought tacky pornographic souvenirs, whose nature will be familiar to anyone who has browsed a postcard rack or gift shop anywhere in the modern Aegean. All this licence was – perhaps predictably – too much for the Byzantine Christians, who destroyed Praxiteles' Aphrodite along with the temple, though the aptly named Iris Love, chief of the American archeological team, claims to have discovered the goddess's head in a vault at the British Museum. Copies and incomplete versions of the statue still exist in New York, Paris, Rome and Munich.

Your overwhelming impression will be of an enormous, weedy mess, booby-trapped with deep, unguarded trenches – you may derive more satisfaction from the windswept, dramatic setting.

Most of Knidos's public buildings were on the mainland side and of these the **Hellenistic theatre**, overlooking the south anchorage, is the best preserved. A military watchtower on the ex-island confirms that most of it is off-limits; visit instead the two **Byzantine basilicas**, one huge with extensive mosaics, overlooking the north harbour. Hellenistic Knidos was laid out in a grid pattern, though the hilly site necessitated extensive terracing, retaining walls and stairways. Clambering along these, you can take a self-guided tour by following arrow-signs to the agora (by the north port), the bouleuterion, a Corinthian temple, a purported sundial and an unidentified mosaic floor. Of the Aphrodite shrine, on the very highest terrace, there remains only the circular foundation of either an altar or perhaps the tholos (round portico) where the image of the goddess was displayed.

Inland Caria

Away from the coastal regions, the major settlements in ancient Caria tended to be concentrated along the upper reaches of the Meander River, now the Büyük Menderes, and its tributaries, particularly the Marsyas – today's Çine Çayı (Çine River). Its old name, the **Marsyas**, commemorates a legend concerning the satyr Marsyas, a devotee of the mother goddess Cybele. Upon finding a deer-bone flute discarded by Athena, he became entranced by its sound as he played in Cybele's processions, and was so bold as to challenge Apollo to a musical contest. The god accepted on condition that the winner could impose the punishment of his choice on the loser. Marsyas lost; Apollo tied him to a pine tree near the source of the stream that would bear his name, and flayed him alive.

Aydın, a pleasant town easily reached from Kuşadası, is the base of choice for visiting ancient **Nyssa**, and also **Alinda**, **Alabanda** and **Gerga**, the archeological sites of the Çine valley. Of these, only Alinda is anything like required viewing, and it is also the easiest to reach by public transport. The other two are pretty remote and for most visitors don't repay the effort involved in driving (or, in the case of Gerga, walking) out to them. Further east, **Aphrodisias**, on a high plateau south of the Büyük Menderes, is similarly isolated, but buses are more obliging since it's fast becoming the archeological rival of Ephesus in the southwest Aegean.

Still further inland, the functional city of **Denizli** has transport connections in every direction, most obviously with **Hierapolis/Pamukkale**, an ancient site cum geological prodigy that's the star of every other Turkish tourist poster ever produced. Whether it figures as the high or low point of your stay depends on your temperament, but if escape becomes imperative, minor attractions such as **Laodiceia** and **Akhan** are conveniently close.

Aydın and around

Aydin is a modern provincial capital, with clean, tree-lined main boulevards and a smattering of older buildings in the centre. Despite its rather dowdy accommodation choices, its excellent dolmuş services make it the obvious jump-off point for the area's ancient ruins – Nyssa to the east, and the sites of the Çine valley (Alinda, Alabanda and Gerga), scattered either side of the scenic road south to Muğla.

Aydın

AYDİN started life as Tralles, the distinguished ancient town founded, according to legend, by colonists from the Greek Argive and Thrace; the site of the original settlement was a plateau northwest of today's city. Despite its good natural defences Tralles submitted, or fell, to whichever conqueror was currently traipsing through Asia Minor, but enjoyed a period of prosperity during the Roman imperial period, even eclipsing neighbouring Nyssa.

Contemporary Aydın's biggest attraction is currently off-limits since the site of **ancient Tralles** lies in a military zone at the northern end of Serbetçi Caddesi, 1km north of town. For the time being visitors will have to make do with **Üçgöz**, literally "three eyes" ($1 when staff present), three arches situated on a small hillock just outside the military zone. Excavations here have yet to be carried out, but according to locals it is all that remains of three vaults, themselves part of the gymnasium of Tralles.

On Gazi Bulvari, next to the sports centre, lies Aydın's other main pull, the **museum** (daily except Mon 8am–noon & 1–5.30pm; free), which has a wide collection of local finds, displayed chronologically. Notable exhibits include a bust of Athena and a statue of Nike, as well as coins, terracotta fragments and idols. The grounds house an extensive range of larger finds from Tralles, including column capitals and parts of recoved statues.

The only other buildings of note are two seventeenth-century mosques: the **Süleyman Bey Camii**, across from the pleasant, mosaic-paved central park, and the **Ahmet Şemsi Paşa Camii** on Adnan Menderes Bulvari. Otherwise, there's nothing to see except the bizarre fig sculpture about 100m west of the *otogar* – Aydın is famous for its figs (and olives) and you'll see dried figs on sale almost everywhere.

Practicalities

The **otogar** is 700m south of the centre on the main highway, just west of a large roundabout and the **tourist office** (Mon–Fri 8am–5.30pm; ☎0256/225 4145), which offers excellent city maps; the *otogar* is connected with the centre of town by complimetary shuttle bus. Adnan Menderes Bulvarı shoots straight up to the heart of town, where the **train station** (services from İzmir and Denizli) and **PTT** face each other, just west of the central square organized around Altsan 1 Caddesi. Hükümet Bulvarı, Menderes's narrower continuation, climbs past the bulk of the hotels and restaurants before intersecting Gazi Bulvarı, Aydın's main east–west thoroughfare and home to the **dolmuş station**.

Accommodation is neither inspiring, nor particularly cheap. The best is found at the *Özlü*, Adnan Menderes Bul 71 (☎0256/213 2988, ℉225 3371; ❸), where rooms come with TV. Otherwise there's the *Kabaçam*, Hükümet Bul, 11 Sok 2/B (☎0256/2252794; ❷), with reasonable en-suites, also with TV; or the similar but slightly more worn *Baltaçı*, Gazi Bulvarı, 3 Sok (☎0256/225 1320; ❷).

You'll find most of the **eating** options tucked in the backstreets around the bazaar, west of Hükümet Caddesi. The Şanlıurfa Kebab Salonu is better than most with standard-issue but well-proportioned şiş and çöp kebaps.

Nyssa

Awash in a sea of orange groves in the hills above the Büyük Menderes valley, ancient **Nyssa** is rarely visited – and except for its theatre, bouleuterion and unusual layout, there is little to interest non-specialist visitors. What's left above ground is mostly numerous arches of inferior masonry.

Originally founded by Peloponnesians, the city flourished from the first century BC until the third century AD, and subsequently remained an important Byzantine community. During the Roman era it was famous as an academic centre, attracting pupils from throughout Asia Minor. Strabo, while not a native, studied here and left detailed accounts of the city, which can still be partly verified, even in Nyssa's present ruinous condition.

The archeological zone lies 2km above **Sultanhisar**, the modern successor to Nyssa, 32km east of Aydın and astride major bus and rail routes; dolmuşes run here every thirty minutes from Aydın. Sultanhisar has simple eateries, but no public transport up to the ruins themselves.

The site

The paved access road from the ticket office (always open; $0.70 during daylight hours) leads into a small car park flanked by picnic tables. Just north of here lies an excellently preserved **Roman theatre** with a capacity of well over 5000 – a structure that is slowly being taken over by wild olives sprouting amidst the seats. The paved road continues another 300m uphill to the start of the 200-metre walk to the **bouleuterion**, where twelve semicircular rows of seats face out onto an area graced with a **ceremonial basin** and **mosaics**.

Strabo described the city as built on both sides of a steep ravine, and some of the monuments that he listed are still clinging to the banks of the canyon. A path just to the east of the theatre descends to the mouth of an enormous, 115-metre-long **tunnel** burrowing under the car park. Beyond the southern exit are the remains of two **bridges** linking the halves of Nyssa, and the virtually unrecognizable rubble of a stadium and a gymnasium, well recessed into the flanks of the gully and both currently off-limits. The tunnel, in addition to functioning as a simple storm drain, could be used to fill the stadium with water for mock naval battles.

To the west of the access road, reached by another path beginning 100m north of the guard post, stand the remains of some **baths** (adjoining the theatre) and a **library**, alleged in many sources to be the most important in Asia Minor after the one in Ephesus. You wouldn't know it from today's muddled, two-storey building, lost in more olives.

Alinda

Alinda, the first and best of the ancient ruins in the Çine valley, south of Aydın, crowns a huge bluff that dominates the area, and is closely linked with a colourful episode in the life of Alexander the Great. Ada, the sister of King Mausolus of Halicarnassus, after losing the battle for succession to the Hecatomnid throne during the middle of the fourth century, was exiled to Alinda, then a mere fortress, where she awaited an opportunity to reverse her fortunes. A few years later, upon the arrival of Alexander, Ada offered to surrender Alinda and all her personal resources in exchange for his aid in regaining her royal position. Her proposal was accepted, and Alexander holed up in Alinda for some time, preparing their combined – and eventually successful – siege of Halicarnassus. During this period they became close friends, and it seems that Ada even adopted Alexander as her son. After their victory Ada was left to rule over most of Caria, but she was the last of the remarkable Hecatomnid line; little of consequence occurred locally after her death.

Getting there

Though the site of Alinda lies 28km off the main highway, a total of 58km from Aydın, public transport connections are decent. There are direct dolmuşes from Aydın to **KARPUZLU**, the fair-sized town at the base of the ruins. Or you can use an Aydın–Çine dolmuş (departing across the road from Aydın tourist office, and from the *otogar*) and change vehicles in Çine town. The last direct service back from Karpuzlu to Aydın leaves at 4pm, to Çine at 5.30pm. If you end up having to stay in **ÇİNE**, the squeaky-clean *Alabanda* (☎0256/711 7949; ❶), opposite the tiny *otogar*, offers en-suite rooms with TV, but no breakfast. In Karpuzlu there are several adequate restaurants, but only one bare-bones hotel.

The site

From the little square where the dolmuşes stop, follow the signs 400m up a dirt track to the unfenced **site** (always open; $0.70 charged during daylight hours) and car park. Close by, the oldest houses of Karpuzlu merge into ancient masonry just below the monstrous **market building**. One hundred metres long, this was originally three storeys high, with hefty interior columns; now only two floors stand, but these are in perfect condition, and, like so much Carian stonework, bear a strange resemblance to Inca construction half a world away. Cross the open agora behind to some courses of wall, where an obvious serpentine path leads up to the well-preserved **theatre**, retaining two galleries and most of its seats. These face south, giving superlative views over Karpuzlu and its valley. From here, continue further north up the hill, where an impressive, two-storey **Hellenistic watchtower** surveys a patchwork of fields and trees, with rings of mountains up to 50km distant. The flat space around the tower is peppered with cistern mouths and partly collapsed tunnels that supposedly once led to the lower levels of the city. Walk west along the neck of the ridge, past the foundations of **acropolis houses**, until you reach a gap in the **city walls**; just beyond are a couple of specimens from Alinda's extensive **necropolis**.

Alabanda

Although originally a Carian settlement, **Alabanda** figures in history only briefly as a Roman city, notorious for its scorpions. Today there is not much on view at all, and the site, 8km west of Çine, is perfunctorily signposted and served only by an infrequent dolmuş from Çine. Only the old **bouleuterion**, north of the road, is obvious, its walls standing up to 6m high. The **theatre**, up in the village across the road, has almost disappeared – houses have been built up against it, and vegetables are being raised in the old stage area.

Gerga

Near the headwaters of the Çine Çayı, the valley narrows to a defile known as the Gökbel pass. The deserted landscape, with the water far below tumbling over huge boulders, is evocative of Marsyas and his fate – and hides **Gerga** (40km southeast of Aydın) the most mysterious ancient site in Caria.

Twelve kilometres south of Eskiçine, the graceful **İncekemer** Ottoman bridge spans the gorge. Dolmuşes from Çine run past frequently, as do buses bound for Muğla, Marmaris and Fethiye, but you'll have to specify carefully that you want to get off at the bridge. There's parking space at the roadside. From here, it's an hour and a half's **walk to Gerga**. Cross the bridge, then another flimsy cement one across a tributary, and stay with the main trail, which soon becomes a dirt track. After 25 minutes you'll reach the village of İncekemer Mahalle, split in two by yet another watercourse. Change to the west bank of this, maintain a northerly course and continue up the small valley between the big ridge and a smaller rock plug to the east. Near the top, make a hairpin left over a slight saddle to reach some drystone walls and thornbush barriers for livestock. Just past this is a small farm at the base of a terraced hillside, on which stand the remains of Gerga.

Virtually nothing is known for certain about Gerga, other than that it is of very early Carian vintage, with crude, monolithic masonry supposedly dating from the Roman era. At first sight it would appear to have not been a town, but a sacred precinct like Labranda. The most conspicuous item is a **tomb-temple** in the form of a house, in perfect condition, despite its current usage as a cowshed. Its stone roof is intact and on the lintel "GERGAS" is inscribed in Greek lettering – which some archeologists theorize is not the place name but that of an obscure Carian deity. You actually enter the site between two upright, flattened **monoliths**, irregularly shaped like African termite nests; adjacent is a large lustral **basin** carved from living rock. A giant headless **statue** lies on the ground beyond the tomb-temple, and at the far edge of the main terrace are two purported **fountains**: one backed into the hillside, the other freestanding and bearing another "GERGAS" legend. While none of the individual structures is that impressive, the total effect and the outlandish location is unsettling.

Aphrodisias

Situated on a high plateau over 600m above sea level, ringed by mountains and watered by a tributary of the Büyük Menderes, **Aphrodisias** is among the most isolated and beautifully set of Turkey's major archeological sites. Acres of marble peek out from among the poplars and other vegetation that cloaks the remains of one of imperial Rome's most cultured Asian cities. Late afternoon visits have the bonus of often dramatic cloud formations, spawned by the elevation, and the attendant dappled lighting.

Some history

Aphrodisias was one of the earliest occupied sites in Anatolia. Neolithic and Bronze Age mounds have been found here, including the artificial hill supporting the theatre. There has also been a **fertility cult** of some sort here for just as long, fostered by the agricultural associations of the river valley. The Assyrian goddess of love and war, Nin, became syncretized with the Semitic Ishtar, whose attributes were eventually assumed by the Hellenic Aphrodite.

Despite a strategic position near the meeting point of ancient Caria, Lydia and Phrygia, and its proximity to major trade routes, Aphrodisias for many centuries remained only a shrine, and never really grew into a town until the second century BC. The citizens of Aphrodisias were amply rewarded for their support of the Romans during the Mithridatic revolt. Many special privileges

– including the right of sanctuary within the Aphrodite temple precincts – were granted, and the rapidly burgeoning city was heavily patronized by various emperors, becoming a major cultural centre. It was renowned in particular for its school of sculpture, which took advantage of nearby quarries of high-grade marble, and Aphrodisian works adorned every corner of the empire, including Rome itself.

Perhaps because of this fixation with graven images, not to mention the lucrative cult of Aphrodite (similar to that at Knidos), paganism lingered here for almost two centuries after Theodosius proscribed the old religions. Even following conversion of the Aphrodite shrine to a more decorous basilica, and a change of name to Stavropolis (City of the Cross), the Christianity professed here tended toward heretical persuasions.

The reputation of its love cult had served to protect Aphrodisias since its inception, but by the fourth century AD a wall had become necessary. This failed singularly, however, to stave off the effect of two earthquakes and sundry raids, and decline was the dominant theme of Byzantine times. The town was abandoned completely during the thirteenth century, its former glories recalled only by the Ottoman village of Geyre – a corruption of "Caria" – among the ruins. Romantic travellers dutifully stopped, sketched and copied inscriptions, but none suspected the wealth of relics hidden from view.

First French, then Italian researchers poked rather desultorily below the surface early last century, but it is only since 1961 that work by a New York University team under Dr Kenan Erim has permitted a fuller understanding of the site. Dr Erim's death in 1990 (he is buried on the site) marked the end of an era; currently no new monuments are being uncovered, with ongoing work concentrating on consolidation, cleaning and documentation of inscriptions. The intention is to render Aphrodisias on a par with Ephesus and the eventual results will certainly be spectacular, though for now some of the site's more interesting areas remain off-limits.

The site

A loop path around the **site** (daily: summer 8am–7pm; winter 8am–5.30pm; $5) passes all of the major monuments, though at the time of writing only the stadium, theatre, odeion, council houses and the temple of Aphrodite have completely unrestricted access.

First stop is the magnificent, virtually intact **theatre**, founded in the first century BC but extensively modified by the Romans for their blood sports three centuries later. At the rear of the stage building are chiselled imperial decrees affecting the status of the town. Still further behind the stage is a large square, the **tetrastoön**, originally surrounded by colonnades on all sides, and one of several meeting places in the Roman and Byzantine city. South of the tetrastoön lies a large baths complex.

The path skirts the north flank of the theatre, right under the the hill's summit; down and to the north you may often see workmen pottering about in the **Sebasteion** – two parallel porticoes erected in the first century AD to honour the deified Roman emperors – and the **double agora**, two squares ringed by Ionic and Corinthian stoas. Numerous columns still vie with the poplars, and the whole area is bounded to the southwest by the **Portico of Tiberius**, which separates the agora from the fine **Baths of Hadrian** (currently out of bounds), preserved right down to the floor tiles and the odd mosaic.

North of the baths, several blue-marble columns sprout from a multi-roomed structure commonly known as the **Bishop's Palace**, from its presumed use during Byzantine times. However, its ground plan, particularly the large audience chamber, is typical of a governor's residence in Roman provinces and that is certainly how the building began life. East of here huddles the Roman **odeion**, with nine rows of seats. Since the many earthquakes have disrupted the local water table, the orchestra is prone to springtime flooding, and today frogs often croak where concerts were once given and the city council deliberated.

A few paces to the north, fourteen columns of the **Temple of Aphrodite** are all that's left of the city's principal sanctuary. The Byzantines mangled not only the idol within but also the ground plan when they converted it to a basilica during the fifth century, so considerable detective work was required to re-establish the first-century BC foundations. Even these were laid atop at least two older structures, with evidence of mother-goddess worship extending back to the seventh century BC. The Hellenistic/Roman sanctuary had forty Ionic columns arranged eight by thirteen, with the cult image erected in the main hall. The Byzantines removed the columns at each end of the temple, fashioning an apse to the east, an atrium and baptistry on the west, and it's this architectural pastiche you see today. Immediately north is the so-called **School**

of Philosophy, tentatively identified, like the bishop's palace, on the basis of resemblance to other such structures elsewhere.

The northernmost feature of the site, 200m off the main path, is the 30,000-seat **stadium**, one of the largest and best preserved in Anatolia. Under the empire, and with official encouragement, many cities of Asia Minor held periodic festivals in imitation of the major Greek competitions. Those at Aphrodisias were a version of Delphi's Pythian Games, with sporting, musical and dramatic events.

Returning to the main loop trail, the last thing you'll notice before exiting onto the museum square is the recently re-erected **tetrapylon**, a monumental gateway with two double rows of four columns, half of them fluted, supporting pediments with intricate reliefs. This second-century AD edifice is thought to mark the intersection of a major north–south street with a sacred way heading toward the Aphrodite shrine.

The museum

An earthquake in 1956 damaged the old village of Geyre, giving the authorities a timely pretext to relocate the villagers 1.5km to the north and begin excavations. The old village square is now flanked by the archeologists' quarters and by the attractive **museum** (daily: summer 8am–7pm; winter 8am–5.30pm; additional $3 admission), whose collection consists almost entirely of sculpture recovered from the ruins.

Given that Aphrodisias met most of the demand for effigies under the empire, even what remains after the loss of originals and the spiriting away of works to city museums is considerable. The so-called "Aphrodite Hall" contains statuary related to the cult, a rendition of the goddess, much defaced by Christian zealots, occupying the position of honour. In the "Penthesileia Hall", a joyous satyr carries the child Dionysos in his arms. The "Melpomene Hall" contains a wrenching version of the muse of tragedy, together with two suitably loutish-looking boxers – ironically lacking their hands – and the completely intact, quasi-satirical portrait of Flavius Palmatus, Byzantine governor of Asia; with a small head and thick body, he was an ugly, malproportioned man, but, judging from the facial expression, one you crossed at your peril. Recent notable additions to the collection include the remounted, so-called "Zoïlos" friezes and portrait busts of various philosophers. The first (or last) notable item you'll pass is a version of Nike carrying a trophy, opposite the souvenir stall.

Practicalities

Aphrodisias is situated 13km southeast of **KARACASU**, the nearest sizable town, which lies 25km from the E24/320 highway between Aydın and Denizli. From the highway, you'll need to change transport at **NAZİLLİ**, whose *otogar* sits just north of the highway on the west edge of town. If coming by train, exit Nazilli station and turn right onto the main town thoroughfare, or follow the tracks southwest – they pass very near the bus stand. **Dolmuşes to Karacasu** depart from the rear of the Nazilli *otogar*; during warmer months the route may extend to Geyre, the village next to the ruins. Best bet for accommodation in Nazilli, if required, is the two-star *Metya Hotel* (℡0256/312 8888, Ⓕ312 8891; ❷), one of two reasonable hotels. In Karacasu there is only the grimmest of dormitories, built directly over the small bus terminal building.

Whatever happens, try to avoid getting stranded at Aphrodisias – a distinct possibility after 6pm, even in summer. A round trip by **taxi from Karacasu** will cost you $13, double that if you have to take it all the way back to the

Nazilli–Denizli highway. If you are going to get stuck, you're best off doing so at **GEYRE**, next to the ruins, which can offer the simple *Chez Mestan pansiyon*-campsite (☎0256/446 8046; ❷), 600m from the site on the main highway and with basic waterless doubles; the more comfortable *Aphrodisias Hotel-Restaurant-Camping* (☎0256/448 8132, ☏448 8422; ❷) is 1km west of *Chez Mestan*, with good en-suite rooms and a rooftop restaurant.

The other option for visiting the site is to take a **tour** organized through one of the pensions in Pamukkale (see p.432), the going rate for which is around $13.

Pamukkale and around

As you approach **Pamukkale** from Denizli, a long white smudge along the hills to the north suggests a landslide or opencast mine. Getting closer, this resolves into the edge of a plateau, more than 100m higher than the level of the river valley and absolutely smothered in white **travertine terraces**. Some are shaped like water lilies, others like shell-bathtubs with stalagmitic feet, with the simplest ones resembling bleached rice terraces out of an oriental engraving. The Turks have dubbed this geological fairyland *Pamukkale*, or "Cotton Castle".

The responsibility for this startling natural wonder rests with a spring, saturated with dissolved calcium bicarbonate, bubbling up from the feet of Çal Dağı beyond. As the water surges over the edge of the plateau and cools, carbon dioxide is given off and calcium carbonate precipitated as hard chalk (travertine). What you see now has been accumulating for millennia, as slowly but surely the solidified waterfall advances southwest. Seen at sunset, subtle hues of ochre, purple and pink are reflected in the water, replacing the dazzling white of midday. The spring itself emerges in what once was the centre of the ancient city of **Hierapolis**, whose ruins would merit a stop even if they weren't coupled with the natural phenomenon of the terraces.

The hotels here at one time siphoned off the precious mineral waters for their own heated pools, thus damaging the terraces further downstream. The waterflow is now strictly rotated in order to preserve the site and also to allow the greatly diminished deposits to "regrow". Present restrictions on access to the travertine terraces mean that visitors are confined entirely to the major pathways around the site and can visit only a handful of the smaller pools on the furthest southern edge of the terraces.

Some history

The therapeutic properties and bizarre appearance of the hot springs were known about for thousands of years before an actual town was founded here by one of the Pergamene kings during the second century BC. After incorporation into the Roman Empire in 129 BC, development proceeded apace, spurred by minor industries in wool and metals, plus a health spa practically the equal of the present one. Hierapolis seems to have enjoyed considerable imperial favour, especially after catastrophic earthquakes in 17 AD and 60 AD. No fewer than three emperors paid personal visits, stimulating local emperor-worship alongside the veneration of Apollo and his mother Leto, who was venerated in the guise of Cybele.

The presence of a flourishing Jewish community aided the rapid and early establishment of Christianity here. Hierapolis is mentioned in Paul's Epistle to the (neighbouring) Colossians, and Philip the Apostle is thought to have been martyred here, along with his seven sons. However, as at Aphrodisias, paganism lingered well into the sixth century, until a zealous bishop supervised the destruction of the remaining focuses of ancient worship and the establishment of nearly one hundred churches, several of which are still visible.

Hierapolis slid into obscurity in late Byzantine times, nudged along by Arab and Turcoman raids. After the Selçuks arrived in the 1100s, the city was abandoned, not to figure much in the Western imagination until Italian excavations began in 1957. A mere six decades have sufficed to re-create, if not the monumental taste, then certainly the commercialism of the Roman period.

Pamukkale Köyü

PAMUKKALE KÖYÜ, a once-sleepy village at the base of the cliff, is where most foreign travellers stay. In recent years, the village has acquired a rash of discos, carpet shops, hustlers (read on) and wretched restaurants in its centre. Despite all this, it's still a rural settlement, partly dependent on cotton; beyond the main drag, especially in the lower neighbourhood away from the travertine, little outward change is evident. For any nocturnal peace, it's better to stay on the outskirts, whose limit seems to have stabilized about 500m west of the road leading up to the south gate of the ruins.

Arrival, information and transport

Most travellers arrive from the agricultural town of **Denizli**, 20km to the south, from where **dolmuşes** labelled "Pamukkale/Karahayat" set off from a rank on the west edge of the *otogar*; the last departure in either direction is around 11pm in summer (9pm for Karahayat), much earlier in the cooler months. A **taxi from Denizli** will set you back $12 per car-load; or consider ringing one of the recommended *pansiyon*s, who are often able to fetch you for free (or at least for a reasonable charge).

There are also **long-distance bus connections** between Pamukkale Köyü and most of the larger resorts – Kaş, Marmaris, Kuşadası and Fethiye, among other places – up to several times daily, although the buses are really minibuses and not air-conditioned. Several bus companies, including Pamukkale, have ticket offices in the village, but be sure that the fare and itinerary include a shuttle to the Denizli *otogar* (you'll rarely get through-service, except perhaps in peak season).

Accommodation and eating

There's been a vigorous winnowing of excess capacity in Pamukkale Köyü, spurred by falling tourist numbers, with substandard (ie non-en-suite) outfits folding. You should still be prepared for the attentions of the notorious local accommodation **touts**, rivalling those at Selçuk and Kuşadası for their aggression and mendacity. An advance telephone call to one of the establishments mentioned below, and a word to the touts that you have prepaid by credit card, should solve any problems. In any case, it's well worth arranging a room in advance as the various establishments, well aware of the touts' ploys, may offer to fetch you from Denizli or meet you in the village if informed of your arrival time. Most lodgings in the village are open all year and advertise the presence of a **swimming pool**, but by the time the mineral water has made the long trip down from the cliff it's distinctly cool and murky – a summertime pleasure only. **Eating out**, the situation is almost uniformly dire. Service is slack and prices nearly double what they'd be elsewhere. You'll usually get better value from your *pansiyon* or motel, some of which offer half-board rates.

PAMUKKALE KÖYÜ

North Gate, Karahayıt ▲   ▲ Plateau

N

▲ Güney Kapısı (South Gate)

Health Clinic

Mosque

Dolmuş stop ★

Bus Company Offices

PTT

Mosque

STAD CAD

TRAVERTEN SOK

KUZEY SOK

ÖZGÜR CAD

BÜLBÜL SOK

BAHÇE SOK

YIĞIK ALİ CAD

BİRLİK SOK

FATİH CAD

FATİH CAD

YÖRÜK SOK

CENGİZ TOPEL CAD

İBRAHİM KALLI CAD

ANA SOK

İNÖNÜ CAD

MENDERES CAD

COŞKUN CAD

KAYALAR SOK

ÖZER SOK

MEHMET AKİF ERSOY BULVARI

KORKMAZ CAD

FEVZİ ÇAKMAK CAD

NAMIK KEMAL CAD

HASAN TAHSİN KUBİLAY CAD

▲ Denizli, Laodiceia & Akhan

❶
❷
❸
❹
❺
❻
❼
❽

ACCOMMODATION

Allgau	8
Aspawa	5
Hal-Tur	1
Kervansaray	3
Koray	6
Meltem	2
Oztürk	7
Weisse Burg	4

0 ————————— 200 m

Allgau Backstreet near junction of Korkmaz Cad and Mehmet Akif Ersoy Bul ☎0258/272 2250, ⓦwww.pamukkale.netfirms.com. At the remote south end of the village, run by the most relaxed, genuine owners in town. Basic rooms overlook the garden and pool, or there are wooden bungalows and tent space. ❶

Aspawa Menderes Cad ☎0258/272 2094. With an off-street mineral pool, a choice of single, double or triple rooms, particularly good breakfasts

($2) and satellite TV. ❷

Hotel Hal-Tur Mehmet Akif Ersoy Bul 45 ☎0258/272 2723, ⓦwww.intergate.com.tr. One of the most prestigious hotels in the village, directly opposite the terraces, with immaculate air-con rooms with satellite TV. It's surprisingly friendly and there's a swimming pool, jacuzzi, sauna and attached restaurant. ❺

Hotel Kervansaray Alley off İnönü Cad ☎0258/272 2209, ℻272 2143. A long-standing favourite, about 200m up the main street, owned by the welcoming Kaya family. Many rooms overlook creek greenery, and there's a pool and a rooftop café-restaurant (though this is closed in winter). **❷**

Koray Otel Pamuk Mah 27 ☎0258/272 2222, ⓦwww.korayotel.com. Popular, small hotel built around a non-mineral pool and garden, with a good restaurant. Well-kept and attractive double rooms (breakfast extra), and full-board options available. **❷**

Meltem Motel aka *Backpacker's Inn*, Kuzey Sok 9 ☎0258/272 3134, ⓔmeltemmotel@superonline.com. Near the top of the village: some of the sim-

ple doubles have air-conditioning, and there's a dorm ($4), satellite TV, internet access and local information. **❶**

Öztürk Pension Pamuk Mah ☎0258/272 2838, ⓦwww.ozturkhotel.com. A quiet off-street location, enclosing a small pool-garden and lovely vined breakfast terrace. Managed by a friendly family. **❷**

Weisse Burg Pension Inönü Cad ☎0258/272 2064, ⓔweisseburg@yahoo.com. Eight basic rooms to choose from, a small pool and a nice rooftop restaurant serving traditional and vegetarian meals. **❷**

Hierapolis and the travertines

The combined site of ancient **Hierapolis** and the **travertines** (daily 24hr, though you'll only be charged admission during daylight hours; $3) has two entrances. One, the signposted "Güney Kapısı" or **South Gate**, is at the end of a 2km road describing a lazy loop up from the village. Here you'll find a rather grandiose "visitor centre" plus a ticket booth and car park. The complex seems, however, a rather futile gesture, as you've a long, shadeless walk to the ruins and terraces from here. Most vehicles – including tour buses - use the other, **North Gate** (where's there's another ticket booth and visitor centre) for access to the central car parks next to the museum. If you plan to visit Karahayıt, beyond Hierapolis, retain your ticket stub so that you don't have to pay again when re-entering the fee zone.

There's also a quite conspicuous **path** up to the plateau (a fifteen-minute hike), from just before the point where the Karahayıt-bound road curls north out of the village. Intended originally to allow the villagers to enjoy the springs, you can also pay to enter the site at the base and walk up – though most people prefer to come down this way.

If you want to take a proper bath in the springs, visit the **Pamukkale Thermal Baths** (daily 8am–8pm; $5 admission for two hours) up on the plateau, which encloses the sacred pool of the ancients, with mineral water bubbling from its bottom at 35°C. Time was when you could discreetly saunter in for an early-morning bath with the staff none the wiser, but admission is now highly regimented; changing rooms are to the right as you enter. Come as early or late as possible; midday is the province of large tour groups.

On your way to the pool you'll have passed the **tourist office** (daily in season 8am–noon & 1.30–7.30pm; ☎0258/264 3971), principally useful for its combined map of the site and village, and the **museum** (daily except Mon 8am–8pm; $0.70), housed in the restored second-century AD baths. Its rather disappointing collection consists primarily of statuary, sarcophagi, masonry fragments and smaller knick-knacks recovered during excavations at Hierapolis. Behind the museum is a large sixth-century **basilica**, probably the Byzantine-era cathedral, with two aisles sandwiching the nave.

Hierapolis: eastern monuments

Access to the **eastern monuments** of ancient Hierapolis is via a narrow road winding up between the main car park and the museum. The first break – it can hardly be called a gate – in the roadside fence gives access to a **nymphaeum**, or fountain-house, the **Temple of Apollo** and the adjacent

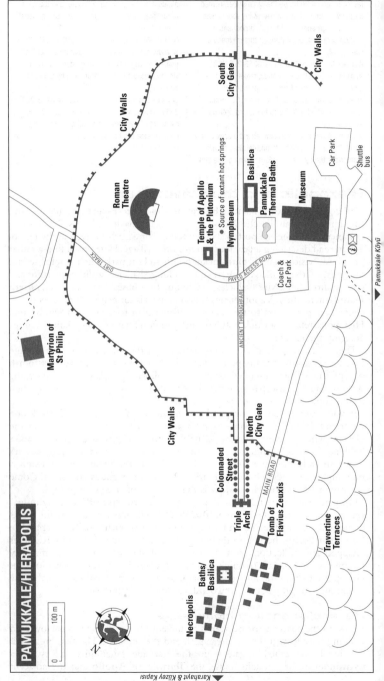

PAMUKKALE/HIERAPOLIS

▲ Visitor Centre & Güney Kapısı

City Walls

South City Gate

City Walls

Roman Theatre

Temple of Apollo & the Plutonium

● Source of extant hot springs

Nymphaeum

Basilica

Pamukkale Thermal Baths

Museum

Car Park

Shuttle bus

 DIRT TRACK

PAVED ACCESS ROAD

ANCIENT THROUGHFARE

Coach & Car Park

▶ Pamukkale Köyü

Martyrion of St Philip

City Walls

North City Gate

MAIN ROAD

Colonnaded Street

Triple Arch

Tomb of Flavius Zeuxis

Travertine Terraces

Necropolis

Baths/ Basilica

0   100 m

N

▲ Karahayıt & Kuzey Kapısı

Plutonium. The Apollo shrine in its present, scanty form dates from the third century AD, though built on a second-century BC foundation. The grotto of the Plutonium, a quasi-oracular site sacred to the god of the underworld, is today a small, partly paved cavity beyond which you can hear rushing water and an ominous hissing – the emission of a highly toxic gas, probably a mixture of sulphurous compounds and carbon dioxide, capable of killing man and beast alike. In ancient times the eunuch priests of Cybele were reputedly able to descend into the chasm with no ill effect; whether this was a result of their anatomical deficiency or some less obvious ruse is unknown. Today, a formidable metal cage-grille keeps daredevils out – before this was installed, two Germans died attempting to brave the cave.

The next feature is the restored **Roman theatre**, dating from the second century AD. Admittedly, theatres are a dime a dozen in Turkey but this one is in exceptionally good shape, including most of the stage buildings and their elaborate reliefs. During the **International Pamukkale Song Festival** (late June) performances are held here: the 46 rows of seats can still hold up to 7000 spectators comfortably, as against the former capacity of 10,000.

After seeing the theatre, return to the dirt track and follow it further east past a stretch of the **city walls**, turning left onto a smaller path and eventually halting before the **Martyrion of St Philip**, built in honour of the apostle, martyred here in 80 AD. This fifth-century structure, comprising many rectangular cells converging on a central octagonal chamber, was almost certainly not Philip's tomb, nor even a church, but probably the venue for festivals and processions on the saint's day.

Hierapolis: northern monuments

Arguably the most interesting part of the city is the **colonnaded street**, which once extended for almost 1km from a gate 400m southeast of the sacred pool to another breach in the north wall. This thoroughfare, parallel to the plateau's edge, unevenly bisected the grid plan of the Hellenistic city and terminated at each end in monumental portals a few paces outside the walls. Only the northerly one, a **triple arch** flanked by towers and dedicated to the emperor Domitian in 84 AD, still stands. The short stretch of intact paved way, flanked by numerous re-erected columns, was the commercial heart of the city.

North of Domitian's triple arch, on the east side of the road, stands the squat bulk of some second-century AD baths, converted 200 years later into a **basilica**. Slightly closer to the archway, west of the asphalt, you'll notice the elaborate **Tomb of Flavius Zeuxis**, a prominent Hierapolitan merchant – the first of more than a thousand tombs of all shapes and sizes constituting the **necropolis**, the largest in Asia Minor and extending for nearly 2km along the road. The more sumptuous ones bear epitaphs or inscriptions warning graverobbers of punishments awaiting those caught, and there are even forecourts with benches for visits by the deceased's relatives. Nowadays, camels and their drovers, instead of tomb-desecrators, lurk among the tumuli.

Karahayıt

Dolmuşes cover the 7km or so from the lower village to **KARAHAYIT**, famous for its *Kırmızı Su* (Red Water). These hot (55°C), iron-rich springs well up from within a single, blunt-topped rock formation and then flow, considerably cooled down, into a large rustic pool flanked by a tasteful tea garden and some small souvenir shops; use of the pool is free.

Karahayıt is a very different experience to Pamukkale Köyü: it's patronized almost exclusively by Turkish families from Konya and other conservative Anatolian cities, intent on finding a thermal cure for various maladies; alcohol is difficult to locate and sunbathing in public is frowned upon. As at Pamukkale, however, overzealous tapping of the thermal springs by the various *pansiyons* has led to a similar reduction in flow and threats by the authorities to close down, or at least regulate, the offending establishments.

The *pansiyons* and **hotels** all offer either en-suite thermal baths or communal pools, the friendliest and cheapest being *Albay Pension* (☎0258/271 4065; ❶). *Yeşil Dere*, which keeps live trout for its **restaurant**, also has the only **campsite** in the area.

Laodiceia and Akhan

Just off the road linking Pamukkale and Denizli are two minor sites, ancient **Laodiceia** and the remains of the Selçuk *kervansaray* at **Akhan** – either worth a short detour if you've time or your own vehicle.

Laodiceia

Thirteen kilometres south of Pamukkale, a black-on-yellow marker points 500m west to a placard detailing the delights of "Laodikya", the site of **ancient Laodiceia**. This covers an elevated tableland squeezed between two river valleys, the bleak melancholy of the meagre remains accentuated by tractor furrows and power pylons. It's a setting redeemed principally by perennially snow-covered Honaz Dağı (2571m) to the southeast, matched in miniature by the white strip of Pamukkale to the north.

Founded by the post-Alexandrian Seleucid kings in the mid-third century BC at the junction of two major trade routes, Laodiceia came under Roman rule at the same time as the other cities of Caria. Under the empire, its prosperity – derived largely from soft black wool – was such that (unlike Hierapolis) it needed no imperial assistance to repair the earthquake damage of 60 AD. As with its northern neighbour, though, the presence of a large Jewish community aided in the rapid adoption of Christianity – albeit half-heartedly according to St John the Divine, whose pungent comment in Revelations 3:15–17 is notorious: "I know your works, you are neither hot nor cold. Would that you were cold or hot! So, because you are lukewarm, and neither cold nor hot, I will spew you out of my mouth" – a metaphor almost certainly derived from John's acquaintance with the springs at Pamukkale. Nonetheless, Laodiceia became an important bishopric during Byzantine times, and only began its final decline after a fifth-century earthquake. Shortly after the Selçuk conquest the city was abandoned in favour of nearby Denizli.

As befits a settlement of mostly Roman importance, the visible ruins date from that era. The track starting at the orientation placard dwindles away in the centre of the plateau, next to the rubble of a **nymphaeum**. Southeast of here, at the edge of the site, is the 350-metre-long **stadium**, the largest in Asia Minor but in parlous condition, constructed in the first century AD under the emperor Vespasian. Overlooking it are the fairly substantial remains of a Hadrianic **gymnasium** and **baths complex**. These, and the archeological zone in general, have suffered from systematic masonry pilferage in recent times; engravings from the 1820s show monuments standing to twice their present height. Return to the nymphaeum once more and cross the rudimentary track to find the foundations of an **Ionic temple**. Continue a short distance north and begin pacing the edge of the upland to find, in quick succession, the **small theatre** – facing northwest and with many seats intact – and the **large theatre**, facing northeast over the modern village of Eskihisar.

Akhan

Its possible to walk the 3km between Laodiceia and the Selçuk *kervansaray* of **Akhan**. Upon reaching the E24/320 highway (the main Denizli–Afyon road), turn left and proceed 1.5km to the lightly restored structure tucked just north of the asphalt, on the west bank of a creek. If you enter the modern village of Akhan, you've gone too far. The rectangular structure encloses a courtyard, with arches to either side, and a covered hall at the rear. An inscription over the front gate, which looks southeast over the stream and a peach orchard, declares that the building was completed in 1252–1253, under the reign of the sultan İzzedin Kaykavuş.

Travel details

Trains

Denizli to: Afyon–Eskişehir–Haydarpaşa–İstanbul (1 daily; 14hr 30min); Afyon (1 daily; 5hr 30min).
İzmir (Basmane) to: Denizli (3 daily, via Aydın & Nazilli; 6hr); Manisa–Balikesir–Bandirma (3 daily; 6hr 30min; ferry connection at Bandırma for İstanbul); Manisa–Balikesir–Kütahya–Ankara (2 daily, both with couchettes or full sleepers; 14–16hr); Manisa–Balikesir–Kütahya–Eskişehir (3 daily; 9hr 30min–11hr); Ödemiş (1 daily; 3hr); Selçuk (2 daily; 1hr 45min); Söke via Selçuk (3 daily; 2hr 15min).
Selçuk to: Aydin (3 daily; 1hr); Denizli (2 daily; 4hr 15min); İzmir Basmane (6–7 daily; 1hr 45min).

Buses and dolmuşes

The schedules below are for the summer season; out of season (Nov–April), the number of buses and minibuses drops drastically.
Aydın to: Alinda via Karpuzlu (hourly; 1hr); Ankara (4 daily; 9hr); Çine (15 daily; 35min); Denizli (every 30min until 7pm; 2hr); Fethiye (hourly; 5hr); Konya (4 daily; 9hr); Marmaris (hourly; 3hr); Nazilli (every 30min; 45min); Söke (every 30min; 50min); Sultanhisar (every 30min; 30min).
Bodrum to: Ankara (4 daily; 11hr); Bitez (every 30min; 15min); Fethiye (6 daily; 5hr); Gölköy (hourly; 30min); Gümbet (every 15min; 10min); Gümüşluk (every 30min; 40min); Gündoğan via Torba (hourly; 25min); İstanbul (20 daily; 12hr); Izmir (hourly; 3hr 30min); Marmaris (hourly; 3hr 15min); Muğla (hourly; 2hr 30min); Ortakent (every

30min; 20min); Pamukkale (2 daily; 5hr); Turgutreis (every 30min; 25min); Yahşi Sahil (every 30min; 20min); Yalikavak (10 daily; 25min).
Datça to: Ankara (several daily; 13hr); İstanbul (several daily; 16hr); Marmaris (9 daily; 2hr); Mesudiye (several daily; 30min); Muğla (11 daily; 3hr 15min).
Denizli to: Antalya via Burdur/Korkuteli (14 daily; 5hr 30min); Bodrum via Kale/Muğla (2–3 daily; 4hr 30min); Konya via Isparta and Eğirdir (several daily; 7hr 15min); Izmir (every 30min; 3hr 15min); Marmaris via Kale/Muğla (8 daily; 3hr 30min); Tavas (hourly until 6pm; 40min); Yeşilova, for Salda Gölü (8 daily; 1hr 30min).
İzmir to: Afyon (5 daily; 5hr); Ahmetbeyli (at least 8 daily; 1hr 20min); Ankara (11 daily; 8hr); Antalya via Aydin and Burdur (hourly; 7hr); Aydin (every 30min; 2hr); Ayvalik (every 30min; 2hr 30min); Bergama (every 30min; 1hr); Bodrum (hourly; 4hr); Bursa (hourly; 7hr); Çandarli (6 daily; 2hr); Çanakkale (6 daily; 5hr 30min); Çeşme (every 15–20min; 1hr 30min); Datça (several daily; 7hr); Denizli (hourly; 4hr); Edirne (6 daily; 12hr); Fethiye (12–18 daily; 7hr); Foça (every 30min; 1hr 30min); Gümüldür (hourly; 1hr 40min); İstanbul (hourly; 10hr); Kuşadasi (every 30min until 9pm; 2hr); Manisa (every 15min; 45min); Marmaris (hourly; 5hr); Milas (hourly; 3hr); Muğla (hourly; 4hr); Ödemiş (every 2hr; 3hr 30min); Salihli (hourly; 1hr 30min); Sart (hourly; 1hr 30min); Seferihisar (at least hourly; 1hr); Selçuk (every 20min; 1hr 40min).
Kuşadasi to: Aydın (hourly; 1hr 15min); Antalya (2 daily; 8hr); Bodrum (4 daily; 3hr); Dilek Yarimadasi National Park (every 30min; 40min); İstanbul (5

daily; 11hr); Menderes airport (every 20min until 9pm; 1hr 30min); İmir (every 30min; 1hr 30min); Pamukkale (12 daily; 3hr 30min); Seferihisar (hourly; 1hr 30min); Selçuk (every 20min; 30min); Söke (every 30min; 40min).

Marmaris to: Akyaka (every 30min; 30min); Ankara (14 daily; 13hr); Antalya (5 daily; 6hr); Bodrum (7 daily; 3hr 15min); Bozburun (3 daily; 1hr 15min); Datça (9 daily; 2hr); Denizli (6 daily; 3hr); Fethiye (hourly; 2hr 45min); İstanbul (4 daily; 11hr); Izmir (17 daily; 5hr); Orhaniye (several daily; 35min); Ortaca (hourly; 1hr); Selimiye (3 daily; 50min); Tavlica (1 daily; 1hr 40min); Turunç (hourly; 20min).

Milas to: Bodrum (hourly; 2hr); Denizli (13 daily; 2hr); Euromos (hourly; 15min); Güllük (every 30min; 35min); İzmir (every 30min; 4hr 30min); Muğla (hourly; 1hr 15min); Ören (at least 6 daily; 1hr); Selimiye (hourly; 20min).

Muğla to: Akyaka (every 30min; 30min); Fethiye (12 daily; 2hr 30min); Köyceriz (hourly; 50min); Marmaris (every 30min; 1hr).

Nazilli to: Geyre (6–7 daily; 50min); Karacasu (6–7 daily; 40min).

Selçuk to: Kuşadasi (every 20min until 10pm; 30min); Tire (every 20min; 40min).

Söke to: Altinkum (hourly; 50min); Bafa Gölü (every 30min; 30min); Balat (several daily; 40min); Didyma (hourly; 50min); Dilek Yarimadasi National Park (every 30min; 40min); Güllübahçe (hourly; 20min); Güzelçamli (every 30min; 40min); Milas (every 30min; 1hr 20min); Miletus (several daily; 40min); Priene (hourly; 20min).

Domestic hydrofoils

All schedules also apply to the reverse itinerary, and are valid during the May–Oct season only. These services are currently operated by Bodrum Express Lines.

Altinkum to: Bodrum (3 weekly; 1hr). $10 one-way, $20 open return. This service usually uses Torba harbour, north of Bodrum; land transfer there included.

Bodrum to: Marmaris (2 weekly; 2hr). $20 one-way, $35 open return.

Datça to: Bodrum (2 daily; 1hr). Services arrive at and depart from Körmen Limani, 9km north of Datça; shuttle bus included in price; $10 one-way, $20 open return.

Domestic ferries

The first two Bodrum-based services are operated by the Bodrum Ferryboat Association, the other by Turkish Maritime Lines. All frequencies are valid

during the May–Oct season only.

Altinkum to: Bodrum–Torba (1 daily; 2hr). $7.50 one-way, $12.50 open return.

Datça to: Bodrum (1 daily; 2hr). Ferries arrive at and depart from Körmen Limani, 9km north of Datça; shuttle bus included in price, $7 one-way, $11 open return, car $27.

İzmir to: İstanbul (1 weekly, usually Sun; 19hr). $30 for a pullman seat, $50 for a middling cabin, $40 for a small car.

Ferries and hydrofoils to the Greek islands

Turkish vessels normally leave in the morning – usually between 8 and 9am – returning from Greece between 4.30 and 5.30pm, depending on the time of year; Greek craft arrive between 9 and 10am and return between 4 and 5pm. For a morning boat you must bring your passport to ticket agencies the evening before – or, failing that, at the crack of dawn – so that your name is recorded on a passenger manifest; for an afternoon boat it should be enough to hand over your papers two hours before sailing time. In high season the boats occasionally sell out a day in advance, and schedules are subject to alteration depending on demand and season.

Fares are overpriced for the distances involved (though there may be significant reductions in slow seasons). This is partly because Turkish ports demand departure and arrival taxes from passengers, while all Greek ports hit any passenger staying overnight with stiff departure taxes. The following prices do not include the cost of Turkish visas required by various nationalities. Taking a small car over on a ferry costs $40–80 one way depending on the port; combi-vans and other overland vehicles can cost almost double. Advance booking is essential, since the boats often hold only two or three vehicles.

Bodrum–Kós (6–12 weekly, dwindling to 1 or 2 weekly in midwinter; 45min; also daily hydrofoils in summer; 20min). Currently the cheapest crossing at $15 one-way, $20 day return, $46 open return (including Greek tax) for ferries.

Çeşme–Híos (May–Oct 2–5 weekly; Nov–April 1 weekly; 1hr). $35 one-way (no Turkish tax), $45 day return, $50 open return (the latter includes Greek tax); cars $70–90.

Kuşadasi–Sámos (daily April to late-Oct, dwindling to 1 weekly midwinter; 1hr 30min; also 2–3 hydrofoils weekly; 45min). Hydrofoils and ferries are much the same price, at $30 one-way, $35 day return, $55 open return (plus $10 Turkish tax, plus $10 if you stay overnight in Greece). Cars around $70.

Marmaris–Rhodes (twice daily hydrofoils May–Oct, down to 1 or 2 weekly in mid-winter; 1hr 15min). $26 one-way (includes Turkish tax), open return $42 (plus $10 Turkish port tax and $10 Greek port tax). Also weekly car ferries (May–Oct 2hr), at slightly cheaper prices. Small car $150.

Ferries to Italy

Çeşme–Ancona (mid-June to late-Sept, weekly on Topaş, usually Wed; 65hr). $185 single ($20 port tax). Small car $185 ($30 port tax).
Çeşme–Brindisi (mid-June to mid-Sept 2 weekly on TML; late June to mid-Sept 2 weekly on Med

Link Lines; 31hr). Sample one-way fares are $138 per passenger for a middling cabin, including taxes and meals, plus $123 for a small car.
İzmir–Venice (at least 1 weekly, usually Wed, & bi-weekly in Dec, on TML; 67hr). Sample one-way fares: approx $200 per passenger; around $230 for a small car.

Flights

Bodrum (Milas) to: İstanbul (summer 4–5 daily; winter 10 weekly); Antalya (1 daily).
Denizli (Çardak Airport) to: İstanbul (1 daily).
İzmir to: Ankara (5 daily); Antalya (6 daily); Dalaman (1 weekly; 1hr); İstanbul (5 daily).

The Turquoise Coast

CHAPTER 5 # Highlights

✳ **Kaya Köyü** This abandoned Greek Orthodox village near Fethiye is a moving relic of the population exchange of 1923. See p.457

✳ **Paragliding at Ölüdeniz** A thrilling (if pricey) way of appreciating the stunning lagoon and beach. See p.462

✳ **The Lycian Way** The long-distance trail – passing spectacular coves, ruins and mountain wilderness – makes an ideal off-season activity. See p.464

✳ **Dalyan** A laid-back resort where the pace is dictated by the river, which links it with thermal springs, ancient ruins and a long beach. See p.469

✳ **Tlos** Perhaps the most dramatically sited of the numerous ancient cities of Lycia. See p.476

✳ **Patara** Ancient ruins enhanced by an enormous sandy beach, one of the longest in the Mediterranean. See p.487

✳ **Kaş** Opposite the Greek islet of Kastellórizo, this is one of the most congenial resorts on the coast, with some of the best scuba-diving in the Med. See p.494

✳ **Kekova** The eerie seascapes and submerged ruins of the inlet system make an ideal sea-kayaking venue. See p.507

The Turquoise Coast

urkey's southwesternmost shore is dominated by the Baba, Akdağ and Bey ranges of the Toros mountains, which drop precipitously to a road running mostly parallel to the sea, its curves sometimes skimming just above the water; this is the **Turquoise Coast**, noted for its fine beaches and beautiful scenery. Here, and some distance inland, lay the ancient kingdom of **Lycia**, peopled by an independent race who bequeathed a legacy of distinctive rock tombs to Turkish tourism.

Until the late 1970s there was no continuous paved road through these parts, and most seaside settlements were reachable only by boat. Many of the most attractive bays and islands are still inaccessible to vehicular traffic, with yachting accordingly popular. But roads in the area have been vastly improved in recent years, penetrating to hitherto idyllic, isolated bays such as Kekova, Adrasan and Çıralı. However, there's a chance that the impact of large-scale development will be minimized by official decrees – certainly, the height of new buildings has been restricted, nearby archeological sites and wildlife habitats often prompt special protection measures, and touting in the streets and at *otogar*s is not yet at the level of Kuşadası, Selçuk or Pamukkale. And the increased overland accessibility is a blessing if you're reliant on public transport rather than a yacht.

The usually excellent **Highway 400** runs from Marmaris to Antalya, linking most of the major sights along the way, and offering occasional panoramic views. A bypass between Göcek and Patara has diverted traffic away from intervening villages and shaved the travel time between Fethiye and Patara to about an hour, though petrol stations are not yet common on this stretch. Arrival on the Turquoise Coast is typically at **Dalaman airport** (in preference to Antalya), to which there are regular direct international flights from April to November, as well as domestic flights from İstanbul.

At the far west of the region, **Dalyan** is renowned for its sandy beach – a breeding ground of loggerhead turtles – as well as being an attractive small resort with a bit more than lip-service paid to preserving the profile of the area. It's also an excellent base for visiting nearby **Köyceğiz Gölü** and the ruins of **Kaunos**. East of here **Fethiye** is the Turquoise Coast's most central resort and, along with the nearby lagoon of **Ölüdeniz**, well placed for visiting some of the best of the area's numerous and spectacularly sited Lycian ruins. **Oenoanda**, **Pınara**, **Tlos** and **Sidyma** lie close to Fethiye in dramatic mountainous locations, while further southeast **Patara** abuts one of Turkey's best beaches, making it easy to combine a sea-and-sun holiday with cultural forays to the **Letoön** sanctuary and **Xanthos**. Other convenient bases for outings are the resorts of **Kalkan** and **Kaş** to the east, both far smaller than Fethiye and pitched at slightly different clientele.

To the east, **Finike** is the next major town; although far less successful than Fethiye as a tourist centre, it still makes a good starting point for a precipitous inland route that takes in the sites of **Limyra** and **Arykanda** on the way up to the high plateau of **Elmalı**. The rarefied air and marvellous setting repay the trip, especially if a return loop to the coast is made via **Gömbe**, jump-off point for the alpine attractions of **Akdağ**.

Beyond Finike, the scenery becomes increasingly spectacular as you enter a densely forested area on the slopes of **Tahtalı Dağ**, officially designated a national park, before passing the sites of ancient **Olympos** – set close to more good beaches at **Adrasan** and **Çıralı** – and ancient **Phaselis**. Thereafter, however, a string of functional (not to say dreary) purpose-built resorts dominated by German holiday-makers lines the approach to Antalya and the Mediterranean Coast (see Chapter 6).

Some history

The mountainous, rugged territory of **Lycia** (Likya in Turkish) lies south of a line drawn roughly between Antalya and Köyceğiz Gölü. The peaks of the Bey Dağları and Akdağ, each exceeding 3000m in altitude, form the core of the region, and have always isolated it from the rest of Anatolia. Relatively secure in their mountain fastness, the Lycians – now thought to be an indigenous, pre-Hittite people rather than (as previous theories held) Cretan immigrants – hold a distinctive place in ancient Anatolian history. Their notoriously fierce desire for independence prompted the citizens of Xanthos on two separate occasions to make a funeral pyre of their own city and burn themselves alive, rather than be conquered. They also had their own language and customs: for example, Herodotus wrote that (unusually) "they reckon their lineage not by their father's but by their mother's side". The main ancient cities or conurbations of smaller towns organized themselves together against external authority as the **Lycian Federation**. This was a democratic grouping consisting of 23 voting units, charged with electing national officials and municipal authorities and, until control of Lycia was assumed by imperial Rome, making decisions of state. The Lycians are first mentioned in Homer's *Iliad*, in which they fought as allies of the Trojans. Later, in the sixth century BC, the region was subdued by the Persian general Harpagus, but was then largely left to govern itself.

From 454 BC, after the Athenian general Kimon had cleared all Persian garrisons from the Mediterranean coast, the Lycians became members of the Delian League, a maritime alliance that required them to pay tribute to Athens. The League ceased to exist after the Peloponnesian War ended in 404 BC and Lycia again fell under Persian domination, although this did not mean that it entirely accepted vassal status. Alexander the Great arrived in 333 BC and, after the conquest of Halicarnassus, secured the surrender of Lycia without further trouble; following his death Lycia was ruled by Alexander's general, Ptolemy, also king of Egypt. During **Ptolemaic rule** in the third century BC the native Lycian language was replaced by Greek and the cities adopted Greek constitutions. The Ptolemies were defeated by Antiochus III in 197 BC, who in turn was bested in 189BC by the Romans, who handed the kingdom over to the Rhodians. The Lycians bitterly resented Rhodian control and succeeded in 167 BC in having this administrative relegation revoked.

Thereafter, the Lycians enjoyed over two centuries of semi-independence, during which time their Federation came back into prominence, resisting attack once again by the Pontic (Black Sea) King Mithridates in 88 BC and being subsequently rewarded by Rome for their loyalty. During the Roman civil wars, Lycian reluctance to assist Brutus led to the destruction of Xanthos, and although Antony later reconfirmed the autonomy of Lycia, in 43 AD the region was joined to Pamphylia in a larger Roman province. **Roman imperial rule** was not unduly harsh. Indeed, the area reached its maximum ancient population of about 200,000, a figure not again equalled until the twentieth century, and the cities were graced by the Roman civic architecture that constitutes most of the ruins on view today.

During the fourth century the province was divided by Diocletian and a period of Byzantine-supervised decline set in, a process helped along by Arab raids in the seventh and eighth centuries. From this point on, the history of the region resembled that of the rest of western Anatolia, where, after the establishment of Selçuk Turk sovereignty during the eleventh and twelfth centuries, and an interlude of minor emirates, a more durable Anatolian Muslim state was installed by the **Ottomans**. They continued a pattern of moving nomadic Turkic tribes into the Lycian uplands, leaving the coast to pirates and local chieftains, until in the eighteenth century the sultan ordered its settlement by more tractable, productive Greek Orthodox colonists from the offshore islands.

Fethiye

FETHIYE is advantageously situated for visits to some of the Turquoise Coast's more fascinating sites and, although adjacent beaches are now much too crowded for comfort in season, the town itself still has qualities that set it apart from most other Mediterranean holiday centres. Fethiye remains a lively, Turkish-feeling market town of nearly 60,000, utterly unlike Marmaris, Bodrum or Kuşadası; in contrast to nearby Kaş, Fethiye has been able to spread north along the coastal plain here. The transport and marketing of oranges and tomatoes is on an equal footing with tourism, though chromium ore – is a major Fethiye-hinterland product – is no longer shipped from here but from nearby Göçek. Fethiye occupies the site of the ancient Lycian city of **Telmessos**, and some impressive rock tombs are an easy stroll from the centre, itself enlivened by a recently excavated Hellenistic theatre.

Fethiye also makes a convenient base for the nearby beaches at Çalış, Ölüdeniz and Kıdrak, while a short drive or long walk out of Fethiye brings you to the ghost village of Kaya Köyü – all destinations covered in "Around Fethiye" (p.455). There's also a good supply of rugged, boat-accessible, local coastline; the **Gulf of Fethiye** is speckled with twelve islands, and a favourite strategy is to embark on a one-to-four-day boat tour from Fethiye harbour, in search of secluded coves in which to swim, fish and anchor for the night.

Some history

Nothing much is known of the **origins of Telmessos**, except that it wasn't originally part of the Lycian Federation; indeed, in the fourth century BC the Telmessans actually fought against the Lycians. It may be that Pericles, a Lycian dynast, subsequently subdued the Telmessans and allowed them into the Federation – Lycian inscriptions have been found in the city, and it is known that during the Roman imperial era the city was part of the Federation, if unique in having good relations with Rhodes.

Like most Lycian cities, Telmessos was captured by Alexander in 334–333 BC, but lost not long after. The city was recaptured by one of Alexander's companions by a famous ruse: Nearchus the Cretan asked permission to leave a number of captive women musicians and boys in Telmessos, but the women concealed weapons in their musical instrument cases, and the prisoners' escort used them to seize the acropolis. In the eighth century, the city's name was changed to **Anastasiopolis** in honour of a Byzantine emperor. This name gave way to **Makri** in the following century (Meğri in Turkish), and – after the expulsion of the predominantly Greek Orthodox population – became Fethiye during the 1930s, in honour of a local pilot and war hero named **Fethi Bey**. Uniquely on the south Turkish coast, a small local Jewish community remained here undisturbed well into Republican times, though they had mostly died out or emigrated to Israel by the 1950s. Hardly anything now remains of the ancient or medieval city, partly because it suffered two immense **earthquakes** in 1857 and 1957, which toppled much of the town – whose rubble lies compacted under the present quay and shoreline boulevard.

Arrival, transport and information

The **otogar** is over 2km east of the town centre at the junction with the Ölüdeniz road. Short-haul **dolmuşes** run almost constantly from here as far as the popular accommodation district of Karagözler, sparing you the necessity of a three-kilometre-plus walk, or shelling out for a taxi. Other dolmuşes to Ölüdeniz, Göcek, Saklıkent, Çalış beach and Kaya arrive at and leave from underneath wooden marquees at the **minibus garage**, about 500m east of the central market area, south of Çarşı Caddesi on 136 Sokağı. The main **taxi ranks** are found near the PTT, and beside şehit Fethi Bey Parkı, in front of the ancient amphitheatre. Seasonal **hydrofoils** to Rhodes dock at the main marina jetty, while **dolmuş boats** link Fethiye and Çalış regularly in season (daily 9.30am–midnight; $0.85), departing from the seafront behind the *Belediye*.

Driving your own vehicle, you're forced to adhere to what is in effect a one-way system: westbound on **Atatürk Caddesi**, the main road leading toward the harbour, lined with most services and official buildings, and eastbound mostly along inland **Çarşı Caddesi**, which threads through the heart of the commercial district. **Parking** can be nightmarish, so you'll probably want to patronize the handful of fee-paying *otopark*s rather than risk being towed.

The **tourist office** (May–Sept daily 8am–noon & 1–7pm; Oct–April Mon–Fri 8.30am–noon & 1–5.30pm; ☏0252/614 1527), near the harbour at ıskele Meydanı 1, is, alas, next to useless.

Accommodation

Fethiye has an abundance of lodging for all tastes and budgets, so unlike in other coastal resorts, you *will* eventually find something – even in high summer – though perhaps after considerable trudging or phoning around. Unless otherwise stated, recommended accommodation is open (or claims to be open) all year round.

Divided into Birinci (First) and İkinci (Second) **Karagözler**, this desirable and quiet neighbourhood is home to the oldest enclave of hotels and *pansiyon*s in Fethiye, with most premises enjoying a view of the bay. The only drawback is that it's a fair distance west of the transport terminals and restaurants, though parking your own vehicle is no problem. Fethiye's **bazaar area**, extending roughly two blocks to either side of Çarşı Caddesi, can be noisy, especially when competing sound systems from assorted bars and clubs raise a din; accordingly there are very few accommodation options left hereabouts. A few paces toward the **water**, and then north along the shoreline of **Dolgu Sahası** district, are some quieter, more expensive choices.

Hydrofoil to Rhodes (Greece)

FETHİYE

RESTAURANTS

Liman	A
Meğri I	H
Meğri II	G
Mutfak	D
Nefis Pide	E
Özlemızgara	F
Şamdan	C
Sedir	C
Yelken	B

HOTELS AND PANSIYONS

Atapark	14
Çetin	3
Farah	15
Fethiye	16
Horizon	12
Ideal	10
Kemal	6
Köln	1
Mara	5
Mer	2
Plaza	7
Savaşçı	11
Sesa Park	4
Telmessos	17
Yacht	8
Yeni Yacht	9
Yeşilçam	13

BARS

Car Cemetery	a
Ottoman Bar	b
Türkü Evi	c
Yasmin	d

0   100 m

Kaya Köyü

Karagözler

Atapark Hotel Shore road, İkinci Karagözler ☎0252/612 4081, ⓦwww.atahotels.com. Considered the best hotel in town, with hamam, fitness centre, restaurant, small pool and internet café, though only the larger, pastel-coloured sea-view rooms are worth the money. ❺

Ferah Pansiyon Ordu Cad 21, İkinci Karagözler ☎0252/614 2816, ⓕ612 7398. Part of a chain of Turkish backpackers' hostels, with dorm beds ($6), basic double rooms, roof terrace, small pool and hamam. There's a sea view, despite its location one block inland. ❷

Fethiye Hotel Ordu Cad 16, İkinci Karagözler ☎0252/614 6813, ⓕ614 3663. Fairly comfort-able, small hotel with bay views and a large pool-garden, though it's dominated by tour companies most seasons. ❹

Horizon Hotel On the back road to Kaya, Birinci Karagözler ☎0252/612 3153, ⓕ612 3154. Small, slightly odd hotel (there are portholes instead of windows in the rooms), but well renovated in mar-ble and pastel trim, with all-new bathrooms, TV and air-con fitted throughout. A small pool and rooftop bar-restaurant clinch the deal. ❸

Ideal Pension Zafer Cad 1, Birinci Karagözler

℡0252/614 1981, ⓦwww.idealpension.net. A quiet, well-sited budget outfit, whose small, basic en-suite rooms have carpets and balconies, and double beds for couples. A roof terrace serving Western-style breakfasts, an on-site laundry and internet service, plus friendly family management, complete the profile. Per-person charges $6.50, or $10 half-board (reduced to $7.50 Dec–March). **Savaşcı Pansiyon** (aka *Feridun's Place*) On the back road to Kaya, Birinci Karagözler ℡0252/614 6681 or 614 4108. This perennial favourite with backpackers has well-worn facilities, but compensates with a rooftop breakfast-terrace, good views

and hospitable management. **①**

Telmessos Pansiyon Shore road, İkinci Karagözler ℡0252/614 1042. A 1970s-vintage building, right opposite the *jandarma* post, with somewhat small rooms, but comfortable enough. It's run by an elderly couple whose daughter, a travel agent, is a mine of good advice. **②**

Yacht Hotel Opposite the yacht marina, Birinci Karagözler ℡0252/614 1530, ⓕ614 5354. Rooms decorated in pleasant pastels, featuring new bathrooms, though it's still only worth the money if you can score a sea-view unit (about two-thirds of the rooms). Small pool with bar-restaurant, and a 15-percent discount for no-view rooms. ❸

Yeni Yacht (Yacht Plaza) Hotel Opposite the yacht marina, Birinci Karagözler ☎0252/612 5067, ⓦwww.yachtplazahotel.com. The closest thing in Fethiye to a self-contained seaside resort, with its private jetty, lush bay-side breakfast garden and fair-sized pool. Rooms are plainer than the common areas, but perfectly serviceable. ❹

Yeşilçam Pansiyon Above yacht harbour on hillside, Birinci Karagözler ☎0252/612 3518, ⓔyesilcampension@hotmail.com. Tottering 1970s building with fairly garish en-suite rooms in various sizes, and rather sullenly staffed by Turkish "Generation X" types. The steep, rickety entrance stairs, not for the drunk or acrophobic, end at a panoramic roof terrace. All that said, still a good-value budget choice. ❶

The bazaar and waterfront

Çetin Pansiyon 510 Sokağı, Dolgu Sahası ☎0252/614 6156, ⓕ614 7794. Oblique sea views and a ground-floor terrace-bar at this welcoming *pansiyon*, run by brothers Şaban and Ramazan, more or less opposite the DSİ (Water Board) building. Rooms without breakfast or air-con are a category cheaper. ❷

Kemal Hotel Behind the PTT ☎0252/614 5010, ⓕ614 5009. Cheerful, air-conditioned rooms, many with sea views; doubles are small but balconied, suites larger but balcony-less. Excellent restaurant (see p.454) on ground floor. ❸

Köln Motel 534 Sok 1, off Sadi Pekin Cad, Dolgu Sahası ☎ & ⓕ0252/614 3373. Rooms with balconies in a well-kept building, with helpful, English-speaking management and rooftop terrace restaurant. The price is for half-board accommodation. ❹

Mara Hotel Kral Caddesi, Yalı Sok 2 ☎0252/614 6722, ⓕ614 8039. Comfortable, well-run, three-star outfit with swimming pool, air-conditioned rooms of good size, furnishings of high standard and tubs in all the bathrooms. That said, it's overpriced – bargain them down a category. ❻

Mer Pansiyon Akdeniz Cad, Dolgu Sahası ☎0252/614 1177. More modest than the nearby *Sesa Park*, but adequate rooms in a 1970s low-rise, with air-conditioning. ❷.

Plaza Hotel Corner Atatürk Cad and Çarşı Cad ☎0252/614 9030, ⓕ614 1070. Quite good fallback hotel, amenable to bargaining at slow times. Rooms have all mod-cons, including double glazing (essential for the noise downtown). ❸

Sesa Park Hotel Akdeniz Cad 17 ☎0252/614 4656, ⓕ614 4326. Well-run two-star waterside hotel, convenient for the museum, *otogar* and bazaar, with public parking out front. More the haunt of travelling salesmen than foreign tourists and under the same management as the excellent *Liman Restaurant*, a few steps away. ❸

The Town

The remains of ancient **Telmessos** are immediately obvious as soon as you arrive in Fethiye. Covering the hillside above the bazaar area are a number of Lycian rock tombs, striking in their proximity to the city and in the grandeur of their setting. Most notable – and worth a closer inspection, despite swarms of children who will offer to guide you there unnecessarily and then demand money – is the **Amyntas Tomb** (daily 8.30am–sunset; $2), so called because of the inscription *Amyntou tou Ermagiou* (Amyntas son of Hermagios) carved in Greek letters on the wall of the tomb. To get there, take any of the lanes leading south from Kaya Caddesi (cars can make it up), which give onto 115 Sokağı running along the base of the fenced-in archeological area. The tomb porch consists of two Ionic columns surmounted by a triangular pediment, carved in close imitation of a temple facade – even down to simulating the bronze nails with which the door frames were studded – giving an excellent impression of what the original wooden temple porches would have looked like. The tomb would have been entered through the bottom right-hand panel of the doorway, but this was broken by grave robbers long ago.

Behind the tourist office and main quay sprawls the conspicuous Hellenistic **theatre**, excavated only since 1994. Much of its masonry was carted away after the 1957 earthquake for construction material, so it's rather frayed at the edges. Benefit concerts are often staged here in season to help raise funds for a complete restoration of the stage building and seating, though the process is completely stalled at present.

There's not all that much else to see in Fethiye, although you can visit the remains of the medieval fortress, the so-called **Knight's Castle**, on the hillside behind the harbour area. The path to the castle leads off Çarşı Caddesi through backstreets up to the acropolis, affording good views of the town on the way. The fortress is attributed to the Knights of St John, but a variety of architectural styles suggests additional work on the part of Lycians, Greeks, Romans, Byzantines and Turks. The Gypsy shantytown formerly built around the walls has been cleared to make way for a future park, whilst the walls themselves will be restored if an EU grant materializes.

In the centre of town, off Atatürk Caddesi, Fethiye's **museum** (Tues–Sun 8.30am–5pm; $0.70) is poorly labelled and very small, but some of the exhibits help to enhance nearby archeological sites by contributing an element of human interest. The most compelling exhibit is the stele found at the Letoön (see p.482), dating from 358 BC, which was critically important in deciphering the Lycian language. This stone slab is covered in a trilingual text in Lycian, Greek and Aramaic concerning a sanctuary in Xanthos dedicated to the mythical god-king, Kaunos, supposed founder of the city of that name. Other finds include a beautiful gold-leaf headdress dating from the third century BC, unearthed at the site of Pınara.

Finally, a huge stele – or rather nocturnally illuminated **obelisk** – of a different sort dominates waterfront Uğur Mumcu Parkı. A pet project of the MHP (nationalist)-run municipality, it was erected in 2001 to honour locals killed during the long-running PKK insurrection. Local outcry converted it to a general servicemen's memorial for all recent conflicts.

Boat tours and cruises

The standard-issue, multi-island, one-day **boat tours** cost about $10 a head and are well promoted at the quayside. Departures are daily between May and October, usually leaving at around 10am and returning at 6pm; just turn up at

---

Scuba-diving at Fethiye

After severe over-hyping of the sport during the early 1990s, when fourteen dive schools competed here, reality has prevailed and there remain just a handful of bona fide **scuba-diving operators** in Fethiye. Despite optimistic brochure promotion, there are few if any fish to be found in local waters; ruthless over-fishing with dynamite and drag-nets has seen to that. What the gulf *can* offer is reasonable visibility, coral and other invertebrates, walls and rock formations, and submerged ruins, artefacts and caves.

Prices for trips and courses are usually quoted locally in sterling. Most long-lived of local companies is British-run **European Diving Center** (℡0252/614 9718, ⓦwww.europeandiving.com.tr), with premises at Atatürk Cad 6–8/A. However, their two-dive days are fairly pricey at £45 (PADI 5-day courses are £265, CMAS two-star £275) and there have been persistent reports of large group sizes and a generally impersonal approach. **Diver's Delight**, Dispanser Sok 25, Cumhuriyet Mahallesi, near the Liman Restaurant (℡0252/612 1099, ⓦwww.diversdelight.com) is currently more service-oriented, with two-dive day rates starting at £39, and PADI five-day courses for £235, and CMAS two-star certification for £230.

A one- or two-week **live-aboard charter** will allow you to dive at seldom-visited, less spoiled sites well beyond the picked-over confines of Fethiye Bay. For these, Axel Lipke's *M/S Sharazan* (℡532/246 9509 or 0252/614 1676, ⓦwww.sharazan .com) comes recommended.

the quayside. However, the one-day trips tend to be rushed, taking in a set repertoire of relatively spoilt islands, with little time at each. It's far better to rent your own boat and crew to take in just one or two selected islands, or sign on for one of the so-called "**cabin cruises**" which depart every other day in season. Recommended boats, popular with backpackers, include the *Murat II* and *Pınar 3*, both of which offer three-day cruises through the "Twelve Islands" of the Fethiye Gulf to Göcek, and back; allow for $75–100 per head, including full board, depending on season – contact Garfield Tourism on Fevzi Çakmak Caddesi, opposite the marina (☎0252/614 9312, ⓦwww.fethiye-achting.com). A similar, five-cabin craft is operated by V-Go, almost adjacent opposite the yacht marina (☎0252/612 2113, ⓦwww.boatcruiseturkey.com). This runs a four-day cruise east, with overnights at Gemile Adası, Kalkan and Kekova before a final minibus shuttle from Demre to the treehouse lodges at Olympos (see p.523); typical cost is $135.

Eating

Especially compared to unadulterated resorts such as Dalyan and Göcek, the eating situation in Fethiye is quite satisfactory. The main thing to watch out for is the oft-used ploy of bringing you, or charging you for, items you haven't ordered – check bills carefully. Fethiye is well supplied with *pideci*s, each with their partisans, while for a tasty blowout (by Fethiye standards), head towards Uğur Mumcu Parkı, at the east end of the waterfront, where two rival eateries specialize in fish.

Liman Uğur Mumcu Parkı. The newest (and arguably best) in-town restaurant, on the far side of the park. From the open-plan kitchen issues artistically garnished grilled meat and palpably fresh fish, mostly un-farmed; a top-drawer wine list and polished service complete the picture. Expect to pay $13 a head in a group.

Meğri Lokantası Çarşı Cad 13, also Likya Sok 8–9. The long-running doyen of Fethiye eateries has two licensed branches: 24-hour premises at Çarşı Cad, best at lunchtime and specializing in home-style Turkish dishes you'll see nowhere else, plus lovely puddings; and a more blatantly tourist-oriented and expensive outlet at Likya Sok, where service can be haphazard but the food is still tasty.

Mutfak Cumhuriyet Cad. Tiny, very friendly stall-premises (the name means "Kitchen"), mobbed at lunch thanks to its limited but inexpensive selec-

tion of fast-food snacks, including *mantı* and *tantani kebap* (diced meat in a roll of *dürüm* pita).

Nefis Pide Eski Cami Sok 9. Eat at outdoor tables beside the mosque – three courses with non-alcoholic drink won't exceed $5, and they also offer a range of excellent cheap kebabs and meat dishes.

Özlem Izgara & Pide Çarşı Cad, opposite 96 Sokağı. The oldest and one of the more reliable *pideci*s, where a couple of bucks gets you somewhat more limited fare than at *Nefis*.

Sedir Tütün Sok 3. A good range of grills, *hazır yemek* and puddings; the adjacent Şamdan has similar fare.

Yelken Ground floor, *Kemal Hotel*, behind the PTT. Justifiably popular with locals, especially during the off-season. Two *meze*s per person and a fish main course, with a modest intake of drink, is yours for about $18 per couple.

Drinking and nightlife

There are plenty of outdoor **drinking venues** between Atatürk and Çarşı caddesis, as well as further west along and above the waterfront. A long-lived favourite is the always busy *Car Cemetery Bar* at the south end of Hamam Sokağı. Nearby on Karagözler Sokağı, the *Ottoman Bar* offer *nargile*s (hookahs) for toking as well as drinks and dancing. Up on the hillside above the theatre – itself an occasional venue for live spectacles – state-of-the art Yasmin sometimes has live **Turkish music**. If you're after authentic Turkish folk performances Türkü Evi, above the *Efes Pub* on Çarşı Caddesi, is the place to go; it runs until 3am and thus far has a largely local clientele.

Listings

Airline THY, c/o Fetur, opposite the yacht marina, ☎0252/614 2034, next to Hi-Car; the agency also runs a service bus to Dalaman airport ($6.50).
Banks and exchange Beware souvenir shops and storefronts that promise cash advances on credit cards – short-changing is common. Stick to the usual venues, such as the PTT, banks and *döviz* dealers – four of five of the latter near the market square, including Dikmen at Atatürk Cad, Belediye İşhanı 21. ATMs that accept foreign cards include those of Yapı Kredi, Koçbank, Garanti and Akbank, all within a few yards of each other at the west end of Atatürk Cad.
Books Imagine, Atatürk Cad 18/B, which lately has as much or more of a stock of very mainstream cassettes and CDs – Richard Clayderman, Bon Jovi, Madonna and the like.
Car rental Active, next to the theatre ☎0252/612 3525; Europcar, Atatürk Cad 40, ☎0252/614 4995; Hi-Car, at the yacht marina ☎0252/614 7434; Intercity, Atatürk Cad 106/B ☎0252/612 2281; Light Tours, Atatürk Cad 104 ☎0252/614 7161; Sixt, Hillside Club Resort, ☎0252/614 7593;Telmessos, Dispanser Sok 24/A ☎0252/614 6223, ⓦ www.telmessos.com.
Hamam At Hamam Sok 2 (daily 7am–midnight; $9); lukewarm, overpriced and touristy, this is not a particularly good introduction to Turkish baths.
Hydrofoil From May to October, hydrofoils run two or three selected days of the week (typically Wed & Fri) directly to Rhodes in Greece (journey time 1hr 30min). For schedules and ticket prices see "Travel details" at the end of this chapter, and contact designated agent Lib Tour (see below).
Internet Most central internet cafés are Inn-ter-net, Atatürk Cad 18/C, and Line Bilgisayar, on 500 Sok, near the *Mara Hotel*.
Laundries Several on Fevzi Çakmak Cad, opposite the yacht marina.
Motorbike rental Abalı ☎0252/614 1597, just behind the theatre roundabout, rents out four or five different motorbike models.
Post office Main PTT is on Atatürk Cad (Mon–Sat 8am–midnight, Sun 9am–7pm).
Shopping Fethiye is excellent for shopping, with a marvellous food market located between Çarşı Cad and Tütün Sok in the centre of town – also plenty of fake Calvin Klein jeans, Chanel scent and a few pickpockets. Main market day is Tuesday, when villagers from surrounding districts flood into town with their produce; peak hours 10.30am–1pm. The place to hunt for carpets, leather and silver is Paspatur district, especially to either side of Hamam Sokağı. Supermarket chains Tansas and Migros have small branches just inland from Atatürk Caddesi, near the PTT.
Travel agents Light Tours, Atatürk Cad 104 (☎0252/614 4757), plus a branch at the yacht marina, handling "Blue Cruises" and jeep safaris; Lib Tour, Fevzi Çakmak Cad 19/A (☎0252/612 1981), is the cheapest outlet for hydrofoil tickets to Rhodes.

Around Fethiye

Easily reached on a day trip from town are a variety of attractions: an ancient Lycian city (**Kadyanda**) recently opened to tourism, the huge abandoned village of **Kaya Köyü**, and a handful of popular if variable beaches, ranging from long **Çalış** to tiny **Gemiler**. Most of them are well connected by public transport in season, and some can even be reached on foot from Fethiye.

Kadyanda

Under an hour's drive north of Fethiye, the ruined mountain-top city of **Kadyanda** dates back at least 2500 years, but has only seen tourists for the last decade or so. It's accessible on a broad, well-marked road from a roundabout on the new highway, northeast of Fethiye, and the initial, paved 16km to **ÜZÜMLÜ** village (served by sparse public transport) are quickly covered. This attractive village has so far made little of its proximity to the ruins, other than an acceptable **restaurant** opposite the mosque. At the crossroads here, turn left at the usual black-on-yellow sign, then proceed 3.5km more on a narrow paved road to just beyond the summit of a pass with a view of Akdağ. Now bear right, following another "Kadyanda" sign, to negotiate well over 5km of

AROUND FETHİYE

widened, improved dirt track to a small car park in the pines below the site. With local assistance you might be able to find the old direct **path from Üzümlü** (1hr-plus), which shortcuts all but the last 2km of the road and goes via some little-visited rock tombs.

At **the site** (unfenced, always open; $2 if warden present), an arrow points you to the start of a self-guided tour along a graded loop path. First you bear south, past numerous vaulted tombs of the **necropolis**, then close to presumed bits of the city wall on the left, followed by a climb to a false summit with a long, partly preserved **agora**, and the first views of Fethiye.

At the true top of things, matters fall into place with the highlight of the site: a long, narrow **stadium**, with seven rows of its seats surviving. Steps in the seats lead up to a huge jumble of masonry, all that's left of a **temple** to an unknown deity. On the opposite side of the stadium stand the substantial **Roman baths**, with their polygonal masonry and entry archway. At the northeast edge of the stadium, a flat expanse is pierced by the mouth of a deep cistern that supplied the city with rainwater – one of many, so beware holes in the ground.

Finally the path angles south to the best-preserved stretch of **city wall**, punctuated by windows and affording incomparable views of the mountains on the horizon and the forested valleys in between. Crossing the top of a square bastion, you look down into the **theatre**, which retains its rear facing and stage wall (doubling as part of the city fortification), plus many of its seats – though like most of the site it's only partly excavated. The descent to the road completes a leisurely 45-minute walk through superb mountain scenery – good reason alone for a visit.

Çalış beach

If you're here specifically for a beach holiday, **Çalış**, some 5km north of central Fethiye, might do the trick. There's a direct road there from town along the coast, as well as boat dolmuşes, though ordinary dolmuşes arrive there in a roundabout way from the main highway via Günlükbaşı suburb. Their final stop is way at the north end, near the *Seril* hotel; the Çalış esplanade itself is off-limits for cars. The gravelly sand of Çalış extends for 2km, with views over the bay islets to the sunset, but it's prone to pummelling in summer from wind and waves, making the water very murky when not downright filthy.

Çalış itself is essentially a tourist ghetto of leather shops, mini-markets, mediocre restaurants and downmarket hotels, overrun in season by a somewhat elderly British and Dutch clientele, who often subsequently return to buy retirement homes here. The navigable channels and marshes just inland are picturesque but breed swarms of mosquitoes. There's almost no **accommodation** here that isn't monopolized by tour operators: exceptions include *Fiesta*, about 200m inland from the central junction at Çalış (☎0252/613 2871; ❺), which compensates for its location by providing attentive service and a pool; and the *Kumsal Pansiyon*, right at the central junction (☎0252/613 1265; ❸), somewhat noisily situated above two bars, whose basic, tile-floored rooms do have balconies. A quieter beachside option, but still too modest to appeal to tour operators, is the *Aytur* (☎0252/622 1177; ❹).

Kaya Köyü

The deserted settlement of **KAYA KOYU**, the largest late-medieval ghost town in Asia Minor, is located on the side of a hill southwest of Fethiye, near the site of ancient Karmylassos. It was known as **Levissi** after the eighteenth century, when it was settled by Greek Orthodox Christians from the Dodecanese islands just offshore; the present appellation is taken from the rather inappropriately named Kaya Çukuru or "Stone Gulch", the small but fertile adjacent upland (altitude 200m) that partly supported a local population of over 6000 before 1923, and still produces substantial crops of tobacco and grain – and, after autumn or spring rainstorms, spectacular mass migrations of toads.

The place has been abandoned since then, when its Christian inhabitants were exiled, along with more than a million others, to a country that had never been their homeland. Kaya is one of the most dramatic and moving sites on the Turkish coast, and puts into painful relief the human suffering involved in the compulsory **population exchange**. Despite the horrors of the 1919–1922 Greco–Turkish war, relations between Christian and Muslim remained good hereabouts, with local "Turks" accompanying the "Greeks" to the dock at Fethiye to bid them farewell. Tales still circulate of the Greeks having entrusted their neighbours with treasure chests against their possible return; of course they never did come back, but the caskets remain unopened. Macedonian Muslims were sent here to occupy the abandoned buildings but, for the most part, they didn't stay, considering the land poor in comparison to Macedonia and emigrating to points as far-flung as Australia instead. In any event, most locals currently live in the hamlets of Keçiler and Kınalı, at the far fringes of the Kaya Çukuru plateau, overlooked by the ruins.

All you can see now of Kaya is a hillside covered with almost a thousand ruined dwellings and the attractive **Panayia Pyrgiotissa** basilica, the most important of three churches here, to the right of the main path, about 200m up the gentle slope from the road. The church, dated 1888 by a floor mosaic, retains some of its marble altar screen and murals, including faces of Christ and the apostles over the altar, but the general state of dereliction merely serves to highlight the plight of the village. A particularly grisly item in the southwest corner of the church precinct is the **charnel house**, piled high with human leg bones; the departing Greeks took the exhumed skulls of their ancestors away with them.

As with most other remote, abandoned Greek villages, proper title deeds for individual Kaya properties were never issued by the Republican Turkish government. In 1988, mass acquisition of the village houses for package-holiday accommodation was threatened, though development plans have been withdrawn and a preservation order slapped on the valley to protect it. Nowadays, only five percent of agricultural land area may be built on and only archeologically approved restoration – including, potentially, two of the churches – is allowed. The old village remains the focus of Greco–Turkish **reconciliation festivals**, with its Greek diaspora visiting regularly from Greece; Orthodox Patriarch Vartholomeos himself stayed here at the start of the new millennium.

Practicalities

A paved seven-kilometre road – plus a much shorter cobbled **path**, still two-thirds intact, which vastly shortcuts it – climb up from behind the castle in Fethiye towards Kaya Köyü. By **dolmuş** from the main terminal, however, it's a fifteen-kilometre journey, taking a roundabout route via the twin resorts of Ovacık and Hisarönü, whose tendrils end around 4km to the east of the village. You can easily continue on foot **from Kaya Köyü to Ölüdeniz**; see the box on p.463 for directions.

There are a number of **accommodation** choices at the edge of the village or slightly beyond. Cheapest is the simple *Selçuk* (☎0252/618 0075; ❷), south of the mini-roundabout beside the central teahouse. Some 500m along the road to Kınalı, in lovely grassy grounds, you'll find *Villa Rhapsody* (☎0252/618 0042 or 618 0049, ⓦwww.villarhapsody.com; closed Dec-April; ❹), where the starkness of the variably sized rooms is softened by pale carpets. There's also English-speaking management, and a bar-restaurant around the large pool. Between these two stands *Les Jardins de Levissi* (☎0252/618 0188, ⓦwww .lesjardinsdelevissi.com; ❺), offering four suite-like rooms in a restored stone house, with an annexe under construction; the French–Turkish management provides evening meals on request.

With more advance planning, the best of several local restoration projects is Jon and Niki Bowker's *Kaya Cottages* (☎0252/618 0168 or 0533/513 5117, ⓦwww.kayacottages.com; closed Jan & Feb), in **Kınalı** hamlet, 2km west of Kaya Köyü, where six old houses have been exquisitely refurbished with many original features preserved. Although these units are contracted exclusively to UK package companies from April to September, from October to May they're available to all-comers by the night (**❺**) or by the week (£220). The Bowkers also manage the local croquet club (open Wed to the public), offer **guided walks** across the entire Kaya peninsula, and helped to prepare the 1:25,000 sketch map of the area provided free locally.

Central Kaya has about a dozen **cafés** and simple **restaurants**, many strategically straddling the paths into the ruined town, but none are particularly memorable. *Bülent'in Yeri*, on the through-road near the colonnaded cistern, is all right for a quick snack of *saç böreği*. For a superlative, not-for-the-squeamish carniverous feed (plus limited *mezes*), head for *Cin Bal* (closed Dec–Feb), well-signposted at the east edge of the village, where whole hung sheep form much of the indoor decor; seating is in the attractive outdoor garden. This is a *kendin pişin kendin ye* place, where you buy your meat by weight and then cook it yourself at a tableside barbeque. Incidentally, the name ("Honey Gin") comes from the late founder's variety of bootleg hooch. A good nearby alternative, with more indoor seating and thus open through the year, is *Oba Kebap Evi*, where a meal of *tandır kebap*, trimmings and copious drink will run to about $7.50 a head in a group. *Deniz Kuşu*, the remotest building in Kınalı (look for the kitsch seagull statue and the roadside wooden dining-kiosk) does superb fresh fish, as owner Tahir dives for them himself or gets a supply from his relatives. Wild boar, chips, salad and a full wine list complete the menu, and there's a sister restaurant on Göbün Adası out in the Gulf of Fethiye.

Af Kule, Gemiler and Aya Nikola

The *Deniz Kuşu* stands just north of the turning west for the isolated ruined monastery of **Af Kule**; the sign says "800m" but it's more like 1km to the road's end, where you bear up and right onto the broad, obvious donkey track. Alternating blue paint arrows and red dots encourage you on the climb west-northwest until you top a ridge, 25 minutes from the Gemiler-bound road, and then plunge down five minutes more in zig-zags to the roofless but otherwise intact monastery on its terrace, overawed by a cliff. Wedged into this are a couple of chapels; stone steps lead to the higher hermitage, which though now without any frescoes is well worth the ascent.

Isolated **Gemiler** beach lies 8km southwest of Kaya Köyü along a well-marked dirt-surface track, not served by any public transport. Despite what you may read elsewhere, it is not possible to walk directly from Kaya to Gemiler – the intervening terrain is steep and dangerous. Instead, you first proceed past Kınalı, and then use the paint-blob-marked trail down from the top of the gully, 200m past the point where the road starts its descent.

After repeated skirmishes throughout the 1990s between the police, forest service and would-be developers, the only amenities remaining at Gemiler are half a dozen semi-legal shack **snack-bars** – none of them up to more than *gözleme* and soft drinks except for genial Robinson's. This, the leftmost as you face the sea, does fresh, cheap fish and salads, and is the most likely to survive as proprietor Ahmet Cafer actually has proper title to his land. The beach itself (not always clean) is divided up by small jetties and sun-bed concessions; the water can be murky, but offers decent snorkelling in autumn

Just offshore at Gemiler looms a prime destination of local boat trips: **Aya Nikola (Gemile) Adası** ($2 admission if warden present), an island and yacht anchorage on which stand prominent remains of several eras, including a few rock tombs, a seventh-century Byzantine monastery and a later, ruined hamlet complete with a nineteenth-century church. The island's environs, along with Ölüdeniz, were used in the late 1990s as the location for a satellite-TV-movie version of *The Odyssey*, with Greta

Scacchi for star appeal. Without a boat, all you can do is walk from Kaya Köyü to the bay of Soğuk Su directly opposite Gemile island, over the obvious saddle with the little white chapel, in about forty minutes – see p.463 for more walk directions.

Ocakköy, Ovacık and Hisarönü

More or less due south of Fethiye are a string of resorts that, despite inland settings, now get the lion's share of tourist overnights in the Fethiye area. **Ocakköy** has some claims to architectural distinction, but **Ovacık** and **Hısarönü** are functional dormitories at best, with water in this arid environment pumped up a pipeline from the plain around Fethiye.

Ocakköy

The main road southeast out of Fethiye climbs to a pass, where a signposted dirt-track leads 2km west to an abandoned Ottoman shepherd's hamlet, **OCAKKÖY**, which served as the winter quarters for the village of Ovacık (see below). The ex-hamlet has metamorphosed into *Ocakköy* (☎0252/616 6157, ⓦwww.ocakkoey.com; closed late-Oct to April except winter hols), a development of some thirty individually styled, self-catering, restored stone cottages dotting the hillside, plus more conventional rooms or apartments set around three swimming pools. The cottages enjoy commanding views over the agricultural plain to Baba Dağı, the ancient Mount Antikragos, and make for a wonderfully peaceful stay, aside from the occasional disco-thump from Hisarönü. This is one of the few resorts in Turkey that actively caters for disabled clients, with wheelchair ramps and harness slings for lowering yourself into one of the pools, and it's also good for kids, as there's a crèche. Most units are available exclusively through Tapestry Holidays from early May to late-October, though the remaining few are available to walk-in guests (❻); the resort is open to all comers at Christmas and New Year, and whenever the major Turkish *bayram*s fall in winter.

Ovacık and Hisarönü

Just beyond the pass, the straggly, linear village of **OVACIK** seems to consist entirely of about a hundred *pansiyon*s and small hotels that have been largely snapped up by tour operators – surprisingly, in view of its inland, roadside location and the decidedly modest endowments of many of these establishments. Folk tend more to stay in Ovacık and do their partying in **HİSARÖNÜ**, which (with fifty or so more lodgings) nominally lies 1.5km along the side road to Kaya and Gemiler. Once a tiny hamlet, it has spread to be almost contiguous with Ovacık and now offers all the dubious delights of a landlocked concrete resort: pulsing sound systems, lanes pedestrianized by night, and a remarkable number of walk-in, 24-hour clinics with English-speaking staff for attending to those afflicted by "Turkey tummy" or who fell asleep drunk in the sun.

Some of the highest standard **accommodation** here, well south of the "seething" zone and thus calm, is at the four-star *Montana Pine Resort* (☎0252/616 7108, ⓦwww.montanapine.com; ❺; closed Dec-March). It's a sympathetically designed complex, with large rooms and good bathrooms (though the bedroom fittings are showing their age), one of the best breakfasts

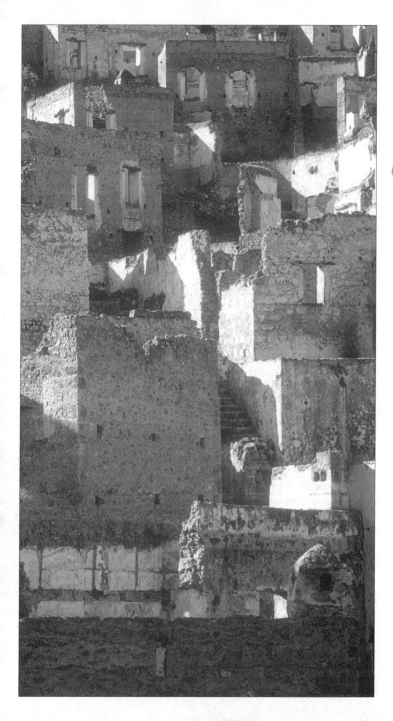

on the Turquoise Coast and no fewer than three pools. Just about the south-ernmost building here – catering to a vastly different market – is the *Sultan Motel* (☏0252/616 6261, ℻612 3998; ❷), built right at the start of the Lycian Way (see box p.464) and acting as a **lodge** to trekkers at the start or end of their journey; stone cottages are arrayed as twin, triple or dorms.

Given the quick-buck nature of the place, few **restaurants** stay in business more than a season, and the general profile is of bad, identikit places serving "steak & chips" priced in pounds, and bars with names such as *Delboy's* and *Hamish McTurk*. However, fairly safe recommendations for eating out include *Our Place*, a decent vegetarian restaurant near the eastern edge of the development, and *The Olive Tree*, at the western edge, for an approximation of Turkish fare. If you're staying at Kaya Köyü or Ölüdeniz (see below), Hisarönü's main utility is the presence of a free-standing bank **ATM**, and competitive **car rental** outlets: Explora (☏0252/616 6890) is particularly recommended for the good condition of its cars.

Ölüdeniz and beyond

ÖLÜDENIZ, 10km south of Fethiye, is the azure lagoon that features on every second Turkish travel poster. Its warm, if occasionally turbid, waters (dawn to dusk; $1 per person, $4 per car, for admission to the fenced "nation-al park") make for pleasant swimming even in April or May, or serve as a pro-tected venue for a spin in a rented kayak. However, the environs of this once-pristine lagoon, whose name translates as "Dead Sea" in Turkish, rank as one of the country's most popular resorts, and since the late 1980s its beaches – both the spit enclosing the inlet (mostly Turks) and the more exposed strand of **Belcekiz** (mostly foreigners) – reach saturation level on summer weekends. At such times, perhaps it's worth avoiding Ölüdeniz altogether in favour of the **Kıdrak** forest service beach (admission charged as above), 3km east of Belcekiz beside the ultra-posh *Club Lykia World* (German tours only). Kıdrak is cleaner and less commercialized than Belcekiz, with just a small snack bar and no sunbed/umbrella concessions.

Both Belcekiz and Kıdrak serve as landing-pads for **paragliders**, who are kit-ted out by several beachfront outfits for a hefty $90–105 and taken to a point near the summit of 1976-metre Baba Dağı for launching – best visibility is in autumn. Despite frankly inflated rates owing to road tolls that must be paid to the forest service, and some gruesome fatalities before stringent safety practices were implemented, the sport goes from strength to strength locally, as this is said to be the second best spot worldwide to indulge. Among the operators, Ölüdeniz Tandem Paragliding Centre (☏0536/315 5388) comes recommend-ed, though Sky Sports (☏0252/617 0511, ❂www.skysports-turkey.com) is the most heavily publicized outfit.

A more predictable repertoire of **boat trips** – to remote coves, islets and Byzantine ruins – is also on offer, though beware limp lunches, guide fatigue or stops missed out. The cheapest ($3; 2–3 daily dolmuş boats) and most pop-ular destination is the beach and limestone canyon just inland dubbed **Butterfly Valley** (Kelebek Vadisi in Turkish) after the many species that flutter about during the right seasons. At all times you'll see a waterfall ($0.70 admis-sion, 20min inland) and the beach itself, frequented by an uneasy mix of day-trippers and time-warped hippies staying in the primitive tree-house and indoor accommodation here.

Practicalities

By far the most attractive approach to Ölüdeniz is **on foot from Kaya Köyü** (see box below), though frequent **dolmuşes** (every 15min) make the trip here from Fethiye until late at night, a fifteen-minute journey. The dolmuşes drop you just behind the beach, between the *jandarma* post and the pedestrian promenade of Belcekiz.

A walk from from Kaya Köyü to Ölüdeniz

This mostly downhill walk takes you from Kaya village to the northwest shore of the lagoon in about an hour and a half, with another half-hour separating you from the dolmuş stop. The route begins in Kaya from the easterly Yukarı Kilise, and is fairly well marked by rust-red paint blobs; don't trust blue ones, nor those leading you over the pass with a windmill and chapel. The proper path climbs somewhat faintly to a plateau within fifteen minutes, then levels out through pine woods for another twenty minutes, before reaching fine overviews of Aya Nikola and Soğuk Su, and a stretch of well-engineered, cobbled, descending path. This ends at some charcoal-burners' flats, with a less distinct path to a large rectangular cistern just beyond, before the head of a ravine. Here the trail appears to split; the left-hand option is easier going. Just under an hour along both routes converge before you reach an obvious pass with some pine-studded rocks on the right, affording the first eye-full of the lagoon. From here you've an uncomplicated, if sharp, drop to the first umbrella-and-sunbed concession on the shore.

Accommodation

Most accommodation clusters behind the gentrified Belcekiz beach; the old car park has been transformed into a broad, landscaped promenade, and virtually all of the rough-and-ready **bungalow-campsites** that set up shop here for the hippie vanguard during the late 1970s have been swept aside by more permanent, lucrative developments. There are just two survivors: *Deniz Kamp* on the promenade (☎0252/617 0045, ⊛www.oludenizbeach.com; ❶), offering somewhat noise-plagued garden-shed-type accommodation, behind the attached *Buzz Grill Restaurant* with its upstairs *Buzz Bar* (also an internet café) and a travel agency; and the quieter *Oba* (☎0252/617 0470, Ⓔobamotel@superonline.com), about 300m directly inland, with a variety of better-standard budget accommodation – either plain cabins and a dormitory "treehouse" ($6 each) or en-suite chalets (❷), as well as internet facilities.

Tent/caravan **campsites** have been exiled to the north shore of the lagoon, where the *Ölüdeniz Camp* (☎0252/617 0048), 1km past the official day-use entrance to the lagoon, is the grassiest of several sites here, with its own little beach and restaurant, plus another dorm "treehouse" ($6) and bungalows (❷).

The nominally four-star *Hotel Meri* (☎0252/617 0001, ⊛www.hotelmeri .com; ❸; closed Nov–March) is the only bona fide hotel **around the lagoon** itself, sited on a forested hillside overlooking Ölüdeniz. Cog-and-pinion elevators take you up from the level of the private beach, annexe buildings and heart-shaped pool, through the gardens to the main body of rooms. Redone in 1998, these mostly have sea views and large balconies; room rates, though steep, are for full board. You may beat rack rates by arranging a stay through various UK tour operators, or by coming in April or October (❻) or May, June or September (❼).

At Belcekiz, you might plump for the comforts of the package-dominated *Belcekiz Beach Club* (☎0252/617 0077, ⊛www.belcekiz.com; ❺ half-board only; closed Dec-March), a pastel-painted compound with attractive mock-rustic units, on-site hamam and masseur, and a huge pool much frequented when the afternoon surf outside hurls egg-sized pebbles at bathers.

Besides the waterfront establishments, there must be three score other motels, hotels and makeshift camps crammed into the former orchards **behind Belcekiz**, and on the slopes flanking the road in. Peaceful, good-value choices include the *Hotel Bronze*, near the shore between the *Deniz* and *Oba* bungalow-camps (℡0252/617 0107, ℻617 0182; ❹), its simple but air-conditioned rooms arrayed around the pool terrace; and the *Aygül Hotel* halfway back to Ovacik (℡0252/617 0086, ℻617 0610; ❸), where the plain rooms are offset by the eyrie-like hillside setting and large pool.

Eating and drinking

Eating out in the Ölüdeniz area is generally bland, forgettable and (predictably) not cheap. Honourable mentions, however, go to durable *Kumsal Pide*, a back-packers' hangout at the east end of the pedestrianized esplanade; the restaurant attached to the *Oba*, which is tasty enough, gets some local patronage and isn't

---

The Lycian Way

Inaugurated in 1999, the **Lycian Way** is a long-distance trail running parallel to much of the Turquoise Coast. It begins above Ölüdeniz, at Ovacik, and ends just shy of Antalya, taking in choice mountain landscapes and seascapes en route, with many optional marked detours to points of interest, typically Roman or Byzantine ruins not found in any conventional guidebook. In theory it takes about **a month to complete** – though it's expected that walkers will sample it in stages rather than tackling the whole trail at one go. Some of the wildest sections are between Ovacik and Gavurağili, above the Yediburun coast, and between Kaş and Üçağiz; descriptions of the best of these routes are given opposite and on p.502. **Elevation** en route varies from sea level to 1800m on the saddle of Tahtalı Dağ. October (pleasantly warm) or April and May (when water is plentiful and the days long) are the best **walking seasons** along most of the way, with summer out of the question.

The Lycian Way uses an assortment of **surfaces**, from cross-country boulder-hopping to brief stretches of asphalt, by way of forested paths, cobbled or revetted Byzantine/Ottoman roads and tractor-tracks. While the entire distance is **trail-marked** with the conventional red-and-white blazes used in Europe, plus occasional metal "street furniture" giving distances to the next key destination, waymarks are often not there when you need them most. Some patches have not been entirely cleared of fast-growing scrub, and may close up again within a few years unless used; additionally, some villagers have taken to maliciously blocking the route with piled, cut gorse.

Kate Clow, who marked the Lycian Way in 1998–99, also adapted the Turkish military's ordnance survey 1:50,000 maps, so a reasonably accurate **guide booklet-with-map** called *The Lycian Way* is available, which indicates points for water, camping, and (somewhat obsolutely) overnighting indoors. The map often saves the day, as trail descriptions can be vague at precisely the points where waymarks are mising; also be aware that elapsed timings in the text are for those with a full pack, so deduct about 25 percent when doing sections as day-hikes. The English-language version is on sale at select outlets such as Imagine Books in Fethiye, the lone computer/CD shop in Hisarönü, Bougainville Travel in Kaş and (overseas) at specialty travel stores like Stanford's in the UK. A **website**, ⓦwww.thelycianway.com, offers updates on route conditions and the opportunity to add comments of your own.

vastly overpriced as long as you avoid the fish; the diner of the *Blue Star Hotel*, where Turkish holiday-makers down passably authentic Turkish cuisine; and the *Beyaz Yunus*, just below the start of the road to Kıdrak, with some of the best (and priciest) seafood in the area, accompanied by *meze* and desserts.

Nightlife tends to be late and loud. The most obvious beachfront spots are *Sugar Shack/Help*, a Siamese-twinned brasserie and bar, and the nearby *Buzz Bar* at *Deniz Camp*.

Beyond Öludeniz: walking the Lycian Way

South of Kıdrak lies some of the least exploited coastline in Turkey: the **Yediburun** or "Seven Capes" headlands, with a number of isolated villages just inland. Since the early 1980s dirt roads have been pushed to most, though not yet all, of them, and for many points the **Lycian Way** long-distance trail remains the best method of access. Below, we cover the first 25km of the route between Ovacık and Kabak, at the current end of the dirt-road system, though the directions are given in the reverse order to those in the Lycian Way guide booklet – ie, *from* Kabak. This makes for a lengthy, lightly laden **day-walk** of six-and-a-half hours, though with rests, lunch stop and safety margin for getting lost you'd be wise to allow eight. To reach Kabak and the start of the walk, you'll need to get the earliest of the three daily **minibuses from Ovacık** to Kabak via Faralya, a hair-raising forty-minute journey careering partly along the edge of the Kelebek Vadisi.

Kabak to Farlaya

The bus will drop you off at the roadhead/turnaround in **KABAK**, from where a spur path leads down from *Mama's* (℡0252/642 1071; **❶**) – a pension and on-site restaurant run by the characterful "Mama" herself – to the sandy beach of **Gemile Liman** and *Turan's Treehouses* (℡0252/642 1227 or 0543/591 6655; **❶**).

Begin your Lycian Way hike with a steady twenty-minute path-climb north past fields and through open woodland to a track; bear right and carry on 25 minutes more, with little altitude change, through high grain fields (and no shade) before dropping to a canyon with a powerful spring draining past **BELEN** hamlet (which isn't shown on the Lycian Way map). Just past the spring, bear right and up onto the resumed path, climbing twenty minutes to the last saddle between Belen and Faralya village. From the pass you've a fifteen-minute descent to the road again – there's a sharp elevation drop, but along a gorgeous forest path with cobbled surface.

Turn right and continue another quarter-hour along the dirt road through the Hisar *mahalle* of Uzunyurt, still known universally by its Ottoman name of **FARALYA**, set magnificently part way up the slopes of Baba Dağı. Along the way you'll pass the non-vehicle lane leading downhill to *George House* (no phone; **❶**), providing basic treehouse-style **accommodation** and meals pitched at trekkers, and – 500m further – the *Gül Pansiyon* (℡0252/642/1145; **❷**), by the bus stop, which also does slightly pricey trout meals. You're far more likely to get a meal or bed on spec at either of these places than at the area's most prestigious accommodation, just up the resumption of the trail proper: *Değirmen/Die Wassermühle* (℡0252/642 12 45, Ⓦwww.natur-reisen.de; **❻**; closed early Nov-Feb), where you're lulled to sleep by the sound of mill-race water. Seven comfortable apartments and two conventional rooms are grouped around a restaurant (meals usually for guests only), the restored mill and a stone-crafted swimming pool; minimum one-week stays are usually required and, as the name and web address suggest, most of the clientele is German.

All three establishments are perched just above "Butterfly Valley", difficult to reach from this upstream end unless you're an experienced and non-agoraphobic scrambler; the path – such as it is – is much easier climbed from the day-trippers' beach.

Faralya to Ovacık

The LycianWay continues sharply uphill and north from *Değirmen*, leaving the stream canyon after twenty minutes; then it's ten minutes more along a steadily broadening forest track, through welcome shade, to a fountain. Some 45 minutes from Faralya, having passed fields on the left, a goat-pen and a second cistern-spring, the path resumes to bring you to the mosque at the centre of **KİRME** village (no facilities), flanked to the east and north by pine-flecked cliffs but open to the south.

It's a ten-minute climb up to the spring and mulberry trees by the road serving the village, where you turn left (north) and then are obliged to follow the road for more than an hour to the next village of **KOZAĞAÇI** – there's a fifteen-minute path shortcut at one point, but the red-and-white waymarks are generally deficient.They continue to be so around Kozağaçı (last spring water) where, once clear of the village, it's vital *not* to be lured into following a green-dot-marked path up Baba Dağı, but stay with the trail that contours around the hillside, past a modern house, to a saddle and spectacular views over the whole coast from Ölüdeniz to the Dalyan area.

From this point a well-engineered **corniche route**, partly cobbled and doubtless of medieval vintage, drops sharply along fairly shadeless hillside – 45 minutes, an hour, and 75 minutes along respectively you'll pass *sarnıç*s or rain cisterns (for emergency use only).About an hour and a half from Kozağaçı, the route flattens out and even climbs momentarily, but there's shade once again.Two hours from Kozağaçı another cistern marks the trailhead where a track system stops and vehicles can pick you up; otherwise it's another 900m to the paved **Ovacık-Ölüdeniz road**, and *Sultan Motel*, the trekkers' lodge noted on p.462.

Göcek and around

Set at the far northwest corner of the Gulf of Fethiye (formerly the Gulf of Skopea), **GÖCEK** is an obligatory stop on yacht or *gület* tours despite some rather off-putting industrial installations to one side of the bay. It has become very trendy indeed among both foreigners and Turks, with the late President Özal himself vacationing here on occasion during the 1980s (the main street is now named for him).While there's no beach to speak of, the passing boat trade has resulted in an astonishing concentration of facilities for such a small place: laundries, a chandlery, a half-dozen posh souvenir shops and several bank ATMs along, or just off, the main inland commercial street, much of which is permanently closed to traffic.The meticulously landscaped, lawn-fringed shore esplanade is car-free too, and venue for one of the best-attended evening promenades on this coast.

The nearest proper beaches lie some 10km east of Gocek along Highway 400 at Küçük Kargı. Here two pebble bays, **Günlüklü** and **Katrancı**, are served by the Kargı–Yanıklar–Fethiye minibuses and have forest backdrop, rudimentary snack bars and no-frills campsites.

Practicalities

About a half-dozen daily **dolmuşes** link Fethiye with Göçek, leaving you at the main car park just off the inland shopping street. If you are seized by the urge to stay – and it does makes a convenient last overnight stop before a flight home from Dalaman – you have some ten **pansiyons** to choose from, plus several **hotels** or apart-hotels. Basic *pansiyon* digs include the air-conditioned *Ünlü* (☎0252/645 1170; ❸) and the nearby, plain *Tüfan's* (☎0252/645 1334; ❷), overlooking the less busy, west end of the quayside. For a better standard, go for the *Yıldırım Pansiyon* (☎0252/645 1189; ❹), further west; the *A&B Home Hotel* (☎0252/645 1820; ❺), on the inland side of the same main street, with a pool and superior breakfasts; or, best of all – though well inland behind the *Nirvana* complex – the *Yonca Resort* (☎0252/645 2255, ☏645 2275; ❹), an intimate, antique-furnished eight-room inn with a small pool and rustic impedimenta in the garden. Other comfortable lodgings here tend to be the exclusive province of UK package companies.

The trendy set has had a deleterious effect on many of the half-dozen, occasionally precious waterside **restaurants**, with obligatory service charges and miniature portions even by Turkish resort standards – this tends to be accentuated the closer you get to the Port Göcek Marina. However, *Nanai* on the western half of the pedestrianized front (relative to Port Göcek) boasts elegant cooking with French flair – about $18 a head for a high-toned meal, but worth it. Nearby *Özcan* is considered tops for a *meze*-based meal but unhappily raises touting for custom to a coarse art. Just inland, but still in the pedestrian zone, prices dip at *Pelin* without a corresponding drop in quality, though if you're really counting the pennies then it has to be kebabs at *Antep Sofrası*, between *Ünlü* and *Tüfan's pansiyons*.

Among a handful of **bars**, the most civilized is *Dr Jazz* next to *Nanai*, with poster decor and a jazz soundtrack. *Blues Bar* by the *Deniz Hotel* is the younger, livelier alternative. Yachties demand **internet cafés** and there's always at least one operating here – currently it's *Sim*, near the *Deniz Hotel*.

Dalaman and Sarıgerme

The main town west of Fethiye is bleak, dusty, grid-planned **Dalaman**, home to the southern Turkish coast's main airport, one of the country's two open prisons and little else. Visitors flying in for resort holidays will see little of the town, and the sole reason for anyone to pass through is to reach **Sarıgerme** beach, 15km southwest of Dalaman. Even then there's a more direct side road from Highway 400, just east of Ortaca, marked with the regulation black-on-yellow signs.

Dalaman

Dalaman airport (flight enquiries ☎0252/792 5291) has a 24-hour tourist information desk and round-the-clock banking facilities, including a Yapı Kredi ATM, as well as two **car rental** booths: Avis (☎0252/792 5118) and Europcar (☎0252/792 5117). Be aware that domestic flights and international charters arrive at separate buildings. There are no public transport links from the airport, so barring a transfer coach or rental car you'll have to take a taxi 5km along Kenan Evren Bulvarı into town (about $8).

With both Göcek (see opposite) and Sarıgerme (see overleaf) so close, there's absolutely no reason to patronize either the handful of shabby *pansiyons* in town – whose numbers diminish yearly – or the overblown businessmen's hotels lining Kenan Evren Bulvarı. As part of their "rehabilitation", low-risk convicts from the local prison get to run a clinical-decor **restaurant** attached to a chicken farm (it's on the right as you enter town from the north) – so the menu's strictly roast chicken and rice, at rock-bottom prices with friendly service.

Another establishment worth sending your custom to is the **travel agency** Steelbird Aviation, on the airport approach road (☎0252/692 3671, ℱ692 3669); as station managers for many foreign airlines flying into Turkey, they can arrange one-way and return charters and scheduled flights back to the UK from Dalaman, Bodrum, İzmir or Antalya.

Sarıgerme

Sarıgerme is not quite as long as İztuzu beach near Dalyan but just as scenic, fringed at its western, developed end with pines and offering sweeping views east past the mouth of the Dalaman Çayı toward the mountains near Fethiye. Just offshore, **Baba Adası**, capped by a crumbling, tree-obscured stone pyramid thought to be an ancient lighthouse, only partly protects the beach from the prevailing strong southwesterly winds that make Sarıgerme better for sailing sports than swimming. The water is likely to be cleaner than at İztuzu, though colder too owing to freshwater springs that dribble into the sea near the westernmost cove.

The fact that several enormous luxury complexes are set well back from the sand confirms that Sarıgermi is a loggerhead-turtle-nesting beach, though new construction on the ridge overhead makes a mockery of the Environment Ministry's guidelines for such protected areas. Cars are banned from the attractively landscaped park in the pines just behind, to which entering pedestrians are charged a fee ($0.50) during daylight hours. But sunbeds and umbrellas there are a-plenty (most of them affiliated with the tour-group-dominated hotels inland), as well as watersports and diving on offer at two outlets (pitched in German and priced in euros). Aside from a drinks stall and rudimentary snack cantina in the park, there's no food, so it's best to bring a picnic to spread on the tables provided.

If you want to stay independently, or eat more substantially, head for the village of **OSMANİYE**, 2km inland along the road and served by regular dolmuş from Ortaca (not Dalaman, as you'd think). A forest of signs in German suggest who's principally catered for here, and the main drag is a tacky and not particularly enticing strip of trinket shops and estate agents, but you might try the *Şahin Otel* (☎0252/286 8284; ❹), the calmest of about ten here, on the slope west of the high street.

Dalyan and around

The landscape to the west of Fethiye more than holds its own in scenic appeal, and the newly widened and straightened Highway 400 has reduced access times. Westbound buses from Dalaman continue to Ortaca, from where plentiful minibuses make the twenty-minute journey to the little town of **Dalyan**, 13km off Highway 400 and a good base for the surrounding attractions: the ancient site of **Kaunos** downriver from Dalyan, **İztuzu beach**, the beautiful freshwater lake of **Köyceğiz**, and the remote but increasingly frequented bay of **Ekincik**.

Dalyan

DALYAN first achieved a measure of international fame in 1986, when its "turtle controversy" blew up into a major battle against developers, who wanted to build a luxury hotel on nearby İztuzu beach, a breeding ground for the loggerhead turtle (Carretta carretta). Conservationists succeeded in halting the scheme, and now the beach is statutorily protected between May and October, when the eggs are laid.

In the wake of this campaign, the town likes to present itself as ecologically correct, but its mess of *pide salonları*, carpet shops, T-shirt vendors and loud bars has proved little different from most other mainstream resorts. The **turtle motif** has been commercially harnessed ad nauseam: there's a turtle statue in the main square; restaurants, car-rental outfits and *pansiyon*s are named after the creatures; they appear on postcards, T-shirts and taxi doors; and you can even buy ceramic statuettes of the infant turtles hatching.

Otherwise life in Dalyan revolves around the **Dalyan Çayı**, the river that flows past the village linking the Köyceğiz lake and the sea. Many choice *pansiyon*s line the east bank of the river, and the boats that putt-putt up and down it – navigating swathes of reeds reflected bright green in the water – are the preferred means of transport to all of the major local sites. Craft heading downstream pass a series of spectacular fourth-century **rock tombs** set into the cliff on the west bank, many of them temple-style with two Ionic columns, similar to those at Fethiye.

Arrival, information and transport

Arriving **dolmuşes** from Ortaca – and far less frequently from Marmaris or Fethiye – drop you at the terminal just behind the centrally placed **PTT** (daily: June–Sept 8am–10pm; Oct–May 8am–7pm). Near the PTT on Gülpınar Caddesi, there are two bank **ATMs** (Yapı Kredi and İş Bankası). There's also a moderately useful **tourist office** housed in a tiny storefront opposite the mosque (April–Nov Mon–Sat 8.30am–noon & 1–6pm).

Dolmuş boats to the river end of İztuzu beach ($2.50; 40min) depart from Kordon Boyu, opposite the mosque. In season, most have left by 10.30am, though there may be one more at 2pm. They return every half-hour or so between 3pm and sunset. Otherwise, there are **minibuses** (every 30min; $0.75) along the thirteen-kilometre road to the east end of the strand. Many of the *pansiyon*s along the river (see "Accommodation" below) also have their own small motorboats providing a once-daily service to the beach for a nominal fee.

Renting a **mountain bike** in town is another possible strategy for getting around, at least in the cooler months. They're available for rent both at the better package hotels and at certain travel agents, for no more than $6 per day. Best route for a **bike ride** is to İztuzu beach: there's one nasty hill en route, with *ayran* and *gözleme* stalls to pause at for refreshment in the hamlet of Gökbel. This land route is recommended at least once, as you loop around the Sulungur lake and get glimpses of marsh and mountain not possible amid the claustrophobic reed beds of the Dalyan Çayı. The unpublicized **rowboat ferry** ($1.25 round trip) at the river end of Yalı Sokağı provides access to the ruins at Kaunos – not a bad target for a sunset stroll. You could take a bike across too – the rowboat ferry should take you after some grumbling – in order to cycle to Kaunos and beyond along an extensive system of dirt tracks.

Accommodation

Many of the most desirable *pansiyons* are scattered around a swelling in the river locally referred to as the "*göl*" (lake), though you'll have little hope of a vacancy in high season without calling well in advance. They're on or just off **İskele (Maraş) Caddesi**, which heads from the middle of town to a dead end nearly 2km south, opposite the fish processing plant. A second cluster of *pansiyons* lines **Ada Sokağı**, the dirt side-track off İskele Caddesi, leading west through the area known as Maraş Mahallesi. All of the options here, except for the *Palmyra*, are set in beautiful "lake-front" orchard-gardens, with breakfast served at riverside terraces, and hygienic river swimming off the same structures. To reach either of these areas, take the signposted **İztuzu road** – home to most of the more comfortable hotels – and then bear right at the second junction (this gets you around nocturnal street closures for pedestrians).

Mosquitoes are a major plague everywhere, so bring anti-bug juice, an electrification mat or a mosquito net, since your accommodation may not have window screens or provide such repellents. Very few places are open all year – most accommodation **closes from November to March** – while anything styling itself a hotel is likely to be monopolized by tours for much of the year.

Riverview establishments

Hotel Caria Yalı Sok, off İskele Cad ☎0252/284 2075, ℻284 3046. Near the rowboat ferry – about half the large, air-conditioned rooms here have river views, and there's also a rooftop breakfast terrace overlooking the rock tombs. **❸**

Çınar Sahil Pansiyon Yalı Sok, off İskele Cad ☎0252/284 2117. Across the street from *Hotel Caria*, set in a small citrus grove and perhaps the best budget choice for the sake of its clean, airy one, two- or three-bedded rooms and rooftop breakfast terrace. **❷**

Göl Hotel North of the central park; follow Kordon Boyu ☎0252/284 20 96, ℻284 2555. Plain, medium-sized rooms in a pleasant environment, with the usual roof terrace. Room balconies allow a partial river view, and there's street parking. **❸**

Prince of Kaunos Hotel Upriver from the mosque; follow Kordon Boyu past the *Göl Hotel* ☎0252/284 5230, ℻284 2604. A kitsch lobby belies cheerful air-conditioned rooms, most with mountain or river views, decked out with coloured curtains and pastel furniture. An overhaul of basic bathrooms is promised. Some tours stay here, but on-spec clients are welcome to try their luck. **❸**

İskele Caddesi

Aktaş Pansiyon 400m south of Yalı Sok ☎0252/284 2042, ℻284 4380. Half the rooms have views of the rock tombs across the river, though top-floor ones lack balconies and, despite air-conditioning, can get oven-like in summer. Self-catering kitchen facilities available. **❸**

Asur Oteli/Assyrian Hotel South end of İskele Cad ☎0252/284 3232, ⊛www.asurotel.com. Dalyan's best hotel is a landscaped complex popular with tour companies. Award-winning architecture and pleasant, if small and slightly dark hexagonal rooms, some with double beds and all with air-con, updated bathrooms, and river and mountain views. There's a private beach-shuttle boat and decent food at the open-buffet restaurant, while an annexe of two-bedroom apartments is available just inland. Rates drop sharply in low season. Rooms **❻**, apartments **❼**

Miletos Pansiyon 600m south of Yalı Sok ☎0252/284 2532. Garden-set outfit with just three basic rooms, two with showers, and a kitchen down the hall. **❷**

Ada Sokağı

Happy Caretta Hotel ☎0252/284 2109. Somewhat bumped-up rates, though you'll appreciate the thick walls on the oldish building (which keep the rooms cool in summer – there are fans but no air-con), and a kind managing family. Proprietress İlknur speaks English. **❹**

Lindos Pansiyon ☎0252/284 2005, ℮lindos@superonline.com. Well-appointed rooms with rare double beds and proper shower cabins, as well as a family studio; rooms with air-con are priced a category higher. Also a pleasant lounge for cool weather, free canoes available and genial management by English-speaking Levent Sünger. İztuzu-bound boats can be flagged down here. Open out of season on demand. **❷**

Midas Pansiyon ☎0252/284 2195, ⊛www.turkeyguide.com/homepages/midas.htm. Just beyond *Lindos Pansiyon*, and with a slightly bleaker setting, this has a German-dominated clientele. The upstairs rooms are the best appointed, but under-roof situation means required use of air-con. **❷**

Palmyra Hotel End of Ada Sok ☎0252/284 4550, ⊛www.Pansion_Palmyra.com. Partly air-con, well-appointed rooms set back slightly from the river, but the rural grounds have their own dock. ❸

İztuzu road

Binlik Sulungur Sok 16 ☎0252/284 2148, ⓦwww.binlik.com. Three-star hotel, currently dominated by UK packages, featuring unusually large air-conditioned rooms and two pools (one with a bar), though breakfasts are poor and the solar-powered hot water can run out. ❹

Kervansaray Arıkan Karakol Sok ☎0252/284 2487, ⓔhotelarikan@hotmail.com. Mock-Ottoman-style three-star with variable rooms – doubles to apartments, and an on-site hamam. Enlargement of the tiny pool is planned. ❹

Manzara Villas Eastern edge of town, 1km from centre; ring for directions ☎0252/284 4465, in UK ☎020/8447 5411, ⓦwww.manzara.co.uk. Three well-designed six-person villas around a pool-garden, set in open country with a view of the "Sleeping Giant" mountain, make an excellent self-catering choice for families, though good breakfasts are available. Genially run by expatriate Clare Baker, whose UK branch will provide help in securing flights and car rental. Rates are quoted weekly, from £200/week for double room, £450/week for 6.

Metin Erkul Sok 14, continuation of Yalı Sok, east of İskele Cad ☎0252/284 2040, ⓦwww.turkuaz-guide.net/metin/. Newish two-star, with spacious fanned or air-con rooms (though views only of the pool court), large common areas (including sauna) and claimed year-round operation. It's currently UK-package-dominated, though you might strike lucky if you ring independently. ❹

Eating and drinking

As a rule, **restaurants** in Dalyan are fairly indistinguishable; don't expect much in the way of Turkish culinary authenticity or portion size, though matters have improved since the mid-1990s.

If you're on a tight budget, check out any of a number of cheaper eateries away from the waterfront, for example in the grid of lanes behind the PTT building. *Metin Pide*, at the start of the İztuzu road, has big portions of meat, fish and *meze* as well as the namesake *pide*, served either in the spartan indoor premises or in the garden across the street. The *Golden Crab*, immediately behind the PTT, features outdoor seating, crab croquettes and crab crêpes as well as standard *sulu yemek* (*kuru fasulye, patlıcan güveç*) at lunch. Or there's the *Atay Dostlar Sofrası*, just shy of the river and diagonally across from the boat co-op office, an inexpensive, licensed *hazır yemek* place with a number of grilled dishes.

On the central waterfront park, the *Köşem* is a decent enough waterfront venue, where you can bargain over the autumn fish specialty *akya* (mock amberjack), as well as wild *mercan* (bream) and semi-farmed *levrek* (bass); the adjacent *Kordon* is comparable in popularity and quality, though based on experience we suggest you count your change carefully here.

If main courses can be less than inspiring, better **breakfasts and sweets** are available down İskele Caddesi at *Fruit Bar*, the place for all manner of fresh fruit concoctions and crêpes with *dondurma*, as well as souvenir homemade jams. An alternative is German-run *Gerda's Waffles*, a little booth with outdoor seating near *Metin Pide*.

Nightlife in the handful of bars along the upper reaches of İskele Caddesi, and around the town centre, is fairly self-evident; as format and ownership changes almost yearly, just choose according to the noise level and the crowd. One of the more durable ones is *Blues Bar*, on the river side of İskele Caddesi, south of Yalı Sokağı, with live music most nights in summer. There's generally at least one **internet café** taking its chances – currently the one opposite the Acarlar supermarket, towards the İztuzu road.

Tours and activities

The most popular local outing is the **day-tour** offered by the motorboat cooperative based on the quayside. These excursions – usually departing at 10.30am – take in thermal springs on Köyceğiz lake, Kaunos ruins and the beach, and are good value at about $5.50 a head (assuming twelve passengers), but a bit rushed for a return by 6pm. If you prefer to dictate the pace, you can **custom-rent** a whole boat, which costs around $70 for an entire day for groups of up to a dozen or so. Half- or two-third day-trips – say for a visit to the ruins and the Ilıca mudbaths – can be arranged for about $40, slightly less for a shuttle to the beach if you've missed the morning dolmuş boats.

Many of the riverside *pansiyon*s will take you on **evening boat trips** upriver to sit and watch for the silent dark shapes of freshwater terrapins surfacing for air. You can sometimes get such boats on a self-skippering basis; usually, though, you'll only be entrusted with a canoe or rowboat.

Kaunos Tours near the PTT (℡0252/284 2816, Ⓦwww.kaunostours.com) **rents cars** and organizes **adventure trips** – canyoning, cascade-swimming, scuba-diving (at nearby Ekincik, p.475), horse-riding and river-rafting on the Dalaman Çayı (aka Akköprü Çayı) – one of the best such rivers in the country – though all of this is subcontracted to Alternatif Turizm in Marmaris (see p.416). Prices per person for rafting are $68, including lunch and transfers.

Kaunos

The excavation of ancient **Kaunos** began in 1967 and still takes place each August, sometimes using labour from the low-security prison at Dalaman. While the ruins are minimally labelled and by no means spectacular, the site is one of the most pleasant and underrated minor attractions on this coast, swarming with wildlife (not least mosquitoes), including herons and storks in summer, flamingos in winter, and small terrapins, tortoises, snakes and nodding lizards in all seasons.

Arriving by **tour boat**, you disembark either at the fish weir or at another jetty on the opposite side of the rock outcrop supporting Kaunos' acropolis. The fish caught (*dalyan* means weir) are mostly grey mullet and bass, and a fragmentary inscription found at Kaunos suggests that the river has been exploited for food since ancient times. From either landing point it is a ten-minute walk up to the **site** (daily dawn to dusk, but unenclosed; $2 when warden present).

It's also easy to walk to Kaunos, using the **rowboat ferry** from Dalyan (see p.469), which lands just under the cliff-hewn temple tombs on the west bank. The ferry is intended mostly for the inhabitants of Çandır, the closest village to ancient Kaunos, itself perhaps a quarter-hour's stroll distant from Dalyan. It is also possible to **drive to Kaunos** from Köyceğiz via the Sultaniye baths and Çandır; but the road beyond the hot springs, while paved, is potholed, meandering and indirect.

Some history

Although Kaunos was a Carian foundation of the ninth century BC, the city exhibited various Lycian cultural traits, not least the compulsion to adorn nearby cliffs with typically Lycian rock-tombs. Kaunos was also closely allied to the principal Lycian city of Xanthos, and when the Persian Harpagus attempted to conquer the region in the sixth century BC, the two cities were the only ones to resist. Kaunos began to acquire a Greek character under the influence of the Hellenizing Carian ruler Mausolus – an apparently successful campaign, since no Carian words have been found on inscriptions here. Subsequently, the city passed from one ruler to another: to Ptolemy after Alexander's death; then to the Rhodians; and finally, after fierce resistance to Rhodes, to indirect Roman imperial administration.

5

Besides its fish, Kaunos was noted for its figs, and for the prevalence of malaria among its inhabitants; the fruit was erroneously deemed to be the cause of the disease by outsiders, rather than the anopheles mosquitoes that, until 1948, infested the surrounding swamps. Another insidious problem was the silting up of its harbour, which continually threatened the city's substantial commercial interests. The Mediterranean originally came right up to the foot of the acropolis hill, surrounding Kaunos on all sides apart from an isthmus of land to the north. But the Dalyan Çayı has since deposited over 5km of silt, leaving an expanse of marshy delta in its wake.

The site

Much of Kaunos is yet to be unearthed, despite the long-running excavation, and not every individual monument is labelled. North of the city extend well-preserved stretches of **defensive wall**, some of which is thought to have been constructed by Mausolus early in the fourth century BC. Just below the **acropolis** outcrop, crowned by a medieval and Hellenistic fortified area, the second-century BC **theatre** is the most impressive building here. Resting against the hillside to the southeast, in the Greek fashion it's considerably greater than a semicircle and retains two of its original arched entrances. Between here and the Byzantine church, a **temple to Apollo** has recently been identified.

Northwest of the theatre and Apollo temple, closer to the upper ticket booth, the **Byzantine basilica** and the city's **Roman baths** are also in excellent condition, and an observation platform has been erected near the basilica. A paved stone street leads downhill from the baths to an ancient **Doric temple**, consisting most obviously of an attractive circular structure, possibly an altar, sacred pool or podium, flanked by bits of a re-erected colonnade. A path continues to the **agora**, on the lowest level, which boasts a restored **fountainhouse** bearing an inscription to Vespasian, at the end of a long **stoa**. The ancient **harbour** is now the Sülüklü Gölü, or "Lake of the Leeches". According to ancient observers the lake was barred by a chain in times of danger; nowadays it's merely dive-bombed by feeding waterbirds.

İztuzu beach

Tourism and turtles have been made to coexist uneasily at superb, packed-sand **İztuzu beach**, which stretches southeast from the mouth of the Dalyan Çayı. You should remain wary of **turtle nests**, which are easily trampled on. Turtle tracks – scrapings in the sand where the creatures have hauled themselves up onto the beach to lay their eggs – are visible in June and July. The beach and marshes immediately behind are often alive with other wildlife too, including lizards, snakes, crabs, terrapins and tortoises, and its approach road is lined with profusely flowering oleander bushes, as well as deformed trees showing the effects of high winter winds.

Whether you go to the road's end ($1 car-park fees May–Oct; barrier, 2km before booth, shuts at dusk) or the river-mouth end of İztuzu beach, the biggest problems are the lack of shade and the poor eating options. Bring some sort of sun protection and consider renting an umbrella from one of the drink-*gözleme*-and-ice-cream kiosks. There are only a few kiosks, at either end of the beach, and their menus are expensive as well as limited, so you'll probably want to bring some food, too. Umbrellas, whose masts damage the turtle nests, are not permitted from a line of squat marker stakes down to the sea, and all access to the beach is banned between 8pm and 8am in summer – though these rules appear to be flouted regularly.

During the day the entire, four-kilometre length of the beach is open to the public (it takes about half an hour to jog it from end to end); owing to wind exposure the water can be choppy and murky, but the gently shelving seabed makes this spot excellent for children. Alternatively, you could be ferried across the river mouth to a smaller, more peaceful beach shaded by some pines (swimming in the current-laced river mouth is discouraged).

Ilıca and Sultaniye Kaplıcaları

Ten minutes upriver from Dalyan in the direction of Köyceğiz are the **Ilıca thermal baths**, a series of open-air mud pools ($0.70) worth investigating on a boat trip. These springs are supposed to increase male potency and cure rheumatism or gynaecological problems; temperatures approach 40°C. Note, however, that the total area is small, and in season gets packed during the day with tour groups – you're better off going at an odd hour, or convincing your skipper to take you to a second, more remote set of hot springs, further upstream toward the lake.

These, the **Köyceğiz Sultaniye Kaplıcaları**, are also accessible by a paved, eighteen-kilometre road from Köyceğiz (see below); follow signposting for Ekincik on the west side of Köyceğiz town, and then veer left to follow signs for Çandır and the Sultaniye Kaplıcaları. The **main baths** themselves ($1), housed in a conspicuous white-domed structure right on the lakeshore, are claimed to be open around the clock despite the nominal posted hours of 6am to 10pm. However, 11am to 6pm is set aside for *tur* (ie foreigners), while at other times there are roughly alternating hours for men and women. The dome shelters a large round pool with a naturally rocky and uneven bottom, from which the water wells up at 39–41°C; it's best appreciated at night or during the cooler months, otherwise you'll be needing to dive into the adjacent lake periodically. The modern chamber has walls marble-lined to waist height, but ancient masonry at the pool rim is evidence that the baths have been present in some form at least since Roman times.

Around the dome structure are scattered a number of **open-air pools** (also $1): one hot (beside the bar), one cold, and one muddy-bottomed (beside the snack-café). If you can't tear yourself away, it's also now possible to stay the night at basic **chalets** (❷) up in the hillside pine trees – ask the attendant.

Köyceğiz

With only its lakeside setting to recommend it, **KÖYCEĞİZ**, 23km north of Dalyan, is a sleepy little town that's pretty much been written off the tourist agenda by its quicker-developed rival. Nevertheless, it boasts a healthy economy, based on local cotton, olive, logging and citrus cultivation, while its position on the scenic, ten-metre-deep **Köyceğiz Gölü** – once a bay open to the Mediterranean that became dammed by silt deposits – gives it a further source of income in the shape of the fish who swim up the Dalyan Çayı to spawn here.

Practicalities

There's no great advantage in staying here, other than the better transport connections – Dalyan, Muğla and Marmaris are served by regular minibus – though you could use it as an alternative base for visiting the ruins at Kaunos. There's a PTT, an internet café just opposite, and at least one bank ATM. The **tourist office** on the main square (Mon–Fri 8.30am–noon & 1.30–5pm; ☎0252/262 4703) can advise on excursions and accommodation.

The three obvious central **lakefront hotels** are, in two cases, overpriced and fairly grim. The happy exception is the welcoming *Alila Hotel* (☎ & ⓕ0252/262 1150; ❸), with carved ceilings in the well-kept and common areas, varied bedroom formats (including family suites sleeping five), heating/air-con, and a decent lakeside restaurant. Alternatively, choose from among a handful of establishments **west of the centre**, listed in ascending order of price and remoteness. First there's the *Tango Pension* on Aliihsan Kalmaz Caddesi (☎0252/262 2501, ⓦwww.tangopension.com; ❷), on the "Fez Bus" circuit of backpackers' hostels, with minimalist rooms or $5 dorms; second, the older, less jolly (and less noisy) *Fulya Pansiyon* on the same street, within sight of the lake (☎0252/262 2301; ❷); next, the slightly more elaborate rooms of the waterside *Flora Motel & Pub*, Cengiz Topel Cad 110 (☎0252/262 3809; ❸), with a lakefront terrace, free airport transfers and river-rafting arrangements; and finally the nearby waterside, German-owned, *Panorama Plaza Hotel* at Cengiz Topel Cad 69 (☎0252/262 3773, ⓦwww.panorama-plaza.net; ❹), with the best-standard units – including large, fancy bathrooms and tiny balconies – a pool and water sports on the lake. The staff seem rather unused to non-German visitors, though this will change if (as promised) they sign a contract with Fez Bus.

There are a bare handful of **restaurants** in the centre, but these are so dire that you should arrange evening meals with your *pansiyon* – both the *Tango* and the *Flora* are particularly geared up for this.

Ekincik

The idyllic **bay of Ekincik** lies 38km southwest of Köyceğiz, the road there mostly paved and wide except near Hamit Köy. There are several daily minibuses from Köyceğiz, but most visitors arrive by boat – either on their own yachts, or with craft of the motorboat co-op based here. As part of the conservation measures instituted at İztuzu beach, boats of any sort were forbidden to anchor the night at the river-mouth there, and Ekincik was chosen both as a yacht anchorage and as a base for shuttling yachties to the Kaunos ruins. This, and the new road in, have spurred development in the Ova *mahalle* of very scattered **EKİNCİK** village, mostly in the form of a cluster of beachfront **hotels**. Best, oldest and most aesthetic of three here is the *Ekincik* (☎0252/266 0203, ⓕ266 0205; ❹) at mid-beach, where the fair-sized, pine-and-white-tile rooms have air-con, balconies and sea, hill or garden views. Inland, but still with sweeping sea views (especially from the rooftop restaurant), top choice is the *Akdeniz* (☎0252/266 0255; ❷), with large if eccentrically laid out rooms and a kindly managing family who may open off-season (they live on site).

The tan-sand **beach** itself is superb, another turtle-egg-laying venue, with good snorkelling and scuba-diving at **Maden İskelesi**, on the far eastern end of the beach near a system of submarine caves. Another favourite local activity is the walk to or from **Çandır village**, on a mostly preserved old trail affording spectacular sea views, which takes under three hours. The only catch is getting back to your start-point, done either by retracing your steps or getting a (stiffly priced) ride with the boatmen's co-operative.

The Xanthos valley

East of Fethiye lies the heartland of ancient Lycia, home to a number of archeological sites, including the two ancient citadel-cities of **Tlos** and **Pınara**, on opposite sides of the **Xanthos river valley**. They were both important settlements, having three votes each in the deliberations of the Lycian Federation, but Tlos had the geographical advantage, lying above a rich, open flood-plain and sheltered to the east by the Massicytus range (today's Akdağ); Pınara's surrounding hilly terrain was difficult to cultivate. Even remoter and less fertile is mysterious **Sidyma**, up on the ridge separating the valley from the Mediterranean. All these cities were unearthed by the English traveller Charles Fellows between 1838 and 1840, during the same period as his work – or pillaging, as some would have it – at **Xanthos**, though he seems to have left unmolested the nearby religious sanctuary of **Letoön** and the naval fortress of **Pydnae**.

The seventy-kilometre stretch of road as far as Kalkan, for the most part following the valley of the ancient Xanthos River (now the Eşen Çayı), is still an immensely fertile area, home to fields of cotton and maize and a wide variety of fruit. Plans for a local airport have thankfully never been realized and this, in tandem with archeological restrictions, has helped to keep growth at **Patara**, the main resort here, modest by Turkish coastal standards. Between Tlos and Patara, the magnificent river gorge of **Saklıkent** is easy to visit by dolmuş or with your own vehicle, though of late it's become something of a tourist circus. Isolated-ruins buffs can instead visit the unpromoted, unspoilt but soon-to-be-excavated Lycian city of **Oenoanda**, high in the mountains north of Tlos.

Tlos

One of the most ancient of the Lycian cities, **Tlos** is situated beside the modern village of Asarkale. It is referred to in Hittite records of the fourteenth century BC as "Dalawa in the Lukka lands", and the discovery on the site of a bronze hatchet dating from the second millennium BC confirms the long heritage of the place. However, little else is known about its history, although it was numbered among the six principal Lycian cities.

The ruins themselves, while reasonably abundant, are confusing and barely excavated – densely overgrown or farmed, in fact – so that the precise identification of buildings is debatable. But the setting is impressive, a high rocky promontory that affords excellent views of the Xanthos valley. The acropolis hill is dominated by a Turkish fortress from the Ottoman period, the residence of a nineteenth-century brigand and local chieftain, Kanlı ("Bloody") Ali Ağa, who killed his own wayward daughter to defend the family reputation. Now used as a football pitch and pasture, it has obliterated all earlier remains on the summit. On its northeast side, the acropolis ends in almost sheer cliffs; on the eastern slope are traces of the Lycian city wall and a long stretch of Roman masonry.

There's patchy **public transport** the full distance to Tlos, provided by Saklıkent-bound minibuses from Fethiye, which occasionally detour to the site. Tlos is, however, now firmly established on the organized-excursion circuit, so you shouldn't have to shell out for a private taxi. Under your own steam, **from Fethiye** veer left 22km out of town towards Korkuteli, and once over the Koca Çayı bridge, bear immediately right onto the marked side road to both Tlos and Saklıkent. Some 8.5km along, turn left (east) onto a signposted paved minor road; it's 4km up here to the base of the acropolis hill – which stays in constant view. In spring the route up, with snow-streaked Akdağ as a backdrop for the purple of flowering judas trees, is spectacularly beautiful. Coming **from Patara**, at Alaçat take the eastbound road marked "Saklıkent 15km"; when you reach a T-junction, with "Saklıkent" signposted opposite a mini-market for the right turning, bear left (north) instead for just over 2km until a "Tloss" sign points up the 4km of final approach.

The site

Entry to **the site** (unenclosed; $2 admission when staff present) is via the still-intact northeastern city gate, next to the guard's Portakabin.

Cobbled stairs ascend to the main **necropolis**, consisting of a few free-standing sarcophagi and a complex of rock-cut house-tombs. If, however, you walk along a lower, level path from the gate, outside the city walls, you reach a second group of rock tombs; dip below and right of these along a zigzagging trail to reach the best of the graves, the **Tomb of Bellerophon**, at the northern base of the hill. Its facade was carved to resemble that of a temple, with roughly hewn columns supporting a pediment, and three carved doors. On the left wall of the porch is the relief that gives the tomb its name, representing the mythical hero Bellerophon riding the winged horse Pegasus, while facing them over the door is a lion – probably meant to stand guard over the tomb. Apparently one of the ruling families of ancient Tlos claimed descent from Bellerophon, so it can be assumed that this was the burial place of royalty. Be warned, however, that it's a fifteen-minute scramble down, requiring good shoes, with a ladder ascent at the end, and both figures, especially the lion's head, have been worn down by vandals and the elements.

Between the east slope of the acropolis hill and the curving onward road is a large open space seasonally planted with peas and hay, thought by some to be the site of the **agora**. Close to the base of the hill are traces of seats that were a part of a stadium, which unusually lay parallel to the marketplace. The opposite side of the agora is lined by a long, arcaded building presumed to be the **market hall**, with vines festooning its interior arches.

Well beyond this, reached by a broad path off the main eastbound road, lie the **baths**, where the sound of running water in nearby ditches lends credence to its identification. This is a romantic vantage point, and perhaps the best bit of Tlos: two complete **rooms** and an apsidal projection known locally as **Yedi Kapı** (Seven Gates), after its seven intact windows, provide an atmospheric view of the Xanthos valley.

Just east of the approach path to Yedi Kapı are the remains of a Byzantine **basilica**, and southeast of this another open space that some believe to be the true site of the city's agora. Just north of the modern through-road stands a magnificent second-century BC **theatre**, with 34 rows of seats remaining. The stage building has a number of finely carved blocks, and its northern section still stands to nearly full height, vying with the backdrop of mountains.

Practicalities

Right opposite the ticket booth there are a couple of simple snack **cafés** run by the villagers of Asarkale. From the theatre just east, the onward road continues 2.5km uphill to several trout restaurants in the village of **YAKA**. Of these perhaps the most intriguing is the *Yaka Park*, formerly a watermill, where at the bar you keep your drink chilled in a sluice through which your potential dinner swims by. There's idyllic outdoor table seating, with the sound of water everywhere, though of course, like the ruins, the restaurant is no stranger to tours.

You can also **stay** overnight locally at the highly recommended *Mountain Lodge* (☎0252/638 2515, ⓦwww.themountainlodge.co.uk; closed one month in winter), just under 2km down the road from the ruins entrance. Choose between well-appointed but bathless rooms in the main house (❸), carpeted, high-ceilinged en-suites in the garden annexe (**④**), or four air-conditioned luxury units (**⑤**) in the wing overlooking the pool and pub. Proprietor Mick (English) is a lively raconteur and knows the area (and its snakes) intimately, whilst his wife Mel (Turkish) prepares fine evening meals in an area thin on non-trout-based cuisine.

Oenoanda

Ancient **Oenoanda**, about 50km northeast of Tlos, was one of the northernmost and highest (at 1350–1450m) of the Lycian cities. Set in wild mountain country, it's one of the more obscure archeological sites in the region but, as an unspoilt example of how all Lycian cities were before tourism, thoroughly rewards the considerable effort involved in reaching it (your own transport is essential).

The **history** of Oenoanda is no less obscure, with no account of it predating the second century BC. It was most renowned as the birthplace of Diogenes the second-century AD Epicurean philospher (not the Athenian cynic); to him is attributed a lengthy inscriptionary discourse, the longest such in antiquity, fragments of which are scattered across the site, most visibly around the agora and "esplanade". Oenoanda was first surveyed by a British archeological team in 1996 and is set for more vigorous excavations in the near future. With luck, the pending digs will be able to find – and reassemble – Diogenes' text to its full estimated length of over 60m, as well as confirm identities of the various structures. Until then, Oenoanda remains a vast, romantic jumble of tumbled masonry, lintels, statue bases, columns fragments, cistern mouths and buried arches, overgrown with a mixed forest of juniper, kermes oak and cedar, frequented only by squirrels and the occasional hunter or shepherd.

The site

To **reach the site**, proceed as if you were travelling from Fethiye to Tlos (see "Tlos" on p.476), but where you would turn right for Tlos and Saklıkent, instead continue straight along Highway 350. Some 34km northeast of the river bridge at Kemer, bear right (east) onto a side-road marked for Seki and Elmalı, where a fine Ottoman bridge in the Seki Çayı by the modern asphalt is the most durable indicator. Exactly 1100m along, turn south on a yet more minor road (the sign is rusted over); 800m down this, veer right at an unmarked fork to proceed 1.5km more to the village of **İncealiler**, visible at the base of the slope to the south. Turn right at the phone box and standard archeological-service sign – do not follow the river further upstream – and park by the **coffee-house** in front of you.

Head up the main pedestrian thoroughfare among the village houses, then near the top of the grade, bear right at two heaped boulders onto a still-narrower track, soon narrowed to a path, running parallel to a tributary stream. Continue west towards the escarpment in front of you, where the first freestanding **tombs** poke reassuringly up. The path describes a broad arc left (south) around the top of the stream valley, forging through the low scrub.

Some 45 minutes from the coffee-house, the trail fizzles out at the ridgeline as you meet the polygonal masonry of the massive south-to-north **aqueduct** that supplied the city, whose bluff-top site inclines gently to the south but is quite sheer on all other sides. Slip through a gap in the aqueduct, with tombs of the **necropolis** flung about on every side, and veer right along the ridge to meet Oenoanda's massive Hellenistic **city wall**, with an arched window; the way through is well to the left of this, by a strong hexagonal **tower** with archers' loopholes. Some ten to fifteen minutes' walk cross-country north from this, keeping just east of the ridge line, brings you to the large flat paved area of the **agora**; just beyond this stands an unidentified structure, possibly a **baths**, with an apse on the northwest wall and an arch dividing two of the rooms. Just northeast of this, a gate in the **Roman wall**, longer but much lower than the Hellenistic one, opens onto vast flat area, tentatively dubbed an "**esplanade**", with traces of stoas to either side. Northwest of the presumed baths, a structure with a three-arched façade – possible a **nymphaeum** or small **palace** – precedes the partly preserved **theatre**, its fifteen or so rows of seats taking in fine views of the Akdağ summits.

Saklıkent

Back on the main country road below Tlos, as you head south, the gauntlet of *saç böreği*, *gözleme* and *ayran* stands confirms that you're en route to the hugely popular **Saklıkent gorge**, the most dramatic geological formation in the Xanthos valley. After 9km, you bear left for just over 3km to the gorge mouth, 44km out of Fethiye. There's a regular minibus service in season – look for vehicles marked "Kayadibi/Saklıkent" at Fethiye's dolmuş *otogar*.

The mouth of the gorge is deceptively modest; to reach it leave the road bridge for a 150-metre pedestrian **walkway** (open during daylight hours; $2) spiked into the canyon walls, ending at the **Gökçesu/Ulupınar springs**, which bubble up under great pressure from the base of the towering cliffs, exiting the narrows to mingle eventually with the Eşen Çayı. It's a magical place, seemingly channelling all the water this side of Akdağ, though made somewhat less so by the tatty tea-and-trout stalls just downstream – and by the regular descent of coached-in tour groups from Fethiye and other resorts. Many of the **restaurants** charmingly suspended on wood platforms above the cascades were heavily rain-damaged in December 2001, and will be slow in rebuilding.

Beyond this point, the water-sculpted chasm extends 18km upstream, though further progress for all except rock-climbers is blocked after about 2km by a boulder slide. If you want to explore up to that point, it's initially a **wading** exercise – take submersible shoes, or rent a pair here for $0.75. In case you're wondering, in 1993 a technically equipped **canyoning** expedition first descended the entire length of the gorge in eighteen hours (bivouacking halfway), which required frequent abseils down dry waterfalls and thirty-metre rock stacks. This trip is now offered on a custom basis, during summer only, by certain adventure outfits in Kaş (see p.501).

With your own vehicle, it's easy to continue from the gorge mouth down the unsignposted road to Xanthos, the Letoön or Patara (all described later in the chapter); proceed over the road bridge past the half-dozen trout restaurants and the treehouse-format *Saklıkent Gorge Camp* (☏0252/659 0074, ✉riverbar@saklikentgorge.com; ❶) to follow the paved road along the left bank of the river. After twelve rather lonely, unmarked kilometres, you reach Palamut village; bear right at the fork immediately beyond Çavdır, the next village, and, 7km past Çavdır, you join the new highway through the Xanthos valley. Bearing left leads to Patara and (eventually) Kalkan; cross the highway and continue on the narrower road to reach Xanthos after a kilometre or so.

Pınara

About 45km southeast of Fethiye on Highway 400 towards Patara, you'll see the well-marked turning west (right) for ancient **Pınara**. Practically nothing is known about this city, inscriptions discovered at the site being singularly uninformative. According to the fourth-century Xanthian historian Menekrates, it was founded to accommodate the overflow from Xanthos. Later on, however, Pınara – whose name means "something round" in the Lycian language, presumably because of the shape of the original, upper acropolis – grew to become one of the larger Lycian cities, minting its own coins and earning three votes in the Federation.

It's just over 3km from the start of the side road to the edge of Minare village (two basic snack bars, but no public transport), from where at least 2km more of signposted but steep dirt track leads to the ruins. You can hike this final distance in about half an hour, though you'll be buzzed by traffic since Pınara is beginning to feature on formal tours. If you're approached by the tall, imposing Fethi Parça, one of the senior uniformed guards, you might take up his offer for a **tour**, as he's been here since 1985 and knows the site in great detail – though he's planning to retire by 2004.

Approaching the site, the **cliff** on which the original city was founded is unmissable, practically blocking out the horizon – indeed it's worth the trip up just to see this towering mass, whose east face is covered in rectangular openings, thought to be either tombs or food storage cubicles. These can only be reached by experienced rock climbers and it's hard to fathom how they were ever cut in the first place.

The site

The main part of the ruins of Pınara (unenclosed; $2 admission when guard present) are situated on the lower acropolis hill, to the east of the cliff, where the city was relocated quite early in its history, when defence had become less of a priority. The **lower acropolis** is overgrown and most of its buildings are unidentifiable.

Pınara's **tombs** are probably its most interesting feature, especially a group on the west bank of the seasonal stream that tumbles through the site. On the east side of the lower acropolis hill, the so-called **Royal Tomb** (now signposted in the plural as the *Kaya Mezarları*) is unique for its detailed if well-worn carvings on the walls of its porch, representing four walled cities with battlements, gates, houses and tombs, plus one or two human figures; a frieze survives above, showing a large number of people and animals in a peaceful scene – perhaps a religious festival. Inside there is a single bench, set unusually high off the ground, suggesting that it was the tomb of just one person, probably of royal blood.

On the same side of this lower hill but higher up, reached by a direct path north from the Royal Tomb, there's a house-tomb with a roof in the form of a gothic arch, at whose point is a pair of stone **ox horns** thought to ward off evil spirits. This stands near the top of the lower acropolis, and at the eastern edge of the presumed **agora**. Just north of the horned tomb, under the welcome shade of a dense growth of pines, the massive foundations of a **temple** to an unidentified god overlook the theatre (see opposite). Hairpinning back south, a level path threads between the pigeonholed cliff and the lower acropolis, first past a very ruinous but engaging **odeion**, then through a chaos of walls, uprights and tombs clogging the flattish area between the heights: there's nothing identifiable, but this was clearly the heart of the city.

At the far south end of this little plateau, two sarcophagi flank a man-made terrace and a sharp drop to the stream valley. About the only building that can be identified here with certainty by its apse is a **church**. Above this juts a strange, intact **tower**, identified by some as a tomb but more likely to have been a guardhouse controlling the way to the upper citadel, and offering a fine vantage point for making sense of the jumbled town. From the terrace, the path descends to the canyon floor, passing more rock tombs and a wonderful permanent spring – which moves down-canyon as the year progresses – en route to the car park.

Northeast of the town, easily accessible along a marked side-track, is the well-preserved **theatre**, backing into a hill and overlooking a tilled field as well as the "Swiss cheese" cliff; small but handsome, and never modified by the Romans (on-site signage to the contrary), it gives an idea of Pınara's modest population.

Sidyma and Karaağaç

Sidyma is the most remote of the Xanthos valley's ancient cities – and indeed, sited halfway up the ancient Mt Kragos (the modern coastal peak of Avlankara Tepesi), is scarcely in the valley at all. Contrary to some reports, it's a rewarding and understated site in a striking landscape astride the Lycian Way. Like most of the region's antiquities, Sidyma was only "rediscovered" by Europeans during the mid-nineteenth century, and has been scarcely visited since – certainly it has never been properly excavated.

From Highway 400 take the turning marked for Eşen and "Sidyma, 13km", just north of a side road for Kumlova and Letoön. Proceed 6km to an unmarked junction on the dirt-road system, and turn left (south); it's just over 2km to the first buildings (including the conspicuous primary school) of **Dodurga** village, and another 3km to road's end in Dodurga's Asar Mahallesi, where two mulberry trees flank the ruins of the agora and a Lycian Way metal signpost. All but the last 2km are paved, and any vehicle should be able to make the climb. Trekking southeast on the **Lycian Way** (see p.464), it's a day-and-a-half's march from Kabak to Sidyma, via Alınca.

The site

The *mahalle*'s mosque occupies the site of the baths, and reuses pillars from the agora's stoa. Indeed the principal charm of the place is the way in which ancient masonry crops up everywhere: incorporated into house corners, used as livestock troughs, or just sprouting incongruously in dooryards next to satellite dishes. An exceedingly ruined **castle**, garrisoned into Byzantine times, sits on a hill to the north; scattered in the fields to the east, and requiring some scrambling over walls to reach, is the **necropolis**, comprising a variety of tomb-types, though most have angular gabled roofs rather than the "Gothic" vaulted ones seen elsewhere. Near the centre of the agricultural plain is a group of remarkable, contiguous tombs: one has ceiling panels carved with rosettes and human faces, while the adjacent tomb has a relief Eros on its lid and Medusas at the ends (a motif repeated elsewhere). Another spectacular cluster, including a two-storeyed one, covers the low ridge beyond the fields. In the middle of the necropolis stands an enormous, fairly intact, square structure – probably a Roman-imperial **heroön** or temple-tomb – with a walled-up doorway on the north side.

Karaağaç

The closest tourist facilities are in the mountain village of **KARAAĞAÇ**, which can be reached by returning to the unmarked junction and heading west through Boğaziçi and then north through Alınca on a steadily worsening road – the village is 3.5km from Alınca, and nearly 20km from the main highway. Here, *Black Tree House* (☎0252/679 1105, ⓦwww.blacktree.net; closed Jan

& Feb) occupies extensive if rather bleak grounds, 1100m up, though rare Baba Dağ cedars grow just overhead. **Accommodation** is offered in a restored old-house trekkers' lodge (16 beds at $8 a head) and nine new free-standing cottages, well-built in local stone and pine, accommodating four to seven people (❺ per couple). There's a swimming pool, tennis courts and restaurant-bar that can do simple lunches if you show up on spec. A decent though unmarked, non-Lycian-Way trail links Karaağaç with Kirme.

The Letoön

The Letoön, shrine of the goddess **Leto**, was the official religious sanctuary, oracle and festival venue of the Lycian Federation, and the extensive ruins remaining today bear witness to its importance. The site lies 16km south of Pınara along the old road (less on the new highway), the turning signposted 1.5km before Kınık. Driving instead **from Patara**, leave new Highway 400 at the Kınık/Xanthos turning, prompted by a "Letoon, 10" sign; clear Kınık town and cross the Eşençay bridge; then descend into pines and take a hairpin left turn marked by a "Letoon 4" marker. There's a **dolmuş from Fethiye** to Kumluova, the nearest village to the site: get off in the village centre near the signposted turnoff to the Letoön, a few hundred metres' walk away.

Some history and mythology

Following the demise of the Lycian Federation, the sanctuary became Christianized during Byzantine times, and wasn't abandoned until the Arab raids of the seventh century. The Letoön was initially re-discovered by Fellows in 1840, although excavations didn't begin until 1962, since when it has been systematically uncovered and labelled, making the ruins easily appreciated even for non-specialists in classical architecture.

The nymph Leto was loved by Zeus and thus jealously pursued by Hera, his wife. Wandering in search of a place to give birth to her divine twins (Apollo and Artemis), Leto approached a fountain to slake her thirst, only to be driven away by local herdsmen. Leto was then led to drink at the Xanthos River by wolves, and so changed the name of the country to Lycia, *lykos* being Greek for wolf. After giving birth to her children, she returned to the spring – on the site of the existing Letoön – to punish the insolent herdsmen by transforming them into frogs.

The name Leto could be derived from the Lycian word *lada* (woman), and it is conceivable that the Anatolian mother goddess, Cybele, was worshipped here before her. Another similarity between the two goddesses is their connection with incestuous mother-son unions – something thought to have been common in Lycian society. Most famous of all the prophecies supposed to have been delivered at the Letoön was that received by Alexander the Great, informing him that the Persian Empire would be destroyed by the Greeks. Encouraged by this, says Plutarch, "he went on to clear the coastline of Persians as far as Cilicia and Phoenicia".

The site

Since excavations of **the site** (daily: summer 8am–7.30pm; winter 8am–5pm; $2) began, the remains of three temples, a nymphaeum and two porticoes have been uncovered, as well as a number of interesting **inscriptions**. One of these lays down the conditions of entry to the sanctuary, including a strict dress code, which stated that clothing must be simple and forbade rich jewellery or elaborate hairstyles. Another important inscription, found on the rock shelf east of the temples, is a trilingual text in Lycian, Greek and Aramaic, referring to the establishment in Xanthos of a cult of the Kaunian deity Basilens ("King"), which proved invaluable in deciphering the Lycian language.

The low ruins of the three **temples** occupy the centre of the site, beyond the relatively uninteresting agora. The westernmost of them, straight ahead as you stand with your back to the entrance, bears a dedication to Leto. Once surrounded by a single colonnade with decorative half-columns around the interior walls, it dates back to the third century BC. The temple in the centre is a fourth-century BC structure, identified by a dedication to Artemis; its northern part incorporates a rocky outcrop. The easternmost temple was similar in design to the temple of Leto, surrounded by a Doric colonnade with half-columns around its interior. The **mosaic** on the floor of this temple – now buried under several inches of protective sand which can, however, be whisked aside – depicts a lyre, bow and quiver with a stylized flower in the centre, which suggests that it was dedicated to Artemis and Apollo, since the bow and quiver were symbols of Artemis, and the lyre that of Apollo. Not surprisingly, these children of Leto, legendarily born in the Xanthos valley, were the region's most revered deities. The style of architecture and mosaic date the temple to the second and first centuries BC.

Beyond the three temples, to the southwest, extends a **nymphaeum**, which consisted of a rectangular structure with two semicircular recesses on either side, with niches for statues. The remains of the building are bordered by a semicircular paved basin with a diameter of 27m, now permanently flooded by the high local water table and full of terrapins and noisy frogs, a fitting reminder of the vengeance of Leto on the herdsmen who wouldn't give her a drink. A **church** was built over the rectangular section of the nymphaeum in the fourth century, and destroyed by Arab invaders in the seventh, so that only its outline is now discernible. Similarly, the notable stork mosaic on its floor is, alas, headless and apt to be covered by grass and sand.

Returning to the car park at the entrance, you'll come to a large, well-preserved Hellenistic **theatre** on the right, entered through a vaulted passage. Sixteen blank plaques, once adorned by now-vanished comic and tragic masks, decorate the southwest entrance to this passage, and nearby is an interesting Roman **tomb** with a relief representation of its toga-clad occupant.

Pydnae

Dolmuşes from Kumluova village (labelled "Kumluova–Karadere" run the 7km southwest to the end of the paved road (and dolmuş stop), where the ancient **fortress of Pydnae** is obvious on the right, on the far side of the Özlen Çayı. To reach the fortress itself, you'll need to continue to the end of the onward mud-and-sand track (best have 4WD) that leads to the beach (no facilities) at the stream mouth. Cross the rickety footbridge here, and head up behind the single dwelling and greenhouses to pick up Lycian Way markers, which lead to – and through – the fortress gate within twenty minutes.

Pydnae was a small naval base at the extreme northwestern end of the much larger, deeper bay that once existed between here and Patara, before the Özlen and Eşen streams silted it up. The irregularly shaped precinct is built of almost perfectly preserved, Hellenistic **polygonal masonry**, with steps leading up to the walls at various points and, every so often, square towers with loopholes for archers. The most recent structure inside, and the only one besides a roofless **cistern** with its walls still rendered, is a Byzantine **church**, its arched apsidal window overlooking the reedy marshes where fleets once anchored.

Xanthos

The remains of the hilltop city of **Xanthos**, with their breathtaking views of the Xanthos River – now the Eşen Çayı – and its valley, are among the most fascinating in the whole of Lycia. The site was first made familiar to the British public in 1842, when traveller Charles Fellows visited and carried off the majority of its movable art works, just four decades after the Elgin marbles had been similarly relocated. It took two months to strip the site of its monuments, which were loaded onto the *HMS Beacon* and shipped to London. The most important construction discovered at ancient Xanthos, the fourth-century Nereid Monument, a beautifully decorated Ionic temple on a high podium, is now in the British Museum, along with many other monuments and sculptures. However, enough was left behind here to require a two-hour visit. Afternoons are scorchingly hot even by Lycian standards – try and go earlier or later in the day.

Buses or (more likely) **dolmuşes** between Fethiye and Patara will drop you off in Kınık, less than 2km beyond the southerly Letoön turn-off, from where it's a twenty-minute uphill walk. Alternatively, Xanthos features in the repertoire of virtually every tour company pitching **organized excursions**, usually in tandem with the Letoön.

Some history

Part of the fascination of a visit to Xanthos lies in the city's history, which was dominated by the mercurial fortunes and unusual temperament of its inhabitants. In mythology the city was connected with the story of Bellerophon and Pegasus (see "Olympos and Çıralı", p.523). King Iobates – who initially set impossible tasks for Bellerophon and later offered him a share in his kingdom – ruled here, and the city was the home of the grandson of Bellerophon, Glaucus, who was described in *The Iliad* as hailing "from the whirling waters of the Xanthos".

Archeological finds from the site date back to the eighth century BC, but the earliest historical mention of the city dates from 540 BC and the conquest of Lycia by the Persian general Harpagus. From Caria he descended into the Xanthos valley and, after some resistance, succeeded in penning the citizens up in their own city. The Xanthians' response was the city's first holocaust, gathering their families and making a funeral pyre with their household belongings. The women and children died in the flames, and the men perished fighting, the only surviving citizens being eight families who were out of town at the time.

The subsequent fate of Xanthos resembled that of the rest of Lycia, with Alexander succeeding the Persians, and in time being succeeded by his general Antigonus and then by Antiochus III. After the defeat of Antiochus, Xanthos was given to Rhodes with the rest of Lycia.

The second Xanthian holocaust occurred in 42 BC during the Roman civil war, when Brutus besieged the city, causing the citizens again to make funeral pyres of their possessions and cast themselves into the flames. Xanthos prospered anew in Roman imperial times, and under Byzantine rule the city walls were renovated and a monastery built.

The site

The **site** is unfenced (except for the theatre area), but officially open 8am to

7.30pm in summer, 8am to 5pm in winter; the warden stationed at the car-park souvenir stall will collect $2 admission, plus any parking fees.

Very close to the entry booth, west of the road, stands the monumental **Arch of Vespasian** and an adjoining **Hellenistic gateway**, the latter bearing an inscription recording that Antiochus the Great dedicated the city to Leto, Apollo and Artemis, the national deities of Lycia. Further up, east of the road, the former location of the **Nereid Monument** is marked by a plaque.

West of the car park, at the top of the access road, the Lycian acropolis and the overgrown Roman agora sandwich the Roman theatre, beside which are two conspicuous Lycian monuments. To the north looms the so-called **Harpy Tomb**, once topped with a marble chamber removed by Fellows; this has since been replaced by a cement cast of the original. The paired bird-women figures on the tomb's north and south sides have been identified as harpies, or – more likely – sirens, carrying the souls of the dead (represented as children) to the Isles of the Blessed. Other reliefs on all four sides portray unidentified seated figures receiving gifts. Beside the Harpy Tomb a **Lycian sarcophagus** stands

New Highway, Saklıkent & Palamut

XANTHOS

N

Walls

NECROPOLIS

Byzantine
Monastery

ROMAN ACROPOLIS

Pillar Tomb

Site of
Lion Tomb

Eşen Çayı (Ancient River Xanthos)

MODERN ROAD

Walls

Xanthian
Obelisk

Café

Roman
Agora

Parking
Area

House Tomb

Sarcophagus

Harpy Tomb
Lycian Sarcophagus

Roman Theatre

Late
Agora

Byzantine
Basilica

Roman Tomb

Lycian
Acropolis

Byzantine
building

Church

LATE STREET

Royal
Terrace

Hellenistic
wall

Walls

Site of Nereid
Monument

Arch of Vespasian &
Hellenistic Gateway

MODERN ROAD

0   100 m

Kınık

on a pillar, an unusual structure thought to date from the third century BC. Traces of a corpse and some third-century pottery were found inside the tomb, along with a sixth-century relief – thought to have been brought from elsewhere – depicting funeral games.

Just northeast of the agora looms what's popularly known as the **Xanthian Obelisk**. It is in fact the remains of another pillar tomb, labelled as the "Inscribed Pillar" and covered on all four sides by the longest known Lycian inscription, which runs to 250 lines and includes twelve lines of Greek verse. Since the Lycian language hasn't been completely deciphered, the understanding of the inscription is based on this verse, and on proper names appearing in the text, which tells the story of a champion wrestler who went on to sack many cities, and generally glorifies his family name.

The nearby **Roman theatre** was built on the site of an earlier Greek structure and is pretty complete, missing only the upper seats, which were incorporated into the Byzantine city wall. Behind the theatre, overlooking the Xanthos valley, lies the **Lycian acropolis**, in whose far southeastern corner are the remains of a square building believed to be the palace of the early Xanthian kings destroyed by Harpagus. Under protective sand you can find patches of sophisticated mosaic, which would seem to indicate Roman or Byzantine use of the acropolis.

Moving east from the car park, paths lead through the residential sections of the Hellenistic, Roman and Byzantine city, where a **Byzantine basilica**, still being excavated and currently fenced off, is distinguished by its extensive abstract mosaics and a *synthronon* in the semicircular apse. On the hill north of here is the **Roman acropolis**, at the eastern side of which are a number of freestanding **sarcophagi**, and above, cut into the hillside, a group of picturesque **tombs** mainly of the Lycian house (as opposed to temple) type. A well-preserved early **Byzantine monastery**, containing an open courtyard with washbasins along one side, is located to the north of the acropolis hill.

Patara and Gelemiş

Patara was the principal port of Lycia, famed for its oracle of Apollo, and as the birthplace during the fourth century AD of St Nicholas, Bishop of Myra (aka Santa Claus). Today, however, the area is better known for its huge white sand **beach**, served by the *pansiyon*s, bars and restaurants in the village of **Gelemiş** almost 3km inland. The beach is a summertime turtle-nesting area, off-limits after dark (May–Oct), while in winter the lagoon behind attracts considerable bird life from inner Anatolia. Conservationists, backed by the Ministry of the Environment, have won the fight to exclude villas from the cape at the southeast end of the strand, while the protected archeological status of the area seems to have put a stop to most new building at Gelemiş – and there have been recent attempts to raze the entire settlement (see opposite). The proposed local airport has also been successfully seen off, with a change of venue to Çukurbağ, above Kaş, contemplated if tourist numbers (and the Turkish economy) ever revive sufficiently. As part of a new-found "green" image, horse-riding and walking in the hills to the east are now promoted, using both the Lycian Way and other trails.

Gelemiş lies south of Highway 400, down a paved side road beginning by a prominent rock outcrop; the turn-off is signposted about midway between the villages of Ovaköy and Yeşilköy. **Minibuses**, stopping at a patch of ground near the PTT, arrive every half-hour from Kalkan – from Fethiye there are around fifteen a day – and many of these continue past the ruins of Patara to the beach at road's end. Be aware that long-haul buses may only call at the junction with the main road, 3.5km north of the village; luckily there's a shaded café at which to wait for transport.

Some history

There are many myths concerning the Greek origins of the city of Patara, but in fact the city was Lycian from the beginning, as evidenced by coins and inscriptions spelt PTTRA. The city was famous for its temple and oracle of Apollo, which was supposed to rival the one at Delphi in accuracy, probably because Apollo supposedly spent the winter months in the Xanthos valley. However, no verifiable traces of this temple have ever been found.

Patara played an important part in Lycian and Hellenistic history, being used as a naval base during the wars between Alexander's successors. Later, in 42 BC, Brutus threatened the Patarans with an ordeal similar to the Xanthian holocaust if they didn't submit, giving them a day to decide. Plutarch wrote that Brutus released the women hostages in the hope that they would lessen the resolve of their menfolk. When this didn't work, Brutus freed all the remaining hostages, thereby proving his amiability and endearing himself to the Patarans, who subsequently surrendered. Whatever his tactics, his chief motive for taking the city was suggested by the fact that he took no prisoners, but merely ordered that all the city's gold and silver should be handed over.

Patara

At the far southern edge of Gelemiş village, a lockable gate and ticket booth controls vehicle access to both beach and **archeological site** (daily: summer 7.30am–7pm; winter 8am–5pm; $7.50, ticket valid for a week) some distance beyond. Although the ruins are unfenced, you are technically not allowed in on foot outside the official opening times.

Most of the site has never been fully excavated, and by and large it presents a spectacle of numerous unidentified and badly overgrown walls in polygonal masonry. Few clear paths link individual ruins, which often means repeated, irritating backtracking to the main road. There are also no facilities or shade – bring water, stout shoes and a head covering during summer.

Two kilometres from the village, the entrance to the city is marked by a triple-arched, first-century AD **Roman gateway**, almost completely intact. To the west of the gate rises a little hill where a head of Apollo was discovered, prompting speculation that this was the site of the temple of Apollo. Just outside the gate, a **necropolis** is currently being excavated every August by a Turkish team from Akdeniz University in Antalya.

South of the hill sits a **baths complex**, similar to the one at Tlos, with numerous arches and five square windows, and the foundations of a **basilica**, to which an exotic touch is lent by a shady palm grove sprouting up from the flooring. To the west of these, tacked onto the longest surviving extent of the **city walls** – and difficult to reach – is an attractive second-century **temple**. While too small and simple to be identified as the city's famous Apollo shrine, it has a richly decorated seven-metre-high doorframe – its lintel long on the point of collapse – leading into a single chamber. Further south, reached by a different track from the main road, are more **baths**, built by the emperor Vespasian (69–79 AD), which impress mainly by their squat bulk. Just west of these is a large **paved area**, either a small agora or a processional street, with its north end partly submerged by the high local water table.

The **theatre** sits southwest of these baths, under the brow of the acropolis hill and easiest reached by yet another track heading off the main road, a few paces before the beach car park. The cavea has been cleaned of sand to reveal eighteen rows of seats up to the diazoma (dividing walkway) and ten more beyond. The partly intact stage building has five doors, with five arched windows above them; on its exterior you can read a Greek inscription ascribing the erection of the stage to a woman, Vilia Procula, and her father, both of them citizens of Patara.

South of the theatre a reasonable path climbs uphill to the city's **acropolis**. At the top lurks an unusual rectangular pit, some ten metres across, with a pillar (for measuring water level) rearing out of the bottom and badly damaged stairs down its side. Since it doesn't overlook the old harbour, the pit is almost certainly a **cistern**, and not a **lighthouse** as originally supposed; that is now thought to be the square, arched tower, its top collapsed, on the west side of the hill, which still has a fine view over the sea, beach and brackish swamp that was once the **harbour**. The last silted up gradually in the Middle Ages and was subsequently abandoned, separated today from the beach by 300-metre-wide dunes stabilized by introduced mimosa and fencing. On the far side of the stagnant port, across the dunes, are the bulky remains of **Hadrian's granary**.

The beach

The **beach** of fine white sand at Patara (same ticket and admission policy as ruins) ranks as one of the longest continual strands in the Mediterranean: 9km from the access road to the mouth of the river (accessible from Gelemiş by a side road labelled "Çay Ağzı"; see below), then almost 6km further to the end. Rather than making the hot, half-hour stroll out from the centre of Gelemiş in summer, most people prefer to flag down a **beach dolmuş** or take advantage of transport laid on by the hotels. Incidentally, parking at road's end is very limited, as the archeological authorities have refused permission to expand the space. Flanking the entrance to the beach is a single **snack bar** serving next to nothing; there is also another wood-built snack-and-drinks stall out on the sand itself, though again the menu is limited, so come prepared.

In season it gets crowded in the immediate vicinity of the beach entrance, but a walk along the dunes toward the river and the Letoön brings you to more than enough solitary spots – and a few unharrassed colonies of nudists. Once away from the road's end, though, there are no amenities, and you're well advised to **rent an umbrella and sunbed** ($3 for both) from the beach snack bar. Spring and autumn swimming is delightful, but in summer the exposed shoreline is sometimes battered by a considerable surf (at least by Mediterranean standards).

If you wish to visit the beach after the Patara gate has closed – to watch the sunset, for example – you'll need to use the side road to **Çay Ağzı** ("River Mouth"), marked inconspicuously between Gelemiş and Highway 400, next to the rock outcrop, where a small sign indicates "Çay Ağzı 5" (km). The beach here isn't as nice as at Patara, nor are there any umbrellas to rent, but you'll find some wooden **tea-and-kebab stalls**, and there are **canoes** available to paddle around the pool which forms at the river mouth.

Gelemiş

GELEMIŞ itself consists of little more than a busy T-junction, with a main, crescent-shaped neighbourhood threaded by a single twisting high street extending west, then climbing northwest onto a small hill. Before 1950, the entire area was highly malarial and the nomadic *Yörüks* who had settled here spent the hottest months up in the healthier mountain village of Islamlar, near Gömbe. Subsequently, a lake immediately northeast of Highway 400 (still erroneously shown on many maps) was drained by a canal, and the Patara swamp shrunk by eucalyptus plantations in the village centre.

It's worth saying at the outset that Gelemiş is threatened by a Turkish Ministry of Culture proposal to evacuate and demolish the entire village, as part of its general policy of "cleaning up" the environs of archeological sites. A petition campaign from hoteliers and satisfied prior clients, and a three-day "strike" by local shopkeepers and taverna proprietors, recently forced the ministry to back down at its first attempt in May 2001, but what's seen locally as a "death sentence" could be revived at short notice.

In the meantime, **accommodation** here is a buyers' market as Gelemiş has an excess capacity of (sometimes shoddy) lodgings, with package allotments relatively scarce. The most desirable premises are either on the ridge to the east of the T-junction, or on the western hill noted above. It is possible to walk from this latter neighbourhood past the west shore of the swamp and Hadrian's granary to the beach in about twenty minutes, but this puts you out on a part of the dunes devoid of facilities, and this route is best used as an interesting alternate return to the village at day's end.

Independent choices for eating out are somewhat limited and you're often best off arranging to be fed at your accommodation; cuisine tends to be sustaining rather than *haute*, but then prices (verify first) are hardly *haute* compared to Kalkan for example. The best **restaurants**, in no preferential order, are those attached to the *Sisyphos*, the *Golden* and the *Flower pansiyon*s. If standard Turkish hotel **breakfasts** don't start the day well for you, you'll do no better than patronizing one of the two unusually tasty *gözleme* stalls next to the *Golden Pansiyon*. On Gelemiş high street are a number of fairly durable **bars** – the best are *Sarpedona*, with a Seventies' and Eighties' soundtrack and a hearth fire in cooler months; the fruit-punchy *Vitamin Bar*; *Medusa*, whose proprietor Pamir is involved with local environmental issues and runs a very basic **campsite** out back; and quirky *Flintstones*, on the beach road a bit before the ticket booth, with cheapish beer, reggae soundtrack and inexpensive snacks. There's even a small local **travel agency** in the basement of the *Golden Pansiyon*: Gelemiş Turizm (☎0242/843 5105), offering trekking trips in addition to the standard Xanthos canoeing and archeological excursions.

Accommodation

Ferah Hotel ☎0242/843 5180, ⓔferahhotel@hotmail.com. On the western hill, with large, well-maintained, partly air-con rooms and an unusually pleasant garden restaurant. ❸

Flower Pension ☎0242/843 5164, Ⓕ843 5034. Among a few establishments along the approach to the village from Highway 400, the only one crying out for consideration – just as you enter Gelemiş, west of the road – is Ayşe Kırca's en-suite *pansiyon*, with breakfast terrace overlooking a lush garden. ❶

Golden Pansiyon ☎0242/843 5162, Ⓕ843 5008. Arif Otlu caters to those on a budget with fairly large rooms (some balconied), located very centrally. The restaurant here sometimes has trout or ocean fish on the menu. Uniquely here, open all year. ❷

Likya 2 Pansiyon ☎0242/843 5211, Ⓕ843 5068. A little way south of the *Patara View Point*, on the eastern ridge, this more basic outfit doesn't have a pool or air-con rooms, but it is set in lush gardens with spacious quarters. ❷

Mehmet ☎0242/843 5032, ⓦwww.hotelmehmet.com. On the eastern ridge, offering plain, medium-sized rooms with balconies, some overlooking a garden-pool and restaurant. It attracts some package tours. ❸

Patara View Point Hotel ☎0242/843 5184 or 0533/350 0347, ⓦwww.pataraviewpoint.com. Muzaffer Otlu's and Anne-Louise's hotel has an unbeatable setting on the easterly ridge. The rooms have mosquito nets and heating/air-con, there's a tractor shuttle to the beach, a pool-bar, internet access and a Turkish-style breakfast terrace. They're open all year by arrangement, with an annexe of several self-catering villas in Kalkan (see below). **④**

Sisyphos ☎0242/843 5043, ⓕ843 5156. Downhill but set well back from the through road, close to the T-junction, offering variable-sized, pastel-decor rooms with kilims and proper stall showers, and a pool-terrace restaurant. **②**

Xanthos ☎0242/843 5015, ⓦwww.xanthoshotel .com. On the eastern ridge north of the *Patara View Point*, with a large garden-pool, air condition-ing and a tennis court. **④**

Zeybek 2 Pansiyon ☎0242/843 5086, ⓔzeybekpension2@hotmail.com. Occupying the best position on the western hill; the rooms have fans. **①**

Kalkan and around

Thirteen kilometres beyond the turnoff for Patara, the former Greek village of Kalamaki, now **KALKAN**, appears to cling for dear life to the steep slope on which it's situated. Occasionally the older, stone-built houses lose their fight with gravity, as happened during the severe 1957 earthquake, traces of which are still discernible in unrepaired buildings of the original village core to the east. Tourism, though now the lifeblood of the place, is a fairly new phenomenon: until the late 1970s both Kalkan and its neighbour Kaş eked out a living from charcoal-burning and olive-growing. The locals benefiting from the recent boom were those too poor to spend the summer tending grain and apples on the huge plateau around the mountain village of Bezirgan, and who therefore were on hand to staff the new establishments. The richer residents sold up their seaside property without realizing its value, and no doubt the speculators will eventually build over most of the olive groves to either side of the village centre. Brazen, often unsympathetic developments sprout both east and west, and two estate agents pitching holiday villas to Brits ensure that more will be built.

Until the mid-1980s, Kalkan had a distinctly bohemian atmosphere and served as an escape from the often oppressive conditions in larger Turkish cities after the 1980 coup. It was the sort of place where Rudolph Nuryev could come ashore from his private yacht one rainy winter night and play a two-hour video of himself dancing naked for those assembled in one of the three exist-ing bar-restaurants of the time. Today, dancing in the buff is probably the last thing on the agenda of a relatively wealthy and sedate clientele, who fuel mutterings that Kalkan is now essentially a toffee-nosed British colony. Compared to Kaş, Kalkan is certainly more exclusive and polished (if not to say twee), something reflected in the high prices and a growing package-tour presence that monopolizes most of the better accommodation. However, despite this (and the resolute lack of a sandy beach) Kalkan still makes a good base from which to explore Patara and Xanthos, or even the Letoön, while **excursions** east along the coast or inland to the Toros mountains can occupy another day or so.

Arrival, transport and services

Minibuses stop near the top of the bazaar, near the taxi rank; long-distance **buses** will leave you at the top of the built-up area, at the junction with the spur road into town. There's no tourist office in Kalkan, and at the time of writing no bank; change money at the **PTT** (open daily in season, also with metered phones until midnight). There are four or five **car rental** outlets, plus a single motorbike franchise, though scooters are only suitable for short jaunts to Patara and Kaş.

In a town where nearly every fourth storefront is a souvenir stall, **shopping** recommendations may seem pointless, but one stands out: Şakir Antik Galery near the top of Yalıboyu keeps an unusual, Arab-influenced collection of antique and new copper and bronze articles.

Accommodation

Some excellent *pansiyons* are located in the converted old buildings lining the central grid of cemented lanes – a district known as **Yalıboyu** – that drops from **Hasan Altan Sokağı** down to the harbour. There is also a district of new modern, purpose-built hotels extending a kilometre or so west from the edge of town along **Kalamar Yolu**, which heads towards Kalamar Bay. Most, though not all, of these establishments are block-booked in season by tour operators; larger room sizes, and usually the presence of a swimming pool, off-set the disadvantage of a hefty walk into town. The closest recommendable accommodation actually on **Kalkan bay** is 3.5km out of town, on the east (left-hand) shoreline.

Yalıboyu

Balıkçı Han On the waterfront, central ☎0242/844 3075, ⓦwww.balikcihan.com. Restored Ottoman house, genially run by Teoman Evci as an excellent tour-free hotel with newly renovated rooms and a roof-restaurant (June–Oct only) for guests on half board; nocturnal noise is dealt with by 11pm bar closure and double glazing. Newer annexes of air-conditioned suites, the *Balıkçı Han 2* and *Balıkçı Han 3*, in the easterly neighbourhood overlooking the ravine and sea, are more tranquil and include two galleried family units. ❹

Çetinkaya Pansiyon On the waterfront, far east end ☎0242/844 3307. Large (for central Kalkan) rooms, with varying numbers of beds and air-conditioning or fan. The breakfast terrace has a harbour view. ❹

Daphne Pansiyon Above the ex-church mosque, opposite fountain plaza ☎0242/844 2788, ⓔdaphne_kalkan@hotmail.com. Five simple but large and tasteful double rooms, all with balconies and partial sea views (but no air-con). ❸.

Kalamaki Pansiyon Süleyman Yılmaz Cad, halfway along the downhill stretch ☎0242/844 3649, ⓔcdusakli@hotmail.com. Run by Durmuş (Turkish) and Christine (Scottish) Uşaklı, the name of this renovated *pansiyon* recalls the original Greek village. Like most conversions near the village centre, the air-conditioned rooms are plain, modern and on the small side, though it's quiet, with a deservedly popular rooftop restaurant. ❸

White House Near top of lane leading up from the east end of waterfront ☎0242/844 3738, ⓕ844 3501, info in winter from UK ☎020/7350 2161. Turkish (Halil)-English (Marion)-run *pansiyon* with large, airy rooms in a variety of formats, from single to quad. Although only four of the ten have balconies, pool privileges are arranged elsewhere and the roof terrace is one of the best in town. Single travellers get a good deal too. ❹

Hasan Altan Sokağı and inland

Çelik Pansiyon Süleyman Yılmaz Cad, one block up Altan Sok ☎0242/844 2126 or 0535/224 3846. Long-established cheapie, with basic en-suite rooms and a dazzling terrace view for breakfast. ❷

Gül Pansiyon Near top of perpendicular lane heading up from Süleyman Yılmaz Cad ☎0242/844 3416. A friendly place, with undistinguished modern architecture, offering a particularly good breakfast and large rooms. ❷

Türk Evi (Eski Ev) Near top of perpendicular lane heading up from Süleyman Yılmaz Cad ☎0242/844 3129, ⓕ844 3492. Wonderfully refurbished old house with welcoming common areas, wooden floors throughout, and rooms with mosquito nets, kilims and (sometimes) fireplaces. Open wintertime by arrangement (there's no other heating – or cooling); the road into town passes just up the hill, for easy car access. ❸

Kalamar Yolu

Aldi Hotels 500m along Kalamar Yolu ☎0242/844 3681, ⓦwww.kalkan.org.tr/aldi. A group of four contiguous, co-managed units at the quiet end of a descending cul-de-sac, furnished to a high standard. All except the *Diva Hotel* (❸) have ample sea views over the surrounding olive groves; you pay extra for an unobstructed panorama at the *Dionysia* (❹). The more sumptuous, self-catering *Diana Aparts* and the one-family *Villa Diana* (both ❺) are usually block-booked by UK package companies.

Kalkan Regency Hotel 1km along Kalamar Yolu ☎0242/844 2230, ⓕ844 3290. Indisputably the town's best hotel, usually dominated by UK packages, but there's some chance of a room if you turn up in April, May or October. Well-laid-out grounds, in a prime position, feature an enormous pool, billiard table, fitness centre, hamam (included in rates) and on-site restaurant. The large rooms are carpeted, with tiny balconies, and tubs in the bath. **8**

Tekinberk Hotel 100m along Kalamar Yolu, seaward side ☎0242/844 3090, ⊕844 3398. Slightly underrated two-star hotel, now free of package-tour business, with partially renovated rooms. These are on small side, but there's an unobstructed sea view, large pool and pleasant lawn-garden. **3**

Mahal Lido

Villa Mahal 3.5km east of town ☎0242/844 3268, ⊕844 2122. Now available on a walk-in basis after some years as an exclusive package venue. A veranda wraps itself around the tasteful, irregularly shaped rooms, while steps lead down to the sea and lido – about the only one in Kalkan directly linked to accommodation – past six new suites furnished in designer-minimalist decor, the stuff of honeymoons. The multi-terrace setting guarantees privacy. **7**

Eating and drinking

Restaurants are scattered fairly evenly throughout town, though bars tend to cluster either just above the front or along Hasan Altan Sokağı, which after dark becomes the main pedestrianized drag linking the bus stop with the village centre. Choose restaurants with care, though – sticking with our recommendations – as there are some rip-off-prone tourist-traps both at the waterfront and the town centre, not to mention the unhygienic *sulu yemek* joints up by the PTT.

Time-tested **waterfront restaurants** include: perennial favourite *Korsan*, near the east end of the front, the second-oldest established here; the *Deniz* (aka *Pala'nin Yeri*), least expensive on the water and open most of the year, though with shambolic service and a limited menu; *İlyada*, specializing in *güveç* and again reasonable for Kalkan, though by no means the best here; and the posh *Aubergine/Patlıcan*, where a quality meal will set you back over $20 a head.

Scuba-diving near Kalkan

Kalkan has three locally based dive operators, all on or near the yacht-harbour quay: Kamil Karayazı's **Dolphin Scuba Team** (☎0242/844 2242 or 0542/627 9757), Fatih Tunalı's **Barrakuda Dive Center** (☎0242/844 3955 or 0536/269 2181, ⓦwww.dive-turkey.com), and the recommended **BT Diving** (☎0242/844 2757, call evenings only, or ⓔdive@bougainville-turkey.com). **Prices** compare well to Fethiye: a two-dive day typically runs £37, a PADI Open Water course £240.

Most of the hundred or so local **dive sites** are a 45-minute boat-ride away, around the islets plainly visible at the mouth of the bay: Yılan Adası (Snake Island), immediately south of Fahre Adası (Mouse Island), and the remoter islets of Heybeli and Öksüz. Beginners dive the shallows at the north tip of "Snake", and virtually the entire perimeter of Heybeli. More advanced divers are taken to a dramatic wall, alive with barracuda, grouper and myriad smaller fish, between 20m and 50m at the south tip of "Snake", to a number of reefs off Heybeli and Öksüz or to sand-bottom caves on the mainland with their entrances at 25m.

But by far the most spectacular calm-weather dive site, for intermediate and advanced divers, is so-called "**Wreckers' Reef**", southeast of Kalkan, off İnce Burun. Here, in 15m of water, are the mangled remains of the *Duchess of York*, built in Hull in 1893 and sunk sometime after 1920 – her bell is on show at Barrakuda Dive Center. However, rather more interesting is another larger, older mystery craft, broken into three sections at depths of 35–60m, and with teak-plank decking, intact winches and a vast cargo of lead ballast. The reef is wrongly marked on most nautical charts and fairly regularly claims new victims.

Except in the caves with their chilly freshwater seeps, **water temperatures** are a comfortable 18–29°C; the sea warms up abruptly in mid-May with a current change, and stays warm into November. **Visibility** is typically 20–30m.

Heading **uphill and inland**, the *Tyche*, run by a young British–Turkish couple, features some unusual dishes from eastern Anatolia, though even a light meal here will set you back about $17. *Ottoman House*, just uphill from the church-mosque, attracts a clientele with its gimmick of a post-prandial hubble-bubble. The *Ali Baba* is the only salubrious joint by the PTT, and popular at lunchtime. Another choice for a limited budget (approximately $12 each) is *Belgin's Kitchen*, popular for its cavernous mock-nomad decor and live Turkish evenings; the limited menu's not bad either, featuring such delights as *mantı* and *çiğ börek* (and, unusually for Kalkan, it attracts a partly Turkish clientele). *Foto'nun Yeri*, just below the taxi rank on Hasan Altan Sokağı, is a somewhat cheaper alternative for similar fare, with platform seating. At the very top of town, near the *jandarma* post en route to the highway, *Hamsi Black Sea Fish* is about as authentic a venue for said cuisine as you'll find at this distance from *hamsi*-land.

Current favourite **bars** include the long-lived and loud *Yalı*, up at the top of Yalıboyu, ideal for a pre-dinner drink, and the *Yacht Point* down on the quay, with variable music but generally hopping late on an August night. At the same elevation, east of Balıkçı Han, the *Koko Bar* has survived several years and attracts a young, largely Turkish clientele with its well-selected soundtrack. Nearby is *Osi's Internet Café*.

The beaches

Kalkan itself has an artificially supplemented **pebble beach**, no less pleasant for that, just at the east edge of town; the water is quite clean and chilled from freshwater seeps. Although bigger than it looks from afar, it will still get hopelessly full in summer, when you'll probably want to use the swimming platforms or **lidos**, with names such as Likya, Kalamar and Mahal, that dot the flanks of the bay – reasonably priced shuttle boats take you to them. The only other bona fide beach within walking distance is a coarse-pebble one well southwest on the coast, which the Lycian Way visits on its course between Gelemiş and the saddle 2km northwest of Kalkan.

The 26km of road east from Kalkan to Kaş follows the harsh karstic coastline, the thin soil stained red from traces of metallic ores, with the Greek isles of Kastellórizo and Rhó increasingly visible out to sea. Just under 6km along you cross the **Kaputaş Gorge**, a deep canyon leading back into the cliffs (canyoning trips are arranged in Kaş). Steps from the roadside parking area take you down to popular **Kaputaş beach**, a 150-metre-long expanse of pebble and sand that is normally fairly crowded, given the poor quality of any beaches closer to Kalkan or Kaş. Bring food and drink, as there are no reliable facilities – the *Ada Fish Restaurant* some 500m further along is usually closed outside peak season.

Inland: İslamlar and Bezirgan

The closest mountain settlement to Kalkan is **İSLAMLAR**, 5km north of Highway 400; make the turn inland at Akbel, with its depressing rows of post-earthquake prefabs. The old name of Bodemya – Ottoman Greek dialect for "rivers" – is still in use, and the high, cool village is indeed alive to the sound of falling water, used to power mills and nurture half a dozen or so trout-farm **restaurants**. Of these, *Değirmen* is about the best set and most atmospheric, with a working mill in the basement grinding locally grown sesame seed, which you can ask to have served with *pekmez* or grape molasses – a high-energy dip. Two grilled trout can be had for about $4, and the wine list is good – and priced accordingly.

Continuing above İslamlar, about 5km along you hit the main Kalkan–Gömbe road; bear right (southeast) for a pleasant forty-odd-kilometre loop back to Kalkan via the upland *ova* (plateau) of **BEZİRGAN**, famous in the past for its horses, but today devoted to sesame, chickpeas and orchard crops – the fertile plain was once a prehistoric lake, and there's a sprinkling of Lycian rock tombs and an ancient citadel on the hill flanking the Lycian Way's entrance to the valley. At the northwest edge of the two-*mahalle* village (and signposted at the *ova*'s north end) is the excellent, 150-year-old village-house **inn**, *Owlsland* (☎0242/843 5214 or 0535/940 1715, ✆owsland@usa.net; ⑤), named after the Scops and little owls resident in the nearby almond trees. It lies about 1.5km off the Lycian Way, making this a logical stage on the trek; proprietors Erol (Turkish) and Pauline (Scottish) stay open most of year, and provide gourmet half-board accommodation (£25/$34 per person) on request.

Alternatively, by studying the Lycian Way map, you can fashion a **loop walk** with the *ova* as pivot; only 1.6km separates the two debouchements of the path onto the ascending road from Kalkan, and indeed this circle-walk is offered locally as an organized outing. If you don't join a tour, you can take a minibus from Kalkan's top junction to Bezirgan – there are two daily from Kınık bound for Gömbe – and then walk back to Kalkan in about three hours.

The main road **north from Bezirgan** makes for a lovely drive, passing great stands of *katran* ("Lebanon" cedar) and the *ova* of Akyazı, comprising the floodplain of the Koca Çayı, which eventually becomes the Saklıkent Gorge, with the three-thousand-metre-high ridge of Akdağ closing the skyline to the northwest.

Kaş

Tourism has utterly transformed **KAŞ**. It sprang to prominence after about 1850, and until 1923 was a Greek-populated timber-shipping port known as Andifli. It's always been beautifully situated, nestled in a curving bay – the name Kaş means "eyebrow" or "something curved" – with a backdrop of vertical, 500-metre-high cliffs peppered with rock-tombs, and startling, head-on views of Greek Kastellórizo. But what was a sleepy fishing village until the early 1980s has become a holiday metropolis, whose permanent population of 8000 is vastly outnumbered in summer by the vacationers on whom locals depend for a living. Attitudes towards outsiders have inevitably hardened – the *otogar* is predictably well patrolled by accommodation touts – though they're not yet like those encountered at Selçuk or Pamukkale. Kaş is less snooty, more youth-oriented and more cosmopolitan than nearby Kalkan; aspiring İstanbul and Ankara yuppies flock here, while amongst foreigners it's still firmly established on the backpackers' trail.

Kaş has long been a major halting point on "Blue Cruise" itineraries, and **yacht and gület culture** is as important here as at Kalkan – with day trips available for the less well-heeled. By 2005 most private yachts should have moved to a new marina being prepared at Bucak Limanı (formerly Vathy), the long fjord west of town, wedged between Highway 400 and the Çukurbağ peninsula, which extends 5km southwest of Kaş. A shipping canal will be cut at the base of the peninsula, sparing craft the long voyage around it.

There's no beach to speak of in Kaş itself, or anywhere nearby, which together with the lack of a really convenient airport, has spared the town the full impact of modern tourism. Indeed, if you're not looking for antiques and carpets, at first glance there seems little to keep you here. However, the town does get lively at night, since shops stay open until 1am in season – and the numerous bars much later than that. If you don't have your own transport, Kaş also makes a handy base from which to reach Kekova and nearby Patara, and local boosters are working hard to make it a major springboard for various types of **adventure tourism** – the new yacht quay will double as a landing-pad for paragliders. The modern town is built atop the site of ancient **Antiphellos**, whose remaining ruins still speckle the streets, as well as covering the base of the peninsula to the west.

Arrival, information and transport

All buses and dolmuşes arrive at the **otogar** at the top inland end of Elmalı Caddesi. The **tourist office** is at waterfront Cumhuriyet Meydanı 5 (April–Oct Mon–Fri 8.30am–noon & 1–7pm, Sat & Sun 10am–noon & 1–7pm; Nov–March Mon–Fri 9am–5pm; ☎0242/836 1238), stocking glossy brochures as well as hotel lists, though rather short on any other information.

Central Kaş is small enough to get around on foot – and **parking** is limited to the harbour quay, to discourage car use. There is a lone public **shuttle service** around the Çukurbağ peninsula's loop road, provided by hourly minibuses labelled "Yarımada-şehiriçi".

Accommodation

Because of the town's nocturnal rhythms, it's worth walking a bit out of the centre – especially away from traffic-clogged Elmalı Caddesi, and the main bar district – in search of calm, views and privacy. Even so, surprisingly few establishments can be recommended with unqualified enthusiasm. The main concentration of desirable hotels and *pansiyon*s within the town-limits lies east of the centre, beyond the main cluster of government buildings and above **Küçükçakıl beach**; an older enclave of budget lodgings lies west of Elmalı Caddesi, along **Hastane Caddesi** and around the hilltop Yeni Cami, formerly a Greek church. The **Çukurbağ peninsula** has since the mid-1990s acquired a crop of multi-starred hotels, but few deserve their rating. Most in-town accommodation is open all year, whilst the Çukurbağ establishments shut down from November to April.

Hastane Caddesi and around Yeni Cami

Andifli Otel Hastane Cad 17 ☎0242/836 1042. Seventies-style outfit with shared bathrooms, though charging contemporary rates strictly by virtue of the wonderful sea-view terrace and sea-facing rooms. ❷

Gülşen Pansiyon Hastane Cad 21 ☎0242/836 1171. Modern affair on several floors; lucky balcony rooms face the sea. ❷

Korsan Karakedi Motel Yeni Cami Sok 7 ☎0242/836 1887, ☎836 3076. Despite the ominous name ("Pirate-Black Cat") this is the pick of half-a-dozen outfits around the Yeni Cami (though it's still too basic for tour companies). There's a tiny pool, roof bar, mossie nets, internet access and a view of the amphitheatre, making it a popular backpackers' hangout. ❷

Meltem Pansiyon Side-street between Elmalı Cad and Yeni Cami ☎0242/836 1055. One of about six *pansiyon*s clustered here and just uphill on Recep Bilgin Cad. This gets the thumbs-up from readers for a warm welcome, sizable rooms and decent breakfasts. ❶

Yalı Pansiyon Hastane Cad 11 ☎0242/836 3226. Slightly more comfortable than its near neighbour the *Andifli*, sharing identical views, with most rooms en-suite, and use of a shared kitchen and fridge. ❷

Küçük Çakıl beach

Aqua Princess Hotel Küçük Çakıl shore road ☎0242/836 2026, ☎www.aquaprincess.com. Large pool terrace and "private" beach are strong points here, as the rooms, while large, are a bit dated and the suites, at the rear of the building, on the dark side. ❹

KAŞ

▲ Friday Market   ▲ Fethiye & Kaputaş Beach   ▲ Antalya

Otogar

Theatre

Doric
Tomb

Yeni Cami

Daily Market

Harbour
Mosque

Hellenistic
Temple

WC &
drinking
water

Boatmen's
Co-op

Swimming
Platform

Dive &
tour boats

Harbour

Lycian
Rock Tombs

Stairs

YENİ YOL

ÇUKURBAĞLI CAD

ELMALI CAD

GÜL SOK

HASTANE CAD

SÜLEYMAN TOPÇU

UZUN ÇARŞI

CUMHURİYET MEYD

Lion
Tomb

Jandarma

Hükümet
Konağı

MEDITERRANEAN
SEA

Küçük Çakıl Lidos

N

0   50 m

(200 m) ⑭ & ⑮ ▲

⑬

⑯

⑫

⑪

Büyük Çakıl Plajı, ⑰ & ⑱ (100 m) ▶

▼ Çukurbağ Peninsula, ③, ④, ⑤, ⑥, ⑦ & ⑧

HOTELS

Andifli	9
Aqua Princess	17
Begonvil	13
Club Antiphellos	7
Club Arpia	6
Club Phellos	11
Ferah	12
Gülşen	8
Hamarat	4
Hera	18
Korsan Karakedi	14
Linda	2
Maki	15
Medusa	16
Meltem	1
Mermaid	3
Villa Hotel Tamara	5
Yalı	10

RESTAURANTS

Acropol	H
Bahçe	D
Chez Evy	C
Don Quixote	E
Naturel	F
Oba	A
Ora	B
Sun Café	I
Sympathy	G

BARS

Deja Vu	f
Magicom	b
Mavi & Abraxas	d
Net-House	a
Red Point	c
Reggae Bar	e

Begonvil Hotel Koza Sok, about halfway along ⊕0242/836 3079, ⑤836 3188. "Boutique" hotel, side-facing at what's currently the end of a terrace, with small-to-medium, cheerfully tasteful rooms; all enjoy some kind of view and are air-conditioned, and some have double beds. ❹

Club Phellos Hotel Doğruyol Sok 4 ⊕0242/836 1953, ⑩www.hotelclubphellos.com.tr. The best-standard town-centre hotel is this 2000-renovated four-star. Medium-sized rooms are all air-conditioned, with sea/island views, terracotta floors and (usually) mini-bathtubs. Facilities include a large pool, sauna/fitness centre, a pool table, and adequate parking out front (a major issue in peak season). Slight discount offered to Rough Guide readers. ❻

Ferah Hotel Küçük Çakıl shore road ⊕0242/836 1377, ⑩www.hotelferah.com. Much better-than-average small hotel, with large air-conditioned rooms, a friendly managing family, and breakfast and evening barbeques served by the pool; open all year. ❸

Hera Hotel Küçük Çakıl shore road ⊕0242/836 3062, ⑩www.herahotel.com. Despite the kitsch Greek facade and lobby, it's considered second only to Club Phellos as prime in-town digs, with a fitness centre and on-site hamam. The rooms vary considerably – go for the larger front-facing units where possible. Open all year. ❼.

Linda Hotel Koza Sok, east end ⊕0242/836 1328, ⑤836 1788. Largish air-con rooms, most with a view, and a tiny pool at this double-winged hotel in a quiet spot. Dutch tours use it, but there's a fair chance of a vacancy on spec. ❹

Maki Hotel Koza Sok, east end ⊕0242/836 3479, ⑤836 1388. Built in 1998 and similar to its neighbour in most respects, though it has an elevator. ❹

Medusa Hotel Küçükçakıl shore road ⊕0242/836 1440, ⓔmedusahotel@e-kolay.net. Well-equipped, well-run three-star hotel with a pool and private lido-beach, though the air-con rooms – some with double beds and island views – are rather small and spartan, with elderly baths. Four-person family suites on roof offer a bit more space. Rooms ❹, suites ❻

Çukurbağ peninsula

Club Arpia North-shore loop road, Gazeteciler district, 7km out of town ⊕0242/836 2642, ⓔarpia@bougainville-turkey.com. Rooms are well-kept, but the place really scores for its sunset views, private shoreline lido and poolside restaurant (there's a better-than-average breakfast for $5.50–7.50 and open buffet supper). Bookable direct or through Bougainville Travel in town (see "Listings"). ❸

Hamarat 3km out on the peninsula road, before the loop-split ⊕0242/836 1547. Cosy if basic eight-room pansiyon with good views over its terraced front garden, kitchen facilities and a swimming platform a few moments down the slope over the road. ❷

Mermaid Hotel South leg of loop road, 5km out ⊕0242/836 2668, ⑤836 2618, winter contact ⊕0312/466 5930. Balconied, limited-view rooms at this self-styled "boutique hotel" are on the small side, but appealingly furnished and have air-con. Common areas, filled with antiques, are grander, while the pool and setting are very pleasant. Closed Nov–April. ❸

Villa Hotel Tamara Southwest end of peninsula before Aquapark Hotel ⊕0242/836 3273, ⑤0242/836 2112. Attractive, stone-clad hotel with eighteen large air-conditioned rooms (plus self-catering villas) in stylishly varied decor. The hot water is reliably boiler-generated (not solar-heated), and there's a salt-water pool in a superb hillside setting. Claimed all-year operation. ❻

Camping

Kaş Kamping Hastane Cad, 1km west of town, just past the amphitheatre ⊕0242/836 1050. Long a favoured link in the Hippie Trail to Asia, the local campsite is perennially for sale, but while it survives in its present format, there's a swimming platform, lively bar-restaurant, caravan space and A-frame cabins (❶) for the tentless.

The Town

Ancient **Antiphellos** was the harbour of ancient Phellos, way inland near the modern village of Çukurbağ and one of the few Lycian cities to bear a Greek name (*phellos* means "cork oak"). Excavations at Kaş have unearthed a settlement dating back to at least the fourth century BC, although Antiphellos only gained importance in Hellenistic times, when an increase in seagoing commerce meant it thrived while Phellos withered. By the Roman era, it was the most important city in the region, famed particularly for its exported sponges, which Pliny mentioned as being exceptionally soft.

Scuba-diving around Kaş

The Mediterranean around Kaş has arguably the best visibility (up to 30m) and greatest variety of sea life of the entire Turkish coast, as well as the shortest transfer times to dive sites. These are facts not lost on Turkey's divers, who descend in force during summer or over any long weekend. There are ostensibly a dozen dive operators in town, many operating out of the basements of Küçük Çakıl hotels, but in terms of boat comfort, safety standards, quality equipment and language/thoroughness of instruction, only two companies really rate consideration: **Sun Diving** at Liman Sok 10, on the west side of the harbour (℡0242/836 2637, ⓦwww.sundiving.de) and **BT Diving**, part of Bougainville Travel, Çukurbağlı (officially İbrahim Serin) Cad 10 (℡0242/836 3737, ⓦwww.bougainville-turkey.com).

Because of the brief shuttle time to sites, it's quite feasible to dive only in the morning or afternoon, and accordingly **prices** are per dive rather than per day. Both recommended operators advertise single dives at £20 (£14 if you bring your own gear except tanks/weights), making this about the least expensive place to dive in Turkey. A PADI Open Water course will cost about £205, Advanced Open Water £140 – again rather less than at Fethiye.

Dive sites

There are close to thirty dive sites in the area, about a third of these on the flank of the Çukurbağlı peninsula, with most of the others around the islets at the marine frontier with Greek Kastellórizo. **Beginners'** dives visit a tunnel at 15m and a shoreline cave fed by an icy freshwater spring in Bayındır Limanı, or the shallower reaches of "Stone Edge", an area off Çukurbağlı. **Moderately experienced** divers may be taken to the site known as "Canyon", where beginning in four-metre depths they drop through the namesake formation past a reasonably intact Greek cotton-carrying freighter that ran aground here in the 1960s. This was later dynamited to remove the navigational hazard, with its stern lodging in 35m of water. Next there's a traverse of a big-wall dropoff, and then a return north with prevailing currents via a tunnel system at 15–18m. Only **advanced** divers using nitrox or triox tanks can visit the wreck of a World War II bomber shot down between Kaş and Kastellórizo, resting nearly intact in 65m of water at the site called "Flying Fish", shortly beyond "Canyon".

Fish you're likely to see – at their best in August or September – includes grouper, barracuda, amberjack and the occasional ray; smaller species typically seen include cardinal fish, damselfish, ornate wrasse and schools of bream or pandora.

The remains of the ancient city are few and scattered, but what's on show is quite impressive. Out of town, 500m along Hastane Caddesi from the harbour mosque, sits a small, almost complete Hellenistic **theatre** with 26 rows of seats. The theatre never had a permanent stage building, but in modern times a curved wall was built in place of a stage to provide a backdrop for local wrestling matches. It's a favourite spot for watching the sunset.

Above and behind the theatre, 100m away on the top of a hill, stands a unique **Doric tomb**, the so-called Kesme Mezar, also almost completely intact. Its single chamber forms a slightly tapering cube cut from the rock on which it stands. The two-metre-high entrance was once closed by a sliding door, but can now be entered in order to examine the bench at the back (on which the body would have been laid out), decorated by a frieze of small female figures performing a dance.

The most interesting of the sarcophagi to have survived local pilfering for building materials is the **Lion Tomb** on Postane Sokak, right at the top of the Uzun Çarşı. This towering structure has two burial chambers, the lower one forming a base for the Lycian sarcophagus above it. On the side of the lower chamber is an undeciphered Lycian inscription, written in a poetic form similar to that of the inscribed obelisk at Xanthos. The tomb's name derives from the four lifting bosses (projecting bits of masonry used to remove the Gothic-style lid from its base) in the shape of lions' heads, resting their chins on their paws.

The beaches

Considering that Kaş is a major Turkish resort, local natural beaches are surprisingly poor; those few on the north shore of Bucak Limanı are muddy and give onto sumpy water. In town itself, **Küçük Çakıl** has been pretty much taken over by the hotels facing it, which have installed snack-bar and sunbed concessions and concreted over the shore as a lido. **Büyük Çakıl**, just over a kilometre east of town, is a small, coarse-shingle cove that nevertheless gets crowded out. Leaving town to the west, along Hastane Caddesi, the **Çukurbağ peninsula** gives good views of the Greek island Kastellórizo, and is lapped by clear, aquamarine water, but again has no beaches to speak of, only hotel-built lidos where you can clamber into the water unmenaced by the ubiquitous sea urchins. The nearest decent beach is **Kaputaş**, 21km towards Kalkan, described on p.493.

Boat tours and Kastellórizo

The local boatmen's cooperative, the *Kaş Deniz Taşıyıcıları Kooperatifi*, offers standard full-day tours from the harbour (depart 10am, return 6pm) to either **Kekova** or to **Patara** (from $10 per person, plus $4 for buffet lunch). **Custom tours** in a boat taking ten to twelve people start at $140 a day at the beginning of the season (April and May), reaching $230 in a busy year by late season (Aug and Sept).

Day- (or one-way) trips to the **Greek island of Kastellórizo** (see below) operate on a demand-only basis, perhaps twice a week at best, although there is usually an extra, unpublicized Greek boat to Kastellórizo on Friday evening. Kaş-based boats have been scared off making the trip by punitive docking fees levied on all non-Greek-registered craft by the Kastellórizo port authorities. Moreover, Kaş is an official entry/exit port for Turkey, but Greek Kastellórizo is not – though the Greek authorities have no basis in law for preventing EU nationals from landing in Greece. Non-EU nationals may be forbidden from leaving Kastellórizo until their personal details are faxed to Athens for confirmation that they aren't heinous criminals; this petty harassment becomes slightly more understandable when you learn that this is a major smuggling corridor. To go across legally, you'll need to surrender your passport to the arranging travel agency the night before; returning to Kaş from Kastellórizo, no fresh visa fee is payable as long as you have time left on your existing multiple-entry visa.

Kastellórizo

The picturesque port of the Greek island of **Kastellórizo**, called Meis in Turkish after the Greek alternate name (Meyísti), lies just over three nautical miles off the Turkish coast. It is among the smallest inhabited islands of the Dodecanese archipelago, a haven for yachties and a favourite place to nip across to for renewing three-month Turkish tourist visas. You'll find complete coverage of the island in *The Rough Guide to the Dodecanese and the East Aegean* but it's worth saying here that there are at least two weekly onward boats to Rhodes most of the year, plus three to seven weekly flights on a puddle-jumper aircraft. If you just miss a departure, a couple of days on the island will be time well spent, with affordable seafood, walking opportunities and adequate nightlife on offer.

Eating and drinking

There are several excellent **restaurants** in Kaş, though few actually face the waterfront, and those that do are prone to scams and ripoffs – two in particular to avoid are *Smiley's* and *Mercan*.

Acropol Çukurbağ peninsula, just before *Club Arpia*. One of the best (and priciest) in the area, in a stunningly renovated venue (formerly the journalists' union club). After a maiden year as an upmarket French eatery, is reportedly set to change over to a posh-Turkish format.

Bahçe Uzun Çarşı. The broadest range of cold *meze*s in town, served in the garden (*bahçe* in Turkish). Also try their annexe, *Don Quixote*, at the base of Uzun Çarşı, a bit livelier and more contemporary in feel.

Chez Evy Terzi Sok 2, off Süleyman Topçu Sok ☎0242/836 1253. A worthwhile splurge ($17 each) sees French country recipes meet Turkish flavours. The result is happier and more generous than you'd expect – the pepper steak and (in autumn) wild boar are to die for – while Evy herself, who used to cook for the rich and famous on their private mega-yachts, is one of the characters of Kaş. Booking for the garden seating is necessary in season; otherwise wait for a table, or have a nightcap, in the rustic bar. Open much of the year.

Naturel Gürsoy Sok, off Uzun Çarşı. Appetizing, inexpensive Turkish snacks such as *mantı*, *su böreği* and *çiğ böreği*, with friendly, low-key service; a good choice for vegetarians.

Oba Çukurbağlı Cad, near the PTT. Locally patronized licensed diner that's ace for simple home-style soups and *sulu yemek*, with an equally pleasant garden or indoor seating.

Ora Northwest corner of daily market. Perched above one corner of the plaza, you can eat well and carniverously at this licensed *ocakbaşı*-type grill for under $10.

Sun Café Hükümet Cad. Big, brilliantly done portions of unusual dishes, such as *ceviz tarama* (walnut dip), *çerkez tavuğu* (chicken in walnut sauce) and *mıhlama kebap* (meat in pitta with spices, walnuts and garlic yoghurt) and fresh fish, at reasonable prices – count on $13 per person with wine, more if you have seafood. Both indoor (winter) and outdoor (summer) seating, plus good music at the bar, which tends to dominate proceedings after 11pm.

Sympathy Gürsoy Sok. Since opening in 2002 this has quickly garnered a reputation for excellent meat dishes accompanied by a few selected *meze*s, such as *arnavut ciğer* and *mücver*, plus four varieties of *rakı*; budget $30 for two with a copious intake of the latter.

Nightlife

A varied, crowded, high-decibel **nightlife** is what makes Kaş for many visitors. *Red Point Club*, which plays taped rock and blues on Süleyman Topçu Sokağı, reigns as the town's premier after-hours pub, packed solid after midnight despite the spacious dance-floor. On Hükümet Caddesi, bars include the aforementioned *Sun Café*, the favourite early-evening bar *Deja Vu*, perfectly situated for the sunset, and what's billed as Turkey's only all-reggae club, logically enough named *Reggae Bar*. On the harbour front, long-established *Mavi/Blue*, which twenty years ago was a coffeehouse where retired fishermen played backgammon, is now musical, young and trendy. Immediately above this, *Abraxas* has a fine-tuned musical sense and two narrow balconies to cling to and take in the town.

Shopping

The upmarket tourist industry in Kaş centres on the **Uzun Çarşı** (Long Market), and that's exactly what it is – an uninterrupted bazaar of crafts and designer clothing shops with a selection (and prices, of course) that would fit right in at London's Covent Garden or San Francisco's Ghirardelli Square. While Naf Naf, Benetton or Quiksilver rags produced under licence are easy to come by, there are also local designers tailoring to order from hand-woven fabrics produced in nearby villages. You can best view such raw cloth at the slightly shabby but lively weekly **Friday market**, now exiled to the edge of town en route to Bucak Limanı. The old market in the town centre has become a park, but still has varied shops surrounding it.

The **antique shops** along Uzun Çarşı are fairly even in quantity, so none are particularly worth singling out; leather is now out of fashion, while carpets and metal antiques predominate. Off Uzun Çarşı, **Kaş and Carry** on Orta Sokağı near the PTT is the longest established in town and has a good reputation for carpets (and lately, ceramics).

Listings

Banks and exchange Yapı Kredi ATM behind the harbour mosque; Halkbank and İş Bankası ATMs on Elmalı Cad; Ziraat Bankası, next to the PTT.

Books and magazines The *Merhaba Café* on Çukurbağlı Cad, towards the PTT end, in addition to gourmet cakes and coffee, sells foreign newspapers and books, as well as quality postcards; Galileo at Süleyman Topçu Sok 9 has a small stock of used books, as well as music cassettes.

Car rental Most travel agencies (see opposite) can oblige. Expect to pay around $37 per day for a car, $225 per week.

Internet Net-House, top end of Çukurbağlı Cad, past the PTT on the right; also Magicom, two doors down.

Laundry Rose, Süleyman Topçu Sok; also Habesos, around the corner on Antik Sok.

Paragliding The cliffs above Kaş are beginning to rival Ölüdeniz as a paragliding venue, and it's marginally cheaper here; contact the local branch of Skysports (☎ 0242/836 3291); expect to pay $80–90.

Travel agents The British/Turkish-run Bougainville Travel, Çukurbağlı (İbrahim Serin) Cad 10 ☎ 0242/836 3737, ⊛ www.bougainville-turkey .com, is the foremost adventure travel agency in the area – this is where you come for diving, mountain treks, canyoning and sea-kayaking, though they also offer more conventional excursions. Simena Tours on Elmalı Caddesi ☎ 242/836 1416 is a more conventional agency, selling air tickets and renting cars.

Water Delicious and potable, straight from the limestone mountains around Gömbe, available free at taps by the harbour mosque; the Saklıkent pipeline water is considered only fit to wash in.

North of Kaş: Akdağ and Yeşil Göl

When sea-level pleasures at Kaş pall, especially in excessively hot weather, there's no closer escape than the cool heights of the **Akdağ range**, which soars to over 3000m in the space of 20km. The standard jump-off point for excursions into the mountains, and one easily reached by public minibus from Kaş, is **Gömbe**, a small town 60km north of Kaş, on the road to Elmalı. This provides access to **Yeşil Göl**, Lycia's only permanent alpine lake, and also serves as a first stop for anyone intending to climb the **peak of Akdağ** itself, a three-hour climb above the lake.

Gömbe

The hour and a half ride up from Kaş is mostly shaded by extensive pine forests, which yield to vast apple orchards as you approach **GÖMBE**. No

A Lycian Way segment: Kaş to Üçağız

The following portion of the Lycian Way (see box, p.464) begins in Kaş and will take most walkers two full days (or three shorter days) to complete. Outside of the spring grazing and charcoal-making seasons, it's one of the lonelier sections of the route, so you need to be fairly self-sufficient (sleeping bag, stove, food, probably a tent), and carry at least two litres of water per person from the outset, topping up at every opportunity. Done as a two-day hike, it's a strenuous 9hr 30min second day from the suggested campsite, with a very early start required to enjoy both the ruins en route and a soft bed in Üçağız before dark.

Take a taxi to the end of the asphalt road at **Büyü Çakıl** and follow the dirt track away from the last houses. Over the first hour this dwindles to a good path leading to a long, flat field above **Bayındır Limanı**, after which there's a rough, overgrown, cross-country hour to the rocky double bay of **Çoban Plajı**, facing Kastellórizo. From here an easier herders' path leads in 45 minutes up to a shady saddle, with a subsequent gradual descent for 45 minutes more, paralleling the coast, to ruined cottages at **Ufak Dere** cove (poor-to-average swimming). This makes a good lunch stop.

From Ufak Dere, ascend 45 minutes on a mix of tracks and paths to another pass where Kastellórizo is visible for the last time, and there's an apparently abandoned, unlocked house with a cistern inside – the first reliable water en route, for which you'll need parachute cord and a container-with-handle to fetch. From here, the trail descends half an hour to a point where you can divert right (seaward) onto a marked-as-"wrong-way" path, which leads quickly to some charcoal-burners' flats under shady pines by the sea. This makes a wonderful **campsite**, with fine swimming in the bay here.

Resuming progress, you've another hour-plus on a sometimes indistinct path to the next "beach", with poor bathing, and the possibility of camping in the olive groves just inland; swimming is better off the rocks some 45 minutes ahead. There the route veers inland up a valley for half an hour to a third pass with a reliable, deep well (equipment required, as above) and the remains of an ancient watchtower. Next

commercial maps yet show the huge **Çaybogazı reservoir** which has re-routed any approach from the south – drivers should avoid the circuitous bypass road by going right over the dam-top road, which may not yet be surfaced or properly signposted. Gömbe, the ancient Comba (nothing remains), is famous for a festival of the local Tahtacıs, which happens in June, and another farmers' fair during the latter half of August.

Around the main square are three simple but adequate **restaurants**, all with similar bean-soup-and-köfte menus (full, if slightly greasy, meals for $4–5 per head), a few dondurma parlours on summer evenings, plus three **pansiyons**, mostly on the hillside south of the square. Of these, fanciest is the en-suite Paşa (☎0242/831 5208; ❷), though the nearly adjacent Akın (☎0242/831 4117; ❶) – enquire at şafak Restaurant – is adequate and clean, with shared bathrooms.

Yeşil Göl and Akdağ

Most people come to Gömbe to visit **Yeşil Göl** (Green Lake), a short distance west and the only permanent body of water in the generally arid, karstic Akdağ sierra. Tucked into the east flank of Akdağ at about 1850m elevation, Yeşil Göl is a large, clean and fairly deep tarn at its best between April and June; the earlier in spring you show up, the finer the **wildflower** displays. The southern shore of the lake has enough (slightly sloping) turf for a handful of tents, should you skirt the hill above, either to its left or right (the waymarks go anticlockwise), to emerge on a jeep track leading to **Boğazcık** village (another hour to get there); there's water here, but no other facilities.

The Lycian Way proper veers off east before actually reaching the village, onto an ancient path giving access within 45 minutes (including a 15-minute detour) to ancient **Apollonia** (see p.509). After visiting Apollonia, continue south on either the marked or "wrong-way" route (they converge) for 2hr 15min to ancient **Aperlae** (see p.508). Do not be surprised if you share the path with a camel or two – the authorities have forbidden road construction in this archeologically rich area, and working (as opposed to tourist-attraction) camels are the most efficient transport for the shepherds who keep animals on the Sıçak peninsula.

From Aperlae, cross the isthmus of the Sıçak peninsula on level ground, arriving after half an hour at the two restaurants at the jetty here – one of them belonging to Ramazan, one of the last local camel-drivers. You could camp behind the buildings, especially if you ate a meal here. The onward trail is initially faint and counter-intuitive, veering briefly northwest away from the water, marked at first only by plain red paint dashes. Subsequently it becomes more distinct in the red dirt, and conventional two-colour blazes reappear. Near some cottages on a ridge, angle towards the northeast edge of the *ova* here – *don't* take tempting traces marching down the centre – to reach simple shelters used by charcoal-burners. Resumed waymarks lead you up onto the true left bank of the ravine draining from the *ova*, about an hour beyond the restaurants, for your first view of the **Üçağız** bay; the *ova* pastures with their cowpats – and flies – are left behind. Go through a fence into olive-grove terraces, where path and waymarks vanish again; make your way, with rough ground underfoot, as best you can, to the shore (1hr 45min from restaurants), making sure to head for the left (north)-most inlet of the double-pronged bay ahead. The route, now essentially cross-country, hugs the shore for the final 45 minutes to the first buildings of **Üçağız** – where some mean-spirited individual has piled gorse in an attempt to hinder walkers.

you wish to **camp** the night – advisable if you plan to traverse Akdağ (see p.504).

To reach the lake, it's best to have your own transport (2WD vehicles passable with care, but best in 4WD), but the following directions apply equally to hikers. Leave the square heading north and turn left immediately after crossing the river bridge, then take the second paved right, and begin climbing. Zigzags take you to the Çukurbağ Köyü mosque; turn left here and keep an aqueduct, and phone lines, parallel to your track – confirm directions by asking for the track to "Subaşı Yayla".

Exactly 6.2km above the central Gömbe bridge, half an hour's low-gear driving around wash-outs, ruts, boulders and treefalls, just above the highest gnarled junipers, you'll reach a widening in the track beside a vigorous stream, near the start of the aqueduct. Some 500m past this widening is another parking place, flanked by a brick privy with four squat-slots; immediately beyond a landslide blocks the track. Down in the stream ravine a cement pedestrian bridge gives the only safe access to the far bank, where faint paths lead up to another non-vehicular track, blocked off by boulders at its turnoff from your original track – assuming the landslip is ever cleared, you could wrestle a car this far as the main motorable track executes a hairpin across the ravine, upstream from the privy. In either case, follow this rougher track past some rudimentary shepherds' huts and corrals; immediately after this leave the track for proper paths over a gently saddle that emerge abruptly at an overlook for the lake (maximum 30min from the privy).

Continuing twenty minutes in the same direction, guided by red paint arrows on rocks, you top another crest from which you can view the not-very-impressive **Uçarsu waterfalls** pouring off the flank of Akdağ summit – more like rapids, these run only during May and June, essentially a snowmelt phenomenon.

Climbing Akdağ

If you intend to **climb the peak** of Akdağ (3024m), retrace your steps to the main motorable track and proceed west; after about ten minutes you pass a quadruple-spouted spring. After a few bends, and now high above the streambed, you adopt the true right bank (facing the direction of flow) of the watercourse. When you reach a tributary coming from the south, turn to follow it, keeping to the true left bank. The summit ridge will be ahead, on your right; soon you should pick up a distinct, cairned path that will take you all the way to the top, a two-and-a-half-hour hike one-way with a daypack, from the spring. The **summit cairn** contains a "guestbook" to sign, and the views over the snow-flecked badlands are superb. An ice-axe is most useful until June or July (depending on the preceding winter), and you'll need an adequate water bottle in any season.

If you wish to do a complete **traverse of the range**, you'll have to plan on an overnight stop somewhere on the mountain. The classic descent is to **Arsaköy** (with a basic village inn) on the west flank of Akdağ, from where a wonderful cobbled path descends for a couple of hours towards Saklıkent before disappearing under a bulldozer track.

Dereağzı

About 30km northeast of Kaş, some imposing ruins at **Dereağzı** – an enormous, half-intact Byzantine church, and a strong Byzantine castle built atop a much earlier fortification – are a worthy destination for anyone with their own transport. The latter guarded a strategic narrows (Dereağzı means "valley mouth" in Turkish) in the easiest route for shipping grain and cedar wood to Andriake (see p.514) from the rich upland plains of Elmalı and Kasaba.

To get there, take the road to Gömbe and turn east at Kasaba village, following signs to Çatallar, and then proceed for just over 8km to Dirgenler village. At a crossroads here, a sign points left to three villages; you go right onto a gravel track towards a pine-studded ridge. After 2.8km, you reach the head of a gorge, with some rock tombs visible, and a small water-pumping station in a concrete shed; this is the point where the Kasaba plateau begins draining towards the sea. The abrupt, roughly triangular hill on your right turns out to be covered in ruins of a castle, barely noticeable from afar.

The castle

From just before the pumping station, faint goat paths angle southwest to become the old Byzantine path – still the only way up – leading within twenty minutes to the overgrown **main gate** in the northwest-facing wall. Once up and in, you fully appreciate the amazing site, not unlike those of the Cathar castles of Languedoc: the southwest-to-northeast ridge is essentially a knife-edge, and the entire fortified hill is lapped by two rivers, the

Kasaba and the Karadağ, which mingle at the southeast tip to form the Demre Çayı.

The ancient Lycians first built this castle during the sixth to fifth centuries BC, using polygonal, unmortared masonry, or occasionally even hewing into the rock strata. After the devastating Arab wars of the eighth Century AD, the Byzantines improved and enlarged it during the ninth and tenth centuries, using their preferred mortared-rubble technique. In particular they added the half-dozen triangular or rectangular **bastions and towers** still visible on the lowest, northwest wall, the castle's weakest side. American surveys and explorations from 1974 to 1981 revealed two more inner layers of defence as one proceeds to the summit, complete with a **church**, plus dozens of **cisterns** and water-collecting channels.

Down in the Karadağ gorge, most of the area's Lycian **rock tombs and sarcophagi** are on the east bank of the stream, near the passage of an **ancient road** with numerous steps. This road can still be trekked along for about 5km, though since the bulldozing of a modern dirt road through the gorge there's less enjoyment to be derived from this.

The church

From the water-pumping station you can walk northwest on a river-bank track along the Karadağ (flippantly called the Boklu or "Shitty" creek by locals, after its algae infestation) to a point just opposite the knoll-top church where channels in the marsh narrow enough for you to cross. The huge **church**, dating from the same time as the castle reconstruction, was clearly funded from the imperial capital, given its size and the richness of its marble decoration (now all in Antalya's archeological museum). Unusual in plan and design, it has two curious, free-standing hexagonal structures, one at the apse end and one where the narthex presumably was. The brick-and-rubble church was the focus of quite a large town, which disappeared within two hundred years of its foundation; oddly neither the Byzantine nor Lycian name for Dereağzı is known, since no identifying inscriptions or coins have been found.

From the pumping station, you can make a circuit back to the coast by following the fairly smooth vehicle track downstream **along the Demre Çayı**; it's 23km, the last 4km paved, and passable to most cars except perhaps at high-water in spring (there's one river ford). Near the end, ancient watchtowers flank the widening valley on either side.

The Kekova region

Some of the most beautifully situated ruins on the south coast are in the area known as **Kekova**, after the eponymous offshore island. It's a stretch of rocky coastline littered with remains of Lycian settlements, some now submerged under the translucent waters of the calm, shallow, almost land-locked gulf here. Since the early 1990s land communications – both by road, and by trail – have been improved, so the region is no longer the exclusive preserve of boat and yacht tours. Many Lycian ruins can be easily visited from the inlet-shore village of **Üçağız**, while inland lie the neglected remains of **Apollonia**, a dependency of coastal Aperlae, and the substantial ruins of **Cyaneae**.

The map shows: Elmalı & Gömbe, Çatallar & Arykanda, Dirgenler, Sion, Karabel, Alakilise, Dereağzi, Kasaba, Muskar, Demre Çayı (Myrus River), Cyaneae, Myra, Yavu, Demre, Hwy 400, Isinda, Sura, Andriake, Çayağzı, Kılınçlı, Uçağız, Teimiussa, Kaş, Boğazcık, Apollonia, Simena, Kale, Batık Şehir, Kekova Island, Çukurbağ Peninsula, Bayındır Limanı, Aperlae, Tersane, Çoban Plajı, Ufak Dere, Sıçak İskelesi, Meis (Kastellórizo), Ulu Burun, MEDITERRANEAN SEA, Fethiye & Kalkan, Finike

THE KEKOVA REGION

Üçağız

The central village for the region is **ÜÇAĞIZ,** 38km from Kaş and connected to Highway 400 by a surfaced, twenty-kilometre road. Thus its quiet days are numbered: already carpet, antique and jewellery shops have sprouted, boat-trip touts swarm around you on arrival (or pretend to be hitchhikers on the road in), and you've little hope of finding one of the hundred-odd beds unoccupied in July or August. Most of the surroundings have been designated as an archeological site, which should protect Üçağız from unseemly concrete expansion by limiting the number of new buildings. And indeed its essential village identity has yet to be completely supplanted – out of season the place is still idyllic.

Practicalities

There's just one daily **dolmuş** from Demre, geared to villagers', not tourists', needs. Üçağız's **pansiyons** are simple, but often fairly pricey considering the remote location and lack of a beach. Although fresh water has been piped in from the environs of Gömbe, hot showers can still be erratic. The best and most secluded places both lie at the west end of the village. The 2001-built, stone-clad *Kekova* (☏0242/874 2259, ℱ874 2039; ❹) has relatively palatial air-conditioned rooms and a shared wrap-around balcony. The *Ekin* (☏0242/874 2064; ❸) just beyond sports a pleasant garden, clean, airy rooms in the original building and newer extension, plus all-important insect screens – and a cultured managing couple with a well-developed service ethic. Runners-up include *Baba Veli* (☏0242/874 2063, ℱ874 2062; ❷), the modern, air-conditioned *Koç* (☏0242/874 2080; ❸), by the first brackish pool-spring, and the *Nergiz* (☏0242/874 2041; ❷), partially en-suite and run by the friendly Alıçavuzoğlu family – it's unmarked, but just opposite the primary school.

None of the seven waterside **restaurants** represents fantastic value, and the most tolerable and durable is the *Liman Marina*, better known as *İbo's*. On its own, five minutes' walk east of the village, the *Kalealtı* (aka *Halil's*), run by the

Kormel family, offers a novel setting: surrounding tombs, castle overhead, shoreline spring flowing through its grounds. It's also marginally cheaper than the harbourside places.

Around Üçağız

Until the road was built, the Lycian remains that surround Üçağız were visited by few apart from hardy goats and archeologists. Teimiussa – and if you like walking, Simena and Aperlae – can be reached on foot from the village, but sooner or later you'll go on a **boat trip**, the main thing to do at beachless Üçağız. Destinations and prices are fairly standard: $10 per person to take in nearby Kale (Simena) and Kekova island; $18 to Andriake port or Aperlae ruins; and $5 for a one-way shuttle to Kale (the walk back takes 45min over rocky terrain, preferably on a cool day).

Üçağız translates as "three mouths" in Turkish, and the old Greek name of Tristomo, meaning exactly the same thing, is still used. The three apertures in question are the straits at each end of the island opposite, plus the entry to the lake-like gulf, at whose rear the village is situated. **Kekova Island** itself boasts the area's only beach, plus the best of the ruins, most of which are submerged but visible below the sea. The ruins of the ancient town of **Aperlae** are found on the other side of a peninsula to the west of Üçağız, while at the east edge of the village stand the fortified acropolis and tombs of another small Lycian settlement – **Teimiussa**. A little way beyond lies the village of **Kale** and the castle at **Simena**, clearly visible on the horizon. Several small islands, quarried in ancient times to near sea level, dot the bay.

Kekova Island

The most romantically situated local antiquities are those submerged along the northern coast of **Kekova Island**, known as Batık şehir (Sunken City) locally, and to date not identified with any ancient city. The underwater remains of stairs, pavements, house walls and a long quay wall can all be seen; however snorkelling or even just swimming are banned to prevent the removal of antiquities from the area, and most boatmen won't approach the rocky shoreline (the best view is from a kayak; see box below). Near the southwest tip of the island, at the spot known as Tersane (Dockyard), looms the apse of a long-vanished church, in whose shadow bathers spread their towels on fine shingle; unhappily, much of the apse collapsed during a particularly violent storm in February 1996.

Sea-kayaking around Kekova

Bougainville Travel in Kaş (see p.501) remains the exclusive organizer of **sea-kayaking day-tours** in the Kekova area, a wonderful, low-impact way of appreciating the eerie seascapes. They have the further advantage of allowing you to approach the shoreline, and the Batık Şehir in particular, much closer than cruise boats do, and also of using narrow, shallow channels off-limits to larger craft – which are, incidentally, your main threat, as you must be wary of their wake. With a suitable head covering and a water bottle secreted under your apron, you'll tolerate all but the hottest summer days, even wrapped inside a life vest. Trips often begin with a motorized tow from Üçağız to the starting point of your choice, for example Tersane; outings can be as long or short as stamina allows. Per-person rates, including a transfer from Kaş to Üçağız and a picnic lunch, are approximately $30 for a day's excursion.

Teimiussa

Ancient **Teimiussa** is easily reached from Üçağız's *Kalealtı* restaurant, immediately below it. Nothing is really known about the history of the settlement, but inscriptions indicate that it was occupied in the fourth century BC. The site, which suggests a settlement without walls and few or no public buildings, consists mainly of a good scattering of rock tombs; some of these have semicircular benches cut into their bases – convenient for pondering mortality as you stare out to sea. On the hill above squats a small fort or tower, about the size of a house, while far below at sea level you can try to hunt for the tiny, rock-cut landing stage.

Kale and Simena

A ruined castle of the Knights of St John – and the village of **KALE** below it – are a ten-minute boat ride, or a longer kayak-paddle or walk from Üçağız. The secluded village itself is the haunt of Rahmi Koç, scion of a wealthy Turkish industrialist family, who donated a school in conjunction with restoring an old house here as a holiday retreat. Even for lesser mortals, Kale makes a lovely place to stay – it's another protected archeological zone, with no permanent new buildings permitted – though some rustic-looking **pansiyons**, overlooking the sea and a marooned sarcophagus, are pricey for what you get. The best three are the *Kale Pansiyon* (☎0242/874 2111, ℱ874 2110; ❹), occasionally monopolized by British package agencies, *Nesrin's Bademli Ev* (☎0242/874 2170; ❹), a charming, three-unit B&B with fireplaces in the wood-and-stone rooms, and, just up the slope from this, the *Mehtap Pansiyon* (☎0242/874 2146, ℱ874 2261; ❸), its rather plain rooms open all year. This also has **camping** space available and good suppers served on the platform-terrace. At the six or seven waterfront **restaurants**, which have had a long and jading acquaintance with the tour-boat trade, the normal routine seems to be charging a set price (around $6) for a fill-your-plate *meze* buffet.

The climb to the acropolis of ancient **Simena** (unenclosed; $2 when warden present) is steep but brief, and worth it both for the views as well as for the mediaval **castle** itself, whose castellated ramparts are in good condition, partly resting on ancient foundations. Inside the Knights' castle is a fifteen-metre-wide **theatre** carved into the living rock, large enough for perhaps two hundred people; on the northern slopes of the hill, off the path, stand some well-preserved **sarcophagi**. Brace yourself for being followed all the way up and down by children peddling printed headscarves, and village women pressing oregano into your hands or offering guiding services in exchange for a consideration.

Aperlae

Southwest of Üçağız lies the site of **Aperlae**, a forty-minute boat ride to a landing stage with two restaurants, followed by a half-hour walk; it's also reachable via the Lycian Way (see p.502 for how). Its remoteness means that the site is practically deserted, though there's a cluster of houses at Sıcak İskelesi, beside the ruins. The remains of the **city walls** are fairly well preserved and easily identified – they bisect the hillside and enclose a rectangular area, with the sea lapping the southern side; the **necropolis**, as is usual, lies almost entirely outside the walls. As at Kekova, subsidence has submerged the harbour quarter, but swimming and snorkelling here is thus far unrestricted. If you follow the line of the old **quay**, now in 1–2m of water and indented at 15-metre intervals for the mooring of ships, you can easily see heaps of pottery shards, amphora necks, terracotta floor tiles and shell-middens from the ancient murex-dye industry, all encrusted together. There are also building foundations in rows divided by narrow **streets**, including a small section of intact pavement near the shore.

In the absence of competing hypotheses, it's assumed that Aperlae was a Lycian city – a theory supported by Lycian coins with inscriptions "APR" and "PRL" that have been found. By imperial Roman times, Aperlae definitely headed a league of four cities – the others being Simena, Apollonia and Isinda (near modern Belenli) – whose citizens were collectively termed "Aperlite".

Apollonia

If Aperlae is neglected, unexcavated **Apollonia** is even more so. It can be reached on foot, either from Boğazcık, by a spur from the Lycian Way (see box on p.502), or part way by a two-kilometre track from the modern village of **Kılınçlı** (alias Sıçak). Kılınçlı lies astride the Üçağız-bound road and is also linked by a direct new road to Andriake.

Apollonia is mainly known for its superb **necropolis**, which spikes the lower northeast slope of the hill on which the city is found, facing Kılınçlı. There is one conventional sarcophagus with extravagant Gothic-type details, but most distinctive are a half-dozen or so **pillar tombs**, considered the ur-burial method of the ancient Lycians, and proving Apollonia's antiquity. Isolated from the other tombs, at the west end of the hill facing Boğazcık, stands an unusual **carved tomb** on two levels. But there is more to see here in the acropolis, which at its east end appears to be double: a much older stockade inside a Byzantine citadel. Particularly on the southwest flank, the **city walls** – made of unusually large quadrangular and pentagonal blocks – are pierced by windows and a gate. From atop the inner, ancient fort, you look west over a well-preserved **Byzantine church**, possibly of the sixth or seventh century; just west of this, overgrown but in a fair state of preservation, is a lovely little **theatre**. The views from the hill, whether inland to the Lycian mountains or out to sea, are the icing on the experience.

Cyaneae

East of the turn-off for Üçağız, Highway 400 enters a stretch of wild, inhospitable countryside, whose bleak aspect appeals only to the herds of sheep and goats grazing it. In antiquity, however, this region was scattered with small settlements, the most interesting nowadays being **Cyaneae** (Kyaneaı in Turkish), 23km from Kaş in the hills above the village of **Yavu**. The name Cyaneae/Kyaneai derives from the ancient Greek for "dark blue" – also the origin of the word cyanide – but it's uncertain why the city was given this name. The contemporary nickname, "city of sarcophagi", seems more apt, since the Lycian and Roman sarcophagi studding the site are the most numerous of any city in the region, and the main reason to visit. Little is known about Cyaneae's **history**, apart from the fact that it was the most important settlement in the region between Myra and Antiphellos (modern Kaş), and linked by a direct road to the harbour of Teimiussa, 12km away as the crow flies. It prospered in Roman times, and was the seat of a bishopric in the Byzantine age.

From Yavu village centre there's a signposted, two-kilometre **path to the site**; the hike up only takes about 45 minutes but the route is extremely steep. Rather easier is an unmarked, four-kilometre **dirt road** that takes off from the north side of Highway 400, precisely 1km west of the side road to Yavu; the last stretch of this track is quite rough, but negotiable with care in an ordinary 2WD car.

It's possible to take a **local guide** along, but not strictly necessary; it is they who've had a hand in misleadingly signposting the slip road to Yavu as "Kyaneai 4", and keeping the dirt track unsignposted. Guides can be found at a marked "tourist office" in the village, and at the *Çeşme* restaurant (see "Yavu and beyond" below); they tend to demand $12 per party – settle on less.

The site
On the left of the path up from the village are some of the oldest and most interesting of Kyaneai's **tombs**, lining either side of a passage that may have been part of the ancient road. The most impressive – a sarcophagus carved completely from the rock on which it stands – lies south of the road. The Gothic-arch "lid", cut from the same piece of rock, has two lions' heads projecting from each side. Near the top of the path, keep an eye out for a subterranean shrine or tomb with six columns.

Below the city, fairly inaccessible on the south face of the hill, stands an impressive **temple-tomb** whose porch has a single free-standing column and, unusually, a recess above the pediment in which a sarcophagus has been installed. According to an inscription, this was reserved for the bodies of the head of the household and his wife, while the rest of the family were buried in the tomb.

The hilltop **acropolis** is surrounded on three sides by a wall, the south side being so precipitous that it didn't need protection. The buildings inside are in a ruined state and covered with vegetation, but several have been more or less tentatively identified, including a library, baths and two Byzantine churches, one with a lengthy inscription by the door. Near the summit is a tomb with a relief of a charioteer driving a team of four horses. The city had no natural spring nearby, so vaulted cisterns and reservoirs square-cut from the living rock are ubiquitous.

To the west of the summit, on the far side of the area used for parking, stands a moderate-sized **theatre** with 23 rows of seats still visible, divided by the diazoma. Its upper rows make ideal vantage points to survey the western walls of the acropolis, the Kekova inlet to the south, and a row of sarcophagi flanking an ancient path linking the theatre and the acropolis. Mainly Roman, these tombs tend to be very simple, with rounded lids and crests, but include a few lion-head bosses too.

Yavu and beyond
Back on Highway 400, about 500m in the Antalya direction, the *Çeşme* is a welcoming **restaurant**, run by an extroverted Turkish woman, Gülay Akkuş. Besides the only decent (and reasonably priced) cooking for 20km to either side, there are four *pansiyon* **rooms** available (☎0242/871 5425; ❶), with more being readied in an old house nearby.

A popular local **walk**, best in winter or spring, involves following the broad, ancient path from here towards Teimiussa: an outing of just under three hours, but sliced now by a minor paved road between Andriake and Kılınçlı, with the last hour unfortunately spent trudging along the paved side road to Üçağız. People at the restaurant can point you to the start of the route.

Demre and around

East of Yavu, Highway 400 swoops down in a well-graded arc towards the river-delta town of **Demre**, focus of some of the more intriguing sites in

Lycia. It's worth pausing for a few hours here in order to see the **Church of St Nicholas** – best observed in peace and quiet before 9am or after 5pm, when Demre is practically empty of visitors. Nearby attractions include the ancient city of **Myra**, just to the north, and the ancient harbour of **Andriake** and Apollo oracle at **Sura**, a little way south (you pass close to both approaching from the west). For the more adventurous, the remote Byzantine churches of **Alakilise** and **Sion** beckon in the hills inland.

Some history

Myra was one of the most prominent members of the Lycian Federation, and retained this importance throughout the Middle Ages because of its associations with the bishop **St Nicholas** (aka Santa Claus). An ancient tradition asserts that the city's name derives from the Greek word for myrrh, the gum resin used in the production of incense. Although no record of the manufacture of this unguent is recorded, the emperor Constantine Porphyrogenitus described the city as the "thrice blessed, myrrh-breathing city of the Lycians, where the mighty Nikolaos, servant of God, spouts forth myrrh in accordance with the city's name". There is also a tale that when the tomb of St Nicholas was opened by Italian grave robbers, they were overwhelmed by the smell of myrrh emanating from it.

Despite its subsequent fame, there is no mention of Myra in records before the first century BC. In 42 BC the city distinguished itself with typically Lycian defiance by refusing to pay tribute money to Brutus; Brutus's lieutenant had to break the chain closing the mouth of the harbour at Andriake – the city's port – and force his way in. Subsequently, Myra had an uneventful if prosperous history until its abandonment in the fourteenth century, treated well by its imperial overlords and receiving its highest accolade when the Byzantine emperor Theodosius II made it capital of Lycia in the fifth century.

By then the city's fame had been much enhanced by one of its citizens, namely St Nicholas, born in Patara late in the third century AD and later appointed bishop of Myra. He is supposed to have slapped the face of the Alexandrian heretic Arius at the Council of Nicaea in 325 AD, although his Western identity as a genial old present-giver is perhaps more familiar, arising from the story of his kindness to the three daughters of a poor man who were left without a dowry. Nicholas is credited with throwing three purses of gold into the house one night, enabling them to find husbands instead of selling themselves into prostitution. Many posthumous miracles were attributed to the saint, but little is actually known about the man. However, it has been established that after his death he was buried in the church in Demre now dedicated to him, and it is also widely believed that in 1087 his bones were carried off to Italy by a group of devout raiders from Bari (although the Venetians and Russians lay dubious claim to a similar exploit). Demre is still proud of its connection with St Nicholas (*Noel Baba* or "Father Christmas" in Turkish), and every December 6 (the saint's feast day) a special mass is held in his church, attracting pilgrims from Greece, Italy and (lately) Russia.

Demre

DEMRE (officially called, and signposted as, Kale) is a rather scruffy little place, too far away from the coast to merit a "seaside" tag, and afforded more mid-day attention by tour parties than it can really handle. Tourism has always been dwarfed by the main local business of growing citrus fruit and tomatoes, whose greenhouses – spread below as you descend the escarpment to the west – make the town seem bigger than it really is. Unlike other non-descript towns on the coast from here to Antalya who juggle sun-and-wave motifs in their municipal logos, Demre is unequivocal about its priorities and self-image: a giant tomato occupies most of its coat-of-arms, though lately a silhouette-bust of Father Christmas has also crept in.

The Church of St Nicholas

The **Church of St Nicholas** (daily: May–Oct 8.30am–7pm; Nov–April 8.30am–5/6pm; $4.50) dominates the centre of Demre, situated on the right of Müze Caddesi as you head west. Despite the erection of a horrible synthetic protective canopy, the building remains evocative of the life and times of its patron saint, even if the myths surrounding him are more romance than fact.

The beatification of Nicholas occurred after visitors to his tomb here reported miraculous events, and Myra soon became a popular locus of pilgrimage. A monastery was built nearby during the eleventh century and, even after the Italian merchants stole the bones of the saint, the pilgrimages continued; indeed, it is thought that the monks simply designated another tomb as that of St Nicholas, and would pour oil through openings in the top and collect it at the bottom, to sell to pilgrims as holy secretions.

The contemporary church has little in common with the fourth-century original, which was first rebuilt by Constantine IX in 1043, probably after its destruction by occupying Saracens. Today's shrine is basically a three-aisled basilica in form, with a fourth added later. In 1862 Tsar Nicholas I had the church renovated, installing a vaulted ceiling instead of a cupola in the central nave, along with a belfry – both unheard of in early Byzantine architecture. Turkish archeologists have carried out more recent restoration in order to protect the building, such as the addition of the small stone domes in the narthex.

Perhaps the most typical Byzantine feature is the **synthronon** or bishop's throne in the apse, a relatively rare sight in Turkish medieval buildings since most were removed when such churches were converted into mosques. **Mosaic floor** panels (many regrettably off-limits), mainly comprising geometric designs, adorn the nave and south aisle, while among the pieces of masonry cluttering the courtyard at the back is one carved with an anchor – Nicholas is the patron saint of sailors as well as virgins, children, merchants, scholars, pawnbrokers and Holy Russia. His supposed **sarcophagus**, in the most southerly aisle as you face the bishop's throne, is worth a look, although not considered genuine. The tomb from which the saint's bones were stolen was reportedly located under a stone pavement – and, more significantly, on this one there are marble statues representing a man and a woman (obviously a couple) on the lid.

Practicalities

All buses and dolmuşes drop you at the fairly central **otogar**. There's a single surviving **pansiyon** out of town on the way to ancient Myra – the *Kent* (☎0242/871 2042; ❷), also with slightly pricier self-contained chalets in the garden. Central **hotels** include the drab *şahin*, on Müze Caddesi towards St Nicholas (☎0242/871 2686; ❷), and the *Grand Hotel Kekova*, east of the centre opposite the PTT (☎0242/871 3462, ℱ871 5366; ❸), which is newer and better value. Among a bare handful of **restaurants** downtown, the *İpek*, on the same side of Müze Caddesi as the church, is acceptable; the locals patronize it, and the bill for two with wine won't exceed $16.

Myra

The remains of ancient **Myra** (daily: April–Oct 8.30am–7.30pm; Nov-March 8.30am–5pm; $3.75) are a two-kilometre walk or drive north of Demre's town centre, and form one of the most easily visited, and most beautiful, Lycian sites. The imagination is captured by the immediacy with which you can walk out of the contemporary agricultural mundanity and into a Greco-Roman theatre or a Lycian rock tomb. Not surprisingly the place can be crawling with people throughout the summer season, when the best times to visit are either early morning or after 5.30pm.

Apart from the highlights – a large theatre and some of the best examples of house-style rock tombs to be seen in Lycia – most of the city is still buried. The **theatre** was destroyed in an earthquake in 141 AD but rebuilt shortly afterwards; the rock face behind it being vertical and unable to support the cavea, the structure had to be constructed with masonry on either side, although its back rests against the cliff. The theatre is flanked by two concentric galleries covering the stairs (still intact), by which spectators entered the auditorium. Lying around the orchestra are substantial chunks of carving that would once have decorated the stage building, including one depicting two theatrical masks (now toppled upside down).

The main concentration of **tombs** is to the west of the theatre, and only accessible by some uphill scrambling. Most of the tombs are of the house type, supposed to imitate Lycian dwelling-places, even down to the wooden beams supporting the roofs. Some are decorated with reliefs, including warriors at the climax of a battle, a naked page handing a helmet to a warrior, and a funerary scene.

The second group of tombs, called the **river necropolis**, is around the side of the second long ridge on the right as you stand with your back to the theatre stage. To get there, leave the main site, turn left off the final access drive onto the main approach road, and continue inland for 1.5km. Here a monument known as the "**painted**" **tomb** (though it no longer retains any pigment) features the reclining figure of a bearded man and his family in the porch, and outside on the rock face what is presumed to be the same family, dressed in outdoor clothes. To the east of the theatre, below the acropolis hill, lie the remains of a brick building whose identity is unknown, although it preserves an inscription on a Doric column concerning a ferry service that operated between Myra and Limyra in imperial Roman times.

Byzantine churches: Alakilise and Sion

In the hills north of Demre are two fascinating early Byzantine churches, rarely mentioned even in archeological manuals, both of them sixth-century constructions by the same architect. The easterly of these, beyond the village of Muskar and in better condition, is that of **Alakilise**, which has no proper automobile access; you get there in four hours via the Lycian Way, which scales the palisade forming the northeast bank of the Demre Çayı via the so-called *Gavur Yolu* or "Infidel's Road", a skilfully engineered cobbled path. Huddled in a valley with some ruinous outbuildings, this was apparently a monastic church dedicated to the Archangel Gabriel; an inscription records its restoration early in the ninth century. The other church, known as **Sion**, is near the village of Karabel, and in not quite as good condition, though you can go most of the distance by sturdy car; a modern road cuts across the Gavur Yolu, linking Demre to Karabel via Muskar.

Andriake and Çayağzı

The port of the ancient city of Myra, **Andriake**, lies well over 2km southwest of Demre, and nearly 5km from Myra itself. To get there (there's no public transport), head west out of Demre towards Kaş, and then bear left, following black-on-yellow signs, when the main highway begins tackling the grade on the right bank of the stream leading down to the sea. Another kilometre beyond the site lies the modern anchorage of **Çayağzı** ("Rivermouth"), site of a reasonable beach and start-point for boat trips to the Kekova region.

Andriake

Ancient **Andriake**, built on either bank of the ancient Androkos River, was the site of **Hadrian's granary**, vital not only to Myra but to the whole Roman world, since its contents were sent to Rome to be distributed around the empire. The substantial remains of the building can still be seen south of today's river, which runs parallel to the road between Demre and the beach. The granary – built on the orders of Hadrian between 119 and 139 AD, and very similar to the one at Patara – consists of eight rooms constructed of well-fitting square-cut blocks. The outer walls still stand to their original height, giving a clear idea of the impressive overall size of this structure. Above the main central gate are busts of Hadrian and what is thought to be his wife, the empress Sabina. Another decorative relief on the front wall, near the second door from the west, depicts two deities of disputed identity, one of whom is flanked by a snake and a griffin, while the other reclines on a couch.

Çayağzı

Çayağzı offers a rather average sandy beach and a half-dozen snack-shacks, though don't count on a full meal here – the lone full-service restaurant on the far side of the pedestrian bridge operates fitfully. This is still a working fishing port, with an active boatyard, and it's possible to get a **boat** from here to the Kekova area, a 45-minute journey, followed by the standard tour of the underwater ruins at Kekova Island. You'll need a boatload (10–15 people) – although some owners (who tout keenly on your arrival) will take individuals or couples for around $10.

The main reason to come to Çayağzı is for a swim. The beach is fairly short, but broad and duney – though also trash-strewn and prone to algae slicks, which, together with the Kaş–Demre highway passing just overhead, perhaps accounts for the minimal development here. However, the beauty of the skyline to the west cannot be underestimated, where parallel ridges – as in a Japanese print – march down to Kekova.

Sura

Marginally more accessible than ancient Andriake is the ancient Apollo oracle at **Sura** (unrestricted access; free), which is reached either from the new Üçağız–Kapaklı–Andriake road, just before it joins the new highway looping high above Andriake en route to Demre, or via the Lycian Way. Sura is little visited and unspoilt, except for a large, illicit rubbish tip by the edge of the road just west, which is slowly polluting the marsh below – and presumably the beach. Incidentally, do not be tempted to try reaching the oracle from Çayağzı beach; you will founder in the marsh, and there is no usable trail along the rocky hillsides enclosing it to either side.

Unlike Patara, Sura was never a city, merely a sacred precinct with only priests resident. The **acropolis**, rising very modestly above the level of a small plateau here, had a square outer perimeter wall (with stubs of watchtowers still visible on the north), and on the west side a peculiar twelve-chambered keep, possibly a hostel for pilgrims. Just southeast of this was a presumed **priestly residence**, today only discernible as a large rock-cut terrace; a few paces west of this, a rock-cut **stairway** (still partly preserved) descended the sheer cliff face beyond the keep to the vicinity of a **sacred spring**, which still flows. Close to this, plainly visible from afar in the mud-flats, is the well-preserved **Temple of Apollo Surios**, together with the spring the focus of the ancient oracle.

This, according to ancient writers, was most peculiar in form and function. Supplicants arrived bearing spits of roasted meat, which they presented to priests awaiting them in a sacred grove by the shore; though the temple is now 1.5km inland, in ancient times the sea came almost up to its door. The priests would then throw the meat into a "whirlpool" in the sand, apparently a place where fresh-water springs welled up in the tidal stream mouth; every surge of the sea would bring numerous fish, attracted by the meat. Then the pilgrims' fortunes would be proclaimed on (accounts differ) either according to whether the fish accepted or rejected the meal, or by the species and behaviour of the fish. The extra springs can still be seen rippling the surface of the stream in front of the temple, and in coastal Turkey quite large ocean fish – sea bass and mullet – are tolerant of brackish conditions, though the "whales and sawfish" of the ancient authors are perhaps fantastic. After the suppression of pagan oracles towards the end of the fourth century AD, two **Byzantine churches** sprung up here: one behind the temple, one up in the acropolis.

Finike

A twisty half-hour drive beyond Demre, the harbour town of **FINIKE**, formerly Phoenicus, no longer preserves evidence of its past, and offers precious little to suggest an illustrious future either. Highway 400 has been a double-edged sword as far as Finike is concerned: its local completion during the 1960s, long before the Finike–Antalya and Kaş–Kınık stretches were opened, provided the town with a much-needed link between the port and inland citrus groves, the mainstay of the local economy (an orange figures in the municipal logo). But this now-busy thoroughfare has also ruined Finike aesthetically by cutting its centre off from the beach and disturbing the peace of this potentially attractive place.

The town used to be deserted in summer as its residents headed for the hills, particularly to the *ova* around Elmalı, but now concrete constructions are beginning to obscure the view of the bay, and they vastly outnumber the few remaining Ottoman houses, now mostly found inland. Finike's **marina** has become very busy, attracting *gülets* and private yachts put off by Antalya's high docking fees and distance from the best cruising coasts. But if you're not on a boat, the only reason to stay is for easy access to a pair of nearby ancient cities: Arykanda and Limyra (see p.516).

Finike's main **beach**, extending east of town for some kilometres, has little to recommend it other than sandiness and length: it's not terribly scenic, clean or protected from wind and waves, and it's backed backed by the suburb of **Sahilkent** with its vast numbers of apartment blocks and lodging pitched at weekending Turks. For calmer swimming, there are a pair of prettier pebble coves – **Gökliman** (4km west) and **Çağıllı** (8km west) – between Finike and Demre.

Practicalities

Finike's **otogar** is centrally situated, just off Highway 400, 300m along the road to Limyra, Arykanda and Elmalı. Those heading east should note that the town has the last **banks** with ATMs before Kemer (bar unsightly Kumluca). The **hamam**, by the bus station, is modern and well maintained.

As at Demre, there's relatively little choice in terms of **accommodation**. Your best option, up a long flight of steps on the hill 150m south of the *otogar*, is the *Paris Hotel-Pansiyon* (℡0242/855 1488; ❷), a pleasant place with some plumbed rooms, and a terrace with a good view of Finike bay. The friendly managing family speaks French and English, and operates a rooftop restaurant in summer, as well as an auxiliary *pansiyon* 4km out along the beach. Otherwise, try the medium-sized, basic *şendil* (℡0242/855 1660; ❷), also with a roof terrace and admirably well signposted at a quiet spot 300m inland from the shoreline park, or – if you require still greater comfort – the *Bahar Otel* (℡0242/856 2020; ❷), right in the town centre. It's quieter but with lesser views than nearby rival *Engin Oteli* (℡0242/855 3040; ❷), half of whose air-conditioned rooms overlook the sea, waterfront park and the main highway.

Eating options in Finike are similarly limited, if mostly licensed: the *Deniz*, a few steps west of the PTT, is an old standby, though portions tend to be small even by Turkish standards. The best all-rounder is *Birlik* (near the *Bahar Otel* across from the Ziraat Bankası), open 24 hours and with good grilled fish plus a few *meze*s and soups (though slightly bizarre service). Certainly the most pleasant environment is provided by the *Petek*, with a summer terrace overlooking the yacht drydock (if not actually the water); the wood-stove-equipped winter salon doubles as the yachties bar and club, and the food's not bad either – $7 a head for wine, salad and farmed bream.

Limyra, Arykanda and Elmalı

The road **inland from Finike to Elmalı** (Highway 635) is an hour and a half's uphill drive along a precipitous mountain route, made especially terrifying by the cavalier attitude of the numerous truck drivers who hurtle up and down it with timber or loads of produce from the local orchards. On the way up it's worth stopping to visit two beautiful mountain sites, **Limyra** and **Arykanda**.

Limyra

The site of **Limyra** is the less impressive of the two, but easily accessible if you have just a cycle or a motorbike. It's about 10km north of Finike, 3km from the Finike–Elmalı highway: turn off at the village of Turunçova and head east down a signposted road. Any Finike–Elmalı dolmuş can drop you off at Turunçova, from where you'll have to walk the remaining distance. There's a car park and village of sorts at the site itself, complete with pesky children.

Limyra had a promising start: founded in the fifth century BC, the city was made capital of Lycia by local ruler Pericles in the fourth century. From then on its fortunes were broadly the same as other Lycian cities, and it didn't make much of an appearance in the history books until 4 AD, when Gaius Caesar, grandson and adopted heir of Augustus, died here on his way home from Armenia. During Byzantine times it became the seat of a bishop, but suffered badly during the Arab raids of the seventh to ninth centuries and was largely abandoned. A peculiar feature of the site, noted in antiquity, is the vigorous spring-fed river, typical of this kind of rock strata, that emerges suddenly at the base of Tocak Dağı; apparently there was a fish-oracle here too, similar in concept to the one at Sura (see p.514).

The main settlement, and consequently most of its public buildings, lay at the foot of the hill, but now few traces of ancient buildings are visible on the flatlands among the branches of the river, and the ruins mostly consist of several hundred **tombs**. The southern slope of the mountain is covered by tombs cut into the rock face; above is a fortified **acropolis**. On the left of the road from Turunçova, the western **necropolis** includes an impressive two-storey tomb in a citrus grove. North of the road looms a **theatre** dating from the second century AD, behind which is a free-standing fourth-century sarcophagus with an inscription in Lycian announcing it as the tomb of Xatabura, thought to have been a relation of Pericles (the founder of the Lycian Federation). Among its abundant relief carvings are a funeral feast, on the south side, and on the west a scene depicting the judgement of Xatabura, pictured as a naked youth.

At the top of Tocak Dağı, north of the site, stands the most interesting **tomb** of all, signposted as the "Heroon" from the theatre. It's about a forty-minute climb to get there, up the path leading from the back of the village, but worth the effort – swarms of local children will offer their unnecessary services as guides. This mausoleum is probably that of Pericles, who saved Lycia from the ambitions of Mausolus in the fourth century. The tomb divides into two parts: a lower grave chamber, and the upper chamber styled like a temple, with a row of four caryatids at front and back. The figures of the frieze, which show the hero mounting his chariot, indicate the blend of Greek and Persian influences on later Lycian art.

Arykanda

Arykanda lies 34km north of Finike, on the right-hand side of the road; if you're coming directly from Kaş, make use of the short cut between Kasaba and Çatallar, 4km below the ruins, which is entirely paved and fairly broad despite pessimistic depictions on obsolete touring maps. Travelling by minibus, you should ask to be dropped off at the village of **Arif**, from whose top end it's a one-kilometre signposted walk to the ruins along a side road passable to any car. At the end of the line you'll find toilets, water taps, and a double parking area, but as yet no fencing or ticket booth (though $2 admission is charged when the warden is present). Individual monuments are scattered and unlabelled, though there is a good site plan by the entrance.

Finds here date back to the fifth century BC, but the typically Lycian "-anda" suffix suggests that the city may have been founded a millennium earlier. Although Arykanda was a member of the Lycian Federation from the second century BC, its inhabitants were chiefly renowned for their sloth and profligacy: when Antiochus III tried to invade Lycia in 197 BC, they reputedly took his side in the hope of reaping financial benefits to help repay their debts. Christianity gained ground here in the third century, as proved by a copy of a petition to the emperor Maximinus, in which the Arykandans request that the "illegal and abominable practices of the godless" be suppressed. The city continued in a much-reduced form until the eleventh century, mainly confined to the area just to either side of today's main through path.

The Tahtacis

The so-called **Tahtacılar** or "Board-Cutters" are a secretive and much-maligned group who are in fact Alevîs, a sect closely related to Shiism and specifically the Bektaşi dervish order. They are descended from remnants of the army of Shia Shah Ismail, who was defeated by Sultan Selim I at the Battle of Çaldıran in 1514. Like all good heretics before and since, the stragglers retreated high into the mountains, out of reach of their enemies, and today occupy villages in a wide montane crescent, extending from Edremit to Adana, with a special concentration in the Toros ranges. Their present name commemorates the professions of logger and wood-carver that many of them have followed in recent centuries; such Tahtacıs are semi-nomadic, under summer contract to the Forest Service, with whole villages sent to fell trees in areas that change from year to year.

While the allied Bektaşis have their spiritual centre at central Anatolian Hacabektaş, the Tahtacıs still maintain a seminary at Narlıdere outside İzmir. Their **beliefs**, which they can be reluctant to discuss with outsiders, share most of the tenets of Alevîsm: stress on inner purity of observance rather than external ritual, or abstention from alcohol; interdenominational tolerance and disdain of materialism; and relatively equal status for women. They are abhorrent to orthodox Sunni Muslims, who in recent decades constructed mosques – often at gunpoint – in previously mosque-less Alevî villages. Their free-thinking has often also brought them into (sometimes violent) conflict with the authorities. The Tahtacı/Alevî attitude towards women has engendered the most scurrilous slanders (principally nocturnal drunken orgies), and for visitors, it is the boldness of the unveiled women – who are not shy about addressing strangers – that is the most reliable clue that you are in a Tahtacı area, and a welcome change after the po-faced sexual segregation of mainstream Turkish village society.

Arykanda's setting is breathtaking, comparable to Delphi in Greece; it occupies a steep, south-facing hillside overlooking the major valley between the Akdağ and Bey mountain ranges. A pronounced ravine and a series of power pylons divide the site roughly in half. The first thing you'll see, beside the lower parking area, is a complex structure variously dubbed "Naltepesi" or "**lower acropolis**"; entered by a right-angled stairway, its function is not yet completely understood, but you can make out a small bath-house and presumed shops. North of the same parking area sprawls a large **basilica** with extensive mosaic flooring under tin-roof shelters posed over each aisle, and a semicircular row of benches (probably a *synthronon*) in the outer apse. Another, smaller one, lying parallel just inside, suggests eighth-century destruction and subsequent more modest rebuilding; on a terrace just below is another, unidentified mosaic-floored building. But the most impressive sight as you arrive, looming to the east, is the ten-metre-high facade of the **baths**, with numerous windows on two levels, and apsidal halls at each end – the westerly one with a still-intact plunge pool, the easterly one with stacked hypocausts; the **gymnasium** lies just beyond.

Other constructions worth seeking out include a small **temple** or tomb above the baths complex (one of three "monumental tombs" on the site plan) that was adapted for Christian worship – on the east wall is the Greek inscription "Jesus Christ is Victorious" and a crude cross; there are more Roman or Byzantine mosaics in the tombs or temples immediately east of the Christianized one. West of the ravine and power lines, and above the agora – whose engaging odeion has been defaced by horrible new marble cladding – an impressive **theatre** retains some twenty rows of seats divided by six aisles, plus a well-preserved stage building. Above this sprawls a short but attractive **stadium**, with several rows of seats exposed.

Elmalı

The 1100-metre-high plain around Elmalı is the biggest stretch of arable land in upland Lycia, an important centre for harvesting apples, potatoes and sugar beets – and, until recent conservation edicts, the cedars of the Beydağları as well. **ELMALI** (literally, "apple-ish"), dominated by nearby snowcapped Elmalı Dağı (2296m), is a town of 12,000, remarkable for its domestic architecture: a large number of houses in the hillside old quarter are beautiful Ottoman timber-framed *konak*s, though many are in precarious condition, and all are greatly outnumbered by the straggly sprawl of the new town. The air is cool and fresh even in summer, with a faint smell of wood smoke, and Gömbe (see p.501) is even easier to reach from here than from Kaş.

Elmalı has a fine Classical Ottoman mosque, the early seventeenth-century **Ömerpaşa Camii** (open prayer times), whose exterior is decorated with beautiful faïence panels and inscriptions; the interior is disappointing, while the mosque *medrese* now serves as a library. Further up the main street is all that remains of a Selçuk mosque, a stubby piece of masonry that was once the base of a minaret. To the west, in the street behind the former *medrese*, you'll find the sixteenth-century **Bey Hamamı**, regrettably poorly run and not recommended.

The town comes alive for its Monday **market**, the best and least touristy in the region, and its notable **wrestling competition**, held in a purpose-built stadium during the first weekend of September. If you were planning on staying – not that there's any need to – a good-value central municipal **hotel** worth trying is the *Belediye Otel* (☏0242/618 6708; ❷), which has comfortable pillows and hot water. In the unlikely event that it's full, your alternative is the *Arzu* (☏0242/618 6602; ❷) just uphill.

With your own transport, you can head northwest beyond Elmalı to the **Güğübeli**, an 1830-metre pass at the north end of the Akdağ massif. The pass provides a worthwhile shortcut west to the Fethiye area, with fine views east to the Beydağları and west to the mountains behind Fethiye. It's a forty-minute climb through a river canyon, past tufts of juniper and the odd pastoral pen, while the descent southwest to Highway 350 via Seki passes the side-turning for Oenoanda (see p.478). Though well-paved, this is considered a minor road, and not kept snow-ploughed from late December to mid-April, when snow chains will usually be needed.

The Olympos coast

East of Finike, the coast road barrels dead straight past the beach before turning ninety degrees to enter Kumluca, a supremely unattractive market town worth a stop only during its late-January camel-wrestling matches. Beyond Kumluca, Highway 400 curls up into the **Beydağları National Park**, comprising a spectacular sequence of densely pine-forested ridges and precipitous bare cliffs. Hidden at the mouths of canyons plunging toward the sea are two of Lycia's more unspoiled beach resorts: **Adrasan** and **Olympos/Çıralı**. If you're heading towards either by car, forgo the main highway in favour of the narrow but paved side-road that veers off at the east edge of Kumluca, signposted "Beykonak, Mavikent". This scenic short cut rollercoasters through forested valleys and along dramatic coastline to **Gelidonya Burnu**, with its lighthouse and scenic flanking sections of the Lycian Way, before emerging at Çavuş, the nearest proper village to Adrasan and Olympos. The only trick en route involves turning left (north) at a signposted junction near the outskirts of Karaöz, the last bay and village before Gelidonya Burnu.

Gelidonya Burnu

From Karaöz, an obvious dirt road beginning at the small pebbly beach heads south towards the cape, parallel to the coast. Taxis or buses won't get any further than about 3.5km along, should you be thinking of arranging a pick-up shuttle later (a popular strategy with walking groups). About 6.5km from Karaöz, leave the track in favour of the marked **Lycian Way**, now a steadily rising path through oaks and pines; from the trailhead it's just under an hour with a daypack (round-trip) to the picturesque **lighthouse** just above Taşlık Burnu (as **Gelidonya Burnu**, the "Swallow Point" of the ancients, has been officially renamed). French-built in 1936, it figures prominently on the back cover of the Lycian Way guidebook. The lighthouse is not currently inhabited, though if you're here at dusk you may meet the keeper who bikes out from Karaöz to light the lamp daily. Beyond the cape straggle the treacherous **Beş Adalar** (Five Islands), shipping hazards that have caused many a wreck, including an ancient one which yielded a vast amount of treasure to archeological divers during the 1960s.

North of the lighthouse stretches a wildly scenic section of the Lycian Way, threading deserted hillside between the sea and a thousand-metre-high ridge, on its six-hour course to Adrasan (path or cross-country except for the last hour). It's probably best not attempted alone, but walking this bit has become a fairly popular organized group outing, so in any case you'll probably have company.

Adrasan

Some 18km beyond Kumluca on Highway 400, the first side road to Olympos (see opposite) provides an alternative route to Çavuş village and the bay of Adrasan. Whether you arrive at the central junction in Çavuş from this direction, or from Mavikent, you'll turn east onto the seaward road (marked "Sahil"), following hotel placards for 4km more to emerge at the attractive, relatively peaceful beach resort of **ADRASAN**. This falls within the confines of the national park, which as much as anything else has acted as a healthy brake on development here.

You can get here directly by a lone late-afternoon **bus from Antalya** (it goes back at 7am), arriving in time to stay at one of the two dozen *pansiyons* and hotels dotted along the length of the beach, or along the stream meeting the sea at the north end, under the shadow of pointy Musa Dağı. Most of the fancier **hotels** (though the term is only relative), formerly aimed exclusively at British package tourists, are sited at the south end of the strand, near the jetty. One of the best, with a large pool and its own patch of beach, is the well-kept *Ford* (T0242/883 1098, F883 1026; ❻; closed Nov–April), the last establishment in the row, with English-speaking management and rooms always held back for walk-ins. Slightly inland along the southerly approach road, on a hillside amidst the pines, the *Eviniz Pansiyon* (T0242/883 1110; closed Nov to mid-May) offers a pleasant pool terrace, indoor restaurant and views over the plain to the sea. At the far north end of the beach, where the road turns inland to become the northlerly access drive following the stream (joining the main

5

road in at the Çakmak Camii), are two more worthwhile choices: *Golden River Hotel* (☎0242/883 1190, ◍www.goldenriveradrasan.com; ❷), closest to the beach, with large if basic, white-tiled rooms, and (best of all) the much newer *Hotel Aybars* (☎0242/8831133 or 0532/314 1887, ◍www.aybarshotel.com; ❸), with large, air-conditioned, balconied rooms overlooking lush grounds and a decent restaurant. It's open in winter, December to March, by arrangement only; Aysın, on the mobile number given, speaks good English.

The *Golden River* and *Aybars* hotels, and several **restaurants** on the east bank of the enchanting watercourse, are all accessed by wobbly suspension bridges; diners are seated by or even in the streambed, where some of the hundreds of local ducks come to cadge your spare bread. None, aside from *Aybars*, are really worth singling out, but competition also ensures that none are grotesquely expensive or greasy. Back on the south end of the beach, *İrfan Korkmazer'in Yeri* restaurant, on the south esplanade, is about the most locally patronized establishment, and reliably open in spring and autumn.

A popular **boat-trip** destination is **Ceneviz Limanı**, a cliff-girt bay beyond Musa Dağı that's inaccessible on foot. There's also a small, German-Turkish-run **scuba centre** at the north end of the beach, Diving Center Adrasan (☎0532/320 3316, ◍www.Diving-Adrasan.com; closed Nov–April). As throughout coastal Turkey, more local areas were opened to dives in late-2001, but Ceneviz Limanı itself remains off-limits.

Olympos and Çıralı

From Highway 400, two marked side roads provide access to the ruins of the ancient Lycian city of **Olympos**. After 8km, the southerly road (marked "Olympos 11, Adrasan (Çavuşköy) 15") becomes a three-kilometre rough dirt track ending at a car park and inland ticket booth for the ruins (see "The site of Olympos" on p.522). Just upstream from here in the **Olympos valley** are a dozen-plus *pansiyons* or "treehouse" lodges – a popular base with Anglophone backpackers. The northerly turning off Highway 400, 800m north of the southerly one and signposted "Çıralı 7, Yanartaş, Chimaera", leads down to the hamlet of **Çıralı** on the coast, which also has food and accommodation, and easy access to the ruins by a short stroll south along the beach. Above the Çıralı coastal plain, on the toes of nearby Tahtalı Dağ, burns a perpetual flame, fed by natural gases issuing from the ground. Since antiquity this has been called the **Chimaera**, a name it shares with a mythical fire-breathing monster supposed to have inhabited these mountains.

There is a single daily direct minibus **from Antalya** to Çıralı, running Monday to Saturday in the late afternoon, returning the next day at 6.30am, as well as three buses a week **from Kumluca**. Whatever you may be told elsewhere, all other services merely pass by the two turn-offs on the main road. There is no connecting dolmuş service down to either Çirali or Olympos, so you must budget $10–12 for the taxis that lie in wait at the junction, or walk the 7km of paved, steep road down to Çıralı. Alternatively, complimentary **shuttle bus service** is laid on two or three times daily to the Olympos valley accommodation, provided individually by the more commercially minded lodges.

Some history

Nothing is known about the origins of Olympos, but the city presumably took its name from Mount Olympos, thought to be present-day Tahtalı Dağ, 16km to the north – one of over twenty mountains with the name Olympos in the Classical world. The city made its historical debut during the second century

BC, when it was minting its own coins in the manner of the Lycians. Strabo the historian wrote in 100 BC that Olympos was one of six cities in the Lycian Federation that had three votes, attesting to its importance.

The principal deity of Olympos was Hephaistos (Vulcan to the Romans), god of fire and of blacksmiths. He was considered a native of this region, and the remains of a temple dedicated to him can be found near the Chimaera; fines for damage to local tombs were payable to the temple treasury. In the first century BC, the importance of Hephaistos diminished when Cilician pirates led by Zeniketes overran both Olympos and nearby Phaselis and introduced the worship of Mithras, a god of Indo-European origin, whose rites were performed on Mount Olympos. Zeniketes made Olympos his headquarters, but in 78 BC he was defeated by the Roman governor of Cilicia, and again in 67 BC by Pompey, after which Olympos was declared public property. The fortunes of the city revived after it was absorbed into the Roman Empire in 43 AD, and Christianity became prominent. Olympos was used as a trading base by the Venetians and Genoese in the eleventh and twelfth centuries – thus Ceneviz Limanı or "Genoese Harbour" just to the south – but was abandoned in the fifteenth century as the Ottomans dominated the Mediterranean.

The site of Olympos

There are two entrances to the **site of Olympos** (daily: April–Oct 8am–7pm; Nov–March 9am–5.30pm; $7.50, ticket valid for a week): one inland, at the end of the southerly approach road, and another (where the guards are reportedly not as vigilant) about fifteen minutes' walk south along the beach from Çıralı. As at Patara, nocturnal "raids" of the ruins are expressly forbidden. It's potentially an idyllic site, located on the banks of an oleander- and fig-shaded stream running between high cliffs. Alas, a decade or so of backpackers littering or sleeping rough in the site (despite notices forbidding both) has seen the water muddied or worse, and the turtles, ducks and frogs that used to live here now make themselves scarce. The scanty ruins line the banks of the stream, which rarely dries up completely in summer, owing to three freshwater springs welling up on the north bank, quite close to the ocean.

The first things you'll notice are extensive **Byzantine-Genoese fortifications** overlooking the beach from each creek bank, just twenty to thirty metres up the crags. At the base of the fort on the north bank are two "**harbour tombs**", recognizably Lycian in form, with a touching epigraph on one translated for viewers. Further along on the south bank stands part of a quay wall and an arcaded **warehouse**; to the east on the same side lie the walls of a Byzantine **church**; while in the river itself is a well-preserved pillar from a vanished **bridge**. Back in the undergrowth there is a **theatre**, its seats mostly vanished.

The north bank of the river has the most striking ruins. On the hill to the east of the path to the beach looms a well-preserved marble **door-frame** built into a wall of ashlar masonry. At the foot of the carved doorway is a statue base dedicated by an inscription to Marcus Aurelius, with the dates 172–175 AD. East of the portal hide a Byzantine **villa** with mosaic floors, a mausoleum-style **tomb**, and a Byzantine **aqueduct** that carried water to the heart of the city. The aqueduct overlaps the outflow of one of the aforementioned springs; follow it upstream, past the mausoleum-tomb, to the villa. Though paths have been hacked through the jungly vegetation beyond the portal, the aqueduct trough remains your best bet for clear navigation.

The Chimaera

North of Olympos, in the foothills of Tahtalı Dağ, the eternal flame of the **Chimaera** is about an hour's stroll from Çıralı village; it's also possible to drive to the bottom of the ascent and walk from the car park (about 20min). Tracks to the trailhead are well signposted, and the path up (now part of the inland alternate Lycian Way) well marked and well trodden. The climb is most rewarding (and coolest) as dusk falls, since the fire is best seen in the dark; some people make rag-torches and ignite them from the flames, using them to light the path on the way down. Several of the Olympos-valley treehouse-lodges organize recommended nocturnal visits, with transfer by tractor-drawn carriages.

The Chimaera, a series of flames issuing out of cracks on the bare hillside, is one of the most unusual sites in the whole of Lycia. It's not certain what causes the phenomenon; a survey carried out by oil prospectors in 1967 detected traces of methane in the gas but otherwise its make-up is unique to this spot. The flames can be extinguished temporarily if covered over, when a gaseous smell is noticeable, but will spontaneously re-ignite.

What is known, however, is that the fire has been burning since antiquity, and inspired the local worship of Hephaistos (Vulcan), generally revered in places where fire sprang from the earth. The mountain was also the haunt of a fire-breathing monster with a lion's head and forelegs, a goat's rear end, and a snake for a tail: the Chimaera. Its silhouette, incidentally, has become the logo of the state-run *Petrol Ofisi* chain of Turkish filling stations.

Legend relates how **Bellerophon** was ordered by Iobates, king of Xanthos, to kill the Chimaera in atonement for the supposed rape of his daughter Stheneboea. With the help of the winged horse Pegasus, Bellerophon succeeded, killing the beast from the air by dropping lead into its mouth. Later, Bellerophon was deemed to have been falsely accused, and avenged himself on Stheneboea by persuading her to fly away with him on Pegasus and flinging her into the sea. He finally got his own just desserts when he attempted to ascend to heaven on Pegasus, was flung from the magical horse's back and, lamed and blinded, forced to wander the earth as a beggar until his death.

Olmypos valley

The main drawback to basing yourself in the **Olympos valley** is that you're still some way from the beach, and need to keep the current week's admission ticket with you every time you cross the archeological zone for a swim. What's more, it's very much a narrow-minded overlanders' "ghetto", despite pretensions to superiority over conventional package tourists. The chief attraction seems to be the cheap beer, and groups of Aussies duly take their evening promenade along the road, bottles in hand, to a soundtrack of reverberating rock music. During the two weeks before or after ANZAC day, when any self-respecting Ozzie or Kiwi will be paying homage at Çanakkale, don't expect any vacancies. Prices at all establishments listed below are ❷ for a shared-bath treehouse, and ❸ for en-suite bungalows (on a half-board basis); dorms (where available) and camping space usually cost $5–7 per person. Many of the lodgings hire travellers to wash up, make beds and cook on a casual basis – as ever, illegal in Turkey, but a good stopgap if funds are running low.

The most treehouse-like of the **lodges**, and thus the first to fill, are: *Kadir's*, furthest from the ruins (☎0242/892 1250, ⓦwww.olympostreehouse.com), with the liveliest bar in the valley; *Bayram's*, nestled in an orange grove closest to the ruins, with internet access (☎0242/892 1243, ⓦwww.bayrams.com); and *Türkmen*, in between the two, near the stream ford (☎0242/892 1249,

© turkmen@turkmenpension.com), the most comfortable of the trio. Among more upmarket and (relatively) quiet establishments, *Pansiyon Carretta Carretta*, adjacent to the *Türkmen* (☎ 0242/892 1295) has better-built treehouses and bungalows than usual, while *şaban* opposite *Türkmen* (☎ 0242/892 1265, © sabanpension@hotmail.com) doesn't play constant music, but does have better-than-average food, family management and internet access.

Çıralı

Since 1990, tourist development has taken off noticeably at **ÇİRALİ**. Three hotels and about thirty *pansiyons* have sprung up along the approach road and behind the three-kilometre **beach**, between the Ulupınar stream which meets the sea here and the low hills to the east. Loggerhead and green sea **turtles** still use this formerly deserted bay to lay their eggs. The Turkish Society for the Protection of Nature booth that used to be here seems to have vanished, but their message, boiled down to basics, remains: don't camp on/illuminate/dig up/litter the beach during the summer nesting season.

The best **accommodation** is listed below, and it's worth noting that rough camping is now actively discouraged (because of the turtles), especially since the opening of two proper **campsites**. After long-running disputes between the forestry and archeological services on the one hand, and local proprietors on the other, the beachfront **restaurants** have been moved back a token few metres from the sand, and seven or eight survivors – stretching in a line north of the river-mouth – seem here to stay. Of these, the best and most popular are the *Orange Home*, the *Azur* and *Karakuş*; while south of the river-mouth, where parking is incidentally very limited, the most durable establishment is the *Olympos Yavuz*, one of three adjacent rivals strategically straddling the sandy path to the ruins (vehicles not allowed beyond this point).

Hotels and pansiyons

Arcadia, ☎ 0242/825 7340, ⓦ www
.arcadiaholiday.com. Near the campsite, this beachfront Canadian-Turkish-managed establishment has four superbly executed all-wood chalet-suites, with recessed lighting, modern baths and coffee machines. The price is for half-board accommodation. ❻

Arşipel Pansiyon ☎ 0242/825 7169. Female manager Aylin has gone to some trouble to soften the usual concrete-box architecture with a multi-colour paint job, tiled floors and faux-antique decor; there are two family suites as well. It's on the northern half of the beachfront, beyond the *Odile Hotel*. ❸

Barış Pansiyon ☎ 0242/825 7080. Just behind the beach near the restaurants, this has ample parking and a choice of spartan older en-suite rooms and a new wing of half-air-conditioned, half-balconied units (priced a category higher). ❷

İpek Otel ☎ 0242/825 7156, ⓕ 825 7363. South half of the beach, inland from the concrete aque-duct. The most unusual of the three hotels – choose from three tasteful octagonal bungalows built in Nevşehir stone, sort of a cross between a hamam dome and a Selçuk tomb, with ceiling ocu-lus and antique furnishings (❼), four more con-

ventional rooms in the back (❻), and a stoutly built treehouse (❺) ideal for families.

Jasmin Pension ☎ 0242/825 7247 or 825 7325. Characterful rooms with en-suite bathrooms in a 1960s house, or two rooms in a modern annexe. There's a pleasant, wood-floor bar/restaurant /lounge area offering vegetarian suppers, flat bread and home-made apricot jam at breakfast, plus a paperback trading library. ❷, annexe ❸

Odile Hotel ☎ 0242/825 7163, ⓦ www.otel-odile
.com. Just past mid-beach. A bit shadeless until the landscaping takes full root, but with keen management, a mixed clientele and large, decent units around a pool garden. Friendly and good-value. Closed Nov–Feb. ❹–❻

Yavuz Motel ☎ 0242/825 7021. Easiest reached on foot from the row of beachside restaurants – a rather grim-looking two-storey "motel", though quiet, air-conditioned, and appealingly set in a poplar grove. ❸

Campsites

Green Point ☎ 0242/825 7182. Well-maintained site at the north end of the beach. Closed winter.
Olympia Tree House no phone. Fairly basic site by the snooty *Olympos Lodge*. Closed winter.

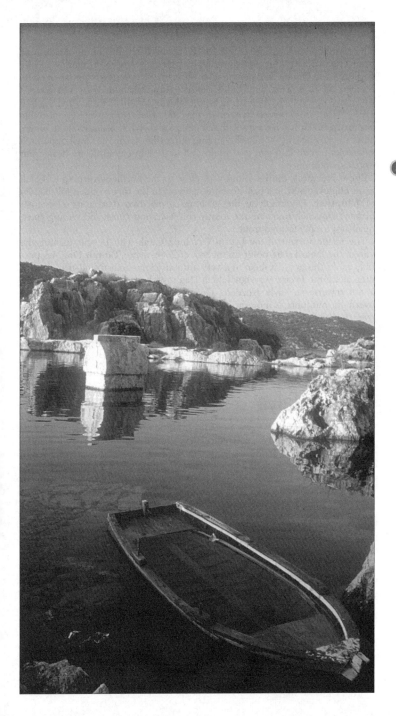

Beycik, Ulupınar and Tahtalı Dağ

The formerly rural village of **BEYCİK**, about 17km inland, up a side-road from Highway 400 just past the Ulupınar turning, has been transformed by wealthy Turks buying land here to take advantage of the superb views – it's currently a bit of a mess, with bulldozer scrapings, half-built villas and gouged pavement everywhere. The main bright spot is *Villa il Castello* (☎0242/816 1013, ⓦhttp://villacastel.hypermart.net; ❹), well-conceived, comfortable **accommodation** with a pool, fitness centre and stylish bar-restaurant, where you can get a decent cappuccino among other things. The nine well-appointed suites can fit two kids and two adults and, at 1000m elevation, are heated but not air-conditioned.

Elsewhere, meals can be found very close to the northerly turning to Çıralı from Highway 400, at a half-dozen restaurants in the tiny, wooded hill-hamlet of **Ulupınar**. Downhill by the gushing spring, two that aren't constantly plagued by coach tours are the jointly run *Yücel* and *Çınar*, and serving *güveç*, quail and locally farmed trout.

The inland variant of the Lycian Way links Çıralı with Beycik, making the village the logical start-point for ascents of 2366-metre **Tahtalı Dağ**. It's possible to do this as a day-hike in a very arduous eight-hour round-trip, continuing along the Lycian Way, but Tahtalı Dağ is such an attractive mountain that a full traverse to Yayla Kuzdere, Gedelme and beyond, with at least one overnight outdoors, is more in order. There are good campsites and water just over the saddle visible from Beycik, at **Çukur Yayla**. The peak itself will have snow from late November through early May in a wet year, and is prone to marine-generated white-outs at any time, so an appropriate level of mountaineering skills and equipment are required for the summit ascent.

On to Antalya

Heading north from Olympos, there is very little reason to stop before Antalya. The overdeveloped and overpriced **resorts** along this stretch of coast – notably Tekirova, Kemer and Beldibi – leave a lot to be desired, and only the ruins of the ancient city of **Phaselis** might tempt you off the main road. With the typical frequencies and travel times of buses out of Antalya in this direction, an overnight hereabouts could only be recommended if you were determined to leave Antalya at, say, 7pm in summer and wanted a base before nightfall.

Phaselis

The ruins of ancient **Phaselis** (daily: summer 8am–7pm; winter 8am–5.30pm; $7.50, plus $1.50 per car), just off the highway, 3km north of the German-dominated resort of Tekirova, are magnificently situated around three small bays, providing ample opportunity to contemplate antique architectural forms from a recumbent position on one of the beaches. The natural beauty of the site, the encroaching greenery, the clear water of the bays, and the seclusion, all make for a rewarding half-day outing – though you may wish to bring a picnic if you don't fancy patronizing the snack-caravans at the beachside car-park.

Some history

Phaselis was not always part of Lycia; situated at the border with Pamphylia, the city at certain points in its history was decidedly independent. According to legend, Phaselis was founded in 690 BC by colonists from Rhodes, and until 300 BC inscriptions were written in a Rhodian variety of the Dorian dialect.

The Phaselitans were great traders; they are supposed to have bought the land on which the city was founded with dried fish, and a "Phaselitan sacrifice" became proverbial for a cheapskate offering. They further earned themselves a reputation as venal scoundrels because at one point, needing funds, they sold Phaselitan citizenship for a hundred drachmas, attracting undesirable elements from all over Asia Minor. The city's trading links apparently stretched as far as Egypt, and their coins commonly depicted the prow of a ship on one side and the stern on the other.

Along with most of the rest of Asia Minor, Phaselis was overrun by the Persians in the sixth century, and was not freed until 469 BC. By that time, they had begun to feel loyalty to their imperial overlord, and it was with some difficulty that the Athenian general Kimon "liberated" them, making the city part of the Athenian maritime confederacy along with Olympos.

In the fourth century, Phaselis demonstrated its autonomy (or perhaps its perversity) by providing help to Mausolus, the satrap – or principal governor – of Caria, in his attempt to subdue the Lycian kingdom. Further evidence of Phaselitan sycophancy in their approach to authority was their behaviour toward Alexander the Great in 333 BC: not content with just surrendering their city to him, they also proffered a golden crown.

Phaselis became part of the Lycian Federation during the second century BC, but was soon, like Olympos, overrun by Cilician pirates. Although it was accepted back into the Federation afterwards, their long occupation of the city reduced it to a mere shell, with a much-reduced, penniless population. After the *pax Romana* came into effect, Phaselis distinguished itself with yet more obsequiousness: when Emperor Hadrian visited in 129 AD during a tour of the empire, statues were erected, a forum was constructed, and a gateway dedicated to him.

The site

The paved, one-kilometre side road that leads to the city from Highway 400 passes under a bluff on the left with a **fortified settlement** enclosed by a wall of Hellenistic masonry, the northernmost section of which has a tower and three archery slits. Though it can't compare in grandeur to several sites on the Pamphylian coast, or even to nearby Arykanda, there's certainly enough to see at the main site, which served as a location for filming *Jason and the Argonauts* in 1999. The most obvious landmark is the substantial and elegant remains of a Roman **aqueduct**. Supposed to have been one of the longest such conduits in the ancient world, it took water from a spring within the northern fortifications almost as far as the south harbour. To one side is a **bath-gymnasium** complex, with a geometric-mosaic floor in one room.

Arranged around a 400-metre-long promontory behind which most of the fan-shaped city is situated, Phaselis's three **harbours** are immediately obvious, and an ideal means by which to orient yourself. They served the city's extensive mercantile activities, particularly the export of local timber and botanical oils. The **north harbour** was too exposed to be used commercially, except in very favourable conditions, but it preserves the remains of an ancient quay on its south side. It offered an easy landing-point for aggressors, however, so the crest of the cliffs above were well fortified. This three-metre-wide wall now lies submerged, but is still intact. The middle or **city harbour** has a strong sea wall, since it is exposed to the north and east, and the eighteen-metre-wide entrance could be closed off. Today it's a sheltered swimming cove with a small beach and shallow water. The largest port, the **south harbour**, was protected by a 180-metre-long breakwater, most of which is now submerged. It provided docking for larger trading ships of up to a hundred tons, and now sees numerous yachts and *gület*s calling for the sake of its fine, large beach.

Between the harbours the promontory **acropolis** is covered in the very overgrown ruins of ancient houses and round cisterns. The main axis of the city is the **paved avenue**, which crosses the neck of the promontory, linking the south and middle harbours; part way along it kinks slightly at a rectangular plaza, thought to be the heart of the **agora**. At the southern-harbour end, a monumental **gateway** was constructed during 129–131 AD, like the agora, in honour of Hadrian's visit. Built of grey-white marble blocks, it bore a dedication to the emperor, though now only the foundations and tumbled masonry survive.

The well-preserved, second-century AD **theatre**, looking towards Tahtalı Dağ from between the acropolis and the main street, could hold around 1500 people. There are three large doors above present ground level, which probably led onto the stage. Just visible below these are a row of five smaller doors that would have opened into the orchestra beneath the stage, and were possibly used to admit wild animals.

Kemer

Some 13km north of Phaselis along Highway 400, **KEMER** is one of the least appealing of the resorts on the Turquoise Coast, and indeed has far more in common with the tone of the Mediterranean east of Antalya – including universal (high) pricing in euros for a largely Germanic clientele, leavened by wealthy Russians who come to shop for leather and jewellery. There was a pre-touristic village here, but you wouldn't know that looking at the white-concrete, government-designed holiday village, dominated by a swanky yacht harbour with overcrowded beaches either side of it. Even the tourist office admits that there's not a lot to do apart from sunbathe and swim, and if you are travelling independently you'd be better off bypassing the place entirely.

Practicalities

There are **dolmuşes** to Phaselis from Kemer, and buses to Antalya's **otogar** every half an hour. It's also possible to rent a **boat** to Phaselis from Kemer harbour, which costs, at most, $20 a day per person, including lunch. The **tourist office** in the town hall, near the harbour (daily 8.30am–6pm; ☎0242/814 1537), can provide a hotel price list and maps.

Villa-style **pansiyons** along the principal, partly pedestrianized, Liman Caddesi include *Esmer* at no. 104/14 (☎0242/814 2506; ❹) and *Erol* at no. 109, Sok 21 (☎0242/814 1755; ❹). But Kemer is not really about roughing it in overpriced *pansiyons*; if you choose to come here, you'll probably want to book in advance at places like the five-star *Türkiz* by the marina (☎0242/814 4100, ⓕ814 2833; ❼), with all creature comforts to hand, or the even smaller four-star *Otem* nearby (☎0242/814 3181; ⓕ814 3190; half-board accommodation ❻), where the service is willing, if not completely devoid of rough edges, owing to its role as the training venue for students at the local tourism vocational academy. Recommendations for the identikit **restaurants** are fairly pointless, though if you're yachting, camping or trekking, it's worth knowing about the the Migros **supermarket**, just off Highway 400 on the approach road (open daily 9am till late) – certainly the largest selection of contemporarily packaged food, sundries, camping gas and the like on view since Fethiye.

The **PTT** on Atatürk Bulvarı changes money (Mon–Sat 8.30am–12.30pm & 1.30–6.30pm), though there are no fewer than four ATMs. It's worth knowing that certain **car rental** chains have bona fide offices in Kemer, so if a car picked up elsewhere is on its last wheels, you could try swapping it here: Europcar is on Akdeniz Cad 14/C (℡0242/814 2909); Hertz, in the Tukan Shopping Centre (no phone); Sixt, Le Jardin Hotel (℡0242/824 7112); and Thrifty/Decar, at Club Zigana (℡0242/824 9177). The Kemer Life Hospital/Özel Yaşam Hastanesi (℡0242 814 6070 for emergencies) nearby provides the best **medical care** this side of Antalya.

Beldibi

BELDİBİ, situated some 12km north of Kemer and 35km short of Antalya, is really just a beach, and not a very good one at that, consisting of watermelon-sized boulders rather than small pebbles; behind it runs the old highway of these parts, 6km of continuous and rather tatty development, whose main virtue is that the small, low-rise hotels at least allow some free access to the shoreline. If you're driving a caravan, head for the popular and well-equipped *Kındılçeşme* forestry **campsite** south of this strip. The main **accommodation** bright spot, about 6km off the Lycian Way but just feasible as an overnight, is the *Naturel Pansiyon* in Çomaklar district (℡0242/824 9695, ⓦwww .natureltrekking.org; ❹), a garden-bungalow format place sympathetic to hikers, with half board available.

Travel details

Buses and minibuses

The schedules below are greatly enhanced in season by the 24-seat minibus service of the Patara Ko-op, which plies the coast between Fethiye and Finike, and of Antalya Tur, which shuttles almost constantly between Kaş and Antalya.

Dalaman to: Antalya (2 daily in summer; 6hr inland route); Bodrum (5 daily; 3hr 30min); Denizli (2 daily; 4hr 30min); Fethiye (twice hourly; 1hr); İstanbul (2 daily; 14hr); İzmir (14 daily; 5hr); Kaş (4 daily; 3hr); Marmaris (12 daily; 2hr); Muğla (18 daily; 2hr); Ortaca (twice hourly; 20min).

Dalyan to: Fethiye (2 daily; 1hr); Göcek (2 daily; 30min); Marmaris (2 daily; 2hr). NB: all these services depart before noon.

Demre to: Elmalı (3 daily; 2hr); Fethiye (6 daily; 4hr); Finike (hourly; 30min); Kaş (hourly; 1hr); Üçağız (1 daily; 45min).

Elmalı to: Antalya (9 daily; 2hr); Demre (6 daily; 1hr 30min); Finike (twice hourly; 1hr 15min); Kaş (3 daily; 2hr 30min).

Fethiye to: Antalya (8 daily; 4hr by inland route, 7hr by coast); Bodrum (6 daily; 4hr 30min); Denizli (5 daily; 4–6hr – ask for express route); İstanbul (3 daily; 14hr); İzmir (twice hourly; 7hr); Kaş (15

daily; 2hr); Marmaris (hourly; 3hr); Pamukkale (several daily; 5hr); Patara (15 daily; 1hr 15min).

Finike to: Antalya (twice hourly; 2hr 15min); Demre (hourly; 30min); Elmalı (twice hourly; 1hr 30min); Fethiye (13 daily; 4hr); Kalkan (2 daily; 2hr); Kaş (7 daily; 1hr 15min).

Kalkan to: Antalya (7 daily; 4hr 30min); Bodrum (1 daily; 6hr); Fethiye (every 30min; 1hr 30min); İstanbul (1 daily; 15hr); İzmir (3 daily; 8hr); Kaş (every 30min; 30min); Marmaris (2 daily; 4hr 30min).

Kaş to: Antalya (6 daily; 4hr); Bodrum (3 daily; 6hr 30min); Fethiye (15 daily; 2hr 15min); Gömbe (3 daily; 1hr 30min); İstanbul (2 daily; 12hr); Marmaris (4 daily; 5hr); Pamukkale (2 daily; 8hr); Üçağız (1 daily; 45min).

Kemer to: Antalya (twice hourly; 1hr); Phaselis (twice hourly; 30min); Tekirova (twice hourly; 30min).

Ortaca to: Antalya (2 daily; 7hr coastal route); Bodrum (5 daily; 4hr); Dalaman (twice hourly; 20min); Dalyan (25 daily; 20min); İzmir (10 daily; 5hr 30min); Kaş (5 daily; 3hr 30min).

Patara to: Antalya (8 daily; 5hr 15min); Fethiye (8 daily; 1hr 15min); Kalkan (10 daily; 30min); Kaş (10 daily; 1hr).

International hydrofoils

Fethiye to: Rhodes (2–3 weekly May–Sept; 1hr 30min). Tickets cost $50, whether one-way or open return, and though this may seem high, there is no departure tax here (as in Marmaris).

Flights

Dalaman to: İstanbul (June–Sept 4 daily, April, May & Oct 2 daily, Nov–March 1 daily; 1hr 20min).

The Mediterranean Coast and the Hatay

CHAPTER 6

Highlights

* **Kaleiçi** Antalya's old quarter, clustered around a charming harbour, is great for nightlife and shopping. See p.539

* **Termessos** Arguably the most dramatically situated of all Turkey's ancient sites, perched on the edge of a precipitous gorge. See p.546

* **Aspendos** Stunningly preserved Roman theatre, the impressive venue for an annual opera and ballet festival. See p.552

* **Köprülü Canyon** Spanned by a graceful Roman bridge, the Köprülü river gorge is ideal for novice white-water rafters. See p.554

* **Side** Watch the sun set behind the elegant columns of the Athene temple on Side's seafront. See p.555

* **Göksu Delta** The atmospheric flatlands of the delta are a haven for the Dalmatian pelican and loggerhead turtle. See p.572

* **Antakya's Archeological Museum** Don't miss the immaculately preserved collection of Roman mosaics. See p.594

* **Regional cuisine** For a taste of the Hatay try the unique fiery *muhammara,* served with flat-bread and a chilled beer. See p.595

6

The Mediterranean Coast and the Hatay

T
he **Mediterranean coast** of Turkey, where the Toros (Taurus) mountain range sweeps down to meet the sea, broadly divides into three parts. The stretch from Antalya to Alanya is the most accessible, with the looming presence of the Toros range separated from the sea by a fairly broad coastal strip. Although undeniably beautiful, intensive agriculture, particularly cotton growing, and package tourism have both taken their toll on the environment here. East of Alanya, the mountains meet the sea head-on, making for some of Turkey's most rugged stretches of coastline, where hairpin bends and mountain roads can make travel an agonizingly slow process. As a result, this is the least developed and unspoiled section of Mediterranean coastline. Further east the mountains finally recede, giving way to the flat, monotonous landscape of the Ceyhan River delta, made even more dreary by relentless urban and industrial sprawl. South and east of here, turning the corner towards Syria, the landscape becomes more interesting, as the Amanus mountain range dominates the fertile coastal plain, with citrus crops and olives the mainstay of the economy.

The bustling, modern city of **Antalya** is the region's prime arrival and junction point. East of here, in the ancient region of Pamphylia, the ruins of four cities – **Perge**, **Sillyon**, **Aspendos** and **Side** – testify to the sophisticated civilization that flourished during the Hellenistic period. Perge and Aspendos, in particular, are both well-established day-trip destinations from Antalya, while the modern town of Side has become a package-tour resort, albeit a highly enjoyable one.

Seventy kilometres east along the coast, the former pirate refuge of **Alanya** – now a bustling tourist centre – is set on and around a spectacular headland topped by a Selçuk citadel. Continuing east, the best places to break your journey are **Anamur**, where a ruined Hellenistic city abuts some of this coast's best beaches, and **Kızkalesi**, whose huge Byzantine castle sits 100m from the shore of a sandy bay. Kızkalesi also makes a good base from which to explore the ancient city of **Uzuncaburç**, a lonely ruin high in the Toros mountains.

Beyond Kızkalesi is the fertile alluvial delta known as the **Çukurova**, where the Ceyhan River spills down from the mountains and meanders sluggishly into the eastern Mediterranean. This end of the coast – characterized by concentrations of industry and low-lying cotton plantations – has very little to recommend it. **Mersin** has regular ferry connections to northern Cyprus; **Tarsus**, the birthplace of St Paul, has few surviving reminders of its long history; while **Adana**, one of the country's largest urban centres, is a hectic staging post for journeys further east.

From Adana, routes head north to the central Anatolian plateau (see Chapter 7) or east to the Euphrates and Tigris basins (Chapter 11), though this chapter turns its attention south, towards the area formed by the curve of the coast down towards Syria. This is the **Hatay**, a fertile, hilly region where different cultures have met – and often clashed – in their efforts to dominate the important Silk Route trade. **Antakya** is the Hatay's main centre and the best starting point for exploring the region, though cosmopolitan **Iskenderun** makes for a surprisingly agreeable base. From Antakya there are frequent dolmuş connections to **Harbiye**, site of the Roman resort of Daphne, and to the town of **Samandağ**, from where you can visit Armenian **Vakıflıköy** and what's left of the ancient Roman port of **Seleucia ad Piera**.

Antalya to Alanya

The western part of the Turkish Mediterranean coast – between Antalya and Alanya – is the most popular with tourists, with long stretches of sandy beach that have, in places, fallen foul of over-development. The cotton-rich coastal margin covers what was the ancient region of **Pamphylia**, a loose federation of Hellenistic cities established by incomers from northern Anatolia. According to ancient Greek sources, Pamphylia was settled by a "mixed multitude" of peoples following the fall of Troy around 1205 BC. It played a relatively minor role in the history of Anatolia, never even attaining local military significance, and the Pamphylian cities were fought over for centuries by stronger neighbours, amongst them the Lydians and Persians. To an extent, the Pamphylians profited from this, playing off one would-be invader against the next, while continuing to run their own affairs, regardless of who exercised ultimate control. In later years, Mark Antony was sent to take charge of the region, treating it as his personal domain until defeated by Octavius Caesar at the battle of Actium in 31 BC, after which Pamphylia was formally absorbed into the Roman Empire under the pax Romana.

You're most likely to start your explorations at **Antalya**, a booming place that over the last ten years or so has turned into a fully fledged resort, worth visiting for its restored old town and marvellous archeological museum. The nearest (and most fascinating) ruined city is **Termessos**, perched on the saddle of Mount Solymos overlooking the Antalya gulf. The four surviving ruined cities of Pamphylia also rival the beaches as tourist magnets, with **Perge** and **Aspendos** the best-preserved and most evocative sites. In between these two, the less intact, earthquake-wracked remains of **Sillyon** are harder to reach. Further along the coast, **Side** is one of the region's major resorts, but sadly, the striking ruins of its ancient city are fast being overshadowed by the rapidly growing tourist facilities. It remains, however, the ideal place if you're after beach action and holiday nightlife.

Alanya, the next sizeable centre, has also seen an explosion of hotel building and tourism-related commerce over the last few years, but so far, the development has managed to retain some sense of proportion. As for less well-trodden tourist paths, the **Köprülü Kanyon** national park and the ruins of ancient **Selge**, not far inland from Antalya and Side, make a delightful day's excursion.

Antalya

Turkey's fastest growing city, **ANTALYA** is blessed with an ideal climate (except during the searing heat of July and August) and a stunning setting atop a limestone plateau, with the formidable Beydağları looming to the west. In the heart of town, the pretty yacht harbour huddles below the Roman walls, while behind the new buildings the crescent of Konyaaltı Bay curves to the industrial harbour 10km west of town. Despite the sometimes grim appearance of its concrete sprawl, Antalya is an agreeable enough city to live in, but the main area of interest for outsiders is confined to the relatively tiny and central old quarter within the Roman walls, known as the Kaleiçi (or "within the castle"). Three or four days in town – including half-day excursions to the nearby ruins of Termessos, Perge and Aspendos – should be sufficient.

Antalya was founded as late as the second century BC by Attalus II of Pergamon, and named **Attaleia** in his honour. The Romans did not consolidate their hold on the city and its hinterland until the imperial period, at the conclusion of successful campaigns against local pirates. Christianity and the Byzantines got a similarly slow start, though because of its strategic location and good anchorage Antalya was an important halt for the Crusaders. The Selçuks supplanted the Byzantines for good early in the thirteenth century, and to them are owed most of the medieval monuments visible today (albeit some built on Byzantine foundations). Ottoman Antalya figured little in world events until 1918, when the Italians made it the focus of their short-lived Turkish colony.

Arrival, orientation and information

Both **buses** and inter-town **dolmuşes** use the *otogar*, about 9km north of town on the Ankara road; bus companies have their own service buses, which will deliver you to the town centre, and there is also a municipal bus marked "Terminal" linking the *otogar* with the centre. Whichever you use, alight either near the Atatürk statue for pensions on the west of the old city, or at the Belediye (Town Hall) corner for pensions on the east side.

Buses for Kemer and the westbound coast road for Kaş and Kalkan arrive at and depart from opposite the *Falez Hotel* on 100 Yıl Bulvarı, 2km west of the centre. Inbound buses arrive just around the corner near the Devlet Hastane (State Hospital), and from the intermediate roundabout frequent dolmuşes take you to the town centre – look out for those marked "Kale Kapası" and "Işıklar".

West of the *Falez Hotel* is the main harbour and dock where **ferries** arrive from Venice – it's 10km from the centre of town and there is no dolmuş service, so you'll have to take a taxi to the centre. Antalya's lushly landscaped **airport** stands at the centre of a maze of motorways some 12km east of the city. Taxis into town cost about $12 per car during the day and $18 at night, or take the Havaş airport bus (see "Listings"), from outside the internal flight terminal ($3), which terminates at the THY office on Cumhuriyet Caddesi, 600m west of Kaleiçi. If you arrive from abroad, via Istanbul, with THY, you will land up at "International Arrivals", from where a taxi is the only option.

Orientation and information

The main entrance – the **Kalekapısı** (literally, "the gate of the city") – to the **Kaleiçi** (old quarter) is marked by the Saat Kulesi (clocktower). The clocktower itself lies opposite a pool and fountain at the southern end of **Şarampol**

▲ Ankara, Termessos & Otogar (7 km)

ANTALYA

FAHRETTIN ALTAY CAD

Murat Paşa Camii

Cinema

Friday Market

MILLI EGEMENLIK CAD

SARAMPOL (KAZIM OZALP) CAD

SUBAŞI CADDESI

İSMET PAŞA CAD

Ⓐ

HÜKÜMET CAD

TAHIL PAZARI SOK

BAZAAR

İki Kapılar Hanı

THY ⓘ

CUMHURIYET CAD

Yivli Minare Complex

Atatürk Statue

Saat Kulesi Ⓑ

Mehmet Paşa Camii

Dönerci Çarşısı

FAL ERENLER SOK

MARBEL SOK

UZUN ÇARŞI SOK

PAŞA CAMII SOK

HIDIRLIK SOK

Ⓕ

Hadrian's Gate ④

Plaza Cinema

KALEKAPISI

Ⓘ Ⓙ

③
⑤

Ⓚ

Mediterranean Civilisations Research Institute ⑨

ATATÜRK CAD

Antalya Lisesi (High School)

Old Harbour

⑦

⑧

⑩

MEMERLİ BANYO SOK

ÇIVELEK SOK

HESAPÇI SOK

⑪

⑫

Medieval Walls Ⓛ

Ⓜ

⑬

N

Mermerli Beach

⑭
⑮
⑯

Kesik Minare

Ⓝ

Ⓞ

Nexus

@

Ⓟ

⑲ ⑱ ⑳
㉑ ⑳
㉒
Ⓠ

Hıdırlık Kulesi

Ⓡ

North Shield Pub

Ⓢ
Ⓣ

Belediye

YENİKAPI SOK

ISIKLAR CAD

Adalar Swimming Platform

Mermerli & Karaalioğlu Parks

FEVZI ÇAKMAK CAD

MEDITERRANEAN SEA

㉓ ▼   Lara & Düden Waterfalls ▼

0   200 m

CAFÉS & RESTAURANTS

Aytek 2	R
Baro	C
Cafe Iskele	I
Castle	P
China Garden	E
Gül	L
Güneyliler	A
Hasanağa	F
Kismet	H
Koru	J
7 Mehmet	D
Mustafa's	B
Salman	T
Seden Osmanlı Mutfağı	M
Sev-et	G
Shanghai Chinese	O
Sirri	K
Stella's Bistro	S
St Paul's Place	N
Villa Park	Q

ACCOMMODATION

Abad	16
Alp Paşa	11
Antique	5
Atelya	6
Dantel	20
Dedekonak	14
Ertan	2
Hıdırlık	22
Kandiler	4
Kardelen Evi	13
Keskin	19
Marina	10
Naturel	7
Ninova	12
Özmen	18
Perge	23
Sabah	17
Senem Family	21
Sheraton Voyager	1
Türk Evi	8
Tuvana	3
Villa Perla	9
White Garden	15

◄ Akm, Aqualand & Devlet Hastane (State Hospital)
◄ Main + r.r. Archeological Museum, Konyaaltı; TML Agent, C D & E
Bar Sok

Airport ►
Halk Pazarı (Permanent Market) G & H ►

⑥

THE MEDITERRANEAN COAST AND THE HATAY | Antalya

537

(Kazim Ozalp Caddesi), now a pedestrian shopping area. A tramway circles the old quarter and runs along the sea front; **tram services** are every half-hour ($0.25) and departure times are posted at the tram stops. South from Kalekapısı, the Kaleiçi's labyrinthine alleys lead to the most desirable pensions and downhill to the harbour. To the west along the waterfront is **Cumhuriyet Caddesi**, later Akdeniz Bulvarı, which gives access to the newly landscaped park behind **Konyaaltı** beach.

The **tourist office** is beside the THY office at Cumhuriyet Cad 91 (Mon–Fri 8am–noon & 1–5.30pm, Sat & Sun 9am–5pm; ☎0242/243 4384). Free city maps are available, but there's little in the way of accommodation listings.

Accommodation

Most travellers stay in the old quarter of **Kaleiçi**, in houses restored as *pansiyons*. These offer competitive prices for variously sized en-suite rooms set around characterful garden courtyards – rates are normally open to negotiation. Ignore the touts at the *otogar*, who work on commission, and choose your own from the lists below, which represent only a selection of what's available; there are dozens of similar options with equally attractive features. Most of the places listed include breakfast in the price, but make sure that you ask first.

Camping is not an option within the city limits. *Camping Bambus*, 3km along the road to Lara (☎0242/321 5263), and *Parlar Mocamp*, 12km along the Ankara road, are both expensive and oriented toward caravanners. However, *Bambus* has its own beach and both have decent facilities.

Between the old harbour and the Saat Kulesi

Antique Pension Paşa Camii Sok 28 ☎0242/242 4615, ✉antique@ixir.com. Unlike many Kaleiçi pensions, the rooms have not been over-restored, though they are let down a little by the dated furnishings. Some rooms have fans, others with air-conditioning fall into the next price category. ❷

Ertan Pansiyon Uzun Çarşı Sok 9 ☎0242/241 5535. Plain but cheap, clean rooms in a modern building. The front rooms are noisy but have great views over the old town and mountains; rear rooms over the garden are quieter. ❶

Marina Residence Mermerli Sok 15 ☎0242/247 5490, ⓦwww.marinaresidence.com. The last word in luxury, murals and marble. It's a tasteful place with excellent views over the harbour, a raised glass-walled pool alongside the garden bar, and appetizing food. ❼

Naturel Pansiyon Mermerli Banyo Sok 8 ☎0242/243 3990, ✉naturelpansiyon @mynet.com. Comfortable, traditionally furnished rooms with fans, and a shady garden with a small pool. This is very good value. ❸

Türk Evi Otel Mermerli Sok 2 ☎0242/248 6591, ✉turkevi@tutavturkevi.com. Top-of-the-range but over-restored luxury hotel with perfect views, pool and sauna, and a dignified but pricey bar and restaurant. ❼

Tuvana Hotel Karanlık Sok 18 ☎0242/247 6015, ⓦwww.tuvanahotel.com. Hotel fashioned from a beautifully restored series of old houses. The characterful rooms are individually furnished and come with satellite TV, minibar and air-conditioning. ❻

Between Hadrian's Gate and the Kesik Minare

Alp Paşa Hotel Hesapçı Sok 30–32 ☎0242/247 5676, ⓦwww.alppasa.com. Lush conversion of an Ottoman mansion, set around a cramped garden with a tiny pool. The cheapest rooms are nicely furnished; pay more and you'll get antique fittings and marble bathrooms. Excellent buffet meals attract non-guests in the evenings. ❼

Atelya Pansiyon Civelek Sok 21 ☎0242/241 6416, ⓕ241 2848. Excellent restoration of two connected houses set around a courtyard. Rooms are furnished in the traditional Ottoman style, while two tastefully built adjacent houses have been added, substantially increasing capacity. ❸

Kandiler Pansiyon Kandiler Sok ☎0242/243 1407, ⓦwww.hotelcandlehouse.com. A new house built in Ottoman style with small but well-furnished, air-conditioned rooms. ❸

Ninova Pension Hamit Efendi Sok 9

⏱0242/248 6114, ✉ninovapension@ttnet.net.tr. Very quiet elegantly restored house with a pleasant garden. Tastefully furnished rooms with wooden ceilings, bare-boards with kilims and air-conditioning. ❹

Villa Perla Hesapçı Sok 26 ⏱0242/248 9793, ✉villaperla@hotmail com. Very authentic Ottoman building, with antique furnishings in individually styled rooms, plus a garden with small pool. ❻

Between the Kesik Minare and the Hıdırlık Kulesi

Abad Otel Pansiyon Hesapçı Sok 52 ⏱0242/247 4466. Smart, converted house with a garden-restaurant and pleasant staff; ask for one of the quieter back rooms. ❶

Dantel Pansiyon Zeytin Geçidi 4 ⏱0242/247 3486, ✉dantelhotel@hotmail.com. Immaculate conversion buried under overgrown bougainvillea, with a rooftop terrace and garden. Rooms with air-conditioning are more expensive. ❷

Dedekonak Pansiyon Hıdırlık Çarşısı Sok 13 ⏱0242/248 5264. Attractive old building whose original Ottoman rooms are marred by modern furniture. Quiet, though, and with a shady garden. ❷

Hıdırlık Pansiyon Hıdırlık Sok 56 ⏱0242/247 4746. Right on the cliff edge, with superb views over the bay, but small and spartan rooms. ❶

Keskin Pansiyon Hıdırlık Sok 35 & 37 ⏱0242/244 0135. Two houses with well-furnished rooms of varying sizes; meals are served in the garden or on the mountain-facing terrace. ❷

Özmen Pansiyon Zeytin Çıkmazı 5 ⏱0242/241 6505, ⊛www.ozmenpension.com. Turkish-German run *pansiyon* with airy, spotless rooms and a lovely breakfast terrace. The owner will collect you from airport or *otogar* free of charge. ❷

Sabah Pansiyon Hesapçı Sok 60 ⏱0242/247 5345, ⊛www.sabahpansiyon.8m.com. Friendly and well-run backpacker joint offering an informal information service (in English), car rental, tours, good food, cheap beer, email access and satellite TV. Standard rooms are simply furnished; rooms with private bathroom and air-conditioning fall into the next category up. ❶

Senem Family Pansiyon Zeytingeçidi Sok 9, near Hıdırlık Kulesi ⏱0242/247 1752. Modern and clean rooms with flexible prices and a family touch; sea views from the rooftop breakfast bar. ❷

White Garden Pansiyon Hesapçı Geçidi 9 ⏱242/241 9115, ✉whitegardenantaly@yahoo .com. IYHF-affiliated and backpacker-orientated – the modern rooms are fairly small but the staff is very helpful and there's a quiet garden. ❷

East of Atatürk Bulvarı

Kardelen Evi Haşim İşcan Mah, 1297 Sok 14 ⏱242 2431148, ✉nicholas66@e-kolay.net. Two self-contained apartments in a restored house in the quiet back streets off Atatürk Cad. Both accommodate up to four people in traditionally furnished and decorated rooms. Weekly rental from $100 per apartment.

South of Karaalioğlu Parkı

Hotel Perge Gençlik Mah, Sok 5 ⏱0242/244 0025, ✉hotelperge@sistemd.com. Situated right on the cliff, just south of Karaalioğlu Parkı, the front rooms have superb views over the bay. The hotel's biggest plus is its own swimming area at the foot of the cliff. ❺

West of the city centre

Sheraton Voyager 100 Yıl Bul ⏱0242/243 2432, ⊛www.airliner.de/ittantalya.html. By far the best of the swanky hotels spread out along the coast from Konyaaltı beach to Lara. Lush gardens surround an ocean-liner style curve of concrete, the foyer glitters with polished brass, glass and crystal, and the huge rooms are marvellously opulent. Two restaurants, two pools, sauna, jacuzzi and every other facility you'd expect for the price (which is a minimum of $180, rising to $250 for some rooms). ❽

The City

The best place to start exploring the old town, Kaleiçi, is from the old harbour, where the once-crumbling quays have been rebuilt, gardens laid out and the harbour walls and a mosque restored. Most attractions are within walking distance of each other, though you will need to jump on a dolmuş to visit the excellent archeological museum.

Kaleiçi

Inevitably, the authentic atmosphere of the **old harbour** has been sacrificed to the redevelopment – the harbour is now mainly home to day-trip boats, some charter *gülets* and a very few fishing boats – but on balance, the venture seems to have been a success, reflected in the fact that half of Antalya now turns out for an evening promenade on what was once a gravel foreshore.

From the harbour, head uphill along Uzun Çarşı Sok, past souvenir and carpet shops and the eighteenth-century **Mehmet Paşa Camii**. Along the way, you might want to stop off at the tiny garden of the local arts society, known as **ANSAD**, for a cool drink or to check notice boards advertising concerts, slide shows and even Sunday treks. At the northern end of Uzun Çarşı Sok is **Kalekapısı** (Castle Gate), where the **Saat Kulesi**, a Selçuk tower with inset Roman column drums, is built into a section of the old walls. Kalekapısı is overlooked by the **Yivli Minare** or "Fluted Minaret", erected during the thirteenth-century reign of the Selçuk sultan, Alâeddin Keykubad, and today something of a symbol of the city. The adjacent mosque is still in use, with the area in front doubling as an informal bazaar and open-air café, with good views over the bay. Facing the café is an early, plain **Selçuk han** whose crumbling walls have just been "restored", a rather grand term for encasing the ruins in glass. Above this area, but accessed from Cumhuriyet Caddesi, is an old baths, now the Fine Arts Gallery, which sometimes hosts interesting exhibitions; the original foundation was built on top of a church. Next door is a **türbe** (tomb) from 1377.

From Kalekapısı, bear right and right again onto Atatürk Caddesi, and you'll soon draw even with the triple-arched **Hadrian's Gate** (Üç Kapılar), recalling a visit by that emperor in 130 AD. Hesapçı Sokak, the quietest entry to Kaleiçi, also begins at Hadrian's Gate and if you follow it through the old town, you'll pass its restored Ottoman houses, many of which have been turned into pensions, craft/antique shops or restaurants and bars. Some are still inhabited by local families, while others appear abandoned and are crumbling to dust under the cypress trees. Right off Hesapçı Sokak, on Kocatepe Sokak, is the well-signposted **Mediterranean Civilisations Research Institute** (Mon–Sat 9am–5.30pm; donation requested), set in two restored Ottoman houses built around courtyard gardens. Behind one house is the restored garden church of St George, which is used for exhibitions often made up of items from the private collection of the Koç family, Turkey's richest, who sponsor the institute. The second house contains a marvellous library of books on archeology and antiquities; treasures include original editions of the engravings made by the archeologist-cum-explorer Texier when he investigated Asia Minor for the French government in the 1840s. There are also excellent reference materials and yearbooks on local archeological activities and projects sponsored by the institute. Experts will want to spend some time here nosing through the rarities, but even amateurs will find the English-speaking archeological staff helpful in finding books about local sites.

About halfway along Hesapçı Sokak stands a tower and attendant buildings known collectively as the **Kesik Minare** (Broken Minaret), an architectural anomaly that's done successive duty as temple, church and mosque: compare the reused Roman capitals with later Byzantine ones. Unfortunately, railings prevent you from getting up close.

Beyond the Kesik Minare, you emerge above the sea and turn left to reach the adjoining **Mermerli** and **Karaalioğlu** parks, which contain a number of tea gardens as well as the **Hıdırlık Kulesi** in the northwestern corner. This round Roman tower is occasionally used as a theatre, and it's the best place in town to watch the frequently spectacular sunsets over the snow-capped mountains across the gulf of Antalya. Return to the harbour past the *Mermerli* café, which has a private staircase down to the only city-centre beach, **Mermerli**, where you can swim for a small fee. The **Adalar** swimming area, reached via steep steps from Karaalioğlu park, with decking on the rocks and ladders into the sea, is a nearby alternative, though it is badly signed and erratically managed.

Antalya's two permanent markets are the **Pazar**, at the southeast corner of Şarampol, selling mainly gold, clothes and shoes, and the **Halk Pazarı** (People's Market), a permanent market a ten-minute walk east of Hadrian's Gate, selling a fantastic array of fresh fruit, vegetables, herbs and spices, as well as fake designer clothes. The **Altın Pazarı** (Gold Bazaar) in the İki Kapılı Hanı, behind the Pazar, has been restored and is now open for business, selling local cotton fabrics and furnishings as well as gold.

The Archeological Museum

The one thing you shouldn't miss while in Antalya is the city's **Archeological Museum** (Arkeoloji Müzesi; Tues–Sun 9am–6pm; $6), situated on the western edge of town at the far end of Kenan Evren Bulvarı. It's one of the top five archeological collections in the country, and it's well worth spending half a day or so nosing through the exhibits. To get there from the city centre, take any dolmuş labelled "Müze" or "Liman" – departing from any of the "D" signs along Cumhuriyet Caddesi – or take the westbound tramway to its last stop, Müze.

At the museum entrance, a small children's section, primarily used for school groups, provides the opportunity for play with old tools and pots, and past this, the well-lit galleries are arranged both chronologically and thematically. Standing out among the early items are a cache of **Bronze Age** urn burials from near Elmalı, and finds from an unusually southerly **Phrygian tumulus**, with the trademark Phrygian griffin head much in evidence. Ancient metal-working skills are also showcased in some fine silver plate, three superb belts and several silver and ivory Phrygian figurines sporting droll yet dignified expressions. All date from the eighth and seventh centuries BC and are among the museum's worthiest treasures.

It's quite a jump in time to the next galleries, which contain many second century AD **statues from Perge**: a complete pantheon in unusually good condition has been assembled. Opening off from here is a room filled with smaller pieces, including perfume flasks, bronze statuary and lamps, and an underwater case showing miscellaneous finds from wrecks, as well as yet more Perge statuary honouring the various demigods and priestesses of the Roman imperial cult. Best exhibits of the adjoining sarcophagus wing are two almost undamaged coffers depicting the **life of Hercules**. In the building's corner hall, mosaics, including one depicting Thetis dunking Achilles in the Styx, are in fair to good condition but crudely executed; a **gaming board** nearby, recovered from Perge, is more unusual. The corner hall leads into a gallery dedicated to **theatre friezes** and statues from Perge. The all-over marble tiling doesn't show them off to their best advantage, but the display, which includes statues of gods and emperors and a frieze showing battles between heroes and sea monsters, is marvellous.

A narrow room adjoining the mosaic hall is devoted to **icons** recovered after 1922 from various churches in the Antalya area. They're mostly of recent date, and popular in style, but unusually interesting for their rarely depicted themes and personalities. At the centre of the collection is a reliquary containing what are purported to be the bones of **St Nicholas of Myra** (see p.512). Near this is a case containing early Byzantine church silver, including a gilt thurible from the monastery of Sion in the hills behind Myra, found in 1963 by villagers at Kumluca after presumably being hidden or lost during a pirate raid. However, the majority of the unique hoard discovered by the villagers was taken abroad in somewhat clandestine circumstances, and is now on show at Dumbarton Oaks Research Library in Washington DC, USA.

The collection is rounded out by an **ethnography** section, a hotchpotch of İznik ceramics, kitsch glass lamps, smoking and writing implements, household goods, weapons, dress and embroidery, weights and locks, musical instruments and a fine Arabic map of the Middle East. A diorama of nomad life is followed by a collection of socks and carpets.

Besides the collections, there's a bookshop, a **café** and a pleasant shady garden scattered with some fine overspill sculptures and tombs. Crossing the road from the museum reveals wide views of Konyaaltı bay and a precarious path that leads down to Konyaaltı beach (see below).

Boat trips, beaches and waterfalls

Boats by the harbour in Kaleiçi offer a variety of half- and full-day local tours, all of which take in the best views of the Düden waterfalls (see below), plus a combination of local beaches, swimming, cruising the gulf and a barbecue lunch. Some also offer evening entertainment in the shape of moonlit buffets and belly-dancing. Prices vary according to the number of people, season and itinerary, but you can expect a half-day trip to cost from around $10 per person, more for evening cruises with entertainment. It is best to check out the trips the day before by wandering down to the harbour, where the touts will accost you as you try to read the itineraries posted on boards on the quayside. Haggle hard as there is plenty of competition.

Antalya's lengthy western beach, **Konyaaltı**, now spruced up, is finally beginning to live up to its dramatic situation between Antalya's cliffs and the Beydağları mountains. It's shingle, rather than sand, but it's clean and well maintained. Entry to the beach is free, and loungers and umbrellas are available for a modest fee. Those with children should be aware that the beach shelves quite steeply and there is a slight tow from west to east. A pleasant **promenade** lined with palm trees and cafes backs the beach and once the new bypass is complete the coastal road will be closed, improving the seafront even further. Konyaaltı is easiest reached by the west-bound tram – get off at the terminus (just past the Archeological Museum) and follow the road down the steep hill (five minutes' walk) or take the curiously converted tractor down (high season only; $0.30).

Lara beach, 10km southeast of town and reached by dolmuşes running along Atatürk Caddesi, has fine sand but is enclosed by a forbidding fence and accessible only for a small fee. The lower **Düden waterfalls** reach the ocean at Lara, though to see them to full advantage you'll need to take a boat tour from the old harbour. The upper cascades, some 9km northeast of town, are served by dolmuş but are barely worth visiting.

The secluded **Kurşunlu waterfalls** (daily 9am–8pm; $0.50), 18km northeast from Antalya off the Isparta road, can be reached by dolmuş or *Belediye* bus from a bus stop on the northern edge of the Halk Pazar. The green pool into which the high falls cascade is forbidden to swimmers, so you wouldn't want to stay here long in the height of summer. An unmarked, but easy-to-follow, walking trail from here follows the riverside in a two-hour circular loop, passing the fishing retreat of one of Turkey's ex-presidents.

Eating

Antalya is full of cafés and restaurants and good places can be found all over town, but especially in **Kaleiçi** and along **Atatürk Bulvarı** and **İşıklar Caddesi**. We've picked out some of the best choices, across all budgets, below. For the local speciality – *tandir kebap*, clay roasted mutton – visit **Eski Serbetçiler İçi Sokak**, a narrow street running down the west side of the Dönerci Çarşısı (see "Atatürk Bulvarı and İşıklar Caddesi", below), crammed with restaurants, many with pavement tables. The mutton (something of an acquired taste) is sold by weight and not especially cheap – a 300-gramme portion will set you back $6. Much better value are the *döner* kebabs, also sold by weight.

Local street markets are open nearly every day in some part of the city and have a staggering array of fresh local produce at knock-down prices. The biggest is the **Friday market** off Milli Egemenlik Caddesi, while on Sundays, head northwest of the main PTT and ask for the *Pazar Pazar* – **Sunday market**.

Kaleiçi

Aytek 2 Bufe Karaalioğlu Parkı. Near the Hıdırlık Külesi, this stand serves excellent spicy *karaşık tost* (toasted sandwich with a cheese, spicy sausage and hot sauce filling) and *köfte* (griddled meatballs), both for under a dollar, which you can eat on the viewing point overlooking the bay.

Café İskele Old harbour. Adjacent to the fountain, good for inexpensive burgers and beer.

Castle Restaurant To the right of the Hıdırlık Külesi, on the cliff edge. A café-bar serving *mezes*, kebabs and cold beer, much favoured by Antalya's young lovers. A meal with beer will set you back around $3.

Gül Kocatepe Sok. Foreign-owned bar next to the taxi stand, serving fresh *mezes* and casseroles, plus beer and a range of wine.

Hasanağa East of Paşa Camii Sok, near Hadrian's Gate. Good for buffet *mezes*, meat and fish grills and frequent traditional live music sessions.

Koru Old harbour. For a bit of a splurge – around $12 – try the mixed grilled fish. The restaurant is adjacent to *Café İskele*.

Mustafa's Under the Saat Kulesi, at the entrance to Kaleiçi. Only in business here between midnight and 5am, this mobile stall sells tasty *köfte* and *kokoreç* (rolled lambs intestines, grilled, heavily spiced and far tastier than you might expect). Help yourself to the array of tomatoes, onions, parsley, lettuce and rocket. With an *ayran* or two it makes for a perfect stop after a night on the town.

Shanghai Chinese Restaurant Yeni Kapı Cad. The service can be slow and the food only average, but if you have been in Turkey a long time you may feel a need for some different flavours. Serves beer.

Sirri Restaurant Uzun Çarşısı Sok. Atmospheric courtyard restaurant specializing in fish dishes and

guveç, an appetizing meat and vegetable casserole served piping hot in a clay bowl. A full meal will cost around $9.

St Paul's Place Just off Yenikapi Sok. Attached to the American-run evangelical church, a fine café serving delicious coffee, cookies and cakes. You can also check out their extensive library (not all of it religious). Closed Sun.

Villa Park Just north of Karaalioğlu Parkı. Cheap and cheerful place directly behind Hıdırlık Kulesi, with a range of grilled meats, kebabs and burgers, fine views and cold beer.

Atatürk Bulvarı and İşıklar Caddesi

Dönerci Çarşısı Corner of Atatürk Cad and Cumhuriyet Cad. A "*döner* sellers' market" – fast-food joints under one roof, devoted to kebabs, *köfte* and *kokoreç*. Some sell *midye* (mussels) in season. A meal here should cost less than $3.

Salman İşıklar Cad. Air-conditioned coffee bar-patisserie at the Atatürk Bul end of the street, with a good range of *poğça* (plain and filled savoury breads), cakes and a salad bar.

Seden Osmanlı Mutfağı Atatürk Bul 52. Partly outdoor restaurant/café, decked out in Ottoman style. Fine range of traditional dishes, including *erikli kebap* (with plums) and *yörük kebap* (shepherds fare), both served with *perde pilav* (seasoned rice in a pastry parcel) and good salads. Excellent puddings and ice cream, and traditional fizzy sherberts served in copper beakers. Full meal for around $7. No alcohol.

Stella's Bistro İşıklar Cad. Close to the *Salman*, and one of the few places in Antalya with a non-Turkish menu: pastas and steaks for lunch and dinner, and afternoon teas with cream cakes. Prices are high, but service is immaculate.

North of the centre

Güneyliler West of Şarampol, just north of the *Kışlıhan Hotel*. This spotlessly clean restaurant serves excellent *lamacuhn* and kebabs and is always packed with locals. A substantial meal can be had for under $3.

West of the centre

Baro Cliff-top park south of Cumhuriyet Cad. A popular restaurant offering a huge range of buffet *mezes*, a good *Osmanli Tabagi* (casserole) main course and live folk music on Friday and Saturday evenings.

China Garden Just off Cumhuriyet Cad, on the way to the archeological museum. Antalya's best

Chinese restaurant. A set meal will cost around $6, a beer $2, and the views from the cliff edge terrace are breathtaking.

7 Mehmet Western side of AKM park. Good for *mezes* and traditional grills but prices are a little above average; count on around $8 for a two course meal with a drink.

East of the centre

Kismet Halk Pazarı. Basic décor but with a good reputation for fish, especially *hamsi* (sardines) in season.

Sev-et Halk Pazarı. With a name meaning "love meat", it's no surprise that this simple restaurant specializes in kebabs of all varieties, fresh made from the butchers next door.

Drinking and nightlife

Much of Antalya's **nightlife** is concentrated around the harbour area, with its myriad bars, clubs and discos. Places further out of the centre, such as Discoland and the Olympos, have their own, fairly inexpensive buses to get you back to your accommodation; just give the driver your destination. Bars are often open all day and keep going until 4 or 5am, discos from around 8pm to 4am. There are also plenty of places to listen to live **Turkish music** in Antalya, particularly *halk*, *türkü* and *özgün*. At these venues you sit at a table and a waiter will take your order for drinks and *çerez* (a mix of salted nuts, sunflower seeds and roasted chick-peas). Keep an eye out for fly posters advertising the concerts of the bigger stars of the Turkish music scene, who often play the **Açık Hava Tiyatro** (open-air theatre) situated at the eastern end of Konyaaltı beach. Tickets can be bought from an open-air stall at the northeast end of Ataturk Bulvarı, priced from $8 and upwards depending on the popularity of the act.

Bars and clubs

Ally Kaleiçi. A complex of bars and a disco on the Roman walls, with an impressive laser show cutting the night sky across the water; but it is prohibitively expensive ($10) by local standards.

The Bar, aka **Rock Bar** Uzun Çarşışı Sok. Reached via a rickety staircase from a side street just below the Mehmet Paşa Camii. The $2 entry fee includes the first beer, which you'll drink in the company of students from the local university and Antalya's grunge contingent. Surprisingly passable live rock acts play weekends.

Club 29 Kaleiçi. Affluent dance club on the west side of the harbour, an open-air affair on a terrace overlooking the sea.

Discoland Aqualand, 3km west of town. Glitzy club in the waterpark on the west side of the AKM complex; leave your camera at home as you're bound to get wet.

Gizli Bahçe Kaleiçi, off Paşa Sok. Well-hidden student-oriented bar (ask for the Karatay Medresesi to locate it), with cheap beer ($1.50),

rock music and shady garden.

Han Bar Paşa Camii Sok. Upmarket bar where a beer will cost at least $3.

King Bar Kaleiçi. Just behind the waterfront – a good bet for those whose tastes fall between low rock dives and large dance venues, with varied music, a small dance floor and beers for around $3.

North Shield Karaalioğlu Parkı. Upmarket English-style pub (part of a chain) in a restored old house, tucked away in the trees at the entrance to the park. An imported beer will set you back $3, so you'll be mixing with Antalya's well-heeled.

Olympos *Falez Hotel*, 100 Yıl Bul. The huge club in the hotel basement has a superb laser show and trilingual DJs playing mostly Eurodisco to a smart Turkish clientele.

Turkish music

Çiçek Pasajı Uzun Çarşısı Sok. The best place in town to catch live Turkish music; it's a couple of hundred metres down from the clock tower. There's a small terrace with views over Kaleiçi and the bay.

Entertainment and festivals

The Hasan Subaşı Kültür Parkı – also known as AKM or **Atatürk Kültür Merkezi** – is a complex of two theatres and a pyramid-shaped glass exhibition centre set in a cliff-top park, 3km west of the centre. It's about 300m down 100 Yıl Bulvarı past the *Sheraton* and *Falez* hotels; dolmuşes from the town centre marked "Adliye" or "AKM" pass the gates. With its tea gardens and children's playgrounds, the park is a favourite spot for joggers, roller-bladers and Sunday strollers, while the theatre complex stages the occasional classical concert and shows American films; programmes are advertised on notice boards in the town centre.

Antalya also has two waterparks with numerous slides, chutes and wave pools. **Aqualand** (May–Oct 9am–dusk; $11), on the southwestern edge of the Kültür Parkı, is reached by the same dolmuşes; while the original **Aquapark** (daily 9am–dusk; $11), behind the *Dedeman* hotel, east of the centre, is reached by Lara-bound dolmuşes.

The most convenient **cinema** is the Plaza, under the Antalya 2000 building, between Hadrian's Gate and the Halk Pazarı, which has three air-conditioned screens. The Prestige on the Lara road has five screens, but for the ultimate experience the eight-screen cinema in the new Migros centre out beyond the Kültür Parkı has double and reclining seats. Check film schedules on notice boards near the THY office or at Hadrian's Gate.

Antalya plays host to the **Golden Orange Film Festival** in September and October, when cinemas show the films entered for the various categories and the Kültür Parkı hosts receptions and parades of the stars. Antalya is also crowded during the **Aspendos Opera and Ballet Festival** (see box on p.553 for details).

Listings

Airlines THY, Özel İdare İşhanı Altı, Cumhuriyet Cad, next to the tourist office ☎0242/243 4384.

Airport General information ☎0242/330 3030, flight enquiries ☎0242 330 3600. The Havaş bus departs from outside the THY office on Cumhuriyet Cad (9 daily; 30min; $3), 1hr 15min before each THY flight, returning straight after each flight lands.

Banks and exchange There are banks and *döviz* offices throughout the city, and some *döviz* offices on Şarampol even open on Sundays (though most open Mon–Sat 9am–7pm). You can also exchange currency at the PTT (see overleaf).

Books The Owl Bookshop, Akar Çeşme Sok 21, off Hesapçı Sok in the old town, has an excellent selection of mainly English-language second-hand books. D&R, Işıklar Cad, is the best place to buy foreign-language newspapers and magazines, and also has English-language guides and novels, music CDs, cassettes, and an upstairs café.

Buses You can reach almost all provincial capitals in Turkey direct from Antalya *otogar*. Major companies such as Kamil Koç, Akdeniz and Metro, have ticket offices in town, especially on Subaşı Cad, and their own shuttles servicing the *otogar*. Minor companies such as Göreme Tur (for Cappadocia)

are "minded" by the majors; see the destinations and company logos on the bus office windows. Important local companies are Antalya Tur (Fethiye and Kaş/Kalkan; ☎0242/331 1086) and Gürman (Eğirdir/Isparta ☎0242/331 1050). Some pensions in the old town sell or book bus tickets.

Car rental It seems every old building in Kaleiçi that's not a *pansiyon* or a rug shop is a car-rental agency; most of the rest line Fevzi Çakmak Cad, on the way to Lara beach. In July and August, book your car well in advance; at other times, bargain hard. Companies include: Avis, Fevzi Çakmak Cad 67/B ☎0242/242 1772; Budget, Ağustos Cad, Atılgan Apt 7/2 ☎0242/242 6220; and Europcar/InterRent, Fevzi Çakmak Cad 14/A ☎0242/241 1260. All three have outlets at the airport as well. Mithra Travel (See "Tours" below) also provides reliable cars at reasonable rates.

Consulate UK, 1314 Sok 6/8, Gençlik Mahallesi ☎0242/244 5313.

Ferries The Turkish Maritime Lines office, for tickets for the fortnightly ferry to Venice, is at Konyaaltı Cad 40/19 ☎0242/241 1120.

Hamams In Kaleiçi, try Nazır on Hamam Aralığı Sok, behind the Mehmet Paşa mosque (daily: men 6–10am; women 10am–5pm; mixed 5pm–midnight; $2.50 bath, $2.50 massage). The new, prettily tiled Demirhan on 35 Sok, east of Güllük, has two separate sections (daily: men 6am–11pm; women 9am–7pm; around $7 for the works).

Hospital State Hospital (Devlet Hastane) and outpatients' clinic, Soğuksu Cad ☎0242/241 2010; University Teaching Hospital (Tıp Fakültesi), Dumlupınar Bul ☎0242/227 4480.

Internet There's a clutch of internet cafes behind Antalya Lisesi (Antalya High School), just down from the Plaza cinema, or try Nexus, at the southern end of Atatürk Bul.

Laundry Both Sempatik and Mutlu Çamışırhane are on Sakarya Sok, facing the Kesik Minare.

Left luggage There's a 24-hour office marked "Emanet" at the *otogar*; items priced by size and value.

Police Tourist Police, Emniyet Müdürlüğü, Yat Limanı, Kaleiçi ☎0242/243 1061.

Post office The main PTT is at Güllük Cad 9 (daily 9am–5pm for exchange and letter service; 24hr for phones). A kiosk near the clocktower in the old city caters to tourist needs.

Shopping Although traditional take-home items are rugs and leather, you'll find that jeans, gold and designer-label clothes and shoes are a better bet these days. Check out the boutiques along Atatürk and Işıklar *caddesis* and in the new Migros centre for the real thing; and Cumhuriyet Cad (past Güllük Cad) or the Halk Pazarı for fakes.

Tours Whitewater rafting on the Köprülü River is a full-day excursion from Antalya, with either Medraft (☎0242/248 0083), or Antalya Rafting (☎0242/321 8631). A day's rafting, including transfers and meal, costs $25–45 depending on company, time of year and your bargaining skills, or book through travel agents – try Akay on Cumhuriyet Cad, Maki on Uzun Carşi Sok, as well as many Kaleiçi pansiyons – for around $40 per person. Mithra Travel, Hesapçi Sok (☎0242/248 7747, ⊛www.mithratravel.com), in the old city, organizes one- or two-day treks (from about $20 per person per day) in the limestone massifs overlooking Antalya, and can also arrange self-guided walks where they book the accommodation and provide you with maps and instructions; prices vary according to group size.

Yachting Some yachts are open to charter for groups of four to twelve. Ask around at the harbour during the slow spring season and you could get a bargain cruise for the same price as hotel bed and board.

Termessos

After a couple of nights spent in Antalya you may well be in a hurry to move on, heading east or west along the coast in search of better and quieter beaches. But before you head off, consider staying in town for another night and having a look inland, where the ancient site of **Termessos**, situated over a thousand metres above sea level, is one of Turkey's prime attractions. Indeed, its dramatic setting and well-preserved ruins, tumbling from the summit of the mountain and enclosed within the boundaries of a national park – the Güllük Dağ Milli Parkı – merit a considerable journey.

Despite its close proximity to Lycia, Termessos was actually a Pisidian city, inhabited by the same warlike tribe of people who settled in the Anatolian Lakeland, around Isparta and Eğirdir, during the first millennium BC. The inhabitants of Termessos originally named themselves after the nearby mountain of Solymus – today's Güllük Dağ; their language, of which no surviving inscriptions remain, was a dialect of Pisidian, which Strabo called Solymian. The first mention of the Solymians comes in the ancient myth of Bellerophon and Pegasus, when Bellerophon, after defeating the monster of the Chimaera, was sent to fight them. The first appearance of the Solymians in history proper was in 333 BC, when Alexander the Great made an attack on the city and was repelled. Fourteen years later, Termessos played an interesting part in the history of the region when Antigonus – one of Alexander's successors – was challenged by Alcatus for command of the region. The Pisidians supported Alcatus, and he took refuge in Termessos. The elders of the city, however, saw the possible dangers involved in defying Antigonus and laid a trap for Alcatus, preparing to take him captive. Alcatus committed suicide; his body was delivered to Antigonus, but after three days it was rescued and reburied in Termessos.

Unlike that of its Lycian neighbours, much of the history of Termessos is characterized more by attack than defence, and in the third and second centuries BC the Termessians first took on the Lycian Federation, then their neighbours in nearby Isinda. The city's position, commanding the road from the Mediterranean to the Aegean, gave Termessians the opportunity to extract customs dues from traders; a wall across the valley is believed to be the site of their customs post. Later, in 70 BC, Termessos signed a treaty of friendship with Rome, under which they were exempted from the jurisdiction of the governor – an independence that they proudly expressed by never including the face or name of a Roman emperor on their coinage. The city must have been abandoned quite early, probably after earthquake damage in 243 AD, and has only been surveyed, never excavated.

The site

Even if you don't have to walk the final 9km through the national park (see "Practicalities" overleaf), the approach to the **site of Termessos** (daily 7.30am–7.30pm; $2) can seem a stiff one. Walking shoes and a supply of water are advisable, as is a visit sensibly timed to avoid the midday sun. After checking the site map at the car park you'll need to climb a good twenty minutes before you reach the first remains of any interest, although on the way you'll pass a number of well-labelled, though mainly inaccessible, ruins; including the aqueduct and cistern high on the cliff-face to the left of the path.

The second-century AD **King's Road** was the main road up to the city, close to which the massive lower and upper **city walls** testify to a substantial defence system. The central part of the city is beyond the second wall, to the left of the path. Its surviving buildings, formed of square-cut grey stone, are in an excellent state of repair, their walls standing high and retaining their original mouldings. In part, this is due to the inaccessibility of the site; it's difficult to imagine even the most desperate forager coming up here to pillage stone.

The first building you reach is the well-preserved **gymnasium**, with a baths complex alongside. This, however, is far overshadowed by the nearby **theatre**, one of the most magnificently situated in Turkey, with the mountain climbing behind and a steep gorge dropping to its right. Greek in style, it had seating space for 4200 spectators, and wild animals were released into the orchestra from a basement under the later, Roman-built, stage. Some of the seats are missing, but otherwise it's in a good state of preservation.

To the west of the theatre is the open grassy space of the **agora**, at the far end of which is a **mausoleum**, approached up a broad flight of steps, with a six-metre square platform – at the back of which a grave pit is sunk into the rock. Its unusual position on the marketplace suggests that the tomb belonged to an extremely eminent citizen, and it has even been suggested that this could be the tomb of Alcatus, the pretender to the governorship of Pisidia – though the tomb on the hill above (see overleaf) is generally accepted as more likely. On the far side of the agora from the theatre stands a smaller theatre or **odeion**, which, according to inscriptions, was used for horse and foot races, races in armour, and – by far the most frequently held – wrestling. The walls of the building stand to almost ten metres, although the interior doesn't amount to much more than a heap of rubble. Surrounding the odeion are four **temples**, only one of which – that of Zeus Solymus, god of war and guardian of the city of Termessos – is in a decent state of repair, with walls standing to over five metres and a bench at the back for statues. Two of the other three temples on the southeast side of the odeion – the two with portals still standing – were dedicated to the goddess Artemis.

Following the trail up the hill from here brings you to a fork, the left-hand path of which continues on to the **necropolis**, where you'll see an incredible number of sarcophagi dating from the first to the third centuries AD. Most are simple structures on a base, though there are some more elaborate ones, with inscriptions that describe the penalties for their violation. If you climb as far as the fire lookout tower, you're rewarded with incredible views over the adjoining valley, rumoured to be the stopping place of Alexander the Great when he planned his assault on Termessos.

Returning downhill, take the left-hand fork for several hundred metres to the so-called **Tomb of Alcatus** – widely accepted as the mausoleum of the general. The tomb itself is cave-like and undistinguished, but the carvings on its facade are remarkable, particularly one depicting a mounted soldier, with a suit of armour, a helmet, a shield and a sword – the armour of a foot soldier – depicted lower down to the right of the figure. The tomb and reliefs are consistent with the date of Alcatus' death, and the figure in the carving wears armour identical to that of Alexander the Great in a mosaic of the battle of Issus in the Naples archeological museum.

Practicalities

Antalya, 30km northwest, is the most obvious base for visiting Termessos, whether you're travelling by public transport or in your own vehicle. To get there **by car**, take the Burdur road out of Antalya, turning left after 11km towards Korkuteli. The left turning to Termessos is marked off the Korkuteli road after about 14km, from where a track leads 9km up through the forested national park (entrance $0.50 per person, $1 per car) to the site. Using **public transport**, you need to take a bus (hourly) headed for Korkuteli as far as the beginning of the forest track, from where you can take one of the taxis (around $10 including waiting time and return to main road) that tout for business here.

The Pamphylian cities

The twelfth century BC saw a large wave of Greek migration from northern Anatolia to the Mediterranean coast. Many of the incomers moved into the area immediately to the east of Antalya, which came to be called **Pamphylia**, meaning "the land of the tribes", reflecting the mixed origins of the new arrivals. Pamphylia was a remote area, cut off from the main Anatolian trade routes by mountains on all sides; nevertheless four great cities grew up here – Perge, Sillyon, Aspendos and Side.

The first recorded mention of the region dates from the sixth century BC, when Croesus, the last king of Lydia, absorbed Pamphylia into his realm. When Croesus was defeated by the Persians in 546 BC, the Persians assumed control of the area. This alarmed the Greeks, who attempted to gain control of Pamphylia, resulting in a series of wars, with the Pamphylians fighting on the side of the Persians. With the exception of Sillyon, Pamphylia eventually fell to Alexander the Great, after whose death the region became effectively independent, though nominally claimed by the various successor kingdoms that inherited Alexander's realm. During the first century BC the Romans, annoyed by the activities of the Cilician pirates operating from further along the Mediterranean, took control of the coast, ushering in three centuries of stability and prosperity, during which the Pamphylian cities flourished as never before.

If you want to visit the main Pamphylian sites in a single day a **taxi** is the best option, and should cost around $60 for the day (check out the rank at the southern end of Atatürk Bulvarı in Antalya, which lists prices for various destinations on a wooden board). The bus tours ($25–40) organized by various agents in Antalya's Kaleiçi district seldom include Selge (see p.555), but do include tedious stops at out of town gold and carpet shops.

Perge

About 15km east of Antalya, the ruins of **Perge** can be reached by taking one of the frequent dolmuşes or *Belediye* buses (every 20min or so) to the village of Aksu on the main eastbound road; these are best boarded at the roundabout at the north end of Dr Burhanetin Onat Caddesi, a five-minute walk east of the Halk Pazarı. From the village it's a fifteen-minute walk to the site itself, though you may be able to flag down a dolmuş from the village if you don't want to walk.

At the top of the hill is the **site entrance** (daily 9am–noon & 1.30–5pm; $9) and car park, marked by a cluster of souvenir stalls and soft drinks stands. It's an enticing spot, the ruins expansive and impressive, and you could easily spend a long afternoon looking around. Substantially more of the city survived until 1922, when, according to some accounts, the theatre was more or less intact. However, a 1920s construction boom in the nearby village of Murtunas led to the readily available supplies of stone at Perge being pillaged by local builders.

Some history

Perge was founded around 1000 BC and ranked as one of the great Pamphylian trading cities, despite the fact that it's nearly 20km inland – a deliberate defensive siting so as to avoid the unwanted attentions of the pirate bands that terrorized this stretch of the Mediterranean. Later, when Alexander the Great arrived in 333 BC, the citizens of Perge sent out guides to lead his army into the city. Alexander was followed by the Seleucids, under whom Perge's most celebrated ancient inhabitant, the mathematician Apollonius, lived and worked. A pupil of Archimedes, Apollonius wrote a series of eight books describing a family of curves known as conic sections, comprising the circle, ellipse, parabola and hyperbola – theories that were developed by Ptolemy and later by the German astronomer Kepler. Most of the city's surviving buildings date from the period of Roman rule, which began in 188 BC. After the collapse of the Roman Empire, Perge remained inhabited until Selçuk times, before being gradually abandoned.

The theatre and stadium

Just beyond the site entrance, the **theatre** has been closed for repairs for some time. It was originally constructed by the Greeks, but substantially altered by the Romans in the second century AD. Built into the side of a hill, it could accommodate 14,000 people on 42 seating levels rising up from the arena and was the venue not only for theatrical entertainment, but also for gladiatorial displays. You can peek through the grating and look out for the fragmentary remains, though the best pieces are in Antalya's archeological museum.

PERGE

ACROPOLIS

NECROPOLIS

Palaestra

Nympheum

Colonnaded
Street

Roman
Walls

Hellenistic
Gate

Roman Baths

Agora

Byzantine
Basilica

Roman
Gate

Ticket Office

Tomb of
Plancia Magna

Stadium

Car Park

Theatre

N

0   100 m

Main road

To the northeast of the theatre is Perge's massive horseshoe-shaped **stadium**, the largest in Asia Minor at 234m by 34m, with a seating capacity of 12,000. Because the stadium was built on level ground it was necessary to provide massive supporting pillars and arches. The spaces between these arches were divided into about thirty huge rooms (housing shops and businesses), many of which are still intact, giving a good impression of the scale of the whole stadium complex.

The walled city

In places, stretches of the Seleucid walls have survived, giving some indication of the extent and ground plan of the original city. Just in front of the outer gates is the **Tomb of Plancia Magna**, a benefactress of the city, whose name appears later on a number of inscriptions. Passing through the first **city gate**, you'll see a ruined **Byzantine basilica** on the right, beyond which lies the fourth-century AD **agora**, centred on a ruined temple. To the southwest of the agora are the excavated **Roman baths**, where a couple of the pools have been exposed. Across the cracked surface of the inlaid marble floor, the original layout of frigidarium, tepidarium and caldarium can – with the help of a few signs – still be discerned. Also visible in places are the brick piles that once supported the hypocaust floor of the baths, enabling warm air to circulate underneath.

At the northwest corner of the agora is Perge's **Hellenistic Gate**, with its two mighty circular towers, the only building to have survived from the Hellenistic period. Behind, the horseshoe-shaped court and ornamental archway were both erected at the behest of Plancia Magna, the former once adorned with statues – the bases of a number of which were found during excavations carried out during the mid-1950s. Beyond is the start of a 300-metre-long **colonnaded street**, with a water channel running down the middle and the shells of shops to either side. Walking along it, you'll be able to pick out the ruts made by carts and chariots in the stone slabs of the roadway. Also visible are a number of reliefs near the tops of the columns, just beneath the capitals, one of which depicts Apollo, while another shows a man in a toga, offering a libation at an altar. At the end of the street is the **nymphaeum**, an ornamental water outlet from where a stream splashes down into the water channel below. Above here is the **acropolis** – probably the site of the original defensive settlement, of which little has survived. To the west of a crossroads just before the nymphaeum is a **palaestra**, dating from 50 AD, according to an inscription found on its south wall. West of here, archeologists have found a **necropolis** leading from one of the city gates, sarcophagi from which can now be seen in the Antalya archeological museum.

Sillyon

About 7km east of Perge are the ruins of the ancient city of **Sillyon**, also dating from about 1000 BC, although much less intact than those at Perge. Situated on top of a table-like hill, its strategic position enabled it to repulse an attack by Alexander the Great, who never succeeded in capturing it. These days, it doesn't seem to attract as many visitors as some of the other Pamphylian sites, partly because it's impossible to reach by public transport, and perhaps because of the landslide in 1969 which swept about half of it away.

To get there by car **from Perge**, head back to Aksu village and follow the coastal road, taking a signposted left turn about 7km east of the village. From here a road leads 8km inland to the small modern settlement of **Asar Köyü**, from where an un-signposted dirt track leads to the site itself. It's possible that some of the villagers may offer to guide you around, which can be quite useful as they will alert you to the presence of hazardous unfenced cisterns.

The site

The site is unfenced and entry free. You can climb up to the acropolis by way of a ramp leading from the **lower gate** up the western side of the hill. To the left of the gate are the foundations of a **gymnasium**, used as a bishop's palace in Byzantine times and now home only to sheep. At the top of the ramp you'll find a large and well-preserved city gate and, scattered around the rest of the hilltop, a number of buildings of indeterminate age and function. The largest is a late **Hellenistic structure** with several arched windows in its upper storeys that later served the Selçuks as a fortress. Just to the south is a long hall-like building, possibly a former gymnasium, in which you can see the slots and holes used to hold wooden shutters in place in the window frames. East of here lies a building with a 37-line **inscription** carved into its stone doorjamb – the only surviving written example (apart from a few coins) of Pamphylian, the Greek dialect spoken in this area until the first century AD.

The most interesting part of the acropolis is the area around the ruined **theatre**, which offers graphic visual evidence of nature's erosion of the man-made past. Following the 1999 earthquake, only the top few seats remain, the rest of the structure now lying scattered across the plain below – the huge blocks you can see were once part of the seating terraces. Further east are the foundations of a number of **houses** and part of a **temple**, which, judging by their precarious state, seem destined to follow the theatre terraces over the edge of the hill.

Aspendos

Returning to the main road, head east for **Aspendos**, whose theatre is proba-bly the best preserved in Asia Minor – it's still used to stage the annual Aspendos Opera and Ballet Festival. In summer, there are regular **dolmuşes** from Antalya to the village of Serik (every 2hr), a ten-minute drive from the site, and for a couple of dollars the driver will usually take you on to Aspendos, a total of 45km southwest of Antalya. If you're here out of season you will have to rely on the buses plying the main coastal highway, which will drop you at the signposted turning just before the humpbacked Selçuk bridge, a few kilo-metres east of Serik. From here you should be able to get a ride to the site, although it's only a three-kilometre walk. Just before Aspendos, the village of **Belkis** has several eating places, including the pleasant riverside *Belkis Restoran*. About half a kilometre northeast of the village lie the car park and Aspendos **site entrance** (daily 8am–7pm; $9).

Some history

Aspendos first came to prominence in 469 BC when the Persian wars culmi-nated in a huge and bloody naval battle at the mouth of the nearby Eurymedon River. The Greeks won and went on to defeat the Persians again in a land bat-tle, when, heavily outnumbered, they outwitted their opponents by coming ashore disguised as Persians, using the element of surprise to stage a successful attack.

This wasn't the end of Persian influence in Pamphylia. The locals, particular-ly the people of Aspendos, weren't any keener on the Greeks and, in 389 BC, they murdered an Athenian general sent to collect tribute, after which control of the area passed to Sparta. The Spartans proved to be ineffective rulers and by 386 BC the Persians were back, staying until the arrival of Alexander the Great in 333 BC. On hearing of Alexander's approach, the rulers of Aspendos agreed to surrender but asked Alexander not to garrison soldiers in the city. Alexander accepted their terms on condition that they paid him a tribute of money and horses, and went off to lay siege to Sillyon. After his departure he was angered to learn that the citizens of Aspendos were busy fortifying the city and he returned demanding a larger tribute and hostages. His demands were met, and Aspendos had to accept a Macedonian governor into the bargain.

After Alexander's death in 323 BC, Aspendos became part of the Seleucid kingdom and was later absorbed into the realm of the kings of Pergamon. In 133 BC, the city became part of the Roman province of Asia. Roman rule consisted mainly of a succession of consuls and governors demanding protection money and carting off the city's treasures. Only with the establishment of the Roman Empire did the city prosper, growing into an important trade centre, its wealth based on salt from a nearby lake.

Aspendos remained important throughout the Byzantine era, although it suffered badly from the Arab raids of the seventh century. During the thirteenth century the Selçuks arrived, followed a couple of hundred years later by the Ottomans, who ruled here until the eighteenth century, when the settlement was abandoned.

The theatre

The Aspendos **theatre** was built in the second century AD by the architect Zeno. He used a Roman design, with an elaborate stage behind which the scenery could be lowered, instead of allowing the natural landscape behind the stage to act as a backdrop, as had been the custom in Hellenistic times.

The stage, auditorium and arcade above are all intact, as is the several-storey-high stage building, and what you see today is pretty much what the spectators saw during the theatre's heyday – a state of preservation due in part to Atatürk, who, after a visit, declared that it should be preserved and used for performances rather than as a museum. A dubious legend relates that the theatre was built after the king of Aspendos announced that he would give the hand of his beautiful daughter to a man who built some great work for the benefit of the city. Two men rose to the challenge, one building the theatre, the other an aqueduct, both finishing work simultaneously, with the result that the king offered to cut his daughter in two, giving a half to each man. The builder of the theatre declared that he would rather renounce his claim than see the princess dismembered and he was, of course, immediately rewarded with the hand of the girl for his unselfishness. Later, the theatre was used as a Selçuk *kervansaray*, and restoration work from that period – plasterwork decorated with red zigzags – is visible over the stage. There's also a small **museum** to the left of the entrance, exhibiting pictures of theatre "entrance tickets" and coins.

Aspendos Opera and Ballet Festival

The **Aspendos Opera and Ballet Festival** is staged in the theatre every year, from mid-June, over a three- to four-week period. Both Turkish and foreign companies perform, and the programme consists of popular and experimental opera, ballet and classical concerts. With an inflow of choreographers and musicians from the ex-Soviet Union, Turkish opera and ballet companies have improved out of all recognition, and stage design and costumes match the standard of the performers.

Tickets (a reasonable $12 for foreigners, less for Turks) are available both in advance and on the night from the theatre, and you can also buy them in Antalya, though the booking office seems to switch venues each year – ask at the tourist office. Programmes are usually advertised at the last minute on notice boards in Antalya, and cheap city buses run here from outside the Antalya archeological museum, and from near the Atatürk statue on Cumhuriyet Caddesi, between 6.30pm and 7pm. You might want to follow the example of most Turkish patrons and take along supper to while away the time between the arrival of the bus and the start of the performance, as well as cushions to sit on, and an umbrella or waterproof in case of a thunderstorm.

The acropolis and aqueduct

Many visitors leave Aspendos after visiting the theatre, not realizing that there's more to see on the hill above. To the right of the theatre door, a path leads up to the **acropolis**, built, like the one at Sillyon, on a flat-topped hill. The site is a little overgrown, but a number of substantial buildings are still in place, foremost among them being the **nymphaeum** and **basilica**, both 16m in height, as well as sections of the main street and a drainage system in good condition.

To the north of the acropolis, on the plain below, stretches a Roman **aqueduct**. Originally 15km long, it brought water to Aspendos from the mountains above and incorporates an ingenious siphonic system that allowed the water to cross the plain at low level; you can still (with care) climb the towers. The aqueduct and towers can also be reached by taking a left turn down a dirt track just outside Belkis, skirting around the western side of the hill.

Köprülü Kanyon national park and Selge

Inland of Aspendos, the **Köprülü Kanyon national park** (Köprülü Kanyon Milli Parkı) and its Roman bridges, with the sparse ruins of **Selge** high in the mountains above, make a good full-day outing with a leisurely lunch stop, provided that you have a sturdy vehicle. There is little public transport to Selge or to the national park – one elusive afternoon dolmuş passes by each day between Serik, on the coastal highway, and the village of Zerk at the very top of the Köprülü valley. However, several companies operate enjoyable half-day **rafting trips** down the Köprülü River, allowing time for a stop en route for a swim and lunch. Contact a tour operator in Antalya (p.546) or Side (p.556) for bookings.

The national park

The turn-off for both the national park ("Milli Parkı") and Selge (see opposite) is signposted 48km east of Antalya on Highway 400; past Sağgırınköyü is a left turn over the river, but you should pass this and continue straight on the asphalt road to **Beşkonak**, a straggly village. Five kilometres or so further on, you reach the *Kanyon restaurant*, with treehouse-type seating in some giant plane trees overhanging the swift-flowing river. It's a popular spot, both with Turks and bussed-in foreigners, but the farm-raised trout awaiting you in the tank under one of the several gazebos is expensive at $4 a shot. Ironically, the Köprülü River itself teems with brown trout, but it's illegal to catch them.

Just above the treehouse restaurant the road narrows; take the left fork, and inch across the first of two Roman spans, the **Oluk bridge**. You can park here and walk into the canyon via a footpath just after the bridge. From here, it's 13km up to Selge, reached by taking the right fork just after the bridge. Return on the west bank past the **Böğrüm bridge**, which has a huge, popular picnic and swimming area just downstream from it. Past here are a couple more trout restaurants and pensions and the river crossing back to the tarmac. In all honesty the bridges are nothing special, little different from hundreds of others in Turkey, and it's only the setting that makes Köprülü stand out.

Selge

Since the final stretch of road up to **Selge** has been widened and improved it's passable to most cars. As you climb to an eventual altitude of 900m, the panoramas become more sweeping, the thickly wooded countryside more savage, and the 2500-metre Kuyucak range ahead more forbidding. At the scattered hamlet of **ZERK** (also known as Altınkaya), some 400m before the Selge ruins, signs beckon you to park near the *Café Dallas,* which can provide cold drinks, food, a guide (around $10 for a couple of hours), information on walks in the mountains and even a place to crash for the night (bring your own sleeping bag and/or tent) – ask for İsmail or Davut. You may also eventually be collared by the site attendant and sold a ticket for the ruins ($2).

The main track, now suitable only if you're travelling by jeep, continues toward the theatre that dominates **ancient Selge**, but your guide will probably take you on a faint path left and south to the ancient agora and two hilltop temples. The **agora** will excite amateur archeologists with its part-visible paving, jumbled masonry and chunks of unexcavated inscriptions. The foundations of a **Byzantine church** sit up on a hill to the southeast and enjoy panoramic views down the valley and up to the snow-streaked peak of Bozburun, while the jumbled remains of a temple of Zeus and a large water cistern lie to the northwest along the ridge. From here you can catch views to the ruined temple of Artemis and old city wall to the northwest and to the stoa in the valley below. Returning to the main track via some village farmyards, you'll pass the **stadium**, of which only the western ranks of seats are left; the sporting area itself is now a wheat field. The theatre, partly cut into living rock, is impressive, but would be more so if the stage building hadn't been pulverized by lightning some decades ago and if the highest tier of seats hadn't sustained rain damage in 1989. Three of the five doors giving access backstage still remain.

Little is known for certain of the origins of Selge; it only left the realm of mythological ancestry and anecdote to enter history – and the Roman Empire – in the first century AD. The city was famous for its storax gum, made from a local shrub, and was inhabited until early Byzantine times. The site has always been arid – only recently did modern Zerk get a permanent spring – and the ancient town must have been abandoned when the aqueduct supplying it with water collapsed. The overwhelming impression you'll have is of the determination necessary to keep a city of 20,000 thriving in such a godforsaken wilderness.

Side

About 25km east of Aspendos, **SİDE**, one-time trysting place of Antony and Cleopatra, was perhaps the foremost of the Pamphylian cities. The ruins of the ancient port survive, but over the last few years Side has changed almost beyond recognition. These days, the resort has one of the highest tourist densities of any town in Turkey, and local people are beginning to recognize that their home has been ruined by indiscriminate development. However, many improvements have been made recently, and work is currently underway restoring the colonnades of Roman shops that flank the main street leading to the city gate. Despite the effects of package tourism, which have pushed up the prices of accommodation and food, Side remains a very attractive resort, especially if you can avoid the peak months of July and August. The beaches are superb, the ruins evocative and the nightlife lively.

Some history

Side (meaning "pomegranate" in an ancient Anatolian dialect) was founded in the seventh century BC, its colonists attracted by the defensive potential of the rocky cape. It grew into a rich port with an estimated 60,000 inhabitants during its peak in the second century AD. Initially a significant proportion of Side's wealth rested on the slave trade, with the city authorities allowing pirates to run an illegal slave market inside the city walls, in which thousands of human beings were bought and sold every day. This trade was later outlawed, and after the collapse of the western Roman Empire, Side survived only until the Arab invasion during the seventh century AD. The Arabs put the place to the torch, driving out the last inhabitants, and Side was abandoned until the beginning of this century, when it was resettled by Muslim fishermen from Crete, who built a village known as Selimiye among the ruins. Despite later attempts by the Turkish government and various archeological agencies to evict them, these villagers stayed, and by the 1980s their descendants were starting to reap the rewards of Side's tourist boom.

Arrival, information and services

Most buses run past the turning for Side, leaving you to find a passing dolmuş into town. However, Manavgat Seyahat runs a direct service from Antalya, which takes you to a small *otogar* a five-minute walk north of Side's main ruins. For those who can't face the walk, tractors drag wagons full of tourists to the entrance to the town at the top of the main street.

Side is effectively **pedestrianized** and cars can only enter the town between 7am and 10am, 3pm to 6pm, and again after midnight. The **car park** is just outside the barrier and a modest daily fee is charged – don't make the mistake of parking anywhere along the approach road as towing is vigorously carried out.

Side's **tourist office** (Mon–Fri 8am–5pm, Sat 10am–2pm; ☎0242/753 1265) is on the main road into town, just before the *otogar*, though like most Turkish tourist offices, it won't overburden you with information. **Banks** and a **PTT** can be found on the square at the southern tip of the promontory. **Car rental** places are ubiquitous, with outfits on the road approaching the main town entrance: Europcar (☎0242/753 1764) is next to the car park; Avis is just off the approach road at Fatih Cad 25 (☎0242/753 1348). There are a couple of **internet** cafés – *Side* and *Chips* – near the *Pettino Otel* on Cami Sokak. **Tours** from Side include outings to Aspendos, Manavgat and, most interesting, rafting on the Köprülü River. Air Raft (☎0242/746 0414) runs a good beginners' outing, using a "friendly" stretch of the river, and includes an excellent lunch

Accommodation

Even in the height of the season it is possible to find a room in the village, as the package operators are put off using the smaller hotels and pensions within the walls because of airport transfer difficulties. Staying here puts you right among the ruins, surrounded by eateries and entertainment. Bear in mind, though, that while the western section within the walls affords sunset views, it's noisier and hotter than the east, which is cooled by onshore breezes. There are some basic **campsites** around the PTT on the western beach.

Within the walls

Evin Pansiyon Lale Cad ☎0242/753 074. This recommended, family-run establishment has clean, bright rooms and a pleasant garden. It's reached from the footpath running behind the theatre. ❷

Family Pansiyon Gül Sok ☎0242/753 1026. Run by an eccentric Turk, this spartan backpacker-oriented pension is the cheapest in town, with drably furnished, waterless rooms set around a scruffy courtyard. ❶

Ilhan Motel ☎0242/753 1099. Well-decorated rooms with balconies overlooking a verdant garden, in a very quiet location.

Lale Park Lale Sok 5 ☎0242/ 753 1131, ⓔhotellalepark@hotmail.com. A new but traditionally stone-built hotel, with tastefully decorated rooms and quality furnishings, some with shared balconies overlooking the garden. Recommended. ❹

Marina Bar Café Apollon Tapanağı ☎0242/753 2097. Well located next to the Temple of Apollo, this garden bar-cum-restaurant has six simple bungalow-style rooms with fans. ❶

Mine Motel Gül Sok 8 ☎0242/753 1869, ⓔjph281@hotmail.com. An Anglo-Turkish establishment with clean rooms with fans, a friendly atmosphere and a shady courtyard garden. ❷

Özden Pansiyon Gül Sok ☎0242/753 1337, ⓔnorthozden@hotmail.com. A cheap option, with small rooms attractively set around a courtyard. ❶

Pettino Otel Cami Sok 9 ☎0242/753 3608, ⓔPettino@superonline.com. Australian-Turkish venture aimed at the backpacker market, the *Pettino* has small but homely rooms with air-conditioning, running around an L-shaped balcony above a courtyard. ❷

Yükser Pansiyon Sümbül Sok ☎0242/753 2010, ⓕ753 4297. Small but well-appointed rooms with fans in a very attractive stone building. The garden is beautiful and the location very quiet. ❷

Outside the walls

Güven Motel Barbaros Cad ☎0242 753 1099. Right on the seafront and aimed more at the domestic market, it has clean, but characterless rooms with fans. ❷

Hanımeli Pansiyon Turgut Reis Cad ☎0242/753 1100. A very attractive stone building, with a sunken seating area and garden given over to barbecue-style meals. The comfortable rooms are currently being upgraded by the ambitious new owner so prices may rise. ❹

Kale Motel ☎0242/753 147. Just before the city entrance, the *Kale* has attractive chalets set around a large garden, and a bar and restaurant. ❸

Kleopatra Hotel Turgut Reis Cad ☎0242/753 1033, ⓕ753 3738. Situated on the western seafront, this has large, comfortable air-conditioned rooms and access to the beach from the restaurant.

Selen Motel Barbaros Cad ☎0242/753 2730. Basic rooms with superb sea views, plus three self-contained apartments, which can sleep four people. The establishment is favoured more by Turks than foreign tourists. Rooms ❷, apartments ❸

Soundwaves Beach House Hotel Barbaros Cad ☎0242/753 1607. Pretty rooms with balconies facing the sea and an excellent restaurant. ❹

Yaşa Motel Turgut Reis Cad ☎0242/753 4024. Friendly, helpful, management and cool rooms in a wooden building ranged around a garden. ❷

Ancient Side

Ancient Side has been almost overwhelmed by the modern town, but fortunately even the inroads of mass tourism have been unable to smother the grandeur of its buildings and monuments. The road into town actually passes through the **city gate**, although this is in such a bad state of repair you could be forgiven for not noticing it. The **city walls** have fared better, the section running east from the city gate is particularly well preserved, with a number of towers still in place.

The agora and museum

From the city gate, a colonnaded street runs down to the **agora**, the site of Side's second-century slave market, today fringed with the stumps of many of the agora's columns. It's a popular spot with nomads who hang around trying to tempt people into taking camel rides. The circular foundation visible at the centre of the agora is all that remains of a **Temple of Fortuna**, while in the northwest corner, next to the theatre, you can just about make out the outline of a semicircular building that once served as a public latrine, seating 24 people.

SİDE

N

ACCOMMODATION

Evin	7
Family	4
Güven	12
Hanımeli	13
İlhan	5
Kale	1
Kleopatra	3
Lale	8
Marina	16
Mine	10
Özden	9
Pettino	14
Selen	11
Soundwaves Beach House	15
Yaşa	2
Yükser	6

MEDITERRANEAN SEA

Western Beach

ℹ

SORGUN YOLU

Otogar

Ancient Walls

City Gate

Ancient Walls

Museum

Monumental Gate

Agora

Byzantine Basilica

Car Park

Theatre

Antique Baths

TURGUTREIS SOK.

LIMAN CAD.

CAMI SOK.

Eastern Beach

RESTAURANTS

Aphrodite	C
Ayişiği	D
The End	B
Gama	F
Orfoz	A
Soundwaves	E

Temples of Apollo & Athena

0   200 m

Sorgun

Campsites

Opposite the agora is the site of the former Roman baths, now restored and home to a **museum** (daily 8am–noon & 1–5pm; $2.50). It retains its original floor plan and contains a cross-section of locally unearthed objects – mainly Roman statuary, reliefs and sarcophagi. If you find yourself wondering why many of the statues are headless, it's because they were decapitated in an out-break of religious zeal during the early days of Christianity.

The monumental gate and theatre

Just south of here, the still-intact **monumental gate** now serves as an entrance to the town's modern resort area. To the left of the gateway is an excavated monument to Vespasian, built in 74 AD, which takes the form of a fountain with a couple of water basins in front. Inside the gate is the entrance to Side's stunning 20,000-seat **theatre** ($3), the largest in Pamphylia, and different from those at Perge and Aspendos in that it was built as a freestanding structure supported by massive arched vaults, and not into a hillside. The two-metre wall surrounding the orchestra was built to protect the audience from the wild animals used during gladiatorial shows.

Other ruins

From the monumental gate, modern Side's main street leads down to the old harbour and turns left toward the **temples of Apollo and Athena**. The Athena temple has been partly re-erected, and its white portico is becoming Side's trademark and a favourite place to take sunset photographs. Both temples were once partially enclosed in a huge Byzantine basilica, parts of which gradually disappeared under the shifting sand; the still-visible section now provides a home to birds and bats.

In the days when Side was an important port, the area to the west of the temples was a harbour. Even in Roman times it was necessary to dredge continuously to clear silt deposited by the Manavgat River, and it soon became clogged up after the city went into decline. Elsewhere, you'll find a number of other buildings, including the city agora, on the eastern side of the peninsula just a stone's throw from the sea, and, a little inland from here, a ruined **Byzantine church** that's gradually disappearing under the dunes. Off Camii Sokak, behind the Nilgin market, are the remains of **antique baths** where Cleopatra is supposed to have bathed, which include several separate rooms, baths, a garden and even a marble seat with a dolphin armrest.

The beaches

Given Side's fine sandy **beaches**, it's not surprising the resort has developed so rapidly. To the west, the ten-kilometre stretch of beach is lined with expensive hotels, beach clubs and outlets renting windsurfing boards for about $2.50 per hour; the crowds, however, can be heavy during the high season. **Sorgun** beach, 3km to the east, is well maintained by the local authority and is quieter and less tacky than Side's beaches. A dolmuş runs there every half an hour from Side.

Ten kilometres from Side, beyond the western beach, is **Kumköy**, with nearly as much in the way of beachside development as Sorgun, but again, its beaches aren't as crowded as Side's. Some of the buses and dolmuşes that run between Antalya and Side now go via Kumköy.

Eating, drinking and nightlife

There's no shortage of places to **eat and drink** in Side, with what seems like hundreds of establishments up, down and around the main street catering to all tastes (particularly German ones).

Down on the **old harbour**, try *The End*, where you can sample reasonably priced fish dishes on the terrace dining area, or the nearby *Aphrodite*, which has excellent swordfish. On the **east side**, food is cheaper and the restaurants quieter. The *Gama* (☏0242/753 4219) is set in an old-fashioned house with lots of pie-edge woodwork; the speciality (for which you'll need to call ahead to order) is a clay-pot fish stew – the pot is brought flaming to your table and broken open to reveal your meal. *Soundwaves*, at the other end of the east beach, is not as expensive as it looks (around $10 for a full meal) and nice little extras, such as liqueurs, are thrown in; ask the charming waiting staff for advice about

the extensive menu. *Ayışığı*, reached from Cami Sokak, is a garden restaurant with sea views from the terrace; it isn't cheap but service is good and the food, *mezes* and grills, above average. The *Orfoz*, near the *Lighthouse* disco, has a large outdoor seating area under palms, with great sunset views. Prices are fairly high (around $15 for a full meal), but the food is excellent.

Turn left at the harbour and you'll pass a line of chic seafront **bars**. From here, walk through the Apollo and Athena temples to the southeast corner of Side, where music-led bars, such as the *Happy Days*, *Stones Bar* and *Barracuda*, offer **dancing** and fine views out onto the Mediterranean. The *Blues Bar* on Cami Sokak is also worth a look. To save money, you can cruise the staggered happy hours that run in different bars between 6pm and 9pm.

The *Lighthouse,* just west of the harbour, plays a variety of (mainly dance) music, with Russian podium dancers as a diversion and beers at around $3. The smaller *Underground*, also on the western seafront, plays a wider range of music. Some 3km out of town on the west beach is the popular *OXYDisco* ($3 entry fee), a huge, 3000-capacity laser-lit rave venue. It has its own pool, more podium dancers and $3 beers.

Manavgat and around

Fifteen minutes east of Side by dolmuş, the small town of **MANAVGAT** is not especially alluring, though it does explode into life each Monday when hundreds of merchants head in from the surrounding countryside for the local **market**. The only real reason to stay here, though, is for a river-boat tour up to the rather overrated Şelale or Manavgat waterfalls nearby or to visit the isolated ruins of Seleucia, 20km inland, a Macedonian foundation that was rebuilt in Roman times (see below). The 8km roundtrip to the **waterfalls** will set you back around $5, boats leaving from a landing opposite the *otogar*. However, a longer trip offered in Side to the falls and Manavgat costs around $20, and is far more interesting

To reach **Seleucia**, take the dolmuş from the northwest corner of the Manavgat *otogar* (see below) by the bridge to the Oymapınar Baraj. Alight at a left-hand turn signposted for Seleucia, from where it's a walk of 5km to the ruins. You will probably be able to hitch the first 4km to the nearest village, from where it's an uphill walk along a tractor track through pretty farmland. Set on a slope in pine forest, Seleucia itself is secluded but nothing special: the tractor path leads through a city gate to some baths and an agora, the most obvious surviving structures. In spring, a pretty little waterfall cascades past the baths to a stream in the valley below.

If you have a car, another worthy excursion from Manavgat is to head inland along the signposted Akseki road east of Manavgat, a recently constructed switchback that runs through beautiful country between the **Ahmetler canyon** and the **Alara River**. Any left or right turn-off takes you through wooded gorges to villages of antiquated stone houses with cedar balconies and vine-wreathed terraces.

Just under 30km east of Manavgat, a road spears off north to **Alarahan**, with its quirky thirteenth-century Selçuk *kervansaray* built for the benefit of traders operating between the Selçuk city of Konya and the port of Alanya. It was the creation of Sultan Alâeddin Keykubad – also responsible for the castle at Alanya – and is particularly impressive, nestling in the tranquil river valley. Further up the same road, ranged around a pyramidal hill, there are the ruins of an ancient

castle, scarcely discernible against the stony backdrop but accessible by way of steep stairs in a tunnel fifteen minutes' walk on from the *kervansaray*. Returning to the main road and continuing east for about 8km, you'll come to another Selçuk *kervansaray*, the **Şarapsa Hanı**, now being used as a disco.

Practicalities

Dolmuşes and buses shuttle between Manavgat and Side (every fifteen minutes), Antalya (every half-hour) and Sorgun (every now and then). It's worth noting that Alanya-bound dolmuşes depart from Manavgat more frequently than from Side. Manavgat town centre is five minutes' walk west of the **otogar**. From the *otogar*, walk over the bridge, passing a 24-hour soup joint, and turn left for the many waterside **restaurants** catering mostly to cruise customers, with identical menus and similar prices, or turn right for the town's few **hotels.** The *Otel Kervan* (☎0242/746 4400; ❸), 200m downstream, has clean rooms, some of which overlook the river. Better than the *Kervan*, though, is the *Otel Nil* (☎0242/465 289; ❸), with clean rooms and balconies facing the river.

Alanya and around

Not so long ago, **ALANYA** was just another sleepy coastal town with just a handful of flyblown hotels to its name. These days, it's one of the Mediterranean coast's major resorts, a booming and popular place that has expanded beyond all recognition along its sandy beaches. Most visitors enter the town from the west, an approach that shows Alanya at its best, the road passing through verdant banana plantations on the outskirts and suddenly revealing a rocky promontory, topped by a castle, rearing out of the Mediterranean.

Little is known about Alanya's early **history**, although it's thought that the town was founded by Greek colonists who named it Kalonoros, or "beautiful mountain". Things were pretty quiet until the second century BC, when Cilician pirates began using the town, known by now as Coracesium, as a base to terrorize the Pamphylian coast. Eventually, the Romans decided to put an end to the activities of the pirates and sent in Pompey, who destroyed the pirate fleet in a sea battle off Alanya in 67 BC. In 44 BC, Mark Antony gave the city to Cleopatra as a gift. Romantic as this might sound, there was a practical reason for his choice: the area around the city was an important timber-producing centre, and Cleopatra needed its resources to build up her navy. In 1221, the Byzantine city fell to the Selçuk sultan Alâeddin Keykubad, who gave it its present name and made it his summer residence. It's from this period that most buildings of historical importance date.

Arrival, orientation and information

Most of **old Alanya** is set on the great rocky promontory that juts out into the sea, dominating the **modern town**, which spreads to the north. Apart from the hotels and restaurants, and the Alanya Museum, there's little to see in the modern town.

It's about a twenty-minute walk to the town centre from Alanya's **otogar**, but there are plenty of *servis* minibuses to shuttle bus passengers in. If you're coming to Alanya on a through-bus heading for Adana or Mersin, you'll probably be able to get off in the centre of town anyway. Dolmuşes operating from the central terminal will take you to many of the local beaches.

The **tourist office** is opposite the Alanya Museum on İsmet Balcı Caddesi (April–Oct daily 9am–noon & 1–5.30pm; Nov–March Mon–Fri 9am–noon & 1–5.30pm; ☎0242/513 1240).

Accommodation

Despite the boom in package tourism it should be no problem finding a room in Alanya, even in high season, and competition has kept the prices manageable. If you've come primarily for the beach scene, then you might want to choose from one of the hotels on Meteorologi Sokak, near the *otogar*, from where it's an easy walk to the west beach. Keykubat Caddesi, the extension of Atatürk Caddesi, leading off to Mersin and backing the eastern beach, is Alanya's out-of-town resort strip, lined with more upmarket hotels. There are a couple of good **campsites** west of Alanya on the Side road: the *Alanya Motorcamp*, about 25km out, just before a large hotel complex, has good facilities including a restaurant and shops. There's also the *BP-Kervansaray Motorcamp*, a little closer, where you get roughly the same deal.

Around Damlataş Caddesi

Pansiyon Alanya Nergis Sok 4, Güzelyala Cad ☎0242/513 1897. Clean, airy, modern rooms with well-appointed bathrooms and balconies. ❸

Pension Best Alaaddinoğlu Sok 23 ☎0242/513 0446, ✉bestapart@hotmail.com. On the fourth floor of an apartment block, just off Damlataş Cad, the rooms here are kept spotless. Four- and six-person apartments with bathroom, living room and kitchen are also available. Rooms ❷, apartments ❹

Çınar Otel Damlataş Cad ☎0242/512 0063. Near where the street becomes İskele Cad – basic but clean en-suite rooms at bargain prices. ❶

Tayfun Pension Damlataş Cad ☎0242/513 0938. Good-value and friendly, with en-suite rooms. ❶

İskele Caddesi

Hotel Kaptan İskele Cad 70 ☎0242/513 4900, ☏513 2000. Comfortable, central and reasonably classy, with its own pool and two restaurants, one overlooking the harbour. ❺

Hotel Temiz İskele Cad ☎0242/513 1016. Lives up to its name (*temiz* means clean) and has a very impressive reception. Rooms at the back are quiet, the breakfast terrace has a lovely view and guests have use of the nearby sister hotel's pool. ❸

Meteorologi Sokak

Hotel Hermes Meteorologi Sok 2 ☎0242/513 2135. Closest to the beach, with a small pool and appealing rooms. It's well run and popular with Scandinavians. ❺

Üstün Aile Pansiyon Meteorologi Sok 4 ☎0242/513 6525. Run by a charming retired bank manager – spacious rooms with balconies and a communal kitchen. ❷

Keykubat Caddesi

Hotel Banana Keykubat Cad, 2km east of town ☎0242/514 1111. The best of a dozen similar options on this strip, with simple but tasteful rooms around garden pools, and its own well-tended beach. ❺

Kale district

Bedesten Kale ☎0242/512 1234, ☏513 7934. The most interesting hotel in Alanya is a thirteenth-century former *kervansaray* near the Süleymaniye mosque, on the winding road up to the castle. Most of the well-furnished rooms lie around a courtyard, with a couple of suites above, and there's a network of huge underground cisterns and a harem room to explore, as well as a pool. ❼

The Town

Guarding the harbour on the east side of the promontory stands the **Kızılkule** – the "Red Tower" – a 35-metre-high defensive tower of red stone built by Alâeddin Keykubad in 1226 and restored in 1951. Today it houses a pedestrian **ethnographic museum** (Etnografya Müzesi; Tues–Sun 8am–noon & 1.30–5pm; $1.25), and has a roof terrace that overlooks the town's eastern harbour. Old wooden houses cling to the slopes above the tower, and you can

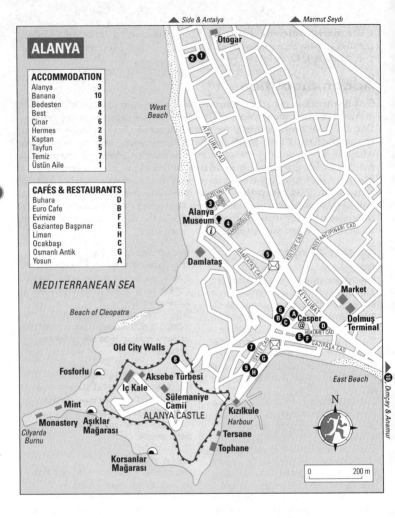

follow the old coastal defensive wall along the water's edge to the **Tersane**, an Ottoman shipyard, consisting of five workshops linked by an arched roof. Beyond here is a small defensive tower, the **Tophane**.

Alanya castle

It's a long, winding climb up to **Alanya castle**, which takes about an hour, assuming you're averagely fit – set off early in the day before it gets too hot, or better still do it in the late afternoon and catch the sunset from the top. There are lots of restaurants and little cafés to stop off at on the way up, often little more than a table and an awning in someone's garden. If you can't face the walk, catch the hourly bus (on the hour) from the junction of İskele and Damlataş *caddesi*s.

The castle itself is a huge fortification system, with walls snaking right around the upper reaches of the promontory. A huge archway (bearing an inscription in Persian) leads into an area that demarcated the original limits of Alanya back in Selçuk times. In among the foliage off the road is an area known as **Ehmediye**, a small village with a few old Ottoman houses clustered around the dilapidated sixteenth-century **Süleymaniye Camii**, a *kervansaray* and the **Aksebe Türbesi**, a distinctive thirteenth-century tomb.

At the end of the road is the **İç Kale**, or Inner Fortress (daily 9am–8pm; $3), built by Keykubad in 1226. Inside the gates, local women sell tablecloths and lace and the smell of lavender hangs in the air. The fortress is pretty much intact, with the shell of a **Byzantine church**, decorated with fading frescoes, in the centre. Look out for the **cisterns** that supplied the fortress with water and to which it owed much of its apparent impregnability. In the northwestern corner of the fortress, a platform gives fine views of the western beaches and the mountains, though it originally served as a point from which prisoners were thrown to their deaths on the rocks below. These days tour guides assure their wards that it's customary to throw a rock from the platform, attempting to hit the sea rather than the rock below – an impossible feat supposed to have been set for prisoners as a chance to save their necks.

Alanya Museum

On the western side of the promontory, the **Alanya Museum** (Alanya Müzesi; Tues–Sun 8am–noon & 1–5pm; $0.70) is filled with local archeological and ethnological ephemera, including finds from (and photographs of) several small Pamphylian sites in the region. Most unusual is an inscription in sixth-century BC Phoenician, a sort of halfway house between cuneiform writing and the alphabet as the Greeks developed it. There's also a mock-up Ottoman living room complete with a beautiful carved ceiling, shutters and cupboards, and a model of a village wedding. The best thing about the museum, though, is the garden, a former Ottoman graveyard in which you can take refuge from the heat in summer; re-creations of grape presses and other farm implements share space with a gaggle of peacocks and chickens.

Incidentally, don't be taken in by signposts pointing to a museum in the back-streets, away from the shore – they in fact lead to a house Atatürk stayed in for exactly three days in 1935, which is, frankly, not very interesting.

The beaches

Alanya's **beaches** are extensive, stretching from the town centre for a good 3km west and 8km east. However, the sand is not the finest and little effort is made to keep the beaches clean, so it's well worth heading out of town for 23km on the Side road to **İncekum** ("fine sand"), a three-kilometre stretch of sand backed by pine forests that does live up to its name, even though it has been voraciously gobbled up by big hotel complexes in the last few years. Frequent dolmuşes make the run from Alanya's dolmuş terminal.

Alanya offers a range of **watersports** and the outlets along the west beach offer jet skis rental ($25 for 15min), parasailing ($25 for 15min), water-skiing ($19 for 30min) and banana-boat rides ($6). If you fancy some scuba-diving, head to Dolphin Dive, by the harbour, the biggest school in town. You can even go bungee jumping ($60) in the east bay around from the harbour.

The caves and boat tours

Not far away from the museum, accessible from behind the *Damlataş Restaurant*, you'll find the **Damlataş**, or "Cave of Dripping Stones" (daily 10am–sunset; $1.25), a stalactite- and stalagmite-filled underground cavern with a moist, warm atmosphere said to benefit asthma sufferers. There are other caves, dotted around the waterline at the base of the promontory, and various local entrepreneurs offer **boat trips** around them, charging about $10 per person for a five-hour trip, or $20 for a longer excursion that includes dolphin-watching. Boats leave from the harbour near Kızıl Kule, usually departing around 10am,

The first stop is usually the **Fosforlu** (Phosphorus Cave), where the water shimmers green; then it's on round the **Cilyarda Burnu**, a long spit of land that is home to a ruined monastery and former mint. It's not actually possible to go ashore, but on the other side of the skinny peninsula is the **Aşıklar Mağarası** (Lovers' Cave), in which, according to a bizarre local story, a German woman and her Turkish boyfriend were stranded for three months in 1965 while the police and army mounted searches for them. A little further round is the **Korsanlar Mağarası**, which, according to more believable stories, is where the pirates of yesteryear used to hide out. You will also be taken to **Cleopatra's Beach**, where the legends claim the queen used to descend to bathe while staying here with Mark Antony.

Eating and drinking

Finding a decent meal is easy in Alanya. The small streets running between Gazipaşa and Hükümet *caddesi*s are lined with *pide* and kebab places where you'll be able to fill up for $5 or thereabouts. There are also plenty of cheap, touristy restaurants and café-bars along Damlataş Caddesi, where you can get a meal for around the same price. Better, more expensive restaurants lie along the seafront (on the street parallel to Gazipaşa Caddesi), most of them serving fish – expect to pay at least $10 a head. The weekly **market**, with masses of fresh provisions, is held every Friday, next to the dolmuş station, north of İsim Tokuş Bulvarı.

There are not as many **bars** in the centre as you might imagine, since most of the nightlife is based around the larger, out-of-town hotels, but the *Efes* at the town-centre end of Damlataş Caddesi is good for cold beers and cocktails, whilst the *Barracuda Bar* near the tourist office is usually lively.

Buhara In a side-street leading to the mosque. The place to come for good *lahmacun* and *sulu yemek*.

Euro Café Damlataş Cad, near the Çınar Otel. Fresh juices, *köfte*, kebabs and burgers at budget prices.

Evimize Next to the Yeni Cami, just behind the waterfront. Good for home-style Turkish food, including *dolma* (stuffed peppers) and *yaprak dolması* (stuffed vine leaves). Some tables are set out on the pavement. A full meal costs around $5, but no alcohol served.

Gaziantep Başpınar Kebap ve Lahmacun Salonu Between Gazipaşa and Hükümet Cad. The huge green-and-yellow fronted restaurant serves

good stews with flat bread, *lahmacun* and kebabs; a filling meal will set you back $3–5.

Liman Overlooking the harbour. Pleasant decor and cheaper prices than the other fish restaurants in town.

Ocakbaşı Müftüler Cad, Kalgıdım Sok. On a side-street behind the police station, the only place in Alanya where you can get traditional Turkish soup, ideal after a night on the town.

Osmanlı Antik Restaurant Just behind the seafront. Eat *mezes*, casseroles and grills sprawled on cushions around *sofra* tables.

Yosun Pastanesi Müftüler Cad. Good for early morning *poğaça* (breakfast buns), as well as ice-cream and coffee throughout the day.

Listings

Banks and exchange There are several banks with ATMs on Atatürk Cad and Hükümet Cad.
Bicycle and motorbike rental Bikes cost $6 per day, mopeds $15 and motorbikes $35, available

from numerous outlets around town.
Buses Regular buses link Alanya with destinations east and west, including Antalya, Mersin and Adana, as well as north to Ankara, İstanbul and

Konya. Most of the buses, however, start their journey elsewhere, so make sure you book your departure seat well in advance.

Car rental There are numerous operators in Alanya; try several places and bargain hard as prices are higher than Antalya. Main agencies, including: Avis, Atatürk Cad 53 ☎0242/513 3513; and Europcar, Keykubat Cad 21/A ☎0242/513 1929. Cheaper is Force Rental, Damlataş Cad 68/A ☎0242/519 6262.

Hospital The State Hospital (Devlet Hastane) is on the bypass, east of the centre.

Internet Casper Internet Café, behind the Yeni Cami on the waterfront.

Post office The PTT, Atatürk Cad, opposite Kültr Cad (daily 8am–midnight), sells phone cards.

There are also PTT caravans scattered about the town during the summer.

Shopping Touristy silverware and carpets are on sale in İskele Cad, and there are yet more shops on the side streets between Gazipaşa Cad and Hükümet Cad. Genuine and fake designer label clothes are better purchases, and if you are looking to add to your collection of soccer replica shirts, Alanya is the place to do it.

Tours and travel agents FAM Tour, Damlataş Cad (☎0242/511 1527), Indiana Tour, Keykubat Cad (☎0242 512 4454), and Mem-Tours, Gazipaşa Cad (☎0242/511 4450), all offer trips to Cappadocia, Pamukkale or the Pamphylian cities (from $25), as well as jeep safaris and boat tours; often they'll pick you up at your hotel.

Around Alanya

Alanya's tourist office distinguishes itself by its dearth of information about sites in the region, and even archeological sites are not signposted from the road, so haphazard is tourism development here. Private tour operators are helping to fill the gap, with trips to Alanya's nearby mountain villages and to the Dimçay River, but otherwise you'll need a good map and a car to get the most out of the town's surroundings.

The Dimçay River

The **Dimçay River** is 6km from the centre of Alanya, but still within the boundaries of the modern city. Take an hourly "Dimçay" or "Banana" dolmuş out of town from along Keykubat Caddesi to the bridge signposted "Dimçay". From the bridge, the riverbanks, especially along the western side, are lined with restaurants offering fresh trout or kebabs at tables actually in the shallow river – you can cool your feet as you eat. Further up, as you near the Toros mountains, the scenery becomes more spectacular, and the most impressive location is about 8km from the bridge. Here, the river deepens into a beautiful green pool where you can swim in the freezing mountain-spring water. Further up the Dimçay is a dam creating an even deeper pool and the *Pinarbaşı* and *Dündar Yıldız* fish farms

If you stay on the "Dimçay" dolmuş past the bridge, as the road climbs the right side of the valley and traverses a new dirt road, you arrive at the **Damlataş Mağarası** (May–Oct daily 10am–5pm; $1), a 300-metre deep illuminated cave lined with stalactites and stalagmites and with a pool at the end. Outside is the cheerful *Sultanyar* restaurant, which affords spectacular views over the river. You could visit both the cave and the river in a combined daytrip; a board outside the cave gives dolmuş times.

Mahmut Seydi

Alanya's principle *yayla* or summer mountain retreat is **MAHMUT SEYDİ**, an attractive village a tortuous 25km out of town. Minibuses aren't designed to meet the needs of tourists, since they arrive in the evening and leave the following morning, and there's no accommodation. To get there by car, take Yayla Caddesi off Atatürk Caddesi and head for the hills.

It's worth renting a car to get to Mahmut Seydi, partly to escape from Alanya's oppressive summertime heat, but also to visit the town's thirteenth–century

mosque. The exterior of the building is modern, but most of the interior fittings, including the woodwork of the ceilings, doors, cupboards and galleries, are original. Unfortunately, the woodwork was painted in recent restorations, but its former glory can still be appreciated, especially in the fine work of the ceiling. In the courtyard is part of the original fountain and a 650-year-old fir tree. From viewing platforms next to the tree and the mosque, the valley, its surrounding mountains and village houses are visible, as well as the distant beach of İncekum. Also visible is the town's real pride and joy – a two-storey public toilet.

Opposite the mosque on the other side of the street, a local family keeps a grocer's **shop** and provides hospitality for visitors in a little shed full of paraphernalia, such as an Ottoman chimney-piece adorned with a 1950s alarm clock and a Selçuk sword with silver inscriptions. *Toros Piknik*, a romantically situated **restaurant** 3km below the village, will serve up a good spread while you admire the mountainside views.

Alanya to Adana

The region between Alanya and Adana formed ancient **Cilicia**, settled by refugees from Troy at the same time as Pamphylia further west, but its remoteness meant that it was never as developed and, although it had a couple of significant centres, the region seems to have been largely wild and lawless. In ancient times it was divided between Cilicia Tracheia (Rough Cilicia) – Alanya to the western edge of the Çukurova – and Cilicia Campestris (Smooth Cilicia), comprising the dull flatlands of the Ceyhan delta.

Cilicia Tracheia, with its rugged, densely wooded coastline, was a haven for pirates, whose increasingly outrageous exploits finally spurred the Romans into absorbing Cilicia into the empire in the first century BC. Today, it retains a wild appearance, and travel through it involves some frighteningly daring drives along winding mountain roads that hug the craggy coastline, traversing the rocky coves that once served as pirate hangouts. All this is to the good if you're trying to escape the crowds further west, since far fewer people make it along here. There are some decent stretches of beach around **Anamur**, overlooked by an Armenian castle and a partially excavated Greek site, while in the mountains above **Silifke** – the next major town – the abandoned city of **Uzuncaburç** is perhaps the most extensive of the region's ancient remains. After **Kızkalesi**, where two huge castles break up the shoreline, there are more good beaches and weird ruins, running through flatter land into the outskirts of **Mersin**. This marks the beginning of what was Cilicia Campestris, and the end of the area's real touristic interest, with ferries to northern Cyprus but nothing else to stop for. Similarly, **Tarsus**, a little further on, has little to betray its former historical importance; while **Adana**, Turkey's fourth largest city, contains few remains of any era despite a venerable history, but does have excellent market shopping.

Alanya to Silifke

Heading east from Aanya, the road starts to cut through the mountains, traversing occasional valleys planted with bananas but rarely losing sight of the sea. On the way, you'll pass odd little wayside restaurants and campsites, often tucked under the old plane trees that indicate the presence of underground water reserves, and sheltered but difficult-to-reach sandy bays, which are guaranteed to be almost empty even at the height of summer.

To make the most of this stretch of coastline you really need your own transport, as only the beaches around the tiny resort of İskele (Anamur) merit a longer stay, and the few sites are difficult to reach by public transport. Taşucu, near to Silifke, is the best place to cross to Northern Cyprus.

Iotape

The first place of real interest after leaving Alanya's hotel sprawl behind is **Iotape**, around 45km away. Oddly situated on a rocky promontory between the road and the sea, this ancient site was named after the wife of the Commagenian king Antiochus IV (38–72 AD), and struck its own coins from the reign of Emperor Trajan until that of Emperor Valerian.

The ruins are mainly very tumbledown apart from a fairly impressive triple-arched bath-house, which can be clearly seen from the road. Closer inspection uncovers drainage and heating systems. The acropolis is on the promontory out to sea and a colonnaded street runs east–west along the valley linking the promontory to the mainland. Also visible from the road are statue bases giving information about successful athletes and philanthropists of the city, and there are frescoes to be seen inside the niches of a small, single-aisled church. The **beach** below Iotape is idyllic: if you're lucky you might get it to yourself.

Gazipaşa

The first significant settlement after Alanya is **GAZİPAŞA**, about 50km to the east, an aspiring resort with a new yacht harbour approaching completion. The *Selinus Hotel* (℡0242/572 1986, ✉info@selinushotel.com.tr; ❹), 3km southwest of the town centre, is worth considering if you want a few days on a quiet beach. It has bright, spacious rooms, a decent pool and loungers and umbrellas on the beach; the price is for half-board accommodation. Better value, though, are the bungalows of the *Belediye Dinlenme Tesisleri* (℡0242/572 1631; ❷), also right on the beach, which have a small kitchen with a fridge, a double bedroom and a living room. There is a large swimming pool here, and a couple of places to eat and drink, though the units are often fully booked in July and August by Turkish families. To get here, take a dolmuş from outside Gazipaşa's *Belediye* offices on the main coastal highway. The ruins of ancient **Selinus** sprawl across the hillside east of the beach.

Anamur, İskele and around

There's little of interest in **ANAMUR** – 80km east of Gazipasa – but its small harbour suburb, **İSKELE** (*İskele* means quay), 4km away, is slowly developing as a fully fledged, but unpretentious resort, packed in summer with holidaying Turks. It's reached via an unmarked road south from Anamur's *otogar*, which is at the junction of the main street and the coast road. İskele's small **museum** (Tues–Sun 8am–noon & 1–5pm; $0.70), just west of the town centre, contains some fine *Yörük* kilims and saddle-bags, and finds from nearby classical sites, best of which is a Hellenistic-era cylindrical pottery burial cask.

If you arrive in the early hours at Anamur *otogar* try the nearby *Saray Hotel* (☎0324/814 1191; ❶), east of the town centre, as after 11.30pm you won't find a dolmuş into İskele. In İskele itself, the cheapest **accommodation** is the *Meltem Hotel* (☎0324/814 1191; ❶), but by far the best budget choice is the *Eser Pansiyon*, a block back from the sea (☎0324/814 2322; ❷), which offers clean rooms, either en-suite or a bathroom shared between two rooms, and a vine-shaded rooftop terrace. The owner and his son both speak very good English and know the local area extremely well. They can arrange boat trips to Anemurium and a taxi or dolmuş to Mamure Kalesi (for both see below), or even a jaunt into the mountains. To the west, on the seafront, the *Yan Hotel* (☎0324 814212; ❷) is built around an atrium, with dark but comfortable rooms; breakfast and dinner is included in the price. The *Ünlüselek* (☎0324/814 1973, ✉unluselk@hotmail.com; ❷), 1.5km west of Iskele, has large air-conditioned rooms, its own stretch of beach and a seaside restaurant. There's also the *Kap Anamur* (☎0324/814 5007; ❷), just off the central square, which has small but comfortable rooms and possibly the best restaurant in town. Other simple **restaurants** line the beach, best at night when tables are laid out on the sand right to the water's edge.

Anemurium

Six kilometres southwest of modern Anamur, but without a local dolmuş service, is the ancient settlement of **Anemurium** (Tues–Sun 8am–8pm; $2.50), on the eastern side of a headland formed where the Toros mountains jut out into the sea. An access road leads down to the partially excavated site from the main road (look out for the yellow sign). Anemurium was at its peak during the third century AD, and most of what remains dates from this period. As you approach you'll see two parallel **aqueducts** running north to south along the hillside to the right. Below these, a sun-baked **necropolis** contains numerous free-standing tombs whose cool interiors harbour murals of mythological scenes on the walls; however, the most notable tombs have been barred off with locked gates. To the right of the road are the hollow ruins of three **Byzantine churches**, set starkly against the blue backdrop of the Mediterranean.

Further down towards the beach you'll see the crumbling remains of a **bath complex** and a desolate **palaestra** or parade ground. Southwest of here is a ruined but still identifiable **theatre** set into the hillside of the headland. Above the theatre on the slope, between the lower and upper aqueduct, are the remains of a number of houses, some of which have intact vaulted roofs, and east of here is the shell of a building containing sixteen curved rows of seating and a mosaic floor, thought to have been either a **council chamber** or **concert hall** (possibly both). Returning towards the theatre and heading south, you'll come across another **baths complex**, a two-storey vaulted structure with discernible traces of decoration and tile-work on the interior walls.

With time, you might want to clamber up the scrubby slopes of the headland to what was once Anemurium's **acropolis**. There isn't a lot to see here, but the promontory is **Turkey's southernmost point**, and on a clear day gives views of the mountains of Cyprus, 80km to the south.

Mamure Kalesi

In the opposite direction from Anamur, a couple of kilometres east of İskele, is **Mamure Kalesi** (daily 8am–7pm; $1), a forbidding castle built by the rulers of the Cilician kingdom of Armenia on the site of a Byzantine fort. It was later occupied by Crusaders, who had established a short-lived kingdom in Cyprus and used Mamure Kalesi as a kind of bridgehead in Asia. Used by successive rulers of the area to protect the coastal strip, it was most recently garrisoned by the Ottomans, who reinforced it after the British occupied Cyprus in 1878, maintaining a strong presence here during World War I. Constructed directly above the sea, its stark facade of crenellated outer walls and watchtowers are certainly impressive, and they hide an interior of languorously decaying buildings that has formed a backdrop to many Turkish films – local people are used to doubling as extras. The whole effect is quietly atmospheric, worth an hour of idling if you've time on your hands.

From İskele it is possible to walk the 2.5km along the seashore to the castle, though this requires being ferried across the Dragon River by boat for around $1. Alternatively, take a dolmuş from İskele to the BP garage on the main road, then another east along the coastal highway to the castle.

Opposite the castle are a couple of small fish **restaurants** and a few noisy pensions, while a couple of kilometres east there's a good forested **campsite**, the *Pullu Mocamp*, which has a beach and an excellent restaurant.

Taşucu

Moving on, there are a couple of quiet bays with sandy beaches, but most people push straight on to the scruffy port of **TAŞUCU**, from where there are frequent ferry and hydrofoil services to Cyprus. Crossing the next day is the only reason you would choose to stay the night here. Of **accommodation** options, the *Hotel Fatih* (☎0324/741 4125; ❷), just beyond the ferry offices, is friendly and nicely furnished. On the east of town near the harbour, try the *Tuğran Pension* (☎0324/741 4493, ❷), a single-storey building in a garden set back from the beach. Just down from the *Tuğran*, the German-Turkish-run *Holmi Pansiyon* (☎0324/741 5378; ❷) has spotless and cheerful rooms with fans and a pleasant breakfast area. Best in town is the *Lades Motel*, Atatürk Cad 89 (☎0324/741 4008; ❸), with a swimming pool and fine sea view.

Ferries and hydrofoils to Cyprus

The cheapest way to the Turkish Republic of North Cyprus (TRNC) is by ferry (daily at midnight; 6hr) to Girne/Kyrenia, though as these are packed with heavy lorries and their drivers, women travellers may feel uncomfortable. A much more pleasant alternative is to take the hydrofoil (*denizotobüsü*; daily at midday; 2hr). **Tickets** for both services are available from Fergün Deniz Otobüsü (☎0324/741 3711) and Akgünler (☎0324/741 3711), both on the waterfront; for further schedules and prices, see "Travel details", p.599. At present, EU, US, Canadian and Australasian citizens require only a valid passport, on which your Turkish entry visa has not expired, for entry into the TRNC. It's not possible to enter southern (Greek-speaking) Cyprus from the TRNC.

Silifke

About 10km east of Taşucu, **SİLİFKE** was once ancient Seleucia, founded by Seleucus, one of Alexander the Great's generals, in the third century BC. Nowadays, it's a quiet, fairly undistinguished town, relatively untouched by tourists – who, if they come here at all, do so only on their way to the ruins at Uzuncaburç. Nevertheless, the very ordinariness of Silifke has its own appeal; many of the town's inhabitants still sport traditional baggy trousers and the streets are full of three-wheeled motorcycles, which seem to be the main means of transport. You may also notice that the food here starts getting spicier, hinting at even hotter things to come in the east of the country.

Silifke Kalesi, a Byzantine castle, dominates the local skyline though it looks a lot less spectacular close up. It's about a twenty-minute walk southwest of town and at the top there's a café and a great view. On the way up you'll pass an old **cistern** – the so-called *tekir ambarı* or "striped depot" – which kept Byzantine Silifke supplied with water. Other sights include the second-century AD **Jupiter Tapınağı** (Temple of Jupiter) on İnönü Caddesi, which comprises little more than a pile of stones and one standing pillar with a stork's nest on top. On the main road to Taşucu and Antalya, about half a kilometre from the turnoff to Silifke, there's an **archeological museum** (Arkeoloji Müzesi; Tues–Sun 8am–noon & 1–5pm; $0.70) containing the finds from excavations at Meydancıkale, a fourth-century BC temple site in the mountains above the coast. Relics include two enormous caryatids, huge, shapeless stone blocks with human-looking feet carved into the bases, and a horde of 5,200 silver coins dating from the reigns of Alexander and his generals in Egypt, Syria and the province of Pergamon.

The Göksu delta

Of Turkey's twelve designated areas of outstanding environmental importance, the **Göksu delta** is one of the largest, its 14,500 hectares comprising most of the flat lands east of the Göksu river and south of Silifke. The southern portion of the delta has been designated as the **Kuşcenneti bird reservation** and boasts a tremendous variety of flora and fauna, most notably millions of water birds who inhabit two natural lagoons enclosed by a huge sand spit which juts into the sea. Despite Göksu's protected status, the area is under long-term threat by the proposed construction of an upstream dam at Kayraktepe, and the battle between environmentalists and the developers continues.

The best place to start an exploration of the area is **Akgöl**, the westerly lagoon, where viewing platforms and huts are under construction. Bird species on Akgöl include pygmy cormorants, Dalmatian pelicans, marbled and white-headed ducks and even the practically extinct black francolin and purple gallinule, two huge birds that have traditionally been shot for food. The **sand spit** is a nesting ground for loggerhead and green turtles as well as a home to sea daffodils and Audouin's gulls. East of this, reached by an access road halfway between Taşucu and Silifke, are extensive ditches where you'll see kingfishers (including the rare chestnut brown and white Smyrna variety), coots, wagtails, spoonbills, egrets and grey, purple and squacco herons. Marsh harriers circle lazily and, in season, migrating vultures and eagles feed in the lush hunting grounds here, gathering strength for their journey north or south. Still further east, the huge natural fishpond of **Paradeniz lagoon** and the flats beyond it harbour waders, ospreys and terns; more viewing platforms are being installed.

You'll see the highest number of birds during the **nesting and migration seasons**: between February and May in the spring (with a peak between late March and early April), and in October, though the storks will have left by autumn. Information leaflets on the delta are available from the **Özel Çevre Koruma Kurumu** (Special Environmental Areas Protection Agency; ☎0324/713 0888), 5km west of Silifke, near the church of Aya Tekla, in the grounds of the DSİ waterworks complex; if you contact them in advance you can also arrange an English-speaking guide for group trips. If you want to go independently, you'll need your own car or a taxi.

Incidentally, it was near Silifke that **Frederick Barbarossa**, the Holy Roman Emperor, met his end: he drowned while fording the Calycadnus (now Göksu) River about 9km north of town, en route to Palestine with the Third Crusade; today a plaque marks the spot. Otherwise, heading 4km west of Silifke and then 1km north takes you to Meyemlik and the early Christian site of **Aya Tekla** (open daily, assuming the warden is around; $1). There's little to see except the underground chapel (bring a torch) used in secret by the early Christians, including Tecla, the first female Christian teacher.

Practicalities

The centre of town is Menderes Caddesi, around fifteen minutes' walk from the **otogar** along İnönü Caddesi. Silifke's helpful **tourist office** is at Veli Gürten Bozbey Cad 6 (Mon–Fri 8am–5pm; ℡0324/714 1151), reached by way of the Roman bridge spanning the Göksu River.

Hotel possibilities are limited. A basic option in the centre is the spotless but soulless *Hotel Akdeniz*, Menderes Cad 76 (℡0324/714 1285; ❶). Another is the *Arısan Pansiyon* on İnönü Caddesi (℡0324/714 3331; ❷), not far from the otogar, whose rooms are bright and come with a fan; you pay a little more for an en-suite bathroom. Best-positioned hotel in town is the *Göksu Hotel*, Atatürk Cad 16 (℡0324/712 1021, ℻712 1024; ❸), on the north riverbank, with large, well-furnished rooms with air-conditioning and TV, and wonderful views over the river, bridge and castle. The two-star *Otel Ayatekla*, opposite the otogar (℡0324/714 392; ❸), is comparable to the *Göksu*, with an excellent restaurant and bar.

There are lots of basic places to **eat and drink**, but most close after dark, leaving you with only a few options for an evening meal. Best bet is the *Babu Oğlu*, opposite the *otogar*, which has medium-priced grills but expensive fish. The *Göksu Hotel* serves excellent food and beer in its waterside garden, though you'll need to book in advance, as they cook to order.

Inland: Uzuncaburç and Alahan

A single dolmuş bound for the ancient city of **Uzuncaburç** departs daily from Silifke *otogar* around 1.30pm. However, as it's not possible to return from the site by dolmuş on the same day, it's much safer to go by taxi, which costs about $20 for the return trip, though this is highly negotiable. The 30km ride to Uzuncaburç is spectacular, taking you through a jagged gorge and a couple of villages that time seems to have forgotten. Beyond Uzuncaburç, drivers can loop back to the main highway to Konya, calling in at the Byzantine site of **Alahan** en route.

Demircili

If you have your own transport, you might care to stop off in the village of **DEMİRCİLİ** 7km north of Silifke, known in ancient times as Imbriogon, where there are six **Greco-Roman tombs** spread out on either side of the road among the olive trees. They are unattended and unrestored – looking more like long-vacated houses than tombs – and it's hard to believe that they have survived the depredations of time and stone plunderers. The first is a simple one-storey affair just to the right of the road; a little further along, there's a larger two-storey structure. To the west of the road is the **Çifte Anıt Mezarları**, or "double mausoleum", consisting of two linked tombs, the right-hand one of which contains three sarcophagi with various decorative features: one with a relief of a lion and another featuring a man's head, the nude figures of two women and the heads of two women.

Uzuncaburç

From Demırcılı, the road continues uphill and then turns off to the right towards the ruins at **Uzuncaburç**, originally a Hittite settlement that was known to the Greeks as Olba and to the Romans as Diocaesarea. A small, modern village has grown up in haphazard fashion around the ruins, but few concessions have been made to tourism. Uzuncaburç is famous for leather bags and handmade rugs known as *çul*; examples are often sold at makeshift stalls. Local culinary specialities include *kenger kahvesi* (coffee made from acanthus) and *pekmez* (grape molasses). The *Burç* café offers simple **meals** and soft drinks, but there isn't anywhere to stay.

The main site
The main **site of Uzuncaburç** (always open; $0.70 when the site guardian is around) lacks the size and scale of Perge and Aspendos, but is atmospheric enough in its own way, if only because of its relatively neglected state. Although the area was first settled by the Hittites, they left little behind and the most impressive ruins that survive date from Hellenistic times.

It is usual to start your explorations at the overgrown Roman **theatre**, overlooked by a couple of beautiful houses whose walls are chock-a-block with

Classical masonry. From here, pass through an enormous five-columned **monumental gateway**, beyond which a colonnaded street, once the city's main thoroughfare, runs east to west: keep your eyes open for what look like small stone shelves on the columns, which once supported statues and busts. On the northern side of the street is a **nymphaeum**, now dried up, which once formed part of the city's water-supply system. This was part of a large network of pipes and tunnels, built by the Romans nearly two thousand years ago, that still supplies water to the modern village and others around.

To the south, the **Temple of Zeus Olbios** is one of the earliest examples of the Corinthian order, erected during the third century BC by Seleucus I, of which only the fluted columns now remain intact. Look out for the fine sarcophagus carved with three Medusa heads and a sarcophagus lid depicting three reclining figures. At the western end of the colonnaded street is the **Temple of Tyche**, dedicated to the goddess of chance, reckoned to date from the second half of the first century AD. Five marble columns still stand, joined by an architrave bearing an inscription stating that the temple was the gift of a certain Oppius and his wife Kyria. From here a right turn leads to a large three-arched **city gate**, which, according to an inscription, dates from the fifth century AD and is home to nesting owls.

Other ruins

The majority of Uzuncaburç's remaining attractions lie to the north of these ruins. Walk from the drop-off point as far as the *Burç* café and turn right for the **High Tower**, a 22-metre-high, five-storey Hellenistic structure that once formed part of the city wall and which today gives its name to the modern town (Uzuncaburç means "high tower"). An ancient Greek inscription above the entrance gives details of repair work carried out during the third century AD. Today, it looks in danger of imminent collapse. It is believed that in addition to playing a defensive role this tower was also part of an ancient signalling network, whereby messages were relayed by flashing sunlight off polished shields.

Just outside the modern village, past the *Burç* café as far as the Atatürk bust (heed the signs for the "Antik Mezar" and follow the curve to the right), is a **necropolis** used by Greek, Roman and Byzantine inhabitants of the area. It has three basic types of resting place: sarcophagi, graves carved into the rock and cave-tombs housing whole families. Most of these are clearly visible, and it's even possible to enter some of the cave-tombs, though they have long since been cleaned out by grave-robbers.

About 1km south of Uzuncaburç, 500m west of the main road, is another **mausoleum**, this time with an eye-catching pyramid-shaped roof, dating from Hellenistic times. Inside, the tombs were hidden under the floor and, outside, the rim of the roof was lined with statues of the deceased.

Another possible excursion from Uzuncaburç is to the ruins of **Olba** (present-day Ura), 5km to the east, a similar but less impressive ancient city which was the third-century BC capital of a temple state run by a powerful priest caste. At the village crossroads you will find a nymphaeum, cistern and theatre nestling at the base of an acropolis. Five hundred metres further northeast you can see the aqueduct built to feed the nymphaeum, and the watchtowers built to protect the aqueduct.

Alahan: the road to Konya

Some 110km northwest of Silifke, and reached by a spectacular road cutting through the Toros mountains en route for Konya, lies **Alahan**, a well-preserved monastic complex in a beautiful mountain setting. The site is well signposted, 2km to the east of the main road (Highway 715). Intact buildings at the site include two late fifth- and sixth-century basilicas, one sporting elaborate relief sculptures of the Evangelists and the two archangels, and a baptistery. Alahan is best reached using your own transport, though the buses plying between the coast and Konya will drop you at the turn. Following your explorations you'll have to chance your luck on flagging down a Karaman/Konya bus

East from Silifke

East of Silifke the coast road winds above the ocean to Kızkalesi, dropping occasionally to small villages where you'll be alone on the sands, though a rash of development is rapidly despoiling this stretch of coastline. Although there are some interesting sites, particularly the Roman baths at **Narlıkuyu** and the caves of **Cehennem** and **Cennet**, you need your own transport to make the most of them. Anyone with a special interest in exploring more ruins off the beaten track should buy Celal Taşkiran's *Silifke and Environs*, an exhaustive guide to all the sites between Anamur and Mersin, available at many of these sites for about $10.

Karadedeli and around

About 7km east of Silifke, **KARADEDELİ**, a small village settled by former tent-dwelling Turcoman nomads, makes a good starting point for a walking tour of some ruined sites to the north. A series of pathways connects these sites, and it may be possible to hire a donkey in the village to make the trek (details from the tourist office in Silifke). The sites themselves are hardly breathtaking, but make an interesting enough target for some gentle hillwalking. First stop, 2km north of the village, is **Yalak Taş**, where there are some Greco-Roman foundations and the ruins of a cistern, together with what's thought to be an olive-oil factory. Another 2km to the north brings you to **Dılek Taş** and a few more ancient cisterns. The largest ruins are at **Karabaklı**, where there are a few Greco-Roman houses, some of them two storeys high.

About 5km east of Karadedeli is **SUSANOĞLU**, the site of the ancient port of Corasium, but now an ugly mass of concrete hotel and apartment buildings lining the coastal road. A number of Roman remains are scattered through a valley running north from the beach, which is actually a silted-up Roman harbour. About half a kilometre east of the village itself is **Yapraklı Eşik** ("the cove with leaves"), a once quiet inlet whose waters are claimed to have curative properties.

Inland from here – reachable if you have your own transport – the ruins of another ancient settlement signal a two-kilometre diversion to the east down a dirt road to the third-century **Mezgit Kalesi**, or "mausoleum of the fearless satrap". This is similar in appearance to those at Demırcılı, but a carving of a phallus adorns the exterior. The phallus represents Priapus, the well-endowed son of Dionysus and Aphrodite, and is supposed to signify that the occupant of the tomb was courageous and valiant, as well as being hung like a horse.

Heading eastwards along the coast from Susanoğlu you'll come across a number of bays with beaches. The best place to stay in this area is the four-star *Altınorfoz Banana Hotel* (☎0324/722 4211; ❼), just a short distance past the village of Atakent.

Narlıkuyu and Akkum

A little way beyond Atakent, **NARLIKUYU** lies on the fringes of an exquisite bay with a handful of restaurants and a couple of basic *pansiyons*. There's a
small car park in the centre of the village, next to which are the remains of a
Roman bath-house, known after its founder as the **Bath of Poimenius** ($1).
Inside, there's a dusty mosaic depiction of the well-rounded nude forms of the
Three Graces, the daughters of Zeus and companions of the Muses. The bath
was fed from the limestone caves above by an ancient Roman spring that supplied a celebrated fountain, the waters of which were supposed to confer wisdom on those who drank from them.

A kilometre or so further down the road is the village of **AKKUM**, again
with a few *pansiyons* and a good stretch of beach. The *Kökler*, not far from the
beach (☎0324/723 3214; ❷), is clean and friendly and has an English-speaking
proprietor.

Cennet ve Cehennem

From Narlıkuyu, a narrow paved road winds 3km northwards into the hills
through groves of olive trees to **Cennet ve Cehennem**, or the "Caves of
Heaven and Hell" (open in daylight hours; $1) – some of the most impressive
of the many limestone caverns scattered along this coast. At the end of the road
there's a car park and a cluster of tea shops and souvenir stands.

The site consists of a series of three caves, and local kids are usually quick to
offer their services as guides, though their assistance isn't really necessary.
Immediately adjacent to the parking space, the largest and most impressive
cave is **Cennet Deresi** (Cave of Heaven), actually a seventy-metre-deep
gorge formed when the roof of an underground canyon collapsed. You enter
via 452 steps cut into the rock on the eastern side of the canyon. On reaching the bottom, head south towards the entrance to the **Tayfun Mağrası**
(Cave of Typhon), a *bona fide* cave of some depth, at the end of which runs a
stream of drinkable water from the same source as the spring water in
Narlıkuyu. As you go further in, it gets progressively more difficult to breathe
and it's best not to hang around too long, a fact recorded by Strabo, the
ancient geographer, leading some historians to believe that this cave may have
been considered one of the mythical entrances to Hades. According to the
legend, Typhon, after whom the cave is named, was an immense hundred-
headed fire-breathing lizard, the father of Cerberus – the three-headed dog
who guarded the entrance to Hades on the banks of the River Styx, allowing
only the souls of the dead to enter and refusing to let them out. At the
entrance to the cave is the **chapel of the Virgin Mary**, a well-preserved
Byzantine church built over the former temple of Zeus and still containing a
few frescoes.

About 100m to the north of "Heaven", the **Cehennem Deresi** (Cave of
Hell) is impossible to enter, as its sides are practically vertical. According to
legend, Zeus imprisoned Typhon here, before banishing him forever to the
depths of the earth or, as one legend goes, trapping him underneath Mount
Etna in Sicily. This gorge is supposed to be another of the entrances to
Hades, and local people used to tie rags to surrounding trees to placate evil
spirits.

About 500m west of "Heaven" is a fourth cave, the **Dilek Mağrası**
(Wishing Cave), the opening of which has been specially widened and a spiral
staircase provided for ease of access. Down below, solid pathways connect a

number of subterranean halls, with a total length of about 200m. The main chamber is filled with stalactites and stalagmites, and the air down below is supposed to be beneficial for asthma sufferers.

Kızkalesi and around

A few kilometres east of Narlikuyu, and about halfway between Silifke and Mersin, **KIZKALESI** ("Maiden's Castle") is the longest established resort along this stretch of coastline. It has scores of hotels, *pansiyons* and restaurants, and the fine sandy beach slopes gently into the sea, making it ideal for kids (camels provide an alternative to donkey rides). The more active can parasail and jet-ski from the pier in front of the *Albatros Restaurant Café Bar*.

Known as Corycus in ancient times, Kızkalesi changed hands frequently until the arrival of the **Romans** in 72 BC, after which it prospered, becoming one of the most important ports along the coast. Roman-period relics still survive in the area, notably a series of mysterious rock reliefs north of town and the carvings at the chasm at Kanlıdivane to the east. Kızkalesi continued to thrive during the Byzantine era despite occasional Arab attacks – against which the town's defences were strengthened with two **castles** constructed during the twelfth and thirteenth centuries – before falling to the Ottomans in 1482.

The Town

The town's most compelling feature is the thirteenth-century **sea castle**, the *Kızkalesi* or Maiden's Castle (daily dawn–dusk; $1.25), on an island lying about 200m offshore. The story (examples of which are found all over Turkey) goes that one of the Armenian kings who ruled the region in medieval times had a beautiful daughter. After it was prophesied that she would die as the result of a poisonous snakebite, the king had the castle built and moved the girl out to it, imagining that she would be safe there. One day one of the king's advisers sent a basket of fruit out to the island for her, out of which slid a snake that killed the girl. According to local stories, the snake still lives on the island, and the only people who venture out to it are tourists, for whose benefit boat services operate ($2 return trip) from the western end of the beachfront. The unadorned walls and sturdy towers still stand, but apart from masonry fragments and weeds there's little to see within.

Opposite the sea castle, the overgrown ruins of the mighty **land castle** (*Korkyos Kalesi*) at the eastern end of the beach ($1.25, if there's anyone around to collect it) are easily explored and its battlements make a good venue for some sunset-watching, provided you can stand the mosquitoes. The main gate, constructed from ancient stones, bears various Greek inscriptions. The western gate was originally a Roman structure, built during the third century AD and later incorporated into the castle.

Immediately northeast of the town, across the main road from the land castle, is a **necropolis**, dating from the fourth century AD and containing hundreds of tombs and sarcophagi, some of them beautifully carved. Many of the epitaphs give the jobs of the occupants – weavers, cobblers, goldsmiths, vintners, olive-oil manufacturers, ship owners and midwives, who all had their last resting places here. Also scattered around this area are the remains of a number of Byzantine churches and cisterns.

Practicalities

Orientation is simple, as **buses** plying the coastal road to and from Mersin will drop you on the main road in the town centre. Nearly all the **accommodation** is found between the main road and the beach to the south. It is possible to find somewhere to stay here, even in the very crowded months of July and August, while out of season you'll be able to negotiate a substantial discount. It's worth noting that all the hotels may be subject to thudding music coming from beachfront bars.

Running from east to west along the beachfront, furthest east is the *Hulya Pansiyon* (☎0324/523 2067; ❷), run by a friendly family, offering good home cooking and nice rooms. The German package-oriented *Hotel Peyda* (☎0324/523 2607, ✉HotelPeyda@hotmail.com; ❸) has clean, spacious air-conditioned rooms, while further west the cheerful *Motel Gold* (☎0324/523 2322; ❷) is good value. Carrying on west the *Hantur* (☎0324/523 2322; ❸) has well-appointed rooms with balconies, some with superb views out to sea. Northwest of the *Hantur*, set back from the beach, is the swanky *Club Barbarosssa* (☎0324/523 2364, ✉chbarbarbarossa@ttnet.tr; ❺) – the air-conditioned rooms here have satellite TV, and the price is for half-board accommodation. The *Hotel Eylul* (☎0324/523 2416; ❹), on the main road, has top-notch facilities but is noisy and lacks sea views.

There are plenty of places to **eat and drink** and, generally speaking, the further away from the beach they are the better the value. The grills, *mezes* and fast-food places offer better value than those serving seafood. There are also a few beachfront bars and a couple of discos.

Around Kızkalesi

Really only practicable with your transport, or by taxi, are three nearby sites: the **Adam Kaylar rock reliefs**, and the ancient cities of **Elaioussa Sebastae** and **Kanytelis**. You could see them all in a day away from the beach.

Adam Kaylar rock reliefs

Most intriguing side-trip from the town is to the series of **rock reliefs** in a valley about 6km to the north (the turning is near the PTT), marked by a sign bearing the legend "Adam Kayalar" (Man's Rocks). Follow the path indicated from here for about a kilometre until it starts to dip down into a valley, where steps cut into the rock lead down to a platform from which you can view a series of Roman men, women and children carved into niches in the wall. There are seventeen human figures and a mountain goat. Unfortunately, extensive damage has been caused to one of the figures by treasure hunters who used dynamite in the hope of finding booty supposedly secreted inside the statue. It's not clear who the figures are, or why they might have been constructed, and the fragmentary inscriptions below most of them offer few clues.

Elaioussa Sebastae

East of Kızkalesi, on both sides of the road, various ancient ruins stretch as far as the village of **Ayaş**, 3km away. This was the site of the settlement of **Elaioussa Sebaste** (currently under excavation), which in the time of Augustus was important enough to coin its own money. Below the village is a theatre, and below that baths, a city gate and possibly a nymphaeum. An aqueduct leads to an underground cistern near the baths, although villagers are still ploughing on top of this area. Above the site is a prominent house-tomb in remarkably good condition, dedicated by a mother to her husband and two sons. On the south side of the road is a Byzantine church, almost on the beach, while scattered around the area are numerous tombs, many of them richly decorated with reliefs.

Kanytelis

About 7km east of Kızkalesi, a signposted turnoff leads 3km north to the village of **Kanlidıvane**, literally "place of blood". This, the site of the ancient city of **Kanytelis**, is where locals used to believe condemned criminals were executed by being thrown into a huge chasm and devoured by wild animals. A car park and ticket seller's hut mark the entrance to the **chasm** (daily 8am–7pm; $0.70), which is certainly large and frightening enough to have given rise to the legends – at 90m long by 70m wide and 60m deep, it forms the core of the ancient city. Visitors descend into it by way of a partly eroded staircase. On the southern and western sides of the chasm there are a number of carvings in niches, one a portrait of a family of six and one of a Roman soldier. On its southwestern edge near the car park, a seventeen-metre-high tower, dating from Hellenistic times, bears an inscription on the southwestern corner next to a three-pronged triskele, a symbol that links the region to the nearby state of Olba. Near the tower are a number of large Byzantine basilicas in various states of collapse, of which the best preserved is the Papylas church. There's another big cluster of tombs northeast of the chasm, with numerous ancient sarcophagi and a few modern graves.

Mersin

The largest Mediterranean port in Turkey, with a population of 1.5 million, **MERSİN** is the first of the three large cities that gird the Ceyhan delta. It's a modern harbour city that – aside from its regular ferry connections to Cyprus – is almost entirely without interest, despite being inhabited since Hittite times. Until the beginning of the twentieth century the settlement was little more than a squalid fishing hamlet. However, over the last century rapid growth and industrialization, coupled with Mersin's role as an international free-trade zone, have turned it into a model, if soulless, example of contemporary Turkish urban planning.

If you do find yourself with time on your hands, the only real diversion is the local **museum** on Atatürk Caddesi (Tues–Sun 9am–5pm; $1.25), which offers a small but well-presented collection of local archeological finds and ethnographical knick-knacks, though you may find the confusion of stone-carvings strewn about the garden more inspiring.

Practicalities

The city's **otogar** is some way out of town and you'll need to take a service bus or a dolmuş into the centre. Unfortunately, the dolmuşes don't pass directly in front of the *otogar*, and it's a five-minute walk to the dolmuş stop on Gazi Mustafa Paşa Bulvarı, the major road one block northwest of the *otogar*. The **train station** (services to and from Adana) is very central and convenient for the listed hotels. The **tourist office** is by the harbour just off İsmet İnönü Bulvarı (Mon–Fri 9am–5pm; ☎0324/238 3271). There's also a **UK Honorary Consulate** in town, c/o Catoni Maritime Agencies, Mersin Orta Okulu Sok 3/B, Çakmak Caddesi (☎0324/232 1248).

On Ismet İnönü Bulvarı, opposite the tourist office, *Olcartur,* sells **THY** plane tickets. **Car rental** companies include Avis, at Ismet İnönü Bulvarı, Uysal Apt 100 (☎0324/232 3450); Esin, at Uray Caddesi, Güvenç İş Merkezi; and Europcar, at Uray Caddesi, Güvenç İş Merkezi, B Block (☎0324/232 0017).

Accommodation

As an important port, Mersin supports plenty of hotels, but the **budget** choices are limited. Best is the *Hotel Melida* (☎0324/231 4084; ❶), just off İstiklal Caddesi, with basic but clean rooms. On Soğuksu Caddesi, the *Hotel Hitit* (☎0324/231 6431; ❷) is another option, with air-conditioning and TV in the rooms. **Mid-range** possibilities include: the *Aktaş Hotel,* İstiklâl Cad 152 (☎0324/233 7007, ⓕ232 3168; ❸) – rather noisy but with an English-speaking manager; the air-conditioned *Hotel Gökhan,* Soğuksu Cad 20 (☎0324/231 6256, ⓕ237 4462; ❸); and the *Hotel Derman,* İstiklâl Cad, İleri İlkökülü Yanı 15/37 (☎0324/237 5028, ⓕ233 3824; ❹), with a swimming pool. **Top-of-the-range** business hotels include the *Mersin Hotel,* in the centre of town on Gümrük Meydanı (☎0324/238 1040, ⓕ231 2625; ❻), and the towering *Mersin Merit* at Hastane Cad 165 (☎0324/336 1010, ⓕ336 0722; ❼), easily visible to the north.

Eating and drinking

The **Balık Pazarı** (fish market) off Uray Caddesi is the best option in town for cheap fish, and opposite, off Silifke Caddesi, the *Mavi Köşe Ocak Başı* is a tiny outlet serving up filling *durum* (meat-filled pastry) and *güveç* (casserole). The *Ali Baba*, off Atatürk Cad at Çankaya Mah 93, Sok 7, is well known locally for its fish dishes and *mezes*, and has a reasonably pleasant interior. The *Kervan* restaurant is central and serves beer. The young crowd meets out at the fast-food joints in the western suburbs, including *McDonalds* and *Tatlises Lahmacun,* or at the *Burger King*, near the museum.

Ferries to Cyprus

Ferries depart from Mersin to Mağosa (Famagusta) in Northern Cyprus on Mondays, Wednesdays and Fridays at 8pm. Buy tickets from the TML office at the harbour. At the moment, EU, US, Canadian and Australasian citizens require only a valid passport on which their Turkish entry visa has not expired to enter the TRNC; bear in mind that it's not possible to enter southern (ie Greek-speaking) Cyprus from the TRNC.

In Mersin, the **TRNC consulate** is at Hamidiye Mahalle Karadeniz (☎0324/237 2482). You can also buy tickets in Mersin for the **Taşucuu–Girne ferry and hydrofoil** (see p.599) – a much faster crossing – from Fergün Denizcilik Şirketi, on Ismet İnön Bulvarı (☎0324/238 2881).

Tarsus

About 30km east of Mersin, across the factory-dotted cotton fields of the Çukurova, lies **TARSUS**, birthplace of St Paul and the city where Cleopatra met Mark Antony and turned him into a "strumpet's fool". St Paul was born as Saul in Tarsus about 46 years after the meeting between Cleopatra and Antony. He returned after his conversion on the road to Damascus, fleeing persecution in Palestine. He seems to have been proud of his roots and is described as having told the Roman commandant of Jerusalem: "I am a Jew, a Tarsian from Cilicia, a citizen of no mean city." Nowadays, however, few reminders of the town's illustrious past remain. Indeed, Tarsus is spectacularly ugly, with pot-holed streets, crumbling buildings and a skyline festooned with electricity pylons and telephone cables. Only the very centre, around the Kancık Kapısı, has any charm or order.

Near the main bus drop-off point, the **Kancık Kapısı** ("the gate of the bitch") is a Roman construction, also known as Cleopatra's Gate. Although it doesn't actually have any known connection with the Egyptian queen, she is thought to have come ashore for her first meeting with Mark Antony somewhere in the vicinity (at that time Tarsus was linked to the sea by a lagoon which has since silted up).

From Cleopatra's Gate, go south to a roundabout flowing with fountains and turn right; a hundred metres west, the Cultural Centre (Kültür Merkezi) houses a fairly mundane **museum** (Tues–Sat 9am–5pm; $0.30), with an unexplained mummified lower arm of a woman and the odd case of jewellery. Immediately opposite the museum and down a sidestreet is Cumhuriyet Alanı, where the **Antik Şehir** or "old city" has been exposed by excavations. A good section of black basalt main street and associated stoas and temples lie well beneath present-day ground level.

Make your way through the backstreets to **St Paul's well**; you'll have to ask for "Sen Pol Kuyusu". It may be something of a disappointment, since it's just a borehole in the ground covered by a removable lid. However, as it's said to be on the site of St Paul's house, the steady stream of visitors gladly pay $0.20 for a sip of water from a bucket hauled up from the depths. North of the well, past the Hükümet Konağı (law courts), is a large mosque and local landmark known as **Makam Cami**. Opposite is the **Eski Cami**, a mosque that started life as a church, and, next door, the Roman baths.

From the Eski Cami it's a few minutes by dolmuş to **Şelale**, a waterfall in a park on the banks of the Tarsus Çayı, just within the town limits, with tea gardens and restaurants. On the hill above is a cave, **Eshabi Kehf** (unrestricted access), reputed to be home to seven sleepers, whose hands clutch Byzantine coins to enable them to buy bread when they awake. This legend is associated with St Paul and Mary Magdalene and repeated in Ephesus, her reputed final home. It's a hot trek up the sign-posted path that leads to the cave and, once there, there's not much to see save the view over town.

Practicalities

Tarsus' **otogar** is near Cleopatra's Gate, right in the town centre. **Accomodation** possibilities are limited, with only two central hotels: the *Hotel Zorbaz* (☎0342/622 1623; ❶) is large and drab, although clean, while the *Cihan Palas Oteli* (☎0324/624 1623; ❷), 400m to the south, almost opposite the *otogar*, has been decorated and modernized, and the air-conditioned rooms have fridges. Out of town, the monstrous *Tarsus Mersin Oteli* (☎0324/614 0600; ❻) overlooks the Şelale waterfall. It has its own pool and large air-conditioned rooms, while the astronomical prices listed at reception can be ignored and a double room negotiated for around $35.

Adana

Forty kilometres east of Tarsus sprawls **ADANA**, Turkey's fourth largest city with 1.5 million inhabitants, a modern place, which has grown rapidly since the 1918–1920 French occupation. Today, as in the past, Adana owes much of its wealth to the surrounding fertile countryside of the Çukurova, with a textiles industry that has grown up on the back of the local cotton fields. It is also an important centre for the trade in gold.

Despite its contemporary, metropolitan feel, Adana has historical roots going back to 1000 BC. The arrival of the Greeks precipitated an on–off power struggle between them and the powerful Persian Empire to the east that was to last for a thousand years, ending only with the arrival of the Romans during the first century BC. Under the Romans the city became an important trading centre, afterwards passing through various hands before falling to the Ottomans during the sixteenth century. Despite all this, Adana has few sites of real interest, but if you are here between buses (it is an important communication hub) there is sufficient to keep you occupied for a few hours.

Arrival and information

Adana's **otogar** is located about 5km west of town on the E5. Frequent dolmuşes run from here to the town centre, and your bus company will probably lay on a *servis* minibus to their office in the centre (see "Listings" on p.586). The city's **train station** is at the northern end Atatürk Caddesi, about twenty minutes' walk north of the town centre, though there are dolmuşes from town.

To get into town from the **airport**, 4km from the centre, don't take a cab from outside the door unless you want to pay double; instead, walk another 50m to the street and either catch a dolmuş into the centre or a normal cab. A THY shuttle bus leaves the city centre THY office an hour and a half before departure, and there is (theoretically) a THY bus awaiting arrivals.

The local **tourist office** is at Atatürk Cad 13, near the roundabout junction with the E5 highway (Mon–Fri 8am–5pm; ☎0322/359 1994).

Accommodation

Adana's accommodation is uninspiring and tourists are a rare sight in the city's hotels. On and around Saydam Caddesi and Özler Caddesi, you'll find some cheap hotels, with mid-range places on İnönü Caddesi. The best options are listed below. Adana's single **campsite**, on the eastern edge of town just off the main eastbound road, is *Green Club Camping*, Girne Bulvarı, İskenderun Yolu – take the İnciler dolmuş from the roundabout next to Çetinkaya shopping arcade, at the junction of Kurtuluş and İnönü *caddesi*. The site is on the small side and noisy, but the facilities, including a restaurant and pool, are reasonably priced.

Ak Özler Cad 19 ☏ 0322/351 2603. Very basic rooms, some waterless, and carpets and curtains of dubious cleanliness, but undeniably cheap. ❶

Duygu İnönü Cad 14/1 ☏ 0322/363 1510. Unfashionable decor, though the small rooms have TV and air-conditioning. ❸

İpek Palas İnönü Cad 103 ☏ 0322/363 3512. Dull rooms with ceiling fans and TV. ❸

Mercan Melek Girmez Çarşısı ☏ 0322/351 2603. Traditional businessman's hotel with clean en-suite rooms with fans and a friendly atmosphere. Recommended. ❶

Selibra İnönü Cad 50 ☏ 0322/363 4283 ☏ 363 4283. Good value with neat, clean and tastefully decorated rooms with air-conditioning, minibar and TV. ❹

Sürmeli Çukurova Özler Cad ☏ 0322/352 3600. Comfortable rooms with air-conditioning, TV and nice bathrooms in a modern building. Luxuries include a decent sauna and well-stocked bar. ❽

Turistik Hotel Koza Özler Cad 103 ☏ 0322/3525857 ☏ 359/8571. Large hotel with clean but basic rooms with air-conditioning and TV. Front rooms are noisy. ❸

Zaimoğlu Özler Cad 22 ☏ 0322/3635353 ☏ 363 5363. Large, elegant rooms with air-conditioning, TV and minibar. Friendly staff help make it a recommended option. ❻

The City

The city is divided, by the E5 Highway, into the swanky north, with its cinemas and designer malls, and the more traditional bustling south, with the markets, mosques and hotels of the old town. Traffic is uniformly helter-skelter and, as there are no pedestrian bridges or underpasses, you have to jaywalk to reach many of Adana's sights.

Start off with the **Archeological Museum** (Arkeolji Müzesi; Tues–Sun 8.30am–noon & 1–4.30pm; $0.70) on the north side of the E5 Highway, containing predominantly Hellenistic and Roman statuary, plus some fine sarcophagi and Hittite statues. The **Sabancı Merkez Camii** next door – with a 28,500 capacity and the highest dome in Turkey – is the third largest mosque in the world and a testament to the continued strength of Islam in the southeast. It was built mainly by subscription, but finished with the aid of the Sabancı family, local boys made good and now the second richest family in Turkey.

One hundred metres southeast, the city's most substantial ancient monument is the **Taş Köprü**, an impressive sixteen-arched Roman bridge built by Hadrian to span the Seyhan River and still carrying heavy traffic. Not far from the bridge in the centre, the **Ulu Cami**, on Abidin Paşa Caddesi, was built in the Syrian style out of white and black marble in 1507, the sole legacy of Halil Bey, Emir of the Ramazanoğlu Turks, who ruled Adana before the Ottoman conquest. Inside the mosque, Halil Bey's tomb has some fine tilework and beautiful mosaics.

South of Ulu Cami, the large clocktower, **Büyük Saat Kulesi**, is at the edge of a bazaar area, where the sound of metalworking echoes through the air. Nearby, **Çarşı Hamam** (see "Listings" on p.586), with a beautiful doorway, is reputed to date back to the time of Piri, son of Emir Halil Bey. Walking west towards the Atatürk statue, you'll see the **Yağ Cami**, accessed across a courtyard; unusually, one bay of the mosque was a church until it was incorporated into the main structure in 1502. A peculiar square building in the courtyard has

6

an interesting domed roof supported by a line of slabs with Selçuk decoration; its original purpose is unknown. Another old building just off İnönü Caddesi, first a church, then a mosque, now houses the **Ethnography Museum** (Etnografya Müzesi; Tues–Sun 8.30am–noon, 1–4.30pm; $0.70), full of carpets and weaponry, with a nomad tent and its contents as an added attraction.

If you are weary of the heat of the city, about 5km north of Adana, is the **Seyhan Barajı**, a huge artificial lake along whose shores bathing (though not at the southern end due to strong currents) and sailing are permitted. It's a popular weekend retreat for overheated city dwellers, who come here to picnic or enjoy the many fine lakeshore restaurants and bars. The reservoir supplies the area with fresh water, and there's a bird sanctuary immediately to the west. Dolmuşes marked "Baraj" or "Universite" go there from Füzuli Caddesi near the museum.

Eating and drinking

Adana has plenty of cheap places to eat, but the food is not wonderful and outside the smarter hotels, women travelling alone may well feel less than comfortable. The local speciality is the spicy *Adana kebap* – minced lamb and pepper wrapped around a skewer and grilled – but frankly, you can eat better ones outside Adana. Pavement **food stalls** selling sandwiches and pastries abound, as do hole-in-the-wall *börek* and kebab places near the central PTT. Of various cheap and cheerful **restaurants**, the *Onbaşılar* on Atatürk Caddesi, opposite the tourist office, is fine for a kebab and a beer. The *Rose* **café** next to the Ethnographic Museum is also recommended, with beer and light food served in a friendly, homely atmosphere at reasonable prices.

Listings

Airlines THY, Prof Dr Nuşret Fişik Cad 22 ☏0322/457 0222, for flights to Ankara, İstanbul and İzmir; KTHY, Atatürk Cad, near the tourist office, has five direct flights to Cyprus per week.
Banks and exchange Most banks are located near the tourist office, and almost all will cash travellers' cheques; Vakıf and Garanti Banks have ATM machines. There are also several *döviz* offices around Saydam Cad and Özler Cad.
Buses Most of the major bus company offices are concentrated on Ziya Paşa Cad, just north of the E-5. When you want to leave town, buy a ticket from one of these and a *servis* bus will take you to the *otogar*, from where you can reach virtually every city in the country.
Car rental Avis, Ziyapaşa Bul, Nakipoglu Apt 9/A ☏0322/453 3045; Budget, Gazipaşa Bul 274, Sok 3/19 ☏0322/457 0754; Europcar, at the airport ☏0322/433 2957; and Talay Turizm, Gazipaşa Bul

46/B ☏0322/457 1712.
Cinemas Try the Metro, a couple of blocks south of the *otogar*, or the Galleria Cinema in the shopping complex of the same name on Fuzulı Cad.
Hamams Çarşı Hamam, Büyük Saat Civari (daily: women 9.30am–3pm, men 5–11pm; $4–8 depending on level of service).
Hospital State Hospital (Adana Devlet Hastane) is on Riza Cad ☏0322/321 5752.
Newspapers and magazines Yolgeçen Kitabevi, 64 Atatürk Cad.
Post office The main PTT office (8.30am–9pm) is on Ulu Cami, the street running parallel to Abdin Paşa Caddesi, sells phone cards and *jetons*.
Shopping For foodstuffs, clothing and toiletries etc, head for Çetinkaya shopping arcade at the roundabout at the western end of İnönü Cad. Also try the huge Galeria Shopping Mall, nearby on Fuzulı Cad.

East of Adana

Heading east from Adana, towards İskenderun and Antakya (referred to as "Hatay" at the *otogar*), the first town you reach, after 20km, is **YAKAPİNAR** (also known as Misis), just south of the main road. This has a small **mosaic**

museum (Tues–Sun 9am–5pm; $0.70), worth a quick look for its examples of locally unearthed Roman mosaics. Beyond here you'll see an Armenian castle on top of a mountain, 3km to the south of the main road – the **Yılan Kalesi**, or "Snake Castle" (always open; $0.50). If you're travelling with your own car, you can drive up to the top to admire the view of the meandering Ceyhan River.

About 12km further on is **CEYHAN**, which, despite the colourful-looking old houses in the town centre, doesn't rate more than a cursory look. Thirty-five kilometres south of here, at the end of a winding and at times hilly road, is the resort of **YUMURTALIK**, reachable from Adana by taking a bus to Ceyhan (1hr) where you'll have to catch a dolmuş (irregular out of the summer-holiday season). There's a small ruined castle here, built by the Knights of St John, and the place is something of a weekend destination for the people of Adana. The best hotel in town is the *Hotel Öztur*, on the beachfront (☎0322/671 2167; ❸), some of whose rooms have rudimentary cooking facilities. During the late summer, en route to Yumurtalık, you'll see how the other half of the Adana population lives – the roadside embankments are lined with tents used by nomads employed to pick cotton.

About 40km east of Ceyhan the main road forks. Due east leads to Gaziantep and beyond, while the southern fork heads towards Antakya. The black basalt castle you can see towering above the road junction is **Toprakkale**, much fought over by the Armenians and Crusaders during medieval times, but abandoned since about 1337. You can visit Toprakkale, but be careful – much of it is very unstable and there are numerous concealed rooms and cisterns waiting for unwary people to fall into them.

Karatepe Arslantaş National Park

If you have your own transport you might want to consider a seventy-kilometre detour to the **Karatepe Arslantaş National Park** (Karatepe Arslantaş Milli Parkı), with its fine neo-Hittite stone-carvings. The route is via Osmaniye on the main highway, where you turn north, crossing the Ceyhan River and passing the columned Hellenistic ruins of Hierapolis Castabala, before following signs up to the green pines and turquoise waters of the park – the **Arslantaş dam** that surrounds Karatepe's stranded site provides the perfect venue for a picnic or a barbecue. Park your car at the entrance ($1) and walk up to the gatehouse where you will be sold a ticket (Tues–Sun 8.30am–noon & 2–5.30pm; $0.70) and escorted on a tour of the site.

Karatepe is thought to have been a frontier castle or summer palace of the neo-Hittite King Asitawanda, whose capital at Pahri near modern Yakapınar reached its peak around the ninth century BC before finally being sacked by the Assyrians. Little of the building complex remains, but the real reason to come is to see the eloquent stone-carvings arranged around the two entrance gates of the former palace. The designs at the first gate depict sacrificial, hunting and feasting scenes, all guarded by sphinxes, horses and lions tattooed in hieroglyphics. The second gate has similar statues of winged sphinxes, one with eyes of ivory, and other fine carvings. Look out for a mini-pantheon of Hittite gods, including Bez the monkey god and a Hittite sun god. There is also a spread of more personal carvings in an almost cartoon style, including one of a woman suckling her child under a date tree.

Dörtyol and Yakacık

South of Toprakkale, the Antakya road is rather nondescript, and the first major town, **DÖRTYOL** ("crossroads"), does little to break the monotony. It was about 10km north of Dörtyol that Alexander the Great defeated the Persian king Darius at the **battle of Issus** in 333 BC. After being outmanoeuvred on the enclosed coastal plain, Alexander's army of about 35,000 took on a Persian force of over 100,000, but despite these unfavourable odds Alexander carried the day by personally leading an attack against Darius and his entourage. Darius panicked and fled, only narrowly avoiding capture (though he was forced to leave his wife and three children behind); Alexander's supply route was saved and the route south was opened up for him and his army. Today, the exact site of the engagement is uncertain, and the task of identifying it from contemporary accounts has been made harder by the fact that, due to earthquakes, the physical appearance of the landscape has changed over the intervening two thousand years.

At **YAKACİK** (Payas) about 10km south of Dörtyol, the little-visited **Sokullu Mehmet Paşa** complex, dating from the early sixteenth century, incorporates a *kervansaray* with kitchens and dining hall, a hamam half-walled in marble, a *medrese* and a mosque surrounding a courtyard where there's a huge gnarled olive tree rumoured to be as old as the mosque. There are plans to reopen the huge bazaar here, as a series of shops. A well-preserved former Genoese **fortress**, with views of the mountains from its battlemented walls, completes the complex. It's well worth making a detour to come here; once you arrive, you'll usually find the site guardian in the bazaar arcade opposite the hamam.

The Hatay

The **Hatay**, which extends like a stumpy finger into Syria, is an Arab enclave and has closer cultural links with the Arab world than with the Turkish hinterland. There has been some separatist tension in the area, but these problems are unlikely to affect visitors and indeed the Hatay's multi-ethnic, multi-faith identity gives it an extra edge of interest. **Antakya**, the largest town, is set in the valley of the Asi River separating the Nur and Ziyaret mountain ranges. The city, which dates back to Seleucid times, was an important centre under the Romans, and although little has survived from its ancient past, Antakya's cosmopolitan atmosphere, its excellent museum and great food make it worth a day or two on anyone's itinerary. The Hatay's other main centre is **İskenderun**, a heavily industrialized port that has more to offer than might appear at first sight.

The Hatay only became part of modern Turkey in 1939, having been apportioned to the French Protectorate of Syria following the dismemberment of the Ottoman Empire in the aftermath of World War 1. Following the brief-lived independent **Hatay Republic** of 1938 it was handed over to Turkey after a plebiscite. This move, calculated to buy Turkish support, or at least neutrality, in the imminent world war, was successful. It was Atatürk, in a move to "Turkify" the region, who dreamt up the name "Hatay", supposedly based on that of a medieval Turkic tribe. The majority of people here speak Arabic as their first language and there's some backing for union with Syria, which in 1983 led to serious unrest in Antakya. For its part, Syria is keen to see the

Hatay returned, or at least to use its avowed irredentist policy as a bargaining chip with Turkey. Tensions between the two countries eased considerably in 1998, when the Syrians expelled the PKK leader Abdullah Öcalan from Damascus and ended their covert support for the Kurdish rebels. Cross-border trade is steadily increasing following normalization of relations between the two countries.

In fact, Arab influence in the Hatay goes back to the seventh century AD, when Arab raiders began hacking at the edges of the collapsing Byzantine Empire. Although they were never able to secure long-lasting political control over the region, the Arabs were able to establish themselves as permanent settlers, remaining even when the Hatay passed into Ottoman hands. Prior to the arrival of the Arabs, the area had been held by the Romans and before that the Seleucids, who prized its position straddling trading routes into Syria.

İskenderun and around

İSKENDERUN was founded by Alexander the Great to commemorate his victory over the Persians at the nearby battle of Issus (see opposite) and, as Alexandria ad Issum, it became a major trade nexus during Roman times. Under the Ottomans, İskenderun became the main port for Halab (Aleppo), now in Syria, from where trade routes fanned out to Persia and the Arabian peninsula. The town was known as Alexandretta during the French mandate era and is now essentially an industrial, military and commercial centre. Although there is little of historical interest left to see in İskenderun, the town centre is visually appealing, with its broad promenade and the magnificent backdrop of the Amanus mountains. A group of churches provides the main focus of a visit, while trips into the surroundings – to the hill town of Belen or the beach at Uluçinar – can be made by anyone with their own vehicle and a bit more time on their hands.

The Town

Traces of the town's cosmopolitan Levantine trading past survive amongst the new apartment buildings. The offices of the Catoni shipping line are housed in a crumbling nineteenth-century building just behind the seafront – the upstairs suite once housed the British vice-consulate and, though now abandoned, is still filled with 1930s furniture and a forlorn framed print of a young Queen Elizabeth II. The **Adliye Sarayı** (courtroom) at the junction of Şehit Pamir Caddesi amd Atatürk Bulvarı is an imposing French mandate-era building, neo-Oriental in style but sporting Lyon-made clocks in its twin towers.

İskenderun, like the rest of the Hatay, prides itself on its tolerance, a virtue that can be seen most clearly by visiting the town's churches. Smallest of these is the **Surp Karasun Manuk Ermeni Kilisesi**, situated on a sidestreet off Şehit Pamir Caddesi, more or less opposite the *Açikalın Hotel*. Built in 1872, but very recently restored, this small, plainly decorated church serves an Armenian community of around eighty families. It's usually locked, though the key is held at an Armenian accounting business whose office is reached via a flight of steps to the right of the church – look for the sign *Serbest Musabeci*. A member of the family will be only too pleased to show you around.

Further away from the seafront, on the opposite side of Şehit Pamir Caddesi, is the pastel-coloured Greek Orthodox Church of **St Nicholas**, built in 1876, while a little more difficult to find is the older, but smaller, whitewashed

St George's, opposite the *jandarma* post on Denizciler Caddesi. This is the most atmospheric of the town's churches, with a walled garden of palm and cypress trees, in which gravestones bear inscriptions in Greek, Arabic and even French. Families live in houses adjoining both the Orthodox churches and they are usually willing to let you look around. The largest of Iskenderun's churches is Catholic **St Mary's,** a substantial nineteenth-century building behind the tourist office.

Practicalities

Buses to all major towns, including Adana and Mersin, drop you at Pac Meydanı on Muammer Aksoy Caddesi, near the *Ontur Hotel.* **Trains** also run daily to Adana and Mersin and are much safer but slower than the road. The station is 1km east of the town centre, reached by following 5 Temmuz Caddesi and then Bahçeli Sahil Evler Caddesi. Buses to Antakya leave hourly from Karaoğlanoğlu Caddesi, a twenty-minute walk back from the waterfront, following Şehit Pamir Caddesi, and take an hour.

The helpful local **tourist office**, at Atatürk Bul 49/B (Mon–Sat 8am–noon & 1–5pm, ☎0326/614 1620), is on the waterfront, a couple of hundred metres west of the junction of Şehit Pamir Caddesi and Atatürk Bulvarı. The manager speaks good English and will furnish you with a reasonable city guide, including a street plan locating the churches and train station.

Accommodation

Most of the town's cheaper **pansiyons and hotels** are centrally located. The best of the inexpensive places is the *Hotel Açıkalan*, Şehit Pamir Cad 13 (☎0326/617 3732; ❷), with clean and airy rooms including some good-value singles. Practically next door is the *Altındişler Oteli* (☎0326/617 1011; ❸) – slightly more upmarket, with primitive but still-functioning air-conditioning in its plain but spacious rooms. The traditional rooms of the *Hotel Cabir* at Ulucami Cad 16 (☎0326/612 3391, ℗ 612 3393; ❸) are rather worn, but the service is good, the atmosphere friendly and there's an American-style bar and a disco. The *Belediye* **campsite** is southwest of town, reached by dolmuş (marked "49 Evler/Sahil Evler") from Şehit Pamir Caddesi.

Eating and drinking

The best **restaurant** is the *Saray*, near the tourist office, with tables set out on the broad pavement. The *mezes* include *cevizli biber* (or *muhammara* in Arabic, a paste of walnuts, chilli peppers and wheat), tender grills for the main course and, of course, cold beer. The *Hasan Baba* at Ulucami Cad 43/E has excellent İskender *kebap* (which originates in Bursa, not here), while round the corner towards the *Hotel Açıkalan*, more *lokantas* – such as the *Şehir* – serve cheap but tasty meals.

Café Körfez on Şehit Pamir Caddesi is good for **breakfasts**, including *menemen* (scrambled omlette with tomatoes). A hole-in-the-wall juice stand just up from the church of St Nicholas whips up delicious fresh juices; try the *Atom*, a local speciality mix of banana, milk, peach, cherry, apricot and pistachio. Several **patisseries** serve excellent *karışık dondurma* (mixed ice cream decorated with loads of fruit) at ridiculously low prices. The promenade area is home to several *gazinos* where you can enjoy a beer overlooking the sea.

Uluçınar

Dolmuşes run regularly from Atatürk Bulvarı in İskenderun to the small resort and fishing town of **ULUÇINAR** about 40km to the southwest, where there are some decent stretches of beach (often charging for entry), very popular with both Syrian tourists and people from İskenderun. Of a number of hotels in town, best is the *Motel Yunus* on Akdeniz Caddesi (☎0326/643 2088; ❷), opposite the post office. Just up the road, another recommended place is the three-star *Arsuz Turistik Hotel* (☎0326/643 2444; ❷). The best place to eat, meanwhile, is the waterfront *Plaj* restaurant, which does good seafood dishes.

Belen

The road southeast from İskenderun rises up into the mountains, passing through the small hill town of **BELEN**, 13km away, where a pair of cafés and some fruit stalls make it a good place to break the journey. It's a quiet, unspoilt place, with a few springs gushing curative water. From here, the road strains and curves through the **Belen Pass** (Belen Geçidi) – of great strategic importance during Roman times, when it was known as the *Pylae Syriae* or "Gates of Syria". For a week or two in early October (if the winds are right), Belen becomes the most important **migration route** on the western Palearctic corridor for birds of prey; an observation post has been recording sightings for the last few years and a photo safari is organized each year. If you want to witness the spectacle, get here early; after midday, all the birds have flown through.

About 5km beyond the Belen Pass you'll come to a major road junction, from where a right turn leads towards Antakya. After a few kilometres a sign marks the road to **Bakras Kalesi**, an imposing medieval castle about 4km off the main road and a fifteen-minute climb from the village below. The first castle to be built on this site was erected by the Arabs during the seventh century and destroyed during the First Crusade. Later the Knights Templar built a new fortress, which became an important link in their defensive system, and which forms the basis of the impressive remains you see today. It was much fought over, and in 1156 a bloody battle took place here between the Templars and the soldiers of Thoros, ruler of Cilician Armenia. In 1188 the castle fell to Arabs but possession was fiercely contested until the Ottomans took over during the sixteenth century.

Antakya

ANTAKYA, 45km south of İskenerun, stands on the site of ancient Antioch and, although there's little sense of historical continuity, the city's laidback pace, cosmopolitan outlook and subtly Arab atmosphere make it unique in Turkey. Flanked by mountains to the north and south, it sits in the bed of a broad river valley planted with olive trees, providing a welcome visual relief after travelling from the drab flatlands surrounding Adana. Although little survives from the city's Seleucid and Roman past, it has enough attractions to merit at least an overnight stop, including an excellent archeological museum and an unusual cave church from which St Peter is said to have preached. The food in Antakya is some of the most varied and best in Turkey, thanks to the city's Arab heritage.

Some history

The city was founded as Antioch in the fourth century BC by Seleucus Nicator, one of the four generals among whom the empire of Alexander the Great was divided. It soon grew into an important commercial centre and by the second century BC had developed into a multi-ethnic metropolis of half a million – one of the largest cities in the ancient world, a major staging post on the newly opened Silk Road trade routes from the Mediterranean to Asia, and a centre of scholarship and learning. It also acquired a reputation as a centre for all kinds of moral excess, causing **St Peter** to choose it as the location of one of the world's first Christian communities in the hope that the new religion would exercise a restraining influence. Indeed, the patriarchy of Antioch became one of the five senior official positions in the early Christian Church organization.

Despite being razed by a series of earthquakes during the sixth century AD, Antioch was able to maintain its prosperity after the Roman era, and only with the rise of Constantinople did the city begin to decline. In 1098 the Crusader kings Bohemond and Raymond took the city in the name of Christianity after a vicious eight-month siege and a savage massacre of Turks, imposing a Christian rule in Antioch that lasted until the city fell to the Mamluks of Egypt, who sacked it in 1268. By the time the Ottomans, under Selim the Grim, took over in 1516, Antioch had long since vanished from the main stage of world history, and by the turn of the last century the city was little more than a village, squatting amid the ruins of the ancient metropolis. After World War I, Antakya, along with most of the rest of the Hatay, passed into the hands of the French, who laid the foundations of the modern city.

Arrival and information

From the **otogar**, it's a ten- to fifteen-minute walk south to the town centre. As well as domestic services, there are regular daily departures to towns in Syria (see box on p.596), while buses also travel several times a week direct to Amman in Jordan, from where you can get to Israel and Saudi Arabia (though you need a transit visa to pass through Syria). Antakya's **tourist office** (Mon–Fri 8am–noon & 1–5pm; no phone) is rather inconveniently sited on a roundabout fifteen minutes' walk northwest of the bridge. Yılmaz, who works at the office, speaks good English and may be able to help you locate some of the area's more obscure sights.

Accommodation

Antakya has a good range of hotels across every price range, including some uninspiring cheapies on and around İstiklâl Caddesi.

Antik Beyazit Hotel Hükümet Cad 4 ☎0326/216 2900. The town's most appealing hotel is this French colonial-style building, a restored former government building with well-furnished rooms. ❺

Büyük Antakya Oteli Atatürk Cad 8 ☎0326/213 5860, ℗213 5869. Flashy four-star, worth the splurge if you're looking for comfort and a range of amenities. ❼

Jasmin Hotel İstiklâl Sok 14 ☎0326/212 7171. A good budget choice, where rooms and shared showers are clean, and you get access to the communal kitchen and all the hot water or tea you can drink. The only drawback is that some of rooms are windowless while others, on the front, are affected by street noise. ❶

Onur Hotel İstiklâl Sok ☎0326/216 2210. Pleasantly furnished, air-conditioned rooms, good service and a bar. ❺

Hotel Saray Hurriyet Cad 3 ☎0326/214 9001, ℗214 9002. The best-value deal in Antakya with spotlessly clean rooms with TV and fans. Good views from the rear rooms over the old quarter and the hillside beyond. ❷

The City

Antakya is cut in two by the **Asi River**, known in ancient times as the Orontes. Once a sizeable river, it's now a brown and sluggish shadow of its former self, its flow depleted by water backed up in dams and drawn off for irrigation. The eastern bank is home to **old Antakya** – a maze of narrow streets,

Map labels:

Adana

Reyhanlı & Kale

Dolmuşes to Samandağ, Reyhanlı, Harbiye

Sen Piyer Kilisesi

Asi River

İSTİKLAL CAD

ATATÜRK CAD

Otogar

KURTULUŞ CAD

Konak Sineması

Bizim

ATA KÖPRÜSÜ

CUMHURİYET CAD

Archeological Museum

GUNDUZ CAD

Asi River

İSTİKLAL CAD

İSTİKLAL SOK

BAZAAR SELÇUK CAD

Ulu Cami

KEMAL PAŞA CAD

Moda

RIHTIM CAD

HÜRRİYET CADDESİ

Greek Orthodox Church

YALI GEN BUL

Habibi Neccar Camii

Turkish Catholic Church

Sermaye Camii

Habibi Neccar Cave

ACCOMMODATION

Antik Beyazit	5
Büyük Antakya	2
Jasmin	3
Onur	1
Saray	4

RESTAURANTS

Antakya Evi	E
Antik Han	D
Şamlıoğlu Künefe	B
Saray	C
Sultan Sofrası	A

6

Dolmuşes to Harbiye

Aqueduct of Trajan

0   500 m

N

ANTAKYA

Harbiye

---

backed by the rocky cliffs of the Ziyaret Dağı range (ancient Mount Sipylus). It's well worth spending an hour or two wandering around the bazaar and market areas north of Kemal Paşa Caddesi (running from west to east just north of the Ata Köprüsü). The **Kurşunlu Han** incorporated in the bazaar, offers a shady courtyard for a tea stop. At the edge of the bazaar close to the bridge, the **Ulu Cami** mosque is an early Ottoman construction with a squat minaret. Far more recent is the **Gunduz** building, at the western end of the Ata Köprüsü. Resembling a typical 1930s suburban cinema, with its graceful curves, geometric friezes and porthole windows, it was actually the Parliament building of the short lived **Hatay Republic**. There are plans to turn it into a cultural centre and house the tourist office there.

At the junction of Kemal Paşa Caddesi and Kurtuluş Caddesi is the **Habibi Naccar Camii**, a mosque incorporated into the shell of a former Byzantine church, which was in turn built on the site of an ancient temple. The distinctive pointed minaret was added during the seventeenth century and is not – as you might be tempted to imagine – a former church tower. Over a kilometre to the east of here, in the hillside above the town, is the **Habibi Neccar Cave** (Habibi Neccar Mağrası), a minor Muslim holy place that was once home to a solitary prophet. Habibi Naccar was violently done to death by the Christians: his head is said to be entombed under the mosque, his body in the cave.

The Hatay has a long history of tolerance, and some 10,000 Christians live in the region, most of them of **Greek Orthodox**. Their substantial nineteenth-century church in Antakya is on Hükümet Caddesi, and contains some beautiful Russian icons. The **Catholic church**, just off Kurtuluş Caddesi, is built around a pretty courtyard filled with orange trees and the resident Italian nun is very friendly. Antakya is also home to a **Protestant church**, established by a Korean mission and housed in the imposing former French Consulate building. Links between Turkey and Korea go back to the 1950s, when Turkish troops formed part of the NATO forces ranged against the Communists. Not far from the Catholic church, on Kurtuluş Caddesi, is a small **synagogue** much visited by Israeli tourists, but identifiable only by the Star of David above its inconspicuous doorway.

The Archeological Museum

From the Ata Köprüsü, it's a quick hop across to the western side of the river and the **Archeological Museum** (Arkeoloji Müzesi; Tues–Sun 8.30am–noon & 1.30–5pm; $3), whose collection of locally unearthed Roman mosaics ranks among the best of its kind in the world. Imaginatively lit and well laid out in the first four rooms of the museum, they are in a state of near immaculate preservation – bar the odd bare patch where the *tesserae* have fallen off – and mostly depict scenes from Greco-Roman mythology.

The majority were unearthed at the suburb of Daphne (now Harbiye), which was Antioch's main holiday resort in Roman times, and this is reflected in the sense of leisured decadence that pervades many of the scenes. A good example is the charming **Narcissus and Echo** (room 2, no. 3), which depicts Narcissus gazing admiringly into a pool of water, in love with his own reflection, as an unrequited Echo looks on in sadness. One of the finest in terms of size and scope is the so-called **Buffet Mosaic** (no. 4), a vivid depiction of the rape of Ganymede, abducted by Zeus in the form of an eagle, and a banquet scene showing different courses of fish, ham, eggs and artichokes. Memorable images in room 3 include bouncing baby **Hercules** strangling the serpents sent to kill him by jealous Hera (no. 4), and a fascinating depiction of the **Evil Eye** – a superstition that still has remarkable resonance in modern Turkey – being attacked by a raven, dog, scorpion, snake, centipede, panther, sword and trident as a horned goblin looks away (no. 6). Room 4 continues with an inebriated Dionysos, too drunk to stand (no. 12), Apollo capturing Daphne as her clothes conveniently fall off (no. 14), Orpheus surrounded by animals entranced by the beauty of his music (no. 23) and a fine portrait of **Thetis and Oceanus** (no. 24), the latter recognizable by the lobster claws protruding from his wet hair, one of many water-inspired motifs that decorated the floors of public and private baths.

After the mosaics, the rest of the museum seems a little mundane, with only a couple of first-century AD statues of Venus in the entrance hall, a fine statue of Hades and Cerberus in the penultimate hall, and some Hittite and Assyrian reliefs and idols recovered from funeral mounds on the Amık plain, to write home about. Among the last, look out for the two stone lions, which were used as column pediments during the eighth century BC.

Sen Piyer Kilisesi

At the northeastern edge of Antakya is the **Sen Piyer Kilisesi** (Tues–Sun 8am–noon & 1.30–6pm; $0.70), the famous cave church of St Peter, from which it's said that the apostle preached to the Christian population of

Antioch. It's reached by following Kurtuluş Caddesi in a northeasterly direction for about 2km until you come to a signposted right turn. Follow the road towards the mountains and after about five minutes' drive you come to the church, set into the hillside just above. It's about a forty-minute walk if you're in the mood and it's not too hot, or you can flag down a dolmuş on Kurtuluş Caddesi, which will take you as far as the turnoff.

Whether St Peter really did preach from the Sen Piyer Kilisesi is – like the exact dates of his stay in the city – open to question. All that theologians seem to be able to agree on is that he spent some time in Antioch between AD 47 and 54, founding one of the world's first Christian communities with Paul and Barnabas. Indeed, the church must have been one of the first ever built and quite possibly the place where the term "Christian" was first heard (in other parts of the Middle East Christians were known as "Nazarenes"). Inside, water drips down the cave walls and the cool atmosphere provides a welcome break from the heat of summer. Beneath your feet you'll be able to discern traces of **mosaic** thought to date from the fifth century AD, while to the right of the altar is a kind of font set in the floor and fed by a spring with reputed curative properties. Left of the altar is a blocked tunnel down which the early Christians could flee in the event of a raid. A special **service** is held here on June 29 to mark the anniversary of St Peter's death, attended by members of Antakya's small Christian community, while Sunday afternoon Mass is held every week at the tiny Catholic church on Kurtuluş Caddesi.

Neatly incorporated into walling around the church are a few **sarcophagi**, and if you follow the new path around to the left of the church for 200m and then clamber up the hillside, you'll find a relief thought by some to be of Charon, ferryman of the River Styx at the entrance to the underworld – though the portrait is more likely the face of a veiled woman, with a tiny man (probably the second-century BC Seleucid emperor Antiochus Epiphanes IV) perched on her shoulder. With your own transport it's possible to drive the 15km – along Kurtuluş Caddesi and around the back of Mount Sipylus – up to the ruined *kale* (castle), from where there are fine views over the city.

Eating and drinking

Antakya's food is wonderful and shows its Arab influence with **regional specialities** such as: *muhammara,* a fiery puree of walnuts and hot pepper, *Şam orouğu,* an egg-shaped case containing minced meat and walnuts, *içli köfte,* similar but without walnuts, *serimsek börek,* a sort of chicken-filled samosa, *kağıt kebap,* kebabs cooked in greased-paper packages, *künefe,* a sweet dessert made with soft, mild cheese and served hot, and *Haleb Burmasi* (Aleppo roll), a sweet confection stuffed with pistachios, which makes a welcome change from baklava.

Antakya Evi Silhali Kuvvetler Cad. Antakya's best eating place, whose intimate, upstairs rooms of a nineteenth-century town house have been tastefully restored. The food is excellent and a full meal with beer should set you back no more than $6. A speciality is the Antioch *kebap*, a *köfte* of minced lamb stuffed with cheese, walnuts and olives.

Antik Han Hürriyet Cad. The unprepossessing exterior hides a walled garden courtyard and rooftop terrace. This is the place the locals come to drink *rakı* and beer, so the *mezes* are particularly good (the humus is a meal in itself, or try the *muhammara*) and the *ızgara* (grills) better than

average. Check the cost before ordering, though, as the menu lacks a price list.

Şamlioğlu Künefe Salonu Next to the Ulu Cami. Run by a portly film actor who has pasted snaps of his co-stars on the walls – this is the place to try the ubiquitous *künefe.*

Saray Restaurant Hürriyet Cad. Cheap and cheerful place for kebabs and *sulu yemek.* A filling meal should cost about $3

Sultan Sofrası İstiklâl Cad. Serves all the regional dishes, as well as excellent soup and main courses, at bargain prices.

Crossing into Syria

A number of bus companies operating out of Antakya offer services to cities in Syria; the better operators are Has and Güney. Several buses depart daily from the Antakya *otogar* for **Halab** (Aleppo; $7) and **Şam** (Damascus; $12). Both services cross the border to the east of Antakya at Cilvegözü/Baba al Hawa, and delays can be considerable. A quicker option to Halab might be to get a dolmuş to Reyhanlı and then make your own way by shared taxi to the border, 5km away, from where you can pick up an onward Syrian microbus. There is also a daily bus to **Laskiye** (Latakia; $6) on the Syrian coast.

There are several **other border crossings** between Turkey and Syria, but the only public transport currently running on any of these routes is the bus from Kilis (south of Gaziantep) to Halab via Azaz. Crossings are also possible, in theory, at Akçakale (from Şanlıurfa), Ceylanpınar and Nusaybin (from Mardin).

For current **visa** regulations, enquire at the Syrian embassy in your home country before departure. It's best to arrange a visa before you leave home as it takes longer and costs more to get one from the visa office at the Syrian Embassy in Ankara. You may also have to name the border you intend to use in advance

Listings

Banks and exchange There are several banks on İstiklâl and Atatürk Cad, and you can change money at the weekends at the *döviz* on Kurtuluş Cad.

Car rental From Titus Turizm, under the *Büyük Antakya Oteli*, Atatürk Cad 8 ☎0326/613 4232; from $30 a day.

Cinema Konak Sineması, 100m east of the Ata Köprüsü, behind the PTT, has four screens showing first-run Western movies.

Hospital The Devlet Hastane (State Hospital) is a couple of kilometres south east of the centre

Internet Modanet, on Hürriyet Cad, and Bizim, between the PTT and the Konak Sineması, on the west bank of the river.

Police Selçuk Cad; emergency number for foreigners is ☎0326/ 213 5953.

Post office The PTT is northwest of the roundabout at the western end of the Ata Köprüs (daily 9am–8pm).

Swimming There's an open-air pool on Günduz Cad (summer daily 10am–3pm; $1.50) with lockers where you can leave your gear if you are heading out on an evening bus.

West of Antakya

There are a number of interesting places to visit in the fertile, hilly countryside to the west of Antakya. The **Saint Simeon monastery** is the most renowned destination, while other other local sights can be visited from the nearby resort of **Samandağ**. If you want to see all of the places in a day from Antakya, it's worth renting a car or taking a taxi and driver, as public transport is limited.

Saint Simeon monastery

One of the more bizarre aspects of early Christianity was the craze for pillar sitting, which developed in Antioch during the fourth century. The trend was started by Simeon Stylites the Elder, whose basilica still stands at Qala'at Samaan near Halab in Syria, and was perfected by **Simeon Stylites the Younger**, whose **monastery** perches on a high ridge southwest of Antakya, 7km south of the road to Samandağ.

Simeon the Younger first chained himself to a rock in the wilderness in an act of ascetic retreat and then ascended progressively higher pillars before reaching a final height of some thirteen metres. He lived chained to the top of this pillar for 25 years, meditating and making sporadic pronouncements castigating the citizens of Antioch for their moral turpitude. The base of the pillar still remains, surrounded by the complex octagonal layout of the monastery that grew up around Simeon as he began to attract growing numbers of curious pilgrims eager to share in his enlightenment. About 250 followers mounted pillars of their own throughout the Middle East. Just south of the pillar you can still see the steps that pilgrims would climb to gain audience with the holy man. It's possible to climb on top of the diminutive pillar, which is just wide enough to lie down on and reap the same views of the Orontes valley and of Mount Cassius looming out of the Mediterranean that Simeon must have enjoyed over fifteen centuries ago.

To reach the monastery, turn south off the main Antakya–Samandağ road at **Uzunbağ**, just past Karaçay. Continue uphill along a good road for about 4km, before branching off to the right, by a white Muslim shrine, and following a bad dirt track for another couple of kilometres. There is no public transport at all to the monastery, but you should be able to find a taxi in Karaçay willing to take you.

Samandağ

About 25km southwest of Antakya, **SAMANDAĞ** is an Arabic-speaking resort town of about 30,000 people. The town is currently undergoing something of a building boom, financed in part by local boys made good in the Gulf, displaying their new-found wealth with gaudy villas and four-wheel-drive utility vehicles. It is served by regular dolmuşes from Antakya *otogar,* which will deposit you in the town's unprepossessing centre, a couple of kilometres inland. Here you'll find a few shops and restaurants and a couple of banks.

To get to the **beach**, take any dolmuş heading for "Deniz" (the sea) – although swimming here is not really recommended because of pollution from İskenderun, 50km or so up the coast. There are a couple of **hotels** close to the beach, best of which is the colonial-style *Dervişhan Tesisleri* (℡0326/512 1656; ❷). The hotel also has a **restaurant** that serves good food and acts as a social focus for the area. Next door at the *Dönmez Hotel Restaurant* (℡0326/512 1841; ❷), the emphasis is more on the restaurant side of the operation than the six very basic rooms up on the roof.

Vakıflıköy

The tiny village of **VAKIFLIKÖY**, with its apparently unremarkable mix of dilapidated mudbrick and timber houses and modern concrete villas, is in fact unique. For this is Turkey's sole surviving **Armenian village**, set amidst orange groves on the lush lower slopes of Musa Dağı. Armenian settlement of this region is said to predate that of neighbouring Cilicia. At the heart of the village is the recently restored and extended **Surp Asdvadzadzin Kilisesi**, to which the village *muhtar* (headman) has the key, though the church is not always locked. The congregation is made up of the 32 Armenian families who live here year round (though the population swells in summer when relatives and friends descend from the Armenian community in İstanbul). During the Turkish deportations and massacres of the Armenians in 1915 the inhabitants of Vakıflıköy, along with the Armenian population of five nearby villages, held out against the Turkish forces until they were evacuated to Port Said by French and British warships. Most of the villagers returned in 1919 when the Hatay became part of French mandated Syria. It wasn't until the Hatay joined the

Turkish Republic in 1939 that the Armenians, bar the inhabitants of Vakıflıköy, decided to leave, most of them ending up in Lebanon's Bekaa valley.

Dolmuses from Samandağ travelling the six or so kilometres to the village don't tend to leave till mid-afternoon (after the villagers have travelled into Samandağ and completed their shopping and errands), so it is best reached with your own transport or by taxi. If you do choose to visit the village, remember that it is a living community and not a mere curiosity.

Çevlik

A few kilometres north of Samandağ is the village of **ÇEVLİK**, easily reached by dolmuş from Samandağ town centre. In ancient times, Çevlik was the port of **Seleucia ad Piera**, serving Antioch, and it is from here that Paul and Barnabus are thought to have set off on their first evangelical mission to Cyprus. There are still a few ruins scattered around, including the 130-metre-long **Titus ve Vespasiyanus Tüneli** (open dawn–dusk; $0.35), a huge channel carved out of the hillside to prevent flooding and silting of the harbour. It's usually easy to find someone who will assist you to scramble around the huge gorge-like site (expect to leave a tip); two inscriptions at the upper end give details of its construction. Also scattered around you'll see foundations, sections of ruined wall and Roman tombs. Swimming is probably unwise, although the village beach is popular with local fishermen.

Çevlik has a few *pansiyons* and a campsite, and you can also camp on the beach, although strictly speaking this is illegal and you might get moved on.

South: Harbiye and the road to Syria

About 10km south of Antakya is **HARBİYE**, the ancient and celebrated suburb of Daphne, a beautiful gorge to which revellers and holiday-makers flocked in Roman times, drawn by shady cypress and laurel groves dotted with waterfalls and pools. Those who could afford to built villas here, while lesser mortals had to content themselves with a day-trip. Today, Antakya's modern citizens follow their example, while Arab tourists have their summer residences in the village. To get there, flag down a dolmuş in Antakya (travelling southwest along Kurtuluş Caddesi), but note that the gorge is really not worth visiting unless the heat in Antakya is absolutely unbearable or you have been invited by the locals to join in a picnic.

The Romans built a temple to Apollo here, since it was generally held to be the setting for the god's pursuit of Daphne. According to the myth, Daphne, when seized by amorous Apollo, prayed for deliverance; in answer to her prayers, Peneus transformed her into a laurel tree. Another legend relates that the resort was the venue of Paris's gift of the golden apple to Aphrodite, indirectly precipitating the Trojan War. Later, and with possibly more basis in fact, Mark Antony and Cleopatra are said to have been married here. Harbiye was also home of the Antioch Games, which were in their day more spectacular than the ancient Olympics, and a haven for escaped slaves and prostitutes, who ran a brisk trade among the laurels. In later years local Christians pulled down the temple of Apollo and used its stone to build their churches. With the departure of the Romans the place went into decline, a process compounded by the destructive attacks of the Persians and Arabs during the sixth and seventh centuries. Now Harbiye is famous for Defne soap, made from the fruit of the laurel tree and doubling as shampoo.

From the dolmuş drop-off point follow a road past modern houses until you come to a waterfall. From here, a litter-strewn path runs down into the gorge, where a number of shady and shabby tea gardens and trout **restaurants** (but not much else) await amid a landscape that has been constantly eroded by the river since Roman times. Several resort **hotels** ring the gorge, including the comfortable *Çağlayan* (☎0326/231 4011; ❸) and the cheaper *Hotel Çınar* (no phone; ❷).

About 8km south of Harbiye lies **Qalat az Zaw**, a ruined fortress originally built to defend the southern approaches to Antioch and much fought over by Crusaders, Arabs and Mamluks. Twenty-odd kilometres further on, close to the Syrian border, is the village of **YAYLADAĞİ**, a quiet spot that has a pleasant picnic area, set in mountain woods down towards the frontier – a good point for a break if you're en route to the border itself.

Travel details

Trains

Adana to: Ankara (1 daily, overnight; 14hr); Gaziantep (4 weekly; 3hr); İskenderun (3 daily; 2hr 30min); Mersin (6 daily; 1hr 15min).
Mersin to: Adana (6 daily; 1hr 15min).
İskenderun to: Adana (3 daily; 2hr 30min); Mersin (3 daily; 3hr 30min).

Buses and dolmuşes

Adana to: Adıyaman (7 daily; 6hr); Alanya (8 daily; 10hr); Ankara (hourly; 10hr); Antalya (3 daily; 12hr); Diyarbakır (3 daily; 10hr); Gaziantep (5 daily; 4hr); Kahta (2 daily; 7hr); Kayseri (3 daily; 7hr); Konya (hourly; 7hr); Malatya (3 daily; 8hr); Şanlıurfa (4 daily; 6hr); Van (1 daily; 18hr).
Alanya to: Adana (8 daily; 10hr); Ankara (8 daily; 10hr); Antalya (every 30min; 2hr); Diyarbakır (1 daily; 14hr); İstanbul (4 daily; 18hr); Konya (8hr); Mersin (8 daily; 9hr); Samsun (1 daily; 24hr); Silifke via Taşucu (8 daily; 7hr).
Antakya to: Adana (hourly; 3hr); Aleppo, Syria (4 daily; 4hr); Amman, Jordan (3 weekly; 12hr); Ankara (1 daily, 13hr); Antalya (3 daily; 14hr) Damascus, Syria (2 daily; 8hr); Gaziantep (8 daily; 5hr); İskenderun (hourly; 1hr); İstanbul (3 daily; 22hr); Riyadh, Saudi Arabia (3 weekly; 20hr); Samandağ (hourly; 1hr); Şanlıurfa (daily; 8hr).
Antalya *otogar* to: Adana (several daily; 11hr); Afyon (hourly, 5hr); Alanya (hourly; 2hr); Ankara (24hr service; 10hr); Antakya (3 daily; 14hr); Denizli (6 daily; 5hr 30min); Diyarbakır (1 daily; 16hr); Fethiye, by inland route (6 daily; 4hr); Isparta (hourly; 2hr 30min); İstanbul (24-hr service; 12hr); İzmir (6 daily; 9hr 30min); Konya/Eğirdir (6 daily; 6hr 30min).

Antalya (Devlet Hastane roundabout) to all destinations southwest of Antalya: Camyuva (10 daily; 1hr 20min); Fethiye by coastal route (7 daily; 8hr); Finike (9 daily; 2hr); Kalkan (9 daily; 5hr); Kaş (9 daily; 4hr 30min); Kemer/Beldibi/Göynük (every 30min; 1hr); Tekirova/Phaselis (10 daily; 1hr 30min).
İskenderun to: Adana (3 daily; 2hr 30min); Antakya (hourly; 1hr); Antalya (4 daily; 13hr).
Silifke to: Adana (every 15–20min; 2hr); Alanya (8 daily; 7hr); Antalya (8 daily; 9hr); Konya (12 daily; 5hr); Mersin (every 20min; 2hr).

Ferries

Antalya to: Venice (1 fortnightly; 71hr). One-way pullman seat costs $250.
Mersin to: Mağosa/Famagusta, North Cyprus (3 weekly; 10hr), with an onward service to Syria during summer. Tickets cost $22 one-way and $42 return, cars $75 return.
Taşucu to: Girne/Kyrenia, North Cyprus (daily except Fri & Sat; 6hr). Tickets cost $21 one-way, $32 return, cars with 4 passengers around $270.

Hydrofoils

Taşucu to: Girne/Kyrenia, North Cyprus (daily; 2hr 30min). Tickets cost $27 one-way, $32 return.

Flights

Adana to: Ankara (2 daily; 1hr); İstanbul (6 daily; 1hr 15min); İzmir (3 weekly; 1hr 30min); Lefkoşa/Nicosia, North Cyprus (5 weekly; 1hr).
Antalya to: Ankara (2 daily; 1hr); İstanbul (6 daily).

South Central Anatolia

CHAPTER 7

Highlights

٭ **Walking in Lakeland**
The lofty peaks of
Davraz, Barla and
Dedegül offer stunning
views over the region's
lakes. See p.606

٭ **Eğirdir** Eat fillets of
crisply fried lake fish as
the sun sets over Lake
Eğirdir. See p.615

٭ **Whirling dervishes,
Konya** Watch the
dervishes whirl each
December in their spiri-
tual home. See p.628

٭ **Hot-air ballooning** An
unforgettable experience
– the interplay of light
and shadow over
Cappadocia's geological
fairy tale landscape,
seen from the basket of
a balloon. See p.647

٭ **Göreme Open-Air
Museum** The frescoes
inside Göreme's cave
churches are a vibrant
reminder of the region's
Christian past. See p.650

٭ **Esbelli Evi** Immaculately
run hotel, elegantly fashioned from a series of
old village houses locat-
ed high above the
Cappadocian town of
Ürgüp. See p.657

٭ **Mustafapaşa** One of
Cappadocia's most
attractive villages sports
a wonderful concentra-
tion of old Greek houses.
See p.660

٭ **Ihlara valley** Don't miss
the natural beauty of this
fertile gorge, enhanced
by its rock-cut Byzantine
churches. See p.669

South Central
Anatolia

The **central Anatolian plateau** seems at first sight to be an unpromising prospect. A large area around the lake of Tuz Gölü is virtual desert, while much of the central plateau is steppe, suitable only for the grazing of livestock. During summer, water is scarce except in the river valleys and in areas that have been artificially irrigated, and in winter the region is blitzed by cold and heavy snowfall. Gertrude Bell recorded the impressions of a European traveller approaching the central plateau in 1909:

Before him stretch wide plains, corn-growing where rainfall and springs permit, often enough barren save for a dry scrub of aromatic herbs, or flecked with shining miles of saline deposit; naked ranges of mountains stand sentinel over this featureless expanse; the sparse villages, unsheltered from wind or sun, lie along the skirts of the hills, catching thirstily at the snow-fed streams that are barely enough for the patch of cultivated ground below; the weary road deep in dust or mud according to the season, drags its intolerable length to the horizon. It is Asia, with all its vastness, with all its brutal disregard for life and comfort and the amenities of existence; it is the Ancient East, returned after so many millenniums of human endeavour to its natural desolation.

The "shining miles of saline deposit" constitute part of the Turkish **Lakeland**, the region south of **Afyon** and west of **Konya**, largely ignored by the Turkish tourist industry. These stretches of azure and silver waters stand out against the grey plateau, or appear suddenly between mountains to startling effect. Many of them, like **Çavuşçu Göl** or **Acı Göl**, have a high salt content, which discourages aquatic life and human settlement alike; others are avoided by would-be settlers as their flat shores are liable to flood. But around the main plateau, forest cloaks the slopes of the mountains around the western lakes of **Beyşehir**, **Eğirdir** and **Burdur**. The residents of their namesake towns, and of the small community on the banks of **Akşehir Gölü**, manage to make a tenuous living out of fishing or reed-cutting, and Eğirdir is an increasingly popular stopover for passing tour parties and backpackers.

To the east of the lakes, the plateau rises gradually towards the highlands. **Tuz Gölü** to the north is little more than a vast salt-producing basin, and aridity in the region is increased by the underground dissipation of water. The light forest that once covered this land was destroyed between 5000 and 1000 BC by herds of livestock that grazed the steppe.

Despite the inhospitable nature of this region, it has been populated as long as anywhere in Anatolia. From the early Paleolithic age man was drawn to the lakes, which provided a livelihood for primitive hunters and fishermen, and during the Bronze Age the **Hittites**, a race who once rivalled the Egyptians, chose the plateau as their homeland. By the early historical period, northern Lakeland had been settled by the **Pisidians**, mountain people with a reputation for fierce independence who worked as mercenaries throughout the eastern Mediterranean. Their strategically situated settlements were difficult to subdue, and Xenophon described them as obstinate troublemakers, who managed to keep their towns independent despite the encroachments of the Persian Empire.

Further east, the area between the extinct volcanoes of **Erciyes Dağ** and the Melendiz range is **Cappadocia**, whose legacy of compacted lava-ash soil is favourable to vine-growing and horse-breeding. Water and wind have created a land of fantastic forms from the soft rock known as tuff, including forests of cones, table mountains, canyon-like valleys and castle-rocks, all further hewn and shaped by civilizations that have found the region particularly sympathetic to their needs. Rainfall is low, but Cappadocia is nevertheless extremely fertile compared to the rest of South Central Anatolia, and it became an important crossroads and home to a politically autonomous state between the third and first centuries BC. From the seventh to the eleventh centuries AD, it was a place of refuge during Arab and Turkish invasions into the steppe. Today its churches and dwellings carved from the rock, particularly by monastic communities, and its unearthly landscapes make an irresistible tourist draw.

Lakeland

After years of isolation, Turkish **Lakeland** is just beginning to be discovered by plant enthusiasts, birdwatchers, trekkers and winter sports aficionados. Other tourists, meanwhile, stop off here at **Eğirdir** on the route from Cappadocia and Konya to the south coast around Antalya or Fethiye. At present, facilities are unevenly spread and not luxurious, but the various Lakeland attractions make it ideal for quiet, unhurried holidays away from the seething coastal resorts. As well as the eye-catching **lakes** themselves, there are the remains of Pisidian cities to see (most impressively at **Sagalassos** and **Antioch ad Pisidiam** near Yalvaç), and largely unspoilt provincial towns, notably **Ayfon**, to explore.

Access to the lakes is from Antalya in the south, over the Taurus range to Isparta; from the plains of Konya in the east, over the Sultan Dağları to Eğirdir; and from Eskisehir or Kütahya in the north via the main north–south road to Afyon and İsparta. All routes are well served by buses.

Afyon and around

Dominated by a tall and imposing rock on which stands a powerful ancient citadel, **AFYON** certainly leaves a vivid impression. The town remains impressive on closer inspection: it is clean and relaxed, retaining much interesting Ottoman architecture as well as a number of attractive mosques. A few reasonably priced hotels make it a good choice for a night's stopover en route to the lakes, and there are several interesting side-trips that can be made from town if you have a bit more time to spare.

In honour of the fortress, and the 200-metre-high dark rock on which it's built, the city until recently bore the resounding name of Afyon Karahisar, or **"Opium Black Fortress"**. The rock is believed to have first been fortified by the Hittite king Mursil II, and remains have also been found dating to the Phrygian era. The Romans and Byzantines – who called the city Akronium or "High Hill" – also occupied the city, the Byzantines building the greater part of the present-day fortress, which was subsequently used as an imperial treasury by both Selçuks and Ottomans.

For three weeks leading up to August 26, 1922, Afyon was Atatürk's headquarters, prior to the last, decisive battle of the independence war, fought against the Greeks at nearby Dumlupınar. The town's statue commemorating the Turkish victory – depicting one naked man towering over another in an attitude of victory – is one of the most moving memorials to Atatürk.

Today, Afyon is a relative backwater, noted for its production of *sucuk* (sausage), *pastırma* (pastrami) and *kaymak* (clotted cream) – and its role as a stronghold of fundamentalists and right-wing nationalists. When Elia Kazan, the noted American film-maker of Anatolian-Greek descent, was looking for a location in western Asia Minor in the mid-1980s to shoot a historical extravaganza, he approached the city fathers for permission to use Afyon's exquisite old town as the setting – and was told in no uncertain terms to go elsewhere.

The Town

The best way of establishing what's where on arrival is to head for the highest point in town: the **fortress** on its 226-metre-high black monolith, which is scaled via some 700 steps on the southern face of the rock (a twenty-minute hike best avoided in the heat of the day). On the way up look out for hoopoes among the varied birdlife, and at the top for votive rags, representing wishes, tied to trees by petitioners. At prayer time, the calls to prayer from as many as eighty minarets resound and echo off the rock to dramatic effect. The fortress itself is thought to stand on the site of the Hittite fortress of Khapanouwa, built around the middle of the second millennium BC. The rock was subsequently fortified by the Phrygians, the Byzantines and the Turks, but all that remain are a few crenellated walls and towers.

Immediately surrounding the fortress rock is the **old town**, a warren of tiny streets frequented by rather polite gangs of street urchins speaking the central Anatolian dialect and a few words of English. Afyon's domestic **Ottoman architecture** is renowned in Turkey; the half-timbered houses here all support overhanging upper storeys, some even complete with a *kafes*, the wooden latticework on the windows designed to protect the chastity of a household's womenfolk.

There are a number of impressively well-preserved mosques near the citadel, with many more somewhat less distinguished ones in the bazaar proper. Opposite the base of the steps leading up the side of the rock stands Afyon's most ancient mosque, the **Ulu Cami** (outside of prayer time wait for the caretaker to let you in; small donation). This typically square Selçuk construction, built between 1272 and 1277, has been restored, so its originally flat roof is

Opium

A town called **"Opium"** (the translation of *Afyon*) could hardly be accused of reticence concerning its most controversial claim to fame. This region produces 25 percent of the world's legal opiates: it used to be almost half, but in 1971 the United States forced Turkey to impose a ban on production because of the extent of illegal drug trafficking. Nowadays, although poppy seeds are sprinkled liberally on bread loaves and the leaves of the plant are used in salads, all of the 20,000 tonnes of capsules processed around Afyon must arrive at the factory intact, and the poppy fields are regularly patrolled by government officials, who check if the seed heads have been illegally "bled" for heroin. If you want to take a look at the crop, in May/June head out of town for around 5km on the Sandıklı road, and the open fields of poppies are clearly visible from the road. Much more grows arund Yalvaç and in the Toros mountains.

While the authorities may be circumspect about touting the city's eponymous enterprise as a tourist attraction, there are still telltale signs of civic pride in the traditional industry: a close look at the fountain in the town square reveals that it is a graceful bronze sculpture of poppy seed-pods.

now pitched, but it retains forty original carved wooden columns with stalactite capitals and beams supporting a fine geometric ceiling.

Slightly downhill from the Ulu Cami, the **Mevlevi Camii** is a double-domed mosque noticeable for its pyramid-roofed *son cemaat yeri*, a porch in which latecomers pray – literally the "place of last congregation". The adjoining *semahane*, or ceremonial hall, has a walnut-wood floor on which Mevlevi dervishes once performed their whirling ceremony. The building has now been converted into the **Mevlevi Museum** (Mevlevi Müzesi; open at prayer times or on request to the *imam*), with exhibits of musical instruments and the ceremonial costumes of the dervishes. Afyon became the second largest centre of the Mevlevi order after the branch of Islamic mysticism was introduced to the city from Konya by the son of the Mevlana, Sultan Veled.

The **Archeological Museum** (Arkeoloji Müzesi; Tues–Sun 8.30am–5.30pm; $0.70), 1km east of the centre on Kurtuluş Caddesi, warrants a visit: the collection is housed in a light, airy building and the objects are well displayed. The most interesting finds are Roman, excavated at nearby Çardalı and Kovalık Höyük, dating from the third and fourth centuries AD. Exhibits from this period include a small marble statue of Diana and a price list from an agora, outside in the covered gallery. The adjoining local ethnographic museum concentrates on locally produced felt, displaying a Turkmen *topakev* (nomad's tent), a shepherd's cloak and a reconstruction of a local feltworks.

Also on Kurtuluş Caddesi, but nearer the centre in its own patch of parkland, the **Gedik Ahmet Paşa Külliyesi** was built for one of the viziers of Mehmet the Conqueror in 1477. Adjoining it are a stone *medrese* and a functioning hamam – the original marble floors are in good condition, but it's otherwise in a bad state of repair. The complex's mosque, identified as the **İmaret Camii**, has a fluted minaret dashed with zigzagging blue İznik tiles.

Atatürk's brief stay in Afyon is commemorated in a museum, the **Zafer Müzesi** (daily 9am–5pm; free), opposite the tourist office on Milli Egemenlik Caddesi. This is the building in which he planned his victory at Dumlupınar: his office has been preserved, and weapons and other paraphernalia from the war, as well as old photos of Atatürk and Afyon, are on show.

Practicalities

The **train station** is at the far north end of Ordu Bulvarı, about 500m from the centre, while the **otogar** is about the same distance east of town on the *çevre yolu* (ring road). Both terminals are linked with the middle of town by a dolmuş service marked "Sanayi/PTT", though if you arrive by bus there should be a free service to the town centre from the *otogar*. Towards the end of the dolmuş-service's run, it passes close by all the city's best hotels, coming to rest at a terminal on Ambaryolu, two blocks behind the main **PTT** (which stands on the main north–south street, Milli Egemenlik Caddesi).

There is a **tourist booth** (Mon–Fri 8am–noon & 1.30–5.30pm; ☎0272/215 6525) in Hükümet Meydani, and a larger **tourist office** (Mon–Fri 8.30am–5.30pm; ☎0272/213 5447) in the Hükümet Konağı building, opposite the Belediye Parkı, off Milli Egemenlik Caddesi. The major **banks and ATMs** are on Bankalar Caddesi.

Accommodation

The cheapest **hotel** is also one of the best, the centrally located *Hotel Soydan* at Turizm Emeksiz Cad 2 (☎0272/215 6070, ℻212 2111; ❷), a friendly place with small, prettily furnished rooms with bathrooms and TVs. It also has a restaurant serving traditional dishes. The relaxed *Sinada*, at Ambaryolu 25 (☎0272/215 6530, ⓕ213 6165; ❷), has some singles and triples as well as double rooms; most have bathroom and TV, and some have views of the citadel. The pleasant *Otel Naman* (☎0272/212 0948, ⓕ211 1249; ❸) is close to the train station, opposite the hospital on the Ankara-İzmir road, and therefore handy for late arrivals.

Eating and drinking

The old-fashioned *İkbal Lokantası*, close to Hükümet Meydanı on Uzun Çarşı, ranks as the most famous **restaurant** in town, with such arcane specialities as bull's bollocks (*billur*, meaning "crystal", is the menu euphemism). With its canopied exterior and well-furnished interior, the *Adem Usta*, on Ordu Bulvarı, looks pricey but is in fact excellent value for filling rice and vegetable broth, *izgara* (grilled meats) and a selection of ice creams to follow: a three-course meal for two will come to around $7.

Around Afyon

The most interesting side-trip from Afyon is to see a series of sixth-century **Phrygian sites**, notable for their stone-carvings, in the vicinity of İhsanıye. The Afyon region is also well known for its **hot springs**, whose waters bubble up at temperatures between 60 and 80°C and have a high content of fluoride, bromide and calcium salts. Mineral water from this region is bottled and sold all over Turkey.

Ayazın, Kaya and Döğer

The trip to see the **Phrygian sites** is best done with your own transport, but there are three convenient daytime trains from Afyon to **İhsaniye**, as well as dolmuşes that leave from a garage at Ordu Bulvarı 11/A, opposite the tourist office. It's about a forty-minute journey, and beyond İhsaniye it's necessary to rent a dolmuş to take you to Döğer (about 10km north of İhsaniye) or Ayazin (about 15km east of İhsaniye, 30km from Afyon). You can also get a bus straight to the village of Kunduzlu, near Ayazin, from Voyvoda Gazlıgöl Caddesi, opposite the *Belediye* building in Afyon.

Best of the remains are those of a Phrygian town located in the modern-day village of **AYAZİN**, reached via a right turn off the minor Afyon–Eskişehir road at Kunduzlu. **Cave houses** and a well-preserved ninth-century **Byzantine church** are visible across fields of opium poppies on the road to the village. Closer observation reveals lion reliefs and the scars from excavations by locals and archeologists, who have found coins and other objects in the rooms.

The rock-cut tomb of **Arslantaş** (Lion Stone), near the village of **KAYA** (formerly Hayranveli), is flanked by another relief of lions, two enormous beasts snarling at each other with bared teeth. This should not be confused with another Phrygian cult monument called **Arslankaya** (Lion Rock), featuring a high relief of the goddess Cybele flanked by two more enormous lions. Arslankaya is near Lake Emre in the village of **DÖĞER**, where the remains of a fifteenth-century Ottoman *kervansaray* can also be found.

Local spas

Fourteen kilometres north of town on the Kütahya road, is the massive *Termal Resort Oruçoğlu* (☎0272/251 5050, ⓕ251 5060; ❾), a **thermal hotel** offering half-board accommodation in luxurious rooms with air conditioning and balconies, and thermal water on tap. The price also includes use of the hamam, sauna, indoor and outdoor pools and a jolly water slide; various massages and treatments are extra, and it's a good way to wind down and recover use of your muscles after a trek.

Hudai Kaplıcılari, 48km south of Ayfon, beyond Sandıklı off the Denizli road, is worth a visit if only for a wallow in its deep mud baths. It's hard to get there without your own transport, however, as there's a further six-kilometre hike from the turning 6km beyond Sandıklı. The *Yeni Kaplıcı Oteli* at Hudai (☎0272/512 6947, ⓕ512 5014; ❹) has comfortable rooms, thermal pools and treatment facilities. The spring waters of the thermal pools all have their own specific properties, which are used as curatives for a variety of ailments – rheumatism especially, but also kidney stones, neuralgia and chronic period pains. The mud baths are believed to help remedy joint and spine calcification.

İsparta

Set on a flat plain dominated by 2635-metre Mount Davraz to the south, **İSPARTA** doesn't have the attractions of neighbouring Eğirdir but it's a likely stop on the way into the heart of the Lakeland region. It's a mostly modern town whose only suggestion of romantic appeal lies in its chief industries: rosewater, distilled here for over a century, and carpets, manufactured in industrial quantities. But there's efficient transport in and out and some good-value, comfortable hotels.

It's perhaps hard to believe, given the paucity of monuments, but İsparta has long been an important city. In its early years it was occupied by Hittites and Lydians, before being ruled briefly by the Macedonians. After Selçuk occupation in 1203, İsparta, like Eğirdir, was one of the cities that came under the control of the Hamidoğlu emirs towards the end of the thirteenth century, and was capital of a territory delimited by the four great lakes of Beyşehir, Burdur, Akşehir and Eğirdir. In the face of Ottoman expansion the Hamidoğlu emir cut his losses and sold the kingdom to the Ottoman sultan Murat I in 1381, and thereafter its star waned. Only when Eğirdir lost its importance did İsparta and neighbouring Burdur regain significance as market towns in their respective areas. This process gained impetus towards the end of the twentieth century, when large numbers of Muslim refugees from the Balkans settled in the area, particularly Bulgarians who brought their rosewater-distilling skills with them. The local carpet industry dates from approximately the same era.

The Town

Although uninspiring at first sight, there are still a few things to see and do in İsparta. On Kaymakkapı Meydanı, the **Ulu (Kutlubey) Cami** dates from 1417, its size and grandeur attesting to the importance of the town in Ottoman times; but the terrible late-Ottoman restoration with arabesque painting and light-green walls doesn't do it justice. Up until the 1923 exchange of populations many **Greeks** lived in İsparta, and their old residential quarter is a fifteen-minute walk from the town centre, near the Devlet Hastanesi (State Hospital). Today an impoverished part of the city, its once handsome lath-and-plaster houses are now crumbling, but a couple of substantial nineteenth-century churches have recently been restored.

Near the train station is a collection of **retired steam locomotives** manufactured in various corners of the world, including one that took Kemal

Atatürk on a triumphal tour. Meanwhile, the town's **Archeological Museum** (Arkeoloji Müzesi), on Kenan Evren Caddesi, 500m northeast of the *Belediye* building, is currently closed for renovation. It would be a shame if it hasn't reopened by the time of your visit, not for its shakily labelled Bronze Age, Roman and Byzantine remains, but because of the İsparta **carpets** usually exhibited upstairs. Many of those carpets are machine-woven and thus not really refined collector's items; they're instead meant to cover large floor areas decoratively but economically. You can see and buy them best in the **Halı Sarayı**, a wholesale and retail bazaar just behind the *Belediye* building. İsparta's **market** day is Wednesday, when people come in from the surrounding rural areas to sell agricultural produce and stock up on necessities.

Gölcük is the closest local attraction, 13km to the southwest, a tiny crater lake surrounded by trees, with a picnic area nearby in a clearing. In the summer, buses go from opposite the *Büyük İsparta* hotel, passing through beautiful fields of cultivated roses en route.

Practicalities

The **train station** is at the far north end of Hükümet Caddesi from the town centre, a 500-metre walk, and the *otogar* is 5km west of town on Suleyman Demirel Bulvarı – free service buses run in to the centre. There is also a **minibus terminal** in the middle of town, about 200m east of Hükümet Meydanı, from where you can take a dolmuş to Burdur, Eğirdir, Ağlasun or Atabey, all around half an hour away.

İsparta's regional **Directorate of Tourism** is on the third floor of the Valikonağı, or governor's building (Turizm Müdürlüğü; Mon–Fri 8am–noon & 1.30–5pm), next to the main square, the Kaymakkapı Meydanı. Tourism manager Resul speaks good English and will give you a street plan. **Money exchange** is best done at any of the *döviz* offices on Mimar Sinan Caddesi, where there are also several **ATMs**. The **PTT** (Mon–Sat 8.30am–noon & 1.30–5.30pm) is near the Valikonağı on Hükümet Caddesi. There's a simple, clean (men-only) **hamam**, Yeni Hamam in the town centre, opposite the Müftülüğü (Religious Affairs Directorate) on the corner of Zübeyde Hanım Caddesi and Eski Tabakhane Caddesi.

Cheapest **hotel** is the *Hotel Artuğ,* off Mimar Sinan Caddesi on 1738 Sok (☎0246/232 2624, **❶**), and even this has TVs in the scruffy en-suite rooms, but it's a bit of a last resort. A recommended place, popular with the French, is the *Hotel Artan*, in a quiet sidestreet at Cengiz Topel Cad 12/B (☎0246/232 5700, ❊218 6629; **❷**). The well-furnished rooms have central heating and satellite TV, and they serve a good buffet breakfast. The larger *Hotel Bolat*, off Kaymakkapı Meydanı at Suleyman Demirel Bul 67 (☎0246/223 9001, ❊218 5506; **❸**), is a little more expensive and similarly equipped, but has both air-conditioning and heating. The *Büyük İsparta* (☎0246/232 4422, ❊232 4422; **❸**) on Kaymakkapı Meydanı is the town's most prominent hotel, with a lobby and bars where the business community meets, and contemporary-styled rooms with TVs.

The *Artan, Bolat* and *Büyük İsparta* hotels all have **restaurants** with reasonably priced à la carte menus, serving the local professional clientele as well as their guests. For more of a local experience, try one of two decent restaurants on Kaymakkapı Meydanı: the *Hacı Benlioğlu* and the *Kebabçı Kadir*. Both serve excellent grills and fine desserts, and are better value and more atmospheric than the hotel restaurants.

Burdur and around

Lying 50km southwest of İsparta, **BURDUR** town is situated some way from its lake. It is known to Turks as the location of an army camp where privileged youths, with the money and connections to buy out of most of their military service, do a token, two-month stint. Despite its status as a provincial capital, flat-roofed village houses are in evidence and the only impressive monument is the fourteenth-century mosque, the **Ulu Cami**, a relic of the Hamidoğlu dynasty.

Frequent dolmuşes cover the scenic hour's drive from İsparta to Burdur, and there are regular onward services towards the lake itself, which is just as well, as you're hardly likely to want to linger in town. If you do get stuck, there are overnight options. The *Hotel Özeren,* Gazi Cad 51 (☎0248/233 9607, ☎234 1600; ❷), near the otogar, includes a buffet breakfast in the price, while the *Emniyet Lokantası* at Cümbüzlü Cad 9 is recommended for its steamtray food.

The lake, **Burdur Gölü**, northwest of town, is most easily reached along Highway 330 to Denizli and Acıpayam. Dolmuşes will drop you 5km from Burdur at its most popular lakeside picnic area, the five-kilometre-long **Çendik beach**, though swimming may prove difficult if the winter has been dry. The 200-square-kilometre lake is extremely saline and is encompassed by desert-like badlands. The area of water is receding annually, as the sources are diverted for irrigation, so the flamingos only appear as hazy dots in the extreme distance and the famous white-headed duck is only present in winter.

İnsuyu Mağarası

Best excursion from Burdur is to the 600-metre-long cave, **İnsuyu Mağarası**, signposted off the Burdur–Antalya road, 14km from Burdur and easily reached on any Antalya-bound bus. The cave (daily 8.30am–6pm; $0.70) is well organized with lighting and footpaths, and features a series of seven beautiful underwater lakes, the largest of which, Büyük Göl, measures 150m by 30m and can attain a seasonal depth of 15m. Its mineral-rich water is phosphorescent blue, warm and supposedly therapeutic for diabetics. Be warned that the lakes are prone to dry up, especially in late summer, in which case the cave itself will be much less impressive.

Salda Gölü

Continuing 70km west from Burdur brings you to **Salda Gölü**, which lies about halfway to Denizli, 6km from Yeşilova, where you will have to change dolmuş; there are regular services from Burdur to Yeşilova and in the summer season you shouldn't have to wait long for an onward dolmuş to the lake.

The westernmost of the lakes, Salda Gölü is a crystal-green expanse, its water lightly alkaline but pleasant to swim in. A succession of simple **campsites** and basic **restaurants** line the shore road, with the scenery becoming more appetising as you proceed from east to west. There's also a forestry service picnic area, and **rooms** available at the traditional, Turkish family oriented *Hotel Şahman* (☎0248/618 0480; ❸), which also has its own restaurant.

Eğirdir and around

EĞIRDIR is the natural focus of Turkey's Lakeland, boasting an astonishingly beautiful setting, clinging to a strip of flat land between the Toros (Taurus) mountains and Turkey's second largest freshwater lake (488 square kilometres). Lying around 900m above sea level, air temperatures are warm in summer (around 30°C), while the clear waters usually remain swimmable until the end of September (though sudden storms can cool things off at any time of year). In April the lake basin's numerous apple orchards bloom and in August/September the apples are harvested.

The lakeside town tends to suffer from its convenience as a stopover between the coast and Cappadocia, and most travellers stay only a night or two. This is a pity as **Yeşilada**, a tiny island connected to mainland Eğirdir by a kilometre-long causeway, is a wonderfully relaxing place to stay. It has many excellent *pansiyons* and makes a useful base from which to explore the region's natural and historic sights. **Watersports** are in their infancy in Eğirdir, though it is possible to rent small sailing dinghies and windsurfing is beginning to take off. Tandem paragliding is on offer for the more adventurous, but Eğirdir is best suited to its role as the Lakeland's **trekking** centre (see box on p.618).

Some history

Founded by the Hittites, Eğirdir was taken by the Phrygians in 1200 BC, but it was not until Lydian times, when it straddled the so-called King's Way from Ephesus to Babylon, that the town became famous for its recreational and accommodation facilities.

Early in the thirteenth century the town came under the control of the Konya-based Selçuks, who refortified it in its role as a gateway to Pisidia. Shortly thereafter the city reached the height of its fortunes as capital of the **emirate of Felekeddin Dündar**, remaining prominent during the reign of the Hamidoğlu clan. In 1331 the geographer Ibn Battuta could still describe Eğirdir as a rich and powerful city; when the Ottomans took over fifty years later, however, its strategic significance – and opulence – disappeared. The Byzantines knew the place as **Akrotiri** ("promontory" in Greek) after its obvious geographical feature; this name was originally corrupted in Ottoman times to **Eğridir** (meaning "it's bent"), but was changed again in the mid-1980s to **Eğirdir**, meaning "s/he's spinning", which officialdom apparently thought more dignified.

Opposite the town is the island of **Yeşilada**, until 1923 home of a Greek community over a thousand strong. Unfortunately, the Turks missed the opportunity of putting a preservation order on the beautiful stone and timber houses that they left behind and, when the causeway was built in the late 1980s, many of them were "redeveloped" as concrete hotels or pensions.

Arrival, information and services

The **train station** is 3km out of town just north of the İsparta road, but unless you are heading to İstanbul (departures at 7pm daily) or arriving from there or from İsparta (2 trains daily) you are unlikely to use it. To get into town from the station, take a blue "Altınkum" bus or a white "Yazla–Nizamiye–İstasyon-Plaj" dolmuş. The **otogar** is right in the town centre, opposite the Hızırbey Camii, from where there are eight daily buses (five in low season) to Yeşilada, the last one at 9pm; alternatively it is only a fifteen-minute walk across the causeway – head east, passing the **harbour** (with its fishing boats, day-trip cruisers and dinghies) on your right and the castle on your left.

The **tourist office** at 2 Sahil Yolu 13 (Mon–Fri 8.30am–noon & 1.30–5pm; ☎0246/311 4388) is by the lakeside, a five-minute walk out of town on the İsparta road. They can suggest hotels or *pansiyons* and give limited advice on trekking. **Getting around** this compact market town is easy on foot as everything lies within five minutes' walk of each other. There are a couple of **ATMs** in the town centre, and several **banks** where you can change money. Some of the pensions on the Kale and Yesilada have **internet** access.

Accommodation

Room prices in Eğirdir and on Yeşilada are reasonable, partly because of cutthroat competition, partly through *Belediye* control. It's best to stay on **Yeşilada** in order to take full advantage of the lake's charms, though rooms in town are more convenient for the shops, restaurants and Selçuk remains. The **Kale** district on the tip of the peninsula has a few more *pansiyons* and has been less developed than the island.

The town and Kale

Çetin's Pansiyon Backstreet east of the castle ☎0246/312 2154. Small, friendly and family-run, with clean rooms overlooking the lake and Mount Barla. ❷

Eğirdir Hotel Poyraz Sahil Yolu ☎0246/311 4992, ☏311 4219. A few minutes' walk north of the *otogar*, this bland three-star is a large modern building with comfortable, centrally heated rooms with TVs. ❹

Lale Pension Kale ☎0246/311 2406, ⒲www.lalehostel.com. The cheapest option in town, with dorms ($4 per person) and en-suite doubles. There's a top-floor terrace restaurant with harbour views and a wide choice of breakfasts including pancakes (from a dollar or so), plus internet access, beer and bike rental. İbrahim, the friendly proprietor, and his brother Mustafa offer an overnight fishing/camping trip and treks on Barla Dağı (negotiable prices depending on numbers). ❷

Yeşilada

Adaç At the island end of the causeway ☎0246/312 3625. Clean rooms with wonderful views. Also offers free use of their rowing boat. ❷

Ali's Pension Eastern side of the island ☎0246/312 2547, ⒲www.alispansion.com.tr. The most hospitable place in town, located on the sunrise-facing shore. Rooms are spotlessly clean, have hot water, central heating and bare wooden floors; the home cooking is wonderful and Ali takes tourists out in his boat at 7am to fish for crayfish and carp. ❷

Big Apple Western side of the island ☎0246/331 4555. Restaurant-pension facing the sunset, with seven pleasant rooms, some with balconies overlooking the lake. ❷

Göl Pension Southern side of the island ☎0246/312 2370. Serves breakfast beside the lake and has extremely well-kept rooms with balconies; pricier rooms on the terrace offer the best views of all. ❷

Halley Pension On the south shore ☎0246/312 3625. A popular option with European backpackers – the rooms are nothing special, but they're overseen by a friendly family. ❷

Mavigöl Western side of the island ☎0246/311 5383, ⒲www.mavigolhotel.com. A step up in quality from the rest, the hotel's rooms are, nonetheless, fairly cramped but good buffet breakfasts served. ❹

Sehsuvar Peace Pension Eastern side of the island ☎0246/311 2433 ⒺSehsuvar-o@hotmail .com. Just behind *Ali's*, with clean, simple rooms. The location is peaceful and the family very friendly. ❷

The Town and Yeşilada

Eğirdir's secular architecture was largely damaged by Byzantine–Selçuk conflict, but the religious edifices survived and have been incorporated in the modern town centre. On a preliminary wander the most obvious remains are of the **Dündar Bey Medresi**, which began life in 1218 as an inn, was converted into a *medrese* by Felekeddin Dündar in 1281 and now serves as a shopping precinct. The adjoining **Hızırbey Camii** has also been nicely restored; the roof is supported by Selçuk wooden pillars and it has an ornately carved door, wooden porch and İznik-tiled *mihrab*. The earliest building in the *medrese* complex is Eğirdir's six-domed **bathhouse** (1202) which retains its sixteen original washing basins. It provides six rooms for men and a large separate room for women (daily 8am–11pm). Nearby, overlooking the approach to the island, are the ramparts of the Byzantine and Selçuk **citadel** (*kale*) on which an imposing cannon is still perched as a reminder of the importance of the trading interests that were once protected.

Across the causeway, **Yeşilada** itself boasts the twelfth-century Byzantine church of **Ayios Stefanos**, now re-roofed and with restoration almost compete. The remaining Greek houses are mainly set in the centre of the island in walled gardens dominated by mulberries and grapes, accessed by tiny cobbled lanes. The small pebble **beaches** that border the island are hard on the feet, but the convenience of being able to take a dip from your pension before breakfast compensates.

Back on the mainland the **Belediye Plajı**, 750m from the town centre in the Yazla district, is the least attractive of the town's beaches. Much better is **Altınkum**, out by the train station, a sandy pay-beach ($1), great for children because of the shallow waters and offering umbrellas, pedal-boats and camping. However, its charm is diminished by a holiday-camp ambience and the modern housing development that backs it.

Eating and drinking

Not surprisingly, **lake fish** – especially carp (*sazan*), zander and crayfish – figure prominently on local restaurant menus. On the island, many *pansiyon* owners double as fishermen and offer fresh-caught lake fish presented either as batter-fried fillets, grilled or poached in tomato sauce (*bulama soslu*). Prices are reasonable, and a meal including fish, French fries and salad should cost between $3 and $5; most of Eğirdir's restaurants serve alcohol.

Especially recommended **on Yeşilada** is the *Big Apple* restaurant near the causeway, with indoor and outdoor tables, sunset views and a huge variety of *meze*s. On the opposite side of the island, the *Sunrise* restaurant serves simple but well-cooked food at waterside tables. If you prefer a conventional restaurant, head for the *Melodi* at the southeastern tip of the island, which sells reasonably priced carp, crayfish and zander. The top-floor restaurant at the *Mavigöl* serves attractively presented Turkish food and has a good range of wines; booking is recommended as they often have groups. The poshest restaurant in town is the *Kervansaray*, on Atayolu near the island causeway, where generous portions of fish and seafood are surprisingly reasonable, given the pleasant waterside terrace and smart white-tablecloth interior.

In the town centre a couple of simple, decent *lokantas* offer budget-priced food but no beer. The *Çinar* on Posthane Caddesi has good soups and a delicious *İskender kebap*, but no desserts; while the *Kemer* near the Hızırbey Camii offers a wider variety of meals than most provincial restaurants. The *Kaltre* **bakery**, on a side street opposite the football courts, is excellent for picnic food; they have a wide range of fresh cakes and pastries to take away. If you want a cup of tea or coffee with your cake, head for the *Sedir Pastanesi* on the northwest corner of Hükümet Meydanı, whıch has been remodelled in folksy style and offers ice cream as well.

Excursions from Eğirdir

Many of the *pansiyon*s in Eğirdir offer half- and full-day **boat trips** out on the lake (from about $8 per person) and the fishermen who take you usually know the best swimming and barbecue spots. There's also a range of minibus and taxi excursions to points of interest within a few hours' journey of the town. Unless you have a car, it's worth signing up for these, as you'd otherwise never get to many of the places described below. Rather unusually in Turkey, *pansiyon* proprietors often co-operate, pooling clients to fill vehicles. Prices vary between $8 and $15 per person for a typical day-trip, depending on whether it is a taxi or minibus, the distance and the number of people sharing.

Atabey and Barla

Midway between Eğirdir and İsparta, the village of **ATABEY** is set on the flat İsparta plain in a lush agricultural landscape. Of most interest to visitors is the **Medrese of Dündar Bey**, built in 1224, and the wooden-porched mosque next to it.

Virtually the only settlement of any size near the lakeshore (other than Eğirdir itself) is the old village of **BARLA**, 25km northwest of Eğirdir, which spills down a hillside about 200m above the water level. It makes an excellent starting point for day walks, and you can see the roofless remains of the church of **Ayios Georgios** (dated 1805 but perhaps earlier) and a far older rock-cut tomb and cyclopean walls in the valley above the village.

Prior to 1923 Barla had a mixed Greek and Turkish population, but many of those now living here are descendants of Kurdish villagers – moved here in the turbulent years following the proclamation of the republic – from the east of Turkey. Barla was also the home for a short time of the controversial religious figure **Sait Nursi**. The wooden house where he lived and preached is something of a shrine for the *Nurculuk* ("followers of light") who admire his interpretations of the Koran.

Barla can only be reached by public transport via İsparta, a time-consuming process. However, it would make an excellent day's cycle ride, perhaps combined with a swim at **Bedre** beach, some 13km from Eğirdir en route to Barla. **Camping** is possible at Bedre and there is a seasonal **restaurant** with toilet facilities for campers.

Antioch ad Pisidiam

Almost equidistant (75–80km) from Eğirdir whether you travel via the east shore road past apple orchards, or make the complete circuit of the lake via Barla, the ancient city of **Antioch ad Pisidiam** (Tues–Sun 8.30am–5.30pm; $0.70) lies about 2km northeast of the modern town of Yalvaç, itself at the head of a valley draining southwest into the lake.

The city was originally a Hellenistic foundation of the late third century BC, later becoming a part of the Roman province of Galatia and eventually, around 25 BC, a Roman *colonia* settled by legionary soldiers from Gaul. Following the creation of the province of Pisidia at the end of the third century AD, Antioch became its capital and remained important well into Byzantine times, finally being abandoned and lost to history in the eleventh century AD. Historically, the city is important as the place where the apostle **St Paul** first attempted to convert pagans to Christianity.

The most unusual extant remains are of the sizeable **temple**, at the highest point of the city, built in a semicircular colonnaded precinct in honour of the Emperor Augustus. Situated just below the temple is the toppled three-arched **propylon** (gateway) dedicated to Augustus, where the Tiberius and Augustus squares meet; most of the blocks lie scattered along the line of the road. Even more substantial are the remains of the **baths** fed by an **aqueduct**. There are also surviving sections of flagged Roman **street**, which once linked the various parts of this walled city and was once spanned by a wing of the **theatre**.

At the lower end of the site, a few courses of monumental stone blocks belonging to the fourth-century **Church of St Paul** (on the site of the synagogue) still stand, but little else can be seen except for the ground plan and some small areas of mosaic floor.

If there are insufficient people to warrant a taxi or minibus tour, you can take a **bus** instead to Yalvaç from Eğirdir, departing at 10.30am and returning from Yalvaç at either 3pm or 5pm – the journey takes an hour and a half. This would give you the opportunity to take a quick look at the small but fine **Yalvaç Museum** (Yalvaç Müzesi; Tues–Sun; $0.70), which houses finds from the site. From Yalvaç you'll have to walk or, more sensibly given the time constraint, take a taxi the 2km on to the site.

Kasnak forest, Kovada Gölü and the Kral Yolu

Twenty kilometres south of Eğirdir lies **Kasnak forest**, reached by a dirt road through the village of Yukara Gökdere and past the dam above it. The park is famous for the single large specimen of *quercus volcanicus*, the volcanic oak, only found here. The beautiful mixed oak, juniper and cedar forest also contains orchids, iris and the deep red wild peony, *peonia maculata*, which flowers in May. Native birds include three species of woodpecker, as well as many tits, shrikes and nuthatches.

Continuing south, and taking the road on the left marked Sütçüler, the lake, marshland and forests of **Kovada Gölü**, 35km from Eğirdir, form a carefully tended and hardly visited national park. Animals found in the reserve supposedly include wolves and bears, though more certainly there are wild boar and snakes – and swarms of butterflies, which attract aficionados in springtime. The lake itself, teeming with fish, receives the outflow of Eğirdir Gölü. The limestone shore is harsh and the lake itself weedy so it is not particularly good for swimming. However, there's a picnic place with fresh water and seating.

Most tours continue another 30km south on the main road through a gorge towards **Çandır** (signed Yazılı Kanyonu), passing a series of icy but scenic pools and waterfalls, crisscrossed by bridges and best sampled at the height of summer. Here, too, are identifiable, well-preserved stretches of the road locally known as the **Kral Yolu**, or "King's Way", an ancient road that threaded through Pisidia. Just outside the park, and reached by a footbridge, is a **trout restaurant**, the *Baysallar Dinleme Tesisleri*; the adjoining pension might now be ready for occupation.

Adada and the Zindan Mağarası

Signposted off the Aksu road, 65km from Eğirdir, **Adada** is another ancient town cut from grey stone. Although there is a warden, no admission is charged and, as the site lies along both sides of a minor road, it is permanently open to visitors. It has never been excavated, but was recently surveyed and mapped by İsparta University students. History books are strangely silent on the place, even to the extent of its original name, but judging from coins found in the area, the place was thriving during imperial Roman times. Visible remains include a particularly well-preserved Corinthian temple, plus two other small temples, a forum with unusual seating along one side, a badly preserved theatre, a church, and various Hellenistic buildings. Tumbled statue bases with inscriptions lie along the main road through the site. If you follow the stream-bed between the acropolis hill and the adjacent hill, heading southwest behind the forum, it's possible to trace the original Greco–Roman road from the south; below the city this contours the hillside on an impressive line of enormous slabs. This is almost certainly the original road that St Paul walked on his first missionary journey from Perge to Antioch in Pisidia.

The northwest Toros mountains dominate the Lakeland landscape, forming a compact arc around Eğirdir lake. They are far more accessible than the better known Kaçkar and Aladağlar ranges and offer activities ranging from day walks up pretty gorges to a tough ascent of **Dedegül**, a peak just eight metres short of 3000m.

Other than Dedegül, the **Barla** and **Davraz** massifs present the greatest challenge, but **Sivri Dağı**, overlooking Eğirdir makes a good day walk. Mounts Davraz and Dedegül are attractively forested with pine and cedar to the treeline at 1800 metres, while wildflowers, including crocuses and tulips, carpet the bare slopes in spring. Wild boar forage in the forests around Davraz and Dedegül, but the mammals you are most likely to see are foxes, hares and marmots.

From early June onwards, the nomadic **Yörük** – descendants of the first Turkic peoples to arrive in Asia Minor from Central Asia – move their flocks of sheep and goats up the limestone slopes. Their black goat-hair tents dot the mountains in the summer months. As a traveller hereabouts, you will be treated as a *Tanrının misafiri* (or "guest of God") and offered sweet black tea, yoghurt and paper-thin *yufka* bread – the staple diet of a proud but poor people.

Practicalities

Eğirdir pension owners are unlikely to have any first-hand information about hiking routes, but they will probably be able to help you sort out the relevant dolmuşes, negotiate car rental or taxi hire and let you store unwanted gear until your return from the hills. Ask about the weekend outings organized by the Eğirdir Tourism and Outdoor Sports Society (ETUDOSD) – a welcoming bunch of local trekking enthusiasts with headquarters near the harbour in Eğirdir. If you trek alone, remember that these are remote mountains where mapping is inadequate; they should be treated with respect.

Bare requirements for the peaks are robust boots, tent, stove, all-weather clothing, compass, food and water (though less is required for lower altitudes). The best months to reach a summit with minimum gear are June to September, as the snows have receded and the weather is generally stable. The Donatım Ticaret shop near the Dündar Bey Medresi, Belediye Cad 15, Sok 7/A (☎ & ℻0246/311 6080) has a wide range of **outdoor equipment** and may provide maps. **Guides** can be arranged by Ibrahim at *Lale Pension* (see p.614). Kate Clow, who originated Turkey's first long-distance trekking route, the Lycian Way, is now working on a long-distance walk following the **route of St Paul** from Perge to Antioch in Pisidia. This route will include optional climbs of the Lakeland peaks and preliminary information and route maps are available at ⊛www.stpaultrail.com.

The Davraz Massif

The usual starting point for hikes on and around 2635m **Mount Davraz** (Davraz Dağı) is Külova Yayla, a half-hour's drive southwest of Eğirdir. The *Davraz Kayak Merkezi* ski lodge there (☎0246/264 2020; $15 per person full board) has comfortable rooms, but ring first to check that it is open.

From the lodge head southwest, then cut back on the path that runs southeast up steep scree slopes. Slip through a narrow notch in the rocky ridge and continue to

Easily visited on the same tour is the **Zindan Mağarası**, a sizeable cave beyond the village of Aksu. It's 27km from Eğirdir – go straight up Cumhuriyet Caddesi in Aksu until you come to the river, crossed by an attractive Roman bridge: the entrance to the cave is in the rock face opposite. At present, workmen are installing electric light and flooring, but you are still free to explore.

a campsite with a spring (3hr). Next day head west along the broad ridge top, leading you to the summit (2hr). Either retrace your steps to the lodge or, to make a circular walk, drop down the western slopes of the ridge before turning north and then east to reach the lodge via moraines huddled in the shadow of Davraz's north face.

The Barla Massif

Rising from the western shore of Lake Eğirdir, 25km northwest of Eğirdir town, lies 2799m **Mount Barla** (otherwise known as Gelincik Dağı or Poppy Mountain to the locals). Take a taxi or local bus to Bağören village and walk to the pretty lake formed by the new dam. A walk along a tractor road leading west past the lake brings you to Kocapınar Yaylası (2hr). Continue west to Kalkan Geçiti (Shield Pass). Turn north then northeast following the course of the obvious valley. There is water and, in season, a *Yörük* encampment at Çukur Yaylası (1hr 30min). The summit climb the next day takes a couple of hours, leaving you plenty of time to break camp and return to Eğirdir the same day.

Dedegül

The highest, most extensive of the Lakeland massifs, 2992m **Dedegül**, is also the least accessible from Eğirdir. The base camp at Melekler Yaylası (Angels' Pastures) is an hour and a half's drive southeast across the Toros. Wildflowers carpet the camp ground in May and June, and there are many interesting walks in the pine forests. Pinargözü (Spring Eye), where cool waters from an underground lake spout out of the mountain, is a thirty-minute stroll east down the forest road from Melekler Yaylası.

The summit is a steep five-hour ascent from the *yayla* at 1700m. Head more or less due south from the *yayla* and ascend a dry valley to a ridge, which joins the true summit to the slightly lower Kartal Tepesi (Eagle Hill). Turn right for the summit, left for Kartal Tepesi. The views of Beyşehir lake and Dedegül's steep and stark satellite peaks are impressive. Dedegül means "Grandfather's Rose" and refers to an unusual pink flower that blooms on the peak in summer. The descent to base takes three to four hours.

The Yaka canyon, on the stream below the forest road returning from the *yayla* to Eğirdir, makes a pleasant two or more hours' walk with a wide range of flowers in spring; be prepared to get your feet wet.

Sivri Dağı

Directly behind Eğirdir, **Sivri Dağı** (1600m) affords excellent views of the town, island and lake. Climb from the road behind the hospital; turn right just behind the graveyard and follow the pylon line to the ridge below the summit. Here are ruins of an old fortification, and a pit that was once a theatre. The peak is reached by a narrow path from this ridge. The north face (strictly off-limits) is dominated by the slogan *Kommandoyuz, Guçluyuz, Cesuruz, Hazırız* ("We are commandos, we are strong, we are brave, we are ready") painstakingly painted in enormous letters and maintained by the thousands of recruits who pass through the commando training camp at the foot of the peak.

Inside, the cave has everything from bat colonies and guano stench to stalactites and stalagmites. When the lighting is finished, the excitement of commando-type adventuring will be eliminated, but at present a lamp and old clothes are essential if you intend to plumb all 2500m of the cave's depths; the first kilometre is the best.

Sagalassos

Although nearer İsparta, the Pisidian site of **Sagalossos** is a popular organized trip from Eğirdir, 55km to the northeast. It's by far the most impressive Pisidian site and is undergoing extensive excavations undertaken by a team that stays on site all summer. Material removed from the site is presently under wraps in the museum at Burdur and at the team's headquarters in Ağlasun, the small town en-route to the site; there are plans to open a large museum here. The site is well signposted from Ağlasun, has picnic tables at the entrance and the helpful guardian will probably sell you a map and, if asked, open up the building housing the restored library.

The remote site – 1400m above sea level and tucked onto the two thousand-metre flank of Akdağı – was found by P. Lucas in 1806; he later translated an inscription, which identified it as the first city in Pisidia. Alexander the Great, of course, stormed the town with a frontal assault in 333 BC. Sagalassos then settled down to life under Macedonian garrison and then as part of Roman Asia Minor. In 25 BC Sagalassos was made a metropolis and free city by Augustus, who also put retired legionaries in it, as a type of *colonia*. Most of the site dates from Roman Imperial times. The population of Termessos (see p.546) probably moved to Sagalassos in 244 AD after an earthquake, though the site was abandoned soon after, when the population moved downhill to the present town.

The **site**, at present free and open during daylight hours (though this may change depending on the state of excavations), is well labelled with illustrations of the buildings in their original state. To the right of the entrance is the 96-metre wide **theatre**, just as the earthquake left it, with seating mostly in place, but the stage building rather more wrecked. Two restored **nymphaea** (fountain-houses) are here: the smaller is a three-sided roofed trough with flat column mouldings, encased in a protective building. The restoration shows both early and Byzantine phases; the floor mosaic is almost intact, as are the alcoves and a major inscription. Walking west you come to the **upper agora**, of which the second, huge nymphaeum formed one side, two ceremonial arches opened off and there was a pagoda-like monument in the centre.

Just above, north of the upper agora, is one of the oldest parts of the site, a Doric **temple** of the second century BC, built of massive blocks still standing on two sides; it was later incorporated into the city walls and you can spot the joins. Walking down from the upper agora you'll see fragments of beautiful Roman friezes laid out like a giant jigsaw. Turn right on the level track through the site for **graves** cut into the rock face; they contained cremations. Below the main track is the **lower agora** with adjacent baths. Earthenware pipes and hypocausts reveal how water was distributed and heated. Beyond this area is a temple with Corinthian columns dedicated to Antonius Pius, now in rubble, but an informative contrast to the Doric one.

Straight ahead down the steps is the **necropolis** containing many graves, and a hill which locals say is the site of an Alexander monument – they believe that a gold statue dedicated to Alexander is waiting to be discovered.

Beyşehir and its lake

Leaving Eğirdir in the direction of Konya the next major lake you come to is Beyşehir Gölü. The town of **BEYŞEHİR** – on its eastern shore – sees a lot of through traffic heading in this direction, and its attractive lakeside position and historical legacy make it a good prospect for at least a day-trip.

Judging by the Neolithic remains found in the region, there has been human settlement here since the sixth or seventh millennium BC. There is also extensive evidence of Hittite settlement around the lake. The town itself was originally Byzantine, known as Karallia, and in Selçuk times was surrounded by walls, as well as acquiring a citadel, mosques and hamams. The local golden age, though, came under the Eşrefoğlu dynasty (1277–1326), and its best building dates from that time.

There are a number of attractive monuments in the town, and a lovely weirbridge, built by German workers in 1902, across the lake's outlet. From here you can watch locals throwing their nets out for the evening catch of *sazan* (carp) in defiance of the "No Fishing" signs.

The Town

The most important monuments in Beyşehir are situated right on the lakeshore to the northwest of the modern town. Finest of these is the **Eşrefoğlu Camii** (most reliably open at prayer time), built by Eşrefoğlu Seyfeddin Süleyman between 1297 and 1299. This large, flat-roofed stone building surmounted by a typical Selçuk flat-sided cone, is an exceptional example of a medieval wooden *beylik* mosque – the *beyliks* being the minor Turkish principalities that ruled Anatolia before the Ottomans gained supremacy. Restoration carried out in the 1950s explains the ugly concrete blocks at the base of the minaret, but otherwise the mosque is in a remarkable state of preservation. There's an especially beautiful carved main north portal (albeit partly marred by a modern pine porch), typically Selçuk in its geometric ornateness.

The effect inside is incredibly forest-like: not only are the columns and capitals wooden, but also the rafters, the galleries, the furniture and the balustrades. Adding to the sylvan effect, light plays on the columns from a central aperture, now glassed over, and from high-set windows. Below this is a deep pit, which (according to the *imam*) once held ice for preserving food and cooling the mosque. The *mihrab* is decorated in typical Selçuk style, its turquoise, black and white tiles being almost the last surviving of their type, and the *mimber* is also a lovely period-piece of woodcarving, echoing the star motif apparent throughout the mosque.

The **Eşrefoğlu Türbesi**, the conically roofed building attached to the east side of the mosque, dates from 1302, and was also built for Eşrefoğlu Seyfeddin Süleyman who died in that year. It's worth asking the *imam* if he'll open it up for a look at its beautifully tiled interior, one of the most ornate surviving examples of its type.

Behind the mosque, to the south, stands a small *medrese* with an almost equally ornate portal. To the north of the mosque there's the late thirteenth-century **Dokumacılar Hanı** (Cloth Hall), also originally built during the Eşrefoğlu period, with six domes recently restored in brick; again, you'll need to ask permission to see it. It's one of the earliest remaining domed bazaars; unlike the Byzantines, and the Ottomans after them, the Selçuks tended to use domes in secular business buildings rather than in their monumental religious architecture. To the northwest of the hall there's a double **hamam**, dating from 1260, usually open, but in poor and dilapidated condition. Outside, at the door, there's a pipe that is said to have supplied milk for bathing purposes.

Practicalities

The **otogar** (regular services from Eğirdir, Konya, Antalya and elsewhere) is 2km out of town, but a regular service bus links it with the centre, dropping you near the weir-bridge.

Beyşehir's only decent central **hotel** is the characterful *Beyaz Park* (☎0332/512 4535, ℱ512 3865; ❷), an imposing stone building overlooking the weir at Atatürk Cad 1. Built in the early twentieth century, it has pleasantly furnished rooms; for period atmosphere and coolness, ask for the old building (as opposed to the modern extension), preferably overlooking the river as the roadside is noisy.

The best **restaurant** in town is at the *Beyaz Park*, with reasonable food (including lake fish) and drinks, served in the riverside garden, weather permitting. The surprisingly homely *Café Yaren*, behind the *Beyaz Park*, is the favoured choice of the town's students, and offers **internet access** and kitsch wall decorations. Opposite the *Beyaz Park* is a **carpet and antique dealer's** called Ceylanlar Sarraf, which sells a good selection of kilims, copperware, Ottoman handguns and old jewellery.

Around the lake

Religious and civic architecture aside, the most obvious local lure is the shallow, freshwater **Beyşehir Gölü**; although Turkey's largest lake in surface area, its 650 square kilometres average a mere 10m in depth. The number of its islands is a hotly disputed topic among the locals, which may be explained by the fact that smaller ones appear and disappear according to the water level (presently very low), but the named ones – many with ruined Byzantine monasteries upon them – number about twenty. The best beach on the lake is **Karaburnu**, 18km from Beyşehir on the Yeşildağ road, then signposted 500m off to the right. It's possible to rent a boat here and explore the islands and the lakeshore.

You can **circumnavigate the lake** by car (rental can be arranged through Muhitten at the *Beyaz Park* hotel) and the little-visited west shore is beautiful. Alternatively, rent a **boat** from Gedikli Köy, on the northwest shore, and visit the once magnificent Selçuk island palace of **Kubadabad**, whose unique tiles can be seen in the Karatay museum in Konya.

More easily accessible on the main, east shore road towards Eğirdir is the **Eflatun Pınar** (Violet Spring), a thirteenth-century BC Hittite shrine initially signposted 15km northwest of town, just before a petrol station. Turn right, following a paved side-road for 5km, then bear left for 2km more along a dirt track to the eponymous village.

At the outskirts, a large, walled pond filling a natural depression in the hummocky countryside receives the flow of vigorous springs. At one corner stand huge carved blocks bearing four relief figures with winged sun discs (symbols of royalty) carried by semi-human monsters. To either side at water level are statues of seated divinities. Unfortuantely, you won't be able to make out much detail without wading boots or binoculars, since the figures face the water and the pond is surprisingly large.

Konya

Focus of Sufic mystical practice and teaching for the Middle East, **KONYA** is a place of pilgrimage for the whole of the Muslim world. This sprawling city has overrun the surrounding mud-walled villages and at its heart is the medieval Selçuk capital, which tugs at the hearts of all pious Turks and is often spoken of with more pride than the better-known tourist resorts. This was the adopted home of Celaleddin Rumi, better known as the Mevlana (Our Master), the Sufic mystic who founded the **whirling dervish** sect, the

Mevlevi; his writings helped reshape Islamic thought and modified the popular Islamic culture of Turkey.

In western Turkey, Konya has a reputation as one of the country's most religious and conservative cities, and while the teachings of Sufic mystics like the Mevlana and of Hacı Bektaş are still important in Konya, it is also a stronghold of Islamic fundamentalists, suggesting a strong current of mainstream Islamic thought. An episode stuck in the minds of western Turks is that of a local severely beaten for smoking in the street during Ramadan during the 1980s; foreigners, however, are treated with more forbearance. In their defence, the citizens of Konya point out that while the place may appear underdeveloped, with poorly equipped schools and people more dour and less sophisticated than those nearer the Aegean, this is partly because they are not allocated their fair share of resources by Ankara. Even the city's obligatory Atatürk statue faces north – towards Ankara and away from the city centre – which locals claim is symbolic of the fact that they have been ignored since the establishment of the Turkish Republic.

The "backwardness" in fact goes some way to creating what for many visitors is Konya's charm. This may be Turkey's eighth largest city – with a population of over half a million – but there are relatively few private cars on the road and bikes have a higher profile than in İstanbul and Ankara. Konya is surrounded by some of Turkey's most fertile countryside (the region is known locally as "the breadbasket of Turkey"), and its parks add a splash of greenery to the ubiquitous light-coloured stone. However, the city can seem bleak in winter and sun-bleached in summer, and you'll find this contrast the rule rather than the exception for Turkish inland towns.

Some history

Konya boasts a history as long and spectacular as that of any Turkish city. The earliest remains discovered date from the seventh millennium BC, and the acropolis was inhabited successively by Hittites, Phrygians, Romans and Greeks. **St Paul** and **St Barnabas** both delivered sermons here after they had been expelled from Antioch and, in 235 AD, one of the earliest Church councils was convened in the city – known then, under the Byzantines, as Iconium.

It also took a central role during the era of the western Selçuks, becoming the seat of the **Sultanate of Rum**. After they had defeated the Byzantine army at the battle of Manzikert in 1071, the Selçuks attempted to set up a court in İznik, just across the Sea of Marmara from İstanbul. They were expelled from there by the combined Byzantine and Crusader armies, but still ruled most of eastern and central Asia Minor until the early fourteenth century.

While the concept of a fixed capital was initially somewhat alien to the Selçuks, Konya became the home of their sultans from the time of Süleyman Ibn Kutulmuz, successor to Alparslan, the victor at Manzikert. **Alâeddin Keykubad**, the most distinguished of all Selçuk sultans, established a court of artists and scholars in Konya early in the thirteenth century, and his patronage was highly beneficial to the development of the arts and philosophy during the Selçuk dynasty. Many of the buildings constructed at this time are still standing, and examples of their highly distinctive tilework, woodcarving, carpet-making and masonry are on display in Konya's museums. All of these art forms later served as the basis for their Ottoman counterparts.

Arrival, orientation and information

Konya's **otogar** is 2km out on Ankara Caddesi; take the "Konak–Otogar" dolmuş into town or the **tramway** ($0.25) to Alâeddin Parkı. The **train station**

▲ *Koyunoğlu Museum*

KONYA

0 — 200 m

- - - - Tramway

N

ACCOMMODATION
Balıkçılar	8
Bey	6
Çatal Aile	3
Hüma	1
Mevlana Sema	5
Tur	4
Turistik Konya	7
Yeni Köşk	2

RESTAURANTS
Çatal Lokantası	A
Gülbahçesi Konya Mutfağı	C
Halil İbrahim Sofrası	F
Mevlana Sema	E
Mevlevi Sofrası	B
Sifa	D
Villa	G

▲ Otogar

State Hospital

NALÇACI CAD

SULTAN ŞAH CAD

SULTAN CEM CAD

KÂZIM KARABEKIR CAD

İHSANİYE CAD

Fairground

ANKARA CAD

SULTAN VELED CAD

İSTANBUL CAD

AZİZİYE CAD

Karatay Medresesi

Küçük Karatay Medresesi

THY

Selçuk Palace

Alâeddin Camii

Alâeddin Parkı

ALÂEDDİN BUL

İnce Minare Medresesi

St Paul's Catholic Church

Dilara @

ATATÜRK CAD

AMBERREIS CAD

FERİT PAŞA CAD

Şerafeddin Camii

SERAFEDDIN CAD

ALÂEDDİN CAD

HÜKÛMET ALANI

İplikçi Camii

BAZAAR

TEVFİKİYE CAD

SIRCALI MEDRESE CAD

Sırcalı Medrese

SAHİP ATA CAD

Sahip Ata Külliyesi

Archeological Museum

SAİT PAŞA CAD

LARENDE CAD (MERAM ESKİYOL)

MEVLANA CAD

NAZİMBEY CAD

TÖRBE CAD

Selimiye Camii

Mevlâna Museum

AZİZİYE CAD

Azîziye Camii

KARAMAN CAD

SELİMİYE CAD

MENGENÇ CAD

TOPRAKLIK CAD

Cemetery

▲ Train Station

▲ 0

is slightly closer, at the far end of Ferit Paşa Caddesi, connected to the centre by dolmuş or by taxi (around $2). A THY shuttle bus links the city centre with Konya's **airport**.

Buses arriving at the *otogar* – not to mention strolling tourists – will probably be met by hotel touts, carpet-shop hustlers and self-styled guides, many having only a hazy idea of the location and history of Konya's monuments. In any case, orientation should not present serious difficulties, despite the absence of detailed, accurate maps. The town centre consists of a large roundabout – encircling the hillock of **Alâeddin Parkı** – and one main street, first called **Alâeddin Caddesi** and, later, **Mevlana Caddesi**, leading southeast from the hill to the Mevlana museum. The city's preferred hotels and restaurants are all situated in this central area, and all of the monuments and other attractions are within walking distance.

The **tourist office** (Mon–Fri 8am–5.30pm; plus discretionary weekend hours May–Sept; ☎0332/351 1074) is at Mevlana Cad 21. This handles bookings for the December **dervish festival** (see box on p.628), for which you should contact them well in advance, as seats for the ceremonies always sell out.

Accommodation

Most of Konya's **hotels** are located on or just off Alâeddin/Mevlana Caddesi. Finding a room shouldn't be a problem, except during the December festival, when Konya fills up and an advance booking is an absolute necessity. Rooms are often surprisingly expensive, but there is a large choice and most are prepared to haggle. There are also some fairly basic, unlisted, bazaar hotels, though none that we can in all honesty recommend.

Balıkçılar Mevlana Karşısı ☎0332/350 9470, ℱ351 3259. If money's no object and you want an excellent location, try this flashy three-star hotel opposite the Mevlana complex, which has air-conditioning, satellite TV and balconies with views over the museum. **7**

Bey Ayanbey Sok ☎0332/352 0173. Clean and quiet; it's worth asking for one of the two top rooms, which have balconies and excellent views of the town. **3**

Çatal Aile Naci Fikret Sok, off Mevlana Cad ☎0332/351 4981, ℱ351 4981. The friendly management makes it popular with both Turks and backpackers; quiet, plain rooms and a roof terrace. **2**

Hüma Alâeddin Bul 8 ☎0332/350 6618, ℱ351 0244. This low-rise balconied neo-Selçuk building, very handy for transport and the sights of Alâeddin Parkı, has tasteful, air-conditioned rooms, a relaxing dining room and bar, and a disco for night-owls. **6**

Mevlana Sema Mevlana Cad ☎0332/350 4623, ℱ352 3521. Centrally heated, with air-conditioning and minibar – the smallish rooms have been tastelessly refurbished, with garish bedspreads and wallpaper, but are at least comfortable. **4**

Tur Esarizade Sok ☎0332/351 9825, ℱ352 4765. A useful fallback if the nearby *Çatal Aile* is full. Similar facilities, but not so helpful management. **2**

Turistik Konya Mevlana Meyd 8 ☎0332/351 9212, ℱ352 1003. Very popular with Turkish families, this tall building has a pleasant rooftop breakfast terrace offering views of the Mevlana complex, but the rooms are a bit dowdy. **2**

Yeni Köşk Esra Kadalar Sok 28, off Aziziye Cad ☎0332/352 0671, ℱ352 0901. Small, quiet and well-maintained, receiving uniformly positive reviews for its clean, air-con rooms with TVs and baths. **4**

The Mevlana Museum

A visit to the **Mevlana Museum** (Mevlana Müzesi; May–Oct Mon 10am–6pm, Tues–Sun 9am–6pm; Nov–April Tues–Sun 9am–5.30pm; tickets sold until 20min before closing time; $2.50) is among Turkey's most rewarding experiences. It's housed in a former *tekke*, the first lodge of the Mevlevi dervish sect, at the eastern end of Mevlana Caddesi, and can most easily be found by

The life and teachings of the Mevlana

Celaleddin Rumi, later known as the **Mevlana**, was born in Balkh, a central Asian city, in 1207. Various prodigies attended his infancy and a wandering dervish prophesied that the boy was destined for greatness. At the age of 20, vouchsafed a warning vision, the young man convinced his father to flee Balkh with him for western Asia, which they did just in time to avoid being massacred with the rest of the town by marauding Mongols.

They settled in Konya, where the reigning sultan Alâeddin Keykubad received them cordially. Poised on the marches between Byzantium and the young Turkish principalities, the city had a cosmopolitan population, whose beliefs were not lost on the young man; it was almost inevitable that he should emerge as a leading heterodox mystic or Sufi. In 1244 came a fateful meeting with **Shams-i-Tabriz**, a wandering dervish from Iran, whom Rumi immediately recognized as a spiritual mentor. For several years the two men kept near-constant company until some of Rumi's followers, jealous of the interloper's hold on their teacher, plotted to have Shams murdered.

Until the 1250s Rumi remained inconsolable, and apparently only reconciled himself to his companion's death in the process of composing a masterpiece of Persian devotional poetry, the **Mathnawi**. A massive work covering several volumes (see p.1085 for a recommended translation of excerpts), it concerns the soul's separation from God – characterized as the Friend – as a consequence of earthly existence, and the power of a mutual yearning to bring about a reunion, either before or after bodily death. The Mevlana – as Rumi was by now widely known – himself died on December 17, 1273, a date subsequently referred to by his followers as the Wedding Night.

On a practical level, the Mevlana instructed his disciples to pursue all manifestations of truth and beauty, while avoiding ostentation, and to practise infinite tolerance, love and charity. He condemned slavery, and advocated monogamy and a higher prominence for women in religious and public life. The Mevlana did not advocate complete monastic seclusion – the Mevlevis held jobs in normal society and could marry – but believed that the contemplative and mystical practices of the dervish would free them from worldly anxieties.

The teachings of the Mevlana were an exciting departure from Islamic orthodoxy, and they're still one of the most attractive aspects of the religion to Westerners and liberal Muslims alike. Although his ideas have never been fully accepted as Islamic orthodoxy, it's reassuring that a man who was expressly opposed to religious bigotry, while advocating song, dance and humility as a means to divine union, should still have a dedicated following among devout Muslims.

locating the distinctive fluted turquoise dome that rises directly above Celaleddin Rumi's tomb.

The site of the *tekke* is thought to have been presented as a gift to the Mevlana's father, Bahaeddin Veled, by the Selçuk sultans. Bahaeddin Veled was certainly buried here in 1232, and his tomb stands upended beside that of his son. According to popular myth, Veled's tomb rose until it stood upright when the Mevlana was buried alongside in 1273, a measure of the unusual respect held by the father towards his son. (Conversely, the custom of a son rising to his feet when his father enters a room is still prevalent in Turkey.)

The structures adjacent to the tomb were subsequently enlarged by the *çelebis* (literally "nobility"), the disciples of the Mevlana who took over leadership of the order after his death. They served as a place of mystical teaching, meditation and ceremonial dance (*sema*), from shortly after Rumi's death in 1273 until 1925, when Atatürk banned all Sufic orders. Over the centuries the various dervish orders had become highly influential in political life and thus could pose a threat to his secular reforms.

Most of the **buildings** in the compound, including the *tekke* and *semahane*, were built late in the fifteenth and early in the sixteenth centuries by the sultans Beyazit II and Selim I. Opposite the entrance a *şadırvan*, or fountain for ritual ablutions, still plays. Along the south and east sides of the courtyard are the **cells** where the dervishes prayed and meditated, today containing waxwork figures dressed in the costume worn during the whirling ceremony. Before they were allowed the privilege of seclusion in the cells, the novices had to spend a period of a thousand and one days in manual labour in the **soup kitchens**, which are also open to the public. After the novitiate they could return to the community and take jobs, even marry, while retaining membership of the order. Next to the quarters of the *şeyh* (head of the dervish order), now the museum office, is a **library** of five thousand volumes on the Mevlevi and Sufic mysticism.

Across the courtyard in the main building of the museum is the **mausoleum** containing the tombs of the Mevlana, his father and other notables of the order. You should leave your shoes at the door and shuffle along in a queue of pilgrims, for whom this is the primary purpose of their visit. Women must cover their heads, and if you're wearing shorts you'll be given a skirt-like affair to cover your legs, regardless of sex. The measure of devotion still felt toward the Mevlana is evident in the weeping and impassioned prayer that takes place in front of his tomb, but non-Muslim visitors are treated with respect and even welcomed. This is in strict accordance with Rumi's own dictates on religious tolerance:

Come, come whoever you are, whether you be fire-worshippers, idolaters or pagans. Ours is not the dwelling-place of despair. All who enter will receive a welcome here.

If you're a lone *gavur* (infidel) in a centre of Islamic pilgrimage this sentiment is surely one to be cherished.

The semahane

The adjoining room is the original **semahane** (the circular hall in which the *sema* was performed), considered the finest in Turkey. Exhibits include some of the musical instruments of the original dervishes, including the *ney* (reed flute). Novice dervish-musicians did not, and still do not, buy a *ney*, but are given one by their *murşid* or spiritual (and music) teacher, who fashions it for them. The reeds for these flutes are still grown throughout southeastern Turkey; it is said that the sound they make is a cry for their nursery reedbed. An analogous but more esoteric explanation in the *Mathnawi* describes it as the lament of the human soul for reunion with the Friend, the dervish epithet for the Godhead. The instrument indeed has the same range as a human voice, and in the hands of a virtuoso the sound is extremely poignant. A tape of dervish music plays continually in the museum, and the "voice" of the *ney* is clearly distinct above the other instruments.

Other exhibits include the original illuminated *Mathnawi* – the long devotional poem of the Mevlana now translated into twelve languages – and silk and woollen carpets, some of which form part of the great body of gifts received by Celaleddin Rumi from sultans and princes. One 500-year-old silk carpet from Selçuk Persia is supposed to be the finest ever woven, with 144 knots to the square centimetre; it took five years to complete. The Selçuk rugs on

The dervish festival and ceremony

Since Konya is the spiritual and temporal home of the whirling dervishes, the city plays host to the annual **dervish festival** every December 10–17, during the week prior to the anniversary of the Mevlana's death. Unfortunately this is not the best place or season to witness a dervish rite: with sub-zero temperatures, doubled hotel rates and shops full of whirling dervish lamp stands and other kitsch, Konya is probably at its worst.

Moreover, the troupe that performs the ritual in an indoor basketball court does not profess to live as Mevlevis; before you fork out for the ticket it's worth remembering that the best place to witness a ceremony is probably in the restored *semahane* in İstanbul, the Galata Mevlevihane (see p.164). The group there has official recognition as a dance troupe, but its members are also practising dervishes who have undergone the novitiate and live according to the teachings of the Mevlana on a daily basis.

Contrary to the main body of Islamic belief, the Mevlana extolled the virtues of music and dance, and the **whirling ceremony** – more properly the *sema* – for which the Mevlevi dervishes are renowned is a means of freedom from earthly bondage and abandonment to God's love. Its ultimate purpose is to effect a union with God.

The **clothes** worn by the Mevlevis during the observance have symbolic significance. The camel-hair hat represents a tombstone, the black cloak is the tomb itself, and the white skirt the funerary shroud. During the ceremony the cloak is cast aside, denoting that the dervishes have escaped from their tombs and from all other earthly ties. The **music** reproduces that of the spheres, and the turning dervishes represent the heavenly bodies themselves. Every movement and sound made during the ceremony has an additional significance, and is strictly regulated by detailed and specific directions. As an example, the right arms of the dancers are extended up to heaven and the left are pointing to the floor, denoting that grace is received from God and distributed to humanity, without anything being retained by the dervishes themselves.

The **three stages of the dance** are: knowledge of God, awareness of God's presence and union with God. As the dancers turn they repeat a *zikir*, or "chant of remembrance", under their breath, while the musicians sing a hymn expressing the desire for mystic union. In the final part of the ceremony, the *şeyh*, or current head of the order, the incarnation of the Mevlana, joins the dancers and whirls with them.

display here give credence to the theory that their skills were adopted by the Ottomans, since many of the patterns and motifs, previously unique to Selçuk works, recur in subsequent carpetwork throughout Asia Minor, and some of the same knots are used in Selçuk, and later, Ottoman examples.

The latticed gallery above the *semahane* was for women spectators, a modification introduced by the followers of the Mevlana after his death. The heavy chain suspended from the ceiling and the concentric balls hanging from it have been carved from a single piece of marble. In the adjoining room, a casket containing hairs from the beard of the Prophet Mohammed is displayed alongside some finely illuminated medieval Korans.

The rest of the city

The modern city radiates out from the **Alâeddin Parkı**, at the opposite end of Mevlana/Alâeddin Caddesi from the Mevlana Museum. As traffic islands go, it's a lovely, wooded place for a stroll; there are also many outdoor cafés to sit at. The site of the original acropolis, the *tepe*, has yielded finds dating back to

7000 BC as well as evidence of Hittite, Phrygian, Roman and Greek settlers; most of which are now in the museum in Ankara. At the foot of the hill to the north are the scant remains of a **Selçuk Palace**: two pieces of stone wall, incongruously surmounted by an ugly concrete canopy.

The only other surviving building to bear witness to any of the long history of this mound is the imposing **Alâeddin Camii** (daily 9.30am–5pm; donation requested), begun by Sultan Mesut I in 1130 and completed by Alâeddin Keykubad in 1221. Masonry on the northeast facade survives from an earlier, unidentified, Classical construction and comprises a row of marble columns whose varying sizes have been cleverly compensated for in the surrounding stonework and whose diminishing heights echo the slope of the hill. The original building probably consisted of the fan-shaped hall, whose flat mud roof is supported on six more rows of Roman columns.

Its typical plain Selçuk interior contains 42 ancient columns with Roman capitals supporting a flat roof, with a small domed area over the *mihrab*. The beautiful carved ebony *mimber*, dated 1155, is the oldest inscribed and dated Selçuk work of art in existence. A hoard of Selçuk carpets, discovered when the mosque was renovated, has been relocated to the Mevlana Müzesi, but the remains of eight Selçuk sultans, including the warrior Alparslan and Alâeddin Keykubad, are still in a **tomb** located in a separate hall of the mosque interior.

The Karatay Medresesi

The nearby **Karatay Medresesi** on Ankara Caddesi (Mon–Sat 8.30am–noon & 1.30–5.30pm; $0.70) is another important Selçuk monument. Built in 1251, the *medrese*, or school of Islamic studies, now houses a museum of ceramics, but the building itself provides greater interest. The main **portal** is a fine example of Islamic art at its most decorative, combining elements such as Arabic striped stonework and Greek Corinthian columns with a structure that is distinctly Selçuk: a tall doorway surmounted by a pointed, stalactite arch, reminiscent of the entrance of a tent. The features that distinguish Konya's two important Selçuk portals – this and the even more decorative example at the entrance of the İnce Minare Medresesi – from other examples of Selçuk masonry are the use of Koranic script and interlacing, geometric patterns in the decoration.

Inside the *medrese* the most attractive exhibit is again part of the building itself. The symmetrical tiling of the famed **dome of stars** is a stylized representation of the heavens in gold, blue and black monochrome tiles. Painted Ottoman tiles from İznik and Kütahya appear clumsy in contrast with those of this delicate mosaic. Selçuk **ceramics** on display in the galleries bear witness to the fact that pious concerns were overruled by secular taste – not to mention the contributions of conquered Christian and pagan subjects – even in medieval times. The striking images of birds, animals and even angels would have been strictly forbidden in more orthodox Islamic societies.

The İnce Minare Medresesi

Behind its fine Selçuk portal the **İnce Minare Medresesi**, or "Academy of the Slender Minaret" (Tues–Sun 9am–noon & 1.30–5.30pm; $0.70), on the west side of Alâeddin Parkı by the tramway stop, is now being used as a lapidary (gem) and woodcarving museum. The minaret from which it takes its name was severely truncated by lightning in 1901; today the most exquisite feature is the **portal**, even more ornate than that at the Karatay Medresesi.

Most of the exhibits in the museum, like the ceramics in the Karatay Medresesi, came from the ruined Selçuk Palace across the way. The finest individual items on display are Selçuk stone reliefs, explicitly showing the influence of Byzantium. Most prominent are winged angels, bestiary pediments and a two-headed eagle relief, said to be from the vanished walls of the medieval city and now the official logo of the modern town.

The Sırcalı Medrese and the archeological museum

A short walk southeast of Alâeddin Parkı along Ressam Sami Sokak, the thirteenth-century **Sırcalı Medrese** (Mon–Fri 8.30am–5.30pm; $0.70) now houses government offices. Highlights of the building, mostly restored in harsh brick, are the fine blue-glazed tilework in the rear porch, all that remains of what was once a completely ornamented interior, and the handsome portal – all visible even if the gate is locked.

Continuing in the same direction, you'll reach the **Archeological Museum** (Arkeoloji Müzesi; Tues–Sun 9am–noon & 1.30–5.30pm; $0.70), containing the only pre-Selçuk remains in the city. These include the few Hittite artefacts from the nearby site of Çatal Höyük (see p.633) that have not been relocated to Ankara, and three well-preserved Roman sarcophagi from Pamphylia, one of which depicts Hercules at his twelve labours. Just northeast of the museum, the thirteenth-century **Sahip Ata Külliyesi** is semi-ruined but retains its beautiful brick and stone entrance portal, plus a tiled *mihrab*.

Around the bazaar

On Hükümet Alanı, the north edge of Konya's workaday **bazaar** is marked by the brick **İplikçi Camii**, Konya's oldest (1202) mosque to survive intact and still be in use; legend claims that the Mevlana preached and meditated here. It is also worth looking out for the **Aziziye Camii** in the bazaar, an Ottoman mosque easily recognized by its unusual (for Turkey) Moghul-style minarets. The bazaar, like the city itself, is very traditional and surprisingly relaxed. Look out for the alternative healing remedies on sale, from daisy water to leeches.

The Koyunoğlu Museum

Around 1.5km away, on the southeast side of the centre, the **Koyunoğlu Museum**, at Kerimdede Cad 25 (Koyunoğlu Müzesi; Mon–Sat 8am–5.30pm; $0.70), is an eclectic private collection donated to the city by the Koyunoğlu family. Downstairs are black-and-white pictures of old Konya, but the museum is mainly interesting for its ethnographic section upstairs, which consists of a rich collection of embroidered textiles, some Selçuk and Ottoman ceramics and objects from everyday nineteenth-century life, such as bath clogs and musical instruments. There's also a fine collection of antique carpets, which enthusiasts shouldn't miss, including examples from Niğde, Konya and Karaman. Adjoining it is the restored period **house** of the donor family (same hours as museum; free), containing original woodwork and furnishings.

Eating and drinking

Konya's innate religious convservatism has hampered the development of a real "eating out" culture and, although this has begun to change recently, **restaurants** serving alcohol are few and far between, while decor and service are usually strictly functional. The better restaurants are listed below, but if you are after **fast food** check out the numerous places on Atatürk Bulvarı.

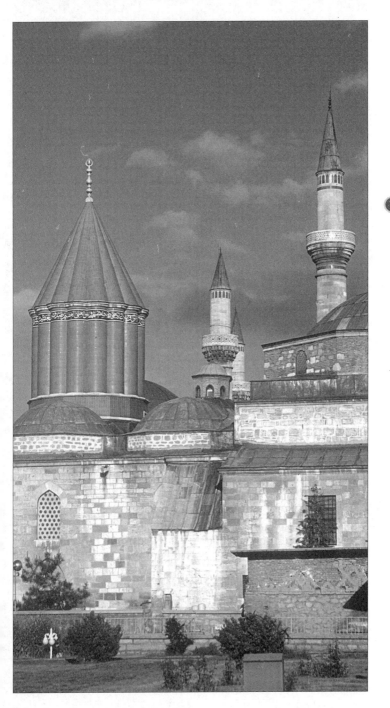

Çatal Lokantasi Naci Fikret Sokak, off Mevlana Cad. Small, homely restaurant that serves a decent, tender version of the local speciality, *fırın kebap* (a small portion of lamb or mutton oven-roasted in a clay dish) for around $2.

Gülbahçesı Konya Mutfağı Nazimbey Cad. Built around the small courtyard of a period house and, like the nearby *Mevlevi Sofrası*, featuring a roof terrace with uninterrupted views of the Mevlana complex and *sofra* tables where you sit cross-legged on cushions.

Halil İbrahim Sofrası Opposite the Mevlana complex. Housed in an old building to the right of the *Balıkçılar Hotel*, and recommended by locals for tender kebabs and crispy *pide*.

Mevlana Sema Mevlana Cad. Rooftop terrace-restaurant of the hotel, offering a standard range of grills and kebabs, but also a delicious green bean stew. Licensed.

Mevlevi Sofrası Nazimbey Cad. North side of the Mevlana complex. Perhaps the best place to eat in town – a restaurant contained within a series of beautifully restored houses, where prices for a wide range of well-prepared Turkish *mezes*, grills and kebabs are reasonable, around $6 a head.

Şifa Mevlana Cad, opposite the *Şifa Otel*. Convenient and well-patronized, with a wide variety of hot and cold *mezes*, plus the standard grills and a *pide* oven.

Villa Restaurant Meram Cad, continuation of Kazım Karabekir Cad. Serves unusual varieties of kebabs, and alcoholic beverages, in a large dining area, but closes around 9pm. It's a good 30min walk west of the centre.

Listings

Airport THY office, Alâeddin Cad 9 ☎0332/351/2000; airport buses leave 45min before flights.

Banks and exchange There are several *döviz* offices and ATMs on Hükümet Alanı.

Car rental Available from Rüya Turizm, Alâeddin Cad ☎0332/352 7228; and Selen, Aziziye Cad ☎0332/353 6745.

Hamam Behind Şerafeddin Camii on Hükümet Alanı. It's everything you could ask of a Turkish bath: white stone and marble with traditional tiny round skylights striping the steam with rays of sunlight. It has separate wings for men and women, and the masseurs are skilled and thorough.

Internet access Dilara, opposite the front entrance of the Catholic church, just off Alâeddin Bul, and another couple of internet cafés near *McDonald's* on Alâeddin Bul.

Police Ferit Paşa Caddesi ☎0332/322 2816.

Post office PTT on Hükümet Alanı (daily 8.30am–midnight).

Tours Selen, Aziziye Cad (☎0332/353 6745), offers city tours and trekking and hunting trips around Beyşehir.

Around Konya

There's little to see in the immediate environs of Konya, save the tumbledown village of **Sille**, though enthusiasts might be persuaded to spend a day or so touring the area's more remote archeological and historical remnants – namely **Çatal Höyük**, possibly Anatolia's earliest settlement; the church of **Kilistra**, with its St Paul connections; and the ruined Byzantine churches and monasteries of the **Binbir Kilise** region.

Everything else to see from Konya is firmly **en route to Cappadocia**, a couple of hundred kilometres to the east. Depending on your available time, and your inclination, the journey can either take in the **Sultanhanı Kervansaray** (on the most direct route east) or, much more roundabout, the crater lake of **Acı Göl** and the isolated ancient site of **İvriz**.

Apart from Sille and (less easily) Çatal Höyük, which can both be visited by public transport, it goes without saying that you'll need your own transport to tour any of the sites scattered across the flat, fertile and relentless Konya plain.

Sille

Hidden in a canyon 8km northwest of Konya, **SİLLE** is accessible by the #64 city bus from the small bus garage on the ring road near the market. With your own vehicle, thread through the village, following the canal spanned by a series of tiny old bridges, until arriving at the bus's final stop, labelled "Son Durak". It's best to show up while school is in session – otherwise the village children can be particularly annoying.

A **Byzantine church** (Tues–Sun 9am–4pm; free), more impressive than handsome, stands visible just to the southwest. The brickwork of the drum dome surmounting the vast, boxy structure is obviously medieval. Inside, however, the naive nineteenth-century decor, collapsed icon screen and fairly well-preserved ceiling murals show that the church was in use until 1923. In the surrounding cliffs you can glimpse some hermitages.

Gökyurt and Kilistra

GÖKYURT, left off the Seydişehir road, 42km southwest of Konya, is a spectacularly situated traditional farming village, with views over a green valley reminiscent of the İlhara gorge. The village overlies **Kilistra** (unlocked; free), a church that has a claim to fame in a visit from St Paul (although it's nearby Lystra, which has less visible remains, that is the place quoted in the texts). On the hill is a charmingly complete rock-cut church of cruciform plan, of the early Byzantine/Christian era, and below it some troglodyte dwellings. It's worth walking down the hill from the village to see the hump-backed bridge carrying a cobbled road that St Paul may have trodden.

Çatal Höyük

Excavations of prehistoric tumuli at the important Neolithic site of **Çatal Höyük** continue under an international team - resident on site during the summer. This is the best time to visit, bearing in mind that there's little to see so you need a lively imagination. There are dolmuşes from Konya to the town of **Çumra**, 48km southeast, from where you will need to take a taxi to the site itself, 10km north of Çumra. With your own transport, leave Konya on the Karaman/Silifke road, Highway 715, and take a left to Çumra 2km before İçeri Çumra. The road to the site is marked in the town.

Discovered by the British archeologist James Mellaart in 1958, **the site** (open daylight hours; free) consists of twin, flattened hills that are supposed to resemble the shape of a fork, hence the name Çatal Höyük, or "Fork Tumulus". A number of exciting discoveries made here gave significant clues about one of the world's oldest civilizations. Thirteen strata have been identified, the earliest dating from 6800 BC, the latest from 5500 BC. Evidence pointed to entire complexes of houses, crammed together without streets to separate them, and entered through holes in the roof. Also found were murals of men being eaten by vultures, animal-head trophies stuffed with squeezed clay, and human bones wrapped in straw matting and placed under the seats in a burial chamber. There is also the world's first landscape painting, a mural depicting the eruption of a volcano, presumably nearby Hasan Dağa.

Most famous of all the discoveries are statuettes of the **mother goddess**, supposed to be related to the Phrygian goddess Cybele and her successor Artemis. The baked earthenware or stone figures are 5–10cm tall and show a large-breasted, broad-hipped woman crouching to give birth. The most interesting pieces are now in Ankara's Museum of Anatolian Civilizations (see p.695).

Binbir Kilise

Binbir Kilise, or "A Thousand and One Churches", is the name given to a remote region directly north of Karaman, itself 107km southeast of Konya.

Scattered across the base of the extinct volcano Kara Dağ are indeed close ›
that number of ruined churches and monasteries, mostly dating from the nin
to the eleventh centuries, when the region was a refuge for persecuted
Christians.

To get there, travel on the paved road 21km north from Karaman via Kılbasan,
and then turn left (northwest) on a rougher dirt track for 10km more towards
the village of **MADEN ŞEHİR**, in the middle of one of the main concentrations of basalt-built chapels. These, many in good condition, are all that's left of
a substantial, unidentified town that flourished from Hellenistic to Byzantine
times. If you're intrigued, and have a tough car, there's another abandoned town
to see, with a cluster of churches, at the hamlet known variously as **DEĞİLE**
or **DEĞLER**, about 8km to the west. Villagers at Maden Şehir may well offer
guiding services, and it's probably a good idea to take them up on it.

❼ Sultanhanı Kervansaray

The **Sultanhanı Kervansaray** (daily 7am–7pm; $0.70), 108km of dull driv-
ing from Konya on the Aksaray road, was one of the many public inns built by
the Selçuks during the reign of Alâeddin Keykubad, testifying to the importance placed on trade and social welfare by this highly cultured society. The
buildings date from 1229, but have been substantially restored, first by Mehmet
the Conqueror, evidence of the continued importance of this east–west trading route in the Ottoman period, and more recently by Turkish Radio and
Television, which used the *kervansaray* as the location for a historical drama.

The emphasis placed on security is clear from the high walls surrounding the
compound, and from the size of the **portal**, truly massive and impressively
ornate. Inside, the most prominent building is the small **mosque**, which takes
a central position raised high above the courtyard on four pillars, away from the
dangers of stray pack animals.

Animals were stabled opposite the entrance, in the enormous hall with five
cradle-vaulted naves divided by huge pillars. The height of this room suggests
accommodation for elephants rather than camels and mules, but it was meant
to convey an impression of might and vigour to the foreign merchants who
would stay here for up to three days completely free of charge. To either side
of the entrance were private rooms and dormitories for servants, a hamam,
workshops, a smithy and storerooms.

Practicalities

The best of the two **pension/campgrounds** in Sultanhanı village, a kilometre
or so southeast, is the *Kervan* (☎0382/242 2325, ✉kervancamping@mynet.com;
❷), run by a friendly, welcoming family; it has comfortable rooms, plus attractive
camping facilities on the lawn (a tent and two people will set you back $2) and
mother cooks a good evening meal, often eaten out in the garden. Much nearer
the *kervansaray*, the unimaginatively named *Kervansaray* (☎0382/242 2429; ❶) is
a little cheaper but not such good value. Both places cater more to groups and
RV-travellers than to independent travellers, though you'll be made welcome
enough.

Acı Göl and İvriz

Ninety kilometres east of Konya, just off Highway 330, there's a very beautiful
crater lake, **Acı Göl**. It lies just east of Karapınar, hidden from the road – the
turn-off is a narrow, unsignposted, white-dirt track a little way east of a
Türkpetrol truckstop on a knoll, about 11km after the Karapınar turn-off. You

Pansiyons and hotels

Almira Kayseri Cad 43 ☎0384/341 8990. Modern high-rise building with three-star hotel facilities, but pretty soulless; of most interest is the pool, which can be used by non-residents for $5. ❻

Asia Minor İstiklâl Cad ☎0384/341 4645, ⓔcappadocia50@hotmail.com. Offers a range of differently priced rooms in one of Ürgüp's oldest and loveliest buildings; there's an attractive garden courtyard. ❹

Elkep Evi 1 & 2 Eski Turban Oteli Arkası ☎0384/341 6000, ⓦwww.elkepevi.com. A recently opened pair of restored cave houses, with extremely comfortable cave or cellar rooms decorated with local handicrafts and antiques. ❼

Elvan Barbaros Hayrettin Sok 11 ☎0384/341 4191, ⓕ341 3455. An atmospheric en-famille experience in an old house up a cobbled side-street. Quiet, clean and characterful. ❸

Esbelli Evi Esbelli Mah 8 ☎0384/341 3395, ⓦwww.esbelli.com. The original features of this collection of village houses have been retained, and the rock-cut rooms are tastefully furnished with period furniture. The owner, Suha Ersöz, is knowledgeable about the area and you're invited to help yourself from the fridge in the kitchen, cook a meal and sit in a communal sitting room, listening to CDs. Breakfast is excellent and the views from the rooftop terrace delightful. ❻

Göreme Şato Şehit Turan Cad ☎0384/341 4022. Set in an old, fairly rundown, but characterful building; double rooms (some with baths) and camping space in the garden. ❶

Hitit İstiklâl Cad ☎0384/341 4481, ⓕ341 3620. A 600-year-old house owned by a charming family. The rooms, looking on to a pleasant courtyard, have attractive vaulted ceilings and Kayseri rugs, but otherwise furniture and fittings, which include central heating, are everyday and practical. ❸

Konak Esbelli Mah ☎0384/341 4667. Well kept and a good choice for families – children will enjoy the beds up on wooden platforms. Balconied rooms with large windows afford views of rock-cut houses and pigeon coops opposite. ❷

Sarıhan Güllüce Cad ☎0334/341 2264, ⓕ341 5820. Plain, simple and very clean rooms in a modern stone-built block, a family-run place in a quiet part of town. ❷

Sun Dead-end street leading off the western edge of the main square ☎0384/341 4493, ⓕ341 4774. Ramshackle affair with a pleasant terrace and a welcoming owner; some rooms are caves, and others have en-suite bathrooms. ❷

Surban Yunak Mah ☎0384/341 4761, ⓕ341 3223. Well-decorated, modern and comfortable, with neat bathrooms. Best-value choice for this price category. ❸

Campsite

Paris Camping Between Ürgüp and Göreme, 3km west of town ☎0384/343 2101, ⓕ343 2214. Has its own pool, restaurant, shop and bar, but is a little exposed.

The Town

Ürgüp may be carefully trimmed with fancy street lighting and cobbles, but before the tourists stir in the morning it is still a rural village, its streets taken over by men and women in traditional working clothes, leading horse-drawn vehicles and donkeys out to the surrounding vineyards, orchards and vegetable gardens. This is the time to explore the **old village**, whose buildings appear to be slowly emerging from the rocky hills into which they have been carved. Some feature stylish pillared and decorated facades of the same stone, others are simple caves with doors and windows cut into the cliffs themselves.

The walk up to the Temmeni "wishpoint" begins with a flight of steps opposite the thirteenth-century **Kebir Camii**. Local children hang around outside the mosque and may offer to act as your guide on the way up. It's worth taking up the offer, as they'll guide you through a 700-metre-long tunnel (original purpose unknown), which leads through the hill to a door and "balcony" on the other side, furnishing panoramic views of the town and surrounding countryside. Continuing uphill, past the former troglodyte town dwellings (now mainly used for storage or abandoned altogether), brings you to a park known as **Temmeni** ("Hill of Wishes"; daily 8.30am–6pm; $0.25), where a Selçuk tomb, the **Kılıç Arslan Türbe**, dating from 1268, is open to visitors. A small renovated *medrese* from the same period is now used as a café.

ÜRGÜP

▲ *Avanos*

◀ *Nevşehir*

OLD ÜRGÜP

AHMET REFIK CAD

Kebir Camii

Kılıç Arslan Türbe

TEMMENI

Museum

(i) **El Sanatlar Çarşısı**

KAYSERI CAD

Hamam

A

Mustafa Ağa Camii

Belediye

CUMHURIYET MEYD.

Otogar

MARKET PLACE

Duayeri Camii

SARAÇOĞLU SOK.

DÜMLÜPINAR CAD.

▶ *Kayseri*

Damsa River

N

RESTAURANTS	
Han Çirağan	A
Karakuş	F
Kardeşler Pizza	C
Ocakbası	D
Sömine	B
Yaprak	E

ACCOMMODATION	
Almira	5
Asia Minor	10
Elkep Evi	1
Elvan	9
Esbelli Evi	2
Göreme Şato	6
Hitit	7
Konak	4
Sarıhan	11
Sun	8
Surban	3

0   100 m

Sanayı Çarşısı

▼ *Mustafapaşa &* **F**

The town's **museum** (Tues–Sun 8am–5.30pm; $0.70) on Kayseri Caddesi is tiny and not particularly well labelled, but the helpful staff are prepared to explain the exhibits. These include a selection of prehistoric ceramics, figurines, lamps, stelae, statues and ornaments found during excavations in the area.

The town's main **shopping** strip, starting at Cumhuriyet Meydanı and continuing down Kayseri Caddesi, has some of the best carpets, jewellery and antiquities in the whole of Turkey. They're not necessarily cheaper here than in İstanbul, but Turkish traders from the east generally make the trip to Ürgüp before starting the journey up to İstanbul, so Ürgüp's shops have first pick of the merchandise. Muammer Sak of Aksa, opposite the tourist office on Kayseri Caddesi, stocks a fine range of antique **carpets and kilims** – among his customers are the Royal Scottish Museum and Liberty's – and is a mine of information on ancient designs and motifs. Other well-stocked outlets in the area include the **El Sanatlar Çarşısı** (the handicrafts market) on Kayseri Caddesi, Le Bazaar d'Orient, Kayseri Cad 32, run by the Güzelgöz, one of Ürgüp's oldest families, and Sultan Mehmet, which also stocks leather, ceramics and hookahs at fixed but reasonable prices. **Antiques**, especially silver, are also readily available, collected from nomad owners in the east of Turkey by Aziz Güzelgöz (also an accomplished *saz* player) of Antikite Aziz Baba, Kayseri Cad 28, and by Veli Kırcı of Antikite Veli Baba, Kayseri Cad 14.

Wine tasting is possible at any of Ürgüp's six wineries, but the best local wines are widely acknowledged to be those produced by the Turasan house in Esbelli, a kilometre northwest of the town centre, and by the welcoming and cheap Taskobirlik cooperative in a former *kervansaray* (also out of town, though they have a town-centre shop). It's worth remembering that white Cappadocian wines are much better than red; the reds are mixed with wines from other regions, and dyes are added. A comprehensive collection of local wine is available from Mahzen Şarap Evi on Cumhuriyet Meydanı.

Eating, drinking and nightlife

There's a decent selection of **restaurants**, from simple places serving traditional dishes to more tasteful places suitable for a night out. For snacks, there are several decent *pastane*s around Cumhuriyet Meydanı. Ürgüp's **nightlife** is also excellent when you consider that this is central Anatolia and there's not a beach in sight.

Restaurants

Han Çirağan Cumhuriyet Meyd. Atmospheric old house with a vine shaded garden. Serves simple regional food, such as *düğün çorbası* (wedding soup), *saç tava* (lamb, tomatoes and onions cooked and served on a wok) and *mantı* (Turkish ravioli). A full meal for around $7–10.

Karakuş Entertainment Centre Pancarlık valley, south of town on Mustafapaşa Cad ℡ 0384/341 5353. An elaborate underground restaurant-floorshow complex hewn out of soft rock. The $15 entrance fee gets you a substantial meal, unlimited wine, whirling dervishes, folk dancing and a disco. If you book with an agency in town (and unless you've got your own transport there's little choice) it will cost closer to $30.

Kardeşler Pizza Restaurant Dumlupınar Cad 9. Serves excellent crusty *pide* and beer, at around $5 for two people. Its sister *Kardeşler* restaurant on Cumhuriyet Meyd is famous for *guveç*, a stew cooked in a clay pot sealed with bread ($3).

Ocakbaşı Near the market place. Unpromisingly located up a flight of steps, serves traditional Turkish kebabs cooked over charcoal, and is very

popular with the locals for its quality food and reasonable prices (allow $5 for a substantial meal).

Şömine Cumhuriyet Meyd ℡ 0384/341 8442. Ürgüp's best restaurant, on a terrace above the main square; the service is friendly and the well-prepared food good value (allow $7–15 for a complete meal). Local specialities include *osbar* (haricot beans with pastrami) and *testi kebap* (a lamb and vegetable stew cooked slowly in the oven).

Yaprak Opposite the *otogar*. Cheap and cheerful restaurant serving *lahmacun*, kebabs and soups.

Bars

Barium Bar İstiklâl Cad 31. Occasional live bands and a good atmosphere.

Kaya Bar Cumhuriyet Meyd. Almost next door to the *Prokopi*, up a flight of stairs and with a pleasant terrace overlooking the square. Internet and *nargile* (hookah) service, and beers for $2.

Prokopi Pub Bar Cumhuriyet Meyd. Using the old Greek name for the town, it has a nice courtyard and cosy cellar bar, though it's rather pricy with beers at $3.

Listings

Banks and exchange Vakıf Bank (summer daily 8.30am–noon & 1.30–9.30pm; normal banking hours in winter), Kayseri Cad 38, opposite the tourist office, has an ATM. The central Ziraat Bankası has a 24hr currency exchange machine.

Bike rental Hepa, in the *otogar* (℡ 0384 341 4543), for mopeds from $18 a day; or Alpin, on Dağıstanlı Sok, for similarly priced scooters.

Car rental Avis, İstiklâl Cad, Belediye Pasajı ℡ 0384/341 2177; Europcar, İstiklâl Cad 10 ℡ 0384/341 4315; Eretna Tour, in the *otogar* ℡ 0384/341 3599; Tonnerre Travel Agency, İstiklâl

Cad, Belediye Pasajı ℡ 0384/341 4879.

Hamam İstiklâl Cad, for men and women (daily 9am–8pm, $6 including massage).

Hospital Posthane Cad ℡ 0384/341 4031.

Internet Kaya Bar on Cumhuriyet Meyd.

Newspapers English-language newspapers from Niyazi Kuruyemiş, on Kayseri Cad near Cumhuriyet Meyd.

Pharmacy Hulya Eczanesi, Açıkpazar Yeri 41, behind the *otogar*, is friendly, with some English spoken.

Police Opposite the PTT, in the centre.

Post office The PTT is on Posthane Cad (daily 8.30am–11pm for phone tokens and cards, 9am–5pm for ordinary business). Tours Most day-long tours covering İhlara and the underground cities are around $45, rising to $150 for three-day-trips to Nemrut/Urfa. Rock Valley, Terminal Karşısı, opposite the otogar (☎0384/341 8813, rockvalley@superonline.com), is a good local operator. Alan Turizm, in the Surban Hotel on the Nevşehir road (☎0384/341 4667), provides

walking tours in Cappadocia from $40, and trekking in the Kaçkar and Toros mountains. Argeus, İstiklâl Cad 13 (☎0384/341 4688, ✆inform@argeus.com.tr), has comprehensive tours to the Ihlara valley and Soğanlı ($70), plus trips to the Kaçkar mountains and winter skiing tours to Erciyes – all its guides speak English. Touring Cappadocia's landscape on horseback can be arranged via Beyaz Yele ($7 an hour, $50 a day; ☎0384/341 5175).

Mustafapaşa and around

The small village of **MUSTAFAPAŞA**, 6km south of Ürgüp, makes for a pleasant excursion. The charm of the place lies in the concentration of attractive carved house facades dating back a century or so, when it was known as Sinasos and home to a thriving Greek community; it is also central to a cluster of little-visited churches. Unfortunately, Mustafapaşa makes an awkward base for the surrounding area, unless you have some way of getting about: it's a nice bike ride, and there are a couple of municipality **buses** to and from Ürgüp, but nothing beyond that to the south.

In the centre of Mustafapaşa an attractively renovated *medrese* has been converted into a carpet workshop and salesroom, the *Kervansaray*. Here you can watch women weaving beautiful **silk carpets**, but in this instance beware of the word "co-operative". The women are low-waged, the work is damaging to their sight and the carpets are overpriced.

The church of **Ayios Vasilios** is located to the north of the village, beyond the *Hotel Pacha*; pick up the key from the makeshift **tourist office** (opening hours variable), next to the *Kervansaray* carpet shop, before setting out. The church has well-preserved frescoes, although the faces are damaged, and four rock-cut pillars. Another church, below Ayios Vasilios in the Üzengı Dere ravine, is the **Holy Cross**, partly rock-cut and partly masonry-built, with pre-Iconoclastic and tenth-century paintings including a most attractive Christ of the Second Coming.

On the other side of the village, passing through streets of houses cut by former Greek occupants into the tuff cliffs, is a monastery complex including the churches of **Aya Nicolas** and **Aya Stefanos**.

Practicalities

Two cheap **hotels** are the *Atasöy Hotel* (☎0384/353 5378; ❷), with comfort-able rooms with showers set round a courtyard, and the basic but clean and pleasant *Monastery* (☎0384/353 5005, ✆monasterypension@yahoo.com; ❷) – named after its original function – with bunk beds or mattresses on the floor and showers. Both lie at the bottom of the village, near the bridge.

Medium-priced options include the *Lamia Hotel* (☎0384/353 5413; ❸), with five homely rooms around a flowery courtyard, perched high above town at the end of a steep cobbled street with fine views. A slightly more expensive option is the wonderfully preserved *Old Greek House* (☎0384/353 5306, ✆353 3141; ❸). More than 120 years old, it was until 1923 the residence of the Greek mayor; several of the rooms have original murals and painted ceilings, and a tiny old chapel off the shady courtyard is now a Turkish bath. The hotel also has its own highly recommend **restaurant** serving Turkish specialities.

Camping is available at the *Pacha* campsite (with pool), attached to the *Pacha Hotel*, above the Üzenge Dere ravine – $2 per person with your tent, $3 with theirs. Turkish village **food** is served, and there's also a well-equipped kitchen for preparing your own.

South of Mustafapaşa

Along the Soğanlı road south from Mustafapaşa – there's no public transport – the fairy chimneys give way to a table mountain formation that is no less fantastic and surreal than preceding landscapes: the red canyon ridge that the road follows could be a backdrop for *Roadrunner*.

About 3km from Mustafapaşa, a precipitous dirt track marked *Alabalık tesisleri* leads to a tiny fish farm and **restaurant** serving oven-baked trout. To the right of the Soğanlı road, 5km from Mustafapaşa, lies the **Damsa Reservoir**, where it is possible to bathe from a small, sometimes crowded pay beach.

The next village along is **CEMİL**, a picturesque hamlet of tuff houses piled up against the cliffside. One and a half kilometres beyond the village, just off the road, lies the **Keşlik Kilesi monastery complex** – three churches, a wine press and a refectory. This is believed to be one of the earliest communal monastic establishments in the region. The watchman, who speaks some English, gives a worthwhile tour of the frescoes in the churches: the first, named after a prominent picture of the archangel Gabriel, includes depictions of the Last Supper, the Annunciation and the Flight to Egypt, all badly damaged and soot-blackened (a torch is essential); the church of St Michael has a wine cellar downstairs; while the church of St Stephen (seventh or eighth century) is the most beautiful of all, elaborately and unusually decorated. Non-figurative ornament includes stylized foliage and interlaced patterns reminiscent of Turkish kilims, and figurative designs include depictions of various fruits and animals, and three peacocks eating grapes.

Four kilometres further along the same road is the village of **TAŞKINPAŞA**. Here a fourteenth-century Selçuk mosque, the **Taşkınpaşa Camii**, is flanked by two hexagonal *türbe* (tombs). The original marble pillars and their disparate capitals are still in place, supporting the twin domes of the mosque, and the old Selçuk minaret can be reached by a set of steps, but the intricately carved *mihrab* and *mimber* for which the building was originally famed have now been removed to Ankara. Just beyond the village, to the left, you can see the remains of another Selçuk building believed to have been a **medrese**, with an attractively carved stone portal.

Ayvalı

Turning right just before Mustafapaşa, coming from Ürgüp, a little-used road leads 10km to the charming village of **AYVALİ**, where you can gain some idea of what Göreme and Ürgüp were like before tourism hit. Built in a narrow valley, it consists of cave houses, a rock-cut Byzantine church and an arched bridge of the same period. The *Gamirasu Hotel* (☎0384/354 5815, ✉gamirsu @hotmail.com; ❺), a combination of cave dwellings and old village houses down in the gorge, is the only place to stay. It's of a very high standard, with an emphasis on organic foods.

The Soğanlı valleys

One of the most spectacular sights this side of Ürgüp are the **Soğanlı valleys** (daily 8am–5/6pm; $1.50), 5km off the road from Taşkınpaşa to Yeşilhisar, and less than 20km from either. **SOĞANLI** itself is an attractive village in two parts, Yukarı (upper) and Aşağı (lower) Soğanlı, set into the side of a table-top mountain. Part of the place's charm derives from its inaccessibility; it's off the tour route of all but small local companies. There are just a couple of simple **restaurants**, a few stalls selling the village-made rag dolls, and one **hotel**; the tiny, basic and friendly *Emek Pansiyon* (☎0352/653 1029; ❶), with one double and one five-bed dormitory room, both fashioned from caves. There's no public transport to the village, and in winter it is often completely cut off by snow-drifts.

The Soğanlı valleys were continuously occupied from early Byzantine times to the thirteenth century, and are remarkable for the architecture of their churches and the beauty of the ninth- to thirteenth-century frescoes they contain. The name is supposed to derive from the Turkish *sona kaldı* (meaning "left to the end"), rather than "with onion", the literal meaning of *soğanlı*. This could be a reference to the fact that this was the last village to be taken during the Arab invasion of Cappadocia led by Battal Gazi in the sixth century.

The most interesting of the churches and monasteries are located in the right-hand valley (as you face Yukarı Soğanlı). To reach the two-storeyed **Kubbeli Kilise** ("Church with the Dome"), follow the footpath across a streambed from the village square, and proceed uphill through the village and along the side of the valley. This has perhaps the most interesting exterior of all the Cappadocian rock churches, its form – a conical dome that is the tip of a fairy chimney resting on a circular drum – being an imitation of a masonry structure. The **Saklı** (Hidden) **Kilise**, with frescoes of the apostles, is 100m before the Kubbeli Kilise, its door facing into the valley.

Descend to the road and then head up the other side of the valley to reach the **Meryem Ana Kilisesi** ("Church of the Virgin"), which has four apsidal chapels with frescoes and Iconoclastic decoration. The **Yılanlı Kilise** ("Church of the Snake") is best seen using a torch, as it is blackened and damaged by Greek and Armenian graffiti. It derives its name from an eleventh-century painting of St George slaying the dragon, to the left of the entrance. Returning towards the village, the **Karabaş Kilise** ("Church of the Black Head") has two adjoining apsidal chapels, the first of which has well-preserved tenth- and eleventh-century frescoes depicting scenes from the life of Christ.

In the second Soğanlı valley, reached by passing the restaurants of Yukarı Soğanlı, the **Geyikli Kilise** ("Church with the Deer") has two aisles that were decorated in the eleventh century, and derives its name from a damaged depiction of St Eustace with a poorly defined deer. Further up the valley the **Barbara Kilise**, a single-aisled basilica divided in two by a transverse arch, has an inscription dating it to the early tenth century.

Avanos and around

The old city of **AVANOS** clambers up hills overlooking the longest river in Turkey, the Kızılırmak. A magnificently "Red River" with a temper to match, the Kızılırmak appears after a good rainfall to be on the verge of bursting its banks. Avanos itself is a town of some character, separated from the rest of

Cappadocia by the river and distinguished from all other towns in Turkey by the distinctive earthenware pottery made here. The same red clay that colours the river has been worked for many centuries, and techniques dating right back to Hittite times are still in use. Strolling through the cobbled backstreets of the old town you'll find superb views out across the river – only slightly marred by the new housing development all too evident on the south bank. Exploration of the fields and hills around the town reveals further attractions: calcium pools and thermal springs, a tiny *kervansaray*, and even an underground city, 14km away at Özkonak.

Arrival, information and tours

Transportation to Avanos is good, with half-hourly **dolmuşes** from Ürgüp, Göreme and Nevşehir. From the **otogar**, cross the bridge into town and the **tourist office** (summer Mon–Fri 8am–noon & 1.30–7.30pm; winter Mon–Fri 8am–noon & 1.30 5pm; ☎0384/511 4360) is more or less immediately on your right. The **PTT** is located just beyond the pottery monument on the main street, Atatürk Caddesi, next to the public toilets. Uğur Mumcu Caddesi runs parallel to the river.

The best stable in the region is located in Avanos, so it's an ideal place to go **horseback riding**. They have twenty locally bred horses, a couple of which are quite sprightly (read "terrifying" if you're not a horsey inclination), though most are gentle and ideal for trekking. Costs are $6 hourly, $18 for a half-day or $30 for a full day; enquire at Chez Galip Pottery (see p.664). Kirkit Voyage, Atatürk Cad 50 (☎0384/511 3259, ⓦwww.kirkit.com), is an excellent **tour operator** that runs horseback trips, as well as bike and snowshoe tours all over Cappadocia.

Accommodation

It's easy enough to find **accommodation**, with a selection of hotels and *pansiyons* catering to most tastes and requirements. The *Venessa Pansiyon*, Atatürk Bul, Hafızağı Sok 20 (☎0384/511 3840, ⓦwww.katpatuka.org.com; ❸), is a rambling building with a bohemian atmosphere and wonderful views over the town and river. *Kirkit Pension*, off Atatürk Caddesi (☎0384/511 3148, ⓦwww .kirkit.com; ❸), belonging to the tour company of the same name, is a series of beautifully converted sandstone houses, decorated with kilims; rooms have either full bathrooms or just a shower. The *Sofa Hotel* (☎ & ⓕ0384/511 5156; ❺) is just next to the Haci Nuri Bey Konağı (an imposing neo-Ottoman mansion highly visible as you cross the bridge). The hotel has been put together from twenty redesigned Ottoman houses, with immaculate rooms, a garden courtyard and a restaurant. More upmarket, the *Irmak Hotel* (☎0384/511 4317, ⓦwww.avanosir-makhotel.com; ❼) makes the most of its secluded setting in extensive riverside gardens, but lacks character. Located a couple of kilometres southwest of the town, it's best reached by taxi.

Mesut **camping** ($2 a head), on the north bank of the Kızılırmak near the footbridge, has a restaurant with a *pide tandır* (an oven cut into the ground) on which the proprietor's wife cooks excellent *bazlama*, a kind of flat-bread sandwich. Another good bet is *Ada Camping* (☎0384/511 2429) on the south bank of the Kızılırmak, with its own pool.

The Town

Though the quaint, cobbled backstreets and rustic, tumbledown Ottoman, Armenian and Greek buildings are enjoyable, Avanos's real tourist attraction is pottery. The monument on the main street – a clay sculpture depicting a potter and, beneath it, a mother and daughter working a loom – is the town's celebration of its art (and of the other local craft of weaving), while the potters' square and the streets that surround it contain numerous tiny workshops where the Cappadocian potter's techniques can still be observed or even attempted. To reach this quarter, carry on walking past the monument for a few minutes, then turn right into the quarter at the Şanso-Panso restaurant.

Perhaps the most famous of all the Avanos potteries is **Chez Galip** (☎0384/511 4240, ℉511 4543), belonging to master potter Galip. It's generally thronged with groups, but if you arrive at a quiet time you may be shown into one of the back rooms where Galip stores hair collected over the years from his female visitors – countless locks trail from the ceiling and walls of a musty cave. A tour of the workshop reveals a cellar where some fifty to sixty tonnes of local red earth, collected from dried-up beds of the Kızılırmak, is stored awaiting the water that will transform it into malleable clay. The clay is worked on a wheel, turned by the foot of the potter, in natural light from the open doorway. Afterwards, the polished finish on the pots is achieved by a laborious process using the rounded end of a piece of metal, a technique thought to date back to Hittite times. The pots dry slowly in a storeroom upstairs, above the workshop, and later more quickly out in the open air. They are then fired in a wood-fired furnace at 950–1200°C for ten hours, and sometimes the firing is repeated to produce the distinctive blackened colour of some of the pots.

Galip is also involved in a movement to revive the production of fine ceramics in Turkey. His workshops, where young people are learning to throw, fire and decorate a range of designs, are called **Çeç**, and are located near the *Motif Restaurant* (see "Eating, drinking and nightlife" below); if you are interested in seeing the process, enquire at the main pottery. Chez Galip also runs **pottery and weaving courses** through the winter, with participants lodged in typical village houses and taught by local craftspeople. It's an excellent way of becoming acquainted with the Cappadocian lifestyle, and Galip and his wife are very welcoming.

Chez Güray, opposite Alâeddin Camii and the Atatürk statue, and **Chez Ömurlü**, adjacent to Chez Galip, have a mixture of avant-garde and traditional pottery, though the best – such as waist-high water coolers – are too difficult to take home.

Another local craft that deserves a mention is **knitting**. The shops in Uğur Mumcu Caddesi are full of beautiful, brightly coloured hand-knitted sweaters as well as a good selection of *şalvar* (harem pants), silver and carpets. The best selection of sweaters is at no. 66, at the Butik Famex, while silver, *şalvar* and semiprecious stones can be found further along towards the bridge at Chez Efe.

Eating, drinking and nightlife

Sofra, on the main street near the PTT, is a reasonably priced **restaurant**, serving *döner* and steamtray food in a friendly atmosphere. The *Tafana Pide Salonu*, Kenan Evren Cad 47, is also cheap, and serves a local speciality called *kiremit kebap* (lamb cooked on a pottery dish), as well as excellent *pide*. *Kibar Restaurant* on the south bank of the Kızılırmak has good food and great river views, as does the *Çalı* near the wooden bridge (Tahta Köprüsü). *Bizim Ev*, just behind the *Sofa Hotel*, is an atmospheric restaurant located in a well-restored Greek house. Specialities include *Bostan kebap*, a mix of aubergines, lamb and cheese cooked in a clay pot.

One of the best **nightclubs** in the region, the *Dragon* (☎0384/511 4486), is located in the area called Bezirhane, signposted off the Gülşehir road. The evening's programme is a familiar one, consisting of Turkish folk dancing and oriental (belly) dancing, followed by a disco. The caves are huge but popular with groups, so it's worth booking in advance. The caves here have been painstakingly carved out of tuff by another famous local potter, Mehmet İpekdere, who has a large and impressive pottery next door to the *Dragon*, where you can sup local wine from tiny clay vessels and watch Mehmet deftly throw another pot.

The *Motif Restaurant* (☎0384/511 2048), on the other side of the river from the town, signposted off the Nevşehir road beyond the *Irmak Hotel* at Hasan Kalesi Mevkii, has a well-established reputation for its **folk-dancing** programme and good food: $24 for meal and entertainment in a pleasantly relaxed atmosphere. For a less organized evening, the *Kervanhan Disco-Bar* off the main square has nightly *saz* and *özgün* music. The *Duygu Bar* on Atatürk Bulvarı plays good *halk* music and is popular with the locals, with beers around $1.50. The *Labirent*, set in the crumbling old houses above the town, occasionally sees sets from Erkin Koray, one of Turkey's most famous guitarists.

Özkonak

Özkonak (daily: summer 8am–7pm; winter 8am–5pm; $2.50), 14km north of Avanos off the Kayseri road, is one of the least-known and least-excavated underground cities in the Cappadocia region. Dolmuşes from Avanos leave hourly from beside the PTT.

In its present state it's not as interesting as Derinkuyu or Kaymaklı, but by the same token it's not as crowded. The city was discovered in 1972 by a muezzin, Latif Acar, who was trying to find out where the water disappeared to when he watered his crops. He discovered an underground room, which, later excavation revealed, belonged to a city with a capacity for sixty thousand people to exist underground for three months. Ten floors descend to a depth of 40m, though at present only four floors are open (to 15m), but throughout the village can be seen parts of rooms belonging to the first and second levels. These first two levels were used for food storage and wine fermentation, and a press and reservoir are labelled, as are mangers for stabled animals. Another typical feature is the stone doors, moved by wooden levers; above them was a small hole, through which boiling oil would have been poured on an enemy trying to break the soft sandstone door.

Southern Cappadocia

The majority of Cappadocia's visitors never get beyond the well-worn Nevşehir–Avanos–Ürgüp triangle, leaving **southern Cappadocia** far less charted and trampled. Although there's a consequent feeling of excitement about explorations made in this area, there's also less to be explored. The two major towns, **Aksaray** and **Niğde**, leave a lot to be desired as tourist centres, and the scenery is generally scrubby, barren steppe, more prone to cause depression than to recharge your holiday spirits.

The area does have its peculiarities and fascinations, however, and these are worth a degree of discomfort to experience. On the way to Niğde you can stop off at the underground cities of Derinkuyu and Kaymaklı (see p.644), located in a rain-washed basin between the central Anatolian plateau and the valleys of cones. Southwest of here is the **Ihlara valley**, where the Melendiz River, running between Aksaray and Niğde alongside the Melendiz mountain range, has created perhaps the most beautiful of all Cappadocian landscapes, a narrow ravine with almost vertical walls being cut ever deeper by the river that runs through it. Also easily accessible from Niğde is a small enclave of beautifully painted rock-cut churches belonging to the **Eski Gümüşler** monastery. South and east of Niğde the spectacular limestone spires of the **Aladağlar mountains** rear up from the plateau, affording excellent trekking and climbing.

Niğde and around

Despite a long history spent guarding the important mountain pass from Cappadocia to Cilicia, the small provincial town of **NİĞDE** has few remaining monuments of any great interest. Apart from a Selçuk fortress perched above the main street on a hill of tuff, and a couple of medieval mosques, the town looks as if it has been thrown together by people who were more interested in nomadic wandering than town planning. Nearby, however, is the Eski Gümüşler monastery complex, with its impressive, well-preserved frescoes – the only real reason for coming to Niğde unless you are en route to the Aladağlar mountains.

Niğde's **history** really began in the tenth century, when Tyana, the town that formerly controlled the pass between the Melendiz mountains to the west and the Toros mountains to the east, was ruined by Arab incursions. From then on Niğde – mentioned as early as Hittite times by the name of Nakida – took on the defensive role. Conquered by the Selçuks towards the end of the eleventh century, it was endowed with some attractive buildings during the reign of Alâeddin Keykubad. When the Arabian geographer Ibn Battuta visited the town in 1333, it was in ruins, probably as a result of the wars between the Mongols and the Karamanoğlu, the great rivals of the Ottoman dynasty. The Ottomans finally moved in in 1467, since when the town has been little more than a landmark on the Kayseri–Adana road.

The Town

The **citadel** was originally founded by the Selçuk sultan Alâeddin at the end of the eleventh century, but was restored by Işak Paşa in 1470, and the keep, all that remains today, probably dates from that time. On a mound to the south of the castle stands the **Alâeddin Camii**, dating from 1203 and later restored by Sultan Alâeddin. The facade is striped grey and yellow and there is a beautiful portal to the east, richly decorated with arabesques and sculpted designs. Below the mosque is the eighty-metre-long **bedesten**, a covered market street dating from the sixteenth and seventeenth centuries, and opposite this, on Nalbantlar Önüat at the foot of the citadel hill, is the fourteenth-century **Sungur Bey Camii**. Its portal is framed by geometrical mouldings, and above the door to the east of the prayer hall a rose window gives the mosque a Gothic look. At the other end of this street, approaching Vali Konağı Caddesi, is the **Akmedrese**, built in the Selçuk open-courtyard style with a white marble portal. It now serves as the town's **museum** (Tues–Sun 8.30am–5pm; $0.70); it's most famous for the Byzantine mummy of a nun, which is exhibited in a glass case to full hideous effect.

Practicalities

The **otogar** is 1km from the centre, off the Nevşehir-Adana highway, on Emin Eşirgil Caddesi, and there are frequent dolmuşes from here into town.

The **train station** is right on the highway, within sight of the citadel's clock-tower, a convenient marker for the centre. To get into town from here, cross the highway and take İstasyon Caddesi into the centre, a walk of ten minutes or so. The **tourist office** (Mon–Sat 8.30am–noon & 1.30–5.30pm; ☎0388/232 3393) is at Atatürk Meydanı 16, right in the town centre. To book a **trek in the Aladağlar mountains** (see p.668) go to Sobek Travel on İstasyon Caddesi (☎0388/213 2117, ✉sobek@kaynet.net), a well-established, reputable company, mainly dealing with package groups, so pre-booking would be sensible.

Reasonable **hotels** include the *Murat* at İstasyon Cad 46 (☎0388/213 3978; ❸), or the *Otel Nahita* on Terminal Caddesi (☎0388/232 5366; ❸), which is a little bit rundown, but has the advantage of being near the *otogar*. The *Otel Şahin,* El-Haci Mahmut Caddesi (☎0388/232 0951; ❹), is not worth the extra money, so if you're looking to spend a bit more try the *Yeni Otel Evim* on Hükümet Meydanı (☎0388/232 3536, ☎232 1526; ❻), which has reasonable rooms with showers, and offers substantial discounts if you're prepared to bargain.

Niğde's **restaurants** are very basic, concentrating on kebabs, *pide* and soups, with most of them clustered on the streets radiating out from Atatürk Meydanı and on the road leading to the railway station.

Eski Gümüşler monastery

The **Eski Gümüşler monastery** (daily: summer 9am–noon & 1.30–6.30pm; winter 8am–12.30pm & 1.30–5.30pm; $1) lies 6km east of town, off the Yeşilhisar road. To get there, take the white *Belediye* bus that leaves the Niğde *otogar* every 45 minutes for the village of Gümüşler. Gümüşler itself is attractively set in a valley surrounded by cherry orchards, but for the monastery you stay on the bus past it.

The monastery, rediscovered in 1963, has a deserved reputation for the excellent state of preservation of its paintings, which seem to have escaped Iconoclastic and other vandalism through the ages. Even the faces are intact, providing some of the finest examples of Byzantine painting yet to be discovered in Cappadocia.

The **main church**, with its tall, elegant pillars, is entered through an almost circular arched doorway opposite the entrance to the courtyard. Decorated with black-and-white geometric designs, the church contains beautiful frescoes in the most delicate greens, browns and blues. They include a Nativity scene complete with tiny animal heads peering in at the swaddled Jesus and the Magi, off to the left, and a tall, serene Madonna, framed in a rock-cut niche. The linear stylization of the figures is marked, the features are drawn boldly and simply, and the light and shade of draperies is reduced to monochrome.

The upstairs **sleeping quarters** were formerly reached by means of niches cut into the side of a shaft; now a metal ladder has been provided. The walls of the bedroom, which is complete with rock-cut beds, are decorated with a wolf, a deer, a lion, and a flamingo, being hunted by men with bows and arrows; there's also a depiction of a Roman soldier.

Connected to the church is a **wine press**, complete with metre-wide wine vats, and outside in the central courtyard there's a skeleton in its grave, protected under glass. Next to the graves are round holes in which precious belongings would have been buried. Other rooms excavated to date include a kitchen and underground baths reached down a set of steps, while below ground level are various chambers and a water reservoir.

The Aladağlar mountains

The **Aladağlar mountains** are part of the Toros range at the point where it swings north of the Mesopotamian plain. Occupying a north–south rectangle 35km by 20km, they are accessed by a minor road from Niğde to Pozantı via Çamardı; on the west they drop away to the Zeyhan River, but there is no access road from this side. Approached in the afternoon, the mountains form a spectacular pink skyline above the poplars of the valley. The six main summits are Büyük and Küçük Demirkazık (3756m and 3490m respectively), Embler (3723m), Kızılkaya (3725m) amd Kaldı (3736m) in a north–south line, and Vayvay (3600m), set back to the east.

The isolated gorges and lakes of the Aladağlar are a birdwatchers' paradise; best during the autumn migration – when the snow has melted and access is (relatively) easy – day-trips can be arranged via the *Şafak Pansiyon* (see below). *Yayla*s (mountain pastures) are used after snowmelt by nomad families and their flocks; black tents dot the upper valleys from June to September. The *Yörük* here are used to tourists and less welcoming than elsewhere in the Toros; you may, however, be able to buy yoghurt and cheese.

Practicalities

Access is by **minibus from Niğde** to Çamardı; there are four daily services from the *otogar* in summer, taking about an hour. Ask for the Demirkazık road or the driver will automatically put you off at the *Şafak Pansiyon*. If you have your own transport you could drive from Adana via Pozantı – look for the turning marked to Kamızlı. Otherwise, take one of the occasional dolmuşes that run from Pozantı to Çamardı. The best **trekking season** is May to June followed by September, when the weather is at its most dependable.

Accommodation close to the trailhead, just off the Niğde road, is provided by *Şafak Pansiyon* (☎0388/724 7039; ❶), in the hamlet of Çukurbağ, 4km east of Çamardı, which provides half-board in small rooms with bathrooms and with unreliable hot water but with excellent cooking. Close by, the *Öz Şafak* (no phone; ❶) offers similar facilities – a family feud having led to the setting up of this second *pansiyon*. The state-owned *Demirkazık Dağ Evi* (☎0388/724 72; ❷), a ski lodge at Demirkazık, is a few kilometres nearer the mountains (ask the dolmuş to drop you at the signed turn, from where it's a 3km walk) and provides larger rooms and dormitories ($5), though with less enjoyable catering. Coastal football clubs use it for high-altitude training, so it can be fully booked, especially just before the season starts. Prices depend very much on supply and demand; negotiate hard and if you feel they are overcharging, you can always use their **campsite** instead.

As soon as you have stocked up with food (preferably in Niğde) you can head off into the hills and camp near any suitable spring. Note that the Aladağlar mountains form a national park, and you will be charged an **entrance fee** ($0.35 per person, plus $0.60 per tent) if you enter on one of the major tracks when there is a warden about. It is better to pay up as the authorities are then more likely to be able to find you should you fail to emerge.

By far the most popular way up to the peaks is via the **Embler valley**, where, in season, there are permanent base camps run by Sobek Travel (see "Niğde: Practicalities" on p.666). From here you can take day walks up many of the peaks, and also cross into the **Korokot valley** on the east, or walk the north–south section of the range, emerging on the **Aciman plateau**. At the end of both these routes you have to hitchhike or catch a rare dolmuş to Adana.

For walking alone, the tourist office in Niğde has some acceptable **maps**, while a technical **guide** (see Contexts, p.1082) in English and Turkish is published by Redhouse and available from Redhouse Books in Turkey. Ali Şafak, owner of the *Şafak Pansiyon*, can arrange guided **one-day walks** or transport by tractor for groups of birdwatchers, but people have reported being asked in excess of $100 for the trip.

Aksaray

Huddled in an oasis on the Melendiz River, on the far side of the Melendiz mountain range from Niğde, **AKSARAY** is a market town with no real interest except as a base for reaching the Ihlara valley. Although no trace of the ancient city survives, Aksaray probably occupies the site of the Byzantine town Archelais. It was captured by the Selçuks in the eleventh century, then passed to the Mongols in the middle of the thirteenth century, but when the power of the Mongols began to wane the Karamanoğlu took possession in the fourteenth century. After the fall of Constantinople in 1453, part of the population of Aksaray was transferred to the capital, a repopulation programme that was a measure of how weak the Byzantine city had become before the final collapse of its empire. The displaced people named the district of İstanbul in which they settled after their hometown, a name which that lively suburb still retains.

The main square, with its Atatürk statue and restored public buildings, is the only really impressive sight in town, the rest is a mere sprawl of apartment buildings with some evidence of local wealth.

Practicalities

Aksaray is linked by regular bus with Niğde, 110km southeast (2hr), and Nevşehir, 85km north (1hr 30min). The **otogar** is some 6km west of the town centre, linked by service bus or the blue *Belediye* bus. If you arrive late, you may have to take a taxi into town. The **tourist office** (Mon–Sat 8am–noon & 1.30–5.30pm; ☎0382/213 2474), at Kadioğlu Sok 1, is in a nicely restored Ottoman building a couple of minutes' signed walk from the main square.

Accommodation is limited, but you might need to stay over before making the onward trip to Ihlara. A couple of simple options, both en-suite, are located behind the *Vilayet* building off Hükümet Meydanı: *Otel Çakir Ipek* on Kizilay Caddesi (☎0382/213 7053; ❷), and the nearby, clean *Hotel Yoğuran* at Hükümet Cad 3 (☎0382/213 5490; ❸). The *Tez Canlar Hotel* on Kızılay Caddesi (☎0382/213 8482, ☏215 1234; ❷) has TVs in the rooms, but given the prices you may as well trade up to the best hotel in town, the *Otel Yuvam* (☎0382/212 0024; ❸). The *Yuvam* occupies a renovated old town house next to the Kurşunlu Camii at Eski Sanayı Caddesi; rooms are attractively furnished and clean, with modern bathrooms. There is nowhere exciting to eat in Aksaray; try the basic **kebab places** around Hükümet Meydanı.

The Ihlara valley

A fertile gorge cut by a deep green river between red cliffs, the **Ihlara valley** is as beautiful a place as you could conceive. If you add some of the most attractive and interesting churches and rock-carved villages in the Cappadocia region, it's hard to believe that the valley hasn't been touristed off the map. It may be that the end of paradise is already in sight: telltale litter is starting to appear on the riverbanks and frescoes have suffered terrible damage in recent years. Restraint and common sense may prevail, but if you want to be sure of seeing the place before things get out of hand, try to visit now.

Minibuses to Ihlara village leave from Aksaray *otogar* three times daily, passing Selime and the turn-off to Belisırma, and returning the same day. A **taxi** from Aksaray to Ihlara costs $15 (round trip, $25) – you can also arrange to be picked up in Belisırma or Selime after you have completed your walk. In addition, there are six dolmuşes daily from Aksaray to Güzelyurt, and frequent dolmuş connections between Güzelyurt and Ihlara. A large enough group could rent a whole minibus either from the drivers in Aksaray *otogar* or from Ürgüp (you'll need about ten people to make it viable). There are three **entry points to the valley**, at Ihlara village, Belisırma and Selime (each open daily 8am–6pm; $3). It's possible to gain entry outside these times, in which case you should pay on exit.

If you have time, it's satisfying to do the trip **independently**, taking a dolmuş to Selime and walking the 6km to Belisırma for an overnight stop, then completing the 10km to Ihlara village via the majority of churches the following day, and catching the dolmuş back to Aksaray from Ihlara. If you're returning to central Cappadocia, you could try asking a private tour bus from there for a lift back, for which they should ask only a small fee. Most of the **tour operators** in the Cappadocia region offer day or longer trips to Ihlara, but there is no reason why you shouldn't base yourself in either Selime or Ihlara and do your own thing.

Selime

One of the most beautiful parts of the whole valley, the troglodyte village of **SELİME** has previously been passed over in favour of the better-known, more frequented Ihlara village area. It's the first village you pass on the way to Ihlara or to the official entry to the valley, and it's worth at least a couple of hours' visit, if not a stopover in one of the valley's best **hotels**. The *Piri Motel and Camping* (☎0382/454 5114; ❷) offers spotless, comfortable rooms, and its owner Mustafa is willing to act as a guide to the surrounding churches. The less conveniently located *Çatlak Pension* (☎0382/454 5065; ❷) has reasonable rooms and offers **camping**, but is a long walk from Selime's attractions.

A number of massive, rather squat **fairy chimneys** dot the valley at Selime, many of them containing churches, and there's even a rock-cut cathedral, divided into three aisles by irregularly shaped pillars. Locals will also show you where a few minutes of footage from the original *Star Wars* movie were shot. The village takes its name from a Selçuk **mausoleum** in the village cemetery, with a pyramidical roof inscribed "Selime Sultan", a dedication of unknown origin.

Belisırma

The troglodyte village of **BELİSIRMA** blends in with the tawny rock-face from which it was carved to such an extent that in a bad light it can all but disappear from view. Its tranquil riverside location provides the opportunity to rest at a table in the water at one of the simple tree-shaded restaurants on the west bank.

Access to Belisırma from the Ihlara–Selime road is complicated by the fact that the sign is frequently removed: just over a kilometre south of Yaprakhisar, turn off to the left down a winding two-kilometre-long asphalt road. The most rewarding way to reach Belisırma, however, is to **walk along the valley**, either from Selime (1.5hr) or from Ihlara village (2hr) – from the latter, you can take in the majority of the valley churches.

Belisırma village is home to two primitive **campsites**: *Valley Anatolia* has tents for rent and an excellent **restaurant** where you can eat trout or *saç*

THE IHLARA VALLEY

Aksaray

Selime

Yaprakhisar

Aksaray & Güzelyurt

Ziga Hamam

Melendiz River

Belisırma

Direkli Kilise
Bahattin Kilisesi
Church of St George

Karagedik Kilise

Yılanlı Kilise
Bridge
Sümbüllü Kilise   Steps
Ağaçaltı Kilise   Pürenli Seki Kilise

Kokar Kilise

N

Ihlara

Güzelyurt

0   1 km

kavurma very cheaply, while the *Aslan* (☎0382/213 3780) also has a riverside restaurant. There is a small **pension** in the village, the *Ev* (☎0382/457 3037; ❶), near the mosque. From Belisırma, it's another 2.5km to the village of Ziga, where hot springs feed a **hamam** (daily 8am–10pm; $1).

Around Belisırma, the eleventh-century **Direkli Kilise** ("Church with the Columns") has fine examples of Byzantine frescoes, including a beautiful long-fingered Madonna and Child on one of the columns from which the church takes its name, and a picture of St George fighting a three-headed dragon.

The **church of St George**, 50m up the cliffside, a half-kilometre south of Belisırma and 3km from the stairs at the main entrance, was dedicated to the saint by a thirteenth-century Christian emir, Basil Giagoupes, who was in the army of Mesut II. It bears an inscription expressing Christian gratitude for the religious tolerance of the Selçuk Turks. St George is depicted in armour and cloak, holding a triangular shield and flanked by the donor and his wife Tamara, who is handing a model of the church to the saint. To the right of this oblation scene, St George can be seen in action, killing a three-headed serpent, with an inscription above that reads "Cleanse my soul of sins."

Ihlara village

Best known of the quaint villages in the valley bottom, **IHLARA** is slightly more developed than its rivals. However, its few *pansiyons* are still devoted to the kind of backpacking tourists who have scant regard for such luxuries of life as hot water, towels and carpeted rooms – an asceticism that keeps the large commercial tour parties away, at least after dark.

Set by the river in the centre of the village, the *Star* (T0382/453 7676; **②**) is overpriced for its clean, but waterless, rooms. To compensate, its location is the best in İhlara. On the lip of the valley are four more **pensions**. The modern, well-built *Akar Pansiyon* (T0382/453 7018, F453 7511; **②**), just off the road to the main valley entrance, is the best – clean and quiet, with comfortable doubles and a basic restaurant attached. The owner speaks good English and will arrange for you to be picked up from the Selime exit of the valley. Nearer to the valley entrance, the friendly *Anatolia Pansiyon* (T0382/453 7440, F453 7439; **②**) also makes a comfortable base. Both these *pansiyons* offer **camping** in their gardens.

The **hamam** (daily 10am–10pm; $0.50), reached down a set of steps behind the mosque on the road out of the village, is served by natural hot springs.

The main churches

The monastic occupation of the Ihlara valley, or **Peristrema** as it was originally known, seems to have been continuous from early medieval times until the fourteenth century, a long period of use reflected in the numerous adaptations and restorations of the churches. It would seem from the decoration of the churches, whose development can be traced through pre- and post-Iconoclastic periods, that the valley was little affected by the religious disputes of the period. Paintings show both eastern and western influence, so that some figures wear Arab striped robes, whereas others resemble those in Byzantine frescoes in Europe.

Descending from the **main entrance**, midway between Ilhara and Belisırma, down several hundred **steps** to the valley floor 150m below, is precipitous, but manageable. The most interesting of the churches are located near the small wooden **bridge** at the bottom of the flight of steps. It's also possible to walk from Ihlara village along the southwest bank of the river to the bridge, or from Belisırma to the northwest keeping to the same side of the river. Walking from either village to this point takes about an hour and a half, a fairly straightforward hike that's well worthwhile for the tremendous sense of solitude.

At the bottom of the steps is a plan showing all the accessible churches, most of which are easy enough to find. To the right of the bridge, on the same side as the steps, is the **Ağaçaltı Kilise** ("Church under the Tree"). Cross-shaped with a central dome, the church originally had three levels, but two of them have collapsed, as has the entrance hall. The most impressive of the well-preserved frescoes inside depict the Magi presenting gifts at the Nativity, Daniel with the lions (opposite the entrance in the west arm) and, in the central dome, the Ascension. The colours are red, blue and grey, and the pictures, naive in their execution, suggest influence from Sassanid Iran, particularly in the frieze of winged griffins. Unfortunately, in recent years these frescoes have suffered serious damage.

The **Pürenli Seki Kilise** lies 500m beyond this, also on the south bank, and can be seen clearly from the river, 30m up the cliffside. The badly damaged frescoes here mainly depict scenes from the life of Christ. Another 50m towards Ihlara, the **Kokar Kilise** is relatively easy to reach up a set of steps. Scenes from the Bible in the main hall include the Annunciation, the Nativity, the Flight into Egypt and the Last Supper. In the centre of the dome, a picture of a hand represents the Trinity and the sanctification.

One of the most fascinating of all the churches in the valley is located across the wooden footbridge, about 100m from the stairs. The **Yılanlı Kilise** ("Church of the Snakes") contains strikingly unusual depictions of sinners suffering in hell. Four female sinners are being bitten by snakes: one of them on the nipples as a punishment for not breast-feeding her young; another is covered in eight snakes; and the other two are being punished for slander and for not heeding good advice. At the centre of the scene a three-headed snake is positioned behind one of the few Cappadocian depictions of Satan; in each of the snake's mouths is a soul destined for hell.

Another church worth exploring is **Sümbüllü Kilise** ("Church of the Hyacinths"), just 200m from the entrance steps. The church shows Greek influence in its badly damaged frescoes and has an attractive facade decorated with blind horseshoe niches.

Güzelyurt

GÜZELYURT, the nearest small town to the Ihlara valley, 13km northeast of Ilhara village, provides an opportunity to catch a glimpse of the old, untouched Cappadocia, and to stay in the best hotel in the region. If that isn't enough incentive, there are good dolmuş connections with Aksaray and Ihlara, and plenty of sites worth visiting in the town and within easy walking distance.

The beautiful *Karballa* **hotel** on the main square (☎0382/451 2103, ⓦwww.kirkit.com; ④) occupies a nineteenth-century Greek monastery. The monks' cells are now bedrooms, with central heating and individual bathrooms now added, the refectory has become an excellent **restaurant**, and there's a small pool. The *Hotel Karvallı* (☎0382/451 2736, ⓔkhl-turizm@superonline .com; ❸), on the southern outskirts of the town, has comfortable rooms in a new, but traditionally styled, building that has stunning views over a small lake, Yüksek Kilise (see overleaf) and Hasan Dağı. Near the *jandarma* post in the town *Halil's Family Pension* (☎0382/451 2707; ❷) has a couple of spotless rooms in a genuine Turkish home, where you eat from a *sofra* table with the welcoming family. It's great value as the price includes breakfast and an evening meal.

The important religious community of Güzelyurt was established by St Gregory of Nazianzen in the fourth century, and a church dedicated to him, called **Cami Kilise** by locals, is located a short walk from the main street, past the PTT and mosque, on Kör Sokak. Renovated several times by the town's Greek community, the church is now in line for further work, with plans to turn it into a museum. A golden bell given to the church by a Russian Orthodox community in Odessa is now in Afyon museum, but other items of interior decor, such as a carved wooden iconostasis and chair, gifts from Tsar Nicholas I in the eighteenth century, can still be seen *in situ*. In place of the bell-tower now stands a brick minaret, dating from the church's conversion to a mosque after the departure of the Greeks in 1923. Elsewhere on Kör Sokak and in the **old town** around it are still-inhabited troglodyte dwellings and old Greek houses with beautifully carved facades.

The most impressive sight in the Güzelyurt area, however, has to be "**Monastery Valley**", below the town to the northeast, approached by taking a right turn out of the village after the Cami Kilise. The valley is riddled with over fifty rock-cut churches and monastery complexes – some dating from the Byzantine era – of which the most attractive is the nineteenth-century **Yüksek Kilise** ("High Church"), dramatically located on a high rock. A walk up the entire 4.5-kilometre-long valley takes about two and a half hours, and brings you to the village of **Sivrihisar**. From there, a signposted fifteen-minute walk south leads to a freestanding church of note, the sixth- or seventh-century **Kızıl Kilise** ("Red Church"), one of the few remaining churches containing masonry in the whole of Cappadocia.

⑦ Kayseri and around

Green fields, wooded hills and a snow-capped volcano surround the modern-looking concrete that is today's **KAYSERI**, encircling an old Selçuk settlement of black volcanic stone. The city has a reputation for religious conservatism and ultra-nationalism; it's the heartland of the Milli Hareket Partisi, the nearest thing there is to a fascist party in the country. In spite of this, there's a gentle acceptance of the waywardness of foreigners. It's also a thriving business centre, where traditional commerce, particularly raw textiles and carpets, still flourishes in the medieval *hans*. The long history and strategic importance of the town have left it with a littering of impressive monuments, while two nearby attractions are Sultansazlığı bird sanctuary and Mount Erciyes, ideal for picnics in summer and skiing in winter.

Some history

Ancient civilization in the region dates back to the fourth millennium BC and a Chalcolithic site at **Kültepe**, 21km from Kayseri on the road to Sivas. During the early Hittite period the site was composed of two settlements: **Kanesh**, the capital of the kingdom of the same name, probably the most powerful in Anatolia in its time; and **Karum**, which was established by Assyrian merchants as a bazaar, one of the oldest in the world.

The site of present-day Kayseri was originally called Mazaka. Its origins are unknown, but the city gained importance under the rule of the Phrygians. In 17–18 AD it was named **Caesarea** in honour of Emperor Tiberius, and at the same time it became the capital of the Roman province of Cappadocia. Captured by the Persians after the battle of Edessa (Urfa), it was quickly regained by the Romans. As part of the Byzantine Empire, Caesarea was relocated 2km to the north of the ancient acropolis, allegedly around a church and monastery that had been built by St Basil, the founder of eastern monasticism and a bishop of Caesarea in the fourth century. The position was strategic in terms of both trade and defence, and it soon became a leading cultural and artistic centre, though always vulnerable to attack from the east. The Arab invasions of the seventh and eighth centuries were particularly threatening, and in 1067 it finally fell to the great Selçuk leader Kılıç Arslan II. The town became capital of a powerful Danişmend emirate, which included Cappadocia, Sivas and Amasya. In 1097 the Crusaders were in brief possession and it was ruled equally briefly by the Mongols in 1243. Passing through the hands of various Turkish chiefs, it came into the possession of Beyazit I in 1397, but when he was defeated by Tamerlane at the battle of Angora the city was occupied by the

ACCOMMODATION

Burç	3
Grand Eras	5
Hunat	1
Kadıoğlu	4
Titiz	2

CAFÉS & RESTAURANTS

Bebek Et Lokantası	D
Bizim Sofra	A
Divan Pastanesi	F
İskender Kebab Salonu	E
Sultanahmet Köftecisi	C
Tuana	B

KAYSERI   0   100 m

Karamanoğlu and then the Mamluks before finally becoming part of the Ottoman Empire in 1515, under Selim the Grim.

The City

Part of the delight of Kayseri is that its beautiful old buildings still play an important part in the everyday life of the place, their very exsistence witness to the social conscience of the Selçuks. Koranic teaching forbade excessive concern with private houses, so public figures poured money into buildings for public welfare and communal activities.

Other buildings still integral to Kayseri's life are the covered markets; there are three in the town centre, all dating from different periods. The **Bedesten**, built in 1497, was originally used by cloth-sellers but is now a carpet market; the **Vezir Hanı**, built by Damat İbrahim Paşa in 1727, is where raw cotton, wool and Kayseri carpets are sold, and leather is prepared for wholesale; while the recently restored **covered bazaar** in the same area, built in 1859, has five hundred individual shops. Bargain hard: stories can be heard all over Turkey about how hard-nosed the businessmen of Kayseri can be. (The one about a Kayseri man stealing a donkey, painting it and selling it back to its owner has become even more hostile in recent years: the man now abducts his mother, paints her up and sells her back to his father.)

The towering crenellated walls of the **citadel**, built from black volcanic rock, are a good place to start exploring, since the life of the town seems to centre

675

on this point. A sixth-century fortress erected in the reign of the emperor Justinian once stood here, but the citadel you see was built in 1224 by the Selçuk Sultan Keykubad, and has been much restored since, particularly by Mehmet II, who also built the **Fatih Camii**, the small mosque near the southwest gate.

Near the citadel, **Hunat Hatun** *külliye* was the first mosque complex to be built by the Selçuks in Anatolia (construction began in 1239). It consists of a thirteenth-century mosque and *medrese*, the latter one of the most beautiful examples of Selçuk architecture in Turkey. This former theological college has an open courtyard and two *eyvans* (vaulted chambers open at the front). A wooden box containing a hair reputed to be from the Prophet Mohammed is to be found near the beautifully decorated *mihrab*.

Beyond the market area is the first of several ancient mosques in the city, the **Ulu Cami**, or Great Mosque. Constructed under the Danizmend Turkish emirs in the first half of the thirteenth century, the mosque, which can be entered from three sides, is still in remarkably good condition. Its roof is supported by four rows of stone pillars with varied marble capitals, and it retains its original carved wooden *mimber*, although the central dome is modern.

Kayseri has been described as the **city of mausoleums** because of its large number of tombs: curious, squat, beautifully carved bits of masonry known as *kümbets*, dating from the twelfth to fourteenth centuries, which can be found scattered about in the most unlikely places – a couple of them are on traffic islands on the main highway to Mount Erciyes. They are graceful constructions, generally two-storeyed, with the burial chamber and sumptuous coffin located in the upper storey. It is supposed that the design was modelled on the *yurt*, a conical tent imported from Central Asia. The best known of them in Kayseri is the **Döner Kümbet**, "turning tomb", a typical example probably dating to around 1275, built for Shah Cihan Hatun. The tomb is decorated with arabesques and palmettes, and a tree of life with twin-headed eagles and lions beneath.

The Gürgüpoğlu House

The **Gürgüpoğlu House** (Gürgüpoğlu Konağı; daily 8.30am–noon & 1.30–5.30pm; $0.70), just inside the city walls off Turan Caddesi, is a restored, half-timbered fifteenth-century Ottoman family home used as a museum of ethnography, complete with tableaux of wax dummies. The first room is a typical Turkish salon, its walls intricately painted using natural dyes, with models seated on low divans, holding musical instruments. The guest room upstairs has a beautiful carved and painted wooden ceiling. You'll also be escorted round a bride's room (labelled in Turkish but the scene is fairly self-explanatory) and the kitchen. Ethnographic exhibits include beautiful Selçuk tiles from the Hunat Hatun, carpets and kilims and a *topak ev*, or nomad's tent.

Kayseri Museum

Kayseri Museum on Kışla Caddesi (Kayseri Müzesi; Tues–Sun 8.30am–5.30pm; $0.70) contains important finds from Kültepe (see p.680) and is extremely well labelled in English. The first room deals with the Hittites, their cuneiform writing and hieroglyphics, and includes a fascinating Hittite rock relief from Develi and the head of a sphinx. Items from Kültepe include early Bronze Age depictions of the mother goddess, Assyrian bowls and jugs in the shape of animals, dating from the second millennium BC, and a collection of clay tablets in their clay envelopes – essentially small cheques – from the same period.

In the second room are finds from around Kayseri itself, including Hellenistic and Roman jewellery, and grave gifts from a Roman tumulus, among them highly worked pieces in gold and silver. In the garden is a pair of lovely seventh-century BC Hittite lions, with all their own teeth, from Göllüdağ near Niğde.

Surp Krikor Lusuvoriç

The substantial Armenian church of **Surp Krikor Lusuvoriç**, a half-hour walk out of town on the Hacılar/Erciyes road (ask the tourist office for directions), is the last architectural reminder of just how important Kayseri was in the Byzantine Christian world. Dating from around 700 AD, it is said to be Turkey's largest consecrated church, and can hold a congregation of a thousand, though at present services are held just twice a year, on March 16 and June 16. The worshippers are largely diaspora Armenians from İstanbul and elsewhere (only around fifty Armenians still live in Kayseri), who hold this church in high regard as Surp Krikor (St Gregory), the first bishop and official founder of the Armenian Church, spent much of his early life here. The church is easily recognizable by its large dome and cross, though the old Greek and Armenian houses that surround it are being bulldozed for new apartment buildings and a road. To gain entry, ring the bell and the caretakers, a friendly Armenian family from İstanbul, will be happy to let you look around.

Practicalities

To get into town from the **otogar**, take the "Terminal" dolmuş from the opposite side of Osman Kavuncu Caddesi. Minibuses to and from Ürgüp use the minbus station instead, a few hundred metres down the road towards town. The **train station** is 1km out of town at the end of Atatürk Bulvarı: "Terminal" dolmuşes into town – and to the *otogar* in the other direction – pass frequently. THY (Turkish Airlines) has an office at Yıldırım Cad 1 (☎0352/222 3858), with a service bus to and from the **airport** ($0.70), 15km southeast of town, which leaves 45 minutes before check-in time. An Argeus tour agency minibus (see "Ürgüp: Listings", p.659) also meets flights if requested and will deposit you in the village of your choice in Cappadocia. This costs $5 per person to Ürgüp, for example, otherwise you'll be at the mercy of Kayseri's taxi mafia.

The central **tourist office** (daily: summer 8.30am–noon & 1–5.30pm; winter 8am–noon & 1–5pm; ☎0452/222 3903) is next to the Hunat Hatun complex. They have train, plane and bus timetables, hotel and restaurant lists, and the latest on the Mount Erciyes ski resort. The **banks**, **ATMs** and *döviz* are mainly found on Nazmi Toker (Bankalar) Caddesi, though Iş Bankası has an ATM on Sivas Caddesi.

Accommodation

The *Hunat Otel*, behind the Hunat Hatun complex (☎0352/232 4319; ❶), is the best budget option. Quiet, convenient and clean, its en-suite rooms have pleasant views of the mosque and the management is very friendly. Mid-range hotels include the *Kadıoğlu Oteli* on İnönü Bulvarı (☎0352/231 6320, ℻222 8296; ❸), a noisy option, though some rooms have mountain views. The good-value *Hotel Titiz*, Maarif Cad 7 (☎0352/222 5040, ℻222 5542; ❸), has small but nicely furnished rooms, with TVs, fridges and tiny bathrooms. Or try the *Hotel Burç*, on Çevik Sokak (☎0532/2224364, ✉Burcotel@ttnet.net.tr; ❸), which has clean, comfortable rooms and is very central.

A luxury choice, a little way out of the town centre en route to the Armenian church, is the *Grand Eras Hotel* (☎0532/330 5111, ⓦwww.granderashotel.com;

❸), with all the four-star facilities you'd expect, if rather more glitz than perhaps you'd want.

Eating, drinking and entertainment

Although more famous for its spicy, garlicky *pastırma* (cured meat), *sucuk* (a kind of sausage-like salami) and *mantı* (perhaps the original ravioli) than for its actual **restaurants**, Kayseri does have some decent eateries.

First stop should be the *Bizim Sofra* on Ahı Evran Caddesi, opposite the Onay Sinemasi (from Sivas Caddesi, turn left opposite the Atatürk stadium and cut down an alley past the Melikgazi Hastanesi). Unusually for anywhere in Turkey, never mind conservative Kayseri, you'll be cooked for, and served by, women. The *Kayseri mantı* with yoghurt and garlic is delicious (eat it sprinkled liberally with *sumac*, mint and crushed chilli; *yaprak sarması* (grape leaves stuffed with spicy rice, served in a rich tomato sauce) is another speciality, and you won't spend more than $3. The immaculately clean, air-conditioned *Tuana Restaurant* near the PTT on Sivas Caddesi, serves reasonably priced kebabs, fresh fish, *mantı* and desserts, and has good views across to Mount Erciyes. The *Bebek Et Lokantası*, Nazmi Töker (Bankalar) Cad 9, is a more upmarket option, very popular with the locals and offering the widest variety of dishes in town. The *günün yemeği* (speciality of the day) is reasonable value at $1.50, but portions are small. Otherwise an old favourite is the *İskender Kebab Salonu* at Millet Cad 5, across from the Hunat Hatun complex. Near the *Tuana*, *Sultanahmet Köftecisi* is good for *köfte*, kebabs and burgers, while the air-conditioned *Divan Pastanesi* on Millet Caddesi is the place to eat ice cream and cakes.

A fifteen-minute walk out of town along Sivas Caddesi (or a two-minute bus ride) will bring you to the gleaming **Kasseria shopping centre**. Here, films (usually the latest Hollywood fare, in English) are shown at the four-screen **Kasseria Sinemaları** (performances start at around 11.30am, with last showings at about 9pm).

Erciyes Dağı

Erciyes Dağı, the 3916-metre-high extinct volcano dominating the city to the southwest, is one of the greatest pleasures the area offers. If you have transport, take a packed lunch and head for the foothills of Erciyes, a twenty-minute drive out of town. Otherwise, the Develi-bound dolmuş, which you can catch from near the Han Camii on Talas Caddesi, will take you to Tekir Yaylası, at an altitude of 2150m. Here you'll find *Kayak Evi*, a **ski lodge** run by Kayseri council (℡0352/342 2031; $10 per person in summer, including breakfast; $15 during ski season). The *Dedeman* chain also has an expensive hotel on the mountain (℡0352/342 2116, ℻342 2117; ❸) – closed for restoration at the time of writing. **Ski season** runs from December to May, and there's a chair lift from the *Kayak Evi* to the slopes. **Ski rental** is under $10 per day (ski clothes also available).

Once you get beyond the foothills, Erciyes is a harsh mountain, with little vegetation to soften its contours. For potential climbers, the two most reasonable routes start at the *Kayak Evi*, but even in summer Erciyes can be difficult and dangerous, with snow frozen solid in the early hours but mush by midmorning, and stonefall from the loose volcanic rock common. Crampons, ice axe and helmet are essential and a guide is advisable – either *Kayak Evi* or the tourist office in town should be able to find you one. More worrying than the natural dangers of the mountain, early in August each year the vast upland meadow of Tekir Yaylası becomes a tent city of up to 50,000 flag-waving ultra-nationalist supporters of the Milli Hareket Partisi.

Sultansazlığı

Beyond Erciyes Daği the countryside around the Kayseri–Niğde road becomes flat, dull steppe, which you might well assume was as barren of bird or plant life as the fairy chimneys of Cappadocia. Consequently, the oasis of the **Sultansazlığı** bird sanctuary is easy to miss in the small back lanes that wind around the tiny lakes in the region, but it's worth the effort of hunting out.

The complex of wetlands at the bottom of a closed basin comprises two main lakes – **Yay Gölü** and the smaller **Çöl Gölü** – and about two thousand hectares of surrounding marshes, covered in reed and cane. The lakes are saline, while the marshland is entirely fresh water, and this particular combination of lakes, marshland, mudflats and steppe makes for an enormous variety of ecosystems. This, allied with the fact that the area is positioned right at the crossroads of two large bird migration routes, make Sultansazlığı an extremely important wetland for breeding migrant and wintering birds.

Although no really detailed ornithological research has so far been carried out, at least 250 **species** have been recorded here, 69 of which breed in the area. Most excitingly for the lay bird-watcher, visiting species include flamingos (particularly in the Yay Gölü region), pelicans, storks, golden eagles from the surrounding steppes, herons, spoonbills and cranes.

There's a **watchtower** in the hamlet of Ovaçiftlik, which can provide very good viewing as long as the water isn't too low (as it may well be in the height of summer), and a little thatched **museum** exhibiting stuffed examples of the feathered species found in the region. There are also various good bird-watching opportunities to the northeast of Ovaçiftlik, near the small village of Soysallı.

Practicalities

The marshes, also known as Kuş Cenneti (Bird Paradise), are easily accessible **from Kayseri**: take the Yahyalı bus (8 daily until 5pm from the *otogar*) and get off at Ovaçiftlik (1hr), from where it's a one-kilometre walk to the water.

The best time to **birdwatch** is at dawn, so it's worth staying in one of Ovaçiftlik's two **pansiyons** with camping facilities. *Sultan Pansiyon and Camping Restaurant* (℡0352/658 5549) can offer dormitories with bunkbeds ($5), with hot showers outside, and plates of *saç tava* (wok-fried lamb). They run expensive **boat trips** in a flat-bottomed punt (be prepared to haggle) and organize tours around Yay Gölü. *Atilla Pansiyon* next door (℡0352/658 5576) has similar dormitory-style rooms ($5) and a boat for rent.

Kültepe

Twenty-two kilometres northeast of Kayseri the important archeological site at what is now known as **Kültepe** (Tues–Sun 8.30am–5.30pm; $1) was, before excavation, the largest artificial mound in Turkey. The primary importance of this site, however, derives from the fact that the earliest written documents of Anatolia were found here, in the ancient city called Kanesh. Nearby is the **Karum of Kanesh**, a sort of chamber of commerce, where a colony of Assyrian traders lived and worked controlling commerce between Assyria and Anatolia. To get there by **public transport** you'll have to take a bus, from Sivas Caddesi in Kayseri, along the main eastern highway headed for Bünyan. After some 20km the site is signposted, near a petrol station, but it's a 2km hike from the bus drop-off.

Some 15,000 clay tablets and a well-preserved selection of household furnishings, including human and animal statuettes, have been discovered here. Most of these are now scattered throughout the various museums of Turkey, with particularly good collections in Kayseri and Ankara, but the site at which they were originally found has been impressively and efficiently excavated to give some idea of building plans and street layouts, as well as construction techniques that are still prevalent in Anatolia.

Some history

The walled city of Kanesh was inhabited continuously from the fourth millennium BC to the Roman era, but its golden age was in the second millennium BC. At that time, the Karum of Kanesh – the most important of nine Assyrian *karum*s (trade centres) in Anatolia, importing tin, fine garments and other textiles in exchange for cattle, silver, copper and skins – was inhabited by the Assyrian trading colony and the lower classes, while Kanesh itself was reserved for royalty of Anatolian stock. The thin layer of ash covering the site (the origin of the name Kültepe, "ash hill") dates from two massive conflagrations, the first in around 1850 BC, when the *karum* was also destroyed, and the second between 1200 and 1180 BC. After the first, the *karum* was rebuilt and continued to trade until 1780 BC, when, it would appear, the traders departed in a hurry, leaving behind numerous personal belongings, including large quantities of earthenware vessels, many with graceful or comical animal forms. The city lost its importance during the Hittite age, but was still settled during the Hellenistic and Roman periods (a square building with towers at the corners was probably a Roman temple). Large quantities of ceramics from these later periods have been unearthed, and are now in museums, including that of Kayseri.

The sites

Excavations labelled "level II", from the second millennium BC, dominate the upper site of Kanesh, especially the Large Palace, which covered an area of 3000 square metres and included a paved central courtyard, and the **Palace of Warsana**, king of Kanesh. Walls were generally of large mud bricks with stone foundations, though the Large Palace had long storage rooms with stone walls.

The **Karum** is a five-minute walk further down the country lane that leads past the entrance to Kanesh. Here, excavations have revealed the foundations of shops, offices, archives and storerooms, all packed closely together inside a defensive wall. Houses from this period had one or two storeys built of mud bricks resting on stone foundations, like the palaces of Kanesh. The dead were buried together with precious gifts under the floors of their own houses in stone cist graves, some of which can be seen on site. Upstairs were the living quarters, while downstairs were workrooms, stores and, in some houses, ovens for baking tiny

clay tablets, the records of all business transactions at Kanesh. In one archive alone, 1500 of these tablets were stored, recording the import of lead, cloth and garments, and the export of metals, mainly copper, to Assyria. The tablets also reveal that the Assyrians and Anatolians had friendly relations, and even intermarried.

Travel details

Trains

Afyon to: Denizli (2 daily; 5hr); Gaziantep (3 weekly; 19hr); İsparta (2 daily; 5hr); İstanbul (4–5 daily; 8hr 30min); Konya (4–5 daily; 5–6hr).
Eğirdir to: Afyon (1 daily; 6hr); İsparta (4 daily; 1hr 10min).
İsparta to: Afyon (2 daily; 5hr); Denizli (1 daily; 5hr); Eğirdir (2 daily; 1hr 10min); İstanbul (1 daily; 13hr); Konya (3 daily; 1hr 10min).
Kayseri to: Adana (2 daily; 7hr); Ankara (1 hourly; 8hr 30min); Diyarbakır (4 weekly; 20hr); İstanbul (2 daily; 12hr); Malatya (1 daily; 6hr); Kars (1 daily; 24hr); Van (3 weekly; 22hr).
Konya to: Adana (3 weekly; 8hr); Afyon (4–5 daily; 5–6hr); Gaziantep (3 weekly; 13hr); İsparta (3 daily; 1hr 10min); İstanbul (2 daily; 14hr).
Niğde to: Adana (2 daily, 4hr); Kayseri (2 daily; 3hr).

Buses

Afyon to: Adana (3 daily; 10hr); Alanya (5 daily; 6hr 30min); Ankara (5 daily; 4hr); Antalya (5 daily; 5hr); Aydın (4 daily; 5hr); Bursa (3 daily; 5hr); Fethiye (2 daily; 7hr); İsparta (3 daily; 2hr); İstanbul (4 daily; 8hr); İzmir (4 daily; 6hr); Konya (3 daily; 3hr); Kuşadası (2 daily; 7hr); Kütahya (5 daily; 1hr 30min); Marmaris (1 daily; 9hr).
Aksaray to: Ankara (4 daily; 4hr 30min); Konya (6 daily; 2hr 30min); Niğde (6 daily; 2hr).
Avanos to: Göreme (half-hourly; 30min); Nevşehir (half-hourly; 40min); Özkonak (half-hourly; 30min); Ürgüp (half-hourly; 30min).
Beyşehir to: Alanya (6 daily; 4hr); Ankara (4 daily; 5hr); Antalya (4 daily; 4hr); Eğirdir (6 daily; 1hr 30min); İsparta (6 daily; 2hr 30min); İstanbul (3 daily; 10hr); İzmir (5 daily; 8hr); Konya (hourly; 1hr 15min).
Eğirdir to: Ankara (5 daily; 7hr); Antalya (hourly; 3hr); Beyşehir (6 daily; 1hr 30min); Denizli (8 daily; 3hr); Göreme (3 daily; 8hr); İstanbul (1 daily; 10hr); Konya (hourly; 4hr).
Göreme to: Alanya (2 daily; 12hr); Ankara (5 daily; 4hr); Antalya (2 daily; 10hr); Denizli (2 daily; 10hr);

Eğirdir (3 daily; 8hr); İstanbul (3 daily; 11hr); İzmir (1 daily; 11hr 30min); Kayseri (6 daily; 2hr); Konya (3 daily; 3hr); Marmaris (2 daily; 15hr); Ürgüp (every 20min; 30min).
İsparta to: Afyon (3 daily; 2hr); Beyşehir (6 daily; 2hr 30min); Kayseri (3 daily; 9hr); Konya (2 daily; 4hr).
Kayseri to: Adana (10 daily; 5hr 30min); Adiyaman (1 daily; 8hr); Afyon (6 daily; 9hr); Ankara (hourly; 4hr 30min); Antalya (4 daily; 12hr); Bursa (4 daily; 11hr); İsparta (3 daily; 9hr); İstanbul (7 daily; 12hr); İzmir (3 daily; 12hr); Konya (8 daily; 4hr); Niğde (hourly; 1hr 30min); Ürgüp (7 daily; 1hr 30min).
Konya to: Afyon (2 daily; 3hr); Ankara (hourly; 3hr); Antalya (4 daily; 5–6hr); Beyşehir (every 30min; 1hr 15min); Bursa (1 daily; 10hr); Göreme (3 daily; 3hr); İsparta (2 daily; 4hr); Kayseri (8 daily; 4hr); Silifke (5 daily; 4hr).
Nevşehir to: Adana (1 daily; 5hr); Ankara (4 daily; 4hr); Antalya (2 daily; 11hr); Fethiye (1 daily; 12hr); Göreme (every 30min; 30min); İstanbul (3 daily; 10hr); Kayseri (8 daily; 2hr); Konya (4 daily; 3hr); Mersin (2 daily; 5hr); Ürgüp (every 30min; 30min).
Niğde to: Aksaray (7 daily; 1hr 30min); Alanya (1 daily; 12hr); Ankara (8 daily; 4hr 30min); Antalya (2 daily; 10–12hr); Çamardı (summer 4 daily; 1hr); Derinkuyu (hourly; 45min); İstanbul (3 daily; 12hr); Kayseri (12 daily; 1hr 30min); Konya (5 daily; 3hr 30min); Mersin (5 daily; 4hr); Nevşehir (hourly; 1hr 30min); Samsun (1 daily; 8hr); Sivas (2 daily; 6hr).
Ürgüp to: Adana (2 daily; 5hr); Ankara (4 daily; 5hr); Antalya (2 daily; 11hr); Denizli (2 daily; 12hr); Göreme (half-hourly; 20min); İstanbul (1 daily; 13hr); Kayseri (hourly; 2hr); Konya (4 daily; 3hr); Marmaris (2 daily; 15hr); Mersin (3 daily; 5hr); Nevşehir (half-hourly; 30min); Side (2 daily; 13hr).

Flights

Kayseri to: İstanbul (2 daily; 1hr 20min).
Konya to: İstanbul (1 daily; 1hr 15min).

North Central Anatolia

CHAPTER 8

Highlights

✳ **Museum of Anatolian Civilizations, Ankara** A treasure-hoard of arte-facts contained in one of the most prestigious museums in Turkey. See p.698

✳ **Sheraton Open-Air Cinema, Ankara** Turkey's most stylish cinema at the top of the *Sheraton* tower – Hollywood block-busters with great city views. See p.711

✳ **Safranbolu** Ancient pastel-coloured timber houses in a town where the old way of life has stayed remarkably intact. See p.723

✳ **Hattuşaş** Enclosed by six-kilometre-long walls, the Hittite capital was an immense city and its scale is still awe-inspiring today. See p.730

✳ **Yazılıkaya reliefs** The thirteenth-century BC rock-hewn reliefs pay homage to nearly a hun-dred Hittite gods. See p.734

✳ **Rock tombs of Amasya** Massive rock tombs of the Pontic kings carved into a cliff-face and lit up at night to great effect. See p.736

✳ **Harşena Otel, Amasya** Sleep in low-slung Ottoman beds in a stun-ningly restored half-tim-bered house with creaky floorboards and authen-tic antiques. See p.738

✳ **Sivas's Selçuk monu-ments** Mongol-inspired architecture with highly decorative facades and beautiful mosaic work. See p.747

8

North Central Anatolia

W hen the first Turkish nomads arrived in Anatolia during the tenth and eleventh centuries, the landscape must have been strongly reminiscent of their Central Asian homeland. However, the terrain that so pleased the tent-dwelling herdsmen of a thousand years ago has few attractions for modern visitors. There are monotonous, rolling vistas of stone-strewn grassland, dotted with rocky outcrops and hospitable only to sheep. In winter it can be numbingly cold, while in summer temperatures rise to almost unbearable levels.

It seems appropriate that the heart of original Turkish settlement should be home to **Ankara**, the political and social centre of modern Turkey. This European-style capital rises out of a stark landscape, a symbol of Atatürk's dream of a secular Turkish republic. Though it's a far less exciting city than İstanbul, Ankara does make a good starting point for travels through Anatolia. And even if it's a city more important for its social and political status than for any pronounced architectural or aesthetic merit, it does have great moments. A visit to the Museum of Anatolian Civilizations is an essential way of gaining some impression of how Anatolia has developed since it was first settled during Neolithic times.

North Central Anatolia also boasts the remains of **Hattuşaş**, one of the earliest known cities in Turkey. Located near the village of **Boğazkale**, Hattuşaş was once the capital of the Hittite Empire. East of here, several later cultures and civilizations have left their successive marks: at **Amasya**, the rock-cut tombs of the pre-Roman Pontic kings tower over a haphazard riverside settlement of Ottoman wooden houses; **Tokat** has a fine Selçuk seminary; while **Sivas** displays some of the finest Selçuk architecture found in Turkey. Hidden away in the mountains to the north of Ankara you'll find **Safranbolu**, an almost completely intact Ottoman town, whose wooden houses are tucked into a narrow gorge. North of Ankara and east of Safranbolu is **Kastamonu**, home to a couple of interesting mosques, which fall under the shadow of the town's huge citadel.

Attractions in the less accessible west of the region are sparse. High points are the remains of the Phrygian capital of **Gordion** and the Roman temple site of **Aezani**. Situated between these two, the Phrygian temple-city of **Pessinus** and the sacred site at **Midaş şehri** are places worth visiting if you have your

own transport. En route you'll invariably pass through **Sivrihisar**, with its appealing Selçuk Ulu Cami, and **Seyitgazi**, with its dervish monastery built around the tomb of a legendary Arab warrior. **Eskişehir** is the largest city hereabouts, but has little of intrinsic interest. It functions principally as a staging post on the way to Bursa, Bandırma and the Sea of Marmara, or to **Kütahya**, from where there's access to Aezani.

All the region's towns, set within the forbidding northern Anatolian landscape, bear witness to nearly ten thousand turbulent years of human settlement, punctuated by the complexities of war and waves of conquest. Anatolia was the Roman front line against the Persians, and in a sense it's still an arena where the conflicting currents in Turkish society are played off against each other. The clash of the traditional and the new is immediately apparent in cities such as Ankara, where radically different ways of life are set side by side. Here sizeable European-oriented middle-class populations coexist with people from the countryside who, only a decade or two ago, adhered to a centuries-old peasant existence.

Ankara

ANKARA is really two cities, each of which seems to exist as a distinct entity with its own separate time zone. The double identity is a result of the breakneck pace at which Ankara has developed since its declaration as the capital of the Turkish Republic in 1923. Until then Ankara (formerly known as Angora) had been a small provincial city, almost lost in the midst of the steppelands and known chiefly for its production of angora, soft goats' wool. This older city still exists in and around the citadel, which was the site of the original settlement. The other Ankara is the modern metropolis, Atatürk's capital, which has grown up around the original city, surrounding and almost swamping it – a carefully planned attempt to create a seat of government worthy of a modern, Westernized state.

For visitors, Ankara is never going to be as attractive a destination as İstanbul, and the couple of excellent museums and handful of other sights that it can offer are unlikely to detain you for more than a day or two (note that most of the museums are closed on Mondays). Even so it's worth the trip just to find somewhere as refreshingly forward-looking as Turkey's administrative and diplomatic centre.

Some history

It was the **Hittites** who founded Ankara around 1200 BC, naming it Ankuwash. Under them the town prospered due to its position on the royal road running from Sardis to their capital at Hattuşaş. The Hittites were succeeded by the **Phrygians**, who called the city Ankyra (and left a significant reminder of their presence in the shape of a huge necropolis uncovered near the train station in 1925), and they, in turn, by the **Lydians** and the **Persians**. Alexander the Great passed through on his way east, while in the third century BC invading **Galatians** (Gauls) held sway for a while, renaming the city Galatia.

By the beginning of the first century BC the **Romans** had made substantial inroads into Asia Minor, and in 74 BC their fourteen-year campaign against the kingdom of Pontus culminated in the defeat of Mithridates the Great by the Roman general Pompey. This event opened up central Anatolia to Roman control and in 24 BC Ankara was officially absorbed into the Empire under Augustus and renamed Sebaste (Greek for Augustus). Ankara thrived under the Romans, thanks to its location astride major trade routes, and by the third century AD it had developed into a flourishing city of 200,000 inhabitants. The later Byzantine era ushered in a period of decline and sporadic attack at the hands of whoever happened to be waging war in the area. Arabs, Persians, Crusaders and Mongols stormed the city en route to greater prizes, but only the **Selçuks** were to settle, taking control of the city in 1071.

By 1361 Ankara had been incorporated into the burgeoning **Ottoman state**, briefly occupying centre stage when the Mongol ruler Tamerlane defeated the army of Beyazit Yıldırım 30km north of the modern city in 1402. The defeat precipitated several years of dynastic in-fighting among the Ottomans as Beyazit's sons fought it out among themselves for the succession. With the eventual restoration of Ottoman rule, Ankara went into something of a decline, with only its famous wool to prevent it from disappearing altogether.

After Atatürk's final victory, Ankara was made the official **capital of the Turkish Republic**, a decision that was ratified by parliament on October 13, 1923. Atatürk chose Ankara for its strategic central location during the Turkish War of Independence, and out of personal preference (between 1919 and 1927 he never set foot in İstanbul). However, at this time the city was little more than a backward provincial centre. The majority of its population lived in mud-brick buildings, and electricity or running water were almost unheard-of luxuries. Turkey's vociferous pro-İstanbul lobby was dismayed by the choice of Ankara as capital and many foreign governments also baulked at the idea of establishing embassies here. Gradually, however, the lure of free land for the building of embassies and a softening of opposition to Atatürk's republic lured in the diplomatic corps, with the British, who had been vocal denigrators of the new capital, snapping up one of the best sites.

The government recruited German and Austrian town planners to transform the city. New streets, public buildings and parks were established – matching Atatürk's vision of a modern, Westward-looking capital – while tens of thousands of people were soon drawn to Ankara from the Anatolian countryside in search of work and a higher standard of living. The planners reckoned on the city's **population** swelling from 30,000 to about 800,000, but the influx far exceeded their expectations and the total number of inhabitants now stands at well over four times that figure. Incomers took advantage of an old Ottoman law, stating that anyone who could build a house in a single night on an unused plot had the right to legal ownership. *Gecekondu* **squatter settlements** now ring the city as, over the decades, what were originally shantytowns have become established as legitimate communities.

The city authorities are working hard at expanding Ankara's infrastructure and there have been concerted efforts to woo foreign investment. Since the terrorist attacks on the United States and elsewhere, the **diplomatic corps** in Ankara has increased its presence dramatically, as Turkey is a key ally in the "war against terrorism". The likes of the Ankara *Hilton* and *Sheraton* have benefited from the new influx of foreign political and military visitors; another five-star hotel is under construction in the city; while upmarket restaurants, bars and Western-style shops are starting to feature heavily in the wealthier suburbs. Other **international organizations** represented in Ankara include the

United Nations, the World Health Organization, the World Bank and the UN Commission for Refugees, and, with Ankara vying for a position in the EU, there's also a Representative for the European Union. Ankara, it would seem, ultimately wants to become a credible regional centre, taking maximum advantage of its traditional East–West links in the redefined post-Cold War world.

Orientation

The city is neatly bisected along its north–south axis by the five-kilometre **Atatürk Bulvarı**, and everything you need is in easy reach of this broad and busy street. At the northern end is **Ulus Meydanı** – usually known simply as **Ulus** ("Nation") – a large square and an important traffic intersection, marked by a huge equestrian Atatürk statue. The square has lent its name to the surrounding area: not a particularly attractive one, dominated by the sprawling PTT sorting offices and rundown shopping centres, but the point to which you'll probably gravitate on arrival as it's the home of cheap hotels and well positioned for both sightseeing and city transportation. About 1km east of here, up Hisarparkı Caddesi, stands the **Hisar**, Ankara's old fortress and citadel, not far from the famous **Museum of Anatolian Civilizations**.

Heading south down Atatürk Bulvarı from Ulus brings you to the main west–east rail line, beyond which lies **Sıhhıye Meydanı**, an important junction marking the beginning of **Yenişehir** ("New City"). A ten-minute walk south of Sıhhıye brings you to **Kızılay**, the busy square that is the main transport hub of the modern city, and shares its name with the surrounding shopping and restaurant district. Keep going south and you'll pass the **Parliament** building on the right, thereafter moving into the **Kavaklıdere** district, home of several major embassies and upmarket hotels. At the bottom of Atatürk Bulvarı is **Çankaya**, Ankara's most exclusive suburb and location of the **Presidential Palace**.

Arrival and information

Ankara's **Esenboğa airport** is 33km north of the city. Green-yellow-and-white Havaş buses from the airport into the centre ($4) tend to depart about half an hour after flights land. These will drop you off at the Havaş bus stop by the train station (see below). A taxi into the centre of Ankara from the airport will set you back about $20 (double this between midnight and 6am).

If you arrive at the **city otogar** at Aşti in the western suburbs, there will be a free *servis* minibus into the centre from the car park out front. Just show your bus ticket to the helpful attendants carrying clipboards who will point you to the right company bus. These run through to the plush hotels in Kavaklıdere, but for Ulus the drop-off point is on the corner of Cumhuriyet Caddesi and Istiklâl Caddesi, from where it is a short five-minute walk or taxi ride to the hotels around Ulus Meydanı. Alternatively, catch the Ankaray (LRT light railway) from Aşti station at the *otogar* to Kızılay, where there is a metro connection to Ulus and buses to Kavaklıdere.

The **train station** is close to the heart of things at the bottom of Cumhuriyet Bulvarı, with frequent buses from outside the main entrance to Ulus and Kızılay – check the signs on the front of the bus. Or you can walk

ANKARA

HOTELS

Aldino	6
Best	5
Büyük Grand Ankara	4
Dedeman	3
Elit	1
Eyüboğlu	2
Hilton International	9
Sheraton	8
Tunalı	7

Airport

Roman Baths

Column of Julian

Haci Bayram Camii

Temple of Augustus

HISARPARKI CAD

İnönü Parkı

Hisar

Aslanhane Camii

Museum of Anatolian Civilizations

BENTDERESİ CAD

ULUCANLAR CAD

Yeni Ankara Hamamı

TALAT PAŞA CAD

Dikimevi Ⓜ

ANAFARTALAR CAD

HASIRCILAR CAD

Hacettepe Hospital

CEBECİ

Ⓜ Kurtuluş

Kurtuluş Park

KOÇATEPE

HASAN ALİ YÜCEL CAD

LİBYA CAD

SÖKÜP CAD

ZİYA

GÖKALP CAD

KOLEJ

KIZILAY

KARANFİL

ATATÜRK BUL

Ⓜ Kızılay

MİTHAT PAŞA CAD

CEMAL GÜRSEL CAD

Abdi İpekçi Park

SIHHİYE

SIHHİYE MEYD

Ⓜ Sıhhiye

Ethnographic Museum

OPERA MEYDANI

ULUS MEYDANI

ÇANKIRI CAD

 İSTİKLAL CAD

Ⓜ Ulus

ULUS

ATATÜRK BUL

CUMHURİYET BUL

Gençlik Parkı

Opera House

State Orchestra Concert Hall

TALAT PAŞA CAD

Train Station

19 Mayıs Stadium

KAZIM KARABEKİR CAD

İSTANBUL CAD

Ⓜ Kültür

HİPODROM CAD

Tandoğan Ⓜ

TANDOĞAN MEYD

CELAL BAYAR BUL

GAZİ MUSTAFA

Ⓜ Demirtepe

Ⓜ Kemal BUL

KEMAL BUL

MALTEPE

Ⓜ Maltepe

ⓘ

AKDENİZ CAD

ANIT CAD

Anıt Kabir

RESTAURANTS, CAFÉS & BARS

Arpien	M
B-Trip	B
Budakatti Brasserie	N
Cafes des Cafes	D
Gitanes	H
Guangzhou Wuyang	E
Hacı Arif Bey	F
Imatti	Q
Ivy Californian Brasserie	P
Japon Mutfağı	R
Jazz Time	G
Kebab 49	C
Kuğulu Park Café	K
Lord Kinross	V
Mado Ice Cream Bar	I
Marilyn Monroe's	A
Mest	S
Q-Wreck	O
Salata Bistro	T
Trilye	J
Yakamoz	L
Yosun	

Kocatepe Camii

see 'Central Ankara' map

Küçükesat Hamamı

BAKANLIKAR

Parliament

US Embassy

United Nations

Kavaklıdere Cinema

Iranian Embassy

Canadian Embassy

Karum Shopping Centre

THY Head Office

Russian Embassy

New Zealand Embassy

Australian Embassy

Segmenler Parkı

British Embassy

Presidential Palace

ÇANKAYA

GAZİOSMANPAŞA

AŞAĞAYRANCI

▼ Otogar (5km)

▼ , Simon Bolivar Cad, Atakule Mall & Tower & Çankya Hospital

691

through the tunnel under the railway line to Maltepe Ankaray (LRT) station, close to the tourist office.

For all **departure and ticket details**, see "Listings", p.711.

Information

Ankara has two tourist offices: at Esenboğa **airport** (daily 9.30am–6pm; sometimes later depending on the time of flight arrivals; ☎0312/398 0348); and in **Maltepe** at Gazi Mustafa Kemal Bul 121 (summer Mon–Fri 9am–6.30pm, Sat & Sun 10am–5pm; winter Mon–Fri 9am–5pm; Sat 10am–5pm; ☎0312/231 5572). The latter is generally more helpful, is easy to get to from the train station via an underground tunnel, and is close to the Maltepe *Ankaray* (LRT) station. Both offices will provide you with a city plan.

City transport

Buses run the length of Atatürk Bulvarı from Ulus to Kızılay, and then either branch off to Maltepe under a tunnel or continue to Çankaya via Kavaklıdere. Check the destinations on the front of the bus – most useful is the #391, which runs the length of Atatürk Bulvarı from Ulus Meydanı to the Atakule Mall and Tower in Çankaya. The bulk of buses are blue-and-white EGO municipality buses, though a substantial number are privately run. For all municipality buses you'll need to buy an EGO **ticket** in advance, which you then deposit in the green machine next to the driver on boarding the bus. EGOs are sold at ticket kiosks next to main bus or metro stops and at some *büfes* (newsagent's stands). Sometimes you may board a privately run bus (usually older and shabbier looking) where you pay the conductor – seated to the left of the front entrance – in cash. Routes overlap with those of the municipal services and prices are the same (a flat fare of \$0.50 a journey).

There are two city **metro lines** with modern stations and efficient trains running at regular intervals throughout the day until around 10.30pm. One line is called the **Ankaray** or LRT (light railway), which runs between the *otogar* at Aşti and Dikimevi in the eastern suburbs. It joins the second line – simply called the **metro** – at Kızılay, where there is a huge underground station under Güven Parkı. The metro runs north from Kızılay to Sıhhiye, Ulus, and then through the northwest suburbs to Batikent. EGO **tickets** for both lines (\$0.75) are available at booths at the stations, which are then deposited into turnstiles. You can also buy a computer-generated **EGO card** from \$2.50, accredited with up to ten standard fares, which can be used on the two metro lines as well as the buses.

Taxis are plentiful and can be flagged down just about anywhere, with \$1 (double between midnight and 6am) as the minimum fare. A trip such as Ulus to Kavaklıdere works out at about \$4.

Accommodation

Accommodation covers the full price and quality spectrum, and finding a room is rarely a problem, given the relative absence of tourists. There are plenty of decent possibilities offering doubles for under \$20. It's worth bearing in mind that the cheapest hotels often charge a couple of dollars for the use of the communal bath, which can make the total cost comparable to a room with bathroom at a far nicer establishment.

Most of the cheaper hotels are in **Ulus**, centred on the streets east of Atatürk Bulvarı **between Ulus Meydanı and Opera Meydanı**, around the main PTT (post office) and close to the Museum of Anatolian Civilizations and the castle. Most are presentable but pretty featureless options where the most you can expect is a bed in a plain room with or without plumbing. More expensive two- and three-star options can be found around **Çankırı Caddesi**, north of Ulus Meydanı, but the traffic is horrendous on this road so ask for rooms at the back. Moving down into **Sıhhiye** and **Kızılay** will take you up another notch or two, and then prices and standards steadily increase as you move further south and into **Kavaklıdere**, home to top-of-the-range places such as the *Hilton* and *Sheraton*. In the highly unlikely event that you draw a blank in these areas head for **Maltepe** where Gazi Mustafa Kemal Bulvarı (running northwest from Kızılay) and the surrounding streets offer everything from fleapits to classy comfort.

A little **haggling** can go a long way, even at the more expensive establishments (though perhaps not the *Hilton*), particularly out of season. At the very least you can try to get the seventeen-percent **KDV** (local sales tax) knocked off your bill if you offer to pay cash.

Hotels in Ulus (between Ulus Meydanı and Opera Meydanı, and around Çankırı Caddesi), and in Sıhhıye and Maltepe, are marked on our "Central Ankara" map (see pp.696–697), those in Kızılay and Kavaklıdere on our main "Ankara" map (see p.690–691).

Between Ulus Meydanı and Opera Meydanı

Otel Akman Opera Meyd, Tavus Sok 6 ☏0312/324 4140, ⓕ324 0161. Clean and bright rooms with spacious wall-to-ceiling tiled bathrooms – for which you pay an extra $6 – and a convenient and inexpensive *pide* restaurant attached. ❷

Otel Buhara Sanayi Cad 13 ☏0312/310 7999, ⓕ324 3327. Centrally located renovated hotel, whose immaculate rooms have satellite TV and giant fridge. A good mid-range choice with friendly English-speaking service – one of the few places to provide parking in the area. ❸

Otel Devran Opera Meyd, Tavus Sok 8 ☏0312/311 0485. Well-run, cheap and friendly, with small but decent rooms. You'll get a bathtub if you're lucky. Lone women may feel a little exposed as this corner of the square is frequented by large groups of men drinking tea. ❷

Farabi Oteli Denizciler Cad 46 ☏0312/310 0777. One of Denizciler Cad's better choices, with helpful staff and a spread of plain singles and doubles with shower. It's good value for lone travellers and convenient for Ankara's museums. ❷

Otel Fuar Opera Meyd, Kosova Sok 11 ☏0312/312 3289. Bare but quiet rooms with washbasins only, but adequate for the budget-minded who can sleep for under $6 a night. Showers cost an additional $1.50. ❶

Hisar Oteli Hisarparkı Cad 6 ☏0312/310 8128. A popular budget option with presentably clean rooms with washbasins only (though there's a hamam in the basement where for an extra $3 you can get a head-to-toe bath). ❶

Otel Sipahı Opera Meyd, Kosova Sok 1 ☏0312/324 0235. Clean rooms adorned with some great tourism posters from the 1960s, and reliable hot water. One of the better budget choices on this street. ❷

Around Çankırı Caddesi

Canbek Hotel Soğukkuyu Sok 8 ☏0312/324 3320, ⓕ311 1373. Fancy two-star down a side street off Çankırı Cad, with a spacious lobby and bar, and quiet air-conditioned rooms away from the traffic. Favoured by Eastern European coach parties, though some English is spoken. ❸

Otel Çevikoğlu Çankırı Cad, Orta Sok 2 ☏0312/310 4535, ⓕ311 1940. Spotless two-star in a quiet back street just north of Ulus. Simple whitewashed rooms have TV and minibar. ❹

Hotel Selvi Çankırı Cad 16 ☏0312/310 3500, ⓦwww.selvihotel.com. Presentable possibility just above Ulus, with a large ornate lobby with barbershop. Some attempt has been made at updating the old-fashioned rooms, and extras include air-conditioning, a phone in the bathroom and hair dryer. Rooms at the front can get noisy, though there is a swimming pool, so all-in-all, not bad value. ❹

Turist Hotel Çankırı Cad 37 ☎0312/310 3980, ✉turisthotels@superonline.com. On the main road, but with double-glazed front windows to keep out the noise. The grand lobby aside, the rooms are in need of modernizing, but have TV, minibar and balcony. Other conveniences include hairdresser, Turkish bath, gym, room service and indoor parking – the last a real boon. ❼

Maltepe

Otel Örnek Gülseren Sok 4 ☎0312/231 8170, ✉229 0352. With only thirty-odd rooms, a friendly intimate hotel in a boxy bright blue building down a side street off Gazi Mustafa Kemal Bul, close to the tourist office. Neat rooms with TV, hairdryers, minibars and 24hr room service. ❺

Sıhhiye

Büyük Sürmeli Hotel Cihan Sok 6 ☎0312/231 7660, ⓦwww.surmelihotels.com. The works, as you'd expect for around $150 a double, including a lovely outdoor pool surrounded by sun loungers, a fabulous kidney-shaped indoor pool, gym, Turkish bath and assortment of restaurants and bars. The huge rooms are very modern, with cable TV and minibar, though the decor is somewhat frilly. ❽

Kızılay

Elit Otel Olgunlar Sok 10 ☎0312/417 4695, ✉417 4697. Nicely decorated with bright duvets and curtains, and equipped with heating and air-conditioning, minibar and TV. There's a simple restaurant/bar in the lobby and it even has a garden out back – a rare find. ❹

Eyüboğlu Otel Karanfil Sok 73 ☎0312/417 6400, ⓦwww.eyubogluhotel.com. Expensive, but at the quieter end of this busy street, whilst still being close to the cinemas and bars. The rooms are nothing special but are adequate and modern – a regular venue for Turkish coach parties. ❻

Kavaklıdere

Otel Aldino Tunalı Hilmi Cad, Bülten Sok 22 ☎0312/468 6510, ⓦwww.hotelaldino.com. Prime location for dedicated shoppers, with a Turkish bath, two restaurant/bars, and useful garage park-

ing. Air-conditioned rooms are bright and spacious with satellite TV, minibars and hairdryers. Friendly for a high-end place and rates are negotiable. ❼

Hotel Best Atatürk Bul 195 ☎0312/467 0880, ✉446 8090. Plush enough – with Turkish bath, flowery decor and teak furniture in the rooms – and one of the cheaper business hotels in town, but it's opposite the US embassy and next door to the United Nations so you'll need to book. ❼

Büyük (Grand) Ankara Oteli Atatürk Bul 183, ☎0312/425 6655, ✉425 5070. The city's third-choice luxury hotel (after the *Hilton* and *Sheraton*), with open-air pool, poolside cocktail bar, health club and rooftop restaurant. It's rumoured to be the subject of a takeover bid by an international chain, when a complete re-fit is expected. For now it's one of the cheaper five-star options. ❽

Hotel Dedeman Büklüm Sok 1 ☎0312/417 6200, ✉417 6214. A luxury place in a residential area, with pool, baby-sitting service, beauty salon and gym. Modern functional rooms go from $140, but when there are no businessmen around you may be able to negotiate a worthwhile discount. ❽

Hilton International Hotel Tahran Cad 12 ☎0312/468 2888, ⓦwww.hilton.com. Luxury rooms on 16 floors, decorated in Anatolian stone and lots of plants, with individual air-con/heating systems and laptop connections. For those on a generous expense account – the presidential suite is a mere $1000 a night – though discounted weekend packages (Fri–Sun) weigh in at around $140 per person per night. ❽

Sheraton Noktalı Sok ☎0312/468 5454, ⓦwww.sheratonankara.com. Enjoy a pampered existence in this newly restored cylindrical concrete monolith. There's a friendly atmosphere for a five-star hotel, a great view of the city from the top, plus various restaurants, a pool and open-air cinema. Five of the rooms have been designed specifically for left-handed people. Doubles from $240 and no shortage of people prepared to pay. ❽

Otel Tunalı Tunalı Hilmi Cad 119 ☎0312/467 4440, ⓦwww.hoteltunali.com.tr. A good upper mid-range option run by the same family for thirty years, cheaper than most places in Kavaklıdere and close to all the nightlife. Rooms are ordinary but functional with fridge, satellite TV and huge windows overlooking busy Tunalı Hilmi Cad. Coffee shop and formal dining room attached. ❼

The City

For most visitors, the first taste of Ankara is **Ulus Meydanı** and it's none too enticing. Ulus once marked the westernmost limits of pre-Republican Ankara, which occupied the area between here and the citadel. Today, the streets are lined with drab, concrete stacks and only the occasional Ottoman-era survivor breaks the monotony. There is also a serious rubbish problem in this part of town, which in turn attracts street kids and hawkers late at night raking through in search of anything to take home or sell. Despite these unpromising looks, the area does hide a couple of **Roman monuments**, offering a hint at the depth of history beneath the prevailing modernity. East of Ulus Meydanı, the **Hisar** is the oldest part of the city: a Byzantine citadel whose walls enclose an Ottoman-era village of cobbled streets, below which lies the excellent **Museum of Anatolian Civilizations**. The long Atatürk Bulvari runs south from Ulus down through **Kizilay**, Ankara's business and shopping district, and on to the increasingly upmarket suburbs of **Kavaklıdere** and **Çankaya**; haunts of the international community, embassies, and best of the restaurants and nightlife.

Around Ulus Meydanı

At Ulus Meydanı, a towering equestrian **statue of Atatürk** – flanked by threatening bronze soldiers in German-style coal-scuttle helmets – gazes out over the busy intersection of Cumhuriyet and Atatürk *bulvar*s. The former president faces the building that housed the Turkish Grand National Assembly, the provisional parliament convened by Atatürk and his Nationalist supporters on April 23, 1920. This modest, late-Ottoman schoolhouse building is also where the Turkish Republic was declared on October 29, 1923, and it served as the parliament building until 1925. Today it's home to the **Museum of the War of Independence** (Kürtülüş Savaş Müzesi; Tues–Sun 9am–noon & 1–5pm; $0.70), devoted to the military struggle that preceded the foundation of the modern republic. An extensive collection of photographs, documents and ephemera covers every detail of the various campaigns and, though captions are all in Turkish, much of the material speaks for itself. Visitors can also view the chamber where delegates sat in small school desks, illuminated by candle- and oil-light, with Atatürk overseeing from the vantage point of a raised platform. Opposite the museum stands Ankara's first hotel, the **Ankara Palas**, once again serving as a government guesthouse for visiting dignitaries.

The **Republic Museum** (Cumhuriyet Müzesi; Tues–Sun 9am–noon & 1.30–5pm; $0.70) is on Cumhuriyet Meydanı, the next road junction west along Cumhuriyet Bulvari from the Museum of the War of Independence. The emphasis here is on the achievements of the Turkish Republic, but Turkish-only captions make everything fairly impenetrable for non-linguists. The museum is housed in the post-1925 headquarters of the Grand National Assembly and you can take a look at the delegates' chamber, which looks like a lecture hall – a natural progression perhaps from the schoolroom layout of the original building.

From Ulus, Hisarparkı Caddesi leads east to the Hisar. On the way, make a quick diversion south down Susam Caddesi, followed by a fork to the left, to reach the **Yeni Hallar**, the city's premier fruit and veg market. Just behind here on Konya Sok is the **Vakıf Sultan Çarşısı**, a restored *han*, now home to multitudes of cheap clothing shops.

Roman Ankara

What's left of Roman Ankara lies just north of Hisarparkı Caddesi. Following Hükümet Caddesi and taking the first right fork leads to the remains of the **Temple of Augustus and Rome**, Ankara's most important ancient monument. Built in honour of Augustus between 25 and 20 BC, after Ankara was made the provincial capital of Galatia, its main claim to fame is an inscription

CENTRAL ANKARA

RESTAURANTS, CAFÉS & BARS

Altin Şiş	P
Akman	D
Black Eight	S
Boyacızade Konağı	I
Bulvar	A
Büyük Ekspress	K
Büyük Pastane	B
Fuaye Cafe	R
Gaziantep Fethi Bey	J
Göksu	M
Hosta Piznik	G
Kebabistan	C
Kale Washington	E
Köşk	L
Mudurnu	N
Paris Aile	O
Pizzeria Tempo	Q
Tapi Tavuk	F
Zenger Paşa Konağı	H

HOTELS

Akman	8
Buhara	6
Büyük Sürmeli	13
Canbek	4
Çevikoğlu	3
Devran	7
Farabi	10
Fuar	11
Hisar	5
Örnek	12
Selvi	1
Sipahi	9
Turist	2

Kurtuluş

Kurtuluş Park

CEMAL GÜRSEL CAD

Abdi İpekçi Park

LIBYA CAD

Kolej

GÖKALP CAD

ZIYA CAD

KOCATEPE

Kocatepe Camii

Kızılırmak Cinema

KIZILIRMAK SOK

MEŞRUTIYET CAD

Metropol Cinema

Hatti Monument

MITHAT PAŞA CAD

BAYINDIR SOK

SAKARYA SOK

TUNALI CAD

YÜKSEL CAD

SELANİK

Gima Department Store

KONUR SOK

KARANFİL SOK

CAD

Megapol Cinema

Esca Cat Speedy

Internet Club Cafe de Net

Andalu Net

SIHHIYE

Şihhiye

ATATÜRK BUL

KIZILAY

Kızılay

Güven Parkı

MÜDAFAA CAD

ADAKALE SOK

İZMİR CAD

STRAZBURG CAD

CİNLİ SOK

SEZENLER SOK

İZMİR CAD

SÜMER SOK

Yenişehir Hamam

Demirtepe

NECATIBEY CAD

Maltepe Camii

GAZİ MUSTAFA KEMAL BUL

SUYOLU SOK

KUBILAY SOK

Maltepe

MALTEPE

TURGUT REIS CAD

SÜLEYMAN BEY SOK

GENÇLIK CAD

AKDENİZ CAD

Anıt Kabır

N

250 m

0

on the outer wall. Detailing the *Res Gestae Divi Augusti* (Deeds of the Divine Augustus) this was the emperor's political testament, which was carved on every temple of Augustus in the Roman world after his death. The Ankara version is the only one that survives in its entirety. The temple, whose walls alone have endured, was converted into a Christian church around the fifth century AD, and during the fifteenth century it became the *medrese* of the **Hacı Bayram Camii,** named after Bayram Veli, founder of the Bayrami order of dervishes and Ankara's most celebrated Muslim saint. His body is buried in the tomb in front of the building.

A couple of hundred metres to the southwest on Hükümet Meydanı is the **Jülyanüs Sütunu** (Column of Julian), commemorating a visit to Ankara by the Byzantine emperor Julian the Apostate, chiefly remembered for his short-lived attempt to revive worship of the old Roman gods in the fourth century. The column's stonework is characterized by a strange, layered effect rather like a long, cylindrical kebab. Once memories of the Byzantine Empire had faded, the locals took to calling the column Belkis Minaresi, "the Queen of Sheba's Minaret".

Ankara's other main Roman remains, the **Roma Hamamları,** or Roman Baths (daily 8.30am–12.30pm & 1.30–5.30pm; $0.70), are about ten minutes' walk north of here on the western side of Çankırı Caddesi. The baths are set in a large *palaestra* (exercise field) scattered with overgrown truncated columns and fragments of cracked masonry. Of the baths themselves, which date back to the third century AD, only the brick pillars that supported the floors – and allowed warm air to circulate and heat the rooms above – survive.

Museum of Anatolian Civilizations

From İnönü Parkı, at the eastern end of Hisarparkı Caddesi, a sharp right turn leads to the **Museum of Anatolian Civilizations** (Anadolu Medeniyetleri Müzesi; Mon 9.30am–5pm, $9; Tues–Sun 9am–5.30pm, $5), an outstanding archeological collection documenting the peoples and cultures of Anatolia from the late Stone Age through to Classical times. When you see a replica artefact at an archeological site elsewhere in Turkey, you can bet the original is here. Housed in a restored fifteenth-century *bedesten*, this unmissable museum is, for most visitors, the highpoint of a visit to Ankara.

Its vast cache of artefacts is laid out in chronological order, clockwise from the entrance, with large stone reliefs dating from the Hittite and Phrygian periods in the central chamber. Most exhibits are clearly labelled in English and German. As you enter, you may be approached by an **official guide** offering to accompany you on your tour. If you have $15 or so to spare, and like the look of whoever approaches you, this can be worth doing – many of the guides are moonlighting academics and correspondingly well informed.

The collection concludes with a look at finds from the most **recent excavations,** and then spills Greek and Roman statuary over into the **café** and outdoor garden. The museum **bookshop** offers a fine catalogue, postcards and some useful introductory history books.

Paleolithic (Old Stone Age) section

An assortment of bone fragments and primitive stone tools and weapons from a cave-site at Karain, 30km northwest of Antalya, bear witness to the two-million-year period of hunter-gatherer development that ended about ten thousand years ago. Later finds from Karain include more sophisticated bone awls, needles and ornaments that are a foretaste of the more complex artefacts found in the following sections.

MUSEUM OF ANATOLIAN CIVILIZATIONS

Entrance

Palaeolithic Section

Neolithic Section

Phrygian Reliefs

Temporary Display

Chalcolithic Section

Late Hittite Reliefs & Statues

Urartian Section

Early Bronze Age

Hittite Empire Reliefs

Phrygian Section

Assyrian Trading Colony Section

Old Hittite Section

Neolithic (7000–5500 BC) and Chalcolithic (5400–3000 BC) sections

Objects found at Çatal Höyük, a settlement of New Stone Age mud-brick houses 52km north of Konya, have yielded significant evidence about the Neolithic period. It was then that settled agriculture began, accompanied by a refinement of tool-making techniques and the appearance of handmade pottery. One of the most interesting features here is the re-creation of a room from a Çatal Höyük dwelling, complete with characteristic bull's-head emblem and wall paintings. The importance of agriculture in this era may account for the abundance of fertility goddess figures – represented by baked clay female forms of ample proportions – that reappear in various forms throughout the museum. Later evidence of a more sophisticated lifestyle emerges in finds dating back to 5700–5600 BC from a settlement at Hacılar in southwest Anatolia. Vessels in the shape of animals, and a red cup in a stylized female form, reveal improvements in pottery-making methods. Other objects on display include simple bead jewellery, and tools and weapons made from obsidian and flint.

Further finds from Hacılar are displayed in the Chalcolithic section, including simple copper implements, the first use of metal in Anatolia. The pottery is decorated with geometric designs that become more complex as the centuries go by. Stone seals suggesting formal property ownership bear witness to an increasingly well-organized society.

Bronze Age section (3000–2000 BC)

Hammering and casting techniques were greatly refined during this period, with the methods used to work not only bronze but also gold, silver and electron (an alloy of gold and silver). This era was characterized by large settlements of mud-brick houses built on stone foundations and surrounded by defensive walls. Most of the objects here come from Alacahöyük; among the most striking exhibits are the pieces of gold jewellery unearthed in the royal tombs. Other memorable objects are cult symbols featuring stags, bulls and the sun. The pottery is plainer than that of the preceding Chalcolithic period but better made, with obvious spouts and handles. This was a time when Anatolia reached an advanced level of civilization, with well-established trade links between the various settlements. One symbol of continuity, the mother goddess figure, was now slimmed down or transformed into a distinctive violin shape.

Assyrian Trading Colony section (1950–1750 BC)

Included here are some well-preserved examples of the earliest written records in Anatolia in the shape of cuneiform tablets produced by the Assyrians. Also striking are the libation vases in the form of birds and animals, and vases made of obsidian and rock crystal. This period saw Assyrian traders from northern Mesopotamia establishing a trading network that covered most of Anatolia, importing tin, goat-hair felt, cloth, garments, ornaments and perfumes, and establishing markets called *karum*s outside their cities. The central one was at Kaniş (Kanesh), outside Kültepe, and it's from this *karum* that most of the objects on display in this section are drawn.

Old Hittite section (1700–1450 BC)

The Hittites left behind spectacular sites at Boğazkale and nearby Yazılıkaya, east of Ankara; most of the objects on display are from Boğazkale and Alacahöyük. Hittite pottery is similar to that found in the Assyrian Trading Colony period, the most sophisticated example here being a vase with a relief depicting a lively wedding procession. There's also some well-executed metalwork, including statues of gods and goddesses in bronze. Also included are a number of stelae carved with hieroglyphics that have proved a valuable source of information about the Old Hittite kingdom.

Hittite Empire (1450–1200 BC) and Late Hittite section (1200–700 BC)

This period of expansionism and warfare, particularly against the Egyptians, represents the zenith of Hittite power. The large and elaborate reliefs from Alacahöyük in the central hall indicate the sophistication of Hittite culture during this time. Most depict religious themes: a king and queen offering libations to a bull, and an elaborate festival scene with a juggler, acrobat and musician stand out in particular. If you're planning to visit Hattuşaş, look out for the lion and sphinx figures from the city gates and the bearded, hook-nosed figure of the weather god Teshuba. The originals are here, replaced with replicas at the site itself.

The main Late Hittite sites were at Kargamiş, Karatepe and Malatya-Aslantepe. A number of well-preserved and detailed reliefs from this period are in the central hall. One of the most vivid is a battle scene depicting a chariot carrying an archer running over a dead man. Others show the children of the Hittite king Araras at play, a procession of three women in mourning and the Hittite mother goddess Kubaba in various poses.

Phrygian section (1200–700 BC)

Most of these objects were recovered from the royal tumulus at Gordion, capital of Phrygian Anatolia after the fall of the Hittites. The timber-framed chamber at the heart of the tumulus has been re-created and objects from it are on display nearby. Most impressive are a wooden table of intricate design and skilfully wrought bronze vessels. Other exhibits attest to cultural sophistication: pottery with stylized animal reliefs and a translucent glass bowl, one of the earliest known examples of glasswork.

Urartian section (1200–700 BC)

Main rivals of the Phrygians and descendants of the Hurrians, the Urartians established a vast empire centred on Van and extending from Sivas and Erzincan to Iran, held together by a series of fortified citadels. Most of what is known about the Urartians derives from clay tablets listing military successes. On the evidence of those artefacts on display here their culture was less sophisticated than that of the Phrygians, though the large bronze cauldron resting on a tripod with cloven bronze feet is austerely beautiful.

The citadel and old town

A pathway leads steeply up through İnönü Parkı between the inner and outer walls of the **Hisar**, the Byzantine citadel whose walls enclose the oldest part of the city. It's an Ottoman-era village of cobbled streets and ramshackle wooden houses that of all Ankara's districts most fully rewards a relaxed and aimless stroll. Most of the area is defiantly un-restored, not to say verging on the squalid, and at times the old-world atmosphere is pungently authentic with the stench of rotting rubbish and bad drains hanging heavy in the air. All this is changing, though, and a number of grand Ottoman mansions have been renovated, decked out with carpets and antiques, and transformed into restaurants or carpet shops geared towards the tourist trade. Some succeed in recapturing the atmosphere of times past, while others are just hopelessly kitsch.

Ankara's **city walls** were probably first constructed by the Hittites over three thousand years ago when they recognized the defensive potential of the citadel outcrop. The walls that are seen today are much more recent, built on the orders of the Byzantine emperor Michael III (remembered as "Michael the

Sot") in 859, who updated defences built by the Roman emperor Heraclius (who in turn had used earlier Galatian fortifications as a foundation).

At the northern end of the citadel is the **Ak Kale** (White Fortress), presenting tremendous views of Ankara. The northeastern edge of the city, just about visible from here, is the approximate site of the battlefield where Pompey defeated the Pontic king Mithridates the Great in 74 BC. **Şark Kulesi**, a ruined tower rising out of the eastern walls, also has a panoramic outlook, as well as being a favourite kite-flying spot for local children. It's from here that you can best appreciate the impact of the squatter settlements that have grown up around modern Ankara.

At the southern end of the citadel is the **Güney Kapı** (South Gate), with two vast towers flanking a twin portal. Embedded in the wall connecting the towers are various fragments of Roman masonry, including altars supported by recumbent statues of Priapus. Just inside the gate is the **Alâeddin Camii**, a twelfth-century mosque, much restored in later years, whose unexceptional exterior conceals a painstakingly carved Selçuk *mimber*.

An unadulterated example of Selçuk architecture can be found a few streets to the southeast in the shape of the **Aslanhane Camii** (Lion-House Mosque), Ankara's oldest and most impressive mosque. The Aslanhane Camii is a "forest mosque", so called because of the 24 wooden columns (arranged in four rows of six) that support the intricately carved wooden ceiling. The astonishingly detailed walnut *mimber* dates back to 1209 and is one of the last examples of Selçuk decorative carving. It's well complemented by the stucco and tile *mihrab*, another outstanding piece of work. Ahi Zerafattin, the founder of the Aslanhane Camii, is buried opposite the mosque in Ankara's sole surviving Selçuk **tomb**, with its distinctive octagonal plan and pointed roof.

There's another forest mosque, the **Ahi Elvan Camii**, a few minutes' walk southwest of here. It's an Ottoman example of the style, dating from the late thirteenth century and, though not as impressive as the Aslanhane Camii, still worth a look. This particular mosque was founded by the Ahi brotherhood, a medieval guild associated with the dervish orders. The carved *mimber*, though overshadowed by the example up the road is, nonetheless, a fine piece of work.

Between these two mosques, off At Pazarı Sok and Can Sok is the **Pirinç Han**, built beneath the walls of the citadel in the eighteenth century as an inn for travellers to provide protection from bandits. It was the first inn in Ankara, constructed with a wooden frame filled in with sun-dried bricks, and was used as such until the War of Independence in 1921, when it was taken over by the military and, because of its strategic position on top of the hill, served as a command post. It's been fully restored since as a shopping centre, with forty shops selling an assortment of carpets, paintings, antiques, spirit lamps, glass, copper and silverware. You can stop by for a glass of tea in the cool courtyard, where you'll hear the gentle sound of craftsmen tapping hammers on copper drifting from the inner rooms. A little further to the east, in front of the Museum of Anatolian Civilizations, the old shops on **Çıkrıkçılar Yokuşu Sok** are also worth a browse for copper, carpets, antiques, costumes and embroidery.

South to Kızılay

It's roughly a two-kilometre walk south from Ulus Meydanı to the centre of Kızılay, or fifteen minutes on the bus (though heavy traffic makes progress by bus slow). Immediately south of Ulus you pass Ankara's main PTT, on the east side of Atatürk Bulvarı, and thereafter comes a succession of banks. Look out for the entrance to **Gençlik Parkı** (Youth Park) on the right after the roundabout. The park was built on the orders of Atatürk to provide a worthy recreational spot for the hard-toiling citizens of his model metropolis. The park's strangely named Monument to a Secure and Confident Future bears his words: "Be proud, hardworking, and believe in yourself". On most summer evenings, the park is packed with families strolling around the artificial lake and enjoying the numerous teahouses. Occasional outdoor concerts are held here and there's also a Luna Park funfair full of antiquated rides. The **State Opera House** (Devlet Opera), looking like a dark-pink Art Deco underground station, stands near the entrance and was built at Atatürk's behest – he developed a taste for opera while serving as military attaché in Sofia in 1905.

Heading on down Atatürk Bulvarı you pass the **Ethnographic Museum** on Talat Paşa Cad (Etnografya Müzesi; Tues–Sun 9am–noon & 1–5pm; $1.50), a grandiose white marble building that was the original resting place of Atatürk before the construction of the Anıt Kabir mausoleum (see p.706) – hence the equestrian statue of Atatürk out front. The museum contains an extensive collection of folk costumes and artefacts from Selçuk times onwards, and is packed with carpets, furniture and domestic utensils, alongside a number of re-created Ottoman household interiors. There are also some fine examples of Selçuk woodcarving, including a *mihrab* from a village mosque near Urgüp that must represent thousands of hours of carving.

A little way further south of the museum, beyond the rail and road bridges and past the Abdi ıpekçi Parkı, **Sıhhiye Meydanı** announces the beginning of modern Ankara. Here the road branches in three directions, while at the centre of the square stands the **Hatti Anıt** (Hatti Monument), with a statue based on the Bronze Age Anatolian stag symbol. Staying with Atatürk Bulvarı leads you into **Kızılay**, the centre of the modern city, which turns out to be yet another immense traffic junction with a small park, **Güven Parkı**, and a mighty Atatürk statue. It's a useful orientation point: the Gima department store on the eastern side of Atatürk Bulvarı, with a restaurant and café society in the parallel pedestrian precincts; and numerous fancy clothes shops along Atatürk Bulvarı to the south.

Kocatepe, Kavaklıdere and Çankaya

Real estate values increase exponentially as you move south of Kızılay towards Çankaya. A few blocks east of the main thoroughfare, the minarets of the massive **Kocatepe Camii** tower above the surrounding streets. This neo-Ottoman structure, finished in 1987 after twenty years of building, and complete with shopping centre and car park underneath, is Ankara's largest mosque and, indeed, one of the biggest in the world.

Half a kilometre or so beyond Kızılay is the Grand National Assembly, Turkey's functional modern **Parliament** building. It's the prelude to a strip of well-appointed embassy buildings and glossy hotels that stretches all the way to the Presidential Palace. About halfway along is the innocuous little **Kuğulu Parkı**, so packed with trysting couples that you'll feel like a voyeur as you stroll through it. At the eastern side of the park is the gleaming **Karum shopping centre**, which, with its air-conditioning and mall kids, comes as something of a culture shock after the crowded streets of Ulus and Kızılay. The area hereabouts is **Kavaklıdere**, one of the capital's smartest suburbs and also one of the liveliest. It is the place to come for Western-style nightlife and designer stores, both of which you'll find in abundance along **Tunalı Hilmi Caddesi**, running north from the Kuğulu Parkı roundabout.

Modern Turkey is largely the creation of one man, **Mustafa Kemal Atatürk**. A complex and often contradictory figure, driven by fervent patriotism and blinding ambition, he salvaged the Turkish state from the wreckage of the Ottoman Empire and defined it as a modern, secular nation. The omnipresent public statues and portraits are not merely symbols of the personality cult that has been built up around him; they also reflect the widely held conviction that without him Turkey in its present form simply would not exist.

Born in 1881 in Salonica (Thessaloníki), on the fringes of the declining Ottoman Empire, Atatürk set his sights on a military career from an early age. After the death of his father, a minor civil servant and unsuccessful businessman, he persuaded his reluctant mother to let him attend military school where he proved to be an excellent pupil.

Early career

In 1902 his military education took him to the Staff College in İstanbul. By now, popular feeling thought that it was time to replace the decay of the old regime with a democratic structure. Atatürk was soon involved in anti-government political activities, which continued after his commission into the regular army. In 1906 he helped form a revolutionary patriotic society called *Vatan* (Fatherland), which in the following year became part of the **Committee of Union and Progress** (CUP), a radical political organization set up by supporters of the Young Turk revolutionary movement.

In April 1909, Atatürk played a key role in the CUP **coup** that deposed Sultan Abdülhamid, leading the "Army of Liberation" into İstanbul and securing the city for the revolutionaries. Despite his prominent role in these events, political and personal differences with the increasingly authoritarian CUP leadership led to his political sidelining (and a couple of unsuccessful assassination attempts). Appointments in distant parts of the empire, followed by a posting to Sofia as military attaché, served to keep him out of the way until the outbreak of World War I.

Gallipoli victory

In February 1915, Atatürk was sent to **Gallipoli**, where an Allied landing was imminent. It was to prove a highly significant posting in terms of both Atatürk's own career and the Turkish war effort. When the Allied assault came in April he organized a daring counter-attack, preventing the Allies from breaking out of the Arıburnu (Anzac Cove) bridgehead. His skill as a commander, coupled with his willingness to put his own life at risk, galvanized the Turkish troops into fierce and heroic defence, and he was rewarded with promotion to colonel and given command of the army corps controlling the strategically vital Anafarta ridge. In this role he was successful at repulsing a second major attack in August, in which he was wounded. Atatürk's key role in the defence of Gallipoli established his military reputation and, more significantly, brought him a nationwide respect that he would put to good use after the 1918 armistice.

As a result of his Gallipoli successes, Atatürk was promoted to general. There was little he could do to turn the wider tide of defeat about to engulf the Ottoman Empire and he spent the remainder of the war taking part in rearguard actions on the southern fringes of the empire. When the armistice was signed on October 30, 1918, he began the task of trying to preserve the demoralized army, knowing there were further battles to come.

Battle for independence

Recognizing that the victorious World War I Allies were about to carve up the empire, and that Sultan Mehmet VI's government wasn't going to do anything about it, Atatürk decided to organize **Turkish resistance** from Anatolia, where Nationalist guerilla bands were already active. In May 1919 he secured a posting to Samsun, ostensibly to restore order in the region. His arrival there can be seen as the beginning of the Turkish struggle for independence. In the words of Atatürk's biographer, Patrick Kinross, he had "set up his standard of liberation on the shores of the Black Sea".

He came out into the open on June 21 in the town of Amasya, delivering a speech that called for national resistance to outside attempts at dismembering Turkey, which as the recent Greek occupation of İzmir had shown were now well under way. Thus Atatürk and his followers became embroiled in open rebellion against the government. He went on to preside over Nationalist congresses at Erzurum and Sivas, which launched a political manifesto known as the **National Pact**, calling for the preservation of Turkey's existing frontiers and the establishment of a provisional government.

With growing support for the Nationalists, the Allies occupied İstanbul and, a month later, the sultan suspended parliament. The time was right for Atatürk to realize his plan to create an alternative Anatolian-based government and, on April 23, 1920, the first session of the **Grand National Assembly** opened with him as president. A month later the sultan's goverment condemned Atatürk and some of his followers to death. Turkey was now split in two and Atatürk was the undisputed figurehead of the Nationalist cause.

Birth of the Republic

In his role of Nationalist leader, Atatürk oversaw a series of complex political and military manoeuvrings, most significant of which was the repulsion of the Greek invasion of Anatolia in 1921. This culminated in the epic **Battle of Sakarya**, which took place 100km west of Ankara between August 23 and September 13. Atatürk took personal command in the field, smashing the Greek advance, and the following summer he directed a lightning offensive that drove the Greeks from Anatolia, culminating in the sacking and burning of İzmir. On October 11, 1922, an armistice agreement was signed with the Allies and on November 1 the Nationalists abolished the sultanate.

The following year saw the consolidation of Atatürk's gains. The Treaty of Lausanne, signed on July 24, 1923, established Turkey's borders and in October the Allies withdrew from İstanbul, allowing the Nationalist troops to occupy the city. In the same month Ankara was officially made capital, and on October 29, Turkey was declared a **Republic** with Atatürk as its president.

Reforms

Having achieved his wider political and military objectives, Atatürk turned his attention towards **internal reform**. His main aim was to transform Turkey into a modern, Western-oriented society, and between 1923 and 1934 he introduced dramatic reforms that touched upon every aspect of Turkish life. Among the most significant of these were the separation of religion and state with the abolition of the caliphate in 1924, the adoption of Latin script in 1928 and the establishment of full suffrage for women in 1934. In the same year, it was decreed that all Turks should adopt surnames. Atatürk's own name, meaning "**Father Turk**" dates from then – previously he had been known only as Mustafa Kemal.

Despite a reformist strategy, Atatürk's style of rule is best described as **benign despotism**. For example, he used a Kurdish revolt in 1925 as a pretext to ban Turkey's sole opposition party and institute censorship of the press. The revolt itself was suppressed with mass hangings of the ringleaders in Diyarbakır. The following year an amateurish plot against Atatürk's life was uncovered, an event that was

continued overleaf

blown up into a full-scale conspiracy and provided a convenient excuse for hanging several members of the former CUP leadership who had been vocal opponents of Atatürk. The 1926 purge succeeded in muting the opposition and was not repeated.

Atatürk and his associates pursued a policy designed to create a self-sufficient industrial base for Turkey, along the lines of fascist Italy. It proved a failure, as massive subsidies crippled the rest of the economy. Atatürk's foreign policy dealings met with greater success, and his resolute non-interventionism kept Turkey out of the impending European conflict.

By the mid-1930s, it was clear that Atatürk's greatest achievements were behind him and his **final years** present a sad picture of decline. Bad health accelerated by heavy drinking made him increasingly unpredictable and irascible. By the winter of 1937 it was evident that he was seriously ill. He survived long enough to oversee the first stages of the transfer of the Hatay from France to Turkey, the last political action in which he took a personal hand. He died of cirrhosis at İstanbul's Dolmabahçe Palace on November 10, 1938, and was succeeded the next day by İsmet İnönü.

At the end of Atatürk Bulvarı is Çankaya Caddesi, beyond which lies the **Presidential Palace** (Çankaya Köşkü; open Sun and national holidays only 1.30–5pm; free), Atatürk's Ankara residence, to which he moved in 1921. A visit here is something of a reverential pilgrimage for Turks, but if you want to go you must arrange a visit in advance with the tourist office, which will fax ahead a day or two beforehand – on arrival, check in at the guardhouse and surrender your passport before joining a group tour. The house itself is a reasonably modest affair, a largish two-storey villa set in formal grounds, but by no means a palace. The ground floor is furnished in the Ottoman Baroque style, with much heavily carved and inlaid dark wood furniture in evidence. Upstairs in Atatürk's living quarters the decor is a little more relaxed, with personal touches, such as a billiard table, on display.

Back on Çankaya Caddesi, at the junction with Atatürk Bulvarı is the unmissable **Atakule Mall and Tower**, a vast mushroom of a tower in reinforced concrete and mirror glass, with another smart shopping centre at its foot. It's worth shelling out a dollar for the lift ride (daily 10am–10pm) up the 125-metre-high structure to enjoy an unbeatable view of the city and an expensive drink in the revolving bar.

Anıt Kabir

Anıt Kabir (Mon 1.30–5pm, Tues–Sat 9am–5pm; winter closes 4pm; free), Atatürk's mausoleum, is a national shrine to the memory of the man who shaped modern Turkey. The main entrance to the mausoleum is reached by travelling up Anıt Caddesi from Tandoğan Meydanı (at the northwestern end of Gazi Mustafa Kemal Bulvarı), and it's this approach that reveals the place at its most impressive (though you can also enter the grounds of the mausoleum from a rear entrance on Akdeniz Caddesi). Bus #265 runs from Ulus Meydanı, dropping you at Tandoğan Meydanı, or alternatively catch an *Ankaray* (LRT) train to Tandoğan.

A flight of steps at the main entrance leads up to a colonnade, guarded by Hittite-style stone lions, which in turn leads to the central courtyard of the mausoleum. The entrance to the colonnade is flanked by two towers: the **Independence Tower** on the left and the **Freedom Tower** on the right. Inside the towers you'll find a scale model of the Anıt Kabir complex, a selection of before-and-after aerial shots of its construction from 1944 to 1953, and some intriguing runner-up designs that never quite made it off the page.

At the head of the central courtyard lies the **mausoleum** itself, a squared-off Neoclassical temple with huge bronze doors. Visitors wearing hats must remove them as they enter and soldiers stand guard to ensure that everyone evinces the appropriate degree of respect. The mausoleum interior is almost completely bare – the only decoration is some discreet mosaic work – so that all attention is focused on the plain sarcophagus. Atatürk's body was brought here in 1953 from its original resting place in what is now the Ethnographic Museum.

On the opposite side of the courtyard is the **tomb of İsmet İnönü** (1884–1973), Atatürk's old comrade and long-time supporter, who served as first prime minister of the Turkish Republic and became president after Atatürk's death. Three large halls are positioned around the courtyard. The largest of these, on the southern side, houses the **Atatürk Museum** in which you'll find everything from Atatürk's evening dress to the rowing machine he used for exercise. Among the most eye-catching exhibits are a gun disguised as a walking stick, of which Ian Fleming would have been proud, and the gifts of a diamond-encrusted sword from the shah of Iran and an elegant toilet set from the king of Afghanistan. An adjacent hall contains Atatürk's cars, namely a couple of Lincoln limousines used for official business and an imposing black Cadillac (reputedly still in working order) for personal use. In the nearby information centre there's not much in the way of information, but fans of esoteric **souvenirs** will appreciate the selection of Atatürk key-rings, ashtrays and wall-clocks that propel the Atatürk personality cult into the same league as Lenin and Chairman Mao.

Eating

Although there's no shortage of standard kebab and *pide* places in Ankara, and an abundance of good sweet and cake shops, on first appearance there seems to be very little else. In fact there are decent **restaurants** in Ankara, they just take a little finding, and the good ones are tucked up back streets in the leafy suburbs, catering to the diplomatic corps and embassy staff. As with hotels, the further south you move the more expensive places tend to become. Ankara also has a better range of foreign (non-Turkish) restaurants than anywhere else in the country and with a little exploration you'll find excellent and authentic Chinese, Japanese, Mexican, and Italian food.

Ulus is your best bet for cheap eats, **Kızılay** has most of the mid-range places (particularly on and around Karanfil and Selanik *sokak*s), and the more classy restaurants can be found in **Kavaklıdere** and **Çankaya**. The exceptions to this general rule are the restaurants that have opened up in restored Ottoman houses in the **Hisar** (citadel) over the last few years.

Workers' cafés and *lokantas*, particularly in the commercial district of Ulus, tend to open early at 6am, closing at around 4pm (and all day Sunday). Other cafés generally **open every day** between 9am and 9pm; restaurants open for lunch and dinner, with last orders at 10/11pm, though the more popular restaurants and bars in Kavaklıdere stay open until the early hours. We've included **telephone numbers** for places where you might need to book in advance.

Hisar, Ulus and Kızılay restaurants are marked on our Central Ankara map (pp.696–697), those in Kavaklıdere and Çankaya on the Ankara map (pp.690–691).

Hisar

Boyacızade Konağı aka *Kale Restaurant* Berrak Sok 9. Spread across several floors of a rambling mansion house, decorated with carpets and bric-a-brac, and specializing in traditional cuisine. There's a good wine list and prices are surprisingly reasonable, from around $15 a head. The separate fish restaurant on the second floor lacks atmosphere, though the dishes are tasty. Closed Sun.

Kale Washington Kale Sok 1. Atmospheric restaurant with a view-laden terrace perched on top of the old city walls. A good place for a cool beer, or for a dinner of the usual Turkish staples or something a little different, such as beef stroganoff or chicken Kiev. Closed Sun.

Zenger Paşa Konağı Doyran Sok 13. Restored mansion offering traditional Anatolian fare and packed with Ottoman-era ephemera. *Kuzu kapama* (a spicy lamb dish) and *gözleme* (filled pancake) are recommended, as is the enormously long *pide*, all at reasonable prices with fabulous views over the city. Expect to pay $12 a head. Closed Sun.

Ulus

Akman Boza ve Pasta Salonu Atatürk Bul 3. In a shopping plaza just south of the Atatürk statue and underneath *Kebabıstan*. Serves light meals, pastries and *boza* (a refreshing millet-based drink) - the open-air seating makes this a popular breakfast spot.

Bulvar Işkembecisi ve Lokantası Çankırı Cad 11. Excellent *İskender kebap*, *fırın sutlaç* (baked rice pudding) and other trusty favourites in a round-the-clock dining operation. It's next to the *Hotel Selvi*.

Büyük Pastane Atatürk Bul. In the shopping centre opposite the Museum of the War of Independence. Milk puddings, *baklava* and chocolate pastries served in a shady courtyard adorned with pot-plants and a fountain.

Gaziantep Fethi Bey Sanayi Cad 31. Simple, cheap worker's canteen, with soups soaked up with plenty of bread, meat and vegetable stews and *baklava* to follow. The cooking's not great but you can't beat the prices.

Hosta Piznik Posta Cad 10. Ulus branch of the fast-food chain, with *doner* and *ayran* for $1 and a busy *sandviç* trade at lunchtimes. There's another branch in Kızılay, at the corner of Sakarya and Selanik Sok.

Kebabıstan Atatürk Bul 3. Very popular family-run joint, in a shopping plaza above the *Akman Boza*, for hearty lunchtime portions of *kebap* and *pide*. It attracts nearby bank workers so come early for a better choice of dishes, each costing little more than $1.50. Closed Sun.

Tapi Tavuk Posta Cad 7. Good value canteen-style cafeteria where what you see is what you get. A wide selection of vegetable side dishes combine well for a filling meal. Closed Sun.

Kızılay

Altin Şiş Karanfil Sok 17. Reasonably priced kebab place with good puddings; a favourite with local office workers.

Göksu Bayındır Sok 22 ☏0312/431 2219. Upmarket Turkish dishes in authentic surroundings. There's a huge menu of excellent kebabs, grills and fish (including salmon, trout and sea bass), with main courses from $7.

Köşk Tuna Cad, İnkılap Sok 2. The best *İskender kebap* and *inegöl köfte* in Ankara, and despite its well-earned reputation prices are still low – $5 for a plate of succulent *köfte*. Eat on the lovely terrace from crisp white tablecloths, or inside the spotless two-storey restaurant decorated with chandeliers, gleaming brass and even ornate cages of songbirds.

Mudurnu Selanik Cad 14. A busy café opposite the flower market – $2 will get you a portion of spit-roast chicken and a soft drink.

Paris Aile Salonu Selanik Cad 32. A surreal Wild-West-style gaming den packed to the gills with old men arguing about politics, or playing cards, dominoes, pool, chess or backgammon. There are snacks available, open-air seating and primitive internet access upstairs. Women are seated separately on the mezzanine level at the back, from where they keep a close eye on their husbands below.

Pizzeria Tempo Corner of Meşrütiyet Cad and Karanfil Sok. Very popular pizza-and-pasta place, with a reasonably authentic Italian atmosphere and moderate prices. Pizzas are generally a safer bet than the pasta dishes, which can miss the mark slightly, but service is quick and lone travellers – particularly women – will feel comfortable here.

Kavaklıdere

Arpien Arjantin Cad 17. Ankara's only Mexican restaurant, with a cosy bar area serving up margaritas in a congenial atmosphere, and a menu big on *nachos*, *tortillas* and the like – though prices reflect its popularity as an embassy hangout.

Budakatti Brassiere Budak Sok 6. Pleasant bar-café with garden tables, serving an excellent Sunday brunch of omelettes, toast, ham and cheese (alas no bacon) between 10am and 2pm. There's another branch on the sixth floor of the Beymen clothes shop on Tunalı Hilmi Cad, where Ankara's wealthy shoppers meet to drink tea.

Guangzhou Wuyang Bestekar Sok 33. In a back

street behind Tunalı Hilmi Cad, serving good, budget-priced Cantonese cuisine.

Hacı Arif Bey Güneş Sok 48. One of the oldest and most established eateries in town, for succulent kebabs in *bona fide* restaurant surroundings (rather than the usual canteen ambience). Expect to pay in the region of $15–20 per head and to battle it out with occasional mass invasions by Turkish families here for weddings or birthdays.

Imattı Arjantin Cad 34. Good-value Italian place with home-made pasta, pastries, pizza and authentic Italian coffee. This is where to come for a late-night *latte* and to watch Ankara's bright young things attempt to negotiate their BMWs into the tight parking spaces outside.

Japon Mutfağı Arjantin Cad 30 ☎0312/467 3344. Excellent, expensive sushi prepared by Japanese chefs – the cutting-edge decor attracts diplomats and five-star hotel guests in abundance, none of whom baulk at paying $35–40 a head for admittedly great food.

Kebab 49 Bestekar Sok 13/A. Kebabs and tablecloths under the same roof in a fashionable part of town. It's a popular spot for family dinners.

Mest Attar Sok 10 ☎0312/468 0743. A classy Kavaklıdere venue boasting outside tables in the garden. Huge menu of pasta, meat and fish, and a good selection of Turkish and French wines.

Trilye Reşit Galip Cad, Hafta Sok 11 ☎0312/447 1200. Superb fish restaurant set in a lovely garden lit by twinkly lights and candles. Treat yourself with lobster thermidor – though the chef's special of oven-baked seafood comes in much cheaper at around $6.

Yakamoz Tunalı Hilmi Cad 114/J 2–3. You'll find surprisingly well-priced fish dishes from the Black Sea and elsewhere in this busy seafood restaurant, hidden in the verges of Kuğulu Park.

Yosun İran Cad 27 ☎0312/509 5464. Customers return again and again for an authentic Turkish night out – start with *meze*, then move on to fish (red mullet, sea bass or bream), while Tolon, the aged owner, provides the entertainment by singing and playing the piano and accordion. Expect to pay around $18 with a half-bottle of wine or *rakı* thrown in.

Çankaya

Lord Kinroos Green Garden Bar & Restaurant Cemal Nadir Sok 18 ☎0312/439 5252. Located in a house on a back street off Simon Bolivar Cad, this rather exclusive white-tablecloth affair serves an interesting mix of Italian and Turkish dishes. Reservations advised; closed Sun.

Drinking and nightlife

For drinking you'll have to head south from Ulus; it's a commercial district and apart from the odd hotel bar and kebab restaurant, shuts up at night after the shops and banks close. The *meyhane*s (taverns) on and around Bayındır, Karanfil and Selanik *sokak*s in **Kızılay** make a good starting point, and although these are largely male-dominated haunts, female visitors shouldn't attract too much unwelcome attention. For something more trendy head for the bars of **Kavaklıdere**, particularly on Tunalı Hilmi Caddesi or the swisher Arjantin Caddesi, near the *Sheraton*, which is the city's main see-and-be-seen strip.

Bars and cafés

Most **cafés** open during the day to offer food, tea, and obligatory backgammon boards, some serving alcohol as the evening progresses. Not many of Ankara's **bars** feature live music, but those that do attract a cover charge when a band is on and generally go on a bit later than most, until 1 or 2am. The Kızılay cafés and bars are marked on the Central Ankara map (pp.696–697), the Kavaklıdere ones on the Ankara map (pp.690–691).

Kızılay

Black Eight Selanik Cad 76. Just at the entrance of the Metropol cinema. Fat sofas, stripped-wood floors and doors combined with hi-tech furniture, beer on tap and live music at weekends.

Büyük Ekspress Bayındır Sok 11. Expat and student haunt that looks a bit rough and ready but is a good place for a beer. Greasy burgers and kebabs complement the serious drinking.

Fuaye Cafe Selanik Cad 69. Atmospheric live-music bar belting out a mix of Western pop and traditional songs. It's one of several places near

8

the Metropol cinema that makes a good venue for an after-film drink.

Kavaklıdere

B-Trip Bestekar Sok 59. Simple pub with high stools along a well-kept bar featuring a range of international schnapps and brandies, plus a vast CD collection of Western pop and rock.

Cafés des Cafés Tunalı Hilmi Cad 81. Although the bar serves food this joint primarily provides an ideal resting place for a caffeine and nicotine fix. Despite looking like a pub, there's no alcohol.

Gitanes Tunalı Hilmi Cad, Bilir Sok 4/3. An intimate candlelit bar with regular live music performances – often attracting the better-known Turkish jazz bands. As good a starting point as any for your in-depth exploration of the Tunalı Hilmi scene.

Ivy Californian Brasserie Iran Cad 35. Huge terrace-bar opposite the *Seğmenler Parkı*. Order a frozen margarita, accompanied perhaps by something from their vast home-made cheesecake menu. It's a perfect spot for a sundowner, and there's a good selection of English-language magazines.

Jazz Time Tunalı Hilmi Cad, Bilir Sok 4/1. A friendly bar with live music (usually Turkish pop) until at least 1am every night, always packed to the gills.

Kuğulu Park Café Kuğulu Parkı. Pleasant open-air retreat from the traffic, serving pastries, snacks and non-alcoholic drinks by the fountain until around 10pm.

Mado Ice Cream Bar Tunalı Hilmi Cad, Kuğulu Parkı. Swanky modern place full of young people on first dates sampling every flavour of ice cream under the sun.

Marilyn Monroe's Tunalı Hilmi Cad 71. Rather tacky, as the name suggests, but immensely popular with ex-pats, mostly engineers who come to play darts. Drink at balcony tables or the street-side terrace.

Q-Wreck Arjantin Cad 34. Modern, spacious bar where Ankara's bright young things like to be spotted sitting on the terrace. Full bar menu of omelettes, burgers and sandwiches.

Salata Bistro Reşit Galip Cad 57, Gaziosmanpaşa. Café-bar popular with the student crowd, serving snacks. There's outside seating in the garden during summer, and in winter they warm things up inside with a log fire.

Clubs

Nightlife in Ankara is limited and the only places that stay open late are a series of seedy *gazino*-type joints along Gazi Mustafa Kemal Bulvarı in Maltepe, and a few tacky clubs in Kavaklıdere and Kızılay. Foreigners are more likely to feel at home in the couple of upmarket venues where the music is influenced by the current MTV playlist, but they don't come cheap. There are some studenty late-night venues hidden away in the back streets of the university district, Cebeci, but you really need to find a local to guide you to them.

Arpej Selanik Cad 28, Kızılay. Dingy basement dance hall frequented by Turkish university students on binge nights, when drinking here takes on an illicit feel. Daily 1pm–3am.

Club House *Sheraton Hotel*, Noktali Sok, Kavaklıdere. Newly renovated super-club frequented by ex-pats and diplomats. One of the few places in Ankara where you can successfully order a gin & tonic, but except to pay through the nose for it. Live music nightly from 10pm to 2am, closed Sun.

My Way Corner of Selanik Sok and Ziya Gökalp Cad, Kızılay. Average fish restaurant on a balcony with *fasıl* music and plenty of *rakı*, with a down-

stairs disco playing Turkish pop daily until 4am, attracting die-hard clubbers still hanging around Kızılay after other places have closed.

Opera Konur Sok 6, Kızılay. Café-bar during the day, Turkish dance music on a tiny overcrowded dance floor at night. Open until 2am, closed Sun.

Rush Filisten Sok 28, Gaziosmanpaşa. Ankara's trendiest club, an intimate place in a shaded garden with a nice terrace and wooden dance floors out back. Frequented by a young international crowd and embassy workers, and with a reasonably priced menu of Thai snacks and good vegetarian options. Daily except Sun noon–4am.

The arts and entertainment

With Ankara's designation as capital of the new republic, the city then had the responsibility of becoming the cultural capital of Turkey, supported by the opera-loving Atatürk. While İstanbul is Turkey's more culturally diverse city, Ankara holds its own as home of the prestigious **State Opera and Ballet** and **Presidential Symphony Orchestra**, as well as hosting a large number of state theatres that feature the work of Turkish playwrights. Concerts, and in particular the opera, are well worth attending here if you can. The atmosphere is refreshingly informal and as concerts are subsidized by the government, tickets are cheap. Otherwise, there are plenty of **cinemas** (*sinemasi*) found all over Ankara.

Classical music and opera

A visit to Ankara's Opera House is a unique experience if you are in town at the right time of year. Otherwise, there are classical music performances by the State Orchestra at the State Concert Hall and at various venues across the city. The main season starts in earnest in October and runs through to March, and monthly programmes are listed in the Sunday edition of the *Turkish Daily News*. The city hosts the **International Ankara Music Festival** during May (information on ⓦ www.ankarafestival.com).

State Opera (Devlet Opera) Atatürk Bul, just south of the entrance to Gençlik Parkı ☎0312/324 2210. Performances of classics such as *Tosca, La Boheme* and *Madame Butterfly*, as well as occasional piano recitals and classical concerts. Tickets ($6–10) are available from the box office in season (9.30am–5.30pm, 8pm on performance days), up to a month in advance and from the Dost bookshop in Kızılay (see "Listings" below).

State Orchestra (Devlet Orkestrasi) Talat Paşa Cad 38, just south of the Opera House and Gençlik Parkı ☎0312/309 1343. The Presidential Symphony Orchestra performs here twice weekly at 8pm on Fri, and 11am on Sat during season, showcasing classical music by Turkish and foreign composers. Tickets ($3–5) are available from the State Opera box office (see opposite).

Film

Recent international releases are usually in the original language with Turkish subtitles, and tickets cost around $3, with discounts before 6pm and for students. The tourist office can supply details of Ankara's **film festivals** – the International Film Festival in March, and the International Cartoon Film Festival in May.

Kavaklıdere Tunalı Hilmi Cad 105, Kavaklıdere ☎0312/468 7193. Several screens showing up-to-date Hollywood films, popular with students and situated amongst several cafés.
Kızılırmak Kızılırmak Sok 21, Kocatepe ☎0312/425 5393. Small and intimate three-screen theatre with frequently changing new releases.
Megapol Konur Sok 33, Kızılay ☎0312/419 4493. More arty than the *Metropol*, which it backs onto, screening anything from Japanese to Eastern European films. Look out for the occasional English-speaking classic.
Metropol Selanik Cad 76, Kızılay ☎0312/425

7479. Hugely popular multi-screen cinema showing new releases and special screenings of classic movies and foreign films. There's a coffee shop inside, a beer garden outside and any number of cafés and bars along this street.
Sheraton Open-Air Cinema Noktalı Sok, Kavaklıdere ☎0312/468 5454. If you're going to watch a film do it in style: the *Sheraton Hotel* has a unique rooftop open-air cinema with fabulous city views, a giant screen showing the latest Hollywood films, and a bar service. Two screenings at approximately 6pm & 8pm on summer evenings, weather permitting; $12 and first drink is free.

Listings

Airlines Most airline offices are in Kavaklıdere or Çankaya. THY (ⓦ www.turkishairlines.com) has offices at the airport ☎0312/398 0100; at Atatürk

Bul 154, Kızılay ☎0312/428 0200; and Atatürk Bul 231, Kavaklıdere ☎0312/468 7300. Others include: Aeroflot ☎0312/440 9874; Air France

⑧

☎0312/467 4400; Austrian Airlines ☎0312/433 2533; Delta ☎0312/468 7805; Lufthansa ☎0312/398 0374; Singapore Airlines ☎0312/468 4670; and Swissair ☎0312/468 1144.

Airport Esenboğra airport, general enquiries and flight information ☎0312/398 0100. Havaş buses for the airport (every 30min; daily 4am–11pm; $4) leave from the Havaş bus stop next to the train station.

Banks and exchange Banks and ATMs are available all over the city, though the biggest concentration is south of Ulus along Atatürk Bul. Outside banking hours you can exchange cash (not travellers' cheques) at PTT branches (see "Post office" below). For travellers' cheques, try the number of *döviz* offices along the Kızılay section of Atatürk Bul, or the cashiers at the big hotels, though they are often reluctant to cash cheques for non-residents. The airport also has several places to change money.

Books Tuhran, corner of Konur Sok and Yüksel Cad, Kızılay, has a good selection of books in English, French and German, plus contemporary books on Turkey, and guide and phrase books. Dost, Karanfil Sok 11, Kızılay, has English novels and a good selection of pricier coffee-table books – the English section is downstairs.

Buses The *otogar* at Aşti (☎0312/224 1000), 5km west of the centre, is a monster housing over 150 bus companies, with transport running to almost every conceivable destination, even as far away as Moscow. Buses and minibuses marked "Yeni Garaj", "Yeni Otogar", "Terminal" or "Aşti" leave for the station from the minibus terminal 300m southwest of Ulus Meyd; the "Ankaray" (LRT) runs directly to Aşti from Kızılay. Bus companies normally provide a bus transfer if you buy your ticket in their town offices, most of which are situated on Gazi Mustafa Kemal Bul or Ziya Gökalp Cad. For popular destinations (such as İstanbul) try the larger companies such as Varan (booth 12; ☎0312/426 9753), Ulusoy (booth 13; ☎0312/440 1468), Pamukkale (booth 58; ☎0312/224 0024), or Kamil Koç (booth 18; ☎0312/224 1700). Other specific destinations include: Adıyaman (booths 36 & 48), Amasya (booths 23 & 28), Bursa (booths 17, 35, 41, 45 & 72), Erzurum (booths 36, 40, 68, 73 & 80), Hatay (booths 55 & 67), Kastamonu (booths 38 & 65), Konya (booths 39, 42, 54 & 74), Kütahya (booths 22 & 30), Nevşehir (booths 50 & 61), Polatlı (booth 28), Safranbolu (booths 4, 14 & 27), Sivas (booths 27, 32 & 74), Tokat (booths 6 & 60) and Trabzon (booths 9, 13, 24 & 41). Note that the ticket booth number is *not* necessarily the same as the *peron* (departure bay) number.

Car rental Atak, Cinnah Cad 42, Çankaya ☎0312/441 9000; Avis, airport ☎0312/398 0315, and Tunus Cad 68, Kavaklıdere ☎0312/467 2313;

Best, Büklüm Sok 89/9, Kavaklıdere ☎0312/467 0008; Budget, Tunus Cad 39, Kavaklıdere ☎0312/417 5952; Europcar, airport ☎0312/395 0506, and Koza Sok 154, Gaziosmanpaşa ☎0312/398 0503; Hertz, airport ☎0312/398 0535, and Atatürk Bul 138, Kavaklıdere ☎0312/468 1029; National Car Rental, Tunus Cad 73, Kavaklıdere ☎0312/427 6453.

Cultural centres British Cultural Institute, Bestekar Sok 32, Kavaklıdere ☎0312/419 1844; French Cultural Association, Ziya Gökalp Cad 15, Kızılay ☎0312/431 1458; German Cultural Centre, Atatürk Bul 131, Bakanlıklar ☎0312/425 1436; Turkish American Association, Cinnah Cad 20, Çankaya ☎0312/426 2648.

Embassies Australia, Nenehatun Cad 83, Gaziosmanpaşa ☎0312/446 1180; Canada, Nenehatun Cad 75, Gaziosmanpaşa ☎0312/436 1275; Iran, Tehran Cad 10, Kavaklıdere ☎0312/468 2820; New Zealand, Iran Cad 13, Kavaklıdere ☎0312/467 9056; Russian Federation, Karyağdi Sok 5, Çankaya ☎0312/439 2122; USA, Atatürk Bul 110, Kavaklıdere ☎0312/455 5555; UK, Şehit Ersan Cad 46/A, Çankaya ☎0312/455 3344.

Emergencies Ambulance ☎112; Fire ☎110; Police ☎155.

Football Local teams Ankaragücü and Geçerbitliği play on Saturday or Sunday afternoons during season (Aug–May) at the 35,000-capacity 19 Mayıs stadium, behind Gençlik Parkı.

Hamams Karacabey Hamamı, Talat Paşa Cad 101, Ulus, is the oldest in town, built in 1445 (daily 10am–10pm; bath $6, massage $3). Otherwise, there's the Yeni Ankara Hamamı, Talat Paşa Cad 166, Cebeci (men only; daily 8am–7pm; $4); Küçükesat Hamamı, Esat Cad 81/A, Kavalkıdere (daily: women 8am–2pm, men 6pm–10pm; $4); and Yenişehir Hamam, Sümer Sok 16/A, Kızılay (men only: daily 9am–9pm; $3 bath, massage $3). More tourist friendly are the baths at the *Büyük Sürmeli Hotel*, Cihan Sok 6, Sıhhiye ☎0312/231 7660 (daily 10am–10pm), where a bath with massage will set you back around $8.

Hospitals Hacettepe Hastanesi, just west of Hasırcılar Cad in Sıhhiye (☎0312/466 5858 or 5859), should have an English-speaking doctor available at all times. You may be treated more quickly at one of Ankara's private hospitals: Çankaya, Bülten Sok 44, Çankaya (☎0312/426 1450), is the most central.

Internet Andalu Net, Atatürk Bul 107, Kızılay (9am–9pm), on the second floor of a shopping mall just south of the Gima department store – a red sign on the pavement on both Atatürk Bul and Karanfil Sok points it out; Café de Net, Karanfil Sok 18, Kızılay (daily 9am–11.30pm); Internet Club,

Karanfil Sok 18, Kızılay (daily 7.30am–midnight). On Konur Sok in Kızılay there are three in a row: Speedy at no.5, Cat at no.7 and Esca at no.8, all open to at least 10pm.

Laundry All but the cheapest of hotels offer a reasonably priced laundry service, but if you get stuck try the Yimpaş department store on Sanayı Cad in Ulus – on the second floor is a laundry and dry cleaners.

Left luggage At the train station (daily 7.30am–10pm; $2–4 depending on the declared value of your bag).

Pharmacies In each neighbourhood pharmacies take turn in providing a 24hr service called *Nöbetçi*, the information posted on the window of the other pharmacy shops. Most central is Ülkü, Meşrütiyet Cad 23, Kızılay.

Police The tourist police (☎0312/384 0606), are located in Ankara's main police station (Emniyet Sarayı) in the district of Akköprü, a short walk south of the Akköprü metro station, two stops northeast of Ulus. If you need to file a complaint, the tourist office will provide an interpreter.

Post office Ankara's main PTT is on Atatürk Bul in Ulus (open 24hr) for international calls and to buy stamps, phonecards, *jetons* etc. You can also place transfer charge calls here. There's also a PTT at the train station (7am–11pm), and one on Gazi Mustafa Kemal Bul (8.30am–7pm) near the tourist office.

Shopping Antikite, Cinnah Cad 32, Çankaya, has general antiques and bric-a-brac, marginally cheaper than you might expect to find at home. The old shops in Çıkrıkçılar Yokuşu are worth a browse for copper, carpets, antiques, costumes and embroidery, as is the Pirinç Han at the citadel. There are shopping centres at Atakule, Cinnah Cad/Çankaya Cad, Çankaya; Beğenik, Kocatepe (beneath Kocatepe Camii); and Karum, Aran Cad, Kavaklıdere. Western and Turkish cassettes and CDs are available from the Supersonic Music Centre, Tunalı Hilim Cad, Kavaklıdere, and from Dost, Karanfil Sok 11, Kızılay, and adjacent shops.

Swimming Some of the big hotels open up their pools to non-residents. The cheapest option is the *Büyük Şurmeli Hotel* (Mon–Sat 10am–7pm; $8 weekdays, $10 Sat). Swimming at the *Sheraton* ($15 on weekdays; $23 at weekends) works out a little more expensive but includes full use of their health club. There's also an open-air pool, Tursan, at Karakusunlar Mevkii 14/1, Balgat, in the western suburbs (June–Sept only; $6; bus #132 from Kızılay).

Trains For schedules see "Travel details", p.752. The train station has an enquiries number, ☎0312/311 0602, but don't expect anyone to speak English.

Travel agents General travel agents can be found in Kızılay and around Tunalı Hilmi Cad in Kavaklıdere. Most can book flights and car rental though English is rarely spoken (better to go directly to the airline/car rental offices). There are English-speaking services at Cherokee Tourism & Travel, Guniz Sok 29, Kavaklıdere (☎0312/468 6572 ⊛ www.cherokee-travel.com); and Yanki Seyahat Acentasi, Atatürk Bul 169/65, Kavaklıdere (☎0312/417 6855); both can arrange half-day tours of Ankara ($50) and day-trips to Gordion or Hattuşaş ($130).

West of Ankara

Attractions west of Ankara are few and far between and, with one exception, probably best treated as stop-off points on the way to or from the Aegean coast. The exception is the Phrygian capital of **Gordion**, which lies 90km or so west of the capital, making it a feasible day-trip destination. Beyond Gordion are a number of less accessible sites really only worth tackling if you have your own transport – these include **Sivrihisar** with a fine Selçuk mosque, and the nearby temple city of **Pessinus**. Even further off the beaten track, towards Eskişehir in the west of the region, are the small town of **Seyitgazi**, with its atmospheric dervish monastery, and the important Phrygian centre of **Midas şehri** – again, you're only really going to be able to visit either if you're driving yourself across country. **Eskişehir** itself is on main train and bus routes but is primarily an industrial centre with little to offer other than meerschaum souvenirs. It's a better bet to press on in the direction of **Kütahya**, a relaxed city famed for its ceramic tiles and a good base for excursions to the eerie temple ruins at the Roman site of **Aezani**.

Gordion

After the collapse of the Hittite Empire the Phrygians briefly dominated Anatolia, and their capital, **Gordion**, is one of western Anatolia's most important archeological sites. It's a name of much resonance, associated not only with the eponymous knot, but also with king Midas and his golden touch. The first things you'll see as you approach are the immense royal tumuli scattered across the drab, steppe-like landscape. Inside these, archeologists found a wealth of stunning artefacts indicating the sophisticated nature of Phrygian culture. Nearby, the foundations of the Gordion acropolis have been uncovered.

There are **buses** every half-hour from Ankara's *otogar* to the town of **Polatlı**, 18km southwest of Gordion. From Polatlı *otogar*, take a *servis* minibus into town and seek out one of the dolmuşes (every couple of hours depending on demand) to the village of **Yassıhüyük**, just short of the site itself. A taxi to and from the site from Polatlı will cost around $20.

Some history

The original settlement at Gordion dates back to the Bronze Age and the site was certainly occupied during the Hittite period. The Phrygians probably took up residence during the middle of the ninth century BC and a hundred years later the settlement became capital of the empire founded by the Phrygian king **Gordios**. The history of Gordion under the Phrygians mirrors the history of the Phrygian Empire itself – a brief flowering followed by destruction and protracted decline. There's little left in the records, save for the myths and legends associated with the empire (see box opposite), though some concrete information survives about the final king of the Phrygian Empire. He is referred to in Assyrian records as Mitas (Midas) of Mushki, who paid tribute to the Assyrians after being defeated in battle by them. He is thought to have reigned from 725 BC to 696 BC and the Greek historian Herodotus describes how he dedicated his throne at the Delphic shrine of Apollo and married the daughter of one of the Ionian kings.

Phrygian prosperity stemmed from the abundant natural resources of the region and the fact that their empire straddled major east–west trade routes. Ironically it was another set of invaders, the **Cimmerians**, who laid waste to the Phrygian Empire, destroying Gordion, and though the Phrygians made a comeback and rebuilt their capital, their power had been irreversibly reduced. In 650 BC the city was occupied by the **Lydians** and then it fell in turn to the **Persians** just over a century later. In 333 BC, **Alexander the Great** wintered here during his great march east, managing to sever the Gordian Knot during his stay. The arrival of the **Galatians** (Gauls) in Asia Minor in 278 BC was the final chapter in the long decline of Gordion, precipitating the flight of the city's population.

The acropolis

From the dolmuş drop-off point in Yassıhüyük village it makes sense to head first for the eighth-century BC **acropolis**. This raised area was the heart of the

8

The myths and legends of Gordion

The name Midas is inextricably associated with Gordion. A number of Phrygian kings bore this name, and over the centuries a kind of composite mythical figure has emerged around whom a number of legends have grown up. The best known of these is that of **Midas and the golden touch**. According to the story Midas captured the water demon, Silenus, after making him drunk by pouring wine into his spring. In ransom for Silenus, Midas demanded of Dionysos the ability to turn all he touched into gold. Dionysos granted this wish but Midas was dismayed to find he had been taken quite literally, and his food and even his own daughter were transformed. He begged Dionysos for release from the curse and was ordered to wash his hands in the River Pactolus. The cure worked and thereafter the river ran with gold.

Another tale tells of how Midas was called upon to judge a musical contest between Apollo and the satyr Marsyas. Midas decided in favour of Marsyas and in revenge Apollo caused him to grow the ears of an ass (Marsyas came off even worse – the god skinned him alive). To hide his new appendages, Midas wore a special hat, revealing them only to his barber who was sworn to secrecy on pain of death. Desperate to tell someone the king's secret, the barber passed it on to the reeds of the river who ever after whispered, "Midas has ass's ears".

Another story may have some basis in reality. It tells how, during the reign of Gordios, an oracle foretold that a poor man who would enter Gordion by ox-cart would, one day, rule over the Phrygians. As the king and nobles were discussing this prediction, a farmer named Midas arrived at the city in his cart. Gordios, who had no heirs, saw this as the fulfilment of the prophecy and named Midas his successor. Subsequently, Midas had his cart placed in the temple of Cybele on the Gordion acropolis, where it was to stand for half a millennium. Somehow the belief arose that whoever untied the knot that fixed the cart to its yoke would become master of Asia. During his stay in the city Alexander the Great took it upon himself to undo the **Gordian Knot**, severing it with his sword.

city, location of the royal palace, temples and administrative buildings, the foundations of which have been revealed by excavations. Substantial remains of the huge Phrygian-era **town gate** survive on the southeastern side of the acropolis. This must have been a formidable structure in its day: even in its present truncated state it's over ten metres high, making it one of the largest surviving pre-Classical buildings in Anatolia. The outer portal was flanked by twin towers, from which defenders would have been able to inflict heavy casualties on attackers in front of the gate. The foundations of what are thought to have been storage rooms stand on either side of the inner portals – the remains of *pithoi*, or stone storage jars, were found in the right-hand one when it was excavated.

The **palace** at the heart of the acropolis consisted of four *megara*, or large halls with vestibules. The second of these is the most impressive, with the remains of red, white and blue mosaics forming geometrical patterns still visible on the floor. When it was excavated, charred fragments of wooden furniture inlaid with ivory were found in the rubble, suggesting that this could have been the central hall of the palace. The fourth *megaron* was probably a temple to Cybele, the Phrygian incarnation of the mother goddess. If this is the case, then it's here that Alexander the Great **cut the Gordian Knot** (see box above). Behind the palace are the foundations of eight more large *megara*, thought to have been the quarters of palace servants.

The royal tombs and museum

The main concentration of the huge and inscrutable tumulus tombs of the

Phrygian kings is at the eastern end of Yassıhüyük, but only the **Midas Tümülüsü** (Royal Tomb) near the museum is likely to attract your attention. At 300m in diameter and over 50m high (reduced by erosion from its original height of around 80m), the Royal Tomb dominates the vicinity, and with these dimensions it's easy to see why it was originally thought to house the remains of either Gordios or Midas. However, material found in the burial chamber dates the tomb to somewhere between 750 and 725 BC, too late for Gordios or his successor and too early for the last king Midas. It is thought instead to be that of a Phrygian king, his identity unknown, curiously buried without weapons or ornaments – though the burial chamber itself, made of gabled pine logs, is reputed to be the oldest wooden structure in Anatolia. The tumulus was excavated during the early 1950s, when American archeologists bored a sixty-metre excavation tunnel through to its centre and discovered the intact wooden chamber. Inside they found the skeleton of a man in his 60s on a wooden couch surrounded by grave objects. Among these were three exquisitely crafted wooden tables, inlaid wooden screens, large numbers of bronze clasps for garments and 178 bronze vessels of various sizes, including three large cauldrons.

Just southeast of the acropolis is the **Köçük Höyük**, a clay mound that's actually higher than the citadel itself. The Köçük Höyük was originally a fortified suburb of Gordion, which was destroyed when the Persian army of Cyrus marched through the region en route to Sardis, and was later turned into a tomb for the defeated ruler of Gordion. It's also worth dropping in on the small **museum** (Tues–Sun 8am–noon & 1.30–5pm; $2), which contains some of the items recovered from the tombs and some attractive mosaics, though inevitably the best of the finds are in Ankara's Museum of Anatolian Civilizations.

Sivrihisar and Pessinus

About 60km to the west of Polatlı, along the E90 highway, is the town of **Sivrihisar** (Byzantine Justiniapolis), with a fine Selçuk forest mosque and access to the Phrygian temple city of **Pessinus**. These two destinations only really make sense if you have your own transport and are looking for a place to break your journey – and even then you have to be a devotee of Selçuk architecture or the history of the Cybele cult to get much out of them.

SİVRİHİSAR itself is a torpid little place, overlooked by a ruined Byzantine fortress perched on a crag high above. In such an ordinary town, the interior finery of the **Ulu Cami** ("Great Mosque"), built by the Selçuks in 1274, seems to belong to another world. There are 67 painstakingly carved wooden columns supporting a timber ceiling, and the walls are decorated with colourful Turcoman motifs. A typically Selçuk feature is the incorporation of stone capitals from ancient columns into the structure of the building.

The ancient temple city of **Pessinus** is in the modern village of **Balihisar**, about 13km southeast of Sivrihisar down a rutted, winding road. The temple was founded by the Phrygians in honour of the earth goddess Cybele. The priests of the cult were eunuchs and the orgiastic rites associated with worship sometimes culminated in self-castration by over-enthusiastic adherents. Though the site fell to the Galatians after their invasion of Anatolia, the temple was maintained and a steady stream of pilgrims ensured that the town prospered. The main symbol of the cult at this site was the Baitylos, a black meteorite that was transported to Rome in 205 BC at the behest of King Attalus I of Pergamon, who had formed an alliance with the priests of Pessinus.

As a result, when the Romans defeated the Galatians, Pessinus became part of Pergamon, and it's from this period that the buildings near the temple date. The **temple** site was excavated during the 1970s to reveal extensive foundations, and features a perfectly square inner sanctum with 7.5-metre-long walls. Nearby are the remains of the town **odeion**.

Seyitgazi

SEYİTGAZİ sits in a fertile valley set incongruously amid the rolling Anatolian steppe. To get there turn off the E90 at the signpost for Hamidiye, around 60km west of Sivrihisar, and take the first right, which will bring you to your destination after 25km. It's little more than a sprawling village, and your arrival may take the tractor-driving farmers by surprise.

Seyitgazi takes its name from Şehit Battal Gazi, the commander of one of the Arab armies that forayed into Anatolia during the eighth century, around whom an unlikely legend has grown up. The story has it that he was killed during the siege of Afyon and buried with a Byzantine princess who had pined away through love for him. The site of their resting place was revealed to the mother of the Selçuk sultan Alâeddin Keykubad, who promptly built a *türbe* (tomb) for the gazi. It became a popular place of pilgrimage and during the thirteenth century Hacı Bektaş Veli, founder of the Bektaşi dervish order, established a *tekke*, or monastery, here. During the sixteenth century, the complex was thoroughly restored on the orders of Selim I, a ruler who numbered among his other contributions to religious life in Anatolia the massacre of 40,000 Shi'ites.

The **türbe–tekke complex**, on the slopes of the valley above the town, seems nothing more than an agglomeration of sandy walls topped by grey-white domes when seen from the distance. The ground plan is roughly horseshoe-shaped, open towards the valley slope with a Byzantine church and a Selçuk mosque by the entrance. The former is a reminder that a Christian convent originally stood on the site, while the latter contains the outsize sarcophagus of Şehit Battal, which measures just under seven metres in length. Next to it is the more modest sarcophagus of his princess. To the rear of the complex is an Ottoman mosque dating from Selim's restoration, with adjacent dormitories and ancillary buildings for the monastery.

Midas Şehri

The major Phrygian site of **Midas Şehri** lies about 30km due south of Seyitgazi. To reach it, head in the direction of Afyon and take the first left turn towards the village of Yazilikaya. The unmetalled road is pretty abysmal but the landscape, with its eerie rock formations, makes up for the discomfort. This whole area is dotted with Phrygian tombs, temples and fortifications, but those at Midas Şehri are by far the most accessible and substantial.

The **site** itself (always open; free) comprises the sketchy ruins of a Phrygian city set on top of a thirty-metre-high plateau whose steep rock sides have been carved with elaborate decorative facades. Despite the fact that Midas Şehri means "City of Midas" in Turkish, there's no specific Midas connection, though for a while it was supposed that one of the Phrygian kings of that name was buried here.

The carved facade on the northwestern face of the plateau has come to be known as the **Midas tomb**. From a distance this huge expanse of tufa, measuring about 15m by 17m, resembles the interior wall of a house that has had a large fireplace cut into it a few metres above ground level. Closer up you can see the rectilinear bands in raised relief that crisscross the facade, topped by a decorative pediment. An early Western visitor to the site in 1800, William Martin Leake, concluded that the "fireplace" niche had to let onto a concealed entrance to a tomb. Attempting to decipher the Phrygian inscription on the monument, he mistranslated one word to read Midas and assumed it was a royal tomb. It's now known that the word Leake took to mean Midas actually reads "Mida", another name for Cybele, and it's probable that the niche housed a cult statue of the goddess. Following the plateau sides round to the west from here leads to more niches carved in the rock, a number of rock tombs and an incomplete relief.

Access to the upper part of the plateau and the remains of the Phrygian **citadel** is via a flight of steps on the eastern side. Near the top of the steps are a number of altars and tombs, some of which bear inscriptions and decorative reliefs. In the southwestern part of the citadel is a **rock throne**, a kind of stepped altar on which the figure of a deity would have been placed. The upper part of this throne has a clear **inscription** and crude decorative scratchings. Elsewhere a few fragments of the citadel's defensive wall survive.

Eskişehir

ESKİŞEHİR – 233km west of Ankara – is a modern industrial city, primarily given over to the construction of railway locomotives and fighter aircraft, but also a hub for the textile industry, cement manufacture and even chocolate production – approaching from the east you might get a welcome whiff from the vast chocolate factory. Out of town to the west, on the E90, is a park with some fifteen to twenty retired light aircraft and fighter jets.

Most visitors, however, come because of the **meerschaum** (literally "sea foam" in German), a porous white stone, large deposits of which are mined in the surrounding villages. While wet, the soft stone is carved into all manner of ornaments, but it's the smoke-cooling properties of a meerschaum pipe that is the most highly prized item. The mineral is worked in a number of shops around town and with a little haggling it should be possible to pick up some bargains. Eskişehir's most famous **pipe shop** is Işık Pipo, Sakarya Caddesi, Konya İşhani 12/6, where you can watch the craftsmen at work.

Despite appearances, Eskişehir has a long history, the modern town having been grafted onto an ancient settlement. Its origins go back at least to Greek times, when it was known as Dorylaeum. Some relics of this old city can be seen in the local **archeological museum** (Arkeoloji Müzesi; Tues–Fri 9.30am–noon & 1.30–4pm; $0.50), midway between the *Soyiç Oteli* and the *otogar* on Yunus Emre Caddesi, which houses a few Roman statues and mosaics. For a taste of the more recent past head for the old quarter in the northwestern corner of town, centred on an unremarkable Selçuk **castle**. On the opposite, eastern edge of the city stands the sixteenth-century **Kurşunlu Cami**, attributed to Sinan.

Practicalities

Eskişehir's sights do not amount to a great deal, and it's not a place you'd want to hang around in for more than a few hours. Fortunately, there are good road

and rail connections, with trains running to Ankara, İzmir and İstanbul, and frequent buses and dolmuşes on the same routes.

The **otogar** is on Yunus Emre Caddesi, near the river, and the **train station** is on the northwestern edge of the city centre. Both are within walking distance of the not-very-useful **tourist office** in the *Valilik* building at İki Eylül Cad 175 (Mon–Fri 9am–noon 1.30–4.30pm; ☎0222/230 1752). It's unlikely you'd want to stay, but the best budget **hotel** is the *Sale Oteli*, İnönü Cad 17/1 (☎0222/231 4144; ❷), while moving up a notch there's the *Soyiç Oteli*, Yunus Emre Cad 101 (☎0222/230 7190, ☏230 5120; ❸).

If you have some time to spare, you might want to sample **nuga helvasi**, the nougat-like local delicacy available at every self-respecting *pastane* in town, or visit the excellent **thermal baths** at the corner of Hamamyolu Caddesi and Sairtekin Sok.

⑧ Kütahya and around

Dominated by an Ottoman fortress, **KÜTAHYA** is famous above all for its fine tiles, which are used throughout Turkey, especially in restoration work on Ottoman mosques, replacing the İznik originals (just as Kütahya has replaced İznik as the country's leading tile-producing centre). Many modern local buildings, including the *otogar*, are entirely covered in tiles; and there are ceramic shops on virtually every street, selling tiles, dinner services and vases – not to mention toilets, of which Kütahya is the nation's largest producer.

Kütahya's earliest recorded inhabitants were the Phrygians and thereafter the city endured the usual Anatolian round of conquest and occupation, coming to the fore briefly when Alexander the Great established his headquarters here en route to Gordion. The town was occupied by the Selçuks after the battle of Manzikert in 1071, but then lost to the army of the First Crusade. The Selçuks returned in 1182 and a century or so later the city became capital of the Germiyanid, a Kurdo–Turkish tribe who had been brought into the area from the east. They were ousted by the Ottomans, only to make a brief comeback after Beyazit Yıldırım's defeat at the hands of the Mongol ruler Tamerlane. The Germiyanid emirate survived until 1428, when Kütahya fell permanently into Ottoman hands.

It was under the Ottomans that Kütahya enjoyed its golden age as a **tile-making centre**. Sultan Selim I forcibly resettled tile-workers from Tabriz here after defeating the Persians at Çaldıran in 1514. He dispatched some of their colleagues to İznik, instigating a two-hundred-year rivalry between the two cities that only ended when the İznik industry was transferred to İstanbul. Contemporary Kütahya tiles look a little garish and crude in comparison with Ottoman-era examples – the secret of the pigment blends that gave the original Kütahya tiles their subtle and delicate lustre has been lost with the centuries.

During the War of Independence, the Greek army occupied the city during its advance on Ankara. The invaders were defeated twice in battles at the defile of İnönü, northeast of Kütahya, in January and April 1921. They managed to break out in the summer of the same year, capturing Eskişehir and Afyon and launching an offensive that took them to within striking distance of Ankara. The following year the Turkish offensive that was to throw the Greeks out of Anatolia once and for all began at Dumlupınar, midway between Kütahya and Afyon.

The Town

A number of well-preserved Ottoman-era houses in the immediate vicinity of the main square, **Belediye Meydanı**, set the tone for Kütahya. The rest of the city's attractions, however, lie at the end of Cumhuriyet Bulvarı, which runs west from Belediye Meydanı. After about 500m, at the point where the road splits off in several directions, you'll find the **Ulu Cami**, an attractive but unexceptional fifteenth-century mosque that stands in the midst of Kütahya's lively **bazaar** area, which extends over several streets in the vicinity.

Just next to the Ulu Cami is the town **museum** (Tues–Sun 8.30am–noon & 1–5.30pm; $0.70), with a collection of archeological finds from the area, including a beautiful sarcophogus found at Aezani (see overleaf) depicting a heroic battle between the Greeks and Amazons. The contents of the museum are considerably less interesting than the building that houses them, the **Vacidiye Medresesi**, a fourteenth-century *medrese* built by the Germiyanid Emir Bey Bin Savcı as an astronomical observatory and school of science and mathematics. The highpoint of the interior is the central marble pool beneath a dome with glass skylights.

Beyond the Ulu Cami and museum, signs point out the way to the **Kossuth Evi** (Tues–Sun 8.30am–noon & 1.30–5.30pm; $0.70), a few minutes' walk to the west. This was home to Lajos Kossuth (1802–1894), the Hungarian patriot who fled to Turkey after the failure of the 1848 uprising against Habsburg rule. The immaculate house has been preserved much as it must have been when he lived there in 1850–1851, although it's the nineteenth-century Ottoman ambience of the rooms, rather than the Kossuth connection, which will be of interest to most visitors.

Kütahya's **kale** towers above the Kossuth house and signposts point you in the right direction should you wish to wander up to the summit, from where there are predictably impressive views of the city below. The fortress was originally built by the Byzantines and extended by their successors, but these days only the western walls survive in anything like their original state.

Practicalities

If you're coming in by bus from Eskişehir you'll be dropped off at Kütahya **otogar** (known as Çinigar, or "Tile Station") on Atatürk Bulvarı, just to the northeast of the centre. Turn right out of the *otogar* and it's a short walk up the main road, Atatürk Bulvarı, to reach Belediye Meydanı, the town's main square, distinguished by a fountain with a huge ceramic vase as its centrepiece. Kütahya's **tourist office** (Mon–Sat 9am–5pm; ℡0274/223 1078) is located in the Vilayet building on the north side of Belediye Meydanı. Emails can be sent from any one of a string of **internet** joints along Atatürk Bulvarı en route to the *otogar*, including Milenyum at no.45, Y@ğiz at no.51 and Kaptan at no.55.

Accommodation

Pick of the budget hotel options is the *Hotel Yüksel*, Belediye Meyd 1 (℡0274/212 0111, ℻212 1562; **❶**), which is plain but clean and about as central as you could hope for. The *Otel Kösk*, Lise Cad 1, just north of the square towards the bazaar district (℡0274/216 2024; **❷**), has spacious doubles, though you share a less than salubrious bathroom. Kütahya suffers from a dearth of mid-range options: there's only the *Gönen Otel* (℡0274/224 7799, ℻224 7801; **❸**), offering overpriced rooms on the southern side of Belediye Meydanı. For considerably more you can enjoy the tiled comfort of the *Hotel Gül Palas*, on Belediye Meydanı (℡0274/216 1233, ℱ216 2135; ❺), or the *Hotel Erbaylar*, Afyon Cad 14 (℡0274/223 6960, ✉erbaylar@superonline.com; ❺), the latter with a pleasant terrace-bar and restaurant, just off the main square. If you arrive late at the bus station you may want to consider the traditionally decorated *Hotel Bakırsözer* (℡0274/224 8146, ℱ224 8149; ❹) or the slightly plusher *Otel Tahya* (℡0274/224 3070, ℱ224 3074; ❺), which charges the same rate for singles and doubles; both are right next to the *otogar*.

Eating and drinking

For eating and drinking try *Cınar Köfte*, Lise Cad 7, where you'll get a couple of courses for next to nothing. Across the road from the *Hotel Yüksel*, the *Kervan* serves a good range of cheap food, as does the smarter *Urfa Damak Kepap Sarayi*, under the *Otel Köşk*. Afterwards, you could sample the chocolate cake at the *Inci Pastanesi* just off the square at Atatürk Bulvarı 11, and a beer further down at *Nezih Café Bar*, Atatürk Bul 24. There are several sprawling **teahouses** on the main square, where Kütahya's youth go to keep a watchful eye on each other.

Yoncalı

There are several thermal resorts near Kütahya, the closest and largest being **YONCALİ**, 18km west on the Balikesir road. Yoncalı is a simple village dominated by the plush four-star *Yancalı Tütav Termal Otel* (℡0274/249 4212, ℱ249 4215; ❻), which taps into the hot springs and channels them into a variety of outdoor and indoor pools and steaming hot baths. The water is rich in magnesium and calcium and is exaggeratedly claimed to be beneficial for a whole series of complaints, from insomnia to backache. Come by dolmuş from Kütahya (hourly; 20min) and it's possible to use the facilities as a day visitor for around $8. There are also a couple of cheaper **pansiyons** in the village.

Aezani

Easily reachable, 60km or so southwest of Kütahya, is the site of Roman **Aezani** (always open; free), famed for its atmospheric Temple of Zeus, one of Anatolia's best-preserved Roman buildings. To get there, take a Gediz-, Samav- or Emet-bound **bus** from Kütahya *otogar* or, more conveniently, from the ticket office on Afyon Caddesi, and ask to be let out at **Çavdarhisar** (journey time approximately 1hr) – the site lies just 1km north of this tranquil village. The most convenient buses leave Kütahya at 9.30am and return at 1pm.

The site

The **Temple of Zeus**, built by Hadrian in 125 AD, occupies a commanding position on top of a large, rectangular terrace. To reach it walk up the side-road that leads from the main road in Çavdarhisar in the direction of Emet, and cross the Koca Çay over the Roman bridge, with its marble frieze commemorating the successful sea passage of its sponsor, Marcus Eurykles. On the north and west sides of the main temple building double rows of columns topped by a pediment survive, but elsewhere the columns have largely collapsed and their broken fragments are scattered on the ground nearby; three on the eastern side were repositioned after falling in the Gedız earthquake of 1970.

At the heart of the temple is the **inner sanctum**, once dominated by a magnificent statue of Zeus. Its walls, made of rectangular stone blocks, are largely intact, but the roof has long since caved in. Beneath there's a subterranean **sanctuary** dedicated to Cybele, which the affable site attendant will open up on request. Back outside just northeast of the building, a fallen but well-preserved bust of Cybele – not, as locals will tell you, Medusa – surveys the landscape.

From the temple, you can walk north past the baths to the remains of the uniquely combined **stadium–theatre**. Paths lead up from the fine inscriptions of the southern gate between ruined stadium seats to the backdrop wall of the theatre and the fallen remains of its marble facade. East of the temple stand the arches of the ruined **agora**, and from here the old ceremonial road leads south over a second Roman bridge to the enigmatic **macellum** (marketplace), whose walls carry a fourth-century decree from Emperor Diocletian fixing market prices in an attempt to stop rampant inflation. Complete your circular tour by heading back to the first Roman bridge and ask the site guardian to open up the nearby second set of **baths**, with their satyr mosaic and statue of Hygeia, goddess of the baths.

North of Ankara

The mountain ranges that lie between Ankara and the Black Sea are rugged and pine-clad, forming a landscape that at times becomes almost alpine in flavour. They are undeniably appealing yet, scenery aside, there is little to attract the traveller. Only **Safranbolu**, with its Ottoman mansions of timber construction, set in a steep-sided gorge, rates a visit on its own merits. Other places in this direction – notably **Kastamonu** – are no more than potential stopovers en route to different destinations.

Safranbolu

SAFRANBOLU is a stunning town of half-timbered houses some 220km north of Ankara, approached via the transport hub of Karabük, which is overshadowed by a vast steelworks and perpetually shrouded in a film of industrial grime. Fortunately, many buses from Ankara now go all the way through to Safranbolu in around four hours. If not, you'll have to cover the last 10km in a dolmuş from the *otogar* on the edge of Karabük, though your bus company may well provide a free *servis* bus for the last leg of the journey. After passing through a landscape of rocks and stunted trees, you'll reach **Kıranköy**, the modern section of Safranbolu. If you're dropped off here, you'll need to take one last dolmuş for the final couple of kilometres to the old town. The road descends into a steep-sided valley, snakes up the other side and finally drops again into the ravine, where you'll find **Eski Safranbolu** (also known as Çarşı), a town far removed in time from its modern counterpart.

SAFRANBOLU

Old Government Building

0 — 200 m

HÜKÜMET SOK

Kazdağlı Camii

Dolmuş stop ★

Cinci Hamamı

Dolmuş stop ★ ❺

KALEALTI SOK

KARAÜZÜM SOK

❸

ℹ

Ⓐ ❹

Ⓑ

❻

HAMAMÖNÜ SOK

N

Belediye

Arasta

Ⓒ

Köprülü Mehmet Paşa Camii

Cinci Hanı ❼

ESKİ HAMAM SOK

ARASTA SOK

MANİFATURACILAR SOK

NAİPLER SOK

HIDIRLIK SOK

Ⓓ

Kaymakamlar Evi

İzzet Mehmet Paşa Camii

Hıdırlık Parkı

HOTELS

Arasna	4
Çarşı	5
Hatice Hanim Konaği	7
Havuzlu Konak	1
Konak	2
Paşa Konağı	6
Tahsin Bey Konaği	3

CAFÉS, RESTAURANTS & BARS

Beyaz Evi	D
Boncuk Café	C
Kadioğlu	A
Merkez	B

Eski Safranbolu

Ancient houses line the slopes of the ravine on the descent into town, presenting a smudge of dirty pastel-coloured timber and red-tiled roofs. Although tourism is established in Safranbolu – it's a summer coach-trip destination for Turks – the old way of life stays remarkably intact. Apart from a bazaar of souvenir shops, few concessions have been made to the twenty-first century: come here out of season and you might well be the only visitor. Various restoration projects are underway, but most of the town remains slightly run-down and it is all the better for it.

Adjoining the town square, the seventeenth-century Ottoman baths of the **Cinci Hamamı** (separate men's and women's sections; daily 6am–11pm; $4) have been fully restored so that you can relax in comfort surrounded by their marble splendour. Past the hamam, old streets lead towards the **Cinci Hanı**, a huge, crumbling *kervansaray* dominating the town centre.

Roughly northwest of the Cinci Hanı is the unexceptional seventeenth-century **Köprülü Mehmet Paşa Camii**, whose courtyard leads to its restored **arasta** (bazaar). This is where the day-trippers are brought to browse at the well-stocked souvenir and antique shops. The bazaar is completely covered by a magnificent vine with bunches of grapes hanging so close above your head you will be tempted to pick them – there are notices telling you not to. South of the *arasta* lies the old bazaar district, where traditional stalls of blacksmiths, cobblers, leatherworkers, tanners and saddlemakers once serviced the needs of Black Sea traders, beyond which lies the **İzzet Mehmet Paşa Camii**, an elaborate, late-eighteenth-century mosque. Past here, the town slides into dilapidation, with a ravine now used as a household dump and, further downstream, women washing clothes in the stream. If you walk down here, though, there's a stunning view back towards the mosque, whose domes and minarets seem to hover above the surrounding houses.

Back in town, immediately beneath the southeastern walls of the Cinci Hanı, there's an open-air market, from where a narrow street to the immediate left of the Ziraat Bankası leads up the side of the valley to the **Kaymakamlar Evi**, the "Governor's House". It's an Ottoman mansion, or *konak*, typical of many around the town, built in 1904, though severely damaged by fire in 1976. Currently under restoration, it will eventually be reopened as a museum and cultural centre. A traditional conservatism dominates the *konak* design: the ground floor, devoid of external windows, would have been used as a stable, while on the upper floors the *selamlık* (male guest rooms), overlooking the street, would have been divided from harem quarters, with a separate entrance and lattice windows looking onto interior courtyards. Each room has a distinctively carved wooden ceiling and furniture would have been sparse, with personal items stored in decorative wall niches, and bedding in cupboards doubling as bathrooms.

If you make your way from here to the hilltop **Hıdırlık Parkı**, vantage points let you look down over the whole town, which appears at its best in the late afternoon light. The palatial-looking edifice above the town, on the opposite side of the ravine, is an old government building, long since derelict.

Practicalities

The **dolmuş** drop-off point in Eski Safranbolu is on the sloping square next to the Kazdağlı Camii. The **tourist office** (daily 9am–noon & 1.30–5.30pm; ☎0372/712 3863) is close by, in the main square between the *arasta* and Cinci Hamamı. It sells a locally produced brochure and map ($0.50), detailing the town's Ottoman architecture, and can help with booking bus tickets.

Accommodation

There's little reason to stay in modern Kıranköy, since there are several good **accommodation** possibilities in Eski Safranbolu. The best budget option in the old town is the modern, bright and clean *Çarşı Pansiyon*, Bozkurt Sok (☎0370/725 1079; ❷), which has rooms with basic private bathroom (upstairs) or sharing a nice communal bathroom (downstairs) for the same price; the main road can get noisy at night so it's best to get a room at the back. West of the old town, *Otel Tahsin Bey Konağı*, Hükümet Sok 50 (☎0370/712 6062, ☎712 5596; ❺), and the affiliated *Paşa Konağı*, on Kalealtı Sok (☎0370/712 8153, ☎712 5596; ❺), are two charming, individual houses with good views of the old town and authentic touches such as bathrooms housed inside step-in cupboards. Another option is the friendly *Hatice Hanim Konağı*, behind the Cinci Hanı at Naiptarla Sok 4 (☎0370/712 7545; ❹), where rooms are named according to the layout of a traditional Ottoman house. Those who like their style a little cheaper should try the *Arasna Otel*, on Arasta Sok, near the Cinci Hamamı (☎0370/712 4170, ☎712 4811; ❸), though be aware that the creaky original floorboards struggle to screen out noise from the thumping bar below.

Half a kilometre from the bus stop **towards Kıranköy** is *Havuzlu Konak* (☎0370/725 2883, ⓦwww.turing.org; ❼), with eleven immaculately restored rooms, a basement restaurant and a fine tearoom arranged around a central pool. And if you really can't find any accommodation in Eski Safranbolu, try the *Konak Pansiyon*, Kaya Erdem Caddesi, Sağlık Sok (☎0372/725 2485; ❷), on the edge of Kıranköy – at the top of the hill before the road descends towards Eski Safranbolu – which offers cool and clean rooms in a family house with a shared bathroom.

Eating and drinking

There are a few cheap *lokanta* places on the main drag in the new town, though the nicest places to **eat and drink** are all found in the old town. The pleasant

Boncuk Café in the *arasta* does tea, coffee, soft drinks and snacks, including burgers, while the *Merkez Lokantası*, next door to the Cinci Hamamı, offers basic dishes. The *Kadıoğlu şehzade Sofrası* by the *Arasna Otel* is classy, yet inexpensive, and has a garden area, while the restaurant at the *Havuzlu Konak* hotel weighs in as the most costly place in town with good food, a decent wine list and a refined atmosphere.

The **bar** in the *Arasna Otel*, or the *Beyaz Evi*, on the south side of the Cinci Hanı, are the best places to grab a beer. Sanfrabolu is famous for its *lokum* and *helva* **sweets**, which you can sample in Eski Safranbolu's *arasta* or at *pastanes* in either the new or the old town.

Kastamonu

It was in **KASTAMONU** – 245km northeast of Ankara – that Atatürk made his first speech attacking the fez in 1925, during his campaign against traditional religious headgear. Little has happened here since, and it's quite a conservative town, though a couple of venerable mosques, some fine Ottoman houses and a crumbling castle make the place worth a half-day visit on the way to the Black Sea coast.

The Town

On the town's main square you'll find the **Nasrullah Kadi Camii**, Kastamonu's largest and most distinguished mosque, built in 1509 and sporting six domes. The attractive undercover fountain at the front draws the townfolk for a gossip. At the western end of the square, the **Asirefendi Han** is still used for commercial purposes, while a street runs south up to the **Yavapağa Camii**, a modern building screened by the ruins of a larger, much older mosque complex. The same street curves off up to the west, in the direction of the *kale*, and along the way you'll pass the **Atabey Camii**, a rectangular stone building with a very low interior, built in 1273 but much repaired and restored since.

Just above is the **kale**, unsignposted but hard to miss. It was built under Tamerlane, a ruler more famous for destruction than construction, and time hasn't been kind to it. Only the massive walls and main gateway are wholly intact, but its grassy grounds are a favourite trysting spot. The other town landmark is the **İsmailbey Camii**, a fine twin-domed medieval mosque set atop a plug of rock, adjacent to a small park. It's near the *otogar*, on the western side of the river. The town **museum** (Kastamonu Müzesi; Tues–Sun 8.30am–4.30pm; $0.70), meanwhile, site of Atatürk's anti-fez speech, is about ten minutes' walk south of the *Rugancı Otel,* with the usual collection of local miscellanea.

Practicalities

The **otogar** is a ten-minute walk north of the town centre (if your bus is coming from the south, ask to be let out in the centre), on the eastern bank of the stream that cuts the town in two from north to south. From the *otogar*, turn left onto Kastamonu's main street, Cumhuriyet Caddesi, and follow it south to the main square. There's a more convenient ticket office and pick-up point for Özlem (Kastamonu's bus company) opposite the *Otel Mütevelli* on Cumhuriyet Caddesi, useful to know if you're heading on to Ankara or İstanbul. Next to the Nasrullah Kadi Camii, at Havaalanı Yanı 15, is the **tourist office** (erratic opening hours; ☎0366/244 3598).

There are quite a few **hotels** around town, but standards are not particularly high. Still, you might have to spend the night if you're travelling by public transport as Safranbolu – the nearest nice town – is another three hours away. At the budget end of the market, the *Otel Ilgaz*, Belediye Cad 4 (☎0366/214 1170; ❶), off Cumhuriyet Caddesi just south of the square, has basic waterless rooms, with the nearby *Otel Selvi*, Banka Sok 10 (☎0366/214 1763; ❷), a slightly better option. The passable *Rugancı Otel* is at Cumhuriyet Cad 27 (☎0366/214 9500; 🖷212 4323; ❷), while moving up another notch is the two-star *Otel Mütevelli*, Cumhuriyet Cad 10 (☎0366/212 2018, 🖷212 2017; ❸), overlooking the main square. This offers clean rooms with excellent showers, but the staff are not particularly friendly and the building suffers from damp.

There aren't too many places to **eat and drink** in town after dark, and your best bet is the *Uludağ Pide ve Kebap Salonu* at the corner of Belediye and Cumhuriyet *caddesi*s, a white-tablecloth establishment that does excellent *pide*. For dangerously addictive chocolate mousse, simply move next door to the *Segün*. If you're desperate for a **beer**, head for the couple of seedy male-dominated *bira salonu* on the other side of the stream from the *Otel Mütevelli*.

East of Ankara

East of Ankara, prospects improve considerably, with numerous places worth going out of your way for. Just three hours from Ankara lies the ancient Hittite capital of **Hattuşaş**, near the modern village of **Boğazkale**. The sheer size of the place is perhaps more astonishing than the ruins themselves, but there's no mistaking the importance of Hattuşaş or the surrounding sites of **Yazılıkaya** and **Alacahöyük**.

Northeast of the Hittite capital is the ancient and atmospheric city of **Amasya**, with its spectacular Pontic rock tombs and riverside quarter of Ottoman houses. This easily warrants a day or two of exploration. Southeast of Amasya, **Tokat** has a couple of interesting buildings, including the striking Gök Medrese, and **Sivas**, further southeast, has a profusion of fine Selçuk architecture, though neither of these places invites a long stay.

Sungurlu, Boğazkale and the Hittite sites

The **Hittite sites** centred on the village of **Boğazkale** are the most impressive and significant in the whole of Anatolia. This area was once the heart of the Hittite Empire and Hattuşaş, spread over several square kilometres to the south of the modern village, was its capital. A few kilometres to the east is the temple site of Yazılıkaya, while Alacahöyük, a smaller Hittite settlement dating back to 4000 BC, 25km north of Boğazkale, is further off the beaten track, but worth the trip if you have your own transport. Excavation here began in earnest in 1905 and many of the objects unearthed are now housed at the Museum of Anatolian Civilizations in the capital. If you've already seen the museum, a visit to the original excavations is doubly interesting.

Visiting the sites

Access to Boğazkale and the sites is via the small town of **Sungurlu**, lying just off the main Ankara–Samsun road. Theoretically, Hattuşaş and Yazılıkaya can be covered on foot **from Boğazkale** if you're reasonably fit. However, it gets very hot here in summer and there are some steep hills to be climbed. You might therefore want to **tour the sites by taxi**: various characters in Boğazkale will offer all-in deals ($15, but haggle), and in the unlikely event that they don't seek you out you'll probably be able to find them at the *Aşıkoğlu Motel* (see "Boğazkale", opposite). A good compromise is to take a taxi to Yazılıkaya and then on to the Aslanlıkapı (Lion Gate) at Hattuşaş, from where you can walk around the site and back to Boğazkale, taking in the ruins at your leisure.

If you don't want to spend the night in either Boğazkale or Sungurlu, then it's also possible to get a **taxi from Sungurlu** around all three sites in a few hours, arriving back in time for an onward bus. This will set you back about $20, though all prices are negotiable. Alternatively, if you're prepared to spend a few more dollars, contact either English-speaking Deniz at the *Aşōkoğlu Motel* or Mustafa and Ahmed at the *Hattuşaş Motel & Pansiyon*, both in Boğazkale, and they will arrange a half day **guided tour** of the main sites from around $25 per person, with pick-up and drop-offs in Sungurlu to time with the buses.

Sungurlu

You have to pass through **SUNGURLU** when you're heading for the Hittite sites, but there's no other reason to stop here. Sungurlu-bound buses depart roughly every hour from Ankara's *otogar* on a three-hour journey across the rolling treeless, landscape of central Anatolia.

Sungurlu does have a tiny *otogar* but through buses will probably drop you off on the main road at one of two service stations, one kilometre west and east of town respectively, where most of the buses coming from Ankara stop for a break at the adjoining restaurants. Direct services will take you into the town centre, a five-minute walk north of the highway. The departure point for **Boğazkale-bound dolmuşes** is the main square in Sungurlu, though you should be able to pick one up from one of the service stations – particularly from *Mavi Ocak* to the east, which is only one kilometre from the Boğazkale turnoff. There is also a good restaurant here. The **journey to Boğazkale** (29km) takes about thirty minutes, with the last departure at 5pm (last return from Boğazkale to Sungurlu is roughly 5.30pm). Taxi drivers usually hang around the square in Sungurlu, and at the bus drop-off point, looking for tourists. They'll ask for $10 to take you to Boğazkale, although you should be able to beat them down to about half that.

If you miss the last Boğazkale-bound dolmuş you might need to stay overnight in Sungurlu. The cheapest of the three friendly **hotels** here is the very basic, waterless *Ferhat*, Kahraman Sok 2 (℡0364/311 8067; ❶), 100m east of the clocktower. More expensive (but still good value) is the immaculate

Hotel Fatih, Cengiztopel Cad V.D. Karşişi 23 (℡0364/311 3488; **❷**), which is run from a shop next door to the hotel. Otherwise, try the *Hittit Motel* (℡0364/311 8409, ℻311 3873; **❸**) on the main road through town, 1km west of the *otogar*, which claims to have put Prince Charles up while he was on a private visit here many years ago.

Boğazkale

BOĞAZKALE, 5km east and then 24km south of Sungurlu, is at the end of a surfaced road cutting across rough pastureland. It's a modern village, with the ancient Hittite capital of Hattuşaş fanning out from its southern rim. Finding your way around is fairly straightforward; there's basically one street, running about half a kilometre from a welcome arch, up a hill, to the main square. The only attraction in the village itself is a small **museum** (daily 8am–noon & 1.30–5.30pm; $0.70) on the left-hand side of the street on the way up to the village square. It has a small collection of objects (mainly cuneiform tablets and pottery) from the Hattuşaş site, some useful books for sale and a large-scale map that sets the scene for what's to come.

Practicalities

Dolmuşes from Sungurlu drop you in the village square, from where the ticket office and entrance to Hattuşaş is just ten minutes' walk to the southeast. There are four **hotels**, often block-booked by tour groups, so it's worth making an advance reservation. Two lie out of the village, on the road leading from Boğazkale to Yazılıkaya, there's one at the entrance to the village, and another right on the village square. The hotels are also the only options in the village for **eating and drinking**. For local **information**, check the website ⓦ www.hattusas.com.

Aşıkoğlu Motel At the entrance to the village ℡0364/452 2004, ℮ hotelasikoglu@hotmail.com. Slightly overpriced modern rooms but with immaculate bathrooms and superb buffet breakfast. A cheaper extension has smaller rooms with older bathrooms (priced a category lower), and there's a rarely used campsite at the back (it's better to go to the *Başkent*). The busy restaurant (sometimes swamped with tour groups) has tables under shady pine trees, and the food is excellent. Closed Nov–Feb. **❹**

Başkent Tourist Motel ve Camping Yazılıkaya Yolu Üzeri ℡0364/452 2037, ℻452 2567. The better of the two options perched on a hill on the outskirts, with large sunny rooms overlooking tractor-laden fields, new plumbing in the bathrooms, and a serene campsite for $2 per person per night (tent rental available). The restaurant, with a view of the ruins of the Great Temple, is good value. **❸**

Hattuşaş Motel & Pansiyon Next to the PTT on the village square ℡0364/452 2013, ℮ ahattibaykal@hotmail.com. Ahmed and Mustafa Baykal, friendly English-speaking brothers, run this converted traditional Turkish house (and obligatory carpet shop). *Pansiyon* rooms are clean and spacious, mostly with showers (discounts for those without), and with kilim-strewn common rooms on each floor. Also ten comfortable double/triple rooms in the motel at the back, with cool granite floors, smart bathrooms and a promising garden (once it has taken root). The restaurant is a plastic-tablecloth affair dishing up economical dishes of the day. Pansiyon **❶**, motel **❸**

Kale Otel Yazılıkaya Yolu Üzeri ℡0364/452 2189, ℻452 2189. In a pretty location, with simple whitewashed rooms and adequate bathrooms, but lacking atmosphere and a little bare of furnishings. There's no real restaurant – though you may get a meal if the hotel is already catering for a tour group – otherwise walk down the hill to the *Başkent*. **❸**

Hattuşaş

Enclosed by six-kilometre-long walls, **Hattuşaş** was, by the standards of the time, an immense city, and its scale is still awe-inspiring today. The site was

BOĞAZKALE AND HATTUŞAŞ

Sungurlu

Museum

MAIN SQUARE

Boğazkale

Ticket Office

Büyük Mabet

Büyük Kale

Nişantepe

Sarıkale

HOTELS
Aşıkoğlu 2
Başkent 3
Hattuşaş 1
Kale 4

Aslanlıkapı (Lion Gate)

Yenicekale

Kralkapı (King's Gate)

Yerkapı (Sphinx Gate)

Yazır Stream

Old City Walls
Restored City Walls

0   200 m

Tunnel

N

originally occupied by the Hatti, who established a settlement here around 2500 BC. The Hittites moved in after their conquest of central Anatolia, making it their capital from about 1375 BC onwards, during the period when their empire reached its greatest extent. By 1200 BC the influence of the Sea Peoples had put an end to Hittite dominance of the region. Hattuşaş was destroyed and later the Phrygians built a large city on the site.

The Hittite city was unearthed by archeologists during the first half of the nineteenth century. It occupies a steeply sloping expanse dotted with rocky outcrops, to the southwest of modern Boğazkale. Of the numerous buildings once scattered over a wide area, only the limestone foundation blocks survive. The vulnerable upper parts, originally consisting of timber frames supporting clay brick walls, have long since vanished. The main points of interest, all conveniently linked by a metalled road, are the Büyük Mabet (Great Temple), just outside the modern village, the section of wall with three gateways at the southern extremity of the site and the Büyük Kale (Great Fortress).

Approaching the site from the village square leads to a **ticket office** (daily 8am–5.30pm, 7pm in summer; $2 joint ticket for Hattuşaş and Yazılıkaya, $3 per car).

The Büyük Mabet

Beyond the ticket office is the **Büyük Mabet**, or "Great Temple", also known as Temple I, one of an original seventy on the site. The largest and best-preserved Hittite temple in existence, it was built around the fourteenth or thirteenth century BC and dedicated to the storm god Teshuba and the sun goddess Hebut. It consisted of a central temple building surrounded by 78 storage rooms laid out in an irregular plan.

As you enter the site through the main gate, you'll be assailed by local men masquerading unconvincingly as archeologists. They will offer to guide you through the ruins and try to sell you little Hittite-style figures carved from local stone, some of which are surprisingly attractive. Such locals are pretty persistent and you may well meet them again later because of their tendency to pursue tour groups around the rest of Hattuşaş by motorbike.

After running the gauntlet of would-be guides, you pass between two large stone blocks, remnants of the **ceremonial gateway** that let on to the temple precincts. Nearby is a stone lion that originally formed part of a cistern and, a little further on, a large, green cubic stone, which was reputedly a wedding present from Ramses II of Egypt. In Hittite times the king and queen, in their roles as high priest and priestess, would have led processions through here on holy days. Today most visitors end up following the route they took, along a clearly defined processional way of uneven slabs. The thoroughfare is flanked by the foundations of many storerooms and after about 30m swings round to the right, opening up on the temple proper.

The **temple** consisted of about twelve small chambers around a central courtyard, with the rooms that would have contained the cult statues of Teshuba and Hebut at the northeastern end – the god on the left and the goddess on the right. In the latter room is a small stone slab, which may well have supported the statue of Hebut. In some of the storerooms adjacent to the temple you can see *pithoi*, or earthenware storage vessels, that have been exposed. Some are complete, pieced together by archeologists, with distinctive zigzag markings running round them. In other cases only the jagged shards remain, sticking out of the ground. Just below the Büyük Mabet, archeologists have identified an early Assyrian **merchant quarter**, which held the Hittite equivalent of the Rosetta Stone, a parallel Hittite hieroglyphic and Akkadian inscription instrumental in the final cracking of the hieroglyphic code.

The Yenicekale and the Aslanlıkapı

About 350m beyond the Great Temple, on the site of the original Hattic city, the road forks. Taking the right-hand branch leads you up a steep hill. After about 800m (this is the worst foot-slogging section), the **Yenicekale**, a ruined

The **Hittites** appear to have been an Indo-European people who moved into Anatolia around 2000 BC. Where exactly they came from remains unclear, though the Caucasus and the Balkans have been suggested. They entered the territories of the Hatti, an indigenous people, and though no records survive of how the Hittite rise to dominance came about, archeologists have found layers of burned material in most Hatti settlements that can be dated to around 2000 BC, indicating that there was at least some degree of violence involved. However, the fact that the Hittites also absorbed important elements of Hatti culture suggests that a more complex interaction may have taken place.

Initially the Hittites set up a number of **city-states**. These were drawn together during the mid-eighteenth century BC under King Anitta. According to cuneiform tablets found at Hattuşaş, he transferred his capital from the city of Kushara (possibly modern Alişar) to Nesha (Kültepe), and destroyed Hattuşaş, cursing any Hittite king who might attempt to rebuild the place. A century or so later his successor Labarna returned to Hattuşaş and did just that. The Hittites came to regard Labarna and his wife Tawannanna as founders of the Hittite kingdom and their names were adopted as titles by subsequent monarchs. Labarna's son, Labarna II, took the name Hattuşaş and launched a number of military campaigns against his neighbours, extending Hittite territory into modern-day Syria and western Anatolia.

Hittite expansion was not a uniform process and over the centuries the boundaries of their territories ebbed and flowed across Anatolia. In 1595 BC, Mursili I succeeded in capturing distant Babylon, but his successor Hantili (who gained power by assassinating Mursili) lost many previous gains. This early period, known to historians as the **Old Hittite kingdom**, ended with a descent into succession-related strife. Stability was restored under Tudhaliyas II around 1430 BC, and he re-established the Hittite state as an empire. An important period of expansion followed under King Suppiluliuma (1380–1315 BC), who secured the northern borders of the empire and conquered the Hurrian kingdom of Mitanni, which had exerted an important cultural influence on the Hittites. This achievement raised the Hittites to superpower status, equal with Egypt, Assyria and Babylon. The Egyptians even asked Suppiluliuma to send one of his sons to marry the widow of Tutankhamun (the union never took place as the boy was murdered en route). After Suppiluliuma's death, Hittite expansion continued and in 1286 BC, during the reign of Muwatalli II, a Hittite army defeat-

fortress, is visible about 50m to the left of the road. Although little remains, its construction was clearly a considerable achievement as Hittite engineers had to create an artificial platform out of the uneven and rocky terrain before they could even start building.

A little higher up is the **Aslanlıkapı** or "Lion Gate", one of the three gateways that studded the southern section of the city wall. The Aslanlıkapı takes its name from the two stone lions that flank the outer entrance, symbolically guarding Hattuşaş from attackers and evil spirits. The lions you'll see are actually fairly convincing copies of the originals, which now reside in the Museum of Anatolian Civilizations in Ankara. The Aslanlıkapı marks the beginning of the surviving section of dry-stone **city wall**, which runs along the top of a massive sloping embankment ten metres in height and surfaced with irregular limestone slabs. Rectangular towers were placed along it at regular intervals and the foundations of some of these are still visible.

The Yerkapı

The road follows the embankment to the **Yerkapı**, or "Earth Gate", more ed the Egyptians at the battle of Kadesh, an empire-shaking event that was carved into the columns of Luxor.

Following the conflict, peace between the two empires was established, cemented by the marriage of one of the daughters of Ramses II to Hattuşiliş III. However, the Hittite Empire had less than a century left. The arrival of the Sea Peoples in Anatolia ushered in a period of instability that was to erode Hittite power, culminating in the **destruction of Hattuşaş** around 1200 BC, roughly the same time as the fall of Troy. The Phrygians replaced the Hittites as the dominant power in central Anatolia, taking over the ruins of Hattuşaş and other Hittite cities.

Hittite culture survived in a number of small successor kingdoms established in southeastern Anatolia and northern Syria, most notably around Carcemish (Kargamiş), Malatya and Karatepe. These Neo-Hittites are mentioned in the Bible, in conjunction with Abraham and David, and endured until around 700 BC when they were finished off by Assyrians, after which the Hittites disappeared from history completely until their rediscovery this century.

Hittite civilization was highly advanced with a complex **social system**. The Hittite kings were absolute rulers, but there was an assembly called the *panku*, which at times appears to have wielded considerable influence. The major division in Hittite society was between free citizens and slaves: the former included farmers, artisans and bureaucrats, while the latter, although they could be bought and sold, probably had the right to own property and marry. Society was regulated by a legal code of two hundred laws under which defiance of the state, rape and bestiality were all punishable by death. Murder and assault, on the other hand, were punished by fines that varied according to whether the victim was free or a slave. For property offences there was a compensatory system of fines.

Hittite **religion** seems to have been adopted from the Hatti, with the weather god Teshuba and the sun goddess Hebut as the two most important deities. Up to a thousand lesser gods also played a role in the beliefs of the Hittites, who were in the habit of incorporating the gods of conquered peoples into their own pantheon. Evidence for all this comes from large numbers of cuneiform tablets found by archeologists. These were kept in chambers maintained specifically for that purpose and subsequently unearthed at various sites.

popularly known as the Sphinx Gate after the two huge sphinxes that once guarded its inner portal, but which now live in museums in İstanbul and Berlin. The most striking feature of the Sphinx Gate is the seventy-metre **tunnel** that cuts through from the city side of the walls to the exterior. The tunnel was built using the corbel arch technique, a series of flat stones leaning towards each other creating its triangular profile. One theory about its purpose is that it served to let the defenders of the city make surprise attacks on besieging enemies. However, its obvious visibility from the outside and the presence of two sets of monumental steps leading up the embankment on either side of the outer portal cast doubt on this, and a more ceremonial function has been suggested.

It's possible to walk through the tunnel to the outer side of the city walls. From here you can scramble up the embankment to examine the scant remains of the Sphinx Gate and also enjoy the view of the rest of Hattuşaş. The sphinxes that stood on the inner side of the gate were found in fragments, but archeologists pieced them back together to reveal imposing leonine figures complete with wings. The outer side of the gate was also flanked by sphinxes – one survives, but prolonged erosion by the elements has made it virtually unrecognizable. The scattered foundations visible on the far side of the road immediately to the north of the Sphinx Gate are the remains of seven large temples.

The Kralkapı, the Nimantepe and the Sarıkale

Following the road east from the Sphinx Gate leads to the **Kralkapı**, or "King's Gate", named after the regal-looking figure carved in relief on the left-hand pillar of the inner gateway. This actually represents the god Teshuba and shows him sporting a conical hat while raising his left fist in the air as though holding an invisible sword. Again, what you see is a copy – the original is in Ankara's Museum of Anatolian Civilizations.

Further down the hill lies the **Nişantepe**, a rocky outcrop with a ten-line Hittite inscription carved into its eastern face. The thirty-centimetre hieroglyphs are badly weathered but enough has been deciphered to suggest that it's a memorial to Suppiluliuma II, last of the Hittite kings. To the immediate southwest of the Nizantepe is the **Sarıkale**, the foundations of a Phrygian fort built on the site of an earlier Hittite structure.

The Büyük Kale

From the Nişantepe the road leads down to the **Büyük Kale**, or "Great Fortress", which served the Hittite monarchs as a fortified palace during the fourteenth and thirteenth centuries BC. The palace consisted of three courtyards, each higher than the previous one, meaning that any attacker would have had to capture it piecemeal. The lower and middle courtyards are thought to have been given over to servants and aides of the royal family, while the upper courtyard was the palace proper. It's easy to see why they chose to reside at this wild and windswept location on the very eastern edge of Hattuşaş. In effect, it was a citadel within the city, protected on all flanks by steep drops. On the outer side to the east these are natural, but the inner side was originally a man-made construction with a series of terraces supported by retaining walls made of vast limestone blocks.

Access today is via a flight of steps leading up to what was the southeastern gate of the palace. On the site of a building near this entrance archeologists found three thousand **cuneiform tablets**, which, when deciphered, yielded important clues about the nature of Hittite society. Among them was the Treaty of Kadesh, signed in around 1270 BC by the Hittite king Hattuşiliş II and Ramses II of Egypt, the earliest surviving written treaty between two nations. The lower parts of walls and some masonry fragments are all that survive of the Büyük Kale, offering few clues as to the original layout. But it's worth coming up here to wander among the weather-battered remnants and take in the stunning view of the Great Temple. The eastern end of the site, where the ground falls away sharply into a ravine below, is particularly atmospheric.

Yazılıkaya

From the Hattuşaş ticket office, signs point to the temple site of **Yazılıkaya** with its famous reliefs, about 3km (or under an hour's walk) to the east. The route there, which more or less follows the Hittite processional course from city to temple, dips down into a river valley then up towards the *Başkent Turist Motel*, from where further signs point the way onwards and then left (the road right continues to Yozgat). When you arrive you'll have to fight your way through the inevitable crowd of would-be guides and souvenir-sellers to reach the **ticket kiosk** (normally unmanned as joint tickets are now sold at Hattuşaş).

Archeological evidence suggests that a temple of some sort existed on the site as early as 1500 BC, but it wasn't until the thirteenth century BC that the two small ravines cutting into a rocky outcrop at the rear of the site were decorated with reliefs (hence Yazılıkaya, Turkish for "inscribed rock"). At roughly the same time a **gateway** and the **temple buildings** were constructed. Today, a few sketchy foundations are all that remain of these ancient structures and attention is focused on the two "galleries" of reliefs depicting nearly a hundred figures, mostly gods from the vast array of Hittite deities.

The reliefs

The entrance to the **larger ravine** of the two is on the left behind the temple foundations. The left-hand wall is lined with images of gods moving from left to right, and the right-hand one with images of goddesses wearing identical long, pleated dresses and conical headgear. A number of the figures on the male side of the ravine stand out, in particular the group of twelve war gods bringing up the rear of the procession. Further along are two figures with human bodies and bulls' heads. The deities seem to rise in rank as the procession progresses, and towards the front are the conspicuous figures of the moon god Kusuh, with a crescent moon, and the sun god, seemingly balancing a winged sun symbol on his head.

The two lines of deities meet on the far wall of the ravine. The scene carved here depicts Teshuba astride a couple of mountain peaks facing Hebut, who is standing on a panther. Behind her is their son Sharruma, also standing on a panther, with two lesser goddesses nearby. All are identified by hieroglyphs written above an uplifted hand. Just behind the procession of goddesses near the ravine entrance is a well-preserved image of a male figure. This represents Tudhaliyas IV (1250–1220 BC) who is thought to have built the temple. He is holding a standard in his left hand and a winged sun-disc in his right. Hittite accounts of religious rituals seem to suggest that this gallery was used for new-year celebrations, which probably coincided with the beginning of spring.

The **smaller ravine** lies over to the right and can be reached via the short flight of steps that leads up to a cleft in the rock. The entrance to the ravine is guarded by two sphinx reliefs, which can be hard to spot, while a group of twelve figures armed with swords lines the left-hand wall. These are similar to the warrior-god figures seen in the first ravine but are much better preserved. Opposite this group are two separate reliefs. One shows an unusual figure that has come to be known as the "Sword God", a blade with a human torso and head where the handle should be. To add to the already strange effect, lions' heads, instead of arms, sprout from the torso shoulders. This vaguely disturbing image is thought to represent Neargal, the Hittite god of the underworld. Next to it is a relief depicting the god Sharruma embracing Tudhaliyas IV. The god is shown as a giant figure in a conical headdress with a protective arm around the slightly built king. The discovery of the remnants of cremations in niches in the rock, next to the gods armed with swords, suggests that this part of the temple may have been used for the funerals of Hittite kings.

Alacahöyük

After Hattuşaş, **Alacahöyük** 25km north of Boğazkale, is the most important Hittite site in existence. Originally a major Hattic settlement, it was taken over by the Hittites during the early stages of the second millennium BC and, as at Hattuşaş, the Phrygians seem to have taken over the site for a while after the demise of the Hittites. The ruins that remain are mainly Hittite, but a number of extensive archeological digs have unearthed a vast array of Hattic artefacts, including standards featuring stags, bulls, sun-discs and statues of the earth goddess, from a number of tombs on the site.

From Boğazkale head back in the direction of Sungurlu and turn right at the road signposted for Alacahöyük. After about 11km take a signposted left turn for the remaining 12km to the site. By public transport, you should be able to pick up a **dolmuş** from Boğazkale or Sungurlu to the village of Alaca, about 10km southeast of the site, but from there you'll have to hitch. The only other alternative is to take a **taxi from Boğazkale or Sungurlu**, which will set you back at least $15.

The hamlet of **HÖYÜK** next to the site is small, but it does have a basic shop and a PTT. In theory there's also a *pansiyon* with a restaurant, the *Kaplan Restaurant ve Hotel* (no phone; ❷), but don't bank on it being open.

The site

Next to the **site** (daily 8am–noon & 1.30–5.30pm; $0.70) is a small **museum** (same hours, but closed Mon), which, for once, is well worth investigating, as it includes some striking Hattic standards and pottery with elegant designs. There's a less inspiring ethnographic section downstairs devoted mostly to farm implements.

The site is entered via the southern **Sphinx Gate**, named after the large sphinxes that guard it. These eerily impressive figures, stained ochre by lichen, have blunted faces with empty eye sockets, and sweeping headdresses. There's a double-headed eagle at the right-hand base of the gate, a symbol that appears on seals found at the Assyrian trading colony at Kültepe. Either side of the gate are **reliefs** (copies of originals now in Ankara), depicting religious ceremonies. The left-hand section is the more lively of the two, showing a procession moving towards the god Teshuba – shown here as a slightly comical-looking bull with outsized sex organs. Approaching him are a king and queen, followed by sacrificial animals and priests, with a group of what look like acrobats bringing up the rear.

The Sphinx Gate opens onto a pathway with excavated areas on either side, all well signposted in English. Immediately behind the gate are vast irregular blocks, the remnants of the city walls, followed by the foundations of storage buildings. Beyond the storage areas, a few metres below ground level to the left of the path, are thirteen **tombs**. These date from the Hattic period and yielded much of the vast hoard of archeological treasure now in the Bronze Age section of the Museum of Anatolian Civilizations in Ankara. Judging by the opulence of the grave goods found in them, these were the tombs of Hatti monarchs. The two largest tombs are set on raised platforms and the timber cladding that covered them has been re-created.

To the right of the pathway are the foundations of what may have been palace buildings, while the tumble of ruins at the head of the pathway was almost certainly a temple. Beyond the tombs are a series of irregular mounds identified only as "Hittite building levels". The foundations of the west gate of the settlement entrance survive, as do the beginnings of a tunnel system, similar to the one under the Sphinx Gate at Hattuşaş.

Amasya

The journey to **AMASYA** does little to prepare you for the charm of the place. Along the E80 highway (the main approach road if you're coming in from points west), the landscape is thoroughly uninspiring until just a few kilometres before the town itself, when you suddenly find yourself amid the lush farmland and orchards of the Yeşilırmak valley. Even arriving at the *otogar* or train station, both well outside the town centre, Amasya doesn't seem especially impressive.

Once you've made the dolmuş trip into town, however, Amasya turns out to be one of the high points of North Central Anatolia. It occupies a point in the river valley so narrow that it's almost a gorge, and is blessed with a super-abundant historical legacy. Most people come here to see the rock tombs hewn into the cliffs above the town by the kings of Pontus over 2000 years ago, but Amasya also harbours some truly beautiful Selçuk and Ottoman architecture, and a multitude of colourful, restored nineteenth-century wooden houses.

Some history

According to some accounts, including that of the locally born geographer and historian **Strabo** (64 BC–25 AD), Amasya was founded by the Amazon queen Amasis. In reality it's more likely that the town began life as a Hittite settlement, later falling to Alexander the Great. The decades of upheaval that engulfed Anatolia after the death of Alexander resulted in the creation of a number of small kingdoms. One of these was **Pontus**, established by Mithridates, a refugee-adventurer from Cius (a Greek city-state on the shores of the Sea of Marmara), who fled east after his city fell to Antigonus. Mithridates arrived in Amaseia (as the town was then known) in 302 BC, setting himself up in the local castle and in time establishing a kingdom. Pontus survived for two hundred years and, at its height, occupied a mountainous region roughly bounded by the Kızılırmak and the Yeşilırmak rivers. The downfall of Pontus began when Mithridates VI Eupator reputedly ordered the massacre of eighty thousand Romans in one day and plunged his kingdom into a series of wars, which culminated in its being absorbed by Pompey into the Roman sphere of influence around 70 BC.

The best description of Amasya during ancient times comes from the writings of Strabo, who compiled a description of the then-known world in seventeen volumes called the *Oikomene*. Of his own town he wrote:

My native city is located in a deep and large valley through which flows the River Iris. It has been endowed in a surprising manner by art and nature for serving the purpose of a city and fortress. For there is a lofty and perpendicular rock, which overhangs the river, having on one side a wall erected close to the bank where the town has been built, while on the other it runs up on either side to the summits of the hill. These two are connected to each other and well fortified with towers. Within this enclosure are the royal residence and the tombs of the kings.

Under the Romans, and through the succeeding centuries of Byzantine rule, the town prospered, and it continued to do so after falling to the **Selçuks** in 1071 – who later left their distinctive architectural mark on the town. In the mid-thirteenth century, Amasya was caught up in the first Mongol invasion of Anatolia, part of the catastrophic irruption begun by **Genghis Khan** and continued by his successors. The Selçuk realm was reduced to a Mongol vassal-state and Amasya apportioned to the Il-khan Empire, one of the several huge khanates into which the Mongol Empire split after the death of the Great Khan Möngke in 1259.

With the waning of Mongol power in the late thirteenth century, the **Ottomans** emerged as a force to be reckoned with in Anatolia, and Amasya soon became part of their burgeoning state. It became a training ground for crown princes, who would serve as governors of the province to prepare them for the rigours of statesmanship at the Sublime Porte. Amasya enjoyed great prosperity under the Ottomans during the Middle Ages and it's from this period that some of the town's most imposing monuments date. It also developed as a theological centre, boasting eighteen *medreses* with up to two thousand students by the eighteenth century.

Like most prosperous towns of the period, Amasya had a wealthy Armenian trading class until World War I. Most of its members disappeared in one way or another after the **pogroms** of 1915. Amasya then became a vital staging post en route to the creation of modern Turkey. On June 21, 1919, Atatürk delivered a speech at Amasya that was in effect a call to arms for the coming **War of Independence**. Afterwards, he and a group of supporters drafted a Declaration of Independence, a document that presaged the establishment of the provisional government in Ankara, and ultimately the Turkish Republic itself. Since then – apart from a severe earthquake in 1939 and a number of bad floods – things have been quiet.

Arrival and information

Amasya is 306km northeast of Ankara. The **otogar** lies well to the east of the town proper and you'll need to take a dolmuş into the centre. When leaving town you can buy your ticket from the bus offices on Atatürk Caddesi, which might well provide transport to the *otogar*. The **train station** (services from Samsun and Sivas) is about 1km to the west, also connected to the centre by regular dolmuşes.

A **tourist information kiosk** (May–Oct daily 9am–noon & 1–6pm; ☎0358/218 7428) stands on Mustafa Kemal Bulvarı, by the riverbank, just north of Atatürk Meydanı. The helpful staff can arrange a two- to three-hour **walking tour** with English-speaking Ali for a few dollars, though you'll need to give them a bit of notice. Out of season, when the kiosk is closed, information can be had from the **Provincial Tourism Directorate** on Atatürk Caddesi (Nov–April Mon–Fri 9am–noon & 1.30–4pm; ☎0358/218 5002).

There's **internet** access at the *Nokta Internet Café* on Ziya Paşa Bulvarı, across the street from the tourist kiosk.

Accommodation

Recently a clutch of antique-decorated, kilim-strewn *pansiyons* has opened in the restored Ottoman houses, with more doubtless to follow, making Amasya an essential overnight stop. At the time of writing, rates were more than reasonable but this is bound to change. Otherwise, apart from an honourable exception or two, Amasya's budget options are fairly unprepossessing.

Apple Palace Hotel 3km south of town ☎0358/219 0019. Amasya's newest hotel, perched right at the top of the southern hill – you'll have to take a taxi. It's three-star standard, with modern rooms, aimed at tour groups; there are plans for a pool, nightclub and internet café. Its undisputed advantage is the spectacular view from the front balconies and the vast restaurant terrace overlooking the Amasya valley. ❻

Emin Efendi Pansiyon Hazeranlar Sok 73 ☎0358/212 0852, ☎212 1895. The downstairs tearoom attracts Amasya's students, and there are a few simple rooms up the rickety stairs, some overlooking the river, with bathrooms in cupboards in the corridor. Breakfast is served to you on the *sedir* in your room – the giant wall-to-wall Ottoman couch under the windows. ❸

Harşena Otel Across the Alçak footbridge ☎0358/218 3979, ☎www.harsena.com. Stunning former Ottoman residence with creaky floorboards and rooms furnished with period antiques, lace and linen curtains, and low-slung Ottoman beds.

Some overlook the river, where you can breakfast on the balcony, but the best rooms are at the back under the floodlit rock tombs where you can sleep to the sounds of gentle guitar music from the garden below. **④**

İlk Pansiyon Hittit Sok 1 ☎0358/218 1689, ☎218 6277. Down a narrow street more or less opposite the tourist kiosk. Faultlessly restored eighteenth-century Armenian mansion, retaining much of the original decor and period antiques. Reservations advisable as there are just six rooms, some of which are priced a category higher. **④**

Melis Hotel Yeniyol Cad 135 ☎0358/212 3650, ✉melishotel@hotmail.com. A modern building in a back street on the south side of town, stuffed full of antiques and interesting bric-a-brac. Rooms are pleasant, if slightly overpriced, with satellite TV

and central heating, and there's a rooftop bar and internet access. **⑤**

Yuvam Pansiyon Atatürk Cad 24/1 ☎0358/218 1342, ☎218 3409. Backpacker-friendly establishment above a pharmacy on the town's main street – excellent value, with reliable hot water, cooking and laundry facilities, and a roof terrace. The owners operate another *pansiyon* south of Atatürk Cad where prices are slightly higher, but it's much quieter and more homely, with a pleasant garden where you can camp for $4 a night. For both places, ring the bell or enquire at the pharmacy. **②**

Zümrüt Hotel 100m east of the Hazeranlar Konağı ☎0358/218 2657. Best of a poor budget bunch, though it's clean and has a fine location in the heart of the old town. **②**

The Town

At the centre of Amasya, the riverfront Atatürk Meydanı commemorates Atatürk's 1919 visit with an equestrian statue of the hero surrounded by admirers. At the eastern end of the square, the creamy yellow **Gümüşlü Cami**, or "Silvery Mosque", was originally built in 1326 but has been reconstructed at various intervals since. Its almost pavilion-like oriental exterior and carved wooden porch overlook the river, and there's an unusual tall brick minaret.

There's another architectural oddity on the south side of the square in the shape of the **Pir Mehmet Çelebi Camii**, which dates from 1507. It's an extremely small *mescit*, or mosque without a minaret, the Islamic equivalent of a Christian chapel. The carved facade of this particular example has been decorated with ochre paint, and it's improbably tiny, almost as though it were a play mosque built for children.

West to the Gök Medrese Camii

West of the square, Atatürk Caddesi runs off through the town. Two hundred metres or so along, on the southern side, is the **Kileri Süleyman Ağa Camii**, an imposing but conventionally designed Ottoman mosque, built in 1489. Behind it lies the eighteenth-century **Taş Han**, a crumbling old brick and stone structure that is now home to a metal workshop. To the rear of the Taş Han is the **Burmalı Minare Camii** (Twisted Minaret Mosque), named after the spiral effect of the stonework of its minaret. The compact building was erected in 1242 but heavily restored in the eighteenth century following a fire.

Back on Atatürk Caddesi, a twin-domed **bedesten** in grey stone stands opposite the Kileri Süleyman Ağa Camii, still home to various shops and businesses. Continuing west brings you to the **Sultan Beyazit II Camii**, set in a spacious rose garden on the northern side of the street. Built in 1486, this is Amasya's largest mosque, laid out on a symmetrical plan with two large central domes flanked by four smaller cupolas and two slightly mismatched minarets. Though some of Amasya's other mosques beat it for sheer whimsicality, none of them can quite match it for structural harmony. The front of the mosque faces the river, flanked by two plane trees thought to be as old as the mosque itself, and it's from this side that the whole is best appreciated. The five-domed porch runs along the facade protecting a minutely carved entrance portal. Either side of this are two marble columns, which though they appear to be

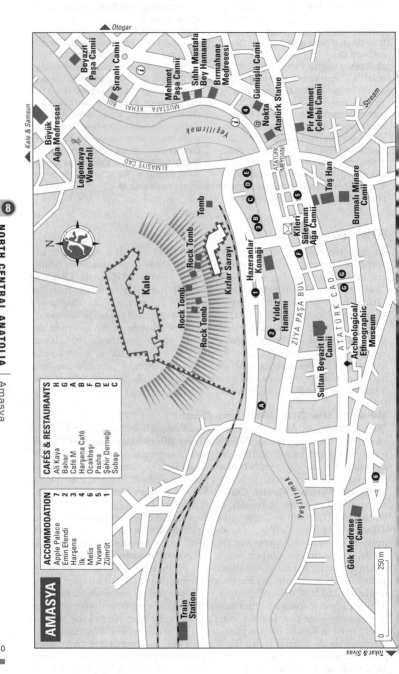

AMASYA

ACCOMMODATION	
Apple Palace	7
Emin Efendi	2
Harşena	3
İlk	4
Melis	6
Yuvam	5
Zümrüt	1

CAFÉS & RESTAURANTS	
Ali Kaya	H
Bahar	G
Café M	A
Harşena Café	B
Ocakbaşı	F
Pasha	D
Şehir Derneği	E
Subaşı	C

▲ Otogar

◀ Kale & Samsun

Beyazit Paşa Camii

Şıralı Camii

Büyük Ağa Medresesi

Leğenkaya Waterfall

Sıhhı Mustafa Bey Hamamı

Mehmet Paşa Camii

Birmahane Medresesi

Gümüşlü Camii

Atatürk Statue

Pir Mehmet Çelebi Camii

Stream

Yeşilırmak

MUSTAFA KEHAL BUL

ELMASİYE CAD

ATATÜRK MEYDANI

Nokta

Kale

Rock Tomb

Rock Tomb

Rock Tomb

Rock Tomb

Tomb

Kızlar Sarayı

Hazeranlar Konağı

Yıldız Hamamı

Kileri

Süleyman Ağa Camii

Taş Han

Burmalı Minare Camii

Sultan Beyazit II Camii

ZİYA PAŞA BUL

ATATÜRK CAD

Archeological/ Ethnographic Museum

Yeşilırmak

Gök Medrese Camii

Train Station

0   250 m

▼ Tokat & Sivas

fixed are in fact free to rotate in their housings. Any shift in their position (after an earthquake for example) gives warning about the mosque's structural state. Adjoining the mosque are a multi-domed *medrese* and a library housing some fifty thousand volumes, including three thousand ancient manuscript copies of the Koran.

Continue west along Atatürk Caddesi, past the museum (see below), and it's a five-minute walk to the **Gök Medrese Camii**, the thirteenth-century Selçuk "Mosque of the Blue Seminary", with a particularly intricate carved doorway (the actual door is in the museum). This doorway was once covered in blue tiles – hence the name – but time seems to have taken its toll and today there's little trace of them. The **türbe** beside the mosque, with traces of turquoise tiles on its octagonal turret, is that of Emir Torumtay, a Selçuk governor of the town. The tomb is reputed to be haunted by the ghost of the Selçuk sultan, Kılıç Aslan, who appears on horseback holding a sword that drips blood.

Archeological and ethnographic museum

Amasya's **Archaeological/Ethnographic Museum** (Arkeoloji/Etnografya Müzesi; Tues–Sun 8.30am–noon & 1.30–5.30pm; $0.70) is a gem among Turkish municipal museums, well worth an hour or so of your time. Archeological finds dating back as far as the Bronze Age are represented by some practical-looking pottery and a caseful of rather unwieldy tools. Hittite relics include beak-spouted jugs, some with what look like built-in filters, and there's also a bronze statue of the storm god Teshuba – though this tends to get loaned out to other European museums. From here things jump forward to ornate Roman glassware and coins recovered from burial sites complete with clay containers.

Centre of attraction, however, is the door of the Selçuk Gök Medrese Camii, on the second floor, a riot of arabesque geometrical patterns enclosing lattice-reliefs. The rest of the floor is devoted to Ottoman times, with a comprehensive selection of costumes, weapons, astronomical instruments and mother-of-pearl inlaid wooden items, including some fetching hamam clogs. There are some excellent carpets (a vivid nineteenth-century prayer rug from Avanos stands out), and a number of studded wooden cupboard doors from Ottoman-era homes. Along one wall is a line of Anatolian handicraft scenes, where dummies toil over antique looms, ploughs, saddles and blacksmith's anvils. A morbid curiosity is the tomb in the museum grounds labelled "Mummies", containing eight desiccated human husks that were found underneath the Burmalı Minare Camii. These are identified as the remains of two Mongol governors, a "concubine" and the children of a Selçuk family.

North of Atatürk Meydanı

The **Bırmahane Medresesi** was built by the Mongols in 1308 as a lunatic asylum. The popular image of the Mongols as a brutal, destructive people makes the presence of this abiding monument to their occupation of Amasya something of a surprise. But the heirs of Genghis Khan were more settled than their forebears, and the Bırmahane Medresesi is a typical example of the way in which they adapted the architectural styles of their subjects, with heavy Selçuk influences in its design. The Mongols used music therapy to pacify the lunatics in the asylum and throughout the centuries the *medrese* has been used as a music school. Today it's a conservatory with a kilim-covered stage against the far wall and a manager who is a famous *fasıl* musician. Students here study original written sheets of *sema* (religious) and *sanat* (classic) scores and learn to play traditional instruments, notably the *darbuka* (goblet drum), *klarnet* (clarinet) and *ud* (lute). There's a lovely atmosphere in the courtyard and it's well worth asking if you can step inside – you may be offered tea – to listen to the impromptu practice sessions. Around the walls are framed pages from a book on rudimentary medical instruments, written by şerateddin Sabmicioğlu in Amasya in the mid-nineteenth century. As the formidable doctor used graphic, naked illustrations in order to explain how to use the instruments – as you will see from the pictures – the head *imam* at the time banned it, though the book was in use elsewhere in Europe in the late-nineteenth century.

Further on is the **Sıhhi Mustafa Bey Hamamı** (daily: men 7–10am & 5–11pm; women 10am–5pm; $2 for bath, $2 extra for massage), very old but very much in use, as the wreaths of vapour emerging from its chimneys testify. Next comes the **Mehmet Paşa Camii**, constructed in 1486 by Mehmet Paşa, who was the tutor of Prince Ahmet, son of Sultan Beyazit. It's a sizable place, with a guesthouse, soup kitchen and *medrese*, and boasts a finely decorated marble pulpit.

A little further along is the **Şıranlı Camii**, built little over a hundred years ago though it looks far older. According to a sign outside, it was constructed using money that had been raised by Azeri Turks, although it's not at all clear why they should have paid to build a mosque in Amasya. The final mosque of any importance is the early fifteenth-century **Beyazit Paşa Camii**, whose leafy riverbank location enhances the quiet beauty of its architecture.

From here a bridge crosses the Yeşilırmak River to the **Büyük Ağa Medresesi**, a seminary/university founded in 1488 by the Chief White Eunuch of Beyazit II. This roughly octagonal structure of stone and brick is nowadays a Koran school. Although it's not officially open to the public, no one seems to mind if you take a look inside the courtyard where the boys who study here play football between lessons.

Across from the *medrese*, on the right hand side of Elmasiye Caddesi, is a tiny garden at the bottom of a sheer cliff. On the cliff-face is an **Arabian inscription** that mentions a field, a mosque and a caravan stop, thought to have been inscribed by Amasya's Hittite founders. To the left of this is the man-made **Leğenkaya waterfall**, a modern addition to Amasya's attractions, where water is pumped down the rock face between 3pm and 10pm each day and lit up very effectively after dark.

The rock tombs

The massive **rock tombs** of the Pontic kings are carved into the cliff-face on the northern bank of the Yeşilırmak. To reach them follow Ziya Paşa Bulvarı west along the riverbank from Atatürk Meydanı. After about five minutes you'll come to a footbridge – the four Roman arches at water level are topped by Byzantine pillars and spanned by a wrought-iron bridge that replaced the original wooden slats. Cross this and follow the signs bearing the words "Kral Kaya Mezarları", under the railway line and through narrow streets of yellow walls, wooden beams and terracotta tiles, to the **Kızlar Sarayı**, or "Palace of the Maidens". This erstwhile Ottoman palace is named after the harem once housed within its walls. Today, little more than a few ruined walls, a ruined bath-house and a crumbling tower remain, with a café built amongst the surviving walls.

There are two main clusters of tombs, and bearing right from the Kızlar Sarayı will bring you to the most accessible group, as well as to a café and toilet. You may want to clamber up inside some of the tombs through the raised stone doorways, but if you find the doorways padlocked you will need to rouse the site guardian to open them. Passages cut out of the rock run behind two of the tombs and you can only marvel at the work that must have been involved in excavating them. Bearing left will bring you to two larger tombs; beside the entrance to one of them is the mouth of a tunnel, thought to lead to the river. More tombs can be found with a bit of effort – there are a total of eighteen throughout the valley – but none is as impressive as these. At night, the rock tombs are lit up to give the city a spectacular backdrop.

Ottoman houses

Below the rock tombs, on the narrow strip of land between the railway line and river, is Amasya's other big attraction, the half-timbered **Ottoman houses** that contribute so much to the atmosphere of the town. While there are still a few dilapidated structures with preservation orders pasted on what is left of their doors, almost all the houses here have been superbly restored with funding from the Ministry of Culture (and free wood from the Ministry of Forestry). Since the buildings have been put to some use again, there's now a wonderful atmosphere in this old quarter, with many of the houses opening as authentic and atmospheric antique shops, *pansiyons* and restaurants, in keeping with the general Ottoman theme.

A good starting point for explorations is the nineteenth-century **Hazeranlar Konağı** (Tues–Sun 9am–noon & 1.30–5pm; $0.70), an imposing mansion at the river's edge. The heavily restored interior has been turned into a convincing re-creation of a nineteenth-century family home, liberally decked out with carpets (shoes are removed at the door), period furniture and domestic artifacts. It incorporates typical features of the time: wall niches for oil lamps, bathrooms secreted away behind cupboard doors, and *sedirs* or divan seating running along the walls, all of which reflect the nomadic distaste for cumbersome furniture. In the basement of the house, accessed by a separate entrance, there's a small **art gallery** (Mon–Fri 8am–5pm, and daily for the first two weeks of a new exhibition; free). Paintings by local artists are displayed (with prices ranging from $150 to $600) and it's often possible to watch artists at work.

Follow the street west from the Hazeranlar Konağı to the **Yildiz Hamami** (daily: men 7–10am & 5–11pm; women 10am–5pm; $2 for bath, $2 extra for massage), built in 1270, making it the oldest in town, though it's been thoroughly restored. Continue westwards as far as the footbridge leading across to the Sultan Beyazit Camii and it'll take you through the heart of the old house district.

The kale

In the crags high above the rock tombs is Amasya's sprawling citadel, or **kale**, a structure that dates back to Pontic times, though the surviving ruins are of Ottoman vintage. The *kale* is difficult to reach, but well worth the effort for the stupendous views of the town below. The most straightforward way to get there is to follow the Samsun road out of town from near the Büyük Ağa Medresesi until you spot the "Kale" sign hidden in a backstreet to the left. From here a steep dirt road winds its way up to the summit for about 2km. It's quite a climb on foot (reckon on an hour or two), so if you're not up to the trek, consider taking a taxi – $4 for the journey there and back.

At the top, the outer walls of the *kale* have been rebuilt in bright, modern stone, but beyond you'll find the crumbling remains of the Ottoman-era fortress. Nothing is signposted and there are no clear paths through the ruins, so much of the time you'll find yourself scrambling over rocks and rubble and through undergrowth. At the southeastern extremity of the ruins, you'll find a rough breeze-block shed containing an old cannon that's discharged to thunderous effect at sundown during Ramadan. Beware of a large unfenced hole hidden in the undergrowth nearby. The best views are to be had from the western end of the *kale*, where the Turkish flag flies.

Eating and drinking

With a riverside setting and the rock tombs above lit up at night, dining out in Amasya provides unbeatable ambience. Classical music is a feature here, too, with many of the **cafés** catering to the students from the town's music *medresesi* who meet to practice their instruments. Cheap eats can be found at a number of *lokanta*-style joints around Atatürk Caddesi on the south side of the river, or for $8–10 you can enjoy a traditional meal in one of the Ottoman-house **restaurants** on the north side.

Ali Kaya On the hill on the south side of town; look up and you'll see the sign. Owned by the same people and with a similar menu as the *Bahar*, though more expensive. Magnificent views, attentive service and tables under shady pine trees. You might want to get a taxi there and back.

Bahar Sadikesan Sok 3 & 6. Sister restaurants, popular with locals; one located below a block of residential flats (no alcohol), the other (licensed) across the street. Both supply large portions of kebabs, grills, roast chicken and good vegetarian options.

Café M 150m west of the wrought iron bridge, near the old city walls. Serves up a cheap, filling Anatolian dish-of-the-day to pull in the student contingent.

Harşena Otel Across the Alçak footbridge. The café-bar here is a fine Ottoman restoration overlooking the Roman bridge, offering cold beer on tap, *nargiles* and backgammon boards to while away hours in the kilim-covered booths. More of Amasya's formidable musicians play in the garden every evening.

Ocakbaşı Restaurant Ziya Paşa Bul 5. Popular place with outdoor seating area but surly waiters.

Inexpensive and piping hot selection of stews, soups, *pides*, and more Westernized dishes such as pizzas and lamb burgers.

Pasha Across the bridge from the main square ⊤0358/218 6269. Stylish venue with bare wooden floors, rustic furniture, exquisite antiques and kilims, a pretty walled garden with wishing well, and a riverside balcony. À-la-carte menu is typically Turkish, and there's an atmospheric basement bar, with tiny wooden tables and cushions set into stone walls, that stays open until 5am if the demand is there.

Şehir Derneği In the Öğretmen Evi (House of Teachers), across the bridge from the main square. Actually a local civil service club, mostly full of men from the town council, but its restaurant seems to be open to whoever wants to try out the exceptionally good food. Fresh Black Sea fish from $5.

Subaşı Café Across the bridge from the main square. Ottoman-inspired teahouse with stone floors, wooden beams and a terrace over the river, attracting earnest-looking university students. No alcohol.

Tokat

TOKAT clusters at the foot of a jagged crag with a ruined Pontic fortress on top. Despite its undeniably dramatic setting, it comes as something of an anticlimax after Amasya, with none of the soothing riverside atmosphere and much less to see – the local claim to fame is the Gök Medrese, another Selçuk "Blue Seminary", now used as a museum. Nonetheless, Tokat makes a good stop-off when travelling between Amasya and Sivas.

The journey from Amasya, 103km away, takes about an hour and a half, with a couple of ruined *kervansarays* en route. The first – after about half an hour – is at **Ezinepazarı**; in the days of the great caravans, this was a day's ride by camel from Amasya. The second is at the signposted village of Pazar, about 26km short of Tokat, where you'll find the well-preserved Selçuk **Hatun Hanı**.

Some history

Tokat first came to prominence as a **staging post** on the Persian trans-Anatolian royal road, running from Sardis to Persepolis. Later it fell to Alexander the Great and then to Mithridates and his successors. In 47 BC, **Julius Caesar** defeated Pharnaces, son of the Pontic king Mithridates VI earlier Eupator, who had taken advantage of a period of civil war in Rome to attempt to re-establish the Pontic kingdom as an independent state. Caesar's victory in a five-hour battle at Zile, just outside Tokat, prompted his immortal line "Veni, vidi, vici" (I came, I saw, I conquered).

Under **Byzantine rule**, Tokat became a frontline city in perpetual danger of Arab attack, a state of affairs that continued until the Danişmend Turks took control of the city after the battle of Manzikert in 1071. Less than one hundred years later the İlhanid Mongols arrived, ushering in a period of war and uncertainty that finally ended in 1392 when the citizens of Tokat, tired of the endless strife, petitioned Sultan Beyazit Yıldırım to be admitted to the Ottoman Empire. Their request was granted and peace returned until the arrival of the second great Mongol wave under **Tamerlane**. On this occasion the town was sacked, but the castle survived a lengthy siege.

With the departure of the Mongols and return of the **Ottomans**, life returned to normal and a period of prosperity ensued. In time, though, trade patterns shifted, the east–west routes to Persia lost their importance and Tokat became the backwater it remains today.

The Town

The real reason to stop is to visit the **Gök Medrese** on the main Gazi Osman Paşa Bulvarı, a squat, rectangular building with a portal whose recessed arch resembles a picturesque cluster of stalactites. Built in 1275 by the Selçuk emir Mu'in al-Din Süleyman (also known as Pervane, or "butterfly", an epithet given to advisers of the Selçuk sultans), the *medrese* was named for the turquoise tiles that once covered its entire exterior. Most of these have unfortunately vanished, but a few still tenaciously grip the walls of the inner courtyard.

Today the Gök Medrese is home to the town's **museum** (Tues–Sun 8.30am–noon & 1–5pm; $0.70), a repository for local archeological finds and various unusual relics collected from the churches that served the town's sizable Greek and Armenian communities before World War I. Typical of these is a wax effigy of Christina, a Christian martyred during the rule of the Roman emperor Diocletian. The ethnographic section features examples of local *yazma*-making – printing on cloth by means of wooden blocks to produce colourful patterned handkerchiefs, scarves and tablecloths.

Keep walking down Gazi Osman Paşa Bulvarı, past the *Belediye Oteli*, and you'll come to the **Taş Han**, originally called the Voyvoda Han, built in 1631 by Armenian merchants. A large, rectangular building of two storeys, it houses a collection of shabby shops centred on a weed-infested courtyard. On the other side of the street is a market area, and on the street behind is the **Hatuniye Camii**, an impressive Ottoman mosque with an adjoining *medrese*, built in 1485 during the reign of Sultan Beyazit II.

A number of Ottoman-era half-timbered houses survive in the sidestreets of Tokat, but most are in states of advanced decrepitude. One exception is the

Latifoğlu Konağı (Tues–Sun 9am–noon & 1.30–5pm; $0.70) on Gazi Osman Paşa Bulvarı, a couple of hundred metres past Cumhuriyet Alanı. Heavily restored, it stands out a mile from the surrounding modern buildings with its plain white walls, brown-stained woodwork and low-pitched roof. The interior is opulent almost to the point of tastelessness, but gives a good impression of how a wealthy nineteenth-century family would have lived. High points are the Paşa's Room upstairs, with its exquisitely carved ceiling and elaborately decorated fireplace, and the Women's Room with garish floral motifs on the walls and windows that incorporate Star of David designs. The pleasant *Konak Café* in the garden is a good place for a break.

Tokat's **kale** dominates the town from its jagged eminence northwest of Cumhuriyet Alanı. Originally a Pontic fortress (although its exact construction date is unknown), it was later used by the Selçuks and Ottomans who added to the existing defences. You might be able to find a way up to the top if you are keen to view the town from on high, but the surviving walls enclose only rubble.

Practicalities

Tokat's **otogar** is a little way outside town on the main road. It takes about fifteen minutes to walk to the centre – head for the roundabout near a bridge flanked by cannons and turn left down Gazi Osman Paşa Bulvarı. Pressing on straight down the main street eventually brings you to busy **Cumhuriyet Alanı**, the town's central square, location of the **PTT** and an underground shopping mall.

Tourist information is available from a kiosk on Gazi Osman Paşa Bulvarı, at the southern corner of the Taş Han (May–Sept daily 9am–6pm), but you'll need a phrase book to extract any information and there are no maps or leaflets to collect. There's also a year-round government-run office on the third floor of the *Vilayet* building on Cumhuriyet Alanı (☎0356/214 8624), but as they'll only direct you on to the Taş Han kiosk during summer, there's little point in going there.

Finding a **place to stay** should present few problems. The best budget option is the friendly, modern and clean *Hotel Çağrı*, Gazi Osman Paşa Bul 92 (☎0356/212 1028; ❷), which offers a spread of rooms with or without shower. Other cheap places on this street aren't nearly as nice, though the *Plevne Otel*, Gazi Osman Paşa Bul 83 (☎0356/214 2207; ❷), isn't bad. There are inexpensive rooms at the tired *Temar Turistik Otel*, central enough at Cumhuriyet Alanı 10 (☎0356/214 7755; ❶), but it's seen grander days. A jump up in quality is the refurbished two-star *Hotel Burcu*, Gazi Osman Paşa Bul 86 (☎0356/212 7570, 🖷212 2894; ❹), whose comfortable, nicely furnished rooms and roof terrace are set off from the main street, a couple of hundred metres south of the square. Or there's the semi-luxurious *Büyük Tokat Oteli* (☎0356/228 1661, 🖷228 1660; ❺), a couple of kilometres northwest of the town centre. The magnificent reception hides rather less impressive rooms, but a swimming pool goes some way to compensate.

There are cheap **restaurants** on virtually every street in town. If the weather's good, head for the tea-garden in the Dudayev Parki, next to the Vilayet building on Cumhuriyet Alanı. To sample the local specialty, *Tokat kebap*, a mouth-watering and very filling combination of roast lamb, potatoes, aubergine, tomato and peppers, head for the *Sofra Restaurant* at Gazi Osman Paşa Bul 8 (just south of Cumhuriyet Alanı); portions tend to be gargantuan. If you're driving and don't want to stop in town, try the rooftop restaurant of the *Yimpaş* department store, on the approach road from Amasya, which serves up good *Tokat kebap* for around $3.

Sivas

As much as any other city in Turkey, **SIVAS** has been a battleground for the successive empires struggling to rule central Anatolia. Now this well-planned city of 200,000 people wouldn't figure on anybody's itinerary were it not for a concentration of Selçuk buildings – among the finest in Turkey – conveniently located in a town-centre park. The 113km journey southeast from Tokat is uninspiring, over barren hills that rise to 1600m metres, with the presence of snow poles giving some indication of what this region looks like in winter.

Sivas has been settled since Hittite times and according to local sources was later a key centre of the Sivas Frig Empire (1200 BC), which seems to have been consigned to historical oblivion. Under the Romans Sivas was known as Megalopolis and then Sebastaea, which in later years was corrupted to Sivas. The town's real flowering came during **Selçuk** times, after the battle of Manzikert (1071), and Sivas intermittently served as the Selçuk capital during the Sultanate of Rum in the mid-twelfth century, before passing into the hands of İlhanid Mongols during the late thirteenth century. The Ottomans took over in 1396 only to be ousted by the Mongols four years later under Tamerlane, who razed much of the city after an eighteen-day siege and put its Christian inhabitants to the sword. The Ottomans returned in 1408 and Sivas pretty much faded out of history until the twentieth century.

On September 4, 1919, the **Congress of Sivas** was convened here when Atatürk arrived from Amasya, on his mission to rally resistance against Allied attempts to carve up the Ottoman Empire. Delegates from all over the country came to Sivas, and the congress was a milestone on the way to establishing modern Republican Turkey.

Arrival, information and services

Buses from Ankara and beyond arrive at the new **otogar**, 1.5km south of town at the junction with the main Erzurum road. From here *servis* buses run to Sivas's old *otogar* (now a dolmuş stop) on Atatürk Cadsesi, 800m from Konak Meydanı. Unfortunately, there's no dolmuş service between the old *otogar* and Konak Meydanı so you may end up having to walk or hail a taxi. The **train station** is 2.5km west of town, but municipal buses and dolmuşes run down İstasiyon Caddesi (later İnönü Bulvarı) to Konak Meydanı.

The centre of Sivas is Konak Meydanı, location of the main municipal buildings and **PTT**. The local **tourist office** is housed in the Vilayet Konaği (Mon–Fri 9am–noon & 1.30–5pm; ☏0346/221 3535), on the north side of the square – you may throw the German-speaking staff into a panic by actually asking for some information. You can **rent a car** from the THY agent, Sivas Turizm Seyahat, at İnönü Bul 50 (☏0346/221 1147). **Emails** can be sent from the *Blue Moon, Ezgi,* and *Rehber* cafés on Kurşunlu Caddesi, as well as from the *Café Rock* (see "Eating and drinking" on p.749). Just past the Yimpaş department store on Atatürk Caddesi is a line of small **shops** selling traditional instruments and *nargiles* – if you want to take a hubble-bubble pipe home as a souvenir you are likely to get one here at a realistic price.

Accommodation

Hotels are plentiful, but unfortunately most are pretty dismal. Even spending a bit more money than usual doesn't guarantee you a decent bed for the night.

Starting 500m southeast of the square, the *Otel Tüğba* on the corner of Atatürk and Kurşunlu *caddesi*s (℡0346/225 0686; **❷**), has recently seen a lick of paint and the installation of miniscule bathrooms. Across the road here are the adjacent *Otel Fatih*, Kurşunlu Cad 15 (℡0346/223 4313; **❷**), and the *Çakır*, Kurşunlu Cad 20 (℡0346/222 4526; **❷**), which both have rooms with television and shower. At either end of the same building, they're pretty similar to each other and in fierce competition, so you're in a good position to haggle for a discount. Nearer Konak Meydanı, the two-star *Otel Madimak*, Eski Belıdiye Sok 2 (℡0346/221 8027; **❸**), and the *Hotel Köşk*, Atatürk Cad 7 (℡0346/221 1150, ℻223 9350; **❹**), are probably the best mid-range options in town, though even these are a little past their sell-by date. The top end is represented by the four-star *Büyük Sivas Oteli* on İstasyon Caddesi (İnönü Bulvarı), a few hundred metres west of Konak Meydanı (℡0346/225 4762, ℻225 0020; **❻**), now also starting to fade with time, though the truly awful, usually empty, dining room is one of the few places in town that serves alcohol.

The Town

Most of Sivas's Selçuk monuments were built during the Sultanate of Rum and in the period of Mongol sovereignty that followed under the İlhanids. With their highly decorative facades and elaborately carved portals, the buildings epitomize Selçuk architectural styles, and nearly all are conveniently grouped together in and around a small park just off **Konak Meydanı**.

Closest to the *meydan* is the **Bürüciye Medresesi**, founded in 1271 by the İlhanid emir Muzaffer Bürücirdi. The building consists of a series of square rooms laid out to a symmetrical ground plan around a central courtyard. As you pass through the entrance, the *türbe* of the emir and his children is to the left. The *medrese* ostensibly houses an archeological collection, which in fact consists of three lonely pieces of stonework; more worthy of attention are the carpet-sellers, who hang their wares from the walls, a small bookshop, and a café that spills out into the open. Nearby is the **Kale Camii**, an oddity in this area as it's a straightforward Ottoman mosque, built in 1580 at the behest of Mahmut Paşa, a grand vizier of Sultan Murat III.

South of here is the stunning **Çifte Minare Medrese** (Twin Minaret Seminary), also built in 1271. The facade alone survives, adorned with tightly curled relief filigrees, topped by two brick minarets, which are adorned here and there with pale blue tiles. Behind, only the well-defined foundations of student cells and lecture halls survive. Directly opposite is the **Şifaiye Medresesi** (1217), a hospital and medical school built on the orders of the Selçuk sultan Keykavus I. Inside are a bazaar, selling everything from kilims to hats, and a delightful tea-garden bedecked in traditional rugs and kilims. Easily overlooked amid all the commercial activity is the **tomb of Keykavus** to the right of the entrance. A number of glazed tiles with eight-pointed star motifs cling to the brickwork and the sarcophagi within are also tiled. In its heyday, the Zifaiye Medresesi was a centre for the treatment of psychological disorders and apparently music therapy and hypnosis were among the healing techniques employed.

The rest of the town's Selçuk monuments lie outside the park. If you turn on to Cemal Gürsel Caddesi (just south of the park), you'll find the **Ulu Cami**, the oldest mosque in Sivas, built in 1197. This is an unattractive building,

❽

SİVAS

KONAK MEYDANI

Kale Camii

THY Agent

Çifte Minare Medrese

Cafe Rock

Bürüciye Medresesi

Şifaiye Medresesi

Ulu Cami

Meydan Hamamı

Ezgi Rehber

Blue Moon

Gök Medrese

N

Old Otogar

ACCOMMODATION	
Büyük Sivas	3
Çakır	5
Fatih	6
Köşk	2
Madimak	1
Tüğba	4

CAFÉS & RESTAURANTS	
Merkez Lokantası 1	C
Merkez Lokantası 2	B
Niyazibey Iskender	A
Şehir Lokantaşı	D
Seyidoğlu Baklava ve Pasta Salonu	E

Train station & Tokat

0   200 m

Erzurum & new otogar ▼

topped by an ugly corrugated-iron roof punctuated with equally displeasing chimneys; but if you step inside the northern entrance you will enter the subterranean cool of a hypostyle mosque, supported by fifty wooden pillars. The peaceful silence is broken only by the murmur of boys reading from the Koran.

A right turn from Cemal Gürsel Caddesi will take you onto Cumhuriyet Caddesi where, on the left after a couple of hundred metres, you'll find the **Gök Medrese**, with its ornate tile-studded minarets. This could well be the most attractive "Blue Seminary" you've yet seen, particularly if you catch it during the afternoon, when the absence of shadows reveals the best of the brickwork, carving (tree-of-life and star symbols are recurring motifs) and tiles that embellish its stunning facade. It was built in 1271 by the Selçuk grand vizier Sahip Ata Fahrettin Ali, who was also responsible for buildings in Kayseri and Konya.

Eating, drinking and entertainment

There are a number of cheap **kebab places** lining the road behind the PTT, and some **teahouses** in the park serving up snacks. The *Şehir Lokantaşı*, just around the corner from the Meydan Camii, and the plusher *Niyazibey Iskender* next to the *Hotel Madimak* do tasty cheap *pides* and kebabs.

Sivas also has plenty of sweet and **pastry shops**, including the Seyidoğlu Baklava ve Pasta Salonu on Atatürk Caddesi, opposite the Meydan Camii. Alternatively, if you don't want to change venues just for dessert, you'll find both courses under one roof at the two branches of the *Merkez Lokantası* on Atatürk Caddesi.

One of the funkiest **internet cafés** in Turkey is opposite the THY office on Inönü Bulvarı. The interior of the *Café Rock* is decked out like the inside of a castle, turrets and all, with moody lighting and even moodier music – think "Stairway to Heaven" and "Hotel California". There's a small kilim-decked coffee bar and $1 will buy you over two hours of internet time. Since Sivas is practically a dry town, this is not a bad place to spend the evening, catching up with emails. Or you could see a **movie** at the Klas Sinemaları, further up at Inönü Bulvarı 6, opposite the park. Finally, up a side-street leading off Atatürk Caddesi, stands the **Meydan Hamamı** (daily 7am–10.30pm; $2 for bath, $2 extra for massage), which has been hissing and steaming for over four centuries and is still going strong.

Divriği

Stuck in the middle of a mountainous nowhere, on a hill overlooking a tributary of the young Euphrates, 162km southeast of Sivas, **DİVRİĞİ** merits a visit for the sake of a single monument, the whimsical and unique Ulu Cami and its dependency, the Darüşşifa (Sanitorium). These date from early in the thirteenth century, when the town was the seat of the tiny Mengüçeh emirate; the Mengüçehs were evicted by the Mongols in 1252, who demolished the castle here but left the religious foundations alone, and the place was not incorporated into the Ottoman Empire until 1516.

The main drawback to stopping in Divriği is the poor state of the hotels – and transport schedules virtually dictate an overnight stay unless you've a car. If dependent on public transport you'll probably arrive from either Sivas or Erzurum, most pleasantly by train.

The Town

Sleepy Divriği lives off the nearby iron and steel works, but retains a ramshackle bazaar crisscrossed by cobbled lanes and grapevines. Architecturally the town sports distinctive wooden **minarets** and old houses with inverted-keyhole windows, neither of which are seen elsewhere in Anatolia.

The conspicuous mosque and sanitorium, joined in one complex at the top of a slope 250m east of town, command a fine view. The **Ulu Cami**, dedicated in 1228 by a certain Ahmet Şah, is remarkable for its outrageous external **portals**, most un-Islamic with their wealth of floral and faunal detail. Rather far-fetched comparisons have been made to Indian Moghul art, but a simpler, more likely explanation is that Armenian or Selçuk craftsmen had a hand in the decoration. The north door, festooned with vegetal designs, is the most celebrated, although the northwestern one is more intricately worked – note the pair of double-headed eagles, not necessarily copied from the Byzantines since it's a very old Anatolian motif. Inside, sixteen columns and the ceiling they support are more suggestive of a Gothic cloister or a Byzantine cistern. There's rope-vaulting in one dome, while the northeastern one sports a peanut-brittle surface, in terms of both the relief work and variegated colouring; the central dome has been rather tastelessly restored. The *mihrab* is plain, flanked by an extravagant carved wooden *mimber*.

The adjoining **Darüşşifa** was also begun in 1228 by Adaletli Melike Turan Melek, Ahmet Şah's wife. Its portal is restrained in comparison to the mosque's, but still bears medallions lifted almost free from their background. The sanitorium complex is theoretically open daily 8.30am to 5pm, but in these lean tourist times the gate is usually locked, so you must find the caretaker to gain admission – easiest just after prayers next door. A $1 donation is requested after signing the guest register at the conclusion of the tour.

The caretaker proudly points out some of the more arcane features of the interior, which is asymmetrical in both ground plan and ornamentation, and even more eclectic than the mosque. Of four dissimilar columns surrounding a **fountain**, two are embossed; the eight-sided pool has a curlicue drain hole as well as two more conventional feeder spouts. Overhead, the dome has collapsed and been crudely replaced in the same manner as the mosque's, but four-pointed **vaulting** graces the entry hall, with even more elaborate ribbing over a raised platform in the *eyvan*, or domed side-chamber, at the rear of the nave. The fan-reliefs on the wall behind this once formed an elaborate **sundial**, catching rays through the second-floor window of the facade; the caretaker claims that the suspended carved cylinder in front of this opening once revolved, though it's unclear how this helped the sundial function – perhaps there was a prism mounted in it. Musicians may once have played on the raised platform to entertain the patients, whose rather poky bedrooms on both ground and upper storeys you're allowed to visit. One of the side-rooms contains the **tombs** of Ahmet Şah and his father Süleyman Şah.

Practicalities

The **train station** for the rail line to Sivas and Erzurum is down by the river, a twenty-minute walk from the bazaar; taxis meet most arrivals and don't cost more than a couple of dollars. The **otogar**, essentially a dirt car park, is 400m south of town on the road to Elazığ; a Sivas-bound bus departs at 9am, another at noon and a few dolmuşes later on as far as Kangal.

There are only two basic **hotels**, the vastly preferable being the government-run *Belediye Hotel* (☎0346/418 1825; ❶), a little out of the centre towards the station. Here the rooms are large, passably clean and come with showers (though the solar hot-water supply means you only stand a chance of a warm shower in the middle of the day); stay on an upper floor to avoid the noise from the downstairs restaurant. **Eating** options are a little better, with a *kebap salonu* and an oven-food place near the hotels, the *Üçler Pide Salonu* in the bazaar and the licensed *Belediye Restaurant* on the main square, below the Mengüçeh monuments.

Travel details

Buses and dolmuşes

Amasya to: Ankara (hourly; 6hr); İstanbul (12 daily; 12hr); Kayseri (3 daily; 8hr); Malatya (5 daily; 9hr); Samsun (10 daily; 3hr); Sivas (6 daily; 3hr 30min); Tokat (10 daily; 1hr 30min).

Ankara to: Adana (12 daily; 8hr); Adıyaman (hourly; 13hr); Amasya (10 daily; 6hr); Antalya (12 daily; 9hr); Bodrum (10 daily; 10hr); Bursa (hourly; 6hr); Diyarbakır (6 daily; 14hr); Erzurum (4 daily; 15hr); Eskişehir (5 daily; 5hr); Gaziantep (12 daily; 12hr); İstanbul (every 30min; 7hr); İzmir (hourly; 8hr); Karabük (6 daily; 4hr); Kastamonu (9 daily; 4hr); Kayseri (14 daily; 5hr); Konya (14 daily; 3hr 30min); Kütahya (5 daily; 7hr); Mardin (3 daily; 16hr); Nevşehir (12 daily; 4hr 30min); Polatlı (every 30min; 1hr); Safranbolu (9 daily; 4hr); Samsun (10 daily; 8hr); Sivas (hourly; 8hr); Sungurlu (hourly; 3hr); Şanlıurfa (4 daily; 12hr); Trabzon (5 daily; 12hr).

Eskişehir to: Ankara (4 daily; 5hr); Bursa (6 daily; 1hr); İstanbul (4 daily; 4hr); Kütahya (12 daily; 1hr).

Kastamonu to: Ankara (9 daily; 4hr); İnebolu (6 daily; 2hr); Safranbolu (hourly; 3hr); Samsun (3 daily; 6hr).
Kütahya to: Afyon (14 daily; 1hr 45min); Antalya (5 daily; 5hr); Balikeşir (4 daily; 5hr); Bursa (12 daily; 3hr); Eskişehir (10 daily; 1hr); İstanbul (14 daily; 6hr); İzmir (12 daily; 6hr); Uşak (5 daily; 1hr 15min); Yoncalı (hourly; 20min).
Sivas to: Amasya (10 daily; 4hr); Ankara (12 daily; 8hr); Divriği (2 daily; 3hr); Diyarbakır (12 daily; 10hr); Erzurum (12 daily; 9hr); Kayseri (10 daily; 3hr); Malatya (12 daily; 5hr); Tokat (10 daily; 2hr).
Tokat to: Amasya (12 daily; 2hr); Ankara (12 daily; 8hr); Erzincan (1 daily; 8hr); Erzurum (2 daily; 11hr); Sivas (10 daily; 2hr).

Trains

Ankara to: Adana (1 daily; 11hr50min); İstanbul (6 daily; 8–9hr 30min); Izmir (1 daily; 15hr); Sivas, Erzurum & Kars (1 daily; 8hr); Sivas, Malatya & Diyarbakır (Mon, Wed, Fri & Sat; 6hr 30min); Zongulak (1 daily; 12hr 15min)

Divriği to: Erzurum (1 daily; 8hr); Sivas (2 daily; 4–5hr).
Sivas to: Divriğl (1 daily); Diyarbakır (1 daily); Erzurum (1 daily); Samsun (1 daily).

Flights

Ankara to: Adana (at least 5 daily; 1hr); Ağri (2 weekly; 1hr 40min); Antalya (8 daily; 1hr); Batman (1 daily; 1hr 30min); Bodrum (at least 4 daily; 3hr); Dalaman via İstanbul (3 daily; 3hr); Denizli via İstanbul (5 weekly; 3hr); Diyarbakır (at least 2 daily; 1hr 20min); Elaziğ (1 daily; 1hr 45min); Erzincan (2 weekly; 1hr 25min); Erzurum (1 daily; 1hr 25min); Gaziantep (3 daily; 1hr 20min); İstanbul (at least 12 daily; 1hr); İzmir (8 daily; 1hr 20min); Kars (1 daily; 1hr 40min); Kayseri via İstanbul (3 daily; 3hr 30min); Malatya (2 daily; 1hr); Mardin (5 weekly; 1hr 30min); Muş (4 weekly; 1hr 30min); Şanlıurfa (5 weekly; 1hr 30min); Trabzon (2 daily; 1hr 15min); Van (2 daily; 1hr 40min).

9

The Black Sea coast

CHAPTER 9

Highlights

* **Black Sea coast ferry** Admire the scenic coastline on the three-day long cruise from İstanbul to Rize. **See p.755**

* **Tatlıca valley** Take a ramble through the valley near Sinop, where twenty-eight waterfalls tumble down hillsides covered in beech forest. **See p.766**

* **A coastal drive** Cruise the little-used coast road from Sinop to Amasra, where sharp switchbacks lead to peaceful bays and long beaches. **See p.767**

* **Amasra** Enjoy the small town charm and historical pedigree of Amasra, with its old cobbled streets, Byzantine gateways and Genoese castle walls. **See p.768**

* **Aya Sofya** Thirteenth-century frescoes in this Byzantine monastery at the edge of Trabzon are among the most vivid sacred art in Anatolia. **See p.786**

* **Sumela** Cliff-clinging thirteenth-century monastery in a superb forested setting. **See p.790**

* **Uzungöl** Large natural lake in the foothills of the Pontic range, the focus of a popular resort. **See p.800**

* **Hemşin valleys** This lushly forested and pastured district is home to a colourful, outgoing people with their own tenaciously preserved culture. **See p.801**

9

The Black Sea coast

Extending from just east of İstanbul to the frontier with Georgia, the **Black Sea** region is an anomaly, guaranteed to smash any stereotypes held about Turkey. The combined action of damp northerly and westerly winds, and an almost uninterrupted wall of mountains south of the shore, has created a relentlessly rainy and riotously green realm. It's not unlike North America's, or Spain's, northwest coast. The peaks force the clouds to disgorge themselves on the seaward side of the watershed, leaving central Anatolia beyond the passes in a permanent rain shadow.

The short summer season means there is little foreign tourism and no UK package operators currently serve the area (though Trabzon airport gets a few summer charters from Germany). However, in those months when the semi-tropical heat is on (July and August), you'll certainly want to swim. The sea here has its own peculiarities, just like the weather. It is fed huge volumes of fresh water by the Don, Dnieper and Danube rivers to the north, and diminished not by evaporation but by strong currents through the Bosphorus and the Dardanelles. The resulting upper layer is of such low salinity that you could almost drink it, were it not for the pollution of recent decades – much of which has been carried down the Danube from as far afield as Germany and Austria. Each year around fifty thousand tonnes of oil and huge quantities of phosphates are discharged into the Black Sea's waters. All of this has had a predictably devastating effect on aquatic life. Attempts to formulate an effective environmental policy for the region have been hampered by the sheer number of countries involved, and chaotic conditions in Russia and the recently independent Caucasian republics.

The coastal ranges begin as mere humps north of Ankara but attain world-class grandeur by the time the Georgian border is reached. Until recently they made land access all but impossible, and provided redoubts for a complex quilt of tribes and ethnic subgroups. Many of these are still there, making the Black Sea one of Turkey's most anthropologically interesting regions. Even so, travelling around largely consists of soaking up the atmosphere. You rarely need worry about missing important sights, as there really aren't many. A particularly relaxing, not to say stylish, way of touring the coast is to take the Turkish Maritime Lines' **ferry from İstanbul to Rize**, which cruises there and back once weekly between early July and mid-September, calling in at Zonguldak, Sinop, Samsun, Giresun and Trabzon on the way (see "Travel details" at the end of the chapter).

The region divides neatly into western and eastern halves, with the former comparatively lacking in character. Everything between the coal-mining town of **Zonguldak** and İstanbul is essentially a beach suburb of the latter. Between

Zonguldak and **Samsun**, the largest and most featureless city of the region, only the Byzantine/Genoese harbour of **Amasra** and the historic, evocatively located town of **Sinop** deserve a special trip. The **beaches** between Amasra and Sinop are generally quiet and magnificent, but the road on this stretch will probably remain substandard for some years yet, with the infrequency of bus and dolmuş links sheltering the area from mass tourism. Travelling by car, or even cycle touring (as long as you have the stamina), is likely to be more rewarding than taking the bus.

East of Samsun, beach tourism has clearly taken a back seat to infrastructure development, as the new four-lane highway from the Georgian border to Sinop (and soon possibly beyond) irrevocably cuts off towns from their shore. Under the onslaught of ambitious tunnelling, sea-walls and revetments, many formerly popular beaches have shrunk or simply disappeared; the coast is further disfigured by enormous T-shaped breakwaters built with small craft, rather than bathers, in mind. Surviving decent swimming opportunities along this entire stretch can be just about counted on one hand, fortunately at or near potentially pleasant stopovers in the old mercantile towns of **Ünye**, **Giresun**, **Perşembe** or **Tirebolu**. Beyond **Trabzon** (Trebizond) – along with the nearby **monastery of Sumela**, the only established tourist destination on the Black Sea – beaches diminish as the scenery inland becomes more imposing. Other than the **Hemşin valleys**, though, there are few specific destinations to point to.

Some history

With much trepidation, the ancient Greeks ventured onto the Pontos Euxine (as they called the Black Sea) at the start of the first millennium BC. They tilted with the local "barbarians" and occasionally, as in the semi-legendary tale of Jason and the Argonauts, got the better of them. Between the seventh and fourth centuries BC numerous colonies of the Aegean cities were founded at the seaward ends of the trade routes through the Pontic mountains. These became the ancestors of virtually every modern Black Sea town, whose name often as not is a Turkification of the ancient moniker. The region had its first brief appearance on the world stage when one of the local Pontic kings, **Mithridates IV Eupator**, came close to expelling the Romans from Anatolia. Even after the suppression of the several Mithridatic rebellions, the Romans concentrated on the western section of the Black Sea and its hinterland, leaving the portion from Trabzon eastwards in the hands of vassals. This, and the climate's heavy toll on all but the stoutest structures, accounts in part for the near-total absence of ancient ruins here.

With the arrival of Christianity, relations between natives and imperial overlords hardly changed at all. Only the Byzantine urban centres by the sea became thoroughly Hellenized, while subjects with grievances embroiled the Byzantine Empire in continual wars by appealing for aid to the neighbouring Armenian and Persian empires. The Byzantine defeat at Manzikert in 1071 initially meant little to the Black Sea, safe behind its wall of mountains; the fall of Constantinople to the Fourth Crusade in 1204 had far greater immediate effects, prompting the Black Sea's second spell of historical prominence. The empire-in-exile of the Komnenos dynasty centred on **Trebizond** (today's Trabzon) exercised influence grossly disproportionate to its size for two-and-a-half cultured (and ultimately decadent) centuries.

After Manzikert, Turkish chieftains had begun to encroach on the coast, especially at the gap in the barrier ranges near Sinop and Samsun; the Trapezuntine dynasty even concluded alliances with them, doubtless to act as a counter to the power of the Genoese and Venetians who also set up shop hereabouts. Most of this factionalism was brought to an end under the **Ottomans**, though even they entrusted semi-autonomous administration of the Pontic foothills to feudal *derebeys* (literally "valley lords") until the early nineteenth century. This delegation of authority, and the fact that the usual replacement of Christian populations by Muslims took place only in the vicinity of Trabzon, meant that the region remained remarkably poor in Ottoman monuments and that until early this century many towns were almost half Greek or Armenian.

The equilibrium was upset when the Black Sea area entered the history books for the third time as a theatre of war between imperial Turkey and

Russia. These two clashed four times between 1828 and 1915, with the Tsarist regime giving active aid and comfort to various separatist movements in the region after 1877. Between 1918 and 1922, Greeks attempting to create a Pontic state fought with guerrillas loyal to Atatürk's Nationalists. Following the victory of the **Republic**, the Greek merchant class was expelled along with the rest of Turkey's Greek Orthodox population, and the Black Sea experienced temporary economic disarray, verging on famine during the 1930s.

Most of the credit for the recent **recovery** must go to the *hamsi*s, as the locals are nicknamed (after the Black-Sea anchovy formerly caught here in large numbers during winter). Enterprising, voluble and occasionally scandalous, they have set up mafias in the shipping, property and construction industries throughout the country, much of which is funded by remittances from industrious *hamsi*s overseas.

All of the above goes some way towards explaining why most Black Sea towns are so hideous. In the old days the shore was the province of Christian businessmen, who were largely responsible for the little attractive architecture that has survived. The scattered dwellings of inland villages tended to be connected only tenuously to a single store and mosque; the idiosyncratic and independently minded hill people were freed of any constraint to cluster by abundant water and arable fields. In short, there was little indigenous tradition of town planning, so when the boom hit, concrete blight set in as everyone did what they pleased. The re-opening of the Georgian border since 1990 has triggered new spasms of urbanization and lorry traffic, which has provided the main pretext for improving the coast road.

The coast from Samsun west to Zonguldak is perhaps the least visited part of the entire Turkish shoreline. This neglect is a joint result of poor communications

Black Sea trade

Since the opening of Turkey's eastern border, large numbers of Caucasians and Russians regularly visit the region. Every town of any size has its *Rus Pazar* or *Avrasya Pazar* (Russian Bazaar/Eurasian Bazaar), where **traders** sell everything from cigarettes to car parts and ceramics, raising hard currency to buy clothing and leather goods for later resale back home. Convoys of battered buses and arthritic cars stream along Black Sea roads heading to and from these symbols of long-severed trade routes in revival. Markets in larger cities are well-organized affairs overseen by the *Belediye Zabitası*, or market police, but in smaller towns they resemble roadside car boot sales.

An equally important aspect of cross-border economic activity has been a boom in **prostitution** with so-called *natasha*s (also sometimes called *madam*) plying their trade in many local hotels. Considered exotic by their Turkish clients, Western-looking women from Russia and elsewhere in the former Eastern Bloc are much in demand and have become an underclass in much of northeastern Turkey. This can cause problems for women travellers in the region, as local men tend to assume all foreign women are here on "business". Brothels are notoriously hard to spot. One general guideline worth remembering is that the presence of a *mescid* (prayer room) or a few words of Arabic script above the door tend to indicate a pious management with a strict *"madam yok!"* policy. To minimize the likelihood of hassle try to check out which hotels are currently OK with local tourist offices, though many might deny a problem exists in their town. It should be said, however, that with Turkey's current economic woes the extra disposable income to indulge in such extracurricular activities has all but dried up for most locals, and prostitution is much less prevalent along the coast than it was during the 1990s.

and the relative lack of tourist facilities and specific attractions. **Samsun** makes a dreary and discouraging gateway to the region, but matters improve as you head northwest to **Sinop**, a more interesting place than any other Black Sea town except Trabzon. Beyond Sinop the coast road west is tortuous and slow, but spectacular scenery, scattered, unspoiled beaches and small ports do something to compensate. The only place that gets much custom is **Amasra**, an old medieval stronghold at the western end of this beautiful stretch. **Zonguldak** has little to detain you, and with its good transport connections is of most use to travellers as an alternative entry and exit point to the region.

As a rule, the **beaches** are cleaner and the weather drier along this section of the Black Sea than further east. Figs and olives attest to the mild climate, and if you just want to laze on the sand without any other stimulation, then you'll find plenty of opportunity. Sparse **bus** and **dolmuş** schedules are the only drawbacks; check frequencies to avoid getting stranded.

Samsun

Despite its long and turbulent history **SAMSUN** has absolutely no remaining historical or scenic attractions. This thoroughly modern city of 330,000 people, laid out on a grid plan, with seemingly endless unruly suburbs stretching some 30km along the east–west coast road, is the centre of Turkey's tobacco industry. Most of the locals work directly or indirectly for the Tekel (state monopoly) cigarette factory. It's also a busy port and centre for the processing of local agricultural produce. Any spare time you have is likely to weigh heavy on your hands – though for a town with so little to see or do, Samsun has a fair amount to offer in terms of food and lodgings.

For the record, Samsun – like several of its neighbours – began life as a colony of Miletus in the seventh century BC. Because of its strategic location, the place changed hands frequently over the centuries; besieged, captured (and usually sacked) by the Pontic kings, Romans, Byzantines and several tribes of Turks. The final insult came in 1425, when the Genoese – who had a major trading station here – torched the town rather than hand it over to Ottoman control.

With the advent of the railway, which facilitated the transport of tobacco to Ankara and beyond, Samsun's flagging fortunes revived and by 1910 it was a thriving city of 40,000 inhabitants. Atatürk's arrival here on May 19, 1919, after fleeing İstanbul, further boosted the town's prominence, and can be said to have marked the start of the War of Independence. Rather than disbanding the groups of Turkish guerrillas who had been attacking Greeks in the area, as he had been ordered to do, he began organizing them into a cohesive national resistance army.

Arrival and information

The **otogar** lies 2km east of the city centre on the main Trabzon road, but just about all the bus companies have ticket offices on the east side of Cumhuriyet Meydanı on 19 Mayıs Bulvarı, from where service buses run to and from the *otogar*. The **train station** is halfway towards the centre; buses #2 and #10, as well as dolmuşes marked "Garaj", link both with Cumhuriyet Meydanı, the town's hub. The İstanbul–Rize **ferry** docks at the Turkish Maritime Line's terminal, north of the centre. Tourists unable to get seats to Trabzon often fly in to Samsun instead; the **airport** is 8km out of town on the road to Amasya and linked to the town centre by a service bus.

Samsun's **tourist office** (daily 8am–noon & 1–5pm; ℡0362/431 1228) is in a kiosk on Atatürk Bulvarı next to the Archeological Museum. There are a range of maps and booklets to pick up but the staff speak little English.

The number of hotels is a result of the tobacco trade rather than either tourism or prostitution. Samsun's hoteliers go to some lengths to keep their town "respectable", so single women may be asked of their intentions and couples shouldn't be surprised if they're grilled on their marital status before being given a room key. You're advised to book ahead in July, when Samsun hosts an international trade fair lasting the whole month, and possibly during the national folk dance festival in the last week of March. The better and more expensive hotels are around Cumhuriyet Meydanı, whilst there are numerous dives located in the streets around the *Altay Hotel*, some verging on the unhygienic.

Anakent Sosyal Tesisleri Atatürk Bul, Doğu Parkı ℡ & ℻0362/228 1470. Best-value hotel in Samsun, with quiet and comfortable rooms with balconies, most overlooking the sea, plus a restaurant and tennis courts. Drivers should go past the *otogar* as if heading out of town and at the first roundabout turn back towards the centre along a small unmarked road on the shoreside of the main road. ❸

Altay Hotel Meşrütiyet Sok 5 ℡0362/431 6877. Budget option with fairly comfortable, clean rooms, but the showers are down the corridor and you could get en-suites for the same price at the *Anakent Sosyal Tesisleri*. ❸

Büyük Samsun Oteli Atatürk Bul ℡0362/432 4999, ℻431 0740. Samsun's four-star offering, overlooking the harbour, with outdoor pool, 24hr restaurant and "American" bar, though relatively mediocre rooms. ❻

Otel Kaya şeyhhamza Sok 9 ℡0362/432 4664, ℻432 4903. Well-furnished, centrally heated rooms with minibars and TVs, heading towards two-star status. ❸

Otel Necmi Kale Mah 6, Bedesten Sok ℡0362/432 7164. Spartan but functional and clean single, double and triple rooms with shared bathrooms, where a night's sleep costs little more than $7 per person. It's in the Tarihi Bedestan Çarşişi (Cloth Bazaar), right by the post office. ❶

Vidinli Hotel Corner of Cumhuriyet Meyd and Kazimpaşa Cad ℡0362/431 6050, ℮vidinli@ttnet.net.tr. Three-star option that has the edge if you're after extras such as satellite TV, restaurant and terrace-bar – though charges the same for singles and doubles. ❹

Otel Yafeya Cumhuriyet Meyd ℡0362/435 1131, ℻435 1135. Imposing building on the corner of the square with large, comfortable rooms, bar and restaurant, and spacious air-conditioned lobby favoured by businessmen conducting earnest meetings. ❹

The City

In the city centre lies **Cumhuriyet Meydanı**, with a statue of Atatürk on horseback and some wilting foliage, beneath which you'll find an uninspiring underground shopping arcade. The rest of the city is largely concrete, though there are a couple of unremarkable fourteenth-century mosques, Hacı Hatun Camii and Pazar Camii.

Well labelled in English, the **Archeological Museum** (Arkeoloji Müzesi; Tues–Sun 8.30am–noon & 1.30–5.30pm; $0.70), off Atatürk Bulvarı, is probably the best place to fill time. The main exhibit is a Roman mosaic found in Karasamsun, site of the ancient acropolis (now a military area), jutting out to sea 3km to the west of Samsun. Thought to have been repaired by the Byzantines, the mosaic is almost complete, and depicts the Four Seasons and a struggle between Triton and nereids; it's not well lit, but you can approach fairly closely to examine it. Other finds are from an early Bronze Age settlement, İkiztepe, 55km northwest of Samsun, including a skull that bears witness to the performance of cranial surgery in the third millennium BC.

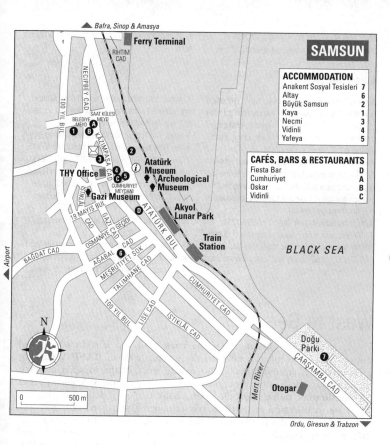

ACCOMMODATION
Anakent Sosyal Tesisleri	7
Altay	6
Büyük Samsun	2
Kaya	1
Necmi	3
Vidinli	4
Yafeya	5

RIHTIM CAD

NECIPBEY CAD

100 YIL BUL

SAAT KÜLESI

BELEDIYE MEYD

KAZIMPAŞA CAD

THY Office

CUMHURIYET MEYDANI

Gazi Museum

ISTIKLAL CAD

19 MAYIS BUL

GAZI BUL

OSMANIYE Ç GEÇIDI

AĞABAL CAD

MESRUTIYET SOK

TALIMHANE CAD

100 YIL BUL

LISE CAD

ISTIKLAL CAD

Atatürk Museum

Archeological Museum

Akyol Lunar Park

Train Station

ATATÜRK BUL

CUMHURIYET CAD

BLACK SEA

Airport

BAĞDAT CAD

N

0   500 m

Doğu Parkı

ÇARŞAMBA CAD

Mert River

Otogar

Next door, the **Atatürk Museum** (Atatürk Müzesi; Tues–Sun 8.30am–noon & 1.30–5.30pm; $0.70) has a large collection of weapons, clothes and photographs of Turkey's most famous citizen. The **Gazi Museum** on İstiklâl Caddesi (Gazi Müzesi; Tues–Sun 9am–5pm; $0.70) is the former *Mintika Hotel*, where Atatürk stayed on his visit to the city in May 1919. It's now a second museum to Atatürk's memory, with his bedroom, study and the hotel's conference room all preserved as he left them.

For food and drink head for the area around Saat Külesi Meydanı, the clocktower square, where there are reasonably priced possibilities. Otherwise you can take your pick from the *kebap* joints and *pastane*s along Cumhuriyet Caddesi to the south of the main square.

Cumhuriyet Restaurant Şeyhhamza Sok 3, off Belediye Meyd. A very good local reputation for fish, *mezes* and every imaginable grilled item. A big portion of *İskender kebap* and *lahmacun* will set you back about $6.

Fiesta Bar Atatürk Bul, opposite the museum. Atmospheric English-style pub – though women should avoid drinking on their own here.

Oskar Restaurant Şeyhhamza Sok 3, off

Belediye Meyd. Downstairs and through a different entrance to the *Cumhuriyet*. Highly recommended for surroundings, service and food, offering *mezes*, a variety of meat and fish dishes, and sweets to follow.

Vidinli Hotel Corner of Cumhuriyet Meyd and Kazimpaşa Cad. A break from Turkish fare, the licensed hotel restaurant serves up well-priced dishes on bone china crockery, including lentil soup, beef stroganoff and mixed grills. A three-course meal with wine will cost around $15 per

head and lone women can eat quite comfortably here.

Listings

Airport Enquiries on ☎0362/440 1488. THY office is in the Ulusoy Travel Centre, Kazımpaşa Cad 18/A (☎0362/435 2330), for direct flights to İstanbul, and Ankara, Antalya, and İzmir via İstanbul; a service bus ($0.75) runs to the airport.

Banks and exchange Banks are located all over the city; there are several on Gazi Cad offering foreign exchange and ATMs. Outside banking hours you can exchange cash (not travellers' cheques) at PTT branches (see below).

Car rental Budget, Lise Cad 17 (☎0362/231 5300), also with a desk open at the airport during arrivals and departures; and Yaşar, Lise Cad 24/B (☎0362/233 3288), easily spotted by the car door hanging over the entrance.

Cinema Hollywood movies with Turkish subtitles are screened at the Konak Sineması on 19 Mayıs Bul, just north of Cumhuriyet Meyd.

Ferries The Turkish Maritime Lines (TDİ) agency is at the ferry terminal, off Rıhtım Cad (☎0362/445 1005 or 445 1605). Karden (☎0362/432 2387) runs twice-weekly catamarans to Sochi in Russia and also has offices by the harbour. See "Travel details" at the end of the chapter for schedules and prices.

Police Tourist Police kiosk at the TDİ Terminal (☎0362/445 1592).

Post office Samsun's main PTT is centrally located on Kazımpaşa Cad (8am–midnight for telephone calls, 8.30am–6pm for counter services).

West to Gerze

Head west out of Samsun along the coast road and it soon cuts inland through extensive tobacco fields to the market town of **BAFRA**, an ugly, grimy town of around 80,000 who mostly work in the tobacco industry. There's no reason to stop, though the surrounding countryside encompasses the **Kızılırmak delta**, also called Bafra Balık Gölleri ("Bafra fish lakes"), a 56,000-hectare region of wetlands, lakes, flooded forests, reed-beds and sand dunes formed by the Kızılırmak River as it falls into the Black Sea. In the delta plain, located to the north of the Samsun–Sinop highway, over 310 bird species have been recorded (there are only 420 throughout Turkey), including pelicans, herons, storks, eagles and falcons. Over 100,000 birds spend their winters here. There is no visitor centre as yet, but there is a road that follows the course of the Kızılırmak River directly north for about 10km from Bafra right to where the mouth of the Kızılırmak River hits the sea. When driving out of Bafra, look for signs for the villages of Koşu, Karıncak and Karpuzle.

Continuing west from Bafra, the road returns to the sea, passing some stunning sandy beaches and pastoral scenery a few kilometres before **GERZE**, a pretty village with many handsome old buildings in a reasonable state of repair. Its handful of hotels – the pick of which is the *Ermiş* (no phone; ❷) overlooking the harbour – and restaurants are flanked by stony, not too crowded beaches. In the third week of July, the **Gerze Festival of Culture and Arts** is a mass circumcision of local boys, who are distracted by international folk groups, the nomination of a local beauty queen and round-the-clock revelry. Outside festival time most people will press straight on to Sinop, 26km further west, though there is a bizarre petrol station on the coast road as it runs past Gerze with over two hundred small "petting" animals – for those that may have an overpowering desire to hug a bunny.

Sinop and around

Blessed with the finest natural harbour on the Black Sea, **SINOP** straddles an isthmus at the foot of an exposed, eastward-jutting headland. The town does some justice to its fine setting, with a clutch of monuments bestowing a real authority on the place. However, it's a sleepy town, where development has not caught up with its potential as a holiday resort, despite the best efforts of the local tourist office to promote it. The port, long outstripped by those of Samsun, Trabzon and Zonguldak, is now dominated by fishing, which along with tourism provides most of the local income for the 30,000 inhabitants. This also used to be the location of a NATO listening post: the Sinop peninsula is just about the northernmost point of Anatolia, less than two hundred nautical miles from the Crimea, and this formerly US-run base played a front-line role in the Cold War.

Sinop takes its name from the mythical **Sinope**, an Amazon queen and daughter of a minor river god. She attracted the attention of Zeus, who promised her anything she desired in return for her favours. Her request was for eternal virginity; Zeus played the gentleman and complied.

The site's natural endowments prompted Bronze Age settlement long before the city was founded as an Ionian colony during the eighth century BC. The first famous native son was **Diogenes the Cynic**: Alexander the Great is said to have visited the barrel in which he lived and been sufficiently impressed to claim, "If I were not Alexander, I would rather be Diogenes." (He had earlier asked if there was anything he could do for Diogenes, to which the cynic replied, "Yes, stand aside, you're blocking my light.")

In 183 BC the indigenous Pontic kings made Sinop one of their main cities, and later that century Mithridates Eupator, the future terror of the Roman republic, was born here. After making the city his capital, he adorned it with splendid monuments, but of these, and of the Roman structures built after the general Lucullus captured the place in 63 BC, virtually no trace remains.

Sinop declined during the Byzantine period, and sixth- and seventh-century attempts to revive the town's fortunes were thwarted by Persian and Arab raids. The Selçuks took the town in October 1214, converting a number of churches into mosques and erecting a *medrese*, but after the Mongols smashed the short-lived Selçuk state, Sinop passed into the hands of the İsfendiyaroğlu emirs of Kastamonu until Ottoman annexation in 1458. Thereafter the town was rarely heard of, except on November 30, 1853, when the Russians destroyed both Sinop and an Ottoman fleet anchored here, thus triggering the Crimean War, and again on May 18, 1919, when Atatürk passed through en route to Samsun.

Arrival, information and services

Sinop's **otogar** is adjacent to the prison, at the end of Sakarya Caddesi, on the western edge of the town centre. It's either a short walk to the centre, or you can take the "Karakum" dolmuş and get off at the stop behind the *Hotel Melia ve Kasım*. Next door, just to the north of the hotel, you'll find the friendly **tourist office** (June–Aug daily 9am–11pm; ☎0368/261 5298) where, for $1, you can buy a whole information pack on Sinop, a useful investment if you are going to stay for more than a day or two. Just to the east of here is the harbour, where the Black Sea Coast **ferry** arrives.

There are two **PTTs** in town: one on Atatürk Caddesi near the harbour, the other on Kurtuluş Caddesi (both open 8am–11pm for phone calls, 8.30am–5pm for full counter services).

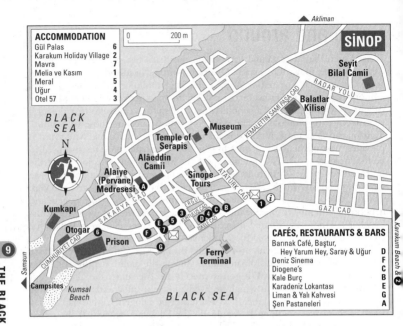

SİNOP

ACCOMMODATION

Gül Palas	6
Karakum Holiday Village	2
Mavra	7
Melia ve Kasım	1
Meral	5
Uğur	4
Otel 57	3

CAFÉS, RESTAURANTS & BARS

Barınak Café, Baştur,	
Hey Yarum Hey, Saray & Uğur	D
Deniz Sinema	F
Diogene's	C
Kale Burç	B
Karadeniz Lokantası	E
Liman & Yalı Kahvesi	G
Şen Pastaneleri	A

Accommodation

Sinop has a reasonable selection of town-centre **hotels**, mostly in the streets behind the harbour, but they tend to fill up in summer. In recent years many small *pansiyon*s have sprung up at Karakum beach near the large *Holiday Village*, a couple of kilometres east of the centre, though these are mostly private homes offering their spare bedroom to rent for the night and you will have to look carefully for the signs. **Camping** facilities are located at Kumsal beach, about five minutes' walk from the *otogar*. Here you'll find both *Öztürkler Kamping* (no phone; ❶) and the nearby *Yuvam Dinlenme Tesisleri* (☎0368/261 7414; ❶), which has a basic restaurant.

Gül Palas Oteli Cumhuriyet Cad 13 ☎0368/261 1737. Clean and presentable, though not quite as central as its rivals. Nevertheless, a good choice, with dorm rooms sleeping four ($5 per person) and basic doubles with shared bathrooms; garden and cheap restaurant. ❶

Karakum Holiday Village Karakum beach ☎0368/261 2693 or 2694. Choice of (not very inspiring) options: camping facilities, bungalows for two ($5 per person), cheap *pansiyon* accommodation and the more comfortable *Ada* hotel up on the cliff, with sea views and en-suite rooms. Only open in summer, when tour groups arrive by the bus-load and their grimy private beach gets very crowded. Pension ❶, hotel ❸.

Mavra Pansiyon Kurtuluş Cad 13 ☎0368/260 5457. Opposite the Ziraat Bankası – nothing special, but good value for neat rooms with or without

showers. ❷

Hotel Melia ve Kasım Gazi Cad 49 ☎0368/261 4210, ℗261 1625. Old, shabby rooms, some with en-suite baths and TV, suffering from the noise of the tacky *gazino* (nightclub) downstairs, but all with great views overlooking the sea and harbour. ❺

Otel Meral Kurtuluş Cad 1 ☎0368/261 3100. Bare but functional rooms, with or without plumbing, plus great harbour views. Twenty percent student discounts offered. ❷

Uğur Pansiyon Kurtuluş Cad 4 ☎0368/260 0978. The cheapest doubles in town are at this tidy backpacker-friendly pension close to the waterfront restaurants, though you may be put off by the caged monkey in the lobby.

Otel 57 Kurtuluş Cad 29 ☎0368/261 5462, ℗261 6068. Currently best value in town for very comfortable air-conditioned rooms with balconies. ❸

The Town

The first thing you'll notice on entering the town is a small **prison** (Tues–Sun 9am–5pm; $0.70) out near the *otogar* on Sakarya Caddesi. The building was put to this use in 1882; before that it was a dockyard and a bastion of the citadel, and local tourist officials assure visitors that this means its walls are unscalable. There's little to see inside except a courtyard surrounded by small dark cells, a couple with their doors hanging open so you can pop in if you have the urge to experience what a nineteenth-century prisoner felt like.

The **city walls** are still highly prominent and, although time has inevitably taken its toll, they remain by far the most atmospheric thing about Sinop. The first defences were built by the original colonists back in the seventh century BC; during the Pontic kingdom more fortifications straddling the isthmus were added, and every subsequent occupier enlarged, strengthened and adapted the whole, until they reached a length of over 2km under the Byzantines. Most of the present structure dates from Byzantine/Genoese times, with Selçuk modifications. Considerable chunks are now missing, but much is still intact, in particular the **Kumkapı**, which juts out bastion-like into the sea on the northern shore. Down near the harbour, a hefty square tower offers good views out to sea (and of the development swarming up onto the headland), and you can stroll along nearby sections of wall. Watch out, though, for the vicious ravens who seem to regard this as their personal territory and can swoop down and deliver a swift peck on the back of the head to unwary visitors.

Heading east from Kumkapı, Sakarya Caddesi leads to the **Alâeddin Camii**, a mid-thirteenth-century Selçuk mosque that's the oldest in town. Entry is via the tree-shaded courtyard with a central *şadırvan*, where a blue-painted porch lets onto a plain interior enlivened by a fine *mimber*. Behind the mosque is the **Alaiye Medresesi**, which also dates from the 1260s. The most notable feature is a marble-decorated entrance portal, relatively restrained by Selçuk standards. It's also known as the Pervane Medresesi after its founder, Mu'in al-Din Süleyman. The Selçuk sultans conferred the title of *Pervane* ("butterfly") on their viziers, and this particular chief minister became so powerful that he did away with his sovereign in 1264, ruling as the virtual autocrat of this area until dispatched in turn by the Mongols in 1278.

Heading north down one of the side-streets at the end of Sakarya Caddesi leads to Sinop's recently restored **museum** (Tues–Sun 9am–5pm; $0.70), which has an array of objects from the Bronze Age onwards. Many of the oldest exhibits were unearthed at Kocagöz, an archeological site a few kilometres southwest of Sinop. Look out also for the Roman amphorae (there are more of these in the museum gardens), a reminder of the days when Sinop was an important trading centre, with ships unloading and loading wine and olive oil. All this, however, is fairly predictable stuff, and only the upper-storey icon display constitutes a departure from the usual Turkish small-town museum fare. Most of the icons are painted in Byzantine style, but actually date from the nineteenth century; scanty labelling makes their exact provenance uncertain, but it's a safe bet that they come from local Greek churches abandoned after 1923, including the Balatlar Kilise (see below). In the museum grounds are the sparse remains of the Hellenistic **Temple of Serapis**, excavated in 1951. A number of objects dug up on the site – including a fourth-century clay mask of the god (Serapis was the Egyptian form of Apollo) complete with long hair and beard – are now housed in the museum.

Following Kemalettin Sami Paşa Caddesi onto the headland will bring you to the forlorn **Balatlar Kilise**, a ruined seventh-century Byzantine church with scant traces of frescoes inside. There are a few mosques out here, too, flanked by tombs, though only the hilltop **Seyit Bilal Camii**, with its decorative tiles, is worth seeking out.

The town beaches

Sinop's main beaches are **Kumsal**, under a kilometre southwest of the bus station, and a pay beach at **Karakum** (meaning "black sand", which is a fairly honest description). They are connected with each other, via the *otogar* and the town centre, by twice-hourly dolmuşes. Kumsal beach is smaller, and backed by untidy campsites, but the sand is lighter and the sea rather more enticing than at Karakum. The best beach on the northern side of the peninsula is **Akliman**, a twenty-minute *dolmuş* ride from town, where a fine stretch of white sand is backed by pine forests and picnic areas, but it's less frequented than the other beaches as unpredictable currents make swimming here dangerous.

Eating and drinking

For food and drink, there are plenty of options down by the harbour on İskele Caddesi. The picturesque wooden *Yalı Kahvesi* and the *Liman*, in a restored stone house next door, are the most popular of the many **teahouses**, with chairs on the waterfront and a fine view of the boats in the harbour. The obvious **restaurants** are the *Saray*, *Uğur* and *Hey Yarum Hey*, in a row just a few steps east of here. They're all pretty similar, with fish *şiş*, *midye tava* (fried mussels) and salmon for around $6 a dish served out on little floating piers. Slotted amongst them is the *Barınak Café*, which serves just three cheap and filling staples – spaghetti, pizzas and burgers. Moored in front of the line of restaurants is the *Baştur*, a fish restaurant on a fishing boat. One street back from the waterfront the *Karadeniz Lokantası* is a what-you-see-is-what-you-get canteen. The *Şen Pastaneleri* at Sakarya Cad 34 sells a wide variety of gooey desserts in air-conditioned comfort.

For a taste of local **bar** life, head for the popular but badly signposted *Diogene's Disco-Bar* next to the Ayhan boat shop off İskele Caddesi, or to the *Kale Burç Café* on top of the massive stone tower by the waterfront, where folk music plays well into the night. Alternatively, if you're in the mood for a drink and evening **film**, check out the arty *Deniz Sinema Cafe* (shows at 6.30pm and 9.30pm), up a side-street north off Kurtulus Caddesi near the *Otel Meral*.

Around Sinop

If you have your own wheels, the pretty **Hamsilos Bay**, 11km up the headland to the west, is worth the drive out for a swim. The bay's entrance is so narrow, it's almost a fjord. A little further west, 24km from Sinop is the **most northerly point in Turkey**. There's nothing to see except the functioning Inceburun lighthouse marking the spot, but birdwatchers may appreciate the two-kilometre long **Sarıkum lake**, which attracts pelicans, herons and storks. The lake is separated from the sea by a ribbon of land, where (supposedly) a herd of wild horses resides.

Forty-two kilometres south of Sinop, and 14km south of the village of Efelek, lie the **Tatlıca waterfalls**. Here, twenty-eight large and small waterfalls tumble down a narrow two-kilometre valley, flanked by an attractive beech forest. Whilst some are quite dramatic, most are little more than mountain streams, but it's a lovely area and worth making a trip out for a couple of hours if you fancy a hike. The site has only just opened to tourists and has been designated a national park – though plans to develop campsites and picnic grounds here will doubtless lead to despoliation. Go while Tatlıca is still a rare untouched corner of Turkish countryside. Without any signposting the falls are almost impossible to find on your own, so the best way to visit is with Sinope Tours, Kibris Caddesi 3 (☎0368/261 7900, ⓦwww.sinopetours.com.tr), which offers a **day trip** from Sinop, including a picnic lunch and plenty of time for rambling, for $8 per person.

West of Sinop: the coast to Amasra

Most public transport from Sinop heads either east towards Samsun or inland to Kastamonu. There are dolmuşes plying the little-travelled coast **west to Amasra**, but none provides a direct service. Expect to travel from village to village and change frequently. Because of this the nine hours' total driving time will probably have to be spread over two days due to infrequent departures. However, with your own vehicle you can explore the coastline's empty coves and sleepy villages at your leisure. Low mountains hedge the sea and force the road to wind around their knees. The region has always been a backwater, home in ancient times to the "barbarian" Paphlagonians and only lightly garrisoned by the Romans. It's still thinly populated, with many residents working overseas for ten months of the year.

The coast road and the scenic but narrow inland route converge just south of Ayancık, reaching the coast again only at **HELALDI**, a pleasant fishing port with a decent beach and a couple of *pansiyons*. **ABANA**, a small resort 40km to the west, is the next place you might consider breaking the journey – a somnolent town with a decent, albeit shingly, beach.

Most, however, will press on to nearby **İNEBOLU**, the biggest place between Sinop and Amasra, but still a sleepy resort mustering only nine thousand inhabitants. A few isolated Ottoman houses grace the web of narrow streets, which is bisected by a river and wedged between the hills and the sea, with a long, empty shingle beach. Two cheap **accommodation** options are the *Otel Özlü* at Cumhuriyet Cad 42 (☎0366/811 4198; ❶) and the *Otel Altınöz* a few doors along at Cumhuriyet Cad 47 (☎0366/811 3352; ❶), on a street running inland from the waterfront just east of the PTT; both have basic en-suite rooms. Between the coast road and the sea, on the western approach to the centre via Ismet Paşa Caddesi, are a couple of beachside resorts. The *Huzur Motel* (☎0366 811 4502; $5 per person sharing a cabin) is the better of the two, offering accommodation with showers for half the price of its nearby neighbour, *Yakamoz Tatil Köyü* (☎0366 811 4305, ⓕ811 3100; $10 per bed). Both have rambling beachside tea gardens where women holiday-makers sit and knit while their husbands throw pebbles into the sea. As for **eating and drinking**, start with a beer at the *Samata Bar* on the front next to the *Huzur Motel*, and then head to the *Liman*, a pale blue harbour building just east of town, where fish, salad and a beer will still leave you with change from $10. The *Dilek Lokantası*, a few doors down from the *Otel Özlü*, does good fish for a bit less money and the *Kristal*, one street east on Hacinuman Caddesi, is excellent value for roast chicken, *kebaps* and pizza. *Root Internet Café* is a few doors along at Hacinuman Cad 38, back towards the seafront.

West of İnebolu, the clifftop road winds its way through a succession of sleepy little havens, including Doğanyurt, İlyasbey (with two *pansiyons*), Akbayır and Çayyaka, where you might want to break your journey for an hour or so.

DOĞANYURT, in particular, just north of the road, is well off the beaten track and worth a look for precisely that reason; it also boasts a friendly restaurant.

The constant curves mean that it takes a good two hours to drive to **CİDE**, where the town centre is actually a couple of kilometres inland, basically a one-street place with a PTT, a range of banks, an internet café and tiny *otogar*. The *Alkan Otel* at Fatimbey Cad 7 (☎0366/866 3143; ❷), south of the *otogar*, represents excellent value for very clean, well-furnished doubles with or without bathrooms. Most arrivals take the "Sahil" bus from the *otogar* to the harbour at the east of the shorefront esplanade and stay at the *Yalı Hotel* (☎0366/866 2087, ⓔinfo@yaliotel.com), where there's a choice between standard accommodation with baths (❷) and better-furnished rooms with fridges, TVs and balconies (❸); a basic restaurant downstairs serves alcohol and overlooks the quiet little harbour. The nearby *Ece Motel* is something of a concrete prison (though it does have a swimming pool), and you'd do better a little way west along the shore at the comfortable *Hotel Yeni Ece* (☎0366/866 4040, ⓕ866 1195; ❸). The **beach** near here is pebbly but extends for nearly ten uncrowded kilometres to the west of the harbour. It's lined with an expanding ribbon of development that provides more simple *pansiyon* rooms during the summer months, including those at the tidy *Kaptan Aile Pansiyon* (☎0366/866 3658; ❶).

GİDEROS, 15km west of Cide, is a small cluster of houses surrounded by green cliffs, where a friendly harbourside fish restaurant serves fried red mullet (*barbunya*) and offers lodgings for the night. Swimming is a possibility from rocks next to the pretty natural harbour, overlooked by a ruined medieval castle.

The road continues up a few steep grades and through a number of small villages with boatyards. The next popular stop is **KAPISUYU**, an idyllic village where a mountain stream enters the Black Sea. The river's bank is shaded by trees and, at its mouth, a fine stretch of sand has accumulated. It's a quiet place with just a single small *pansiyon* and restaurant, but many people camp along the beach.

Just a few kilometres ahead lies **KURUCAŞİLE**, long renowned as a boatbuilding centre. After centuries of turning out oak-timbered fishing and cargo boats, craftsmen can still be seen hard at work on the eastbound road, making pleasure boats for customers from all over Turkey and northern Europe. The town's *Hotel A*, pleasantly located at İskele Cad 18 on the harbour (☎ & ⓕ0378/518 1463; ❷), is the biggest outfit between Cide and Amasra.

A final, slow series of switchbacks brings you to **ÇAKRAZ**, whose good beaches and scattering of *pansiyons* do little to disturb a splendid torpor. The best local strand is at **BOZKÖY**, nestled at the bottom of cliffs out of sight of the road, a couple of kilometres west. It can get crowded at holiday time, when infrequent dolmuşes on the Kurucaşile–Amasra run are jammed to sardine-can density.

Amasra

AMASRA brazenly flaunts its charms to new arrivals. Approached from any direction, the town suddenly appears below you, swarming up onto a rocky headland sheltering two bays. Amasra's historical pedigree and colourful atmosphere make it worth at least an overnight stop. During the day it is a quiet place, full of shady corners to sit and contemplate; by night it's much livelier and the old walls are lit up rather attractively, though it doesn't lose its small-town charm.

Originally called Sesamus – mentioned in Homer's *Iliad* – it was colonized by Miletus in the sixth century BC. The name Amasra derived from Queen

Amastris, a lady of the court of Alexander the Great, who, after the death of her husband, acted as regent for her young son, only to be repaid with murder at his hands. The city then passed rapidly through the grip of a succession of rulers, until avid letter-writer Pliny the Younger was appointed Rome's special commissioner of the region in 110 AD. From the ninth century, after a barbarian attack, the town declined in importance, though the Byzantines maintained a garrison here. The Genoese took over when Byzantine strength began to decline, and held the city until the Ottomans assumed control in 1460.

The Town

The modern town occupies a headland; a narrow stone bridge links the main town to the island of Boztepe further out. The headland shelters the west-facing Küçük Liman (Little Harbour) on one side and the east-facing Büyük Liman (Big Harbour) on the other. Both the main town and island are scattered with stretches of ancient fortifications from two Byzantine/Genoese **castles** near the tip of the peninsula. One of these is situated in the modern town above Büyük Liman, and a short walk in this area, above the *Amasra Oteli*, reveals old cobbled streets straddled by Byzantine gateways. The other castle is reached by following Küçük Liman Caddesi across the bridge to **Boztepe**, where a ruined watchtower on a piece of land jutting out into the harbour is still visible. Boztepe's heavy-duty walls, pierced by several gates, are still largely intact. The **inner citadel** is studded with towers and the Genoese coat of arms; of the two **Byzantine churches** that you can hunt down in the maze of alleys on Boztepe, the larger was converted to a mosque after the Ottoman conquest, while the ruined smaller one was in use until 1923.

Amasra also boasts a good **museum**, located at the inland extremity of Küçük Liman (Tues–Sun 8.30am–5.30pm; $0.70). It contains locally unearthed archeological finds, mainly from the Roman period. Pride of place is given to the torso of an emperor, with Romulus and Remus carved on his tunic, discovered in the citadel area in 1995. Eighteenth- and nineteenth-century woodcarvings demonstrate a quality of craftsmanship sorely lacking nowadays; throughout town, you'll come across the hopelessly kitsch objects – goblets, ashtrays and back-scratchers, as well as more useful kitchen utensils – which local workshops churn out by the thousand for the tourist market.

The ancient mole of the Küçük Liman across the isthmus, near the watchtower, is the most likely spot for a quick **swim** (if the jellyfish aren't too numerous). Elsewhere, the water is seriously polluted, particularly at the deceptively attractive town beach fronting the eastern fishing port, and it's best to regard Amasra as a base for forays to better beaches further east.

Practicalities

The **dolmuş and bus terminal** is near the **PTT** on the small Atatürk Meydanı, near the middle of the main part of the headland. From here everything is in easy reach, including a small **tourist information kiosk** at the harbour, which is open whenever they can find someone to staff it.

Accommodation

The cheapest **accommodation** is found overlooking the eastern beach on the Büyük Liman side of town, reached from Atatürk Meydanı by taking Büyük Liman Caddesi. The *Huzur Otel* (☎0378/315 1082; ❶) is a family-run place with simple rooms and shared bathrooms; if this is full simply carry on walking east along the front where there are a line of un-named *pansiyons,* often only open in the summer – there will be a sign out front. Further east, and a better bet for drivers since it has parking, is the *Sahil Otel*, Büyük Liman Cad 82 (☎0378/315 2211; ❷), though the central ventilation shaft shared by all the rooms may mean that you will hear more of other people's ablutions then you want. Breakfast is served on the rooftop terrace.

One block back from the eastern beach, the *Amasra Oteli* at Büyük Liman, İskele Cad 59 (☎0378/315 1007, ℱ315 1722; ❸), has sea views, while the nearby *Otel Timur*, Çekiciler Cad 57 (☎0378/315 2589, ℱ315 2590; ❷), is deservedly popular (and often full) on account of its comfortable rooms and professional management. Just to the northeast of the main square, the bright pink *Hotel Türkili*, Özdemirhan Sok 6 (☎0378/315 3750, ℯturkilihotel @ttnet.net.tr; ❺), is the plushest in town with modern air-conditioned comfort though no views. On Çamlı Sokak, near the museum, the newly renovated *Nur Turistik Pansiyon* (☎0378/315 1015, ℱ315 2525; ❺) boasts stylish, comfortable rooms with great views across the bay from the front balconies, and a reasonable terrace restaurant and bar. For something a little quieter, there are numerous small *pansiyons* among the alleyways between the fortresses. Pick of the bunch are the lovely *Emek* (☎0378/315 3548; ❶) and *Kale* (☎0378/315 1251; ❶), practically built into the city walls on Topyanı Sokak above Büyük Liman, where you'll get clean sheets, hot water and a spectacular cliff-top view. In summer you can **camp** on the harbour front, near the Bartın road, but be prepared for traffic noise.

Eating, drinking and entertainment

The *Mustafa Amca'nin Lokantasi* is easily Amasra's most colourful establishment, a 60-year-old fish **restaurant**, with terraces on the water side of Küçük Liman Caddesi, with booze and *istavrit* (Black Sea mackerel) dished up in abundance by a suitably piratical-looking "uncle" Mustafa. Drop in at the *Han Bar* a few doors north for more drinking (and probably some singing) or make your way to the *Karadeniz Pide Salonu*, Hamam Sok 9, which serves up hot *pide*. On the eastern beach, near Büyük Liman, there are two excellent restaurants: the *Çeşmi Cihan*, a three-storey affair at the harbour entrance with wraparound balconies and commanding views (around $10 for fish, salad and a beer); and the smartest place in town, the *Liman Restaurant,* right on the harbour, with an impressively long fish menu including salmon (*saumon*), turbot (*kalkan*) and crayfish (*ıstakoz*), plus a bar stocked with champagne and scotch whisky, and a rooftop terrace.

After dark the town takes to the streets along both harbour fronts. Büyük Liman boasts the tacky *Bedenaltı* music café near the excellent **waterside food stalls**, while the *Nür Taverna*, a family affair, is the big draw across the headland on Küçük Liman, with traditional **music** and lots of *rakı*-induced dancing.

Beyond Amasra

Southwest of Amasra, Highway 010 leaves the coast, dipping inland to **BARTIN**, a large town of Ottoman wooden houses (most of which are sorely in need of restoration), with superior bus connections to Safranbolu and Ankara.

If you want to continue along the coast, or demand sleeper-train comfort for travelling to Ankara, you'll have to make for the provincial capital of **ZONGULDAK**, nearly 100km away. Bang in the heart of Turkey's main coal district, it's a surprisingly attractive city, approached from the south through a steep, tree-lined gorge, where towering pitheads seem to complement the dramatic valley scenery. If you spend much time in the city, however, you may find your eyes stinging from the almost palpable pollution in the air; downtown Zonguldak is fittingly marked by a lump of metal from which figures (representing coal miners) are hacking out their exit. The *Hotel Ay*, Gazipaşa Cad 61 (☎0372/251 1310, ℻251 1357; ❸), opposite the giant mosque, has decent rooms with TVs, but its inflated prices reflect Zonguldak's importance for travelling businessmen. A cheaper option is the tidy *Otel Emniyet*, Aralık Sok 31/C (☎0372/251 1051, ℻253 6588; ❷), with a simple restaurant downstairs. **EREĞLİ**, 60km further west, is rather more unpleasant: the largest steelworks in the Middle East dominates the town, and hotels are even more overpriced than in Zonguldak.

AKÇAKOCA, well on the way to İstanbul, has one last Genoese fortress, a seven-kilometre-long sandy beach and hotels jammed with clients from the nearby metropolis. The town has grown into a glitzy Mediterranean-style resort, with a lively promenade – a tractor and trailer cunningly disguised as a steam train chugs tourists up and down the front during summer. The *Sezgin Pansiyon* at Atatürk Cad 44 (☎0308/ 611 4162, ✉sezginpansiyon@hotmail.com; ❷) is the best-value **accommodation** in town (you'll pay $5 extra for an en-suite room), though you could just as well try your luck in the many *pansiyon*s on the streets inland. There's a spattering of adequate **restaurants**, while the nicest place for a beer is the *Türkü* with tables on the sand. Emails can be picked up at *Café Ar-Net* near the new mosque. The best of the local **campsites** is *Tezel Kamping & Pansiyon* (☎0308/611 4115, ✉tzicamping@yahoo.com), about 2km west of town on the road to the Genoese castle, in an idyllic spot with shady sites next to the sea, clean washing facilities and a small restaurant. Simple rooms with shower up the hall go for $6 per person.

A thirty-kilometre drive through hazelnut groves to the west is **KOCAALİ**, with more sandy strands but no shade. Beyond Kocaali, there's so much sand on the stretch of road to **KARASU** that the fields bordering the dunes are desert-like, used as campsites by groups of nomads. Karasu itself is a drab town set back from the sea; the beach is full of sun brollies as far as the eye can see, with a massive campsite, the *Öz-su*, which also offers bungalow-style rooms (no phone; ❶). West of Karasu, it's best to ignore Kandira in favour of Ağva or Şile, both attractive resorts with a number of accommodation possibilities.

The eastern Black Sea

The eastern coast of the Black Sea sees far more visitors than the western half, partly because there's more of interest here, partly because it's easier to get to. **Trabzon**, with its romantic associations and medieval monuments, is very much the main event and, as it's located at or near the end of plane, ferry and bus services, makes a logical introduction to the region. It's also the usual base for visits to **Sumela monastery**, the only place in this chapter that you could describe as overwhelmed by tourists. Other forays inland, however, are just as rewarding – particularly the superlatively scenic **Hemşin valleys**, home to a welcoming, unusual people, and the northern gateway to the lofty Kaçkar Dağları, covered fully in Chapter 10.

Other than Trabzon, the coast itself between the Georgian frontier and Samsun offers little apart from fine scenery and increasingly restricted swimming opportunities – **Perşembe**, **Giresun** and **Ünye** being the most attractive and feasible bases for exploration. All this is best appreciated with your own transport, but even without this you'll face few problems. The towns are close together, served by seemingly endless relays of dolmuşes, and as just about every journey is covered, you can safely ask to be set down at an isolated beach in the near-certainty that another minibus will be along to pick you up when necessary.

East of Samsun: the coast to Trabzon

Just east of Samsun, the Black Sea coastal plain, watered by the **Yeşilırmak delta**, widens to its broadest extent. The area was once thought to be the land of the **Amazons**, a mythical tribe of men-hating women who cauterized their right breasts to facilitate spear-throwing and arrow-shooting, and who only coupled with men – their neighbours the Gagarians – during two months of the year, sending male babies to the Gagarians to rear. Nowadays the delta is home to rather more conventional Black Sea Muslims, who are welcoming enough to members of either sex.

The road, slightly elevated to avoid flooding, heads well inland, across one of the most fertile patches along the coast. South of the highway, tobacco is the main crop. North of the asphalt the landscape becomes a morass of channels, copses and lagoons, teeming with wildlife pursued by the local fishermen and hunters; if you're interested in exploring, a canoe might be of more use than a car or local bus.

Ünye and around

ÜNYE, the ancient Oinaion, is a small, friendly place just over 100km east of Samsun that makes for a thoroughly pleasant overnight stay. Inland from the busy shore highway, the town has a few grand buildings dating from Byzantine times and its eighteenth-century heyday as a regional port, including a former Byzantine church that now serves as a hamam (men only most days, women Sat) on the main square, Cumhuriyet Meydanı. The Black Sea "renovation" craze has not yet hit Ünye; its fine buildings, many of them on Kadılar Yokusu, leading uphill from just behind the church-hamam, are rotting, and most are occupied by squatters. It's worth coinciding with the burgeoning **Wednesday market**, where you'll see gold-toothed farm women selling hazelnuts (harvested in August) and unusual edible plants (described under the catch-all term of *salata*), alongside churns full of farm-produced milk and cheese.

Ünye also profits from its status as a **beach resort**. You see the best strands approaching from the west, where the highway is lined by ranks of motels and *pansiyon*s of a concentration not seen since the Aegean or the Marmara regions. The luckier of these give onto aptly named **Uzunkum** (Long Sand) beach, though signs warn you not to bathe when the sea is rough, and there's no consistent life-guard presence.

The only specific local sights are each well inland from town, reached by different roads. The medieval **fortress of Çaleoğlu**, badly signposted as "Ünye Kalesi", lies just off the minor 850 road to Niksar and Tokat. Just over 5km from the coast, turn left (south), following signs for the *Kaledibi* streamside teahouse/grill; 1.2km along, turn right at a junction and proceed 1.3km more to track's end at the base of a natural pinnacle crowned by the fortifications. The Byzantine ramparts around the south-facing gateway have been restored, but the adjacent rock-cut tomb, of Roman or Pontic-kingdom vintage, suggests that one or the other originally fortified the site. Beyond the gate little remains intact, though you can follow a slippery, usually damp path to the summit, with the final approach by steps cut into the rock and – at the last moment – a rickety ladder to scramble up. Your reward is the view south over an exceptionally lush valley, and north to the Ünye coast.

For the rock-cut **tomb of Tozkoparan**, head east out of Ünye and, just over 4km from the centre, turn south onto a minor road signposted "Tozkoparan Mezarı". Pass the giant cement plant, which employs a good many locals, and, 1.5km along, where a two-tap fountain stands by the roadside, bear right up a dead-end cement drive leading to a group of three houses. The rock-tomb stands in private land, in a low cliff at the top of the hazelnut grove behind the leftmost house; the owners are happy to point the way.

Arrival and information

Ünye's minuscule **otogar** is at the eastern edge of town, by the road to Niksar; there's a separate stop for minibuses to Tokat. The usually enthusiastic **tourist office** (June–Aug daily 8am–6pm; Sept–May Mon–Fri 8am–noon & 1–5pm; ☎0452/323 4952) is housed in the ground floor of the *kaymakamlık* (county administrative offices) building at the rear of central Cumhuriyet Meydanı, though offerings are limited to a single Turkish-text-only leaflet with a useful sketch map.

Accommodation

If you want to stay **in the town centre** and savour the bourgeois atmosphere, try one of three tolerable backpackers' options just east and south of the main square. The *Otel Güney*, Belediye Cad 14 (☎ & ☎0452/323 8406, ❶) offers small, mostly en-suite, double-glazed rooms, but they smell of damp, have no air-conditioning, and the roof-terrace café is currently closed. A few doors down at Belediye Cad 4, the *Otel Burak* (☎0452/312 0186; ❶) has functional rooms with TVs and very small bathrooms that are prone to plumbing problems. You might just get a better view and more calm (*ezan* moments excepted) at the friendly *Otel Kılıç*, Cumhuriyet Meydanı, Hükümet Yanı 6 (☎0452/323 1224; ❶; breakfast not included), to the right of the *kaymakamlık* as you face it. Most of the 1960s-style en-suite rooms (cheerier than the grim lobby promises) have balconies – not that laundry ever dries completely in the muggy climate.

If you're determined to stay **near the beach**, it's best to do it west of town in Gölevi district, along the Samsun road; green-and-white dolmuşes marked "Curuderesi" leave every few minutes from the town centre. The *Belediye Çamlık Moteli* (☎0452/323 1085), located in a little pine forest 2km from town, is a slice of 1970s Turkey, offering either ordinary doubles (❷) or self-catering cottages (❸), though bathrooms underwent a year-2000 makeover and kitchens have marbles sinks and counters; Uzunkum is still a way off, but below the motel grounds there are picturesque, surf-lashed rocks serving as perches for the ubiquitous Black Sea cormorants.

For accommodation backing onto **Uzunkum**, continue 2km further west, where the three-star *Ünye Park Hotel* (☎0452/323 2738, ℉323 7032) keeps a pool table in the bar and serves seaside breakfast on the lawn garden. The standard rooms (❹) are fairly well-equipped (with fridges), but the balcony-less suites (❺) are more worth the splurge. The nearby *Ankara Oteli* (☎0452/324 1013, ℉324 2751; ❷) has somewhat bleaker rooms but nice balconies and a similarly pleasant garden-restaurant overlooking perhaps the best patch of Uzunkum beach. A kilometre or so beyond, just before the town limits, stands the two-star *Otel Kumsal* (☎ & ℉0425/323 4490; ❷), where the wood-trim rooms, sparsely but tastefully furnished, vary; the best and quietest have oblique or full-on sea views.

There is also a handful of cheaper *pansiyon*s, most marooned on the inland side of the highway, as well as a few beachside **campsites**, the latter actually welcoming tents and caravans for overnighting. The most convenient sites are the *Gülen* (☎0452/324 7368) and the adjacent, better-equipped *Uzunkum* (☎0452/323 2022), both sheltering in the pines west of the *Belediye Çamlık Motel*.

Eating and drinking

All the hotels mentioned, as well as the campsites, have **restaurants** of some sort, though the *Kumsal*'s cool-case fare might be a bit long in the tooth and you're well advised to check seafood prices beforehand at the barn-like *Belediye Çamlık*. You'll do better in town itself, though even here there are too many *pide salonları* and not enough proper *lokanta*s or *meyhane*s. The moderately priced *Park* on the shore road, the only "family" restaurant serving alcohol, has a fairly limited menu of seafood, *meze*s and grills, plus a popular summer roof terrace. At the *Çakırtepe Sami Soysal Parkı*, excellent *pide* is on an equal footing with the lovely wooded surroundings and sweeping views; it's well signposted along a street leading inland from near the *Belediye Çamlık* – take any dolmuş labelled "Cakırtepe/D. Hastanesi" from Cumhuriyet Meydanı to the end of the line.

Fatsa to Perşembe

FATSA, 21km east of Ünye, is a shabby mess with polluted beaches and a sad recent history. Like nearby Bolaman, it is populated by Alevîs, a sect closely allied to Shi'ism and the Bektaşi Sufi order, and during the late 1970s the inhabitants took the opportunity to put the radical political beliefs that often accompany this affiliation into action by electing a Marxist city council. A Paris-style commune was established, its mayor a tailor popularly known as Terzi Selim; as a run-up to the coup of September 1980, the army sent in tanks to close down the experiment. Locals erected barricades to no avail: an undetermined number of activists were killed or imprisoned, and Terzi Selim subsequently died in jail. Today the place is subdued as well as unattractive, with locals still reluctant to discuss these traumatic events.

Near the western town limits, difficult to spot coming from the west, the *Dolunay Oteli* (☎0452/423 1528, ℉423 1633; ❸) has a fine seaside setting, though the nearest proper beach is some distance east, and the hotel itself has definitely seen better days. The attached restaurant is still good though, and your best bet for a meal locally.

At **BOLAMAN**, the ancient Polemon, 10km east on the same bay, the so-called "castle" of the Haznedaroğlu clan overlooks the harbour. The clan, de facto rulers of the area during the eighteenth and nineteenth centuries, called themselves the governors of Trabzon, in defiance of the Ottomans. A wood superstructure, whose restoration is indefinitely stalled, perches atop a Byzantine/Genoese fortress. Tiny Bolaman merits a stop if you're in your own vehicle: alongside the castle, the pretty harbour is fringed by Ottoman houses, the beach is set back from the busy road, and there are a couple of restaurants and a tea garden.

The coast highway winds on northeastwards past more sandy coves to an inconspicuous sign at Yalıköy pointing towards **Yason**, a cape where mariners once sacrificed at a temple of Jason (the Argonaut) before venturing further on the temperamental waters of the Black Sea. The temple was replaced in due course by a medieval church, 500m off the road, still well preserved except for a chunk missing out of the dome.

Once past Yason, the scenery regains the drama of the stretch between Sinop and Amasra, as the hills tumble down directly into the water. **ÇAKA** has one of the eastern Black Sea's prettiest white-sand, forested beaches – **Beyzakum** – but there's no place to overnight indoors, only Turkish-style *kampings* next to restaurants hiding under the mulberry trees.

Just the other side of Çam Burnu sprawls **PERŞEMBE**, the first substantial place since Fatsa, a pretty fishing port where the two-star *Hotel Vona* (☎0452/517 1755; ❸) fronts a small beach just east of town. With fair-sized, well-furnished rooms, all with balconies and sea views, and its own pool and playground, it's a surprisingly upmarket establishment for a town so small.

Ordu

Called Kotyora by the ancients, **ORDU** is now an undistinguished city of 117,000, with just a few older houses scaling the green slopes of Boztepe to the west, above the recently restored nineteenth-century Greek Orthodox cathedral. The only other historic remnants are in the **museum** in the Paşaoğlu Konağı (daily 8am–5pm; $0.70), signposted off Hükümet Caddesi, past the main PTT. Once home to a leader of the Muslim immigrants fleeing the Caucasus in 1877–1878, this typical example of nineteenth-century Black Sea architecture is well worth a look if you have the time. Downstairs there's a fairly dull museum of ethnography, but upstairs the two bedrooms and their original furnishings have been beautifully restored.

The **otogar** is 2km east of the centre on the Trabzon-bound highway, while the **tourist office** (summer Mon–Sat 8.30am–noon & 1–5.30pm; winter Mon–Fri 8.30am–noon & 1–5.30pm; ☎0452/223 1606) is located in the *Belediye* building a little to the east of the Atatürk statue, also on the main highway (called Atatürk Bulvarı while threading through the town centre).

There are few really appealing or decent-value **hotels** in or around Ordu. The outstanding exception, just uphill from the Greek cathedral, is the *Karlıbel İkizevler Hotel* (☎0452/225 0081, ☏223 2483; ❺), occupying two surviving old mansions. Both the smaller doubles and larger suites (sleeping three) offer wooden floors and good bathrooms with shower cubicles. A cheaper, passably comfortable alternative is the two-star *Turist Otel*, Atatürk Bul 134 (☎0452/225 3140, ☏214 1950; ❸), some of whose rooms have balconies and sea views. Nearly 1.5km west of town, the *Belde Hotel* (☎0452/214 3987, ☏214 9398; ❺) presents an odd mix of new and faded decor, but comes with a comprehensive range of three-star comforts including a pool, satellite TV, restaurant, Turkish bath and sauna.

Stopping for **lunch** is probably more rewarding than staying the night. Dead central, at Atatürk Bul 1, opposite the great man's monument, stands *Ayışığı*, a combination restaurant and events centre; local dishes, based for example on chard and beets, are featured, and events include an annual Volkswagen bug rally. The *Midi*, sitting on a pier jutting out from Sahil Caddesi, is the best option for fish, including salmon, trout and *mezgit* (whiting). Cheaper, more Westernized food, such as chicken *şiş*, hamburgers and Italian pizzas, can be had in congenial, clean surroundings at *Café Bulvar*, Atatürk Bul 98. On the shoreline roundabout closest to the church the *Pikola Cinema Café* has weekly quality **film screenings**. Ordu is most famous for its hazelnut-in-chocolate products produced by Sağra, and there's a whole shop full of the stuff, called **Sağra Nuthouse**, at Süleyman Felek Cad 95, the road that runs parallel to Atatürk Bulvarı and perpendicular to Hükümet Caddesi.

Continuing east towards Giresun, you'll find no more appealing **beaches** until just before Piraziz, 14–16km out of Ordu; the best ones are marked at weekends by knots of parked cars.

Giresun

Tucked on both sides of a steep, fortified bluff 31km east of Ordu, **GİRESUN**, with its mix of old and new buildings and converted churches, must be a nice place to live – but you wouldn't necessarily visit, as there's precious little in the way of sights. The town entered history as Pharnacia, a second-century BC foundation of the Pontic king Pharnaces, but the name was soon changed to Kerasos, the root of the word for cherry in virtually all Western languages. It was from here in 69 BC that the Roman gourmet-general, Lucullus, first introduced the fruit to Europe, and cherry orchards still flourish all around. However, these days hazelnuts are the main local cash crop – at the base of Gazi Caddesi, there's a statue of two hazelnut gatherers, standing back to back and bowed by the weight of three giant sculpted nuts emerging from their characteristic calyces.

The grounds of the **castle** on the bluff, nucleus of the earliest settlement, are today the main city park. Partly overgrown, they're wild and satisfying in a way that normally more regimented Turkish parks rarely manage, and the locals picnic here en masse at weekends. At the foot of the ramparts on Sokakbaşı Caddesi, an eighteenth-century Greek church has been pressed into service as the **Giresun Museum** (Giresun Müzesi; daily 8am–5pm; $0.70), a mixed archeological and ethnographic collection containing a number of ancient wine and olive oil amphorae from ships that sank off the Black Sea coast. To complete the rather threadbare picture, there's a Turkish wooden printing press, some heavy *bindallı* embroidery on velvet traditional costumes and a corner display of fine kilims.

Further east, a nautical mile or so offshore, lies **Giresun Adası**, the only major island in the Black Sea. In pre-Christian times it was called Aretias, and was sacred to the Amazons who dedicated a temple to the war god Ares on it. Jason and his Argonauts supposedly stopped here to offer sacrifice, but were attacked by vicious birds. The islet is still the venue for fertility rites on May 20, dating back four thousand years to the celebration of Priapus and Cybele, respectively the phallic god and Anatolian mother goddess, and described in one 1990s tourist-office handout as a festival of "abundance and male procreative power". Any village woman who doesn't have babies yet is ritually passed through a trivet (a hoop-like affair on legs); this is followed by a boat tour of the island for a large part of the population of Giresun, and then pebbles (representing troubles and misfortunes) are cast into the sea. Finally, upon return to the mainland, general inebriation ensues. Otherwise, there's nothing in particular to see on the island, except the scant ruins of a Byzantine monastery, and in any case, the former passenger ferry service from the jetty east of town is currently suspended.

Arrival, orientation and information

Giresun's **otogar**, with frequent services east to Tirebolu and Trabzon and west to Ordu, is 3km west of the centre. If you're coming in from the east, have the bus drop you on the west flank of the castle bluff, at the central dolmuş drop-off point beside the Atapark; most companies have their ticket offices in this area. If you're coming from the west, there's a dolmuş between the *otogar* and the seafront Atapark, marked "Beyaz Baş". Turkish Maritime Lines no longer operates a ferry service to or from Giresun.

Gazi Caddesi is the main commercial street leading inland from the Atapark, past the statues and fountain. The **tourist office** (summer Mon–Sat 8.30am–6pm; winter Mon–Fri 9am–5pm; ☎0454/216 3007) is in a booth in the park. The most central **internet café** is *Pota*, at Gazi Cad 54.

Accommodation

Most of the **accommodation** in Giresun clusters in the lanes east off Gazi Caddesi. Supply usually exceeds demand, and prices are realistic, so it's worth avoiding the grungiest dives.

Budget travellers might start their search at the *Otel Bozbağ* (☎0454/216 1249; ❶), a rambling place at the junction of Eskiyağcılar Sokak 8 and Arif Bey Caddesi (head up Gazi Caddesi from the waterfront and take the second left), but despite a 2001 makeover it's still dingy and jail-like. It's certainly poor value compared to the nearby one-star *Er-Tur Oteli*, off Osmanağa Caddesi at Çapulacılar Sok 8 (☎0454/216 1757, ℗216 7762; ❷), a modern, comfortable affair with updated bathrooms and a private car park. Near the disused ferry dock and the pedestrian flyover, the two-star *Giresun Oteli*, Atatürk Bul 103 (☎0454/216 3017, ℗216 6038; ❷), is also a bargain, with friendly staff and a sixth-floor restaurant – although the decor's aging, the air-conditioned rooms have bathtubs and double-glazing against the traffic noise. The similarly equipped three-star *Kit-tur Otel*, Arifbey Cad 27, off Gazi Caddesi (☎0454/212 0245, ℗212 3034; ❹), has proper shower cubicles in the rooms, plus a sauna and gym in the basement (and another rooftop restaurant), but isn't really worth the extra outlay. Top standard in Giresun is the four-star *Hotel Başar* (☎0454/212 9920, ⓦwww.hotelbasar.com.tr; ❺), on the waterfront next to the *Giresun Oteli*. Entry is via a vast atrium with a glass elevator swooping up the central well as far as a top-floor restaurant and attic bar; the rooms almost do this justice, with terracotta floors and shower-tub stalls in the baths let down by harsh furnishings, though the four-person suites are a bit jollier, with giant bathrooms.

Eating and drinking

You certainly won't starve in Giresun – the area around the Atapark swarms with decent **restaurants**. Although the Left-leaning town is hardly a fundamentalist stronghold, it can still be difficult to get a "wee drop" with your food. The *Deniz Lokantası*, on Alpaslan Caddesi, at the far side of Atapark from the sea and next to the *Belediye*, is the locals' favourite for steamtray food; no booze is served but it's open all day. Behind the *Otel Bozbağ*, Köprülühan Sokağı is a narrow pedestrian lane crowded in summer with the outdoor tables of three competing *kebap/pide salonları*; currently *Yetimoğlu Meydan Sofrası* has the edge. On the same lane, but upstairs, is the licensed *Yöremiz Restaurant*, with a summer roof terrace; portions are on the small side but the fare – savoury vegetable *meze*s, perfectly fried breaded *mezgit* – is very good and won't exceed $6 with a beer. The only other central licensed premises, and reckoned to have the best cooking in town, is the *Tibor Sosyal Tesisleri*, behind the *Belediye* at İncedayı Sok 4, but hours are restricted to noon–2pm and 6.30–10.30pm; take the lift to the fourth floor (lunch) or roof terrace (supper), and budget $9 for a meal. Up in the castle, there's a *pide salonu* plus stalls selling ice cream, drinks and *mısır* (roast corn), but no proper eateries.

The area's best beaches lie about 5km west, backed by four **disco-bars**, which provide the town's nightlife. However, both sand and clubs seem threatened by the soon-to-be-completed highway widening, so check they still exist before setting out specially.

Tirebolu to Akçaabat

TİREBOLU, curled above a bay enclosed by two headlands 41km east of Giresun, is an attractive spot. A Greek Orthodox community until 1923, it's virtually unique hereabouts in not having been entirely overrun by concrete atrocities. On the easterly promontory stands the intact **castle of St John**, built for a fourteenth-century Genoese garrison. A nocturnal tea garden operates on the lawn inside the castle – pleasant except for the blaring pop music, and your only chance to see the fort's interior.

However, there are few other amenities in town, and all told there's not really enough here to make it worth an overnight stop. The most tolerable **accommodation** is the *Eren Pansiyon* (☎ 0454/411 4600; ❷), opposite the sandy but often crowded westerly *Belediye* beach. **Eating** is equally problematic: there are no waterfront fish restaurants, so you'll have to make do with the reasonable *Tütüncüoğlu* on Gazipaşa Caddesi, or the standard *Rıhtım* by the otogar. You can get a beer and *çerez* at *Tosun Fıçı Bira* by the fishing port.

Tirebolu lies at the heart of the *fındık*- or **hazelnut-growing** area, which extends roughly from Samsun east to the Georgian frontier. During late July and August you'll see vast mats of them, still in their husks, raked out to dry. Impatient locals perversely insist on eating them slightly green, when the taste resembles that of acorns.

Besides the *Belediye* beach, Tirebolu has a much larger if more exposed sandy **beach** stretching to the east, which has emerged unscathed from the roadworks. There are more decent beaches between Tirebolu and **ESPİYE**, 12km back towards Giresun. A sign just west of Espiye points to the hill, less than a dirt-track kilometre inland, on which stands **Andoz Kalesi**, the westernmost of the three Genoese strongholds in the area – but it's badly overgrown and crumbled. East of Tirebolu you'll see more of the numerous **castles** built, mostly by the Genoese but occasionally by the Byzantines, during the thirteenth and fourteenth centuries to protect the sea approaches to Trabzon. One well-preserved stronghold lurks 15km inland, up the Harşit Çayıat Bedrama; this river, just east of Tirebolu, marks the furthest line of advance by the Tsarist army in 1916.

Nearby **GÖRELE** boasts a fine collection of Black Sea houses, more apparent than Akçaabat's (see opposite), but only really worth the effort for buffs of vernacular architecture with their own cars. The town's name is an obvious corruption of nearby Coralla citadel, just before Eynesil. At **BEŞİKDÜZÜ**, the three-star *Hotel Bestt* (☎0462/871 3944; ❸), on the ocean side of the highway, offers the best standard on this coast, with comfortable, centrally heated rooms and clean, tiled bathrooms with tubs. Another Byzantine castle at

AKÇAKALE, close to the road, is the best preserved between Tirebolu and Trabzon; the fortress on **Fener Burnu** is less obvious. In addition to fortresses, there's a final flurry of wide beaches – especially between Vakfıkebir and Fener Burnu – but they're generally unshaded, functional at best and lacking in charm.

If you're depressed by the relentless drabness of Black Sea coastal architecture, then **AKÇAABAT**, 15km west of Trabzon, may serve as a partial antidote. From the looks of the shore districts it would seem to be more of the same, but **Ortamahalle** (Middle Neighbourhood), on the central of the three ridges behind the modern town, features a dense concentration of the wood-and-stucco houses once prevalent throughout the region. Russian naval shelling in 1916 devastated much of Akçaabat, however, and only one medieval church out of three dozen survived the war. You can reach Akaabat easily by red-and-white *Belediye* buses plying frequently to and from Trabzon.

Trabzon

No other Turkish city except İstanbul has exercised such a hold on the Western imagination as **TRABZON** (ancient Trebizond). Travel-writers from Marco Polo to Rose Macaulay have been enthralled by the fabulous image of this quasi-mythical metropolis, long synonymous with intrigue, luxury, exotic customs and fairy-tale architecture. Today the celebrated gilded roofs and cosmopolitan texture of Trebizond are long gone, replaced by the blunt reality of an initially disappointing Turkish provincial capital of over 200,000 people. But a little poking around the cobbled alleyways will still turn up tangible evidence of its former splendour – not least the monastic church of **Aya Sofya**, home to some of the most outstanding Byzantine frescoes in Anatolia.

Some history

The city was founded during the eighth century BC by colonists from Sinope and Miletus, who settled on the easily defensible bluff isolated by today's Kuzgun and Tabakhane ravines. From the promontory's flat summit – *trapeza* or "table" in ancient Greek – came the new town's original name, Trapezus, and all subsequent variations. Under the Romans and Byzantines the city continued to prosper, thanks to extensive patronage by Hadrian and Justinian, and its location at the northeast end of a branch of the Silk Route.

Trabzon's romantic allure is derived almost totally from a brief, though resplendent, **Golden Age** during the thirteenth and fourteenth centuries. A scion of the royal Komnenos line, Alexios, managed to escape the Crusaders' sacking of Constantinople in 1204; shortly after, he landed at Trebizond in command of a Georgian army and proclaimed himself the legitimate Byzantine emperor. Despite the fact that there were two other pretenders, one in Epirus and the other at Nicaea (it was the latter's descendants who eventually retook Constantinople), it was the pint-sized Trapezuntine Empire that was arguably the most successful.

The empire owed its unlikely longevity to a number of factors. Mongol raiders of the mid-thirteenth century swept across the Middle East, accentuating the city's importance by forcing the main Silk Route to divert northward through Tabriz, Erzurum and ultimately Trebizond. The empire's diplomats, hampered by few scruples and with the survival of the state as their only aim, arranged short- and long-term alliances with assorted Turcoman and Mongol chieftains manoeuvring at the borders. In this they were aided by the preter-natural beauty of the Komneni princesses, who were given in marriage to any expedient suitor, Christian or Muslim. Accordingly, garbled tales of Christian princesses languishing in the grasp of the infidel reached Western Europe and, among other literature, apparently inspired Don Quixote's quest for Dulcinea.

Someone had to transport all the goods accumulated at Trebizond's docks and this turned out to be the **Genoese**, followed soon after by the Venetians as well. Each demanded and got the same maritime trading privileges from the Trapezuntine Empire as they did from the re-established empire at Constantinople. Western ideas and personalities arrived continually with the Latins' boats, making Trebizond an unexpected island of art and erudition in a sea of Turkish nomadism, and a cultural rival to the Italian Renaissance city-states of the same era.

Unfortunately, the empire's factional politicking was excessive even by the standards of the age. In this respect they managed to outdo even the Medicis, lending extreme meaning to the disparaging adjective "Byzantine". The native aristocracy fought frequent pitched battles with transplanted courtiers from Constantinople, and the Italian contingents rarely hesitated to make it a three-or even four-sided fray. One such civil war in 1341 completely destroyed the city and sent the empire into its final decline.

It was Mehmet the Conqueror, in a campaign along the Black Sea shore, who finally put paid to the self-styled empire; in 1461 the last emperor, David, true to Trapezuntine form, negotiated a more or less bloodless surrender to the sultan. Under the Ottomans the city became an important training ground for future rulers: Selim the Grim, while still a prince, served as the provincial governor between 1490 and 1512, and his son Süleyman the Magnificent was born and reared here until his accession in 1520. Given these early imperial associations and the sultans' vigorous local Turkification programme, Trabzon, as it was renamed, was and still is a relatively devout place.

In late Ottoman times the city's Christian element enjoyed a resurgence of both population and influence. The presence of a rich merchant class justified the foundation of numerous European consulates in Trabzon and a spate of sumptuous civic and domestic building. But it was a mere echo of a distant past, soon ended by a decade of world and civil war and the foundation of the Republic. Shipping dwindled after the construction of the railway between Ankara and Erzurum and roads beyond into Iran.

Today the outlook is still uncertain: though there was a brief boom during the Iran–Iraq war, both port and town have been overtaken by Samsun to the west. Trabzon now makes much of its living as a trans-shipment point for lorries taking goods to the recently independent Caucasian republics.

Arrival, orientation and information

Trabzon's **airport** is 7km away at the eastern edge of town, connected by frequent dolmuşes to a town-centre stop near the *Horon Oteli*; the **otogar** is closer, 3km out, near the junction of Highway 010 with Route E97/885 (heading towards Sumela and Erzurum) and served by dolumşes marked "Meydanı". All services, whether long-distance coaches or short-hop minibuses, use this terminal now that the old mid-town minibus stand has been abolished. The Turkish Maritime Line **ferry port** is huddled at the base of the medieval shore bastion pierced by the coast-highway tunnel, just off our map. **Parking** is a trial anywhere in congested Trabzon – the closest legal car park to the centre is near the İskender Paşa Camii.

9

All roads converge on **Atatürk Alanı**, also called "Meydanı" or "Parkı". This tree-shaded square is the hub of both Trabzon's social life plus endless dolmuş, bus and taxi traffic. Major bus company ticket offices also congregate at the corners of the square. Most of Trabzon's sights are within walking distance of Atatürk Alanı, though you'll need a dolmuş (here often a saloon car rather than a minbus) to get to Aya Sofya, and a bus or taxi to reach the Kaymaklı monastery behind Boztepe.

From Atatürk Alanı, İskele Caddesi winds down to the port, while the city's two major longitudinal avenues lead west towards the old town. **Kıbrıs Şehitler Caddesi**, becoming **Uzun Sokak**, the pre-Republican high street, cobbled and narrow, heads off from the southwest corner; **Kahraman Maraş Caddesi** (shortened in addresses to Maraş Caddesi), the modern boulevard carrying most traffic, from the northwest corner. **Taksim Caddesi** (also known as Şehit Sani Akbulut Caddesi) leads from the southeast angle up toward **Boztepe**, the hill dominating Trabzon.

Information

The **tourist office** (March–Nov daily 8am–7pm; Dec–Feb Mon–Sat 8am–5pm; ☎0462/321 4659) is located on a side street just east of Atatürk Alanı, opposite the İskender Paşa Camii. The staff here are friendly, helpful and English-speaking. They keep a broad range of fairly useful brochures to hand, are eager to suggest excursions into the mountains (particularly *yayla*-based tourism and, crucially, can advise as to which (if any) of our recommended hotels have slid down the slippery slope to brotheldom.

Accommodation

Given Trabzon's status as the first major stop-off after the ex-Soviet border, many of the city's hotels spent the 1990s doubling as brothels. With the recent economic crash in Turkey, this activity has been relatively subdued of late, but could revive in the future. The traditional red-light district lies along İskele Caddesi and the streets immediately off it, right down to the port; Güzelhisar Caddesi just west is more wholesome. Those on the latter street that we've mentioned below are reputable and unlikely to deteriorate unless they change owners; in any case you might want to choose a hotel in a more salubrious area.

But charm in Trabzon is only relative – it's a big, gritty city, with many new arrivals repulsed by the traffic, noise and subtropical mugginess. Particularly if you have transport, you might consider nearby recommendations on the way to Sumela, at Uzungöl or between Maçka and the Zigana pass. This may prove a necessity in mid-summer, when the more comfortable lodgings in Trabzon are often block-booked by tour groups.

Anıl Güzelhisar Cad 10 ☎0462/326 7282. Clean, small, plain rooms with TV. Sea breeze (and coast-road noise) in lieu of air-conditioning. Ground-floor breakfast salon, and help with arranging excursions. ❷

Horon Oteli Sıramağazalar Cad 125 ☎0462/326 6455, ⓦwww.otelhoron.com.tr. Don't be scared off by the rack rate – staff readily offer big reductions, even in summer. Rooms are on the small side, but they're furnished in some style, with superior bathrooms (including American-style shower nozzles), air-conditioning and double-glazing. Also a rooftop sea-view bar/restaurant, relatively easy street parking, and nearby fee car-parks. ❻

Nur Cami Sok 15 ☎0462/323 0445, ⓕ323 0447. Small, well-worn but decently equipped rooms with fridge, TV and double-glazing. Good-natured management, used to foreign guests. ❷

Sankta Maria Katolik Kilisesi Sümer Sok 28 ☎0462/321 2192. The most characterful and cheapest place to stay in Trabzon is this French Capuchin church and monastery, built around two courtyards just north of Atatürk Alanı. The welcoming voluntary staff offer spacious double rooms

TRABZON

BLACK SEA

TDİ

Otogar (3km), Airport (7km), Rize & Artvin

Sahil Paşa
İskender Paşa Camii

Russian Market (Avrasya Pazarı)

Georgian Consulate
Airport dolmus
Sumela dolmus taxi

City Bus Stop
THY Office

BOZTEPE

Trabzon Museum

Kızlar (Theoskepastos) Monastery

Kaymaklı (4km)

Kaymaklı & K

BEDESTEN

Taş Han

Küçük Ayvasıl Kilisesi (St Anne's)

Fatih Hamamı

Yeni Cuma Camii (St Eugenius)

PAZARKAPI

Çarşı Camii

Sekiz Direkli Hamam

Walls

Tabakhane Bridge

ORTAHISAR

Ortahisar Camii

Russian Consulate

Zağnos Bridge

Byzantine Palace (ruins)

Kuzgun Deresi

Walls

Zağnos Tower

Gülbahar Hatun Camii

N

0   200 m

Atatürk Köşkü (4.5km)

Hospitals ▲ Aya Sofya (1.5km)

Giresun & Samsun

9

THE BLACK SEA COAST | Trabzon

782

and hot showers down the hall to guests of any religion in return for a reasonable donation (say $10–20) at the end of a visit; kitchen, washing machine and garden are all available, free of charge.

Hotel Usta Teleğrafhane Sok 3 ☎ 0462/326 5700, ⊛ www.ustahotel.com.tr. Veteran three-star, whose rooms – lightly refreshed since the mid-1990s – are bigger than *Horon*'s, with small tubs in most bathrooms. Formal but pleasant ground-floor restaurant; fee car-park adjacent. ❹

Yuvan Güzelhisar Cad 10B ☎ 0462/326 6823. A

plain, if clean and apparently *natasha*-free, ensuite cheapie, probably as basic as you'll want to be in Trabzon. ❷

Zorlu Grand Hotel Kahraman Maraş Cad 9 ☎ 0462/326 8400, ⊛ www.zorlugrand.com. Rooms are plush, with marble-clad bathrooms, but you're really paying for the facilities – especially the massive atrium, two restaurants, "English pub", gym and indoor pool. Rack rates are massively overpriced (from $195), but advance booking/bargaining may or may not be productive. ❽

The City

Trabzon straggles along the coast and penetrates inland for several kilometres, presenting you with the choice of short rides or substantial walks to get to many points of interest – a characteristic aggravated by the modern city centre being a full kilometre from the ancient and medieval focus of settlement. On foot, you can see most of the in-town sights in a day; the suburban monuments require both extra time and use of public transport for access. If time is limited, concentrate on the two remote monasteries of Aya Sofya and Kaymaklı.

Around Atatürk Alanı and Uzun Sokak

An east-to-west walk along the seaward portion of town begins unpromisingly: the Genoese bastion straddling the coast highway tunnel, approached along Güzelhisar Caddesi, is an officers' club, off-limits to the public; detour slightly left instead, to the flyover taking you to a tea garden and small park on the west flank of the castle. This seems to be Trabzon's sole acknowledgement of its seaside location, since – apart from the Russian market – the shoreline in general is amazingly dead, with the city introverted up on its plateau. The **Catholic church of Sankta Maria** (Tues–Sun 2–3pm), a few alleys west of the ramparts, is the last surviving reminder of the western powers' former pivotal role here.

If you visit one **Russian market** on the Black Sea it should be that of Trabzon, which – labelled "Avrasya Pazar" – occupies a long covered area at the foot of the cliff occupied by the İskenderpaşa Camii. The nominal entrance fee will be waived if they realize you're not Turkish: hard currency is always welcome. Stalls display an amazing array of Eastern European memorabilia, from inter-nesting *matryushka* dolls to balalaika maestros immortalized on vinyl (sadly, the sale of vodka is forbidden in the Russian markets).

Shifting northwest of Atatürk Alanı, pedestrianized **Kunduracılar Caddesi** (Shoemakers' Street) is the usual entry to Trabzon's **bazaar**. Ironically just about everything *except* shoes can be found on this avenue, with a special emphasis first on pharmacies and doctors, then gold jewellery. Once past Cumhuriyet Caddesi, Kunduracılar veers right to become **Semerciler Caddesi** (Saddlers' Street), devoted to a mix of factory-made clothing and the electrically coloured, striped *keşans* (shawls) and *peştemals* (waistbands) that are standard issue for so many Trabzon-province women. Copper merchants and tin-platers cluster on and just off Alacahan Sokak, which leads downhill from Semerciler to the water.

Sooner or later you'll stumble upon the monumental heart of the bazaar, where the **Çarşı Camii**, largest mosque in town, is handsome on the outside but garish late-Ottoman inside. Just behind it, the sixteenth-century **Taş Han** is a rather standard tradesmen's hall, still the location of retail outlets and (inside the courtyard) tailors' workshops. The **Bedesten**, below the mosque, was built by the Genoese in the fourteenth century, and revamped by the Ottomans. Square-seeming from the outside, the interior is actually octagonal, but the four pillars were evidently insufficient to support the dome, which has long since fallen in. After decades of dereliction, and use as a lumber mill, the *bedesten* has been restored as a somewhat touristy crafts bazaar, with a small café-restaurant on the top floor.

Leave the bazaar going uphill, cross Kahraman Maraş Caddesi, and you can't miss the ninth-century Byzantine **Küçük Ayvasil Kilisesi** just the other side. Also known as St Anne's, the diminutive shrine is permanently locked – little matter as its frescoes have been obliterated since 1923. A stroll along Uzun Sokak, lying to the southeast and dotted with imposing *belle époque* mansions, may be more satisfying. There's no real concentration of old houses in Trabzon; the appeal of leisurely strolling lies partly in the unexpected confrontation with a creaking masterpiece on an otherwise unremarkable block.

One of the best examples of this is the Italian-designed Kostaki Theophylaktos Konağı, just south of Uzun Sokak on Zeytinlik Caddesi, newly opened as the **Trabzon Museum** (Trabzon Müsesi; Tues–Sun 9.30am–noon & 1–5.30pm, $0.70). The ground-floor rooms, with their parquet floors, painted ceilings, fancy drapes and plush armchairs give a good idea of life amongst the *belle époque* Ottoman bourgeoisie. There's a rather perfunctory ethnographic collection upstairs, while the basement is devoted to the archeological collection, where pride of place is given to a complete but slightly crushed bronze, life-sized statue of Hermes. This was found during excavations in 1997, smashed into several pieces by a fallen column on the grounds of his presumed temple in the Tabakhane district, and meticulously reassembled.

The old town

Following Uzun Sokak further west soon brings you to the **Tabakhane Deresi** (Tannery Ravine) and the namesake bridge spanning it. On the other side sprawls the fortified old town on its "table", but before crossing you should make a detour left along the east bank of the ravine, being careful to bear onto **Bilaloğlu Sokak** (from the bridge, follow the hamam sign and then take a sharp right at the first turning – there is a street sign but it's hard to spot), away from markers pointing to the Fatih Hamamı. After about 350m you'll come to the thirteenth-century **Yeni Cuma Camii**, formerly the church of St Eugenius, patron saint of Trabzon. There may have been a shrine of sorts here as early as the third century, when Eugenius disrupted the cult of Mithra at Boztepe and was martyred by Diocletian for his pains. As so often happened in these cases, his skull was found on the spot within a few years of the arrival of a new ruler, Alexios Komnenos, and the present church was erected to house the holy relic. The saint's intervention supposedly spared the city from the Selçuks in 1222, but he let the side down in 1461; Mehmet the Conqueror offered up his first Friday prayers here after capturing Trabzon, and immediately reconsecrated the church and added its minaret. You'll need to time your visit to the plain but relatively undisturbed interior around the daily cycle of prayers.

Crossing the Tabakhane bridge you arrive in the **Ortahisar** (Middle Castle) district of the old town; further upstream, at the steepest point of the gullies flanking it, is the upper citadel, while below, tumbling off the tableland, sprawls the less defensible lower town, huddled behind a third circuit of walls that reach the sea. The walls are in variable condition but at their crenellated and vine-shrouded best give some idea of Trabzon's skyline in its heyday.

The highlight of Ortahisar is the former church of Panayia Khrysokefalos, now the **Ortahisar Camii** (usually open) and also referred to as the Fatih Camii. As in the case of the Yeni Cuma Camii, there was almost certainly a church on this site from the third century, but the present building dates mostly from the thirteenth century, with massive renovation after a fire set during the 1341 civil war. This was the main cathedral of the Trapezuntine Empire, and most royal weddings, funerals and coronations took place here; the epithet *Khrysokefalos* or "Golden-Headed" recalls the zenith of the dynasty, when the Komneni could afford to plate the dome with gold. This is, of course, long vanished and the Byzantine frescoes inside, smothered under layers of Islamic whitewash, and a thirteenth-century mosaic floor, cemented over during the 1980s, are equally unavailable for viewing, though some fine Byzantine *opus sectile* stonework remains visible in the apse. Today it's the volume of the soaring basilica, with its massive interior columns, that impresses.

From the apse end of the former church you can bear south, uphill, about 400m along Kale Sokağı, through a gateway astride the street, to enter the upper citadel. Of the glittering Komnenos **Byzantine palace**, in the southwest corner of the highest terrace overlooking the Kuzgun Deresi (Raven Canyon), nothing is left but battered masonry. From the eastern ramparts, dominating the Tabakhane Deresi, there's a fine view across to the Yeni Cuma Camii. Some careful navigating could get you through the maze of shacks and market gardens in the ravine bottom and up the other side.

Heading west from Ortahisar Camii, the **Zağnos bridge**, built by a Greek convert who was one of Mehmet the Conqueror's chief generals, leaves Ortahisar over the Kuzgun ravine where dilapidated Greek mansions are steadily losing ground to contemporary tenements. On the far side, the **Zağnos Tower**, the southernmost dungeon in the outer boundary walls, sports the ornate, late-Ottoman Abdullah Paşa fountain at its base.

Across a busy boulevard and a swathe of parkland from the tower squats the **Gülbahar Hatun Camii**, the most important Ottoman monument in Trabzon. However, its background is more fascinating than the run-of-the-mill mosque you see now. The mother of Selim I and wife of Beyazit II – known in later life as *Gülbahar* or "Spring Rose" – was originally a Komneni princess famous for her piety and good works among Christians and Muslims alike. She died in 1512, the first year of Selim's reign, and he completed the mosque and her adjoining tomb by 1514.

From just in front of the Gülbahar Hatun complex, Soğuksu Caddesi heads up toward the finest surviving example of the palatial bourgeois follies that sprouted locally at the end of the nineteenth century.

The Atatürk Köşkü

Set in immaculately maintained gardens, the **Atatürk Köşkü**, or Atatürk Villa (daily 8am–7pm; winter closes 5.30pm; $0.35), began life in 1903 as the property of the Greek banker Karayannidhis, who was obliged to abandon it two decades later. Atatürk stayed here on the first of three occasions in 1924, and the city formally presented it to him a year before his death. As another example of patrician Black Sea architecture, the mansion is more compelling than the contents – which include a bevy of photos of Atatürk, plus a map bearing his strategic scribbles during the Kurdish Dersim revolt of 1937.

Both dolmuşes to the "Köşk" stop and red-and-white city buses marked

"Park-Köşk" serve the villa – which is 6.5km southwest of Atatürk Alanı, so you wouldn't want to walk. You can also catch the bus as it passes Gülbahar Hatun.

Aya Sofya

Alone on a park-like bluff overlooking the Black Sea west of the city, the monastery **church of Aya Sofya** (Haghia Sophia) is one of the most romantically set of Byzantine remains, and even the fact that Trabzon's suburbs have long since overtaken it does little to detract from the appeal. It seems certain that there was a pagan temple here, and then an early Byzantine chapel, long before Manuel I Komnenos commissioned the present structure between 1238 and 1263. The ground plan and overall conception were revolutionary at the time, successfully assimilating most of the architectural trends, Christian and Muslim, prevalent in contemporary Anatolia. Aya Sofya's role as a model for many later Byzantine churches will be evident if you've already seen St Saviour in Hora (Kariye Camii) or the Pammakaristos church (Fethiye Camii) in İstanbul. Converted to a mosque after 1461, Aya Sofya subsequently endured some even leaner and more ignominious times as an ammunition store and then as a hospital. Between 1957 and 1964, technicians working under the supervision of David Talbot Rice and David Winfield rescued the building from certain oblivion, in particular restoring dozens of frescoes to their former glory. Well-lit and accurately labelled in English, these are compulsory viewing even if you've only a passing interest in religious art.

From Atatürk Alanı infrequent **dolmuşes** labelled "BLK Sigorta/Aya Sofya" cover most of the 3km to the monument, dropping you 300m south of Aya Sofya, with the way onwards fairly well signed.

The site

The **church** (April–Oct daily 8am–6pm; Nov–Feb Tues–Sun 8am–4pm; March Tues–Sun 8am–5pm; $0.70) is laid out along a greatly modified cross-in-square scheme, with a dome supported by four columns and three apses at the east end of the triple nave. At the west end of the building a narthex extends across the full width of the nave; barrel-vaulted porticoes adorn the north, west and south sides of the exterior. Before rushing inside to view the famous frescoes, take a moment to study the finely sculpted, albeit weather-worn, **frieze** illustrating Adam and Eve in the Garden of Eden, which surrounds the south portal, the only one of the three not tampered with by the Ottomans when they re-consecrated the church. This relief work is the most obvious evidence of the strong Armenian, Georgian and even Assyrian influence on the craftsmen – who left, in lieu of signature, the single-headed eagle of the Komnenos dynasty over the biblical work of art.

In their fluidity, warmth and expressiveness, Aya Sofya's **frescoes** represented a drastic break with the rigidity of prior painting, and compare well with the best work of their century, and the next, in Serbia and Macedonia as well as in Constantinople itself. The most important compositions are in the apse and the narthex, as well as in the north porch – which many people miss.

In the central **apse** a serene Ascension hovers over The Virgin Enthroned between the two Archangels; on the north wall of the same apse appears *The Miraculous Draught of Fishes*. The southeast apse is thought to have once been the location of Manuel I's tomb. The Pantocrator in the **dome** was unhappily beyond repair, but a host of angels swirls around him, just above the apostles.

The **narthex**, whose ceiling is divided into three sections by stone ribs, is almost wholly devoted to scenes from the life of Christ. The central zone exploits its complicated quadruple vaulting by depicting each of the Tetramorphs, symbols of the Evangelists, accompanied by seraphim. Alongside, such miraculous episodes as *The Wedding at Cana*, a decidedly adolescent *Child Jesus Teaching in the Temple, Healing the Blind Man at Siloam* and *Healing the Canaanite's Daughter* (complete with vomited demon) fill the south vault, while *Feeding the Five Thousand* and *Calming the Storm on the Lake of Galilee* grace the north vault. The north portico is taken up mostly by Old Testament scenes, including *The Sufferings of Job* and *Jacob's Dream*.

Just north of the church an ensemble of sunken masonry was once the baptismal font; the square belfry to the west is a 1443 afterthought, indicative of the strong Italianate flavour of the waning empire. If the tower is open – a rare event – you'll find that the frescoes within are not nearly of the same quality as those in the church proper.

In the garden opposite the ticket office is a small **museum** (same days and hours as Aya Sofya; separate $0.70 admission), consisting of a village house built and furnished in typical Black Sea style, and a 1920s-vintage *serender* or grain crib on stilts, with wooden disks at the top of the stilts, to prevent mice attacking the stored grain. A pleasant adjacent café offers light snacks and drinks.

Boztepe

Boztepe, the hill dominating Trabzon to the southeast, has always been held in religious esteem. In olden days it was the site of the amalgamated cults of the Persian sun-god Mithra and the Hellenic deity Apollo, an ironic dedication when you consider how little unfiltered sun this coast receives. This reverence persisted into Christian times, when the hill was studded with churches and monasteries. Two of the latter still stand – after a fashion – and one at least is well worth the effort to visit.

Theoskepastos Convent

The ruined former **Convent of the Panayia Theoskepastos** or "God-protected Virgin" (in Turkish, Kızlar Manastırı) backs into the rocky slope 1.5km from Atatürk Alanı, reached by following Taksim Caddesi south and then bearing left when you see the shell of the building on the hillside. Dolmuşes marked "Boztepe" leave from Atatürk Alanı.

Though founded in the fourteenth century, and in continuous use by the Greek Orthodox church until 1923, few internal frescoes or other artistic details remain, and in any case the place has been securely locked since the early 1990s while the Ministry of Culture deliberates how or whether to restore it. Just above the convent an appealing picnickers' park, a tea-garden and a single restaurant (see "Eating" on p.788) share the view over the city with a military base and the locked **mosque and tomb of Ahi Evren Dede**, a target of pilgrimage for Trabzon's faithful.

Kaymaklı monastery

The former Armenian **Kaymaklı monastery** (dedicated to the Saviour), reached by a 900-metre sidetrack 3.5km beyond the turnoff for Theoskepastos, is in an altogether different league, containing as it does the finest frescoes in the region after those of Aya Sofya and Sumela. It's too far to walk, so take a taxi, or a bus marked "Çukurçayır" from Atatürk Alanı. The bus will drop you at the Mısırlı Cami, out by the local prison on the flat summit of Boztepe;

100m past the mosque, turn left (east) and down onto an unsigned but paved lane. Bear right at a fork 250m along, then keep right again a similar distance along, soon reaching concrete's end next to an ugly green-and-cream house with a garage underneath. When the ground is dry you can continue by vehicle another 150m along dirt track to the proper "car park" in the centre of a farmyard.

What's left of Kaymaklı studs a green plateau overlooking the highway to Erzurum; today the monastery grounds are a farm, and the resident family is used to showing visitors around. Much of the place dates from the mid-fifteenth century, though more recent tenants have wedged a concrete dwelling into the former cells on the east edge of the courtyard. The subsidiary chapel or baptistry is bare, but the main *katholikon* is a marvel, its interior protected until the early 1990s by its use as a hay barn, now lying roofless. This current exposure means that all frescoes are easily seen, but also – in the determined absence of any official recognition or protection for the site – that they are unlike to survive much beyond 2010 or so.

The **west wall** bears a Bosch-like conception of the Last Judgment, complete with a *Four-Headed Cerberus*, *The Whore of Babylon Riding the Beast of the Apocalypse* and *The River of Fire* draining into Hell; adjacent hagiographies and admiring angels are less lurid, especially the stoning of a halo-ed, unidentifiable saint on the **north wall**. In the badly damaged **apse**, you can still make out a *Dormition* and *The Entry of Christ into Jerusalem*, with the Saviour riding a horse rather than an ass. None of the frescoes dates from earlier than the seventeenth century, but they are far more sophisticated in concept and execution than you'd expect for such comparatively recent work.

Eating

There are plenty of places to eat in central Trabzon, but few of them are really outstanding. Booze in this conservative town is hard to come by, as is (surprisingly for a port) fish. The almost uninterrupted line of **restaurants** on the north side of Atatürk Alanı gets most of the tourist custom, though not all of the places here deserve to. Most restaurants offer at least some **desserts** – the confectioners of Hemşin (see box on p.804) aren't far away – but some exclusively sweet-dedicated venues are worth seeking out.

Restaurants

Boztepe Gasinosu İran Cad 14, Boztepe, 4km from centre. Two *meze* plates, a beer, trout, service charge and "*garsoniye*" (mandatory tip) work out at nearly $8 – expensive for Trabzon – but the food's not at all bad and the setting, on a sloping lawn with sweeping views of town, idyllic.

Çardak Pide Salonu Corner Uzun Sok and Atatürk Alanı. Excellent, very cheap *pide* in an arbour-shaded courtyard, away from the traffic. Better for lunch as it shuts by 8pm most nights.

Gelik Lokantası Uzun Sok 84/B, by the police station. The city's best all-rounder; unusual vegetarian *meze*s such as mushroom salad, corn and other novelty breads, assorted meat-based steam-tray dishes, *döner* and sweets, served on two floors.

Kebabland Maraş Cad 30. Diagonally opposite the *Zorlu Grand Oteli*, this is the most savoury and

hygienic of the city's all-too-numerous *kebap* houses, with an unusually good selection of puddings too.

Kıbrıs Restaurant East side of Atatürk Alanı. An upstairs, indoor *meyhane*, more salubrious than rival *Şişman* across the square, with food on a more equal footing with drink.

Murat Balık Salonu Atatürk Meyd, north side. Tiny hole-in-the-wall joint doing inexpensive grilled *hamsi* (anchovy) in winter, otherwise *mezgit* or *uskumru* (mackerel), accompanied only by salad and soft drinks. Closes 9.30pm.

Sweets and desserts

Beton Helva Uzun Sok. Huge blocks of *helva* on display – thus the somewhat off-putting name, "Concrete Helva" – but also good *dondurma* (ice cream) and *sıra* (half-fermented grape must), in wonderfully retro 1950s surroundings, next to

Seyitoğlu Lahmacun.

Palet Patisserie Cumhuriyet Cad 2/C, corner Uzun Sok. The most popular of three in a row here; famous for its *dondurma* and *profiterol*. Stiff competition for a table in summer.

Selim Gazipaşa Cad 11/A. A wide range of *dondurma*, milk-based sweets, pastry and *boza* (a millet-based drink), served in airy surroundings; open from 7am until nearly midnight.

Drinking and entertainment

Apart from the **bars and clubs** of the three most upmarket hotels, women will have difficulty finding anywhere to drink comfortably in the evening. Given Trabzon's conservative ethos (and contemporary hard times), various discos and clubs opened for the university-student clientele have quickly come to grief. The *birahane*s on and off İskele Caddesi are predictably late-night pick-up joints for prostitutes and their clients, and probably best left to the imagination if signs seen in the area ("Entry with Loaded Weapons Forbidden") are anything to go by.

The wittily named *Trabira-zon*, one floor below the *Şişman Restaurant* at Maraş Cad 5, is a fairly savoury (if still not wildly female-friendly) bar that gets a cross section of local men in to watch footie on the TV and sip a vast range of imported bottled beers, plus Efes on tap. In the basement of the shopping mall opposite the *Zorlu Grand* on Maraş Caddesi, *Magic World* offers "cosmic" bowling on five lanes, six billiard tables and three dart boards – plus a snack-type café-restaurant open until late. The *Saray Sineması*, about 400m west of Atatürk Alanı, then south of Uzun Sokak, on Kasımoğlu Çıkmazı, shows slightly dated Hollywood **films**, often with the original soundtrack.

Listings

Airlines Azerbaijan Airlines, Sıramağaalar Cad, opposite Ustatour Travel agency ☎0462/326 2497; THY, corner Uzun Sok and Atatürk Alanı ☎0462/321 1680.

Airport There are frequent dolmuşes marked "Havaalanı" from a small plaza one block north of Atatürk Alanı, just off Siramağazalar Cad near the *Horon Oteli*.

Banks and exchange For after-hours encashment of travellers' cheques, try the *Hotel Usta*, Teleğrafhane Sok 3; the PTT and Akbank may also oblige. There are *döviz* offices all over the centre, particularly on Atatürk Alanı Kahraman Maraş Cad, and Kunduracılar Cad. All banks have ATMs taking the usual range of plastic.

Camping gas Small cartridges for French-made Bleuet stoves can usually be found at Milangas, Gazipaşa Cad 21.

Car rental In summer, when Trabzon swarms with locals returned from northern Europe, getting any kind of vehicle can be nearly impossible; you'll need to start your search weeks in advance and contact all the multiple numbers given to find anyone responsible (English is not widely spoken). Companies with both in-town offices and airport booths include: Avis, Gazipaşa Cad 20/A

☎0462/322 3740, ☏326 3520; Cande, Atatürk Alanı, southwest corner ☎0462/321 6289 or 0532/745 2135; Ceyhun, Atatürk Alanı, southwest corner ☎0462/326 8014 or 0542/396 8484, ☏321 7507; and Decar/Thrifty, airport ☎0462/321 6289.

Consulates Georgia, Gazipaşa Cad 20, 3rd Floor ☎0462/326 2226; Russia, opposite Ortahisar Camii ☎0462/326 2600.

Ferries Turkish Maritime Lines (TDİ) (☎0462/321 7096) occupies a huge warehouse with a crossed-anchors crest behind the harbour tourist police, heading east from the bottom of ıskele Cad. See "Travel details" at the end of the chapter for schedules and ticket prices. Apolloniya Tur (☎0462/326 4484), Karden Tur (☎0462/321 3479) and Gürgen Tur (☎0462/321 4439), all along İskele Cad, have current details on sea travel to Russia.

Hamams Much the best on offer is Sekiz Direkli Hamam, Pazarkapı 8, Direkli Hamam Sok 1 (daily 7am–11pm; women only on Thurs, men only all other days; $4.50). Second choices include Fatih Hamamı, three blocks south of Uzun Sok, a little to the east of the Tabakhane bridge (daily 8am–10pm; women on Wed; $1.50), and the Meydan, located just off Atatürk Alanı on Kahraman

At present, all non-Turkish travellers should buy a **visa for Russia** in their country of nationality in order to go from Turkey into Russia. Changing circumstances may permit the granting of visas in İstanbul or Ankara, but it's best not to count on this. **Visas for Georgia** are obtainable the same day from the Georgian consulate, Gazi Paşa Cad 20, in Trabzon ℡0462/326 2226 (Mon–Fri 9am–5pm), and in Ankara; they cost $20 for a transit visa, $40 for a single-entry visa (valid for 15 days), and $50 (valid for 30 days) for a multiple-entry visa.

In the wake of severe economic conditions affecting all countries concerned, **trans-Black-Sea services** to both Russia (Sochi) and Georgia (Poti) have been severely reduced; see "Travel details" at the end of this chapter for specimen frequencies/prices, and contact one of the ferry agencies in Trabzon (see "Listings" on p.789) for the most current information. Azerbaijan Airlines may still offer twice-weekly **flights to Baku** in Azerbaijan.

Overland **bus services** have been less affected; the main operator out of Trabzon is Göktaş Ardhan Tur (℡0462/325 0411), with offices in Çömlekçi Mahallesi, under the *Kardelen Oteli*. They run daily services in the afternoon and evening to Georgia and (indirectly) Armenia and Azerbaijan (again see "Travel details" on p.807), but some buses originate in Samsun and can arrive at Trabzon's *otogar* full. The **Georgian frontier** is crossed either at Sarp, or (for onward connections to Armenia and Azerbaijan) Posof, which only opened in 2001 for non-local traffic. It's easy enough to do the trip to Georgia in smaller chunks, taking a dolmuş or taxi from Sarp to the border and then arranging local transport on to Batumi on the Georgian side.

Maraş Cad (men and women, daily 6am–10pm; $1.50).

Hospitals The Özel Karadeniz (private), Reşadiye Cad (℡0462/229 7070), and SSK (Social Security), Trabzonspr Bul (℡0462/230 2285), are both out near Aya Sofya. However the biggest hospital in the region is the KTÜ's medical-school teaching hospital, or Tıp Fakültesi Hastanesi (℡0462/325 3011) – buses and dolmuşes marked "KTÜ" run from the centre.

Internet access The most central of a half-dozen or so are *World*, above McDonald's on the south side of Atatürk Alanı, and *Ortam* and *Limit* nearby, inside the arcade at Uzun Sok 32.

Laundry Pak Çiti, Zeytinlik Cad 18/B, off Kıbrıs şehitler (daily 8.30am–9.30pm). Dry cleaning at Galip, Uzun Sok 30.

Newspapers and magazines Very limited

foreign-language selection (no books) at Aksakal, opposite the THY building at the corner of Uzun Sokak and Atatürk Alanı.

Police Tourism Police, at the harbour customs-zone gate, and on the east side of Atatürk Alanı (daily 9am–7pm; ℡0462/326 3077).

Post office PTT at Posthane Sok, corner of Kahraman Maras Cad (post and exchange daily 8am–7pm); also a booth at southeast corner of Atatürk Alanı. Payphones and card sales on the south side of Atatürk Alanı.

Travel agencies Two reputable agencies are Afacan, İskele Cad 40/C ℡0462/321 5804; and Ustatour, İskele Cad 3–4 ℡0462/326 1870. Both offer day tours to Sumela, Ayder, assorted caves in the mountains, and Uzungöl, while Ustatour also sells air tickets and rents cars.

The monastery of Sumela

At the beginning of the Byzantine era a large number of monasteries sprang up in the mountains behind Trabzon; this tendency was reinforced during the life of the Trapezuntine Empire, when many of them also played a military role near the tiny realm's southern frontier. The most important and prestigious monastery – and today the best preserved – was **Sumela** (increasingly sign-posted as Sümela), clinging to a cliff-face nearly a thousand feet above the Altındere valley, the sort of setting that has always appealed to Greek Orthodox monasticism. Despite the habitual crowds, often rainy or misty weather – and

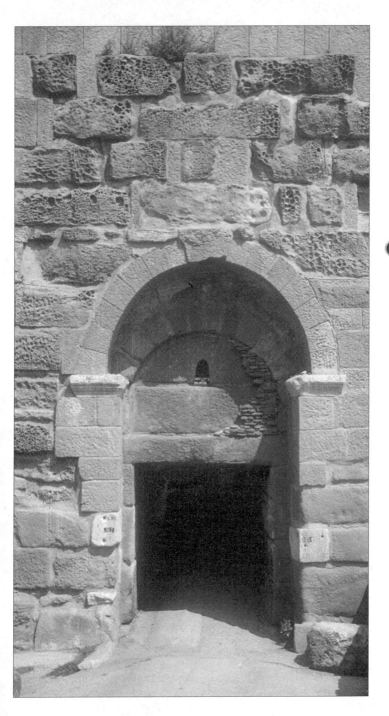

rather battered condition of the frescoes – Sumela still rates as one of the mandatory excursions along the Black Sea.

The name *Sumela* is a Pontic Greek shortening and corruption of *Panayia tou Melas* or "Virgin of the Black (Rock)", though some translate it – taking a few more grammatical liberties – as "of the Black Virgin". She has been venerated on this site since at least the year 385, when the Athenian monk Barnabas, acting on a revelation from the Mother of God, discovered an **icon** here said to have been painted by St Luke. He and his nephew Sophronios found the holy relic on a site that matched the one in his vision – a cave on a narrow ledge part of the way up the nearly sheer palisade – and installed the icon in a shrine inside.

A **monastery** supposedly grew around the image as early as the sixth century, but most of what's visible today dates from the thirteenth and fourteenth centuries, when Sumela was intimately linked with Trebizond's Komnenos dynasty, several of whose rulers conducted their coronations at Sumela rather than in the imperial capital. Over the centuries the icon was held responsible for numerous miracles, and the institution housing it shared its reputation, prompting even Turkish sultans to make pilgrimages and leave offerings.

Sumela was hastily evacuated in 1923 along with all other Greek Orthodox foundations in the Pontus; six years later it was gutted by fire, possibly set by careless squatters. In 1931 one of the monks returned secretly and exhumed a number of treasures, including the revered icon, from their hiding place. The Virgin's icon is now housed in the new monastery of Sumela, in northern Greece; unfortunately, when the other reliquaries were opened on arrival in Greece, precious illuminated manuscripts from the Byzantine era were found to have rotted away during their damp eight years underground.

Since 1996, the monastery of Sumela has been undergoing **restoration**, set to finish in 2003. The aim has been to shore up what was left standing and rebuild the rest; by the standards of often brutalist Turkish public renovations, the work done thus far is in reasonable taste, even extending to proper ceramic canal-tiles for the roof. Most important of all, the surviving frescoes have been consolidated and cleaned.

The buildings

However you arrive, all paths converge at the **ticket booth** by the monastery gate (daily: June–Sept 8.30am–6pm; Nov–Feb 9am–3pm; March–May & Oct 9am–4pm; $2.50).

Sumela actually occupies a far smaller patch of level ground than its five-storeyed facade would suggest. A climb up the original entry stairs, and an equal drop on the far side of the gate, deposits you in the central courtyard, with the monks' cells and guest hostel on your right overlooking the brink, and the chapel and cave sanctuary to the left. Reconstruction of most of the former living areas is complete, though there are still a number of off-limits areas and unsightly scaffolding. The degree of vandalism and decay is appalling: sophisticated art thieves were caught levering away large slabs of the famous frescoes in 1983, and any within arm's reach have been obliterated by graffiti-scrawlers – much of the graffiti is pre-1923 vintage Greek, but Turkish, European and North American visitors have also left their marks.

The main grotto-shrine is closed off on the courtyard side by a wall, from which protrudes the apse of a smaller chapel. A myriad of **frescoes** in varying styles cover every surface, the earliest and best ones dating from the fourteenth or fifteenth century, with progressively less worthwhile additions and re-touchings done in 1710, 1740 and 1860. The highest cave paintings are in good condition – ceilings being harder to vandalize – though the irregular surface makes for some odd departures from Orthodox iconographic conventions. The Pantocrator, the Mother of God and various apostles seem to float overhead in space; on the south (left) wall is an archangel and various scenes from the Virgin's life (culminating in *The Virgin Enthroned*), while *Jonah in the Whale* can be seen at the top right.

Outside on the divider wall, most of the scenes from the life of Christ are hopelessly scarred. Among the more distinct is a fine *Transfiguration* about ten feet up on the right; just above sits *Christ in Glory*, with two versions of the *Ascension* nearby. At the top left is *Christ Redeeming Adam and Eve*. On the apse of the tiny chapel the *Raising of Lazarus* is the most intact image. Next to it is the *Entry into Jerusalem*, with the *Deposition from the Cross* just right of this. On the natural rock face north of all this appears the *Communion of Saints in Paradise*. When craning your neck to ogle the surviving art gets too tiring, there is (mist permitting) always the spectacular view over the valley – and the process of imagining what monastic life, or a stay in the wayfarers' quarters, must have been like here in Sumela's prime.

Practicalities

Without your own transport, you have three ways of getting to Sumela from Trabzon: **taxis** from a rank signposted "Sumela Manastırı'na" on the south side of Atatürk Alanı, which charge $34 return for a carload of four people; a **minibus** to Sumela, from next to the taxi rank, for $6–7 per person return; or an **organized tour**, run at 10am daily by the Afacan and Usta travel agencies in Trabzon (see "Listings", p.790) and costing $5 per person for a return minibus seat (you pay the admission fee), with a stop for tea thrown in en route. However you arrive, you should make it clear that you're interested in a very full half-day out, since the distance, frequent road blockages from landslips and the final walk in dictates two hours thirty minutes for the return trip, and you'll want nearly as much time at the ruins.

Driving, it's 43km in all from the coastal junction of highways 010 and E97/885, 3.5km east of central Trabzon, to the main parking lot for Sumela; after 26km you turn off Highway E97/885 at Maçka to follow the Altındere valley upstream. This side road provides a stunning approach to the monastery; as you climb, the habitual cloud ceiling of these parts drifts down from the equally dense fir forest to meet you. In exceptional circumstances you may catch an advance glimpse of the monastery's faded, whitewashed flank soaring above the trees at the top of the valley, at an altitude of 1200m.

The monastery proper is linked to the valley bottom by the most commonly used, often slippery woodland **trail** (30min). Those with their own car may prefer to use the steep, initially paved track (no buses) that lurches up the valley for 3.5km to a point about level with the monastery; park where you can before a shed used by the restoration crew and cover the last ten minutes on foot. There's a third approach, less busy than either of these two options; about 1km along the cement drive, keep an eye out for a wood bridge over the stream – this path, going via an abandoned chapel, joins the more usual trail just below the monastery.

Accommodation and eating

By far the best local **accommodation** option, an attractive alternative to staying in Trabzon, is the *Kayalar Turistik Dinleme Tesisleri* (☎0462/531 1057, ℗531 1054; ❸), about 3km before the admission booth (see opposite). All rooms in this charming, rambling, wood-floored building have balconies and en-suite plumbing (some with bathtubs), plus there are a few family suites – and the inevitable trout farm/restaurant on site.

The environs of Sumela have been designated a national park (admission $2 per private car), which means a picnic area, a **snack bar** (the *Çardak*) and a full-on **restaurant** (the *Sümela Sosyal Tesisleri*), which, though not brilliant (chaotic service, bumped-up prices and mandatory ten-percent service charge), does have a lovely setting and a token nod towards regional cooking, with such dishes as *lahana sarması* (stuffed baby cabbage leaves). Also on the Altındere valley floor are some basic but attractive **bungalows** (reserve on ☎0462/230 2179 or 531 1061) that can be rented for $10 per person. Further downstream, the valley teems with **trout farms** of variable quality – *Sumela Çiftlik Restaurant*, 2km beyond Maçka, comes recommended for good *meze* as well as fish.

Vazelon and Peristera monasteries

So many monasteries are crumbling away in the Pontic foothills that some may never be documented before they disappear forever. Two of the more famous ones, relatively close to Sumela, are best visited with your own transport – but in all honesty they will appeal only to committed enthusiasts.

To reach the cloister of **Vazelon**, dedicated to St John the Baptist, proceed 7.5km south of Maçka on the road to Erzurum, until a black-on-yellow sign reading "Vazelon Manastırı, 3" points to a track up and right (the "3" may be defaced to a "7"). Some 1.5km along this reasonable track, bear left at a junction; the track worsens before reaching, just over 3km along, a trout farm (rarely open) and car park. It's prudent to leave non-4WD vehicles here and continue on foot for half an hour up the even rougher track heading east. Make a hairpin right (west) at the fork; any vehicle must halt at a massive washout over a concrete culvert some 2km beyond the trout farm. The monastery will be visible from here, like a mini-Sumela on the cliff-face ahead, but the final path approach is not obvious – it starts inconspicuously on the uphill side of the track about 150m past the culvert.

In fact Vazelon once ranked second to Sumela in wealth and ecclesiastical clout, but its deterioration since the mid-1980s has accelerated alarmingly. Frescoes exclaimed over in the past have vanished under the ministrations of rain, campfire smoke and vandals, and within a few more years all will have disintegrated. For the moment, the side chapel outside the walls contains a *Dormition*, a *Raising of Lazarus* and a *Baptism*, each dating from the sixteenth century and in fair-to-poor condition. A rockfall from the palisade above smashed the roof at some point during the 1990s, so these images are doomed to disappear within a decade or two. The *katholikon*, or main sanctuary, reached by much crawling through rubble and nettles, has collapsed; only the northern exterior wall bears bits of a naive, eighteenth- or nineteenth-century Last Judgement.

There is good, *yayla*-based **accommodation** in the hills just northwest of Vazelon; take the signposted dirt track, heading west of Highway 885 between Maçka and the Vazelon turning, to the *Lişer Yaylası Dinleme Tesisleri* (☎0456/553 1104; ❸), a fourteen-bed inn serving meals.

The monastery of **Peristera** (in Turkish, Hızır İlyas Manastiri) is somewhat easier to reach but in no better condition. From Km 22 of Highway 885 bound for Maçka, bear left (southeast) onto a minor road signposted as "Şahinkaya" and proceed 14km on poor surface to the village of Şimşirli, formerly Kuştul. More nettles await the intrepid scaler of the nearby crag on which perch the monastery walls. No art remains here; the view is the main thing, especially the view to the monastery from across the valley – most people don't actually bother with the climb up.

The Zigana Pass and environs

Highway E97 continues southwest towards the Trabzon provincial border at the fabled (but rather anticlimactic) **Zigana pass** (2025m), 60km from the coast, though the modern highway now goes 200m under the pass via a 1990s-built tunnel and the 883 bypass road. First-time visitors might prefer to use the old 885 highway, which winds through the dispersed village of **HAMSİKÖY**, famous for its ultra-rich *sütlaç* (rice pudding) sold by the roadside. This old route carries on over the pass proper, from where, in 339BC, the remains of Xenophon's army, retreating from a disastrous campaign in Persia, first caught sight of the Black Sea, raising the legendary cry of relief "**Thalassa, thalas-sa!**" (The sea, the sea!) – though the ancient Greek would probably have been pronounced *thalatha*, and the sea is not actually visible from any point of either existing road.

Between the pass and "downtown" Hamsiköy, at Bekçiler, awaits the most ambitious and luxurious of the area's *yayla* **accommodation**, the *Zigana Yayla Tatil Köyü* (☎0462/542 6115 or 326 5815, ⓦwww.ziganatatil.sitemynet.com; ⑤), a wooden bungalow complex (two- and four-person units) at the edge of the forest, complete with enormous restaurant. It's open all year, with heating and a small cross-country ski centre nearby during winter. At just 50km from the airport, the holiday village could make an excellent and relatively convenient alternative to staying in Trabzon.

East of Trabzon

The shore **east of Trabzon** gets progressively more extreme as you approach the Georgian border – if the Black Sea coast as a whole is wet, here it's positively soggy. The mountains increasingly impinge on the sea and soar ever more steeply upward, and the people match the landscape in their larger-than-life qualities. Natives of this area have long exercised a disproportionate influence in national politics, the best current example being Rize province's Mesut Yilmaz, once foreign- and prime minister, whose 1990s patronage of local prestige projects has done as much to raise the area's profile as the important local tea industry (see box on p.797).

Civics and commerce aside, however, the coast route has remarkably little to offer travellers. Visually, the only colour is lent by the uniformly red, black and white-striped **keşans** (shawls), **dolaylıks** (vertically striped skirts) and multi-coloured **peştemals** (waistbands) worn by women between Tirebolu and Çayeli. Another exotic touch is lent by occasional roadside signs in Georgian and Russian, aimed at visitors from the former Soviet Union – 1990 marked the first time either language appeared publicly in print in Turkey since 1923. If you happen upon a summertime knees-up, the **music** will be that of the *kemençe*, the Pontic (and rather monotonous-sounding) three-string spike fiddle, and less often the *tulum*, the slightly more versatile local goatskin bagpipe.

Arakli to Çamburnu

For a swim and a half-day out from Trabzon, the first decent, unpolluted beaches are found between **ARAKLI** and **SÜRMENE**. The towns themselves are nothing to write home about, and the only point of cultural interest hereabouts is the late eighteenth-century mansion of the Yakupoğlu clan, the *derebey*s, or feudal overlords, of these parts. Otherwise known as the **Kastel**, or the Memişağa Konağı, this squats above the west bank of the Kastel Çayı, 4km east of Sürmene, opposite a seashore teahouse, the *Kastel Restaurant*. Abandoned in 1978 by the Yakupoğlus – whose ranks once included one of the richest men in the country, Cevher Özden, and for contrast Zeki Baştımar, former head of the Turkish Communist Party – it's locked and beginning to decay, but is still impressive. Four stone bulwarks guard the tapered centre of the ground plan; the lightness of the wood and stucco-work on the upper storey, and the whimsical toadstool roof, seem incongruously wedded to the forbidding lower level.

It would only really be worth stopping at these places if you had your own car, and the same goes for the boatyards with their colourful, top-heavy *taka* fishing boats at **ÇAMBURNU**, 3km east. A much-touted pay beach is tucked at the base of the cliff just beyond the port, but equally good or better free beaches line the road to Of.

Rize

A modern Turkish city of over 70,000 in a grand setting, **RİZE**'s name at least will be familiar to every traveller who's bought a souvenir box of "Rize Turist Çay". Of its ancient history as Rhizos nothing survives, and of its role as the easternmost outpost of the Trapezuntine Empire hardly more than a tiny, eighth-century castle. If you do pause it would be to visit the **Tea Institute**, a combined think-tank, botanical garden, tasting and sales outlet on a hill overlooking the town; follow the signs to the "Çay Araştırma Enstitüsü".

There are two main streets, Atatürk Caddesi (inland) and Cumhuriyet Caddesi which runs parallel to the sea; the town square, **Belediye Parkı**, lies between them. The PTT here has been smartened up with wooden trimmings, complementing the two nineteenth-century restored **wooden houses** and the barn on stilts that are visible on the hill behind. East of the square lies Rize's major **tea garden**, which, not surprisingly, is the focus of the town's social whirl. Surrounding shops sell Rize tea in every conceivable packaging, plus the unlikely spin-off product of tea cologne.

Practicalities

The **otogar** is 800m to the west of town, with service buses bringing you into the centre. However, minibuses heading east and west also leave from the main highway, the shore road. The Turkish Maritime Lines agent is Riport, down at the quay, 1km west of the centre (☎0464/223 4568), where the İstanbul–Rize **ferries** dock. The main **long-distance coach** company operating from Rize is Ulusoy, which has offices on Cumhuriyet Caddesi off the northwest corner of the square. International **buses to Georgia** are dealt with by Aybakı Tourism on Tophane Karakolu Yanı (☎0464/217 3763) in the Rus Pazar: walk five minutes east of the square along Cumhuriyet Caddesi and turn right at the roundabout and you'll find the office 100m along on the left. There's at least one bus daily to Batumi and Tbilisi (Georgian visas obtainable in Trabzon, see p.789).

East of Trabzon, thanks to a climate ideal for its cultivation, **tea** is king. The tightly trimmed bushes are planted everywhere between sea level and about 600m, to the exclusion of almost all other crops. Picking the tender leaves is considered women's work, and during the six warmer months of the year they can be seen humping enormous loads of leaves in back-strap baskets to the nearest consolidation station. The tea, nearly a million raw tonnes of it annually, is sent more or less immediately to the cutting, fermenting and drying plants whose stacks are recurring landmarks in the region.

Oddly, tea is a very recent introduction to the Black Sea, the pet project of one Asim Zihni Derin, who imported the first plants just before World War II to a region badly depressed in the wake of the departure of its substantial Christian population in 1923. Within a decade or so tea became the mainstay of the local economy, overseen by Çaykur, the state tea monopoly. Despite the emergence of private competitors since 1985, and the Chernobyl accident, which caused condemnation of the 1986 crop, Çaykur is still the major player in the domestic market. Export, however, seems unlikely since supply can barely keep pace with domestic demand.

On the north side of the park, near the mosque, there's a helpful summer-only **tourist office** usually staffed by eager local English students. Ritur, off the northwestern corner of the square, at Cumhuriyet Cad 93 (℡0464/217 1484), organizes **tours** into Georgia and the Kaçkar mountains. The *Rize Dedeman* hotel (see below) is the local outlet for Decar/Thrifty **car rental**.

Most **hotels** stand on or near Atatürk Caddesi and Cumhuriyet Caddesi running east of Belediye Parkı. Many double as brothels, though a good exception is the *Otel Akarsu* behind the ornate, twin-minareted Hükümet Konağı on the square (℡0464/217 1779; ❶), which has plain but clean rooms, with or without bathroom, and tries a little harder than most budget hotels. A worthwhile notch up is the *Otel Efes* at Atatürk Caddesi, 100m east of the square (℡0464/214 1111; ❷), where all rooms have balconies. The two-star *Otel Keleş*, off Cumhuriyet Caddesi at Palandöken Cad 2 (℡0464/217 4612, ℻217 1895; ❸), has fairly comfortable rooms with fridges and TVs. Towards the top end of the range, the better value of two three-star establishments is the newish *Asnur* at Cumhuriyet Cad 165 (℡0464/214 1751; ❻), with all mod cons in the rooms, plus a sauna and gym. For the full treatment, go to the luxurious, four-star *Rize Dedeman* (℡0464/223 5344, ℻223 5348; ❼) on Alipaşa Koyu, at the western outskirts of town.

For **food**, the *Kuğu 2 Kebab Salonu*, Cumhuriyet Cad 229, is clean and cheap with friendly service and wide-ranging menus of soups, fish (including grilled trout), chicken and kebabs. You will also find several other simple but hearty *pide ve kebap salonları* along Cumhuriyet Caddesi – for example *Huzur* at no. 111 and *Bekiroğlu* next door. The *Lale Restaurant*, on the east side of the central square, is an "*aile*" (boozeless), multi-leveled institution famous for its *etli kurufasulye* (white haricot bean stew with chunks of lamb). The *Müze Kafeteriya*, a converted Ottoman house behind the PTT, is a little more atmospheric than the foregoing, and features regional cooking.

Hopa

HOPA, which used to be the end of the road until the nearby frontier was opened and the route to it was militarily declassified, is a grim industrial port, devoted to shipment of the copper mined slightly inland. The **otogar** is just on the east bank of the Sundura Çayı, which laps the west side of Hopa.

Lazland

Thirty to forty kilometres beyond Rize you pass the invisible former eastern limit of the Trapezuntine Empire and enter the territory of the **Laz**, the Black Sea's most celebrated minority group – erroneously much of the time, since other Turks have an annoying habit of stereotypically classing anyone from east of Samsun as "Laz". Strictly speaking, the Laz are a Caucasian people speaking a language related to Georgian, 150,000 of whom inhabit Pazar, Ardeşen, Fındıklı, Arhavi and Hopa, plus certain inland enclaves. The men, with their aquiline features and often reddish hair, particularly stand out; they also distinguish themselves by an extroversion unusual even for the Black Sea, a bent for jokes – practical and verbal – and an extraordinary business acumen that's the source of envy and of so much of the Laz-baiting and misidentification further west. A fair chunk of Turkey's shipping is owned and operated by Laz, who recruit crews from improbably small villages. The wealth so generated makes them relatively progressive in outlook; the women are out and about in Western garb from Fındıklı east, and the men, too, seem better dressed in the latest styles, though "progress" has also been translated into making the five municipalities listed some of the ugliest on the Black Sea – which is saying a lot.

From Ardeşen east the coast has absolutely no plain. Instead, the imposing mountains, shaggy with tea and a few lingering hazelnut trees, drop directly into the sea. These natural defences have helped the Laz maintain a semblance of independence throughout their **history**. It seems most likely that they're descendants of the ancient Colchians (from whom Jason supposedly stole the Golden Fleece). The Laz accepted Christianity in the sixth century and almost immediately got embroiled in a series of protracted wars with the Byzantines, whose governors had managed to offend them. No power managed fully to subdue them until the Ottomans induced conversion to Islam in the early sixteenth century. Like their neighbours the Hemşinli (see box on p.804) they don't lose too much sleep over their religious affiliation, though with their peripatetic habits and far-flung enterprises the Laz are now well integrated into the national fabric.

Perhaps too well integrated – **Lazuri**, the spoken language, is under threat, as until recently no systematic transcription system existed. The Turkish authorities have strongly discouraged any attempts, declaring persona non grata one Wolfgang Feurstein, a German linguist studying the language *in situ*. Working abroad thereafter, Feurstein finally compiled the first Turkish–Lazuri dictionary, complete with specially devised alphabet, in 1999.

If you have to stay here – and this would only happen if you were en route to Georgia and arrived too late to get an onward connection – head for one of several reasonable, relatively *natasha*-free **hotels** within walking distance of the *otogar*, almost all of them on the coast road, Ortahopa Caddesi. Just on the far side of what passes for the central *meydan* and tiny adjacent park stands the helpful, clean one-star *Cihan* (☎0466/351 2333, ⓕ351 4898; ❸), though despite the presence of fridges and TVs, the baths are more contemporary than the rooms; there's also an on-site restaurant and a small car park in front. The two-star *Papila* (☎0466/351 6120, ⓕ351 2975; ❷), about 300m further east – there's no sign, look for the mosaic frieze and gaudy portico – constitutes excellent value, though a 2001 refit was directed mostly at the lobby and the bathrooms; furnishings in the pink, balcony-less rooms are still severely dated, though the beds are OK. Almost 1km west of the *otogar*, and impossible to approach unless you're driving east or walking – the highway is divided at this point – is the three-star *Hotel Terzioğlu* (☎0466/351 5111, ⓕ351 5115; ❺), where most rooms have balconies. Vying with it for top billing is the 2001-built *Otel Peronti*, just east of the

Papila but one block inland at Turgay Ciner Cad 78 (☎0466/351 7663, ⓦwww.peronti-otel.com; ❹). It has almost no balconies, but some of the modern rooms have air-con and small tubs in the baths; there's off-street parking and a slightly gloomy breakfast salon.

There's just one **restaurant** not affiliated with a hotel – the *Beslen*, between the *meydan* and the coastal highway by the park, but fortunately it's pretty good: generous portions of *sulu yemek*, *pide*, *döner* and desserts in salubrious surroundings, though no fish or booze – three courses will cost about $3.50.

On to the Georgian border

Ten cliff-hemmed, twisty kilometres northeast of Hopa, **KEMALPAŞA** is the next-to-last Turkish village on the Black Sea, with a huge pebble beach, still known by its pre-1923 name of **Makriyalı**, on the seaward side of the four-lane blacktop. The highway has done for most of the makeshift Turkish "*kamping*s" that used to be here, and there's no other accommodation, but you won't starve thanks to a handful of restaurants.

Minibuses cover the 20km from Hopa to the **Turkish–Georgian frontier**, set by the Turkish and Soviet revolutionary governments in 1921 at the stream dividing the previously insignificant village of **SARP** (rather than more logically at the Çoruh River by Batumi). The crossing was virtually inactive between 1935 and 1988, a casualty of Stalinist, then Cold War, paranoia, but since the gates have opened, Turkish Sarp has become a busy 24-hour way-station. Convoys of Georgians and Russians head through here for the markets of Turkey's Black Sea cities and towns. If you intend to do more than just ogle the colourful spectacle, show up with your Georgian visa. Minibuses to Batumi leave early evenings from Sarp.

Inland: the foothills from Trabzon to Rize

While Sumela is a hard act to follow, there are a number of other possible destinations in the hills southeast of Trabzon. The valleys leading to and past them are also useful alternative routes toward Erzurum, avoiding some or all of the often congested E97/885 Highway.

Of, Çaykara and around

The coastal starting point for excursions up the valley of the Solaklı Çayi is **OF** (pronounced "oaf", the ancient Ophis). Both Of and **ÇAYKARA**, around 7km south, the unexciting main town of the lower valley, are renowned for their devoutness, with the highest ratio of *kuran kursu*s (Koran schools for children) per capita in the country, and phalanxes of bearded and skull-capped *hoca*s and *haci*s striding about in the shadow of huge, ever-multiplying mosques. A further peculiarity is that anyone over 50 speaks the Pontic dialect of Greek as their first language. It seems probable that the tribes of this valley were Hellenized (along with others such as those around Maçka) at some point during Byzantine rule, though they never lost their reputation as fierce brigands. Upon conversion to Islam at the end of the seventeenth century, their ferocity was transmuted into piety; as the saying goes, when the devil grows old he becomes a monk. It should come as no surprise, then, that you haven't a prayer of anything stronger than a fruit juice between Of and Uzungöl.

Sixteen kilometres inland stands the covered wooden bridge of **Hapsiyaş** (Kiremitli), photogenic despite its prosaic setting. The present structure dates from only 1935, and was badly damaged to the point of collapse by floods in 1998, but it seems likely there's been a span here for several centuries.

Uzungöl and around

From Çaykara, it's 45km on a paved road up to **Uzungöl** (Long Lake), the main attraction of this area. After Sumela, it's the second most popular excursion out of Trabzon, and especially at weekends the place is a bit too popular for its own good. Frequent dolmuşes make the hour and a half trip up from Of, and tours (about $10 a head, transport only) are laid on daily according to demand by Trabzon travel agencies (see p.790). The lake, at just under 1100m, is only averagely scenic, with a bazaar district around its outlet; the remaining wooden houses of the namesake village, clustered on the slope above, are more picturesque, though again outnumbered by modern concrete and brick structures.

In line with its mushrooming popularity as a destination, **accommodation** here is plentiful, with five licensed "motels" and a handful of *pansiyons*; among foreign travellers it's a popular overnight stop en route to or from Trabzon airport. The *İnan Kardeşler Tesisleri* (☎0462/656 6021; ❸), at the high south end of the lake, where most minibuses end their run, is the oldest hotel in town, a combination trout farm/restaurant/wood-bungalow complex where the menu consists of reasonable trout, salad and pudding – and no alcohol. The *Sezgin Motel* (☎0462/656 6175; ❸) is also a safe bet, not nearly as crowded, again with wooden cabins and trout-based cuisine. The *Huzur Pansiyon* (☎0462/656 6095; ❷), downstream from the village on the hillside, is a more homely option. If you're here on a weekend, you might well be better off at **Sultanmurat Yaylası**, reached by a different road 45km southwest of Çaykara, where the well-regarded *Taşkın Hotel* (☎0462/326 9335; ❸) is typical of the new wave of lodging that has sprouted at formerly primitive pastoral communities.

Uzungöl is an ideal base for rambles southeast up to the nearby peaks of **Ziyaret** (3111m) and **Halizden** (3376m), with a chain of glacier lakes at the base of the latter. It's a very long day's hike there and back – though you can go part way by car to save time – so take a tent and food for two days if at all possible.

The right-hand turning above Çaykara leads after 3.5km to **ATAKÖY**, formerly one of the better preserved of the Black Sea foothill villages. Don't expect a museum piece like Safranbolu, but there are still scattered clusters of half-timbered farmsteads above the main street. The municipality runs its own occasional bus between here and Of. With your own 4WD vehicle the 70km from here to Bayburt, via the 2330-metre **Soğanli pass** at the head of the Solaklı valley, makes for a very scenic and challenging drive – the road was opened by the Russians in 1916, hasn't been much improved since, and features 22 switchbacks to get up a 700-metre cliff.

The İkizdere Valley

The next major valley east of Uzungöl, the **İkizdere Valley**, holds no special attraction to stop for, but the scenery along the way is memorable and the road eventually winds up to the highest drivable pass in the Pontic ranges – one of the three loftiest in all Turkey. The place is mostly worth knowing about as an alternative route to Erzurum, or as an approach to the Kaçkar range (see Chapter 10).

İKİZDERE, with frequent minibuses from Rize, is the main town, and the transfer point for the 27-kilometre trip up the Yetimhoca valley to Başköy, the westernmost trailhead for the Kaçkar Dağları. Watch out though: there are at least three other Başköys or Başyaylas in a thirty-kilometre radius, so don't let yourself or your driver get confused. A better alternative, if possible, is to arrange transfer to Saler, the highest village in the valley with road access.

Beyond İkizdere, the main road soon finds itself between jagged peaks and the *yaylas* gathered at the 2600-metre **Ovitdağı pass** (only negotiable May–Oct), marking the edge of Rize province and far more alpine than the overrated Zigana pass to the west. On the way up you'll pass various grill and trout **restaurants**, and even a small, concrete-block **hotel** in the middle of nowhere, the *Genesis* (☎0462/476 8090; ❷).

The Hemşin valleys

The most scenic and interesting of the foothill regions east of Trabzon are the valleys of the **Fırtına Çayı** and its tributaries, which tumble off the steepest slopes of the Pontic ranges, here known as the Kaçkar Dağları. Between the mountains and the sea lie a few hundred square kilometres of rugged, isolated territory that have been imperfectly controlled at best by the prevailing imperial, or regional, powers of every era.

The area is known simply as **Hemşin**, a word whose etymology encapsulates local history: "–eşen" is a local dialect suffix, derived from Armenian, meaning "population" or "settlement", as in "Hamameşen" or "the settlement around the baths" (the hot springs at today's Ayder). Over time this was abbreviated to Hemşin, and came to describe the triangular zone with its base against the mountains and its apex at Pazar, and by extension the people in it.

Çamlıhemşin

ÇAMLIHEMŞİN, 21km upstream from the mouth of the Fırtına Çayi, is still too low at 300m to give you a real feel for the Hemşin country, but offers a hint of what's to come. It's the last proper town before the mountains, utilitarian and busy, with a constant chaos of minibuses (hourly from Pazar, mid-June to mid-Sept) and shoppers clogging its single high street.

There's a **bank** with an ATM, a **PTT**, stores for last-minute hiking supplies, and a recommended **travel agency** at no. 47 on the main street, Türkü Tourism (☎0464/651 7230, ⊛www.turkutour.com). Proprietor Mehmet Demirci is among the most genial and knowledgeable local mountain guides, and offers a variety of five-to-seven-day treks (early June to late Sept), starting at $280 per person, either tent-based (camping equipment provided) or *pansiyon*-based.

To either side of Çamlıhemşin, along both the main stream and the tributary flowing down from Ayder, you begin to see some of the two dozen or so graceful **bridges** that are a regional speciality. Their age and attribution are both subject to debate, but many have been dated to the eighteenth century (one, controversially, to 1696) and credited to Armenian craftsmen. Just before one of these bridges, at Yolkıyı Köyü, is the rambling, somewhat institutional *Otel Doğa*, 4.5km uphill on the way to Şenyuva (☎0464/651 7455; ❸, half-board only), offering one-, two- and three-bed rooms, plus family suites, mostly with baths and river-view balconies. Owner İdris Duman speaks English and French, and is a mine of information about the area.

Şenyuva

One of the most gravity-defying bridges, the **Taş Kemer**, spans the Fırtına Çayı at **ŞENYUVA** (Şinçiva in Hemşinli; 450m), a typically dispersed community of occasionally impressive farmstead dwellings 6–8km above Çamlıhemşin. These date principally from the late nineteenth and early twentieth centuries, the result of locals working in Russia and upon returning building these mansions as a gesture of wealth. Many of these farms have no road access, but are still served by *teleferikler* (motorized pulleys), which winch supplies – and occasionally people – up the rankly vegetated slopes.

Currently the only **accommodation** in Şenyuva is at the *Fırtına Pansiyon* (☎ & ⓕ0464/653 3111 or 0532/783 2708, ⓦwww.firtinavadisi.com), opened in 2000 and housed in the former schoolhouse. It's basic – one shower and one small hamam make up the bathing facilities – and a bit pricey for what's on offer, but is friendly and very trek-savvy, with route knowledge and an excellent sketch map to consult (also shown on their website). Sleeping facilities consist of three conventional rooms in the rear building, a free-standing chalet sleeping six at a pinch, and a five-person dormitory ($6.50 per person). Room and chalet rates are either charged on a bed-and-breakfast (❸) or half-board (❹) basis.

A short trek: Pokut and Amlakit

If your level of commitment isn't up to multi-day treks involving camping out in the high mountains, consider the track that heads southeast from Şenyuva via Sal to Pokut *yayla*. **POKUT**, three hours' walk from Şenyuva, is fairly representative of the more substantial Black Sea *yayla*s, with handsome woodwork capped by mixed tin-and-timber roofs rising from stone foundations. For the first night's **lodging**, Pokut has the rather pricey *Demirci Pansiyon* (☎0464/651 7495; ❸), offering half-board accommodation.

The following day you hike east to **Hazindag** (Hazıntak), a handsomely clustered settlement just above the tree-line, and then briefly follow a majestic river canyon on a corniche route south before veering up and southeast to the primitive rock-and-sod cottages of **Samistal**. From the ridge above Samistal, weather permitting, you'll have spectacular views of the main Kaçkar summit ridge. You then double back west to **AMLAKİT**, with its *Amlakit Pansiyon* (book through Türkü Tourism in Çamlıhemşin, see above; ❷), or drop in stiff zig-zags from Samistal to Aşağı Kavron and minibus service down to Ayder (see p.804).

If you stay in Amlakit, a final day of walking would see you use a direct trail north to Hazindag and thence back to Pokut and Sal (a steep path northeast through cloud forest direct to Ayder exists, but it's presently in bad condition). Alternatively, keener trekkers can carry on south from Amlakit for 45 minutes on a rough road to Palovit (2300m), and thence to Apevanak Yayla (2500m) en route to the true alpine zone. For details on the rest of the Kaçkar, refer to Chapter 10.

The upper Fırtına Valley

Above Şenyuva, along the main branch of the Fırtına Çayı, the road steadily worsens while the scenery just as relentlessly becomes more spectacular. Below, the water roils in chasms and whirlpools that are irresistible to the lunatic fringe of the rubber-rafting fraternity – as well as the central government, which in the face of local opposition plans to divert most of the river's flow into assorted hydroelectric projects.

Some 12.5km from Çamlıhemşin, the single-towered castle of **Zilkale**, improbably sited by either the Byzantines or the Genoese to control a decidedly minor trade route, appears at a bend in the track. The tree-tufted ruin, more often than not garnished with wisps of mist, today dominates nothing more than one of the most evocative settings in the Pontus. No such lonely castle would be complete without its resident ghosts, and the locals claim that after dark it's haunted by the shades of its former garrison and their horses – so don't get left behind if your minibus pauses to let you snap a picture. Under your own power, you can conduct a more leisurely survey of the various castle bastions (free, may be locked after dark) dating from the thirteenth to fifteenth centuries.

Çat and around

After another 15 or 16km of violent abuse to your vehicle's undercarriage – rental sedans will lose their mud flaps at the very least – you'll arrive at **ÇAT**, 1250m up. Despite the horrid road in, there is now a fairly regular – at least daily – dolmuş service from Çamlıhemşin, but it's more comfortable to use your own transport, whether mountain bike or 4WD. This is another classic base for rambles in the western Kaçkar, though there seems not to be much to the village beyond a few scattered buildings and a final, exquisite bridge leading seemingly nowhere, just upstream.

The most conspicuous building is a surprisingly good combination **hotel/restaurant** (and general store/souvenir shop), the *Cancık* (☎0464/654 4120; ❶), with six clean wood-trim rooms upstairs, and a hot shower on demand down the hall. Half-board accommodation is also available (❷), though food, served in a gazebo by the stream, is limited to trout, salad, *muhlama* (fondue-like dish) and a meat dish of the day. If the *Cancık* is full, your fallback is the concrete *Toşi Pension*, 1km downstream (☎0464/654 4002 or 0535/621 5215; ❸), again with a riverside terrace. The price is for half-board and here, too, rooms – doubles, triples, quads – can be packed out by organized trek groups.

At Çat the upper reaches of the Firtina divide. A road running parallel to the main fork heads 30km due south to Ortayayla or Başhemşin, passing Zilkale's sister fort of **Varoş** (Kale-i-Bala) at Kaleköy, where yet another sideroad winds up to an alternative trailhead for the western Kaçkar mountains at Kale Yayla. Don't try to walk any more of these tracks than you have to – between Kale Yayla and Çat, for example, you've a very boring three-to-four-hour slog in either direction – but wait for the one daily minibus at the junction in Çat.

The other turning above Çat bears almost due east, still on a poor surface; minibuses ply the 7km up to **ELEVİT** (1800m), a surprisingly substantial place with summer villas multiplying where there were only pastoral huts until the road was opened in 1989. This is as far as ordinary cars will prudently go – the road, braved by a few jeeps, three or four weekly minibuses and reckless non-4WD vehicles, continues east to Karunç, Tirovit and Palovit, but it's hardly worth the risk to your suspension. Elevit, like its nearest neighbour Tirovit, an hour and a half's walk east, is a Laz *yayla*, an enclave of sorts in Hemşin territory. It's also high enough to be a good trek-from-your-doorstep base, but there's only the exceedingly basic *Otel Kartal* (no phone, no sign – look for the eagle statue; ❷), with half-board **accommodation**, and a slightly seedy independent restaurant, *Aruçoğlu/Naci'nin Yeri*.

The Hemşinlis and their yaylas

The **Hemşinlis** are, according to competing theories, either ethnic Armenians who arrived here at or before the time of the Georgian kingdoms, or natives descended from the Heptacomete tribesmen of old, who, through contact with "true" Armenians, adopted a dialect of Armenian and were nominally Christian or pagan until the early nineteenth century. In any event, religious affiliation did not much trouble these people; there is no evidence of either church or mosque in these hills before the twentieth century. Curiously, there also exists a group of Islamic Armenian-speakers south of Hopa who call their dialect Hemşince and claim origins in Hemşin proper.

Certainly the main body of Hemşinlis – strong-featured and fair-complexioned women and Caucasian-looking men – appear anything but mainstream Turkish, and these outgoing, merry, occasionally outrageous people are diametrically opposite in behaviour to the more serious central Anatolians. This has a lot to do with wearing their Islam lightly; there's none of the overt piety of the Çaykara valley, and you're unlikely to be blasted out of bed at dawn by a muezzin for the simple reason that most communities are too small to support a mosque. Despite stern little signs in local shops warning that "alcohol is the mother of all ills", the men in fact are prodigious drinkers, a tendency aggravated by the **environment**. This is by far the dampest and mistiest part of Turkey, with the sun in hiding two days out of three and up to 500cm annually of rain in some spots. It doesn't take a genius to predict cloud forest vegetation, with everything from moss-fringed fir and alders down to marsh species and creeping vines clinging to the slopes, as well as moods swinging wildly between moroseness and euphoria among the inhabitants.

Like the nearby Laz, whom they dislike being mistaken for (the feeling is mutual), the Hemşinlis are intrepid and independent. They also have a special genius for the profession of **pastry chef and pudding-maker**: the top sweet shops (*pastanes*) of major Turkish cities are usually owned and/or staffed by natives of these valleys. The number of Hemşinlis living in diaspora, a process begun under Russian rule last century, far exceeds the 10,000 permanently inhabiting this rather compact domain.

You know you've left the Laz coastal zone when, a little way inland from Pazar or Ardeşen, you begin to see the brilliant yellow, black and red **scarves** (called *puşi* or *poşi*) of the Hemşin women, skilfully worn as turbans and contrasting with

---

For the lightly equipped, there are several possible day-hikes from Elevit, most rewardingly the three-hour walk up to **Yıldızlı Göl** (Starry Lake) at the top of the vale opening to the south of Elevit. You won't appreciate the name unless you camp overnight there, for just after sunrise little scintillating points of light flash briefly – for perhaps twenty minutes – on the surface of the water.

The properly outfitted can continue along a superb **three-day traverse** southwest across the western Kaçkar, taking in Başyayla, Çiçekliyayla, the 2800-metre-high lakes at the base of Tatos and Verçenik peaks – all potential campsites – and finishing at Başhemşin at the head of the Fırtına valley. If necessary you can "bail out" at Çiçekliyayla, which has a road in.

Ayder

The busiest, most trout-farm-laden road above Çamlihemşin – heavily storm-damaged in June 2002, and slow going until repaired – ends after 17km at **AYDER**, the highest permanently inhabited settlement in the Hemşin valley system. (At Km13, all cars pay a toll of $1.75.)

Ayder has long since given up the struggle to be a genuine village or *yayla* the drabness of the men's garb. Curiously, the scarves are not local but imported from India, perhaps a relic of the days when Trabzon was a terminus of the Silk Route.

As in attire, so in **housing**, the mix of vernacular and borrowed styles and materials reflecting wealth earned outside the area. Some positively baronial residences preside over tea terraces and cornfields at lower elevations (Hemşin, incidentally, is one of the few places in Turkey where corn is made into food for human consumption rather than fed to animals). But to fully understand the Hemşin mentality you need to visit at least one *yayla*, or summer pastoral hamlet.

Yaylas are found throughout Turkey in the uplands, but in the Kaçkar in general – and especially Hemşin – they are at their best. Tightly bunched groups of dwellings, usually stone-built to waist height and chalet-style in timber thereafter (but with metal roofs), they begin just at tree-line and recur at intervals up to 2700m. They're inhabited only between late May and early September, when the snow recedes and their tenants come from as far away as Holland or Germany to renew attachments to what they consider their true spiritual homeland. At the more primitive, roadless *yayla*s, sanitary mod cons don't come to mind – shrouded in acrid smoke, awash in mud and nettles, these seem more part of, say, Nepal than a country with EU candidacy – but provision of a road usually brings electrical power, satellite dishes, sundecks with parasols sporting "Coca-Cola" and "Tamek" logos and even the odd phone hook-up in its wake.

Traditional **summertime activities** include the making of yoghurt, butter and cheese (though much less so now that flocks are diminished), and (increasingly) catering to trekkers' needs – which has inevitably put a commercialized tinge to the formerly spontaneous provision of hospitality to wayfarers.

There is wide variation in the spelling of **Hemşinli place names**, especially the *yayla*s, as this Armenian-derived language isn't yet written, doesn't observe vowel harmony and thus isn't particularly amenable to attempts at Turkified standardized spelling. Thus you will see Apevanak or Apıvanak, Palovit or Polovit, Hazindag or Hazıntak, Tirovit or Tirevit, and so on. In this book, we have opted for the more regional rendering, as used by local trekking maps.

and now revels in its role as a spa resort and showcase for Hemşinli culture. Commercialized it may be, but the displays of ethnic pride during August – spontaneous outbreaks of *horon* (dancing) on the central meadow; the skirling of *tulum*s until late from most of the restaurants, and Hemşinli women normally resident in İstanbul or Rotterdam striding about in full regalia – seem genuine. For some years concrete tattiness threatened to overwhelm the indigenous stone-and-wood structures, but this cellblock architecture has happily been checked by municipal edict and all new building must be in traditional style, with stone foundations and Olde Worlde wood higher up. That said, the surrounding scenery – a narrow, sharply inclined valley with waterfalls pouring off the sides – has always been the main attraction, but with roads being pushed ever higher, Ayder can no longer rate as a genuine trekking trailhead. Every walk necessitates a minibus transfer, even the relatively close (and thus popular) day-jaunt to the Çengovit lakes above the Laz *yayla* of Yukarı Avusor.

Arrival, orientation and services

In season (mid-June to mid-Sept), hourly **minibuses** depart from Pazar (between 10am and 6pm) for the one-hour-plus trip to Ayder; you may have to change vehicles in Çamlıhemşin, and out of season you may have to stump up $15 or so for a taxi beyond. Back down to the coast from Ayder, there are hourly departures to Pazar, three daily to Rize and one to Trabzon. You can descend from Ayder to pick up the single daily minibus going up the Fırtına valley toward Çat and Elevit without having to return all the way to Pazar, but you'll need to be in Çamlıhemşin by noon or so.

Ayder is divided into two *mahalle*s or districts: **Birinci** (Lower) Ayder at about 1250m, and İkinici (Upper), better known as **Yukarı Ambarlık**, at about 1350m elevation. Birinci has the spas, **dolmuş stop** and most of the considerable high-season noise and congestion; Yukarı Ambarlık is loads calmer and has most (but not all) of the more desirable accommodation. There's a rudimentary **PTT** booth in Birinci Ayder, but no banking facilities, so get any money you need in Pazar or Çamlıhemşin.

Accommodation

Most establishments are open April to October only, though a bare few trade all year round; showing up on an August weekend without a reservation is not recommended. Owing to the proximity of the spas, it used to be that all local hotels were decidedly basic, with showers (if any) down the hall. However, the writing is on the wall for these old-fashioned inns, and conversion to en-suite facilities is the new order at the better establishments.

Birinci Ayder

Çağlayan Oteli At the very top edge of Birinci ☎0464/657 2073. Not really the same since Kadir Sarı, grandson of the founder of the oldest wooden hotel in Ayder, leased the business out and moved on – a relatively quiet if spartan fallback for the impecunious, with double rooms off long corridors. **❶**

Fora Pansiyon First, highest building on left hillside as you enter town ☎0464/657 2153; or book through Türkü Tourism in Çamlıhemşin. Excellent choice for its bohemian, trek-friendly atmosphere, with on-site sauna, *teleferik* to hoist up your packs and a lovely terrace for grilled suppers prepared by welcoming hosts Mehmet and Kader Demirci. Mostly double en-suite rooms (though a few triples); the Demircis also manage a four-person chalet, the *Sincina*, near Çamlıhemşin, plus the *pansiyon* in Amlakit. Half-board **❹**

Otel Yeşilvadı Just below the road ☎0464/657 2050. Tidy, efficient and salubrious modern structure; currently half bathless and half en-suite, with total conversion to the latter foreseen by 2004. Breakfast served at the adjacent affiliated restaurant. Standard rooms **❶**, en-suite rooms **❸**

Yukarı Ambarlık

Ahşap Pansiyon North hillside, path-only access ☎0464/657 2162, ℗657 2212. All-wood (*ahşap* in Turkish) outfit, built in 2000, with smallish en-suite rooms, a couple of large self-catering apartments and good cooking (sometimes even running to fried *hamsi*) at the view-terrace restaurant. Advance booking advisable, as it's popular with tour groups. **❷**, half-board **❸**

Koru Oteli On the through road between *Ahşap* and *Kuşpuni* ☎0464/657 2083, ℗657 2010. A bit impersonal, but the rooms are 2000-vintage and at present it's just one of four establishments in Ayder that's completely en-suite. **❸**

Kuşpuni Downhill from *Koru* ☎0464/657 2052, ℗657 2151. The highest-standard establishment, open all year, popular with city professionals and expatriate Turks. Centrally heated rooms vary from doubles to family suites. The regional food – inevitably trout, plus salads, *muhlama* at breakfast and home-made desserts – is abundant and deftly executed. Half-board **❺**

Serender Pansiyon Near top of Yukarı Ambarlık ☎0464/657 2201. Decent wood-trim rooms in varied formats, set to convert to en-suite by 2003; peaceful location, lots of common sitting areas and a self-catering kitchen. **❷**

Eating and drinking

Most people arrange half-board with their *pansiyon*s and local **cuisine** tends to be limited and repetitive, based largely on farmed trout, salad and *muhlama* (a fondue-like dish of cheese, butter and corn flour), the last scooped up with corn bread.

The best placed **restaurant**, and one of the few licensed ones, is the *Dört Mevsim* between Birinci and Yukarı Ambarlık, just above the river. Up in Yukarı Ambarlık, the only option is the *Huzur Ocakbaşı* near the *Kuşpuni* and *Koru*, with a strong line in grilled meat. One of the better eateries in Birinci Ayder is the prosaically set *Nazlı Çiçek*, with a steady clientele and thus a healthy turnover in food such as grilled chicken and trout (no alcohol available). It's also one of the more reliable venues to witness the *horon* outside of August; supposedly the dancers' limb-movements, the rhythm set by the *tulum*, imitate those of the Black Sea waves, boats and *hamsi* fish.

The spas

Ayder once had two old *kaplıcalar* or sulphurous **hot springs**, one on each bank of the stream. Those on the far (south) side – incidentally marking where the muddy, slippery, little-used path descends from Hazindag – shut down in the mid-1990s. The north-bank premises (daily 5am–10pm; men dawn & evenings, women all day; $1), just downhill from Birinci's main mosque, carry on the tradition of a stone-and-concrete lined communal *havuz* (pool) fed by scalding water (close to 60°C) spurting from an overhead pipe; a shower on entry is mandatory before joining the venerable townsfolk, lounging like Roman senators. The huge, modern **upper bath complex** built in the early 1990s (separate sections for men and women, 8am–7pm; $2) is predictably sterile, with even hotter water filling rectangular, tiled group pools, more expensive private tub-rooms available and safe-boxes for your valuables.

Travel details

Trains

Samsun to: Amasya (1 daily; 4hr 30min); Kayseri (4 weekly; 19hr); Sivas (1 daily; 12hr).
Zonguldak to: Ankara (1 daily, overnight; 9hr 10min).

Buses and dolmuşes

Amasra to: Bartın (every 30min; 25min); Sinop (6 daily; 6hr); Zonguldak (3 daily; 1hr 45min).
Ayder to Pazar (hourly; 1hr); Rize (3 daily; 1hr 45min).
Bartın to: Ankara (5 daily; 5hr); Safranbolu (8 daily; 1hr 30min); Zonguldak (hourly; 1hr 20min).
Giresun to: Ordu (every 30min; 30min); Tirebolu (every 45min; 45min); Trabzon (every 45min; 2hr 15min).
Hopa to: Artvin (hourly 7am–5pm; 1hr 30min); Rize (hourly; 1hr 45min).
İnebolu to: Kastamonu (10 daily; 1hr 45min).
Ordu to: Giresun (every 30min; 1hr); Perşembe (every 30min; 20min); Samsun (hourly; 2hr 45min); Ünye (hourly; 1hr 20min).
Rize to: Ankara (3 daily; 14hr); Ayder (1 daily; 2hr); Bursa (2 daily; 18hr); Erzurum via İspir (4–5 daily; 6hr); Hopa (hourly; 1hr 40min); İkizdere (hourly;

1hr); İspir (5 daily; 4hr); İstanbul (4 daily; 18hr); Samsun (every 30min; 7hr); Trabzon (every 30min; 1hr).
Samsun to: Afyon (4 daily; 10hr); Amasya (10 daily; 2hr 30min); Ankara (5 daily; 7hr); Artvin (4 daily; 10hr); Balıkesir (1 daily; 14hr); Erzurum (2 daily; 10hr); Giresun (4 daily; 3hr 30min); İstanbul (10 daily; 11hr); Rize (every 30min; 7hr); Sinop (every 30min; 3hr); Sivas (3 daily; 6hr 30min); Trabzon (4 daily; 6hr); Van (2 daily; 23hr).
Sinop to: Ankara (9 daily; 9hr); İstanbul (5 daily; 10hr 30min); Kastamonu (9 daily; 2hr 30min); Samsun (every 30min; 3hr).
Trabzon to: Ankara (7 daily; 12hr); Artvin (5 daily, may have to change at Hopa; 5hr); Bayburt (5 daily; 4hr 30min); Erzurum (6 daily; 6hr); Giresun (hourly; 2hr 15min); Hopa (every 30min; 3hr); İstanbul (10 daily; 18hr); İzmir (3 daily; 23hr); Kars (2 daily with change at Erzurum or Artvin; 12hr); Of (every 30min; 1hr); Rize (every 15min; 1hr); Samsun (hourly; 6hr).
Zonguldak to: Ankara (hourly; 5hr 30min); İstanbul (6 daily; 6hr).

International buses

Rize to: Batumi, Georgia (1 daily; 3hr 30min);

Tbilisi, Georgia (1 daily; 14hr); Erevan, Armenia (1 daily; 14hr).

Samsun to: Tbilisi, Georgia (1 daily; 21hr).

Trabzon to: Baku, Azerbaijan (1 daily via Georgia; 30hr, $45); Batumi, Georgia (1 daily; 4hr 30min, $15); Erevan, Armenia (15hr, $35); Posof, Georgian border (daily at 7.30pm; 7hr; $20) and on to Erevan, Armenia (15hr, $25); Tbilisi, Georgia (1 daily at 1pm; 15hr, $25).

Black Sea Coast ferry

Turkish Maritime Lines (TDİ) runs a ship **from İstanbul to Rize** and back on a five-day cycle, between late June and early September (total one-way journey time from İstanbul to Rize about 46hr). **Prices** vary considerably depending on the class of cabin or seat required, but to give some idea, a Pullman seat from İstanbul to Trabzon costs $16, a single berth in the cheapest cabin $23, while a luxury-class cabin goes for $114; four-berth second-class cabins suitable for families are relatively economical at $111 for the group. Pullman seats on short hops, for example from Trabzon to Rize, are negligibly priced at under $2. The tariff to take a car from İstanbul to Trabzon is $32, from Trabzon to Samsun $10. **Meals** are served on the boat, though they're exorbitantly priced in comparison; do as the Turks do and take picnic fare, and/or disembark wherever there's a long layover for a meal on shore.

In recent years the schedule has been:

Depart İstanbul Mon 2pm, arrive Zonguldak midnight.

Depart Zonguldak Tues 12.30am, arrive Sinop Tues 1.30pm.

Depart Sinop Tues 2pm, arrive Samsun Tues 8pm.

Depart Samsun Tues 8.30pm, arrive Trabzon Wed 8.30am.

Depart Trabzon Wed 9am, arrive Rize Wed 12.30pm.

Depart Rize Wed 2pm, arrive Trabzon Wed 5.30pm.

Depart Trabzon Wed 6pm, arrive Samsun Thurs 6am.

Depart Samsun Thurs 6.30am, arrive Sinop Thurs 12.30pm.

Depart Sinop Thurs 1pm, arrive Zonguldak Fri 2am.

Depart Zonguldak Fri 2.30am, arrive İstanbul Fri 12.30pm.

International ferries/catamarans

Samsun to: Sochi, Russia (twice-weekly catamarans; 7hr). Around $75 one-way.

Trabzon to: Sochi, Russia (2–4 weekly ferries, 18hr; departures typically around 6pm, budget $60 one-way for a cabin berth).

Flights

Samsun to: İstanbul (2 daily; 1hr 20min).

Trabzon to: Adana (2–3 daily via İstanbul or Ankara; 3hr 30min–4hr); Ankara (1–2 daily; 1hr 30min); İstanbul (3 daily; 1hr 50min); İzmir (3 daily via İstanbul; 3hr 30min–4hr).

Northeastern Anatolia

CHAPTER 10 **Highlights**

✳ **Erzurum** The twelfth- to fourteenth-century monuments of the Saltuk, Selçuk and İlhanid emirs at Erzurum comprise the finest collection of Islamic architecture in the northeast. See p.815

✳ **Ani** Don't miss the ruined medieval capital at Ani, site of the region's densest concentration of Armenian churches and castles. See p.829

✳ **Georgian churches** The early medieval Georgian churches in the river valleys between Erzurum, Artvin and Ardahan spawned the Romanesque churches of Western Europe and retain superb relief decoration. See p.843

✳ **Whitewater rafting on the Çoruh River** Yusufeli is the base for a sport that draws hundreds of enthusiasts during May and June. See p.849

✳ **Kaçkar Dağları** The glacially sculpted, wildflower-carpeted Kaçkar mountains rank as the most versatile and popular alpine trekking area of Turkey. See p.853

✳ **Kafkasör festival** One of the most authentic folkloric expressions in the country can be witnessed every June outside Artvin. See p.859

10

Northeastern Anatolia

Bleak, rugged and melancholy, **northeastern Anatolia** is Turkey's version of Siberia or the Australian Outback. Much of it is a high, windswept plateau segmented by ranks of eroded mountains that seem barely higher, despite impressive altitudes on the map. Four great rivers – the Çoruh, Kura, Aras (Ahuryan in Armenia) and Euphrates (Fırat in Turkish) – rise here, beginning courses that take them to scattered ends in the Black, Caspian and Persian seas. Their sources almost meet at the forbidding roof of the steppe near Erzurum, but as the rivers descend through warmer canyons and valleys at the edge of the uplands, oases and towns appear, lending much of the interest and attraction of the region.

A great deal of governmental attention, both military and civilian, has been lavished on the provinces of Kars, Artvin and Erzurum, which form the heart of the region. But despite ambitious development projects, most of the terrain will never be suited to anything except cultivating grain, hay and sugar beets (between May and September), or the grazing of livestock. The area and its farms remain stubbornly poor, with horse-drawn harrows and hand tools still just outnumbering combine harvesters and tractors. Huge flocks of sheep are tended by men, while the herding of gaggles of geese in every village is considered women's work. Given the treeless landscape, the making and stacking of cow-dung patties (*tezek* in Turkish) for fuel becomes a conspicuous necessity for villagers unable to buy coal, the dung vying in height with the equally ubiquitous haystacks. The harsh, seven-month winters dictate a troglodytic architecture of semi-subterranean burrow-houses – and a stoic, self-contained character to go with it. Only the relatively prosperous and forested valleys around Yusufeli and Artvin have a lighter atmosphere and quasi-Mediterranean climate, as a tangible Caucasian influence begins to be felt.

As a traveller, you will probably have the place largely to yourself, except for the mountainous areas bordering on the Black Sea. Tourism, never exactly booming elsewhere in the region, was hobbled by the long-running Kurdish troubles in the adjacent southeast. Although these have now abated, the aftermath of a Georgian civil war to the north and an Azeri–Armenian war nearby in Nagorno-Karabakh – the latter closing until further notice the land frontier between Turkey and Armenia – have combined to choke off any subsequent recovery.

However you approach – from central Anatolia, the extreme southeast of Turkey, or the Black Sea – your first stop is likely to be **Erzurum**, long a goal of armies and merchants and the only real urban centre. Today it's the main jumping-off point to just about anywhere else in the region, with a clutch of post-Selçuk Turkish monuments to distract you. To the northeast, **Kars**, the last major town before the Armenian frontier, is a dreary disappointment for most travellers, but serves as the base for visits to the former Armenian capital of **Ani** and less heralded, isolated **Armenian churches** and **castles** in the province, together comprising the biggest tourist attraction in the region. North of Erzurum, the southernmost **valleys of early medieval Georgia**, now part of Turkey, hide nearly a dozen churches and almost as many castles – enchantingly set, little visited and arguably the most rewarding targets in this area. The provincial capital of **Artvin** and the pleasant town of **Yusufeli** are the logical overnight stops while in search of Georgian monuments, and Yusufeli also sits astride the most popular southern approach to the magnificent **Kaçkar Dağları**, a trekker's paradise that separates northeast Anatolia from the Black Sea.

Some history

Perhaps because of the discouraging climate and meagre resources, this corner of the country was thinly settled until the second millennium BC. The **Urartians** had their northernmost city at today's Altıntepe, near Erzincan, between the ninth and sixth centuries, but the next real imperial power to make an appearance was the **Roman** Empire, succeeded by the Byzantines and **Armenians**. The eleventh-century undermining of the Armenian state and the Byzantine defeat at Manzikert marked the start of a pattern of invasion and counterattack, which was to continue until 1920. The **Selçuks**, their minor successor emirates and the newly ascendant **Georgian** kingdom jockeyed for position in the territory until swept aside by **Mongol** raids in the early thirteenth century and Tamerlane's juggernaut in the early 1400s; the **Ottomans** finally reasserted some semblance of centralized control early in the sixteenth century.

Just as the northeast had been a remote frontier of the Byzantines, so it became the border of this new Anatolian empire, confronting an expansionist Tsarist Russia, which effectively ended what remained of Georgia's autonomy in 1783. As the Ottomans declined, **Russia** grew bolder, advancing out of its Caucasian fortresses to lop off slices of the region on several occasions during the nineteenth century, though they got to keep their conquests only in 1829 and 1878. Until 1914 nearly half of the sites described in this chapter were under Russian rule, with additional conquests up to 1917 nullified by the Bolshevik Revolution and the collapse of the Caucasian front. Between 1915 and 1921 the area was the scene of almost uninterrupted **warfare** between White Russian, Armenian Dashnakist and Turkish Nationalist armies, and of massacres among the mixed civilian population that had historically been over a third Armenian and Georgian-Christian.

By 1923 the northeast was all but prostrate, with ninety percent of its former population dead or dispersed. The present international boundaries between Turkey and Georgia or Armenia are the result of treaties between Atatürk and the **Soviet Union** in March and October 1921, and don't necessarily reflect historical divisions (indeed as late as 1945 Stalin was still demanding that Kars and Ardahan be returned to the "Russian motherland").

Towards Erzurum: the Euphrates valley route

Coming from the west, many travellers cover the lonely stretch of Highway 200/E88–100/E80 between Sivas and Erzurum in one day – easily done and certainly recommended if you're in a hurry. With more time at your disposal, a leisurely approach via the valleys of the **Euphrates River** and its tributaries is preferable. Most of the countryside between Kangal and Kemah is all but trackless, the railway still the most dependable link to the rest of Turkey; during daylight hours a **train trip** through the spectacular, ruddy river gorges flecked with oases is certainly the most enjoyable and scenic introduction to northeastern Turkey. The river itself, green and opaque, is warm enough above the giant Keban Dam to support carp – an anomaly in a region famed for trout. In addition to the long-distance expresses between Ankara and Erzurum, a local "milk run" train sets out most days early in the morning **from Divriği** in central Anatolia to Erzincan and Erzurum.

With more advance research and a taste for adventure, you can explore the river even more thoroughly by **kayak** or **raft**, albeit in the opposite (downstream) direction. The favourite stretch, with highest water between May and July, is the two-day run between Erzincan and Kemah. Continuing further downstream is complicated by the difficulty of meeting a support vehicle on the largely roadless banks; the next place you could try is Ilıç, another two days' float beyond Kemah and accessible via a side-road from Refahiye.

Kemah and Alpköy

If you don't mind the risk of being stranded for half a day, you could get off the train at **KEMAH**, a historic town perched over a picturesque reach of river. There's a complex of tombs from different eras perched above the river, and a huge Byzantine/Selçuk castle with cellars to explore. The place is fairly small, however, and can muster just a few tiny shops and one unmarked, rudimentary hotel. Except at weekends, dolmuşes along the paved 50km to Erzincan are fairly regular.

Kemah is theoretically a major trailhead for treks across the **Munzur Dağları**, which tower snow-streaked above the Euphrates' south bank, but there have been sporadic Kurdish-related troubles since the 1930s – which may or may not have subsided since the capture and imprisonment of PKK leader Abdullah Öcalan. If you inform the *jandarma* post of your intention to go mountaineering you may still be prevented from doing so. **ALPKÖY**, twenty minutes further east along the tracks, is a better place to start – nobody will stop you here, and a giant canyon leading straight up to the heart of the mountains opens out very close to the station.

Erzincan

ERZİNCAN – once one of the most elegant cities in Turkey, with several Armenian monuments on the outskirts and dozens of mosques and *medreses* in the town – was devastated by earthquakes in 1939 and again in 1983. It's now a dull, semi-planned low-rise city of a 100,000 or so, its wide, bleak boulevards enlivened only somewhat by students at the local university. So there's no reason to linger longer than the time it takes to change buses (the **otogar** is at the far eastern end of town) or trains (**train station** at the southwestern edge) – connections on to Erzurum are frequent, but transport to Divriği only gets going in the afternoon. There's a wide choice of slightly overpriced **hotels** on Fevzipaşa Caddesi, the city's main drag in from the *otogar*. The friendly *Hotel Burcu* at Fevzipaşa Cad 29 on the north side of the boulevard (☎0446/223 8360, ℱ214 6781; ❷) offers the best value among a half-dozen lodgings here, within easy reach of the *lahmacun*, *pide* and *kebap* outfits that line the same street.

Tercan

Exactly halfway between Erzincan and Erzurum, near the head of the Euphrates valley, you should try and break the journey at **TERCAN** (not so easy on public transport), graced by a *türbe*, *kervansaray* and bridge erected by the Saltuk emirs of Erzurum at the beginning of the thirteenth century. The **Mama Hatun Türbesi** in particular is bizarre, built to a design found elsewhere only in Central Asian Turkestan and signposted pessimistically as "1km" northeast from the through highway (it's more like 500m). The west-southwest portal, with its stalactite vaulting, Kufic inscriptions and flanking false columns with intricate relief (including an interlocking five-pointed star motif on the false capitals), runs a close second to the Divriği monuments for extravagance. The tomb itself, inside the circular outer enclosure elaborated into a dozen *eyvans*, has eight lobes (in which are interred other members of the Saltuk dynasty) and a conical "witch's hat" roof. The complex is unfortunately locked while its environs are being rather desultorily groomed and landscaped; the **kervansaray** just opposite is also locked at the moment but it would seem that shops inside will be rented out soon.

Retracing your steps through the lively contemporary bazaar with its simple **restaurants** to the main highway junction, you'll find a single basic **hotel**, the *Kervansaray*, available in the *Belediye* building (☎0446/441 2588; ❶), for emergency use if you get stranded.

Erzurum

Nearly 2000m up, its horizons defined by mountains a further 1000m above, and rocked by frequent earthquakes, **ERZURUM** is Turkey's highest and most exposed city. Because of a strategic location astride the main trade routes to Persia, the Caucausus and western Anatolia, its sovereignty has always been contested, and today it's still a major garrison town of over 300,000 people. All told, the combination of history, climate and earthquakes has resulted in a bleak, much-rebuilt place where sunlight can seem wan even in midsummer, and where the landscaped, broad modern boulevards often end abruptly in literally the middle of nowhere.

In this conservative backwater, far from the freedoms of Ankara, many women wear gunny-sack-like *çarşafs* (full-length robes with hoods and veils) tinted the same dun colour as the surrounding steppe, and some even wear the black *chador*, a cultural import from nearby Iran; men often wear skullcaps, not just the ubiquitous Turkish bobble-hat. Compared to points west, poverty is shockingly obvious: just south of the main thoroughfare a huge shantytown persists, home to legions of beggars, bootblacks, small boys selling packs of tissues and self-styled adolescent "guides" relying on pidgin (or slightly better) English.

While it spent the 1960s and 1970s as a transit stop for overlanders on the way to Iran, Afghanistan and India, Erzurum never really made the transition to mass tourism, though it gets some trade in winter thanks to the excellent skiing facilities at **Palandöken** just to the south (see p.820). During summer, the city serves as an occasional base and staging point for mountaineering and rafting expeditions bound for the Kaçkar Dağları, but it also deserves a full day in itself to see a compact group of very early Turkish monuments.

Some history

Although the site had been occupied for centuries before, a city only rose to prominence here towards the end of the fourth century AD, when the Byzantine emperor Theodosius II fortified the place and renamed it **Theodosiopolis**. Over the next five hundred years the town changed hands frequently between Constantinople and assorted Arab dynasties, with a short period of Armenian rule.

After the decisive battle of Manzikert in 1071, Erzurum – a corruption of Arz-er-Rum, or "Domain of the Byzantines" in Arabic – fell into the hands of first the Selçuks and then the Saltuk clan of Turks. These were in turn displaced by the İlhanid Mongols during the fourteenth century, forerunners of Tamerlane himself, who used the city as a springboard for his brief blitzkrieg into western Anatolia.

Erzurum was incorporated into the Ottoman Empire by Selim I in 1515, where it remained securely until 1828, after which the Russians occupied it on three occasions. With the memory of the last Russian tenure (1916–1917) still fresh in their minds, and the city held by renegade General Kâzım Karabekir, supporters of the Nationalists convened a congress here in July 1919, at which the present borders of the Turkish Republic were put forth as the minimum acceptable.

Arrival, transport and information

Erzurum has two main bus terminals: the long-distance **otogar**, located almost 3km northwest of the city centre (taxis into the centre won't exceed $2), and the **Gölbaşı Semt Garajı**, for Yusufeli and Artvin, much more conveniently situated just over 1km northeast of downtown. Many, though by no means all, long-distance buses stop at both of these stations – when it's time to move on from Erzurum, make sure you know exactly which one your vehicle starts from. This is easily enough checked when you buy tickets at the terminals or at the numerous ticket offices scattered around town.

The **train station** is over 1km north of the centre, close to a concentration of inexpensive accommodation. If you fly into the **airport**, 10km northwest of town at the end of the same road serving the *otogar*, try and catch the THY bus ($1.50) into town – a taxi will set you back $5.

Aside from walking, **taxis** are really the way to get around Erzurum. There are municipal **buses** – particularly useful is the #2, which links the *otogar* with Cumhuriyet Caddesi, the main east–west thoroughfare – but it's tedious to hunt down ticket sales points, and taxi ranks are everywhere. For drivers, **parking** is difficult, made more so by ongoing sewer works, which have entailed excavation of the entire centre – best prospects are on the broad streets south of the PTT.

ERZURUM

Artvin & Yusefeli ▲

Exhibition Grounds

Otogar

Stadium

Train Station

Gölbaş Semt Garaji (for Artvin & Yusefeli)

Bayburt ★ Dolmuş Terminal

Hamam

Dolmuşes to İspir

Boyahane Hamam

Rüstem Paşa Bedesteni

Citadel

Cumhuriyet İş Merkezi

Yakütiye Medresesi

Lala Mustafa Paşa Camii

Çifte Minareli Medrese

Park

THY

Ulu Cami

Üç Kümbetler

Atatürk Üniversitesi

Archeological Museum

N

0   200 m

10

NORTHEASTERN ANATOLIA | Erzurum

Ağrı & Kars

Ağrı & Kars

HOTELS		
Akçay	**5** Oral	**4**
Dedeman Palandöken	**7** Polat	**2**
Dilaver	**3** Polat Renaissance	**9**
Kardelen	**8** Sefer	**1**
Kral	**6** Tourinn Palan	**10**

EATING & DRINKING		
Erzurum Evleri	**F** Salon Asya	**B**
Güzelyurt	**E** Salon Çağın	**C**
Kılıçoğlu Sütiş	**A** Serender	**D**

▼ Elâzığ, Bingöl & Palandöken   Palandöken, ▼ **7**, **8**, **9**, **10**, Iranian Consulate & Research Hospital

The **tourist office**, at Ömer Nasuhi Bilmen (ex-Cemal Gürsel) Cad 9, 500m west of the centre, is beyond doubt one of the most useless and poorly stocked in Turkey, with only a cyclostyled city plan from the late 1980s and a single vague regional brochure available; give it a miss.

Accommodation

The supply of **accommodation** in Erzurum usually exceeds demand, and you should have no trouble finding a decent room to suit any budget without resorting to the city's surviving fleapits. If you're on a long haul overland, it's wise to break the journey here, since there's nowhere else as good to overnight for hundreds of kilometres. With your own vehicle, it makes most sense to stay south of town at the base of **Palandöken** ski resort, where four hotels (three open all year) offer unregulated parking, comfort and quiet at affordable rates.

City centre

Akçay Hotel Kâmil Ağa Sok, off Cumhuriyet Cad 2 ☏0442/235 3264. Fairly quiet spot, with off-street

parking, but about as basic as you'll want to be in Erzurum: 1970s-decorated rooms that vary in plumbing arrangements, but all tend to be dank, with lurid hospital-green walls and muddy-coloured carpets. ❷

Dilaver Hotel Pelit Meyd, Aşağı Mumçu Mah ☎0442/235 0068, ℻218 1148. Despite a rooftop view-restaurant, tubs in the bathrooms and BBC/CNN on the telly, this three-star has one star too many. Breakfast served in the mezzanine bar. Ignore the ridiculous rack rates of ❼; they'll generally part with rooms for ❺

Kral Otel Erzincankapı 18, near southwest corner of the central park ☎0442/234 6400, ℻234 6474. Don't let the dire exterior fool you – this was almost completely overhauled in 2001 and now offers the best budget value in town. The most striking rooms feature mock-İlhanid-Mongol decor in their mosaic-tiled baths – even the tubs – and marble sink-surrounds, paired with double-glazing and carpets. Multi-person suites also available. ❸

Oral Otel Terminal Cad 3 ☎0442/235 2500, ℻235 2600. On a quiet, almost leafy (for Erzurum) street, this worthy three-star is a 1970s period piece (albeit a well-kept one), from the lobby with its white-leather armchairs to the individual room decor, most charitably described as "eclectic", though bathrooms have been updated and fridges added. Decent on-site restaurant, money exchange at near-bank rates, street parking possible. ❹

Polat Otel Kâzım Karabekir Cad 2 ☎0442/235 0364, ℻234 4598. Renovated in 2000 (and now two-star), but most of the money was spent on modernizing the half-tub bathrooms, and fitting double-glazing and heating, rather than upgrading the rather plain rooms themselves (some with balconies). There's a roof restaurant, though breakfast is served in the lobby. ❷

Sefer Hotel İstasyon Cad ☎0442/235 0818, ℻235 0831. Old warhorse one-star, much better than the *Akçay* but not great value compared to the nearby *Polat.* The 1970s-vintage rooms with

baths to match are musty and cheerless, with fake double-glazing; the only really selling point is the busy, well-regarded ground-floor restaurant, which makes it worth considering half-board. Rooms ❷, half-board ❸

Palandöken

Dedeman Palandöken 8.5km from Erzurum ☎0442/316 2414, ℻316 3607. Four-star hotel in an alpine bowl at 2450m, pitched at doorstep skiers who want to be right at the heart of the action. Large if spartan rooms and wooden mock-chalet common areas. Closed mid-May to Nov. ❽

Kardelen Oteli 5km from Erzurum ☎0442/316 6851, ℻316 6070. Definitely the runt of the litter of the Palandöken hotels, this three-star is the least expensive up here but fairly basic, barely functioning in summer and with a management somewhat suspicious of foreigners. ❹

Polat Renaissance Erzurum Oteli 5km from Erzurum ☎0442/232 0010, ✉palandoken @polatholding.com. Turkey's most comfortable hotel east of Cappadocia, built in 2000, this five-star at 2200m is a bit remote from most of the ski slopes – a private chair-lift bridges the gap – but compensates with cheerful, fair-sized rooms with cable TV and internet access. Palatial common areas include a pleasant indoor pool, hamam and gym. Discounted packages available during ski season. Winter ❽, summer ❻

Tourinn Palan Otel 6.5km from town ☎0442/317 0707, ⊛www.palanotel.com. Second-best all-year choice here, at about 2250m; rooms – try not to get one facing the often noisy car-park – are on the large side, decorated in shades of beige, with tubs in the baths. Breakfasts are disappointing for a four-star, but there's an indoor pool, gym and sauna. ❻

The City

All features of interest in Erzurum lie along – or just off – Cumhuriyet Caddesi, and a leisurely tour shouldn't take much more than half a day. Start at what is the de facto city centre – the Yakutiye Parkı – a landscaped area with benches and a tea garden around the Yakutiye Medresesi.

Yakutiye Medresesi and around

The **Yakutiye Medresesi** was begun in 1310 by Cemaleddin Hoca Yakut, a local governor of the İlhanid Mongols, and with its intricately worked portal, and truncated minaret featuring a knotted lattice of tilework, it's easily the most fanciful building in town. The minaret in particular seems displaced from somewhere in Central Asia or Persia – not such a far-fetched notion when you learn that the İlhanids had their seat in Tabriz. The beautiful interior of the *medrese* – note especially the stone stalactite carvings of the central dome – now holds an excellent **Museum of Islamic and Turkish Arts** (Türk-İslam Eserleri ve Etnografya Müzesi; Tues, Thurs, Fri & Sat 8am–noon & 1.30–5.15pm; $0.70), nicely arranged around the student's cells. Exhibits include displays of local *oltu taşı* jewellery (see p.820), various dervish accessories, *ehram* (woven waistcoats for pilgrims to Mecca) and a selection of interesting old prints of Erzurum, among them a fine photograph taken from the roof of the old British consulate (Britain had a commercial agent in Erzurum as early as 1690). A **türbe** at the east end of the *medrese* was intended for Yakut but never used. Just behind the tomb squats the uninspiring, mid-sixteenth-century **Lala Mustafa Paşa Camii**; it was supposedly designed by the famous architect Sinan, but you'd never guess it.

Ulu Cami, Çifte Minareli Medrese and Üç Kümbetler

Continuing east about 300m along Cumhuriyet Caddesi, past an obscure *türbe* jostled by the surrounding shops, you pass the **Ulu Cami**, erected in 1179 by Nasirüddin Muhammed, third in the line of Saltuk emirs. Like most mosques of that age, it's a big square hall, with dozens of columns supporting bare vaults; the one note of fancy is a wedding cake of stalactite vaulting culminating in the central skylight. At the *mihrab* the orderly rows of columns – seven aisles of six each – break up around an odd wooden dome built of overlapping timbers and pierced by two round windows.

Immediately adjacent stands the **Çifte Minareli Medrese**, the purported main tourist attraction in Erzurum. The name – meaning "double-minareted" – derives from the most conspicuous feature of the seminary, two thirty-metre-high towers curiously devoid of a balcony for the muezzin to sound the call to prayer. There is some dispute about the structure's vintage, but the majority opinion holds that Hüdavend Hatun, daughter of the Selçuk sultan Alâeddin Keykubad II, commissioned it in 1253, making it a contemporary of the similar Gök Medrese in Sivas. In conception the Çifte Minareli was the boldest and largest theological academy of its time, but was never finished. The stalactite portal, whose carved dragons and double-headed eagle designs hark somewhat un-Islamically back to an earlier nomadic animism, gives onto a vast, bare courtyard, with stairways at the front corners leading to an upper storey of cells (alas, rarely open). At the back looms an unusual cylindrical or *kümbet*-style tomb, thought to be that of the foundress; the sarcophagus, which may in fact be empty, lies in a separate subterranean chamber below the dome.

A cluster of less enigmatic mausoleums, the **Üç Kümbetler**, graces another small park about 250m directly south. The oldest of the three tombs, and the most interesting, is probably that of the first Saltuk emir and dates from the early twelfth century, its octagonal base of alternating light and dark stone breached by half-oval windows demonstrating the mutual influence of Georgian, Armenian and early Turkish architecture. The other two *kümbets* in the ensemble date from at least a century later and aren't nearly as compelling.

The citadel and Rüstem Paşa Bedesteni

On the opposite side of Cumhuriyet Caddesi from the Çifte Minareli Medrese, a narrow lane leads past some of the oldest houses in town and a handful of carpet/antique shops to the **citadel** or *kale* (daily 8am–5.30; $0.35), whose vast rectangular bulk was originally laid out by Emperor Theodosius II. The interior is bare except for a shoebox-like *mescit*, or small mosque, capped by an afterthought of a *kümbet*-style dome. The adjacent free-standing **Tepsi Minare** now doubles as a clock-tower; like the mosque it's mostly twelfth century, though the superstructure (which can be climbed) was added by the

Russians during one of their occupations. Stairs on the east side lead up to the ramparts, and while the citadel is no longer the highest point in town since Erzurum began to spread to its rim of hills, it still lends the best view over the city – and the great, intimidating vastness of the plateau beyond.

Just northwest of the castle, but easiest reached by retracing your steps along Cumhuriyet Caddesi to descend Menderes Caddesi, stands the **Rüstem Paşa Bedesteni**, the covered bazaar, endowed by Süleyman the Magnificent's mid-sixteenth-century grand vizier. Erzurum owed much of its wealth to transcontinental trade routes and even in the nineteenth century some forty thousand laden camels were passing through the city every year. Today trade is almost totally monopolized by **oltu taşı**, an obsidian-like material mined near Oltu, 150km northeast, and most frequently made into *tespih* (prayer beads), *kolye* (necklaces) and *küpe* (earrings). Prices start at about $6 for a tiny, ten-centimetre *tespih*; silver clasps cost $2–3 extra. Earrings go for anything between $3.50 and $11, depending on the size and number of stones, but most importantly whether the setting is gold or silver; a longish necklace with a silver chain will run about $14.

The Archeological Museum

Erzurum's least compelling sight is the **Archeological Museum** (Arkeoloji Müzesi; Tues–Sun 8am–noon & 1–5pm; $0.70), 400m south of Havuzbaşı roundabout. The ground floor has assorted Urartian and Caucasian pottery, plus some Roman and Hellenistic glassware and jewellery. There is also a rather unedifying "massacre room", containing items removed during the 1980s from two mass graves in the province – the property, it is claimed, of Turks and Kurds slaughtered by Armenians between 1915 and 1918.

Palandöken: skiing

Palandöken, stretching 5–6.5km south of town, offers far and away the best skiing in Turkey, more than adequate compensation for being stuck in Erzurum during its habitually arctic winters. With largely north-facing slopes ranging from 2300m near the *Tourinn Palan Hotel* up to Point 3125 on Mt Ejder, excellent conditions (essentially nice dry powder on a two-metre base) are just about guaranteed. Pistes total 35km at present, with 10km more (and the lifts to serve them) projected; currently seven chair-lifts, two drag-lifts and a telecabin give access to seven easy, five intermediate and two advanced runs, as well as four recognized off-piste routes.

Eating and drinking

Restaurants in Erzurum tend to offer good value, with a concentration of sorts on or around Cumhuriyet Caddesi and the central park; thanks in part to the local student contingent, they're also open later than you'd expect for the Anatolian interior, serving until 11.30pm or midnight in most cases. Not surprisingly in this devout town, licensed places are rare.

Restaurants

Erzurum Evleri Yüzbaşı Sok 18, south of Cumhuriyet Cad. Eight old dwellings knocked together to make an institution that's equal parts funhouse maze, folklore museum and restaurant. Antique displays comprise everything from Ottoman houseware to 1950s portable gramophones. The food's only just better than average, from a very limited menu, but the price ($5 for three courses and a juice) is right, and the seating, shoeless on cushions around low tables occupying various alcoves with fireplaces and skylights, highly atmospheric.

Güzelyurt Restaurant Cumhuriyet Cad 54/C. One of the oldest (founded 1928) restaurants in town, and one of the few licensed ones, where women can dine comfortably with friends or significant others. Erzerum's *beau monde* retire behind curtained windows for a nip of *rakı* (in small-measure pitchers), wine or beer to accompany good vegetable *meze* and less exalted grilled mains. Budget $6–10 depending on how much booze you have; price includes *garsoniye* charge for obsequious service and muzak covers of greatest (Western) classical hits.

Salon Asya Cumhuriyet Cad 27. Ace for kebabs and a full soup menu, with willing service, dazzling (read migraine-inducing) lighting and contemporary decor; you can fill up for under $4.

Salon Çağın Cumhuriyet Cad 18/C. Fusty subterranean environment with contrastingly good food, including *mantı* (Asian ravioli) on Sunday and trout daily in summer; a big meal will set you back $6.

Desserts

Kılıçoğlu Sütiş Cumhuriyet Cad 20. The main branch of three in town for this premier pudding shop and nemesis of dieters: two dozen flavours of *dondurma*, all other milk sweets, plus profiteroles, biscuits and every imaginable sort of oriental sticky cake.

Serender Pastanesi Cumhuriyet Cad 32. Cheaper but less varied offering offering than *Kılıçoğlu*; open until after midnight.

Listings

Airport bus Departs 2hr before flight time from in front of the THY office, Cumhuriyet Cad, Eren İş Merkezi 88/3 ☎0442/218 1904.

Banks and exchange The only relatively efficient banks in town prepared to accept travellers' cheques are the Türk Ticaret Bankası branch situated near the Gürcü Kapı roundabout up at the top of İstasyon Cad, and the Garanti Bankası near THY. You're better off using the three İş Bankası ATMs opposite the Yakutiye Parkı or the scattering of *döviz* stalls, such as Cihan Döviz, on the west side of Çaykara Cad, or Erzerum Döviz next to the *Salon Asya* on Cumhuriyet Cad.

Camping gas For those bound for the Kaçkar mountains, small 190-ml cartridges are usually available at İpragaz, İstasyon Cad 12/A.

Car rental Avis, Terminal Cad, Mavi Site, Birinci Blok ☎0442/233 8088; Evis, Terminal Cad 13/A ☎0442/234 4400, airport ☎0442/327 1377; Decar/Thrifty, airport only ☎0442/233 3560.

Cirit This is a sort of cross between polo and a jousting tournament, with the players on horseback eliminating opponents from the field by thrusts of a blunted javelin. Ask at the tourist office during spring and summer if a match is scheduled nearby.

Consulate Iran, Ülçer Apartments, Atatürk Bul, Yeni Şehir Girişi, on the minor road to Palandöken ☎0442/316 2285, ⊕315 9983 – and read the box on p.708 for details on crossing into Iran before you leave Erzerum.

Hamam Most historic and salubrious is probably the Boyahane Hamamı, in the warren of lanes west of the Rüstem Paşa Bedesten.

Hospitals One is north of Havuşbaşı on Hastaneler Cad, another south of Havuzbaşı on Yenişehir Cad, and still another (probably the best), the research and teaching hospital, south of the Ağrı- and Kars-bound highway in Yenişehir itself.

Internet access Internet cafés are found on or just off Cumhuriyet Cad – try the side street heading south from the *Serender Pastanesi*, where there's the *Konak* at no. 9.

Supermarket Migros, by the train station, for "European-packaged" goods, especially trek-suitable fare.

Northwest of Erzurum: Çoruh River citadels

As you head west out of Erzurum on the way to the Black Sea, you'll follow either of two roads away from the lorry route to Ankara. One follows the old Silk Route northwest down to Trabzon via **Bayburt**; the other leads north to Rize via **İspir**. After scaling the first range of peaks beyond Erzurum, both routes drop dizzyingly from 2300-metre passes to the **Çoruh River**, which flows through a deep trench that lies well below the level of the Anatolian plateau. This remote valley, reminiscent of deeper Central Asia or the American Southwest, was the ancestral homeland of the Bagratid clan (see box on p.846), who went on to furnish early medieval Armenia and Georgia with so many of their rulers.

Bayburt

BAYBURT is dwarfed by the largest **fortress** in Turkey, its history virtually synonymous with the town. Thought to have been erected in the sixth century during Byzantine emperor Justinian's skirmishes with the Laz tribe from the Black Sea, it was later appropriated by the Bagratids, until being taken and renovated by the Saltuk Turks early in the thirteenth century. The citadel was a much-coveted prize in the Russo-Turkish wars of the nineteenth and twentieth centuries, so it's something of a miracle that the perimeter walls are in such good condition – though this isn't true of the interior, where there's not much to see apart from the view.

Little else redeems Bayburt other than its position astride the young Çoruh River, best enjoyed at one of several riverside **restaurants** or **cafés** with wonderful views of the castle. There are thirteenth- and fourteenth-century **mosques** founded by Saltuk Turks and the İlhanid Mongol governor Cemaleddin Hoca Yakut – he of the *medrese* in Erzurum – but these fall squarely in the category of time-filling exercises, and the main reason to pause here is to break a journey between Trabzon and Erzurum. Otherwise content yourself with a glance at the fort while in transit.

Practicalities

Bayburt's small **otogar** is 500m south of the centre on the main highway, but buses to and from Erzurum often begin and end in the bazaar. If you need to stay, your best bets are two **hotels** on Cumhuriyet Caddesi, the main drag aiming right for the castle. The budget *Saracoğlu* at no. 13 (☏0458/211 7217; ❶), has rooms overlooking the river, en-suite showers but toilets down the hall; across the road, a little way towards the *otogar*, the two-star *Hotel Adıbeş* (☏0458/211 5813; ❸), is clean and comfortable, with large doubles and an attached restaurant.

For **eating out**, the enclosed *Yeni Zafer*, next to the central vehicle bridge over the Çoruh, is more appealing in winter, but the *Çoruh Lokantası* upstream, with riverbank seating under willow trees, has the edge during the warm months. For summer dessert, good ice cream is dispensed on the quay between the two. Abandon all hope of a stiff **drink** in this conservative backwater – Bayburt is still the sort of place where half the women shuffle about in all-enveloping gunny-sacks, and transgressors of the Ramazan fast are apt to be dealt with summarily by the offended religious.

İspir

İSPİR, the Byzantine Hyspiratis, once rivalled Bayburt in importance, but has precipitously declined. The setting, overlooking a bend of the Çoruh, with a monument-crowned acropolis, promises much but disappoints up close. There's not even a proper gate left to the Bagratid **castle**, which hardly rewards a climb through the town's shanties; inside there's a squat, little-used mosque from the Saltuk era, and a badly ruined Byzantine church. The town itself is shabby, the only foreigners passing through are those en route to the scenic Salaçur Mountains just to the north. The two or three **hotels** and **restaurants** are among the most loathsome in Turkey, so it's a very good idea to avoid getting stuck here.

If you've arrived by **bus** from Rize on the way to Erzurum, or vice versa, you can get an onward bus the same day as long as you've made an early start. The last ones can be as late as 2.30pm, but it's safest to get a through service. If you deliberately alight here, one of the most interesting things to do is to cover the rough but scenic 91km of partly paved Highway 50 to Yusufeli, sometimes by public transport (dolmuşes run almost half way, as far as Çamlıkaya) but more often than not by thumb.

Northeast of Erzurum: the road to Kars

Convoys of lorries often clog the heavily travelled Highway E80/100 beyond Erzurum, bound for Iran and (in peaceful times) Georgia. Once past Pasinler, the road follows the increasingly scenic valley of the infant Aras River, an excellent backdrop should the hard-pressed Turkish cinema industry ever crank out a string of "*pilav* Westerns".

Pasinler and around

PASİNLER, 41km along, is distinguished only by the crumbled citadel of **Hasankale**, an originally Bagratid stronghold taken over by the Akkoyun Turcomans during the fifteenth century, and by its famous hot springs and mud baths. However, the town itself is shabby and the bath-building sterile and regimented, while the spa-side "two-star" *Kale Hotel* (☎0442/661 4994; ❷) has been awarded two stars too many, though it makes a feasible emergency overnight stop.

Twenty kilometres east, just past Köprüköy, the graceful thirteenth-century **Çobandede bridge**, the finest medieval bridge in Turkey, spans the Aras River in six arches near the beginning of its course, a particularly bewitching sight in late-afternoon light. The road, railway and river stick together until **Horasan**, where the E80/100 to Iran – via Ağrı and Doğubeyazit – peels off to the southeast, and the train tracks and Highway 80 meander north.

Sarıkamış

At Karakurt junction the river forsakes Kars-bound Highway 957, and starts a sharp descent toward the Caspian Sea. The next place of any consequence, nestled 6km off the main road amidst an unexpected forest of conifers, is **SARIKAMIŞ**, subject to the coldest climate in the country. The winter of 1914–1915 proved lethal here for the Ottoman Third Army under the command of the megalomaniac Enver Paşa, when – in one of the worst Turkish defeats of World War I – 75,000 men froze to death, died of typhus or were killed attempting to halt a Tsarist force of roughly equal size; in the wake of the debacle the Russians advanced to Erzurum and beyond, and you can still see their vast barracks, built to garrison troops at the then-frontier from 1878 until 1917.

Today the thick seasonal snow supports the very good **Cibiltepe ski resort**, 3km back east towards the main highway. Thus far, facilities comprise just two chair lifts from 2150m up to 2700m, serving two advanced runs, two intermediate ones and one novice piste threading the trees. At the foot of the lifts, the ostensibly three-star *Çamkar Sarıkamış "Motel"* (☎0474/413 5259, ✉camkar@domi.com.tr; ❺ half board) offers medium-sized standard units with small, dated, shower-only bathrooms in a chalet-style structure with a sauna and licensed restaurant. Unfortunately, it only pretends to be open during summer, when the hot water works sporadically, the food on the two-item menu is dismal, and the motel's principal function seems to be as watering hole for locals, since it's the only licensed spot for miles around. A *Dedeman Hotel* is currently under construction next door, which should provide some much-needed competition.

If you intend to ski here, the budget alternative would be to arrange rental of equipment, lift passes and instruction at the lift offices and stay instead at the *Sarıkamış Turistik Otel* at Halk Cad 64 in the town centre (℡0474/413 4176; ❷), with its funky rustic-style lobby and spacious rooms. Other **hotels** on the same street are fleapits, and there's only one proper **restaurant**, *Dönerci Canbaba*, one block over at Belediye Cad 245; happily it's excellent and inexpensive, with a broad selection of kebabs, *pide*, soups and baked puddings.

The Kümbet Kilise

North of Sarıkamış, the scenery becomes humdrum again as the mountains level out onto the high, grassy steppe that surrounds Kars. About 9km before Kars, 200m northwest of the road near the village of Kümbetli and a smoking beet-sugar refinery, you'll glimpse the ruined, tenth-century Armenian church known as the **Kümbet Kilise**, the first of various such monuments in the province. The church was reported destroyed as long ago as 1830, and its original name forgotten. Far more interesting inside than its battered exterior suggests, this four-apsed, octagonal rotunda is essentially a miniature of the Holy Apostles church in Kars proper (see below). In the fan-top niches between the column capitals are four little relief gargoyles representing the Evangelists: the man of Matthew (southeast), the eagle of John (northeast), and the lion of Mark and bull of Luke (northwest/southwest), so badly worn as to be indistinguishable.

Kars

Hidden in a natural basin on the banks of the Kars Çayı, **KARS** is a fairly dour town with only a few terraces of Russian *belle époque* buildings to cheer it up. Although a couple of hundred metres lower than Erzurum, the climate is even more severe; the potholed streets never quite recover from the fierce winters; and when it rains, which it often does, the outskirts become a treacherous swamp. There are a few sites in town worth dallying for, but most visitors have made the long trek out here for the sole purpose of visiting the former Armenian capital of Ani (see p.829).

Rain and mud remain big factors – with the advent of global warming, summers seem to have got even wetter – but Kars has improved beyond all recognition since the early 1990s, even if poverty and beggars are nearly as evident as in Erzurum. Central streets are well signposted, and/or repaved in cobbles or bricks, with even a designated pedestrian zone or two. Something approximating a local middle class, and the establishment of the Kafkas Üniversitesi, have prompted the emergence of better lodging, eating, drinking and shopping options.

Some history

Originally founded by the Armenians who knew it as Kari, Kars became the capital of their Bagratid dynasty early in the tenth century when the citadel, which still dominates the town, was substantially improved. Later in that century the main seat of Armenian rule was transferred to nearby Ani, and Kars lost some of its importance. The Selçuks took it along with almost everything else in the area during the mid-eleventh century, but devastating Mongol raids made a mockery of any plans the new overlords had for Kars. In 1205 the Georgians, profiting from the wane of both Selçuk and Byzantine power in the area, seized the town and held it for three centuries until displaced by the Ottomans.

Kars defends the approaches to Erzurum just as the latter is the key to the rest of Anatolia; the Russians tried repeatedly during the nineteenth century to capture the place. Sieges in 1828 and 1855 were successful – the latter during the Crimean War, when a British and Turkish garrison was starved out of the citadel after five months – but on both occasions Kars reverted to Turkey by terms of peace treaties. Not so in 1878, when, after a bloody eight-month war between the two powers, Kars was finally awarded to the Tsar. It remained in Russian or Armenian hands until 1920, a period that bequeathed both the unusual grid layout of the city centre and the incongruous *belle époque* buildings found here. Today Kars is, not surprisingly, still a major forward military position, swarming with soldiers who supplement its native population of 90,000.

Arrival and orientation

In the northeast of the town and within walking distance of most points of interest, the **old otogar**, on Küçük Kâzımbey Caddesi, now houses only dolmuşes to nearby Yusufeli, Ardahan, Posof (for Georgia) and Iğdır (change there for Doğubeyazit). For major towns such as Erzurum and beyond, you'll need the **long-distance otogar**, 5km east of the town centre – *servis* buses link it with bus company ticket offices in the town centre. Daily flights from Ankara land at the **airport**, 6km south of town beyond the bypass highway; a shuttle-bus service runs you into the centre, stopping at the THY office (see "Listings" on p.829). The **train station** lies 1km southeast of the centre, off Cumhuriyet Caddesi, on the way to the museum.

The Russian grid **street-plan** makes central Kars easy to navigate, and the general broadness of the thoroughfares makes life easier for **parking**. The most important southwest-to-northeast streets are Faikbey Caddesi, essentially the continuation of the Erzurum–Armenia highway, and three parallel avenues immediately northwest, which bracket the central business district. Lined with both humble and grandiose Russian structures, Gazi Ahmet Muhtar Caddesi, Atatürk Caddesi and Kâzımpaşa Caddesi lead approximately southeast–to–northwest until the river, on the far bank of which huddles the medieval settlement – now a shantytown. Most items of interest cluster near this district, a few hundred metres north of the modern city centre.

Information and tours

The principal duty of staff at the **tourist office**, on the upper floor of the grey stone structure on the corner of Atatürk and Karadağ *caddesi*s (daily 8.30am–5.30pm; ☎0474/212 6817), is to issue Ani-visit applications (see p.831 for more on this); they speak little English, and thus can tell you equally little about the province's assorted churches and castles, snaps of which are tantalizingly pinned to the wall. They may, however, refer you to the local English-speaking "fixer" and knowledgeable **guide** Celil Ersözoğlu (☎0532/226 3966, ℗0474/212 4445), who arranges reliable group taxi-tours to Ani and remoter monuments – though he will probably find you first.

Accommodation

Accommodation options in Kars have improved immeasurably from the years when the "mid-range" establishments offered backpacker standards and the "budget" choices were unspeakable. Even so, most ultra-budget places remain beyond the pale (we've had a report of theft from a room at an unlisted dosshouse) and the following are the current sum total of safe and salubrious recommendations.

Asya Oteli Küçük Kâzımbey Cad 50 ☎0474/223 2299. The only passable budget hotel in town, thankfully in a quiet location. Slightly musty-smelling, 1980s-vintage rooms, some en-suite, with blue carpet. **❶**

Güngören Oteli Millet Sok 4, just off Halitpaşa Cad ☎0474/212 5630, ☎223 4821. Large rooms with shocking colour schemes but modernized baths, plus decent ground-floor restaurant and a hamam. **❸**

Hotel Karabağ Faikbey Cad 142 ☎0474/212 3480, ⊛www.hotel-karabag.com. A 1994-built, slightly overpriced three-star whose decor and furnishings are already ageing. Rear rooms are the largest and quietest, with tubs in large bathrooms; heating and fridges throughout. There's a laughably naff bar-with-disco-ball just off the lobby, itself the smoky meeting place of local worthies at all hours, but the mezzanine breakfast

salon/restaurant (see "Eating and drinking") is OK. Rooms **❹**, half-board **❺**

Sim-Er Hotel West edge of town on the old Erzurum road, Haydar Aliyev Bul ☎0474/212 7241, ☎212 0168. An externally grim high-rise, built in 1999 as a four-star, with most effort devoted to the common areas. The sharply overpriced, pastel-coloured rooms have poor bathrooms, though the four-person suites are worth the extra outlay. Limited off-street parking, pleasant lawn-seating restaurant. Rooms **❺**, suites **❼**

Temel Yeni Pazar Cad 9, just off Halitpaşa Cad ☎0474/223 1376, ☎223 1323. A thorough year-2000 refit and still-modest prices have vaulted this old standby into best-value ranking for Kars. All pastel-blue-decor, cutting-edge rooms with mini-bars (and most with tubs in the bathrooms) and a pleasant first-floor breakfast salon. **❷**

The Town

The obvious **Church of the Holy Apostles**, just the other side of the Kars Çayı on the way to the castle, was erected between 930 and 937 by the Armenian king Abbas I. Crude reliefs of the twelve apostles adorn the twelve arches of the dome, but otherwise it's a squat, functional bulk of dark basalt; the belfry and portico are relatively recent additions. A church when Christians held Kars, a mosque when Muslims ruled, it briefly housed the town museum before being reconsecrated in 1998 as the Kümbet Camii. Just before or after prayer times, you can slip inside to view the elaborately carved altar screen.

Before climbing the short distance to the *kale*, or castle, detour slightly up the tributary of the Kars Çayı to see the **Taş Köprü**, or "Stone Bridge", made of the same volcanic rock as the nearby church and restored during the 1580s by order of Murat III. A few **hamams**, none dating from before the eighteenth century, huddle nearby: the still-functioning **İlbeyoğlu**, the **Mazlutağa** (in ruins) and the **Topçuoğlu** (still in use); see "Listings" on p.829 for details.

There has been a fortress of some kind on the hill overlooking the river confluence for well on two millennia. The Armeno-Byzantine structure was maintained by the Selçuks but levelled by the Mongols; the Ottomans rebuilt it as part of their late sixteenth-century urban overhaul, only to have the Russians blast it to bits, then put it back together again during the nineteenth century. On October 30, 1920, an Armenian Dashnakist army besieged in the castle surrendered to Turkish general Halitpaşa (he of the street), and with that went any hopes of an Armenian state straddling both banks of the Ahuryan River.

KARS

Main Otogar, Çıldır Gölü, Ardahan & Artvin

EATING & DRINKING
Antep	C
Aspava	H
Eylül	J
Güzelyurt	I
Hukukçular	G
IL & KE	F
Karabağ	K
Konak	A
Ocakbaşı & Marmara	E
Planet	B
Şirin Anadolu Mutfağı	D

HOTELS
Asya	4
Güngören	1
Karabağ	5
Sim-er	2
Temel	3

Kars Çayı
Kars Museum

Kızlay Hamamı

Train Station

Old Otogar

Ruined Hamam
İlbeyoğlu Hamamı
Kale
Topçuoğlu Hamamı
Taş Köprü
Church of the Holy Apostles

Army Camp

Fethiye Camii

Police

Sports Stadium

Kars Çayı

HALIT PAŞA CAD
KÖÇÜK KAZIMBEY CAD
KARADAĞ CAD
YENİ PAZAR SOK
KAZIM PAŞA CAD
FAIKBEY CAD
ATATÜRK CAD
GAZI AHMET MUHTAR CAD
GAZI AHMET MUHTAR CAD
ŞEHIT YUSUF BEY CAD
ZÜBEYDE HANIM CAD
CUMHURIYET CAD
İSTASYON CAD
DUVAY AKSU CAD
MEŞRUTIYET CAD
KURBAN ALI SOK
ORDU (ALIBEY) CAD
LISE SOK
INÖNÜ CAD
BORSA SOK
HAYDAR ALIYEU BUL (ERZURUM CAD)

İğdır & Doğubeyazit

Ani

Erzurum
Erzurum & Airport

After decades as an off-limits military reserve, **Kars Kalesi** as it's officially known (daily 9am–7pm; free), is now open as a park. Locals come to pay their respects at the tomb of Celal Baba, a holy man of the fourteenth century, and to enjoy the panorama over Kars, but there's little else to see other than the black-masoned military engineering.

The only other compelling attraction in Kars is the excellent **Kars Museum** (Kars Müzesi; daily 8.30am–5.30pm; $0.70), a fifteen-minute walk out to the east end of town, whose ethnographic section includes such curiosities as a ceramic *yayık* (butter churn) and a cradle, as well as jewellery, leatherwork and extensive exhibits on local carpets and kilims. Downstairs is given over to ancient pottery, and ecclesiastical artefacts of the departed Russians and Armenians, particularly a huge church bell inscribed "This Tolls for the Love of God", and a pair of wooden doors, which graced one of the cathedrals before 1920. On the way back pay a visit to the **Fethiye Camii**, a converted nineteenth-century Russian Orthodox church.

Eating and drinking

Fortunately the **restaurant** scene in Kars is a bit more promising and fairly priced than the hotel prospects. It's also easier than in Erzurum to get alcohol with your meal, though be aware that the after-hours *müzikhols* (sic, "music-halls") along Halitpaşa Caddesi are haunted by a certain *natasha*-influenced, vodka-soaked sleaziness – and often knots of police cars parked in readiness outside. The limited number of youth-oriented **bars** are better bets for a night out, especially for women; doyen of these is the *Planet* at Atatürk Cad 108, which has occasional live music at weekends as well as pastries, fast food and a full range of hard drinks (about $4 each).

Antep Pide ve Lahmacun Atatürk Cad. The most varied and best-executed *pide* and *lahmacun* in the city. Unlicensed.

Aspava Lokantası Faikbey Cad 74, corner Ordu Cad. Never mind the lurid lighting and kitsch decor, this is the best of a handful of a 24-hour soup and *sulu yemek* kitchens in town – a god-send if you've arrived on a late bus; chunky, reviving *İşkembe* a speciality. The name, incidentally, is an anagram of the popular prayer *Allah Sıhhat Para Afiyet Versin Amin* (God Grant Truth, Money and Health, Amen).

Eylül Kâzımpaşa Cad, just south of Faikbey Cad. The most appealing and quietly set of a handful of *pastanes*, with milk-based sweets, wood-panelled decor and an upstairs gallery. Try the famous local honey (*bal*) with a continental breakfast.

Güzelyurt Lokantası Faikbey Cad, corner Kâzımpaşa Cad. Large, basic cheapie, surprisingly enough licensed, featuring soups in the morning and wraparound windows for you to watch the world (and vice versa).

Hukukçular Ordu Cad 218, corner Faikbey Cad. Upstairs *meyhane* that's better (and friendlier) than it looks from outside. Full booze list but the menu is limited to a half-dozen vegetarian *mezes* of the day, and a range of grills. Budget $5 for a meal with beer.

Karabağ *Karabağ Hotel*, 1st Floor, Faikbey Cad 142. This is the spot for white-tablecloth service and a full wine list, though the food (only *mezes* and grills after the few ready dishes run out) does-n't really rate the prices asked – $11 or so each with a modest intake of drink.

Konak Halitpaşa Cad, north corner with Kâzımpaşa Cad. One of the oldest restaurants in Kars, lodged in a Russian-era building; modest but well-priced *meyhane*-style fare. It's licensed, but best go at lunchtime as it tends to close evenings.

Ocakbaşı Atatürk Cad 176. Not to be confused with a namesake two doors down, this unlicensed outfit gets a brisk trade for the sake of its good kebabs and *pide* (if not the often shambolic serv-ice) in a mock-troglodytic/Flintstones environment.

Şirin Anadolu Mutfağı Karadağ Cad 5. Despite the name ("Amiable Anatolian Cuisine"), this mere-ly offers standard *pide* and *kebap* – but very well done. It's in the heart of Kars's first pedestrian zone, opposite the fountains, with ground-floor seating in a contemporary environment and a pleasant nocturnal-café-only section upstairs for dessert and non-alcoholic drinks.

Listings

Airport bus Shuttle-bus ($1.50), departing 1hr 45min before flight time from the THY agent, which is Sınır Turizm, Atatürk Cad 86 ℡0474/212 3838.

Banks and exchange There are several ATMs attached to, among others, the İş Bankası (corner Atatürk and Halitpaşa *caddesi*s), Akbank and Vakıf Bank (Halitpaşa Cad 117); otherwise use several efficient *döviz* on Kazımpaşa Cad.

Hamams Two of these are near the Taş Köprü: the İlbeyoğlu (men 8–10am & 6–11pm; women noon–6pm; $1.75); the Topçuoğlu (Muradiye on some maps), on the far side of the bridge, is for women only. The *Güngören Hotel* has an attached hamam for men only, but the newest is the Kızılay Hamamı (men 6.30am–11pm; women noon–5pm), about 500m northeast of the town centre on Faikbey Cad.

Hospital Near army camp and sports stadium on İnönü Cad.

Internet access Try the *Marmara*, also with pool tables, directly above the listed *Ocakbaşı* restaurant, or the *IL&KE Café* on the first floor of Kâzımpaşa Cad 152.

Post office Main PTT branch (open late into evenings) is a bit out of the way on Ordu Cad; there's also a useful *çarşı* branch on Kâzımpaşa Cad.

Ani

Once the capital of Bagratid Armenia, **ANİ** is today a melancholy, almost vacant triangular plateau, divided from Armenia by the stunning Arpa Çayı (Ahuryan River) gorge and very nearly separated from the rest of Turkey by two deep tributaries. The site is mainly an expanse of rubble, but from it rise some of the finest examples of ecclesiastical and military architecture of its time. The Armenians were master stoneworkers, and the fortifications that defend the northern, exposed side of the plateau, and the handful of churches behind, are exquisite compositions in a blend of ruddy sandstone and darker volcanic rock. These, and the cliffs fringing the river, are the only vertical features here, dwarfed by an evocative but relentlessly horizontal landscape. It is worth putting up with Kars for a couple of nights to make the trip out, and inconceivable that you'd venture east of Erzurum or Artvin without fitting Ani into your plans.

Some history

There was a settlement here before Christian times, centred on the citadel near the southern tip of the upland; the name Ani is perhaps a corruption of "Anahit", a Persian water goddess who was one of the chief deities of the pagan Armenians. The city first came to prominence after the local instalment of the Armenian Gamsarkan clan during the fifth century. Situated astride a major east–west caravan route, Ani prospered, receiving fresh impetus when Ashot III, fifth in the line of the Bagratid kings of Armenia, transferred his capital here from Kars in 961. For three generations the kingdom and its capital, under the successive rule of Ashot, Smbat II and Gagik I, enjoyed a golden age. Beautified and strengthened militarily, with a population exceeding a hundred thousand, Ani rivalled Baghdad and Constantinople themselves.

By the middle of the eleventh century, however, wars of succession and the religiously motivated enmity of the Byzantines (the Armenian Apostolic Church was deemed heretical) took their toll. The Byzantine Empire, having neutralized Bagratid power, annexed the city in 1045, but in the process dissolved an effective bulwark against the approaching Selçuks, who took Ani with little resistance in 1064. After the collapse of the Selçuks, the Armenians returned in less than a century, this time with the assistance of the powerful Georgian kingdom. The Pahlavuni and Zakhariad clans ruled over a reduced but still semi-independent Armenia for two more centuries, continuing to endow Ani with churches and monasteries. The Mongol raids of the thirteenth century, a devastating earthquake in 1319 and realigned trade routes proved mortal blows to both Ani and its hinterland; thereafter the city was gradually abandoned, and forgotten until noticed by European travellers of the nineteenth century.

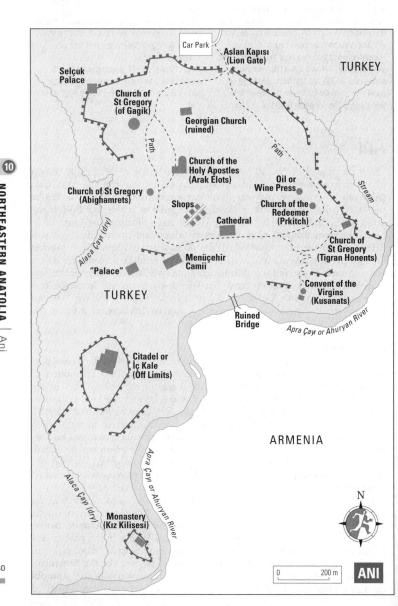

Visiting the site

Ani lies 45km southeast of Kars, just beyond the village of Ocaklı. Without your own transport, you could take the early afternoon bus service between Kars and the ruins, but this vehicle overnights in Ocaklı, leaving you stranded. The more common alternative is a **taxi tour** for about $36 a vehicle. Solo travellers typically band together at the tourist office; the taxis hold four passengers, and minibuses carrying up to nine customers ($8–9 each) are also available. The ruins are scattered, and many monuments are absorbing, so allow a good two-and-a-half to three hours at Ani, plus two hours for going there and back – make sure your driver agrees to a **five-hour** stint. Mid-summer is usually very **hot**, so you're advised to bring a hat, sun cream and water to tour the site – as well as some snack food, as the massively ugly restaurant outside the entrance has shut down and may not re-open.

Permits and admission

Because of its location in a restricted zone, Ani would ordinarily be closed to visits, but in view of its artistic and historical interest both the Armenian and Turkish governments have made an exception in this case. It's **open daily** (8.30am–5pm; $3.50) though you'll still need a **permit**, routinely granted and requiring less than an hour to issue. Fill in a petition at Kars tourist office, have this endorsed at the Security Police two blocks away (first office on the right, ground-floor corridor), and proceed to the Kars museum to buy **tickets**. Tickets are usually *not* sold at the site, a measure designed to prevent people showing up unvetted. There is talk of this complicated procedure being superseded in 2003 by a one-stop petition/police stamp/ticket process at the Kar tourist office – you'll be told if this has been implemented. **Photography** at Ani is prohibited in theory by the military, but this edict is laxly enforced – even the civilian site-guards furtively encourage visitors to take snaps with small cameras, and it's foreseen that any lingering bans (except for photographing the Armenian bank of the river) will be swept aside in 2003.

The site

The vast **boundary walls** of Ani, dating from the late tenth century and studded with countless towers, are visible from several kilometres as you approach past villages teeming with sheep, buffalo, horses, donkeys and geese. After handing over your ticket and permit, you enter via the **Aslan Kapısı**, so named because of a sculpted Selçuk lion on the wall just inside, and sole survivor of the four original gates.

Once beyond the inner wall you're confronted with the sight of the vast forlorn, weed-tufted plateau, dotted with only the sturdiest bits of masonry that have outlasted the ages. A system of **signposted paths**, many of them remnants of the former main streets of Ani, lead to or past all of the principal remains.

Church of the Redeemer

Bear slightly left and head first about 500m southeast to the **Church of the Redeemer** (Prkitch), built between 1034 and 1036. In 1957, half of the building was sheared away by lightning, so that the remainder, seen from the side, looks uncannily like a stage set, albeit one with the carved filigree crosses and Armenian inscriptions. Three metres up on the exterior wall you can see a frieze of a cross on an ornate rectangular background; this is a fine example of the typically Armenian *khatchkar* (literally "cross-stone") carvings that gave their name to the Kaçkar mountains. Adjacent are the labelled remains of an **"oil press"** – more likely a wine press, as even a millennium ago the climate here would not have been mild enough to support olive cultivation.

Church of St Gregory and Convent of the Virgins

Some 200m east, tucked down a stair-path by a course of wall overlooking the Arpa Çayı, the charming monastic **Church of St Gregory the Illuminator** (Tigran Honents) is the best preserved of Ani's monuments, and somewhat confusingly one of three dedicated to the saint who brought Christianity to Armenia at the start of the fourth century. The pious foundation of a merchant nobleman in 1215, it's unusually laid out in a rectangle divided width-wise into three (though a colonnaded narthex and small baptistry have mostly collapsed). The ground plan reflects the prominent Georgian influence in thirteenth-century Ani, and the fact that the Orthodox, not the Armenian Apostolic, rite was celebrated here. The church still sports delicate exterior relief work, including extensive avian designs.

But Tigran Honents is most rewarding for its **frescoes**, the only ones surviving at Ani, which cover most of the interior and spill out around the current entrance onto what was once the narthex wall, giving the church its Turkish name *Resimli Kilise* or "Painted Church". They are remarkable both for their high degree of realism and fluidity – especially compared to the static iconography of the contemporaneous Byzantines – and for the subject matter, depicting episodes in early Armenian Christianity as well as the doings of ordinary people. As you enter the first of the two nave compartments, you'll see in the lower two rows of images on your right *The Trial of St Gregory by King Trdat III*, *The Martyrdom of Hrpsime* (an early female convert) and *The Torture of St Gregory*. All these events took place before Trdat's repentance and conversion, the earliest sovereign to do so; to the left are secular vignettes from the life of King Trdat. The transept is taken up by scenes from the life of Christ; on the south wall are *The Annunciation*, *The Nativity*, *The Entry into Jerusalem* and the *The Dormition of the Virgin*. To the north is *The Raising of Lazarus*, with *The Apostles* ringing the drum of the dome. On the upper level of the apse is shown *The Communion of the Apostles*, depicting Christ dispensing the Host. All images have had eyes and faces vandalized by pious Muslims.

From Tigran Honents, a narrow trail leads past the Selçuk baths and skims the tops of the cliffs above the Arpa Çayı before finding a steep way down to the thirteenth-century **Convent of the Virgins** (Kusanats), perched on a ledge even closer to the river. A minuscule, rocket-like rotunda church, contemporary with Tigran Honents, is flanked by a smaller chapel or baptistry, and the whole enclosed by a perimeter wall. Just downstream are the evocative stubs of the ruined medieval **bridge** over the Arpa, though it's unwise (if not actually forbidden) to approach it – the Turkish bank of the river is stoutly fenced and probably mined as well.

The cathedral and around

Rejoining the main plateau trail heading west from Tigran Honents, you reach the elegantly proportioned **cathedral**, completed between 989 and 1010. The architect, one Trdat Mendet, could present rather impressive credentials, having very recently completed restoration of the earthquake-damaged dome of Aya Sofya in Constantinople. However, this is a surprisingly plain, rectangular building, with just the generic blind arcades of Armenian churches and no external apse; the dome, once supported by four massive pillars, has long since vanished. The main entrance was – unusually – not to the west, opposite the apse, but on the side of the nave, through the south wall.

A little to the west, within sight of the cathedral, is an excavated area, apparently a medieval **street lined with shops**. Just beyond stands what's known as the **Menüçehir Camii**, billed as the earliest Selçuk mosque in Anatolia, though its lack of *mihrab*, its alternating red and black stonework and its inlaid mosaic ceiling, invite suspicions of mixed antecedents. Certainly the view from the ornate gallery over the frontier river fits more with use as a small palace. The truncated minaret was briefly off-limits for a while after a tourist committed suicide by leaping off, though the daring may now clamber up the eroded steps for an unrivalled aerial view of the site. Slightly southwest, the foundations of a purportedly verified **"palace"** have been exposed.

At the southern tip of the triangular site lies the inner **citadel** or İç Kale, which has long languished in a forbidden zone and is likely to remain so. Beyond the fortress at the far south end of the city, also off-limits but visible from many points of the riverbank escarpment, perches the fairy-tale monastery of **Kız Kilisesi**, spectacularly sited above a sharp curve in the river gorge. Should you be allowed out here by lenient *jandarma* personnel, the view back towards the main site gives an insight into the defence of the city, with steep gorges protecting the east and west flanks of the city, and high walls linking the two sides.

The northerly churches

North of the Menüçehir Camii stands the second **Church of St Gregory** (Abighamrets), begun in 1040 by the same individual responsible for the Church of the Redeemer. This rotunda is like no other at Ani – instead of just merely blind arcades in a flat surface, the twelve-sided exterior is pierced by functional recessed vaults, which alternate with the six rounded interior niches to lend extra structural stability. The east side of the building is slowly but surely losing its dressed stone.

The nearby, so-called "Kervansaray" began life as the eleventh-century **Church of the Holy Apostles** (Arak Elots), and despite ruinous first impressions proves a rewarding hybrid Selçuk–Christian monument. At first the church seems to have an odd south-to-north orientation, with a rounded apse at the north end – then you realize that this is the *kervansaray* bit added at a later date, and that the western half of the church nave is three-quarters crumbled but still discernible. Copious Armenian inscriptions confirm the building's original use, while overhead in the nave, superb four-way ribbing arcs cross an intricate ceiling in a two-colour mosaic pattern, culminating in a stalactite-vaulted dome

The main circuit continues north to the sparse ruins of a third **Church of St Gregory of Gagik**, begun in 998 by Trdat, architect of the cathedral. Intact, it would have been one of the largest rotundas in medieval Armenia proper, but the design, based on the three-storey, seventh-century rotunda at Zvartnots in Armenia, collapsed almost immediately, so that today only man-high outer walls, bases of the dome piers and giant column stumps remain.

Before completing your tour at the Aslan Kapısı, you can stop in at the **Selçuk Palace**, the only indisputably Islamic item at Ani, tucked into the northwest extremity of the ramparts. Since 1988, this has been meticulously rebuilt – the only structure to receive any degree of archeological investigation and maintenance, and a striking example of ultranationalist archeology in action.

Other churches and castles around Kars

The present-day province of Kars formed an important part of the Bagratid kingdom between the sixth and the eleventh centuries, and of the Zakhariad clan's holdings during the thirteenth century, so it's not surprising that there are numerous local **churches and castles**, mostly Armenian, besides those at Ani. The Armenians had a particular flair for poising their churches on sheer rock-faces overlooking river canyons, and many of the remains detailed below adhere to this pattern; even in their ruinous state they are still among the most impressive sights in northeastern Turkey.

Visiting them is not always straightforward, however: some are in bad condition, others accessible only by atrocious, poorly marked roads or on foot, or else they lie in military security zones – sometimes all three. You'll really need your own transport or a cooperative taxi-driver, enough Turkish to ask directions from villagers, and one of the two most detailed **maps** available – the 1:800,000 GeoCenter/RV "Turkey East", or the Reinhard Ryborsch 1:500,000 Karayolları Haritası no. 6, "Rize-Kars-Erzurum-Muş-Diyarbakır-Van" – though even these are full of serious, potentially time-wasting errors.

The only useful **public transport** in the area described below are the daily minibuses from Kars to Iğdır and from Kağızman to Çengilli, and the more regular Kars–Digor and Kağızman–Tuzluca minibuses.

Access, restrictions and information

The **border region** abutting Armenia is generally subject to strict army or *jandarma* control in a zone varying in width from a few paces (as at Ani) to several hundred metres; if you actually approach the Arpa (Ahuryan) stream, which forms the frontier until its union with the Aras River, you may well spark off an international incident. At times in the past, the entire region between the Digor–Tuzluca highway and the frontier was a no-go area after dark – even the villagers were not allowed to move about. The main road between Digor and Tuzluca still has at least two *jandarma* **checkpoints**, but upon presentation of ID foreigners are waved straight through.

At the time of writing, only two of the monumental zones described below – Horomos and Bagaran – remain absolutely **off-limits**, though Magazbert fortress will require a parley (and thus a local taxi driver's assistance) with the *jandarma* detachment stationed nearby. To visit Horomos or Bagaran, contact the central military command in Ankara several weeks in advance, presenting yourself as a high-level university student of medieval art or architecture, with supporting documents; permission is more often denied than granted, and in practice most tourists simply don't have the time. Don't just head off hoping for the best; you'll certainly be detected by the military and turned back, and should you somehow slip through, be aware that the area around Horomos in particular is known to be mined.

For many years the tourist information authorities in Kars were markedly disinclined to help visitors find these monuments; this becomes more understandable once you accept that the past treatment of these churches is as sensitive a topic as the alleged mistreatment of the Armenians themselves in 1895 and 1915. Officially Armenians don't exist historically, and any archeological evidence of their past rule is either ignored or misattributed to Islamic builders. The continued presence of recognizable churches in this part of Turkey con-

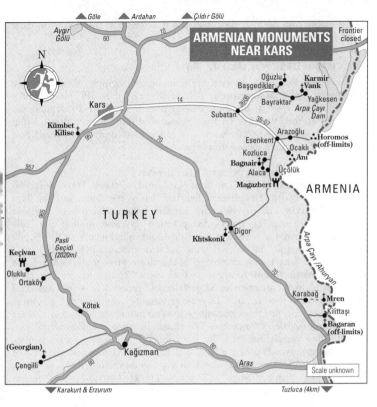

Map labels: Göle, Ardahan, Çıldır Gölü, Aygır Gölü, 60, 10, Frontier closed, N, Oğuzlu, Başgedikler, Karmir Vank, Kars, 14, Yağkesen, Bayraktar, Arpa Çayı Dam, Subatan, 36-07, Kümbet Kilise, 957, Arazoğlu, Esenkent, Horomos (off-limits), Ocaklı, Kozluca, Ani, Bagnair, Üçölük, Alaca, Magazbert, ARMENIA, TURKEY, 957, Digor, Khtskonk, Pasli Geçidi (2020m), Keçivan, Oluklu, Ortaköy, Arpa Çayı (Ahuryan), 70, Kötek, Karabağ, Mren, Kilittaşı, Bagaran (off-limits), (Georgian), Çengilli, Kağızman, Aras, 80, Scale unknown, Karakurt & Erzurum, Tuzluca (4km)

stituted a major inconvenience to most post-1923 Turkish governments, which saw them as the basis for potential Armenian territorial claims and demands for reparations. Certain entities would rather that outsiders did not see the churches, and would probably be relieved if they disappeared altogether. Several sources claim that army demolition units have helped the process along with dynamite or bulldozers since the 1950s – compounding extensive damage done between 1914 and 1923 – and while this is debatable, it's certainly true that nothing is being done to preserve these monuments.

Since the late 1990s, however, Kars tourism honchos have had a change of heart, correctly reckoning that tourists would stay an extra night or two in town if they had a good reason besides Ani to do so. There are now pictures of all the monuments noted below prominently posted in the tourist office as well as the museum, and there are indications that civilian authorities are preparing to request that the Turkish military declassify Horomos in particular. Matters can only improve as some of the local bitterness engendered by the long Armenian-Azeri war abates.

Once you show up at a remote church or castle, **local villagers** are generally only too happy to point the way to the ruins. They have no ethnic axe to grind and are honoured that someone should bother to visit what for them is a barn – or a quarry for building stone. Incidentally, some degree of attention from outsiders is often enough to stop any ongoing vandalism, not so much in anticipation of the monetary benefit of increased tourist traffic, but because the village elders consider that they lose face if a "cultural" institution on their patch deteriorates.

Monuments around Ani

A number of churches and castles in the immediate vicinity of Ani are easily visited with your own transport or a cooperative taxi; they will enjoyably fill a day already half-spent at the more extensive ruins. Be warned that there are absolutely no formal tourist facilities near any of those remote sites – bring picnic fare or trust in village hospitality (often forthcoming, in conjunction with a lot of curious attention from the locals).

Oğuzlu, Karmir Vank and Horomos

Just before Subatan, itself 27km from Kars, head northeast 11km along the minor 36-06 road to Başgedikler, then bear left at the T-junction, for 2km more to **Oğuzlu**. The massive, tenth-century hilltop church here is visible from some distance, but proves disappointing up close; roofless and half-collapsed, it's devoid of ornament other than some blind niches on the exterior, flanking the apse. The original name and dedication are unknown.

Much more intact and interesting is the thirteenth-century **church of Karmir Vank** (in Turkish *Kızıl Kilise* – both mean "Red Monastery"), reached by returning to the junction at Başgedikler and proceeding 4.5km east on a now-dirt road to the hamlet of **Bayraktar**, looping around on its right, forking left (northeast) just above the village and continuing for 3.2km more to the westernmost *mahalle* of **Yağkesen**. The church is helpfully visible on the final stretch, often protruding vertically from the flat Kars steppe; it's a beauty, despite being currently used as a barn, with hay and *tezek* patties stacked to one side and the land sloping gently down to a stream on the other. This compact, cross-in-square-plan building of 1228 was well restored in 1887 and still retains its dome and checkerboard-patterned cladding stone. The apsidal end is flat; ornamentation is confined to *khatchkars* and inscriptions on the west facade, simple carvings over the windows, and blind niches on the north and south walls.

About 5km northeast and upstream from Ani via the village of Arazoğlu, just below the Arpa Çayı dam, the intriguing monastic complex of **Horomos** (sometimes Köşe Vank) huddles on a secluded terrace above the river; it's currently off-limits to tourists. Founded in the tenth century, Horomos comprises a church (complete with a delicate lantern over the dome), a *zhamatoun* or chapter house, and various Selçuk and Armenian mausoleums in a walled enclosure at the brink of the Arpa Çayı. Because of its tucked-away location, Horomos never got much press from nineteenth-century travellers compared to Ani, but locals who were able to visit before the checkpoints and mines went in say it runs a close second in interest to its neighbour – and is worth pestering the authorities over, to see if the no-access policy has changed.

Bagnair and Magazbert

These two monuments are both south of the 36-07 provincial road linking Kars with Ani. Just 6km before the ruins, there's a right-angle intersection at the edge of Esenkent village; go south onto the side-road and after 6km more turn right (west) towards the village of **Kozluca**, 2km further on. The two churches of Bagnair should be in plain sight. Incidentally, disregard all maps which show Bagnair by the village of Bulanık, about 15km northwest. Fork right at Kozluca's lowest buildings to proceed directly to the smaller church;

the other track leads to the larger structure, though it's easy enough to walk the 200m between them.

The larger monastic church at **Bagnair** (or Bagnayr) was founded between 1010 and 1012 by the Armenian prince Smbat, supplanting the smaller church, which had already existed here for some decades. The latter continued as a dependency of the new monastery, which vanished from history after the 1200s, though travellers reported the buildings largely intact until early in the twentieth century. Today the main *katholikon*, consisting of a shrine to the Mother of God abutting a *zhamatoun*, is two-thirds vanished; the *zhamatoun* retains a dome, fine stalactite vaulting in the ceiling, and several massive columns, and still dwarfs the church abutting it, of which only the west nave remains. Across the ravine, the **smaller church**, like its neighbour used as a hay-barn, has fared much better; its twelve-sided dome-drum crowns a hexagonal structure, with five internal apses and a west portal (difficult to reach through all the hay) in lieu of a sixth.

To reach the Armeno-Byzantine fortress of **Magazbert** (aliases Mağazbert, Magarsbert), return to the side road from Kozluca and drive 3km south to the turning east for the village of **Üçölük** – and in all probability a detachment of *jandarma* at the junction, who will quiz you as to what you're up to (a local escort is helpful here) and consult by walkie-talkie with their HQ. Assuming you get permission, head 1.3km towards the village – don't actually go to the central "roundabout" unless you want a guide – and find another track heading south from near the *jandarma* post; non-4WD cars must be left at a huge, suspension-destroying rut. The track descends into a mostly dry ravine draining to the Arpa Çayı, crossing to the far bank and giving a good view of Cappadocian-style fairy chimneys on the north flank on its progress (35min on foot) to the base of the fortress.

What impresses on approach are the three western bastions, like elephant's toes, fronting a long, narrow, internally desolate **castle** dominating a sharp S-bend in the frontier river – be sure to come in the late afternoon as they catch the sun's last rays. Originally erected during the late tenth or early eleventh century, the fortress was taken in 1579 by the Ottomans, who made some modifications around the gateway (commemorated by an inscription), but abandoned it within a few decades as part of a truce with the Persians.

From the *jandarma*-manned junction it's possible to continue about 20km more, via Âlem, to Digor.

Monuments around Digor

The two currently visitable churches covered below are even more architecturally and historically significant than those around Ani, but require fairly long walks to reach and together will occupy nearly a full day in themselves, even with your own transport. **Dıgor** (Tekor in Armenian), 40km southeast of Kars, is the closest large village but has few amenities other than fairly frequent dolmuşes to and from Kars.

Khtskonk

The closest monument to Digor is a dramatically set church at **Khtskonk** (Beşkilise), a few kilometres upstream along the Digor Çayı; ignore all maps, which erroneously show a "Chtskonk" northeast of the highway. If you don't want to walk a fairly taxing hour up the gorge from the village, have the bus set you down, or drive, 4.5km north of town along Highway 70, near the top of the pass. Leave the vehicle here and turn onto a rough dirt track veering southwest from the asphalt, heading some 600m towards the gorge of the Digor Çayı. Walk behind the white pumice quarry and uphill, west-northwest, for 200m and then turn left down a dry ravine. The path follows the right-hand bank downhill and then curves northwest to enter the gorge. Continue along the path, midway between the valley floor and clifftop above, for twenty minutes to reach the church (a total of 35–40min from your start point).

There were originally five churches (*beşkilise* in Turkish) perched at the Khtskonk monastic complex on the rim of the narrow canyon, but the rotunda of **St Sergius** (Sargis), founded in 1029, is the sole survivor. All five were restored in 1878, but at some time between 1920 and 1965 the other four were destroyed either by rolling boulders onto them or with explosives. St Sergius' side-walls are rent by fissures, but the dome is still intact and the west wall is covered in intricate Armenian inscriptions, making it the equal of any single monument at Ani.

Mren and Bagaran

From Digor, Highway 70 continues just under 45km to the intersection with Highway 80, passing the side roads for two important Armenian monuments. The only one currently accessible is the seventh-century Cathedral of Mren, a unique specimen even in a region rich in such art and well worth the long trip out.

Some 21km southeast of Digor, keep an eye peeled for a dirt road heading east, rustily signposted for the village of **Karabağ**; if you overshoot the turnoff, you'll know it, as the cathedral also shows clearly to the east from the main road, after about 10km further on. After 2km along the proper detour, Mren appears on the horizon beyond the village. Keeping the church in sight, drive through Karabağ, adopting the onward track between a sheet-roofed mosque and the livestock wallow-pond; about 700m beyond these – roughly 5km in total from the highway – non-4WD vehicles must be left at track-side, on a slope above the Digor Çayı. From here it's fifty minutes' walk east-southeast at an average pace to the church, which is bigger (and further away, at 4.5km) than it looks. The track first descends to the stream, which has both a jeep ford and narrow pedestrian bridge, and then curls up the far bank of the valley before dwindling on the far side as it crosses a volcanic plateau within sight of two military watch-points (whose occupants, if any, make no attempt to stop passers-by).

Once the focus of a fair-sized town, **Mren** (Mirini) stands atop a very slight rise on this desolate plateau, near the confluence of the Digor and Arpa streams, which both flow out of sight. The town was abandoned at some point in the fourteenth century amidst İlhanid Mongol raids, but its rubble still litters the immediate surroundings. The cathedral itself was completed in 639–640 by David Saharuni, Prince of Armenia, and as one of the earliest examples of Armenian architecture it exhibits a marked Byzantine influence with its elongated cross-in-square, three-aisled ground plan and octagonal dome supported by four pillars. The structure, built of alternating red and dark basalt blocks, weathered the centuries remarkably well before 1920 – the dome still retains most of its tiles – though the southwest corner and south transept vault have collapsed since then. A fissure is threatening to detach the north wall and the floor has been completely dug up by treasure-hunters.

The most outstanding **decorative features** include numerous, extravagant *khatchkars* on the inner and outer south wall; the outer apse and north wall are by contrast featureless except for a somewhat defaced lintel relief over the north door, showing the *Restoration of the Cross* at Jerusalem in 630, following its removal by the Persians in 614. The Byzantine empereror Heraklios, on the left, walks from his horse towards a young man steadying the Holy Rood,

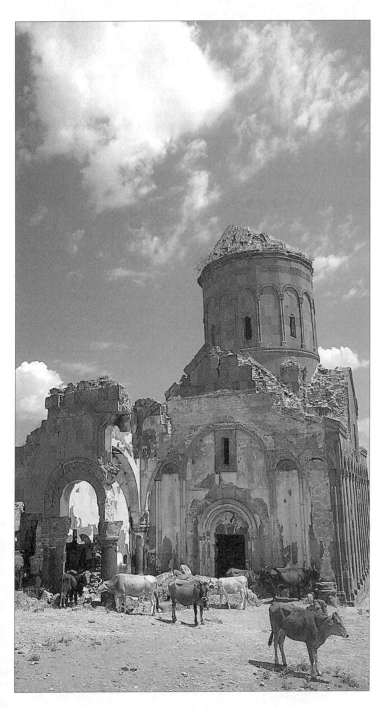

while to the right stands Modestos, Bishop of Jerusalem, and a Tree of Life. Much clearer is the relief over the west door: here two angels hover above Christ (centre), St Peter and St Paul, in turn flanked by the donors of the church – Sarahuni and the bishop Theophilos (right), and the clean-shaven princeling Nerses Kamsarakan (left). This kind of relief ornamentation continued to be used in the Caucausus long after it passed from favour in Byzantium.

The ninth-century Bagratid citadel-town of **Bagaran** (or Pakran) incorporates an earlier seventh-century square four-apsed cathedral, but unless Armeno-Turkish relations improve dramatically, the site will remain off-limits. The adjacent modern village is Kilittaşı, to which an unmarked side-turning 5.5km south of the Karabağ access road leads after a like distance to a road-block manned by *jandarma* – who will curtly send you back the way you came, so don't bother trying.

Çengilli and Keçivan Kalesi

Just south of the confluence of the Aras and Arpa rivers, right on the Armenian border, Highway 70 joins Highway 80 – the latter leading south to Tuzluca and Iğdır (see below), or west to Kağızman. Just below Kağızman – which is 4km uphill off the main highway – a bridge over the Aras carries Highway 965 north back towards Kars. Some 800m past this bridge, the first dirt road to the left (west) follows a rutted, jeep-only 25-kilometre route up into the mountains, through three timeless villages, to finally arrive at **ÇENGİLLİ**, home to an anomalous thirteenth-century **Georgian monastery**. Not only was the contemporary population of the area largely Armenian, but the architecture apes the tenth- and eleventh-century styles of Georgian specimens further north – specifically Tbeti (see p.862). Unlike Tbeti, the enormous church here has survived fairly intact to this day. Public transport from Kağızman is limited to a single daily minibus, departing from the main square at about 3.45pm – enforcing an overnight stay in primitive Çengilli.

From the Kağızman bridge, Highway 80 scenically follows the Aras west and upstream as far as Karakurt on the Erzurum–Kars road. It's a colourful journey in an often otherwise drab area, where the green and blonde of hay-fields and apricot orchards contrast with the tones of the volcanic rock comprising the valley flank. In the relatively tidy riverside villages, satellite dishes jab the skyline along with poplars and pyramids of hay or dung.

Returning north from the Kağızman bridge towards Kars via Kötek, after about 20km a choice of side-roads lead west towards **Keçivan Kalesi** (Geçvan in Armenian). Access is either via Ortaköy, 3.5km off the asphalt, with a subsequent hour-and-a-half's walk, or by a rough twelve-kilometre drive, the first 5km to Oluklu and then 7km southwest from there. The castle's western ramparts and gates are in fair condition, though little else remains of the third-century Armenian fortified town sacked by the Persians after a year's siege. Back on the main road, the route back to Kars crosses the **Paslı pass** (2020m) and the ensuing plateau, before dropping back into the valley of the Kars Çayı.

Tuzluca to Iğdır

Frequent buses from Kars to Iğdır follow the Digor–Tuzluca–Iğdır route, with the Digor Çayı or the Aras River for company much of the way; at Iğdır you must change vehicles to reach Doğubeyazit.

TUZLUCA itself, 8km south of the Highway 80/70 junction, is a pretty dire place, notable only for some salt-bearing caves in the bluff immediately east; apparently the stuff is still mined, and you can see white streaks where it's leaching out of the rock. If you've visited Mren cathedral you might schedule a lunch-stop here, but neither of the main-drag **restaurants** (the *Turistik* and the *Hayat*) is particularly recommendable, and you'll do much better in Iğdır.

Beyond Tuzluca, the road skirts the Armenian frontier (if not quite so closely as near Bagaran), with watchtowers plainly visible to the north, before dropping sharply into a basin only 850m in elevation. The more temperate climate here permits the cultivation of rice, cotton, and grapes; the inhabitants are mostly **Azeri Shi'ites**, resettled here during the nineteenth century. They used to – and may still – indulge in a bizarre rite during the first ten days of the Islamic holy month of Muharrem, in which frenzied worshippers flagellated themselves to bloodiness.

Should you need to break the journey to Doğubeyazit, **IĞDIR** – a pleasant though unremarkable provincial capital at the southern corner of the valley – would be the place to do so. There are a handful of decent **hotels**, including the two-star *Azer* off Atatürk Caddesi at Cırcır Mevkii 13/15 (☎0476/227 7190, ℱ227 9753; ❷), with an attached restaurant, and the slightly more comfortable two-star *Parlar*, İrfan Cad 14, Söğütlü Mahallesi (☎0476/227 7199, ℱ227 6451; ❷). The best **eating** in the area is at the western edge of town, at the *Ağırkaya Petrol Dinleme Tesisleri* – filling stations in eastern Turkey aren't generally the best source of *haute cuisine*, but this one whips up patently fresh, traditional fare, served in a lush orchard-garden.

North from Kars: Çıldır Gölü and Ardahan

From Kars most travellers will want to move northwest towards Ardahan and Artvin without making the lengthy detour through Erzurum. There are basically three routes to consider: first via **Çıldır Gölü** and Şeytan Kalesi to Ardahan and then Şavşat; second via Susuz to Ardahan and Şavşat; third via Göle to Ardahan. The first, most northeasterly route is the scenically superior but it's difficult without your own vehicle: minibus services to **Ardahan** short-cut via the dull Susuz–Hasköy route, and while the Göle route is initially enlivened by picturesque little Aygır Gölü, the Göle–Ardhan road is a narrow, dug-up mess and likely to remain so until 2005. Two **dolmuşes** a day run from Kars to Çıldır town, but only one morning minibus connects Çıldır to Ardahan, 47km further west.

Çıldır Gölü

The slate-like expanse of **Çıldır Gölü**, nearly 2000m up, is the primary source of the Arpa Çayı/Ahuryan River, and the highest sizable lake in Turkey; only during the summer – when hay and grain are growing by the shore – is there a hint of colour. Men on horseback, wielding scythes, rakes and other farming implements, canter splendidly across the steppe against the backdrop of 3197-metre Kısır Dağı, but their families live like moles, with houses burrowed even deeper than the norm for this province. The shallow lake itself is frozen over for six months of the year, but it's an important **bird habitat** during the warmer months, when handsome falcons and hawks swoop over your vehicle, while migrating waterfowl include pelicans and more mundane gulls.

This region was an extension of medieval Georgia rather than Armenia, and most of the decidedly minor local monuments are of recent vintage compared to those at Ani. At **DOĞRUYOL** (Djala in Georgian), the only substantial town on the lake's eastern shore, the thirteenth-century hilltop church masqueraded until recently as a mosque; there are other eleventh-to-thirteenth-century churches on the lake's southwest shore at the villages of **GÜLYÜZÜ** (Pekreşin; badly ruined) and **GÖLBELEN** (Urta; in a better state, still used as a mosque). A few kilometres beyond Doğruyol, the islet of **Akçekale** (Argenkale) is crisscrossed by crumbled walls and linked to the semi-fortified village opposite by a causeway. There is also a fragmentary eleventh-to-fourteenth chapel on the far end of the islet, above the football pitch and last streetlights, with only the northwest walls and part of the apse surviving; of uncertain date is the crudely built fortification tower on the point to the south, opposite some islets. With its birds, fishing boats and changeable weather the lake here bears an uncanny resemblance to a Scottish highland loch.

The town of **ÇILDIR** is an unprepossessing place north of the lake, out of sight of the water; the single commercial street is hard-pressed to muster a proper restaurant, and the only grubby "hotel" is best left unpatronized. Çıldır serves as the theoretical jumping-off point for **Şeytan Kalesi** (Satan's Castle), but local taxis are pricey and it's more usually visited on a group tour from Kars, which takes in the lake as well. Perched on a precipitous bend of the Başköy gorge, the castle lies a thirty-minute walk downstream from Yıldırımtepe village, itself 3.5km northwest of Çıldır: 2km on the highway, then 1.5km north on an unmarked but obvious dirt road. A path winds into the gorge from just above the village and leads up to the brooding medieval keep and watchtower.

Ardahan

From Çıldır town you've a fairly bleak stretch west to **ARDAHAN**, one of the smallest Turkish provincial capitals, faintly reminiscent of Kars with its Russian grid-plan and fin-de-siècle architecture – and a pervasive military presence. There's nothing in particular to see in Ardahan except a fine old **bridge** over the Kura River, just opposite the massive **citadel**, originally Georgian but restored by Selim the Grim early in the sixteenth century. It's still an army camp, so no photography is allowed.

From town, regular buses run to Erzurum and Yusufeli, departing from the **otogar** near the citadel; for Kars or Çıldır you'll have to seek out the **dolmuş depot** in the centre. Ardahan has around ten **hotels**, but the more basic among these may be occupied by prostitutes, who cross the Georgian border beyond nearby Posof. Preferable are the *Belediye Turistik Otel* (☎0478/211 6506; ❷), right in the centre, with off-street parking but well-worn rooms, or the 1999-built *Büyük Klas* or "Grand Class" at Atatürk Cad 23, the onward Şavşat road (☎0478/211 3458, ℗211 5426; ❷). Here, the spartan rooms with small baths belie three (self-awarded) stars, and there's little "class" apparent in the bizarre management. There appears to be only one full-service **restaurant** in town, the unlicensed *Karadeniz* at no. 47, on the east side of the main commercial street, but luckily it's pretty good, with $2 fetching you an *İzmir köfte* and an *aşure*; only *sulu yemek* is offer at lunchtime, while grills predominate by night.

The route northwest out of Ardahan leads through a vast plateau of hayfields and huge mossy boulders, as you begin the climb up to the **Çam pass** (*Çamlıbel* in Turkish; 2640m), northeastern gateway to the Georgian valleys.

North from Erzurum: the southern Georgian valleys

Highway 950 heads north out of Erzurum across the steppe, aiming for a nearly imperceptible gap, too trivial to call a pass, in the surrounding mountains. Almost without noticing it you're across the watershed, and as you begin a slow descent the landscape becomes more interesting, with the Tortum Çayı alongside and trees appearing for the first time in a long while. Most buses bypass the nondescript town of Tortum, 57km from Erzurum; 15km beyond here, a pair of **castles** to left and right, crumbling away atop well-nigh inaccessible pinnacles, announce more effectively than any signpost that you've now reached the southern limits of **medieval Georgia** (see box on p.846).

Bağbaşı and the church of Haho

Twenty-six kilometres north of Tortum, turn off to the west over the Taş Köprü humpback bridge, obeying signposting for "Taş Camii, Meryemana Kilisesi", keep left in the first large village you come to, then take another left towards İspir, a few minutes later by a modern mosque. Finally, take a right at the next, well-marked junction; it's 8km in total from Highway 950 to the main square of **BAĞBAŞI**, a large community dispersed in a fertile valley. Two minibuses a day make the trip from the Gölbaşı Semt Garajı in Erzurum out to the village, but that's a lot of to-ing and fro-ing just to see Bağbaşı's only sight. Beyond the streamside square – really just a handful of minibuses loitering by a widening in the road, with shops, teahouses and the *Belediye* opposite – bear left 200m past the football pitch, and after another 500m you will find, hidden behind some ablution toilets to the right, the dome of the late tenth-century **church of Haho** (Khakhuli).

This is the first of several institutions that were constructed by David Magistros (the Great), ruler of Tao between 961 and 100. For once, most of the monastery complex – the boundary wall and gate, and three satellite chapels – is in good condition, the effect spoiled only by aluminium corrugated sheets on the roof, though the conical-topped dome is still covered in multicoloured tiles. Over the south transept windows, a vigilant stone eagle grasps a doe in his claws, before a fan of alternating light and dark masonry.

An arcaded, barrel-vaulted narthex on the west side of the nave still exists (you gain entry by crawling in a window), but the doors to the nave have been blocked off. Entry to the church proper is now through a gallery on the south, a skilful addition of the thirteenth century that appears at first glance to be part of the original building. On either side of the old south entrance, now inside the **gallery**, there's a lion and a chimera in relief; on the right a whale that looks suspiciously like a dog devours Jonah, while below struts a cock (presumably the one of obstinate Pride, such as Jonah's). Inside, a small but well-executed swathe of frescoed angels and apostles set on a blue background hovers over what was once the apse.

Haho's excellent state of repair is owed to its continual use as a mosque since the eighteenth century. Entry is only possible on Friday around prayer time, or by tracking down the key-keeper in the village. After your visit, sign the "guest register" and make a donation.

Öşk Vank

Downstream from the Haho turning, the Tortum valley widens appreciably. The side road to the monastery church of **Öşk Vank** (Oshkhi), 15.4km from the Haho turning and just before Tortum lake, is prominently marked with a white-on-brown archeological-site sign. It's an easy, mostly paved 7.2km straight run up to **Çamlıyamaç** village, but the church, with houses built up to the very walls, seems initially the least evocative of all in the area. Given the good road in, this is also the one Georgian monument that's the target of coach tours – though a small teahouse near the south door sees little trade in these depressed times.

None of this should deter you, since Öşk Vank is the most elaborate example of Georgian Gothic in these valleys. Another late tenth-century foundation of David Magistros, it represents the culmination of Tao Georgian culture before the Bagratid dynasty's move northeast and the start of the Georgian "Golden Age" after 1125.

A protruding porch shelters the main entry through the **facade** of the south transept; blind arcades, topped by scallop-shell carving, flank it, with reliefs of the archangels hovering high overhead. Alternatively, you are able to enter from the southwest corner of the building, through a triple-arched **narthex** with an engaging zigzag roofline. The interior colonnade – with no two columns alike – exudes a European Gothic feel with its barrel-vaulted, coffered ceiling; the most westerly column capital sports sculpted angels. The roof over the nave, elongated to the west, has fallen in, leaving the dome stranded atop four essential **pillars**, two of which have their massive bases intricately worked in sinuous geometric designs. Halfway up the south transept wall, the vanished wooden floor of the mosque that once occupied the premises acted as protection for a stretch of **frescoes**, the best preserved in any of the Turkish Georgian churches. Bracketing half a dozen ethereal saints in hieratic poses are a vivid scene to the north, possibly from the Life of Christ, and on the south a model of the church, with its presumed congregation assembled outside.

Tortum Gölü and falls

A little way past the turnoff for Öşk Vank lies the inlet end of **Tortum Gölü**, a substantial body of water, roughly 10km long by 1km wide, that forces the road up onto a corniche bypass above the western shore. The water is by turns muddy green, milky beige and dull slate even on a bright day, so a swim doesn't necessarily appeal, though the locals try from the stone beach below the village of Balıklı, or from the relatively secluded far end of the little peninsula 8km north of the Öşk Vank side-road. Here, too, is by far the best **lunch** option while touring the churches: the İskele *Alabalık Tesisleri*, simple but salubrious, serving salad, trout and nothing else – three small fish make a tasty meal for about $4, and the restaurant may also have rowboats to rent.

The lake was formed by a landslide blocking the north end of the valley between two and three centuries ago. The famous *şelale* or **falls of Tortum** are today its natural outlet, accessible by a signposted side road 12km north of the Öşk Vank turning. TEK, the Turkish Electric Foundation, has supplemented the natural dam with an artifical one and a turbine; you leave the asphalted highway where you see the power plant, and then proceed as indicated by a "Tortum Şelalesi" sign for just over a kilometre, until glimpsing a vast rock ledge with its 48-metre cascade on your left. You'll have to scramble down a path to the left to get a good look, and you won't see much except in spring, since during the summer the TEK diverts most available water for power generation later. Below the falls the valley narrows to an impressive canyon as the various arms of the Kara, Aksek and Dutlu ranges start to tighten their embrace.

İşhan

Fifteen kilometres below the falls there's an important intersection in the steadily descending highway; continuing straight ahead will lead you to Yusufeli (see p.849). Bearing right instead towards Olur, you reach, after 6km, an archeological-service sign pointing to **İŞHAN** (Ishani), a bluff-top oasis village 5.7km up a partly paved road; the crumpled hills of a heavily eroded, lifeless moonscape contrast sharply with the apple, mulberry and walnut groves in the village. At the central two-spouted fountain and teahouse-with-satellite-dish, bear left and down on a 300-metre track, passing some attractive vernacular houses to arrive at the environs of the sanctuary, where there's ample parking and another fountain.

Georgians have lived in the valleys of the Çoruh, Tortum, Kura and Berta rivers, now in Turkey, since the Bronze Age. Like the neighbouring Armenians, they were among the first Near Eastern nations to be evangelized, and were converted rapidly to Christianity by St Nino of Cappadocia in the mid-fourth century. Unlike the Armenians, they never broke with the Orthodox Patriarchate in Constantinople, and maintained good relations with Byzantium.

The Georgian kingdoms

An effective Georgian state only entered the local stage early in the ninth century, under the auspices of the **Bagratid** dynasty. This clan contributed rulers to both the Georgian and Armenian lines, and hence the medieval history of both kingdoms overlapped to some extent. They claimed direct descent from David and Bathsheba, which explains a preponderance of kings named David, a coat of arms laden with Old Testament symbols and curiously Judaic stars of David embossed on many of the churches they built.

Feudal Bagratid lords initially emerged in the nominally Byzantine-ruled districts of Tao (centred around today's İspir, Yusufeli and Oltu) and Klarjeti (Ardanuç and Ardahan), from where **Ashot I Kuropalates** began the first stages of territorial aggrandizement at the expense of Byzantium and the Arab Caliphate – and the initial wave of church-building in the area, under the guidance of the monk **Gregory Khantzeli**. Ashot's descendants included **David Magistros ("the Great")** of Oltu, a late tenth-century ruler responsible for several of the churches described on these pages, and Bagrat III, who in 1008 succeeded in unifying the various Georgian principalities into one kingdom with a capital at Kutaisi.

A decade or so later the Byzantines compelled Bagrat's successor, Georgi I, to evacuate Tao and Klarjeti, making it an easy matter for the Selçuks to step in during 1064. They ravaged Georgia and all of eastern Anatolia, but as soon as they turned to confront the crusaders a Bagratid revival began. **David the Restorer** not only managed by 1125 to expel the Selçuks, but moved the Bagratid court to newly captured Tblisi, and reunited the various feuding principalities ruled by minor Bagratid warlords.

Under the rule of David's great-granddaughter **Tamara**, medieval Georgia acquired its greatest extent and prestige, controlling most of modern Georgia, Armenia and Azerbaijan from the Black Sea to the Caspian, as well as the ancestral Georgian valleys. The queen was not only a formidable military strategist and shrewd diplomat, but displayed a humanity and tolerance in her domestic administration unusual for the era. Many churches and monasteries were repaired or re-endowed by Tamara, and despite being a woman and a non-Muslim, her name still elicits respectful compliments and even a proprietary pride in the now-Turkish valleys of southern Georgia.

Following Tamara's death the Georgian kingdom began a slow but steady decline, precipitated by Mongol and Persian raids in the mid-thirteenth century but most of all by Tamerlane's apocalypse early in the 1400s. Tamara's Georgia was effectively partitioned between the Ottoman and Persian empires, and although Bagratids continued to occupy thrones in Tblisi, they were essentially puppets. The

---

The imposing **church**, originally dedicated to the Virgin, was constructed in stages between the eighth and eleventh centuries, ranking it among the oldest extant sacred Georgian architecture. The semicircular colonnade lining the apse, with superb carved capitals, is the earliest surviving portion of the building, and was modelled consciously after the church at Bana (see p.848); great chunks of the roof are now missing, meaning that the 42-metre-high dome, rise of imperial Russia was a mixed blessing: while it prevented further Muslim encroachment, it signalled the end of any viable Georgian state, and the last semi-independent king effectively surrendered what was left of his autonomy to Catherine the Great in 1783.

Georgian monuments

Tangible evidence of the Georgian heyday is still abundant in the northeastern parts of Turkey, not least in the common prefix "Ar-" (as in Ardahan, Artvin, Ardanuç and so forth), equivalent to "-ville" or to "-burg".

The Bagratids were a prolific bunch, and their princelings stuck **castles** on just about every height; generally a passing glance is what you'll have to be satisfied with, since access to many of these eyries has long been impossible except for technical climbers. Most remarkable, however, are the early Bagratid monastic **churches**, all dating from before the move northeast to the Caucasus proper, and most sited amid oases at the heads of remote valleys. As a rule, the core conventions of Armenian religious architecture – domes supported on four freestanding columns, a cruciform east–west ground plan with prominent transepts, blind exterior arcades and intricate relief work – were borrowed wholesale, and it takes a trained eye to distinguish the two styles, though in general the Georgians rarely attempted the rotundas or multi-lobed domed squares beloved of the Armenians. Georgian building has, however, been pinpointed as one of the major vehicles by which church architecture was transported to Russia, and together with Armenian structures directly spawned the Romanesque and early Gothic churches of western Europe.

There's not been nearly the degree of official stonewalling about Georgian Christians as there is concerning Armenians, and the churches have become recognized as tourist attractions. We've only detailed the most intact examples; there are numerous unsung others, slowly collapsing in isolated settings, that villagers will be happy to show you. Virtually every church has suffered some damage from dynamite- and pickaxe-wielding **treasure-hunters**: the locals have an unshakeable conviction that all of the Christians who left the area in 1923 or before secreted precious items in or under their churches before departure in the mistaken belief that they'd eventually be able to return.

You'll need your own vehicle, or a lot of time for walking and hitching, to visit most of the sites. There's usually a small village nearby, or even surrounding the monument, but invariably **bus services**, where they exist, arrive in the afternoon and depart for the nearest town in the morning – exactly the opposite of tourist schedules. Some of the roads are bad, but if you can assemble a group and find a **taxi** driver willing to risk his undercarriage, this can end up being far cheaper than renting a vehicle in Erzurum or Trabzon. Even with a car or taxi **three days** will be required to see all of the monuments detailed in this text; for example, a loop south out of Artvin, taking in Öşk Vank, Haho, Bana and İşhan is only really possible with an early start during the long days of May to July, and judicious use of the short-cutting Highway 25-03 from Highway 950 to Oltu.

built in a similar fashion to Öşk Vank's, rests in isolation on four columns. The acoustics, however, remain superb, as you can hear for yourself if you stand directly beneath the dome. There are some patches of fresco to be seen high up on the surviving walls of the south transept, portraying portions of the *Vision of Zacharias*, and in the cupola, there's an abstract cross from the Iconoclastic era. The external eleventh-century **relief work** is far more interesting, though, particularly on the small baptistry with its bestiary and semicircular inscription commemorating King Bagrat III (ruled 1000–1014), opposite a bricked-up southern portal where a lion and snake are locked in combat above an upper window to the right. Sadly, however, the church in general was much tampered with as part of its conversion during its decades as a mosque, particularly on the northwest corner – defaced with ill-advised masonry – and in the nave, completely blocked by a modern wall.

Oltu and Bana

A detour from Tortum via Narman and Oltu on Highway 965 is time well spent, especially if you have your own vehicle. Invariably dismissed in other sources, this alternate approach to İşhan and Yusufeli compares well to similar landscapes in Afghanistan and the American Southwest. Stands of poplars and green fields are juxtaposed against a cobalt sky and reddish bluffs, often crowned with crumbling Georgian castles. If you're travelling on a day-circuit out of Artvin, similar scenery (and 22km less driving) can be enjoyed on Highway 25-03, linking Sevenyurt with Oltu and far better than depicted on touring maps.

Oltu

Beside the river at **OLTU** stands the first of the citadels – well restored by the Ottomans and again in 2002. A further 18km north brings you to the junction with Highway 80; continue left for 4km to the confluence of valleys as the Penek Çayı joins the Narman Suyu to become the Black-Sea-bound Oltu Çayı. Here on either side of the strategic Y-fork rise two castles – one backed into the cliff, the other freestanding and flanked by a small church. Continuing towards İşhan takes you past yet another redoubt, atop a rock spur by the minor road to Olur.

Bana

Bearing right (east) instead onto Highway 80 leads towards Göle and Kars; 28km beyond Oltu (or 37km southwest of Göle) you'll see, just before the river valley narrows drastically, the seventh-century Armenian **church of Bana** on the north bank of the Penek (Irlağaç) Çayı. Its original name is "Banak", which lives on in the Turkified village name of Penek. To actually get to Bana, carry on 4km further east from your first glimpse of it – 14.5km in total from the junction – to take the side track that hairpins off left just before the gorge, just past where the main road crosses the river. Continue through the village of **Penek**, branching left after 2.8km to approach the church – in sight much of the way – from the northeast; depending on ruts and mud an ordinary car can drive with care almost up to Bana.

Perched on a knoll surveying water-meadows, and dominated in turn by tawny crags, the church enjoys a commanding position. A century after local Christians abandoned it, the Ottomans accordingly fortified Bana during the Crimean War, adding the crude bulwark still visible on the south side. The Russians blasted the upper levels off during the 1877–1878 war, and later carted away much of the masonry to build a turn-of-the-nineteenth-century church in Oltu.

What remains – the first floor of an originally three-storeyed, vast rotunda half-submerged in its own ruins – is still impressive. The original plan was identical to (and of the same vintage as) the massive rotunda at Zvartnots in eastern Armenia – hardly surprising, since the two had the same builder, the

Katholikos (Bishop) Narses I, who built this church during a six-year (653–658) local exile. The east apse retains a colonnade virtually identical to the later one at İşhan, with an equally generous ambulatory behind, though only one column survives with its carved capital.

The western Georgian valleys

The area around the confluence of the **Barhal and Çoruh rivers** is scenically and climatically one of the most favoured corners of the northeast. During the balmy summers, every sort of fruit ripens and you're treated to the incongruous spectacle of rice paddies (and further downstream, olive groves) by the Çoruh, within sight of parched cliffs overhead. Functional **Yusufeli** is gateway to these river valleys, which in their lower reaches can offer **Georgian churches** near **Tekkale** and **Barhal**, plus trekkers' trailheads higher up at **Hevek** and **Meretet**, as well as Barhal.

The rivers themselves are a magnet for visitors, making Yusufeli a popular base for **whitewater rafters** finishing the challenging runs from İspir or Barhal upstream. Highest water is between early May and late June, when the overseas adventure companies (listed in the "Getting there" section of Basics) run their trips, but there is always at least one local outfitter arranging days out on the spot from May to September. Downstream runs towards Artvin are pretty much a thing of the past, killed off by the growing number of hydroelectric projects on the Çoruh.

General tourism has never really taken off in the area, and the stark simplicity of local facilities will appeal mostly to the hardier breed of traveller. Even if you're not an outdoor sports enthusiast, you'll need a steady hand at the wheel – or a strong stomach if you're a minibus passenger – for the often bumpy, steep rides out to the local Georgian churches.

Yusufeli

Straddling the Barhal Çayı just above its junction with the Çoruh, **YUSUFELİ** is a gritty, rather time-warped town living under a death sentence; if funds ever permit construction, it will disappear under the waters of the highest Çoruh dam, and accordingly nothing new has been built here since the 1970s. Yusufeli constitutes a fairly conservative and devout anomaly in the secular, relatively progressive, province of Artvin, a situation partly explained by the fact that a high proportion of the inhabitants are descended from Bulgarian Muslim settlers of the 1890s. Traveller opinion on the place is sharply divided: some can't wait to see the back of it, hitching out at dusk to avoid staying the night, while others, en route to or from the Kaçkar mountains, end up spending a few nights here and make a day-trip up one of the nearby river valleys.

Arrival, onward transport, and services

If you're unable to get a direct **bus** service to Yusufeli from Erzurum, ask to be set down at Su Kavuşumu junction, 10km below the town centre. The last Artvin–Yusufeli bus doesn't roll past the turnoff until about 4pm, but if you've missed it, or your heart is set on being in Barhal that evening (see below for onward schedules), **taxi** shuttles up to Yusufeli from the junction are available for about $6 per car. Heading in the other direction, the junction is also a good place to pick up transport to Ardahan and Kars, and the aforementioned sights along the way.

Yusufeli marks the start of **dolmuş routes** to various villages further upriver, including Barhal and Hevek. Service to these two high settlements is available daily all year, since both are inhabited in winter, but adheres to a somewhat informal schedule. The four Barhal vehicles leave Yusufeli from the **otogar** or the main road outside the *Çiçek Palas Oteli* between 2 and 5pm, the first and last departures going all the way to Hevek. In theory all are linked to the arrival of afternoon buses from Artvin.

The most active **rafting** outlet in Yusufeli is Antalya Rafting (☏0466/811 2393, ⓦwww.antalyarafting.com), with offices under the *Çiçek Palas Oteli*. They offer five-hour outings from an appropriate point upstream: an hour for the land transfer, an hour's lunch break, and three hours actually on the water. Rates begin at a whopping $120 for two people, though outside peak season prices drop by half.

Three **banks** (with ATMs), a **PTT** and **shops** with basic trekking staples round out the list of essential services. For trekking in the Kaçkar mountains (see p.855), local **guides** Sirali Aydın (☏0466/811 3893, ⓔsirraft@hotmail.com) and Özkan Şahin (c/o *Çiçek Palas Oteli*) rent equipment and arrange expeditions.

Accommodation

The rather basic style of **accommodation** does nothing to encourage lingering, and few can be recommended with much enthusiasm; hot water, for instance, is rarely reliable anywhere in Yusufeli. **Hotels** are all grouped within 200m of each other, and when business is slack – generally the case except during May and June – it may be possible to get a three- or four-bed room for the same price as a double. Best of the lot is probably the *Barhal Hotel* (☏0466/811 3151; ❶), near the pedestrian suspension bridge, with small, cleanish, en-suite rooms, though attempted overcharging here is common. Alternatively, try the *Çiçek Palas Oteli* (☏0466/811 2102; ❶) at Halitpaşa Cad 8/A, with shared showers.

Of the two **campsites** about 700m upstream from the foot bridge, on the far side of the river, the leafier, remoter *Greenpeace* (☏0466 8112271; $2.50 per person) is to be preferred, having double rooms (❶) and an attached restaurant with riverside seating.

Eating and drinking

The *Çınar Restoran* under the *Barhal Hotel*, with a terrace overhanging the river, offers the highest-drawer **eating** in town – strictly *meze*s and grills; three can eat well with a beer apiece for $12. Runner-up is the *Mavi Köşk*, just off İnönü Caddesi (the main drag), opposite Halkbank. Just downstream from the *Çınar* on the opposite bank, the *Mahzen Fıçı Bira* used to offer worthy competition, but of late there's a rather belligerent atmosphere here as its trade in draught beer has eclipsed any food offerings. During springtime all three places are likely to be packed out by rowdy, carousing rafters unless you arrive early in the evening.

Tekkale and its churches

Sleepy **TEKKALE** lies 7km southwest of Yusufeli on the same bank of the Çoruh, connected by dolmuşes heading to either Kılıçkaya or the remoter Köprügören, 27km further upriver and the last point served by public transport. The road to Tekkale passes two ruined chapels (one perched above the Çoruh in Yusufeli town, the second on the far side of the river 2km upstream) and a vertiginous castle guarding the valley road, before curving the last 2km into the village.

The only **accommodation** is at Cemil Albayrak's *Dört Kilise Resting Camp,* aka *Cemil's Pansiyon* (℡0466/811 2908, ℻811 2105; $10 half-board per person), with a choice of simple doubles downstairs or sleeping-bag space on the wooden terrace; there's a single communal hot shower, pitches for tents, and a tank full of trout. Unlike many other backpacker havens it's fairly pleasant, without being a "scene", attracting a widely varied clientele; Cemil may play his *saz* for you after nightfall, and also offers useful sketch maps and guiding services for an unusual trekking approach to the Kaçkars (see p.855).

Dörtkilise and Bayırkilise

From Tekkale, just a few paces upstream from *Cemil's Pansiyon*, a dirt side road heading uphill and away from the Çoruh allows you to walk or drive the 6.3km further to **Dörtkilise** (Otkhta Eklesia; the road sign says "7"). En route, ignore the first two bridges spanning the stream to the right, and find the church a bit uphill to the left on a grassy hillside at 1140m, just beyond the third bridge over a tributary. Despite the name – meaning "Four Churches" – only one is found intact, but it's very fine and unlike most other Georgian places of worship. Domeless, with a steep gabled roof and relatively plain exterior, Dörtkilise is a twin of the church at nearby Barhal, though built several decades earlier and later renovated by David Magistros. Since the closest *yayla* is about 3km away, Dörtkilise was never reconsecrated as a mosque, and is now home only to bats, swallows and occasionally livestock. Inside, a double line of four columns supports the barrel ceiling hiding under the pitched roof; some traces of fresco persist in the apse, while an unusual choir takes up much of the west end. The large half-ruined building to the northeast, arcaded and double-vaulted, was the monastery refectory, joined to the main body of the church by an equally decrepit gallery that served as a narthex.

The adventurous – equipped with anti-bug juice – can continue west on foot to the remote chapel of **Bayırkilise** (elevation 1680m); it's a tough ascent, with a proper path for only about two-thirds of the way. The route begins at a jeep "ramp" and culvert by a power pylon, 150m north of Dörtkilise; an initially broad path dwindles as it climbs, changing banks of the adjacent stream and fizzling out completely about 45 minutes along, just after re-crossing the stream. Thereafter you face an increasingly steep, trackless half-hour scramble on unstable surface, though the church – outrageously perched on a seemingly inaccessible pinnacle rearing above the canyon – is in distant view just long enough to give you bearings. In fair-to-middling condition, Bayırkilise has a gabled roof like its lower neighbour, with a single barrel vault and traces of frescoes inside; the views, and the sense of accomplishment in arriving, are the main rewards. The downhill return takes just under an hour, for a two-hour-plus round trip; Cemil's sketch map traces the route more or less correctly.

Barhal

The most popular route out of Yusufeli follows the valley of the Barhal Çayı north through a landscape straight out of a Romantic engraving, complete with ruined Georgian castles on assorted crags overlooking the raging river. After 18km of one-lane asphalt, the road surfaces changes to dirt at river-straddling Sarıgöl; **BARHAL** (1300m), officially renamed Altıparmak after the mountains behind, is reached 11km beyond, an-hour-and-a-half's drive in total from Yusufeli.

With its scattered wooden buildings peeking out from lush pre-alpine vegetation, Barhal conforms well to most people's notions of a mountain village.

There are several **accommodation** options, for which advance booking is strongly advisable in July or August. Mehmet Karahan's *Karahan Pansiyon* (☎0446/826 2071 or 212 1800; $14 per person half-board), 1.2km out of the centre on the Altıparmak-bound turning and then uphill, is the most characterful: choose between treehouse-type double chalets or mattresses on the airy terrace-dorm. The roadside *Barhal Pansiyon* (☎0466/826 2031; ❶) by the dolmuş stop is an acceptable alternative, one of the first establishments encountered on the right as you enter Barhal. Just uphill and slightly more comfortable are the clean double/triple/quad rooms (sharing bathrooms) of Ahmet Pehlivan's three-storey *Marsis Village House* (☎0466/826 2026; $10 per person, $14 half board). A *teleferik* winch hoists your bags up the slope from the roadside; suppers are large but strictly vegetarian, with beer available. You'll wake early here, as every footfall reverberates from the upper floors to the lower ones. Village facilities are completed by a **bakery**, well-stocked **shop** and well-attended **teahouse**.

Barhal church

The tenth-century **church of Barhal** (Parkhali), the final legacy of David Magistros, is a twenty-minute walk up the secondary track toward the Altıparmak mountains (not the main one headed towards Hevek and the central Kaçkar); follow signs for the path to the *Karahan Pansiyon*, which climbs a lushly vegetated slope. Set in a hillside pasture next to the *mahalle's* school, it's virtually identical to Dörtkilise, except for being somewhat smaller – and in near-perfect condition owing to long use as the village mosque. It's now only used for Friday prayers, but it's worth securing admission (try the school for keys) to appreciate the sense of soaring height in the barrel-vaulted nave – and the debt European Gothic owed to Georgian and Armenian architects. The interior is now bare and whitewashed, but frescoes may be hiding underneath; painted grafitti in Georgian along the exterior roofline dates only from the nineteenth century and supposedly contains an admiring reference to the local mountains.

Hevek

HEVEK (Yaylalar) lies another hour-and-a-half's drive from Barhal along a scenic 21-kilometre dirt road. At over 2000m, this fairly substantial if remote village has one place to stay – the 25-bed *Altunay Pansiyon* (☎0466/832 2001 or 832 2087, ✉ismail@kackar3937.com; $6 room only, $12 per person half-board), with brightly coloured, traditionally decorated double, triple and quad rooms; there's also an overflow annexe, cooking facilities, a washing machine and two hot showers. Genial manager İsmail also runs a large food shop and the village **bakery** downstairs, hires out mules for $25 per day and generally arranges **trekking expeditions** (more information on ⓦwww.kackar3937.com). Architecturally the village varies from new concrete to century-old houses, though the only specific sight is an Ottoman **bridge** just downstream at the mouth of the Körahmet valley. If you're leaving by dolmuş, rather than on foot, there's usually one departure a day at dawn for the spectacular ride to Yusufeli.

Meretet

MERETET (officially Olgunlar), currently road's end and the highest trailhead for the Kaçkar at 2200m, is a three-kilometre hike southwest of Hevek, though private cars regularly make the journey in dry conditions, and the dolmuş calls once daily in summer. The spartan but clean *Olgunlar Pansiyon* (☎0466/832 2044; $6 per person bed only, $11 half-board) with its communal balcony, self-catering kitchen and reliable hot water provides an even more scenic alternative to a night in Hevek. The little ground-floor **teahouse/restaurant** is inexpensive but sustaining, with trout prominent on the menu; proprietors Osman Alkan and İbrahim Bayram are experienced trek outfitters.

The Kaçkar Dağları

A formidable barrier between the northeastern Anatolian plateau and the Black Sea, the **Kaçkar Dağları** are the high end of the Pontic coastal ranges – and Turkey's most rewarding and popular trekking area. Occupying a rough rectangle some 70km by 20km, the Kaçkars extend from the Rize–İspir road to the Hopa–Artvin highway, with the more abrupt southeast flank lapped by the Çoruh River, and the gentler northwest folds dropping more gradually to misty foothills. At 3972m, their summit ranks only fourth highest in Turkey after Ararat, Gelyaşin peak in the Cilo mountains and Süphan Dağı, but in scenic and human interest they fully earn their aliases "the Little Caucasus" and "the Pontic Alps".

"Kaçkar" is the Turkish spelling of *khatchkar*, sculpted Armenian votive crosses or gravestones once abundant in eastern Turkey – perhaps a reference to the complicated and tortured outline of the range, with multiple hanging valleys and secondary spurs. In addition to the principal summit area, several other major massifs are recognized: the Altıparmak and Marsis groups of about 3300m, at the north end of the Bulut ridge, which links them with Point 3932; and the adjacent Tatos and Verçenik systems of about 3700m, at the extreme southwest of the chain. Exceptionally for Turkey, the Kaçkars are a young granite-diorite range instead of the usual karst, and were much transformed by the last Ice Age; there are still remnants of glaciers on the north slope of the highest peak, and hundreds of lakes spangle the alpine zone above 2600m.

Partly because of intensive human habitation, the high Kaçkars support relatively few large **mammals**; bear and boar prefer the forested mid-altitude zones, while wolves and ibex are ruthlessly hunted in the treeless heights. **Birds** of prey and snow cocks are more easily seen and heard, while the summer months witness an explosion of **wildflowers**, butterflies – and vicious deer flies. Between May and September, migration from the nearby lowlands to the *yayla*s, or summer pastoral settlements is the norm: the lower, more substantial ones are occupied first, the higher ones once the snow recedes.

Given the ethnic variety here, it's no surprise that local **place names** are similarly tangled – a discerning glance at the map will turn up plenty of Georgian and Armenian words, plus Turkified versions of same. Thus Pişankara (the original form) has become Pişenkaya (Turkish for "the cooking rock"), while other more provocatively foreign ones such as Sevcov lake are camouflaged outright as Deniz Gölü. The recurring suffix "-evit" is an Armenian dialect particle meaning "*yayla*".

Practicalities

The six most popular **trailhead villages** are – on the Black Sea slopes – Çat and Ayder (see Chapter 9), and on the Çoruh side Barhal, Hevek, Meretet and Tekkale (see "The western Georgian valleys" starting on p.849). The approach

KAÇKAR DAĞLARI

from the Black Sea hills is gentler, with clearer trails, but the paths and villages can be crowded, and the almost daily mist rising up to 2900m is a problem. Hiking grades are tougher on the Çoruh flank, but the weather is more dependable. The main **season** is June to September, with the mists less of a hazard as autumn approaches; if you show up earlier than late July, you may need crampons and an ice axe to negotiate some of the higher passes. If you're hardy, it gets warm enough in midsummer for a quick swim in most of the lakes.

In terms of **itineraries**, the Kaçkars are infinitely versatile. The manic and the pressed-for-time cross from Hevek to Ayder via certain passes in two gruelling days, but there's little pleasure in this, and a more reasonable minimum time to switch sides of the mountains would be three or four days, and most people are happy to spend a week or even ten days trekking around. The Kaçkars are lately enjoying a vogue amongst Turkish and Israeli trekkers, with just a token presence of British, Dutch, German and Spanish hikers in most years. Total numbers are in fact slightly down from the early-to-mid 1990s, but you wouldn't know that from the abundant rubbish at over-subscribed campsites such as Dilber Düzü and (to a lesser extent) Kara Deniz Gölü. Purists and misanthropes may prefer less frequented routes in the far southwest, or the southerly approach from Tekkale.

Guides and treks

If you'd rather go with a **guide**, there are a number of helpful individuals in Ayder and Şenyuva, as well as in Yusufeli, Hevek and Meretet. Otherwise most of the adventure travel companies listed in the Basics section of this book run some sort of Kaçkar group itinerary, almost always subcontracted to a Turkey-based **expedition outfitter**. With advance notice from within the country, two of these are particularly worth contacting for fully outfitted treks: Ogzala Turizm, İstiklâl Caddesi, Bekar Sok 16/4, Beyoğlu, İstanbul (℡0212/293 9195, ⓦwww.ogzala.com), and Bukla Seyahat, Yeniçarşi Cad, Gür Han 28/1-2, Galatasaray, İstanbul (℡0212 245 0635, ⓦwww.bukla.com). Both companies offer regular one-week trips from June to September under the supervision of keen mountaineers who often grew up in the area; English-language guiding cannot be guaranteed, but you'll be trekking with sophisticated city Turks, and land-only prices are pitched at the local economy.

Equipment, local conditions and hazards

You'll need a **full trekking kit** appropriate to similar conditions in the Scottish Highlands, the Pacific Northwest or the Pyrenees: quick-draining, non-rotting, heavy-duty boots, wool socks, waterproof trousers or gaiters, a backpack cover and/or cagoule, and a proper, free-standing tent. A camp stove and ample backpacking food are also essential – and you should bring ten to twenty percent more **supplies** than you think you'll need for the projected length of the trek, to allow for being stuck for an extra day by thick mist. Pure **water**, available everywhere from springs, is never scarce.

The lack of good-quality, large-scale **maps** is a major drawback, but some thorough route descriptions are available in mountaineering books (see p.1083) – though they don't offer cartography much better than the sketch map in this book. Even though no compatible maps exist, a GPS device is still very useful: the integral altimeter function will be a godsend in the typically unstable weather conditions where conventional barometric altimeters are useless.

Paths are not waymarked or signposted, but cairns may be present at ambiguous points. Otherwise, there are few specific **dangers**, besides the absolute necessity of crossing all tricky passes early in the day – certainly by noon – before they're shrouded in mist or storm cloud. Territorial domestic bulls are also a nuisance, far more likely to charge a tent than any wild beast. It's useful to know that the ubiquitous Pontic azalea, from whose blossoms the notorious hallucinogenic *deli bal* is made (the "mad" honey that gave Xenophon's soldiers chronic diarrhoea), contains sufficient flammable resin to ignite even in damp conditions. The mountain people consider it a pest and uproot it with little compunction.

Routes in the northern Kaçkar

Starting from **Barhal** (1300m), most trekkers head west to the top of the valley walled off by the Altıparmak chain, finishing a tough first day either near **Karagöl** (2800m) or the nearby **Satibe** meadow (2450m). The following day usually involves a drop down to the Kışla/Önbolat valley just south, threading through the *yayla*s of Borivan, Binektaşı and Pişkankara before making camp higher up. If you pitch tent at **Libler Gölü** (2700m), near the top of the main valley, the next day will see you over the tricky Kırmızı Gedik saddle for an easy descent to **Avusor**, end of the road up from Ayder.

Alternatively, you can bear south from Pişkankara up to a camp in the Bulul valley, at the head of which is the wonderful **Öküz Gölü** (Ox Lake, 2800m) and an initially easy – but later steep – pass giving on to the **Körahmet valley**, still on the Çoruh side of the range. From an overnight next to **Satelev** *yayla*, you can choose between crossing the Bulut ridge via the Baber pass, dropping down to **Balakçur** just above Ayder; or rolling down-valley to **Hevek** via Körahmet (now served by a dirt road), with the option of ending your hike or stocking up to continue through the central Kaçkar.

Routes in the central Kaçkar

Above Hevek, two more valleys lead up to the base of the highest Kaçkar peaks. At **Meretet** (2200m) the split occurs. Bearing right (northwest) takes you within three-and-a-half hours to camping spots near spectacular wild-flowers high up in the Düpedüz valley, just below the **Çaymakcur pass** (3230m), the easiest in the entire Kaçkar range. You should leave for the pass (1hr 30min further) early the following morning, when you'd camp at **Kara Deniz Gölü** a hour beyond, with plenty of time for a day-hike south up to a group of three lakes at the top of the Cennakçur valley (see opposite) – and from a nearby overlook, your first, spectacular nose-to-nose view of Point 3932's north face. From Kara Deniz Gölü you can reach **Ayder** in another long walking day north, via the upper and lower **Çaymakcur** *yayla*s, which may have minibus service.

The path through the other valley follows the Büyük Çay southwest and upstream to the apparent cul-de-sac of the meadows at **Dilber Düzü** (3050m, 3hr from Meretet), a popular (and oversubscribed) camping venue at the formidable base of Point 3932 itself. Despite appearances there is a way up and out: first to the lake of **Sevcov** (Deniz Gölü; 3400m; 1hr 45min more), with just two or three cramped sites for tents, and then over the low crest just south to **Peşevit** (Soğanlı; 3377m; 2hr 15min from Dilber Düzü) lake with much better camping. Try to get an early enough start out of Meretet to make one of the lakes before dark, in preference to Dilber Düzü. Sevcov, where ice floes last into August during many summers, is the veering-off point for the moderately difficult, five-to-six-hour return climb north to the **summit**, where the climbers' register is hidden underneath a rubble cairn.

From Peşevit lake you've a path-less scree-scramble west up to a false pass, then an even more miserable scree descent, another climb and a final drop to some water-meadows near the top of the **Davali valley**, where a faint cairned path takes you up to the **Kavron pass** (3310m; 2hr 45min from Peşevit). Because of the rough terrain, no organized expeditions or pack animals come this way, and you'll need some sort of self-arrest device to save your knees – and yourself from a nasty fall.

Once on the Black Sea side of the pass, the most popular choice involves following the distinct path north an hour to another col (3200m) overlooking the **Kavron valley** – and allowing superb afternoon views of Point 3932's west flank. The trail, fainter now, drops within 45 minutes to **Derebaşı lake** (2885m) where you'll prudently camp. There are limited sites at the inflow, and a few better ones by the lake's exit, where you scout around for the easiest cross-country route down to the floor of the U-shaped, glacial Kavron Deresi. After two hours, the latter half of this on a clear, right-bank trail, you'll reach a roadhead at the busy, electrified *yayla* of **YUKARI KAVRON** (2350m), a quite substantial place with daily minibus service down to Ayder, a central teahouse where you can get basic supplies and the more trekker-friendly *Şahin Pansiyon/Kamping/Kafeterya* (no phone; ❶) at the outskirts, with double chalets.

From just past the *Şahin Pansiyon* on the access road, a sporadically cairned route leads west-southwest up the **Çennakcur valley** to the lakes at its head (2hr 30min; ca. 2900m). There are at least three lakes here – **Kavron Gölü**, right by the path with emergency camping, and **Büyük Deniz** and **Meterel** off to one side – Meterel is the highest and, in summer, often the driest. Another hour over a saddle behind Kavron Gölü will take you to Kara Deniz Gölü, and usually a lot of company. From here it's simple enough to reverse the directions given above for traversing the Düpedüz valley and Çaymakcur pass from Meretet, and complete a three-day, three-night circuit around Point 3932 – an excellent plan if you've left a vehicle or stored extra gear in Meretet or Hevek.

Another possibility from the ridge above Derebaşı lake is to veer west, initially cross-country, to Apevanak *yayla*, which is linked by path or track to the *yayla*s of Palovit and Tirovit; the latter gives access to the western Kaçkar.

Routes in the western Kaçkar

Elevit *yayla* (see p.803) is roughly midway between Tirovit and Çat, and is the starting point for the march up to **Yıldızlı Gölü** (Star Lake; good camping), just across the top of the valley from Haçevanag *yayla*. The nearby, gentle Capug pass allows access to the headwaters of the Fırtına Çayı, though the onward route is briefly confused by the maze of bulldozer tracks around Başyayla (2600m) and Kaleyayla. At the latter, bear south up toward campsites by a lake at the foot of Tatos peak; the following day you'd cross a saddle to another lake, Adalı, at the base of 3711-metre Verçenik.

From this point you'd either descend to Çat via Ortaköy and Varoş, using a morning bus if possible part of the way, or continue walking west for another day, past other lakes just below the ridge joining Verçenik to Germaniman peak. A final 3100-metre pass just north of Germaniman leads to the valley containing Saler and Başköy *yayla*s, linked by daily bus to **İkizdere**.

Routes in the southern Kaçkar

Starting from Tekkale, the same dirt road that serves Dörtkilise continues another 3km to Bölükbaşı *yayla* and the start of a two-to-three-day traverse finishing in the Hevek valley. The weather is more reliable (and also hotter) than elsewhere in the Kaçkar, but this route is thus far relatively unspoilt; sketch map and arrangements are available from Cemil at his *pansiyon* in Tekkale (see p.851).

From **Bölükbaşı** (1400m), a path heads west via the *yayla*s of **Kusana** (1630m) and **Salent** (2400m), before reaching a pair of **lakes** (imaginatively dubbed Küçük – "little" – and Büyük – "big"), below a 3300-metre pass. You'd prudently overnight east of the pass, possibly beside **Büyük Gölü** (2900m), before descending a valley northwest to **Modut** *yayla* (2300m) and then **Mikeles** (1700m), on the side of the Hevek Deresi, about 5km downstream from Hevek itself.

Artvin province: the northern Georgian valleys

The northerly Georgian valleys form the heart of the **province of Artvin**, lying within a fifty-kilometre radius of the town of the same name. Nowhere else in Turkey, except for the Kaçkars, do you feel so close to the Caucasus; ornate wooden domestic and religious architecture, with lushly green slopes or naked crags for a backdrop, clinch the impression of exoticism. Here, too, you may actually encounter native **Georgian-speakers**, though they're mostly confined to the remote valleys around the towns of Camili, Meydancık and Posof, and the immediate surroundings of Şavşat. Whatever their antecedents, the people here are remarkable for their high literacy rate and left-of-centre polling practices – and their seasonal presence. Disgusted by the lack of local opportunities, many have emigrated internally to work ten months of the year at the factories around Bursa and İzmir, to the extent that there are now more *Artvinli*s out west than in the province itself. This situation may or may not change upon completion of the ambitious local hydroelectric schemes (see box below).

The region, with its wet, alpine climate on the heights, formerly had potential as a winter sports playground, but global warming – and the fact that, in Turkey's current economic straits, existing ski resorts can barely cope – scotched such hopes. For the moment most tourists come in summer to see the local **Georgian churches**; individually these are not as impressive as their southern relatives, but their situations are almost always more picturesque.

The Çoruh River hydroelectric schemes

The Çoruh, hitherto one of Turkey's few remaining wild rivers, became the target during the late 1990s of the country's most ambitious **hydroelectric schemes** – far less publicized than the controversial İlisu Dam on the Tigris. Three dams are currently under construction, with two more planned should the cost–benefit ratio ever permit; local sentiment seems guardedly in favour, even though the boost in local employment will be mostly transient. A 40-metre dam is going up at the Georgian border, with Austrian contractors; they're also responsible for a 160-metre dam just above Borçka, scheduled to come on-line in 2004. The mammoth, 210-metre-high dam for the **Deriner Reservoir**, being built by a Swiss–Russian consortium just south of Artvin, has proven more problematic, but should be ready by 2008. By inundating a critical stretch of Highway 10, the Deriner project has added 22 very steep kilometres to the journey into Artvin from all points south or east; no commercial maps as yet show the new route correctly.

French contractors are contemplating two further dams: one in the canyon narrows at Narlık, roughly halfway between Artvin and Yusufeli, and another just below Yusufeli itself, which will drown that town as well as Tekkale. While the lower three projects were in regions where the riverbank was largely uninhabited and non-arable, the mooted upper two would entail expensive compulsory purchase of real estate at a time when the country is effectively broke. Though the main pretext for the projects – the constant shortfall in power to supply Turkey's heavy industry – has evaporated with the parlous state of said industry, ongoing works are being justified by the proposed sale of surplus electricity to the neighbouring Caucasian republics and even Russia. What remains to be seen is whether the proceeds of such sales would be ploughed back into the impoverished northeast, or spent elsewhere by the central government.

Artvin

As your vehicle winds up several kilometres' worth of zigzags from the Çoruh River, you begin to wonder just where **ARTVİN** is, especially if you've approached from the Black Sea, without the benefit of the broadside views from the new southerly highway. Suddenly the town reveals itself, arrayed in sweeping tiers across a steep, east-facing slope, seeming much higher than its actual 500–600m of elevation. Unusually, the medieval **Livane Kalesi**, now occupied by the army, is down low by the river; the only other buildings with a patina of history are houses from the Russian era, tucked here and there on the hill above the centre, but falling increasingly victim to the wrecker's ball. Certainly it has the least flat ground of any Turkish provincial capital, and – within the city limits at least – perhaps the fewest specific attractions. But Artvin is pleasant enough for a night or two, and becomes a destination in its own right for several days over the third or fourth weekend in June, when the **Kafkasör festival** takes place at a *yayla* above town. Highlight of this has traditionally been the pitting of bulls in rut against each other, but since the opening of the nearby frontier the event has taken on a genuinely international character, with wrestlers, vendors, jugglers, musicians and dancers from both Turkey and Georgia appearing among crowds of over 50,000. It's one of the last genuine folk fairs in the country, unlikely to be mucked about with by tourism officials, so be there if you can.

Arrival and services

The **otogar** is way down by the river in the suburb of Köprubaşı, so the three main bus companies all run a shuttle van up to town. If you get left behind, you'll have to take one of the municipal buses, charging about $0.50 for the ten-minute crawl up. All the bus companies have ticket offices along **İnönü Caddesi**, the single high street running past the Hükümet Konağı (Government Hall), where you'll also find the **PTT**, various **banks** with ATMs, and a handful of **internet cafés** whose identities change yearly.

Accommodation

Things have improved slightly since the 1990s when nearly every **hotel** featured hot and cold running *natashas* as standard and Artvin ranked as the hooker capital of Turkey. Even so, there's still only one passably comfortable place, the two-star *Karahan* at İnönü Cad 16 (☏0466/212 1800, ⓦwww.hotelkarahan.com; ❺ during Kafkasör, otherwise ❸). Access from İnönü Caddesi is up a concrete stairwell in a grim shopping centre just downhill from the hotel sign; if you're driving, swing around behind to the tiny, controlled-access parking lot. The rooms, with mostly showers in the bathrooms, are overdue for updating, but about forty percent have air conditioning ($6 extra supplement).

The promising *Çağdaş Oteli*, immediately opposite the *Karahan*, experienced a devastating fire in 2002 and may not re-open. For the moment the best budget alternative is the *Otel Kaçkar*, Hamam Sok 5 (☏0446/212 9909, ℻212 8315; ❶), which has a sign visible from İnönü Caddesi but is actually in an alley parallel and downhill from the main road. Fair-sized rooms, with a variety of views and bed formats, were redone as cheerful en-suites with TV and central heating in 1999. Most of the other "hotels" in Artvin remain little more than brothels and are best given a wide berth.

During the festival it may be more convenient to stay at the municipally run *Kafkasör Tatil Köyü Dağ Evleri* (☏0466/212 5013; ❷), which offers en-suite bungalow rooms up on the Kafkasör meadow, 10km out of town – though you must book months in advance to secure a vacancy.

Eating and drinking

The **restaurant** of the *Hotel Karahan* is one of just three licensed places in town, acceptable and not too overpriced. At the very base of İnönü Caddesi, where the curvy access road straightens out, the *Nazar Restorant* plugs its "million dollar view", but the *meyhane*-format food's not bad or expensive either, running to $6.50 for a couple of *mezes*, a *bir buçuk* portion of chicken and a couple of drinks. Among **unlicensed eateries**, the *Dostlar Sofrası*, upstairs at İnönü Cad 36 near the *meydan* and government buildings, has all the usual *hazır yemek* dishes in a cheerfully contemporary environment. *Bakıroğlu Kebap Salonu* opposite has a stronger stress on grills, served on an outdoor terrace. Breakfast-time *börek* and the usual range of **puddings** are on offer at the competing cake-shops *Köşk* and *Sedir*, more or less opposite each other near the top of İnönü Caddesi.

Borçka and İbrikli

Some 30km downstream from Artvin on Highway 10 en route to Hopa, **BORÇKA** is a nondescript market town of interest only for its riverside setting – and a decent, three-star **hotel**, the *Demirkol* (☎0466/415 3660; ❷) overlooking the Çoruh River. Room furnishings are a bit well-worn, and disco noise can reach everywhere except the fourth floor, but all units have balconies and tubs in the bathrooms, and there's nothing else between Artvin and Hopa. Independent **restaurant** options around Cumhuriyet Medyanı, the main square with a taxi rank, are limited – the *Sofram* is better than the poorish *Gizem Pide/Lahmacun Salonu*.

Borçka is, however, the reference point for visits to **İbrikli**, the only frescoed medieval church in Artvin province, completely absent from most archeological surveys or manuals. It is in fact "Greek" in origin rather than Georgian, as there were always small Greek Orthodox communities inhabiting the northern and western Caucausus until well into the twentieth century.

On Highway 10, 6.3km southeast of Borçka, head up an unsigned, appalling dirt track on the inland (northeast) side of highway, away from the reservoir. Ignore hairpin turns to the left at 200m and 1.5km along; after 5.2km, you'll reach the village of İbrikli, whose use of ceramic roof tiles lends it a Mediterranean feel. Bear left and up at the first possible junction, away from the mosque, then 200m later ignore another track right towards mosque and village centre, but 300m further along do go right and down onto an even steeper descending side-track. You may have to park at a cluster of houses 300m from this last junction. The quickest path to the church – whose dome can be glimpsed in the pastures and hazelnut groves below – begins 200m uphill, at a sharp curve where you may also be able to leave a vehicle.

This access trail goes straight down past, but not to, the **church** – after 200m hop the field boundary fence to approach the utterly crumbled exterior, overgrown with wild fig and bracken. Crudely built to a cross-and-square plan with a brick dome, this diminutive country chapel – for it was never more than this – retains the most complete cycle of **frescoes** this side of Ani, but they're predictably badly damaged. Greek lettering makes identification of some scenes just possible, and they would seem to date from the fourteenth century at the earliest.

Ardanuç and Yeni Rabat

The river valleys east of Artvin are no less spectacular than their counterparts around Yusufeli. The approach to **ARDANUÇ**, once the capital of Klarjeti

Georgia, is through the spectacular, high-walled gorge of the Köprüler Çayı, defended by the **Ferhatlı Kale**, 5km along. **Dolmuşes** from Artvin do the 45-minute trip all morning, starting at 8am, with the last one back at 5pm. The dwindling, slightly shabby old quarter of Ardanuç, 10.5km from the main highway, crouches at the foot of a giant wedding cake of crumbling orange rock, on top of which sits the giant Bagratid **castle of Gevhernik**. With an early start to beat the heat, you can climb it on foot or (part way) by car, but to do that and see the church up the valley in one day you'll need your own transport.

The newer bazaar cantonment, a kilometre or so further, is arrayed around a pleasant, plane-tree-studded "village green" – a legacy of the Russian occupation – with teahouse tables in the middle and a few *döner/pide salonları* at which to stop for a **snack**. All hotels here – which were never up to much – have closed down, so don't get stranded.

Yeni Rabat

The 08-05 road east of Ardanuç is being widened and paved, eventually all the way to its junction with the 955 above Ardahan; beyond some messy and ambitious tunnel works, the scenery is idyllic and gets ever more so as the dirt road worsens. Just under 26km from the main highway, a sign points left (north) towards "Yeni Rabat Kilisesi 6" and the village of "Bulankık/Lengetev" (in a burst of ethnic pride, Georgian place-names are now commonly indicated in this region). Despite the horrid surface, one daily Ardanuç-based dolmuş lurches along, bound for Bulanık and Tosunlu, across the valley.

From the *meydan* in "downtown" **Bulanık**, 1km along and distinguished by fine vernacular log cabins, an onward dirt track leads off slightly down and left (east-northeast) for the remaining 2.5km (best done in a 4WD) to the tenth-century monastery church of **Yeni Rabat** (Shatberdi), nestled in the vegetable gardens of its four-house hamlet, with an idyllic setting up the slopes of one of the loveliest Georgian valleys. The long-vanished monastery, founded a century earlier by Gregory Khantzeli, was renowned as a school for manuscript illuminators. The dome, nave and transept are still virtually intact, with extensive relief carving on the south and east facade, but the exterior has been stripped of most of its dressed stone.

The lower Berta valley: Dolishane and Porta

From the Ardanuç area, retrace your steps to the junction with Highway 10 linking Artvin and Şavşat, which parallels the Berta River (Imerhevi in Georgian). Exactly 300m upstream from the Ardanuç turning, a fine stone **bridge** leaps over the water, and directly opposite this the new bypass highway begins its tortuous journey to Artvin.

Dolishane

Some 3.5km above the stone bridge (or 2.5km from Köprübaşı at Artvin), a badly marked dirt road (there may be some hand-painted signs reading "Dolishane Kilisesi" up on the rock face) leads within 2.5km more to the village of Hamalı. The dome of the tenth-century church of **Dolishane** peeks above the lush vegetation of this oasis village; most ordinary cars will have to stop at the base of the final grade up. The church has not fared well since it ceased serving as the village mosque (when the new adjacent one was built in the mid-1990s); the interior is now being used as an agricultural tool shed. The exterior is more rewarding, the south facade window surrounded by such reliefs as the Bagratid builder-king Smbat I (954–958) offering the church to Christ, a Star of David and an archangel.

Porta

Twelve kilometres above the turning for Artvin, or 26km downstream from Söğütlü Kale (see below), an easily missed yellow metal sign – posted by the management of the *Otel Karahan* – points to the start of the direct path up to **Porta**, modern name for the ninth-century monastery of Khantza, home to the architect-monk Gregory Khantzeli. It's an enjoyable but steep 45-minute climb up to the Bağcılar district of Pırnallı village, though you'll need stout, treaded shoes and preferably a self-arrest device, since the trail is very slippery; for the same reason reckon on the same amount of time down. Some ten minutes up the hill, you need to go up and left very briefly where a newer bulldozer track disrupts the path. The seasonally inhabited hamlet, an oasis tucked into a side ravine of the main canyon running up to Pırnallı, is built higgledy-piggledy around and up against the dilapidated monuments; it's an excellent example of the rural "chalet-style" architecture of these valleys, wooden upper floors on stone-built ground floors, garlanded here with utility wires and the odd satellite dish.

The main tenth-century **church**, still impressive despite gaping holes in the dome and walls, is similar in plan to the one at Haho, with low-ceilinged, arcaded aisles flanking the nave. To the west stands a separate, smaller sixteen-sided **cupola**, once part of a belfry or (less likely) a baptistry. A Georgian inscription is chiselled across its two-toned masonry, still in good condition. Of the monastery quarters themselves, oriented west to east, only the southeastern corner remains. Beside the path in, the eastern wall of an isolated chapel shelters an **ayazma**, or sacred spring, which supports the local walnut groves – a contrast to the endemic scrub oak (*pırnal*) that gives the main village its name.

The upper Berta valley: Tbeti, Meşeli Karagöl and Şavşat

Georgian vernacular architecture reaches its apotheosis along the upper reaches of the Berta stream and its tributaries, most notably in the intricately carved chestnut-wood balustrades of the houses' wraparound balconies. The saturated greens of the lower hillsides rival those around Bulanık, while higher up dense forest cover evokes the alps of central Europe.

Tbeti

The last local Georgian church lies 10.5km off the Artvin–Şavşat road, starting from the compact fortress of **Söğütlü Kale**. Turn up the paved but one-lane side-road marked for Veliköy, and follow the Kaleboyu stream valley for 7km to the village of Ciritdüzü. Bear left here by a "mini-market", following signs for Cevizli village and "Tibet (sic) Kilisesi"; just over 9km from the highway, by the Cevizli "city limits" sign, bear right with the asphalt, then left beside the school for the final short distance to the church.

The remains of the tenth-century monastic **church of Tbeti**, peeking out of the trees at the head of a beautiful valley, are visible at a distance to the sharp-eyed, though up close the building – extensively damaged by local treasure-hunters a few decades ago – is heartbreaking. Tbeti was unique in its non-elongated cross-in-square ground plan, with only the church in far-off

Çengilli (see p.840) approximating it. Now, only the south transept and east apsidal facade retain any relief work, with particularly fine carved windows and medallions at the base of the capitals of false columns on the south facade. According to tradition the great medieval Georgian poet, Shota Rustaveli, studied here for a time; he is said to have fallen hopelessly in love with Queen Tamara while serving as one of her ministers and, being briskly rejected, ended his days in a Jerusalem monastery.

Meşeli Karagöl

The only tourist facility in the area is found at **Meşeli Karagöl**, 20km beyond Ciritdüzü via Veliköy and Meşeli villages, and so qualified to distinguish it from the five thousand others called "Karagöl" (Black Lake) in Turkey. The last 4km of road beyond Meşeli are atrocious, but your reward is the slightly reedy lake, set in dense spruce forest on the lower slopes of Cin Dağı – and the simple but salubrious, four-room *Karagöl Pansiyon* (☎0466/537 2137 or 537 2300; ❷), an ex-Forest-Service **lodge** now run privately by Atanur "Babo" Şahin, one of the characters of the district. It's popular in summer, so reservations are suggested unless you don't mind camping – though note that bears, wild boar and deer roam hereabouts at night.

Şavşat and beyond

Back on Highway 10, Söğütlü castle, just west of the town-limits sign, heralds your arrival in **ŞAVŞAT** (Shavsheti in Georgian), but there's little to stop for in this thoroughly modern, grubby town; the local carpet-weaving tradition has died out and prositution is prominent at most local **accommodation**, though the *Gökçe Pansiyon* at Yeni Cad 13 (☎0466/517 2126; ❷) may be an exception.

The road east from here to Ardahan proves wonderfully scenic if steep. Just 4km east of Şavşat, the idyllic hay meadows of **Yavuzköy** look like they've escaped from the cover of a Swiss chocolate box, but the first facility – and more appealing than any eatery in Şavşat, Ardanuç or Ardahan – is a licensed **meat-and-trout grill**, above a curve in the road some 10km east of Şavşat. A mixed coniferous forest persists until about 2350m elevation, while sinuous switchbacks lead up to a final picturesque *yayla* of log cabins and sheet metal roofs, just below the **Çamlıbel pass**, at the border between Artvin and Ardahan provinces.

Travel details

Trains

Erzurum to: Ankara/İstanbul (daily at noon & 8pm; 24hr/35hr); Divriği (1 daily; 7hr); Kars (daily at 7.30am & 5.20pm; 5hr).
Kars to: Erzurum (daily at 7.10am; 5hr).

Buses and dolmuşes

Artvin to: Ardahan via Şavşat (10 daily; 3hr); Ardanuç (6 daily until 4pm; 45min); Erzurum (4 daily; 4hr 30min); Hopa (hourly until 3pm; 1hr

30min); Kars (1 daily at noon; 6hr); Rize (hourly until 3pm; 2hr 15min); Şaşvat (7 daily; 2hr); Trabzon (5 daily; 4hr); Yusufeli (4 daily; 1hr 45min).
Erzurum to: Ankara (6 daily; 13hr); Artvin (5 daily; 4hr 15min); Bayburt (hourly; 2hr); Doğubeyazit (4 daily; 4hr); İspir (3 daily; 2hr); Kars (6 daily; 3hr); Rize (2 direct daily; 6hr); Sivas (5 daily; 7hr 30min); Trabzon (3 daily; 5hr); Van (1–2 daily; 6hr); Yusufeli (3 direct daily; 3hr).
Kars to: Ardahan (hourly; 1hr 30min); Artvin via Göle (1 daily at 8.30am; 5hr); Çıldır (2 daily at 11am & noon; 1hr 30min); Digor (hourly; 45min);

Erzurum (6 daily; 3hr); Iğdır (hourly; 3hr); Trabzon (1 daily at 8.30am; 7hr).

Yusufeli to: Artvin (5 daily; 1hr 45min); Barhal (4 daily; 1hr 30min); Erzurum (2 daily in the morning before 1pm; 3hr); Hevek (2 daily; 3hr); Tekkale (1–3 daily; 15min).

Flights

Erzincan to: Ankara (2 weekly; 1hr 20min).
Erzurum to: Ankara (1 daily; 1hr 30min); İstanbul (2 weekly non-stop; 2hr).
Kars to: Ankara (1 daily; 1hr 50min).

Travel to Armenia

The Turkish–Armenian border at Doğukapı east of Kars has been closed since 1994, due to diplomatic wranglings and historical enmity between the two nations. Through trains, as well as vehicle transit, from Kars to Gyumri (ex-Leninakan), the first major Armenian city, is thus suspended until further notice. Oddly, it is still possible to fly from İstanbul to the Armenian capital of Erevan – currently the only way to travel between the two countries.

The Euphrates and Tigris Basin

CHAPTER 11

Highlights

✳ **Gaziantep's old Christian/Jewish quarter** This warren of steep streets contains the magnificent former Armenian cathedral, once a jail, now the Independence Mosque. See p.873

✳ **Şanlıurfa's "pizza"** Home of the spicy dish, *lahmacun*, best eaten amidst the hustle and bustle of one of Turkey's best bazaars. See p.880

✳ **Nemrut Dagı** The massive stone heads of Hellenistic deities glare out from a remote mountain-top. See p.889

✳ **Diyarbakır** Walk around the mighty basalt walls of this predominately Kurdish city, high above medieval alleys teeming with street kids. See p.896

✳ **Mardin** A hilltop town of beautiful Arab-style houses interspersed with graceful mosques and solid churches. See p.905

✳ **Syrian Orthodox Church** Catch a service in Diyarbakır, Mardin or Midyat, and experience a liturgy that has remained virtually unchanged for 1500 years. See p.910

✳ **Hasankeyf** A once grand city, spectacularly situated on a soaring cliff overlooking the green Tigris. See p.913

The Euphrates and Tigris Basin

ast of the Mediterranean coast, you leave touristic Turkey behind and the going gets harder: there are no full-scale resorts, scarce travelling companions and only a few items of conventional interest. Yet for many, the **basin of the Euphrates and Tigris rivers**, a broad, fan-shaped flood plain ringed on three sides by the mountains containing their headwaters, is the most exotic part of Turkey, offering a number of compelling ancient sites and some fascinating, isolated towns.

Historically, this has always been a border zone where opposing empires and civilizations have met and often clashed. Settlements on the Euphrates formed the eastern boundary of the Roman Empire against the Parthians, and subsequently the Byzantines pushed their frontier further southeast against the Persian heartlands. With the birth of the new religion, Islam, in 632 AD, Byzantine authority began to crumble under pressure from the Arabs to the east and south. Thereafter, almost everybody of any import in Middle Eastern affairs seems to have passed through at one time or another: Arabs, Crusaders, Armenians, Selçuks, Turcomans, Mongols and finally the French, who invaded southeastern Turkey as part of a wider attempt by the victorious World War I Allies to break up the defeated Ottoman Empire.

Today a frontier atmosphere persists and you'll notice that ethnic Turks are in the minority in most places. Close to the Syrian border, **Arab** influence is strong, but the further east or north you go, particularly into the remoter valleys of the Tigris and its tributaries, you'll find an ever-increasing proportion of the population is made up of **Kurds**. The potential volatility of this racial mix has been exacerbated by the fundamentalist or separatist sympathies of some of the population, not to mention the occasionally heavy-handed tactics of the Turkish authorities – a consequence of the primitive structure of society. Traditionally, smallholding farmers and herdsmen have barely scratched a living from the rocky and unrewarding land, and the new dams of the Southeastern Anatolian Project (see box on p.869) have only improved farming in the west of the area, where water finds its way to the fields via huge irrigation tunnels. Outside this area, high pastures are being abandoned due to drought and low farm prices, and, in spite of the cessation of PKK activities, population drift to the big cities continues.

Coming from the west, most visitors pass first through **Gaziantep**, the last outpost of Europeanized Turkey and a cheerful, booming city benefiting from

11

N

0   50 km

▲ Van

Kurtalan

Ilisu
Dam

Dargeçit

Tür Abdin
Churches

Mar
Gabriel

Mar Augen

Girmeli

Batman

Hasankeyf

Mardin   Midyat

Deyr-az-Zaferan

Nusaybin

Diyarbakır

Dicle (Tigris River)

Ceylanpınar

Pertek

Harput

Elazığ

Hazar
Gölü

Siverek

Soğmatar

Suayb

Keban Barajı

Eski Malatya

Aslantepe

Nemrut Dağı

Atatürk
Barajı

Şanlıurfa

Harran

Han-el-Ba'rür

Akçakale

S   Y   R   I   A

Malatya

Adıyaman

Kâhta

Fırat (Euphrates) River

E90

Karkamış
Dam

S   Y   R   I   A

Gölbaşı

Birecik

Belkıs/
Zeugma

Karkamış

▲ Kayseri

K. Maraş

Gaziantep

Kilis

Halab (Aleppo)

Toprakkale

İskenderun

Antakya

Asi River

▲ Kayseri

▲ Adana

its new-found industrial wealth. From Gaziantep a narrower road leads across the Euphrates to **Şanlıurfa**, an ancient city mentioned in the Bible as the birthplace of Abraham. It's one of the region's most rewarding destinations – and a convenient staging post for Nemrut-bound travellers – and also makes an ideal base for an excursion to **Harran**, with its mud-brick beehive houses.

The Southeastern Anatolian Project

The *Güneydoğu Anadolu Projesi* (GAP), or **Southeastern Anatolian Project**, was begun in 1974 with the construction of the Keban Dam across the upper Euphrates near Elazığ. Upon completion (originally scheduled for 1997, but unlikely to happen within the next few years) the scheme will total no fewer than 22 **dams** in the ring of foothills around the joint Euphrates–Tigris basin. A series of large-bore tunnels leading to spots as far-flung as Harran and Ceylanpınar near the Syrian border have begun to irrigate 1.6 million hectares of what was previously partial wasteland. Moreover, 17 of the dams will generate **electric power**, for a total hourly capacity of 26 billion kilowatts – a third of this from the massive **Atatürk Dam**, fourth largest in the world at 80m high and 800m broad at the base, tapering gradually to 20m at the top. As evident from the mind-boggling numbers, the GAP is an undertaking of pharaonic confidence and ambition, intended to be a panacea for most of the southeast's economic and social ills, although Syria, Turkey's southern neighbour, has complained bitterly that its share of water from the Euphrates has been halved since the completion of the Atatürk Dam.

In conjunction with tax incentives offered by the government to companies who move their operations here, hydro-electrification has also triggered some rapid **industrialization** to the west of the basin. Proprietors of textile mills in western Turkey have even gone so far as to dismantle loss-making plants and machinery and ship them for reassembly in the GAP area, where the cheap power and huge pool of inexpensive labour will allow them to run at a profit. Promoters of the scheme plan to send any excess power to western Turkey, though the inefficiency of Turkey's national grid makes this difficult at present.

In terms of the local benefits of GAP, the improvement to agriculture is apparent from the main road. Eastwards from Gaziantep, the area has greened – new pistachio and olive plantations flourish, cotton is being grown around Harran, and many fruits and vegetables are under seasonal cultivation. A new university has emerged at Şanlıurfa to investigate the application of new agricultural methods and provide trained experts. However, only **large landlords** are able to qualify for credits from the state bank to purchase the fertilizer and machinery necessary to engage in large-scale agribusiness. Smaller farmers are being forced off the land as small fertile riverside plots are submerged under the rising waters. Many of these smallholders have migrated to the cities to seek work in factories, which has contributed to the creation of *gecekondu*, or **slum areas**, populated by a permanent urban underclass of unskilled or semi-skilled labourers.

Rural depopulation aside, the other major effects of GAP have been on the region's archeological and natural heritage. Immense efforts have ensured that artefacts from many sites in the Euphrates have been saved, with the finds taking pride of place at local museums. However, major settlements such as Samsat, occupied since pre-Roman times, proved too big a challenge to the overworked international teams and have vanished forever beneath the waters. The dam reaching completion on the Euphrates at **Birecik**, as well as drowning part of the Roman frontier town of Zeugma, has caused severe environmental disruption as endemic populations of animals, birds and plants are threatened by the disappearance of their habitat. The lower dam at **Karkamış** also threatens an important archeological site. However, it seems that, at least temporarily, the **İlisu** project, the first of a series of dams planned on the Tigris, has been abandoned.

11

In the mountains to the north of Gaziantep, the spectacular temple and tomb of **Nemrut Dağı** fully justifies a pilgrimage. **Kâhta**, the closest village, is a scruffy development that concentrates on servicing the Nemrut Dağı tourism trade. The two nearest towns, **Adıyaman** to the south and **Malatya** to the north, are not particularly enticing either, although the former has an interesting old quarter and the latter offers easy access to the nearby attractions of **Eski Malatya** and **Aslantepe**.

From either Şanlıurfa or Malatya, it's a journey of half a day or less to **Diyarbakır**, a teeming city built on the banks of the River Tigris. South of Diyarbakır, the other major destination for travellers in the Tigris region is **Mardin**, with its atmospheric collection of beautiful vernacular houses set on a crag overlooking the Syrian plain. To the east of Mardin, the isolated **Tür Abdin** plateau is home to most of the remaining Syrian Orthodox Christian population of Turkey and to a scattering of monasteries and churches. At its heart lies **Midyat**, a town of elegant mansions, once the equal of those in Mardin but now crumbling into almost irredeemable abandonment. Finally, following a different route back to Diyarbakır, the breathtakingly sited village of **Hasankeyf** has been temporarily reprieved from being swallowed up by the waters of the proposed İlisu Dam, planned to block the Tigris near the Syrian border. Swayed by protests on social, environmental and historical grounds and, more prosaically, by the likelihood of the Turks defaulting on repayment, the British government have withdrawn its support for the project.

Travelling around presents few problems, with good bus links between all the major towns. The once pot-holed roads in the eastern part of the region have been patched up and are generally in excellent shape. Hotel facilities have improved steadily, and only in the small towns, such as Midyat, will you have trouble finding a reasonable hotel. In summer, the harsh terrain bakes in an intense heat, though the lack of humidity does something to mitigate the fierce temperatures. To enjoy the region at its best, try to visit during spring or autumn.

It's worth bearing in mind that the main jumping-off point for **crossing to Syria** is not, in fact, in this region, but Antakya in the Hatay (see p.591).

The Euphrates basin

As you approach from Adana, the **floodplain of the Euphrates** opens out to the east and northeast, reaching the southern fringes of the Anatolian plateau, from which the Euphrates River itself (Fırat in Turkish) winds its turbid way into Syria. The broad alluvial plain has been inhabited for several millennia and was once a lush, fertile region; indeed, remains of some of the world's oldest known human settlements have been discovered here. Unfortunately, the thirteenth-century Mongol destruction of the intricate irrigation canals that had existed since ancient times, aggravated by the depredations of flocks of goats, have reduced much of the area to dusty steppeland.

Approaching from the west, the first major centre is **Gaziantep**, where the narrow lanes of the old quarter make a sharp contrast to the modern, shop-lined boulevards. East of Gaziantep, the road shoots across the plain of the Euphrates, crossing the river at bleached, sandy **Birecik** before cutting through rocky uplands to the venerable town of **Şanlıurfa**, well worth a couple of days' sightseeing on its own as well as making a good base for exploring **Harran**, a village continuously inhabited for over 6000 years.

For many visitors, though, the region's main attraction is the Commagene mountain-top temple of **Nemrut Dağı**, Eastern Turkey's most photographed and publicized site. It was badly hit by the perceived threat from the PKK (who were never really active in this area), but tourists are now returning in droves. Nemrut Dağı can be approached from **Adıyaman** to the south or from the north via **Malatya**, a civilized, rather bland town set in the middle of the rolling, gorge-cut plateau that divides İç Anadolu (Inner Anatolia) from Doğu Anadolu (Eastern Anatolia). From Malatya, it's also a fairly easy matter to make your way to **Elazığ**, an ugly, modern place notable only for its archeological museum and the presence of the ruined city of **Harput** just outside town.

Gaziantep

GAZİANTEP, a lively, crowded modern city, has the largest population in the region: over a million at last count, all seemingly bent on seeking the good things in life. It's one of the main beneficiaries of the GAP dams project and has a prosperous air. Progressive local government has overseen the construction of an industrial quarter separated from the city by a belt of forest (some of which belongs to the military) and the various town-planning strategies and investment incentives have been a palpable success. Gaziantep boasts some fine domestic architecture, especially in the Christian/Jewish quarter, as well as several mosques (one of which was originally a cathedral) and a ruined castle. It's a handy staging post on a journey to more exotic destinations to the north or further east, and an excellent base for rest and recreation, with the cinemas, bars and shops that are almost unknown further east. Gaziantep is also famed for its incredible pistachio nuts – properly *şam fıstığı* but often referred to as *Antep fıstığı* – some of the best you'll taste anywhere in Turkey.

The city is known by local people (and, significantly for visitors, by most bus companies) as "Antep", a corruption of the Arab *ayn teb* ("good spring"); the prefix "Gazi" ("warrior for Islam") was only added in 1920 after Nationalist forces defending the city withstood a ten-month siege by the French, who had advanced up from their Syrian protectorate in an attempt to seize a portion of defeated Turkey.

Arrival, information and services

Gaziantep's old quarter is built on a hill; it's linked by Hürriyet Caddesi/İstasyon Caddesi to the museum (1.5km downhill) and *otogar*, via a large park surrounding the river. Atatürk Caddesi/Suburu Caddesi crosses this main artery just north of the old city and Sinema Bowling complex, the latter a local landmark.

The **otogar** lies 5km northwest of the centre, so you'll need to take a service bus or dolmuş into town. Get off at Hükümet Konağı (the Sinema Bowling complex), near the junction of Suburcu and Hürriyet *caddesi*s, where you'll find most of the city's hotels and restaurants. The **train station** stands at the north end of İstasyon Caddesi, 2km from downtown; dolmuşes shuttle up the hill into town. There are daily flights from Ankara and İstanbul to **Sazgan airport**, 10km southeast; Havaş buses ($1.50) meet arrivals and will shuttle you to the **THY terminal** at Atatürk Bul 30/B (℡0342/230 1565), west of Sinema Bowling.

Gaziantep's helpful **tourist office**, in Yüzüncü Yıl Park (Mon–Sat 9am–noon & 1–5pm; ℡0342/230 5969), lies a kilometre northwest of the junction of Suburcu and Hürriyet *caddesi*s. Staff can provide printed maps of the town and lists of accommodation, but speak only basic English. The main **PTT** is 100m south of the Sinema Bowling, and there's **internet** access at the *Metpas Internet Café* on Atatürk Bulvarı. Finally, there are a number of **car rental** outfits in town: Met-Kar, Atatürk Bul 90/A (℡0342/232 0021), and Al-Ser, Gazı Paşa Bul 19/B (℡0342/234 3084), are likely to be cheaper than Avis, Ordu Cad 15/A (℡0342/336 1194), and Hertz, Ordu Cad 92/C (℡0342/336 7718).

Accommodation

There are scores of hotels in Gaziantep, with many top-of-the-range business-oriented outfits but few good-value mid-range or budget options. The only decent inexpensive option is the clean and friendly *Evin*, Kayacak Cad 11, 50m southwest of Sinema Bowling (℡0342/231 3492; ❶), where breakfast isn't included. The slightly seedy but nonetheless spacious *Hotel Petek* (℡0342/231 1982; ❷), on Suburcu Caddesi opposite the Büyk Pasaj shopping centre, is next best bet.

In the medium range, a good choice for both rooms and location is the comfortable and quiet *Katan*, 100m from the archeological museum at İstasyon Cad 58 (℡0342/230 6969, ℻220 8454; ❸). The prominent, three-star *Belkiz*, on a sidestreet off Suburcu Caddesi (℡0342/220 2020, ℻234 2675; ❹), is a smart new option; it lies 300m east from Sinema Bowling and is not marked on the tourist-office map. West of the centre are the tower block of the modern *Gap Hotel* at Atatürk Bul 10 (℡0342/220 9690, ℻230 2091; ❺), and the five-star *Hotel Tuğcan*, Atatürk Bul 34 (℡0342/220 4323; ❽), with a smart restaurant where the town's bosses wine and dine. A more sober-minded luxury choice would be the plush four-star *Hotel Tilmen*, on the corner of İnönü and Hürriyet *caddesi*s, 500m south of Sinema Bowling (℡0342/220 2081, ℻220 2091; ❻), with comfortable air-conditioned rooms.

The City

Gaziantep was first occupied during Hittite times and has since experienced the familiar round of occupations – Assyrian, Persian, Alexandrine, Roman, Selçuk, Crusader, Byzantine, Arab – shared by so many places in this part of Turkey. Industrialization based on textile mills has brought a degree of prosperity to the city, along with an influx of country people looking for a better standard of living. They tenant the maze of multi-storey buildings and slums, which spread up the surrounding hills.

A worthwhile starting point is the **Archeological Museum** on İstasyon Caddesi (Arkeoloji Müzesi; Tues–Sun 8.30am–4.30pm; $0.70), south of the park and opposite the football stadium. This contains a number of draft Hittite reliefs from Yesenek, 100km west of Gaziantep, once one of the main open-air stone-carving centres of the entire Hittite empire. The museum also has a well-labelled seal collection from the Hittite and Urartian period, some made from precious stones, and displays finds from the most important of local excavations, the Roman border city of Zeugma (see p.874). Mosaics from Zeugma illustrate the hedonistic lifestyle at the border city; mythological characters dine extravagantly or disport gaily in states of *deshabille*. There are also animal mosaics from other sites.

The most prominent survivor from Gaziantep's past is the **kale**, which dominates the town from the eastern hill – an artificial mound formed by layers of accumulated debris from thousands of years of human occupation. The castle dates back to late Roman times, but the present structure, with its 36 towers, owes more to the Selçuks. To reach it, take any road running east from İstasyon Caddesi; bear right at the square and you'll come to a ramp that leads up to the main doors. The castle is not officially open, but a foreman will probably turn up and show you the excavated baths, which have a hypocaust floor and a domed roof, and a sizable medieval tunnel.

From the *kale*, Gümrük Caddesi takes you through the surrounding **bazaar quarter**, where several *han*s are today used for metalwork. In some workshops you might find craftsmen manufacturing the local speciality: furniture inlaid with *sedef* (mother-of-pearl), although lately it's just as likely to be plastic. Other local souvenirs include copperware, such as *samovars*, *mangals* (braziers) and *ibriks* (ewers), *yemeni* (all-leather slippers) and *aba* (embroidered vests), now usually adulterated with synthetic fibres. Beyond the bazaar is an area of modern pedestrian shopping streets.

To the southwest of Sinema Bowling, behind the *Gül Palas* hotel, is the former **Christian/Jewish quarter**, where the inward-looking houses with their black-and-white arched gates were each once a fortress in themselves. In readiness against the attempts of successive invaders, each had its own well, food cellars and stabling, as can be seen at the well-signed **Hasan Süzer Ethnography Museum** (Hasan Süzer Etnografi Müzesi; daily 8am–noon & 1–5pm; $0.70). If you ignore the fading mannequins and peeling paint, the house itself is compelling enough, with a garden and *selamlık* (mens' reception room), and a crypt-like basement used originally for food storage and still some thirty degrees cooler than the surroundings. From the top floor you can glimpse the former Armenian cathedral, an imposing domed box, although you will probably have to get local help to find it in the confusing maze of streets; ask for its new name, the **Kurtuluş Camii** (Independence Mosque). This hilltop building served as a prison during the War of Independence and after and then stood empty until its conversion to a mosque. The facade, with black and white stone trim and restrained carvings around the windows, would do credit to a French city square. Inside, Corinthian columns support the porch, while the main space is covered by a huge cleverly constructed dome. Persistent visitors are allowed to climb to the top of the minaret, which is paired with a square bell-tower, from where there are extensive views of the dome and the city behind.

The same architect built the **Alauddevle Camii**, on the north side of Eski Saray Caddesi, which runs east from Sinema Bowling. There is also another church, the **Kendirli Kilisesi**, just north of Atatürk Bulvarı, but although it's an imposing building and scheduled for conversion to an arts centre, it's not currently open to the public.

Eating and drinking

Gaziantep is noted for *içli köfte*, a cracked-wheat case filled with minced meat and nuts and served as a delicious starter. Another delicacy, *Ciğ* (raw) *köfte* is also made from cracked wheat, flavoured with pepper and tomato, and served with lettuce and lemon juice.

The town has about as many **restaurants** as it does hotels, but many of them are somewhat overpriced. Scores of cheerful grills and *lokantas* vie for your custom around the Atatürk Bulvarı/Hürriyet Caddesi junction. Recommended is the *Ekim 29 Lokantası* on Gaziler Cad, Çekemoğlu Çikmazı, a cul-de-sac off the main street in the pedestrian area, which sometimes has live Kurdish music. In the fairground opposite the archeological museum, the *Fuar* lays on a live music programme alongside the food, though the volume and general tackiness may have you running for cover. It's worth considering the rooftop restaurant at the *Hotel Kaleli*, 200m south of Sinema Bowling, which is not as expensive as you might imagine – you should be able to eat a two-course meal with a beer for about $10.

As for **drinking,** the *English Pub*, on the corner of Suburcu Caddesi, in the same building as Sinema Bowling, has a good range of beers, but the first-floor *Kantara* opposite is considerably cheaper.

East of Gaziantep: towards Şanlıurfa

Travelling east of Gaziantep can be hellishly uncomfortable, despite the new road, with temperatures in summer edging into the mid-forties centigrade. If you're travelling by bus, try and make sure you get a seat in the shade when buying your ticket. With your own car you'll be able to call in at two intriguing archeological sites en route to **Birecik**, though dam development at **Karkamış** and ongoing excavations at **Zeugma** affect access.

Karkamış

About 30km from Gaziantep, just before the Euphrates bridge at Birecik, amid a landscape of pistachio and olive groves stippled with hilltop villages, there's a turning for **Karkamış**, the ancient Hittite city of Carchemish. It's 25km south of the highway, situated just south of the railway bridge at the junction of the Euphrates and a tributary. A number of important reliefs (including scenes from the Assyrian epic of Gilgamesh) were unearthed here by British archeologists (Leonard Woolley and T.E. Lawrence among them) during excavations financed by the British Museum between 1910 and 1915, and again in 1920. In those days, access was by train from Beirut and the railway line to the east was still under construction, so the British excavators disputed various piles of stones with the German railway builders.

Many of the finds have been removed to the Museum of Anatolian Civilizations in Ankara. The **site** itself, in principle always freely open, is subject to dam construction and military restrictions, as it lies just a few kilometres north of the border with Syria and adjacent to the new Karkamış dam. It's difficult to reach except by car, though an adventurous alternative is the one daily train from Gaziantep (leaves 7am, returns 2pm), to Barak, a kilometre from the site. Ask at Gaziantep tourist office for the latest information.

Zeugma

From Nizip, on the same highway, it's 9km to the waterside excavations at **Zeugma**, just northwest of Birecik. Zeugma, originally known as Seleucia, was founded by Seleucius Nicator, one of Alexander the Great's generals and, due to its strategic position as a major crossing point of the Euphrates, it thrived. Roman border troops, especially from the Scythian legion, were stationed here and the town merchants built sumptuous villas between the town and the Euphrates. However, the city was devastated, first by Sassanid raids in 252 AD, then by an earthquake, although the site was partly resettled in the Byzantine and Abbasid eras.

More recently the site has been threatened by mosaic thieves and by the rising waters of the Birecik dam, which have now submerged around a third of the site. Consequently, Zeugma was the scene of a massive archeological rescue mission in 2000, when many mosaics were recovered by international teams working hastily as the waters rose below them; even so, many beautiful examples were lost. The surviving mosaics have been reassembled in Gaziantep museum, while the upper part of the extensive site is still undergoing excavation. At the time of writing, the site museum was not open and before making a visit you should enquire at the Gaziantep tourist office (or check the extensive website ⓦ www.zeugmaweb.com), as it is not possible to explore the site unless archeologists are in residence.

Birecik

The highway crosses the Euphrates River and the provincial border at the shabby town of **BİRECİK**, around 40km from Gaziantep, where all Urfa-bound buses stop. The town is of interest mainly to ornithologists as one of the few places in the world where you're likely to see the **bald ibis**, a relative of the stork, that once nested wild on the castle walls but are now confined to a **breeding station** (April–Oct daily during daylight hours; $0.35; 1km north of town on the east river bank. Excess birds are released into the wild every year, but so far none has migrated back. **Storks** themselves are far more in evidence and here (as elsewhere in both the Euphrates and Tigris basins) large numbers can be seen occupying their untidy nests in the spring and summer months. The Birecik environs are also home to several other bird species; you might see eagles and Bruce's Scops owls (the latter a regular visitor to the *Belediye* tea garden on the east riverbank in town), yellow-throated and pale rock sparrows, menetries warblers, see-see partridges and sand grouse.

Birecik's ruined **castle** was founded during the eleventh century as a frontier outpost for the Crusader state of Edessa, but isn't worth going out of your way to inspect closely, though its entourage of old houses backed into the cliff-face are appealing from a distance. If you want to stay in the area, there's the bland but clean *Mirkelam Tesisleri Motel* (Ⓣ 0414/652 1178, Ⓕ 652 3047; ❸), set amongst the last petrol stations before the bridge over the Euphrates. In Birecik itself, the *Deniz Restaurant*, north of the bridge on the east bank, serves excellent, reasonably priced food, including river fish and a good range of *mezes*.

Şanlıurfa

The name of **ŞANLIURFA**, or "Glorious Urfa" (most of the locals just say Urfa), commemorates resistance to the French invasion and occupation of 1918–1920. It's a place of pilgrimage for many religions; you could easily spend a day taking in the local monuments, which include the reputed birthplace of the Prophet Abraham and a mosque complex of some beauty, reflected in the limpid waters of the town's famous lakes.

Just as compelling is Urfa's Middle Eastern atmosphere. A significant proportion of the population is Kurdish: women are veiled and often tattooed with henna, and men wear baggy trousers and traditional headdresses. Amongst the

Arab population, women tend towards brightly coloured clothes and rich fabrics, while visiting pilgrims are often fully veiled and clad in black from top to toe. For visitors coming from western Turkey, the traditional dress of women in Urfa's bazaars make this seem like the place where "the Orient" really begins, but to the north, around the university, students are smartly dressed in western fashions. In Turkey this so-called "city of the prophets" has gained notoriety as a focus for Islamic fundamentalism, which means that alcohol has almost disappeared from restaurants and that the good citizens retire early to bed. The poorest inhabitants, despite the supposed wealth generated by the GAP project, can still be seen queuing at the east end of the Şurkav Çarşısı for cooked rice and bread distributed by the local governor.

Some history

Even by Turkish standards, Urfa is an old city. According to both Jewish and Muslim sources, Abraham received his summons from God to take himself and his family to Canaan while living in Urfa. Other stories record that the prophet Job was a resident for a while, though claims that the Garden of Eden was somewhere around here are probably based more on wishful thinking.

Whatever the factual basis of these legends, it's certain that people have been living on the site for thousands of years. The first settlers were the Hurri, members of one of Anatolia's earliest civilizations, who built a fortress on the site of the present citadel around 3500 BC and controlled much of the surrounding area. The Hurri, who probably named the place Orhoi – corrupted in modern times to Urfa – were followed by the Hittites and Assyrians, the latter remaining in control until Alexander the Great swept through after his victory at Issus. Renamed Edessa, after the Macedonian town, the place was an important eastern outpost for the Romans against the Persians.

From the second century AD, Edessa was a thriving centre of Christianity, the Nestorian variant of it particularly taking root. The city changed hands between Byzantine and Arab several times; according to Syriac legend it was once ransomed for the "mandalyon" (see box on the Syrian Orthodox Church p.910). When Byzantine power finally collapsed, the Arabs moved in permanently, staying until the eleventh century, when, during the First Crusade, a French count, Baldwin of Boulogne, stopped off en route to Tripoli and the Holy Land to establish the county of Edessa, a short-lived Christian state. In 1144 the Arabs recaptured Edessa, giving the rulers of Europe a pretext to launch the Second Crusade, although the city was soon forgotten and never wrested back from the Arabs. In 1260 it was put to the sword by the Mongols and never really recovered, declining into obscurity before being absorbed (as Urfa) into the Ottoman Empire in 1637.

Arrival and information

Şanlıurfa's **otogar** is more than a kilometre west of the centre, so take a dolmuş into town (or bargain for a taxi if arriving late at night – you shouldn't pay more than $5). Head for the *Hotel Harran* on Köprübaşı Caddesi, which makes a good orientation point, as most of the hotels and other tourist facilities can found around here. The **airport** is about 6km south of town, on the road to Harran, with a THY bus to take you into the centre; the **THY office** is at Sarayönü Cad 74/A (☎0414/215 3344).

The **tourist office** is in the Şurkav Çarşısı behind the Rizvaniye Camii (summer Mon–Fri 8am–noon & 1.30–5.30pm; winter Mon–Fri 8.30am–noon & 1–5pm; ☎0414/215 2467); they hand out almost illegible provincial and city maps.

ŞANLIURFA

0 — 200 m

N

▲ Diyarbakır

▶ Mardin

Stadium

Archeological Museum

Vilayet

Ş NUSRET CAD

ATATÜRK CAD

KÖPRÜBAŞI CAD

◀ Gaziantep

Karakoyun River

Otogar

ASFALT CAD

KÖPRÜBAŞI CAD

② THY
④
③

Şanmed Hospital

★ Harran Dolmuş

SARAYÖNÜ CAD

ONIKI EYLÜL CAD

Haci Hafiz Efendi (Fine Arts Gallery)
⑥
KARA MEYDANI

Döviz (Money Changers)

Ulu Cami

Bey Gate

Fırfırlı Camii

VALİ FUAT BEY CAD

Selahattin Eyubi Camii

Medieval Houses

DİVAN CAD

GÖL CAD

⑦

Şurkav Çarşısı

Gümrük Hanı

ℹ ⑨

Abdürrahman Camii

Rızvaniye Camii

GÖL CAD

Hasan Paşa Camii
⑧

Narinci Camii

KAPALI ÇARŞI

Gölbaşı

Halil-ür Rahman

Ayn-i-Zeliha

Mevlid-i-Halil-Camii

Yeni Camii

Cave of Abraham (Ibrahim Haliullah Dergahı)

Kale

▶ Harran & Airport

ACCOMMODATION

Doğu	4
Edessa	9
Gül Palas	6
Güven	2
Harran	5
Köran	1
Şafak	8
Şanliurfa Valiliği Konuk Evi	7
Uğur	3

11

THE EUPHRATES AND TIGRIS BASIN | Şanlıurfa

877

Accommodation

Urfa's popularity as a prime destination for Middle Eastern tourists on religious quests means that accommodation at the cheap end of the market is plentiful. Budget hotels all have shared bathrooms, but even so tend to offer far better value for money than the town's three mid-range hotels – breakfast isn't included at any of these places. If you don't shrink at the idea of sleeping on an iron bedstead on a roof, there are also plenty of really cheap (say $2 a night) options that are not listed below – just ask around.

Otel Doğu Sarayönü Cad ☏ 0414/215 2128. Labyrinthine and in need of a lick of paint, some of the basic rooms are en-suite, others have share (squat) toilets down the hall. ❶

Hotel Edessa Göl Cad ☏ 0414/215 9911, ⓦ hoteledessa@superonline.com. Luxurious, elegant rooms around a cool courtyard restaurant, but no swimming pool. ❼.

Gül Palas Beyaz Sok ☏ 0414/215 7201. The most atmospheric of the budget hotels, on a side street past the Hacı Hafiz Efendi art gallery. It's an old, pink-painted house, whose rooms are vast and high-ceilinged but none too clean. ❶

Hotel Güven Köprübaşı Cad ☏ 0414/215 1700. You'll have to endure the alternately offhand and belligerent management to enjoy the power-showers, fluffy towels and air-conditioning of the obsessively clean rooms. ❸

Harran Atatürk Cad ☏ 0414/313 2860, ⓕ 313 4918. Popular with tour groups, this is equipped with its own swimming pool, hamam and top-floor bar, sometimes with a floorshow patronized by local businessmen. ❼

Köran Hotel On the main northern highway, 2km from town ☏ 0414/313 1809, ⓕ 312 1737. If you have your own transport (buses are few and far between in the late evenings), consider staying out here – pleasant air-conditioned rooms with television and refrigerator. ❹

Şafak Oteli Göl Cad ☏ 0414/215 1157. Aimed at migrant workers and less than prosperous businessmen, it offers very basic rooms and only passably clean shared bathrooms, but is very central. ❶

Şanlıurfa Valiliği Konuk Evi Vali Fuat Bey Cad ☏ 0414/215 4678, ⓕ 312 3368. Best of the luxurious hotels, with just six comfortable, traditionally decorated rooms arranged around the *selamlık* section of a restored nineteenth-century mansion; reservations required well in advance. Follow the alley that leads off Vali Fuat Bey Cad, just opposite the Selahattin Eyubi Camii. ❺

Otel Uğur Köprübaşı Cad 3 ☏ 0414/313 1340. Behind the Sanmed Hospital, the Uğur is much favoured by backpackers, with clean rooms and helpful management – it's gradually upgrading its accommodation and prices. ❶

Old Urfa

At the extreme south end of Sarayönü Caddesi is the restored **Hacı Hafiz Efendi** house, which is now a fine arts gallery; take a look at their current exhibition and enjoy the cool courtyard and pretty architecture. Adjacent is the **Kara Meydanı**, boasting a venerable-looking nineteenth-century mosque, the Yusuf Paşa Camii. Past Kara Meydanı, Sarayönü Caddesi becomes Divan Caddesi, where you'll find the twelfth-century **Ulu Cami**, with a design based on that of the Grand Mosque in Halab (Aleppo) in Syria. You can take a look around the courtyard with its octagonal minaret (originally the belfry of an earlier Byzantine church) and graves, though the interior is unexceptional.

East of Divan Caddesi lies an extensive warren of bustling narrow streets boasting examples of Urfa's rather plain, pale limestone **medieval houses**, whose distinctive features include lattice-windowed overhangs supported on ornate corbels. At the end of Divan Caddesi sprawls the **Gümrük Hanı**, a late sixteenth-century *kervansaray*, whose shady courtyard is taken up by the tables of teahouses and watch repairers. This is surrounded by the **Kapalı Çarşı**, or covered bazaar, a maze-like commercial area spilling out into the narrow streets nearby. There are stalls and hole-in-the-wall shops selling everything imaginable, from spices to guns. Traders sell green Diyarbakır tobacco by the kilo out of plastic sacks, and domestic appliances are occasionally auctioned off the back of horse-drawn carts, while the pungent stink of skins from freshly slaughtered sheep vies with the more pleasant odour of various powdered herbs. Exotic fabrics, including velvets in glowing colours and beaded or sequined cloth, are an excellent buy.

Turning right out of the Gümrük Hanı brings you to the *bedesten* next door, beyond which lies the **Hacı Kamil Hanı** and the coppersmiths' bazaar. Further west lie the **Sipahi** and **Hüseyniye** bazaars, both left over from the time when camel caravans moved regularly between Urfa and Aleppo, Palmyra, Mari and Baghdad.

İbrahim Halilullah Dergahı

From the bazaars, make your way west along Göl Caddesi to the Mevlid-i Halil Camii and so into the gardens of the **Hızır İbrahim Halilullah**, a colonnaded mosque and *medrese* complex named after the "Prophet Abraham and Friend of God", which has grown up to serve the large numbers of pilgrims – as have stalls selling religious tracts. The **İbrahim Halilullah Dergahı**, or "Cave of Abraham" (daily 8am–5.30pm; $1.50) is set in the wall of the far courtyard. According to local legend, the prophet Abraham was born here, spending the first ten years of his life in hiding because a local Assyrian tyrant, Nemrut (Nimrod), had decreed that all new-born children be killed.

As Abraham is recognized as a prophet by Muslims, his birth-cave remains a place of worship, the majority of visitors being Muslim pilgrims from all over Turkey rather than tourists. Although there isn't actually much to see inside, the atmosphere is very reverential; there are separate entrances for men and women, dress must be respectful and shoes removed. There is another holy cave nearby, reputed to hold a hair plucked from Mohammed's head, and a recently constructed mosque, the Yeni Cami.

Gölbaşı and the kale

It's a short walk from the cave to **Gölbaşı** – literally "at the lakeside" – where you'll find a shady park, a pair of mosques and two pools filled with fat carp. According to a continuation of the local legend, Abraham, after he emerged from his cave, became an implacable opponent of King Nemrut and tried to smash the idols in the local temple. The tyrant was displeased and had Abraham hurled from the citadel battlements into a fire below. Abraham was saved when, on a command from God, the flames turned into water and the firewood into carp. The carp have long been considered sacred, and it's said that anyone who eats them will go blind.

Beside the first pool, the **Ayn-i-Zeliha** (named after the daughter of Nimrod), are teahouses and restaurants where you can sit in the shade after feeding the carp with bait bought from poolside vendors; you can even take a small rowing boat out onto the water. The elongated **Halil-ür Rahman** or Balıklı Göl is the pool that saved Abraham from a fiery end; it's surrounded by stone arches, its banks usually swarming with pilgrims and the water seething with fish.

The far western end of Balıklı Göl is closed off by the seventeenth-century **Abdürrahman Camii**, which you are free to look around. The present mosque replaced an older twelfth-century building whose distinctive square minaret has survived. The entire north side of the pool is flanked by the **Rizvaniye Camii**, built by an Ottoman governor in 1716, with some intricately carved wooden doors giving onto its peaceful courtyard.

Above Gölbaşı, and reachable via a signed path between the new mosque and the first pool, is Urfa's **kale** (Tues–Sun 9am–6pm; $0.70), a massive citadel whose construction is claimed by everybody who ever occupied the city. A nomad tent, where cold drinks are served, has been set up inside the entrance – very welcome if you've made the ascent in summer. Much of the castle's surviving structure is thought to date from the time of the twelfth-century Frankish Crusader state. The fortifications are completely ruined now, but it's worth climbing up there for the view of the mosques and pools down below. At the top are a couple of massive lone Corinthian columns, thought to be the remains of a third-century Christian chapel. They are referred to as the Throne of Nemrut, and local people will tell you that this is the spot from which Nemrut cast Abraham down into the flames.

North to the Archeological Museum

If you head north from Gölbaşı up Vali Fuat Bey Caddesi, you'll come to the **Selahattin Eyubi Camii**, whose interior layout remains essentially unchanged from its previous incarnation as the Christian church of St John. From here head north again for a glimpse of the former Armenian church of the Twelve Apostles, now converted to **Fırfırlı Camii**. Echoes of former worship can be seen in the star and moon carvings on the old clocktower, which now serves as the mosque's minaret. Continue north to the **Karakoyun River**, the traditional northern boundary of the old town, and if you have time, check out the Byzantine aqueduct, built in 525 and now squeezed between two Ottoman bridges. Some of the ruined old houses above the river still bear pockmarks made by French rifle bullets during the assault on the city in 1920.

The city's excellent **Archeological Museum** (Arkeoloji Müzesi; Tues–Sun 8.30am–noon & 1.30–5pm; $0.70) is just north of the town centre. Walking north to the museum, you'll pass an ancient *kervansaray* on the right, still very much in use, and an old church with belltower (now a mosque) to the left. Inside the museum, there's plenty of jewellery and pottery from funerary tumuli on the Euphrates flood-plain, as well as from the sites of ancient Harran and Lidar. An ethnographic section devoted to more recent local lifestyles includes statuary from the province's vanished Christian communities, plus magnificent carved doors from demolished mansions. The outdoor collection of reliefs, with inscriptions ranging from Hittite to Armenian, is particularly fascinating, thanks to the sharpness and clarity of the carvings. Keep an eye out, too, for numerous carved angels retrieved from caves all around Urfa, and a selection of large amphorae.

Eating and drinking

Spicy and fresh, the food in Urfa is usually pretty good. The town is the home of the **Urfa kebap** (spiced minced meat on a skewer) and of **lahmacun** (a thin, chapati-like bread topped with spicy lamb). Stalls in Urfa bazaar sell it hotter, spicier and cheaper than anywhere else and at the bus station hungry travellers can eat three *lahmacun* and drink an *ayran* for under a dollar. There are numerous simple eateries offering other local specialities based on bulgur (cracked wheat), notably *çiğ köfte* (a pattie of spicy, uncooked bulgur, pepper and spices) and *dolmalı köfte* (stuffed meatballs). **Desserts** such as *dondurma*, *kadife* (shredded wheat with cream cheese and honey) and *baklava* are best sampled from shops or cafés along Sarayönü Caddesi.

Dotted along a terrace opposite and at right angles to the *Harran* hotel on Atatürk Caddesi, a line of **bars** serves alcohol (beer or *rakı*) and snacks such as fruit, yoghurt and nuts, but will also send out for kebabs if you want to eat. The only alternatives for alcoholic drinks are the upmarket bars at the *Harran* and the *Edessa* hotels.

Boğaziçi Off Atatürk Cad. Best of the bars on this strip, recommended for its attentive service and cheap beer.

Kilim Pastanesi Köprübaşı Cad, beneath the *Otel Uğur*. Try *kaymakam* (clotted cream) with honey for breakfast at this café/breakfast shop.

Kızılay Aile Lokantası Sarayönü Cad. Set in its own pleasant garden off the north end of the street – good kebabs at average prices.

Şanlıurfa Valiliği Konuk Evi Vali Fuat Bey Cad ☎ 0414/215 4678. The hotel restaurant offers stylish, romantic Turkish dinners at roughly $10 (phone ahead to book) as well as afternoon coffee.

Sümer Lokantası Köprübaşı Cad. Two branches of this popular chain serve Urfa specialities and kebabs at moderate prices.

Listings

Banks and exchange There are a couple of convenient *döviz* offices and ATMs on Sarayönü Cad.

Buses The usual eastern bus companies have offices all around town, especially on Sarayönü Cad, and provide service buses to the *otogar*. Harran Dolmuş (see "Tours" below) and some hotels will also book tickets for you. Local companies include Urfa Cesur ("Urfa the Brave"), which runs right through to Ankara and İstanbul.

Car rental Harran Dolmuş, and one or two other places, rent cars for $30 daily upwards.

Hospital Özel Sanmed Hastanesi (Şanmed private hospital), Köprübaşı Cad ☎ 0414/216 3616/215 4348; Devlet Hastane ve Polikliniği (State Hospital), Hastane Cad ☎ 0414/313 1928/313 1220.

Internet *Interactive Café*, opposite the Boğaziçi, just off Atatürk Cad. There are others in the student quarter near the stadium.

Police Police station is on Sarayönü Cad.

Post office The PTT is on Sarayönü Cad (Mon–Sat 9am–noon and 1–5pm for money exchange and mail; 24hr for telephones).

Tours Harran Dolmuş (☎ 0414/215 1575), just behind the Şanmed hospital, runs half- and full-day trips to Harran (see below), as well as to Nemrut Dağı ($35), Mardin and Dar el-Zaferan monastery ($20 depending on group size). For $35 per person (minimum four people), Harran can also arrange a two-day monastery tour that includes a night in Midyat and visits to several monasteries on the Tür Abdin plateau as well as Hasankeyf and Diyarbakır.

Harran and around

Some 45km southeast of Urfa, the beehive-style houses in the village of **HARRAN** (also known as Altınbaşak) have become a major tourist attraction in recent years. It's the last surviving such community, the bleak plain around being dotted with the ruins of other mud-built villages in this Syrian-influenced style. Harran has strong biblical links: in Genesis 11:31 and 12:4, the patriarch Abraham is described as having dwelt here for a while on his way from Ur to Canaan, and it's tempting to imagine the place hasn't changed much since – although over the last decade or so, visitors have made big inroads into the traditional way of life.

Harran is thought to have been continuously inhabited for at least 6000 years, which makes it one of the oldest settlements on earth. It first came to prominence under the Assyrians, who turned it into a prosperous trading town, as well as a centre for the worship of Sin, god of the moon; there was a large temple here, later also used by the Sabian cult (see "Soğmatar" on p.883), on the site now occupied by the ruins of a Crusader fortress. In 53 BC the Roman general Crassus's advance east was halted here, where he was defeated, crucified and had molten gold poured into his mouth by the Parthians. Despite this, the Romans were later able to convert Harran into an important centre of learning, a role it continued to play under the Byzantines and subsequently the Arabs, who founded a university in the town. However, the arrival of the Mongols during the thirteenth century meant devastation. Today, the village overlays the scattered ruins; the beehive houses are mainly between the more extensive sections of the walls (east) and the fenced remains of the mosque and university (northwest).

Getting there

The Harran Dolmuş company in Şanlıurfa (see "Listings" on p.881) runs four-hour **excursions** to Harran ($8 per person), departing early or late in the afternoon during summer to avoid the horrific heat. **Dolmuşes** to Harran also run hourly from Şanlıurfa *otogar*; the last return dolmuş is at 7pm. Alternatively, you'll pay the fixed price of $22 to hire a taxi for the two-way trip with waiting time; in slower periods, you should be able to get a cheaper rate. Harran Dolmuş also offers more comprehensive **full-day tours** at $15–20 per person, including stops at the Han-el-Ba'rür *kervansaray*, the ruins of Şuayb and Soğmatar (for all of which see "Around Harran", opposite), and at a nomad encampment.

Tours drop you off at the western end of the village by the *jandarma* post and a small café, adjacent to the ruined Urfa Gate and a small **ticket booth** whose occupant will charge you $1.50 admission if he's around.

If you have your own transport, take the road south from Urfa towards Akçakale for 35km, following irrigation canals that bring water from the Atatürk Dam, until you reach a yellow-signposted turning; Harran is about 10km east of here.

Old Harran

These days, semi-nomadic Arabs and a few Kurds live amid the ruins of old **Harran**, surviving by farming the newly irrigated fields and smuggling sheep (in exchange for instant coffee, Ceylon tea and other foreign luxury goods) across the Syrian border 10km to the south. It is they who have built – and to some extent still live in – the mud-brick beehive-shaped buildings that dot the area, the distinctive shape of which is owed to the fact that no wood is used as support. However, if you're expecting a homogenous community of gumdrop houses, you'll be disappointed, as they're interspersed with conventional cottages and increasingly used for storage or animal – not human – habitation.

Most of the people here are fairly amiable and amused by the fascination their way of life exerts on visitors. Many are likely to want to talk and show you around. If possible try to visit out of season when the heat won't be quite so intense. Soft drinks are available from cafés to the east and west of the main site, and in the dark, cool communal house used as a point of sale for local handcrafts. The *Bazda Motel* on the village bypass road offers overnight **accommodation**; check with Harran Dolmuş that it is open. The locals themselves pass the torrid summer nights outdoors, on peculiar raised platforms.

The site

The enigmatic ruins of old Harran have a kind of tragic grandeur, dwarfing the beehive dwellings, and it's not difficult to picture the town as it must have been before the arrival of the Mongols. Near the *jandarma* is an artificial tumulus thought to mark the site of the original settlement. Just north of here, and surrounded by broken fencing, stands the most impressive of the ruins, the **Ulu Cami**, with its graceful square tower, built by an Arab caliph during the eighth century and mistaken for a cathedral belfry by T.E. Lawrence when he passed through in 1909. Scattered around are broken pillars, a central water pool with carved seats and remnants of the Arab university, which, judging from the surviving fragments, must have been an exceptionally beautiful complex.

By now you'll have been approached by the village kids, who'll beg for *para* (money) and *stilo* (pens). If you take pictures of the little girls in traditional costume they'll demand presents, and throw tantrums if you don't cough up. At this point a couple of them will probably attach themselves to you, offering to be your guides. Some of the older ones are gifted linguists with good twenty-word vocabularies in English, German and French; in addition, they all speak Arabic (their first language), Turkish (learned in school) and often Kurdish.

With your new entourage, make your way to the eleventh-century **Crusader fortress**, built on the site of the ancient moon temple at the eastern end of the village. There are plenty of ruins to scramble around, although much of the structure looks in a dangerous state of near-collapse. Watch out for the distinctive ten-sided tower; part of its ramparts once ringed the city, and a few sections are still visible to the south. Your young guides may also offer to show you the lion relief on the **Aslan Kapısı** (Lion Gate) at the northeast edge of the ancient town.

Around Harran

Northeast of Harran are the **Tek Tek Dağı**, a range of dusty hills dotted with ruins and remains, the most accessible and interesting of which can be reached on the Harran Dolmuş tours or with your own vehicle. Be warned, however, that the dense network of roads makes navigation frustrating.

Twenty-five kilometres east of the uninspiring twelfth-century *kervansaray* of **Han-el-Ba'rür**, itself 23km from Harran, you'll reach **ŞUAYB**, an ancient, partially subterranean, village founded in Roman times and fully inhabited until the Mongol raids. Villagers still occupy many of the caves and chambers, and various lintels and archways remain above ground.

From Şuayb, continue north 17km to the site of ancient **Soğmatar** (Sumatar on some maps), about 65km from Harran and Urfa. Soğmatar was the main centre of the Sabians, inheritors and elaborators of the local moon cult at Harran, who worshipped here from early Christian times onwards. Though nominally monotheistic, referring to the deity as Marilaha, the sect in fact was steeped in ancient Chaldean astrology, revering all the planetary bodies. By most accounts they were a pretty wild bunch, engaging in lurid orgies and performing human sacrifice in the course of their worship of the stars and planets. Even more amazing is the fact that they managed to elude Byzantine Christian censure till well into the ninth and tenth centuries, at which time the Arabs, disgusted by their rites, gave them the choice of death or conversion to Islam.

Ringing the contemporary village are seven circular hilltop ruins believed to have formed the Sabians' principal observatory and temple complex, with some ancient Syriac inscriptions on the walls. There are also carved statues and lunar insignia in a cave near the centre of the village. Local boys are happy to show strangers around and people in this desperately poor Arab settlement will be grateful for any deserving tip.

Adıyaman

If you choose **ADIYAMAN**, 60km northeast of Gaziantep, as an overnight staging post for Nemrut Dağı – and it's the only reason you'd come – there are a few things worth exploring before you leave on your tour. South of the bus station at the far end of town is the **copper bazaar**, where you can watch

Organized **minibus trips** to Nemrut Dağı run in the summer season (May–Oct) from Kahta, Adıyaman, Malatya, Şanlıurfa and Cappadocia and, given the distances involved, these are about the only way of getting there unless you have your own transport. Note that the summit road is only open from April 15 until the first snow-fall of winter, but outside the peak summer months (July and August) there may well be insufficient demand to make up groups each day. For more on the best time of day to visit the site, see p.889.

From Kahta

Khata (p.885), the closest town, would seem to make the best base, but it has its drawbacks. Although there are reputable operators, competition is cutthroat – don't be bludgeoned into taking a tour before you have checked out all the options. Tales abound of dissatisfied customers misled by some hotel proprietors. Theoretically, there are sunrise or sunset tours (sunset trips leave at 1pm and return at 9pm, sunrise tours leave at 3am, returning at 10am). The trips cost about $45 per minibus (seating eight) and should include the subsidiary sites of the Karakuş tumulus, Cendere bridge and the ancient Commagene capital of Arsameia.

From Adiyaman

Adıyaman (p.883) is a more pleasant base than Kahta; the only disadvantage is the additional half-hour journey time. Adıyaman Unal bus company, based in the *otogar*, runs daily daytime tours (8–9hr, early morning departures) for a minimum of three people for around $15 per person; prices are lower for larger groups. Tours take in the subsidiary sites – Karakuş tumulus, Cendere bridge and Arsameia – and the Pirinç prehistoric caves.

From Malatya

Tours from Malatya (p.891), on the north side of the range, may look more expensive, but if you count in the night's stay at the *Guneş Hotel* virtually at the summit, the difference is negligible. The main disadvantage is that you miss out on Nemrut's

old and new copper being tinned over open fires. Behind the bazaar is a *kervansaray*, used for tethering animals and ideal for a cup of tea in the shade. Between the main traffic lights and the bus station, the **museum** (Tues–Sun 8am–noon & 2–5pm; $0.70) houses artefacts from local tumuli, which were excavated prior to submersion under the Atatürk Dam waters. Also notable is the wide collection of Selçuk pottery, some pieces with turquoise glazes and painted decoration, others with embossed inscriptions. Finally, if you call at the office of Adıyaman Unal at the bus garage, you may be able to arrange a visit to the **Syrian/Armenian church** in a green garden in Adıyaman's old quarter; expect to tip the boy who guides you.

Practicalities

The **bus station**, where Nemrut tours are booked, is east of the main traffic lights on Atatürk Bulvarı, and less than 100m north of Harıkcı Caddesi. Adıyaman has a rather sleepy **tourist office** next to the PTT at Atatürk Bul 41 (Mon–Fri 9am–noon & 1–5pm; ☎0416/216 1008).

Inexpensive **hotels** are clustered in the centre of town. A couple of fairly uninspiring options are the *Otel Yoluç*, Harıkçı Cad 26 (☎0416/213 5226; ❷), and the *Unal Turistik Tesisleri*, Harıkçı Cad 14 (☎0416/ 216 1508; ❷), which subsidiary sites (though see below), but on the other hand you view both sets of heads at sunrise and sunset, and you get to stay at the welcoming stone-built *Guneş Hotel*, a well-built hotel with clean and cheerful en-suite rooms and good food. A Kurdish *yayla* (summer tent encampment) lies but a few minutes' walk away.

Bookings are best made the day before at the tourist office. Departures are usually at noon (though can be later), reaching the summit in good time for sunset; the return trip starts at about 7am, having given you time to admire the sunrise, reaching Malatya at about 11am. Assuming a fifteen-person minibus chartered from the tourist office, the cost is a good-value $30 per person for transport, lodging and two meals; the entrance fee is extra. If it suits your onward travel plans, you could walk over to the south side of Nemrut and find a lift to Kahta. This way, you get to see the subsidiary sites – the Malatya operator gives a small discount for this arrangement.

Cheapest way to visit from Malatya is to take a public dolmuş from Malatya dolmuş garage on the ring road to Büyüköz; for an extra fee, the driver will take you right to the *Guneş Hotel,* where you can camp, or sleep in the hotel's mock nomad tent.

From Şanlıurfa

Visiting Nemrut from Şanlıurfa (p.875) has the advantage of cutting out Adıyaman and Kahta, and can include a trip to see the Atatürk Dam, but the 420-kilometre (14-hour) round-trip takes in lots of uninteresting scenery. Harran Dolmuş currently offers these gruelling day-trips: sunrise tours depart Urfa at midnight; sunset tours at 8am, both costing $35 per person (minimum of three) people and including the subsidiary sites.

From Cappadocia

Many operators in Urgup, Göreme and other Cappadocian towns offer tours to Nemrut Daği, usually spanning three days and two nights and including Urfa. It's a long and tiring journey, but all the hassles are removed and, if you're not planning any further eastern travel, they make sense. The all-inclusive price is around $150 per person.

at least have the advantage of being close to restaurants and shops. At the central traffic lights, the *Serdaroğlu* (℡0416/216 4842, ℻216 1554; ❸), has plain rooms and an outdoor restaurant. To the east, past the bus station, the comfortable and quiet *Motel Beyaz Saray*, Atatürk Bul 136 (℡0416/216 4907; ❷), has the unexpected luxury of a garden swimming pool, while a further kilometre east lies the modern three-star *Hotel Antiochos*, Atatürk Bul 141 (℡0416/216 3377; ❸), again with a swimming pool but marred by thumping piped music that may keep you awake if the highway traffic doesn't. Adıyaman's lushest and largest hotel is also on Atatürk Bulvarı, the comfortable but dull *Bozdoğan Hotel* (℡0416/216 3999, ℻216 3630; ❹), also with a swimming pool.

There are plenty of small **kebab houses** around Harıkçı Caddesi, or the *Bozdoğan Hotel* has a pleasant outdoor **restaurant**.

Kahta

From Adıyaman, regular dolmuşes make the half-hour journey to **KAHTA**, 25km to the east, a dusty town of low houses that looks as though it's just heaved itself up out of the earth. It is only about a kilometre from the waters of the Atatürk Baraji, though you can't see the lake from the town.

The obvious budget **accommodation** choice is the *Hotel Kommagene* (☏0416/725 9726, ✉kommagenem@hotmail.com; ❶), at the junction of the town's main street with the road up to Nemrut, which attracts backpackers and relieves them of their money; it also has rudimentary camping facilities. Rooms with air conditioning will put it into a higher price bracket. However, the best of Kahta's inexpensive hotels is the laid-back, refurbished *Mezopotamya* (☏0416/725 5112; ❶) at the west edge of town: rooms have private bathrooms and air-conditioning, and there's a decent restaurant. Another choice is the compact, clean and friendly *Merhaba Hotel* (☏0416/725 7949, ☏725 8055; ❸) in the town centre. Also central, but at the top end of the scale, is the overpriced *Hotel Hans Bardakçı* (☏0416/725 8060, ☏725 5385; ❻), whose large rooms all have TVs. Kahta's most luxurious hotel is the new *Zeus Hotel* (☏0416/725 5694, ⓦwww.zeushotel.net. ❻), with pleasantly landscaped swimming pool, bar-restaurant, and rooms with air-conditioning and foreign-language TV.

There are a few cheap and basic **restaurants** on Kahta's broad main street, though the only one worth specifically recommending, for its leafy setting, is the *Yayla Çay Bahçesi ve İzgara*, south of and well below the main boulevard. A couple of kilometres east of town, overlooking the Atatürk lake is the *Neşetin Yeri* **fish restaurant** which serves excellent-value lake fish and grills on terraces with a view of the mountain and lake, but you really need your own transport or a taxi to reach it.

The road to Nemrut Dağı

The 75-kilometre road from Kahta up the mountain to Nemrut Dağı is mostly paved but potholed and therefore slow going; only the last few kilometres pose any danger to your vehicle's suspension. A road also connects Karakuş to Narince but misses out many of the interesting subsidiary sights on the way. The trip is easily done in your own transport, but make sure you fill up with fuel in Kahta.

Karakuş Tumulus and Cendere Köprüsü

The first attraction is about 9km north of Kahta, where a huge mound suddenly rises up by the roadside, just past a small oil-drilling field. This is the **Karakuş Tumulus**, said to be the funeral mound of Antiochus's wife. It's surrounded by pillars bearing animal motifs, the best of which is an intact eagle that gives the site its name – "black bird". From the top, you can see the waters trapped behind the Atatürk Baraji, and catch views of Nemrut Dağı to the northeast.

Another 9km along, the **Cendere Köprüsü** is a Roman bridge built between 193 and 211 AD during the reign of Emperor Septimius Severus, and still in use after repairs. It's a graceful, single-arched, humpbacked structure with tremendous views all around – especially up the adjacent Cendere canyon. Three of the original four columns at each end are still in place. Just beyond it are a couple of cafés and souvenir stands, where your custom will be assiduously solicited.

Eski Kahta and Arsameia

After another 6km or so you come to the turning for **ESKİ KAHTA**, a traditional village layered onto the hills behind and dominated by the **Mamluk**

Yeni Kale. The castle's fine keep and watchtower are ripe for exploration and give access to several hundred steps chiselled out of the sheer rock-face that once led into the thundering gorge below – however, they are now too dangerous to use. Just past the Eski Kahta turning, an alternative road goes over a Selçuk bridge, from where you can get down into the scenic river canyon below for a dip. From Eski Kahta, the direct road runs some 20km northeast to Nemrut Daği.

Arsameia

Signposts a kilometre or two beyond the Selçuk bridge point the way east to the ancient site of **Arsameia** (unfenced; $0.70 when guard present), the capital of the ancient Commagene kingdom, which lies nearly another 2km away at the end of an unsurfaced track. This was excavated by German archeologists during the 1950s and is worth a quick detour for the chance to admire the mountainous local scenery as well as the site itself. Members of a local family responsible for the site will collect admission and sell you soft drinks, postcards or souvenirs, as well as escorting you around.

From a rudimentary parking space a path leads along the hillside, where steps detour to a truncated relief stele of the god Mithras, before the trail forks left past two fingers of rock (one inscribed) to a cave with a tunnel running to a cistern. Just below the cave is another damaged stele, this one showing Mithridates I Callinicus, the founder of the Commagene kingdom, and perhaps Apollo.

From here the trail proceeds up the hillside to the highlight of the site, a sizable, perfectly preserved **relief depicting Hercules and Callinicus** shaking hands. Next to it is another tunnel with steps leading down into the earth, which terminates in a cave-in after about 150m. It's steep and roughly surfaced inside, and you'll need a torch if you want to take more than a cursory look. Above the tunnel entrance a huge, 25-line inscription tells you that Mithridates I Callinicus, father of Antiochus (founder of the complex at Nemrut Daği), is buried in the vicinity, and that the site is consecrated to him.

Just above the relief depicting Hercules and Mithridates sprawls a plateau with some sketchy foundations – so sketchy that it's difficult to determine what they once were. Also scattered around are fragments of what must have been quite large statues – look out for a giant, sandal-clad foot hiding in the grass. The Germans uncovered a number of mosaics here, but these have all been removed to the Museum of Anatolian Civilizations in Ankara.

Karadüt

Beyond the Arsameia turn-off, the road heads due south, passing the village of Damlacık after a couple of kilometres and then heading east past equally diminutive settlements such as Kuztepe, Tütünocak and Narince, before turning north again for Nemrut Daği. You could come this way directly from Kahta instead, but you'd miss out on the Cendere bridge and Arsameia ruins.

Nine kilometres out of Narince, there's a well-signposted left turning for Nemrut Daği, while three kilometres further on **KARADÜT** is the last village served by local dolmuşes from Kahta. Just above the village is the *Karadüt Motel Pansiyon* (☏0416/737 2169; ❶) and, beyond that, the *Çeşme* restaurant and *pansiyon* (☏0416/737 2032, ❶), the last **budget accommodation** before the summit. Nearer Nemrut Daği, you'll pass the *Hotel Euphrat* (☏0416/737 2175; ❸) and the pleasant *Otel Kervansaray Nemrut* (☏0416/737 2190; ❷), a cheaper, better choice with good bathrooms and a shady pool. Both include half-board in their rates and offer opportunities for high-level walks and exploration.

Beyond the hotels the road deteriorates noticeably, paved with basalt cobbles that guarantee a bone-shaking ride for the final 7km to the summit. Winter frosts have heaved up many of the blocks, whose sharp edges are capable of shredding a tyre, so drive with care.

Nemrut Daği

A day's journey northeast of Gaziantep, the mountain-top sanctuary at **Nemrut Daği** is an unforgettable place, remote and grandiose, drawing visitors who make the long journey up the mountainside by minibus and car. The mighty stone heads adorning the temple and tomb of king Antiochus have become one of the best-known images of Eastern Turkey. They are recycled endlessly on postcards and souvenirs, and if you find yourself anywhere within a couple of hundred kilometres of the place, people will naturally assume that you're here to see them.

You'll be told that the **best time to visit** is at dawn, in order to watch the sunrise. This is debatable, and will probably involve setting out at 2am; upon arriving at the 2150-metre summit you will almost inevitably find that at least several dozen other people are there with the same idea. You might also find that it's quite cold, so come prepared, while if you're visiting out of season check up on weather conditions before you leave, as there's often snow on the ground from late October until May. If you have a choice, it is better to visit at sunset, when it is less chilly and the setting sun illuminates the western terrace in a warm glow.

Finally, if you are here in the last week in June, you can witness the **Commagene Festival**, when folk dancing and music performances take place on the mountain. See posters in Kahta for details.

Some history

The result of one man's delusions of grandeur, the great tomb and temple complex of Nemrut Dağı was built by **Antiochus I Epiphanes** (64–38 BC), son of Mithridates I Callinicus, the founder of the Commagene kingdom. The Commagene dynasty was a breakaway from the Seleucid Empire, covering only a small territory from modern Adıyaman to Gaziantep, and it wouldn't rate much more than a passing mention in histories of the region were it not for the fact that Antiochus chose to build this temple as a colossal monument to himself. Despite having shown early promise as a statesman by concluding a non-aggression treaty with the Romans, Antiochus later decided he was divine in nature, or at the very least an equal of the gods, declaring: "I, the great King Antiochus have ordered the construction of these temples . . . on a foundation which will never be demolished . . . to prove my faith in the gods. At the conclusion of my life I will enter my eternal repose here, and my spirit will ascend to join that of Zeus in heaven."

Antiochus's vanity knew no bounds – he claimed descent from Darius the Great of Persia and Alexander the Great – but eventually he went too far, siding with the Parthians against Rome, and was deposed. This was effectively the end of the Commagene kingdom, which afterwards passed into Roman hands, leaving only Antiochus's massive funeral folly as a reminder of its brief existence.

Even this was forgotten by the outside world until the late-nineteenth century, when Karl Puchstein, a German engineer, came across the site while making a survey in 1881. In 1883 he returned with Karl Humann (the man who removed the Pergamon altar to Berlin) to carry out a more thorough investigation, but it wasn't until 1953 that a comprehensive archeological survey of the site began, under the direction of an American team. Since then Nemrut Dağı, hitherto only reached after an arduous journey of several days, has been put back on the map.

The summit

You may well find yourself travelling the last few kilometres in a convoy of minibuses and, at first sight, **the summit** of Nemrut Dağı often seems to be no more than a parking area full of milling crowds. Just adjacent are a small café, souvenir shop and toilet facilities. The café provides tea, soft drinks and low-alcohol beer, and usually breakfast for groups, but sometimes only has dry biscuits, so it makes sense to bring your own food. They rent out **dormitory beds** here too (❶), but you'd be well advised to bring your own sleeping bag. Far better suited to those ascending from Malatya is **accommodation** at the comfortable *Güneş Hotel* (no phone; ❷), a half-hour walk below the summit site and reachable from the south only on foot. If you are determined, it is possible to visit the site from the Kahta side, then walk down to the *Güneş* to spend the night, and thence onto Malatya.

The site

Behind the car park buildings is the entrance to the **site** ($3), beyond which is a fifty-metre-high tumulus of small rocks, thought to cover the tomb of Antiochus; signs tell you that it's forbidden to climb the mound. In any case you don't need to be at the very top to enjoy the awesome views for hundreds of kilometres around. Antiochus selected virtually the highest peak in his kingdom to give free rein to his megalomania.

A paved path leads along the south side of the tumulus, coming to a terrace area after ten to fifteen minutes' walk, on which stands the **eastern temple** with six decapitated seated statues, each several metres in height. From left to right they represent: Apollo, Fortuna (symbol of the Commagene kingdom), Zeus, Antiochus and Hercules plus an unidentified figure. Scattered in front of these truncated figures are the much-photographed **detached heads**, each measuring a couple of metres in height – just three in the case of the eastern terrace, with Fortuna squeezed behind the bodies, and perhaps a little disappointing after all the hype, but remarkably intact bar the odd missing nose or two.

They were meant to incorporate several similar deities drawn from different cultures, according to the principle of syncretism, which Alexander the Great had promoted to try and foster a sense of unity among the disparate peoples of his empire. On the date of Antiochus's birthday and the anniversary of his coronation, the Commagene people would file up to the mountain-top to witness the dawn sacrifice and make offerings, carried out in strict accordance with the Greek inscriptions carved onto the back of the royal statues. The sacrificial altar still stands in front of the statues, in a space now used as a helipad for VIP visitors.

The **altar** makes a good vantage point from which to admire the statues and wonder at the immense effort that must have gone into their construction. Scattered around about are fragments of a massive stone eagle and a lion, symbolic temple guardians that once stood like bookends at either end of the royal line-up.

A path leads around the northern base of the tumulus to the **western terrace**, lined by slabs once decorated with reliefs. None of the western statues is even partially intact, although the dispersed **heads** here are much less weathered than those on the other side of the tumulus, and there are more statues – a complete set of five, plus two eagle-heads to flank them – which argues in favour of a sunset visit. The line-up is the same, although it's harder to work out who's who. Look out for Fortuna, with a garland of leaves and vines in her hair, and Apollo, claimed by some to be a dead ringer for Elvis Presley.

A number of **reliefs** have, however, survived adjacent to the statuary debris – three depict Antiochus shaking hands with Apollo, Zeus and Hercules. Another shows a lion with the planets of Jupiter, Mars and Mercury and a moon representing the Commagene kingdom draped around his neck; it's thought to be an astrological chart referring to the date of Antiochus's conception.

Malatya and around

MALATYA, 120km north of Nemrut Dağı, is a lively, cosmopolitan city of around 600,000 people. Smart shops line tree-shaded boulevards – the easternmost examples of both in Turkey. There's little to see within the city limits, but it's a pleasant enough place for an overnight stop before tackling Nemrut Dağı, and there are possible excursions out to the old town of Eski Malatya and the nearby site of ancient Aslantepe.

Malatya has always been a political town and is the home of two former presidents of the Republic, General İsmet İnönü (who gets a statue in his honour) and part-Kurdish Turgut Özal (who doesn't). There's a university (a perennial focus of "left versus right" political agitation) and a huge army base. It's also the centre of a fertile fruit-growing region, particularly famed for apricot production – you'll see abundant supplies of dried, unpitted apricots on sale.

Arrival, information and services

Whilst Malatya is pretty large, the centre is fairly compact and most of the hotels and restaurants are within walking distance of each other.

The **otogar** and **train station** (both served by bus #11 from opposite the *Vilayet*) are 7km and 2km respectively west of the centre on the Çevre Yolu (ring road). Service buses run into town from the *otogar*, dropping you at the Çevre Yolu junction closest to the centre. From Malatya's **airport**, 20km northwest of the city, an airport bus meets the two daily flights and ferries arrivals ($3) to the THY terminal at Kanal Boyu Cad 10 (℡0422/324 8001).

There's a helpful **tourist office** (Mon–Sat 9am–noon & 1–5pm; ℡0422/323 3025) in the *Vilayet* (governor's office) building, behind the statue of İnönü in the main square, İnönü Meydanı; ask one of the security men on duty at the door for directions. The office's main function is to sign you up for a **trip to Nemrut Dağı** (see box on p.884). At weekends, the Vilayet Parkı behind the *Vilayet* building hosts an informal tourist office for intended visitors to Nemrut. The **PTT** is near the square at the very start of İnönü Caddesi. You'll find **internet cafés** along and at the south end of Fusili Caddesi near the museum; **banks and exchange facilities** are in the same area.

It's worth noting that the sketch plan of the city handed out by the tourist office doesn't make it clear that the main boulevard is called **İnönü Caddesi** west of the *Vilayet* building, but becomes **Atatürk Caddesi** east of it – and the whole thing is referred to as **İstasyon Caddesi** by some sources.

Accommodation

Malatya's hotels are spread between the ring road and the İnönü statue in the city centre. The best **budget** option is the noisy but spotlessly clean *Otel Park*, Atatürk Cad 17 (℡0422/321 1691; ❶), with some en-suite rooms; you'll need ear-plugs if you're to get any sleep. The quieter *Otel Kantar*, Atatürk Cad 21(℡0422/321 1510, ❶), seems to have cornered the backpacker trade and also has clean rooms, some with showers, but shared toilets. Most **mid-range** options are also near the centre. The *Hotel Yeni Sinan* (℡0422/321 2907; ❷), on Atatürk Caddesi just east of İnönü Meydanı, is excellent value, with good views from the upper floors. The *Hotel Beydağı* on Darbakhane Sokak, on the way into town from the bus stop (℡0422/322 4611 or 323 2258; ❷), runs it a close second. The two-star *Malatya Büyük Hotel*, Yeni Cami Karşısı (℡0422/321

1400, ⓟ321 5367; ❸), has a good view of the main mosque, but the early call to prayer is ear-splitting.

Moving **upmarket**, the *Palancı Hotel* on Turgut Temelli Caddesi (ⓣ0422/325 1003, ⓟ325 1154; ❹) is just north of the centre. Rooms are double-glazed and air-conditioned, and have cable TV. Malatya's best hotel, the *Altın Kayısı*, İstasyon Caddesi (ⓣ0422/238 0533, ⓟ238 0083; ❼), is inconveniently located out of town, near the train station, but is equipped with a mouth watering array of top-notch facilities, including smart restaurant, gardens and a pool.

The City

The **Şire Pazarı**, in the centre between Atatürk Bulvarı and the ring road, is devoted to local agricultural produce, namely cherries, mulberries, apples, walnuts and, especially, apricots. Indeed, the best time to visit town is during the apricot harvest in July, when there's an **apricot festival** (July 15–22) at Mişmiş Parkı, 5km east of the town.

Next to the Şire bazaar is Malatya's **copper bazaar**, giving you an opportunity to watch the craftsmen hammering away or tin-plating surfaces intended for use with food. A bit of scrabbling on the dirty shelves of stalls will reveal old pieces with Armenian inscriptions – antique copper is cheaper and more likely to be genuine here than anywhere else.

On the south side of Malatya, at the end of Fuzuli Caddesi, is a new waterfall feature, with attractive landscaped **gardens** set alongside a stream. Unfortunately, the adjoining **archeological museum** is still closed to the public, although a few Hittite monuments in the garden are visible. The district around the falls is something of an upmarket shopping area, with internet cafés, restaurants, banks and exchange offices.

The only building of any historic interest, situated northwest of the town beyond the ring road, is a neglected **Armenian church** of impressive size, currently closed to visitors.

Eating and drinking

There are plenty of **cafés and restaurants** in Malatya, but few are outstanding; around the bazaars you can eat well for $5. The *Kışla Restaurant* on Atatürk Caddesi near the *Otel Park* is a basic grill redeemed mostly by its nice *sütlaç* (rice pudding). Further east on Atatürk Caddesi is the *Beyaz Sarayi*, good value for *pide*, kebabs and soups – it also serves comb honey and creamy yoghurt for breakfast. For grilled meats there's the late-opening *Güngör*, at the intersection of Atatürk and PTT *caddesi*s; and you can eat late, too, at *Magdalena Burger*, Şehit Hamit Fendoğlu Cad 35, a pleasant café with a range of fast food. The open-air *Şelale* café-restaurant near the (closed) museum has a holiday atmosphere, ducks to feed and Kahramanmaraş ice cream.

The restaurant at the *Hotel Yeni Sinan* (see "Accommodation" above) is open in the evenings and offers **live entertainment**, views of the city and decent grills, as well as serving beer. The *Aspuzu*, opposite the PTT, is another good bet if you want a beer with your meal. For rock-bottom drinking, there is an alley west of Atatürk Caddesi near the *Otel Park* with several **pubs** and a *lokanta*.

Eski Malatya

About 12km north of the modern city, **ESKI MALATYA**, or "Old Malatya", a ruined Roman/Byzantine town, is served half-hourly by blue city buses marked "Batalgazi"; catch them from the northwest side of the traffic lights on the Çevre Yolu, a few hundred metres due east of the city centre. You can return to Malatya via the red *Belediye* bus, which takes longer but makes a scenic tour around local villages.

The old town walls are still visible but much of the original settlement, which boasted 53 churches and a couple of dozen monasteries, has been built over. The local angle on the creation of "Old" and "New" Malatya has it that when the Ottoman army was billeted inside the walls in 1838–39 BC, the citizens, in order to keep their wives and daughters away from the rough soldiery, moved to their summer houses further up the hill at present-day Malatya; most never moved back.

Buses arrive at the main square, where (if you arrive during opening hours) the owner of the bookshop, a retired schoolteacher, will usually appoint a child as your guide in exchange for an impromptu English lesson. It's a 200-metre walk southwest of the square to a partially restored seventeenth-century *kervansaray*, and a further couple of hundred metres south to the Selçuk **Ulu Cami**. This huge mosque complex was commissioned by the powerful Selçuk sultan, Alâeddin Keykubad, who was also responsible for Alanya castle. It was built by Yakub bin Ebubekir around a central *eyvan* and consists of summer and winter mosques. The latter is of plain stonework with massive pillars in the usual Selçuk style, but the former consists of a central bay with a soaring domed roof flanked by two wings, the whole surrounding the *eyvan*. The brickwork of the dome reveals complicated herringbone patterning and inset blue glazed tiles that sparkle like stars. The *mimber* is of intricately carved wood topped by turban-shaped finials. The arches onto the *eyvan* – decorated with intricate turquoise and black tile-work – are still in reasonable condition, although modern glass doors have been installed in them. Just south of the mosque is a ruined *medrese* and the stranded **Melik Sunullah minaret** (1394) with traces of tile-work still clinging to it. Nearby is a saint's tomb with two coffins covered in green silk.

Aslantepe

One of the most actively excavated ancient sites in central Anatolia, Hittite **Aslantepe** lies just over 4km from the northeastern edge of Malatya; city bus #36 from the Çevre Yolu stop, labelled "Orduzu", passes within 800m of the site, or take a bus marked "Bahçebaşı" from opposite the *Vilayet* building.

Like many similar settlements in Turkey, the mound here is largely artificial, raised up a convenient distance from a river in the midst of what has always been an oasis; from up top there's a view over well-watered apricot groves. The name – "Lion Hill" – derives from the stone lions found guarding the north gate of the Hittite city, now in Ankara's Anatolian Civilizations Museum. They, and many other Hittite treasures, were uncovered by French scholars in the 1930s using the now-discredited technique of deep, rapidly cut, exploratory trenches. Since 1962 Aslantepe has been more meticulously uncovered by Italian archeologists, in residence each August to October – the prime time for a **visit to the site** (daily 8.30am–5pm), since at other times tarpaulins shroud much of the area. Members of the team speak good English and will escort you around, making sense of a dig that is otherwise still very much of specialist interest.

The most exciting discovery to date is a vast **palace complex**, the earliest known, built of mud bricks on a stone foundation and dating from the end of the fourth millennium BC. Also unusual are a pair of eerie **wall-paintings** from approximately 3200 BC. The room with the painted wall is flanked by storehouses in which were found pots and clay seals for accounting and administration of foodstuffs, since writing was as yet unknown.

Adjoining the palace to the west is a **temple** to an unknown deity, with concentric oval decorations stamped into its walls. On the northwest of the tumulus, some Neolithic remains predate the palace, while the northeast slope, now overgrown, was the location of the Hittite town and its spectacular finds. Beside the Hittite excavations, you can make out a bit of the Roman village; the Byzantines moved the population to Eski Malatya in the fifth century, ending more than four thousand years of habitation on this spot.

Elazığ and Harput

One hundred kilometres northeast of Malatya, and easily accessible by dolmuş, **Elazığ** is not really on any kind of a normal tourist route. With a population of 300,000, it's a friendly but uneasy mix of Kurd and Turk, Alevi and Sunni, founded in 1862 by Sultan Abülaziz to house the overspill population from the old settlement of **Harput**, wracked by earthquakes and now largely abandoned. It's an important grape-producing town, the centre of an area where *okuzgözü* (ox-eye) grapes, used to produce the red Buzbağ wine, are harvested. Following the lifting of the Emergency Regulations, the local authorities are less suspicious of travellers, but will nonetheless be surprised at your presence in a town with only minor historical interest.

Elazığ

ELAZIĞ is predominantly modern and soulless, but it has a decent **archeological museum** (Tues–Sun 8.30am–noon & 1.30–5pm; $0.70), displaying objects from various local ancient sites submerged after the completion in 1974 of the Keban Dam project, north of town. There's a remarkable collection of Urartian jewellery, as well as an ethnological section with some unexciting costumes and carpets. The museum's opening times chop and change and, as it is on the campus of Euphrates University, it may be closed for periods during the summer recess. To reach it, take a *Universite* bus from opposite the *Polis Evi* (Police House) on the main square and alight at the university gates; enquire here for the museum. Make sure you buy your bus ticket first from a little pavement kiosk behind the bus stand.

If you want to stay overnight, the best-value **accommodation** is at the *Turistik Otel* (☎0424/218 1772; ❶), on Hürriyet Caddesi in the town centre, just east of the main square. It's modern, clean and friendly, and rooms here even have a (noisy) balcony. Opposite the *Turistik* is the *Hotel Çinar* (☎0424/218 1811; ❷), also up-to-date but with better-quality furnishings, TV in the rooms and secure parking.

Elazığ has a number of simple **lokantas**: the *Hacioğulları* on Hürriyet Caddesi is bright and cheerful, and serves excellent *lahmacun* on wooden platters.

Harput

The all-but-abandoned town of **HARPUT** lies a five-kilometre ride to the north of Elazığ, at the end of a road lined by military installations guarding the Keban Dam. It's reached on red city bus #19 or by dolmuş from Elazığ. Harput was a thriving commercial centre of many thousands until the late nineteenth century, when a series of disastrous earthquakes led to mass emigration to Elazığ.

Today, the sleepy town is studded with yellow signs pointing to numerous **mosques**, **hamams** and **tombs** of much-venerated saints, though none is especially distinguished and all told the detour is only advisable if you're looking to kill some time. A tiny **museum** stands at the entrance to Harput, whose friendly keeper will show you the few relics on display. Most interesting is a black-and-white photograph showing Harput in the late nineteenth century, dominated by the massive bulk of the American/French missionary school, which is now totally destroyed.

Well-marked at the northeast edge of the site, the originally Byzantine **castle** is essentially a shell, except for its fine restored gateway and a small church inside. Despite apparent impregnability on top of a rocky outcrop, it was captured by Tamerlane during the second Mongol wave and again by Sultan Selim I in 1515. The view from the top of the citadel is pleasant, with the blue waters of the Keban Dam glinting below the rolling mountains.

Back in the centre of Harput, the still-functioning **Meydan Camii** and its attached hamam are the remaining focus of life in the town. Nearby is the **Arap Baba Türbesi**, housing the body of a local holy man. Once in a while, an attendant at this small mausoleum will raise the lid of the wooden coffin to reveal a startling mummified brown body. The town's oldest mosque is the box-like twelfth-century **Ulu Cami**, with its brick minaret leaning at a crazy angle.

In the blissfully peaceful leafy park adjoining the simple Kurşunlu Cami, you can get ayran, **tea and snacks** including *Harput köfte*, the local meatball dish.

The Tigris basin

Approaching the **valley of the River Tigris** (Dicle in Turkish) from the northwest, from Malatya, the road threads through an Asiatic canyon-riddled landscape, with the scenic Hazar Gölü en route the only natural lake in a land of reservoirs. In contrast, travelling from the east, from Urfa to Mardin or Diyarbakır, you leave the lush green of newly irrigated plantations behind and enter a barren but austerely beautiful landscape that provides a fitting introduction to the underdeveloped provinces of the southeast.

Most points of interest lie on the southwestern banks of the River Tigris. The natural gateway is **Diyarbakır**, a rapidly expanding, predominantly Kurdish city, with a unique cultural mix and character that makes a memorable impact on most visitors. The main road to Iraq from Şanlıurfa heads due east to the stunning architecture and narrow lanes of **Mardin**, a town isolated on a limestone bluff above the Syrian plain and preserving a way of life apparently frozen in the past. Mardin has never been hit by the poverty of Diyarbakır, perhaps because its proximity to the border has allowed the black economy to thrive. East of here, **Midyat** and its hinterland is the traditional home of Turkey's Syrian Orthodox Christian community, who split with the rest of

Christendom 1600 years ago. There are now only six Christian villages on the **Tür Abdin plateau** that extends to the east of Midyat, dotted with semi-ruined churches and monasteries. Some churches still function on a rotational basis, but it is the monastery of **Mar Gabriel**, supported largely by émigrés, that keeps the faith alive. Further north, on the Tigris, are the spectacular medieval ruins of **Hasankeyf**, now reprieved from drowning under the planned İlisu Dam.

Diyarbakır

Superbly positioned at the edge of the Tigris flood-plain, the old city of **DİYARBAKIR** shelters behind huge, ancient walls of black basalt, which enclose a maze of cobbled streets and alleys peppered with beautiful mosques, imposing *hans*, stately mansions and intriguing churches. There's a lively, energetic atmosphere to the place, and on the whole, the residents – who number two million – are generally open, helpful and self-confident. From the west, though, the first sight of Diyarbakır is uninspiring: the modern town has long since burst out of the confining walls, and the soulless multi-storey apartment buildings of the new quarters hide the old city. In addition, there is a major fresh water and drainage project currently underway, funded by the World Bank, and many of the already narrow alleys may be impassable due to pipe-laying. The authorities also seem to be using this upheaval as an excuse to pull down the *geceköndü* (shantytown) dwellings huddled inside the city walls.

Despite the friendly atmosphere, Diyarbakır has something of a bad reputation in other parts of Turkey. Once a hotbed of separatist activity, in fact it's now no more dangerous than any other large Turkish city, although some tourists are intimidated by the constant attention of hordes of noisy children

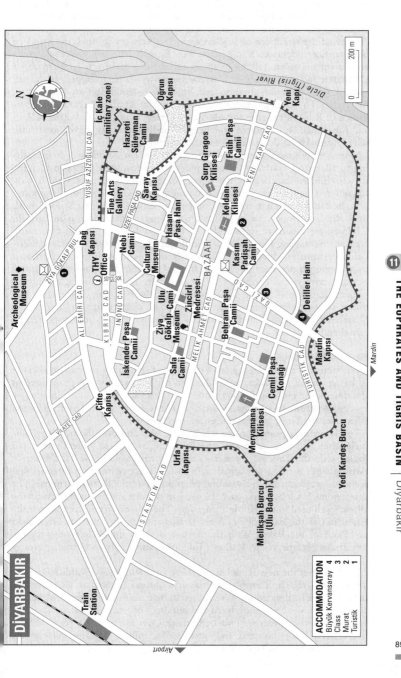

DİYARBAKIR

Train Station

Archeological Museum

İç Kale (military zone)

Hazreti Süleyman Camii

Oğrun Kapısı

Dicle (Tigris) River

Yeni Kapısı

Fine Arts Gallery

Saray Kapısı

Surp Giragos Kilisesi

Fatih Paşa Camii

Keldani Kilisesi

Dağ Kapısı

Nebi Camii

Hasan Paşa Hanı

THY Office

Cultural Museum

Ulu Camii

Zincirli Medresesi

Kasım Padişah Camii

İskender Paşa Camii

Ziya Gökalp Museum

Safa Camii

Behram Paşa Camii

Deliller Hanı

Çifte Kapısı

Meryamana Kilisesi

Cemil Paşa Konağı

Mardin Kapısı

Urfa Kapısı

Yedi Kardeş Burcu

Melikşah Burcu (Ulu Badan)

ZİYA GÖKALP BUL

YUSUF AZİZOĞLU CAD

İZZET PAŞA CAD

YENİ KAPI CAD

ALİ EMİRİ CAD

KIBRIS CAD

İNÖNÜ CAD

SÜTÇÜ SOK

MELİK AHMET CAD

GAZİ CAD

BAZAAR

TURİSTİK CAD

VİLAYET CAD

İSTASYON CAD

0   200 m

N

Mardin

Airport

ACCOMMODATION

Büyük Kervansaray	4
Class	3
Murat	2
Turistik	1

in the slum areas and the general bustle in the streets. The sight of policemen watering the flower-beds outside their city-centre police station should convince you that the authorities are still in control.

To avoid the attentions of hustlers and street kids, try to hook up with one of the many students keen to practise their English, who will give you a guided tour of the town. Talking to these students is a good way to learn about Diyarbakır and pick up a basic Kurdish vocabulary – *sipas* (pronounced "spaas" – thank you) and *rojbaş* (pronounced "rojebosh" – good day) are good words for starters. They will point out the finer points of Kurdish dress, the predominance of Kurdish cassettes for sale and the nuances of the local dialects, Zaza and Kurmancı. This concrete evidence of **Kurdish identity** makes you realize why Diyarbakır has long been a focus of discontent.

Moreover, the rapid population influx over the last decade has done nothing to alleviate Diyarbakır's already precarious **economic situation**: eight-to-ten-children families are the norm, some of the side streets are frankly squalid and beggars are not an uncommon sight. Class sizes in the poorest schools can approach a hundred, and many children starting school speak only Kurdish – not very helpful when the entire curriculum is in Turkish. Children are taught in shifts and the kid that sells you a *simit* at 10am may well not be starting his school day until 5pm. The effect of the recent legislation permitting education in Kurdish is unlikely to have much effect as it only applies to private, fee-paying schools. Unemployment approaches forty percent, with no real industry to speak of; the only significant product is watermelons, grown on the banks of the Tigris with pigeon droppings as fertilizer. Fifty-kilo monsters are the result, but it's claimed that in the old days Diyarbakır melons weighed as much as 100kg and had to be transported by camel and cut using a sword.

Some history

Diyarbakır is not only the capital of the upper Tigris valley, but has some claim to being one of the oldest settlements on earth. Certainly the city existed at the time of the Hurrian Empire, some 5000 years ago, and it subsequently saw successive periods of Urartian, Assyrian and Persian hegemony, before falling to Alexander the Great and his successors, the Seleucids.

The Romans appeared on the scene in 115 AD and over the next few centuries they and their successors, the Byzantines, struggled violently over the town with the Sassanid Persians. The Romans, who knew Diyarbakır as **Amida**, built the first substantial walls around the city in 297 – the ones you see today were erected in Byzantine times on top of the Roman originals. The threatening, basalt bulwarks gave the place its popular ancient name – Amid the Black – still used in the Kurdish languages. The modern name comes from the Arabs: in 638 the Bakr tribe of Arabs arrived and renamed the city Diyar Bakr or "Place of the Bakr". With the decline of Arab influence in the region, Diyarbakır became a Selçuk, then a Turcoman, and finally an Ottoman stronghold.

In 1925, after the new Republican government had dashed Kurdish hopes of autonomy, a rebellion erupted in the area around Diyarbakır. The city was besieged and Turkish troops were rushed in by train through French-occupied territory. The siege was soon lifted and hundreds of rebels were hanged on the spot, though the bloodshed didn't end there. Over the next few years the lives of between forty thousand and quarter of a million Kurdish villagers are thought to have been taken in reprisals.

Arrival, orientation and information

Most of what you need in Diyarbakır is in the old city, within the great walls. The **train station** lies a kilometre west of town at the end of İstasyon Caddesi, the **otogar** 2km northwest at the top of Ziya Gökalp Bulvarı. A new *otogar* is currently under construction further out of town. Dolmuşes are on hand to ferry new arrivals to the centre from either terminal; don't believe any taxi drivers who tell you that there aren't any. You'll be dropped off at **Dağ Kapısı** (formerly known as Harput Kapası), which was once one of several gigantic city gateways. **Dolmuşes from Mardin** arrive at the central crossroads where Gazı Caddesi and Melik Ahmet Caddesi intersect. Kaplaner **airport**, 3km southwest of town, is theoretically served by THY buses, which will drop you at the **THY office** at İnönü Cad 8; if none is available bargain for a taxi, which should cost around $10.

The local **tourist office** (Mon–Sat 9am–5pm; ☎0412/221 2173) on Kıbrıs Caddesi will dole out city plans, and staff are eager to chat in limited English. Finding your way around Diyarbakır is straightforward enough if you keep to the main roads. From Dağ Kapısı, **Gazı Caddesi**, running south to the Mardin Kapısı, bisects the city from north to south, and **Melik Ahmet Caddesi**, later becoming **Yeni Kapı Caddesi**, does the same from west to east. The back streets, however, are a maze of narrow alleys, where it's easy to lose your bearings.

Accommodation

Most of the desirable accommodation in Diyarbakır lies within a short walk of the Dağ Kapısı – the further away from here, the quieter it's likely to be. Many new affordable mid-range hotels have made it easier to avoid staying in the grottiest of the bottom-end hotels – we've only listed the most passable of the budget choices, but bear in mind that in the midsummer heat, paying the small difference in cost of a decent air-conditioned room will considerably enhance your stay. Also, the cheaper hotels don't usually include breakfast in the rates. Accommodation is marked on the "Around Dağ Kapısı" map, except for those few places towards Mardin Kapısı and outside the walls, which are shown on the main Diyarbakır map.

West of Dağ Kapısı

Balkar Hotel Kıbrıs Cad 38 ☎0412/228 1233, ℗224 6936. Beautifully fitted out with nice textiles and paintwork, with a terrace restaurant for breakfast. ❸

Büyük Otel İnönü Cad 4 ☎0412/228 1295, ℗221 2444. Appealing to Art-Deco lovers; old-fashioned rooms marred by awful views of blank walls and fire escapes. ❸

Dicle Oteli Kıbrıs Cad 3 ☎0412/223 5326. Large, airy and popular place, well frequented by locals, but sliding into a state of disrepair. ❷

Hotel Gap İnönü Cad 3, Çıkmaz 3 ☎0412/221 1218. Basic rooms with iron bedsteads, some with ceiling fan, some with air-conditioning (extra), set around a cool courtyard. ❶

Hotel Grand Güler Kıbrıs Cad 13 ☎0412/229 2221 ℗224 4509. Although now a bit dated, this business-oriented hotel has well-fitted air-conditioned rooms. ❸

Hotel Kaplan Sütçü Sok 14 ☎0412/224 9606. Friendly and in a quiet location on a side street to the north of İnönü Cad. All rooms have a TV, fridge and air-conditioning. ❷

Hotel Kristal Sütçü Sok 10 ☎0412/224 1642. Same management and facilities as its sister-hotel, the *Kaplan*, but not quite such good value. ❸

Southeast of Dağ Kapısı

Demir Otel İzzet Paşa Cad 8 ☎0412/228 8800, ℗228 8809. Not much charm, but the rooms are well furnished and there's a flashy mirrored lobby, restaurant and swimming pool. ❺

Hotel Kenan İzzet Paşa Cad 20/B ☎0412/221 6614. Clean, spacious rooms and an attached hamam. Some rooms in the next category have air conditioning. ❶

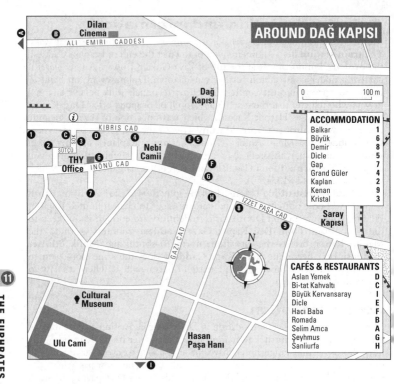

AROUND DAĞ KAPISI

Dilan Cinema
ALI EMIRI CADDESI

Dağ Kapısı

0   100 m

KIBRIS CAD

SÖK

SÜTCÜ
THY Office
INÖNÜ CAD

Nebi Camii

İZZET PAŞA CAD

Saray Kapısı

N

GAZI CAD

Cultural Museum

Ulu Cami

Hasan Paşa Hanı

ACCOMMODATION

Balkar	1
Büyük	6
Demir	8
Dicle	5
Gap	7
Grand Güler	4
Kaplan	2
Kenan	9
Kristal	3

CAFÉS & RESTAURANTS

Aslan Yemek	D
Bi-tat Kahvaltı	C
Büyük Kervansaray	I
Dicle	E
Hacı Baba	F
Romada	B
Selim Amca	A
Şeyhmus	G
Şanlıurfa	H

THE EUPHRATES AND TIGRIS BASIN | Diyarbakir

11

Towards Mardin Kapısı

Büyük Kervansaray Gazı Cad, Deliller Hanı ☎0412/228 9606, ☎223 7731. Smallish air-conditioned rooms, nicely decorated and with new bathrooms, set in a converted *kervansaray* with a shady central courtyard and a large swimming pool. Don't be fobbed off with the *Kervansaray 2*, the sister building in the town centre, which is very poor value. ⑥

Class Hotel Gazi Cad 101 ☎0412/229 5000 ⊛www.diyarbakirclasshotel.com. A modern hotel, with good facilities and value-for-money prices. Behind the flashy facade is the restored courtyard

of a medieval mansion, now with swimming pool, bar and restaurant. ⑥

Hotel Murat Balıkçılarbaşı ☎0412/224 5514/221 2705. Quiet but central place next to the four-legged minaret, with a hamam next door; small, clean rooms overlook a noisy but interesting street. ①

Outside the walls

Turistik Oteli Ziya Gökalp Bul 7 ☎0412/224 7550, ☎224 4274. Spacious rooms with balconies and nice bathrooms. There's a swimming pool and a pleasant restaurant, but less atmosphere than at the *Büyük Kervansaray* or *Class*. Best choice, though, if you have a car to park. ⑦

The Walls

Diyarbakır's six-kilometre-long **city wall**, breached by four huge main gateways plus several smaller ones, and dotted with 72 defensive towers, is the city's most famous attraction. Although the foundations are Roman and Byzantine, most of what can be seen today dates from the eleventh-century Artukid kingdom of Malık Salih Şah.

The obvious place to start would be at Dağ Kapısı, an angular and unbreach-able-looking black tower, and the best preserved of the city gates. However, you can't actually climb up onto the battlements at this point. Elsewhere, note that much of the section between Çifte Kapısı (Double Gate) and Dağ Kapısı no longer exists, that from Dağ Kapısı to Saray Kapısı is out of bounds, and from Oğrun Kapısı to Mardin Kapısı it's currently unusable. In hot weather be sure to take water and a head covering along – there are long intervals where you won't be able to descend for shade or refreshment.

Saray Kapısı to Oğrun Kapısı and the İç Kale

Saray Kapısı marks the entrance to the **İç Kale**, Diyarbakır's citadel and probably the oldest part of town. The section from Saray Kapısı to Oğrun Kapısı is navigable, but take care while ascending the steps. The walls offer a glimpse of local colour: in the early morning, families rise from their rooftop beds and hang strings of peppers and aubergines to dry; later in the day, they dip themselves in a few small swimming pools. The crumbling tower just south of **Oğrum Kapısı** gives fine views over the Tigris valley, spread below you the alluvial plain on which Diyarbakır's famous melons grow in special holes dug in the sandy riverbanks.

The citadel itself is a military zone, its walls patrolled by soldiers, a fact that restricts your wanderings somewhat. The only accessible building is the **Hazreti Süleyman Camii**, a black stone structure with a huge square minaret, built in 1160 by the Artukids, and looking these days rather like a grim Victorian workhouse. The cool spring that supplies the mosque's *şadırvan* is probably the city's original water source.

Mardin Kapısı to Cifte Kapısı

The stretch of wall running between Mardin Kapısı and Çifte Kapısı is the best-preserved and most impressive, although it may be shrouded in scaffolding as repairs progress slowly. Head down Gazi Caddesi until you reach the **Deliller Hanı**, now restored as the *Büyük Kervansaray* hotel. Nearby is the **Mardin Kapısı**, near to which you can ascend the wall – though if you don't feel up to the scramble it's slightly easier to go up at the Urfa Kapısı.

From Mardin Kapısı you can walk west along the battlements, which most of the way are wide enough for three people walking abreast – only in a couple of places do things get slightly hair-raising, requiring sturdy footwear. After about 400m you come to the **Yedi Kardeş Burcu** (Seven Brothers Tower), a huge circular bastion decorated with Selçuk lions and a double-headed eagle, from where there's a fantastic view out towards the Tigris. The view over the town is less inspiring, but enables you to appreciate the way Diyarbakır has developed over the centuries within the city walls, and you can pinpoint the mosques and churches from their minarets and towers. At this point, the walls curve round to the northwest for 300m until you reach another tower, the **Melikşah Burcu** (also known as the Ulu Badan), which is again decorated with Selçuk motifs. From here a path, one of the few running parallel to the ramparts, also leads along them to the **Urfa Kapısı**.

At the Urfa Kapısı you'll have to descend to street level, but you can climb back up a little further north. Continuing, the walls curve around to the northeast over the minor **Çifte Kapısı**, where you have to descend again.

The City

You may not be able to climb up to the walls there, but **Dağ Kapısı** makes a good starting point for an exploration of the city proper. Give yourself the best part of two days to do justice to the city sights and monuments.

Nebi Camii and Hasan Paşa Hanı

Immediately to the south of the gateway, at the intersection of Gazı Caddesi and İnön Caddesi, stands the **Nebi Camii**, or Mosque of the Prophet, a late fifteenth-century foundation of the Akkoyun Turcomans. The mosque's most distinctive feature is the alternating bands of black basalt and white sandstone used in its construction, especially effective in the minaret. You'll come across this striped effect frequently in Diyarbakır, as both stones are quarried locally and their combination is considerably less threatening than the unrelenting black of the walls.

Continuing down Gazı Caddesi will bring you to the **Hasan Paşa Hanı** on the eastern side of the street, and more bands of black and white stone. The *han* dates from the late sixteenth century and is still in commercial use, mainly for carpet and jewellery shops, while the city's **main bazaar** area occupies the narrow, twisting streets all around.

The Ulu Cami and around

Opposite the *han* stands the gatehouse of the **Ulu Cami**, Diyarbakır's most important mosque. The first of Anatolia's great Selçuk mosques, it was probably extended in 1091 by Melik Şah, the Selçuk conqueror of the city, though legend claims that it was built on the site of, and with masonry from, the Byzantine church of St Thomas at the time of the Arab conquest in 639, giving rise to the assertion that this is the oldest mosque in Anatolia. It was gutted by fire in 1155 and extensively refurbished, but has been little altered since. In support of the later foundation date, many have noted that the Ulu Cami closely resembles the Umayyad mosque in Damascus.

On passing through the entrance portal, decorated with bull and lion motifs, you find yourself in a large **courtyard**, perhaps the most impressive part of the building. Two *şadırvans* occupy the centre of this courtyard, with its two-storeyed facades at the eastern and western ends. The north and south sides sport true arcades, constructed using pillars salvaged from earlier Roman and Byzantine buildings; on some of the columns and capitals are visible fragments of Greek inscription. The wing to the east and above the arch, with storks nesting on its roof, is actually a library, incorporating a much earlier stoa beneath it. At the northeast corner of the courtyard is the locked entrance to the **Mesudiye Medresesi**. Built in 1198 by the Artukids, this became the first university of Anatolia and is still in use as a Koran school.

The mosque itself is entered via a doorway on the southern side of the courtyard; a carved white *mimber* graces the cavernous interior. The central bay is of much earlier origin, supporting the theory that the Ulu Cami was converted from what was originally a church, and has a superbly decorated roof in the porch area. The minaret is tall and angular, like many such structures in Diyarbakır.

Leaving Ulu Cami's tiny north gate and following Ziya Gökalp Sokak, you'll find the **Cultural Museum** (Kültür Müzei; Mon–Sat 9am–5pm; $0.35), occupying the former home of Cahit Sıtkı Tarancı, a prominent modern poet. There are exhibits about the man's life and work, as well as ethnographic memorabilia, but the vernacular building itself overshadows the displays.

If you leave the mosque courtyard via a door in the southwestern corner you enter a narrow alleyway. Turn left into the clothes bazaar and then right, and you will eventually come to the **Ziya Gökalp Museum** (seldom open; $0.35), former home of the architect of Turkish nationalism, which houses sections devoted to the man's life and work and an unexceptional ethnographic collection. Another restored mansion is the **Esma Ocak Diyarbakır Evi**, opposite *Surp*

Giragos, a typical black-and-white stone construction around a courtyard. The rooms have been refurbished as they would have appeared in 1899, and there are photographs of the original owners on the walls. The caretaker will open up for you and let you look around in return for a small tip.

Diyarbakır's other mosques

Heading west from the Ziya Gökalp museum brings you to the stunning fifteenth-century **Safa Camii**, a mosque of notably graceful design and construction. Its tall, round minaret, a departure from the city norm, still bears traces of blue tile-work on its white, relief-worked surface. Archway masonry in the courtyard alternates between black and white in the local fashion, while the interior ceiling is accented by blue and green tile-work.

Some way southeast across Melik Ahmet Caddesi stands the **Behram Paşa Camii**, Diyarbakır's largest mosque, built in 1572 by Behram Paşa, the governor, but currently closed for extensive renovation.

Also worth seeking out, east of Gazı Caddesi on Yenikapı Caddesi in the Balıkçılarbaşı bazaar, is the early sixteenth century **Kasım Padişah Camii**, virtually the last Akkoyun monument built before the Ottomans took over. Its tall, square detached minaret, set on four two-metre basalt pillars, is known colloquially as the *Dört Ayaklı Minare* ("Four-Legged Minaret"). According to legend, if you walk around the minaret seven times and make a wish, it will be granted.

Diyarbakır's churches

To reach the **Keldanı Kilisesi**, walk past the Kasım Padişah Camii and turn left down an alley, then immediately right. The church is about 100m down the alley on the right; ring the bell for entry. The church and bell tower date from 1602; the spacious, arched interior contains a rather garish altar with a crucifix and icons. It's a Chaldean foundation (a Catholic schism of the Nestorian church), and there are around thirty Chaldean families left in the city, making them the largest Christian denomination left in Diyarbakır.

A short but confusing hop away (you'll need to get someone to show you the route) is the huge **Surp Giragos Kilisesi**, a once-thriving church in the days when the population of Diyarbakır was one-quarter Armenian. To gain entry, you will have to persuade the rather forcible Kurdish woman caretaker; a little *bakşiş* will not go amiss. Regrettably, the roof fell down in 1992, but the huge shell still contains the gold-painted woodwork of the altar and the building has supposedly been scheduled for restoration.

There's also a Syrian Orthodox compound, the **Meryamana Kilisesi** (Church of the Virgin Mary), southwest of the Behram Paşa Camii; to get there, use the prominent bell-tower as a guide. A small door leads on to a paved courtyard surrounded by buildings that were once part of a seventh-century monastery. The church itself dates from the third century and is thus one of the oldest in the world; it was reconstructed after a fire a couple of centuries ago. Services conducted in either Syriac (a form of Aramaic) or Turkish are still held here at 8am each Sunday morning, but at other times you're free to look around. A contribution should be made to the caretakers and the Syriac priest, who is striving to keep his small community together and is putting himself out especially for you.

The Archeological Museum

Diyarbakır's **Archeological Museum** (Arkeoloji Müzesi; Tues–Sun 8.30am–noon & 1.30–5.30pm; $0.70) lies just outside the old city, near the main PTT. To reach it, head out along Ziya Gökalp Caddesi: you'll see a fairground on the northeastern (right) side of the road, and the typical black-on-brown sign in the vicinity will lead you down a side-street to the museum. As well as early historic carvings, it contains extensive local Roman remains, some from the Akkoyun and Karakoyun Turcoman dynasties that ruled much of eastern Anatolia and western Persia in medieval times, and Korans and ceremonial items from Derviş Tekkes (monasteries).

Eating and drinking

The **local speciality** is lamb *kuburga* (ribs stuffed with rice), available at various restaurants in town. A particular Diyarbakır institution is the pavement liver-heart-and-offal **grill stalls** that set up shop on summer evenings along Gazı Caddesi and Kıbrıs Caddesi. The meat bits are skewered and grilled as you watch, then served up hot and savoury with a raw vegetable garnish. Portions are generous and you can eat well for a couple of dollars, but don't go overboard the first time or you'll regret it the next day. There are several more **grill restaurants** outside the Urfa Kapısı, set in shady gardens under the walls.

Aslan Yemek Salonu Kıbrıs Cad. Welcoming air-conditioned restaurant – try the *yufkalı incik*, lamb on the bone with peas, pepper and tomato, wrapped in pastry.

Bi-tat Kahvalti Salonu Sütçü Sok. A good choice, serving comb honey, butter and honey for breakfast as well as the usual soups or Turkish breakfasts; they also dish up *pide*, *lahmacun* and *kebabs* later in the day.

Büyük Kervansaray Gazı Cad, Deliller Hanı. The courtyard of the hotel hosts the closest thing in the city centre to a nightclub; dinner is served around the pool, and there's live music and dancing most nights.

Dicle Oteli Kıbrıs Cad 3. The cheapest licensed restaurant (and one of the most atmospheric) is attached to the hotel, where tasty, generous portions of kebabs and other grills are served on a rooftop terrace in the summer.

Hacı Baba Kebapcısı Opposite the Nebi Camii. A modest place serving cheap grilled *kebaps* and *sac tava* (meat dish cooked in a wok).

Romada Ali Emiri Cad. A beer, grill and live music joint, though not recommended for unaccompanied women, particularly as the steps to the restaurant lead past a porn cinema.

Selim Amca Sofra Salonu Ali Emiri Cad. Lunch-only place, 5-min walk west of Dağ Kapısı, serving lamb *kuburga*; reservations must be made a day in advance, so go along and book.

Şeyhmus Pastanesi Junction of İzzet Paşa Cad and Gazı Cad. Sweets and pastries to take away or eat in with Turkish coffee or tea.

Şanlıurfa Kebap Evi İzzet Paşa Cad 4. Very popular with the locals for its fast service, tasty food and bargain prices (it's hard to spend more than $3).

Listings

Airport Buses to the airport leave from the THY office, İnönü Cad 8 ☎0412/228 8401.

Banks and exchange Most of the banks and *döviz* offices are on Gazı Cad; Akbank takes most credit cards and travellers' cheques.

Buses The usual eastern bus companies have booths near Dağ Kapısı on Kıbrıs Cad, and service buses run from here to the *otogar*. The Batman/Hasan Keyf/Mardin dolmuşes run from an office and lay-by on the east side of Gazi Cad, at the north end.

Car rental Avis, İnönü Cad ☎0412/229 0275.

Hospital The Devlet Hastanesi (State Hospital) is north of Dağ Kapısı.

Police Police station on Gazi Cad, just north of the main crossroads.

Post office There is a small PTT on Yeni Kapı Cad, near the junction with Gazi Cad (Mon–Sat 9am–noon and 1–5pm for mail; 24hr for telephones). For money exchange, go to the larger PTT on Ziya Gökalp Bul, 300m north of Dağ Kapısı (same hours).

Trains The Güney Ekspresi departs for İstanbul every Monday, Wednesday, Friday and Sunday. Tickets from the station at the end of İstasyon Cad.

Travel agencies Diyarbakir has several reputable agencies, best of them being Bianca Seyahat, İnönü Cad 42 ☎0412/223 14250.

⑪

Mardin

Seen from the south at a distance, **MARDİN** looks spectacular, its tiered layers of houses, mansions, mosques and churches rising out of the endless level plain and clinging to a huge citadel-topped rock. The town itself affords breathtaking views, especially at sunset, over the Syrian plain. Mardin's position has always made it a strategic military outpost – the higher of the two castellated bluffs today sports golf-ball radar domes. Mardin's population is a mix of Kurds, Arabs, Turks and Suriyani Christians, and, like Diyarbakır, the town has had to cope with an influx of people from surrounding villages fleeing the burnt-out shells of their homes. Now that the political situation is stable, Mardin is starting to receive its fair share of visitors. The hotel situation has improved in the town, although many tourists still visit as a day trip from Diyarbakır, 95km and under two hours away by bus to the north.

The town's precipitous location has encouraged local youngsters in the sport of kite-flying (you may well see a few fluttering above the streets in the evenings), while Mardin's close proximity to Syria facilitates the other local hobby – smuggling. In corners of the bazaar, you may be offered anything from coffee to cameras at advantageous prices.

Some history

Mardin's probable Roman origins are lost in the welter of war and conquest that forms this region's historical backdrop, while the town's later history is tied up with the development of early Christianity. The first Christians to settle here were Syrian Orthodox, who arrived during the third century AD. Today, eleven churches are hidden away in the back streets, of which eight still serve the dwindling community on a rotation basis.

The Christians survived the period of Arab occupation from 640 to 1104, and were left largely unaffected by the arrival of the Selçuks and later the Turcomans. From the twelfth century through until the fourteenth century, the citadel served the Artukid Turcoman tribe as a capital. From here they were able to beat off the Arabs and endure an eight-month siege during the first Mongol onslaught, falling only to the second Mongol wave. In 1394, the Mongols under Tamerlane captured the town, doling out death and misery in equal measures to Christian and Muslim alike, before handing Mardin over to the Karakoyun Turcoman tribe in 1408; they built the (now ruined) palace and mosque inside the citadel walls. The town fell to the Ottomans under Selim I in 1517 and an era of torpor began that was not significantly disrupted until the Kurdish rebellion of 1832, when a number of public buildings were blown up. There was a brief Egyptian occupation in 1839–1840, after which the town sank back into somnolence until World War I.

Before and during Turkey's War of Independence, Mardin's Christian population was drastically reduced by massacre and emigration. There were renewed emigrations in the early 1990s and today only a few hundred practising Syriac, Orthodox and Armenian Christians remain – roughly one percent of the town's population.

Arrival, orientation and information

It's not difficult to find your way around old Mardin. The citadel bluff is skirted by one road on the north, leading to Midyat, and another on the southern edge, which heads off to the southeast and the Syrian border. The old town itself lies on the steep southern slopes below the citadel. The principal street, **Birinci Caddesi**, branches off the main road at the western end of town, and rejoins it at the eastern end.

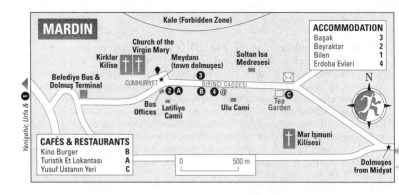

There's no *otogar* as such. Buses for Diyarbakır and other destinations usually depart from the **Belediye bus terminal** at the western end of Birinci Caddesi. For some far-flung destinations, *servis* buses from the couple of coach companies located at the western end of Birinci Caddesi, under the *Bayraktar Hotel*, will take you down into Yenşehir (New City) to board the bus. There is a **dolmuş terminal** at the eastern end of town on the main Syria-bound road, with services to Midyat. City dolmuşes go from Cumhuriyet Meydanı in the city centre to either of these terminals.

Mardin's **tourist office** is in the Valilik Binası, in Yenisehir, 2km from the old city, and the detour there is a waste of time. The *Flaş* **internet café** just east of the *Erdoba Evleri* hotel on Birinci Caddesi, is the most reliable in town

Accommodation

The hotel situation in Mardin is slowly beginning to improve, but for budget travellers the situation is still fairly grim. The *Bayraktar Hotel* (☎0482/212 1338; ❶), at the Cumhuriyet Meydanı end of Birinci Caddesi, has plain but passable rooms with tepid-water bathrooms, though it does command fabulous views of the Syrian plain to the south. The *Otel Başak*, also on Birinci Caddesi (☎0482/212 6246; ❷), is friendly though it doesn't have the *Bayraktar*'s views, the rooms are basic and the shared bathrooms grimy.

If you have your own transport, want better-quality accommodation and don't mind missing the exhilarating view, it's better to stay at the comfortable *Otel Bilen* (☎0482/212 5568, ℗212 2575; ❸), 1.5km out of town at Mardin's northwestern entrance; you should be able to bargain them down. The *Erdoba Evleri Hotel* (☎0482/212 7677, ⓦwww.erdoba.co.tr; ❻) has a main building in Birinci Caddesi, with air-conditioned rooms equipped with fridge and TV, built in "period style" around a courtyard at the rear; there's an upmarket restaurant attached. There's also a separate, associated building with a few more rooms lower down the hill (accessible only on foot), a converted merchant's mansion that has retained much of its character. The owners of the *Büyük Kervansaray* in Diyarbakır are also building a luxury hotel in the old style, set to open during 2003.

The Town

Although there's no shortage of featureless concrete, the architecture of Mardin's old **Arab-style** houses is stunning in places. Following the main street, Birinci Caddesi, east from Cumhuriyet Meydanı leads you to a famous example – a beautiful stone facade with three arches, on the north side of the street. This is one of the finest private houses in town, and now serves as home to an extended family.

Several hundred metres beyond the house, the easterly of two sets of stone steps lead up to the **Sultan İsa Medresesi**, built in 1385, a striking, albeit crumbling, white structure with a magnificent Selçuk doorway, from which you can look out across the town towards Syria. It's possible to take a look inside the building and climb onto the roof.

Above the Sultan İsa Medresesi is the **kale**, or citadel, originally built by the Romans and extended by the Byzantines. You may be able to enjoy the views from the terrace, but the castle interior and the golf-ball-crowned summit are a strictly off-limits military zone. From the terrace you can see the **Hediye Minare**, very similar to that at Hasankeyf, but distinguished by its twin staircases, built so that those ascending do not catch a glimpse of those descending.

East of Cumhuriyet Meydanı stands Mardin's **Ulu Cami**, an eleventh-century Selçuk mosque with a fluted dome, blown up during the 1832 rebellion and much restored since. To the south of Cumhuriyet Meydanı is the **Latifiye Camii**, dating from the fourteenth century. It has a carved Selçuk-style portal, and a courtyard with a shady garden – just the place to escape the blinding summer heat. Around these two mosques lies a maze of streets, forming part of the **bazaar**. At the western end of town, south of the main road (you'll have to ask directions), is the fifteenth-century **Kasım Paşa Medresesi**, similar in design to the Sultan İsa Medresesi.

Immediately above the two car parks at Cumhuriyet Meydanı is Mardin's **museum** (Tues–Sun 8.30am–4.30pm; $0.70), housed in a restored mansion and boasting a small café and gift shop. It contains finds from the Sumerian, Assyrian and Urartian periods, as well as the usual Greek and Roman statuary and coins; an Assyrian excavation near Nusaybin has also provided some interesting finds. Adjoining the museum to the east is the town's largest church, the **Church of the Virgin Mary**, used by five families of Syrian Catholics. If you can gain admission (the door is often locked) to the damp-damaged but handsomely vaulted interior (donations invited), you'll be shown many portraits of saints and an icon of the Virgin. To the northwest are two smaller churches, hidden behind high stone walls; to find them, look for the bell-towers. The Syrian Orthodox **Kirklar Kilise** (Arbin Söhad in Syriac) is the most welcoming to visitors and dates back, in part, to the sixth century. The door is usually open, and the priest speaks excellent English and from him you may be able to learn something of the ancient history of the once-powerful church.

Eating and drinking

There are a few places to eat along Birinci Caddesi, of which the best is *Yusuf Ustanın Yeri*, opposite the PTT, an *ocakbaşı* (charcoal grill) garden **restaurant** serving excellent kebabs but no alcohol. The *Turistik Et Lokantası*, above the bus office by the *Bayraktar Hotel*, serves poorer quality food and you'll pay slightly over the odds for the privilege of being able to drink alcohol. *Kino Burger* on Birinci Caddesi, between the *Bayraktar* and the PTT, is good for fast food; the nearby restaurant of the *Erdobe Evleri Hotel* is the swishest option in town.

Opposite the PTT is a small and leafy terrace **tea garden**, where you can watch the sun set over Syria.

Deyr-az-Zaferan

Six kilometres southeast of Mardin, **Deyr-az-Zaferan** (also known as Deyrülzafran, or the "Saffron Monastery", so named for the yellowish rock from which it's built) is the most accessible of the area's surviving Syrian Orthodox religious communities. Founded in 493 AD, it was, from 1160 until the 1920s, the seat of the Syrian Orthodox patriarch – though he has since relocated to Damascus. A surprisingly large rectangular building of three storeys, set on a low bluff overlooking an approach road, it wouldn't look out of place in southern Italy or Spain and, judging by the different styles of stonework, was built in stages, with frequent pauses for restoration. Now only two monks remain, running a school for about 25 orphans with the assistance of a few lay helpers.

Visiting Deyr-az-Zaferan is easy enough. You can walk to it in an hour and a half from Mardin, following the brown signs leading southeast: first adopt the Nusaybin road, then turn off left following a little brown sign, passing through the village of Eskikale. Eventually you'll come to another signposted turning leading you to the monastery. Failing that, pick up a taxi from Mardin's Cumhuriyet Meydanı or the dolmuş terminal; reckon on paying $10 for a return trip with waiting time, though you'll have to bargain.

From the hills, ancient but still intact rock channels bring water to the Deyr-az-Zaferan monastery, whose **entrance portal** bears an inscription in Syriac. After being greeted and perhaps offered a glass of tea, visitors are usually entrusted to one of the older orphans or visiting students and taken on a guided tour.

First stop is an **underground vault**, said to have been used as a temple by sun worshippers as long ago as 2000 BC. A now-blocked window at the eastern end enabled them to watch the sunrise, while a niche on the southern wall served as an altar (possibly sacrificial). The vault is enclosed by a ceiling of self-supporting stone built without the use of mortar. The room above, entered via huge 300-year-old walnut doors, is a **mausoleum**, whose walls contain the grave niches of seven Syrian Orthodox patriarchs and metropolitans (the equivalent of bishops).

Tours move on from here to the **chapel**, with fine relief-decorated arches and a carved stone altar (replacing a wooden one destroyed by fire fifty years ago), and the patriarch's or metropolitan's throne, on which are carved the names of all the patriarchs since 792 AD. Services in the chapel are held in Syriac, and if you can manage to be here at around 6pm you may be able to attend one of them.

Beyond are a couple of rooms containing sedan chairs once used to transport the patriarchs; you'll also be shown a carved walnut altar, made without using nails, and an ancient mosaic said to come from the grotto of Sen Piyer in Antakya.

Upstairs, across the peaceful courtyard, you may also be shown the monastery's **guest rooms** (it is possible to stay overnight, but bear in mind that the quarters are intended for people visiting for religious reasons) and a more personalized suite intended for the use of the patriarch on his rare visits from Damascus. Lastly, you'll be taken out onto the roof terrace for fine views south into Syria, and the orphans will point out surrounding abandoned cave hermitages and two ruined monastic churches: Mar Yakoub and Miryam Anna.

At the end of the tour you may want to make a donation or perhaps tip your guide, who may refuse your offer at first but will accept if you persist a little.

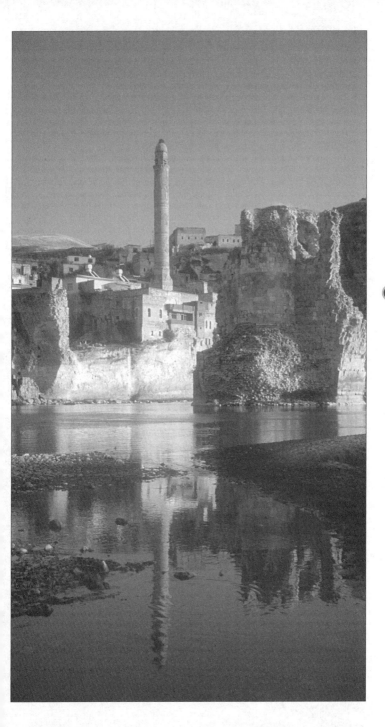

The Syrian Orthodox Church

Syrian Orthodox priests believe that the **Syrian Church** was established in this area during the lifetime of Jesus, when he himself was invited by King Abgar I of Edessa (modern Şanlıurfa) to move his ministry to the area. He refused, but a handkerchief – the *mandalyon* – bearing an imprint, or possibly a painting, of his face was despatched as a gift. This, together with a letter from Jesus, became the most holy relic possessed by the Church until it was lost to Arab conquerors, who passed it on to the Byzantines as ransom for the city of Urfa. According to legend, it ended up in Constantinople, where it was lost in the sack of 1204.

The area around Mardin has been a stronghold of the Syrian Orthodox or Jacobite church since 543 AD, when one Yakoub Al-Bardai (better known in the West as Jacobus Baradaeus), was appointed bishop of Edessa (Şanlıurfa) and revived the persecuted and faltering Church. A native of Mesopotamia, Baradaeus was – like most of the Christians in the eastern and southern reaches of the Byzantine Empire – a Monophysite, subscribing to an anathemized doctrine locked in a century-old theological dispute with the patriarchate in Constantinople about the divine nature of Christ. According to the ecclesiastical Council of Chalcedon, convened in 451 AD, Christ had both a human and a divine nature, but dissenting bishops throughout the Middle East held that Christ had only a divine nature – a creed known as **Monophysitism**, whose adherents risked condemnation as heretics and excommunication.

Present-day Syrian Orthodox Christians deny explicit Monophysite leanings, calling themselves "non-Chalcedonian Orthodox". In fact, the core and uniqueness of Syrian Orthodox observance, which has enabled the Church to endure over time, is its liturgy in the **Syriac language**. Written from right to left in its own script, this had already evolved from ancient Aramaic – the purported mother tongue of Jesus – by the second century, when the first recognizable Syriac New Testament translations appeared. Between 541 and 578 AD, Baradaeus served as an energetic and peripatetic proselytizer throughout what is now the Hatay and Syria, helping to revive his Church as it suffered determined attack by the agents of Constantinopolitan orthodoxy. From the advent of local Arab dominion in the seventh century, Syrian Orthodox Christians enjoyed considerable religious freedom and, by the time of the First Crusade at the end of the eleventh century, the Tür Abdin in particular encompassed four bishoprics and eighty monasteries, the ruins of which are dotted across the plateau. Ironically, it was Christian crusaders from Edessa and Antioch (Antakya) who unleashed a major, determined attack against what they regarded as a heretical Church, forcing abandonment of the traditional Syrian patriarchal seat in Antioch. They were followed by the Mongols whose motives had little to do with religion – they massacred and pillaged everybody regardless of race, colour and creed.

Under the Ottoman Empire, order was restored, and the Christian community once again enjoyed a long period of tolerance and stability. Unfortunately, during World War I, they were tainted by association with Allied plans to dismember the Ottoman Empire and suffered widespread persecution and massacre, a fate they shared with the Anatolian, Armenian and Greek minorities. Today the number of Syrian Christians worldwide totals nearly three million, though this figure may include members of the breakaway **Syrian Catholic (Uniate) Church**, which acknowledges the authority of the Pope. The largest surviving national community is, perhaps surprisingly, in Kerala, India; in Turkey there remain just the bishoprics of Tür Abdin, Mardin (currently vacant) and İstanbul, where many thousands of beleaguered Tür Abdin residents have fled. The seat of the Patriarchy is in Damascus.

Nusaybin and Mar Augen

About 50km southeast of Mardin is **NUSAYBIN**, on the frontier with Syria, from where you can reach the abandoned monastery of Mar Augen. The last 33km of the journey runs parallel to the border, along the main D400 to Iraq. Nusaybin was the site of the **Roman town of Nisibis** and has a triumphal arch. More interesting is a sporadically functioning Syrian Orthodox church, **Mar Yakoub**, and the town's ornate **train station**, built by the Germans just before World War I and the last stop in Turkey on the Berlin–Baghdad railway. There are currently no international services, and just one slow local train daily at dawn to Gaziantep.

The monastery of **Mar Augen** is the most evocatively set and most poignant of all the abandoned monasteries in the area, though only the bare fifth-century monastery church is intact, with all traces of decoration long since erased. With your own car, drive 25km towards Cizre and turn left to the village of Girmeli, 1km away; just past the village take a right turn and follow it 3km to the foot of the cliffs below the monastery. In the absence of your own transport, it is best reached by taxi from Nusaybin (around $30).

The Tür Abdin plateau

Less than 100km east of Mardin spreads the undulating plateau of the **Tür Abdin**, a traditional homeland of the Syrian Orthodox Church – whose independence from the Greek Orthodox Church was formalized by theological disputes of the sixth century (see box opposite). Scattered across the area are numerous churches and monasteries, reflecting the fact that the Tür Abdin is still home to a few Christians, who coexist uneasily with the local Kurds. Aside from a traditional livelihood in grapevines, the rocky, parched plateau is a poor region even by the standards of eastern Turkey, but the Christian villages are supported to some extent by émigrés.

Midyat is the western gateway to the Tür Abdin proper, which still has six villages wholly, and two partly, inhabited by Syrian Orthodox Christians, plus 46 **monasteries and churches** in varying states of repair and use. To reach them, because of the distances and lack of public transport, you'll really need your own transport, or a taxi arranged in Midyat. The positions of several are shown more or less correctly on the GeoCenter/RV map of eastern Turkey.

Midyat

From Mardin, **MİDYAT** is an uneventful journey of just under an hour. It's actually a double town: the westerly, unremarkable, Kurd-inhabited business district of **Estel**, and – 2km east but un-signposted – the originally Christian portion of half-abandoned medieval mansions, known as **Eski** (old) **Midyat**. In theory, old Midyat, with its four churches and intricate architecture, should be a place people head for in droves, but visitors are rare, partly due to a lack of facilities. The one **hotel** on the fringes of old Midyat, the *Metro* (☎0482/464 2317; **❶**), just northeast of the central roundabout on the Hasankeyf–Batman road, offers waterless rooms with metal-framed beds but is friendly enough and reasonably clean. A more pleasant alternative is the *Öğretmen Evi* (Teachers' House) in Estel, which is theoretically available only for those employed in this profession; you can make enquiries and pre-book via the Harran Dolmuş tour company in Şanlıurfa (see p.875), or ask in Estel for directions.

There is no *otogar* in old Midyat; **dolmuşes** stop at a roundabout (signed to Cizre, İdil and Mar Gabriel in the southeast, and to Batman to the north) at the foot of the old town, immediately east of which lies a small **bazaar**. Above this the residential quarter climbs up a slight hill, all cracked streets with open drains and mysterious gateways opening onto the courtyards of imposing mansions, inhabited by extended families of Kurds, Syrian Orthodox Christians and a very few Armenians.

As recently as 1974 there were nearly 5000 Syrian Orthodox Christians in residence here, the men mostly engaged in gold- or silver-smithing, but following PKK extortion of money from the merchants and death threats by Muslim bigots during the PKK war, the population has dwindled to about 300, and all but one of the town's priests have fled. However, because of the changed political climate, the exodus now seems to have halted and conditions improved. The town's **churches** are easily spotted by virtue of their graceful belfries and can all be reached on foot. Of the two upper churches on the hilltop, only one is in use; the other, built as recently as 1912–17, has been taken over by pigeons. A third lies south and downhill – you'll see a doorway with a cross carved above it – where there is a caretaker in residence. He will show you around the simple whitewashed interior with its hand-painted altar curtains and illuminated Syriac missals that are between 300 and 1000 years old. A group of Syriac schoolchildren meets after school in the courtyard schoolroom to have Bible lessons, so if you time it right you may be able to listen to them chanting the liturgy in the language used by Christ. The young people make hand copies of the holy books in Syriac and you may also be offered crocheted handwork – you might want to support their community through a purchase or a donation.

Mar Gabriel

Southeast of Midyat, the monastery of **Mar Gabriel** (Deyrulumur) is the geographical and spiritual centre of the plateau. To get there with your own transport, leave Midyat on the Cizre-bound road; after 20km turn northeast onto a signed tarmac road that leads to the monastery gate in just over 2km. A **taxi** to the monastery gates and back will cost $20, including waiting time. Using **public transport** from Midyat, walk down the Cizre road for about 100m from the roundabout to a dolmuş stop. The Cizre and Idil dolmus will drop you at the signed Mar Gabriel junction, a half-hour journey, from where you will have to walk the final two kilometres.

Founded in 397 AD, Mar Gabriel is not only the oldest surviving Syrian Orthodox monastery, but the most vital in Turkey, with the nineteen resident nuns and monks occupying separate wings, as well as a fluctuating number of local lay workers, guests and students sent by Suriyani emigrants to learn the Syriac language and retie hazy cultural connections. It is also the seat of the metropolitan bishop of Tür Abdin, who speaks good English, and with whom you may be granted an audience.

Compared with the showcase of Deyr-az-Zaferan, Mar Gabriel is a working community, set among gardens and orchards, and somewhat disfigured by a 1960s-vintage hostelry. The monastery's primary purpose is to keep Syrian Orthodox Christianity alive in the land of its birth by providing schooling, ordination of native-born monks, and – if necessary – physical protection to the faithful. You visit for the opportunity to gain some insight into the Church

THE EUPHRATES AND TIGRIS BASIN | The Tür Abdin plateau

through a **guided tour** – visiting hours are 9am to 4.30pm. A lay person will take you around; the teacher of the Syriac language also speaks excellent English and can answer your questions. At noon you are welcome to attend the liturgy conducted in the subterranean church underneath the belfry, a heady mix of Syriac chants, swirling incense and prostration.

Restoration and new building work is in progress and there's a tangible aura of prosperity, a sign that secure times have returned again to the Tür Abdin. The heavy steel gates to the monastery are now locked to protect the gardens from the depradations of goats, rather than protecting the inhabitants from danger.

Village churches

In the opposite direction from Midyat – travelling north 4km towards Hasankeyf, then east along the secondary road to Dargeçit – lie the rest of the Tür Abdin's historic churches.

Finest, though also the most remote, is the monastic church of **Meryemanna** (El Hadra), about 24km away (17km along the road and then a further 7km south) in the village of Anıtlı (Hah). This fifth-century foundation sports a two-storey wedding-cake turret with blind arches atop a pyramidal roof; archways and lintels are also heavily ornamented.

Closer in, 10km along the Dargeçit road and then 3km north on a dirt track, the **Mar Yakoub** monastic church in Baraztepe (Salah) village is similarly ancient and impressive, with its barrel-vaulted nave and intricate relief work. Returning to the Dargeçit road, continuing east for 2km and then turning south for a further couple of kilometres, you reach the slightly later church of **Mar Kyriakos**, with its small courtyard, in the mixed Christian/Kurdish village of Bağlarbaşı (Arnas). Its architect also built the **Mar Azazael** church on a knoll at the edge of Altıntaş (Keferzeh) village, about 7km east of Mar Kyriakos.

Hasankeyf

The spectacular ruined settlement of **HASANKEYF**, built on and around a rocky spur on the banks of the Tigris, contains remarkable medieval remains of Selçuk, Arabic and Kurdish origin. The original settlement was founded by the Romans as an eastern bastion of Asia Minor, and later became the Byzantine bishopric of Cephe. In 640, the conquering Arabs changed the town's name to Hisn Kayfa. During the twelfth century the Artukid Turcoman tribe made it the capital of their realm, which it remained until the Mongols arrived in 1260. Hasankeyf then served as the stronghold of the Ayyubids, a clan of Kurdish chieftains supplanted by the Ottomans early in the fifteenth century.

Hasankeyf was recently threatened by the proposed construction of the **İlisu dam** across the Tigris, which would have drowned the village, bridge and lower part of the site as well as impeding water flow to Syria for a number of years. Fortunately, the international outcry, plus the parlous state of Turkey's finances, reprieved the site for the time being. The Turkish government still intends to proceed if funds become available, leaving the locals suffering from planning blight and still without adequate employment prospects.

The Town

The modern town trails along for several hundred metres, overshadowed by the ruined Artukid city to the southwest, which covers two square kilometres of a clifftop above the right bank of the Tigris River. The **site** (always open; $0.70) is reached by turning west down a narrow paved street, later a dirt track, just west of the modern Tigris bridge. After a kilometre look out for a ruined gateway halfway up the right side of the gorge, beyond which a stone pathway, currently being restored, leads uphill to the twelfth-century **palace of the Artukid kings**, perched high above the Tigris. From here there is a fine view of the Tigris, a sheer drop of several hundred metres below, while behind you stretches the rest of the city. Although they look like standard-issue ruins from the road, many of its skeletal houses contain intricate decorative features. Particularly impressive are the well-preserved **mosque** and a couple of domed **tombs**.

To get a closer look at the Tigris, head back towards town and turn left by a gorgeous carved minaret to drop down to the riverbank, where families come to paddle and wash their cars. The several hundred steps carved into the sheer cliff-face, which give secret access to the Artukid palace above, have been closed on grounds of safety. Just downstream are the four pillars of an old **Artukid bridge** that in its day was apparently one of the finest in Anatolia.

The best single bit of Hasankeyf is the fifteenth-century **Zeyn El-Abdin Türbesi**, a sizable, onion-domed cylindrical building clad in glazed turquoise tiles and red brick, conspicuously isolated in a walled orchard on the north bank. This tomb, perhaps the most Timurid-influenced monument in Turkey, is easily reached on foot, via mud tracks starting opposite a filling station on the main road towards Batman, or via the north bank of the Tigris from the bridge.

Practicalities

The journey north from Midyat to Hasankeyf by local **dolmuş**, or with your own transport, involves a gradual, scenic descent towards the river and provides an excellent return route to Diyarbakır, without having to backtrack to Mardin. The Van-Cizre long-distance bus also runs directly through the village. Regular dolmuşes run from Hasankeyf to Batman, where you change buses for the final leg of the journey to Diyarbakır along an attractive green gorge of the Tigris, but these local buses stop running at about 6pm.

Hasankeyf now has some **accommodation**, and an overnight stay is recommended especially for photographers, as the morning and evening lighting effects are spectacular. The *Öğretmen Evi* on the south side of the bridge is reached by some steps just above the main road. This provides basic waterless rooms with bunk beds for $3 and has a shady courtyard where tea and soft drinks are served. Just below and opposite the *Öğretmen Evi* is the new *Hasankeyf Motel* (❷), with great views over the river from some of the rooms. The *Antik Kent Et Lokantası* on the main street is good for soup, grills and *lahmacun*. Further up is an **internet café**, but there is no bank and no PTT in Hasankeyf.

Travel details

Buses and dolmuşes

Adıyaman to: Adana (4 daily; 6hr); Ankara (5 daily; 13hr); Diyarbakır (1 daily; 3hr 30min); Kahta (hourly; 45min); Kayseri (1 daily; 8hr); Malatya (6 daily; 3hr); Şanlıurfa (8 daily; 2hr 30min).
Batman to: Hasankeyf (6 daily; 1hr); Diyarbakır (10 daily; 1hr 30min).

Diyarbakır to: Adana (4 daily; 9hr); Ankara (5 daily; 13hr); Batman (10 daily; 1hr 30min); Bitlis (5 daily; 3hr 30min); Gaziantep (5 daily; 5hr); Malatya (6 daily; 4hr 30min); Mardin (6 daily; 1hr 45min); Şanlıurfa (6 daily; 3hr); Siirt (hourly, 3hr); Siverek (hourly; 2hr); Sivas (4 daily; 10hr); Tatvan (4 daily; 4hr); Van (4 daily; 7hr).
Gaziantep to: Adana via Mersin (10 daily; 3hr

⑪

30min); Ankara (12 daily; 12hr); Antakya (8 daily; 4hr); Diyarbakır (5 daily; 5hr); Malatya (3 daily; 4hr); Mardin (5 daily; 5hr); Şanlıurfa (10 daily; 2hr).

Hasankeyf to: Batman (6 daily; 45min); Midyat (6 daily; 45min); Van (1 daily; 7hr); Cizre (1 daily; 2hr).

Kâhta to: Adıyaman (hourly; 45min), Karadüt (1 daily in season, 3 hrs); Siverek (several daily; 2hr).

Malatya to: Adana (5 daily; 7hr 30min); Adıyaman (5 daily; 3hr); Ankara (8 daily; 9hr); Diyarbakır (6 daily; 4hr 30min); Elazığ (8 daily; 1hr 40min); Erzurum (1 daily; 7hr); Gaziantep (3 daily; 4hr).

Mardin to: Cizre via Nusaybin (3 daily; 3hr); Diyarbakır (6 daily; 1hr 45min); Midyat (frequently on demand; 1hr); Şanlıurfa (5 daily; 3hr).

Midyat to: Hasankeyf (4 daily; 45min); Batman (6 daily; 1hr).

Şanlıurfa to: Adana (5 daily; 6hr); Adıyaman (6 daily; 2hr 30min); Ankara (3 daily; 14hr); Diyarbakır (5 daily; 3hr); Gaziantep (8 daily; 2hr); Harran (hourly 7am–7pm; 1hr); Mardin (5 daily; 3hr).

Trains

Diyarbakır to: Ankara (4 weekly; 26hr 15min); Kayseri (4 weekly; 18hr); Sivas (4 weekly; 13hr).

Gaziantep to: İstanbul (3 weekly; 29hr); Konya (3 weekly; 16hr); Nusaybin via Karkamiş (1 daily; 6hr).

Malatya to: Adana (daily; 8hr 30min); Ankara (daily; 20hr); Diyarbakır (3 weekly; 6hr 30min); Tatvan (3 weekly; 10hr 30min).

Flights

Diyarbakır to: Ankara (2 daily; 1hr 30min); İstanbul (2 daily; 1hr 55min).

Elazığ to: Ankara (5 weekly; 1hr 15min); İstanbul (1 daily; 1hr 45min).

Gaziantep to: Ankara (1 daily; 1hr 20min); İstanbul (6 daily; 1hr 50min).

Malatya to: Ankara (5 weekly; 1hr 10min); İstanbul (1 daily; 1hr 40min).

Şanlıurfa to: Ankara (4 weekly; 1hr 30min); İstanbul (5 weekly; 2hr).

Lake Van and the southeast

CHAPTER 12

Highlights

* **Nemrut Dağı** This unique mountain habitat shelters migrating birds in May and September, and in between offers the possibility of a dip in the crater lakes. See p.925

* **Van Kalesi** The "Rock of Van" was fortified by ancient Urartians, whose cuneiform inscriptions are inscribed on the cliff-side. See p.933

* **Akdamar Kilisesi** Tenth-century Armenian church with stone-cut friezes, on a tiny island in Lake Van. See p.939

* **Hoşap Kalesi** Picturesque medieval Kurdish castle topping a mound above the main road to Hakkari. See p.941

* **Hakkari** Join in the dancing to fiddle, pipe and drums at a tradition-al Kurdish wedding. See p.945

* **Muradiye waterfalls** The gushing falls near Van boast a twenty-metre drop and a wonderful early summer display of wild flowers. See p.948

* **İshak Paşa Sarayı** An architectural folly of golden limestone, set in a valley of sculpted rocks controlling the silk road to Iran. See p.951

* **Mount Ararat** The high-est mountain in Turkey, like a huge Christmas pudding, topped with snow and a puff of rising smoke. See p.952

Lake Van and the southeast

T he **southeast** of Turkey is a fascinating and challenging place to visit, despite its reputation as one of the most backward and ethnically diverse parts of the country. It is a high, rugged, sparsely populated area with a natural beauty on which people seem to have made little impression (other than deforestation) over the ages. At the heart of it all lies **Lake Van**, a vast inland sea trapped by laval deposits from the dormant or extinct volcanoes that soar over the familiar undulating steppeland of central Anatolia. The volcanoes culminate in the peak of 5137-metre Ağrı Dağ – better known as **Mount Ararat** – while extensions to the Toros range loop around the south and east of Lake Van. The climate is as severe as the terrain, with torrid summers (from June onwards) giving way to freezing winters starting in early November.

The southeast is undeniably much more primitive than other parts of Turkey. Communications are significantly slower and mountain roads are often unsurfaced, although main roads have been improved significantly, often due to military requirements during the PKK troubles (see box on p.896). Restaurant food and many hotels lack any sort of refinement or adornment – and working women are a rare sight except in the fields and villages. But in the end you'll probably feel that the trip here was worth it. The region's monuments and sights are some of the most diverse and impressive in Turkey, and there are fewer tourists in evidence than anywhere else in the country.

You might consider flying into **Van**, long the favoured capital of the region, with its ruined ancient citadel and the atmospheric foundations of Old Van. Modern Van, a low-roofed concrete sprawl set amongst a forest of market stalls, lies a few kilometres inland from the lake, and is a remarkably civilized and welcoming centre for exploration. Overland, the conventional but often bottlenecked approach is by bus from Diyarbakır (see Chapter 11), via the old trade route through the stark hill town of **Bitlis** and rather dreary **Tatvan**, itself a base for seeing the northwestern parts of Lake Van. Further north, a second approach to the region is possible from Erzurum (Chapter 11), from where travellers head straight to **Doğubeyazıt** and its fanciful palace below the dominating bulk of Mount Ararat. The more adventurous, coming from the southeast, might try the approach via Şırnak and the border road to **Hakkari**, previously out of bounds due to PKK activity.

▲ Tehran

ARMENIA

I R A N

Esendere

Şemdinli

▲ Iğdir

Ağrı Dağı
(Mount Ararat
5165m)

Gürbalak

Doğubeyazit

İshak Paşa Sarayi

Çaldıran

Muradiye

Surb Bartolomeos

Albayrak

Yüksekova

Diyadin

Banik
Gölü

Ağrı

Alaköy

Yedi
Kilise

Hoşap

Güzelsu

Çavuştepe

Başkale

Resko
(4136m)

Yeni Köprü

Karadağ
(3752m)

Kochanes

Hakkari

ÇILO-SAT DAĞLARI

Çukurca

I R A Q

HWY E-23

Patnos

Malazgirt

Süphan Dağı
(4434m)

Adilcevaz

Ahlat

Tatvan

Nemrut Dağı
(3050m)

El-Aman
Kervansaray

Bitlis

Ava mis

Çarpanak

Atinsaç

St Thomas

Akdamar

Göründü

Aşağı
Narlıca

Bahçesaray

Andzghonts

Van

Edremit

Gevaş

Çatak

Beytuşşebap

Uludere

Cudi Dağı
(2134m)

Şırnak

Cizre

Biloris
Kaplıcası
(Springs)

Siirt

Kurtalan

Batman

Midyat

Muş

Erzurum

Malabadi
Köprüsü

Silvan

Bingöl

Murat River

Diyarbakır

Lake Van

Gürpınar

Karadağ

Gürpınar

N

25 km

0

Trekking and travelling in the southeast region

From 1992 to 1994, the Van region repeatedly made headlines overseas by virtue of the kidnappings of foreign tourists by Kurdish separatist PKK operatives. The huge response to the insurgency by the Turkish military, culminating in the capture of the rebel leader Abdullah Öcalan in February 1999, resulted in the PKK declaring a unilateral ceasefire on September 1, 1999, and operations against the remaining elements of the PKK are now very rare. The only regions still under **emergency rule** are Diyarbakır and Şırnak, and it is expected that these will be returned to normal civilian rule during 2003. While foreigners, by their rarity, attract attention, the military presence is sufficient to ensure that personal safety from terrorism is the rule.

However, the combination of the Turkish economic crisis, the wild countryside and proximity to international borders has given rise to increased crime, especially the **smuggling** of people (illegal immigrants) and goods (petrol and heroin). This is unlikely to affect tourists, although it has made the military reluctant to grant access to Ararat and other mountainous areas, particularly those close to the borders. Although foreign civilians travelling in public transport are currently allowed access to the mountains, private cars and buses are stopped and checked at **roadblocks**, and sometimes turned back or given an armed escort in remote areas. It is unclear what will happen to these remaining checkpoints: even though emergency rule has been lifted, the rural police (*jandarma*) retain extensive rights to check civilians and regulate movement, though as Turkey seeks entry to the European Union these rights may be gradually dismantled.

For the average traveller visiting major cities and sites, apart from the odd checkpoint, travel is no different from other areas of Turkey. However, circumstances can change at any time, so keep your ear to the ground. The southeast has been unstable for so long that both locals and officialdom are understandably suspicious of all outsiders; but once you gain the trust of the locals, most are extremely friendly and helpful. If you intend to hike in the mountains, birdwatch or botanize, or visit remote rural sites and villages, it's worth heeding the following.

Transport

Most local **dolmuş** services stop running in mid-afternoon; start your journey early in the day to ensure you reach your destination before nightfall. **Car rental** is expensive; by renting a minibus or taxi instead, you have the advantage of a **driver** who knows local conditions and can often get you with minimum delay to your chosen destination.

Travel permission

If, and only if, you intend making forays off the beaten track into the mountains south of Van, it's advisable to reduce the possibility of minor officialdom blocking your path. Make enquiries and get initial clearance at the **Jandarma Hareket Merkezi** (movement centre) at the large barracks on the Hakkari road, about 3km outside Van. Leave your name and your intended purpose and destination, as any patrol that subsequently stops you will have to report to the centre for instructions.

Trekking advice

Forays into the mountains themselves – the real treasure of this region – are becoming possible again, although we recommend taking a local guide. **Permits** for Mount Ararat are now available for foreigners (see p.952), Mount Suphan is unrestricted, and the Cilo Sat mountains of Hakkari, theoretically open, are being monitored. Take **up-to-date advice** from the websites ⓦwww.mountainsofturkey.org and ⓦwwww.trekkinginturkey.org, or other genuine mountaineering sources, rather than tourist offices.

Siirt and around

Heading east of Diyarbakır en route to Tatvan, the first reasonable diversion is provided by the isolated town of **SİİRT** (900m), which lies 40km south of the main highway (99) between Diyarbakır and Van. It's about a three-hour drive from Diyarbakır, with little to stop off for on the way, save the **Malabadi Köprüsü**, 20km east of Silvan, a beautiful stone bridge with an enormous single arch, constructed in 1146 by the Artukids, who also built Hasankeyf. From the bridge it's about 50km to the Siirt turn-off; your progress will be slowed by curvy roads and increasingly reckless driving habits.

Originally settled by the Babylonians, Siirt's heyday was during the period of Arab rule preceding the arrival of the Selçuks. It was the Selçuks, though, who left a lasting impression on the town, which now centres on a major roundabout with an Atatürk statue. Siirt's main attraction, the twelfth-century **Ulu Cami**, is behind the market area, uphill from the roundabout on the Bitlis road, well-hidden amongst mud-brick houses. Its tall, square, brick minaret is adorned with geometrically patterned tiling.

There are a couple of other things to see in town – the thirteenth-century **Cumhuriyet Camii** and the Selçuk-built **Kavvan Hammam** – but it's perhaps more pleasant to escape the confines of this rather claustrophobic town. Seven kilometres east from Siirt by local dolmuş is the pleasant picnic spot of **Aydınlar**, with a tomb of a local saint, İbrahim Hakkı, and there are also hot springs 20km south at **Biloris Kaplıcası**. Buses further south to the small town of **Şırnak** run on winding, but moderately good and empty, roads via green and pleasant valleys with occasionally interesting rock strata and formations. The villages en route, depopulated by the PKK troubles, are beginning to be reoccupied, and the farmland reclaimed.

Practicalities

Siirt has very little experience of tourism and you will probably find that the **local police** take an interest in your presence. You may be asked to show your passport and explain what you are doing there (not easy unless you speak Turkish), or even accompany the police to the station where they will photocopy your passport before sending you on your way.

Minibuses leave daily in all directions from the garage at the roundabout end of Aydınlar Caddesi; there are also a few long-distance bus company offices on the roundabout. There is at least one daily **dolmuş to Van**, which leaves at around 9am and takes three to four hours; otherwise, dolmuşes run north on demand to Ziyaret, at the junction with the main highway, where you change for Tatvan and Van. The main **otogar** is 2km west of town, with services to Diyarbakır, Hasankeyf and Batman. Four mornings a week, currently Monday, Wednesday, Friday and Sunday, **trains** leave Kurtalan (dolmuşes from Aydınlar Caddesi), 30km west of Siirt, for the long trip to Kayseri and Ankara via Diyarbakır; timetables, however, are subject to constant change.

The town has extremely limited **accommodation**. The *Vatan Hotel* (no phone; ❶) on Aydınlar Caddesi, opposite the dolmuş garage, offers only semi-clean doubles with temperamental hot water. A hundred metres further along on the same side of the road, walking away from the junction, you'll find the poor *Büyük Hotel* (no phone; ❶), which is dirtier and more expensive. The surprising best choice is the *Otel Erdef* (☎0484/223 1081; ❷) on Cumhuriyet Caddesi (downhill from the roundabout), with huge, spotless, air-conditioned en-suite doubles, a dainty white-frilled breakfast room-cum-restaurant, comfortable lobby-bar and gardens.

The *Metro* **internet café** is next to the *Vatan Hotel*, and there's a **currency exchange** office opposite. Good, cheap food is served cheerfully in a busy, noisy hole-in-the-wall **restaurant** next to the dolmuş garage, and there are kebab houses and fruit stalls in the **market** area north of Aydınlar Caddesi.

Bitlis

From the Siirt highway turn-off, it's only 44km to **BİTLİS**, but the winding gorge road means that the journey will take an hour. On the way you'll pass a few *han*s and old bridges, the only points of interest in an otherwise bleak landscape.

A strange and atmospheric town, impoverished Bitlis (1545m altitude) is set in a steep-sided valley and famous for its tobacco. Its lack of facilities mean that most people now pass through without stopping, but Bitlis once controlled the pass from Syria to the Van region and Persia and Armenia beyond. Nowadays the population is predominantly Kurdish, unemployed and mainly to be seen aimlessly passing time in the teahouses, but before World War I about half the inhabitants were Armenian.

The Town

Modern Bitlis is essentially a one-street place, threading its way along the banks of a river that's torrential in winter but dries to little more than a sluggish trickle in summer. Its dark stone houses and steep valley setting give it the feel of an isolated nineteenth-century English mill town. The most notable monument is the sixteenth-century **Şerefiye Camii**, with a fine carved portal, echoing the Selçuk style, on the northern bank of the stream. Also of interest are the **Ulu Cami**, an unusual-looking mosque built in 1126 by the Artukids, and the **Saraf Han** *kervansaray*.

Reached by the steps above the Tatvan dolmuş-stop on the main street is a walled complex containing the **Küfrevi Türbesi**, dating from 1316, and a much more modern *türbe* built by Greek craftsmen under the orders of Sultan Abdülhamid in 1898. Together they house the tombs of six Sunni saints, who draw pilgrims from all over the Muslim world. Ring for entry; Mustafa, the caretaker, whose family have lived here for generations, speaks some English and, in the Bitlis trading tradition, he buys tea in Sri Lanka and sells it all over Europe.

A huge **citadel** built on a rock outcrop looms over the north side of the town. You can walk up to it by following a road that snakes around its base to the far side, from where a dirt path continues to the summit. The grass-covered grounds are about the size of a football pitch, and while there are few recognizable remains to be seen, the view is excellent.

Practicalities

The main **dolmuş stop** is to the south of the centre, but some Tatvan dolmuşes depart from the foot of the steps below the Küfrevi Türbesi, on the main road some 400m northeast of the *Hanedan* hotel. The first dolmuş to Tatvan leaves at 8am and they run regularly through the day. Van buses heading west to Diyarbakır pass through Bitlis, but may be full.

The town's parlous economic state is reflected in the fact that there is only one shabby **hotel** remaining – the *Hanedan* (no phone; ❶) – which is less grim than the slog up several flights of stairs through the apparently abandoned Social Security building would suggest.

Bitlis' **food** is equally uninspiring; the local speciality is *buryan kebap*, leg of goat steamed in a *tandır* oven for four hours and served on the bone, but better examples are available in Tatvan. Reasonable *lahmacun* is served at a hole-in-the-wall **café** near the Şerefiye Camii, and excellent *su böreği* (savoury cheese or mince-meat pastries) and *porça* (savoury breakfast rolls) can be found at the **bakery** opposite the Tatvan dolmuş stop.

The El-Aman Kervansaray

Between Bitlis and Tatvan, on the right as the road reaches the plain, just after the turning to Muş, is the **El-Aman Kervansaray**, huddling into the barren ground below the level of the present-day road. A classical Ottoman *kervansaray* built of volcanic black stone by Hüşref Paşa in 1502, it is one of the largest of the period, 90m long and with 160 rooms. Entry is via an enclosed courtyard, where the local kids play football.

The interior is based on the pointed arch, reaching great spans in the hall to the right of the entrance. Passing through the main building, the rear extension is now unroofed, but seems to have consisted of more cell-like rooms. A small mosque and bathhouse adjoined the entrance courtyard. The gently deteriorating building is a reminder of the volume of trade through the Bitlis gap; it's well worth a visit and afterwards you can hail a passing dolmuş to continue your journey to Tatvan, half an hour away.

Tatvan and around

If you're heading for Van and its environs you'll almost inevitably end up in the modern town of **TATVAN**, about 20km northeast of Bitlis. The town itself, squatting between Lake Van and the surrounding hills, has nothing of historic interest, but despite its fairly limited facilities it does make a good base to explore the attractions in the surrounding area. To the north is the massif of **Nemrut Dağı** with its crater lakes, to which it's easy to arrange a local tour; while you could also use Tatvan as a jumping-off point to visit the impressive Selçuk remains at Ahlat (p.927), further around the northwestern lakeshore. To the south are the hills around Hızan, well-watered, forested with oak and hiding remote farming villages and the ruins of several Armenian churches.

Practicalities

Tatvan's streets follow the grid layout common in new developments in Turkey with the main street, **Cumhuriyet Caddesi**, running east to west 100m south of the lake.

The town's **otogar** is 1km along the Bitlis road, but if you arrive by bus you will probably be dropped off in the vicinity of the PTT on Cumhuriyet Caddesi. You can pick up onward **dolmuşes** from in front of the various companies' ticket offices around here. The dolmuş to Van (with one checkpoint possible) follows the main road along the beautiful south shore of the lake; Ahlat dolmuşes leave approximately every 45 minutes from the corner of the PTT, near Cumhuriyet Caddesi, and run along the north shore of the lake.

The **train service** (Van Golu Express) between İstanbul and Tatvan/Van has now resumed; trains for İstanbul depart on Tuesday and Thursday at 7am; the train for Tehran (which involves trans-shipment of the train on the ferry across the lake) is on Wednesday at 10am. All services run from the station 1km northwest of the town centre on the Ahlat road and are subject to hours of delay.

Other boats also ply **across the lake to Van**, a four-hour journey. Supposedly, there is one sailing a day, but in practice the schedules are unpredictable; the very helpful, English-speaking **tourist office** (☎0434/827 6301) – a couple of hundred metres west of Cumhuriyet Caddesi, around the corner from the *Hotel Kardelen* – can advise.

Bang in the middle of Cumhuriyet Caddesi is the **PTT**. There are a few **internet cafés** in town, most central the *Sena Internet Café* (one street south of Cumhuriyet Caddesi from the *Alize* hotel) and the *Edessa* near the PTT.

Accommodation

Opposite the PTT, Belediye Yanı leads south to the town's top-rated **accommodation**, the large *Hotel Kardelen* (☎ & ℗0434/827 9500; ❸), with a restaurant, bar, sauna and very spacious rooms with satellite TV and comfortable beds. A new hotel, the *Alize Hotel*, Cumhuriet Cad 160 (☎0434/828 0020, ℗828 0022; ❷) is better value, offering clean and comfortable accommodation with nicely fitted bathrooms. Some of the balconies have good views of the lake and Nemrut Dağı. Next door, the *Hotel Altılar*, Cumhuriyet Cad 164 (☎0434/827 4096; ❷), has clean, cheap doubles and hot water round the clock. The cheapest option is the shabby *Akgün Otel*, Hal Cad 51 (☎0434/827 2373; ❶), a couple of blocks east of Cumhuriyet Caddesi, catering for the less prosperous male business traveller with small rooms and no breakfast included.

Eating and drinking

On Cumhuriyet Caddesi are a number of **breakfast** places serving fresh bread with comb honey, butter and cheese. The hotels provide the main **restaurant** options: for upmarket dining (around \$7 a head) and alcohol with your meal, the restaurant in the *Alize* is an alternative to the *Kardelen*, while the *Akgün* has a restaurant/bar, frequented by the locals, featuring occasional live music. The *Koşem* restaurant, just east of the *Alize* hotel, serves excellent soup and kebabs and has a big eating salon upstairs. Nearby, the *Şimşek* offers a similar range of food, for around \$3 a head.

Nemrut Dağı

Immediately north of Tatvan, the extinct volcano of **Nemrut Dağı** (no relation to the mountain with the statues), rises to 3050m. Six thousand years ago Nemrut is believed to have been 4450m high; as a result of a huge volcanic explosion, the whole upper section of the peak was deposited in the Van basin, thus blocking the natural outlet and creating the lake. The present day volcanic cone contains two crater lakes, one of which is pleasantly warm.

After snowmelt in May/June, the crater lakes are accessible by car or dolmuş. The tourist office in Tatvan can organize full-day **dolmuş excursions** for groups at $35 per group, including waiting time. This will probably be under the auspices of Mehmet Selinci (℡0542/832 4228), a local guide who speaks reasonable English and who also arranges trips to local villages, *zoma* (the Kurdish for summer pastures) and remote churches. If you're travelling under your own steam, take the Bitlis road out of Tatvan and turn right for Şentepe; it's about 15km to the crater rim.

From the rim, with its unbeatable views of Lake Van, it's another 3km down an ill-maintained dusty track to the shores of the crater lakes. The **crater**, 7km in diameter, seems to have its own microclimate and the lush vegetation (beech, aspen and juniper) contrasts sharply with the bare landscape outside. Water birds that stop off here include gulls, stilts, herons and ducks, notably the rare, black velvet scoter; the crater is also noted for its snowmelt vegetation. The only other inhabitants are transhumant Kurds whose flocks graze the slopes during the summer months. The crescent-shaped **Soğukgöl** (cold lake) occupies the western half of the crater and lives up to its reputation all year round, but there are some hot springs on the east shore that are good for a swim, as well as cold, potable ones. Better still, take a dip in the smaller **Sıcakgöl** (warm lake,) connected to its partner by a narrow path leading east or a branch of the dirt road.

Lake Van and its wildlife

Lake Van, virtually an inland sea of almost 4000 square kilometres, at an elevation of 1750m, is one of the most unusual features of eastern Turkey. Along with Lake Sevan in Armenia and Lake Urumiya in Iran, it is one of a trio of huge upland lakes without outlets in the region. Surrounded on all sides by a narrow but fertile plain, and then mountains, the lake – nearly 200m deep in spots – occupies what was once a lowland basin that was later dammed by lava flowing from Nemrut Dağı. Owing to rapid evaporation in this desert climate, the lake water is highly **alkaline**, rendering it slightly soapy and slimy to the touch, so local people can sometimes be seen washing clothes in it.

Yet **pollution**, plus the summer mosquito population, particularly around Van, has meant that swimming is not recommended close to the major towns. You can **swim** from the stony beaches on and opposite Akdamar Island, and around Edremit, but otherwise the shore remains largely unexploited, with a notable scarcity of boat-rental or watersports facilities. It is also possible to take a dip along the more sparsely populated stretches of shoreline, especially on the north side. Even non-swimmers will float – the water's specific gravity is greater than the sea. Two species of **fish** – one called *dareka*, attaining forearm size – live in the lake, though only near mouths of the streams feeding it, where they are caught for food during spring.

The lake is on the main **bird migration route** to Africa, so is seasonally filled with migrants. Visible populations include a few pelicans, gulls, flamingos and cormorants, and there are kestrel and night heron colonies on Akdamar. Two other forms of local animal life are worth noting. First, there's the famous **Van cat**, a fluffy white beast endowed naturally with one blue and one gold eye, and an affectionate disposition; its pure strain is disappearing from careless interbreeding with ordinary cats, but a few specimens are still kept at local hotels and carpet shops as tourist bait. Less commonly seen is the **Lake Van monster**, or Van Gölü Canevarı – this two-metre long beast was supposedly first spotted in the 1960s and has been growing ever since, but recent reported sightings are of a dinosaur-like monster about the size of a bus . . .

Ahlat and around

Forty-two kilometres from Tatvan along Lake Van's northwestern shore, the small, shabby town of **AHLAT** is known chiefly for its numerous free-standing tombs and cemetery, essentially an outdoor museum of funerary relief-work. The journey from Tatvan takes in some lovely views of Nemrut Dağı and the lake, with marshes full of birdlife and orchids on either side of the road as you approach the outskirts of town.

First an Urartian, then Armenian settlement, Ahlat fell to the Arabs during the seventh century, was retaken by the Byzantines some two hundred years later, and passed to the Selçuks after the nearby battle of Manzikert in 1071. The Mongols arrived in 1244, succeeded by the İlhanids from Persia a century later; by the 1400s Ahlat was the main base of the Akkoyun Turcomans. Even after the local Ottoman conquest of 1548, real power in this remote region remained in the hands of the Kurdish emirs of Bitlis. Throughout its long history Ahlat was a populous, polyglot city, home to both Christians and Muslims until World War I. That it used to be far larger than the modern town is amply shown by the vast extent of the cemetery.

Today Ahlat's famous *kümbet* **tombs** – rivalled in quantity only by those at Kayseri – are scattered about some 2km southwest of the modern settlement's centre. In a typical local *kümbet* (housing one to four persons), the deceased was interred in an underground chamber, beneath a prayer room reached by steps from the outside. It's thought that the traditional nomadic tent inspired the distinctive conical design, executed in purple basalt, often by Armenian stonemasons. Even the word *kümbet* appears to be a corruption of the Armenian *gmbed*, a conical-roofed cupola.

You'll see the first (and largest) of them, the two-storey **Ulu Kümbet** (Great Tomb), in a field just south of the main road as you approach the town. This simple tomb of a late thirteenth-century Mongol chieftain is the largest in the Van region (there are a few more at Gevaş, on the opposite shore of the lake). On the other side of the road, next to one of the entrances to the cemetery, is a small **museum** (Tues–Sat 9am–12.30pm & 1-5pm; $0.70) with stone animals and other monuments standing outside, including an undated stone portraying reliefs of the tombs. Inside, you'll find some Urartian bronze pieces and jewellery, and miscellany from other eras.

The **Selçuk cemetery** covers almost two square kilometres, crammed with tilted, lichen-encrusted headstones dating from the eleventh to the sixteenth centuries. The headstones appear in all shapes and sizes, most covered with floral, geometric and calligraphic decorations staying within good Islamic taste. The language of most inscriptions is not Turkish but – like the town's predominant linguistic profile until the fourteenth century – Persian and Arabic.

Set back outside the wall on the north of the cemetery stands the **Çifte Kümbet** (Twin Tomb), similar to the Ulu Kümbet in age and design (only double) and also a Mongol mausoleum, in this case for two couples. Nearby is the **Bayındır Türbesi**, most impressive of all the tombs hereabouts with its colonnaded upper storey and distinctive *mescit* (oratory); it was built in 1492 to house the remains of the Turcoman chief Bayındır.

Leaving town towards the northeast, you'll notice a ruined **fortress** down by the lake, built during the sixteenth century by sultans Süleyman the Magnificent and his son Selim. Grand as it is, not much apart from the outer walls and two adjoining, crumbling mosques have survived, but it's worth scrambling across the fragmented masonry to view Lake Van from the battlements.

Practicalities

Dolmuşes from Tatvan take fifty minutes. Ahlat's transport hub is near the *Belediye* in the middle of town with something – be it bus or dolmuş – going in either direction (to Tatvan or Ercis/Doğubeyazit) every hour or two.

The *Selçuklu* on Zübeyde Hanım Caddesi (☎0434/412 5697, ℱ412 5699; ❸), at the extreme east end of town, down by the shore, is the better of just two **hotels** in Ahlat; they don't get many visitors, so try to bargain gently. It's gargantuan in scale, a bit dated and has less than spotless rooms with temperamentally-plumbed bathrooms, but there's a pleasant **restaurant** with live music at weekends. Ask for a room with balcony overlooking the overgrown gardens and lake.

Around Ahlat

Continuing 25km northeast from Ahlat will bring you to the attractive modern village of **ADİLCEVAZ**, set amid a fertile lakeside strip and dominated by a mighty Selçuk fortress, which is in turn overshadowed by the 4434m volcano of **Süphan Dağı**. The mountain, Turkey's third highest peak, is not technically difficult to climb, but it is remote, with an unreliable water supply and semiwild sheepdogs on the loose. Below Adilcevaz, look out for the **Tuğrul Bey Camii**, a distinctive thirteenth-century mosque near the shore, constructed using the dark brown volcanic stone typical of the area.

To the north of the village remains of the Urartian citadel of **Kefkalesi** can be seen. The site, at 2200m, is not easy to reach, though you could walk there from the village in a couple of hours or so. In the grounds of the citadel archeologists have unearthed the foundations of a Urartian palace, and at the base of the Urartian settlement are the ruins of an Armenian monastery.

If you don't leave it too late in the day, it's possible to **travel on to Van** following the northern shore of the lake; get off the northbound bus at the major road junction 20km east of Ercis and wave to stop a passing bus or car.

Van

Capital of the region, sited on the eastern side of the lake, **VAN** is by turns impressive and disappointing. The most enduring image of the place is **Van Kalesi**, the so-called Rock of Van, which eighteenth-century artists fancifully depicted as an improbable column of rock rising from the lakeside. Even though it's actually rather more horizontal than portrayed, the Rock, when viewed from certain angles, with the ghostly traces of Old Van at its foot, does almost live up to these flights of fancy. Modern Van, however, with a population of 600,000, is set 4km back from the lake against a mountain backdrop, and is blighted by its concrete construction and grid layout. Both are owed to an earthquake in the 1950s that destroyed what remained of the town's Ottoman architectural heritage. Nonetheless, Van is one of the friendlier cities you'll come across in Turkey and its main virtues are an excellent museum and its handy location as a base for exploring Old Van and the surrounding area.

The most atmospheric way to arrive in Van is by the rusting **boats** that ply the aquamarine waters of Lake Van from Tatvan. These are highly unreliable, though, and it's far more likely that you will reach Van by the scenic **south-**

ern shore route from Tatvan, initially following a pretty willow-fringed valley to the pass of Kusun Kiran, where you are greeted by spectacular views over the eastern lake basin. From here, the road descends through a checkpoint and then follows the lakeshore with vistas of the Armenian island church of Akdamar and Süphan Dağı reflected in the still waters. The road then turns north through the lakeshore town of Edremit, but the ultimate approach to Van itself is disappointing, as unsightly urban sprawl has invaded the lakeside orchards.

Arrival, information and services

The **airport** is 6km south of town, and there's a bus ($1) to the crossroads of Cumhuriyet Caddesi (the town's main drag) and Kazım Karabekir Caddesi, where the main bus companies have their offices. Most of the better hotels are also around this crossroads, as is the **THY agency** at Urartu Turizm (℡0432/214 2020), a minute's walk south of the junction. The cheaper hotels and restaurants are located in the huge market just to the west of the crossroads, in the streets running parallel to Cumhuriyet Caddesi.

The **otogar** is a little way northwest of the centre: dolmuşes and *servis* buses run from here to the busy junction of **Beş Yol**, at the northern end of Cumhuriyet Caddesi. **Trains** arrive at the station 3km northwest of the centre, where you can find a dolmuş or taxi into town. If you do manage to arrive by **ferry**, from the docks you can pick up a dolmuş to take you the 5km into town.

During the season, the **tourist office** at Cumhuriyet Cad 127 (℡0432/216 2018) usually has an English-speaker around to give you a brochure and rudimentary street plan, and details of ferry sailing times.

Almost everything else in Van, such as **banks** and the **PTT**, can be found on and around Cumhuriyet Caddesi. For **internet access**, there's the *Net Café*, halfway along Cumhuriyet Caddesi; alternatively, opposite *Kebabistan* is the *Nokta Internet Café*, and around the corner in the pedestrian precinct are a few more. Hertz's local **car rental** agency is Akdamar Oto Kiralama, Cumhuriyet Caddesi, Ornek Iş Merkezi 1 (℡0432/215 8990 or 0532/596 0144); Avis works with Erek Turizm Şeyahat, Hastane Caddesi, behind the *Büyük Urartu* hotel (℡0432/214 6375 or 214 4333). If you're thinking of moving east, note that there's no **Iranian consulate**.

Accommodation

Van is the largest town in the southeast and most people who visit this part of Turkey usually end up spending at least two nights here. There are therefore plenty of **hotels** at all prices; and for women travelling alone staying in Van is more comfortable and safer than the other towns in the area.

Otel Ağansoy Hastane Cad 23/C ℡0432/2161686, ℻212 0551. A brightly painted building in a quiet cul-de-sac, with a clientele of Turkish student groups; the small clean en-suite rooms have TVs. ❶

Akdamar Hotel Kazım Karabekir Cad 56 ℡0432/214 9923, ℻212 0868. Very friendly, efficient place with restaurant, barber's shop, bar and comfortable lounge; ask for the quieter rooms overlooking the rear. Half-board accommodation, including an excellent buffet dinner, is good value here. ❹

Hotel Aslan Cumhuriyet Cad, Sok 3 ℡0432/216 2469. Slightly more expensive than the neighbouring *İpek*, but better for solo women. Newly decorated, with basins in all the smallish rooms and a shower on each floor. Try to avoid a room overlooking the noisy dancehall opposite. No breakfast. ❶

Beşkardeş Oteli Cumhuriyet Cad 16 ℡0432/215 5030. Good value, with small but TV-equipped en-suite rooms. ❶

Büyük Asur Hotel Cumhuriyet Cad, Turizm Sok 5 ℡0432/216 8792, ℻216 9461. Overpriced accommodation, but the management speaks good English and offers day-trips taking in Hoşap, Çavuştepe and Akdamar for from $30 per person, not including boat tickets. ❸

Büyük Urartu Oteli Hastane Cad 60 ℡0432/212 0660, ℻212 1610. Four-star hotel with rather old-fashioned, though comfortable rooms, plus swimming pool and sauna. ❻

Hotel Fuat Posta Cad 7 ℡0432/214 0780, ℻216 6804. Cavernous rooms, with pretty, fresh linen. It's central but noisy. ❷

Hotel Güzel Paris İrfan Baştuğ Cad ℡0432/216 3739, ℻216 7897. Businessman's hotel a couple of hundred metres east of Cumhuriyet Cad; newly decorated and with impressive marble bathrooms. ❷

Otel İpek Cumhuriyet Cad, Sok 3 ℡0432/216 3033. Clean, simple, but jail-like rooms with high-level windows, with or without attached shower; some include washbasins at no extra cost; no breakfast. ❶

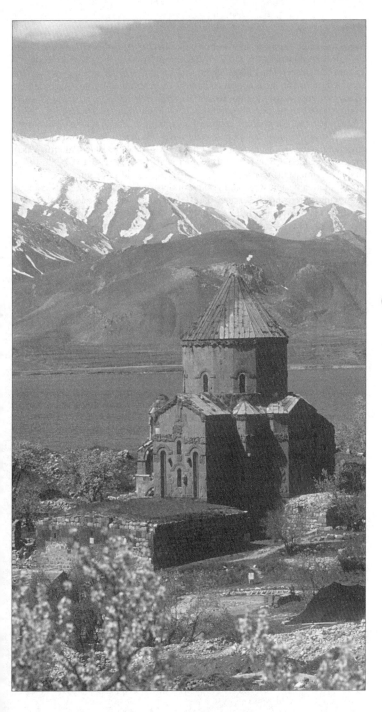

The City

Since the PKK cease fire and more recent liberalizing parliamentary legislation on Kurdish education, the locals are beginning to wear their **Kurdish identity** on their sleeves. The villagers who arrived in the 1990s as refugees from the troubled mountain areas appear to have to been absorbed by the urban culture. Many are just beginning to return to their former homes, some through homesickness and others through the lack of economic prospects in the city.

Van is still the commercial centre of area, with colourful market streets, livestock sales and general lack of commercial rip-offs. If you decide to buy Kurdish rugs here, one place to look is the **Türkiye Eğitim Hizmet Çalışma Vakfi**, on Barış Caddesi, Onur Sokak, Bostaniçi Mah, (☎0432/215 1513), 8km from the city centre. This is a charitable trust set up to aid poor village women by giving them a decent wage and good working conditions, with profits going to improving village heath services. The kilims are woven to traditional designs from the Hakkari region using natural dyed wool and time-honoured methods. The prices are comparable to the huge carpet emporium outside Van, but the product is genuine and profits go to a worthy cause.

Van Museum

Typical black-on-brown signs point the way to the **Van Museum** (Van Müzesi; daily except Mon 8am–noon & 1.30–5.30pm; $0.70), on Cengiz Caddesi just east of Cumhuriyet Caddesi. This is the main attraction of Modern Van, and it's among the best provincial museums in Turkey, with far more than the usual jumble of archeological miscellany.

In a room to the left of the ticket office on the ground floor you'll find displays of **Urartian** gold jewellery, bronze work and terracotta figures unearthed at Çavuştepe, plus some ornate bronze belts and jewelled breastplates. Adjacent to this gallery is a small conservatory, containing various **rock carvings** from Mesolithic times (9000–8000 BC) through to the Bronze Age. Some of these are very primitive representations of stags, which could almost be prototypes of the stag carvings in the Museum of Anatolian Civilizations in Ankara, while others are more sophisticated animal figures. Local ethnologists reckon that many such designs can still be found in local kilim and pottery designs. Also on display are children's sarcophagi from the fourteenth century BC and a number of cuneiform inscriptions.

Upstairs there's an **ethnographic** section displaying some fine kilims from Van and Hakkari provinces, as well as a prominently signposted **Genocide Section**, similar to the one in the Erzurum museum. This, it transpires, is devoted to atrocities committed against Muslims in the area during World War I and features a gory display of cracked skulls, supposedly those of Turks or Kurds killed by Armenians or Russians, though locals will tell you the reverse is true. Nearby a cabinet contains numerous books debunking foreign allegations of an officially sponsored massacre and mass expulsion of the Armenian population. Whatever the true identity of the skulls, no attention whatsoever is given to the fate of Van's Armenians (see box on p.936), making this a rather one-sided corner in an otherwise fine museum. However, the exhibits in the garden outside include a few interesting Armenian gravestones, an evocative reminder of the region's past.

Toprakkale

Van's only other significant site, **Toprakkale**, is situated in a military zone and is off-limits at the time of writing. Toprakkale is a largish rock outcrop just north of town, the location of an eighth-century BC Urartian citadel, which has been identified as the town of Rusahinili, founded by Rusas I in 733 as a counter to Assyrian aggression. You'll be told that there's an underground palace, but in reality the subterranean chamber is just a large cistern. Other than that there's not much about, a temple and its treasures having been destroyed and looted by semi-skilled excavators in the last century.

Van Kalesi: the Rock of Van

From the Beş Yol junction in town frequent dolmuşes ($0.50) run west to the **Van Kalesi**, a narrow outcrop 1.5km long, over 100m tall and perhaps 300m wide at the base. It was just the sort of plug that the Urartians favoured for their strongholds. If it's not too hot, the 3km there make for an easy walk; visit in full daylight and you'll be able to appreciate the ever-changing colours of the lake; go late in the afternoon and you'll be treated to a magnificent sunset. Entry is from the car park and **ticket booth** ($0.70) on the north side.

The dolmuş will drop you at the eastern end of the Rock, from where you follow the road along the northern face towards the lake, passing a mosque and a *türbe* (tomb) that attract many pilgrims. Above these is a terrace, the site of an **Urartian temple**, of which only a couple of arched niches remain. Cuneiform inscriptions on a statue base in one of the niches document the life and works of Menua, an important Urartian king.

Below, the road continues for 500m to a car park and teahouse with a pretty stone bridge and willows. Nearby is a large stone rectangle with an inscription of Sarduri I, originally an **Urartian jetty**. The lake once came right up to this point, but these days a fish farm stands between the erstwhile landing stage and the water, now almost a kilometre away.

The ticket booth leads to a steep path followed by stairways and landings leading to the citadel at the top. As you climb you'll find that the views are increasingly spectacular, sometimes vertiginous. Immediately south of the Rock of Van lies the site of Old Van (see overleaf); beware of the sheer drops on the southern side, which, if you're not careful, could well take you there sooner than you'd anticipated.

What follows is an attempt to guide you through the more salient features, but it's difficult to precisely locate features. In general, the Cyclopean well-cut stone blocks are Urartian; the later poor quality workmanship is Armenian or Ottoman.

On the north face you can walk along what's left of the stone **battlements**. At one point a flight of stairs cut into the rock leads down to a cliff-side terrace from where you can reach the vast rock **tomb of Sarduri II** (762–733 BC), where three chambers lead off from the central one.

Continuing upwards, you pass through an arch onto a ramp, leading up to the **kale** precinct. In Ottoman times the citadel was garrisoned by three thousand janissaries as well as by conventional troops. Today the most prominent building is a **ruined mosque** with a minaret, whose partially intact steps can be climbed; the arched-roofed building is a *medrese* while nearby are barracks. On a large stone block an Urartian cuneiform **inscription** in suitably self-glorifying language credits Sarduri I (840–825 BC) with the construction of the first walls.

Past the *kale*, from the terraces overlooking the old town, steps cut into the strata lead down to the rock-hewn **tomb of King Argishti** (786–762 BC), successor of Menua, but the area has been fenced off. Nearby, on another terrace overlooking Old Van, are two more **rock tombs**, those of kings Ishpuini

(825–810 BC) and Menua (810–786 BC); the latter was the builder of the 65-kilometre aqueduct, portions of which are still used, supplying the dry Rock with water. A little more accessible than that of Argishti, these tombs are reached via a winding path that snakes down from the summit. Each consists of a large central chamber with three smaller chambers branching off. The southern edge of the terrace is marked by the remains of mud battlements.

The huge and famous inscription on the southern face of the rock is only visible from below; it was first recorded in 1827 by the traveller/archeologist Schulz (who was later murdered by Kurdish tribesmen near Başkale), dangling on a rope from the summit. The fifth-century BC **cuneiform inscription** in Persian, Medean and Babylonian celebrates the Persian king Xerxes.

Old Van

The destruction of **Old Van** in 1915 (see box on p.936) was so thorough that today only three mosques and a few other indeterminate ruins remain. The rest is a sea of overgrown, rubble-strewn mounds, with not even the basic street plan discernible. These days, people come here only to pasture their cattle and lounge around on the grassy knolls and appreciate the view of the Rock of Van, the silhouette of which has been likened to that of a kneeling camel. The only other sign of life is Kurdish women washing their carpets and kilims in the nearby stream, which loses itself in marshes towards the lake. In these marshes, one of Turkey's rarest birds, the citrine wagtail, flourishes, alongside the commoner yellow wagtail, which is a far more conspicuous egg-yolk yellow.

It's possible, but hair-raising, to scramble down to ground level at the south-eastern edge of the Rock and walk across the dead town, but far easier to circle the rock on the lakeside. The closest mosque to the rock is the ruined thir-teenth-century **Ulu Cami**, with a minaret that can still, with care, be climbed.

The southern limits of the old town are bounded by a road, near to which stands a pair of sixteenth-century mosques. The easterly one is the **Kaya Çelebi Camii**, a sealed-up shell whose white stone *mihrab* has unaccountably survived; the western mosque, rather more intact and with an attached tomb, is the **Hüsrev Paşa Camii**. The only other significant remnants are some stretches of the medieval wall that once girded the town, a couple of tombs and a ruined hamam.

The rest has vanished forever and it's hard to believe that this was once among the most attractive settlements in Anatolia, its stone and wood hous-es inhabited by some 80,000 people, mostly Armenians and Kurds. Within the walls lay a thriving bazaar, several churches, the government offices and even some foreign consulates. Only a few nearby orchards now give an indi-cation of the once-extensive "garden suburbs" where the bulk of the popu-lation lived, which once extended east from the walls to the site of the pres-ent town.

Eating and drinking

The **restaurant** scene in Van is fairly standard: the regional favourite *Kürt köfte* – a doughy ball of herb-flavoured wheat – only features in home cooking, while *otlu peynir*, a sharp, dry, spiced cheese, is most usually found at the bazaar. Van is noted as being one of the only places in Turkey having specific tiny shops dedicated to **breakfast**. Most of these are on Cumhuriyet Caddesi and serve a selection of cheeses, olives, honey and cream (*kaymak*) with fresh hot bread and gallons of tea; excellent places to set yourself up for the day or buy

VAN

Lake Van

Toprakkale

▲ *Iran*

Train Station

Otogar

See 'Central Van' map

BEŞ YOL

◆ **Museum**

Yeni Cami ◆

YANI MEHMET EFFENDI CAD

SİKKE CAD

KAZIM KARABEKİR CAD

EREK CAD

İPEK YOLU

CUMHURIYET CAD

▷ ⓘ

✉

★

Dolmuşes to Hoşap & Çavuştepe

▶ *Hoşap & Hakkari*

▶ *Airport, Akdamar, Tatvan, Bitlis & Diyarbakır*

İSKELE CAD

Van Kalesi (Rock of Van)

P

Ulu Cami

Hüsrev Paşa Camii

O L D   V A N

Kaya Çelebi Camii

İskele (Docks)

▶ *Tatvan*

▶ *Çarpanak*

N

0   500 m

From the standpoint of the modern Turkish state, the history of Van and its province is sensitive, being inextricably bound up with that of eastern Turkey's now-vanished Armenian population.

Ancient precursors: the Hurrians and Urartians

The earliest inhabitants of the Van region were the **Hurrians**, an expansionist and warlike people who established a kingdom stretching as far south as modern Syria around 1900 BC. Their territorial ambitions brought them into conflict with the Hittites. Eventually the Hurrians were defeated by the Hittite king Suppiluliumas in about 1400 BC.

The fragmented Hurrian kingdom later re-emerged as the **Urartian Empire** during the ninth century BC; Van, now known as **Tushpa**, was its capital. At the empire's peak, under King Argishti I (786–762 BC), it encompassed most of the territory described in this chapter, stretching also into present-day Iran, Iraq and Syria.

The Urartians were great citadel-builders, and remains of their fortified efforts have been unearthed at a dozen sites in southeastern Turkey and in modern Armenia. They were also skilled jewellers, with fine examples of their gold-working visible in Van Museum, as well as in Ankara, and have even been credited with the discovery of wine-making. Eventually centuries of fighting with the Assyrians and later the Scythians took their toll, and the Urartian Empire went into decline at the start of the seventh century.

The coming of the Armenians

After defeating the Assyrians in 612 BC, the **Persian** Scythians and Medes essentially annexed the weakened Urartian state. Around this time **Armenian** settlers began to drift into the Van basin, taking advantage of the Urartian collapse and inter-marrying with the indigenous population. Their origins are unclear, but it's thought that the Armenians probably came from the Caucasus, although Herodotus refers to them as Phrygians from western Anatolia, and Strabo suggested that they were related to the Babylonians or the Syrians. Whatever their provenance, during the reign of the Persian king Darius I (521–486 BC), the Armenians were established enough to count as a vassal principality.

In 331 BC **Alexander the Great** defeated the Persians and granted the Armenians a degree of autonomy, which enabled them to build up an extensive trade network across eastern Anatolia. After Alexander's death Armenian territory became part of the Seleucid Empire before passing into Parthian and **Roman** hands. Between 95 and 55 BC Armenia, under King Tigranes II, "the Great", wrested short-lived independence from the Romans, in alliance with his father-in-law Mithridates of Pontus. After protracted campaigns against both the Pontic and Armenian kingdoms, the Romans effectively re-absorbed the region.

The advent of Christianity

Under the Romans and Byzantines, Armenia was to play an important role in the growth of **Christianity**. Towards the end of the third century, during the reign of King Trdat III, it became the first nation to adopt Christianity officially, thanks to the efforts of St Gregory, known henceforth as "the Illuminator". Following the Edict of Milan in 313 Christianity became tolerated throughout the Byzantine Empire, enabling the Armenian church to consolidate and establish its own identity. By 404 the monk Mesrop Mashtots had devised the **Armenian alphabet**, which except for two later additional letters has endured unchanged to the present day.

The **Armenian Apostolic Church**, as it's technically known, split from the Byzantine Church in 451 after it refused to accept the ruling of the ecclesiastical Council of Chalcedon, which declared that Christ had two equal and co-existent natures. The Armenians, like the Coptic and Syrian Orthodox Christians, retained their monophysite doctrine, maintaining that the human nature of Christ was absorbed in the divine.

The ninth and tenth centuries saw the greatest flowering of Armenian culture, particularly in the Van basin under the **Atzruni dynasty**. But the long-running religious antipathy between the Byzantine capital at Constantinople and outlying provinces such as Armenia fatally weakened the empire. The Selçuks took Van in 1064, even before the fateful battle in 1071 at nearby Manzikert. A brief Armenian revival came during the twelfth and thirteenth centuries, when they were vassals of the Georgians, but subsequently there was little respite from repeated raids by the Turcomans, and the disastrous Mongol and Persian onslaughts of the thirteenth and fourteenth centuries.

Ottoman rule

The **Ottomans** finally assumed control of the traditional Armenian homelands during the fifteenth and sixteenth centuries, snatching Van from the Persians in 1548. Ottoman rule in its initial centuries was tolerant and the attendant stability beneficial for the Armenians, who like the other non-Muslim minorities were conceded substantial control over education and family law, and even earned for themselves the epithet of *sadık millet* (loyal nation). However, in the latter half of the nineteenth century there was an upsurge of **Nationalist** feeling in many Armenian communities, contemporary with similar movements among other Christian subjects of the Ottoman Empire. In the case of the Armenians, this was strongly encouraged by the Russians who had an interest in fragmenting the Ottoman Empire. With the outbreak of **World War I** the Armenians' predicament deteriorated. What happened during these years is still the subject of fierce debate, but it's incontrovertible that by 1918 there were very few Armenians left in the Van area, or indeed anywhere else in Turkey except İstanbul.

The events of 1915–1918

Though thousands of Armenians served in the Ottoman army from 1912 until 1915, many others in eastern Anatolia saw the global conflict as a chance to found an **independent Armenian state** centred on its traditional territories, and went over to the Russian side.

Local Turks and Kurds used this as a pretext to attack Van's Armenian civilians, who barricaded themselves in the old town. The Turkish garrison up on the Rock responded by pulverizing the walled quarter from above with heavy artillery. The bloodshed ceased temporarily when the Russians took the town in May 1915, but when the Ottomans counter-attacked, the remaining Armenian townspeople chose to flee with the Russian army.

The Russians, accompanied by some Armenian regiments, returned to Van and elsewhere in the east that August, remaining until the Tsarist collapse in late 1917. During these occupation years the Armenians and their nominal allies, the Russians, retaliated for the events of 1915 by forcing as many Muslims as possible out of potentially Armenian sovereign territory (a pattern, incidentally, being repeated in the current Armenian campaign to annex Nagorno-Karabağ). Turkish sources estimate that up to **600,000 Turks and Kurds** too slow in leaving were killed at this time – it is these victims who are highlighted by the "Genocide Sections" of the Van and Erzurum museums.

Official Turkish history is more reticent about what happened to the Armenian population during these same years. Few deny that CUP (Young Turk) ruling circles, at the instigation of Interior Minister Talaat Paşa, ordered the **deportation** of all Anatolian Armenians – not just potential combatants in the far east – to the Syrian

continued overleaf

desert. Much harder to prove are allegations that his partner in the ruling triumvirate, Enver Paşa, issued explicit orders for the systematic extermination of Turkey's Armenian population. The CUP's party archives were destroyed in the course of the war and precise attribution of guilt may never be possible.

However, numerous eyewitness accounts describe the rounding up in major towns of Armenian women, children and elderly for transportation to Syria, and the summary execution of any men of fighting age or in positions of authority. Sifting through conflicting claims, it would seem that between **700,000 and one million Armenian civilians** were dispatched in various ways between 1915 and 1920.

When the first census of the Turkish Republic was conducted in 1927, Van town had a population of just a few thousand, as against 80,000 before the war. The annihilation of Old Van had been so complete that it was never rebuilt. Instead Modern Van was founded 4km inland, beyond the "garden suburb" of the disappeared Armenian merchants.

picnic items. Van's other many small and cheap **eateries** are clustered in the streets west of Cumhuriyet Caddesi, behind the *Akdamar* hotel.

The **bars** of the big hotels make reliable if sterile drinking venues; the *Akdamar* is popular with wealthier locals. For an unusual night out, take a look in the nearby side streets where the numerous no-name **teashops** show Digitürk action movies and football matches.

Altın Şiş Salonu Cumhuriyet Cad. Excellent vegetarian *kaşarli pide*, which comes on a round base dripping with cheese ($2); the *kebap*s are good value, too.

Ayça Patisseri Kazım Karabekir Cad. Cakes, sweets and savouries, plus soft drinks, *çay* and *Nescafé*.

Çinar Restaurant Cumhuriyet Cad, next to the *Bayram* hotel. Service and food are a little above the norm and you can get a beer with your meal.

Doylum Lahmacun Beş Yol. Good for a snack of spicy *lahmacun* between dolmuşes.

Güven Pastanesi Cumhuriyet Cad. A central cake shop with a cavernous interior and good quality

cakes, *baklava* and coffee.

Kebabistan Off Kazım Karabekir Cad. A three-storey affair specializing in large, hearty *kebap*s and catering for groups.

Şelale Off Kazım Karabekir Cad. Around the corner from *Kebabistan*, on the new pedestrian precinct, is this third-floor restaurant serving kebabs and other dishes.

Yedisu Börekçi Cumhuriyet Cad. Fresh, tasty *börek*, which can be eaten hot or packed to take on a picnic.

Zaloğlu Café Kazım Karabekir Cad. Serves drinks, hamburgers and desserts to a young crowd.

Around Van

To get the best out of the wild scenery and historic associations of the area, plan to stay in Van for more than a day and enjoy some of the excursions covered below. Most trips can be made by dolmuş, though for some a rental car is necessary. Taking a picnic is advisable as restaurants and cafés are in short supply out of town.

The area to the south of Van is one of the most physically impressive in Turkey, featuring rugged mountains dotted with isolated settlements and stretching all the way to the Iraqi and Iranian borders. The Armenian church on the island of **Akdamar**, the less-visited church of **St Thomas**, the ancient Urartian royal palace at **Çavuştepe** and quaint old **Hoşap** castle all make excellent day-trips from Van. In the rocky foothills east of Van, there are more church remains at **Yedi Kilise**, while two more Urartian sites – the monastery church at **Çarpanak** and **Ayamis castle** – are situated on less spectacular parts of the lake north of town.

Akdamar Kilisesi

On an island just off Lake Van's southern shore stands the justly famous tenth-century Armenian **Akdamar Kilisesi** (open daily dawn–dusk), set against a mountain backdrop. The church itself is an incredible example of Armenian architecture, comparable with anything you'll find around Ani, while the scenery alone warrants a trip.

The ruler of the minor Armenian kingdom of Vaspurakan, Gagik Atzruni, built the church as the cathedral of the royal court on the island between 915 and 921 AD. He also constructed a palace and monastery here, which have not survived, but the church is still intact, a small four-apsed building of only 15m by 12m, but with a central cupola over 20m high. The exterior is covered in profuse **reliefs** depicting biblical scenes, idiosyncratically interpreted by Armenian masons who obviously observed nature with affection. In fact, the reliefs are so distinct and well preserved (the odd target practice session by local conscripts excepted) that you'll have to remind yourself they're over a thousand years old. Three reliefs on the south side describe the story of Jonah and the Whale, one of them showing Jonah being swallowed by a chimeric creature with ears and teeth. Also well represented are episodes demonstrating the rewards of faith: along the southern wall you'll find Abraham and Isaac, and David and Goliath. The most famous panel is on the north wall showing Adam and Eve (inexcusably vandalized) and next to it, a very butch Delilah is cutting off Samson's hair. The west wall is adorned by Gagik the builder-king presenting a model of the church to the clergy, and incorporates some fine **khatchkars** – the Celtic-looking, obsessively detailed carved crosses that the Armenians used both as celebratory or commemorative offerings and as grave markers. Mythical and real animals (at one point being named by Adam, elsewhere placed purely for whimsy, or to illustrate virtues or vices) and inscriptions in the hook-like Armenian alphabet also abound. You'll find more *khatchkar*s beside the church, to the northeast, where a group of handsome specimens date from the thirteenth to seventeenth centuries.

Stretching all around the church exterior, starting from the west wall, is a breathtaking vine-leaf trellis that runs above the reliefs: in the first scene, a prelapsarian woman embraces a beast, while towards the end there's hunting and animals feeding on the vine itself. Unfortunately, the **interior** is more or less gutted, its faded murals daubed with graffiti. The famous golden bell and the illuminated Bible that feature in the reliefs have long since been whisked away to the Moscow museum.

Practicalities

Dolmuşes ($1) run from a yard in Van one minute's walk up Zübeyde Hanım Caddesi, near the junction of Sikke Caddesi, and in high season you shouldn't have too much trouble picking one up to the quay for Akdamar-bound boats. Out of season (before May and after September) the dolmuş may only run as far as the town of Gevaş, and you'll be charged another $2 for the remaining 5km to "İskele".

From the **quay** by the roadside, the boatmen charge $20 per boatload for the round trip, or, if the boat is full, which it normally is in high summer or at weekends, about $1.50 return per person (last outbound departure about 2pm); there's a further charge of $1 for admission to the island. For a few extra dollars you can persuade the boatman to make a circular **tour of the island**, enabling you to view the seabird and night heron colonies on the cliffs and giving alternative views of the church.

Near the quay stands *Akdamar Camping Restaurant*, a large wooden building with a car park. This slightly expensive establishment (serving good fish) is where tour operators usually feed their charges before herding them across to the island; they also have rudimentary **camping** facilities. In season, 200m east on the shore road, you'll find a cheaper, unnamed restaurant, where it's also possible to camp.

The church of St Thomas

The monastic **church of St Thomas** (Kamrak Vank), situated on an isolated promontory in the lake and visible from the island of Akdamar, can be reached with your own vehicle or by taxi; it's about thirty minutes' drive from the main road and two hours from Van, followed by an hour's walk. The church overlooks the bay of Varış from a plateau 5km from the modern village of Altınsaç (formerly Ganjak); alternatively, a zigzag path (2hr) starts from Göründü village, which is quite close to the main road. It's also possible to visit **by boat from Akdamar** (3hr), though you would have to make arrangements at the Akdamar quay (see above) at an off-peak time of day/week.

A monastery existed here as early as the tenth- and eleventh-century Vaspurakan heyday, when it was built to house supposed relics of the apostle to India, and was occupied until the communal troubles of 1895. Most of the compound, enclosed in rectangular walls, is in ruins, though the church itself is still in good condition. Built to a cruciform plan, its sparsely decorated walls uphold a twelve-sided, capped drum; on the west is the building's glory, an extensive covered courtyard added late in the seventeenth century. Much of what you see is original, though restoration work was carried out in 1671 and 1801.

Edremit

On the road between Van and Gevaş, 15km southwest of Van, is the would-be resort of **EDREMIT**, a straggling lakeshore town with a few upmarket hotels and waterside tea gardens, much favoured by Van's barbecue fraternity at weekends. Dolmuşes run here hourly. It's possible to swim from Edremit's mixed sand and pebble **beaches** below the tea gardens. The lakeside *Tuşba Hotel* (☎0432/312 2965, ℻312 2858; ❺) has luxurious rooms with well-fitted bathrooms, a lakeside swimming pool and restaurant, and is a good place to break a driving tour.

Çavuştepe

The village of **ÇAVUŞTEPE**, 28km from Van on the Hakkari road and accessible by the Hakkari or Güzelsu dolmuş or bus, is the site of a **Urartian royal palace**, built between 764 and 735 BC by King Sardur II. To the right of the road is a long hill, on top of which the palace buildings once stood; a brown sign leads you up a single-track road to what remains of the ancient citadel.

When the warden is in attendance you should pay him an entrance fee ($0.70) plus a tip; he also has a few souvenirs and drinks for sale. He will lead you past some sunken grain storage jars to a temple with a number of black basalt blocks covered with cuneiform, which he can read and interpret impressively. There's also a sacrificial altar, several cisterns and even an ancient loo. Beyond here is the palace itself, but extensive excavations have failed to reveal anything much of its structure.

Hoşap Kalesi

Continuing along the Hakkari road from Çavuştepe, and 45km from Van, you pass the lake of Zernek Baraj, where the road winds just above water level. Over a small pass, and around 55km from Van, you arrive at the impressive medieval Kurdish fortress of **Hoşap Kalesi** (daily 8.30am–noon & 1.30–5pm; $0.70), which towers above the squat modern village of Güzelsu (a Turkish translation of *Hoşap*, which is Kurdish for "Beautiful Water"). Dolmuşes heading for Güzelsu depart from the Sevimli office in the bazaar in Van, behind İş Bankası.

The fortress, an extraordinary, now half-ruined, flight of fancy, was constructed at the behest of Sarı Süleyman Mahmudi, a local Kurdish strongman, in the 1640s. According to legend, he was so pleased with the result when the castle was completed that he had the architect's hands lopped off, to ensure that he would never build another to rival it.

To reach the fortress, cross the river either by a bridge with alternate light and dark stone courses and a major inscription, dating from 1671, or a road bridge 100m further on, and follow a dirt track winding around to the far side of the hill. This will bring you to the **main entrance**, set in an immense round tower. If the caretaker is on hand he will let you in and relieve you of the entrance fee; if not, he will send his son running up from the village below. The entrance, above which are lion **reliefs**, a symbolic chain of power and a Persian inscription, opens into a tunnel leading to the interior of the fortress. Originally there were several hundred rooms, including a couple of mosques, three hamams and a *medrese*, but there isn't really a great deal left. The round arena-like structure is said to have been a gladiators' pit, but the best-preserved part is the **keep** – reached by a path from the outer fortress. There is a cooling system built into the walls of the castle, and drainage pipes in the hamam below. Looking east from the fortress you can see the line of mud defensive walls that once encircled the village: aeons of erosion have turned these battlements into a row of rounded plates, reminiscent of a line of browsing stegosauruses.

Yedi Kilise

About 10km east-southeast of Van, in the village of Yukarı Bakraşlı, are the remains of the once-grand monastery of the Holy Cross, founded in the seventh century and beautifully situated in the foothills of Erek Dağı. The locals know the village as **YEDİ KİLİSE** (Seven Churches), or "Varaga Vank" in Armenian, as seven Armenian churches and the monastery once stood here. Unfortunately, most of the structures have been destroyed by earthquakes and vandals, but one remains behind the new village mosque; it has now been locked and you will be charged a small fee for access. This is the once-domed **church of St George**, conforming to a cruciform ground plan, built or perhaps rebuilt during the thirteenth century. The porch is enlivened by intricate stone-carvings, and an arched stone portal with an Armenian inscription leads to the interior, which has retained traces of seventeenth-century frescoes and crosses carved into the walls. A trip here will also give you a glimpse of contemporary Kurdish village life. Take a picnic and share it with the locals, some of whom may invite you to eat in their homes.

The best way to reach Yedi Kilise is by **taxi from Van**. The taxi drivers out-side the *Akdamar* hotel will take you there, find the key to the locked church, wait and bring you back, all for around $15. It's theoretically possible to reach Yedi Kilise by dolmuş, but departures are uncertain.

Çarpanak

The well-preserved remains of the **monastery church of St John** are curious-ly set on the long, narrow island of **Çarpanak** (Ktuts in Armenian), 1.5km off-shore from a promontory some 25km northwest of Van. The most certain way to reach the island is by renting a boat for the hour-and-a-half trip there from Van İskelesi (docks), but you need a Turkish speaker to bargain (and expect to pay at least $20 per person, depending on the size of the group); resist the overcharging of Ercan Bozbay at the *Büyük Asur Hotel*. Alternatively, you could chance your luck at Van İskelesi on a Sunday morning, when locals cross by boat to picnic. There is a huge gull colony on the island, so peace and quiet is not assured.

A monastery grew up here around a twelfth-century church at least as early as 1414, but a disaster befell it during the next century and the present church was heavily restored during the early 1700s. Despite this late date it's a hand-some, rectangular compound, with a shallow dome sporting a pyramidal roof.

Ayamis castle

Ayamis castle is a recently excavated Urartian fortification set on a typical hilltop site right above the lakeside north of Çarpanak. The only access is by private car; drive 20km north of Van on the main road, turn left at the sign-post and, some 8km further on, turn right in the village of **Alaköy**; from here the unsurfaced road rises over hills and approaches the lake, veering right through a small settlement to the obvious hilltop site. There may be a guardian in attendance who will show you around.

A trek to the hilltop is rewarded with views of **excavations** of the perime-ter walls and an impressive central **temple** compound. The temple doorway bears a long cuneiform inscription in excellent condition on both sides of the main entrance. The views of the lake are expansive, and bee-eaters from a colony on the northern slope of the hill whirl over the site.

Bahçesaray

The rural town of **BAHÇESARAY**, 106km southwest of Van, rates at least one TV mention every year, on the occasion of the reopening of the road that links it to the outside world, over the Karabel Geçiti. At 2985m, this is the highest (unsurfaced) road pass in Turkey and usually the last to open after the winter snow (April/May). Bahçesaray was once far more important than its present-day size would suggest, with a population of 12,000 over a century ago (three times today's size), and if you have two days to spare, the long (six-hour) bumpy journey here from Van is better than the trip to Hakkari (see p.944) for the variety of scenery, vegetation and birdlife on display, both up on the pass and in the nearly deserted countryside beyond. On the east slopes of the pass are seasonally scattered **encampments** (*zoma*) of Kurdish transhumant shep-herds and their flocks, forming a colourful complement to the spectacular mountain scenery. The descent west from the pass plunges you down steep slopes towards villages hidden under canopies of walnuts and stands of poplars.

Entering the town, you pass attractive tea gardens at the start of the single main street, which ends at a mosque and welcoming restaurant by the stream. Bahçesaray, still known to most of the locals by the Armenian name of Müküs, has the remains of a small Armenian church, called **Andzghonts**, lying on the eastern slopes above the town. Much damaged by fire in 1805, it still has *khatckars* (stones inscribed with crosses) visible in the exterior walls. Other pleasant diversions are an upstream walk to the underground source of the **Botan Çay**, a tributary of the Tigris, and, a few kilometres downstream, a single-arched brick Selçuk bridge, the **Kızıl Köprü**. However, the Armenian monastery of **Aparank**, in the hills west of the Botan Çay, is impossible to find without a guide (and military permission).

Practicalities

A daily **dolmuş** ($4; bag the front seats) from Van leaves any time after 9am from the *Bahçesaray Çayevi*, a small teahouse opposite the Halk Pazarı (market), off Zübeyde Hanım Caddesi

It's possible to stay the night in Bahçesaray at the local council **visitors' house** (*misafir evi*), which contains a couple of rooms with beds and blankets, and a small washroom; enquire at the **restaurant** by the stream, which – if you're interested – will also find a vehicle to take you to the Selçuk bridge.

If you are rash enough to wish to **drive to Bahçesaray**, enquire first at the *Jandarma Hareket Merkezi* outside Van (see p.921), fill up with petrol and, after Edremit, turn left and then right onto the Çatak road, then right to Aşağı and Yukara Narlıca. At the time of writing there is a major **checkpoint** and barracks at Yukara Narlıca; you may be asked to visit the commanding officer to explain yourself, and he has authority to turn you back.

The route to Hakkari

The three- to four-hour bus or dolmuş trip to **Hakkari**, along the gorge of the Zab River, has spectacular mountain scenery, with amazing stretches around the 2730-metre Güzeldere pass and beyond the town of **Başkale**. Both the Çavuştepe and Hoşap Kalesi excursions from Van are off the Hakkari road and, if you have your own transport, could be visited en route. Hakkari was once Turkey's most active trouble spot, but it is now looking forward to welcoming tourists again.

Head south of Van on the Hakkari-signposted road, not the Gevaş shore road. After a few kilometres it starts to climb and, at an altitude of about 2260m, you traverse the Kurubaş pass. Some 5km beyond here the road forks: a right turn will point you towards the southern shore of Lake Van, while left continues towards Hakkari.

Başkale and around

Past the plains around Çavuştepe and the lake at Zernep, 45km southeast of Güzelsu, and lying at 2500m, **BAŞKALE** is the highest town in Turkey – and that's its only claim to fame. South of here the **Zab gorge** is at its most spectacular and photogenic, but mainly inhabited by sheep and shepherds: look out for the quaint plank and wire bridges that enable the flocks to cross the river. Here and there tracks lead off to medieval-looking settlements, and you may well spot the odd transhumant encampment.

On the way to Başkale, 14km before town, a road leads northeast to the village of Albayrak, where you'll find the old Armenian **church of Surb Bartolomeos**. Once the focus of a monastery, it's now half-ruined, the roof and cupola collapsed, but retaining fine reliefs on what's left of the facade. This area may still be restricted; enquire at Van's *Jandarma Hareket Merkezi* (see p.921) before you attempt to drive there.

Yüksekova and the Iranian border

Some 60km south of Başkale is **Yeni Köprü**, at the time of writing there is a major checkpoint where the road forks: right is to Hakkari, while a left turn in the direction of the yellow sign marked "İran" takes you 35km to **YÜKSEKOVA**. Before the insurrection, this was the favoured base for climbing in the 3794-metre **Sat** range and for **Reşko** (4135m), Turkey's third highest peak, in the Cilo range. From there, a side road continues to Dağlıça, base for trekking in the Sat mountains, where there is a ruined Armenian church.

From Yuksekova it is respectively 40km and 50km to Esendere and Şemdinli, and several kilometres beyond them to the **Iranian border-crossing points**. Foreigners require Iranian visas in order to cross (available in Ankara, Istanbul or before leaving home), although Turks can buy them at the border. Taxis are available at the border crossings, and the attitude to foreigners is now said to be quite friendly.

Hakkari and around

HAKKARİ, 196km south of Van, is sited right in the Kurdish heartland, where the mountain ranges start to sweep down to the northern Iraqi plain. It's a sprawling building-site of a place, due to the influx of villagers forcibly evacuated from their outlying villages during the unrest. Trekking in the mountains – the main reason to come this far off the beaten track – is still an uncertain matter; although the local tourist office claims it is possible, they have no direct experience to base this on. In any case, detailed maps are not available, so before attempting anything, take professional advice as outlined in the chapter introduction.

Hakkari itself is no big deal. The only historic monument is the small square **Meydan Medresesi** in the lower town, just south of the petrol stations. This contains a collection of primitively carved prehistoric statues found in the locality, which alone seem to justify turning the *medrese* into a museum. Pending this conversion/restoration, the key is held by the Culture Ministry office; if you ask at the tourist office (see below) you may be able to arrange a visit.

At the upper end of town is the new **park**, which acts as a summer evening rendezvous for youngsters and their families. It contains swings and amusements, and has striking views down the main street to Sumbul Dağı and, looming behind it, the 4135-metre Cilo range. To the south is a new hilltop complex, which comprises the technical education facilities linked to Van University; unfortunately, the adjoining **castle** remains are closed to the public.

Practicalities

Buses and dolmuşes arrive outside the bus offices on the main street. Hakkari's **tourist office** (Mon–Fri 9am–noon & 1–5.30pm; ℡0544/ 211

Hakkari is one of the few places in Turkey where you might see (and hear) a proper **Kurdish wedding** being celebrated. Celebrations take place at both the bride's and groom's residences before the actual wedding; the groom with his loyal supporters then walks, rides or drives to claim his bride and after a legal ceremony they may go off together for a Western-style honeymoon. The **celebrations** involve much dancing, usually with a paid band of musicians setting up their screeching electrical amplifiers on any suitable piece of level ground. In contrast to Turkish custom, women and men dance together to **traditional music** played on the fiddle, *demblik* (drums) and electric keyboard, and women can lead the dances. **Dancers** link little fingers in a line, before advancing in step with much shaking of the shoulders and intricate footwork. Married women may wear a headscarf, but younger women let their hair fall free; both men and women wear as much gold as they can possibly muster.

The **traditional dress** for women consists of a full-length fitted under-dress with full skirt and sleeves extending well below the hand, usually in a plain colour. Over it is worn a velvet dress (with an embossed pattern) with short sleeves and open front, drawn in tightly at the waist with an antique worked silver belt. Sleeves are tied around the upper arms to prevent them trailing while dancing. Dress colours are chosen in fantastic combinations to stunning effect: for example, a red under-dress can be matched with a white over-dress with scarlet poppies; an older woman might wear a deep red under-dress contrasted with deep green over-dress embossed with crimson roses; a young woman, a black under-dress with silver and black print over-dress.

You will have no difficulty finding the wedding; as well as the music, guns are occasionally fired into the air. The atmosphere is usually very friendly; no-one will object to photographs and **visitors** will be fed and expected to join in the dancing. As is appropriate at a Muslim event, there is no alcohol in evidence, although the old men may sneak off for secret tipples.

6509) is opposite the Turk Telecom building in the side street adjacent to the bus company offices. The **PTT** is in another side street, opposite the Atatürk statue.

For **accommodation**, the basic *Ümit Otel* (☎0438/ 211 2469; ❶) on Altay Caddesi, has a restaurant and clean rooms with patched-up bathrooms and temperamental plumbing. Adjacent to the park on Bulvar Caddesi is the more expensive *Şenler Hotel* (☎0544/211 5512 or 5515, ℻211 3808; ❸), a three-star place with large rooms opening off rambling marble corridors. The rooms and bathrooms are almost luxurious but breakfast does not live up to the promise of the decor. Below is a complex with hamam, sauna and hairdresser.

If you're looking for somewhere to **eat and drink**, you will most likely be led to the *Çiçek Kebap Salonu* or *Derya Kebab Salonu*, where you'll find the usual lamb *kebaps*, beans and bread; the *Diyar 21 Ocakbaşı* near the tourist office also seems promising. The *Damla Pastanesi* has an upstairs tearoom that serves ice cream as well as baklava and other sweets, and there is an **internet café** nearby. There are two other internet cafés near the PTT, and a central covered **market** opposite the park. A street market operates along Atatürk Caddesi on Saturdays.

Around Hakkari

Some 20km north of Hakkari is **Koçhanes** (Quodshanes on some maps), once the patriarchal seat of the Nestorian Christians (see box on p.946). Small and simple in design, the church is beautifully situated on a grassy spur high above the Zab valley. You will only be able to find the church with the help of a local guide and it would be wise to get official clearance before setting out. There are many other Nestorian churches scattered through the surrounding mountains, including one at Diz, in the Zab valley below Hakkari, and at Kursin, a tiny hamlet en route to the glacier at the foot of Reşko (4135m), the highest peak in the Cilo range. How many of the Nestorian churches have survived the burning and levelling of the mountain hamlets by the security forces during the troubles remains to be seen.

Above Koçhanes lies **Berçelan** *zoma*, a huge lush summer pasture; as for most summer grazing lands, the *zoma* was closed to villagers and visitors alike during the unrest. With the lifting of the Emergency Regulations it is once again accessible for day-trips and, with luck, will soon be studded with black goat hair tents from late spring (end of May) through to September. Close to the pastures is a small glacial lake and the 3752m peak of **Karadağ**, suitable for a day hike and giving superb views across the Zab valley to the spectacular **Cilo-Sat** range of mountains. The Cilo-Sat are one of the last remaining strongholds of the rare *fritillaria imperialis* (misnamed in Turkish as *ters lale*, or upside-down

Nestorian Christians

The history of the **Nestorian Church** parallels that of the Syrian Orthodox Church in many ways, although their respective theological positions are completely opposed. **Nestorius**, bishop of Constantinople from 428 to 431, formulated a doctrine that held Christ to be predominantly human in nature and refused to recognize the term "Mother of God" as appropriate for the Virgin Mary. In 431, however, the Council of Ephesus declared his positions to be heretical. The works of Nestorius were burnt and he was deported to the Egyptian desert after suffering hideous tortures.

Despite his fate, Edessa (Şanlıurfa), Antioch (Antakya) and Nusaybin near Mardin became important Nestorian centres, though later the focus of the faith moved to Persia, where the Sassanid emperors officially encouraged it along with Zoroastrianism. After the Mongol attacks the Nestorians relocated again to the inaccessible Zagros mountains of western Iran, and to the equally remote area around present-day Hakkari in southeast Turkey. Isolated in the inaccessible mountains, the Nestorians developed their own ethnic as well as religious identity, with half the population organized into tribes little different from their Kurdish neighbours.

During the nineteenth century, however, serious rivalries developed between the Nestorians and the Kurds. This was due in no small part to the British and American missionaries who had infiltrated the region in search of easy converts. The missions aroused the distrust of the local Kurdish leaders, leading to the **massacre** of Nestorian men around Hakkari and the selling of the women and children into slavery. Their fate was sealed in 1915 when the Nestorian patriarch came out in support of the World War I Allies. When the Russians withdrew from the region in 1918, the Nestorians deemed it wise not to linger as targets for reprisal, but more than half their number perished anyway in the **flight** to Iran and Iraq. A short-lived attempt to resettle their mountain fastnesses was crushed by Atatürk in the early years of the Turkish Republic.

Today just a few tens of thousands survive in Iraq, Iran and Syria, with the patriarchate now in Chicago. There is also a small Nestorian church in Hanwell, West London. In modern times adherents of this sect are confusingly referred to as Assyrians, because – like the Syrian Orthodox – most surviving believers speak Syriac.

tulip), a tall fritillary with a stunning head of hanging orange-red bell-like flowers. Bunches of them may be for sale in the street market in June.

West from Hakkari to Şırnak and Cizre

South and west of Hakkari, a new **border road** has been opened between the Çukurca road and Şırnak, running mainly just south of the mountainous massif. As this road runs parallel to the Kurdish enclave in Northern Iraq (and was built in order to police this volatile border) expect a heavy military presence. One **bus** from Hakkari runs daily at some time after 8.30am and takes about six hours. A separate dolmuş runs at 8.30am on dirt roads for **Beytüşşebap**, an isolated village five hours away on the River Habur, but since there are no hotels or other facilities here, and no regular dolmuş service on to Uludere, there seems no real reason to go. It's also possible to get off the Şırnak bus at the Uludere junction and hitch the 7-8km into **Uludere** village, which has some shops, a teahouse and a bank or two, but again there is nowhere to stay and the police may encourage you to leave.

The border road runs parallel to the rapid-strewn Zab river for about 50km; at a major checkpoint the bus turns right instead of continuing to Çukurca, down on the border with Iraqi Kurdistan. From here, it rises over the Konaklı mountains to a beautiful pass at 2350m, and descends to a junction with the Beytüşşebap road in a gorge. The climate is noticeably warmer here than around Hakkari, with walnuts, poplars and even rice paddies in the valleys. The Egyptian vulture abounds, as do rolls of discarded razor wire in the bushes.

Şırnak

An hour past Uludere is **ŞIRNAK**, perched on a hillside with views over Cudi Dağı. While not being exactly civilized, the town does have two **hotels**. Near the dolmuş stop, the primitive *Otel Menteşe* (no phone; ❶) has tiny rooms with bathroom and, if you can force the balcony door, views as far as Syria. Uphill, on Cumhuriyet Caddesi, the road into the town centre, is the slightly better *Hotel İlkar* (☎0486/216 6464, ☏216 4444; ❷), a modern building with large but already seedy rooms with TV, and a rooftop restaurant/breakfast terrace.

Around Cumhuriyet Caddesi are various **restaurants**, including the cheerful, clean *Merkez* and *Merkez II pide* and kebab joints, doing a lively trade. Nearer to the *Otel Menteşe* is the small, cheap *Dost Lahmacun* restaurant, with fresh salads and friendly service; do not make the mistake of eating at the *Menteşe's* restaurant. The *Atatürk Park* **tea garden** in the town centre has extensive views of the vast cemetery and its blue irises, which dominates the southern slopes of the town. From the corner opposite the tea garden, **buses** leave to Siirt at 8.30am and to Cizre every hour until mid-afternoon. The Hakkari bus leaves from the Uludere road at 8.30am.

Cizre

The traditional resting place of Noah's Ark – and one to which Muslims, Christians and Jews did in fact make pilgrimages before medieval times – is **Cudi Dağ**, a modest 2134m peak above the River Tigris and the town of **CİZRE**, near the point where the modern Turkish, Syrian and Iraqi frontiers meet. The only other reason to go to Cizre is to catch a bus to westward destinations such as Mardin and Diyarbakır. The town is a major truck stop on the route to Iraq, so is well equipped with hotels, but foreigners are not normally permitted to cross the Habur border gate into the Kurdish enclave in northern Iraq.

The road to Doğubeyazıt

Heading **northeast from Van**, the road skirts the lake until it branches north where the encircling mountains open out to a wide valley, which rises gradually from the lake towards the Iranian border. At the north end is the pass over the laval flows from the eruption of Mount Tendurek, with first spectacular views of Mount Ararat. Between these two volcanoes on a major pass from Iran, is Doğubeyazıt (see below), an obvious starting point for any exploration of the Mount Ararat area.

It's three hours from Van to Doğubeyazıt by direct public transport, but it is possible to break your journey at the roadside waterfalls at **Muradiye**. Dolmuşes depart hourly from a side-street leading north off İskele Caddesi, 500m west of Beş Yol in Van, and from the northbound side of the main road in Tatvan. As long as you don't tarry until late afternoon, it's pretty easy to pick up another northbound dolmuş to resume your journey; there are regular services between Muradiye and Çaldıran, a major bus garage, 26km further northeast and from Çaldıran to Doğubeyazıt.

If driving yourself, take the road signed "Ağrı" (D975) out of Van and turn right at the major junction north of the lake.

Muradiye waterfalls

The **Muradiye waterfalls** are signed on the west side of the main Doğubeyazıt road, some 20km north of the junction with the road from Tatvan and past the village of Muradiye, and are entered via a car park with ticket booth ($0.50). A wooden bridge gives good views of the frothing twenty-metre falls, and leads to a large café and kebab house on the far bank. From here there are **riverside walks** along the stream and through cool poplar woods. One kilometre south of the falls is an old bridge known as **Şeytan Köprüsü** (Devil's Bridge), spanning the deep gorge. The valley channels birds migrating north from Lake Van and hundreds of species, some rare, can be observed during a short period in May. In May/June, the fields around also contain two stunning examples of the region's **flora** – a huge chocolate-and-white coloured iris and a brilliant red *phelepya*.

Doğubeyazit

DOĞUBEYAZİT, affectionately dubbed "doggie biscuit" by tourists over the years, has something of the frontier town about it. Lying 185km northeast of Van, and with Iran just half an hour away, the dusty streets are full of cross-border traders and even a few overland travellers en route to India via the Islamic republic. The over-militarized and rapidly modernizing town of Doğubeyazıt is the base for ascents of Mount Ararat and for visits to the fine old fortress of İshak Paşa Sarayı, set on a hill above the town. Tank sheds occupy the back streets and conscripts loiter in the cafés, but tourists are unlikely to have any encounters with either the military or their "opponents".

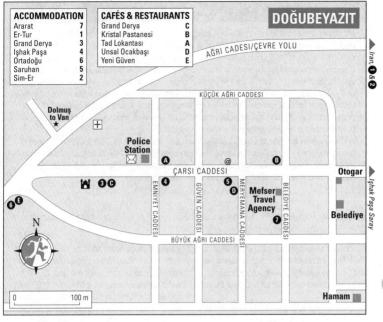

ACCOMMODATION		CAFÉS & RESTAURANTS		DOĞUBEYAZIT
Ararat	7	Grand Derya	C	
Er-Tur	1	Kristal Pastanesi	B	
Grand Derya	3	Tad Lokantası	A	
İshak Paşa	4	Unsal Ocakbaşı	D	
Ortadoğu	6	Yeni Güven	E	
Saruhan	5			
Sim-Er	2			

Arrival, information, services and tours

Dolmuşes drop you on the eastern side of town on Kücük Ağğı Caddesi (this road, with its southern extension, Büyük Ağrı Caddesi, is also known as the Çevre Yolu, or ring road); buses stop at the **otogar**, on the western side of the town centre.

There is no official tourist office, but the various **travel agents** and **bus companies** – mainly on Belediye Caddesi (south of the Atatürk statue) – will be able to tell you about transportation. Mefser Travel Agency on Belediye Caddesi (☎0472/312 6772) offers half- and full-day **tours** from $25, combining visits to the Iranian border, a meteor crater and a Kurdish village. They also arrange ascents of Ararat. The Saruhan brothers at the *Hotel Saruhan* also organize good-value day tours ($25 per person) around İshak Paşa Sarayı, the Iranian border, "Noah's Ark" and a meteor crater.

Doğubeyazit is well supplied with **banks,** there's a **PTT** (Mon–Sat 8.30am–12.30pm & 1–5.30pm) on the main İsmail Beşikçi (Çarşı) Caddesi, and a **hamam** off Belediye Caddesi (men and women; from $4). The best **internet café** is the *Omega* on the second floor of a clothes shop opposite the *Hotel Saruhan*; the alternative is the *Klas* on Emniyet Caddesi.

Accommodation

Accommodation in Doğubeyazit has improved lately with the addition of new hotels at the western end of town and on the bypass. Elsewhere, buildings and furnishings are often a little creaky, but the continuous stream of traffic from Iran creates healthy competition. The town itself caters for border traders

Most people **enter Iran** on a week-long **transit visa** (issued to non-US citizens at major Iranian consulates on proof of a Pakistani visa), which most travellers then extend for up to a month upon arrival in a major Iranian town (Tabriz is a good choice, Tehran and Isfahan can be more problematic). It is generally better to get this visa in your home country as the Iranian consulates in İstanbul, Ankara and especially Erzurum have a reputation for being obstructive – eg, requiring a letter of invitation from Tehran, which can take two weeks to arrive and be processed. If your plans change at the last minute, the Mefser Travel Agency in Doğubeyazit (see p.949) may be able to obtain the visa for you.

The **Iranian border** is at Gürbulak, 34km out southeast of Doğubeyazit, accessible by a dolmuş from Ağrı Caddesi. You can obtain Iranian Riyals at the border; from there, take a taxi to Maku and then an onward Iranian bus to **Tabriz**. Travellers (especially women) should be aware of Iranian dress codes.

---

more than businessmen, but you should have no trouble finding a comfortable double room.

Hotel Ararat Belediye Cad ☎0472/312 4987. Plush three-star hotel with restaurant, sauna, bar and tempting breakfasts. Neat but small rooms, some with double beds; ask for a room at the top for views. ❸

Hotel Er-Tur Ağrı Cad ☎0472/312 7866, ℻312 7868. Clean place, with modern rooms with showers; the restaurant serves breakfast (included) and there's a good set meal for $3.50. ❷

Grand Derya Çarşı Cad ☎0472/312 7531, ℻312 7833. Central, friendly place, almost next door to the mosque (so expect an early awakening), popular with trekking groups. Rooms are a little tatty, but there's a TV lounge with English-language broadcasts. ❸

İshak Paşa Hotel Corner of Çarşı Cad and Emniyet Cad ☎0472/312 7036, ℻312 7644. The dingy rooms have showers, balconies (with street view) and TV. Quiet and good value. ❷

Hotel Ortadoğu Büyük Ağrı Cad 105 ☎0472/312 4225, ℻311 3681. Well-equipped rooms with TV and fridge; some have views of Ararat. ❸

Hotel Saruhan Çarşı Cad ☎0472/311 3097. Best option at the budget end of the scale, with clean, basic but carpeted rooms (charged at $2 per bed if you share) and a 24-hr electric shower; breakfast not included. Owners, Nesim Saruhan and his brother Fetuh, speak English and organize local day tours. ❶

Sim-er Hotel 5km east of Doğubeyazit, Ararat road ☎0472 /312 4842 ℻312 4843. A low, modern hotel with attached restaurant, much used by tour groups. For those with their own transport, it's very tempting – gardens with morning views of Mt Ararat, comfortable rooms with TV and gushing hot water, and generous buffet breakfasts. ❹

Eating and drinking

For **breakfasts and desserts**, try the *Kristal Pastanesi* on Çarşı Caddesi, near the junction with Belediye Caddesi, with a large selection of sweets and savouries. For the most part Doğubeyazit has run-of-the-mill **restaurants** without a great deal of variety, but the *Unsal Ocakbaşı*, Meryemana Caddesi, is recommended as the best place to celebrate an ascent of Ağrı, with huge grills costing $6 a head. The *Yeni Güven*, with *sulu yemek* and grills, near the *Hotel Ortadoğu*, is handy if you are staying in the west of the town. The *Tad Lokantasi* on Çarşı Caddesi, opposite the *İshak Paşa Hotel*, is a good bet for *piliç kebap* and other sundries. The restaurant of the *Grand Derya* is a satisfying, comfortable venue that serves alcohol.

İshak Paşa Sarayı

Six kilometres southeast of Doğubeyazıt stands the **İshak Paşa Sarayı** (Tues-Sun 8am–5pm; $3), a half-ruined seventeenth-century palace set on a 2000-metre-high plateau overlooking the town. It looks as if it could have been built as a film set, epitomizing Western stereotypes of Near Eastern architecture – which is doubtless what makes it so popular with tourists. The designer seems to have taken elements from every architectural style extant in Anatolia and incorporated them into the palace's construction: thus Selçuk, Ottoman, Armenian, Georgian and Persian influences are all clearly evident once you start to examine the building's fabric.

The strategic importance of the site was recognized as far back as Urartian times when a fortress was constructed here, and later the Selçuks and Ottomans built castles to control east–west traffic on the Silk Route. The palace itself, more Xanadu pleasure-dome than military stronghold, dates only to 1785, when work began under Çolak Abdi Paşa, a local chieftain of uncertain (Kurdish, Armenian or Georgian) background; his son İshak Paşa added the finishing touches early in the nineteenth century. According to stereotypical Asian legend, the Armenian architect had his hands amputated once he'd completed the work to prevent him from building anything else as magnificent. Another legend asserts that the palace originally had 366 rooms, one for every day of a leap year. By 1877 the complex was already in decline, being used by the Turkish army as a barracks; subsequent periods of Russian occupation set the seal on its decay.

In recent years the Culture Ministry has carried out a programme of restoration; the halls around the entrance court have been shored up and the foundations on the south side repaired extensively, although the works have been left in an unfenced condition so that it's possible to fall down some very deep pits.

The palace

You enter via a grandiose **gateway**, which once boasted gold-plated doors: the Russians removed these in 1917 during their retreat from Anatolia, and they're now on show at the Hermitage Museum in St Petersburg. From the outer courtyard, an ornately carved portal leads to a smaller, inner courtyard. Straight ahead of you is the harem entrance, while to the right is the entrance to the *selamlık* or men's quarters. The **tombs** of İshak Paşa and his favourite wife stand in a *türbe* in one corner of the inner court.

The **harem** contains fourteen fireplace-equipped bedrooms (in which four hundred soldiers were quartered in 1877) overlooking the valley below, a kitchen and two circular bathrooms. At its centre is a colonnaded dining hall.

The *selamlık* also contains a library, bedrooms and a fine **mosque**, retaining much of its original relief decoration and ceiling painting. You can reach the roof of the chambers adjoining the mosque, giving fine views of the domes and points of the skyline, as well as cocky little rock nuthatches nesting in the eaves. The view across the valley takes in another mosque and the ruins of a fortress. The distant mosque dates from the reign of Selim I, who defeated the Persians at the battle of Çaldıran (70km south of Doğubeyazit) in 1514. The fortress is much older and is thought to date originally from Urartian times, although the visible remains – except for an Assyrian relief on one wall – are more recent. The foundations you can see below on the plain are all that's left of Eski Beyazıt (Old Beyazıt), a city founded by the Urartians. It was inhabited until 1930, when – in the wake of an unsuccessful local Kurdish rebellion – the place was forcibly depopulated and the new Doğu (East) Beyazıt founded in its present location.

Practicalities

To reach the İshak Paşa Sarayı take a **taxi** from Doğubeyazıt's Atatürk statue for about $6 return (this includes waiting time). If you're visiting out of season, ask your hotel or a travel agency to confirm opening times, as these can sometimes be a little erratic. There's a **campsite** on the road below the palace, charging about $1 a tent, and it has a **restaurant** and washing facilities. You'll be a long way from town, however, and it gets very cold in winter.

Mount Ararat

Few mountains west of the Himalayas have as compelling a hold on Western imagination as **Mount Ararat** (Ağrı Dağı in Turkish). And for once this huge volcano – where Noah's Ark supposedly came to rest – manages to deliver that promise in reality. There are two peaks; the larger, 5165m one, is known as **Büyük Ağrı** and the lesser cone, measuring 3925m, is **Küçük Ağrı**. Traditionally, Armenian monks considered Mount Ararat holy and nobody was allowed to climb it, so it was not until 1829 that Dr Johann Jacob Parrot, a German academic, conquered the peak. Numerous other ascents have followed, but even today some villagers believe that it's not possible to climb the mountain, and Turkish officials did not allow it until the 1950s.

Despite the efforts of American astronaut James Irwin and others, no reliable trace of Noah's Ark has so far been found – not too surprisingly given the centuries-long effects of lava and glaciers on wood. Locals however insist that the oval mound of earth spotted by a Turkish airforce pilot on a routine flight over the region is the real thing, and the "Ark", complete with visitor's centre, is routinely included in tours of the area. Ararat of course may simply be the wrong place to look. The passage in Genesis 8:4, which reported the Ark coming to rest on the "mountains of Ararat" is prone to misinterpretation; Ararat was the Assyrian rendition of Urartu, an ancient empire – and by extension, geographical area – extending quite far south of Lake Van as well as north. Mount Ararat is still sacred to the Armenians, who must be content to gaze at it on rare clear days from their capital of Erevan.

Access to Mount Ararat

Unfortunately, the mountain lies in a sensitive military zone, adjoining both the Armenian and Iranian frontiers. However, after a gap of ten years, following the assassination of the owner of a trekking firm, access has just been resumed, though strictly on a permit-only basis.

Many local touts and companies will advise you that they can **obtain a permit** immediately; this is not true and you risk the loss of your deposit at best and, at worst, arrest, if you take their advice. Conditions of granting a permit include the provision of a recognized guide, so you need to apply at least two months in advance through a registered tourism **agency** offering treks. Permits are processed by the Tourism Ministry and, through them, by the local military and civil authorities and it is not possible to shortcut the process. The main **climbing season** is from June to September, so if you intend to be in the area during this time and would like to join a climbing group, then you should start

⑫

to plan several months in advance. See ⓦwww.mountainsofturkey.org, for current information.

Necessary **equipment** includes good winter trekking gear (snow goggles, hat, gloves, down jacket, winter boots, gaiters, crampons and ice axe, plus four-season sleeping bag and mat); you are hardly likely to have this lot with you on a normal holiday and although it may be possible to rent some of it from your trekking firm, you definitely need your own boots. The major problem on the trek is dehydration – caused by altitude and lack of fresh water supplies, not altitude sickness; make sure your company has adequate means to supply you with several litres per day.

The ascent

Currently, ascents are only permitted from the **southwest side** of the mountain; the other faces are sensitively close to Armenia and Iran. **Treks** are normally of five to six days' duration, allowing for acclimatization and two attempts at the summit, and are supported up to Camp 2 by mules. They start from **Eli**, a village on the southern slopes of Büyük Ağrı, a little over 10km north of Doğubeyazıt. From here you head up to **Camp 1** (3200m) at the base of the mountain proper; reckon on an afternoon start to reach this camp by nightfall.

After this **Camp 2**, at 4200m, is a strenuous half-day's march above, so it's wisest to halt the rest of the day there and avoid the risk of altitude sickness. From Camp 2, a dawn start is needed to reach the summit before cloud cover becomes too thick. At around 4900m the stones give way to permanent snowpack and then glacier, where crampons are necessary. Winds can be strong here and your company should have means of roping you together. In the past, most climbers have reached the main summit four hours or so after leaving Camp 2, and the views on a clear day are stupendous, compensating for the hard slog of the ascent.

A ski resort is under construction on the **north side** of the mountain, accessed by a right turn on the road to Iğdır about 15km north of Doğubeyazıt. This may in future provide another starting point for the ascent. Finally, if you ever have the opportunity, ascend from the **northeast flank** of the mountain, using the town of Aralık as a jump-off point – this way at least you may see some ruined Armenian monuments, dramatic evidence of the last (1840) eruption, and a lake, Köp Gölü.

Travel details

Trains

Kurtalan (Siirt) to: Diyarbakır (daily; 2hr 30min); İstanbul (4 weekly at 8.15am, 39hr) via Malatya (10hr), Kayseri (22hr) and Ankara (32hr).
Tatvan to: İstanbul (Tues & Thurs at 7am; 40hr), Tehran (Wed at 10am; 28hr).
Van to: Tehran (Wed at 2pm; 24hr).

Buses and dolmuşes

Doğubeyazıt to: Ağrı (every 30min; 2hr); Ankara

(1 daily at 1pm; 16hr); Erzurum (10 daily; 4hr 30min); Iğdır (every 30min; 45min); Kars via Iğdır (every 30min; 4hr); Van (3 daily; 3hr).
Hakkari to: Beytüşşebap (1 daily; 5hr); Şırnak (1 daily; 8hr); Van (3 daily; 3–4hr); Yuksekova (15 daily, 1hr).
Siirt to: Kurtalan (1hr before train; 30min); Batman (1 daily; 2hr); Diyarbakır (1 daily; 5hr); Van (1 daily; 4hr).
Sırnak to: Hakkari (1 daily; 8hr); Siirt (4 daily; 3hr 30min); Cizre (hourly; 30min).
Tatvan to: Ahlat (every 45min; 30min); Bitlis

(hourly; 30min); Ercis (2 daily; 2hr), Diyarbakır (5 daily; 4hr); Van (5 daily; 3hr).
Van to: Ağrı (every 30min; 5hr); Ankara (12 daily; 22hr); Diyarbakır (6 daily; 7hr); Doğubeyazit (3 daily; 3hr); Erzurum (4 daily; 7hr); Hakkari (3 daily; 3–4hr); Şanlıurfa (6 daily; 9hr); Tatvan (5 daily; 3hr); Trabzon (2 daily; 15hr).

Ferries

Tatvan to: Van and vice versa (1 daily; 4hr).

Flights

Ağrı to: Ankara (1 daily, Tues & Sat; 1hr 45min).
Van to: Ankara (1–2 daily; 1hr 40min); İstanbul (direct service, 1 daily except Sat & Mon; 2hr 15min).

Contexts

Contexts

The Historical Framework

So many cultures and states have held sway on the Anatolian peninsula that a thorough unravelling of its past would demand scholars of comparative religion, linguistics and archeology as well as historians. The present-day Turkish Republic is but the core remnant of a vast, late-medieval empire, which extended at one point from the Indian Ocean almost to the Atlantic – and all of these realms contributed personalities and events. What follows is only the barest outline of a complex subject.

The Earliest Cultures

Discoveries in the heart of modern Turkey – the region known historically as Anatolia or Asia Minor – suggest that there has been settled habitation since the eighth millennium BC, among the oldest on earth. The **earliest finds**, including cave deposits in the region of Antalya, and surface finds from the Ankara and Hatay regions, prove that Anatolia was inhabited in the Paleolithic Age. More extensive discoveries from the **Neolithic** period include entire farming communities, of which the best known is **Çatal Höyük** near Konya (c.6500–5650 BC), demonstrating that early settlers lived in sizable villages surrounded by defensive outer walls. Their tools were made from locally found obsidian and flint; pottery was beautifully burnished, and included stylized figures representing the mother goddess.

Oriental influence brought southeast Anatolia into the **Chalcolithic Age**. The commercial and technical interaction of cultures is particularly noticeable in pottery types and the use of metal tools; shared features are found from Upper Mesopotamia and northern Syria. Sites of this period were more like fortified towns, and frequent evidence of violent destruction suggests that they regularly waged war with each other or with new arrivals. In central Anatolia and the west Anatolian lakeland there was less influence from the east; cultures that developed here are characterized by bright, burnished pottery and idols of local deities.

The third-millennium BC **Bronze Age** witnessed the rise of local dynasties, and the organization of land resources by communities inhabiting fortified settlements. The sophisticated metal equipment found in the royal cemetery of **Alacahöyük** suggests metallurgy was one of the principal reasons for the rise of the early Anatolian kings. Religious art included standards crowned with highly stylized deer and bulls, hoards of gold jewellery, as well as musical instruments were prominent among the finds. It is thought that the Alaca dynasty originated in northeast Anatolia, since their culture shares features of those in the Caucasian and Pontic zones.

Meanwhile, on the south and west **coasts**, trade was becoming increasingly important. On the Aegean, **Troy** was in trading contact with the Aegean islands and mainland Greece, and with other Anatolian rulers in the southeast, around present-day Tarsus and Mersin. Anatolian metals, jewellery, weapons and tableware were exported in exchange for exotic goods such as lapis lazuli, rock crystal and ivory. The material advantages of a coastal situation, which provided naval contacts with the Aegean and the Orient (particularly Syrian trading ports), are obvious from the comparative wealth amassed by the rulers of cities like Troy, for example the so-called "Treasure of Priam", a third-millennium hoard of jewellery and tableware discovered in the late nineteenth century.

The **Middle and Late Bronze Ages**, during the second millennium BC, began with a period of violent destruction and turbulence, out of which a race of people known as the **Hatti** emerged in central Anatolia, whose culture was later to be assimilated by the Hittites. This was an age of highly systematic commerce along fixed trading routes, and many Anatolian cities were annexed by colonies of Assyrian business agents. Their meticulous records have been discovered in many places, including the most famous of all these trade centres, Karum near Kanesh (modern Kültepe) in south central Anatolia. Textiles and tin were the main imports, and the principal export was copper; ornamental pottery for local use was also skilfully crafted.

The Hittites

The first really major civilization to emerge in Anatolia was that of the **Hittites**. Moving into Hatti territory, they seem to have first appeared around 2000 BC, but their so-called "Old Kingdom" is reckoned to have been founded by King Labarnas between 1700 and 1600 BC. The capital at Hattuşaş was created by his son and successor, Hattusilis I, remaining a power to be reckoned with until 1200 BC.

Hattuşaş was a huge city for its time, the kings residing in a citadel located on a rock overlooking a gorge; within were domestic quarters, administrative buildings, storage units and archives. The Hittite artistic style was a direct outgrowth of Anatolian predecessors and, unlike Syrian art, was never overwhelmed by Mesopotamian and Egyptian styles. The principal examples are enormous rock-cut reliefs, including warrior gods and stylized sphinx-like beings, adapted from the Egyptian tradition.

While the warlike, imperialist nature of the Hittite rulers left an enduring impression on a previously non-aggressive Anatolia, the Hittites are also known for the humanity of their constitution and religion, and for a highly developed sense of ethics. Diplomacy was preferred to warfare, and often cemented by royal marriages. Libraries, archives and bureaucracy all had their place in Hittite society, and rulers were not despotic but tied to a constitution like their subjects. The Old Kingdom dynasty lasted several generations before being riven, apparently by succession struggles; after a confused interlude, the state was re-established as the Hittite Empire by Tudhaliyas II, in about 1430 BC. By this time a rival power had arisen in Upper Mesopotamia. The Mitanni, ruled by an Indo-European dynasty, were basically East Anatolian Hurrians. They exerted an important cultural influence on the Hittite Empire before being defeated in battle by the Hittite ruler Suppiluliumas (1385–1345 BC).

Under Muwatallis the Hittites confirmed their military strength at the battle of Kadesh (1290 BC), where they defeated the Egyptians under Ramses II. After the battle, friendship between the two dynasties was cemented by the division of Syria and by the marriage of Ramses II to a daughter of another Hittite ruler, Hattusilis III, in 1250 BC. The real threat to both, however, lay with the arrival of the "**Sea Peoples**", early Iron Age merchants from the Greek archipelagos and mainland, which was to have widespread repercussions. The land-bound Hittite Empire was surrounded by **smaller states**. The southern and western coasts were inhabited by tribes of Indo-European stock, with their own kings, languages and feuds, and a major interest in sea-borne trade. In the southeast Mediterranean, the land later known as Cilicia was taken from the Hittites by Hurrians, and referred to as Kizzuwadna. They remained closely related to the Hittites, however, with regular intermarriage between the respective ruling families.

On the west coast, a greater degree of independence on the part of local dynasties meant that their activities were not well documented in Hittite records, but excavations at the site of Troy show that, simultaneous with the apogee of Hittite power, Troy was being rebuilt by a new dynasty, and great supplies were amassed inside the large citadel. The second-millennium Trojans were serious rivals to the Greeks in the Aegean, and Troy was ultimately sacked by the Greeks around 1200 BC in the **Trojan War**, at about the same time that the Hittite Empire finally collapsed.

The post-Hittite era

Identical factors can ultimately account for the demise of both civilizations: migrations, invasions and sudden increased pressures from all sides. New tribes, of Indo-European origin, poured into Anatolia from east and west. The Hittite capital and other centres of Hittite rule were attacked and burnt as Anatolia entered a long cultural Dark Age.

Small city-states were founded in the southeast by the surviving Hittites and their Anatolian allies, and these **Neo-Hittite** centres, for instance at Malatya, Sakça Gözü and Karatepe, managed to salvage something of the old culture. Neo-Hittite culture was important as a bridge between the Bronze and Iron Ages, rescuing Hittite traditions and at the same time creating lively trading centres for the Greek **Iron Age** merchants. Thus early Greek art was confronted by Hittite reliefs and statuary, and knowledge of oriental mythology and religion was also transmitted to Greece via the Neo-Hittites. The Neo-Hittite city-states were finally conquered and destroyed by the Arameans and the Assyrians in the eighth century BC.

To the east, in the region which was later to be known as Armenia, the kingdom of **Urartu** was founded by a people thought to be descendants of the native Anatolian Hurrian race. Their cities, including the capital at Tushpa near Lake Van, were well engineered, with walled citadels and elaborate tunnel systems for escape or survival under attack. The Urartians extended their power into central Anatolia and northern Syria, before they were curbed, in the second half of the eighth century BC, by the Assyrians. The Urartians specialized in metalwork, and their bronzeware was traded as far away as Greece.

To the west, a new tribe of immigrants who attained some prominence in the eighth century BC, especially under their most famous king Midas, were the **Phrygians**. Their capital was at Gordion, on a strategic east–west trading route, by the River Sangarius (today the Sakarya). **King Midas**, according to Greek tradition, had a Greek wife and dedicated a throne at the sanctuary of Delphi. His kingdom reached its height during his rule, around 725 BC, but when Cimmerian horsemen came to loot and burn Gordion, he is said to have committed suicide in despair, and the Phrygian kingdom came to an abrupt end.

The southwest coast was inhabited during the Iron Age by the **Lycians**, probably the survivors of a nation of sailors and pirates referred to as the

"Lukka" in Bronze Age records. Their language and culture had a local pedigree, suggesting that they were descendants of native Anatolian Luvians. Their architecture – timber forms copied in stone – was strikingly unique. Greek influence on the Lycians is attested to in the Bronze Age by the legend of Bellerophon and the Chimera, and by the later importance of the cult of Apollo, Artemis and their mother Leto.

The country of the **Lydians** was an inland district of western Anatolia, its capital at Sardis in the Hermus valley. The Lydians survived the Bronze Age with a language of Anatolian derivation, emerging from the turmoil of the eighth century BC to dominate western Anatolia, including areas that had previously been Phrygian. Lydian ivories, textiles, perfumes and jewellery were exported to Greece and the East, and their refined and elegant art forms influenced those of Greek Ionia and even Persia.

The Persians and Alexander

Lydian power lasted until 546 BC, when their last king, **Croesus**, was defeated by the newly ascendant **Persian Empire** under **Cyrus**. Over the next half-century, the Persians subdued the Greek coastal trading colonies as well as the entire interior, ending the last vestiges of Anatolian self-rule. **Satraps** (compliant local puppets) were installed in various seats of power and obliged to pay tribute to the self-styled "Great King" of the Persians; even more rankling was the fact that Persian allies, such as the Phoenicians, were favoured at the expense of the Greek Anatolian cities in their role as commercial intermediaries with the west. In 499 BC, western Anatolia, under the leadership of Miletus, **revolted** against Persian rule, but in the absence of massive aid from mainland Greece, the rebellion was doomed to fail.

Enraged by even the token support of the Athenians for the rebels, **Darius I** and his successor **Xerxes** crossed into Greece proper and were soundly defeated at the famous land battles of Marathon and Plataea, and the sea engagements of Salamis and Mykale, the latter in the straits between Samos and Anatolia. This blunting of Persian strength initially availed the cities of Asia Minor little, though as time went on they were able to exploit the growing rivalry between Athens and Sparta to negotiate a bit more autonomy. Indeed by the middle of the fourth century BC, some virtually independent dynasties had arisen in western Anatolia, the most notable being the **Hecatomnid** clan at Halicarnassus, whose more illustrious rulers included the Hellenizing **Mausolus** (377–353 BC) and his wife and successor **Artemisia II**.

In spring 334 BC, a new power swept out of Macedonia and across Asia Minor: **Alexander**, later the Great, possessed of little other than a guiding vision and some Corinthian volunteers to supplement his small Macedonian army. Having crossed the Dardanelles near present-day Çanakkale, he quickly defeated the Persians and proceeded down the west coast via all of the major cities, treating them with lenience or harshness depending on whether or not they rallied to his standard. Having wintered in Lycia, Alexander and his juggernaut rolled on across Pamphylia, inland to Gordion where he cut the eponymous knot with his sword, then crossed the Toros range into coastal Cilicia, intent on attacking the Persian heartland beyond Syria. **Darius III** awaited Alexander at **Issus** (modern Dörtyol), but was soundly defeated by the Macedonians, despite outnumbering them two to one; this conquest of

Muslim before the law. Although the climate engendered by such noble sentiments permitted the founding of newspapers and private, secular schools in the ensuing decades, the proposal of infidel equality deeply offended most of the population.

Foreign economic penetration of the Ottoman Empire increased suddenly, with growing commercial activity in all coastal cities, and massive imports of European products; in the process the Greek, Armenian and foreign-Christian merchant class of the ports benefited in a disproportionate manner. Simultaneously inland centres and traditional bazaar crafts went into precipitous decline, unable to compete with the products of the industrial revolution.

By mid-century the empire had become thoroughly enmeshed in the **power struggles of Europe** – a far cry from the smug aloofness of 250 years before, and a consequence of the fact that England and France had determined that, for better or worse, the Ottomans must be propped up as a counter to Russian expansionism. Thus the empire found itself on the winning side of the 1853–1856 **Crimean War**, which began as a dispute between Russia and France over the protection to be extended by each to respectively the Orthodox and Catholic churches in Ottoman Palestine. The war ended with little significant territorial adjustment, but did bring a twenty-year interval of peace for the Ottomans.

Abdülmecid had been a well-meaning but weak and extravagant ruler, and was succeeded in 1861 by his brother **Abdülaziz**, who combined all of his predecessor's defects with a despotic manner. There sprung up in reaction, from the ranks of the first graduates of the empire's secular schools, the **Society of Young Ottomans**, which strove for the evolution of a constitutional monarchy along British lines. Its most enduring figure was the poet and essayist **Namık Kemal**, and it made extensive use of the newly admitted media of the press, drama and literature to get its points across. Predictably the group aroused the ire of the sultan, who exiled the boldest; undeterred, the Young Ottomans overseas mounted a barrage of written material, much of it smuggled back into the empire to good effect.

Faced with Abdülaziz's flagrant financial irresponsibility in the period preceding the crash of 1873–1875, and his growing mental instability, together with new Russian mischief in İstanbul and brutally suppressed revolts in the Balkans, the Young Ottomans among the bureaucratic elite – particularly **Mithat Paşa** – deposed him on **May 30, 1876**. The sultanate was passed to his promising nephew Murat, but he shortly suffered a nervous breakdown, was declared unfit to rule and in turn placed in seclusion. The next heir apparent was his younger brother **Abdülhamid**, an unknown quantity, who was offered the throne on condition that he accept various Young Ottomans as advisers and rule under a constitution.

Abdülhamid and the Young Turk revolution

The new sultan did in fact promulgate the **constitution** drafted by the Young Ottomans, presided over the opening of the first Ottoman parliament and retained – for a time – his hapless brother's advisers, including Mithat. But Abdülhamid soon moved to forestall a government by ministers, exiling Mithat (and later having him murdered).

As so often in late Ottoman history, the implementation of liberal reforms was interpreted by the Great Powers as a sign of weakness. Accordingly, Russia attacked on two fronts in **1877**, in the Caucasus and in the Balkans, with an explicitly pan-Slavic agenda. The war went badly for the Ottomans, with extensive territorial losses confirmed by the harsh peace treaty of San Stefano (at the ceasefire line just a stone's throw from İstanbul), later modified, under British pressure, at the 1878 **Conference of Berlin**. The final settlement provided for the independence of Romania, Montenegro and Serbia, an autonomous if truncated Bulgaria, the cession of Thessaly to Greece, and Kars and Ardahan districts to Russia, and the occupation of Bosnia and Herzegovina by Austria. **Nationalism** had been unleashed – and rewarded – in the Balkans, and would be a theme for the next forty years, and indeed to this day. Britain, in compensation for fending off further Russian advances, was given the right to "administer" – and garrison – **Cyprus**.

Throughout all this the new **parliament** displayed altogether too much independence for the sultan's taste, criticizing war policy and summoning certain government ministers to answer for their conduct. In early 1878, between the San Stefano and Berlin negotiation sessions, Abdülhamid finally dropped all pretence of consultative government and dissolved the Chamber of Deputies; it was not to meet again for thirty years.

With any restraining influence safely out of the way, Abdülhamid chose to rule despotically and directly. A **police state** emerged, attended by huge numbers of spies and rigorous press censorship; the introduction of a **telegraph network** provided a tremendous boost to the surveillance system. The only clause of the constitution still honoured was the repeatedly invoked one that entitled the sultan to exile troublemakers.

After the disastrous wars marking the start of his reign, Abdülhamid's **foreign policy** was xenophobic and Asia-oriented, espousing Islam as a unifying force and, for the first time in centuries, emphasizing the sultan's second role as **caliph**. This ideology didn't, however, prevent the loss of Tunis and Egypt, and had as a corollary the steadily worsening treatment of the **Armenians** of eastern Anatolia, who began to show the same nationalist sentiments as the Christians of the Balkans. The abuses culminated in the organized pogroms of **1895–1896**, in which nearly 150,000 Armenians died, provoking (albeit short-lived) outrage abroad. In 1897, war with Greece and a revolt on Crete co-incided; even though the Prussian-trained army defeated the Greeks in the field, the Ottomans were forced to grant the island autonomy.

Despite his political obscurantism, Abdülhamid presided over widespread **technological Westernization**; carefully cultivated ties with Germany resulted in much-needed development projects – most famously the German-built **rail system** across Anatolia. Important investment credits were also extended, and a **Public Debt Administration** was created, which gathered revenues of the various state monopolies to service the enormous debt run up earlier in the century. At the same time, secular schooling and technical training were encouraged, as long as they didn't directly challenge the sultan's rule – but the creation of an educated elite inevitably resulted in change.

In 1889 the Ottoman Society for Union and Progress – later the **Committee for Union and Progress** (CUP) – arose, mainly among army medical staff but also drawing on the talents of the huge European exile community. Soon it took strongest root in **Macedonia**, the worst-administered and most polyglot of the Ottoman provinces, and completely infiltrated the officer ranks of the Third Army at Salonica (Thessaloníki), a city where the sultan's repression was less, and where Westernizing Jews, Dönme sect members and

Masons were influential. Threats of further intervention by the great powers in Macedonia – where disorderly Greek, Bulgarian and other nationalist guerrilla bands were rampant – coincided with failure to pay the army, providing the spark for the revolt of the "**Young Turks**", as the CUP plotters were nicknamed. In July 1908, the Macedonian army units demanded by telegraph that Abdülhamid restore the 1876 constitution, or face unpleasant consequences. Abdülhamid's spies had either been oblivious to the threat, or he had chosen not to believe them, and on **July 24**, the sultan assented. There was widespread rejoicing on the streets of the major imperial cities, as *mullahs* fraternized with bishops, and Bulgarians walked arm in arm with Greeks. With the sultan's despotism over, surely a peaceable kingdom was imminent.

After the revolution – the Balkan wars

The euphoria prompted by the re-enactment of the 1876 constitution soon subsided as the **revolutionary government** fumbled for a coherent policy. The coup itself had had as immediate goals the curbing of Abdülhamid's powers and the physical preservation of the empire – but even these limited aims proved beyond it. By October 1908 Bulgaria had declared full independence, and Austria had formally annexed Bosnia and Herzegovina, occupied since 1878. **Elections** for the reconvened parliament were reasonably fair, and the "Young Turks", their CUP newly organized as a political party, gained a majority. Opposition to the Westernization and autocracy represented by the CUP simmered, however, and in spring 1909 a joint **revolt** of low-ranking soldiers, anti-CUP politicians and religious elements ousted the new government and took control of İstanbul. Abdülhamid, overestimating the rebels' strength, unwisely came out in their support. The CUP fought back from its base in Salonica, sending Third Army general Mahmut Şevket to crush the insurrection, and topped this off by **deposing the sultan**, banishing him to house arrest in Salonica. His younger brother ascended the throne as Mehmet V, promising to respect the "will of the nation".

The revolution had been saved, but there was still no agreement on a programme. Three main ideas vied for consideration. **Ottomanism** asserted that a Eurasian empire, federal in stucture, in which all ethnic and religious minorities had equal rights – and who in turn were loyal to the central government – was both viable and desirable. The adherents of **Pan-Islamism**, the pet creed of Abdülhamid, stressed the Islamic nature of the Ottoman Empire and the ties between Muslim Albanians, Caucasians, Kurds, Arabs and Turks. **Pan-Turanism** was more blatantly racial, dwelling on the affinities between all Turkic peoples between central Asia and the Balkans, disproportionately promoted by Caucasian Muslims exiled by the Russians during the 1870s; as time went on it was modified to a more realistic **Turkism**, or the promotion of the interests of the Turkish-speaking Muslims of Anatolia, and it was this notion that would eventually carry the day.

Discussion of these alternatives – and cultural life in general – flourished uninhibitedly for a while. Between 1908 and 1912 the CUP, beset by internal disputes, was by no means monolithic, and parliamentary opposition was not completely quelled until 1912.

The growing **authoritarianism** of CUP rule coincided with renewed **external threats** to the empire. Italy invaded Tripolitania (today's Libya) in 1911, and the next year took all of the Dodecanese islands. In late 1912, the Balkan states of Bulgaria, Serbia, Montenegro and Greece united for the first and last time in history, driving Turkey out of Europe in the **First Balkan War** and indeed approaching within a few miles of İstanbul by the beginning of 1913. Enraged at attempts to limit the army's, and the CUP's, involvement in government, and the unfavourable terms of a pending peace treaty, key CUP officers staged a coup, murdering the minister of war and continuing on the battlefield; when the new grand vizier Mahmut Şevket was assassinated in retaliation soon after, the CUP used it as an excuse to suppress all dissent and establish a **military junta**.

The unlikely Balkan alliance soon fell apart, with Bulgaria turning on Serbia and Greece in the **Second Balkan War**, and the Ottomans taking the opportunity to regain eastern Thrace up to Edirne. This action made temporary heroes of the junta, which by now was in effect a triumvirate: **Enver Paşa**, an officer of humble origins, dashing, courageous, abstemious, as well as vain, ambitious and megalomaniac; **Talat Paşa**, a brutal Thracian civilian who would eventually be responsible for ordering the 1915 deportation of the Armenians; and **Cemal Paşa**, a ruthless but competent professional soldier from an old family.

World War I

The CUP's ideology was now resolutely Turkish-Nationalist, secular and technocratic, as well as anti-democratic – and increasingly pro-German. Public opinion, and the more level-headed CUP members, hoped that the Ottoman Empire would remain neutral in the obviously impending conflict, but Germanophile Enver had signed a secret agreement with the Kaiser on August 2, 1914. By coincidence Britain committed a major blunder the same day, impounding two half-built battleships, which had already been paid for by public subscription in Turkey. The German government pulled off a major public relations coup by sailing two **replacement ships** through the Allied Mediterranean blockade to İstanbul in October, presenting them to the Turkish navy – whose German commander promptly forced Turkey's hand by sending them off to bombard Russian Black Sea ports. By November Turkey was officially at war with the Allies, though various CUP ministers resigned in protest. "This will be our ruin," said one prophetically, "even if we win."

Despite appearances, the CUP did not become puppets of the Germans, nor Turkey a complete satellite; although men and weaponry were diverted to the European eastern front and Anatolia used as a granary by the Central Powers, the Capitulations were unilaterally abolished over German protests (they affected the French and English more anyway), and monetary policy was determined without outside interference for the first time in sixty years. These measures counted on military successes to reinforce them, though, and the **Turkish war effort**, carried out on five fronts simultaneously, was an almost unmitigated disaster. Over the four-year duration, the empire lost all of its Middle Eastern domains, as the Arabs threw in their lot with the British on the promise of subsequent autonomy, thus proving pan-Islamism as dead as Ottomanism. Enver Paşa demonstrated his incompetence by losing an entire army on the Russian front during the winter of 1914–1915; the subsequent Tsarist advance deep into Anatolia was only reversed after the Bolshevik revolution.

The two bright spots from the Turkish point of view were the defeat of a British army at the bloody campaign of Mesopotamian Kut, and the successful defence of the **Gallipoli peninsula**, guarding the Dardanelles and thus the sea approaches to İstanbul. Credit for the successful Turkish resistance belonged largely to a hitherto unknown colonel named **Mustafa Kemal**, later **Atatürk**, ranking Turkish officer in the operations. He had come of age in the midst of the pre-1908 Young Turk agitation, and like many other junior officers had been sent into internal exile for "disloyal" activities. Though an early member of the CUP, he had opposed its autocratic tendencies and entry into the war on Germany's side. The Turkish public craved a hero at this point, but upon Kemal's return to İstanbul the jealous Enver deprived them of this satisfaction, shuttling Kemal between various backwoods commands, until war's end saw him overseeing a strategic retreat to the hills on the Syrian border.

For the Ottoman Empire's **Armenians**, April 24, 1915 was also a fateful day, on which the CUP authorities ordered the disarming of all Armenians serving in the Turkish army, and the roundup of Armenian civilians from Anatolian cities, towns and villages; only those living in İstanbul and İzmir were exempted, for economic and public-relations reasons. Over the next ten months of deportations, the men were usually shot immediately by gendarmes, Kurdish irregulars or bands of thugs recruited for the purpose, while women and children were forced to march, under conditions that guaranteed their abuse and death, hundreds of kilometres towards concentration camps in the Mesopotamian desert. Estimating **total casualties** is difficult and controversial, but Ottoman and foreign censuses at the turn of the century showed nearly 1.5 million Armenians living in Anatolia. Allowing for the roughly half-million refugees who managed to hide in Turkey or escape abroad by 1923, most of the one million difference can be assumed to have perished, making it the first deliberate, large-scale genocide of the twentieth century.

The above scenario is hotly disputed by recent Turkish governments, which deny that any officially sanctioned, systematic expulsion or killing took place, and admit a maximum of 300,000 Armenian fatalities from unspecified causes – but implying that most of these were combatants in treasonous alliance with Russia or France. While it is true that many Armenians, particularly in Van, Kars and Adana provinces, sided with those two powers in the hopes of securing a postwar state for themselves, this happened *after* the deportation and massacre orders were issued, and could be construed as legitimate self-defence. In any event, the issue is still very much alive, with relatively clumsy Turkish propaganda developed since the 1980s to counter vigorous Armenian lobbying for international recognition of the tragedy.

On **October 30, 1918**, Turkish and British officers signed an armistice on the Greek island of Límnos. Two weeks later an Allied fleet sailed into İstanbul, and strategic points around the Sea of Marmara were occupied by the victors, though Turkish civil administration was allowed to continue on condition that no "disturbances" took place. In the interim the CUP triumvirate had fled on German ships, and all met violent deaths in the following years: Talat killed in revenge by an orphaned Armenian in Berlin; Cemal assassinated in Caucasian Georgia; and Enver – dying as flamboyantly as he had lived – as a self-styled emir fighting the Bolsheviks in central Asia.

The struggle for independence

The Allies were now in a position to carry out their long-deferred **designs on the Ottoman heartland**, as per secret wartime protocols. By early 1919 French troops were in occupation of parts of southeast Anatolia near the present Syrian and Iraqi frontiers, the Italians landed on the coast between Bodrum and Antalya, and the Greeks disembarked at İzmir, where Greek civilians formed a large part of the population. The British concentrated their strength in İstanbul and Thrace, and along with the other victors garrisoned in the capital effectively dictated policy to the defeated Ottoman regime. The new sultan **Mehmet VI** was interested only in retaining his throne, and prepared to make any necessary territorial or administrative concessions to that end – including the dissolution of the last wartime parliament.

İstanbul, under de facto occupation, was a poor seedbed for a war of independence. In Thrace and Anatolia, however, various **Committees for the Defence of (Turkish) Rights** – patriotic Turkish guerrilla bands – had sprung up, and a substantial remnant of the Ottoman armies survived at Erzurum, under the control of **Kâzım Karabekir**. Together these would form the nucleus of the liberation forces. All that was lacking was visionary leadership, and further provocations from the Allies; neither was long in coming.

Mustafa Kemal, the hero of Gallipoli and the Syrian front, was the only undefeated Ottoman general at war's end; was not compromised by close association with the CUP leadership; and could hardly be accused of being pro-German. Popular and outspoken, he was considered too dangerous by the Allies to be kept idle in the capital. For his part, Kemal itched to cross over to Anatolia and begin organizing some sort of resistance to the pending imperialist schemes, but dared not do so without a suitable pretext. This was provided in the spring of 1919, when Kemal managed to wangle from the collaborationist war ministry a commission as a military inspector for all Anatolia, empowered to halt the activities of the various Committees for the Defence of Rights and seize their arms. His first stop was to be the Black Sea, where Turkish guerrillas had been fighting it out with Greeks bent on setting up a Pontic republic. On **May 19, 1919**, Mustafa Kemal landed at Samsun, four days after Greek operations began at İzmir – the last straw for many hitherto apathetic Turks. Contrary to his brief, Kemal promptly began organizing and strengthening the Turkish guerrillas. The puppet government in İstanbul, realizing too late what he was up to, attempted to recall him, then summarily relieved him of duties, and finally ordered his arrest; he returned the compliment by resigning his commission. Kemal and Karabekir, along with **Rauf**, **Ali Fuad** and **Refet** – three high-ranking officers of old Ottoman families – drew up a provisional plan for resistance, with the strong support of the Anatolian religious authorities. Two **ideological congresses** were scheduled, one at Erzurum in July, and another in Sivas in September. Both gatherings elected Kemal as chairman, and both ratified the so-called **National Pact**, which demanded viable Turkish borders approximating those of today, an end to the Capitulations and a guarantee of rights to all minorities. At the same time the pact reaffirmed its loyalty to the institution of the caliphate, if not the sultan himself, who was deemed a prisoner of the Allies. It was still far too early in the game to antagonize the religious elements, and indeed secularization was probably still a gleam in Kemal's eye.

Throughout these manoeuvres the **Nationalists**, as they came to be called, made good use of the **telegraph lines** installed by Abdülhamid, often conducting convoluted arguments with the İstanbul regime over the wires. By the autumn of 1919, they forced the resignation of the grand vizier and the announcement of elections for a new parliament. These, in early 1920, returned a large Nationalist majority, which openly proclaimed the National Pact – and created a climate where thefts from Allied arms depots, often with the connivance of the French and Italians who opposed Greek aims in Anatolia, became a routine occurrence. At the instigation of the outraged Ottoman court, the British placed İstanbul under formal military occupation on **March 16, 1920**, raiding parliament and bundling a few score deputies into exile on Malta. Luckier MPs escaped to Ankara, where Kemal and others had prudently remained, and on **April 23** opened the first **Grand National Assembly**, in direct defiance of the sundry Allied encroachments. Turkey's first Ankara-based parliament met in a Wild West atmosphere, lit by oil lamps for several years, while its members tethered their horses to wooden railings out front.

The sultanate reacted vehemently to all this, securing a **fetva** (ruling) from the Islamic authorities sanctioning a holy war against the "rebels" and condemning the Nationalist leadership to death in absentia. Kemal and friends secured a counter-*fetva* from sympathetic religious figures in Ankara, and soon afterwards the head of the Bektaşi dervish order publicly commanded his followers to help the Nationalists.

Such moral support was vital to the beleaguered guerrillas, who were now fighting for their lives in a **multiple-front war**: against the French in the southeast, the Italians in the southwest, Armenians in the northeast, irregular bands supporting the sultan in various locations and – most dangerously – the Greeks in western Anatolia. The only consistent aid came from the newborn Soviet Union, which sent gold and weapons and partitioned the short-lived Armenian Dashnakist republic between itself and Turkey, thus closing that theatre of war by late 1920.

The Allied governments, oblivious of the new reality on the ground in Turkey, attempted to legitimize their claims to Turkish territory by presenting the humiliating **Treaty of Sèvres** to the Ottoman government in May 1920. By its terms, partly motivated by the Wilsonian Fourteen Points, but more by unalloyed greed, an independent Armenia and an autonomous Kurdistan were created, the straits of the Sea of Marmara and İstanbul were placed under international control, Thrace and İzmir and its hinterland were given to Greece, France and Italy were assigned spheres of influence in those portions of Anatolia remaining to the Ottomans, and Turkish finances were placed under Allied supervision, with a revival of the Capitulations. By signing this document, the demoralized sultanate sacrificed its last shred of credibility, convinced any remaining waverers of the necessity of the Nationalist movement – and sparked a predictable Greek response.

The **Greek expeditionary armies**, acting with the authorization of British prime minister Lloyd George, not only pressed inland from İzmir but captured Edirne, İzmit and Bursa, seeking to revive notions of a "Greater Greece" straddling both shores of the Aegean. Only French and Italian objections caused them to halt just short of the strategic Afyon–Eskişehir railway. In early 1921 the Greeks were on the move again, but Nationalist general İsmet Paşa stopped them twice, in January and April, at the defile of **İnönü**, from which he would later take his surname. Both sides had undergone subtle changes: since the fall of the Republican Venizelos government in Greece, and the return of the royalists, the Greek Anatolian armies had become progressively more corrupt, incompetently led and brutal in their treatment of Muslim civilians. Kemal's forces, on the other hand, had become more cohesive and professional, with irregular bands either defeated or absorbed.

But when the Greeks advanced east once more in July 1921, they swiftly captured Afyon, Eskişehir and the vital railway that linked them; the Nationalists strategically retreated east of the Sakarya River, less than 100km from Ankara, to buy time and extend the enemy's supply lines. Panic and gloom reigned in Ankara, with calls for Kemal to be instated as commander-in-chief at the head of the defending army, to share its fate. This was done, and soon the Greeks went for the bait, sniffing an easy chance to finish off the Nationalists. But in the ferocious, three-week **battle of the Sakarya** beginning on August 13, they failed to make further headway towards Ankara. Although most of the Greek army survived, anything less than its capture of the Nationalist headquarters was a decisive defeat. The jubilant Grand National Assembly conferred on Kemal the title *Gazi*, or "Warrior for the Faith".

The victory at Sakarya greatly enhanced the Nationalists' international position: both the **French and Italians** soon concluded peace treaties, withdrawing from southern Anatolia, and contributions from various Asian Muslim countries poured in to finance the "holy war". With remaining support for the Greek adventure evaporating, the British tried unsuccessfully to arrange an armistice between Greece and the Nationalists. Both camps dug in and waited until, on **August 26, 1922**, Kemal launched his final offensive at **Dumlupınar** near Afyon, designed to drive the Greeks out of Anatolia. The Greek lines crumbled and those not taken prisoner or killed, fled down-valley in a disorderly rout towards waiting boats in İzmir, committing atrocities against the Turkish population, destroying the harvest and abandoning Greek civilians to the inevitable Turkish reprisals. The latter included the **sacking and burning of İzmir** within four days of the triumphant entry of the Nationalists.

Despite this resounding triumph, the war was not yet over, and indeed the threat of a prolonged conflict loomed. A large Greek army remained intact in **Thrace**, disposed to fight on, and British contingents guarding the strategically vital **Dardanelles** faced off against the Nationalist army sent north to cross the straits. Some of Kemal's associates even urged him to retake western Thrace and Greek Macedonia, a sure invitation to renewed world war. Cooler heads prevailed at the last minute, however, and at Mudanya on **October 11, 1922**, an armistice was signed, obliging the last Greek troops to depart from eastern Thrace. A week later British premier Lloyd George, his pro-Greek policy utterly discredited, was forced to resign.

There remained just one obstacle to full Nationalist control of Turkey: Sultan Mehmet VI still presided over a diminished realm, consisting of İstanbul alone. Few in Ankara had a good word to say about the man himself, but many expressed reluctance to abolish his office, favouring a constitutional monarchy with royalty exercising a stabilizing influence as in Britain. The Allies themselves helped decide the matter by extending a clumsy double invitation to a final peace conference at Lausanne – one addressed to the sultanate, the other to the Grand National Assembly. The outrage thus provoked in the latter quarters made it an easy matter for Kemal to persuade the deputies to **abolish the sultanate** on November 1, effective retroactively as from March 16, 1920, the date of British direct rule in İstanbul. Within two weeks Mehmet VI, last of the House of Osman, sneaked ignominiously out of the old imperial capital on a British warship, bound for exile in Italy; his cousin Abdülmecid was sworn in as caliph, but with no temporal powers whatsoever.

The **peace conference** at Lausanne was convened immediately, with İsmet Paşa as the sole Turkish representative. If the Allies were hoping to dictate terms as at Versailles and Sèvres, they were quickly disappointed; İsmet soon proved as dogged at the negotiating table as on the battlefield, reducing seasoned diplomats to despair by feigning deafness and repetitive insistence on the tenets of the Erzurum-Sivas National Pact. The conference was suspended for two months in early 1923, the Allies doubtless hoping to wear İsmet down, but in the end it was they who gave in. The **Treaty of Lausanne**, signed on July 24, recognized the frontiers won in the recent War of Independence, abolished the Capitulations, demilitarized the Dardanelles and the islands at its mouth, and postponed a decision on the status of the oil-rich Mesopotamian district of Mosul (now in Iraq).

More drastically, Greece and Turkey agreed to an **exchange of minority populations** to eliminate future outbreaks of communal conflict. Nearly half a million Muslims in Greece were sent to Turkey, and the remaining 1.3 million Greek Orthodox Christians in Turkey were officially despatched to Greece (most had already fled there). The only exceptions were the Turkish minority in western Thrace, and Greeks with Ottoman citizenship resident in İstanbul and on Imvros and Tenedos islands at the mouth of the Dardanelles. The sole criterion was religious affiliation and incalculable suffering was caused, especially among Turkish-speaking Christians and Greek-speaking Muslims who suddenly found themselves in a wholly alien linguistic environment.

The pact marked the true end of World War I, and saw Turkey, alone of the defeated nations, emerge in dignity, with defendable territory and modest demands made of her. Compared to the old empire, it was a compact state – 97 percent Anatolian and Muslim. A new political party, the **Republican People's Party** (RPP), incorporating the resources and personnel of the various Committees for the Defence of Rights, and the precepts of the National Pact, was formed, and a new parliament was swiftly created, its members drawn from the ranks of the new entity.

The young Republic and Kemal Atatürk's reforms

The Nationalists may have won the military battle for political sovereignty in Anatolia, but after ten years of constant warfare the country was physically devastated and economically a shambles. Export agriculture and urban commerce had largely been in the hands of the Greek and Armenian minorities. With their departure or demise, and that of the foreigners who had benefited from the Capitulations, the Turks were obliged to start from the ground up agriculturally and commercially, which they failed to do for many years.

Kemal had little patience for or understanding of intricate economics, and preferred to emphasize sweeping social change by fiat. In October 1923 the Grand National Assembly officially moved the capital to **Ankara** and proclaimed the **Republic**, to which there was little practical obstacle since the last sultan had absconded. Kemal was designated head of state and İsmet İnönü was named prime minister. Though the sultan was gone, the caliph Abdülmecid was still around and very much a public personality – an intolerable situation for Kemal and the other Westernizers; since the war had been won they no longer felt the need for the legitimizing function of Islam. In March 1924 the caliphate was abolished and all members of the House of Osman exiled, the *medrese*s and religious courts closed, and the assets of the *vakıf*s supervized by a new Ministry of Religious Affairs.

Even some of Kemal's long-time supporters were dismayed by his increasingly autocratic ways, and a few – including military men Ali Fuad, Rauf Orbay and Kâzım Karabekir – resigned from the RPP in October 1924 to form an opposition, the **Progressive Republican Party** (PRP). At first Kemal tolerated the new party as a means of blowing off steam, even replacing the unpopular İsmet as prime minister to placate them, but the RPP became alarmed when PRP speakers attracted large crowds and elements of the less supervized İstanbul press began siding with them.

Events soon provided Kemal with a basis for more action. In February 1925 the first of several twentieth-century **Kurdish revolts** erupted at Palu, near Elazığ, under the leadership of a Nakşibendi (Naqshbandi) dervish leader. The revolt was both fundamentalist Muslim and Separatist-Nationalist in ideology, and it took the central government two months to suppress. Kemal, demanding unity in a time of crisis, secured the abolition of the PRP and established a series of sanguinary **Independence Tribunals** invested with summary powers; not only the leaders of the revolt but a few minor members of the PRP found themselves on the wrong end of a rope, and freedom of the press was quickly curtailed. By autumn 1925 all the **dervish orders** had been made illegal throughout Turkey (though they were never completely suppressed), and the veneration of Sufi saints at their tombs was forbidden. Simultaneously, Kemal embarked on a campaign against **traditional headgear**, in particular women's veils, the turban and the fez. Although the caliphate had been dissolved with hardly a murmur, the sartorial laws outlawing the turban and fez, and requiring the donning of the hated European hat, were met with stiff resistance; dress for the Ottomans had always served as a vital indicator of rank. Not a few offenders were hanged from lampposts by the reactivated Independence Tribunals, but the secularists have never to this day succeeded in eliminating the cloaking of women in the rural areas, and there is still no law against it.

More drastic measures followed at a dizzying pace. By 1926, the **Gregorian calendar** had replaced the Muslim lunar one for official use, and the *şeriat,* or Islamic **law code**, was replaced by adaptations of the Western European versions. The same year, the Jewish, Armenian and Greek minorities relinquished the last vestiges of their communal laws; henceforth all citizens of the Republic were to be judged by a uniform legal system. Parallel with the introduction of a secular law code came the relative **emancipation of women**: marriage and divorce became civil rather than religious or customary, polygamy was abolished, and within four years women were given the vote.

Not surprisingly all this inflamed the existing opposition to Kemal, and in mid-1926 a **plot** to assassinate him was uncovered. Those involved were mostly disgruntled minor deputies and ex-CUP men, but Kemal took the opportunity to charge and try most of the former Progressive Republican Party's leadership, including war hero Karabekir. Several, including all the surviving CUP leadership, were hanged, and even those acquitted were effectively barred from public life in the future. This was the last mass purge, however, and soon after, the feared Independence Tribunals were disbanded, having served their purpose. There was to be no more public opposition to Kemal during his lifetime, except for a period in 1930 when a second short-lived opposition party was again judged to be a "premature experiment".

Kemal now felt secure enough to press on with his agenda, and chose as his next field **alphabet reform**. A special commission prepared a Roman script within six weeks in 1928, and by the end of the year its universal use was law, with the Gazi himself touring the country to give lessons in public parks. Reform was extended to the entire language over the next few years, with the founding of a language commission charged with the duty of purging Turkish of its Arabic and Persian accretions and reviving old Turkish words, coining new ones or adopting French words to underline the break with the Islamic past. Nowadays most observers admit that the process was carried too far, with the language soon as top-heavy with borrowed Western words as it had been with Eastern ones, but together with the script change the measures resulted in a substantial increase in literacy and comprehension. (A deliberate side effect of the language reform was to isolate many Turks from their own history; unable to read Ottoman Turkish, they became estranged from their imperial past.)

Less successful, and ultimately embarrassing, were programmes purporting to rewrite history, in which it was variously asserted that all other languages derived from Turkish, that the Turks were an Aryan race (and other racial nonsense uncomfortably close to Nazi theories), or that they were the descendants of the Hittites or Sumerians. Such hypotheses, springing from a mix of inferiority feelings and a need for political legitimacy, lingered on in Turkish schoolbooks into the 1970s. A more constructive move, in 1934, was full **suffrage for women** in national elections and the mandatory adoption of **surnames** by the entire population; previously this had been discretionary. Kemal chose for himself the unique **Atatürk**, "Father-Turk", dropping his first name Mustafa.

Belatedly Atatürk and his associates had turned their attention to the **economic** sphere, where Turkey's weaknesses had been accentuated by the crash of 1929. Despite public discontent at deprivation and stagnation, **Kemalism**, as Atatürk's ideology was named, continued to stress industrial self-sufficiency through state investment in heavy industry with a goal of complete import substitution (except for factory equipment). Development banks had been set up in 1925, and subsequently the strategically important rail network was extended, and mining, steel, cement and paper works heavily subsidized on a pattern modelled on Italian fascism. This paternalistic programme was, however, grossly inefficient, and proceeded at the expense of the agricultural sector, which remained in abject condition until the 1950s. The east of the country was effectively condemned to a subsistence existence – aggravating Kurdish feelings of punitive neglect – a situation unchanged until the massive, controversial irrigation and hydroelectric projects of the 1970s and 1980s.

Turkey's **foreign policy** during the post-independence years was rooted in non-interventionism and isolationism, though the country did join the League of Nations in 1934, and opposed appeasement of the fascist regimes in Europe. Atatürk's slogan "Peace at home, peace in the world" may have had an unfortunate resemblance to Neville Chamberlain's utterances after Munich, but in practice secured for Turkey years of badly needed calm. Though the RPP may have imitated aspects of contemporary European totalitarian systems, Turkey had no wish to follow Germany, Italy and the USSR into the abyss. Atatürk removed a remaining irritant to Anglo–Turkish relations by consenting to the cession of the Mosul region to Iraq, but began in 1936 an ultimately successful campaign to annex the Hatay, part of the French protectorate of Syria with a large Turkish population. Alliances of the 1930s, with Greece, Yugoslavia and Romania to the west, and with Iraq, Iran and Afghanistan to the east, tended to be opportunistic and short-lived, nowhere near as durable as a Treaty of Friendship promulgated with the Soviet Union.

Fortunately for Turkey, Atatürk had accomplished the bulk of his intended life's work by **1938**, for his health, after a lifetime of heavy drinking, was steadily worsening. He died from complications caused by cirrhosis of the liver in İstanbul's Dolmabahçe Palace at 9.05am on November 10, 1938. Thousands of mourners bearing torches lined the route of his funeral cortege-train between İstanbul and Ankara. Fifteen years later he was interred in a mausoleum, the Anıt Kabir, designed by an Italian and a German, and guided by the monumental fascist aesthetic of the 1930s.

Atatürk's **legacy** is a considerable one: unlike the totalitarian rulers of his day, he refrained from expansionist designs and overt racial/ethnic hatred, leaving behind a stable, defensible state and a guiding ideology, however uneven, expressly intended to outlive him. Personally he was a complex, even tragic figure: his charisma, energy and quick grasp of situations and people were unparalleled, but he had little inclination for methodical planning or systematic study. While respected, even revered, he was not loved by his associates or particularly loveable – despite his sponsorship of the advancement of women, he was himself a callous, compulsive womanizer, with one brief spell of unhappy marriage. In his fundamental loneliness, he nursed grudges and suspicions, which often had deadly consequences for those who, as partners, might have been able to extricate Turkey from later awkward situations. By his stature and temperament Atatürk, like a tree allowing nothing to grow underneath, deprived Turkey of a succeeding generation of leadership. The cult of his personality, obvious from the silhouettes and signs on every hillside, is in some ways symptomatic of an inability to conceive of alternatives in ideology or heroes, though since 1983 reverence for the economic principles of Kemalism has fallen completely by the wayside.

World War II and the rise of multi-party politics

Atatürk was succeeded as president by his long-time general and prime minister **İsmet İnönü**, and his policy concerning the **Hatay** was posthumously vindicated in 1939, when annexation of the nominally independent Hatay republic was ratified. France, eager for Turkish support in the impending war, acquiesced, and was apparently rewarded by the Turkish signing of a deliberately vaguely worded treaty of alliance with France and Britain in 1939.

In the event the treaty turned out to be a dead letter: France was swiftly defeated, and German propaganda convinced the Turkish government that Britain was probably doomed as well, and that the Axis would also dispatch Russia, the hereditary Turkish enemy. Accordingly a "Treaty of Friendship" was signed with Nazi Germany in 1941, guaranteeing at least Turkish non-belligerence. Entry into the war on either side had in fact been doubtful from the start, since Turkey's armed forces had become desperately antiquated. Memories of the Ottoman Empire's humiliation at the hands of the World War I Entente powers were strong too. Turkey instead remained **neutral**, selling strategically vital chromium ore to both Germany and Britain. Despite this fence-sitting, the country was essentially on a war footing, with all its able-bodied men mobilized, and the economy subject to the stresses of shortages, black markets, profiteering and huge government budget deficits.

All these, and the partial infiltration of Nazi ideology, provoked the institution in 1942 of the so-called **Varlık Vergisi**, or "Wealth Levy", a confiscatory tax applied in a discriminatory manner against businessmen of Armenian, Greek, Jewish and Dönme (nominal Muslims, ex-disciples of a false Jewish messiah) descent. Defaulters had their property confiscated and/or were deported to labour camps in the interior, where many died. The measure, having in fact raised very little money, was rescinded in 1944, but not before urban commerce had been set back a decade, and the Republic's credibility with its non-Muslim minorities severely damaged.

Even after the collapse of the Italians, Turkey still declined to enter the war, despite assurances of Allied support. Turkey only declared war on Germany in early 1945 to qualify for membership of the UN, not soon enough to prevent the USSR from renewing demands for the return of the Kars and Ardahan districts, and joint control of the straits at each end of the Sea of Marmara. Though these were summarily rejected, Turkey badly needed a protective ally in the international arena, and found it in the **United States**. The arrival in İstanbul of the American warship USS *Missouri* in 1946 was greeted with such euphoria that the city fathers, in a famous instance of Turkish hospitality later worked into popular literature, ordered the local bordellos thrown open for free to the sailors.

The eventual results of the mutual wooing were, first, Turkey's participation in the Korean War, and soon after admission to **NATO** after an initial application had been rejected. This new pro-Western stance had several further consequences: the expulsion from Warsaw Pact Bulgaria into Turkey of vast numbers of ethnic Turks, a harbinger of an identical act four decades later; consistently bad relations with neighbouring Arab states, particularly after Turkey's recognition of Israel and the overthrow of the Iraqi monarchy by the Ba'ath Party; and a short-lived alliance with Greece and Yugoslavia, effectively dissolved by the first Cyprus crisis of the mid-1950s.

On the home front, discontent with one-party rule, secularization and the stiflingly centralized economy came to a head when four politicians – including Celal Bayar and Adnan Menderes – having been expelled from the RPP, formed the **Democrat Party** in early 1946. Despite prematurely scheduled elections of that summer and widespread balloting irregularities, the new opposition managed to gain nearly fifteen percent of the parliamentary seats. The fact that this gain was not reversed by force was due as much to the climate of Turkish public opinion, demanding a change, as to any subtle pressure exerted by the Americans, whose **economic aid** was now pouring into the country.

A showdown could not be long postponed, however, and campaigning for the nationwide **elections of May 14, 1950** was strenuous and unimpeded. The Democrat Party's platform promised an end to anti-business strictures for the embryonic middle class, freer religious observance for the devout and attention to the badly neglected agricultural sector. Though it was a safe bet that the Democrats would win, the scale of their victory – 55 percent of the vote, and, by the winner-takes-all, slate-of-candidates system, over eighty percent of parliamentary seats – caught everyone by surprise. Bayar replaced İnönü as president, and **Menderes** took office as prime minister.

Populist governments

Virtually the first act of the new government was to permit, after a seventeen-year gap, the recitation of the call to prayer in Arabic – a decree neatly coinciding with the start of Ramadan. Simultaneously, rashes of fez- or turban-wearing, polygamy and use of the Arabic script erupted in the provinces (where Atatürk's various reforms had never really penetrated). There followed far-reaching programmes of rural loans and public works, an end to various government monopolies and restrictions on investment by foreigners, plus massive imports of luxury goods and farm machinery, based on the assumption that Turkey's allies would quietly subsidize all this. Many of the projects were controversial, though in retrospect Menderes can be credited with opening up a country where for three decades very little in the way of people, ideas, capital or goods had moved in or out. Despite lip service paid to private enterprise, however, much of this development was unplanned, uncoordinated investment in state enterprises, and most of it took the form of expensive rewards to supporters. Menderes himself, a largely self-taught farmer/lawyer, had his colossal vanity aggravated by the adulation of the peasants, who not only sacrificed livestock in his honour at his public appearances, but went so far as to name boy children after him.

The honeymoon with the electorate continued through the first years of the 1950s, aided by bumper harvests, though by 1954 clouds loomed on the horizon: the **national debt** and trade deficit were enormous, and the black-market value of the Turkish lira was one-fourth the official exchange rate. But the increasingly sensitive Democrats would not tolerate even mutterings of criticism: in 1953 assets and institutions of the ousted RPP had been expropriated and abolished, and the small, right-wing/religious National Party, with its handful of seats in parliament, was proscribed. The first of a series of **repressive press laws** was passed in early 1954, further poisoning the atmosphere just before the May elections. These the Democrats won even more easily than four years previously, but instead of imbuing them with more confidence, they took the result as a mandate to clamp down harder on dissent and to run the country ever more shamelessly for the benefit of their clientele. The economy continued to worsen, with the first bouts of the rampant **inflation**, thereafter to be a constant feature of Turkish life. During 1955 the government, looking for a distraction from, and scapegoats for, domestic problems, found both in the form of the Cyprus issue and minorities – especially İstanbul Greeks. DP-orchestrated street demonstrations got out of hand, ending in destructive **riots** aimed at foreigners and the wealthy in all three major cities.

In the wake of all this, support for the government tumbled, but probably not enough for it to have lost honestly contested elections in 1957. These, however, were heavily rigged, and the results – still trimming the Democrats' strength to just over two-thirds of total – were never officially announced. Turkey thus approached the end of the decade in a parlous state, with a huge, dangerous gulf between the rural, largely pro-DP population and the intellectual/commercial elite in the towns – and, more dangerously, an alienated, antagonized military.

The first military intervention and the 1960s

Nowhere had dismay over the intentions and policies of the Democrat government been felt more keenly than in the military, who considered themselves the guardians of Atatürk's secular reforms. The officer corps, debarred from voting and watching the value of their fixed salaries erode in the face of inflation, felt betrayed and neglected as the new middle class and Democrat apparatchiks surpassed them economically and socially. Cliques of officers had begun to formulate plans for action as far back as 1954, but it was not until May 27, 1960 that middle-ranking officers, enlisting a few commanders as figureheads, staged a **coup** – announced on the radio by a certain Colonel Alpaslan Türkeş (see p.987).

The putsch was bloodless, swift and complete. Democrat Party MPs and ministers were jailed, and there was rejoicing on the streets of the larger cities. For the next sixteen months, a **National Unity Committee** (NUC) ruled the country, and oversaw the preparation of a new, extremely liberal constitution to supersede that of 1924. The ruling committee, however, was an uneasy marriage of convenience, incorporating as it did not only idealistic top brass hoping for a speedy return to civilian rule, but junior officers who wished for an indefinite period of authoritarian military government, and who in fact embarked on disruptive purges of university faculties and the officer corps themselves. Committee chief and acting head of state **Cemal Gürsel** adroitly outflanked this element, exiling their representatives overseas to minor posts and lifting the ban on political activity early in 1961. The new constitution, which provided for a bicameral legislature, proportional representation in the lower house and a constitutional court, was submitted to public referendum in July, with elections scheduled for October.

The **referendum**, which was essentially a vote of confidence in the NUC, showed just 62 percent in favour of the new constitution. This was hardly gratifying to the junta, who panicked at the display of lingering support for the Democrat Party. Since the coup, several hundred leading DP members, including Menderes and Bayar, had been imprisoned and on trial at bleak Yassıada in the Sea of Marmara, on charges of undermining the 1924 constitution, corruption and complicity in the riots of 1955. Upon the return of guilty verdicts and fifteen death sentences, the NUC hastily ratified three of these – against Menderes, foreign minister Zorlu and finance minister Polatkan – while commuting the others, including that of Bayar, to life imprisonment. The three hangings, carried out a month before the elections, backfired badly, making Menderes a martyr and ensuring a long electoral life for the Justice Party (JP), the new incarnation of the now-banned Democrat Party.

The inconclusive **parliamentary elections** proved a further disappointment to the NUC; neither the Justice Party nor a refurbished RPP gained a majority, with the balance of power held by splinter groups. Under threat of another coup, the two major parties were induced to enter into a coalition, with Cemal Gürsel as president and İnönü again prime minister for the first time since 1938. These compromises rankled with certain disaffected junior officers who had hoped to be rid of the Democrats once and for all, and they resolved to clean up the "mess" with two subsequent coup attempts, one in February 1962 and another fourteen months later. The latter, involving the occupation of the state radio station by veterans of May 27, was quelled and its leader executed. There would be no more putsches from below.

Civilian political life settled into a semblance of **normality**, with more unstable coalitions until 1965. In terms of standards of living, the promised economic reforms of the NUC had not borne fruit; the import substitution policies of the old RPP, whereby industrial self-sufficiency – however uneconomic – was subsidized, were quietly revived, while land reform and rural development were again deferred. The first wave of **emigration** to Germany and other Western European countries acted as a social safety valve, and the "guest workers" would return at holiday time with cars, consumer durables and – to a limited extent – European notions and wives. For the first time, independent labour unions began organizing and recruiting inside Turkey, with the right to strike finally confirmed in 1963. The growing urban proletariat found a political voice in the newly formed Turkish Workers' Party (TWP), whose very existence nudged the RPP, now led by future prime minister **Bülent Ecevit**, leftward into a social-democratic mould. **Süleyman Demirel**, who was to emerge as one of the most enduring political figures over the next three decades, became leader in 1964 of the JP, which was obliged to come out strongly for free enterprise and foreign investment. In October 1965, Demirel's Justice Party gained a majority of votes in national elections, with the RPP and TWP together tallying less than a third.

But international events were to assume increasing importance in the Turkish domestic scene. Neighbouring **Cyprus** had gained independence in 1960 by terms of a treaty between the new Cypriot republic and its guarantors Britain, Greece and Turkey. Incorporated in the Treaty of Guarantee and the Cypriot constitution were extensive concessions to the Turkish Cypriot minority, who constituted roughly one-fifth of the island's population. By 1963 Cypriot president Makarios declared these clauses unworkable, and sought to limit the veto power of the Turkish community. Members of EOKA, the right-wing paramilitary force of the Greek population, took this as a cue to commence attacks on Turkish Cypriots, who replied in kind. Virtual civil war beset the island through much of 1964, with the ranks of both sides swelled by illegal, smuggled-in Greek and Turkish troops. A full-scale Greco-Turkish war was only narrowly avoided by US pressure on both countries. The Turkish government had to confine its response to retaliations against the Greek population of their two Aegean islands and İstanbul (including the expulsion of 12,000 resident Greek nationals), while communal violence recurred sporadically across Cyprus, despite the imposition of a UN-supervised truce, for the rest of the decade.

Turkey was also not immune from the spirit of May 1968, which here took the form of increased **anti-Americanism** and leftist sentiments, particularly on and around university campuses. Many Turks felt betrayed by the US's lack of support on the Cyprus issue, having studiously followed the American lead on foreign policy issues since the end of World War II. Even the ruling establishment found the obviousness of American tutelage offensive to sentiments of national independence, and soon most of the half-dozen US military installations were quietly given over either to Turkish sovereign control or alternatively that of NATO. At the same time, relations with the Soviet Union improved dramatically. Ironically perhaps, the most lasting American legacy to Turkey would be swarms of classic automobiles and 110-volt household appliances, provided as part of Marshall Plan assistance during the 1950s or sold off by departing diplomatic and military personnel throughout the 1960s.

Demirel was returned in **1969** for a second term as prime minister, but his majority and authority were soon eroded by the loss of a crucial budget vote and the defection of sixteen percent of the JP to legally reform the Democrat Party. More ominous was the upsurge in **political violence** on the streets and around the universities, which was to be a pervasive feature of Turkish life until 1980. Extreme left-wing groups such as Dev Sol (Revolutionary Youth) fought it out with right-wing and/or Islamist activists such as the notorious Grey Wolves, who had set up paramilitary training camps as far back as 1966, under the tutelage of **Alpaslan Türkeş**, spokesman of the 1960 coup and founder of the fascist Nationalist Action Party (NAP).

The second military intervention and the 1970s

Against this backdrop of domestic unrest, lingering corruption and continued non-productive parliamentary manoeuvres, the generals acted again. On March 12, 1971, they issued a proclamation forcing Demirel and his cabinet to resign in favour of an "above-party" government composed of reformist technocrats. This measure, often called the "**coup by memorandum**", allowed parliament to continue functioning, while stealing the wind from the sails of a considerable body of restive NCOs who had hoped for a full-scale military regime. Martial law was, however, imposed on the major cities and the ever-troublesome southeast, and thousands from the university community, the press and broadcasting were arrested and tried, mostly on charges of inciting violence or class conflict. In September amendments were promulgated to limit the freedoms granted by the 1961 constitution, but soon the "above-party" regime, effectively stymied by JP operatives in the Grand National Assembly, was forced to resign. Despite, or because of, the threat of another putsch, acting premier Nihat Erim managed to cobble together a merry-go-round of successively less radical and more acceptable cabinets, and preserved a semblance of civilian rule for two more years. The army, mindful of the hash that the colonels' junta had made of neighbouring Greece since 1967, decided to let the politicians take the blame for any adverse results in Turkey.

The surprise winners of the freely contested **elections in October 1973** were Bülent Ecevit and his RPP, though they were soon forced into uneasy alliance with Islamist **Necmettin Erbakan**'s National Salvation Party (NSP), which gained control of several ministries. During Ecevit's short but momentous period of office, the economy was savaged by OPEC's oil price hike, which preceded the Turkish **military intervention in Cyprus**.

The military junta then ruling Greece had ousted Cypriot President Makarios in July 1974 and replaced him with EOKA extremists supporting union with Greece. Ecevit's pro forma appeal to Britain to intervene in accordance with the Treaty of Guarantee went unheeded, so he gave the order for Turkish troops to invade the island on July 20. The EOKA regime fell three days later, after the Turks had secured a bridgehead around Kyrenia. A ceasefire was declared while furious negotiations between the Greek, Turkish and British foreign ministers continued over several weeks; on August 14, after the Greek Cypriots refused an ultimatum from Turkey, its army advanced further to occupy the northern third of the island.

Nearly three decades later the situation remains essentially unchanged, though a negotiated settlement is now up for referendum approval by the

Greek-Cypriot and Turkish-Cypriot populations. The **ceasefire** (hostilities have not yet formally ended) is policed by UN peace-keeping patrols along the "Attila Line" between the Greek Cypriot-controlled south and the self-proclaimed Turkish Republic of Northern Cyprus. There was long considerable unity of opinion in Turkey on the Cyprus issue, in that the status quo was seen as the only viable option. But from the mid-1990s Turkey slowly began withdrawing troops from Cyprus and hinting to the intransigent and sometimes ungrateful Turkish Cypriot leadership that some accommodation with the South would end the international isolation of the North if discussed in such international forums as the UN and the EU.

Back on the domestic front, Ecevit – riding a tide "victory" induced of popularity – resigned in September to seek early elections and hopefully a workable parliamentary majority. This proved a major blunder, for opposition footdragging ensured that polling was delayed until April 1975, when Süleyman Demirel was able to assemble a coalition government along with the Islamist National Salvation Party and the fascist Nationalist Action Party, and hung on to power after inconclusive elections two years later.

All this served only to further polarize the country, which from 1976 onwards was beset by steadily increasing political **violence** by extremists at each end of the political spectrum. Annual death tolls escalated from about three hundred during 1976–1977, to over three thousand during 1980, with the number of wounded and bomb explosions during this period well into five figures. While the perpetrators initially confined their activities to each other, a steady deterioration of parliamentary decorum and the politicization of trade unions and the civil service meant that incidents – and victims – were soon almost universal.

Ecevit regained power for about eighteen months beginning at the close of 1977, and attempted to address the **dire economic situation**, which had been aggravated by successive governments' profligate public spending, trade deficits and other inflationary policies. International assistance was secured, but on condition that the budget was balanced, protectionism reduced and the lira devalued, and in the event the political resolve to apply such strict controls was lacking. In December 1978, street battles in the southern city of Maraş between right-wing, fundamentalist Sunni gunmen and left-wing Alevîs claimed more than a hundred lives within a week; Türkeş's NAP were blamed by many for having orchestrated the clashes. Martial law was declared with some reluctance by Ecevit in many provinces, but this failed to prevent the establishment of an Alevî commune in the Black Sea town of Fatsa, where the army eventually sent tanks through street barricades. Against such a background of events, Demirel assumed office again in October 1979, but he also failed to halt the slide into **civil and economic chaos**. Random, tit-for-tat murders in İstanbul reached twenty per day, with various neighbourhoods run by particular factions – entry to these with the wrong newspaper in hand, or the wrong attire and moustache (each faction had a "dress code") guaranteed a beating or worse.

The 1980 coup and its aftermath

The armed forces soon decided that the Republic was facing its gravest crisis yet. A planning group for a military takeover apparently existed as early as 1978, but public rumblings first surfaced in the form of a warning letter to the two major political parties at New Year 1980. By this time **martial law** was in force in all of the major cities as well as the southeast, and an economist and engineer named **Turgut Özal** had been appointed head of the State Planning Organization, in which capacity he jettisoned the import-substitution policies prevalent since the founding of the Republic in favour of an **export-oriented economy**.

Now international events intervened. Turkey's strategic importance to the West had been emphasized by the Iranian revolution and Soviet invasion of Afghanistan, and the Americans in particular were anxious to secure a stable base in the Middle East. After five years of cool relations, prompted by an embargo of arms to Turkey in the wake of the Cyprus action, rapprochement feelers were put forth. By the time the Iran–Iraq war began in April 1980, these began to include signals of tacit approval for a coup. Some sources have also alleged that, given the existing martial law controls, the continued escalation of domestic violence was inconceivable without the military's toleration of it – even to the extent of using *agents provocateurs* to guarantee a solid pretext for a full-scale takeover.

This occurred bloodlessly on **September 12, 1980**, to the initial relief of a vast majority of the population. The frenzied killings ceased; Demirel, Ecevit, Erbakan and Türkeş were detained; all political parties were disbanded shortly after; and all trade unions and associations were closed down. Turgut Özal was, however, left in charge of the economy, since his reforms were seen as both effective and essential to Western support.

It soon became apparent that this coup represented a drastic break from the pattern of the previous two. A junta of generals, not junior officers – the **National Security Council (NSC)** – were firmly in control from the start, and return to civilian rule would be long delayed, and within a new frame-work. Meanwhile, bannings, indictments and purges punctuated the early 1980s, and while the radical Right was by no means immune from prosecution, it became clear that the Left would bear the brunt of the crackdown. Nationalist right-wing beliefs, if not explicitly violent or fascist, were compatible with the generals' agenda – as was an encouragement of mildly Islamic views on society as an antidote to secular Marxism, as long as the fundamentalists stayed out of the military itself.

The new rulers' principal **targets**, which had been relatively untouched in prior putsches, were labour syndicates, internationalist or separatist groups and the left-leaning intelligentsia. DİSK, the far-left trade union confederation, had 1477 of its members put on trial after its dissolution; 264 were convicted, despite lack of evidence of advocacy of violence, though the proceedings dragged on for so long – until 1990 – that many defendants qualified for immediate release on the basis of time served on remand. Even more controversial was the six-year court case against the Turkish Peace Association, with twelve defendants, including a former ambassador, sentenced. An example of the relatively lenient treatment of the Islamists was the acquittal, on appeal, of fundamentalist National Salvation Party leader Necmettin Erbakan, on charges of attempting to create an Islamic state. The Nationalist Action Party was, however, decimated, with eight capital verdicts and dozens of longer prison terms for its members – though Türkeş himself was acquitted.

The military attacked the **universities** and their hotbeds of radicalism less directly, purging 1475 academic staff as of 1984 by outright dismissal, placement on non-renewed short-term contracts or transfer to less desirable positions. All campuses were put under the control of a new body, the Higher Education Council (YÖK), subject to the direct authority of the acting head of state.

A 160-strong Consultative Committee of carefully vetted applicants was convened, which promulgated a new, highly **restrictive constitution** in 1982, expressly reversing most clauses of its 1960 predecessor. This was ratified by ninety percent of the electorate in a controversially coercive referendum, which was also an election for the presidency. No campaigning against was allowed; the only candidate was **General Kenan Evren**, head of the NSC and coup leader, and it was presented as an all-or-nothing package.

Return to civilian rule and the rise of ANAP

Civilian authority was tentatively re-established in the **general elections of November 1983**, although severe controls were placed on parties and candidates. Pre-coup parties and their leaders remained excluded from politics, and only three of the fourteen newly formed parties were allowed to contest the elections, the rest being deemed transparent proxies for banned organizations. Nonetheless, the centrist slate backed by the generals came last, and Turgut Özal's centre-right Motherland Party (initials ANAP in Turkish) won just under half the votes and just over fifty percent of the parliamentary seats.

ANAP was a party of uneasy alliance, incorporating a wide range of opinion from economic liberals to Islamists. Özal embodied these contradictions in his person: though a devout Muslim, ex-member of the NSP and adherent of the still-clandestine but progressively bolder Nakşibendi dervish order, he had strong appetites for booze, tobacco, food and *arabesk* tunes, while his colourful and charismatic speaking manner belied his American training in engineering. As party leader and prime minister, he managed the almost impossible task of balancing the opposing technocratic and traditionalist forces in the new party; simultaneously he set a scorching pace of **economic reform** during his first term, with exports reaching record levels and growth rates averaging more than six percent during the period 1983–1988. Inflation, however, continued to soar, as public budgets were reflated to buy support, especially among the farmers and civil servants; by 1986 foreign indebtedness and spiralling prices were again critical issues.

In retrospect, ANAP (and Özal) during their heyday can be credited with sweeping economic and legal **reforms** bringing Turkey more into line with the international economy – and at the same time blamed for the **vulgarization** of public culture. Under ANAP, money and its ostentation assumed paramount importance, with the exact means of earning it secondary – creating an ethical climate conducive to sharp practice and the growing wave of public scandals. A provincial elite, matching Özal's small-town, lower-middle-class background, came in on his coat-tails, earning an initial reputation of being able to "get things done", in contrast to the fumbling of the 1970s. Though trained abroad (mostly in the US), they hadn't necessarily absorbed Western values, and when they had, their cue was taken from Texas rather than the EC. **English** became the preferred language of this nouveau riche class, and of the best universities, which in the wake of the National Security Council's efforts during the early Eighties had become little more than apolitical polytechnics geared to cranking out technicians. Thatcher–Reaganism was the order of the day, unlike the noblesse oblige of the earlier RPP elite: **large conglomerates** and holding companies, numerous in Turkey, were expressly favoured, and many small businesses were forced to the wall. Along with the export earnings – and mass tourism should be included in this – came a flood of luxury goods that contrasted with the shortages of the 1970s: just about anything became available, for a price, flaunted avidly by the new consuming classes. This of course aggravated the ballooning trade deficit, since Turkish manufactured products – despite vast improvements since the 1970s – were (and are) still not competitive on most markets.

In local elections of 1984 and 1986, opposition parties gained some ground, particularly Erdal (son of İsmet) İnönü's Social Democrat Party (SHP in Turkish), and the True Path (DYP) and Democratic Left (DSP) parties, fronts respectively for the activities of still-proscribed Demirel and Ecevit. Another banned politician to return to the hustings was Necmettin Erbakan, whose old Islamist apparatus regrouped itself as the Welfare Party (*Refah Partisi* in Turkish). Popular pressure grew for a **lifting of the ban** on pre-coup politicians, which was narrowly approved in mid-1987. Parliamentary elections in November of that year showed just 36 percent support for ANAP but, because of the non-proportional-representation system put into effect especially for the occasion, they took nearly two-thirds of the seats in the Grand National Assembly. The SHP emerged as the main opposition, with nearly a quarter of the seats, though their performance was impeded by public perception of **Erdal İnönü**, a university professor turned politician, as a nice but ineffectual individual whom the unkind nicknamed "ET" after his resemblance to Spielberg's hero.

The DYP did badly; Ecevit, his DSP party failing to poll the ten-percent nationwide figure required for parliamentary representation, tearfully announced his (very temporary) retirement from politics.

The late 1980s: trends and problems

Özal's two prime ministerial terms were marked, not surprisingly in view of his background, by a dramatic increase in **Islamic activity**. The Department of Religious Affairs received extra staffing and funding, and the mandatory teaching hours devoted to Muslim issues in schools saw a similar rise. Much of this can be attributed to a conscious effort to offset or channel the influence of Iranian-style fundamentalism, but there seems also to have been a deliberate policy of promoting moderate Islamic sentiment as a safeguard against the resurgence of communist ideology. Outside of the government apparatus, the *vakıf*s, or pious endowments, also grew spectacularly, supported largely by donations from Saudi Arabia. Educational and welfare programmes run by the *vakıf* offered, and continue to offer, some hope and relief to those trapped in the burgeoning *gecekondu*s of the principal cities, where life is most precarious, but the assistance also encouraged fanatical and intolerant elements. On the other hand, the military periodically conducted purges of Islamists who managed to infiltrate the ranks, in a continuation of their post-coup stance.

Kurdish separatism, an intermittent issue since 1925, resurfaced in a violent form in the southeastern provinces. The main group involved, the Marxist-Leninist Kurdish Workers' Party (PKK), was founded in 1978, and based partly abroad in western Europe. Its guerrilla war of attrition against the Turkish government did not initially win it widespread support, but its position was undoubtedly strengthened by the frequent over-zealous reactions of the Turkish authorities.

Ties with Greece were strained not only by the Cyprus issue but by on-going disputes over airspace, seabed exploitation rights and territorial waters in the Aegean, and by the Greek government's maltreatment of and denial of full civil rights to the Turkish minority in Greek Thrace. **Bulgarian–Turkish relations** made international headlines throughout the summer of 1989, as the Communist Bulgarian regime's policy of forced Slavification of the Bulgarian Turkish minority resulted in dozens of deaths and ultimately escalated into the largest European mass emigration since World War II. Between May and August, over three hundred thousand ethnic Turks fled Bulgaria for Turkey, which initially welcomed them (the government had in fact invited them as part of a war of words with Bulgaria) and attempted to capitalize politically on the exodus. The reality of the number of refugees to be settled soon hit home, however, the border was closed, and by 1990 the new government in Sofya had formally renounced the heavy-handed assimilationist campaign of its predecessor, while most of the new arrivals eventually decided to return to Bulgaria or emigrate to Western Europe.

In direct contrast to the Turkish government's concern for the rights of Turkish minorities abroad, there was an ongoing pattern of **human rights violations** at home. This took the form principally of inhumane conditions in prisons but more importantly torture of suspects by law-enforcement agencies, and continual harassment of the press. At various times government spokesmen admitted that torture was practised during the 1980–1983 period of military rule, when hundreds of thousands of individuals were taken into custody, but until recently declined to comment on, or denied, allegations of continuing incidents. In the late 1980s and early 1990s several cases of official torture during the subsequent period of civilian rule were admitted, and some prosecutions of those responsible conducted, but their numbers were token, with the guilty often quietly promoted out of harm's way rather than being jailed.

Abuses continued into the 1990s and Amnesty International claimed that **torture** was still systematic; other monitoring organizations maintained that, while admittedly widespread, it was no longer officially condoned. However, only after the national elections of 1991 was there an official proclamation forbidding the maltreatment of non-political suspects prior to formal charging, the period for which was reduced from two weeks to 24 hours. Simultaneously, the Turkish Human Rights Foundation founded a chain of medical rehabilitation centres where victims of torture could apply for treatment.

If torture may eventually cease to be a feature of Turkish civic life, restrictions on the press show no signs of abating. The record number of prosecutions of journalists, editors and publishers since 1984 may paradoxically be a result of the media's growing boldness in testing the limits of censorship. An unsettling echo of the Menderes years was the increasing sensitivity of Turgut Özal to even the mildest criticism in print, with dozens of libel and slander suits filed by government prosecutors.

Meanwhile, in not entirely unrelated developments, Turkey's Europe-oriented **foreign policy** suffered various setbacks towards the end of the decade. Turkey had been an associate member of the EC since 1964, but her 1987 application for full membership was shelved indefinitely by the Community shortly after, ostensibly because of the need to concentrate on increased integration of the existing Twelve.

At the same time substantial public relations efforts were devoted to beating back repeated proposals in the United States Congress, sponsored by the international **Armenian lobby**, to designate April 24 as a day of "national remembrance" for the alleged genocide perpetrated against the Armenian community in 1915. This marked an increase in the sophistication of the more extreme Armenian advocates, who appeared to have mostly abandoned the policy of terrorist attacks on Turkish diplomats and installations which characterized the years 1973–1982.

Finally, the dramatic changes in eastern Europe further marginalized the country, as Soviet influence in the region nearly vanished and doubts were cast on the future strategic importance of a post-Cold War NATO in general and Turkey in particular.

The presidency and death of Özal

ANAP's influence was also already waning by early 1989, when municipal elections showed strong support for the opposition SHP and DYP. This was due to continuing high domestic inflation, the blatant nepotism benefiting Özal's cronies and large extended family – including his flamboyant, cigar-smoking, whisky-drinking wife Semra – and the inevitable corruption that attended this. Under the circumstances, most observers found Özal's self-nomination for the **presidency** – and election to it in November 1989 by a parliament half-empty owing to an opposition boycott – presumptuous in the extreme.

As prime minister, Özal had skilfully maintained a balance between the religious and secular wings of ANAP; now, as only the second civilian president in Turkish history, he strategically distanced himself from the nationalist/religious wing of the party in favour of the liberal one. Despite his official description as being "above-party", Özal was still widely perceived as the real leader of ANAP. He was instrumental in choosing the next prime minister, **Yıldırım Akbulut**, a lacklustre yes-man unable to command much respect either within the party or in the general population, where the promulgation of jokes at his expense became a favourite pastime. Akbulut's position was repeatedly undermined by Özal himself, who – in apparent contravention of the constitution – assumed many of the executive functions of the prime minister. Özal's continued **interference** – including but not limited to highly quotable, foot-in-mouth utterances that were the despair of his cabinet ministers – prompted the resignations of several of them.

Iraq's **invasion of Kuwait** in August 1990 reinforced Özal's position, and also reminded NATO and the US of Turkey's continuing strategic position. Özal, not the prime minister, contacted other heads of state and was central in defining Turkey's stance as an enthusiastic adherent of the UN sanctions, in anticipation of tangible rewards from the West for such support. He enthusiastically provided the US with landing facilities at İncirlik and Diyarbakır air bases, despite the risk of Iraqi attack, and incurred considerable financial loss by complying with UN sanctions, closing the pipeline which shipped Iraqi oil out through Turkish territory. Later in 1991 he permitted the stationing of coalition troops near the Kurdish "safe haven" across the Iraqi border as part of Operation Poised Hammer.

Özal perhaps entertained hopes that Turkey would be rewarded after the war by the return of the oil-rich province of Mosul. All he got tangibly for Turkey's co-operation was President Bush the Elder's undertaking that an independent Kurdistan would not be set up by dismembering Iraq. In the long term the coalition treated Turkey shabbily, failing to compensate it adequately for its losses – or for its admittedly reluctant hosting of hundreds of thousands of terrified Iraqi Kurdish refugees. Closer to home, participation in the anti-Iraq alliance sparked fundamentalist and leftist **attacks** on American and foreign property and personnel throughout early 1991, and sporadic street demonstrations against the war. A police crackdown on all this ensured a calm environment for President Bush's visit in July, the first of an American leader to Turkey in several decades and growing evidence of Turkey's importance for the US as a reliable regional ally.

Moreover, a nationwide **political vacuum** in terms of maturity and substance was growing both before and after the war. ANAP, beset by resignations, defections and factions, had lost its original energy and direction, but the opposition was not yet able to capitalize on this. The SHP, rent by an internal power struggle in which chairman İnönü ousted general secretary Deniz Baykal, accordingly slipped from its 1989 electoral standing, while Bülent Ecevit's DSP rebounded from a nadir in its fortunes by doing extremely well at the SHP's and DYP's expense in August 1990 municipal elections. İnönü renewed his oft-repeated call for a merger of the two left-of-centre parties but was rebuffed by Ecevit.

Overall the electorate was uninspired by the politics of personalities and almost complete lack of coherent party agendas or manifestos. The only consensus that in fact developed was the posthumous **rehabilitation of Menderes** and his cronies, an act of contrition that has taken the form of naming streets and public facilities after Menderes, and – on the thirtieth anniversary of the hangings of the three ministers – their solemn reburial in a special mausoleum in İstanbul.

By June 1991 Prime Minister Akbulut had been replaced by Ali Bozer, in tandem with Özal's increasing support for ANAP's liberal wing. The new premier and party leader **Mesut Yılmaz** decided to go to the polls considerably earlier than the November 1992 limit stipulated: with the economy worsening, he preferred earlier to later, while some of Özal's postwar support might still rub off on ANAP.

But the **October 1991 elections**, considered the fairest since 1983, produced a surprise result: the DYP was top finisher, with ANAP a strong second, and İnönü's SHP third. The biggest surprise, however, was the Welfare Party's unprecedented seventeen percent of the vote. But since no party secured an absolute majority, a **coalition** was inevitable, and in the event was perhaps the best combination available: between DYP and SHP, forged after several weeks of negotiations. Demirel was designated prime minister, İnönü deputy prime minister, with the various lower ministries divided between their two parties.

The coalition began with considerable optimism and goodwill (or at least forbearance) on all sides, even from the excluded ANAP; both parties pledged to pull together in tackling the country's pressing economic problems. Rapid privatization of the state firms was envisioned, along with a better deal for labour, and tax reform to make the wealthy pay their fair share after the jamboree of the ANAP years. The unenviable task of tackling inflation was assigned to **Tansu Çiller**, state minister for economy and the sole woman cabinet member.

There were also promises to make Turkey a *konuşan* (talking) society, where opinions were freely aired without fear of retribution, in contrast to the intimidated silence of the past. This intention ran into an immediate snag, however, when some of the 22 parliamentary deputies of **HEP** (the Kurdish-dominated Popular Labour Party, accused of ties with the PKK) – legally compelled to run on the SHP ticket but winning a quarter of the party's seats – caused an uproar when they refused to recite the standard loyalty oath upon being sworn in. **Deniz Baykal** further destabilized the SHP by repeatedly challenging İnönü for its top post, branding him responsible for the declining party fortunes since 1989, with the latter defending his position by predicting the demise of the coalition should Baykal replace him.

Legislation **un-banning pre-1980 parties** saw the Republican People's Party revived, setting off a scramble as to who would assume its leadership: 1979 chief Ecevit, İnönü (envisioning its incorporation into the coalition) or his persistent adversary Deniz Baykal. Baykal won, and as defections to his standard from DSP and SHP mounted, coupled with resignations of HEP deputies from SHP, the coalition's governing majority dwindled to a slim three.

Throughout 1992 **Özal** played an increasingly negative, spoiling role, much of it a function of the personal antipathy between him and Demirel, who openly sought a way to have him impeached. Özal also sparred with ANAP leader Yılmaz for influence in a party which as president he constitutionally could no longer head, eventually attempting to unseat his old protégé. When this failed, he flip-flopped again and hinted he would resign the presidency to participate in a party dominated by defected ANAP conservatives. In his capacity as president, Özal delayed the signing of many bills, prompting serious discussion of having him removed from office, a drawn-out procedure requiring a two-thirds majority in parliament. In the event, this proved unnecessary; Özal **died suddenly** of a heart attack on April 17, 1993.

It was impossible for anyone to remain indifferent to Özal, despite his many faults the most eloquent and influential head of state since Atatürk. Respected by many for his energy, courage and vision, despised by an equal number for his overbearing manner and shameless self-aggrandizing, he remains an ambiguous figure who sometimes did the right thing (for example his advocacy of concessions to the Kurds) for opportunistic reasons. His passing incontestably marked the end of an era, but the beginning of another where Turkey would have an increasingly high global profile.

After Özal

Demirel eventually emerged as president, while economic adviser **Tansu Çiller** – not Demirel's favoured candidate – became **prime minister** in June 1993. Like Özal and Demirel on the centre-right of Turkish politics, she was a US-educated academic-technocrat who had been brought into politics by Demirel in 1989 as part of an effort to modernize his party's image. With her assertive style and telegenic manner, she attracted considerable popular support, and her rise to power was initially viewed with optimism both within and without the DYP.

Such hopes, however, were soon dashed as the new prime minister proved herself woefully inadequate to the task at hand. Expectations of a fresh look at the **Kurdish problem** vanished as Çiller relegated all initiative to military hard-liners. Despite repeated assurances that the PKK was on the verge of defeat, the death toll in the undeclared civil war in east Anatolia continued to mount, exceeding three thousand per year. A controversial policy of expulsion of villagers from affected areas resulted in a tide of internal refugees, while efforts to bring about a political solution foundered when the latest pro-Kurdish Democracy Party (DEP) was proscribed and most of its MPs prosecuted.

The government's **economic policy** was characterized by hasty improvization. Inflation shot up from 66 percent in 1993 to a staggering 120 percent during 1994, hovering around 80 percent in subsequent years. During early 1994 the prime minister's confused meddling in monetary policy led to the Turkish lira losing nearly half its value within a month. April stabilization measures managed to contain the crisis at the cost of a year-long recession and a five-percent fall in national income. A boldly announced programme of privatizations and tax reform failed to materialize, since given the complete lack of unemployment or early retirement benefits, or retraining schemes, such moves would have caused enormous social distress and threatened social stability. As it was, a spate of industrial disasters – particularly mine and factory explosions, with large loss of life – made headlines despite a commitment to a better social contract for labour, while massive strikes by public-sector workers in 1994 and 1995 won them only paltry wage increases. In late November 1994, a privatization bill was finally passed by the Turkish parliament, eleven years after being first discussed.

In the matter of **foreign affairs**, hesitation replaced Özal's active (if at times bumbling) intervention in Balkan, Central Asian and Middle Eastern affairs. Seven foreign ministers in thirty months prevented the emergence of a consistent policy direction. A much-heralded project to carry Azerbaijani petroleum to Mediterranean ports through a Turkish-built pipeline was stalled indefinitely by Russian opposition; Moscow's displeasure also resulted in the toning down of noisy public support for the Chechen rebels. Equally vociferous Turkish sympathy for the Muslim cause in Bosnia failed to translate into a coherent policy initiative. Tensions with Greece flared periodically into crises, which were aggravated by demagogic posturing by political leaders in both countries; in February 1996 the two countries nearly went to war over the sovereignty of the Kardak/İmia archipelago, a pair of uninhabited rocky islets in the Aegean Sea.

The only significant – if controversial – foreign policy success of the Çiller-led coalition was the conclusion in March 1995 of a **customs union** agreement with the EU. Overseas, there was considerable opposition in view of Turkey's poor human rights record; within the country, opponents pointed out that billions of dollars in annual import duties were being forfeited, while Turks would still not have freedom of movement to and within Europe. Though falling considerably short of the ideal of full EU membership for Turkey, the agreement, which would take effect incrementally between 1996 and 2000, was still trumpeted as a triumph by the increasingly beleaguered government.

Perhaps the most important civic issue facing Çiller's government was its handling of the major **corruption scandals**, which seemed to erupt almost every week. But as in Italy, no political party was immune from guilt, as all had governed since the 1960s. Most of the scandals concerned public firms and entities such as the PTT, the Health Ministry and the Social Security Administration, whose officials allegedly took kickbacks for the award of contracts to private companies. In the most spectacular case, Özal's widow and daughter were accused of contracting a mafia hit-team to shoot Engin Civan, chairman of a state bank, who allegedly received a $5 million bribe to fix a credit deal but failed to deliver the goods. Another name to figure prominently in graft stories

Uncivil liberties: human rights in Turkey

Turkey's dismal **human rights record** has been a perennial irritant in relations with the EU. Despite Demirel's 1991 election pledge that police stations would have "walls of glass", international human-rights monitoring organizations reported little substantive change in subsequent years, with torture and suspicious deaths in custody routine occurrences. Despite the parliamentary modification during 1995 of many objectionable clauses of the 1982 constitution, and of the notorious Article 8 of the 1991 Anti-Terrorism Law, Turkish prisons still contain over a hundred non-violent political prisoners. The civilian government habitually defers to chiefs of the internal security forces, which, together with elements of the State Security Tribunals, the police and the gendarmerie, form a virtual para-state, accountable to no one.

Between 1990 and 2000 a sharp rise in urban terrorism occurred, with literally scores of **political assassinations** perpetrated by Islamic fundamentalists, far-leftists and possibly rogue civilian operatives of the Special Warfare Department, the common feature being the inability of police to identify or apprehend any suspects. Targets have included American personnel during and after the Gulf War; officers in the army and security forces; secularist professors, including the head of the national bar society, and (after a two-decade respite) members of Turkey's Jewish community.

But it was the demise of **Uğur Mumcu** in an Ankara car bombing of January 1993 that caused the most widespread revulsion. His funeral, attended by hundreds of thousands (including the National Security Council), was the occasion for mass demonstrations of support for his ideals of secularism and pluralistic democracy. As ever, nobody significant has been apprehended in the case, with his relatives alleging a cover-up amidst wider murmurings of involvement by radical fundamentalists, in connivance with elements in the security forces. Meanwhile, police devoted most of their energies to crushing the Marxist terrorist group Dev Sol with a series of spectacular shoot-ups of alleged safe houses in İstanbul and elsewhere. Another feature of the Çiller era was the huge upsurge in the number of **"disappeared" persons** – usually left-wing or Kurdish activists who vanished after being detained by police or by unidentified civilians. From 1995 to 2001, female relatives of "disappeared" persons rallied regularly at İstanbul's Galatasaray Square each Saturday, defying police harassment and occasional mass arrests.

Early 1996 saw the conclusion of year-long court proceedings against the internationally acclaimed novelist **Yaşar Kemal**. He had been charged with promulgating "separatist propaganda" and fomenting "hatred between races", following his January 1995 article in *Der Spiegel* describing the Turkish state as a "system of unbearable repression and atrocity" and claiming that the Kurdish rebellion was a justifiable response to seventy years of official repression (a similar, English-language article appeared in the special "File on Turkey" of *Index on Censorship*, Vol. 24 1/1995). With the eyes of the world on Turkey so soon after the customs union ratification, he was given a suspended twenty-month sentence in March, but not before 99 other prosecutions under Article 8 had been brought against artists and intellectuals who had rallied to his support.

The need for genuine action rather than words was again underlined in May 1998, with the assassination attempt by ultra-nationalist extremists on Akın Birdal, head of the IHD (Turkey's Human Rights Association), who was facing twenty different court cases trying to link him to the outlawed PKK (Kurdish Workers' Party). Despite being confined to a wheelchair after the shooting, Birdal was sentenced to one year in jail for "inciting racial hatred" (ie, acknowledging that there is a Kurdish minority in Turkey), again to the dismay of the EU.

Similar court cases and violent incidents have continued into the new millennium, until just before the unprecedented liberalization laws passed by the Turkish parliament during summer 2002. But human rights guarantees have always existed abundantly in Turkey on paper since late Ottoman times – the EU will only be impressed in the coming years by the practical application of the latest versions.

was that of the prime minister's husband, **Özer Çiller**, a businessman who apparently amassed $50 million worth of real estate (partly in the US) during his wife's term in office. An Associated Press feature in September 1996 listed Tansu Çiller among the world's ten most corrupt politicians of the 1990s, so it was hardly surprising that she did little to combat this endemic feature of Turkish political culture.

Even before mid-1993, there had been widespread public disillusionment with the coalition, and the inadequacies of Çiller's leadership soon also fuelled discontent within the parties concerned. Old DYP bosses led the internal opposition to Çiller with the tacit backing of President Demirel, whose dislike of his former protégée became apparent soon after she had taken office. The anti-Çiller front found a ready ally in ANAP leader **Mesut Yılmaz**, whose opposition strategy seemed motivated principally by intense personal hatred of "that woman".

The junior partner of the coalition fared no better. Shortly after Çiller's elevation, Erdal İnönü announced his **retirement** as leader of the SHP. Former Ankara mayor Murat Karayalçın, who replaced him in September 1993, proved unable either to defuse factional tensions in the party or to subordinate his rivalry with CHP leader Deniz Baykal in the interests of a long-mooted merger with the latter party. By late 1994, paralysed by infighting, saddled with the dismal performance of SHP-led municipalities since 1989 and rent by increased radicalism within the traditionally leftist Alevî community, the SHP disintegrated into its constituent factions. In February 1995, the party formally dissolved and merged with the CHP; a former foreign minister, **Hikmet Çetin**, was designated interim leader of the unified party, and by extension Çiller's newest deputy prime minister. But in September 1995, Deniz Baykal returned as head of the neo-CHP, and after failing to agree with Çiller on several crucial issues, announced the end of the electoral pact. Elections were set for December 24, with the tattered coalition as caretaker government in the interim.

The 1995 elections and the rise of Refah

When they came around, the **elections** provided a rude shock for the established parties of both right and left. DYP did poorly with 19.2 percent of the vote, down eight points from its 1991 performance; the European Parliament's ratification of the customs union agreement just the week before had clearly not benefitted Çiller's party. ANAP, which languished under the lacklustre leadership of Mesut Yılmaz, tied for second place with an almost identical share of the votes, down five points from its showing four years earlier. The CHP, with 10.8 percent of the vote, came within a whisker of failing the statutory ten-percent nationwide minimum for parliamentary representation; the other centre-left party, Ecevit's DSP, performed only slightly better at 14 percent. HADEP, the latest incarnation of the HEP-DEP ethos, failed to gain seats with its 4.8 percent, though it scored a majority in several Kurdish-populated provinces; Turkeş's quasi-fascist MHP also missed the barrier at 8.7 percent. The only clear winner in the election was top-polling **Refah** with 21.3 percent of votes cast, taking 197 out of 550 seats in the recently enlarged parliament, despite assertions by Çiller that a Refah victory would mean a return to the Dark Ages.

The result was hardly surprising, as political Islam had been making impressive gains since the late 1980s, when Özal and the NSC had both given its milder expressions their blessing. Refah had established itself as the most active party in terms of grassroots organization; alone among political groups, it harnessed the energies of women (however conservatively attired) and employed door-to-door canvassing techniques, relying on campaign material that addressed – in however lopsided a manner – social issues such as prostitution and income inequality, rather than stressing personalities and platitudes. In the burgeoning *gecekondus*, it alone seemed to represent the values and aspirations of the newly urbanized underclass, attracting it with populist rhetoric. To the lower-middle-class bazaar craftsman most at risk from the trappings of liberal capitalism, Refah promised protection in the form of a sharply renegotiated customs union. In the conservative east, its Islamic ecumenicism seemed to provide a reasonable alternative to many Kurds alienated by the more usual forms of Turkish Nationalism. Last but not least, many voters threw in their lot with Refah simply in protest at the corruption and inertia of the discredited mainstream parties.

In the March 1994 **municipal elections**, Refah had carried a plurality of cities across the country, including both metropolitan İstanbul and Ankara (by contrast, it did poorly in rural areas and small towns). In İstanbul, initial fears of puritanism run amok – alcohol-free pubs, obligatory gender segregation on buses, *Swan Lake* in harem pants – were quickly dispelled as the administration of mayor Recep Tayyip Erdoğan proved itself pragmatic, efficient and remarkably honest by Turkish standards. Pollution was substantively addressed, extra buses laid on, the rubbish collected regularly and facilities provided for the handicapped. Cynics said the rabbits would stop coming out of the Refah skullcap as soon as clandestine donations from the Saudis dried up; others, and by no means all of them Islamists, pointed out that Refah's success was earned both by their opponents' moral bankruptcy and by their own organizational skill. Relative Refah competence in Turkey's largest city had helped convert many voters in time for the national elections, and seemed to establish young Erdoğan as heir apparent to the party's septuagenarian leader Erbakan, now nicknamed "the Hoca".

The **Islamic revivalism** which has gripped increasingly broader segments of Turkish society from the mid-1980s can just be seen as the latest in successive cycles of reaction against the Atatürkist secular republic. In post-1923 Turkey, "secularism" and "laicism" had always meant subordinating the clergy to a Ministry of Religious Affairs, simultaneously keeping it out of politics, suppressing the public expression of Islam and deeming it strictly a matter of private conscience – quite different from its Western interpretation as freedom of belief and equal treatment for all religions. The longstanding official ban on **traditional Islamic dress** at state functions meant in practice that many young people of conservative social background could never expect to enter a public career, or even be admitted to university. A December 1989 decree empowering individual universities to allow, at their discretion, attendance by women wearing headscarves was viewed by secularists as the thin edge of a wedge of increased religiosity. For them, such garb is not akin to a Sikh train-driver in Britain wearing a turban, but a red flag before the bull of official atheism. But by the mid-1990s, wearers of the scarf or the prophetic beard had grown from an initial radical fringe to include some of the brightest members of the academic community.

The prohibition of **dervish orders** had also begun to grate, as the various mystical brotherhoods emerged from underground and gained renewed popularity in the 1980s. For a majority of the population, Islam remained a much stronger cultural presence than the assertive Westernizing of the elites, and a more homespun expression of the national spirit than the quasi-colonial arrogance often associated with the Atatürkist establishment. On a wider level there was a general **distrust of the West**, regarded as the wellspring of Christian prejudice and capitalist exploitation, sworn enemy of the Muslim world and betrayer of the Bosnians, Azeris and Palestinians. From this posture it was not too far a leap to overt anti-Semitism and hostility towards Israel; opposition to a series of military co-operation agreements signed between Turkey and Israel during the final months of the DYP–CHP coalition formed a key plank in Refah's campaign.

Refah takes power

The political establishment reacted to the December 1995 election results with a hastily cobbled-together **DYP–ANAP coalition** of second-bests, expressly designed to keep Refah from assuming power. But even together they could only muster 267 seats out of the 276 needed for a parliamentary majority, and were forced to put out unsuccessful feelers to both left-of-centre parties in order to form a three-way, right–left coalition. In the event, Mesut Yılmaz presided over an unstable minority government, characterized by intensified mutual loathing between himself and Çiller, and constant sniping from Refah – which felt cheated of its electoral spoils – and from the rest of the opposition, which finally rang down the curtain in June 1996 with a motion of censure.

The annual spring offensive against the PKK and the highly visible Yaşar Kemal case indicated the pervasive, resurgent influence of the ex-security-service chiefs who had infiltrated Çiller's entourage at her express invitation, giving the DYP the nickname of the "Police Academy". But they were unable to protect her against impending investigations into corruption, in particular allegations that she'd helped herself to $6.5 million from the central bank to finance the recent elections. To save her skin, in mid-July she negotiated a **DYP coalition with Refah**, something she'd sworn she would never do, with Erbakan as prime minister and herself as foreign minister and deputy prime minister; her price was the dropping of all proceedings against her, which Erbakan had encouraged. Secularist, professional women, who had believed her claim to be their last line of defence against the *hoca*s, faxed their resentment in plenitude to DYP headquarters; feelings ran equally high in parliament, where punch-ups flared and handguns were drawn as the coalition was approved by a narrow vote of 278 to 265. Lurid press headlines predicted coup and disaster as Erbakan immediately embarked on a series of controversial trips to Iran and Libya, sent emissaries to Iraq and generally made friendly noises towards various global pariahs.

The courtly, soft-voiced Erbakan, with a taste for expensive shoes and ties and 25 pilgrimages to Mecca under his Gucci belt, initially proved nimbler than his detractors. While the secularists conjured up spectres of turbaned *kadi*s (Islamic judges) and obligatorily veiled women, Refah moved quickly to divest itself, in public at least, of its threatening image. Within weeks of taking office, after a discreet word in its ear from the military's US minders, the government meekly signed a new military treaty with Israel, making mockery of its campaign promise to tear up such documents. Authorization for the use by NATO aircraft of two airbases in the southeast as part of Operation Provide Comfort was quietly extended, despite prior characterization of NATO as a "formal occupation". An IMF negotiating team, in Ankara to sort through the morass of Turkish finances (its foreign debt ranked among the top ten worldwide), was pleasantly surprised to hear nothing further about either zero-interest banking or a proposed "Islamic currency". A September party conference jettisoned much of the radical vocabulary that the Islamists had accumulated over 23 years in opposition, and Refah trod softly in the cities that it controlled. Non-veiled wives of Refah MPs began making the social rounds, and soon Erbakan himself was spotted committing the ultimate Islamist sacrilege: laying the customary wreath at Atatürk's tomb. Critics alleged that Refah was merely practicing **taqiya** – the concealment or temporary compromising of one's true aims in the interest of Islam – and that given a clear electoral majority, a radical fundamentalist programme would in fact be implemented. Certainly the party contained, in addition to technocrat renegades from ANAP, a radical fringe eager to embrace Iran-style rule – and, ominously, pump-action shotgun sales burgeoned in Refah-controlled neighbourhoods.

In terms of day-to-day administration, the performance of the new government was disappointing. There were no imaginative policy initiatives against the spectres of hyperinflation and the mayhem in the east, only a proposal for a "M-8" of developing Muslim nations to parley with the Group of Seven. And worst of all, in November 1996, a high-speed **car crash at Susurluk** near Ankara virtually proved the long-muttered assertions of a link between right-wing-nationalist assasins, top police chiefs, the anti-PKK Kurdish drug mafia, and certain elements of the DYP. A representative member of each faction was found dead or dying in the wreckage, along with a fair quantity of weaponry and drugs, and the DYP Interior Minister **Mehmet Ağar** was compelled to resign when his close ties to the group were demonstrated. The assassin, Abdullah Çatlı, long wanted by Interpol for participation in the 1981 attempt to murder Pope John Paul II, was given a state funeral, and even though a desultory investigation sputtered along for two years, Susurluk – characterized as "equal to 100 Watergates" – became a byword for cover-ups, the corruption of most politicians and the strength of the para-state.

Islam under fire

The military's growing unease with Refah came to a head at a marathon meeting of the **National Security Council** on February 28, 1997. The NSC, consisting of Turkey's five top military commanders, plus the president, the prime minister and three leading ministers, meets monthly and is acknowledged by most Turkey observers as the country's final arbiter of power. It stipulated **twenty measures** designed to safeguard secularism and curb the growth of private weapons purchases, Islamic schools, religious brotherhoods and the Islamic media. With European relations at an all-time low and with US support certain in the face of any perceived Islamic threat, the military felt they had little to lose by baring their teeth. Tanks duly rolled through the streets of an Ankara suburb when its Refah mayor and the Iranian ambassador made speeches advocating the introduction of *sharia* law. Yet even in its beleaguered condition Refah managed to secure closure of the country's 79 **casinos**, their billion-dollar annual turnover having acted as a magnet for Turkish, Russian and Israeli mafiosi.

Pressure on Refah increased that spring, with attention focused on the right of female civil servants to wear "Islamic" headscarves at work, and plans to build a series of giant mosques in central Ankara and İstanbul. Two DYP cabinet ministers resigned, calling for fresh elections and another DYP–ANAP coalition to exclude Refah. In late June 1997 the inevitable happened when, under duress, **Erbakan stepped down** and shortly after judicial proceedings were instigated against Refah. This "silent coup" left President Demirel free to invite ANAP leader Mesut Yılmaz to form a new government of "national reconciliation" along with Bülent Ecevit and his DSP, bolstered by defections from the DYP.

One of the new coalition government's first moves to combat the Islamists was a cunning piece of legislation, suggested by the NSC in April, raising the **compulsory secular education** span from five to eight years (from ages 7–12 to ages 7–15). This denied parents the opportunity to send their children to the religious **imam hatip okulları** (religious oratory schools) until they were fifteen rather than twelve, fatally reducing the religious schools' enrolment and income in the process. Legislators claimed that they had acted in the best educational interests of Turkey's youth, while many parents and children (particularly from poor areas) were left to rue the demise of these academically very successful schools, which had burgeoned with official tolerance since 1980, and where only a few hours per week were devoted to Arabic and the Koran.

The secularist establishment scored another victory over the Islamists in January 1998, when **Refah's forcible dissolution** was ordered by the Constitutional Court (for "acting against the principles of the secular Republic"), with Erbakan banned yet again from politics for five years. International condemnation of these anti-democratic moves came from both the EU, which had just rejected Turkey's renewed application to join in December 1997, and the US. The Islamists were far from beaten, however, and a new successor party, **Fazilet (Virtue)** was established immediately. Many former Refah deputies flocked to join it, and Fazilet held the largest number of seats in parliament. Led by former Erbakan aide **Recai Kutan**, Fazilet sought to present a more moderate image than its precursor. Several career women figured on its executive board ("window-dressing", said detractors), while its ostensible policies were pro-EU and stressed the importance of human rights.

In September 1998 the popular Fazilet mayor of İstanbul, **Recep Tayyip Erdoğan**, was jailed for four months for a speech the prosecution claimed "incited armed fundamentalist rebellion"; he had in fact quoted some admittedly provocative lines ("The mosques are our barracks, the minarets our bayonets, the domes our helmets, and the believers our soldiers...") from a poem by Ziya Gökalp, a hard-line Republican nationalist and one of Atatürk's intellectual godfathers. Erdoğan was widely respected for both literally and metaphorically cleaning up the streets of İstanbul, and his brief imprisonment – which attracted huge queues of visiting well-wishers – was widely regarded as a hollow victory by a suspect secular establishment over an honest (albeit "Islamic") politician. As if to prove sceptics right, Prime Minister Yılmaz – who had returned to power on an anti-corruption platform – ironically found himself implicated in a financial scandal revealed by the ongoing investigations of the Susurluk incident. A vote of "no confidence" instigated by the main opposition party, Deniz Baykal's CHP, brought down the coalition in November 1998.

The return and retreat of the Grey Wolves

President Demirel was now obliged to ask his perennial political foe, Ecevit, to form an interim government. The nominally left-wing Ecevit was unsurprisingly reluctant to ask Fazilet to join him; the CHP, led by Ecevit's long-standing rival Baykal, who had a record of breaking agreements when it suited him, was similarly cold-shouldered.

The political squabbling of early 1999 was set against the turbulence following the February **capture** of reviled PKK leader **Abdullah Öcalan** in Kenya. PKK sympathizers demonstrated, sometimes violently, both in Turkey and across Europe; in March, the PKK warned tourists to stay away from Turkey or risk being terror targets. This announcement, the ongoing Öcalan trial and the fire-bombing of stores in İstanbul and Ankara with fourteen fatalities, resulted in mass cancellation of holiday bookings, with dire economic consequences for an economy already hard hit by the Russian financial collapse of autumn 1998.

Despite all this, **elections** were actually held on schedule in **April**. Ecevit's DSP, bolstered by the public euphoria surrounding Öcalan's capture, won the largest number of votes (22 percent) and 136 parliamentary seats. The biggest surprise, however, predicted by none of the political pundits, was the meteoric return of the National Action Party (MHP in Turkish), who finished second with 18.2 percent of the vote (compared to 8.7 percent in 1995), which translated into 129 seats. Notorious founder Alparslan Türkeş had recently died, to be succeeded by **Devlet Bahçeli**, who made valiant attempts to portray the MHP in a more moderate light, while glossing over the party's history of political violence and lurid symbolism of a howling wolf (in Nationalist mythology, a grey wolf had led the first Turkic tribes west out of central Asia). The MHP capitalized on public anger over the seemingly endless war with the PKK and equally futile attempts by Turkey to be accepted for EU candidacy. Fazilet saw its vote share drop to 15 percent (against 21.3 percent polled for Refah in 1995), hardly surprising given the military and secular establishment's vendetta against Islamists. They did, however, manage to retain control of İstanbul and Ankara in the simultaneous municipal elections. The second electoral shock was to find Atatürk's old party, the CHP, with no seats in the new parliament as it had failed to garner the requisite ten percent of the vote. ANAP finished fourth, just over the ten-percent barrier for 86 seats, and together with the two front-running parties formed yet **another coalition** to exclude the Islamists.

The pact between leftist but nationalist Ecevit – wary of the EU, hard-line on the Cyprus issue – and the rightist MHP initially proved surprisingly stable, as MHP leader Bahçeli initially proved willing to compromise on his followers' hot-button issues. As the world watched what it would do with the imprisoned Öcalan, the government declined to ratify the death sentence handed down in July 1999 and allowed Öcalan's appeal to the European Court of Justice to take its course. Action against the Islamists continued, however, and the country's chief prosecutor opened a case in the Constitutional Court aimed at **closing down Fazilet**.

Economic fragility resulting from the worst touristic year in a decade was compounded by the **catastrophic earthquake**, which struck northwestern Turkey on August 17, 1999. Registering 7.4 on the Richter scale, it devastated property in Turkey's most industrialized and heavily populated region, and killed nearly 20,000 people. Survivors were outraged by needless deaths resulting from collapsed apartments built on unsuitable sites and/or with substandard materials. Public anger was directed at local authorities for winking at violations of the zoning and building codes, and at the shambolic response of the emergency services; foreign aid teams were equally appalled, sitting about waiting for directions while trapped victims perished. Even the army, usually either too respected or too feared to be criticized by ordinary Turks, came under fire for saving its own first and failing to help the public. This scapegoat-hunting, in which the housing minister himself was implicated, ignored universal complicity in decades of shoddy building; the blocks of flats were often priced unrealistically cheaply, making them fatally attractive to migrants from the countryside who bought them no questions asked – and got, structurally, what they paid for.

Ironically enough, the earthquake had some lasting **positive consequences**. An outpouring of material aid and sympathy from arch-rival Greece – whose aid teams were first on the scene – heralded a sustained thaw in bilateral relations. In December 1999, after foreign minister İsmail Cem had presented Turkey's case and negotiated several compromises over long-standing problems, Greece dropped its objections and Turkey became an official candidate for **eventual EU membership**; Greece has since in fact become Turkey's major EU sponsor, a not entirely altruistic stance since admission would shift the Union's eastern frontier – and the arduous policing duties that go with it – to Turkey.

At the beginning of 2000, police raids across the country uncovered an alarming network of "safe houses" set up by **Turkish Hizbullah**, an extreme Islamic fundamentalist organization. The most spectacular raid was on the group's HQ in a quiet Istanbul suburb, where a four-hour gun battle ensued between security forces and the terrorists. Found at several of the group's hideouts were the dismembered remains of the group's victims, most of them businessmen of Kurdish origin or members of rival Islamic organizations. Recai Kutan, leader of the beleaguered Fazilet Party, dared to voice what many privately believed – that the state itself had been turning a blind eye to Hizbullah's actions, seeing them as a useful counter to the Marxist PKK, Hizbullah's sworn enemies. Kutan was roundly criticized by the Turkish military, and pressure on moderate Islamists continued; in March, former prime minister and Refah leader Erbakan was given a one-year prison sentence (eventually suspended) and a long-term ban from politics for a speech made in 1994.

In May a constitutional crisis was avoided by the appointment of **Ahmet Necdet Sezer** to the presidency. PM Ecevit had wanted his old rival Demirel to continue in office, but the constitution forbade more than one term as president, and attempts to amend the office to two five-year terms – allowing Demirel to stay on until 2003 – ended in a humiliating parliamentary rebuff for Ecevit. A dark-horse, last-minute compromise candidate and a Constitutional Court judge (rather than a politician or general like all of Turkey's previous presidents), Sezer has acted as an advocate of freedom of expression and a stickler for adherence to the law, as well as proving influential in pushing forward reforms necessary to begin the process of EU accession. However, in July the state prosecutor renewed his call for the closure of Fazilet on the grounds that it was a continuation of the banned Refah. The embattled Islamists got a brief reprieve in July when Sezer, in a principled stand, proved less maleable than anticipated by refusing to sign a government decree sacking hundreds of pro-Islamic civil servants; he has since vetoed other measures which in his opinion violate democratic principles.

Towards the close of 2000, the authorities attempted to introduce so-called "F-type" jails with small one-to-three-person cells to replace dormitory accommodation in the nation's overcrowded and poorly managed **prisons**. While an ostensibly humane move, the real motive was to disperse the dorms, which the government claimed served as "universities for indoctrination" by jailed "terrorists" who effectively ran many of the prisons, and (claimed the affected inmates) make it easier to isolate alleged troublemakers for torture in the privacy of solitary confinement. The prisoners, many of them members of the proscribed Marxist-Leninist Revolutionary Party, responded with **hunger strikes** and barricades, while relatives demonstrated outside in sympathy. December assaults by elite troops on scores of prisons nationwide housing leftist strikers led to the deaths of at least thirty inmates and two soldiers and the mass transfer of the survivors to the F-type jails. This harsh strategy backfired as the number of fasters actually increased from 282 to 353, some of them released MLRP members fasting at home in solidarity. In May 2001, an amendment to the Anti-Terror Law allowed F-cell inmates to mix with others in recreational areas, and soon after civic committees were set up to monitor prisons, but by autumn 2002, over fifty of the hunger strikers had died, with neither the fasters nor government hard-liners inclined to back down on the "F-type" issue.

In the international arena, the controversy surrounding Turkey's **treatment of Armenians between 1895 and 1915** stubbornly refused to go away. During autumn 2000, the Turkish government reacted with anger and a threat to cancel defence contracts worth billions of dollars when the United States House Foreign Relations Committee, after years of lobbying, actually approved a resolution deeming as "genocide" the slaughter of the Armenians in 1915. Outgoing President Clinton, deciding that US-Turkish relations hung in the balance, ensured that the bill never had a floor vote. By contrast **France**, at the instigation of an MP of Armenian descent, had begun the process of officially recognizing the massacres in June 1998, joining Russia and Canada by finally endorsing a resolution on January 18, 2001. In tandem with the recall of the Turkish ambassador to France, mobs attacked the French Embassy and business leaders called for a boycott of French goods. In further retaliation, Turkey cancelled bridge-building and satellite deals with French companies, and refused to accept French tenders for military contracts. On a lighter note, Prime Minister Ecevit, who had given up his Renault in protest, was forced to use it again when his Hyundai broke down.

Economic and political meltdown

After a deceptive smooth economic ride for Turkey from mid-1999 to mid-2000, numerous private **banks** began to fail in late 2000; by the end of this initial crisis, a half-dozen banks had to be wound up or put into receivership of the state-run the **Savings Deposit Insurance Fund**, which had to compensate account-holders who'd lost their savings. The last and most spectacular crash occurred in November, when Demirbank found itself without liquidity after making the classic mistake of borrowing short-term at high rates while lending long; it ended up being rescued by HSBC, which now owns it.

A new economic **crash of late February 2001** was the final straw, sending share prices reeling and a final half-dozen unsteady banks into the arms of the SDIF. After a snap decision by foreign capital to quit the country, compounded by insider trading, the Turkish lira – which had been artificially tied to the dollar through the so-called "crawling peg regime" in an IMF-backed plan to reduce chronic inflation – was free-floated. The exchange rate rocketed as everyone rushed to buy dollars, whose price rose from about 800,000 TL to over 1,200,000 TL overnight, and nearly 1,500,000 TL by April. Inflation stood at 21 percent in February, rising to nearly 50 percent over the next three months. Stoical Turks saw the value of their savings, investments and wages slashed overnight.

In an attempt to limit the damage, **Kemal Derviş**, a Washington-based World Bank vice president of twenty years' standing, was appointed Minister of the Economy as an independent, though with his extraordinary powers he functioned in effect as a "fourth party" in the coalition. Viewed by the desperate Turks as an economic messiah, Derviş managed to persuade the IMF to release billions in aid far earlier than planned. Among his stringent reforms was the overdue decoupling of politics and economics by the privatization or liquidation of the four state-owned banks, which had hitherto acted as conduits for ruling parties to funnel dubious loans to supporters. The only silver lining to the cloud was the cancellation of a $19.5 billion spending spree by the military, at the same time as neighbouring Greece was cutting back on military expenditure.

In June, the Fazilet party was finally **banned** by the Constitutional Court for "anti-secular activities", specifically for inciting protests against the prohibition of headscarf-donning by women in education and government employment, and for backing MP Merve Kavakçı's bid to swear an oath of office wearing said scarf. The futility of banning Fazilet was immediately demonstrated by the rapid formation the AK (*Adalet ve Kalkınma*, Justice and Development) Party, under former Fazilet mayor of İstanbul **Recep Tayyip Erdoğan**; a rival party (*Saadet* or "Contentment") attracted the old Islamist guard, again under Recai Kutan.

Summer 2001 saw parliament working desultorily on a draft package of **constitutional amendments** to bolster Turkey's EU bid, including guarantees for greater freedom of thought, expression and association, and the easing of restrictions on educating and broadcasting in minority languages – specifically Kurdish, Laz and Circassian. The three coalition partners bickered endlessly, with ANAP posing as pro-European and the MHP doing their best to scupper plans without looking as though they were the guilty parties; one of the Nationalists' loopier counter-proposals was to officially replace all "foreign" (ie Greek- or Kurdish-based) place names in Anatolia with purely Turkish ones.

Domestic politics were temporarily overshadowed by the **September 11 terrorist strikes** on the US; the fall-out of the attacks acted as a boost for secularist Turks, as worldwide condemnation of Islamic extremism seemed to justify their own persecution of political Islam. Turkey instantly became the "blue-eyed boy" of the US, as the country's role as the major American ally (along with Israel) in the Middle East was highlighted. The Turks, tired of European criticism over human rights, Cyprus and economic mismanagement, briefly basked in the praise (and, more pragmatically, promises of aid) of a US congressional delegation sent to Ankara in October.

Turkey was brought down to earth with a thump by the end of 2001 by a 10,000-strong rally in Ankara protesting against the economic crisis, which had halved the purchasing power of the average worker. The only potentially good news was an unexpected **thaw in the Cyprus stand-off**, with Greek Cypriot leader Glafkos Clerides and Turkish Cypriot leader Rauf Denktaş renewing negotiations in December under the aegis of the UN, after a four-year gap in communication.

The by-now thoroughly unpopular PM Ecevit was hospitalized in May 2002, and didn't reappear at work for two months; the fragile stock market reacted with a further five-percent drop, and another large bank went into receivership. The only relief amidst the gloom was Turkey's unexpectedly strong third-place finish in football's World Cup. By July, the coalition government began to totter seriously as the coalition partners challenged Ecevit's premiership, amid ongoing revelations of corruption scandals, and an eight-percent contraction in the GDP, with consequent massive unemployment and layoffs. Loans from the IMF since late 2000 now totalled $31 billion, making Turkey the organization's biggest single debtor. Eventually 63 DSP MPs, including seven ministers, **resigned** from the party, leaving it a distant second in the coalition behind the MHP. Among the defectors was highly respected Foreign Secretary İsmail Cem, who formed the *Yeni Türkiye* (New Turkey) Party; everyone expected economy minister Kemal Derviş to join him. The MHP began calling for early elections and, surprisingly, Parliament obliged late in the month by set a date of November 3. Despite the chaos of this parliamentary twilight, legislators **passed the required EU reforms** just before the summer recess. The death penalty was abolished (saving Öcalan from the gallows), education and broadcasting in several minority languages were now theoretically permissible, indigenous Christian religious foundations were allowed freedoms undreamed of earlier, and even the once-sacred military could now be criticized in print.

The next few months were dominated by the possibility of Western strikes against Iraq and the run-up to the November elections. The Turkish military remained terrified that a de facto Kurdish state would emerge in northern Iraq if Saddam Hussein were toppled, leading to Turkey's own Kurds seeking independence or union with Iraqi Kurdistan: a nightmare notion in a state whose "territorial integrity" has been a cornerstone of every constitution. MHP Defence Minister Sabahattin Çakmakoğlu threatened military action if Iraqi Kurds made moves towards independence, and went so far as to describe oil-rich Kirkuk (part of Kurdistan, though it lies outside the protected Kurdish zone) as "Turkish soil". For the first time, the Turkish army admitted what everyone already knew – that they maintained a permanent presence in northern Iraq, ostensibly to control the remnants of the PKK based there. It now seemed clear that the army's true aim was (and remains) preventing the emergence of an independent Kurdistan.

After weeks of press speculation and secret negotiations with potential partners, Kemal Derviş eventually bolted to Deniz Baykal's CHP, seen by most secular Turks as the one group capable of challenging the pro-Islamic AK Party. President Sezer did his best to prevent a showdown between the AK Party and the military by obtaining guarantees from the incoming chief of staff, Hilmi Özkök, that he would respect the peoples' choice. However, the secular judiciary fought a rearguard action to fend off the so-called Islamists, and in August AK party leader Erdoğan was formally re-banned from holding political office (as was pro-Kurdish HADEP leader Murat Bozlak) because of his previous conviction for "inciting religious hatred".

The UN, in particular General Secretary Kofi Annan and Cyprus special envoy Alvaro de Soto, had been attempting to **broker a Cyprus settlement** between Clerides and Denktaş for most of 2002, but progress proved elusive and negotiations stalled as Denktas underwent heart surgery in New York, thus excusing him temporarily from the obligation to respond to Kofi Annan's compromise proposals. On both sides of the island, popular feeling in favour of a settlement rose sharply as the year progressed. On October 9, the EU recommended 2004 admission of ten new member states in 2004, pointedly including Cyprus (whether or not a settlement had been reached), but deemed Turkey as yet unready for membership despite "significant progress".

Islamists redux

Against a background of EU procrastination and continuing economic crisis, it was no surprise that **AK swept to power** on November 3, 2002, garnering 34 percent of the vote and claiming 363 of the 550 parliamentary seats. For the first time in fifteen years Turkey had a majority government, and if AK failed in the tasks ahead it would not be able to blame coalition infighting. Under current electoral law, only parties polling at least ten percent of the vote nationwide are entitled to send MPs to parliament; the single other party to top ten percent was the CHP, who had been excluded in the 1999 election but who now, unsmeared by the sticky mud of the economic crisis, polled twenty percent for 177 seats. The rump of Ecevit's DSP was humiliated, crashing from 22 percent to just over 1 percent. The ultra-Nationalist MHP also fell short of the *baraj* as it's termed, with only 8 percent as against a former 19 percent. ANAP, the third coalition partner, scored well below the 10-percent minimum, while DYP also polled only 9 percent. Smaller personality-centred splinter groups like İsmail Cem's New Turkey Party were utterly buried. DEHAP (a reincarnation of pro-Kurdish HADEP, which had voluntarily closed itself to avoid being banned) increased its share of the vote, but still failed to gain any parliamentary seats, although it had come first in thirteen of the Kurdish-dominated provinces of the southeast.

In all, only 9 million of the registered electorate of well over 30 million voted for the AK Party; abstentions and spoiled papers reached record levels, and – due to the *baraj* system – nearly 46 percent of voters are unrepresented in the new parliament. By European standards, the **10-percent minimum** for party parliamentary representation seems excessively high – it was promulgated in the 1982 constitution to, among other things, exclude "regional" or "minority" (ie Kurdish) parties; the cut-off point in neighbouring Greece, for example, is 5 percent. But curiously it doesn't bother most Turks, and none of the defeated parties of November 2002, having benefited handsomely from this system in the past, were in a position to cry foul.

Since de facto AK Party leader Erdoğan was prohibited from serving as an MP and thus prevented from assuming the position of Prime Minister, President Sezer had to choose an alternative Prime Minister. The position fell (temporarily, it would seem) to deputy leader **Abdullah Gül**, an English-speaking former economics professor widely regarded as a moderate. (By late December the AK Party, with the required two-thirds parliamentary majority, amended the constitution to permit Ergoğan to run in any by-election and thus formally become prime minister as an MP.) General Özkök, on a visit to the United States where he was being briefed on plans to invade Iraq, again pledged to accept the electoral decision; the AK Party hastened to reassure all concerned that they would pursue a moderate programme with the maximum of consultation on all issues, and immediately invited Baykal to join Erdoğan on his victory tour of European capitals.

As Erdoğan commenced canvassing EU heads of state to press Turkey's case for a favourable decision on a date for commencement of accession negotiations, the TL exchange rate reversed its habitual inflationary spiral, the local stock market commenced a steady rise, and the World Bank, business community and political opposition expressed their confidence. The new government's programme was elaborated as part of a package of 36 measures designed to meet the so-called "Copenhagen Criteria" of acceptable civic practice stipulated by the European Union; Erdoğan made the right noises about zero tolerance of torture, but was simultaneously embarrassed by a domestic TV station filming a boy being beaten up by police officers during of a demonstration in Ankara. There has been no showdown to date on the headscarf issue; although most of the party leaders have headscarf-wearing wives, AK is being diplomatic in ensuring that none of its female MPs wear such garb in Parliament.

Recep Tayyip Erdoğan has been brave enough to make the connection, denied by most other Turkish politicians for years, between Turkey's accession to the European Union and an internationally accepted Cyprus settlement. UN Secretary Annan's November 28 deadline for an agreement to his proposals came and went with Denktaş having a relapse. However, one of the first acts of the new Turkish foreign minister was to visit Denktaş in his New York hospital and try to extract a promise to agree to Kofi Annan's proposed settlement of the dispute.

In mid-December 2002, the **EU summit** in Copenhagen announced in a statement that "Turkey is a candidate state destined to join the union"; this text fell rather short of the Turks' desire for a fixed date to begin accession negotiations, and Erdoğan accused the EU of double standards compared to its treatment of central European candidate states who were to be whisked through the door after a mere decade in waiting. The US and Britain, stalwart international supporters of Turkey and anxious not to alienate their crucial Middle Eastern ally in the build up to a possible war against Iraq, were unable to overcome a Franco–German axis resistant to setting a firm date. Despite Turkish disappointment, it was progress of a sort. Providing Turkey passes a human rights review in December 2004, and a solution to the Cyprus problem is found before the Greek-Cypriot government of the island joins the EU in May 2004, it seems likely that Turkey's decades-long effort to join the "European Club" will eventually succeed.

The twenty-first century

The risk of a successful Taliban-style **Islamic revolution** in Turkey has never been high, despite AK's electoral victory – and luridly irresponsible reporting thereof in the Western media. Mainstream Sunni Islam in Turkey is essentially different, long tempered by "heterodox" dervish sects under the leadership of charismatic *şeyhs*, which presided over the peaceful fusing of the original Anatolian Christian population with the Turkish settlers. The Christian minority has now dwindled to a few thousand Greek Orthodox, Armenian Apostolic and Syrian Orthodox adherents, though Alevî (Shi'ite) numbers are variously estimated at between one in seven and one in five of the population, a joint legacy of Turcoman nomadism, medieval Iranian influence and the Bektaşi dervish order. Since 1923, society's upper crust, the so-called "White Turks" – comprising academia, the army, the civil service and (more recently) big business and the media – have ruled the Republic under the ideology of secular Kemalism, and can still be counted on to oppose Gulf-style Islam.

Another military **coup** would have neither public nor overseas support, since such action would scupper Turkey's chances of entering the European Union. Equally important, coups are demonstrably ineffective in the long term; the period since 1987 has witnessed the gradual yet total reversal of the 1980–1983 regime's agenda. Everything and everyone that the generals sought to eradicate has returned either briefly or permanently – including DİSK, which has helped the workforce regain the right to strike. Cynics observe that the army discreetly does as it pleases through the NSC, having grown progressively more sophisticated in using civilian politicians as window-dressing for foreign consumption. But President Sezer is an experienced and adroit constitutional jurist, and under his aegis civilian politicians and the military seem to have agreed to consult and respect each other's views without allowing dangerous rifts to develop.

The stability a **majority government** brings is crucial for Turkey to move forward, implement legislation necessary to satisfy EU criteria, and return hope to ordinary Turks, whose standard of living has plunged dramatically since 1991. Establishment politicians have lamentably failed the poor, presiding over repeated crises, which opened the way for the huge protest vote for AK. This party, most of whose members were until recently devoutly opposed to joining a "Christian" organization, now views EU entry as the best way to raise their voters' standard of living, thus assuring re-election. Increasingly, political debate in Turkey is not about secularism versus Islam, but pro- and anti-EU (the latter banner carried until lately by the now-discredited MHP), and pro- or anti-globalization. The Turkish business sector in particular, having submitted to the customs union and the consequent challenge to their domestic monopolies, is impatient to reap the full rewards of inward infrastructure investment and subsidies.

Despite the economic disaster of 2001, Turkey seems poised to become a major **regional power**, a role not actively played since World War I. On the other hand, Turkish governments since the early 1990s have proven perversely adept at mismanaging the economy. The resulting huge debt burden (over 90 percent of GNP, the result of five effective national bankruptcies since 1950), the new government's lack of experience, and a reliance on the US to ensure the goodwill of the IMF and other lenders makes Turkey highly exposed to both the current global economic slowdown and US political manipulation. Full acceptance into the EU would remove these vulnerabilities, and preclude any anti-democratic backsliding. It's an open question whether the new leadership has the necessary stature and determination to stay the course politically and economically, though the early signs are encouraging.

The EU membership question

Many Turkish intellectuals have long considered **EU membership** a due reward for past services rendered to NATO, or imagine that Turkey will thus be passively insured against further rule by its military or other undemocratic elements. European parliamentarians, however, periodically point out that three EU members – Spain, Portugal and Greece – with a recent history of authoritarian regimes had disposed of them and most of their legacy well in advance of joining, and that more proactive remedial measures on Turkey's part are expected.

Accordingly, MPs are now at work on a **new "European style" constitution**, to replace the 1982 army-drafted model. A new constitution will hopefully deny MPs the immunity from criminal prosecution for non-violent offences (ie corruption) that they currently enjoy. Enhanced police training is also being introduced, and anyone summoned to a police station will now be read their rights before being interviewed.

Europe has already brought pressure on Turkey to effect various other **reforms** in preparation for membership, and if the Ankara parliament approves the measures up for debate, EU sceptics such as the French and Germans will have difficulty refusing Turkey entry when the hour comes. But a substantial body of European opinion still sees Turkey as a Third World country inherently unsuitable for membership in a "white, Christian" club that would be overwhelmed by Turkey's seemingly intractable economic problems and geographically lopsided development. Left unsaid is the threatening prospect of a new member state second in population only to Germany, with concomitant demands for influence in the inner councils of EU power. Though three-fourths of the population in principle favour EU membership, about half the Turkish public remains sceptical, convinced that Turkey – despite "associate membership" since 1964, and customs union membership since the millennium – will be kept waiting indefinitely. There is also deep resentment that so many ex-Communist republics were admitted so readily without a simultaneous firmer commitment to Turkish membership.

The economy

One of the chief **economic measures** required and already implemented has been a sharp reduction in agricultural subsidies. The purchase prices of staple crops handled by government agencies has in consequence dropped, and farmers forced to amalgamate into larger units or quit the land. This, coupled with steadily diminishing water supplies to upland farms, has accelerated urban drift and the growth of a vast underclass of uneducated unemployed; not surprisingly theft, once almost unknown, has become a minor nuisance. The only industrial bright spot is the probability that Turkey may soon become one of the world's leading auto manufacturers, as overseas names set up plants to take advantage of cheap labour. Enhanced social security and unemployment benefits are also due to materialize, but will cost vast sums to fund – most readily done by bringing large numbers of currently non-tax-paying individuals into the revenue net; new income tax legislation is scheduled for 2003. In tandem with all this will be a slimming down of the grossly hypertrophied, inefficient and life-tenured civil service, estimated at one in five of the work force; imminent privatization of Turkish Airlines, Türk Telekom and the last four state-owned banks can only help the country's Euro-credentials.

The results of the old junta's, and ANAP's, 1980s policies are now almost irreversible, insitutionalized as a yawning (and growing) **disparity in incomes** between the top and bottom of the heap, second globally only to Brazil. The changed economic landscape has worked to the advantage of speculators and wheeler-dealers, and to the detriment of farmers, tradesmen and wage-earners;

the rich, ensconced in comfortable suburbs of İstanbul, grow richer as they dabble in government contracts, speculate on the stock exchange or live off their *rentier* incomes. Such inequalities – strongly correlated with a galloping rate of inflation historically been fuelled by the world's largest arms-import programme – will continue to provide grist for demagogues exploiting social discontent if AK stumbles.

A new political era?

It might not be too much to hope that the 2002 elections and EU-prompted reforms will finally stop the chronic and fundamental **immaturity of civilian politics**, long dominated by a coterie of aging dinosaurs who had been around since the 1960s. For years there were few young, outstanding politicians about (apart from Recep Tayyip Erdoğan); everyone knew that ultimately the military called the tune, so ambitious, capable graduates went into business rather than politics. At the same time, there were always far too many parties (32 were officially registered in 1998, and 23 contested the 2002 poll), mostly rump factions of older parties formed by defecting MPs and their cronies, long on personality cults and short on issues.

Since November 3, 2003, the traditional parties now excluded from parliament have all demanded their leaders' heads as the price of failure; Çiller and Yılmaz in particular, both threatened with renewed criminal investigations, are rumoured to be considering prolonged self-exile in countries having no extradition treaty with Turkey. ANAP is now shattered, with no obvious candidate to lead it; many of its former ministers are likely to be tried for corruption, still a debilitating constant in all walks of Turkish life. The DYP is lately the haunt of out-and-out gangsters, and it may now merge with ANAP, now that their two ex-leaders joined in mutual loathing have retired. Only the old and frail Ecevit still heads the ruins of the DSP, poised to die with him; the equally demolished MHP has retreated to its grass roots and is unlikely to contest the next election.

The other potentially important political players are the **Kurds**. Their traditional party, HADEP, has dissolved itself and is further handicapped by having five of its leaders imprisoned for attempting to take parliamentary oaths in Kurdish. The European Union is pressing for a retrial, while the AK Party, having some sympathy with political detainees, could declare an amnesty. This may give HADEP's successor, DEHAP, the boost needed to gain a substantial minority of seats in the next parliament – if AK consents to reduce the minimum nationwide vote percentage from ten to five percent.

The Iraq question

As of writing, all public life in Turkey is being overshadowed by the US **military action in Iraq**. During late 2002, Turkish leaders were feted in Washington, and wooed with promises of arms, cancellation of debts and other compensation for the damage to be inflicted on Turkey's economy, in particular the tourism sector and revived trade with Iraq. US weaponry already accounts for 60 percent, or $2.3 billion, of the Turkish military's annual $4 billion procurement budget.

The local conspiracy-theorist view was that the early 2002 elections were engineered by the US to place the AK Party in power with a full majority, and now AK would have to return the favour by ensuring **full Turkish co-operation** over Iraq. However, war remained deeply unpopular with a basically conservative, Muslim public, and the military and civilian authorities stood in broad agreement on the goals of any involvement. Both had deep reservations about a campaign that could result in a divided Iraq, with a separate Kurdish state created in the former "no-fly zone" north of the 36th parallel.

Since Turkey was never compensated for economic losses – estimated at up to $50 billion – incurred during the 1991 war, the official position was that unless the UN endorsed military action, Turkey would not accept US requests to station 80,000 soldiers on Turkish soil, and to have use of assorted ports, air-bases (specifically İncirilik) and other facilities. The military knew that over-zealous co-operation with the US would be viewed with disfavour by the EU (excepting, perhaps, Britain), and their natural inclination was to participate in the European Defence Force as a way to enhance their prestige at home and abroad prior to EU membership. The future of any Baghdad regime is crucially important to Turkey, whose preference for a unitary, strongly centralized, post-Saddam Iraq stands at odds with the most prevalent model of a weak federal state.

Relations with the Middle East

The untried AK party will have its hands full encouraging the stubborn Turkish Cypriot leader Rauf Denktaş to compromise on the **Cyprus issue** and agree to a settlement for the island's unification. The UN-backed proposals for a federal state seem acceptable (barring a few minor adjustments) to most observers – including the Greek- and Turkish-Cypriot electorate, to whom it will be put as a referedum – though the ailing Denktaş himself has declined to say a good word about them. Since over ninety percent of Turkish Cypriots now demand a durable solution to the long-running conflict – and massive street demonstrations to this effect convulsed Turkish Nicosia throughout early 2003 – he will have difficulty in refusing to sign a treaty unless the Turkish military intervene on his behalf. By February 28, 2003, a "final offer" will have been made to Cyprus to join the European Union, but without a settlement this effectively means the Greek-Cypriot-controlled Republic of Cyprus rather than the entire island.

By contrast, the **European Defence Force** issue has now been resolved with a compromise allowing Turkey some veto rights over the use of the force. However unappreciated it often feels for doing the US's bidding in the region, strategic realities also make it unlikely that Turkey will ever leave NATO; Russia remains an unknown quantity, while relations with Iran and Syria always proceed on a rollercoaster basis.

Simultaneously, Turkey forges an ever-closer **relationship with Israel** – especially militarily, with joint naval exercises and the Israeli air force training Turkish pilots while using Turkish airspace for its own training. Turkey is one of the few Muslim countries that Israelis can visit, and many do (though less so since the casinos closed). These ties have of course done nothing to improve Turkish–Arab relations. The probability of a new, harder-line Israeli government taking advantage of an Iraqi war to utterly crush the Palestinians is something that pre-2003 Turkish governments haven't really pondered; it remains to be seen whether the AK government will consider itself more than sentimentally responsible for fellow Muslims.

Turkish-Arab relations have also been seriously clouded by the highly controversial **İlisu Dam** project on the Tigris River, which – along with the massive Atatürk Dam on the Euphrates – would have deprived downstream states Syria, Iraq and Jordan of even more water in an already drought-prone region.

International lending agencies dropped İlisu after concluding that it would be politically destabilizing and environmentally disastrous, forcing the UK government to withdraw its financial support. Turkey's current shaky financial position should enforce a medium-term moratorium on large new projects; it's also possible that the new government will act more sympathetically towards neighbouring states and reverse the policy of **dam-building** as strategic weapon.

Relations with other countries

If the European customs union and elevation to EU candidacy prove an indefinite limbo, Turkey's century-long commitment to the West will face its most serious challenge since Atatürk's time. Disillusion with his restrictive ideology, if not the cult of his personality, has long been widespread, and since Özal the main question has always been what the change in national direction will be, not whether there will be one. Following the precipitate collapse of the Soviet Union, and the ongoing realignment of the Balkans, wider **regionalist options** have come to the fore as some familiar dynamics of Turkish history reassert themselves.

The independent, ex-Soviet republics of **Central Asia and the Caucasus** were, throughout the 1990s, assiduously courted in mildly **pan-Turkic** terms, and Erdoğan is looking at ways to revitalize these ties. Such overtures, competing with those of fundamentalist Shia Iran, have been quietly encouraged by the US, which seeks a mildly Sunni counterbalance in the region. After a meagre start in the early Nineties, Turkish business investment in Kazakhstan, Uzbekistan, Turkmenistan and Kyrghizia topped $6.5 billion by 1995, with civil engineering projects at the forefront.

Oil pipelines from these regions are the most frequently proposed works: to supply oil-deprived Turkey, to banish messy and dangerous tanker traffic from the Bosphorus, and to enable the country to act as a toll-collecting conduit for petroleum products to the West. Thus far the only project that looks set to get off the drawing board is the Baku-Ceyhan line, moving oil from Azerbaijan and Kazakhstan to İskendurun on the Mediterranean. **Natural gas supply** agreements are far more evolved: besides Russian gas being pumped under the Black Sea to Samsun, Turkey is receiving natural gas from Azerbaijan and Iran, despite US pressure to shun a member of the "axis of evil"; trade with Iran, both official and unofficial, is lively and growing.

In the Caucasus, **Azerbaijan** – the most closely linked to Turkey by language, history and (via Nakichevan) a common border – has seen the greatest direct political involvement by Turkey. Successive Turkish governments have ridden out swells of public opinion calling for active official military assistance to the Azeris in their long-running struggle with the Armenians, mindful since Cyprus of the dire consequences of such an intervention – though "freelance" Turkish volunteers and weaponry have certainly found their way to the theatre of war. Since the late 1990s there has been a slight thaw in Turkish relations with **Armenia**, pending a negotiated settlement of the Nagorno-Karabagh issue; however Turkey's refusal to accept responsibility for the 1895 and 1915 massacres and deportations means that contacts are unlikely to develop further, and this denial gives Turkey's opponents a constant source of ammunition. Should Turko–Armenian relations stay chilly, a direct rail line from Kars to the Georgian capial of Tblisi is planned to bypass the currently disused indirect line through Armenian territory.

Hand in hand with pan-Turkism, there has been a whiff of old-fashioned Ottomanism, as Turkey took an increased interest in its former Balkan possessions, from which the forefathers of many contemporary Turks emigrated and which retain some Muslim population. At Özal's urging, Turkey sent officers to retrain the army of predominantly Muslim **Albania**, as well as civilian economic aid and advisers. Relations with **Bulgaria** are vastly improved since the ethnic-Turkish-dominated DPS party served as a partner in the ruling coalition there. Turkey was among the first countries to recognize the republic of **Macedonia** under that name, much to the outrage of Greece, and the very first to send an ambassador. A Turkish-funded motorway, designed to compete with and bypass Greece's ongoing Via Egnatia project, was mooted to transit Bulgaria, Macedonia and Albania, ending on the Adriatic, but has been shelved indefinitely.

The Kurdish question

The majority of people in the Tigris valley, the Lake Van region and in the mountains between Erzurum, Erzincan and Diyarbakır are Kurds, an originally nomadic people speaking an Indo-European language related to Farsi. They have been here for millennia, though their exact origins are obscure, and it seems most likely that they are the offspring of more than one ethnic group.

Some authorities consider them descended from, or identical to, the "Karduchi" who gave Xenophon's Ten Thousand so much trouble; others have described the nursery of the Kurds as either the Hakkâri mountains in present-day Turkey, or the Zagros range in western Iran. Their traditional **nomadic culture** focused on horse-breeding and pastoralism, practices which brought Kurds into perennial conflict with farmers and town-dwellers; today a far higher proportion have adopted a settled lifestyle.

The Kurds have never been united as a state, owing partly to their traditional organization in **clans** – not unlike Scottish Highland ones – further grouped into tribes headed by all-powerful hereditary ağas, or chieftains. There exist four mutually unintelligible **dialects** of the Kurdish tongue, two of them (Kurmanji and Zaza) spoken in Turkey. Kurds are further subdivided by **religious affiliation**, being both Sunni and Shi'ite Muslim – proportions varying by region – or members of two small heterodox sects, the Yezidis and the Ahl-i-Haqqi. In Turkey, Shi'ite (Alevî) Kurds are concentrated near Erzincan and Tunceli, while in the southeast the Naqshbandi (Nakşibendi) and Qadiri (Kadiri) dervish orders have historically claimed many Kurdish adherents.

The **number** of Kurds in Turkey is a contentious subject, but sober estimates reckon over eleven million out of a population of sixty million, the largest Kurdish population in the Middle East. (Iraqi Kurds – so much in the news recently – constitute, at 23 percent, a greater proportion of that country, but at only four million a much smaller absolute number.) Modern Turkish governments have always disputed Kurdish numbers and their geographic distribution, and indeed have usually denied that Kurds have a distinct ethnic and linguistic identity at all, describing them in official propaganda as "mountain Turks" who have forgotten their racial origins.

The Kurds in pre-Republican Turkey

Under the Ottomans, the majority **Sunni Kurds** were regarded in the same way as other Muslim but non-Turkic subjects, such as the Arabs or Circassians, enjoying no special *millet* (nation) status like the Christian and Jewish religious minorities. The sultans found their warlike qualities useful, using them often as a mobile, irregular raiding force on the frontiers with Russia and Persia. Under Sultan Abdülhamid, they were also allowed to terrorize both Alevî Kurds and the Armenians, their settled neighbours and hereditary enemies across much of eastern Anatolia.

After the Ottoman collapse in 1918, the victorious Allies, in response to pleas from certain Kurdish nationalists, briefly mooted the establishment of a

Kurdish state straddling the current borders of Iraq, Turkey and Iran. Most Kurds, however, continued in their martial tradition, standing by the Kemalists in their struggle against the Armenians in the east and the Greeks in the west, the two greatest threats to a Muslim-dominated Anatolian state. But following the Turkish Nationalist victory in 1922, the Kurds found themselves poorly rewarded for their loyalty, as any special privileges for them were explicitly withdrawn.

The first modern rebellions

At the same time as the abolition of the caliphate in 1924, all Kurdish-interest societies were banned. **Resistance** to these measures was not long in coming, though at first it was Islamic fundamentalist, rather than explicitly Kurdish nationalist, in character. In 1925, a Nakşibendi *şeyh* (dervish leader) north of Diyarbakır mounted a rebellion which took two months for the government to crush; at its conclusion all dervish orders were suppressed nationwide. Almost immediately another insurrection, this time of a more overtly Nationalist and secular character and supported by Iran, broke out near Mount Ararat. Only in 1929 was this completely quelled, when Iranian backing for the rebels was withdrawn. In 1936 yet another revolt, by the Alevî Kurds of Dersim (thereafter renamed Tunceli), took the Turkish army two years to put down. To each of these rebellions the central Turkish government responded harshly with executions and deportations of villagers to the west, as well as suppression of any local Kurdish cultural manifestations. Most of the east was designated as a **military zone** – long before relations with the Soviet Union had soured – in order to give the army a free hand against the Kurds.

Thereafter Kurds could participate in Turkish public life only inasmuch as they **assimilated**. Kurdish concerns had to be addressed under the vaguer rubric of "development of the east" and – after 1960 – in conjunction with generalist left-wing parties where Kurds could have a voice. Before this Sunni Kurdish society had been essentially semi-feudal, subject to the *ağas* who would deliver their charges' vote in return for minimal benefits from Ankara. Alevî Kurds in particular, however, have since the Sixties tended to espouse left-wing beliefs, making them the target of pogroms by Muslim fundamentalist and/or rightist activists, most notably at Kahraman Maraş in 1978. The military interventions of 1971 and 1980 were notably hard on leftist parties in general and anything specifically smacking of Kurdish sectarianism, providing fertile ground for the rise of the PKK (*Partia Karkaris Kurdistan*, the "Kurdistan Workers' Party"). This group therefore represented a continuation, albeit an ideologically extreme one, of Kurdish rejection of forced assimilation or marginalization.

The PKK: beginnings

The **PKK** (pronounced "Peh-Ka-Ka" in Turkey) was founded in November 1978 by **Abdullah Öcalan**, a political science student in Ankara, with the express intent of establishing a Marxist, Kurdist-run state in southeastern Turkey. While other Kurdish-separatist manifestos of the 1970s may have been better articulated, the PKK was able to appeal to numerous poor and badly educated Kurdish youths, without realistic prospects in the underdeveloped southeast, with the possibility of direct guerrilla action.

After the 1980 military intervention, "**Apo**" – as Öcalan came to be known – fled to Syria and established training camps with the assistance of the Syrian government and the PLO; more camps were opened later in Lebanon's Beq'aa valley. By summer 1984, the PKK felt strong enough to begin its **guerrilla campaign**, infiltrating southeastern Turkey and initially targetting isolated *jandarma* posts. The Turkish government responded by declaring **martial law** in the affected provinces, sealing the border with Syria and raiding PKK installations across the Syrian frontier.

The PKK quickly widened its attacks to include civilians it branded as accomplices of the Turkish state and representatives of the old "feudal" order, namely large landowners and conservative tribal chiefs. In 1986 the central government effectively augmented this class by creating the **village guards**, Kurds demonstrably loyal to the government who were provided with antiquated weapons. The better-armed PKK had no difficulty in dispatching them, often massacring their entire families in the process. **Schools**, seen by the PKK as centres for government indoctrination and Turkification, were also routinely destroyed, and teachers targetted, further aggravating the already high local illiteracy rate. Village life in much of the Tigris basin and Van region gradually became unbearable, with populations divided into pro- and anti-PKK factions – often merely covers for pursuing old feuds. Much of the rural population was threatened by each side with dire consequences for co-operating with the other, and both the government and the PKK used increasingly coercive techniques for recruiting young men.

By 1988, the regular **army** had replaced the gendarmerie in the suppression of the PKK, which in turn forged a provisional alliance with urban terrorist groups such as Dev Sol, allowing it to commit outrages in the larger western cities. Apo granted a few interviews to Turkish journalists, publication of which sparked court proceedings and a progressively more stringent **blackout** on media coverage of PKK statements.

The PKK in politics and battle

Between late 1989 and early 1991, the Kurdish question as a whole came increasingly to dominate Turkish public opinion, as well as perceptions of Turkey abroad. By its various actions the PKK succeeded indirectly in splitting both the ANAP government, and the DYP–SDP coalition which succeeded it in October 1991, between those favouring a more conciliatory approach to the Kurds and those advocating the continuation of the iron fist.

October 1989 marked the inauguration of a specifically Kurdish-based parliamentary **political party**, though of course under existing laws it could not (and still cannot) be identified as such. Seven deputies from the opposition SHP (Social Democrat Party), who had attended an international conference on Kurdish affairs, were expelled upon their return to Turkey for "weakening national feeling by appealing to narrow class or ethnic interests". They formed the **HEP** (Popular Labour Party), which drew more defectors from the ranks of the SHP as time went on, especially after the autumn 1991 elections. In June 1993 the HEP was forcibly disbanded, only to quickly reform as the **DEP**

(Democracy Party), with essentially the same personnel and aims. DEP in turn was compulsorily shut down in June 1994, only to be succeeded by the broadly similar **HADEP** (People's Democratic Party). By year's end, ten former HEP deputies and six DEP MPs, stripped of parliamentary immunity, had been tried by State Security Courts and sentenced to terms of up to fifteen years for "separatist activities" (ie clandestine PKK membership) – verdicts widely condemned by American and European parliamentarians. Once in jail, lower-ranking PKK activists or fellow-travellers could expect miserable treatment even by the appalling standards of Turkish prisons; mid-1996 saw hunger strikes by more than two hundred inmates in protest at prevailing conditions.

In the eastern hills, a **yearly pattern** had been established by 1990: the government would announce sweeping military measures to crush the rebels over the winter and early spring, when they were at their most vulnerable, with specially trained commando units wielding increasingly sophisticated hardware. (Purchase of such overseas technology, in defiance of human-rights-group-inspired embargos, has occasionally had international repercussions, as in the 1992 resignation of a German defence minister who had approved the surreptitious transfer of tanks to Turkey; the Turkish reaction has been to conclude arms deals with the less fastidious Russian Federation, and to start constructing its own fighter aircraft.) The PKK in turn would usually "celebrate" **Nawroz**, the Kurdish New Year, by some particularly bloody atrocity, inaugurating the summer season of incidents. As the decade wore on, the PKK grew bolder militarily, mounting attacks not just in the mountains but near and within sizable towns. By 1995 the PKK could muster an estimated 15,000 guerrillas, or *peshmergas*, in the field, plus perhaps 75,000 "part-time" militants. Already by 1992 there had been mass resignations of village guards who no longer wished to risk their lives for an administration that did not protect them adequately. Subsequently there was a marked increase in the severity of the government's punitive responses; by early 1997 **over two thousand villages** in both the southeast and Tunceli had been either bombed or forcibly evacuated, and then burnt to the ground, on suspicion of co-operating with the PKK, or merely for not enrolling in the village-guard scheme. Up to **one million internal refugees**, who filled shantytowns around Diyarbakır and western cities, were thus created.

The two main Iraqi Kurdish factions, hostile to the PKK for various reasons – among them its support for Saddam Hussein – have since 1991 been persuaded to cooperate in regular Turkish cross-border efforts to eradicate PKK bases in **Iraq**. These increased in frequency and magnitude as the US-proclaimed safe-haven zone effectively became a farce; the biggest incursion took place in late March 1995, when 35,000 Turkish troops plus supporting air cover and artillery crossed the frontier in a bid to definitively wipe out PKK training camps in the area. Four months and numerous civilian casualties later, Turkish forces pulled out, though Turkey has since created a permanent "zone of influence" and marked out a "line of control" well inside the Iraqi frontier, similar to the one deployed by the Israelis in Lebanon.

The PKK in turn became more sophisticated in its repertoire of **unarmed actions**, mobilizing large street demonstrations, staging ostentatious funerals of slain HEP, DEP, HADEP or PKK personnel and inspiring shopkeeper strikes in large southeastern towns. The government played into its hands with a string of decrees muzzling press coverage of events and authorizing the deportations of troublemakers or the relocation of villagers from sensitive areas.

Those funerals were evidence of an ominous trend, parallel to a general one in Turkish society at large: the regular **assassination** or "**disappearance**" of non-violent activists and politicians (HEP/DEP/HADEP in these cases), by "unknown assailants", never apprehended or charged, but widely believed to be shadowy, organized groups of Kurdish Hizbullah fundamentalists or far-right Turkish nationalists operating with the indulgence of the army and gendarmerie. Such killings continued unabated through the 1990s, averaging several individuals per month, with corpses often found mutilated by the roadside or buried in rubbish tips.

The PKK further **diversified tactics** between 1992 and 1996, with demonstrations and attacks on Turkish property and diplomatic missions **overseas**, as well as the abduction of numerous foreigners in the southeast. In early 1993 they offered a unilateral ceasefire, to include the traditional Nawroz offensive season. When that did not elicit a matching government response, the PKK announced the targeting of Turkey's **tourist industry**, one of the country's main foreign-exchange earners, with warnings that the battle would be carried to the resorts. Thus numerous bombings in İstanbul, Fethiye, Marmaris, Antalya and Kuşadası were carried out during 1993 and 1994, with 26 fatalities and many more wounded, accompanied by a brief dip in tourist numbers.

The PKK's **inner command circle** was by most accounts a very unpleasant bunch, steeped in Stalinist cant (and methodology) of the 1950s and 1960s, allegedly financing their operations by opium-smuggling in the Van area (as did pro-government Kurds) now that conventional Eastern Bloc support had dried up, and valuing the lives of their ever-younger and more inexperienced recruits as little as those of their victims. Despite all this, Europeans have been apt to romanticize the PKK, thanks partly to its vigorous "public relations" efforts overseas.

Beginning in the mid-1990s, there was a mixed but increasingly hostile reaction by various European governments to the PKK. While the Netherlands, to the considerable ire of Turkey, tolerated the convening of a self-styled "Kurdish Parliament in Exile" in April 1995, and the Greeks provided consistent, surreptitious support for PKK activities, the German and French governments shut down PKK offices in their countries later that year at Turkish diplomatic instigation, and the Belgians, in mid-1996, raided the Brussels-based satellite station **MED TV**, which had been broadcasting in the various Kurdish dialects. MED promptly resurfaced in London, licensed by the Independent Television Commission (ITC), where it gained an audience even amongst non-Kurds for its incisive coverage, despite being jammed by the Turkish authorities.

The war winds down

Throughout 1997 and the first half of 1998, the PKK insurrection appeared to be losing impetus, as the Turkish army's increasingly sophisticated weaponry and tactics took their toll on the beleaguered guerrillas. This weakness was demonstrated by Öcalan's renewed call for a unilateral ceasefire in late summer following the appointment of a new chief of staff, General Hüseyin Kıvrıkoğlu. Öcalan's appeals for negotiation fell on deaf ears, as the army opted for a military rather than a diplomatic solution.

Pressure was exerted on the PKK's main backer, **Syria**, to close down Öcalan's headquarters in Damascus. Turkish troops moved to the Syrian border and threatened invasion; economically, diplomatically and militarily weaker than Turkey, Damascus backed down. Öcalan was **expelled** in late October 1998, and after a short sojourn in Iran and then Moscow, was arrested in Rome in mid-November. The Italians refused to extradite Öcalan back to a country (Turkey) that still retained the death penalty, provoking outrage there. The Italian embassy and consulate in İstanbul were attacked by angry mobs, and an economic embargo was placed on Italian goods. The football association UEFA went so far as to postpone the scheduled cup clash between Juventus and Galatasaray in Istanbul.

In limbo **in Italy**, Öcalan used the opportunity to call for displaced Kurdish villagers to be allowed to return to their homes, for the disbanding of the village-guard system, for local Kurdish autonomy within Turkey and recognition of their cultural identity. Öcalan's pleas were ignored in Turkey, and the war against the PKK if anything intensified. The Italians, in an untenable situation, pressured Öcalan to leave Italy. After more asylum quests to Russia and Greece, he eventually turned up in mid-February 1999 at the Kenyan Greek embassy where, to the jubilation of most Turks, he was **captured** in a secret operation by MIT (Turkish intelligence service) operatives. Both the Israeli secret service, Mossad, and the CIA were thought to have assisted Turkey with tip-offs as to his whereabouts.

Following Öcalan's arrest, more than three hundred **incidents** linked to the PKK and Kurdish sympathizers took place, most seriously the bombing of a shopping centre in İstanbul that caused thirteen deaths. Kurds and their supporters protested, sometimes violently, both within Turkey and in many European cities. In Berlin, three Kurdish demonstrators were shot dead by guards outside the Israeli consulate; in London, a teenage Kurdish girl set herself alight outside the Greek embassy in protest at Turkey's treatment of her people. MED TV, after six months on probation by the ITC, was taken off the air in March 1999, for carrying interview quotes urging violence in Turkey in revenge for Öcalan's capture, and for "breaching the impartiality and incitement sections of the programming code".

In the April 1999 Turkish **general elections**, pro-Kurdish HADEP polled only 4.6 percent of the vote, falling well short of the ten percent needed to send deputies to parliament. HADEP did, however, gain Turkey's most important Kurdish city, Diyarbakır, in the municipal elections. More surprisingly, HADEP almost won Mersin, a Mediterranean city in a predominately Turkish area. This amply demonstrated just how many Kurds have been forced westward by the war in the southeast.

The Turks were left with the problem of what to do with Öcalan. Public opinion demanded his execution, but the more pragmatic realized that eliminating Öcalan could scupper Turkey's chance of joining the EU. After a June **show trial** on the heavily guarded prison islet of İmralı, in which Öcalan cravenly recanted his violent campaign and pleaded to be allowed to live as a force of reconciliation, he was found **guilty** of both murder and treason, both capital crimes according to law and the constitution. The Turkish parliament, however, had to ratify the **death sentence**, and with 47 prisoners ahead of Öcalan on Death Row, it seemed unlikely that the death sentence would be carried out. In what Turkish cynics denounced as a further attempt to save his neck, Öcalan appealed in August for all armed *peshmergas* to leave Turkey for Iraq and Iran; the government dismissed this virtual surrender and beefed up border security with infrared night-vision devices.

The end of the armed struggle

Despite objections from the ultra-Nationalist MHP, and relatives of soldiers killed in battle with the PKK, in January 2000 the Turkish parliament bowed to EU pressure and agreed to delay implementation of Öcalan's death sentence until the European Court of Human Rights had given its verdict on the case. In February the PKK **renounced their armed struggle** (in response to Öcalan's earlier appeal) but this did not prevent the authorities clamping down on more moderate Kurds, and later the same month the HADEP mayors of three southeastern cites were arrested and charged with aiding "separatists", ie the PKK.

In May, Turkish forces launched a major incursion into the Kurdish enclave of northern Iraq, where the majority of the PKK's remaining forces were based; over fifty guerillas were killed. Students of Kurdish history were not surprised to find the Kurds once again indulging in internecine warfare, with KDP (Kurdish Democratic Party) *peshmerga* aiding the Turkish operation. Whether the moderate, pro-Western but essentially tribal KDP leader Masud Barzani was motivated by ideological opposition to the Marxist PKK, or pragmatism – because he realized that a strong PKK presence in Northern Iraq would invite more Turkish army incursions – is uncertain, but this uneasy alliance further weakened the PKK in their last "safe haven".

In June the Turkish military finally appeared to acknowledge what most moderate Turks had known all along – that military muscle may have sufficed to crush the PKK but was not enough to solve the "Kurdish problem" – and pressured Prime Minister Ecevit into announcing an **aid and redevelopment package** for the economically depressed southeastern provinces. Simultaneously, persecution of HADEP continued, with the arrest of 23 party members for protesting against the death penalty. Later in the year, against the background of proposed reforms allowing broadcasting and education in Kurdish, police closed a theatre in İstanbul which was staging a Kurdish-language play.

The year 2001 opened with another major Turkish army operation in Iraqi Kurdistan. On this occasion both Barzani's KDP and Jalal Talabani's PUK (Patriotic Union of Kurdistan) helped the Turks, leaving the beleaguered PKK with nowhere to hide. In Turkey itself the authorities followed up the military's successes against the PKK with further moves against HADEP, long suspected of having links with the PKK. In February police detained sixteen HADEP party members in the town of Batman for staging a protest against the disappearance of two activists – last seen in the hands of the authorities – and in March a state prosecutor sought a four-year jail sentence for the director of a publishing house that had printed a book about Öcalan. In August a Turkish human rights activist was detained following his investigation into abuses in Şırnak, where the military had evacuated two villages in retaliation for the death of a soldier in a landmine explosion, and in September a HADEP demonstration in Istanbul was broken up by police using teargas.

Following the effective **collapse of the PKK** as a viable fighting force on Turkish soil, 2002 saw Turkey's attention centered firmly on worrying developments in northern Iraq. With the increasing likelihood of US strikes on Iraq in the aftermath of the September 11 attack on New York, the Turkish government became increasingly concerned that the collapse of Saddam Hussein's regime would lead to the disintegration of Iraq and the emergence of a de jure independent Kurdish state in Iraq's "safe haven", rather than merely the de facto autonomous zone that had existed up until then. Anything that would indicate that Kurds – any Kurds – were capable of governing themselves was (and is) anathema to the Turkish state, and it became clear that the continuing Turkish military presence in the Kurdish enclave was as much about preventing a truly independent Kurdistan emerging as it was about blocking PKK cross-border raids. In August PUK leader Talabani claimed that the Turkish military had occupied an airfield in the Kurdish enclave; shortly thereafter, KDP leader Barzani called for Turkish troops to leave northern Iraq, and observed that the Turkish military presence in the region had increased significantly since the threat of a US strike on Iraq. In September, the Turkish Defence Minister appeared to revive irredentist Turkish claims to parts of Iraqi Kurdistan, asserting that the Iraqi cities of Mosul and Kirkuk were "Turkish soil". Barzani in turn announced that the Kurds were not aiming for independence, but that oil-rich Kirkuk (then under Baghdad's control) was an integral part of Iraqi Kurdistan.

Domestically, a positive development for Turkish Kurds was legislation passed in August abolishing the death penalty, thus sparing Öcalan, and guaranteeing the right of several minorities (including Kurds) to broadcast and educate in their own language. Until quite recently, such **reforms** – part of a judicial reform package aimed at EU accession – would have been unthinkable in a state that had strenuously denied the existence of the Kurds as a separate ethnic group, and demonstrated to the Kurds (among others) Turkey's apparently sincere desire to join the EU. Later the same month, one of the country's most famous and respected musicians, Sezen Aksu (an ethnic Turk), performed a concert in İzmir in which she sang in Kurdish (as well as Greek, Armenian and Judaeo-Spanish). Although she was predictably criticized by elements in the military and by ultra-Nationalist politicians, the majority of the mainstream press, the Culture Minister and many ordinary Turks applauded her brave attempt to heal the wounds of ethnic intolerance, exacerbated by the bitter insurrection in the southeast. This was more than symbolic progress: many ethnic Turks, particularly in the west of the country, had long nursed a racial hatred towards unassimilated Kurds, and in the past funerals of soldiers killed fighting the PKK had often been pretexts for anti-Kurdish demonstrations or violence. On a practical level, the lives of ordinary Kurds in the southeast have been eased considerably by the lifting – or as of writing, the imminent lifting – of emergency rule in all the "Kurdish" provinces.

With less than ten percent of the nationwide vote in the November 2002 elections, the pro-Kurdish **DEHAP** party, the new successor to HADEP (which had dissolved itself in order to avoid the worse fate of being banned), again failed to claim any parliamentary seats (despite the expected solid support in the southeastern provinces), suggesting that many Kurds elsewhere in Turkey view the moderate Islamists of the triumphant AK Party as more effective representatives of their views than the Kurdish-oriented DEHAP.

Prospects for the future

With the capture of Öcalan and the defeat of the PKK, there is no realistic prospect of an independent Kurdish state emerging in Turkey, and it appears that the Turkish authorities' hard-line stance towards crushing the PKK insurgency has proven successful – at the cost of nearly **50,000 deaths** on all sides, military and civilian, since 1984. Most of the organization's remaining forces are trapped in the Kurdish enclave of northern Iraq, plus a few more in ideologically uncongenial Iran. Öcalan's outdated ideology never really appealed to the proud but conservative rural Kurds, and even the dispossessed Kurds scratching out a living in the *gecekondu* shanties surrounding many of the country's cities were unconvinced by the PKK's Marxist cant. Öcalan's allure was always principally that of the "strong man" – a figurehead ruthless and brutal enough to take on the repressive Turkish authorities and instill some pride into the grindingly poor and downtrodden Kurds, but his capture and subsequent attempts to save himself by renouncing armed insurrection have effectively undermined this "hard man" image. Following the abolition of the death penalty, **Öcalan** will not hang, his remaining supporters will not have a martyr, and the influence he can wield from his prison cell will diminish still further.

Events over the border in **northern Iraq** could well have a bearing on the aspirations of Turkey's Kurds. Following the rapprochement between Masud Barzani's KDP and Jalal Talabani's PUK, the US-protected Kurdish enclave in northern Iraq is beginning to look more and more like an independent state, with its own parliament and proto-governmental institutions, and a healthy economy fuelled by massive western aid. The Turks are worried that should an explicitly Kurdish de jure state emerge – a distinct possibility if Iraq falls apart in the wake of an increasingly probable US-led invasion – Turkish Kurds in the southeast would have a considerable incentive to declare their own independence, or attempt to attach a number of provinces to a "Greater Kurdistan". Turkey is currently lobbying the US and other western allies to ensure the territorial integrity of a post-Saddam Iraq at all costs. Despite their need for Iraqi Kurdish support in the event of war, it is almost certain that the Americans will defer to the wishes of Turkey, their most important ally in the Middle East, and the Turkish military's role in "policing" a post-Saddam Iraq will be crucial. Assuming a successful "regime change" in Baghdad, the Turkish Army – already well ensconced in northern Iraq – will have a strong hand in shaping the future of Iraqi Kurdistan.

With EU accession talks set to begin sometime in 2004, pending a favourable review of Turkey's progress on **human rights**, the widespread and long-running detainment, torture and extra-judicial killing of Kurds must surely end if Turkey's cherished dream of joining the European "club" is to be realized. Now that the PKK is no longer a threat, Turkey will also need to fully accept the legitimacy of Kurdish-interest political parties like DEHAP, and continue to pass legislation enshrining freedom of thought and expression. That Kurds can now broadcast and educate in their own language is a hopeful sign that **cultural repression** of Turkish Kurds is on the wane.

Underpinning these reforms, however, must be a massive **regeneration** of the Kurdish provinces. Despite the end of the PKK insurrection, the economic outlook for millions of Kurds remains appalling. Unemployment is endemic, the infrastructure of the poorer quarters of cities such as Diyarbakır has virtually collapsed under the weight of migrants from the denuded countryside, and social problems have burgeoned as formerly tight-knit families crack under the strain. Despite much government propaganda about rural regeneration, the organization Human Rights Watch claims that only ten percent of the Kurds displaced (estimates vary between 380,000 and one million) during the fifteen-year conflict have returned to their villages. Many sold off their livestock, following bans on access to summer pastures, and now have no funds to renew their herds. Without economic aid to the Kurdish southeast (and assurance that it goes into the hands of the deserving poor rather than local drug-dealers or smugglers) there is always a risk that dispossessed and alienated Kurds will drift once again into extremist Islamic parties or militant Kurdish nationalist organizations such as a resurgent PKK.

For a country struggling with the consequences of chronic economic mismanagement and the crash of February 2001, it will be difficult to find the necessary cash to invest in the southeast, but if Turkey can do so, the outlook for local Kurds seems more hopeful than ever before. As Turkey moves gradually towards the EU, there's a real possibility of the nation's Kurds finally being accepted as ethnically distinct from, yet socially and politically an integral part of, an inclusive Turkish state conforming to European democratic norms.

Turkish music

Outside the country, Turkish music is mostly associated with the Mevlevî ("whirling") dervishes and usually unsuccessful efforts in the Eurovision song contest. Yet it has greatly influenced other music genres across the eastern Mediterranean and Balkans, and still has a huge following amongst the Turkish and Kurdish diaspora in northern Europe. Belying the stereotypes, there's an enticing variety, from refined classical forms to commercial *arabesk* by way of rural bards and fiery Gypsy ensembles.

As with language and ethnicity in Turkey, music has always been a major cultural battlefield. The state devoted great effort to constructing a unitary national culture upon the establishment of the Republic in 1923; Atatürk and others emphasized the purported ancestry of the Turks in central Asia, and conversely the supposed cultural distance of contemporary Turks from neighbouring Middle Easterners. This exercise involved highly implausible flights of historical imagination, and the often brutal repression of rival claims to cultural as well as political legitimacy within Turkey.

Although privately aficionados of Turkey's urban musical tradition, Atatürk and his cohorts deemed it too tainted by Arab civilization and minority contributions to be an exemplar of **Turkish national culture**. "The capacity of a country to change is demonstrated by its ability to change its music," he declared, and he set about doing exactly that by prohibiting the distribution of Arabic-language musical films, and by banning music sung in minority languages from the radio. Genuine folk and Western classical music were decreed to be the oddly twinned musical destinies of the nation. Accordingly, official musicologists fanned out across Anatolia during the late 1920s, charged with the responsibility of collecting, archiving and recording material that would flatter the racially based vanity of Nationalist ideologues. Incalculable harm was done as **melodies were standardized**, lyrics were purged of so-called vulgarities (ie non-Turkish passages) and ensemble playing was mandated. Spontaneity and improvization were banished, as (briefly) was unsupervized folk on the state-controlled radio.

A generation of musicians was trained to propagate folk music in a largely orchestral setting, and some of them still serve as the senior musical policy-makers on **state radio and television** (**TRT**), remaining faithful to the secularist vision of a hybrid Western and Anatolian-based culture. There do exist superb TRT archival tapes from the early 1960s, featuring such master solo practitioners as Niyazi Sayın and Akagündüz Kutbay on *ney*, Necdet Yaşar on *tanbur*, İhsan Özgen on *kemençe* and Hurşit Üngay on *küdüm*; but they were essentially "after-hours" material, not intended for mass broadcast, and the tradition of discipleship on which this type of music depends was very nearly broken.

This policy eventually ran aground. The classical art music genre known as *sanat* or *klasik*, associated mainly with the cosmopolitan Ottoman cities of İstanbul, İzmir and Bursa, underwent a process of recuperation, culminating in the foundation of a **public conservatory** in İstanbul in 1976. Here Turkish classical musicians were given the same quality of training as the previously privileged folk musicians, and orchestras of up to thirty intrumentalists and singers gained an increasing share of radio and television airplay, and the performers cited above were able to teach without hindrance.

A decade later, President Özal began **deregulating the media** as part of his stealthy dismantling of Atatürkist values. Pop, rock and *arabesk* (a supposedly

Arab-inspired popular genre, despised by the republican intelligentsia) began to fill the private FM radio stations, plus the satellite and cable TV channels which burgeoned semi-legally until being officially licensed in 1994. Faced with competition, TRT made efforts to update its large orchestral formats, while still managing to retain and attract charismatic and talented performers. More startlingly, Kurdish-lyrics folk music could be heard either live in trendy İstanbul cafés or purchased on recordings.

The same was true of religious and Sufi music. Following the forcible closure of the dervish *tekke*s in 1925, a widespread base of dynamical classical music was lost, or at the very least driven deep underground. Members of the Mevlevî order in particular had been great patrons of music across the Ottoman Empire, but until the 1980s, the Mevlevî *âyin* (their main musical ritual) was performed in public only as a kind of tourist attraction in Konya, the home of the order. Under Özal, who encouraged a public face for Islam, the Mevlevîs were principal beneficiaries. Not only is religious music now easily available as recordings, but the Mevlevî perform to a new generation of tourists and interested Turks in the restored Mevlevî lodge in Galata, and even occasionally in the Byzantine monuments of Sultanahmet.

Folk music

Turkish folk music is dominated by the **saz**, a long-necked fretted lute with a varying number of strings, played in a variety of styles. Large, heavily amplified orchestras of this instrument dominate **TRT-type folk music**. Performers associated with the TRT studios and the urban folk market can release up to two cassettes a year (often containing the same pieces heard on the radio, but with a few Western rock instruments grafted on), found in their hundreds in music shops and mobile street stalls. All bear the impress of **Belkis Akkale**'s tremendously successful style of the mid-1980s: large, buzzing *saz* orchestras, driving rhythms and a deep, soulful voice singing a *türkü* (folk song). A talented younger generation, including **Güler Duman** (specializing in Alevî music), **İbrahim Can** (from the Black Sea) and **Nuray Hafiftaş** (from eastern Turkey) maintain this tradition, though the TRT's cultural mandate and influence on the musical world was much reduced by the media deregulation of the 1990s.

Played as a solo instrument accompanying the voice, the *saz* has an intricate, silvery tone, providing not just notes and rhythmic patterns, but an ambience; it's a partner in a complex dialogue with the singer. Listen to **Ali Ekber Çicek**'s *Haydar Haydar*, an old recording by a TRT-trained musician that's a complex and dramatic creation largely of his own inspiration, but anchored in the expressive techniques of the *aşık* and Alevî mysticism. It's hard to say whether the instrument is accompanying the voice, or vice versa. Then listen, for contrast, to **Talip Özkan**'s intricate and idiosyncratic solo style, embracing a variety of Anatolian tunings and plectrum techniques, but with each musical phrase embellished to the utmost degree. There are those who favour playing with a plectrum and those who play without, plus many regional styles (*tavır* – literally, "attitudes") of playing and tuning (*düzen* – literally, "order"). Some players strive to maintain the regional *tavır*, others support a national style.

Percussion

Bendir or **bendil** Frame drums of assorted sizes.

Davul or **ramzalla** A large double-sided drum. Each side is used with different-sized sticks to create a bass-and-snare-drum-like effect.

Deblek, **dümbelek** or **dar(a)buka** (*demblik* in Kurdish) A goblet-shaped drum made of pottery, wood or metal and played with the hands.

Def A frame drum with added cymbals or metal rings inside the frame; also, a Kurdish bass drum.

Erbane Kurdish tambourine.

Kaşık A set of wooden or metal spoons, often brightly painted, that are manipulated like chopsticks by placing the handles of the spoons between the fingers.

Küdüm Small kettledrums usually played in pairs, with sticks, restricted to Ottoman classical or Mevlevî music.

Zil A pair of small cymbals.

Wind/reed instruments

Blur A Kurdish shepherd's flute made from a branch of either mulberry or walnut, with seven or nine finger-holes.

Çifte or **arghul** A double instrument sounding similar to the clarinet, with two mouthpieces and two sets of finger-holes on a pair of reed pipes. Often one set is used as a continuous drone. The *arghul* is found only in a small area near the Syrian border, and is related to the *arghoul* played in Egypt and Syria. The *çifte* is particular to the environs of Ereğli on the western Black Sea.

Kaval An end-blown flute made of wood, with seven finger-holes in the front and one thumb-hole at the back, and sometimes another at the side. A favourite instrument of Turkish shepherds.

Klarnet The Western valved clarinet, favoured by the Gypsies (especially the G-tuned), introduced across the lower Balkans by military bands during the 1870s.

Mey and **düdük** These are essentially the same, being called *mey* in most of Turkey but *düdük* in the northeast and in neighbouring Caucasian republics. Both are small and oboe-like instruments with a very large reed and a much sweeter tone than the *zurna*. Confusingly, *düdük* is also the name given to a simple duct flute which you see on sale at markets throughout the country.

Ney An end-blown flute requiring enormous skill to play, despite its simple design.

Regional music

Despite the heavy promotion of *saz*-based music by the TRT, many other varieties of folk music exist in Turkey today, recognizable by their associated instruments and dances. Outside the large cities in western Turkey, or in their shantytown suburbs, one can hear the quintessential **rural Turkish ceremonial music** combination, the *zurna* and *davul* (the shawm-and-drum duo found from the Balkans to as far east as China), at almost any wedding or circumcision celebration. Usually played by Gypsies, their enormous and unamplified volume indicates that something important is taking place – inevitably involving **folk dancing**. Dances are performed by segregated groups of men or women; if you're watching you'll invariably be asked to join. In the east this will most usually be the stately line dance known as *halay* (arms linked or on shoulders); on the Aegean coast the macho *zeybek*; and more or less everywhere the *çiftetelli* and *karşılama*, both couples' dances. Among Black Sea Turks

It is made from calamus reed or hardwood, with six finger-holes in front and a thumb-hole at the back.

Tulum A bagpipe found in Rize and Artvin provinces, near the Georgian border. It generally has two pipes, each with five finger-holes, inserted into a goatskin bag, which the player inflates before he begins. In Turkish Thrace, a nearly identical instrument is called a *gayda*.

Zurna (*zirne* in Kurdish) A very loud double-reed oboe-type instrument with seven finger-holes, made of wood with a conical body ending in a large bell.

String instruments

Cümbüş A fretless banjo-type lute which substitutes for the *ud* when playing with louder instruments. It has a large resonating metal bowl covered with skin or plastic.

Kanun A trapezoidal zither with between forty and a hundred strings, and a system of levers for tuning to different scales quickly.

Keman Originally a round-bodied version of the *kemençe*; now the name refers to a Western violin, preferred for its tone.

Kemençe or **kemançe** A fiddle with three strings, originally used by the shepherds of the Black Sea coast. It has an oblong wooden body and a short neck. The *kemençe* is held vertically and played with a bow of horsehair or, during more recent decades, nylon.

Rebab A pear-shaped relative of the *kemençe* used in classical and Mevlevî dervish music.

Saz A long-necked fretted lute, usually with seven strings (two pairs, and one set of three) played with a very thin plectrum. Variations include: the *divan saz*, with eight strings; the *cura saz*, with six strings; and the *bağlama*, with seven strings on a shorter neck and a large bulbous body.

Saz tambur A smaller fretted version of the *cümbüş*.

Tanbur or **tambur** A very long-necked lute with three strings and a large, almost rectangular body, noted for its very deep tone.

Ud A fretless lute with eleven strings (five pairs and one single), and nearly identical to the oud found throughout the Arab world.

Yaylı tanbur Bowed version of the *tanbur*, its tone somewhere between a cello and double bass.

or Laz people you'll hear a small upright fiddle (*kemençe*), the bagpipe (*tulum*) or smaller versions of the *zurna* and *davul* accompanying the *horon*, whose quick movements are said to imitate the wriggling of the *hamsi* – local anchovies that used to feature conspicuously in the diet. Most of the rural population know, at least passively, these regional dances and their music. In provincial cities, the *elektrosaz* and the *darbuka* (goblet drum) constitute the main proletarian musical fare for ceremonial occasions often held in *düğün salonları* or wedding salons for hire, and electric keyboards are now almost universal.

Cassette recordings of all of these kinds of music can be picked up from roadside stalls; their proprietors are usually well informed on highly rated local musicians. Regional genres and instruments are well represented in this cassette culture: look out for the *sipsi* (a plaintive double-reed mini-oboe) in the southwest; the *mey* in the southeast (lower and more mellow than the *sipsi*); accordion music played by Circassian migrants in the northeast; and Gypsy music to the sound of *darbuka*, valved clarinet, violin and *çümbüş* (a metal-bodied lute) from the west.

Contemporary musicians across the country are updating and reinventing local styles; many are only of specialist interest, but others make universally accessible music. A good example is Laz *kemençe* and *tulum* player **Birol Topaloğlu** from the Black Sea coast, who has collected and arranged regional songs in some striking albums.

Around eleven million **Kurds** live scattered within the political boundaries of Turkey, a fact only minimally acknowledged by the central government, which compulsorily labelled their music and dance as "Turkish" during its 1920s musicological expeditions. Traditionally, Kurdish folklore and national identity have been preserved through the help of the *dengbey* (bard), the *stranbey* (popular singer) and the *cirokbey* (storyteller). A *dengbey* is a singer with an exceptional memory, effectively the guardian of the Kurdish national heritage, since he must know hundreds of songs existing only in oral tradition. *Dengbey*s sing about the Kurdish myths and legends, the struggle for freedom and the successive rulers and occupiers of their land, as well as love songs and lighter entertainment. Sadly, some of the best Kurdish *dengbey*s, like **Şivan Perwer** and **Temo**, now live in exile in northern Europe, though since the late 1990s there has been an incremental relaxation on the ban of public Kurdish musical events and recording sales.

The main instruments used in Kurdish music are reed instruments such as the *blur* and the *düdük* – found in the mountainous regions where the echo from the hills is taken advantage of – and string instruments, such as the *tembur* and the *saz*, used in the towns of the plains.

Ozan or aşık music

There are claimed to be over fifteen million Alevîs in Turkey (out of a total population of nearly seventy million), so it's unsurprising that the best-known regional music, **ozan**, is associated with the **aşıks**, folk bards from these heterodox Muslim communities of inner Anatolia, especially the provinces of Sivas, Tunçeli, Çorum, Erzincan and Kars. These troubadours, literally "the ones in love", sing a repertoire of songs of mystical quest, interspersed with invocation to the various Alevî saints, and to Mohammed's brother-in-law Ali, whom they regard as the rightful heir to the Prophet's spiritual tradition. This makes them Shia Muslims, although with different practices than Arab or Iranian Shi'ites; the Alevî faith and its offshoot the **Bektaşi** dervish order stresses intersectarian tolerance, the teachings of its saints and bards and equality between men and women. *Aşık*s play an honoured role in the regular Alevî religious ceremony (*cem*) which includes prayers, recitations, singing and the culminating circle dance, the *sema*.

Alevî music (and the entire orientation of the sect) is far more rural and folk-based than the classical, high-art Mevlevî ritual. It's possible to attend a *cem* at the Şahkulu Sultan (Merdivenköy) *tekke* or the Karaca Ahmet Sultan (Üsküdar) mosque in İstanbul on Sundays and Alevî holidays. Recently, several commercial cafés featuring singers with *saz* or a small band have appeared in İstanbul, off İstiklâl Caddesi in Beyoğlu.

The **solo saz** is virtually a sacred object to the Alevî, rich in spiritual significance; traditionally they favour the three-string version for its trinitarian symbolism of Allah, Mohammed and Ali. Many of the songs have words by or about **Pir Sultan Abdal**, an *aşık* martyr of the sixteenth century, executed for his associations with a rebellion against the Ottoman authorities; his birthplace, the village of Banaz near Sivas, remains a place of pilgrimage. Alevîs in general and many *aşık*s in particular have been the subject of mistrust and contempt from orthodox Sunni Muslims, often officially condoned. Most blatantly, a Sivas hotel hosting a leftist/Alevî conference was attacked and set alight on July 2, 1993 by a fundamentalist mob; 37 poets and *aşık*s died, and the 128 prosecuted over the incident were either released or given risibly light sentences at their 1994 trial.

This *aşık* revival was encouraged in the early 1970s by opera singer and *saz* player **Ruhi Su**. Though not an Alevî, he was uncompromisingly left-wing and lost his job at the state opera as a result. While mainstream performers had to compromise, the sacking freed him artistically – his albums sold, and still sell, in large numbers, though they remain banned on TRT. Today's top names, **Arif Sağ**, **Yavuz Top**, **Musa Eroğlu** and the late **Muhlis Akarsu** (killed in the Sivas fire) have made excellent recordings both as a group, **Muhabbet**, and individually. *Aşık* music has always had a latent political-protest content. **Ali İzzet** and **Mahsuni Şerif** brought this out in songs ranging from passionate denunciations of social and political injustice to gentle satires on Turkish football. Celebrated by the urban Turkish left in the late 1960s, they still retain some nostalgic cachet today amongst the intelligentsia. **Feyzullah Çınar** is a slightly more recent representative of this tradition.

The politics of others has been more pro-establishment. **Aşık Veysel**, the blind bard from Sivrialan in Sivas province, is still a household name in Turkey though he died in poverty and obscurity in 1974. His most famous songs, such as "Dostlar Beni Hatırlasın" (May My Friends Remember Me), "Kara Toprak" (My Faithful, Beloved Black Earth) and "Uzun İnce Bir Yoldayım" (I'm on a Long Difficult Journey) circulated widely in both written and recorded form, and remain well known. In comparison to harder-biting Şerif and İzzet, Veysel sang a gentler poetry expressing humanistic sentiments. Like many Alevî he strongly endorsed the secularist stance of the young republic, and lent his talents to official efforts to teach and disseminate officially approved music in Anatolia. This assistance was rewarded by honours and a token official pension in 1965, but fellow singer Aşık İhsani, more rigorous about his anti-authoritarian principles, said of Veysel: "He was born one of us, but died one of them."

Aşık music is generally easy to identify, even to those unfamiliar with Turkish music. It is one of the few studio-recorded genres featuring solo voice and *saz*, though there have been a few orchestral experiments, notably by Yavuz Top and Arif Sağ. The *saz* is tuned specially, resulting in a particularly sombre and intense sound, with complex chord patterns emerging from the shifting drones. Elsewhere, the instrument is tuned in open fifths, and played with more attention to flamboyant melodic lines.

One exception worth mentioning is **bozlak**, a style associated with Alevî communities in western Anatolia: free-rhythm, semi-improvized declamations of scorching emotional intensity, somewhat akin to flamenco. The singer sings, literally, at the top of his voice, and the *saz* is tuned in the open-fifths manner, allowing for dramatic melodic flourishes and a sparse, astringent sound. Perhaps the greatest exponent in recent years was **Neşet Ertaş**, from Kırşehir, a person of cultic veneration amongst enthusiasts in Turkey, and son of **Muharrem Ertaş**, another *bozlak* singer of mythic reputation. **Ekrem Çelebi**, an extraordinary virtuoso, is perhaps the best known of the younger generation.

The *aşık* tradition assumes another distinct form in the northeastern district of Kars. Here the singers are considered to have fallen into a trance in which gifts of musical and spiritual knowledge are revealed to them by the prophet İlyas (Elijah), and henceforth wander the countryside in search of their beloved. They make their living as entertainers and storytellers in cafés of the northeast, where audiences particularly enjoy the ritualized exchange of insults between two rival performers, which follows a pre-ordained rhyme and musical scheme. No detail of appearance or character trait is spared, and the contest concludes when one musician fails to come up with a witty riposte, which, by the end, often revolves around graphic sexual innuendo. Even given the language barrier, it's worth attending such events just to enjoy the sense of occasion, and the tears of laughter rolling down the cheeks of the listeners. **Aşık Seref Taşlıova** and **Murat Çobanoğlu** are still recognized as the masters of such events, which can be heard occasionally in İstanbul at the Gülhane Park festival as well as at Çobanoğlu's own café in Kars town.

Classical traditions

Urban Turkish music, the fruit of classical Ottoman civilization, divides into three broad genres: **religious** (*sema*), **classic** (*klasik* or *sanat*) and **nightclub** (*fasıl*), which all share the compositional rules known as *makam*.

The **makam** are musical modes or scales (with associated rules governing melodic flow and prominent notes) in which the musicians compose their songs and instrumental pieces, and, more importantly, weave their improvisations (**taksim**), which are central to classical music performance. The *makam* currently used in Turkey have most in common with those of the Arab world; the Iranian *dastgah* are more distantly related.

The *taksim* improvisation usually precedes, and also punctuates, long suites of music that often begin with an instrumental prelude (*peşrev*), end with a postlude (*saz semaisi*) and consist mainly of "art" songs, known as **şarkı**. Most of those sung today date from the late nineteenth century, the era of one of the great songwriters, **Hacı Arif Bey**, though some are much earlier. The tradition dates back to the fourteenth century, and notational systems appeared with **Abdülkadir Merağı** (died 1435), though its present theoretical bases took shape at the end of the seventeenth century, when a Romanian princely enthusiast, **Dimitri Cantemir**, was resident in İstanbul.

These classical genres are essentially chamber genres, where the instruments play as a loose collection of soloists, each taking turns at improvising *taksim*, and each elaborating the melodic and rhythmic line as they see fit. Songs and instrumental numbers thus differ greatly from performance to performance. Typical **instruments** are the *ud* (lute), the *ney* (end-blown flute), the *tanbur* (long-necked fretted lute), the *kanun* (zither) and *klarnet* (valved clarinet). Rhythm (*usul*) is provided by the *def* (a frame drum) and the *darbuka* (the omnipresent goblet drum). Some of these instruments, in particular the *darbuka* and *klarnet*, are restricted to secular contexts; others are effectively synonymous with spiritual music, in particular the *ney* and *küdüm* drums. Performers themselves were often extremely versatile, so the stylistic distinctions made below and in the discography following are not rigid; *sanat* and *fasıl* practitioners overlapped considerably, and classical musicians would even perform *türkü* on demand, sometimes singing in Anatolian dialect.

Many famous virtuosi composers are associated with particular instruments: **Tanburi Cemil Bey** (1871–1916) and **Necdet Yaşar** (born 1930) on the *tanbur*, **Yorgo Bacanos** (1900–1977), **Marko Melkon Alemsherian** and **Udi Hrant Kenkulian** (1901–1978) on the *ud*, **Tatyos Efendi** (1863–1913),

Kemani Haydar Taltlıyay and Kemani Nubar Çömlekçiyan on violin, Şükrü Tunar (1907–1962) on the *klarnet*, Ahmet Meter (alias Halil Karaduman, born 1959) on the *kanun*. Many players and composers inhabited the world of professional secular music-making, whose profane associations with drink and dance made it the preserve of İstanbul's and İzmir's Armenian, Greek and Jewish minorities, and others, notably Gypsies, who fell outside bourgeois Muslim respectability.

The Ottoman urban repertoire was zealously attacked by Republican ideologues, who considered it thoroughly decadent because of its reliance on Arabic, Byzantine and Persian forms, not to mention its cosmopolitan (ie non-"Turkish") and religious influences. The formal teaching and radio broadcasting of Turkish classical forms was forbidden between 1923 and 1976, with Western classical aggressively promoted instead.

Despite such public strictures, traditional urban genres survived in the private sector, as witness recent, welcome reissues of recordings made between the 1920s and 1950s. Non-Muslim musicians, who continued to dominate urban music until mid-century, were feted by no less than Atatürk himself, and an Armenian *kanun* player, Artaki Candan-Terzian, was head of the *Sahibinin Sesi* (HMV-Turkey) recording studios from 1925 until 1948.

Sanat vocal stars

Classical Turkish music theory is now principally taught in private conservatories, of which the most highly esteemed is the **Üsküdar Musiği Cemiyeti** in İstanbul. There are others in most major cities, where musicians gather to socialize or give regular public concerts. Many, if not all, of the top echelon of instrumental recording artists are trained at conservatories, and singers as well tend to have at least passing connections with them.

The voice lies at the heart of all classical genres. Since the time of **Münir Nurettin** (or Nureddin) **Selçuk** (1901–1981), singers have assumed most of the trappings of the Western star system. He was the first solo artist to stand at the front of the stage, with the other instrumentalists reduced to a backing role; after years of neglect, he is now enjoying a nostalgic reappropriation by the Turkish intelligentsia. Contemporaries of Selçuk's who crop up on archival compilations include **Müzeyyen Senar**, the ethnic Armenian **Ağyazar Garabetyan Efendi**, Jewish cantor **İsak el-Gazi** and Atatürk's favourite female singer, **Safiye Ayla**.

Zeki Müren (1931–1996), perhaps the highest rated vocalist in the latter half of this century, worked extensively with the composer **Muzaffer Özpınar**, who trained at the Eminönü conservatory. Müren first made his name through classical broadcasts during the 1950s, then with versions of Egyptian and Lebanese musicals, and finally by performing in İstanbul's burgeoning *gazino* clubs during the 1970s. He went *arabesk* (see below) with the album *Kahir Mektubu* in the early 1980s, but throughout his career produced austerely classical recordings, and also did Turkish versions of tango and *chanson*. During the 1960s and 1970s, increasingly camp stage decor and personal costuming (he was in fact a gay transvestite) overshadowed musical values, though the 1980s saw such tendencies reined in – and little discernible drop in performance quality. He died dramatically onstage of heart failure while staging a comeback concert in İzmir.

Bülent Ersoy, Turkey's most famous transsexual, studied with Senar, and continues to produce songs in a restrained classical idiom: her recordings on Orkide label are particularly fine examples, as is her striking reinterpretation of the late-nineteenth repertoire, *Alaturka 95*. This outraged devout Muslims by its inclusion of a call to prayer on the opening track (sung by Bülent herself) – the association of religion with this outrageous figure was too much for some, and indeed a right-wing nationalist fired a shot at her during one concert. Following the 1980 operation, Ersoy had been forbidden from performing publicly on moral grounds, but she successfully lobbied then-President Özal (a big fan) to lift the bar both to her stage appearances and to her (and other transsexuals) marrying.

The Mevlevî dervish âyin

Classical religious music is almost the exclusive preserve of the **Mevlevî** (**"whirling"**) **dervishes**. While the order has no official existence (yet), public performances are put on, as indeed they were in Ottoman times, for foreign observers in Konya during the week before December 17, and at the Galata lodge in İstanbul. Mevlevî performances consist of long **âyin**, complex yet delicate compositions, preceded and followed by instrumental and vocal pieces with words from the thirteenth-century Sufi poet **Celaleddin Rumi** (**Mevlâna**), the order's founder, interspersed with *taksims*, particularly on the *ney* and *küdüm* (kettledrum). Other important instruments in the *âyin* are the *tambur, kanun* and *rebab*.

The best-known Mevlevî composers are **Köçek Derviş Mustafa Dede** (seventeenth century), **Dede Efendi** (eighteenth and nineteenth century) and **Rauf Yekta** (nineteenth and twentieth century). Major contemporary musicians associated with the Mevlevî order, notably **Kudsi Ergüner** (born 1952) and **Necdet Yaşar**, live and record outside Turkey, and their recordings reflect Western interest in Sufi and Ottoman high culture more than popular religious expression in Turkey. Versions of the Mevlevî repertory can be heard at the lodges of the Halveti-Cerrahi sect, with a heavier emphasis on the practice of *zikr*, a trance-inducing repetition of various of the 99 names of God, and the collective singing of *ilahi* (hymns). Such practices, while freed from the overt suppression of prior decades, are still somewhat clandestine, though one of the greatest Halveti-Cerrahi *şeyhs* (leaders), **Müzaffer Özak**, made a superb recording of Mevlevî *âyin* with Kudsi Ergüner in the late 1970s.

Gypsies and fasıl music

As so often, Gypsies (*Rom*, or *Roman* in Turkish) have an important local musical presence, particularly in the semi-classical, urban-nightclub style referred to as **fasıl**. This is essentially a vocal suite interspersed with light orchestral ensemble pieces and solo *taksims*, or improvisations; every short rest (*fasıl* means "interval") is filled with flourishes and improvisations from the stars of the orchestra, frowned upon in strictly classical circles. Like *sanat*, this style was also officially discouraged, though privately enjoyed, by Atatürk and his retinue.

Fasıl has continued to suffer somewhat from its association with sleazy *gazino* **nightclubs and belly-dancing** for tourists, but it's also performed in more respectable restaurants. Downmarket *gazinos* still abound, particularly around Beyoğlu in İstanbul, though they've become less seedy since the mid-1990s as a result of the Islamist municipality's efforts to tidy up the city. At the renovated, somewhat touristy Çicek Pasajı and the clubs around it, the music incorporates recent songs, and sticks less assiduously to classical formula – this is, after all, music to drink and dance to.

Though much of the nightclub repertory overlaps with what you might hear on a radio concert, or in a conservatory, *fasıl* is a very different kind of music.

The classical values of precision and dutiful respect to tradition are replaced by a demonstrative, present-tense music. The *klarnet* and *darbuka* dominate the instrumental ensemble, and many if not all of the most noted performers are Gypsies from the Tarlabaşı district, playing with great skill and passion. Tunes are tossed around with breathless, exhilarating ease, long notes are held on the *klarnet* for extended yet exquisitely poised moments during improvisation, *kanun* and violin decorate and interrupt; noise and gestural energy flow across the stage like a torrent, carrying all before it. Violinists spike pieces with lightning-fast glissandos, and clarinetists favour the low G-clarinet for the throaty sound that gives *fasıl* its special character.

Perhaps the most famous of all the clarinetists is **Mustafa Kandırali** (born 1930), who has worked for the TRT and toured and recorded widely. No *fasıl* player approaches his knowledge of the repertoire, or his fiery improvisations, which wring every possible tonal nuance from the instrument. Other celebrated *fasıl* musicians, both living and deceased, include *kanun* player **Ahmet Yatman**, *oud*ist **Kardi Şençalar**, violinist **Kemani Cemal** and *darbuka*-player **Burhan Öçal**, renowned for his epic solos. Vocalists worth looking out for on recordings include **Perihan Altındağ**, **Mahmut Celalettin**, **Denizkışı Eftalya** and **Kemal Gürses**. Another younger player featuring on several recordings is clarinetist **Selim Sesler** (born 1957), who began his career as an İstanbul *fasıl* musician but has since distinguished himself as an interpreter of wedding and dance tunes from his native Thrace and beyond.

Arabesk and pop music

Turkey's dominant popular music, **arabesk** is derived from the folk, classical and *fasıl* traditions, though the name alludes to its predominantly Arabic rather than Turkish melodies. Turkish Nationalists have made, and still make, strenuous efforts to exclude "Arab" history and cultural links, but for most locals *arabesk* remains Turkish music in its most basic and appealing form.

Arabesk is a working-class and, to an extent, outsiders' sound which addresses the everyday realities and problems of the *gariban*, the poor and oppressed. Also known as *minibüs müziği*, after its blaring from such vehicles taking workers into the cities from surrounding slums, *arabesk* is as much a stance towards life – complete with windscreen ornaments, tacky postcards, dayglo coloured stickers and associated melodramatic films – as a music.

Arabesk star Müslüm Gürses once sang, in characteristically self-pitying mode, *Kulak veren yok garibin sesine* ("Nobody listens to the voice of the poor man"). In fact, *arabesk* CDs and cassettes outsell any other genre by far – a star name will reckon on selling a million copies per year – and fill a good half of any street stall. And despite the current, largely bourgeois vogue for Turkish rock and pop, live *arabesk* remains ubiquitous: look out for concerts and festivals, such as that during late August in İstanbul's Gülhane Park, which attracts big names like Gürses or Ferdi Tayfur – plus crowds of eighty thousand from some of the poorest suburbs, despite (intentionally) scanty advertising to prevent stampedes.

"Oriyental" roots

Arabesk has its roots in Egyptian "oriental dance" music – **raks şarkı** or **oriyental**, often vulgarly dubbed "belly-dance" music – which has long been popular in Turkey. It was first introduced in the 1940s by **Haydar Tatlıyay** (1890–1963), who had worked as a musician in Egypt, and returning to Turkey in 1947, set up a large dance orchestra as used in Egyptian film. Indeed numerous classical Turkish musicians worked across the Middle East early in the twentieth century, either as composers for films, as instrumentalists or singers. When the Turkish state attempted to ban Arabic music and film in 1938, and began in earnest to establish a Nationalist alternative through the TRT, people voted with their radio dials, tuning to Radio Cairo.

Turkey's nascent recording and film industry subsequently invested heavily in versions of Egyptian hits, particularly those associated with Mohammed Abd el-Wahaab and Umm Kulthum, and the Lebanese star Farid al-Attrache. **Zeki Müren** and **Münir Nurettin Selçuk** initially made their names as film stars during the 1940s and 1950s, singing solo in front of large string-based orchestras, declaiming abstract but dramatically intense lyrics of unrequited love.

Despite what its detractors say, *arabesk* is not merely Egyptian-derived music, and since the late 1940s its songs have addressed specifically Turkish problems such as rural–urban migration. Many popular films, particularly those of Baha Gelenbevi, began to deal with themes of rural life, accompanied by rural music, and urbanized rural musical genres began to appear in the big city and on recordings. **Diyarbakırlı Celal Güzelses** and **Malatyalı Fahri Kayahan** were amongst the earliest to record popularized folk-based forms for an urban audience, drawing heavily on the musical styles and repertoires of southeastern Turkey.

Ahmet Sezgin took this one step further, bringing urban and rural styles into a creative mix during the mid-1960s. Recordings from this period also illustrate the enduring fascination with the traditional art of vocal improvisation, or **gazel**. Singers such as **Hafız Burhan Sesiyılmaz** and **Abdullah Yüce**, both with electrifying voices, did much to repopularize the genre, which otherwise did not find much favour amongst the reformist intelligentsia.

The arabesk explosion

The 1960s also saw local middle-class listeners embrace imported Ango-American rock, with some musicians and/or singers adopting elements of this style; by the 1970s the instrumental heart of *arabesk* consisted of electrified strings (including an obligatory solo *saz*), keyboards and percussion. The first major figure to do so was **Orhan Gencebay**, born in 1944 on the Black Sea coast, who began his career with Ahmet Sezgin after studying a variety of genres in private lessons, in the military and at TRT. His debut solo recording, "Bir Teselli Ver" (1969) was based on classical forms, but the sobbing intensity of the voice owed much to the *gazel*, and frank lyrics addressed the plight of the lonely lover – a far cry from the involved metaphors and archaic language of the classical song. A more eclectic set of references, particularly rock and flamenco, was displayed in his 1975 album *Batsın Bu Dünyayı* (A Curse on This World), and this creative and playful eclecticism continues to be found on almost any of his albums. Gencebay is perhaps best appreciated for his virtuoso *saz*-playing and for his film-acting skills, rather than for his voice or song lyrics.

Gencebay's colossal status acknowledged, it is indeed the voice which defines *arabesk* aesthetics, and those of **İbrahim Tatlıses**, Müslüm Gürses and Ferdi Tayfur (all film actors too) are the most significant. Their songs, thinly disguised autobiographies, tell of self-pity and humiliation in the big city, experiences close to the hearts of Turkey's numerous internal migrants. Of mixed Kurdish/Arab background, Tatlıses himself migrated from the impoverished southeastern town of Urfa. He was a huge figure during the mid-to-late 1980s, with a series of albums featuring well-drilled orchestras, danceable tunes and his electrifying voice.

Ferdi Tayfur's voice also has strong resonances with southeastern vocal styles, and his reputation, like that of Tatlıses, rests heavily on his portrayal of a poor villager made good in the big city. Adana-born **Müslüm Gürses** is still adored by his fans for his older hits: mournful, fate-obsessed numbers inviting the listener to light another cigarette ("Bir Sigara Yak") or to curse the world ("Yeter Allahim"). His audiences, almost all from the bottom strata of Turkish society, were notorious for their unruly behaviour at concerts; in one bizarre incident, they attacked Gürses for miming to playback rather than actually singing.

Despite being a music with a chequered history and dubious origins, *arabesk* acquired some powerful advocates and defenders during the 1980s, as part of the general "revision" of Republican cultural mores. The late President Özal even used an *arabesk* song as the theme for his 1988 election campaign. Establishment apparatchiks were properly horrified; the tragic lyrics were claimed to encourage the retrograde oriental vices of despair, fatalism and even suicide. Accordingly industrial-strength *arabesk* was banned from the airwaves in 1989, and the minister of culture attempted to promote a sanitized, inherently contradictory alternative, *acısız arabesk* (painless *arabesk*); it flopped spectacularly, and the prohibition was soon rescinded.

Many *arabesk* stars were quick to take advantage of their new legitimacy, and, more particularly, of Özal's deregulation of electronic media. Private FM radio and TV have given the music a new lease of life, and it is now possible to see classic *arabesk* films from the 1970s on a more or less daily basis. Though the Big Four noted above still dominate the scene, some younger stars are getting a look in: sales of **Mahsun Kırmızıgül**'s *Tam 12'den* almost doubled those of İbrahim Tatlıses' *Klasikler* in 1995. Singers with classical backgrounds, notably **Bülent Ersoy**, **Muazzez Abacı**, **Nese Karaböçek** and more recently **Muazzez Ersoy** and **Yılmaz Morgül** continue to flirt with *arabesk*. Many in Turkey assumed that with lionization and patronage in high circles, *arabesk* would lose its *raison d'être* and disappear. But if anything the reverse seems to be the case, with *arabesk* showing no sign of vanishing soon.

Rock, pop and özgün

Turkish rock and pop have leapt to enormous prominence since 1990, part of the revolution of values that has transformed parts of İstanbul and Ankara beyond recognition. Music shops in and around Beyoğlu that used to carry spare strings and tuning pegs for the *saz* now exclusively stock imported electric guitars; there are numbers of live rock clubs catering to moderately well-off students, often around the corner from the *fasıl gazinos*.

That said, rock and pop have a long history in Turkey – and in the Turkish diaspora, where the Ertegün brothers founded the enormously influential Atlantic jazz, rock and blues label in New York. But this is just one aspect of the well-established practice of producing local versions of fashionable international genres. Tango was enormously popular in Turkey (as in Greece) from the 1930s until the 1950s, French *chanson* had its Turkish exponents such as blonde bombshell Ajda Pekkan, and Elvis Presley spawned a wave of imitators in the late 1950s, most notably Erol Büyükbürç. But the Turkish intelligentsia were always saddled with a fear that they could do little more than imitate styles originated elsewhere.

Yet a number of musicians began to try reconciling Anatolian folk with Western rock genres. Most had come up through the fairly exclusive foreign-language schools in İstanbul, many were members of the city's non-Muslim minorities, and a few had the means to travel across Europe in the 1960s. Despite phenomenal difficulties in procuring instruments and recording outside Turkey, an **Anadolu (Anatolian) Rock** movement gathered pace. Domestically, it faced exclusion from broadcast media and general intolerance from the political elite; the new bands' growing identification with the international Left movement was reflected in increasingly politicized lyrics, and many groups promptly disintegrated when the generals took over in 1980.

Cem Karaca, who had worked with nearly every significant Anadolu Rock band (Apaşlar, Kardaşlar, Moğollar, Dervişan), fled to Germany just before the coup, returning only in 1987. His is the most interesting voice of the genre, combining rock histrionics with a cultivated bel canto. His songs combined a taste for highbrow literature with social realism; Dervişan's *Safinaz*, recorded in 1979, was a kind of rock opera about a poor girl's struggle with honour and blood feuds. He has also superbly recorded the poetry of Nazım Hikmet and Orhan Veli.

Today, Karaca performs in small Beyoğlu clubs, with his old accomplice Uğur Dikmen on keyboards. For some observers, Karaca's political integrity was undermined by his overly craven reconciliation with Özal's regime, and he doesn't command the universal attention he once did, though his music has lost none of its jagged intensity and literary intelligence. Moreover, **Moğollar**, under Cahit Berkay, has reformed; politically edged lyrics are still very much to the fore, while the chamber-ensemble lyricism and complexity of their earlier work has been replaced with an up-tempo stadium rock style. Perhaps the most successful of their recent recordings is *Dört Renk* (1996), with catchy tunes, punchy lyrics, and something of the old psychedelia to the keyboard and *saz* sound, despite a predominance of guitar and drums.

CDs of this music are easy to find, since the genre has undergone a nostalgic rehabilitation. Look out for old as well as new recordings by **Erkin Koray**, **MFÖ** (one of the few bands to survive the generals), jazz-influenced drummer **Okay Temiz** (who has emigrated to Scandinavia), **Edip Akbayram** and the late **Barış Manço**, whose politics eventually swung even further right than Karaca's.

A few bands maintained the impetus of the earlier countercultural movement into the mid-1980s, of which Yeni Türkü remains perhaps the best known, and **Bulutsuzluk Özlemi** (Longing for Blue Skies) was the most radical. **Yeni Türkü**, inspired by the Latin American "New Song" movement, was one of the first groups to use traditional Turkish acoustic instruments played in good arrangements, and enjoyed great popularity amongst the intelligentsia from the late 1980s for their versions of old İstanbul songs and Greek *rebetika* numbers, as well as original lyrics with a liberal-to-left stance on topical issues.

During the mid-1980s, there was a distant cousin of mainstream *arabesk* that combined rural melodic forms with guitar- or *saz*-based harmonies and an intimate, mellow vocal style, dubbed **özgün** (original) music. The austere figure of composer and *saz*-player **Zülfü Livaneli** – best known outside Turkey for his work with Greek composer Mikis Theodorakis and singer Maria Farandouri, and for the film music to Yılmaz Güney's film *Yol* – dominated the genre during the 1980s. Born in the eastern Black Sea region, as a leftist intellectual he spent several years during the early 1970s exiled in Sweden, where he first hooked up with like-minded Theodorakis.

As befitted the time, *özgün* lyrics were politically cautious, but **Ahmet Kaya**'s renditions of Communist poet Nazım Hikmet's work had enormous resonance amongst the Turkish Left. Despite the fact that Kaya and many other *özgün* singers were Kurds from an area associated with militancy, any impulse to radical expression fell foul of a conservative recording industry, and didn't get much past sloganeering album titles. The gentle, literary lyricism of Kaya's thoughtful and social-realistic love songs was not, in the end, enough to sustain the genre, and despite some popular 1990s Kurdish practitioners, notably **Hasan Hüseyin Demirel** and **Umut Altınçağ**, *özgün* has practically disappeared. However, recordings by Livaneli, Kaya, Selda and Fatih Kısaparmak can still be found.

Turkish pop, on the other hand, is resolutely mainstream, and at its heart stands one figure: **Sezen Aksu**. She trained as an art music singer in her native İzmir, and her current prominence owes much to her partnership with the late **Onno Tunç**, an Armenian church musician who embraced soul and jazz during the 1960s, and had the unfortunate task of overseeing Turkey's Eurovision song contest entries in the 1980s. Aksu's soulful voice, owing much to traditional Turkish urban musical aesthetics, and Tunç's eliptical arrangements and keyboard-based harmonic style, made for a winning combination from the 1970s onward.

More successfully than the *özgün* stalwarts, Aksu has also been a political figure, embracing concerns and campaigns: Bosnia, feminism, ecology and human rights, and particularly the plight of the *Cumartesi Anneleri*, the "Saturday Mothers" – a long-running, mid-1990s Turkish women's protest in Beyoğlu against the refusal of the judiciary to investigate the disappearance of their sons. Her CDs cleverly anticipated the political zeitgeist, and each one through the mid-1990s was a national media event. When *Işık Doğudan Yükselir/ The Light Rises from the East* came out in 1995, evoking the cultural mosaic of Anatolia in gentle feminist terms, at a time of intercommunal religious rioting in İstanbul and the worsening crisis in the southeast of the country, the album's release was the first item on the TRT's evening news programme. Her 1997 *Düğün ve Cenaze/Wedding and Funeral* was a collaboration with Bosnian Serb musician Goran Bregoviç, reworking a number of popular tunes currently circulating widely around the Balkans – and had considerable resonance in a Turkey regarding the ruins of Yugoslavia, ancestral home to many modern Turks. Since the millennium she has toured overseas with a Macedonian Gypsy brass band, the Koçani Orchestra, to considerable acclaim, and enjoyed stealth exposure in the UK when her song "Sımarık" reached the top of the UK charts repackaged as "Kiss Kiss".

Aksu's disciples dominated the pop scene at the end of the 1980s and early 1990s. **Levent Yüksel**, a multi-talented instrumentalist and singer, has produced carefully crafted CDs (in particular *Med Cezir*), which connect quite explicitly with indigenous Turkish traditions and literature. Amongst more recent singers, **Candan Erçetin** has done most to continue the Aksu tradition, drawing on a wide range of Anatolian, Balkan and Mediterranean influences. **Aşkın Nur Yengi**'s voice is disconcertingly difficult to distinguish from Aksu's, though recent recordings (for instance *2002*) reflect the *arabesk*-pop synthesis of more recent years.

Later in the 1990s, a newer genre of pop came to the fore, with lyrics, driving rhythms and melodic style that are, if anything, closer to *arabesk*, but pitched at youthful, cosmopolitan city-dwellers looking for a hedonistic and extroverted music. **Mirkelam**, **Tarkan**, **Rafet el Roman** and **Mustafa Sandal** produce energetic and danceable sounds in this idiom, while **Volkan Konak** has come up with an engaging hybrid for the large Black Sea community in İstanbul.

Selected discography

In Turkey the leading label for folk and classical recordings is **Kalan** (Ⓦwww.kalan.com), which releases an unrivalled range of archive recordings of classical instrumentalists, contemporary folk and popular singers, *aşık* bards and the music of minority groups in Turkey. Their website has a literate English page that allows you to order their complete backlist as well as new releases at Turkish high-street prices. Outside Turkey, **Traditional Crossroads** (PO Box 20320 Greeley Square Station, New York, NY 10001-9992 US; ☎1-800-422-6282, Ⓦwww.traditionalcrossroads.com) has an excellent catalogue of archive and contemporary recordings; again you can order on-line, and download streaming sound samples. Look out also for Golden Horn Records, which has some interesting and unusual archival recordings. Pressings from American, German or French labels such as Rounder, Music of the World, Ocora, Network or Auvidis can be obtained, often by special order, from major UK/US retail chains such as Tower, HMV or Virgin. Some, though not all, Traditional Crossroads productions are released under licence by Kalan in İstanbul. Turkish-label pressings are available only in Turkey, or overseas in speciality music shops catering to Turkish emigrant communities. Good **shops in İstanbul** include Lale Plak, Tünel, Galipdede Cad 1, Beyoğlu, İstanbul (☎0212/293 7739) and Metropol Müzik, at İstiklâl Cad 140 (☎0212/245 6921). In Britain, there's an excellent Turkish-label CD/cassette shop with a good stock, ten-day special-order service and reasonable mark-up: Melodi Müzik, 121 Green Lanes, London N16 (ask for Salih, who speaks perfect English; ☎020/7359 0038).

All titles below are available on CD unless specified otherwise.

Folk and aşık: compilations

Gaziantep Türküleri (Kalan) An idiomatic collection of songs and instrumental music from the Gaziantep region, performed by local musicians on vocals, *saz*, *zurna* and *davul*.

Music and Throat Playing of the Yörük in Anatolia (Kalan) This covers the music of the pastoral *Yörüks* in the Toros mountains. Beautiful strings and flutes, songs to the animals and throat-vocals (a custom peculiar in Turkey to the *Yörük*) using the fingers to change the note while singing. Notes in English, a rarity for Kalan.

Salkım Söğüt 1 (Metropol, Turkey) Good contemporary acoustic folk samplers of various, often quite young, artists contracted to this label: İlkay Akkaya, Arzu Görücü, Birol Topaloğlu and Alaaddin Us. The first two-named (women) performers make the disc, and invite further exploration of their solo titles.

Salkım Söğüt 2 (Metropol, Turkey) The sequel, as good if not better, with a reprise by Görücü, singing in Laz by Kazım Koyuncu, and central Anatolian pieces interpreted by Mustafa Özarslan and Hakan Yeşilyurt.

Saz (Kalan) Traces examples of the various *saz* types from Central Asia to Turkey and beyond to Greece: Uzbek *dutar*, Tadjik *tambur*, Kyrgyz *komuz*, Kazakh *dombra*, Iranian *tanbur*, Azeri *saz* and various Turkish varieties, including Ali Ekber Çiçek playing "Haydar" on the big *divan saz*. A listenable survey, with photos and a few notes in English.

Turkish Village Music
(Nonesuch/Explorer, US) One of the best field recordings of Turkish rural musics, recorded by ethnomusicologist Laxmi Tewari in two villages in northwest Turkey. Heart-rending *aşık* songs; also good examples of *zurna* and *davul*.

Turquie Aşık: Chants d'amour et de sagesse d'Anatolie
(Inedit/Auvidis, France) Probably the best introduction to *aşık* music, overseen and annotated by Kudsi

Ergüner; well-balanced between the artistry of Nuray Hafiftaş, Ali Ekber Çiçek and Turan Engin, all from the northeast, plus a spectacular *saz* solo by Arif Sağ.

Turquie: Musiques des Yayla
(Ocora, France) Haunting melodies and songs from settled *Yörük* communities near Acıpayam in the southwestern mountains of Turkey. Various types of *saz* and violin predominate, though there's also a sample of the *sipsi* (pine-twig oboe); excellent sound quality and sleeve notes.

Song Creators of Eastern Turkey
(Smithsonian/Folkways, US) An anthology of four contemporary *aşık*s who have set up performance cafés in their hometowns Kars and Erzurum; not quite up to the Inedit disc, but again good notes and lyric translations.

Folk and aşık: artists

Belkis Akkale *Türkü Türkü Türkiyem* (Sembol Plak, Turkey). Possibly the greatest living *türkü* singer at her earthiest, carried along by driving *saz* rhythms – plus almost all of the traditional instruments of Turkey. A second goodie from this TRT stalwart is *Güvercin* (Raks/Midas, cassette only, Turkey), which epitomizes her poised, grave and passionate renditions of the popularized Alevî repertory. Includes the Azeri "Bu Gala Dasli Gala", with its characteristic 6/8 rhythm.

İbrahim Can *Bir Avuç Türkü* (Coşkun Plak, Turkey). Another TRT artist, specializing in Black Sea music, who has done much to tastefully update the folk genre; this 1996 recording reconciles the *kemençe* with rock and mainstream pop in an utterly compelling manner.

Ali Ekber Çiçek *Haydar Haydar: Klasikleri* (Mega Müzik, Turkey). Benchmark collection of old standards; Haydar is an epithet of Ali, meaning the "Lion of Allah".

Neşet Ertaş *Kova Kova İndirler Yazıya* (Raks/Müziksan, Turkey). German-resident Neşet, son of Muharrem, turns in some of the most passionate *bozlak* improvisations ever recorded. A number of classics including the title track, much covered by other singers, plus two *uzun hava* that take that genre to extremes.

Muhabbet *Beş* (Zirve, Turkey) & *Seksensekiz* (Pınar, Turkey). The combined talent of four of the greatest *saz*-players. All have deep, resonating voices, which add soulful respite to the swirling *saz* interludes. Alas, these 1980s cassettes may prove difficult to find, so you may have to make do with the newer *Yedi* (Kalan), Muhabbet as a trio without Arif Sağ.

Talip Özkan *L'art vivant de Talip Özkan* (Ocora). Eight superb tracks encompassing various regional styles and instruments from the large *divan saz* to the small *cura*; if you like this, then go for *L'art du Tanbur* (Ocora), a wonderfully meditative foray into classical *tanbur*, varied by folk melodies and unexpectedly delicate singing. Özkan is a TRT-trained player now long resident in France.

Arif Sağ *Halay* (Nora/ASM, Turkey). This tape by one of the stars of Muhabbet features complex rhythms, superb *saz* playing and solos from many Turkish folk instruments. *İnsan Olmaya Geldim* (Nora/Sembol, Turkey) is more specifically *saz*-based, featuring some choral backings and arrangements by many other *aşıks*, including the late Nesimi Çimen, one of the Sivas atrocity victims.

Ruhi Su *Zeybekler/Ezgili Yürek* (Nepa-İmece Müzik). This label has recently reissued most of Ruhi's output on a series of budget-priced CDs; these, numbers 11/13 in the series, are packaged together rather fortuitously. The 1981 *Zeybekler* – traditional west Anatolian folk epics delivered in Ruhi Su's unmistakeable, dramatically deep voice – ranks among his most famous recordings, though *Ezgili Yürek*, recorded in 1986, a year and a half before Su's death and consisting mostly of readings from his own poetry, is of more specialist interest.

Bayram Bilge Toker *Bayram: Turkish Folk Songs and Sufi Melodies* (Music of the World, US). A riveting collection of folk songs, dances, improvisations and Sufi ritual music sung and played on *saz* by this native of Yozgat.

Birol Topaloğlu *Lazuri Birabape Heyamo* (Kalan). Very listenable album of vocalists from the Black Sea Laz minority, with self-taught Topaloğlu on *kemençe* (he also plays *tulum*) and musicians from folk/protest Grup Yorum. The Bulgarian-sounding title track is a well-known work song. Topaloğlu also compiled the more recent (2001), lavishly annotated double CD, *Lazeburi* (Kalan), a mix of dance melodies, a capella chants, work/love songs accompanied by the *tulum*, laments and poetry recitations: mostly field recorded and not always the best sound quality, but affecting, genuine material, especially the second disc.

Aşık Veysel *Voyages d'Alain Gheerbrant en Anatolie* (Ocora, France). The only field recordings (1957 vintage) of Veysel in a village setting, including his classics "Bülbül" (Nightingale) and "Kara Toprak". Wonderfully supported by his constant companion Küçük Veysel, who sings in imitating unison with the master. (The second disc, less interesting, encompasses Tahtacı/Alevî rituals.) *Dostlar Beni Hatırlasın* (Diskotür, Turkey) is the best of his Radio Ankara recordings; rather sterile sound but it contains many of his most treasured songs.

Classical and devotional music: compilations

The Bektashi Breaths (Cemre, Turkey) The Bektaşi are a mystical, heterodox sect whose musical rituals and dances feature hymns called *nefes*, or "breaths". An extraordinarily powerful disc which exudes ritual solemnity; melodies sigh and droop expressively, with an ensemble of *ney, kemençe, kanun, ud*, cello and percussion.

Gönül Telimizi Titreyenler (Coşkun Plak, Turkey) A compilation from the old HMV-Turkey catalogue, working from some early recordings by one of the first female vocalists, Safiye Ayla, to the pre-

arabesk club stars of the 1950s and 1960s, notably Zeki Müren, Münir Nurettin Selçuk and Suat Sayin.

İstanbul 1925 (Traditional Crossroads) The best *sanat* played by Turkish, Armenian and Greek musicians in the city during the first decades of the Republic, varied by the odd urban *türkü* song and *fasıl* instrumental. Highly recommended, with award-winning notes.

Masters of Turkish Music, Vol. 1 & Vol. 2 (Rounder, US) These remasterings of early recordings make another excellent introduction to genuine *sanat*, and include plenty of *türkü*s and classicized *taksim*s as well. Vol. 1 is half *gazel* or *şarkı*, half instrumental solos, though liner notes are often missing; Vol. 2, starting off with Safiye Ayla's rendition of the famous İstanbul *türkü* "Katibim" (covered bizarrely by Eartha Kitt in the 1950s), is less rigidly divided and has more reliably packaged notes, including translated lyrics, compiled

by the University of Maryland's Center for Turkish Music.

Mevlâna: Music of the Whirling Dervishes (EMI Hemisphere) Worthy, easily available, if slightly dull compilation, based partly on the six 1977 cassettes of *Mistik Türk Müziği Şaheserleri Serisi* (Kent, Turkey). Features Süleyman Ergüner on *ney*, Nizeh Üzel as solo vocalist and conductor.

Mevlâna Beyâti Âyini (Aras/Nora, Turkey) If you can track it down, this is the definitive version of the Mevlevî *sema* accompaniment; far better than the badly recorded schlock usually offloaded on hapless tourists in Konya.

Women of Istanbul (Traditional Crossroads) A companion, all-singing selection to *İstanbul 1925*; as usual with this label, excellent remastering, intelligent notes and lovingly rescued archival photos. All the great female vocalists of cabaret-nightclub style, mostly recorded in the mid-1930s.

Classical and devotional music: artists

Boğaziçi *Türk Müziğinde Rum Bestekârlar* (Columbia, Turkey). A mixture of Greek and Turkish musicians playing music of the Byzantine, Ottoman and Mevlevî traditions. Beautiful, landmark 1987 recording of courtly classical and sacred music.

Tanburi Cemil Bey (Traditional Crossroads/Kalan). Pieces performed on various stringed instruments (including cello) by this composer-virtuoso, a late Ottoman genius, recorded between 1910 and 1914 with fairly primitive acoustic technology. *Tanburi Cemil Bey, Vol. 2 & 3* (double CD; Traditional Crossroads) is more of the same – a very spare, elegant style which valiant remastering has just about made accessible.

Mesut Cemil *Early Recordings* (*Volume 1*); *Instrumental and Vocal*

Recordings (*Volumes 2 & 3*) (Golden Horn Records, US). Mesut Cemil was Tanburi Cemil Bey's son, perhaps the only musician in Turkey to surpass his father as an instrumentalist. He ran the classical musical section of TRT-İstanbul for decades, creating its distinctively ethereal ensemble style. These recordings contain material from the Cairo music congress of 1932, at which Mesut Cemil was one of the Turkish representatives, an extremely rare recording of him singing and TRT archival material interpreted by choirs and ensembles, as well as some definitive *taksim* improvisations by the master himself – and a superb two-*tanbur* recording of Cemil's famous *Nihavent Saz Semaisi*.

Udi Yorgo Bacanos *Udi Yorgo Bacanos* (Traditional Crossroads). If Udi Hrant was the soul of the urban *ud*, then Udi Yorgo was the brains, a master technical innovator; that said, this recording of a "musician's musician" is for the most dedicated fans only.

Kudsi Ergüner *Dervisches Tourneurs de Turquie* (Arion, France). Leading *ney* master Ergüner, resident in Paris since 1975, is closely associated with the music of the Mevlevî dervishes. This disc, featuring the voice of a late *şeyh* of the Halveti order, Muzaffer Özak, covers the entire ceremony, including parts other recordings miss out, like the opening Naat-i Mevlâna recitation and the recitation of the Koran. For a slightly less devotional take on Ottoman music, get *Makam: Ottoman Classical Music* (Al Sur, France), a reissue of a landmark 1971 London session with noted Mevlevî cantor Kani Karaca guesting on vocals, and the great Akagündüz Kutbay on *ney*. Ergüner's *Tatyos Efendi: Vocal Masterpieces* (Traditional Crossroads) is one of the best discs of overtly secular classical Ottoman music, composed by Armenian violinist to the sultan, Kemani Tatyos Efendi (1863–1913). An ensemble of *ney*, violin, *kanun*, *klarnet*, *ud*, *tanbur* and *def* accompanies Tatyos' *şarkı*s, interpreted by Melihat Gülses, interspersed amongst instrumental passages.

Bülent Ersoy *Alaturka 1995* (Raks, Turkey). Interpretation of the popular classics from the 1880s to the 1960s, conceived as a tribute to her mentor, Muzaffer Özpınar. Bülent's best recording in recent years, this recording contains some *gazel*s of scorching intensity. *Seçmeler* (Raks, Turkey) is a collection of all-time greatest hits from Ersoy's prolific *arabesk* output, including "Biz Ayrılamayız", "Geceler" and "Sevgi İstiyorum".

The Golden Horn Ensemble *Sultan Bestekarlar: Turkish Classical Music Composed By Ottoman Sultans* (Kalan). The Ottoman nobility were all taught a fine art or craft as a discipline and "finishing". Those who took up music, including Sultan Beyazit II (1447–1512), Selim III (1761–1808) and deposed Princess Gevheri Osmanoğlu (died 1980) are the basis for this extraordinary double CD that covers Turkish classical music from prehistory to its recent past. The first disc features vocal music, the second contains instrumentals, while both are interspersed with solo *taksim*s which blend formal precision with passion. The Ensemble brings this music to life in brisk though generally conservative performances, appropriate use of Western instruments co-existing with period details like small kettledrums. Accompanied by a beautifully illustrated booklet with informative, scholarly articles.

Udi Hrant Kenkuliyan *Udi Hrant* (Traditional Crossroads/Kalan). The great blind *oud*ist sings on many of these wonderful tracks from a 1950s concert tour of the US. *The Early Recordings, Vols. 1 & 2* (also Traditional Crossroads), made in Turkey during the 1920s, are equally good, with heart-rending vocals chronicling unrequited love, many of his famous *taksim*s and affecting ensemble work with violin, clarinet and piano. As ever, exemplary remastering, liner notes and lyrics translations.

Zeki Müren *Kahir Mektubu* (Türküola, Turkey). Originally recorded in 1979, this was composed by Zeki's long-time associate Muzaffer Özpınar, and heavily influenced by Egyptian star Umm Kulthum's later, monumental style. Simultaneously vast in scope and intimate in style, it was a landmark in *arabesk* history. Remastered from the old HMV catalogue, *Türk Sanat*

Müziği Konseri (Coşkun Plak, Turkey) is a near-perfect example of Zeki's elegant mastery of the classical style.

İbrahim Özgür *Tangolar: The Bel Ami Of Turkish Tango* (Oriente Musik, Germany). After returning from a seven-year tour of Asia, saxophonist and singer Özgür (died 1959) became a fixture on the İstanbul nightclub circuit during the late 1930s. These superb tracks, from the decade after his return in 1938, are some of the best specimens of the tango craze then sweeping Turkey along with much of the Mediterranean, and a snapshot of cosmopolitan İstanbul. The lyrics speak of longing and the agonies of separation; the music – familiar melodies with a haunting, Middle Eastern nuance – is restrained.

Münir Nurettin Selçuk *Bir Özlemdir* (Coşkun Plak, Turkey). One of a series of reissues of the old HMV backlist, this contains some enduring classics: "Aziz İstanbul", "Kalamış", "Endülüste Raks" (a Turkish take on flamenco) and an electrifying semi-improvised *gazel*, "Aheste Çek Kürekleri".

Sufi Music from Turkey (Arc, Germany). Excellent recording by the Turkish Music Ensemble of the State Conservatory of Afyon Kocatepe University, with the talented Tahir Aydoğdu leading from the *kanun*, and Timuçin Çevikoğlu on vocals and *bendir*. Though concentrating on ensemble, rather than vocal repertoire, one gets a strong sense of the continued centrality of Mevlevî mysticism in Turkish classical musical culture. The recording contains an unusual and effective *perde kaldırması*, a group improvisation on ascending degrees of the *makam* scale.

Şükrü Tunar *Şükrü Tunar* (American Recording Productions, Michigan). The only solo disc easily available of the great Gypsy clarinetist from the İzmir region, who served as one of Zeki Müren's first accompanists, and whose repertoire encompassed everything from folk tunes to *fasıl*.

Vosporos *Zontani Ihografisi sto Irodheio* (MBI, Greece). Vosporos is the Greek title and packaging of the identical group Boğaziçi, coordinated between 1987 and 1993 by Nikiforos Metaxas in İstanbul; this records a 1990 concert in Athens. Disc 1 features Greek composers of Ottoman music; disc 2 (more interesting) has songs of the Alevî *aşıks*, with Kani Karaca, Melda Kurt and Sibel Sezal on vocals.

Fasıl and Gypsy music

Kemani Cemal Çınarlı *Sulukule: Rom Music of Istanbul* (Traditional Crossroads). Instrumental numbers and chorus-vocals evoking the earthy character of urban Gypsy music. Centre stage are the soaring violin solos of Kemani Cemal, a native of Thrace and long a fixture on the İstanbul club scene. On-site recording and uneven miking, however, means occasional strange reverb and absolutely thunderous *darbuka*.

Barbaros Erköse Ensemble *Lingo*

Lingo (Golden Horn Records, US). The Erköse Brothers – Barbaros, Ali and Selahattin – at one time "were" Gypsy music in Turkey. Since he retired from the TRT, clarinet player Barbaros has been pursuing a solo career, involving collaboration with Peter Pannke, Anouar Brahim, Craig Harris and others. *Lingo Lingo* is urban folklore at its best, and a superb demonstration of the art of "meyan", improvisation over a rhythmic background. Useful liner notes for those wanting to know more by Sonia Seeman, an authority on Turkish Rom music.

İstanbul Oriental Ensemble
Gypsy Rum (Network, Germany). Led by percussionist Burhan Öçal, this ensemble (traditional line-up of clarinet, violin, *ud*, *kanun* and *darbuka*) delivers fourteen tracks of tight instrumental playing. Emotional twists and lightning virtuosity will have your shoulders shaking; listen for the screaming shrieks from Fethi Tekyaygil's violin. If you like this, try their follow-up album, *The Sultan's Secret Door* (Network).

Mustafa Kandıralı *Caz Roman* (Network, Germany). The great clarinetist Kandıralı's performances have a quiet iconoclasm in their melodic invention. This disc is the epitome of instrumental *fasıl*, including such masters as Ahmet Meter (*kanun*), Metin Bükey (*ud*) and Ahmet Kulık (*darbuka*). The final section of dance tunes is from a concert recorded in 1984.

Karşılama *Karşılama* (Green Goat, Canada/Kalan). İstanbul Gypsy musicians led by Selim Sesler on G-clarinet, with locally trained Canadian vocalist Brenna MacCrimmon, interpret Rom music from western Turkey and the Balkans. Played with real panache,

and good to have some of the vocal repertoire – gleaned from archival recordings and manuscripts – expertly showcased.

The Road to Keşan: Turkish Rom and Regional Music of Thrace (Traditional Crossroads/Kalan). Gypsy music breaks out of its nightclub ghetto and gets a full, thunderously percussive hearing in its native village setting with this superb production overseen and authoritatively annotated by Sonia Seeman. The clarinetist is again Selim Sesler, but all the musicians – including Bülent Sesler on *kanun* and Nüsret Şüte on violin – are excellent. Irresistibly danceable, with plenty of influences (and the occasional melody) from Greece, in particular its Pomak communities.

Hüsnü Şenlendirici and Laço Tayfa *Çiftetelli* (Traditional Crossroads). Mildly electrified Gypsy jazz funk, the Turkish equivalent of Cuba's Irakere, guaranteed to outrage purists, but the musicianship of Şenlendrici – from a clan of hereditary musicians in Bergama – and the Laço Tayfa band ultimately carries the day. When the percussion, keyboard and bass guitar aren't purring along as an undercurrent, there are some wonderful long clarinet solos by Hüsnü on "Harmandalı" and "İzmir'in Kavakları".

Arabesk

Müslüm Gürses *İnsaf/Kahire Resitali* (Uğur, Turkey). Gürses' collaboration with Egyptian musicians, billed as his "Cairo recital", is in fact a tight studio recording. The inspiration of Egyptian dance-orchestra musicians on the genre as a whole is immediately obvious from this recording. Contains perfect examples of his intense vocal style and despairing lyrics. His complete discography would defy compilation, as he's been

recording prolifically since the 1970s; *Sevda Yüklü Kervanlar* and *Bir Kadeh Daha Ver* contain many of his classic hits.

Orhan Gencebay *Yalnız Değilsin* (Kervan, Turkey). This relatively recent recording demonstrates Gencebay's unflagging musical curiosity, taking in Middle Eastern, European and American popular and classical genres in one magisterial sweep. His own virtuoso *saz* playing, as ever, dominates; listen out for the thunderous belly-dance number ("Gencebay Oriyentali") and a mock-Baroque overture ("Nihavent Üvertür"). Most of his early recordings accompanied musical films, and can still be found in either cassette or CD form.

İbrahim Tatlıses *Fosforlu Cevriyem* (Emre, Turkey). This live recording is a rare chance to hear what *arabesk* sounds like in the flesh, with some of his all-time favourites ("Beyaz Gül, Kırmızı Gül", "Fosforlu Cevriyem", "Beyoğlu", "Yeşil Yeşil"), and some superb *uzun hava* semi-improvisations. It was a huge 1990 hit, and gives some sense of Tatlıses' phenomenal vocal presence.

Rock, pop, özgün and crossover

Sezen Aksu *Işık Dogudan Yükselir/The Light Rises in the East* (Foneks, Turkey). An intriguing CD, from the overblown orchestral opening (courtesy Onno Tunç), to the intimate, sparse style that characterizes all of her recent work. Some songs are self-consciously authentic in spirit ("Ben Annemi Isterim", and "Rakkas", based on Black Sea and urban dance styles respectively), others in a more abstract, allusive style ("Halımımı Yaktılar", based on traditional women's laments). *Düğün ve Cenaze* (Raks, Turkey), a collaboration with Yugoslav musician Goran Bregoviç, translated the music from Emir Kusturica's films *The Time of the Gypsies* and *Underground* into Aksu's distinctive idiom, with an opening slow tango and a Serbian brass band thrown in for good measure. Aksu's latest, and arguably best, is *Deli Veren* (Balet, Turkey); her voice continues developing in subtlety, range and lyric control, the song-writing by turns playful and experimental but increasingly her own. "Gidiyorum bu Şehirden" extends her interest in Aegean musical détente, and her ability to forge productive partnerships with musicians from elsewhere in the region, here with Haris Alexiou. "Kahpe Kader" and "Yalancı Dunya" suggest an intriguing rapprochement with *arabesk*.

Cartel *Cartel* (Mercury, Germany). The first recording by, for many, the definitive Turkish–German rap and hip-hop collective. Though almost buried under hype, academic commentary and furious polemic when it was released in Turkey in 1995, its peculiar qualities can perhaps be better appreciated today: a witty and humorous commentary on life on the Turkish–German street, with high-voltage sampling of Turkish folk music sounds.

Kudsi Ergüner *Islam Blues* (Act, Germany). The vocals of Yunus Balcıoğlu, Derya Türkan's *kemençe* and Hakan Güngör's *kanun* blend effectively with Bruno Caillat on percussion, Nguyen Le on guitar, Renaud Garcia-Fons on bass, Mark Nauseef and Karinm Ziad on drums. There's a spiritual intensity to this more successful experiment than his earlier *Ottomania* that's sometimes reminiscent of Coltrane, and sometimes simply its own thing. Perhaps one of the most effective jazz/Middle Eastern crossovers to date.

Cem Karaca *Cemaz ül-Evvel* (Kalan). A retrospective of Karaca's major work with his early groups, particularly Apaşlar and Kardaşlar, and thus traces his experiments with a variety of Western pop and rock genres, plus his emerging political radicalism. Essentially the whole story of Turkish highbrow rock, on one recording.

Ahmet Kaya *An Gelir* (Taç, Turkey). Plangent *saz*, and up-tempo *halay* dance numbers, deep, melancholy vocals; radical in gesture, but social-realist pessimism in content. Nothing that Kaya, the Kurdish "Jacques Brel", subsequently did lived up to the enormous vitality and lyricism of this early album.

Zülfü Livaneli *Maria Farandouri Söylüyor* (Raks, Turkey). From the early 1980s, this was a landmark collaboration between historical enemies: Greek star Maria Farandouri singing Livaneli compositions in both Greek and Turkish. Beautiful, often dark, melodies, exquisitely rendered in fine arrangements. Livaneli has more recently been through a dubious New Age phase, but his 1998 album *Nefesim nefesime* (*Breath to Breath*) showed him back on better form.

Mirkelam *Mirkelam* (İstanbul Plak, Turkey). Featuring the song that launched Mirkelam in 1995, "Her Gece", this CD illustrates all of the virtues and vices of contemporary Turkish pop. This is, effectively, turbo-charged *arabesk*, with a distinctly Turkish sound to the melodic line and vocal style, but a pounding dance/techno pulse.

Şivan Perwer *Chants du Kurdistan* (Auvidis/Ethnic, France). A good introduction to this Kurdish bard's earlier, mostly traditional songs, self-accompanied on *saz*. *Kirive, Vol. 1 & 2* (SES Plak, Turkey) are among nearly twenty Perwer CDs on this label, most of them still banned within Turkey (Şivan himself is now based in Sweden). These "Best of..." titles include many of his most famous political songs, plus some folk songs; *düdük, bloor, ud* and *kanun* in addition to *saz*.

Selda *Selda* (Uzelli, Turkey). Selda is equally at home singing *türkü* or *özgün*. This collection features both and includes the wonderful *Dost Merhaba*.

Tarkan *Karma* (İstanbul Plak, Turkey). Tarkan assembles an exotic team of musicians (including Hossam Ramzy's ensemble, Ruben Harutunian on Armenian *duduk*, Jean-Louis Solon on *didj, sitar* and *sarod*) who promptly disappear into a dance-oriented mix, dominated by Tarkan's voice, which nicely combines rock heroics and Middle Eastern sophistry.

Yeni Türkü *Her Dem Yeni/New Every Time* (BMG, Turkey). The "greatest hits" album, drawing on their various excellent BMG releases, with twenty of their songs.

Martin Stokes, with Marc Dubin

Turkish cinema

The films of Yılmaz Güney aside, **Turkish cinema** is little known outside Turkey, a result perhaps of its historic preoccupations with what most foreign critics have perceived as strictly local issues such as rural to urban population drift and the dislocation of traditional lifestyles. Throughout the 1970s and 1980s, however, Turkish directors produced a number of powerful movies worthy of wider recognition. Since the mid-to-late 1990s, economic problems in the industry, and the country in general, have ravaged the film-making sector, just as Turkish art-house cinema was gaining a growing – if still small – number of followers.

Although cinema as an art form has only emerged in Turkey over the last four decades, the local film industry has been churning out low-budget melodramas for the better part of 75 years, and indeed continues to do so. All forms of film-making have been handicapped by a relative lack of finance and technical resources, and directors and writers wishing to address social or political issues have also had to contend with state censorship in varying degrees over the years, which has given rise to a tendency to portray everyday life lyrically or through allegory.

The growth of the industry

The history of public cinema in Turkey began in 1897 when **Sigmund Weinberg**, a Romanian-Jewish café-owner in the Pera district of İstanbul, staged the city's first film show. It was not until World War I, however, that the government, realizing the propaganda value of film, set up several **army film units**. These units put together a number of documentaries, although the first film ever produced under Turkish government auspices (recording the demolition of a Russian monument in İstanbul) was shot under the direction of an Austrian military crew. A Turkish projectionist, **Fuat Uzkınay**, took the largely symbolic role of holding the camera, under close Austrian supervision.

By the end of World War I, Turkish military film-makers had mastered their trade sufficiently to go on and make documentaries on the War of Independence. With the end of all hostilities a number of **production companies** were set up, including one owned jointly by Sigmund Weinberg and Fuat Uzkınay, and Turkey's feature film industry came into existence.

During the 1920s, a trend for ham-fisted adaptations of works by seventeenth-century French playwrights like Molière was established, a field that was dominated by two companies, İpek Film and Kemal Film. The leading director of the period was **Muhsin Ertuğrul**, who made 29 films between 1922 and 1953. His "backlist" includes a couple of features based on the War of Independence: *Ateş'ten Gömlek* (Shirt of Fire; 1923) and *Bir Millet Uyanıyor* (The Awakening of a Nation; 1932). These films did refer to actual events, but they never sought to challenge the official line of Kemalist Turkey, nor did they break any new ground artistically.

Any attempts to do either would probably have foundered against the government's rigorous **censorship laws**, codified in 1932. All films faced a three-tiered process; first, scripts were censored before filming began, then the police controlled sequences as they were shot, and finally government censors inspected the finished work, excising contentious material. Governmental stifling of creativity was exacerbated by chronic lack of cash and equipment, with the result that by World War II the staple fare of Turkish picture houses was Hollywood productions and risible B-movies churned out in Egypt by a Turkish producer, **V.O. Bengü**.

In quantitative terms the output of the Turkish film industry picked up significantly in the 1950s with the establishment of a genre of mass-entertainment **melodrama** that continues to this day, lapped up by rural and small-town audiences. These films had a very basic premise that was to prove successful time and again: rural boy meets rural girl, the world tries to keep them apart (in more sophisticated variants, one is temporarily blind to the virtues of the other) but, ultimately, they triumph over tragedy and live happily ever after, having achieved fame and fortune along the way.

One positive effect of this increased cinematic activity was that it enabled a **new generation** of young film-makers to master the skills of cinematography, among them Yılmaz Güney and others who, in the 1960s and 1970s, would go on to develop a homegrown Turkish cinematic identity.

The new wave and Yilmaz Güney

During the 1960s, the first attempts were made to produce films that moved away from melodrama into the realm of social criticism. A leading director of the period was **Lüfti Ö. Akad** who, having cut his teeth on melodramas and a few derivative gangster pictures during the 1940s and 1950s, went on to direct *Tanrı'nın Bağışı Orman* (The Forest, God's Gift) in 1964, a documentary study of the feudal hierarchy in Anatolia. In 1966 he made *Hudutların Kanunu* (The Law of the Frontier), a dramatic treatment of similar issues, dealing with the stranglehold of wealthy landlords on the rural population in the southeast. He later directed *Kızılırmak-Karakoyun* (Red River, Black Sheep), based on a play by poet Nazım Hikmet. Between 1973 and 1975 Akad produced an important trilogy, exploring the drift of population from rural Anatolia to the cities, and the conflict between traditional lifestyles and modern, Westernized city life: *Gelin* (The Bride), *Düğün* (The Wedding) and *Diyet* (Retribution).

During the 1970s **Yılmaz Güney** took over as Turkey's leading serious director and became, in the process, the first Turkish director to gain real recognition outside his native land. After serving his apprenticeship on the melodramas of the Fifties, Güney had scripted *Hudutların Kanunu* for Akad and took the lead acting role in *Kızılırmak-Karakoyun*. The first major film he directed, in 1970, was *Umut* (Hope), the story of a taxi driver who loses his house and stakes his remaining money on a mad treasure-hunting venture. Though not an outstanding film, it is indicative of the thematic direction that Güney's later works were to take, and certain scenes, notably the final one where the maddened hero circles a hole in the ground blindfolded, are echoed in later films.

Umut was followed in 1971 by *Ağıt* (Lament), in which a man is forced to resort to smuggling by economic circumstance, and *Acık* (Sorrow), a film about lost love and revenge. Güney was imprisoned after the 1971 coup, remaining in jail until 1974. Upon his release he made the film *Arkadaş* (The Friend), which, like the earlier *Umutsuzlar* (Those Without Hope) and *Baba* (The Father), dealt with the lot of Turkey's urban poor, an area in which Güney was less confident as a director. In the same year Güney was imprisoned again, accused of murdering a judge. He began directing films from his cell, writing scripts and passing on instructions to fellow-directors; paradoxically, he produced some of his finest work in this period.

In 1979 *Sürü* (The Herd), written by Güney with **Zeki Ökten** directing, was released; like Güney's earlier films its theme is rural dislocation. Life among feuding nomadic families in the south is the starting point; with their traditional grazing lands threatened by development, a Kurdish family decide to take their sheep to the markets of Ankara. Visually the film is dominated by the road and rail journey of the shepherds and their flocks, and this is used to highlight the dichotomy between their lifestyle and city ways. The political turmoil that surrounds them, but which they are barely aware of, is suggested by characteristic Güney touches: almost impressionistic sequences of manacled prisoners and a youth being shot for distributing pamphlets.

Güney also worked on his most famous film, **Yol** (The Road), from the confines of his prison cell, with the outside directorial assistance of **Şerif Gören**. It's an extraordinary film, taking an allegorical look at the state of the nation by following the fortunes of five prisoners who have been allowed a week's parole. Even when temporarily released they are unable to make their own way through a society that seems unreal to them, and their behaviour is determined by social conditions over which they have no control. One prisoner, Ömer, returns to his Kurdish village and is faced with a choice between returning to prison or taking to the hills. He eventually opts for the latter but there is a strong sense that the decision is forced on him. The film focuses, though, on Seyit Ali, who returns to his village to find that his wife, who has become a prostitute, is being held by his brothers, who expect him to kill her. He refuses to do so outright, but abandons her in the snow – after a change of heart he returns to save her, only to find that she's dead. Güney, having escaped from jail, was able to edit this film in exile in France, and the final result, released in 1982, is permeated by a strong sense of longing for his homeland. *Yol* shared the Cannes Film Festival's Palme d'Or for that year with Costa-Gavras' *Missing*, greatly elevating Turkish cinema's international standing. Banned in Turkey itself, *Yol* finally made it onto the country's cinema screens in 1999, where it played to packed houses.

Güney's last film was *Duvar* (The Wall), made during his French exile and released in 1983. Unrelentingly brutal, it's a composite portrait of Turkish prison life, focusing on the experiences of a group of young detainees, little more than children. The prison of the film becomes a microcosm of Turkish society as seen through the eyes of its inmates. The prison hierarchy, with the director of prisons at the top, is shown as unmerciful and inflexible; complaints are responded to with violence and the prisoners have no chance of redress for the wrongs done to them. This is graphically demonstrated by the fate of Şabah, one of the young inmates; he is sexually assaulted by one of the guards and, encouraged by his fellow inmates, decides to report the incident to the prison doctor. At the last moment his nerve fails him. His friends ostracize him, and in despair he attempts to escape, and is killed. Güney died of cancer, aged 46, the year after *Duvar*'s release.

An important contemporary of Güney was **Ömer Kavur**, whose first film, *Emine*, was released in 1974. Set in a small provincial town at the turn of the century, the film looked at the role of women in traditional society. In 1979

Ömer directed *Yusuf İle Kenan* (Yusuf and Kenan), the story of two young boys forced to leave their village after their father is killed in a blood feud. An increasingly important element of modern Turkish life, the experience of the migrant worker, was explored in *Otobüs* (The Bus) by **Tunç Okan**. This 1977 film examines the dislocating effect of having to leave the homeland in search of work through the eyes of a group of Turks who, having come to Sweden, find themselves abandoned in Stockholm, ripped off by a fellow countryman.

The 1980s

Turkish film output actually peaked numerically in 1972 with 299 films, but as the decade progressed there was a steady decline amidst the political turmoil and violence preceding the 1980 coup. In that year, however, **Ali Özgentürk** released *Hazal*, a dramatic depiction of life in a spectacularly isolated, semi-feudal village, where a young woman attempts to escape from an arranged marriage to a 10-year-old boy in order to be with her lover, but suffers swift, harsh retribution. In the wake of the 1980 coup, however, the work of many directors was banned, and the Turkish film industry was effectively driven into exile.

The early to mid-Eighties saw something of a revival. In 1982 Ali Özgentürk made *At* (The Horse), a co-production with West German colleagues, which has been aptly described as a bleaker reworking of *The Bicycle Thief*. The film tells the story of a peasant and his son who arrive in İstanbul in search of a better life. The father hopes to be able to earn enough as a street trader to put his son through school, but is inevitably overwhelmed by the big city.

In 1983 *Hakkâri'de Bir Mevsim* (A Season in Hakkâri), directed by **Erdan Kıral** in another German-funded co-production, was released. Arguably the best Turkish film of the Eighties, and certainly the one that won most international acclaim, this visually stunning film examines the experiences of a young teacher sent to a distant Kurdish village to staff the local school. He is shocked by the poverty and isolated from the locals by vast linguistic and cultural gaps. Gradually, however, through his relationship with two local orphans, the girl Zazi and her brother Halit (a smuggler, also excluded from village life), he comes to identify with his surroundings, a process helped when the locals call on his aid during an epidemic. When he receives notice from the authorities that he can leave the village he is reluctant to go, having found a stability previously absent from his rootless existence.

Although many Turkish films of the decade were notably subdued, focusing on themes of individual struggle to skirt direct political comment, a few made after the middle of the decade addressed issues such as social hypocrisy, or the position of women in Turkish society. *Bir Yudum Sevgi* (A Sip of Love), directed by **Atif Yılmaz** in 1984, looks at one woman's struggle to win her personal independence. Related themes emerge in *Asiye*, an unusual musical adapted from a stage play, lambasting the notion of the woman as male property through the tale of a peasant woman who becomes a prostitute and later brothel madam.

The director **Başar Sabuncu** chalked up a number of noteworthy films during the later 1980s. *Çıplak Vatandaş* (The Naked Citizen) is a fairly light-hearted 1986 satire, following the fortunes of a man who, while temporarily deranged by economic misfortune and confrontation with bureaucracy, runs almost naked through his home town, only to be subsequently exploited by an advertising firm who use him in a TV ad for bath salts. *Kupa Kızı* (Queen of Hearts), released the following year, is an acidic reworking of *Belle de Jour*, telling of a woman who turns part-time prostitute and uses sex as a means of revenge. In *Asılacak Kadın* (A Woman to be Hanged), a young woman becomes a judicial scapegoat for the murder of an old man who has sexually abused her. The film fell foul of the censors and its release resulted in the banning of the novel that inspired it, for "offending national morality". Sabuncu's next film, in 1988, was *Zengin Mutfağı* (Kitchen of the Rich), an adaption of a stage play set among the servants in the kitchen of a wealthy family, intended as an allegory of the situation immediately before the 1971 military coup.

Other Eighties films worthy of mention include **Nesli Çölgecen**'s 1986 effort *Ağa* (The Landlord) and Ömer Kavur's 1986 return to the director's chair, *Anayurt Oteli* (The Motherland Hotel). The former examines the struggles of a wealthy landlord in the southeast, unable to come to terms with changes in rural life. Here a severe drought is substituted for the socio-economic forces that might have caused these changes had the film been made a decade earlier. Kavur's film is set in a small town near İzmir where an obsessive and lonely hotel-owner's life falls apart when an attractive female guest breaks a promise to make a return visit. The film breaks new ground for Turkish cinema, exploring psychological and emotive issues with a previously unknown depth. Another important late Eighties film was *Kırk Metre Kare Almanya'da* (Forty Square Metres in Germany), directed by **Tevfik Başer** in 1987, looking at the experience of Turkish migrant workers through the eyes of a village woman brought to Hamburg and confined in a dismal flat while her husband goes off to work.

Films made towards the end of the decade indicated that Turkish directors once again felt secure enough to question openly the way their society functions, and to refer directly to political conditions within Turkey. **Tunç Başaran**'s *Uçurtmayı Vurmasınlar* (Don't Let Them Shoot the Kite; 1989), about the relationship that develops in jail between a sensitive inmate and the 5-year-old son of a woman doing time for drug-dealing, touches on an area of Turkish life that, earlier in the decade, would have been out of bounds to film-makers. *Blackout Nights* (1990), by **Yusuf Kürçenli**, went even further. Based on an autobiographical novel by the poet Rıfat Ilgaz, arrested as a suspected communist at the end of World War II, it questioned the need for censorship and attacked political oppression.

The 1990s

While the rest of the world was celebrating the hundredth anniversary of film in 1995, Turkey's industry remained in crisis. Multinational production companies dominated cinema screens so that independent Turkish operators, whose films were still plagued with technical difficulties, most noticeably their poor sound quality, found it hard to find outlets for their productions. A general lack of interest on the part of the Ministry of Culture, who withdrew funding for the subtitling of Turkish films to be shown abroad, compounded the problems. Despite the difficulties, there were a few notable productions in an otherwise uneventful decade. In 1990, Ömer Kavur managed to release his acclaimed movie *Gizli Yüz* (The Secret Face), based on a story by writer Orhan Pamuk about a nightclub photographer and his pursuit of a beautiful woman who disappears with a watchmaker. In 1994, **Erden Kıral**'s *Mavi Sürgün* (The Blue Exile) gained worldwide attention and was nominated (unsuccessfully) for an Academy Award for Best Foreign Film. Beautifully photographed and acted, it tells of aristocrat Cevat Şakir's 1925 exile to Turkey's then-remote southwestern coast. By the end of his journey, he has come to terms with his past and started a new life based on self-understanding and his role in his adopted home.

One encouraging trend has been the emergence of **women directors**, most notably **Tomris Giritlioğlu**, whose films have received both national and international recognition. Her first, *Yaz Yağmuru* (A Passing Summer Rain), released in 1994, concerns a writer who is overwhelmed by images inspired by a young woman he sees in his garden one day; *80 Adım* (The 80th Step), winner of the best movie award at the İstanbul Film Festival in 1996, is about a committed left-wing political activist released from jail in 1980 as the country reels from the September 12 military coup, and deals with his personal conflicts in a changing society. Another female director, **Biket İlhan**, explores İstanbul's underworld in a thriller made in 1995, *Sokaktaki Adam* (The Man in the Street), about a ship's steward who becomes involved in smuggling and then falls for a famous prostitute.

One of the most highly acclaimed works of the decade was *İstanbul Kanatlarımın Altında* (İstanbul beneath my Wings), made in 1995 by **Mustafa Altıoklar**. Set in seventeenth-century İstanbul during the reign of tyrant Murat IV, four close friends are tussling with the theories of flight while Murat and his janissary guards rampage around the city closing down its more riotous drinking establishments by lynching everyone they discover on the premises. Murat eventually catches up with the four heroes, whose number includes the travel chronicler Evliya Çelebi, and is advised of their appropriate fate by reactionary forces in his divan council. The film, based on a true story, disguises its contemporary political overtones with tongue-in-cheek dialogue and farcical comedy, but its plea for enlightenment in the face of fundamentalist zeal is a timely message in modern Turkey. A joint Turkish–Italian venture, the film's success led to a number of other co-productions, including the acclaimed *Hamam*, made in 1998 by Celhan Özpetek, in which its Italian star inherits a run-down Turkish bath in İstanbul. Through his efforts to restore it, he discovers his own sexuality, making this one of the few Turkish films dealing with gay relationships to have gone on general release.

After the success of *İstanbul Kanatlarımın Altında*, Turkey's filmgoers decided to give the domestic industry another chance in 1996. Financial constraints forced a group of the country's best-known directors to collaborate on two releases made up of five short made-for-TV films, *Aşık Üzerine Söylenmiş Her Şey* (Everything Untold about Love) and *Yerçekimli Aşıklar* (Loves with Gravity). These anthologies are snapshots of contemporary Turkish society, covering domestic themes with little overtly political content.

A minor boom in film production then followed, fuelled by the massive domestic success of *Eskiya* (The Bandit), made in 1996 and directed by **Yavuz Tuğrul**. Telling the tale of a former outlaw released from prison to embark on a search for his lost past, the script touched on a number of social issues while never losing its story-telling drive. As the "bandit" wanders through a modern İstanbul of petty criminals and mafia dons, his outdated rural codes seem more and more at odds with the world he encounters.

Into the new millennium

The late 1990s and the early years of the new century have seen a gradual unwinding of the country's tight censorship laws, with both ethnic Turkish and ethnic Kurdish directors at the forefront of pushing out the boundaries of the permissible. *İşıklar Sönmesin* (The Lights Must Not Go Out), directed by **Reis Çelik** in 1996, was the first action film to deal directly with the war between ethnic Kurdish separatists and the army in the southeast, a subject returned to with increasing skill during subsequent years. **Yesim Ustaoğlu**'s 1999 İstanbul Film Festival winner, *Güneş'e Yolculuk* (Journey to the Sun) dealt with the travails of a Turk whose swarthy looks lead him to be constantly mistaken for a Kurd, while **Kâzım Öz**'s 2001 *Fotograf* (Photograph), shot on a miniscule budget, achieved a breakthrough with its use of the Kurdish language. Also in 2001, **Handan İpekçi**'s *Büyük Adam, Küçük Aşk* (*Hejar* in Kurdish, or "Great Man, Small Passion") pitted itself against the censors by throwing together the only-Kurdish-speaking child of two activists killed in a police raid and an only-Turkish-speaking former judge. Their relationship, replete with total misunderstandings and a thankfully unsentimental ending, unsettled the authorities enough for it to be temporarily banned from screening at the 2002 İstanbul Film Festival.

Portrayals of other sensitive political and social problems have also become more widespread in the last decade. **Mustafa Altıoklar**'s 1997 *Ağır Roman* (Heavy Novel), the first widely released Turkish film to display police torture, was followed by Tomris Giritlioğlu's *Salkım Hanım'ın Taneleri* (Lady Salkım's Jewels), winner of the 1999 Antalya "Golden Orange" Film Festival, which explores the punitive "wealth tax" imposed on the country's non-Muslim minorities during the 1940s. It follows the rise to fame and fortune of an unscrupulous Muslim who exploits the ruination of his Armenian ex-bosses. Also broaching a taboo subject is director **Tayfun Pirselimoğlu**'s *Hiçbiryerde* (In Nowhere Land; 2002), which takes a look at Turkey's "disappeared" – the thousands of people who vanished in mysterious circumstances during the political conflicts of the 1970s, 1980s and 1990s. Cinematically flawed, it is largely saved by the performance of one of Turkey's most talented actresses, Zuhal Ölçay.

With Turkey moving closer to Europe politically and economically, plus commitments by the newly elected government to further freedom of expression, Turkish cinema is likely to continue exploring previously banned themes with increasing daring. Meanwhile, the issue of the country's ethnic diversity promises to also be more prominently featured, with directors such as Kâzım Öz, who are Turkish citizens but ethnic Kurds, creating a completely new genre: Kurdish-language movies from Turkey.

Updated by Jon Gorvett

Turkish writers

T urkish literature, like so much else about the country, is virtually unknown abroad except for the epic works of Yaşar Kemal and the trendy cult novels of Orhan Pamuk. This is regrettable, because Turkish authors particularly excel in the genre of short stories and memoirs. On the whole, writing in the country is heavily biased towards accounts of city life, particularly İstanbul, a reflection perhaps of that city's cultural dominance. The pieces below, however, show more of a cross-section of Turkish society.

İrfan Orga

İrfan Orga was born into a wealthy Ottoman family in old İstanbul in 1908, whose lives were irrevocably shattered by World War I and the Nationalist revolution. Brought up in extreme poverty after 1915, Orga was enrolled as a cadet in the Kuleli military academy, which was seen by his widowed mother as the only way for advancing the family fortunes. Later, as a Turkish air force officer, he arrived in wartime England in 1941 speaking no English, and soon began living with a married woman. Despite the unhappiness and dislocation this precipitated – court cases, trouble with the Home Office, the loss of his officer's commission and eventually a seventeenth-year ban on return to Turkey – Orga quickly learned English and within eight years had penned the memoir excerpted below, currently in print and published by Eland Books. This was phenomenally well received, a success he was never to repeat despite producing numerous subsequent works on Turkish subjects. Orga died in 1970, survived by a son, and was able to live in some semblance of comfort only in his later years.

Portrait of a Turkish Family

I had become very restless at home and was often insubordinate. My mother worried incessantly about my education, but all the schools were still disorganized and many teachers had never come back from the war. I used to haunt the streets, playing a corrupted version of football near the gardens of the Mosque, for I had nothing to keep my mind constantly occupied. My mother and I used to have fierce and bitter quarrels and, because I could not bear being confined to the house, I took to roaming farther and farther away from home. No doubt had I had a father to discipline me I should never have dared to do these things, but I would not listen to my mother or grandmother, flying into a passion if they attempted to interfere with me.

My mother was rebelling against life too – but for a different reason. Her rebellion was, unexpectedly enough, against wearing the veil, for she had noticed that none of the foreign women wore them and that even a few of the more daring Turkish women from good families had ceased the practice also. She used to complain about it to my grandmother, declaring she was sick and tired of keeping her face covered, and I would interrupt, with lordly ten-year oldness, saying I would not have her going about the streets with her face open. I would chastise her too for her many goings-out.

"You are never at home," I would declare and although usually I was told to mind my own affairs, one day I was very surprised when my grandmother actually agreed with me.

"It is quite true," she said heatedly. "You are always out these days. And it is not right for you to complain that you have to wear the veil. Why, many women are still behind the kafes and they never see the colour of the sky, excepting from behind their veils. But at least you cannot complain of that for you tore the kafes from here and it is a wonder to me that you were ever accepted in this street, for you behaved exactly like a fast woman looking for another husband or like a prostitute. Yes, you did!" she assured my mother's astonished face. "And now you talk of leaving aside your veil. Why, I lived for thirty years with my husband and I never went out without his permission and I had to keep my face covered all the time. If I went out in the carriage with Murat, immediately all the windows were closed and sometimes the blinds were drawn too. I say it is a scandal that women are today revealing their faces. God will punish them! Do not let me hear another word from you, my daughter, for surely the sky will open on you for such impiety."

Never had I heard my grandmother talk at such length or with such obvious passion. My mother replied:

"You are talking a great deal of old-fashioned nonsense, mother! My place is not in the home these days. If I were to sit at home all day, or you either for that matter, who would go to market for us? Do you expect me to stay here all day, reading the Koran and wearing my veil for fear the passers-by should see me from the street? I tell you again, from now on I shall go without my veil!"

And she angrily tore the pretty veil from her face and threw it petulantly on the floor.

My grandmother lifted her hands to heaven.

"I never thought I should live to see this day," she said.

"Times are changing," said my mother.

"They will say you are a prostitute!" wailed my grandmother, genuinely distressed, totally incapable of accepting such a fierce gesture as the "opening" of the face.

"If they do, it will not worry me," retorted my mother. "Their words will not bring bread to me. And from now on, you will throw aside your veil too, mother."

"Oh no, no, no!" said my grandmother in superstitious horror. "God forbid I should invite punishment upon me!"

But the next morning when my mother went into Beyoğlu, with a box of embroidered articles under her arm and her lovely face naked to the world, she was stoned by some children near Bayazit and received a nasty cut on the side of her head. After that she was cautious about going anywhere alone, but was adamant about not re-veiling herself; Mehmet or I would go with her to Beyoğlu, my grandmother steadfastly refusing to be seen with her. The reaction to her in the street was mixed. The older ones were stricken with horror, more especially since they had always recognised my mother as a good woman, and now their faith in her was sadly battered. She was still young and attractive – she was twenty-five – and despite the shadows that lingered now and then in her eyes, was so unusually beautiful that people could not help but stare at her, and certain sections of the street wondered if she were trying to catch a husband. They came in their droves, the old men as well, to remonstrate with my grandmother, urging her to put a stop to this terrible thing, and my grandmother, thoroughly enjoying herself, would groan to them that she had no authority left in this wayward family of hers. But the younger women sided with my mother, and some of them even began to follow her example. Their fathers, however, in the absence of dead husbands, took a stick to them muttering piously that no woman in their family would so disgrace themselves. So they put on their veils again in a hurry.

Not a few wished to apply the chastening stick to my mother also. They gave my grandmother sympathy until she was sick of it and prophesied gloomily – but with a little bit of anticipatory relish too, I think – that my mother would come to a bad end.

And indeed she very nearly did!

For one day in Bayazit, when she was alone, an impressionable Frenchman attempted to flirt with her. She tried walking hurriedly on but this had no effect at all, or if anything a worse effect, for the gallant Frenchman became more than ever aware of the swing of her silk skirts and the little dark curls that twined so coquettishly at the nape of her neck. Naturally he followed her. And all the little boys of the district became aware, as is the way of all little boys, of the one-sided flirtation which was in progress. And naturally enough they followed the tall Frenchman, so there was that day in Bayazit the very, very unusual sight of a young Turkish woman, with open face, followed by a foreigner and an innumerable number of small, dirty-nosed boys. When my mother made the mistake of stopping, trying to explain in her totally inadequate French that the gentleman was making a great mistake, he took off his hat, bowed elegantly and declared with obvious feeling:

"Vous êtes ravissante!"

And all the small boys who could not understand a word of what he said, cheered or jeered, according to their several temperaments, and my mother – very properly – hurried on, blushing and breathless and perhaps wishing a little bit for the security of her veil.

So it was that when she came down our street, with her procession behind her, the neighbours were more than ever scandalised and ran into their houses to tell the ones inside. But when my mother called out to them in Turkish that she was being followed, and very much against her will, they set to with a vengeance and brought out sticks and brooms and shooed off the gallant representative of Gallicism in no uncertain manner. Mehmet and I, who were watching the whole proceedings from the window, were bursting with laughter but my poor grandmother was quite ready to die with shame.

"Such a disgrace!" she kept saying. "We shall never be able to live in this street again."

But in this she was wrong for when the street had finally disposed of the amorous Frenchman, and a few old men had in fact chased him half-way to Bayazit with tin buckets in their hands, to break his head, the street settled down again to lethargy, exonerating my mother from all blame. All excepting the old women, that is.

Reprinted by permission of Eland Books.

Sait Faik

Sait Faik was born in 1906, the son of a wealthy Adapazarı businessman, but spent most of his later years at the family villa on Burgazada, one of the Princes' Islands. He was fortunate in being able to rely on a small inheritance, because he was intrinsically unsuited for conventional employment, never holding any job for longer than a few weeks. Nor did he spend much time away from the İstanbul area, except for a brief period of study and travel in Switzerland and France, where he failed to complete university. Instead he spent most of his life strolling the quays and back streets of his beloved city, cultivating friendships with all sorts of people, who were astonished to learn, after his death, of his profession and class, since he kept both a secret – along with his homosexuality. His stories, available in English in the collection *A Dot on the Map*, first published in 1983, are rarely strong on plot, often verging on the indulgent; but they have an unerring eye for characterization, dialogue and description. Faik died in 1954 of cirrhosis of the liver, doubtless caused by long hours of tippling with the fishermen, bootblacks and idlers of İstanbul's *meyhanes* and coffee houses.

The Silk Handkerchief

The broad façade of the silk factory was bathed in moonlight. Several people hurried past the gate. As I was moving listlessly with steps that did not know where they were heading, the gatekeeper called after me, "Where are you going?"

"Just taking a stroll," I said.

"Aren't you going to the circus?"

When I didn't answer, he added, "Everyone is going. Nothing like this has ever come to Bursa before."

"I don't feel like going at all," I said.

He begged and begged, and persuaded me to guard the factory. I sat a little while, smoked a cigarette, sang a song. Then I became bored. "What should I do?" I wondered, got up, took the spiked stick from the gatekeeper's room, and started making the rounds of the factory.

As soon as I passed through the shop where the girls process the silk cocoons, I heard the sound of rapid footsteps. I turned on the flashlight I had been carrying in my pocket and scanned the place. In the bright beam of the flashlight there appeared two bare feet that were trying to run away. I hurried after them and caught the fugitive.

We entered the gatekeeper's room together, the thief and I. I turned on the yellow light. Oh, what a little thief this was! The hand that I squeezed to the verge of crushing was minute. His eyes were shining. After a while I let go of his hand because I had to laugh – to laugh my head off. At this point the tiny fellow rushed at me with a penknife. The rascal wounded my little finger. I firmly grasped the scamp and searched his pockets. I found a handful of illicit tobacco, some contraband cigarette paper, and a fairly clean handkerchief. I pressed some of the tobacco on my bleeding finger, tore the handkerchief, and made him bind my hand. With the remaining tobacco we rolled two thick cigarettes and had a friendly chat.

He was fifteen. Now this kind of thing was not his habit, but there you are, sin of youth. You understand, my friend, someone wanted a silk handkerchief from him, his sweetheart, his beloved, the girl next door. He of course didn't have the money to go and buy it at the market. He thought and thought and in the end hit upon this solution. I said, "All right, but the manufacturing plant is over there, what were you doing over here?" He laughed. How was he to know the location of the manufacturing plant?

Both of us smoked my cheap-brand cigarettes and became good friends. A genuine native of Bursa, born and bred there, he had never been to İstanbul, and just once to Mudanya in his long life – you should have seen his face as he said this.

At Emir Sultan, where we used to go sledding in the moonlight, I had other friends of this same type. I was sure that the skin of this one, just like theirs, turned dark in the pools of Gökdere, whose sound I could hear from afar. I know how they turn the same color as the skin of the fruits according to the season.

I looked and saw that he had a complexion as swarthy as a walnut whose green peel has fallen off. He also had white and brittle teeth like the white meat of a fresh walnut. I know that from the beginning of the summer until the walnut season only the hands of Bursa children smell like plums and peaches, and only the chests that appear through the holes left by the torn buttons of their striped shirts smell like hazelnut leaves.

At that point the gatekeeper's clock chimed midnight. The circus was going to be over any minute.

"I must be off," he said.

As I was thinking, troubled that I had sent him away without giving him a silk handkerchief, I was startled by a noise from outside. The gatekeeper was coming in grumbling. Behind him, the thief. . .

This time I pulled his ears and the gatekeeper gave him a searing whipping with a slender willow branch on the soles of his feet. Thank God the boss wasn't there. Otherwise he would surely have handed him over to the police with the words, "A child this young, and a thief! Sir, let him sit in jail and wise up!"

However much we tried to scare him he did not cry. His eyes took the expression of the eyes of children ready to cry, but not even the slightest tremor appeared on his lips, and his eyebrows remained just as firmly set; they were just a little dishevelled.

When he was let go, he shot out like a swallow that has been set free. Like a sharp wing that swipes at the moonlight and the corn field, he dashed off.

At that time I lived in the upper level of the manufacturing plant where the goods were stored. My room was really beautiful, especially pleasant on moonlit nights. There was a mulberry tree right in front of my window. Moonlight would slip through the foliage of the tree and pour in shafts over the room. Almost invariably, summer and winter, I left my window open. How cool and strange were the gusts that blew in! Because I had often worked on ships, I could tell from their smell which were the southwest, the northeast, the northwest, and the west winds – I knew them all. What winds passed over my blankets, each like an erotic dream!

I was sleeping lightly as usual. Morning was approaching. I could hear a noise from outside. It was as if someone were on the mulberry tree. I must have been frightened, for I did not get up or shout. At this very moment a shadow appeared in the window.

It was the boy, quietly slipping through the window. As he passed by me, I shut my eyes. He rummaged in the closets, searching for quite a while through the stacked goods. I didn't make a sound. To tell the truth, faced with this daring, I wasn't going to utter a word even if he had taken all the goods. I knew that the next day the boss would say, "Idiot, were you a corpse in a grave? You bastard!" He would kick me in the rear and fire me. But I didn't make a peep.

The boy, however, slipped away through the window emptyhanded just as he had come, without a sound. At this moment I heard the cracking sound of a branch. He fell to the ground. As I came down, the gatekeeper and a few other people had gathered around him.

He was dying. The gatekeeper wrenched open his fist, which was tightly clenched. From inside its palm, a silk handkerchief spurted out like water.

Yes, genuine, pure silk handkerchiefs are all like that. No matter how much you squeeze and crease them inside your palm, once the fist has opened, they spurt out of your hand like water.

Translated by Svat Soucek; reprinted by permission of Indiana University Press.

Edouard Roditi

Edouard Roditi was born of Turkish Sephardic Jewish parents, but left İstanbul relatively early in life. Though for many years dividing his time between Paris and California, he still retained an obvious affection for his roots; he died in Spain in 1992 in a motoring accident. Roditi was above all a versatile writer, having translated some of Yaşar Kemal's work into English and penned a history of Magellan's circumnavigation of the globe, in addition to being an important Surrealist poet. The following piece, taken from a collection called *The Delights of Turkey*, first published in the 1970s, demonstrates that he was also an elegant prose stylist.

Three Faiths, One God

In one of the boxes of secondhand books that the Latin Quarter dealers of Paris display on the parapets of the embankments of the Seine, I once picked up an old guidebook of İstanbul. It attracted my attention because it contained more explanatory text and fewer illustrations than those that are now published for hasty semiliterate and camera-clicking tourists who know things only by sight, and, no longer finding enough time for reading, generally remain a mine of misinformation about all that they have seen. To prepare myself for a more thorough exploration of the Byzantine and Ottoman monuments of the former Turkish capital, I therefore began to read this book a couple of months before I was actually able to leave Paris for Turkey. Somewhere among the learned author's very factual descriptions of Byzantine churches and other Greek-Orthodox monuments, I found a story that fascinated me because it contrasted so oddly with the otherwise sober tone of his historical explanations.

In 1453, when the besieged Byzantine capital finally fell to the Turks, it had been resisting their attacks for so long that most of the surrounding territory was already living fairly peacefully behind the Turkish lines. Close to the besieged city, a Greek-Orthodox monastery thus went about its daily business without ever being disturbed by constant warfare which seemed to have become part of the natural order of things. Among its bearded and black-robed brethren, it harbored a particularly lazy, gluttonous, and ignorant monk who never displayed much interest in anything but the immediate satisfaction of his own gross appetite. Brother Dositheos, since we must give him a name, happened one day to be preparing to fry himself some fish in a pan when a breathless messenger reached the monastery, bringing news that the Imperial city had at long last fallen to the Turks.

"Impossible," Brother Dositheos replied, calmly continuing to season his fish, perhaps even sprinkling a pinch of oregano herbs in the pan while the rest of the monastery interrupted their occupations to listen in dismay to the messenger's account of bloodshed, plunder, and rape. "Impossible," Brother Dositheos repeated. "Haven't we all seen them displaying every day for weeks, on their rounds along the top of the city's battlements, all the miraculous icons under whose protection the city has been placed by our saintly Patriarch Gennadios? Haven't we all heard that the Patriarch has revolted against the usurping authority of the new Roman Legate and proclaimed again the full independence of our Church? How can you believe that the Most Holy Virgin and all our Saints have deserted a city thus placed under their protection?"

The messenger and the other monks continued to argue with Brother Dositheos while he began to fry his fish as if nothing of any importance had happened. Finally, he rebuked them: "I'll believe you if the fish that I'm now frying come back to life in my pan."

Immediately, the three fish that he was frying jumped out of the pan, live and unharmed, and fell into the waters of a nearby pool that was fed by a natural spring. But all three fish bore, on one side, black marks where their skin had already been charred by the pan, whereas their other side remained silvery and unharmed. Ever since, there has always been, in the monastery's pool, which has thus become a *haghiasma* of waters that perform miraculous cures, the same number of fish that continue to display the same unique markings.

I decided to investigate this tale in İstanbul and, shortly after my arrival there, repeated it to a friend, a well-known Turkish historian. He too was fascinated by it, but admitted that he had never yet heard of the monastery and its miraculous pool. Inquiries made in various quarters then revealed that a few older people could remember having once heard the legend of the miraculous fish, but nobody that I knew had ever seen them or could tell me where the monastery and its pool might still be found.

In my wanderings in the more distant section of Old İstanbul where the last Byzantine Emperors had lived in the Vlachernae Palace, I asked again and again, in the following weeks, whether anyone there knew where I might find the *balikli kilisi*, the Church of the Fish. Many had heard of it and informed me that it was somewhere beyond the city's battlements, but nobody could tell me near which gate I might find it along the great fortified stretch that protected the city from land attacks all the way from the shores of the Golden Horn to those of the Sea of Marmara, where the city was then defended against attacks from the sea by the sinister Fortress of the Seven Towers.

Though I still failed to find the object of my search, the search itself proved fruitful, however, in that it now led me to discover a number of little-known mosques and Byzantine monuments which I might otherwise have neglected. I was thus encouraged to continue my explorations, especially as the spring weather was ideal for such long walks in little-frequented neighborhoods on the outskirts of Old İstanbul, where the fruit trees were blossoming in the many gardens scattered among almost rural slums and the ruins of abandoned monuments.

Among other monuments, I then discovered, close to the Fortress of the Seven Towers where I had just visited the dungeons and deciphered on their walls some of the messages left there by desperate prisoners, the ruins of what is now called Imrahor Djami, the Mosque of the Executioner. Situated among unidentifiable Byzantine ruins which an old Turkish woman with a passion for flowers, cats, and caged songbirds had transformed into a fantastic garden that she watered diligently with rain from a well-head that still communicated with vast underground Byzantine cisterns, this abandoned Byzantine church had once been rebuilt as a mosque by the pious executioner employed at the nearby fortress. It had previously been attached to the Monastery of Saint John of Studion, reputed in ecclesiastical history to have been the first Christian monastic community endowed with a rule, as opposed to earlier communities of hermits grouped together without having a common rule of life.

One day, close to one of the gates of the Old City, I then discovered another old mosque that was not listed in any of my guidebooks. It had been built to commemorate a holy man who, on the day that Baghdad had fallen to the armies of the Sultan, had stood there proclaiming the great news by the gate of the city, having been vouchsafed a vision of the fall of Baghdad, though the messengers sent to the Ottoman capital to bring the news of victory reached İstanbul only several weeks later, having come all the way from Baghdad by camel or on horseback.

In any other city, this little mosque might have attracted the tourist's attention. Though its proportions were modest, its architecture was in the same delicately classical style as the famous Baghdad Kiosk in the gardens of the Imperial Palace of Top Kapu. Its decoration was more simple, but in exquisite taste, and its *mihrab*, toward which the Faithful turn when they must face the east in prayer, was of finely carved marble and flanked with beautiful flowered panels of brightly colored İznik ceramic tiles. As I was quietly admiring all this, I was approached by the mosque's *Imam*, a surprisingly young Moslem ecclesiastic for these days of weakened faith when so few men of his generation choose a religious way of life. As he greeted me, he seemed to be proud to discover a foreigner visiting his otherwise deserted mosque. In broken Turkish, I told him that I found the *mihrab* truly beautiful, *chok güzel*. Seeing that I was bareheaded but wore an embroidered cap that I always carry in my pocket for such occasions, and that I had dutifully removed my shoes before entering the sacred precincts, he asked me if I was a Moslem. When I told him without further ado that I'm a Jew, an American poet, he remarked that we are all brothers if we still believe in one and the same God, especially in days when all too many men have lost their faith.

Suddenly, it occurred to me that he might know where I could find the *balikli kilisi*. To my inquiry, he replied that he knew it well. One of the Greek priests there was his friend. I would find the monastery only about half a mile from here, just beyond the nearest gate in the Old City's battlements. He then decided to lock the door of his mosque and accompany me to the gate, where he pointed out to me, in the suburban countryside beyond it, a few buildings that were almost concealed behind a slight tree-capped rising that was skirted by a rough road leading from the walled city's gate.

Together, we followed this road till we reached a group of monumental buildings that appeared to have been built in the early nineteenth century, in the Russian neo-Classical style of many Greek Orthodox monasteries that I had already visited on Mount Athos or elsewhere in Greece. Wealthy and pious Russians once devoted vast sums to the task of rebuilding such hallowed ecclesiastical monuments which, since the fall of Byzantium, had slowly been allowed to go to rack and ruin. But these particular buildings now seemed to have fallen on evil days again. At first, they appeared to be deserted, left almost in a state of ruin. Suddenly, a black-robed Greek ecclesiastic appeared in a doorway. Recognizing my guide, he greeted him cordially and volubly in fluent Turkish. I was then introduced to him somewhat abruptly as an American Jew, a poet who believed in God and who had come to visit the *haghiasma*.

The Greek priest led us through a paved yard where grass grew between the disjointed stone flags, to a huge church built in neo-Classical Russian imitation of a pillared Greek temple. Unlocking its main door, he revealed to me its once majestic and splendidly decorated aisles, which now offered every evidence of having but recently been wrecked by a mob of sacrilegious Vandals. From the vaulted ceilings, heavily wrought brass lamps had been torn and still lay scattered on the floor. The painted *iconostasis*, or icon screen, with its neo-Gothic woodwork and its saints depicted in the "Pre-Raphaelite" manner of Russian Romantic painters who studied in Rome instead of remaining faithful to traditional Byzantine styles, was sorely battered. Though much had already been hastily repaired, I could see that great effort and expense would still be necessary in order to restore all that had been so wantonly destroyed or damaged.

We stood there for a while, embarrassed by what we saw and by the Greek priest's silent sorrow as he contemplated the ruin of the splendid church of which he had once been so proud. Then he sighed, shrugged his shoulders and, through another door, led us into a small walled churchyard where all the marble tombs had been desecrated, disfigured, or overturned. From their Greek inscriptions, I was able to read the names of a couple of nineteenth-century Patriarchs of Constantinople as well as of several formerly aristocratic Phanariot families: Photiadis, Zarifi, Eliasco, Mavrogordato. In a corner of the yard, a pile of human bones had been gathered, after the Turkish mob had torn them from their sepulchers and scattered them to the winds during the anti-Greek riots which the Menderes government encouraged, a few years earlier, as an expression of protest against Greek oppression of the Turkish minority in Cyprus.

The Greek priest patted the young *Imam's* shoulder affectionately, then explained to me in Turkish: "When he heard that the mob was coming here, he came and fetched us and hid us all in his mosque. God will remember what he did for us on that dreadful day."

Returning to one of the other buildings of the almost deserted monastery, the Greek priest opened a small and nondescript door, then led us down some steps to a marble-lined and quite undamaged crypt that had escaped the attentions of the mob. In the marble basin of a fountain into which the waters of the natural spring now flowed, the three fish were swimming. They had black markings on one side, as if they had been burned, but their other side was immaculately silvery. The miraculous fish seemed to have lived over four hundred years, ever since the fall of Byzantium, and only recently to have escaped by another miracle the destructive frenzy of a rioting Turkish mob. I felt down my spine a shiver, like the devastating touch of the finger of God in a poem by Gerard Manley Hopkins. We stood there, all three, in silence, each one of us confirmed in his own different faith, but united in our common respect for all who try sincerely to be worthy of their faith.

Reprinted by permission of New Directions Publishing.

Aysel Özakin

Aysel Özakin was born in Şanlıurfa in 1942 and educated in Ankara, teaching French in İstanbul before beginning her career as a novelist and short-story writer. Shortly after the 1980 coup, Özakın moved to Germany where she has lived ever since. The following extract is from the novel she wrote shortly before leaving Turkey, *The Prizegiving* (published in the UK by The Women's Press) – in part an autobiographical work that was one of the first Turkish works of literature to question the institution of marriage.

The Prizegiving

"Is this Polatlı?" asked the young girl sitting next to Nuray.

All the women in the compartment looked outside simultaneously, at the soldiers sitting in groups on the flat ground.

"Yes," said Nuray, "it's Polatlı."

The woman of thirty or thirty-five, with short, blonde hair, who was sitting on the other side of Nuray, next to the window, looked at the soldiers too, in an absent-minded way, and nodded her head. Of all the occupants of the compartment she was the one who had spoken least. She had either leant her head back and slept, or opened and read the notebook which she was holding on her knees. While she was reading she would hold the notebook upright, with the blue plastic cover facing towards Nuray, trying to hide what was written inside. Nuray respected this effort on her part, and refrained from looking into the notebook. Is it a diary? she wondered. Or the draft of a novel? For a moment Nuray looked at her pale face, turned towards the window. It seemed as if deep thoughts and anxieties lay hidden in that face. It looked tired but meaningful . . . From such observations Nuray began to imagine that she and the silent woman sitting next to her had qualities in common. From time to time the woman would raise her head from the notebook and scrutinize the other women in the compartment.

The women had acquired small pieces of information about one another. They had found out in which district of Ankara or İstanbul each lived. In the process, each of them had expressed her views on İstanbul or Ankara as a city. İstanbul was chaotic, dirty, out of control and so on . . . Ankara, for its part, had polluted air, but on the other hand was orderly and easy to live in . . . The conversation dragged on along these lines. The women were more or less equally divided into two camps: those who favoured İstanbul in spite of everything, and those who would not exchange Ankara for any other city. Eventually they tired of this discussion, and remained silent for a long while.

The train stopped at many stations along the way. Village women and men would get on to the train with their baskets, string bags and sacks and would open the doors of the compartments to ask if there were any seats free. The city-dwelling passengers sitting inside would say there were no seats free, even if there were. The villagers would either, with silent stubbornness, come in and sit down, or else travel quietly in the corridors, keeping themselves to themselves. They would get off at another intermediate station. A village girl, wearing a long, loose-fitting coat, *şalvar* (baggy trousers) of floral-printed cotton material and a traditional head-covering, had come in and perched herself beside Nuray. The man waiting outside, with the sun-tanned face, wearing a cloth cap and aged about thirty-five, was her father. The girl was sixteen. She had bound her *yemeni* (headscarf) tightly round her brow. She had a tiny nose, and sparkling, black, childlike eyes. Her father had taken her to a *hoca*. They were on their way back. She pointed to her forehead and the back of her neck. Her head ached constantly. The *hoca* had written her an amulet. She put her henna-dyed, chapped hand down inside her clothing, brought out the amulet, and showed it to them. A small, triangular-shaped object, wrapped in a piece of flannel cloth, had been hung around her neck. One of the women, who was about Nuray's age, immediately reproached the girl.

"What good is a *hoca* going to do your headache? Tell your father to take you to a good doctor." Then, addressing herself to the other women in the compartment, she said, "What age are we living in? They still haven't managed to break away from these absurd things . . . "

The village girl, sitting with her back hunched, like an old woman, looked at her in bewilderment. After that, she did not speak at all until her father opened the door and said to her, "Come on, now." As she left she turned back towards them with a shy smile and said, "Have a good journey."

The train stopped for quite a long time at that station. Was there a mechanical fault, or did the crowd of people on the opposite platform mean another train was expected? Some cloth-capped, dark-skinned, poorly dressed men had gathered round a pillar and were talking idly, puffing at their cigarettes. Two women in black *feraces*, their heads covered in finely embroidered *yemenis*, carrying baskets in their hands and their children on their backs, walked quickly away on to the road behind the station, which led to a village. Three other women, dressed in *çarşafs*, and a man wearing a wide cloth cap and loose-fitting trousers, were squatting on the ground at the foot of the wall, eating food laid out on newspaper. There was a little girl standing waiting, her back leant against the station wall. Like the other women, she was fully covered. Only her small, red-cheeked face was exposed. She was about eleven or twelve. The people who were taking most interest in the train were some thin village youths in blue jeans. They were smoking and walking up and down in front of the windows. One of them was peering impatiently into the women's compartment where Nuray was sitting, as if he wanted to say something, or was waiting for something. He had a pale, spotty face and narrow shoulders. There was a shameless desire and a sad longing in his gaze. A very old man with a white beard, wearing *şalvar* and a green skull-cap, walked on bow legs away from the station, carrying a *heybe* (saddle-bag) on his back.

The young girl sitting on Nuray's right took out of her bag a hardback book with gold lettering on the cover and began to read it. Nuray had a daughter the same age as her; she gave the girl a motherly smile, and asked what she was reading. It was a novel. The title was *When You Choose Freedom*. Nuray looked at the cover of the book. She had never heard of the author before.

The girl was wearing tight-fitting jeans. Her fingernails were painted dark red, and she would frequently insert one of them into her mouth and nibble at it. After discovering the train had arrived at Polatlı, she put the book back in her bag and took out a black metal box, which she opened. There was a mirror in the lid, and the compartments inside contained blue, green, black and grey eyepencils, lipsticks of various shades, powder compacts, tweezers, toilet water and a hairbrush. She started to clean her dark-skinned face with a piece of cotton wool wetted with toilet water. She worked in a bank, and lived in the Ayrancı district of Ankara.

Nuray folded her arms and heaved a sigh. She thought about her daughter, who carried no make-up articles in her bag apart from a comb and a cheap mirror bought from a street stall, and who merely washed her face with soap every morning before going out with a large canvas bag full of books and papers hanging from her shoulder. Nuray felt the pain of her love for her daughter.

Translated by Celia Kerslake; reprinted by permission of The Women's Press.

Celaleddin Rumi

Celaleddin Rumi (1207–1273) was a Sufi mystic who founded the Mevlevî whirling dervish order, and whose writings helped reshape Islamic thought. The Mathnawi, his master work, was composed from 1248 onwards, after the death of his spiritual companion Shams of Tabriz, and so strong is the presence and inspiration of Tabriz that Rumi's work is also often known as the Divan of Shams-i-Tabriz. Written in Persian, the Mathnawi is a sprawling, six-volume epic varying widely in tone, content and style, alternating between prose invocations of Allah, Sufi teaching parables, ecstatic love odes, practical advice for meditation, jokes and frankly raunchy sections (including how to best attempt unnatural acts with a donkey). It is still one of the best-loved pieces of medieval Persian literature. The only complete English translation is the terribly dry one of Reynold Nicholson (8 vols, London: Luzac & Co, 1925–40), but in recent years, more lively and contemporary renderings of selected passages have appeared. The following are versions by Coleman Barks, who has produced nine small volumes in the past decade or so. For more on Rumi, see p.626.

The Seed Market

(Book IV, Stanzas 2611–25)

Can you find another market like this?

Where,
for one seed
you get a whole wilderness?

For one weak breath,
the divine wind?

You've been fearful
of being absorbed in the ground,
or drawn up by the air.

Now, your waterbead lets go
and drops into the ocean,
where it came from.

It no longer has the form it had,
but it's still water.
The essence is the same.

This giving up is not a repenting.
It's a deep honoring of yourself.

When the ocean comes to you as a lover,
marry, at once, quickly,
for God's sake!

Don't postpone it!
Existence has no better gift.

No amount of searching
will find this.
A perfect falcon, for no reason,
has landed on your shoulder,
and become yours.

The Indian Parrot

(Book I, Stanzas 1814–33, 1845–48)

There was a merchant setting out for India.

He asked each male and female servant
what they wanted to be brought as a gift.

Each told him a different exotic object:
A piece of silk, a brass figurine,
a pearl necklace.

Then he asked his beautiful caged parrot,
the one with such a lovely voice,
and she said,
"When you see the Indian parrots,
describe my cage. Say that I need guidance
here in my separation from them. Ask how
our friendship can continue with me so confined
and them flying about freely in the meadow mist.

Tell them that I remember well our mornings
moving together from tree to tree.

Tell them to drink one cup of ecstatic wine
in honor of me here in the dregs of my life.

Tell them that the sound of their quarreling
high in the trees would be sweeter
to hear than any music."

This parrot is the spirit-bird in all of us,
that part that wants to return to freedom
and is the freedom. What she wants
from India is *herself*!

So this parrot gave her message to the merchant,
and when he reached India, he saw a field
full of parrots. He stopped
and called out what she had told him.

One of the nearest parrots shivered
and stiffened and fell down dead.

The merchant said, "This one is surely kin
to my parrot. I shouldn't have spoken."
He finished his trading and returned home
with the presents for his workers.

When he got to the parrot, she demanded her gift.
"What happened when you told my story
to the Indian parrots?"

"I'm afraid to say."
"Master, you must!"
"When I spoke your complaint to the field
of chattering parrots, it broke
one of their hearts.

She must have been a close companion,
or a relative, for when she heard about you
she grew quiet and trembled, and died."

As the caged parrot heard this, she herself
quivered and sank to the cage floor.

This merchant was a good man.
He grieved deeply for his parrot, murmuring
distracted phrases, self-contradictory –
cold, then loving – clear, then
murky with symbolism.

A drowning man reaches for anything!
The Friend loves this flailing about
better than any lying still.

The One who lives inside existence
stays constantly in motion,
and whatever you do, that king
watches through the window.

When the merchant threw the "dead" parrot
out of the cage, it spread its wings
and glided to a nearby tree!

The merchant suddenly understood the mystery.
"Sweet singer, what was in the message
that taught you this trick?"

"She told me that it was the charm
of my voice that kept me caged.
Give it up, and be released!"

The parrot told the merchant one or two more
spiritual truths. Then a tender goodbye.

"God protect you", said the merchant.
"As you go on your new way.
I hope to follow you!"

The Mouse and the Frog

(Book VI, Stanzas 2632, 2665–69, 2681–84)

A mouse and a frog meet every morning
on the riverbank.
They sit in a nook of the ground and talk.

Each morning, the second they see each other,
they open easily, telling stories and dreams and secrets,
empty of any fear or suspicious holding-back.
To watch and listen to these two
is to understand how, as it's written,
sometimes when two beings come together,
Christ becomes visible.

The mouse starts laughing out a story he hasn't thought of
in five years, and the telling might take five years!
There's no blocking the speechflow-river running-all-carrying momentum
that true intimacy is.

The God-Messenger, Khidr, touches a roasted fish.
It leaps off the grill
back into the water.
Friend sits by Friend, and the tablets appear.
They read the mysteries
off each other's foreheads.
But one day the mouse complains, "There are times
when I want *sohbet* (mystical communion), and you're out in the water,
jumping around where you can't hear me.

We meet at this appointed time,
but the text says, *Lovers pray constantly*.

Once a day, once a week, five times an hour,
is not enough. Fish like we are
need the ocean around us!"

Do camel-bells say, *Let's meet back here
Thursday night?*
Ridiculous. They jingle
together continuously,
talking while the camel walks.

Do you pay regular visits to *yourself*?
Don't you argue rationally.

Let us die,
and dying, reply.

Books

There are numerous English-language books about every aspect of Turkey, many published or reissued since the mid-1990s. Three UK publishers specifically or partly dedicated to Turkology, and worth contacting directly for information on their latest offerings, are: I.B. Tauris, 45 Bloomsbury Square, London WC1A 2HY (☎020/7916 1069), and c/o St Martin's Press, 257 Park Avenue South, 18th Floor, New York, NY 10010 (☎212/982-3900); Saqi Books, 26 Westbourne Grove, London W2 5RH (⊛www.saqibooks.com); and The Eothen Press, Huntingdon, Cambridgeshire, PE18 9BX (☎01480/466106, ⊛www.btinternet.com/~theeothenpress). Books with Turkish publishers are rarely available outside Turkey. One particularly reliable retail source for Turk-related literature in the UK is Daunt Books, 83 Marylebone High St, London W1M 4DE (☎020/7224 2295).

Publishers are detailed below, where applicable, in the form British/ American, although not all titles have editions in both the UK and US (but some have the same imprint everywhere); "o/p" means out of print. Retail **websites** such as Amazon or Barnes & Noble are excellent venues for hard-to-find or out-of-print items; almost every book in this bibliography can be found secondhand or on a print-on-demand/special order basis through these sources. Websites also permit you to order US-published items in the UK, and vice versa, so always check both the ".co.uk" and ".com" versions of any on-line retailer if you're after an oddball title.

The star-book symbol marks titles that are particularly recommended.

History

The classics

Herodotus *The Histories* (Oxford UP). A fifth-century BC native of what is now Bodrum, Herodotus is revered as the father of both systematic history and anthropology, providing descriptions of the Persian Wars and the assorted tribes and nations who inhabited Anatolia in his time.

Strabo *Geography* (Harvard UP; multi-volume Loeb Library edition). A native of the Pontus, Strabo travelled widely across the Mediterranean;

our best document of Roman Anatolia.

Xenophon *Anabasis, or The March Up-Country* (order through ⊛www.Indypublishing.com). The Athenian leader of the Ten Thousand, mercenaries for the Persian king Cyrus the Younger, led the long retreat from the Cunaxa battlefield in Mesopotamia to the Black Sea. An ancient travel classic still mined for titbits of ethnology, archeology and geography.

Ancient history and archeology

Ekrem Akurgal *Ancient Civilisations and Ruins of Turkey* (Türk Tarih Kurumu Basımevi, Ankara/University

of Pennsylania Press, US; latter o/p). Excellent detailed survey of Anatolian sites from prehistoric times to the end of the Roman Empire. Includes site plans and interesting graphic reconstructions of monuments, as well as a few dated photos.

O.R. Gurney *The Hittites* (Allen Lane or Penguin, UK). Non-specialist's history of the first great Anatolian civilization.

Ian Hodder *On the Surface: Çatalhöyük 1993–1995* (McDonald Institute of Archeological Research). Neolithic Çatal Höyük is the earliest known proper city in the world, rumoured to contain the secrets of the origins of Western civilization. This volume relates the first two years of a 25-year project to excavate what's arguably the world's most important archeological site.

★ **Seton Lloyd** *Ancient Turkey – A Traveller's History of Anatolia* (British Museum Publications /University of California Press). Written by a former head of the British Archeological Institute in Ankara, this is indispensable on the ancient civilizations. Without sacrificing detail and convincing research, it's written in an accessible, compelling style, avoiding the dull, encyclopedic approach of most writing on the subject.

★ **J.G. MacQueen** *The Hittites and their Contemporaries in Asia Minor* (Thames and Hudson, UK). Well-illustrated general history; more accessible than Gurney's tome.

Otto F.A. Meinardus *St John of Patmos and the Seven Churches of the Apocalypse* (Lycabettus Press, Athens/Caratzas, New York). The Seven Churches were all in western Anatolia, and this volume, though mostly ecclesiastical history, is also a practical handbook to the sites. The same author's *St Paul in Ephesus and the Cities of Galatia and Cyprus* (Lycabettus Press, Athens; o/p) contains copious material on Christianity in Ephesus and is set soon for re-issue.

David Traill *Schliemann of Troy: Treasure and Deceit* (John Murray, UK). The man versus the myth of his self-publicity: not strictly ancient history, but if you're intending to visit the ruins of ancient Troy, this volume, portraying the crumbling edifice of Schliemann's reputation as an archeologist, will certainly help to bring the old walls to life.

Byzantine and early medieval history

Anna Comnena *The Alexiad* (Penguin). The daughter of Emperor Alexius Komnenos I, perhaps the first woman historian, wrote a history of the First Crusade from the Byzantine point of view. Accounts of military campaigns predominate, and it's all a bit dry, but holds its own for historical interest.

★ **Cyril Mango** *Byzantium: The Empire of the New Rome* (Weidenfeld & Nicolson/Phoenix). A single volume that makes a good, accessible introduction to Byzantium, taking in daily life, economic policy and taxation, scholar-ship and universities, cosmology and superstition, among other topics. The newer *Oxford History of Byzantium* (Oxford UP), also edited by Mango, will also be of interest.

★ **John Julius Norwich** *Byzantium: The Early Centuries, The Apogee* and *The Decline* (Penguin/Viking). An astonishingly detailed trilogy, well informed and above all the most readable account of a fascinating period of world history up to 1453 (a single-volume abridged version is also available). His edition of *Liuprand of Cremona* (Everyman) proves a colourful account of an early Lombard embassy to the already declining Byzantine Empire. Liuprand didn't care much for the Byzantines and goes to great lengths to explain why. After reading this account, the Fourth Crusade – diverted by Venice to sack Constantinople instead of Jerusalem – begins to be more understandable.

Procopius *The Secret History* (Penguin Classics/University of Michigan). Often raunchy account of the murkier side of the reigns of Justinian and his sluttish empress, Theodora, from no less an authority than the imperial general Belisarius' official war historian. Besides a demolition job on the grisly royal couple, Procopius' employer Belisarius, one of the greatest Byzantine generals, is also portrayed (like Justinian) as spinelessly uxorious.

Michael Psellus *Fourteen Byzantine Rulers* (Penguin). Covers the turbulent period between 976 and 1078, when the scholarly author was adviser to several of the emperors of whom he writes.

Jonathan Riley-Smith *What Were the Crusades?* (Palgrave Macmillan, UK). A slim, readable discourse on the nature of the Crusades, including recently unearthed material throwing new light on the whole movement.

★ **Steven Runciman** *Byzantine Style and Civilisation* (Penguin, o/p). Eleven centuries of Byzantine art in one small paperback, and still fascinating. Facts are presented in interesting contexts, theories are well argued. His *The Fall of Constantinople, 1453* (Canto/Cambridge UP) remains the classic study of the event, while *The Great Church in Captivity* (Canto/Cambridge UP), a history of Orthodoxy under the Ottomans, continues the saga in a readable if partisan manner.

Speros Vryonis *The Decline of Medieval Hellenism in Asia Minor and the Process of Islamization from the Eleventh through the Fifteenth Century* (University of California Press, UK/US; both o/p). Heavy, footnoted going, but the definitive study of how the Byzantine Empire culturally became the Ottoman Empire.

Ottoman history

Jason Goodwin *Lords of the Horizons* (Vintage). "Popular" history of the Ottoman Empire in the tradition of Noel Barber's long-vanished *Lords of the Golden Horn* – ie a breathless, sensational romp through the era for *Daily Mail* readers.

Halil İnalcık *The Ottoman Empire: The Classical Age, 1300–1600* (Phoenix, US). As the title says; the standard work, not superseded since its first 1973 appearance.

★ **Patrick Balfour Kinross** *The Ottoman Centuries* (Weidenfeld & Nicolson, o/p/Morrow). Readable, balanced summary of Ottoman history from the fourteenth to the twentieth century.

M. Fuad Köprülü *The Origins of the Ottoman Empire* (State University Press of New York, US). Translated by Gary Leiser, early twentieth-century classic covers much the same ground as İnalcık's work.

I. Metin Kunt and Christine Woodhead *Süleyman the Magnificent and His Age* (Longman). Concise summary of the reign of the greatest Ottoman sultan, and of the cultural renaissance over which he presided.

Bernard Lewis *The Emergence of Modern Turkey* (Oxford UP, US). Analysis of the roots of the Republic in the reform movements of the late Ottoman Empire; as such, strong on cultural history, weak on events. His

The Muslim Discovery of Europe (Phoenix/Norton; latter o/p) is arguably Lewis's most enduring work: a detailed exploration of the failure of Islam – essentially the Ottoman Empire – to come to terms with science, technology and the growing power of the West.

⭐ **Philip Mansel** *Constantinople: City of the World's Desire, 1453–1924* (Penguin, UK). Readable, nostalgic, faintly anti-Republican popular history, focusing on the imperial capital and organized topically as well as chronologically. Obscure factoids and scandals are all here, to wit: Boğaziçi University began life as a hotbed of Bulgarian nationalism; Russian floozies have previously (1920–1922) held Turkish men in thrall; coffee-consumption was periodically a capital crime until the eighteenth century.

Philip Mansel *Sultans in Splendour – the Last Years of the Ottoman World* (Parkway/Vendome; latter o/p). The illustrations make this book: a collection of rare photos depicting unbe-lievable characters from the end of the Ottoman Empire. It's also well written, and contains much information not available elsewhere.

Alan Palmer *The Decline and Fall of the Ottoman Empire* (John Murray, UK/Barnes & Noble, US). Particularly good for the manoeuvres and machinations of the European powers vis-à-vis Turkey in the mid-nineteenth century; spotty on the periods before and after.

⭐ **Andrew Wheatcroft** *The Ottomans* (Penguin). Not an event-focused, chronological history but an analysis of trends in Ottoman life, and its stereotypical perceptions by the West – usefully demonstrated by period art, cartoons and photos.

Alfred C. Wood *A History of the Levant Company* (Oxford UP, o/p). Comprehensive account of the foundation and activities of the Levant Trading Company, which controlled British commerce with the Ottoman Empire between the sixteenth and early nineteenth centuries. To be found in major reference libraries.

Modern history

⭐ **Feroz Ahmad** *The Making of Modern Turkey* (Routledge). Not the most orthodox of histories but lively, partisan and replete with wonderful anecdotes and quotes you'll find nowhere else.

Mehmet Ali Birand *Shirts of Steel: An Anatomy of the Turkish Armed Forces* (I.B. Tauris/St Martin's Press). Based on interviews by one of Turkey's top journalists, this gives a good idea of the officer corps' world view and their justifications for the numerous military interventions.

⭐ **Marjorie Housepian Dobkin** *Smyrna 1922: The Destruction of a City* (Faber/Newmark Press, New York; former o/p). Partisan (ie rabid-ly anti-Turkish) but harrowingly graphic account of the sack of İzmir, when approximately 150,000 of the 400,000 Armenians and Greeks trapped in the city met their deaths. Most-original insights are how the US coddled Republican Turkey by massaging press coverage of the incident, in hopes of postwar oil concessions in Mosul, and helping to conceal the cause of the great fire so as to facilitate (ultimately unsuccessfully) insurance claims against a British company. The only people who emerge honourably are American Consul George Horton, Dr Esther Lovejoy and the ordinary seamen who, against orders, fished survivors out of İzmir harbour.

Michael Hickey *Gallipoli* (John Murray, UK). Currently the best single-volume history of the campaign.

Cağlar Keyder *State and Class in Turkey: A Study in Capitalist Development* (Verso, o/p). Intertwined with the Marxist and academic rhetoric is a very useful economic history of the Republic.

Faik Okte *The Tragedy of the Turkish Capital Tax* (Croom Helm/ Longwood; both o/p). Short, remorseful monograph on the discriminatory World War II tax, written by the İstanbul director of finance who was responsible for its implementation.

Hugh Poulton *Top Hat, the Grey Wolves and the Crescent: Turkish Nationalism and the Turkish Republic* (C. Hurst/New York University Press). After some brief operative definitions, Poulton does an excellent, thorough dissection of the "holy trinity" – secularism, ethnically based nationalism and Islam – which jostle for position in Turkey, and also summarizes the fortunes of antecedents such as Pan-Ottomanism. Plenty of asides on the fates of minorities (mostly the Kurds), but marred by numerous typos, and despite the 1997 publication date, stops short of the crucial political-Islam period.

★ **Barry Rubin** *İstanbul Intrigues* (Bosphorus Univeristy Press, İstanbul/St Martin's Press; latter o/p). Un-put-downable account of Allied/Axis activities in neutral Turkey during World War II, and their attempts to drag it into the conflict. Surprising revelations about the extent of Turkish aid for Britain, the US and the Greek resistance, and a wealth of detailed anecdote.

Nigel Steel and Peter Hart *Defeat at Gallipoli* (Pan Macmillan, UK). Uses contemporary accounts to give a vivid impression of the siege.

Richard Tapper, ed. *Islam in Modern Turkey: Religion, Politics and Literature in a Secular State* (I.B. Tauris/St Martin's Press). Short collection of essays by various specialists on the resurgence of religion in Turkish life.

★ **Erik J. Zürcher** *Turkey: A Modern History* (I.B. Tauris/St Martin's Press). If you have time for only one volume covering the post-1800 period, make it this one; it's well written and breathes some revisionist fresh air over sacred cows and received truths. Also with an opinionated, annotated bibliography.

General multi-era histories

Roderic Davison and C.H. Dodd *Turkey, a Short History* (Eothen Press, UK). Non-chronological text that touches on everything up to 1997, particularly good for late Ottoman and early Republican events.

Geoffrey L. Lewis *Turkey* (Ernest Benn/Praeger; both o/p). Hard to find, but a much more witty and readable choice than Davison and Dodd – a little uneven, though, and coverage ceases at 1974.

Richard Stoneman *A Traveller's History of Turkey* (CassellInterlink Publishing Group, Northampton, MA). An easy-reading volume of this small series, and at less than 200 pages inevitably superficial, but it does touch on all salient points from Paleolithic times to 1992.

Minorities and religion

Alexis Alexandris *The Greek Minority of İstanbul and Greek Turkish Relations 1918–1974* (Centre for Asia Minor Studies, Athens). Effectively illustrates how the treatment of this community, whose rights were guaranteed by the Treaty of Lausanne, has functioned as a gauge of general relations between Greece and Turkey during the period in question.

Esther Benbassa and Aron Rodrigue *The Jews of the Balkans: The Judeo-Spanish Community, 15th to 20th Centuries* (Basil Blackwell, UK/US; both o/p). Dense but brief overview of the Sephardic community in the European core of the Ottoman Empire, decimated this century by assorted nationalisms, the Nazis and emigration to Palestine.

★ **William Dalrymple** *From the Holy Mountain: A Journey in the Shadow of Byzantium* (Flamingo/Harper Collins). A witty retracing of a classic sixth-century monkish journey through the monasteries of the Near East. Section II is devoted to Turkey, and he takes a suitably dim view of the sorry history and current poor treatment of Assyrian Christians and Armenian monuments in eastern Turkey.

John Freely *The Lost Messiah: In Search of the Mystical Rabbi Sabbatai Sevi* (Penguin/Overlook). Story of the millennial, seventeenth-century movement in İzmir and Salonica that emerged from Kabbalistic ferment and gave rise to the Dönme, a crypto-Judaic sect disproportionately prominent in modern Turkish history.

John Guest *Survival among the Kurds: A History of the Yezidis* (Kegan Paul Int/Routledge). A very expensive hardback, but the last word on this little-known heterodox sect scattered astride Turkey's eastern borders.

F.W. Hasluck *Christianity and Islam under the Sultans* (2 vols; Oxford UP/Octagon; both o/p). Invaluable if you can find it; ample material on the history of shrines and festivals, their veneration and attendance by different sects at the turn of the last century, plus Christian and pagan contributions to the dervish rites.

★ **David McDowall** *The Kurds: A Nation Denied* (Minority Rights Publications/Cultural Survival). About one-third of this book is devoted to the Kurds of Turkey, though they are now distributed over the territory of several modern states – few of whose governments get high marks here for their treatment of Kurds, up to 1992. Consult also McDowall's more recent *A Modern History of the Kurds* (I.B. Tauris/St Martin's Press), out in paperback.

Yaşar Nuri Öztürk *The Eye of the Heart: An Introduction to Sufism and the Tariqats of Anatolia and the Balkans* (Redhouse Press, İstanbul). A frustratingly brief description of the tenets of mystical Islam and the main dervish orders in Turkey; lavishly illustrated, easily available in the country.

★ **Jonathan Rugman and Roger Hutchings** *Atatürk's Children: Turkey and the Kurds* (Academic & Professional, US). Excellent, even-handed exploration of the topic by (in part) the Guardian's former Turkey correspondent.

Stanford J. Shaw *The Jews of the Ottoman Empire and the Turkish Republic* (New York University Press, US; o/p). The story of the one Turkish minority, which has usually managed to stay on the good side of those in power; pricey in hardback, try for a secondhand paperback copy.

⭐ **Christopher Walker** *Armenia: The Survival of a Nation* (Routledge/St Martin's; former o/p). A far-reaching if partisan histo-ry, with extended discussion on Armenian relations with the Turks – particularly the 1895–1896 and 1915 massacres. His more recent *Visions of Ararat* (I.B. Tauris/St Martin's) is an edited collection of literary excerpts, mostly views of the Armenians by outsiders over the centuries.

Travel

⭐ **Neal Ascherson** *Black Sea* (Vintage/Hill & Wang). Subtitled "The Birthplace of Civilisation and Barbarism", this excellent historical, ethnological and ecological meditation explores these supposed antitheses around Turkey's northerly sea; only two chapters specifically on the Pontus and Bosphorus, but still highly recom-mended.

⭐ **John Ash** *A Byzantine Journey* (I.B. Tauris/Random House). Historically inclined reflections of a poet as he takes in all the major, and some of the minor, Byzantine sites in Anatolia; better than it sounds, and recommended.

⭐ **Frederick G. Burnaby** *On Horseback through Asia Minor* (Oxford Paperbacks). Victorian offi-cer's thousand-mile ride through snowy northeast Anatolia to spy on the Russians in the run-up to the 1877 war. Prophetically observant (especially in light of the Chechen wars) and gruesomely, if inadvertent-ly humorous (sample conversational opener: "Are people ever impaled here?"). Anti-Armenian, conde-scendingly Turkophilic, plus Russophobic appendices.

John A. Cuddon *The Owl's Watch-Song* (Century Pimlico/Random; both o/p). Flanneur's guide to rubbish-strewn, back street "Old Stamboul" of the late 1950s; good on legends and historical anecdotes, but too much of the author's own psyche for most tastes, and ultimately not enough on the soul of the city. The original Barrie and Rockliffe (UK) hardback often turns up in secondhand bookshops.

Laurence Kelly, ed. *İstanbul: A Traveller's Companion* (Constable/ Simon & Schuster; latter o/p). Well-selected historical writing concern-ing various aspects of the city, and fascinating eyewitness accounts of historical events such as the cru-saders' sack of Constantinople.

Patrick Balfour Kinross *Europa Minor* (John Murray/Morrow; both o/p). Good yarns interspersed with a comprehensive coastal ramble from the Hatay to İstanbul during the early 1950s; *Within the Taurus* (John Murray, o/p) is the companion vol-ume covering the interior.

Mary Wortley Montagu *Letters* (Everyman/Oxford UP); *Turkish Embassy Letters* (Virago, UK). Impressions of an eccentric but per-ceptive traveller, resident in İstanbul during 1716–1718, whose disregard for convention and popular preju-dice gave her the edge over contem-porary historians.

Michael Pereira *East of Trebizond* (Geoffrey Bles, UK, o/p). Travels between the Black Sea and northeast Anatolia during the late 1960s, interspersed with readable history of the area. Common in secondhand travel bookshops and on websites.

★ **Brian Sewell** *South From Ephesus: An Escape from the Tyranny of Western Art* (Gibson Square Books, UK). Pre-touristic southwest-coastal Turkey and its ruins during the 1970s and 1980s, when vile hotels, domineering guides and amorous, bisexually inclined villagers were a constant hazard (or attraction, depending on one's point of view). As erudite and curmudgeonly as

you'd expect from the controversial art critic of the London Evening Standard.

Freya Stark *Ionia – a Quest* (Century Hutchinson/Transaction Pubs; former o/p), *Alexander's Path* (Arrow/Overlook Press; former o/p), *Lycian Shore* (John Murray, UK) and *Riding to the Tigris* (John Murray, UK, o/p). Some of the most evocative travel writing available on Turkey, if now inevitably dated.

Views of contemporary Turkey

★ **Tim Kelsey** *Dervish: The Invention of Modern Turkey* (Penguin; o/p). The troubled soul of the country, sought amongst minority communities, faith healers, the bulging prisons, the brothels and the transsexual underground, plus the mystics of the title; bleak and pitiless analysis of Republican Turkish angst, with little optimism for Turkey's future.

James Pettifer *The Turkish Labyrinth: Atatürk and the New Islam* (Penguin/Viking; both o/p). Balkan specialist Pettifer's useful, if literally all-over-the-place interpretations of trends and issues confronting Turkey. Many conclusions are now obsolete or dubious after Öcalan's capture and impending EU candidacy, and it's marred by

numerous typos and factual errors.

★ **Nicole and Hugh Pope** *Turkey Unveiled: Atatürk and After* (John Murray, UK); published also as *Turkey Unveiled: A History of Modern Turkey* (Overlook, US). Probably the best non-academic introduction to the place: a series of interlinked essays, arranged both topically and chronologically, by two foreign correspondents who, after two-plus decades in harness, understand Turkey better than most outsiders. Particularly good grasp of Kurdish- and Europe-related issues, and wonderful anecdotal detail on events and personalities. Despite their affection for and optimism about the country, unflinching description of its many shortcomings.

Biography

Saime Göksu and Edward Timms *Romantic Communist: The Life and Works of Nazım Hikmet* (C. Hurst & Co, UK). Long-overdue English-language biography of Turkey's most controversial modern poet. Banned and imprisoned for seventeen years in Turkey, Hikmet

spent much of his life in the Soviet bloc (he died in Moscow). Though as yet little known outside Turkey, he once rubbed shoulders with such Leftist luminaries as Pablo Neruda, Jean-Paul Sartre and Paul Robeson.

Patrick Balfour Kinross ★ *Atatürk: the Rebirth of a Nation* (Weidenfeld & Nicolson, UK). Long considered the definitive English biography – as opposed to hagiography – of the father of the Republic and still preferred by some to the newer Mango text (see below).

Andrew Mango *Atatürk* (John ★ Murray, UK). Despite massive press acclamation, does not supersede Kinross's more readable tome as the best biography of the man, but merely complements it. Thorough and authoritative, but also steeped in military and conspiratorial minutiae.

Sympathetic to its subject, and the Turkish national project as a whole; the compulsory post-1922 exchange of populations rate hardly a mention and the vicissitudes of the Armenians are also glossed over.

Michael Strachan *Sir Thomas Roe 1581–1644: A Life* (Michael Russell, UK). Biography of an influential Elizabethan statesmen who spent several years as English ambassador to the Ottoman court, and head of the Levant Company. Fascinating insight into the perilous life and intrigues of Europeans in Constantinople.

Memoirs

Shirin Devrim *A Turkish* ★ *Tapestry: The Shakirs of Istanbul* (Quartet, UK). Turbulent chronicle of a vastly eccentric, dysfunctional and talented aristocratic Ottoman family whose exploits, if anything, became even more colourful after 1923. Divorces, affairs, suicide attempts, art exhibits, travels and residence across four continents – and lurking always in the background, the notorious Şakir Paşa murder case of 1914. The author, who is niece and grand-daughter of the respective protagonists, gets as close to the truth as anyone is likely to.

Aziz Nesin *İstanbul Boy* (University of Texas, US; o/p). An autobiography set in the same era and milieu as Orga's first work (see below), and strong on local colour (eg spectacular "Howling" dervish ceremonies), but not such a good read.

İrfan Orga *Portrait of a Turkish* ★ *Family* (Eland, UK). Heartbreaking story following the Orga family from an idyllic existence in late Ottoman İstanbul through grim survival in the early Republican era; some of it is excerpted on p.1056.

His *The Caravan Moves On: Three Weeks among Turkish Nomads* (Eland, UK) is also excellent. Set in the late 1950s, it's a fine snapshot of the Menderes era – and a suitably unsentimental portrayal of a *Yörük* community in the Toros.

Mary Seacole *The Wonderful* ★ *Adventures of Mrs Seacole in Many Lands* (X Press/Oxford UP). This alternative Florence Nightingale was a black Jamaican who, unlike her paler-skinned compatriot, ministered to Crimean War casualties in İstanbul at her own expense. Seacole's bankruptcy touched the British public to such an extent that *Punch* magazine helped raise funds for her, as did proceeds from London concerts (including a sell-out at the Albert Hall). Subsequent history has not done Seacole justice, but her autobiography continues to figure amongst top feminist texts – and has remained in print almost without interruption.

Daniel de Souza *Under a* ★ *Crescent Moon* (Serpent's Tail, UK). Turkish society seen from the bottom looking up: an excellent volume of prison vignettes by a jailed foreigner, and in its compassion the antithesis of *Midnight*

Express. Compellingly written and spiced with interesting prejudices.

Architecture, arts and crafts

Architecture and monuments

John Freely and Augusto Romano Burelli *Sinan: Architect of Süleyman the Magnificent and the Ottoman Golden Age* (Thames & Hudson; o/p). Photographs by Ara Güler complement this reverential catalogue of the great sixteenth-century genius's work; expensive coffee-table volume.

★ **Godfrey Goodwin** *A History of Ottoman Architecture* (Thames & Hudson, UK only). Definitive affordable paperback guide to Ottoman architecture, covering the whole of Turkey and providing a sound historical and ethno-geographical context for any Ottoman construction you care to name. Goodwin's *Sinan: Ottoman Architecture and its Values Today* (Saqi Books, UK) provides fascinating insights into the architect, his life and influences, made eminently readable by the author's passion for his subject.

Spiro Kostoff *Caves of God – Cappadocia and its Churches* (Oxford UP, o/p). Dry rendering of a fascinating subject, but there's still no rival, and it is thorough.

Richard Krautheimer *Early Christian and Byzantine Architecture* (Yale UP). An excellent survey from the Pelican "History of Art" series.

★ **Raymond Lifchez, ed.** *The Dervish Lodge: Architecture, Art and Sufism in Ottoman Turkey* (University of California Press; o/p). Lavishly illustrated essays by specialist scholars on all aspects of the Sufi orders in Turkey. Though

nineteenth-century İstanbul is disproportionately represented, as are the Mevlevî and Bektaşi orders, and the core of the book is the relation between *tekke* layout and function, there's ample material on rural *zaviyes* of the *ahis*, Nakşibendi practice, tomb veneration and pictorial calligraphy. Among pieces on poetry, the symbolism of costumes and gravestones, ritual food and even continuing Sufi influence on contemporary Turkish culture, only a piece on music disappoints.

★ **Cyril Mango** *Byzantine Architecture* (Faber & Faber/Electa Editrice; former o/p). A complete survey of the most significant Byzantine structures, around a quarter of which fall within modern Turkey. Well worth paying the slight premium for the Electa Editrice re-issue.

★ **T.A. Sinclair** *Eastern Turkey: An Archaeological and Architectural Survey* (4 vols; Pindar Press, UK). The standard reference, with copious plans and covering just about every monument east of Cappadocia, but prohibitively priced. Specialist or university libraries usually have copies.

Metin Sözen *The Evolution of Turkish Art and Architecture* (Haşet Kitabevi, İstanbul). Lavishly illustrated, erudite survey of major Turkish monuments by period, followed by detailed discussion of the fine arts.

★ **David Talbot Rice** *Islamic Art* (Thames & Hudson/Oxford

UP) covers an enormous timescale and geographical area, giving useful perspectives on Ottoman and Selçuk art forms alongside those of Persia and Muslim Spain. His *Art of the Byzantine Era* (Thames & Hudson), a chronologically ordered and lavishly illustrated but still affordable study in the same "World of Art"

series, is unlikely to be ever superseded. For specialists, *The Church of Hagia Sophia in Trebizond* (Edinburgh University Press, UK, o/p) remains the last word, from the Talbot-Rice-headed team that restored the frescoes in this landmark church.

Coffee-table illustrateds

Diana Barillari and Ezio Godoli *İstanbul 1900: Art Nouveau Architecture and Interiors* (Rizzoli International). Superbly researched and illustrated account of İstanbul's rich but neglected legacy of Art Nouveau architecture, in particular works of Italian architect and long-time resident Raimondo D'Aronco. A nice corrective to the axiom that the city consists only of palaces, concrete towerblocks and crumbled wood terraces.

★ **Chris Hellier and Francesco Venturi** *Splendours of the Bosphorus: Houses and Palaces of İstanbul* (Tauris Parke/Abbeville Press). Not the usual coffee-table

fare – inviting photographs of interiors you'd never otherwise see are supported by intelligent text that puts the shoreline *yalıs* and opulent palaces into their social and artistic context.

Stephane Yerasimos, Ara Güler and Samih Rifat *Living in Turkey* (Thames & Hudson/Abbeville Press; Dünya in Turkey). Covers some of the same ground as Hellier and Venturi, but with less of a focus on nobility and more on the nouveau riche. Landscapes and interiors to drool over, in photos by Güler and Rifat; a bit prettified but still alluring as an ideal.

Fine arts

Metin And *Turkish Miniature Painting – the Ottoman Period* (Dost Yayınları, İstanbul). Attractive, interesting account of the most important Ottoman art form. Loads of colour plates, mostly excellent production.

Jean Jenkins and Poul Rovsing Olsen *Music and Musical Instruments in the World of Islam* (World of Islam Festival Publications, UK, o/p). Interesting introduction; not too technical, but usefully illustrated with photos and line drawings.

Carpets

★ **Alastair Hull** *Kilims: The Complete Guide* (Thames & Hudson/Chronicle Books). Comprehensive and thoroughly illustrated survey of Turkish kilims. His *Living With Kilims* (Thames & Hudson) is an excellent manual on

how to use and care for (as opposed to museumize) kilims in interior-decorative situations.

James Opie *Tribal Rugs* (Laurence King, UK). Contains examples off Turcoman and Kurdish rugs as part of a general Central Asian survey.

Orient Stars (E. Heinrich Kirchheim and Hali Publications, UK). Despite the silly title, the ultimate rug book; 250 colour plates, with excellent representation of classical Turkish carpets.

Jon Thompson *Carpet Magic: Carpets from the Tents, Cottages and Workshops of Asia* (Lawrence King, UK). A good general introduction.

Kurt Zipper and Claudia Fritzsche *Oriental Rugs: Turkish* (Antique Collectors Club). Volume 4 of the series entitled "Oriental Rugs". Extensive discussion of weaving techniques, symbols and rug categories, and the weavers themselves, along with a regional survey of distinctive patterns.

Specialist guidebooks

Regional guides

⭐ **George E. Bean** *Turkey's Southern Shore* (John Murray, UK, o/p), *Turkey Beyond the Maeander* (John Murray, UK, o/p), *Lycian Turkey* (John Murray, UK, o/p), *Aegean Turkey* (John Murray, UK, o/p). A series of scholarly guides to the archeological sites of Turkey written from the original research of Professor Bean, much of which has never been superseded; thus expect some or all to come back into print soon.

Everett Blake and Anna Edmonds *Biblical Sites in Turkey* (Redhouse Press, İstanbul). If it's mentioned in the Bible (New Testament, that is), it appears here too, with description of sites. Their *Turkey's Religious Sites* (Damko, İstanbul) is more current, better produced and includes Jewish and Muslim sites.

Sevan and Müjde Nişanyan *Black Sea: A Traveller's Handbook for Northern Turkey* (Boyut Yayın Grubu, İstanbul). Covers the Black Sea coast and mountains just inland in greater cultural depth than space allows in this Guide, though few hotel or restaurant recommendations.

⭐ **Jane Taylor** *Imperial İstanbul* (I.B. Tauris). Excellent, stone-by-stone guide, complete with site plans, of the major Ottoman monuments in Bursa and Edirne as well as the old capital.

Nature

Sally Taylor *A Traveller's Guide to the Woody Plants of Turkey* (Redhouse Press, İstanbul; o/p). Coverage of all native trees and shrubs of Turkey, with keying sections and an especially useful glossary of Turkish species names.

Acculturation

Arın Bayraktaroğlu *Culture Shock: Turkey* (Kuperard). A useful volume, especially on a prolonged stay or business trip, which helps make the Turks less inscrutable by explaining some of their more bizarre customs.

Turkish Culture for Americans (International Concepts, US, o/p).

Side-splitting, problem-solution examples of cultural misunderstandings that Americans may experience living in Turkey. Not likely that any book would achieve such comedic heights unintentionally, but this one does. A staple of Turkish secondhand bookstores; to be sought after and cherished.

Hiking/mountaineering

Haldun Aydıngün *Aladağlar: An Introduction* (Redhouse Press, İstanbul; o/p). Details approaches and scrambling routes in this compact karst range near Niğde.

★ **Kate Clow** *The Lycian Way* (Cordee, UK). Hour-by-hour, west-to-east route guide for Turkey's first officially marked long-distance trail; supplied with folding map.

Marc Dubin and Enver Lucas *Trekking in Turkey* (Lonely Planet, o/p). Long and short treks – many still followable as written – in every Turkish mountain range, plus an obsolete section on the Turquoise

Coast; worth trying to get a copy secondhand, as the maps are still among the best available.

Karl Smith *The Mountains of Turkey* (Cicerone/Hunter). Marginally more up-to-date than *Trekking in Turkey*, but hiking accounts – fleshed out with general tourism – are often spotty or secondhand, and the maps are poor.

Ömer Tözel *The Aladağ: Climbs and Treks in Turkey's Crimson Mountains* (Cicerone/Hunter). More technical and much less hike-orientated than the Aydıngün volume, but also much easier to find.

CONTEXTS | Books

Turkish fiction in translation

Sait Faik *A Dot on the Map* (Indiana University Turkish Studies, US; o/p). A large collection of short stories, translated by various scholars, from the acknowledged Turkish master of the genre; most are set in and around İstanbul and the Sea of Marmara during the early Republican years. One of these tales is reproduced on p.1059.

★ **Yaşar Kemal** The best-known Turkish novelist in the West, thanks to English translations by his wife Thilda of virtually every one of

his titles. Except where noted, Harvill do the current editions in the UK, Pantheon in the US. Oldest are the epics, somewhat turgid and folksy, set in inner Anatolia: *Mehmed My Hawk*; its sequel *They Burn the Thistles* (o/p); and *The Lords of Akchasaz*; and *Murder in the Ironsmith's Market* (Koch, Neff & Oetinger, UK). The trilogy *The Wind from the Plain*; *Iron Earth, Copper Sky* and *The Undying Grass*, is strong on human observations and detail rather than plot. Better are some later novels, mostly set in and around İstanbul, including: *The Sea-Crossed Fishermen* (Methuen, o/p), a psychological drama set against the background of an İstanbul sea-fishing village, contrasting an old man's struggle to save the dolphins in the Sea of Marmara with the fortunes of a desperate hoodlum at bay in the city; and *The Birds Have Also Gone* (o/p), a symbolic, gentle story about bird-catchers near İstanbul. In a more recent work, *Salman the Solitary* (Harlan Davidson, UK) Kemal returns to his native Çukurova with a tale of a displaced Kurdish family from the Van area.

Aysel Özakın *The Prizegiving* (The Women's Press, UK, o/p). Interesting insights into Turkish society, but lacks momentum as a novel, and it can be a bit predictable; used copies fairly easy to obtain. The opening passage is given on p.1064.

★ **Orhan Pamuk** The Turkish writer with the largest overseas (and domestic) audience, Pamuk's enduring concerns are Turkey's often corrosive encounter with the West, including its colonization by all forms of media (especially old films and comics), and the irrepressibility of its Islamic heritage. His first work, *The White Castle* (Faber & Faber/Braziller), is an excellent historical meditation in which a seventeenth-century Italian scholar is enslaved in the service of an Ottoman astronomer. His 1994-translated *The Black Book* (Faber & Faber/Farrar Straus Giroux), a mystery set in modern İstanbul, was more convoluted and surreal, and did well in Turkey. But Pamuk's 1998 *The New Life* (Faber & Faber/Farrar Straus Giroux) is, with nearly three quarters of a million copies sold, the most successful Turkish novel ever and had foreign critics falling over themselves hailing the heir-apparent of Calvino and Borges. Many readers will disagree: despite some fine set-piece satires of provincial Turkish life, the narrator is unappealing and the tale slight. His latest *My Name is Red* (Faber & Faber/Farrar Straus Giroux), a late-sixteenth-century Ottoman-set murder whodunnit, is again marred by poor characterization and clunky translation.

Haldun Taner *Thickhead and Other Turkish Stories* (Forest Books/ UNESCO). Mostly set in İstanbul from the 1950s to 1970s, translated by Geoffrey L. Lewis.

Latife Tekin *Berji Kristin: Tales from the Garbage Hills* (Marion Boyars). The hard underbelly of Turkish life, in this surreal allegory set in a shantytown founded on an İstanbul rubbish dump (one of which exploded in 1993 from accumulated methane).

Foreign literature set in Turkey

★ **Maureen Freely** *The Life of the Party* (Penguin/Warner; former o/p). Salacious, desperate cavortings of the Bosphorus University faculty and their families during the Sixties, including a thinly disguised amalgam of the author's father John Freely and others. An excellent read.

Pierre Loti *Aziyade* (Kegan Paul Int/Routledge). For what's essential-ly romantic twaddle set in nineteenth-century Ottoman İstanbul, this is surprisingly racy, with good insights into Ottoman life and Western attitudes to the Orient. Current re-issue is expensive; look for used o/p editions.

★ **Rose Macaulay** *The Towers of Trebizond* (Flamingo/Carroll & Graf). Classic send-up of Low and

High Church conflict, British ethno-centricity and proselytizing naivety, with generous slices of Turkey in the 1950s.

★ **Edouard Roditi** *The Delights of Turkey* (New Directions, US, o/p). Twenty short stories, by turns touching or bawdy, set in rural Turkey and İstanbul, by a Sephardic Jew of Turkish descent long resident in Paris and America. One of the best is reproduced on p.1061.

★ **Barry Unsworth** *The Rage of the Vulture* (Penguin). Set in the twilight of the Ottoman Empire, with the paranoid sultan Abdülhamid during the last year of his reign observed by a troubled British officer-with-a-past stationed in İstanbul.

Poetry

★ **Coleman Barks, trans.** *Like This* (Maypop, US), *Open Secret*, with John Moyne (Shambhala Books, US) and *We Are Three* (Windrush, UK/ Maypop, US). Three of various volumes of Rumi poetry, in lively if not necessarily literal translations. Some selections are reproduced on pp.1066–1070.

Yunus Emre *The City of the Heart: Verses of Wisdom and Love* (Element Books, UK). Along with Rumi, the most highly regarded Turkish medieval Sufi poet; translated by Süha Faiz.

Talat S. Halman *Living Poets of Turkey* (Dost Yayınları, İstanbul). A wide selection of modern Turkish poetry, with an introduction giving the socio-political context. Halman also edited *Yunus Emre and His Mystical Poetry* (Indiana University Turkish Studies, o/p), the works of the medieval Islamic folk poet, with explanatory essays.

★ **Nazım Hikmet** *Poems of Nazım Hikmet* (Norton, US). The newest (2002), most easily available, and reasonably priced anthology by the internationally renowned Turkish Communist poet who died in exile in 1963. *A Sad State of Freedom* (Greville Press Pamphlets, UK, o/p) contains gentle, moving poems also worth keeping an eye peeled for.

Geoffrey L. Lewis, trans. *The Book of Dede Korkut* (Penguin). The Turkish national epic, set in the age of the Oğuz Turks: by turns racy, formulaic, elegant and redundant.

Language

Language

Glossary

Many of the Turkish terms below will change their form according to their grammatical declension (eg ada, island, but Eşek Adası, Donkey Island); the genitive suffix is appended in brackets, or the form written separately when appropriate.

Medieval and modern Turkish terms

Ada(sı) Island.

Ağa A minor rank of nobility in the Ottoman Empire, and still a term of respect applied to a local worthy; follows the name (eg Ismail Ağa).

Ahi Medieval Turkish apprentice craftsmen's guild and religious brotherhood, predecessor of the more conventional dervish orders.

Arabesk Popular, derivative form of Turkish *sanat*, or "art" music.

Ayazma Sacred spring.

Bahçe(si) Garden.

Bedesten(i) Covered market hall for valuable goods, often lockable.

Bekçi Caretaker or warden at an archeological site or monument.

Belediye(si) Municipality – both the corporation and the actual town hall, for a community of under 2000.

Bey Another minor Ottoman title like *ağa*, still in use; follows the first name.

Cami(i) Mosque.

Çarşaf A bedsheet, or the full-length, baggy dress-with-hood worn by religious Turkish women.

Çarşı(sı) Bazaar, market.

Çay(ı) 1) Tea, the national drink; 2) a stream or small river.

Çeşme(si) Street-corner fountain.

Çıkmaz(ı) Dead-end alley.

Dağ(ı) Mount.

Dağlar(ı) Mountains.

Dolmuş Literally "filled" – the shared taxi system operating in larger Turkish towns; some confusing, though decreasing, overlap with "minibus", since not all of the latter are dolmuşes, and vice versa.

Entel Short for *entelektüel* – the arty, trendy set which patronizes Western-style pubs and bars in the larger cities and resorts.

Eski Old (frequent modifier of place names).

Ezan The Muslim call to prayer; these days often taped or at the very least transmitted up to an elevated loudspeaker.

Ferace Similar to a *çarşaf*, but less all-enveloping.

Gazı Warrior for the (Islamic) faith; also a common epithet of Atatürk.

Gazino Open-air nightclub, usually adorned with coloured lights and featuring live or taped *arabesk* or *taverna* music.

Gecekondu Literally "founded-by-night" – a reference to the Ottoman law whereby houses begun in darkness, which had acquired a roof and four walls by dawn, were inviolable. The continuance of the tradition is responsible for the huge *gecekondu* shantytowns around all large Turkish cities.

Gişe Ticket window or booth.

Göl(ü) Lake.

Hacı Honorific of someone who has made the pilgrimage to Mecca; precedes the name, though rarely used conversationally as a term of address.

Hamam(ı) Turkish bath.

Hamsi The Black Sea anchovy; by extension, nickname for any native of this area.

Han(ı) Traditionally a tradesmen's hall, or an urban inn; now can also mean an office block.

Harabe Ruin; *harabeler* in the plural, abbreviated "Hb" on old maps.

Harem The women's quarters in Ottoman residences.

Hastane(si) Hospital.

Hicrî The Muslim dating system, beginning with Mohammed's flight to Medina in 622 AD, and based on the thirteen-month lunar calendar; approximately six centuries behind the *Miladî* calendar. Abbreviated "H." on monuments and inscriptions.

Hisar Same as *kale*.

Hittite First great civilization (c.1800–1200 BC) to emerge in Anatolia.

Hoca Teacher in charge of religious instruction for children.

Ilıca Hot spring.

Irmak River, eg Yeşılırmak (Green River).

İl(i) Province, the largest administrative division in Turkey, subdivided into *ilçes* (counties or districts).

İmam Usually just the prayer leader at a mosque, though it can mean a more important spiritual authority.

İmam Hatip Okulları Religious secondary schools, established in the 1980s as an alternative to secular state schools, ostensibly to train youths for mosque preaching and teach basic Arabic and the Koran.

İskele(si) Jetty, dock.

Kaaba Shrine at Mecca containing a sacred black stone.

Kale(si) Castle, fort.

Kapı(sı) Gate, door.

Kaplıca Developed hot springs, spa.

Kervansaray(ı) Strategically located "hotel", often Selçuk, for pack animals and men on Anatolian trade routes; some overlap with *han*.

Kilim Flat-weave rug without a pile.

Kilise(si) Church.

Konak Large private residence, also the main government building of a province or city; genitive form *konağı*.

Konut Same as *Tatil köyü* (see below).

Lokanta Restaurant; rendition of the Italian *locanda*.

Mağara(sı) Cave.

Mahalle(si) District or neighbourhood of a larger municipality, village or postal area.

Meydan(ı) Public square or plaza.

Meyhane Tavern where alcohol and *meze*-type (see below) food are served together.

Meze Small plate of often vegetable-based appetizer, typically fried, pureed and/or marinated; from the Arabic *maza*.

Miladî The Christian year-numbering system; abbreviated "M." on inscriptions and monuments.

Muezzin Man who pronounces call to prayer (*ezan*) from the minaret of a mosque.

Muhtar Village headman.

Muhtarlık The office of the *muhtar*, both in the abstract and concrete sense; also designates the status of any community of under 2000.

Namaz The Muslim rite of prayer, performed five times daily.

Nehir (Nehri) River.

Otogar Bus station.

Ova(sı) Plain, plateau.

Ören Alternative term for *harabe*, "ruin"; common village name.

Pansiyon Typical budget accommodation in Turkish resorts.

Ramadan The Muslim month of fasting and prayer; spelt *Ramazan* in Turkish.

Saz Long-necked, fretted stringed instrument central to Turkish folk ballads and Alevî/Bektaşi devotional music.

Selçuk The first centralized, Muslim Turkish state based in Anatolia, lasting from the eleventh to the thirteenth centuries.

Sema A dervish ceremony; thus *semahane*, a hall where such ceremonies are conducted.

Şehzade Prince, heir apparent.

Şeyh Head of a Sufi order.

Sufi Dervish – more properly an adherent of one of the heterodox mystical branches of Islam. In Turkey the most important sects were (and to some extent still are) the Bektaşi, Mevlevî, Helveti, Nakşibendi, Cerrahi and Kadiri orders.

Sultan valide The Sultan's mother.

Tatil köyü or **site(si)** Holiday development, either for Turkish civil servants or a private co-operative – not geared for foreign tourists.

Tuğra Monogram or seal of a sultan.

Ulema The corps of Islamic scholars and authorities in Ottoman times.

Vakıf Islamic religious trust or foundation, responsible for social welfare and upkeep of religious buildings.

Vezir Vizier, the principal Ottoman minister of state, responsible for the day-to-day running of the empire.

Vilayet(i) Formal word for province; also a common term for the provincial headquarters building itself.

Yalı Ornate wooden residence along the Bosphorus.

Yayla(sı) Pastoral mountain hamlet occupied only in summer; in the Black Sea region, may have rustic accommodation ranging from simple to luxurious.

Yeni New (common component of Turkish place names).

Architectural and artistic terms

Acropolis Ancient fortified hilltop.

Agora Marketplace and meeting area of an ancient Lycian, Greek or Roman city.

Apse Curved or polygonal recess at the altar end of a church.

Arasta Marketplace built into the foundations of a mosque, a portion of whose revenues goes to the upkeep of the latter.

Bouleuterion Council hall of a Hellenistic or Roman city.

Camekân Changing rooms in a hamam.

Capital The top, often ornamented, of a column.

Cavea The seating curve of an ancient theatre.

Deesis or **Deisis** Portrayal of Christ between the Virgin and John the Baptist.

Diazoma A horizontal walkway dividing the two blocs of seats in an ancient theatre

Exedra Semicircular niche.

Eyvan Domed side-chamber of an Ottoman religious building; also applies to three-sided alcoves in secular mansions.

Göbek taşı Literally "navel stone" – the hot central platform of a hamam.

Halvet Semi-private corner rooms in a hamam.

Hararet The hottest room of a hamam.

İmaret(ı) Soup kitchen and hostel for dervishes and wayfarers, usually attached to a *medrese*.

Katholikon Central shrine of a monastery.

Kemer Series of vaults, or an aqueduct.

Khatchkar An ornate relief carving centred around stylised crosses, on the walls of Armenian churches; also a free-standing cruciform gravestone so carved.

Köşk(ü) Kiosk, pavilion, gazebo, folly.

Kubbe Dome, cupola – as in *Kubbeli Kilise* (the Domed Church).

Kule(si) Tower, turret.

Kurna Hewn stone basin in a hamam.

Külliye(si) Building complex – term for a mosque and dependent buildings taken as a whole.

Kümbet Vault, dome; by analogy the cylindrical "hatted" Selçuk tombs of central Anatolia.

Mabet Temple, at archeological sites; genitive *mabedi*.

Medrese(si) Islamic theological academy.

Mescit Small mosque with no *mimber*; Islamic equivalent of a chapel; genitive *mescidi*.

Mezar(ı) Grave, tomb; thus *mezarlık*, cemetery.

Mihrab Niche in a mosque indicating the direction of Mecca, and prayer.

Mimber Pulpit in a mosque, from where the *imam* delivers homilies; often beautifully carved in wood or stone.

Minare(si) Turkish for "minaret", the tower from which the call to prayer is delivered.

Naos The inner sanctum of an ancient temple.

Narthex Vestibule or entrance hall of a church; also *exonarthex*, the outer vestibule when there is more than one.

Nave The principal lengthwise aisle of a church.

Necropolis Place of burial in an ancient Greek or Roman city.

Nymphaeum Ornate, multistoreyed facade, often with statue niches, surrounding a public fountain in an ancient city.

Pendentive Curved, triangular surface, by means of which a dome can be supported over a square ground plan.

Pier A mass of supportive masonry.

Porphyry A hard red or purple rock containing mineral crystals.

Revetment Facing of stone, marble or tile on a wall.

Saray(ı) Palace.

Sebil Public drinking fountain, either free-standing or built into the wall of an Ottoman structure.

Selamlık Area where men receive guests in any sort of dwelling.

Serender Wooden, enclosed corn-crib on stilts, particular to the Black Sea; sometimes spelt *serander*.

Son cemaat yeri Literally "Place of the last congregation" – a mosque porch where latecomers pray.

Stoa Colonnaded walkway in ancient Greek marketplace.

Synthronon Semicircular seating for clergy, usually in the apse of a Byzantine church.

Şadırvan Ritual ablutions fountain of a mosque.

Şerefe Balcony of a minaret.

Tabhane Hospice for travelling dervishes or *ahis*, often housed in an *eyvan*.

Tapınak Alternative term for "temple" at archeological sites; genitive *tapınağı*.

Tekke(si) Gathering place of a Sufi order.

Tersane(si) Shipyard, dry-dock.

Transept The "wings" of a church, extending north and south perpendicular to the nave.

Tuff Soft, carvable rock formed from volcanic ash.

Türbe(si) Freestanding, usually domed, tomb.

Tympanum The surface, often adorned, enclosed by the top of an arch; found in churches or more ancient ruins.

Verd antique Type of green marble.

Voussoir Stripes of wedge-shaped blocks at the edge of an arch.

Zaviye Mosque built specifically as a hospice for dervishes, usually along a T-plan.

Zhamatoun Chapter (council) hall of an Armenian church.

Acronyms

AK *Adalet ve Kalkınma Partisi* or Justice and Development Party. Islamist movement headed by Recep Tayyip Erdoğan, which swept the 2002 elections and currently dominates parliament with a two-thirds majority.

ANAP *Anavatan Partisi* or Motherland Party. The centre-right party founded by the late president Turgut Özal.

AŞ *Anonim Şirket.* Turkish equivalent of "Ltd" or "Inc".

CHP *Cumhuriyetçi Halk Partisi* or Republican People's Party (RPP). Founded by Atatürk, disbanded in 1980, revived in 1992, headed now by Deniz Baykal; the minority party in parliament at present.

DSP *Demokratik Sol Partisi* or Democratic Left Party. Leftist party long headed by Bülent Ecevit; now out of parliament.

DYP *Doğru Yol Partisi* or True Path Party. Centre-right party long headed by Tansu Çiller; now out of parliament

FP *Fazilet Partisis* or Virtue Party. Formed instantly as a successor entity when Islamist RP (see opposite) was banned; also subsequently banned, but in part gave rise to AK Partisi (see above).

KDV Acronym of the Turkish VAT.

MHP *Milliyet Hareket Partisi* or National Action Party. Originally quasi-fascist group later rebranded, and headed, by Devlet Bahçeli; now out of parliament.

NSC National Security Council. The military-dominated council, meeting monthly, which really runs Turkey.

PKK *Partia Karkaris Kurdistan* or Kurdish Workers' Party. Actually an armed guerrilla movement, formed in 1978 and now on its last legs.

PTT *Post Telefon ve Telegraf.* The joint postal, telegraph and (formerly) phone service in Turkey, and by extension its offices.

RP *Refah Partisi* or Welfare Party. Islamist party headed by Necmettin Erbakan, respectively disbanded and banned from politics in 1998.

SHP *Sosyal Demokratik Halkçı Partisi* or Social Democratic Party. Centre-left party, absorbed into the CHP in 1994.

THY Türk *Hava Yolları.* Turkish Airways.

TIR (pronounced "turr" locally) *Transport International Routière.* Large, slow trucks, your greatest road hazard.

TL Standard symbol for Turkish lira.

TDİ *Türk Denizcilik İşletmesi* or Turkish Maritime Enterprises; TML (Turkish Maritime Lines) in English.

TRT *Türk Radyo ve Televizyon.* The Turkish public broadcasting corporation.

TT *Türk Telekom.* Entity hived off from the PTT, devoted exclusively to telecommunications services.

Index

and small print

Index

Map entries are in colour

INDEX

1115

Twenty Years of Rough Guides

In the summer of 1981, Mark Ellingham, Rough Guides' founder, knocked out the first guide on a typewriter, with a group of friends. Mark had been travelling in Greece after university, and couldn't find a guidebook that really answered his needs. There were heavyweight cultural guides on the one hand – good on museums and classical sites but not on beaches and tavernas – and on the other hand student manuals that were so caught up with how to save money that they lost sight of the country's significance beyond its role as a place for a cool vacation. None of the guides began to address Greece as a country, with its natural and human environment, its politics and its contemporary life.

Having no urgent reason to return home, Mark decided to write his own guide. It was a guide to Greece that tried to combine some erudition and insight with a thoroughly practical approach to travellers' needs. Scrupulously researched listings of places to stay, eat and drink were matched by careful attention to detail on everything from Homer to Greek music, from classical sites to national parks and from nude beaches to monasteries. Back in London, Mark and his friends got their Rough Guide accepted by a farsighted commissioning editor at the publisher Routledge and it came out in 1982.

The Rough Guide to Greece was a student scheme that became a publishing phenomenon. The immediate success of the book – shortlisted for the Thomas Cook award – spawned a series that rapidly covered dozens of countries. The Rough Guides found a ready market among backpackers and budget travellers, but soon acquired a much broader readership that included older and less impecunious visitors. Readers relished the guides' wit and inquisitiveness as much as the enthusiastic, critical approach that acknowledges everyone wants value for money – but not at any price.

Rough Guides soon began supplementing the "rougher" information – the hostel and low-budget listings – with the kind of detail that independent-minded travellers on any budget might expect. These days, the guides – distributed worldwide by the Penguin group – include recommendations spanning the range from shoestring to luxury, and cover more than 200 destinations around the globe. Our growing team of authors, many of whom come to Rough Guides initially as outstandingly good letter-writers telling us about their travels, are spread all over the world, particularly in Europe, the USA and Australia. As well as the travel guides, Rough Guides publishes a series of dictionary phrasebooks covering two dozen major languages, an acclaimed series of music guides running the gamut from Classical to World Music, a series of music CDs in association with World Music Network, and a range of reference books on topics as diverse as the Internet, Pregnancy and Unexplained Phenomena. Visit **www.roughguides.com** to see what's cooking.

Rough Guide credits

Text editor: Jules Brown
Series editor: Mark Ellingham
Editorial: Martin Dunford, Jonathan Buckley, Kate Berens, Ann-Marie Shaw, Helena Smith, Olivia Swift, Ruth Blackmore, Geoff Howard, Claire Saunders, Gavin Thomas, Alexander Mark Rogers, Polly Thomas, Joe Staines, Richard Lim, Duncan Clark, Peter Buckley, Lucy Ratcliffe, Clifton Wilkinson, Alison Murchie, Matthew Teller, Andrew Dickson, Fran Sandham, Sally Schafer, Matthew Milton, Karoline Densley (UK); Andrew Rosenberg, Yuki Takagaki, Richard Koss, Hunter Slaton (US)
Production: Link Hall, Helen Prior, Julia Bovis, Katie Pringle, Rachel Holmes, Andy

Turner, Dan May, Tanya Hall, John McKay, Sophie Hewat
Cartography: Maxine Repath, Melissa Baker, Ed Wright, Katie Lloyd-Jones
Cover art direction: Louise Boulton
Picture research: Sharon Martins, Mark Thomas
Online: Kelly Martinez, Anja Mutic-Blessing, Jennifer Gold, Audra Epstein, Suzanne Welles, Cree Lawson (US)
Finance: Gary Singh
Marketing & Publicity: Richard Trillo, Niki Smith, David Wearn, Chloë Roberts, Demelza Dallow, Claire Southern (UK); Simon Carloss, David Wechsler, Megan Kennedy (US)
Administration: Julie Sanderson

Publishing information

This fifth edition published June 2003 by
Rough Guides Ltd,
80 Strand, London WC2R 0RL
345 Hudson St, 4th Floor,
New York, NY 10014, USA
Distributed by the Penguin Group
Penguin Books Ltd,
80 Strand, London WC2R 0RL
Penguin Putnam, Inc
375 Hudson Street, NY 10014, USA
Penguin Books Australia Ltd,
487 Maroondah Highway, PO Box 257,
Ringwood, Victoria 3134, Australia
Penguin Books Canada Ltd,
10 Alcorn Avenue, Toronto, Ontario,
Canada M4V 1E4
Penguin Books (NZ) Ltd,
182–190 Wairau Road, Auckland 10,
New Zealand
Typeset in Bembo and Helvetica to an
original design by Henry Iles.

Printed in Italy by LegoPrint S.p.A

1136pp includes index
A catalogue record for this book is available
from the British Library

ISBN 1-84353-071-6

The publishers and authors have done their best to ensure the accuracy and currency of all the information in **The Rough Guide to Turkey**; however, they can accept no responsibility for any loss, injury, or inconvenience sustained by any traveller as a result of information or advice contained in the guide.

Help us update

We've gone to a lot of effort to ensure that the fifth edition of **The Rough Guide to Turkey** is accurate and up to date. However, things change – places get "discovered", opening hours are notoriously fickle, restaurants and rooms raise prices or lower standards. If you feel we've got it wrong or left something out, we'd like to know, and if you can remember the address, the price, the time, the phone number, so much the better.

We'll credit all contributions, and send a copy of the next edition (or any other Rough Guide if you prefer) for the best letters. Everyone who writes to us and isn't already a subscriber will receive a copy of our full-colour thrice-yearly newsletter. Please mark letters: "**Rough Guide Turkey Update**" and send to: Rough Guides, 80 Strand, London WC2R 0RL, or Rough Guides, 4th Floor, 345 Hudson St, New York, NY 10014. Or send an email to **mail@roughguides.com**

Have your questions answered and tell others about your trip at
www.roughguides.atinfopop.com

Acknowledgements

Marc Dubin would like to thank Orhan Tung, formerly of the Turkish Embassy in London, for press accreditation; Hülya Soylu and Joanna Marsh at the London Turkish Tourist Office for facilitating travel arrangements; Tapestry Holidays for travel facilities; Nikiforos and Vasiliki in İstanbul, especially for the barbequeing trick and the wild asparagus; Naci for restaurant tips in Fethiye; John and Niki for more recommendations in the Kaya area; Clare for hospitality and updates in Dalyan; Alison for the same in Göcek; Phil, Alison, Ufuk, Tevfik and the dive team of Bougainville Travel, Kaş; Muzaffer and Anne-Louise in Patara; Mick and Melihat at Tlos, for hospitality, the spot height for Akdağ and last word on snakes; the management of *Odile Hotel*; David and Kate for their hard work on *Basics*; Seyifeddin for village lunch, heaving his car out of the ditch and guiding services in Üçölük; and last but not least Susana and Rafi for trekking company and the loan of the ski pole in the Kaçkar.

Paul Sentobe would like to thank the staff of the many tourist information offices, in particular Özgür Bozkurt, Kaan Erge and Cemal Gül from the İzmir and Marmaris offices for their unparalleled help and support. He would also like to express his gratitude to Lisa Lay from *Paşa* in Bozcaada, Aydin and family, *Athena Pension* in Bergama, 'Mr Flash' *Sammy's Place* in Kusadasi, Jesse from *Diana Pension* Selçuk, TJ from Çannakale and finally Merryl from *Şaban Bungalows*, Olympos, for help, advice and homemade cocktails. Finally a big thank you to Tom and Jelena, Dina, Quiteriep and Duncan for friendship on the road.

Terry Richardson would like to thank Kate Clow in Antalya for too much to mention; Atıl, Erdoğan,Talat and Kerem of Middle Earth Travel for their help in Cappadocia, Fritz and Gillian for their hospitality in Göreme; Ismail, Zehra, Berdan, Bager and all their Hakkari clan for looking after him (again) in Van, Birsen and extended family at Ali's Pension in Eğirdir, Esat and Behice for the low-down on Antalya, Yılmaz of the Antakya tourist office for showing him Vakıflıköy, Hulya and Joanne at the Turkish Tourist Office in London; finally his sons Douglas (10) and Jacob (8) for accompanying him to the summit of Davraz.

Lizzie Williams would like to thank İşek, manager of the *Sheraton Hotel* in Ankara, Suat Okay, director of the tourist office in Ankara, Kiros Langston from the British Council in İstanbul, all the helpful staff at the tourist office in Sultanahmet, the waiters at the *Yaga Bar* in İstanbul, Hassan and all the staff at the *History Hotel* in İstanbul, Ali and his family from İznik, Mustafa the director of the archeological museum in Amasya, Ali Fuat from the tourist office in Amasya, all the RG readers she met along the way, and finally her dad and step mum who came out to drink Efes beer with her and reminded her how daunting it was to get around İstanbul by bus.

Finally, many thanks to all the readers who took the time to write in with their comments and suggestions, all of which were of great help in updating this edition.

SMALL PRINT

Photo credits

Cover credits

Main front picture Topkapı Palace © Robert Harding

Small front top picture Ölüdeniz © Robert Harding

Small front lower picture Cappadocia © Robert Harding

Back top picture Nemrut Dağı © Robert Harding

Back lower picture Ölüdeniz © Robert Harding

Introduction

Jewelled heads of girls, İzmir Festival © Yusuf Tuvi

Nemrut Dağı, Zeus head © Marc S Dubin

Fruit stall © İzzet Keribar

Ferry travel on the Bosphorus © Yusuf Tuvi

Fairy chimneys © İzzet Keribar

Carpet shop, Bergama © Mecky Fogeling/ffotos

Child playing in the street © Yusuf Tuvi

Stork and dome, İznik © Marc S Dubin

Traditional Turkish dress © İzzet Keribar

Things Not To Miss

Library, Ephesus © İzzet Keribar
White-water rafting © Terry Richardson
Gulet in a peaceful bay © İzzet Keribar
Hittite capital of Hattuşaş © Yusuf Tuvi
Opera performance at Aspendos © Terry
  Richardson
Oil wrestlers © Terry Richardson
Cappadocian frescoes © İzzet Keribar
Temple of Trajan, Bergama © Yusuf Tuvi
Interior of the Anatolian Civilization Museum
  © İzzet Keribar
Camel wrestling © Yusuf Tuvi
Kumkapı restaurant district area © İzzet
  Keribar
Path through the Lycian Way © Marc S Dubin
Making gözleme © İzzet Keribar
Underground city, Kaymaklı © Ibrahim Zaman
Doric columns, Assos © Marc S Dubin
Beehive houses, Harran © Yusuf Tuvi
İstanbul covered bazaar © Mecky
  Fogeling/ffotos
Ihlara Valley © Yusuf Tuvi
Aya Sofya exterior © Mecky Fogeling
Exterior view of the Sumela monastery ©
  Yusuf Tuvi
Koza Hanı silk market, Bursa © Marc S Tubin
Whirling dervishes, Konya © Robert Harding
  Picture Library
Lagoon Beach at Ölüdeniz © Robert Harding
  Picture Library
Football fans © Lizzie Williams
Fairy chimneys at Goreme © Marc S Dubin
Scuba diver off Turquoise Coast © İzzet
  Keribar
Interior, Topkapi Palace © Mecky
  Fogeling/ffotos
Buzul Lake, Kaçar Dağları © R.
  Lawrance/Ffotograff
Orchids at Lake Van © Terry Richardson
West façade, İşhan © Marc S Dubin
Cağoloğu Hunamı baths, © Adam
  Woolfitt/Corbis
View of İşak Paşa Sarayı & Mount Ararat ©
  Marc S Dubin
Drinking tea in a tea house © Yusuf Tuvi
Roman mosaic, Antakya © Yusuf Tuvi
River scene with houses, Amasya © Lizzie
  Williams
Hot air ballooning © Stuart Turpin/ffotograff

Black & White Images

Fishermen on the Bosphorus © Nick
  Tapsell/Ffotograff (p.94)
Kariye Camii mosaic © İzzet Keribar (p.165)
Pot plants and wooden *yalis* © Lizzie
  Williams (p.204)
Gallipoli memorial site © İzzet Keribar (p.216)
Anzac Cove, Gelibolu © İzzet Keribar (p.239)
Assos harbour © İzzet Kerribar (p.274)
Street scene with cart, Ayvalık © Paul
  Sentobe (p.301)
Restored ancient Aphrodisias © Marc Dubin
  (p.322)
Thermal terraces, Pamukkale © Eric
  Smith/Trip (p.377)
Temple at Priene © Yusuf Tuvi (p.419)
Ruins at Tlos © İzzet Keribar (p.444)
Ghost village at Kayakökü © Ibrahim
  Zarman/İzzet Keribar (p.461)
Submerged ruin, Kekova © İzzet Keribar
  (p.525)
Alanya Castle © Yusuf Tuvi (p.532)
Roman mosaic © Yusuf Tuvi (p.560)
Interior of Eşreyfoğlu Camii © İzzet Keribar
  (p.602)
Mevlana, Konya © İzzet Keribar (p.631)
Hittite capital of Hattuşaş © Yusuf Tuvi
  (p.684)
Façade of Ottoman house, Safranbolu ©
  İzzet Keribar (p.719)
Byzantine mosaic, Aya Sofya, Trabzon ©
  Marc Dubin (p.754)
Citadel gate, Amasra © Marc S Dubin (p.791)
Erzurum Gallery © Marc Dubin (p.810)
Church of St Gregory (Tigran Honents), Ani ©
  Marc S Dubin (p.839)
Nemrut Dağı, west terrace © Marc S Dubin
Hasankeyf © Yusuf Tuvi (p.909)
Lake Van & Hoşap castle © Marc S Dubin
  (p.918)
Akdamar Island & Church of Holy Cross ©
  Adam Woolfit/Robert Harding Picture
  Library (p.931)

SMALL PRINT

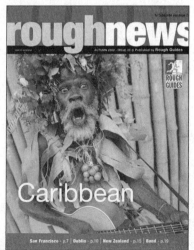

Rough Guides music, reference & CDs

Music

Acoustic Guitar
Blues: 100 Essential
  CDs
Cello
Clarinet
Classical Music
Classical Music:
  100 Essential CDs
Country Music
Country: 100
  Essential CDs
Cuban Music
Drum'n'bass
Drums
Electric Guitar
  & Bass Guitar
Flute
Hip-Hop
House
Irish Music
Jazz
Jazz: 100 Essential
  CDs
Keyboards & Digital
  Piano
Latin: 100 Essential
  CDs
Music USA: a Coast-
  To-Coast Tour
Opera
Opera: 100 Essential
  CDs
Piano
Reading Music
Reggae
Reggae: 100
  Essential CDs
Rock
Rock: 100 Essential
  CDs
Saxophone
Soul: 100 Essential
  CDs
Techno
Trumpet & Trombone
Violin & Viola
World Music: 100
  Essential CDs

World Music Vol1
World Music Vol2

Reference

Children's Books,
  0–5
Children's Books,
  5–11
China Chronicle
Cult Movies
Cult TV
Elvis
England Chronicle
France Chronicle
India Chronicle
The Internet
Internet Radio
James Bond
Liverpool FC
Man Utd
Money Online
Personal Computers
Pregnancy & Birth
Shopping Online
Travel Health
Travel Online
Unexplained
  Phenomena
Videogaming
Weather
Website Directory
Women Travel

Music CDs

Africa
Afrocuba
Afro-Peru
Ali Hussan Kuban
The Alps
Americana
The Andes
The Appalachians
Arabesque
Asian Underground
Australian Aboriginal
  Music
Bellydance
Bhangra
Bluegrass

Bollywood
Boogaloo
Brazil
Cajun
Cajun and Zydeco
Calypso and Soca
Cape Verde
Central America
Classic Jazz
Congolese Soukous
Cuba
Cuban Music Story
Cuban Son
Cumbia
Delta Blues
Eastern Europe
English Roots Music
Flamenco
Franco
Gospel
Global Dance
Greece
The Gypsies
Haiti
Hawaii
The Himalayas
Hip Hop
Hungary
India
India and Pakistan
Indian Ocean
Indonesia
Irish Folk
Irish Music
Italy
Jamaica
Japan
Kenya and
  Tanzania
Klezmer
Louisiana
Lucky Dube
Mali and Guinea
Marrabenta
  Mozambique
Merengue & Bachata
Mexico
Native American
  Music
Nigeria and Ghana
North Africa

Nusrat Fateh Ali
  Khan
Okinawa
Paris Café Music
Portugal
Rai
Reggae
Salsa
Salsa Dance
Samba
Scandinavia
Scottish Folk
Scottish Music
Senegal
  & The Gambia
Ska
Soul Brothers
South Africa
South African Gospel
South African Jazz
Spain
Sufi Music
Tango
Thailand
Tex-Mex
Wales
West African Music
World Music Vol 1:
  Africa, Europe and
  the Middle East
World Music Vol 2:
  Latin & North
  America,
  Caribbean, India,
  Asia and Pacific
World Roots
Youssou N'Dour
  & Etoile de Dakar
Zimbabwe

he very best of uncommercial

GREECE & TURKEY

2003

TAPESTRY

H O L I D A Y S

www.tapestryholidays.com